W9-DDS-309

Government by
the People

National, State, and Local Edition

Government by the People

10th Edition

James MacGregor Burns
Williams College

J.W. Peltason
University of Illinois, Urbana-Champaign

Thomas E. Cronin
University of Delaware

Prentice-Hall, Inc., Englewood Cliffs, New Jersey   07632

Library of Congress Cataloging in Publication Data

BURNS, JAMES MACGREGOR.
   Government by the people: national, state, and
local edition.

   Bibliography: p.
   Includes index.
   1. United States—Politics and government—Hand-
books, manuals, etc.   2. State governments.
3. Local government—United States.   I. Cronin,
Thomas E., joint author.   II. Peltason, Jack Walter,
joint author.   III. Title.
JK274.B855 1978   320.4 '73   78–1260
ISBN 0–13–361147–7

Parts 1–5 © 1978, 1975, 1972, 1969, 1966, 1963, 1960, 1957, 1954, 1952 by Raymond H. Young
Part 6 © 1978, 1975, 1972, 1969, 1966, 1963, 1960, 1957, 1954, 1952 by Prentice-Hall, Inc.,
Englewood Cliffs, New Jersey 07632

Printed in the United States of America

10 9 8 7 6 5 4 3 2

Prentice-Hall International, Inc., London
Prentice-Hall of Australia Pty. Limited, Sydney
Prentice-Hall of Canada, Ltd., Toronto
Prentice-Hall of India Private Limited, New Delhi
Prentice-Hall of Japan, Inc., Tokyo
Prentice-Hall of Southeast Asia Pte. Ltd., Singapore
Whitehall Books Limited, Wellington, New Zealand

Design by Ben Kann
Illustrations by Eric G. Hieber Associates
Cover photo by Stan Wakefield

Photo Credits

Contents

Preface

As we near the 1980s Americans are in a somber mood. Gone is the once reckless but adventuresome notion that we can go anywhere and do anything. We have endured wars, recessions, and a near-impeachment that sorely tested our political system. Today we emphasize not our new frontiers, but our scarcity of resources. We sense the limits of what we can do to bring about change. We content ourselves with slogans such as "Small is beautiful," as we try to conserve energy and water.

Yet there are signs of revitalization of our politics and government. Voters are electing more women and minority members to key offices. Our legislative bodies are more representative and better staffed. Younger persons are playing a bigger role in all levels of government. Some of the secrecy of government has been stripped away. Congress has taken a more active part in national policy-making—and policy-thwarting. The influences of the Carter administration upon the executive branch and Chief Justice Burger's leadership of the judicial system have begun major efforts to ensure that our laws are carried out fairly and effectively.

But the problem of leadership and public policy-making continue to swell, even as we improve the capabilities of many of our political institutions. Inflation, unemployment, poverty, the high costs of medical care, rising taxes, inadequate public transportation, faltering environmental controls, and massive and often conflicting regulations plague the political system. We may have improved the integrity of governmental arrangements, but ultimately the people demand solutions and governmental programs that are responsive to our problems.

The crucial challenge in this new era, just as in the past, will be the ability of our political system to manage the critical policy conflicts of the 1980s. An enduring test of a political system, especially a democratic political system, is its capacity to establish publicly acceptable priorities among the multitude of societal conflicts. Government cannot solve everything at once; it must go forward, step by step, trying to find solutions to the searing problems of the day, in order to shape a more livable, just, and equitable society.

As in the past, we have extensively revised and rewritten this examination of American government and politics. Entire chapters have been added to this new edition. All chapters have been redrafted, and we have added material, such as case studies and a detailed analysis in Chapter 14 of the new balance of powers in congressional—presidential relations. A concise summary section now concludes each chapter. We have added a glossary of key terms, which is found at the end of the book. Words that appear in the text in boldface, color are defined in the glossary.

A conscious effort has been made to write in a style that is readable and clear, without avoiding complexities. Our aim has been to write a book that would be interesting enough for a student to pick up and read without it being a course requirement. The book is designed to introduce political science to beginning students, as well as to guide them through the complexities and practical aspects of the American system of government. The authors' biases support the ideas of democracy, constitutionalism, and an open society. We have tried throughout to summarize and explain the latest research by political scientists.

We wish to call attention to James A. Burkhart's and Raymond L. Lee's, *Guide to "Government by the People,"* designed to give students an opportunity to participate more directly in the learning process. These two authors have also produced a valuable new edition of *A Systems Approach to Teaching "Government by the People."* A completely new test booklet and package prepared by Professor Richard Pious of Barnard College is available as a supplementary aid to instructors.

New editions of this book have always been dependent on a heavy infusion of fresh ideas, criticism, and research findings from some of the ablest people in political science. We are especially grateful this time to the helpful suggestions made to us by Herbert Asher, Thad Beyle, Jonathan Casper, Jeane Kirkpatrick, Kay Lawson, James A. Nathan, Bruce I. Oppenheimer, Carl Stenberg, Paul H. Weaver, and William O. Winter.

We are in debt also to dozens of persons who have written to us or talked with us about ways we might improve the book for this edition. Thus we thank James A. Burkhart, James Cameron, Craig Charney, Robert DiClerico, Roger Haigh, Dennis Ippolito, Alton McIver, Walter Miles, Peter K. Rofes, James R. Soles, Ian Spatz, Rochelle Stanfield, Norman C. Thomas, Walter E. Travis, and Brian Uslan.

Several talented individuals at Prentice-Hall have helped to make this a very special edition of *Government by the People.* We especially thank our political science editor, Stan Wakefield, our production editors, Janet Palazzo-Craig and Natalie Krivanek, as well as Jeannine Ciliotta, Marv Warshaw, Kitty Woringer, Ben Kann, and the other dedicated professionals at Prentice-Hall who have contributed in so many ways to make this a visually attractive book. For encouragement and advice we thank our wives.

James MacGregor Burns

J. W. Peltason

Thomas E. Cronin

P.S.: Please feel free to argue with us. Send comments and suggestions for future printings and editions addressed to us: *c/o Political Science Editor, Prentice-Hall, Inc., Englewood Cliffs, N.J. 07632.*

Part One

Constitutional Democracy in America

A Problem Guide

THE late Mr. Justice Felix Frankfurter of the Supreme Court once observed that "talking constitutionality" was a disease that afflicted many Americans. One may wonder why we should care about what went on in Philadelphia during the summer of 1787. We do care because we are interested in learning about "the rules of the game" that govern who wins and loses in American politics. By finding out about the values and interests that the framers of our Constitution intended to advance, we set the stage to learn what values and interests the American system favors today.

Forty men gathered in Philadelphia to write the Constitution. They faced the problem of how to build a national government strong enough to perform its tasks but not so strong as to scare the people. They also faced the problem of working out compromises among the many different ideas about how government should operate and among the many different political and economic interests of the nation. Chapter 1 describes how the framers met these problems.

Our Constitution both grants and limits power. It gives our government officials enough power, we hope, to meet the nation's needs. But it also places limits on them to prevent, we hope, their abusing their power. The framers knew that government was necessary, but they also knew that it was dangerous. They were especially fearful of the national government. To check its powers they created a constitutional system that relies on two devices: (1) free and fair elections, so nobody could take elective office unless he or she is acceptable to most of the voters; and (2) an elaborate system of balancing power.

This system of balancing power is the heart of our constitutional system. It rests, in turn, on two devices: (1) a *separation of governmental powers* among the several branches of the national government (for example, between president and Congress); and (2) a system of *checks and balances* that makes the branches of government accountable to different sources of political support (for example, senators are elected for six-year terms by statewide electorates; representatives are elected for two-year terms by congressional districts based on population).

Although this system of separation of powers and checks and balances has stood the test of time, it has created a set of difficult problems. Some people are asking whether a system good enough for the horse-and-buggy age is good enough for the space age. Does it make coordinated policies too difficult? Does it allow leaders to "pass the buck" so that the voters have trouble finding out who to blame when things go wrong? Does the system work to the advantage of the rich at the expense of the rest of the people? Chapter 2 takes up this set of problems.

Closely related to these questions is the question of whether the Constitution, drawn up almost two centuries ago, is flexible enough that the government it created is capable of dealing with modern problems. Or should we adopt a new constitution more in line with the needs of today? Chapter 3 discusses these questions too.

Finally, there are the problems created by federalism—the division of power between the national and state governments. Is federalism as desirable today as it was when the Constitution was written? Chapters 3 and 4 deal with this problem.

Examining these and related questions will help us organize our thinking about the basic problem of Part Two. Can we, and should we, maintain a constitutional system largely shaped in 1787 in the face of the urgent demands of the last third of the Twentieth Century?

Chapter 1

The Making of
a Republic

On a bright Sunday afternoon in May 1787, General George Washington, escorted by three other generals and a troop of light horses, rode into Philadelphia to the sound of chiming bells and cheering citizens. After depositing his baggage, Washington went to call on an old friend, Benjamin Franklin. They had vital matters to discuss. For Washington, as a delegate from Virginia, and Franklin, as a delegate from Pennsylvania, were in the vanguard of a group of illustrious men who were to spend the hot summer of 1787 writing a new constitution for the thirteen American states.

Three months later Dr. Franklin, the most venerable of the Founding Fathers, was confronted by a woman as he came from the last session of the Constitutional Convention. "What kind of government have you given us, Dr. Franklin?" she asked. "A Republic, Madam," responded Franklin, "if you can keep it."

Almost two centuries later the question is still a good one; the answer — and the warning — are still valid. How goes the Republic? What are its underlying principles? How is it working? Whom does it serve? These are some of the questions we shall examine in this reappraisal of the American political system.

A constitutional republic — what and why?

The government of the United States is a constitutional republic or a constitutional democracy. Democracy comes from two Greek roots — *demos*, the people, and *kratis*, authority. The word was used by the Athenians to mean government by the many, as contrasted with government by the few (oligarchy) or by the one (autocracy). At one time democracy was used to refer only to *direct* or *pure* democracy of the kind used in some Greek city-states in which all citizens participated directly in making the laws and took turns in carrying them out. Today democracy is more likely to mean a representative democracy, or in Plato's term, a *republic*, in which the people do not actually make the laws or administer them but, choose those who do.

The Founding Fathers preferred the term republic to avoid any confusion with pure democracy. For them, the word "democracy" meant mob rule and demagogues appealing to the "masses." Today democracy, although practiced in only a few nations, is a fashionable word and even a regime like that of East Germany, in which a small group of Communist party leaders run the government, calls itself the German Democratic Republic.

Here we define democracy or a republic to mean a system of government in which those who have the authority to make decisions that have the force of law acquire and retain this authority either directly or indirectly as the result of winning a free election in which the great bulk of adult citizens are allowed to participate.

Ours is not only a democratic system, it is a *constitutional* one. These two concepts are related, but they are different. Democracy refers to how power is *acquired* and *retained*. Constitutionalism refers to how power is *limited.* A government can be constitutional without being democratic—as in seventeenth-century England. It can also be democratic without being constitutional, as in Athens at the time of Pericles.

True, all governments have a constitution in the sense that there are agreed-upon ways by which governments proceed. In this sense both the Soviet Union and the People's Republic of China have constitutions. But the term constitutional government has come to have a more restricted meaning: government in which there are clearly recognized and regularly applied limits on the powers of those who govern. By this definition Great Britain, Canada, and the United States are constitutional democracies but the Soviet Union is not, for the people of that country have few checks on the powers of their rulers.

Our Founding Fathers created a system in which the first great safeguard against abuse of authority was to be a reliance on the *people*—the democratic principle. But this was not to be the only safeguard. They established a variety of checks on the power of officeholders. These are recognized and routinely enforced limits on what public officials may do, even those who are elected by the people.

In the chapters that follow we will look at our constitutional republic in greater detail. We will find that it is a complex system, difficult to describe. It is even harder to operate; constitutional republics such as ours exist in only a few nations. But to democrats, or if you prefer, to republicans, it is a precious thing, precious because our system is committed to protecting and expanding liberty. That commitment rests on certain fundamental convictions.

BASIC PREMISES OF DEMOCRACY

First, democrats recognize the fundamental dignity and importance of the *individual.* This emphasis on the supreme worth of the individual runs unbroken through democratic thought. It is woven into the writings of Thomas Jefferson, especially in the Declaration of Independence—*all* men are endowed by their Creator with certain *unalienable* rights. Individualism makes the person, rich or poor, black or white, male or female, the *central* measure of value. The state, the union, the corporation are measured in terms of their usefulness to individuals.

Not everyone, of course, believes in putting the individual first. Those who believe in statism, which makes the state or community supreme, do not. Democrats, however, consider the state or even the community as being less important than the individuals who compose it.

Second, democrats recognize the right of each individual to be treated as a unique and inviolable human being. They do not insist that all are equal in talents or virtues; they do insist that one person's claim to life, liberty, and property must be recognized as much as any other's. This right raises difficult questions of how equal rights can be secured, but the *principle* of equality of right is clear.

Third, democrats are convinced that freedom is good in itself. *Liberty* or *freedom* (used interchangeably here) means that all individuals must have the opportunity to choose their own goals. The core of liberty is *self-determination*. Liberty is not simply the absence of external restraint on a person; it means the individual's power to act positively to reach his or her goals. Moreover, both history and reason suggest that individual liberty is the key to *social progress*. The greater people's freedom, the greater the chance of discovering better ways of life. Progress is stifled wherever any group—or even rigid social custom—imposes rules that none may question.

These basic values of democracy do not necessarily coexist happily with one another in a particular society. The concept of individualism may conflict with the older tradition of public virtue and collective welfare—of the citizen as a participant in the general welfare. Freedom as the *liberation* of the individual may conflict with freedom as the *alienation* of people from their friends or from their communities. The concept of individual self-determination may conflict with that of collective decision making for the national welfare or the public good. The right of a mill owner to run his factory as he pleases, as compared to the right of a millhand in that factory to join a union, or even to share in the running of the plant, illustrates this type of conflict in everyday life.

Thomas Jefferson's rough draft of the Declaration of Independence.

Democracy, said a former Texas Congressman, is "liberty plus groceries." Probably the single most powerful idea in American history has been that of liberty. It was for life, liberty, and the pursuit of happiness that independence was declared; it was to secure the blessings of liberty that the Constitution was drawn up and adopted. There is no way to prove, of course, that liberty has been this powerful a concept for Americans; we had no scientific polling for the first century and a half of our national existence (even if that would have proved anything). But consider our patriotic anthems—it is to the "sweet land of liberty" that we sing. Or take a coin out of your pocket. Unless something has happened since these words were written, that penny, nickel, dime, quarter, or half dollar proclaims not authority, security, brotherhood, but *liberty*.

Liberty is a fuzzy as well as a compelling concept, of course, and much depends on how Americans would define it as they make practical decisions. During the early decades of the republic, the American concept of liberty was essentially negative. The main aim of Jeffersonian democracy was to throw off the burdens of established governments, churches, and other institutions. These negative liberties were made explicit in the Bill of Rights of the Constitution: free speech, free press, freedom of religion, freedom of assembly. The main role of the Constitution was to remove governmental constraints on individual liberties.

During most of the nineteenth century, liberty as "freedom *from*" meshed with the dominant economic and social doctrine of laissez faire. Under this doctrine, individuals must be freed of governmental impediments that might stop them from reaching maximum efficiency and productivity. The state, it was argued, must intervene no more than was absolutely necessary to protect life and property. Further intervention, such as minimum wages, health protection, or even compulsory vaccination, was both immoral in theory and improper in fact. The idea was simple: the less governmental power, the more individual liberty.

But what was the meaning of liberty when not governments but other individuals—employers, lynch mobs, plantation owners, labor bosses, —deprived persons of their liberties? Slavery forced Americans to rethink their ideas. "The world has never had a good definition of the word liberty," Abraham Lincoln said during the Civil War, "and the American people, just now, are in want of one. We all declare for liberty; but in using the same word we do not all mean the same thing. With some the word liberty may mean for each man to do as he pleases with himself, and the product of his labor; wnile with others the same word may mean for some men to do as they please with other men. . . ."[1] He used the example of the shepherd who drives the wolf from the sheep's throat, for which the sheep thanks the shepherd as his liberator, while the wolf denounces him for the same act as the destroyer of liberty.

With the coming of intensive industrialization, urbanization, agrarian and labor discontent; of unions, depressions, social protest; and of leaders like William Jennings Bryan, Theodore Roosevelt, Robert La Follette, Eugene Debs, and Woodrow Wilson, liberty came to have far more positive meanings. Americans slowly came to understand that men and women, crowded more and more together, lived amid growing webs of all kinds, personal and private, institutional and psychological. To abolish one type

The drafting of the Declaration of Independence.

[1]Speech at Sanitary Fair, 1864.

of restraint such as black slavery might mean increasing another type of restraint such as wage slavery. To cut down on governmental restraint of liberty might simply mean increasing private economic and social power. The question was not simply liberating people from *government;* it was how to use government to free people from *non*governmental curbs on liberty as well.

But what about the idea of *equality,* next to liberty probably the most vital concept in American thought. "All men are created equal and from that equal creation they derive rights inherent and unalienable, among which are the preservation of liberty and the pursuit of happiness." Those were the words of Jefferson's first draft of the Declaration and they indicate the primacy of the concept. Alexis de Tocqueville, James Bryce, Harold Laski, and other foreigners who investigated American democracy were struck by the strength of egalitarian thought and practice, in both our political and social lives.

What did equality mean? What *kind of* equality? Economic, political, legal, social, something else? Equality for *whom?* Blacks, as well as whites? Children and teenagers as well as adults? Equality of *opportunity?* — almost all Americans said they wanted that — but also of *condition?* This last question was the toughest. Did equality of opportunity simply mean that everyone should have *the same place at the starting line?* Or did it mean that there would be an effort to equalize most or all of the factors that during the course of a person's lifetime might determine how well he or she made out socially or economically?

Herbert Hoover posed the issue when he said: "We, through free and universal education, provide the training of the runners; we give to them an equal start; we provide in government the umpire of fairness in the race. . . ."[2] Franklin D. Roosevelt sought to answer the question when he proclaimed first the Four Freedoms — freedom from *want* and *fear* as well as freedom of speech and religion — and later a "second Bill of Rights." Under this second bill of rights, he said, Americans had accepted the idea that a new basis of security and prosperity can be established for all, regardless of position, race, or creed. This meant good housing, health, jobs, social security for all. The New Deal and its successor programs in both their achievements and failures have tried to advance the egalitarian intentions of the second bill of rights.

What has happened is that two concepts once seen as opposites have found a meeting point in a philosophy that calls for government to help broaden people's *social* and *economic* liberties, and to prevent other institutions (corporations or unions or landlords) from infringing on those liberties. At the same time, that government must prevent *itself* from interfering with liberty. This is no small task, and it is not always performed well. But the idea is an exciting one. It means that Americans, perhaps without being wholly conscious of it, have brought together the values of liberty and equality. No longer can one say flatly, "the more government, the less liberty." But neither can one say the opposite. Everything depends on the impact of government and other restraining and liberating forces on a person's sum total of liberties.

That Texas Congressman was only half right, some Americans would contend. The values of American democracy are not only liberty *plus* gro-

[2]Herbert Hoover, *American Individualism* (Doubleday, Page, 1922), p. 9.

ceries but the *interrelation* between the two. Liberty and equality interlock and stimulate each other at some points; they are in a state of opposition or at least tension at other points. And at still other points they do not relate to each other at all. Pushed too far, liberty becomes license and unbridled individualism; pushed too far, equality could mean leveling, a dull mediocrity, and even the erosion of liberty. Just how to strike a balance is a question around which much of our political combat revolves.

Voter registration drive in New York City.

Some favor democracy not only because they believe it stands for goals such as liberty and equality, but also because they see it as the best process available for governing a complex society. If those who admire democracy for the human ends it represents can be called "principle democrats," those who see democracy essentially as a technique of self-government can be called "process democrats." Process democrats grant that democratic processes do not guarantee that "justice will be done," but they contend that the chances are better under "government by the people" than under any other system.

It is important to note what is *not* included in the concept of democracy as a means. "Process democrats" do not judge a democracy by its policy output. Their concern is with the *procedures* for making policy and not with the rightness of the policy that is made.

Their central point is this. Government *by* the people usually will produce government *for* the people. But the very reason they are committed to democratic government is that they reject the notion that it is possible to define "scientifically" what the public interest is. If one believes, as did Plato, that decisions about public policy are of the same nature as, say, a decision as to how to build a boat, then it would follow that the best way to make policy is to turn everything over to a group of specialists or experts. Then like Plato one would favor a system that placed authority in the hands of philosopher-kings or perhaps, in today's terms, in the hands of the "best and the brightest." Process democrats, on the other hand, take their stand with Aristotle, who argued that although an expert cook knows better than the nonexpert how to bake a cake, the person who eats it is the better judge of whether it tastes good.

Most Americans do not trust experts that much. As President Eisenhower stated in his farewell address: "Yet in holding scientific research and discovery in respect, as we should, we must also be alert to the equal and opposite danger that public policy could itself become the captive of a scientific-technological elite." Few democrats—especially process democrats—wish to shift the control of our destinies from voters and their elected leaders to some new priesthood of technocratic systems analysts.

The crucial mechanism in all genuinely popular governments is a system of free, fair, and open elections. Democratic governments take many different forms, but democratic elections have at least four essential elements:

1. *All citizens should have equal voting power.* This does not mean that all must or will have equal political influence. Some persons, because of wealth, talent, or position, have much more power than others. How much extra influence key figures should be allowed to exercise in a democracy is one of the questions that face democrats. But no matter whether one is president or pick-and-shovel laborer, newspaper publisher, or lettuce picker, each casts only one vote at the polls.

"Gad, when I think of the power the people have . . . It just isn't fair."

© 1965 Los Angeles Times; reprinted by permission.

THE AMERICAN SYSTEM:
DEMOCRATIC AND
CONSTITUTIONAL

2. Voters should have the right of access to facts, to criticism, to competing ideas, to the views of all candidates. Here again, the extent to which different ideas actually receive equal attention is a problem because of the nature of the mass media, the special access of the president to television and the press, the inability of many lower-income people to make their ideas known. But the principle of free competition of ideas during an election is essential.

3. Citizens must be free to organize for political purposes. Obviously individuals can be more effective when they join with others in a party, a pressure group, a protest movement, or a demonstration.

4. Elections are decided by majorities (or at least pluralities). Those who get the most votes win, even if the winning side seems to be made up of idiots, and the minority of the wise. The persons chosen by the majority take office. How much power the winners may then have over the losing minority is another problem of democratic government, but there is no question that the winners take office and assume formal authority.

The Founding Fathers were both *principle* democrats and *process* democrats. Their genius lay in their relating the *goals* to the *methods* of democracy. If the Declaration of Independence was more concerned with the *goals* of free men such as liberty and equality, the Constitution focused more on the *processes* that could help realize these goals without sacrificing other values such as controlled power, stability, continuity, due process, balanced decision-making. For two centuries American politicians, jurists, and other leaders have been enormously influenced by the resounding success of the revolutionaries of 1776 and 1787 in working out effective and durable political processes. The Watergate scandals were a dramatic warning, process democrats remind us, that to abuse democratic processes is to threaten both the means and ends of a free people.

The origins of the American republic

The American Revolution was a conservative one in several respects. Certainly it had constitutional goals. Those who declared our independence from England did so reluctantly and in the name of the English Constitution. They sought not to establish a new order but to restore the rights taken from them by the king.[3] As Alexis de Tocqueville, the perceptive nineteenth-century French visitor to the New World observed, "The great advantage of the Americans is that they have arrived at a state of democracy without having to endure a democratic revolution. . . ."[4] Tocqueville had not forgotten our war period, 1775–1781. He meant that the American Revolution was primarily a rebellion of colonies against an empire. But even in this respect, "The Americans [other than blacks] were not an oppressed people; they had no crushing imperial shackles to throw off. In fact, the Americans knew they were probably freer and less burdened with cumbersome feudal and hierarchical restraints than any part of mankind in the eighteenth century."[5] In the modern sense, it was hardly a revolution; there were no sharp breaks with the past and no great social, economic, or political upheavals. Contrast the colonists' demand

[3]See Martin Diamond, "The Revolution of Sober Expectations," *The American Revolution: Three Views* (American Brands, 1975), p. 57.

[4]*Democracy in America,* ed. F. Bowen (Sever and Francis, 1872), II, 13. For other statements of the same view, see Daniel J. Boorstin, *The Genius of American Politics* (University of Chicago Press, 1953), p. 68; and Louis Hartz, *The Liberal Tradition in America* (Harcourt, 1955).

[5]Wood, *The Creation of The American Republic, 1776–1787* (University of North Carolina Press, 1969), p. 3.

for the "rights of Englishmen" with the French demand for the "rights of man" in 1789. "Even the fact that Americans jettisoned a monarch and suddenly and without much internal debate adopted a republican government marked no great upheaval."[6] Thomas Jefferson observed in the summer of 1777 that Americans "seem to have deposited the monarchical and taken up the republican government with as much ease as would have attended their throwing off an old and putting on a new suit of clothes."[7] As a result, the American Revolution did not open class wounds. Neither a radical tradition nor one of reaction developed. The political system based on such a *revolution* centered more on consensus than conflict.

THE NEW GOVERNMENTS

The destruction of English authority was the first step in the establishment of the American republic. The next was to create new state governments to replace the colonial ones and to establish at least a limited central government under the Articles of Confederation.

Although the breaks with the past were not dramatic as compared to the French Revolution of a few years later or the Russian Revolution of this century, the new governments were different from those they replaced. New state constitutions incorporated bills of rights, abolished most religious qualifications, and liberalized property and taxpaying requirements for voting.[8] There were no kings. Power was concentrated in the legislatures. The governors and judges, officials who reminded Americans of royalty, lost influence. Governors were made dependent on the legislature for election, and the legislatures overrode judicial decisions and scolded judges whose rulings were unpopular. The legislative branch, later complained the writers of the *Federalist Papers*, was drawing all power into its impetuous vortex.[9] What about the central government? Having just fought a war against one central government, Americans were reluctant to create another one. The Articles of Confederation when finally approved by all the state legislatures in 1781 more or less legalized the existing arrangements, under which the Continental Congress had assumed power in 1776. The Articles established only a fragile league of friendship, not a national government.

These, in broad outline, were the arrangements under which Americans tried for a decade (1778–1788) to govern themselves. They made some progress. But as we know from our history, the practical difficulties confronting the new nation would have tested the strongest government. The end of the war reduced the sense of urgency that had helped to unite the states, and conflicts among them were frequent. Within the states, economic differences between creditors and debtors grew intense. There were foreign

"You know, the idea of taxation *with* representation doesn't appeal to me very much either."

Drawing by Handelsman;
© 1970 The New Yorker Magazine, Inc.

[6]*Ibid.* p. 10.

[7]Quoted by Wood, p. 92, Jefferson to Benjamin Franklin, August 2, 1777. In Boyd, ed., *Jefferson Papers*, II, 26.

[8]Elisha P. Douglass, *Rebels and Democrats* (University of North Carolina Press, 1955). See also R. R. Palmer, *The Age of the Democratic Revolution* (Princeton University Press, 1959), pp. 217–35; Chilton Williamson, *American Suffrage: From Property to Democracy, 1760–1860* (Princeton University Press, 1960), p. 92; Robert A. Rutland, *The Birth of the Bill of Rights, 1776–1791* (University of North Carolina Press, 1955); Richard Ashcraft, "Locke's State of Nature: Historical Fact or Moral Fiction?" *American Political Science Review* (September 1968), pp. 898–915; Samuel Eliot Morison, *The Oxford History of the American People* (Oxford University Press, 1965), p. 276; Hannah Arendt, *On Revolution* (Viking, 1963), p. 139.

[9]*Federalist* No. 48.

threats as well. The English, French, and Spanish surrounded a new nation which, internally divided and lacking a strong central government, made a tempting prize.

As the problems mounted, many leaders, especially in New York, Virginia, Massachusetts, and Pennsylvania, became convinced that it would not be enough merely to revise the Articles of Confederation. To save republicanism and to create a union strong enough to resist external threats, they wanted to create a stronger central government with adequate powers.[10] They therefore set out to create a republican government that could be made to work by and for *ordinary people.*[11]

Although there was a growing recognition of the need to give Congress authority to regulate commerce and collect a few taxes, many Americans were still suspicious of a central government. But those who felt that we must fashion a truly national government kept working at their objective. Finally, in the late summer of 1786, and under the leadership of Alexander Hamilton, they took advantage of a meeting at Annapolis on problems of trade and navigation, attended by delegates from five states, to issue a call for a "plenipotentiary Convention." Such a convention would have full authority to consider basic amendments to the Articles of Confederation. The delegates to the Annapolis Convention requested the legislatures of their states to appoint commissioners to meet at Philadelphia on the second Monday of May, 1787, "to devise such further provisions as shall appear to them necessary to render the Constitution of the Federal Government adequate to the exigencies of the Union."

A lull followed. Then, in Western Massachusetts that winter some farmers and debtors under the leadership of Daniel Shays, a revolutionary war captain, blocked the entrance to the courthouse in Northhampton and stopped the judges from foreclosing some mortgages. The state militia quickly put down this disturbance, but its message seemed clear. Some kind of action must be taken to strengthen the machinery of government. Spurred on by Shays's Rebellion, seven states appointed commissioners to attend the Philadelphia Convention. Congress, apathetic and suspicious, finally issued a cautiously worded call to the states to appoint delegates for the "sole and express purpose of revising the Articles of Confederation." The cautious legislators specified that no recommendation would be effective unless approved by Congress and confirmed by all the state legislatures as provided by the Articles.

Eventually every state except Rhode Island appointed delegates. (The debtors and farmers who controlled the Rhode Island legislature rightly suspected that one of the major purposes of the proposed convention would be to limit the power of state legislatures to interfere with the rights of creditors.) Some of the delegates were bound by instructions only to consider amendments to the Articles of Confederation. Delaware went so far as to forbid her representatives to consider any proposal that would deny any state equal representation in Congress.

Under the leadership of Daniel Shays, a group of farmers forcibly restrained the Massachusetts courts from foreclosing their mortgages. The uprising was known as "Shays's Rebellion."

The Philadelphia convention

The delegates who assembled in Philadelphia that summer were presented with a condition, not a theory. They had to establish a national government powerful enough to prevent the nation from dissolving. What these

[10]William H. Riker, *Federalism: Origin, Operation, Significance* (Little, Brown, 1964), pp. 18–20.

[11]Wood, *American Republic, 1776–1787*, pp. 122, 612.

men did that summer continues to have a major impact on how we are governed. It also provides an outstanding lesson in political science.

THE DELEGATES

Seventy-four delegates were appointed by the various states, but only fifty-five put in an appearance in Philadelphia, and of these, approximately forty took a real part in the work of the convention. It was a distinguished gathering. Many of the most important men of the nation were there— successful merchants, planters, bankers and lawyers, former and present governors and congressional representatives (thirty-nine of the delegates had served in Congress). As theorists they had read widely in the classics of political science. As activists they were interested in the practical task of constructing a national government. Theory played its part, but experience was to be their main guide.

The convention was as representative as most political gatherings at the time. Of course, there were no women or blacks. The delegates were mainly state or national leaders, for in the 1780s the ordinary person was not expected to participate in politics. (Even today farm laborers, factory workers, and truck drivers are seldom found in the ranks of Congress, although a self-styled peanut farmer has done pretty well for himself in our executive branch).

Although most of the leaders from those days eventually supported the Constitution in the ratification debates, only eight of the fifty-six signers of the Declaration of Independence were present at the Constitutional Convention. Among those who did not come were Jefferson, Paine, Henry, Richard Henry Lee, Sam and John Adams, and John Hancock. Of the active participants at the convention, several men stand out as the prime movers.

Alexander Hamilton had been the engineer of the Annapolis Convention and as early as 1778 had been urging that the national government be made stronger. Hamilton had come to the United States from the West Indies and while still a student at Kings College (now Columbia University) had won national attention by his brilliant pamphlets in defense of the Revolutionary cause. During the war he served as General Washington's aide, and his experiences confirmed his distaste for a Congress so weak it could not even supply its troops with enough food or arms.

From Virginia came two of the leading delegates—General George Washington and James Madison. Although active in the movement to revise the Articles of Confederation, Washington had been extremely reluctant to attend the convention. He accepted only when persuaded that his prestige was needed for its success. He was selected unanimously to preside over the meetings. According to the records, he spoke only twice during the deliberations, but his influence was felt in the informal gatherings as well as during the sessions. The assumption that Washington would become the first president under the new Constitution inspired confidence in it.

James Madison was only thirty-six years old at the time of the convention, but he was one of the most learned members present. He had helped frame Virginia's first constitution and had served in both the Virginia Assembly and in the Congress. Madison was also a leader of those who favored the establishment of a strong national government.

The Pennsylvania delegation included Benjamin Franklin and Gouverneur Morris. Franklin, at 81, was the convention's oldest member and, as one of his fellow delegates said, "He is well known to be the greatest philosopher of the present age." Franklin enjoyed a world reputation unrivaled by that of any other American.

Gouverneur Morris of New York was more eloquent than brilliant. He addressed the convention more often than any other person. The elegance of the language of the Constitution is proof of his literary ability for he was responsible for the final draft. Luther Martin of Maryland, John Dickinson of Delaware, and William Paterson of New Jersey were not in agreement with a majority of the delegates, but they ably defended the position of those who insisted on equal representation for all states.

The proceedings of the convention were kept secret. Delegates were forbidden to discuss the debates with outsiders in order to encourage everyone to speak freely. It was feared that if a member publicly took a firm stand on an issue, it would be harder for him to change his mind after debate and discussion. Also, the members knew that if word of the inevitable disagreements got out, it would provide ammunition for the many enemies of the convention. There were critics of this secrecy rule, but without it, agreement might have been impossible.

CONSENSUS

The Constitutional Convention is usually discussed in terms of three famous compromises: the compromise between large and small states over representation in Congress, the compromise between North and South over the counting of slaves for taxation and representation, and the compromise between North and South over the regulation and taxation of foreign commerce. But this emphasis obscures the fact that there were many other important compromises and that on many of the more significant issues most of the delegates were in agreement.

A few delegates might have personally favored a limited monarchy, but all supported republican government, and this was the only form of government seriously considered. It was the only form that would be acceptable to the nation. Equally important, all the delegates were constitutionalists, who opposed arbitrary and unrestrained government, in whatever form.

The common philosophy accepted by most of the delegates was that of *balanced government*. They wanted to construct a national government in which no single interest would dominate. Because the delegates represented those alarmed by the tendencies of the farmers as an interest group to interfere with property, they were primarily concerned with balancing the government in the direction of protection for property and business.

There was an almost universal concurrence in the remark of Elbridge Gerry (delegate from Massachusetts): "The evils we experience flow from the excess of democracy. The people do not want virtue, but are dupes of pretended patriots." Likewise there was substantial agreement with Gouverneur Morris' statement that property was the "principal object of government."

Benjamin Franklin favored extending the right to vote to male nonproperty owners, but most of the delegates agreed that freeholders (owners of land) were the best guardians of liberty. James Madison voiced the fear that those without property, if given the right to vote, would either combine to deprive property owners of their rights or would become the "tools of demagogues." The delegates agreed in principle on restricted suffrage, but they differed over the kind and amount of property one must own in order to vote. Moreover, because the states were in the process of relaxing qualifications for the vote, the framers recognized that they would jeopardize approval of the Constitution if they made the federal franchise more restricted than the franchises within the states.[12] As a result, each state was left to determine the qualifications for electing members to the House of Representatives, the only branch of the national government in which the electorate was given a direct voice.

Within five days of its opening, the convention, with only Connecticut dissenting, voted to approve the Fourth Virginia Resolve that "a national government ought to be established consisting of a supreme legislative, executive, and judiciary." This decision to establish a national government resting on and exercising power over individuals would alter the nature of the central government profoundly, and change it from a league of states to a national government.

There was little dissent from proposals to give the new Congress all the powers of the old plus all other powers in which the harmony of the United States might be disrupted by the exercise of state legislation. The framers agreed that a strong executive, which had been lacking under the Articles, was necessary to provide energy and direction for the general government. And an independent judiciary was also accepted without much debate. Franklin favored a single-house national legislature, but almost all the states had had two-chamber legislatures since colonial times and the delegates were used to the system. Bicameralism—the principle of the two-house legislature—also expressed their belief in the need for balanced government. The upper house would represent the aristocracy and offset the more democratic lower house. So the delegates established two chambers in the national government too.

CONFLICT

There were serious differences among the various groups, especially between the representatives of the large states, who favored a strong national government they expected to be able to dominate, and the delegates from the small states, who were anxious to avoid being dominated. The Virginia delegation took the initiative. It had met during the delay before the convention and, as soon as the convention was organized, was ready with fifteen resolutions. These resolutions, the Virginia Plan, called for a strong central government. The legislature was to be composed of two chambers. The members of the lower house were to be elected by the voters. Those of the upper house were to be chosen by the lower chamber from nominees submitted by the state legislatures. Representation in both houses was to be on the basis of either wealth or numbers, thus giving the more populous and wealthy states—Virginia, Massachusetts, and Pennsylvania—a majority in the legislature.

The Congress thus created was to be given all the legislative power of its predecessor under the Articles of Confederation and the right "to legislate in all cases in which the separate States are incompetent." Furthermore, it was to have the authority to veto state legislation in conflict with the proposed constitution. The Virginia Plan also called for a national executive, to be chosen by the legislature, and a national judiciary with rather exten-

[12]John P. Roche, "The Founding Fathers: A Reform Caucus in Action," *American Political Science Review* (December 1961), pp. 799–816, emphasizes the importance of such political considerations in the framers' deliberations.

sive jurisdiction. The national Supreme Court, along with the executive, was to have a qualified veto over acts of Congress.

For the first few weeks the Virginia Plan dominated the discussion. But by June 15, additional delegates from the small states had arrived, and they began to counterattack. They rallied around William Paterson of New Jersey, who presented a series of resolutions known as the New Jersey Plan. Paterson did not question the need for a greatly strengthened central government, but he was concerned about how this strength would be used. The New Jersey Plan would give Congress the right to tax and regulate commerce and to coerce states, but would retain a single-house legislature in which all states would have the same vote, regardless of their size. The plan contained the germ of what eventually came to be a key provision of our Constitution—the *supremacy* clause. The national Supreme Court was to hear appeals from state judges, and the supremacy clause would require all the judges—state and national—to treat laws of the national government and the treaties of the United States as superior to the laws of each of the states.[13]

Paterson was maneuvering to force concessions from the larger states. He favored a strong central government but not one that the big states could control. And he raised the issue of practical politics: to adopt the Virginia Plan, which created a powerful national government dominated by Massachusetts, Virginia, and Pennsylvania and eliminated the states as important units of government, would be to court defeat for the convention's proposals in the ratification struggle to come. But the large states resisted, and for a time the convention was deadlocked. The small states argued that states should be represented equally in Congress, at least in the upper house. The large states insisted that representation in both houses be based on population or wealth and that national legislators be elected by the voters rather than by the state legislatures. Finally, a Committee of Eleven was elected to devise a compromise. On July 5 it presented it proposals.

Because of the prominent role of the Connecticut delegation, this plan has since been known as the Connecticut Compromise. It called for an upper house in which each state would have an equal vote, but for a lower house in which representation would be based on population and in which all bills for raising or appropriating money would originate. This was a setback to the large states, who agreed only when the smaller states made it clear that this was their price for union. After equality of representation in the Senate was accepted, most objections to the establishment of a strong national government dissolved.

Slavery was already an issue in 1787. The southern states wanted slaves to be counted in determining representation in the House of Representatives. It was finally agreed that a slave should count as three-fifths of a free person, both in determining representation in the House and in apportionment of direct taxes. Southerners were also fearful that a northern majority in Congress might discriminate against southern trade. They had some basis for this concern. John Jay, secretary of foreign affairs for the Confederation, had proposed a treaty with Great Britain that would have given advantages to northern merchants at the expense of southern ex-

[13]Robert H. Birkby, "Politics of Accommodation: The Origin of the Supremacy Clause," *Western Political Quarterly* (March 1966), p. 27.

porters. To protect themselves, the southern delegates insisted on requiring a two-thirds majority in the Senate for the ratification of treaties.

The delegates, of course, found other issues to argue about. Should the national government have lower courts or would one federal Supreme Court be enough? This issue was resolved by postponing the decision; the Constitution states that there *shall* be one Supreme Court and that Congress *may* establish inferior courts. How should the president be selected? For a long time the convention accepted the idea that the president should be elected by the Congress. But it was feared that either the Congress would dominate the president or vice versa. Election by the state legislatures was rejected because of distrust of these bodies. Finally, the electoral college system was decided upon. This was perhaps the most original contribution of the delegates, and is one of the most criticized provisions in the Constitution.

After three months, the delegates ceased debating. On September 17, 1787, they assembled for the impressive ceremony of signing the document they were recommending to the nation. All but three of those still present signed; others, who opposed the general drift of the convention, had already left. Their work over, the delegates adjourned to the City Tavern to relax and to celebrate a job well done.

THE FRAMERS— WHAT MANNER OF MEN?

Were the delegates an inspired group of men who cast aside all thoughts of self-interest? Were they motivated by the desire to save the nation or by the desire to save themselves? Was the convention the inevitable result of the weaknesses of the Articles? Was it a carefully maneuvered coup on the part of certain elites? Was the difference between those who favored and those who opposed the Constitution mainly economic? Or was the difference mainly regional?

Students of history and government have held various opinions concerning these and other questions. During the early part of our history, the members of the convention were the object of uncritical adulation; the Constitution was the object of universal reverence. Early in the twentieth century, a more critical attitude was inspired by J. Allen Smith and Charles A. Beard. Smith, in his *The Spirit of American Government* (1911), painted the Constitution as the outgrowth of an antidemocratic reaction, almost a conspiracy, against the rule of majorities. Beard's thesis was that the Constitution represented the platform of the propertied groups who wanted to limit state legislatures and strengthen the national government as a means of protecting property. In his influential book *An Economic Interpretation of the Constitution* (1913), Beard described the economic holdings of the delegates and argued that their support or opposition to the Constitution could best be explained in terms of their financial interests. He explicitly denied that he was charging the Founding Fathers with writing the Constitution for their personal benefit. Rather, he contended that men's political behavior reflects their broad economic interests.

More recent historical works have questioned the soundness of Beard's scholarship and challenged his interpretation. Some historians have pointed out that in 1787 there was no great propertyless mass in the United States.[14] Even the poor were interested in protecting property. The Founding Fathers, they argue, were too smart as politicians to think they

[14]Robert E. Brown, *Charles Beard and the Constitution* (Princeton University Press, 1956), pp. 197–98.

could get away with a plan designed merely to protect their own wealth, even if that had been their motive.[15] Certainly they were anxious to build a strong national government so that it could promote economic growth. Such a government would win the support of all classes of people.[16] And these historians contend that the political differences over the merits of the Constitution, just as political arguments of today, cut through economic class divisions. The struggle, it is argued, was more between differing political ideologies.[17]

Political scientist Martin Diamond took issue with those who portray the Constitutional Convention as a reactionary move of aristocrats designed to curtail the brave democratic beginnings proclaimed in the Declaration of Independence, an interpretation he calls the "conventional wisdom of those who give academic and intellectual opinions to the nation." "The fact is," he writes, "The Declaration . . . is neutral on the question of forms of government; any form is legitimate, provided it secures equal freedom and is instituted by popular consent." It was the framers of our Constitution who gave us a democratic form of government. "Of course, the Founders," Diamond comments, "criticized the defects and dangers of democracy and did not waste much breath on the defects and dangers of the other forms of government. For a very good reason. They were not founding any other kind of government; they were establishing a democratic form, and it was the dangers peculiar to it against which all their efforts had to be bent."[18]

The various interpretations of the American Revolution and of the framing of the Constitution, reflect the changing styles of thought as current political debates are read backward into our past. But the various interpretations also reflect the fact that "The American Revolution . . . was so complex and contained so many diverse and seemingly contradictory currents that it can support a wide variety of interpretations and may never be comprehended in full."[19]

Beard himself recognized that men are motivated by a complex of factors, both conscious and unconscious. Self-interest, economic or otherwise, and principles are inextricably mixed in human behavior, and the framers were not much different from today's political leaders. The Founding Fathers were neither gods for whom self-interest or economic considerations were of no importance, nor selfish elitists who thought only in terms of their own pocketbooks. They were, by and large, aristocrats fearful of the masses, but they were committed to an aristocracy of merit, of education, of accomplishment and not of birth or wealth. The framers wanted to protect the nation from aggression abroad and dissension at home. Stability and strength were needed to protect their own interests—

[15]Forrest McDonald, *We the People: The Economic Origins of the Constitution* (University of Chicago Press, 1958), pp. vii, 415.

[16]Gordon S. Wood, *The Convention and the Constitution* (St. Martin's Press, 1965), p. 31.

[17]Wood, *American Republic, 1776–1787*, pp. 484–85.

[18]Martin Diamond, "The Declaration and the Constitution: Liberty, Democracy, and the Founders," *The Public Interest*, 41 (Fall 1975), pp. 40, 50, 52.

[19]Jack P. Greene, "The Reappraisal of the American Revolution in Recent Historical Literature," in Jack P. Greene, ed., *The Reinterpretation of the American Revolution, 1763–1789* (Harper & Row, 1968), p. 2.

but also to secure the unity and order necessary for the operation of a democracy.

**To adopt
or not to adopt**

The delegates had gone far. They had not hesitated to disregard Congress's instructions about ratification or to ignore Article XIII of the Articles of Confederation. This article declared the Union to be perpetual and prohibited any alteration in the Articles unless agreed to by the Congress and *by every one of the state legislatures*—a provision that had made it impossible to amend the Articles. But the convention delegates boldly declared that the Constitution should go into effect when ratified by *popularly elected conventions in nine states.* They had turned to this method of ratification both for practical considerations and for reasons of principle. Not only were the delegates aware that there was little chance of securing approval of the new Constitution in all the state legislatures, but many felt that the Constitution should be ratified by an authority higher than a legislature. A constitution based on popular approval expressed via specified elected ratifying conventions in each state would have a higher legal and moral status. The Articles of Confederation had been a compact of state governments, but the Constitution was to be a "union of people."[20]

But even this method of ratification was not going to be easy. The nation was not ready to adopt the Constitution without a thorough debate, and soon two camps sprang up. The supporters of the new government, by cleverly appropriating the name of Federalists took some of the sting out of the charges that they were trying to destroy the states and establish an all-powerful central government. By calling their opponents Antifederalists, they pointed up the negative character of the arguments of those who opposed ratification.

The split was in part geographical. The seaboard and city regions tended to be Federalist strongholds. The vast back-country regions from Maine through Georgia, inhabited by farmers and other relatively poor people, were areas in which the Antifederalists were strong. But, as in all political contests, no single factor completely accounted for the division between Federalist and Antifederalist. For example, in Virginia the leaders of both sides came from the same general social and economic class. New York City and Philadelphia strongly supported the Constitution, but so did predominantly rural New Jersey.

The great debate was conducted with pamphlets, papers, letters to the editor, and speeches. The issues were important and the interest of those concerned intense, but the argument, in the main, was carried on in a quiet and calm manner. Out of the debate came a series of essays, known as *The Federalist*, written by Alexander Hamilton, James Madison, and John Jay to persuade the voters of New York to ratify the Constitution. The Federalist is still "widely regarded as the most profound single treatise on the Constitution ever written and as among the few masterly works in political science produced in all the centuries of history."[21] The great debate stands even today as an outstanding example of a free people using

[20]Max Farrand, ed., *The Records of the Federal Convention of 1787* (Yale University Press, 1911), II, pp. 93, 476.

[21]Charles A. Beard and Mary R. Beard, *A Basic History of the United States* (New Home Library, 1944), p. 136.

the techniques of discussion and debate to determine the nature of their fundamental laws.

The most telling criticism of the proposed Constitution made by the Antifederalists was its failure to include a bill of rights.[22] The Federalists argued that a bill of rights would be superfluous. The general government had only delegated powers, and there was no need to specify that Congress could not, for example, abridge freedom of the press. It had no power to regulate the press. Moreover, the Federalists argued, to guarantee *some* rights might be dangerous because it would then be thought that rights *not* listed could be denied. Anyway, they pointed out that the Constitution already protected some of the most important rights — trial by jury in federal criminal cases, for example. Hamilton and others also insisted that paper guarantees were weak reeds on which to depend for protection against governmental tyranny.

The Antifederalists were unconvinced. If some rights were protected, what could be the objection to providing constitutional protection for others? Without a bill of rights, what was to prevent Congress from using one of its delegated powers in such a manner that free speech would be abridged? If bills of rights were needed in state constitutions to limit state governments, why was one not needed in the national constitution to limit the national government? This was a government farther from the people and with a greater tendency, it was argued, to subvert natural rights. The Federalists, forced to concede, agreed to add a bill of rights if and when the new Constitution was approved.

THE POLITICS OF RATIFICATION The political strategy of the Federalists was to secure ratification in as many states as possible before the opposition had time to organize. The Antifederalists were handicapped. They lacked access to the newspapers, most of which supported ratification. Their main strength was in the rural areas, underrepresented in some state legislatures and difficult to arouse to political action. They needed time to perfect their organization and collect their strength. The Federalists, composed of a more closely knit group of leaders throughout the colonies, moved in a hurry.

In most of the small states, now satisfied by equal Senate representation, ratification was gained without difficulty. Delaware was the first state to ratify. The first large state to take action was Pennsylvania. The Federalists presented the Constitution to the state legislature immediately after the Philadelphia Convention adjourned in September 1787. But the legislature was about to adjourn, and the Antifederalist minority felt that this was moving with unseemly haste (Congress had not even formally transmitted the document to the legislature for its consideration!). They wanted to postpone action until after the coming state elections, when they hoped to win a majority and so prevent calling a ratifying convention. When it became clear that the Federalists were going to move ahead, the Antifederalists left the legislative chamber. With two short of a quorum, business was brought to a standstill. But Philadelphia, the seat of the legislature, was a Federalist stronghold. The next morning two Antifederalists were roused from their quarters, carried into the legislative chamber, and forced to remain. The resolution calling for election of delegates

[22]Rutland, *Birth of the Bill of Rights.* See also Alpheus T. Mason, *The States Rights Debates: Antifederalism and the Constitution* (Prentice-Hall, 1964), pp. 4, 66–97.

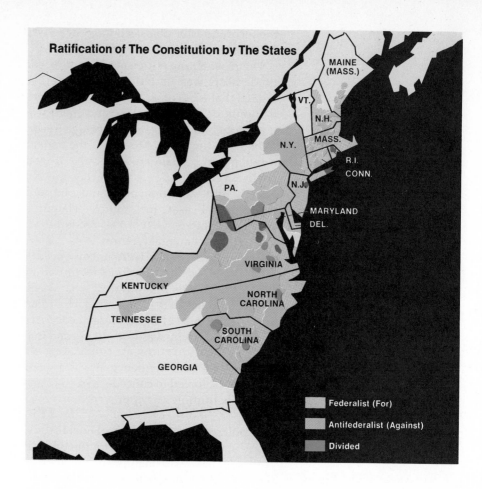

Ratification of The Constitution by The States

to a ratifying convention was adopted.[23] Under the generalship of James Wilson, the Pennsylvania convention ratified by a vote of 46 to 23 in December 1787.

By early 1788 New Jersey, Connecticut, and Georgia had also ratified. The scene of battle then shifted to Massachusetts, a key state and a doubtful one. John Hancock and Samuel Adams had not declared themselves, and these men of '76, with their great popular following, held the balance of power. The Federalists cleverly pointed out to Hancock that Washington would be the first president and that therefore the vice-president would undoubtedly be a New Englander. What citizen of New England was more distinguished than John Hancock? Whether or not this hint was the cause, Hancock eventually came out for ratification, and Adams was persuaded to vote for approval after securing a promise that a bill of rights would be forthcoming after adoption. Even so, Massachusetts ratified by the narrow margin of 187 to 168.

By June 1788, Maryland, South Carolina, and New Hampshire had ratified, so the nine states required to bring the Constitution into effect had been obtained. But neither Virginia nor New York had taken action, and without them the new Union would have little chance of success. Virginia was the most populous state and the home of many of the nation's outstanding leaders, and New York was important geographically.

[23]Julius Goebel, Jr., *Antecedents and Beginnings to 1801* (Macmillan, 1971), p. 267.

The Virginia ratifying convention rivaled the Constitutional Convention in the caliber of its delegates. James Madison was the captain of the Federalist forces, and he had able lieutenants in Governor Randolph and young John Marshall. Patrick Henry, George Mason, and James Monroe within the convention and Richard Henry Lee outside led the opposition. Henry attacked the proposed government, point by point, with great eloquence; Madison turned back each attack quietly but cogently. At the critical juncture, Washington sent a letter to the convention urging unqualified ratification. This tipped the scale, and Virginia ratified. News was rushed to New York.

The great landowners along the Hudson, unlike their southern planter friends, were opposed to the Constitution. They feared federal taxation of their holdings, and they did not want to abolish the profitable tax that New York had been levying on the trade and commerce of other states. When the convention assembled, the Federalists were greatly outnumbered, but they were aided by the strategy and skill of Hamilton and by word of Virginia's ratification. New York approved by a margin of three votes. Although North Carolina and Rhode Island still remained outside the Union (the former ratified in November 1789 and the latter six months later), the new nation was created. In New York, a few members of the old Congress assembled to issue the call for elections under the new Constitution, and then Congress adjourned *sine die*, that is without setting a day for reconvening.

Into the third century — and some questions

A constitution that is to endure must reflect the hard experiences and high hopes of the people for whom it is written. Those who framed our Constitution did not, of course, complete the task of constitution making. That is a process begun long before the Constitutional Convention met and continuing still. Constitutions, even written ones, are growing and evolving organisms rather than documents reflecting a particular moment in time.

The completion of two centuries of self-government — a major accomplishment — *is* a time of national celebration. However, it is also appropriately a time of national questioning. The questions that are being asked have no easy answers. They are questions to which there is no single logical response, no answer that stems easily from an analysis of facts, for they are basic questions that deal with value choices. Here are some of the complex questions that we put forth not to answer at this time, but to help organize your thoughts as we proceed with a more detailed investigation of the operations of the American Republic:

1. Is the system sufficiently *open* to persons of all races, sexes, classes, and political views who wish to participate in the making of decisions?
2. Is the system sufficiently *responsive*? Is the leadership *accountable* to the voters?
3. Is the system sufficiently *representative*? This concept of "representation" is one of the most difficult in political science. Here we mean to focus not on whether those who govern precisely mirror divisions of class, race, interest, and region, but whether those who govern are sensitive to the needs and opinions of differing groups.
4. Is the system sufficiently *responsible*? Does the leadership keep in mind the long-term needs of the entire nation and not merely respond to the short-term demands of the most vocal or the most prosperous special interests?

In considering these questions, we must remember that the framers did not favor a government that would be directly participated in, be representative of, or responsive to the mass of people. They sought to control both the spirit of faction and the thrust of majorities. Their prime concern was how to fashion a viable but limited government. The framers had not seen a political party in the modern sense and would not have liked it if they had. They believed not in an arousing, mobilizing kind of leadership but in a stabilizing, balancing, magisterial leadership—the kind George Washington was expected to supply and did supply. Today we have *high-pressure politics*—strongly organized groups, potent and volatile public opinion dominated by opinion-making agencies, parties vying to mobilize nationwide majorities, celebrity-leaders intimately covered by the media. How responsive are our political agencies to fast-moving changes in public attitudes and moods? Will our Constitution and the system it created be able to deal with the problems of our third century? This and related questions guide our analysis in the chapters that follow.

There are other questions on our national agenda that are more directly related to our constitutional system. The Constitution, as we will note time and again in the coming pages, deliberately fragments powers and divides it among officials because the framers were afraid those in power might try to use it unjustly. The Founders were also fearful of direct democracy and wished to filter public opinion and impose restraints on it. As a result, as James Bryce wrote in his famous commentary, *The American Commonwealth*, in 1888, "There is in the American government . . . a want of unity . . . The sailors, the helmsman, the engineer, do not seem to have one purpose or obey one will, so that instead of making steady way the vessel may pursue a devious or zigzag course, and sometimes merely turn round and round in the water." Such conditions, he felt, were not too dangerous at the time. "Social convulsions from within, warlike assaults from without," he wrote, "seem now as unlikely to try the fabric of the American Constitution, as an earthquake to render the walls of the Capitol. This is why the Americans submit, not merely patiently but hopefully, to the defects of their government. The vessel may not be any better built, or found, or rigged than those which carry the fortunes of the great nations of Europe. She is certainly not better navigated. But for the present at least— it may not always be so—she sails upon a summer sea."[24]

We no longer sail upon that summer sea. And today the question that Franklin put is being asked even more urgently. Can we keep the Republic?

"When my distinguished colleague refers to the will of the 'people,' does he mean his 'people' or my 'people'?"

Drawing by Richter;
© 1976 The New Yorker Magazine, Inc.

Summary

1. Our constitutional democracy is both a process for making decisions and a set of principles, namely, the importance of the individual, the uniqueness of each person, and the desirability of liberty. The process is one in which those who acquire governmental power to make decisions do so as the result of winning a free and fair election. And most important, those defeated in one election are free to use all peaceful means to persuade the voters to vote them into office at the next election.

2. Our constitutional democracy in its basic form rests on English institutions. After the American Revolution, a contained and conservative one, we operated under the Articles of Confederation, which gave us a loose league of states. But many leaders felt that a national government with direct authority over individuals was necessary. They proposed such a form at the Constitutional Convention of 1787.

[24]James Bryce, *The American Commonwealth* (Macmillan, 1911), I, pp. 294, 310.

3. The Constitutional Convention is an outstanding example of a creative political act. What the framers of the Constitution proposed was ratified by the states in special conventions after long debates in which those supporting the Constitution demonstrated considerable skills as politicians.

4. Nearly two hundred years later we continue to live under the Constitution they proposed. But we face the constant necessity of understanding that system and working to adapt it to ever-changing conditions.

Chapter 2

The Living Constitution

For a time, some people were skeptical of the new Constitution. After watching merchants and mechanics march side by side in a parade celebrating ratification, a Bostonian remarked sourly that "it may serve to please children, but freemen will not be so easily gulled out of their liberties." On the other hand, a Philadelphian said that the procession in his city had "made such an impression on the minds of our young people that 'federal' and 'union' have now become part of the household words of every family in the city." This effect on youth was significant, for it was on the younger generation that hopes for the new government depended.

The adoption of the Constitution coincided with the return of prosperity. Markets for American goods were opening in Europe, and business was pulling out of its postwar slump. Such events seemed to justify Federalist claims that adoption of the Constitution would correct the nation's problems. Within a surprisingly short time, the Constitution lost its partisan character; Antifederalists vied with Federalists in honoring it. Politicians differed less and less over whether the Constitution was good. More and more they began to argue over what it meant.

As the Constitution won the support of Americans, it began to take on the aura of natural law:

> Here was the document into which the Founding Fathers had poured their wisdom as into a vessel; the Fathers themselves grew ever larger in stature as they receded from view; the era in which they lived and fought became a Golden Age; in that age there had been a fresh dawn for the world, and its men were giants against the sky; what they had fought for was abstracted from its living context and became a set of "principles," eternally true and universally applicable.[1]

[1]Max Lerner, *Ideas for the Ice Age* (Viking, 1941), pp. 241–42.

This adoration of the Constitution was important as a means of bringing unity into the diversity of a new nation. Like the Crown in Britain, the Constitution became a *symbol* of national loyalty that evoked both emotional and rational support from all Americans regardless of their differences. The framers' work became part of the American creed. It stood for liberty, equality before the law, limited government—indeed, for whatever anyone wanted to build into it.

But the Constitution is also a supreme and binding law that both *grants* and *limits* powers. "In framing a government which is to be administered by men over men," wrote James Madison in *The Federalist*, "the great difficulty lies in this: you must first enable the government to control the governed; and in the next place oblige it to control itself." The Constitution is both a *positive* instrument of government, enabling the governors to control the governed, and it is a *restraint* on government, enabling the ruled to check the rulers.

In what ways does the Constitution limit the power of the national government? In what ways does it create national power? How has it managed to serve both as a great symbol of national unity and at the same time as a somewhat adaptable and changing instrument of government?

Checking power with power

It is strange, perhaps, to begin by stressing the ways in which the Constitution *limits* national power. Yet we must keep in mind the dilemma that the framers faced. They wanted a more effective national government, but at the same time were keenly aware that the people would not accept too much central control. Accordingly, they allotted certain powers to the national government and reserved the rest for the states. They established a system of federalism (the nature and problems of which will be taken up in Chapters 3 and 4). But this distribution of powers, they felt, was not enough. Other ways of limiting the national government were needed.

The most important device to make public officials observe the constitutional limits on their powers is free elections. This means that the voters have the ability to go to the polls and throw out of office those who abuse power. But the framers were not willing to depend solely on such *political* controls, because they did not fully trust the people's judgment. The people might be misled and vote a demagogue into office. Thomas Jefferson, a firm democrat, put it this way: "Free government is founded on jealousy, and not in confidence. . . . In questions of power, then, let no more be heard of confidence in man, but bind him down from mischief by the chains of the Constitution."[2] Even more important, the framers feared that a majority faction might use the new central government to deprive minorities of their rights. "A dependence on the people is, no doubt, the primary control on the government," Madison admitted, "but experience has taught mankind the necessity of auxiliary precautions." Thus the framers made part of the Constitution two interrelated arrangements—*separation of powers,* and *checks and balances*—that they hoped would prevent public officials from abusing their power, or any one group of people, even a majority, from capturing control of the government and tyrannizing the rest of the people.

SEPARATION OF POWERS

The first step was the *separation of powers,* that is, dividing constitutional authority among the three branches of the national government. In *Feder-*

[2]Quoted in Alpheus T. Mason, *The Supreme Court: Palladium of Freedom* (University of Michigan Press, 1962), p. 10.

alist No. 47 James Madison wrote, "No political truth is certainly of greater intrinsic value, or is stamped with the authority of more enlightened patrons of liberty, than that . . . the accumulation of all powers, legislative, executive, and judiciary, in the same hands . . . may justly be pronounced the very definition of tyranny."

But the force of this logic alone does not account for the doctrine of separation of powers being included in our Constitution. This doctrine had been the general practice in the colonies for over a hundred years. Only during the Revolutionary period was authority concentrated in the hands of the legislature, and the experience confirmed the belief in the merits of separation of powers. Many of the framers attributed the evils of state government and the lack of energy in the central government to the fact that there was no strong executive who could both check legislative abuses and give energy and direction to administration.

But separating power was not enough. For there was always the danger—from the framers' point of view—that different officials with different powers might pool their authority and act together. Separation of powers by itself would not prevent government branches and officials from responding to the same pressures—for example, an overwhelming majority of the voters. If separating power was not enough, what else could be done?

CHECKS AND BALANCES: AMBITION TO COUNTERACT AMBITION

The framers' answer was a system of *checks* and *balances*. "The great security against a gradual concentration of the several powers in the same department," wrote Madison, "consists in giving to those who administer each department the necessary constitutional means and personal motives to resist encroachment on the others . . . . Ambition must be made to counteract ambition."

Each branch is therefore given some role in the actions of the others. We have a "government of separated institutions *sharing* powers."[3] Thus, Congress enacts laws, but the president can veto them. The Supreme Court can declare unconstitutional laws passed by Congress and signed by the president, but the president appoints the justices with the Senate's approval. The president administers the laws, but Congress provides the money. The Senate and the House of Representatives have an absolute veto over each other in the enactment of a law, since bills must be approved by both houses.

Not only does each branch have some authority over the actions of the others, *but each is politically independent of the other*. The president is selected by electors (now popularly elected). Senators are now chosen by the voters in each state, the members of the House by voters in their districts. And although federal judges are appointed by the president with the consent of the Senate, once in office they hold terms in practical fact for life.

The framers were also careful to arrange matters so that a majority of the voters could win control over only part of the government at one time. A popular majority might take control of the House of Representatives in an off-year (that is, a nonpresidential election), but the president, representing a previous popular majority, would still have two years to go. And senators are chosen for six-year terms, with only one-third being selected every two years.

---

[3]Richard E. Neustadt, *Presidential Power*, rev. ed. (Wiley, 1976), p. 101.

Finally, if this distribution of powers between the Congress and the president did not work, there were the judges. In fact, so important has the role of the judges become in our system that they deserve special attention.

Judicial review and the "guardians of the constitution"

It was not until some years after the Constitution was in operation that the judges asserted the power of judicial review—the power of a court of law to set aside an act of the legislature that in the opinion of the judges violates the Constitution. But from the beginning the judges were expected to be a check on the legislature and the groups the legislative majority represent. "Independent judges," wrote Alexander Hamilton in *Federalist No. 78*, would be "an essential safeguard against the effects of occasional ill humors in society."

Judicial review is an American contribution to the art of government. If an Englishman or an American is thrown into prison without cause, either can appeal to the courts of his or her respective country for protection. But when Parliament passes a law, no English judge has the authority to declare it null and void because the judge believes it violates the English Constitition. Parliament is the guardian of the English Constitution. In the United States, the courts, ultimately the Supreme Court, are the keepers of the constitutional conscience—not Congress and not the president. How did the judges get this tremendous responsibility, which adds a major dimension to our system of checks and balances?

ORIGINS OF JUDICIAL REVIEW

The Constitution itself says nothing about who should have the final word in disputes that might arise over its meaning. It does not specifically grant such power to the Supreme Court. Whether the members of the Convention of 1787 intended to give the courts the power of judicial review is a question that has long been debated. There is little doubt that the framers intended the Supreme Court to have the power to declare *state* legislation unconstitutional, but whether they intended to give it the same power over *national* legislation is not clear. Edward S. Corwin, an outstanding authority on the American Constitution, concluded that unquestionably "the framers anticipated some sort of judicial review . . . . But it is equally without question that the ideas generally current in 1787 were far from presaging the present vast role of the Court."[4] Why, then, did the framers not specifically provide for judicial review? Probably because they believed the power rested on certain general provisions that made specific statements unnecessary.

The Federalists—the men who wrote the Constitution and controlled the national government until 1801—generally supported the courts and favored judicial review. Their opponents, the Jeffersonian Republicans, were less enthusiastic. In 1798 and 1799 Jefferson and Madison (the latter by this time had left the Federalist party) came very close in the Virginia and Kentucky Resolutions to arguing that the state legislatures and not the Supreme Court had the ultimate power to interpret the Constitution. This would seem to mean that the Supreme Court did not even have the final authority to review *state* legislation, something about which there had been little doubt.

[4]"The Constitution as Instrument and as Symbol," *American Political Science Review* (December 1936), p. 1078.

MARBURY V. MADISON

When the Jeffersonians defeated the Federalists in the elections of 1800, it was still undecided whether the Supreme Court would actually exercise the power of judicial review. "The idea was in the air, the ingredients to support a doctrine of judicial review were at hand, and a few precedents could even be cited;" nevertheless, judicial review was not an established power. Then in 1803 came *Marbury v. Madison,*[5] a case closely related to the political struggles between the Federalists and the Jeffersonians.

The elections of 1800 marked the rise to power of the Jeffersonian Republicans. President John Adams and his fellow Federalists did not take their defeat easily. Indeed, they were greatly alarmed at what they considered to be the "enthronement of the rabble." But there was nothing much they could do about it before leaving office—or was there? The Constitution gives the president, with the consent of the Senate, the power to appoint federal judges to hold office during "good behavior"—virtually for life. If the judiciary were manned by good Federalists, thought Adams and his followers, they could stave off the worst consequences of Jefferson's victory.

The Federalist lame-duck Congress created dozens of new federal judicial posts. By March 3, 1801, Adams had appointed, and the Senate had confirmed, deserving Federalists to all these new positions. Adams signed the commissions and turned them over to John Marshall, the secretary of state, to be sealed and delivered. Marshall had just received his own commission as chief justice of the United States, but he was continuing to serve as secretary of state until Adams' term expired. Working right up to nine o'clock on the evening of March 3, Marshall sealed but was unable to deliver all the commissions. The important ones were taken care of, however, and only those for the justices of the peace for the District of Columbia were left undelivered. The chief justice left the remaining commissions to be delivered by his successor.

Jefferson was angered by this Federalist packing of the judiciary. When he discovered that some of the commissions had not been delivered, he told the new secretary of state, James Madison, to hold up seventeen of those still in his possession. Jefferson could see no reason why the District needed so many justices of the peace, especially Federalist justices.

Among the commissions that were not delivered was one for William Marbury. After waiting in vain, Marbury decided to seek action from the courts. Searching through the statute books, he came across Section 13 of the Judiciary Act of 1789, which authorized the Supreme Court "to issue writs of mandamus, in cases warranted by the principles and usages of law, to . . . persons holding office, under the authority of the United States." A *writ of mandamus* is a court order directing an official to perform a certain act. Delivering a commission is a ministerial act; the secretary of state is a person holding office under the authority of the United States. So why not, thought Marbury, ask the Supreme Court to issue a writ of mandamus to force Madison to deliver the commission? He and his companions went directly to the Supreme Court and, citing Section 13, they so asked.

What could Marshall do? If the Court issued the mandamus, Madison and Jefferson would probably ignore it. The Court would be powerless,

Chief Justice Marshall

[5]1 Cranch 137 (1802).

and its prestige, already low, might suffer a fatal blow. On the other hand, by refusing to issue the mandamus, the judges would appear to support the Republican party's claim that the Court had no authority to interfere with the executive. Would Marshall issue the mandamus? Most people thought so; angry Republicans talked of impeachment.

On February 24, 1803, the Supreme Court published its opinion. The first part was as expected. Marbury was entitled to his commission, said Marshall, and Madison should have delivered it to him; a writ of mandamus could be issued by the proper court against even such a high officer as the secretary of state.

Then came the surprise. Although Section 13 of the Judiciary Act seems to give the Supreme Court original jurisdiction in just such cases, this section, said Marshall, is contrary to Article III of the Constitution, which gives the Supreme Court original jurisdiction in *only* those cases in which an ambassador or other foreign minister is affected or in which a state is a party. This is a case of original jurisdiction, but Marbury is neither a state nor a foreign minister. If we follow Section 13, wrote Marshall, we have jurisdiction; if we follow the Constitution, we have no jurisdiction.

Then, in characteristic fashion, Marshall stated the question in such a way that the answer was obvious—namely, should the Supreme Court enforce an unconstitutional law? Of course not, he concluded. The Constitution is the supreme and binding law, and the courts cannot enforce any action of Congress that conflicts with it.

The real question remained unanswered. Congress and the president had also read the Constitution, and according to their interpretation (which was also reasonable), Section 13 was compatible with Article III. Where did the Supreme Court get the right to say they were wrong? Why should the Supreme Court's interpretation of the Constitution be preferred to that of Congress and the president?

Marshall, paralleling Hamilton's argument in *Federalist No. 78*, reasoned that the Constitution is law, and that judges—not legislators or executives—interpret law. Therefore, the judges should interpret the Constitution. "If two laws conflict with each other, the courts must decide on the operation of each," he said. Obviously the Constitution is to be preferred to any ordinary act of Congress.

Case dismissed.

Jefferson fumed. For one thing, Marshall had said that a court with the proper jurisdiction could issue a writ of mandamus even against the secretary of state, the president's right-hand man. But there was little Jefferson could do about it, for there was not even a specific court order he could refuse to obey. Thus, in a single stroke Marshall had given the Republicans a lecture for failing to perform their duties and had gone a long way toward acquiring for the Supreme Court the power of judicial review of acts of Congress. And he had done it in a manner that made it difficult for the Republicans to retaliate.

Marbury v. Madison is a masterpiece of judicial strategy. Marshall went out of his way to declare Section 13 unconstitutional. He could have interpreted the section to mean that the Supreme Court could issue writs of mandamus in those cases in which it did have jurisdiction. He could have interpreted Article III to mean that Congress could add to, though not subtract from, the original jurisdiction the Constitution gives to the Supreme Court. He could have dismissed the case for want of jurisdiction without

In 1857 the Supreme court denied Dred Scott his freedom, ruling that slaves were property and protected as such, even on free soil, by the Constitution. This decision declared the Missouri Compromise of 1820, an act of Congress, to be unconstitutional.

discussing Marbury's right to his commission. But none of these would have suited his purpose. Marshall was fearful for the Supreme Court's future, and he felt unless the Court spoke out it would become subordinate to the president and Congress.

Marshall's decision, important as it was, did not by itself establish for the Supreme Court the power to review and declare unconstitutional acts of Congress. *Marbury* v. *Madison* could have meant that the Supreme Court had the right to interpret the scope of *its own* powers under Article III but that Congress and the president had the authority to interpret *their own powers* under Articles I and II, respectively. However, Marshall's decision has not been interpreted by court or country in this way (though it was not until the *Dred Scott* case in 1857 that another act of Congress was declared unconstitutional).[6] Had Marshall not spoken when he did, the Court might not have been able to assume the power of judicial review. The precedent had been created. Here we have a classic example of constitutional development through judicial interpretation. There is no specific authorization in the Constitution for the Court's power to declare congressional enactments null and void, yet today it is a vital part of our constitutional system.

Checks and balances — does it work?

Several important consequences followed from the acceptance of Marshall's argument that the judges are the official interpreters of the meaning of the Constitution. The most important of these is that even a law enacted by the Congress and approved by the president under many circumstances may be challenged by a single person. Through a lawsuit, those who lack the clout to get a bill through the Congress or who cannot influence a federal agency may secure a hearing before the courts. Litigation thus supplements, and at times takes precedence over, legislation as a way to make public policy. What people lose or gain in Congress, they may gain or lose in the courts.[7]

What if a majority of the people should get control of all branches of government and force through radical and impulsive measures? The framers knew that if, over a period of years, the great majority of the voters wanted to take a certain step, nothing could stop them. Nothing, that is, except despotic government, and they did not want that. The men of 1787 reasoned that all they could do — and this was quite a lot — was to prevent, temporarily, full control by the popular majority.

It may seem surprising that the people — or at least the large number of them who were suspicious of the new Constitution — did not object to these "auxiliary precautions," which often are barriers to action by a popular majority. But the Antifederalists were deeply suspicious of officeholders and were even more anxious than the Federalists to see the power of national authorities defined and restrained.

Early Americans (and perhaps their descendants two centuries later) did not look on government as an instrument they could seize with their votes and use for their own purposes; they viewed it as something to be handcuffed, hemmed in, and rendered harmless. The separation of powers and

---

[6]*Dred Scott* v. *Sandford*, 19 Howard 393 (1857).

[7]Stuart A. Scheingold, *The Politics of Rights: Lawyers, Public Policy, and Political Change* (Yale University Press, 1974); Karen Orren, "Standing to Sue: Interest Group Conflict in the Federal Courts," *American Political Science Review* (September 1976), pp. 723–41.

the system of checks and balances were intended to make it difficult for a majority to gain control of the government. Equally important, they were intended to keep those who govern from exceeding their constitutional authority.

The framers, distrustful both of elites and the masses, deliberately built *inefficiency* into our political system. These constitutional limitations on the exercise of governmental power still have profound significance. Almost two hundred years after the ratification of the Constitution, Americans continue to debate whether it is desirable to maintain these limits under the vastly different conditions of the 1970s. Crucial questions remain: Are these checks necessary or sufficient to prevent abuses of political power? Is the greater danger that governments will not do the right things or that they will do the wrong things? Do these limitations work to prevent abuses, or do they make coherent governmental action for the general welfare difficult if not impossible?

CHECKS AND BALANCES:
MODIFICATIONS·

Fragmentation of political power remains basic, but several developments have modified the way the checks and balances that the Founding Fathers so carefully placed in our constitutional system actually work.

1. *Rise of national political parties.* Parties have served to some extent as unifying factors, drawing together the president, senators, representatives, and even judges behind common programs. But the parties, in turn, have been splintered and weakened by the necessity of working through a system of fragmented governmental power.

2. *Changes in electoral methods.* The framers wanted the president to be chosen by wise, independent men free from popular passions and hero worship. Almost from the beginning, however, presidential electors have pledged prior to elections to cast their vote for their party's presidential candidate. And senators, who were originally elected by state legislatures, are today chosen directly by the people.

3. *Establishment of agencies deliberately designed to exercise all three functions—legislative, executive, and judicial.* When the government began to regulate the economy and detailed rules had to be made and judgments rendered on complex matters such as policing the airlines or preventing energy shortages, it was difficult to assign responsibility to an agency without blending the powers to make and apply rules and to decide disputes.

4. *Changes in technology.* Atomic bombs, television, computers, instant communications—these and other alterations in our environment create conditions for the operation of governmental agencies very different from those that existed two centuries ago. In some ways these new technologies have added to the powers of the president, in others they have given additional leverage to organized interests working through Congress, in others they have given greater independence and influence to nongovernmental agencies such as the press. Governmental power remains fragmented, but the system of checks and balances operates differently from the way it did in 1789, when there were no televised congressional investigating committee hearings, no FBI using electronic listening devices, no *New York Times* with a national constituency, no presidential press conferences, no live coverage of presidential visits to foreign nations.

5. *The emergence of the United States as a world power and the existence of recurrent crises.* Today crises and problems anywhere in the world become crises and problems for the United States, and vice versa. The need to deal with perpetual emergency has concentrated power in the hands of the chief executive and his immediate staff.

6. *The office of the president has become a force to impose some measure of national unity.* Drawing on constitutional, political, and emergency powers, the presi-

dency has been able to overcome some of the restraints imposed by the Constitution on the exercise of cohesive governmental power, to the applause of some, to the alarm of others.

A STUDY IN CONTRASTS

Although many Americans are raising questions about the usefulness and functions of our institutions, we tend to take the system of checks and balances for granted. The separating and dispersing of power seem to be the very basis of constitutional government. Like Madison, and especially since Watergate, we view the amassing of power by any one branch of government as the way to tyranny. Yet it is quite possible for a government to be constitutional without such an apparatus. In the British system, the voters elect members of Parliament from districts throughout the nation (much as we elect members of the House of Representatives). The members of the House of Commons have almost complete constitutional power. The leaders of the majority party serve as executive ministers, who collectively form the cabinet, with the prime minister as its head. Any time the executive officers lose support of the majority in the Commons, they must resign or call for new elections. The House of Lords once could check the Commons, but now is almost powerless. There is no high court with the power to declare acts of Parliament unconstitutional. The prime minister cannot veto them (though he may ask the Crown to dissolve Par-

American System of Separation of Powers

House of
Representatives
Two-year term

Senate
Six-year term

Judges
Life term

President
Four-year term

Electors

BALLOT

BALLOT

Voters

liament and call for elections for members of the House of Commons). And, of course, the English take their system as much for granted as we do our own.

The British system is based on *majority rule*—that is, a majority of the voters elect a majority of the legislators, who can put through (virtually without any check) the majority's program as long as the parliamentary majority stays together, at least until the next election. Ours usually depends for action on the agreement of many elements of the society. The British system *concentrates* control and responsibility in the legislature; ours *diffuses* control and responsibility among several organs of government.

We have a written document called the Constitution; Britain does not. Yet both systems are constitutional in the sense that the rulers are subject to regular restraints. Clearly constitutionalism requires something much more basic than the existence of a document: There are military dictatorships whose "constitutions" bear no relation to the exercise of political power. The limits that our written Constitution and the conventions of the unwritten British constitution impose on all those who exercise governmental power rest on underlying values, attitudes, and norms (rules) that exist in both societies. One of the major concerns of political scientists today is to identify the social basis for constitutional democracy. Although

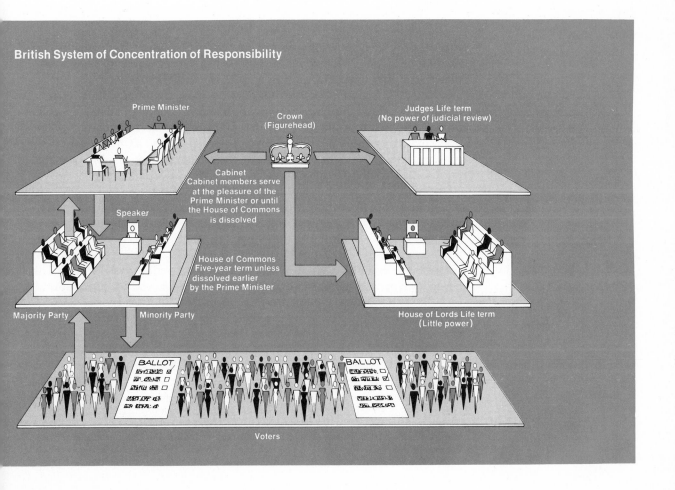

British System of Concentration of Responsibility

Prime Minister

Crown
(Figurehead)

Judges Life term
(No power of judicial review)

Cabinet
Cabinet members serve
at the pleasure of the
Prime Minister or until
the House of Commons
is dissolved

Speaker

House of Commons
Five-year term unless
dissolved earlier
by the Prime Minister

Majority Party

Minority Party

House of Lords Life term
(Little power)

BALLOT

BALLOT

Voters

research in this area is far from conclusive, it seems certain that constitutional government requires more than any one particular set of formal legal rules.[8]

The constitution as instrument of government

As careful as the Founding Fathers were to limit the powers they gave to the national government, the main reason they had assembled in Philadelphia was to create a *strong* national government. They had learned that weak central government incapable of governing, is a danger to liberty. They wished to establish a national government, within the framework of a federal system, and to give it enough authority to meet the needs of all times. They did not try to put down all the rules in black and white. They made their grants of power general, leaving the way open for succeeding generations to fill in the details and organize the structure of government in accordance with experience.

Consequently, our formal, written Constitution is only the skeleton of our system. It is filled in by a number of rules that must be considered part of our constitutional system in its larger sense. Without an understanding of the rules of the "informal" Constitution, we would have an incomplete and even misleading picture of our government, because it is primarily through changes in our *informal* Constitution that our system is kept up to date. These changes are to be found in certain basic statutes and historical practices of Congress, decisions of the Supreme Court, actions of the president, and customs and usages of the nation.

CONGRESSIONAL ELABORATION

Because the framers gave Congress authority over the structural details of the national government, it is not necessary to amend the Constitution every time a change is needed: Congress can act from year to year. Examples of congressional elaboration appear in such legislation as the Judiciary Act of 1789, which laid the foundations of our national judicial system; in the laws establishing the organization and functions of all federal executive officials subordinate to the president; in the development by Congress of the "congressional veto" over presidential and administrative rule making; and in the rules of procedure, internal organization, and practices of Congress itself. (All these will be discussed in later chapters.)

Perhaps one of the most dramatic examples of the role of Congress in constitutional elaboration is provided by its application of its impeachment powers. The constitutional language is sparse: It is primarily up to Congress to give meaning to that language. Article I—the Legislative Article—says that the House of Representatives shall have the sole power of impeachment and the Senate the sole power to try all impeachments. The Senators when sitting for that purpose "shall be on oath or affirmation," with the chief justice of the United States presiding in the event the president is being tried. The article provides that conviction on impeachment charges requires the agreement of two-thirds of the senators present. Judgments shall extend no further than removal from office and disquali-

[8]See Seymour Martin Lipset, *Political Man* (Doubleday, 1959), Chaps. 2, 3; Seymour Martin Lipset, Martin Trow, and James Coleman, *Union Democracy* (Free Press, 1956); Harry Eckstein, *A Theory of Stable Democracy* (Princeton University Center of International Studies, 1961); Charles F. Cnudde and Deane E. Neubauer, eds., *Empirical Democratic Theory* (Markham, 1969); Robert W. Jackman, "On the Relation of Economic Development to Democratic Performance," *American Journal of Political Science* (August 1973), pp. 611ff; Paul H. Conn, "Social Pluralism and Democracy," *American Journal of Political Science* (May 1973), pp. 237ff.

fication to hold any office under the United States, but a person convicted shall also be liable to indictment, trial, judgment, and punishment according to the law. In Article II—the Executive Article—the Constitution provides that the "President, Vice-President, and all civil officers of the United States, shall be removed from Office on Impeachment for, and Conviction of, Treason, Bribery, or other high Crimes and Misdemeanors." The article also excepts cases of impeachment from the president's pardoning power. Article III—the Judicial Article—exempts cases of impeachment from the jury trial requirement.

We have relatively little congressional elaboration to go on with respect to impeachment. As James Bryce wrote in his celebrated *American Commonwealth* (1888), "Impeachment . . . is the heaviest piece of artillery in the congressional arsenal, but because it is so heavy it is unfit for ordinary use. It is like a hundred-ton gun which needs complex machinery to bring it into position, an enormous charge of powder to fire it, and a large mark to aim at."[9]

Prior to 1974, the House of Representatives had investigated for possible impeachment about sixty-five persons, had voted charges against twelve, and the Senate had convicted four (all federal judges). One judge resigned after being impeached and the charges against him were dropped, although resignation does not give immunity from being tried on impeachment charges for acts committed while in office.

By the time of Watergate and the impeachment case against President Nixon, past congressional practices had rejected both the *broadest* view that officers may be removed because of political objections or unpopularity (a view that might have given us a parliamentary type of government) and the *narrowest* construction that the only impeachable offenses are those that involve violations of the criminal laws. Rather, the established position of the Congress is that an impeachable offense, especially for a president elected by a vote of the people for a fixed term, although not necessarily criminal, must relate to improper conduct reflecting serious violation of constitutional responsibilities and a clear dereliction of duty.

Other questions about the impeachment process remain for Congress and the courts to answer. Are persons subject to impeachment also subject to criminal prosecution while they are in office, or must they be removed from office before standing trial? The answer is not likely to be the same for the president, the vice-president, or a federal judge. Judge Otto Kerner was convicted of a criminal offense while holding office as a federal appeals court judge, but this would not necessarily serve as a precedent to be applied to the president. Vice-President Agnew's resignation after deciding not to contest a charge of a criminal offense made it unnecessary to face the question as far as the vice-presidency is concerned. May conduct occurring before occupancy of the office in question be grounds for removal through the impeachment procedures? Again, Vice-President Agnew's resignation made it unnecessary for Congress to face that issue with respect to charges of misconduct stemming from his prior service as governor of Maryland.

If an officer is first tried for a criminal offense, are the House and Senate bound by a finding of guilt or innocence as it applies to impeachment? May the president withhold information the House and Senate

[9]James Bryce, *The American Commonwealth,* 3rd ed. (Macmillan, 1911), Vol. I, p. 212.

believe relevant to the pursuit of their responsibilities under the impeachment clauses? In the *United States* v. *Nixon* (1974) the Supreme Court ignored the question when it ruled that the president's executive privilege did not extend to withholding information needed for a criminal trial.[10] The House Judiciary Committee deliberately chose not to seek judicial enforcement for its subpoenas directed to President Nixon, but it did vote to recommend to the House as one of the articles of impeachment his refusal to supply the committee with requested information. President Nixon's resignation avoided a resolution of this clash between the House Judiciary Committee and the president. But most scholars feel that the president has a constitutional obligation to furnish the House and Senate with the information they request in order to carry out their obligations under the impeachment clauses.

The Nixon affair illustrates the role of congressional elaboration of our constitutional system. It shows that the system is still growing: Congress applied to contemporary conditions the impeachment procedures placed in the Constitution by the framers in the eighteenth century, who in turn were drawing on the experiences of four hundred years of English history.[11]

PRESIDENTIAL REALITIES

The Child Labor Amendment to the Constitution has still not been ratified more than fifty years after its submission. However, the Supreme Court has since changed the construction of the Constitution, and the amendment is no longer needed to outlaw child labor.

Although there has been no change in the formal constitutional powers of the president, the position is dramatically more important and more central today than it was in 1789. Nuclear age realities, for example, force a president to act as the nation's "final arbiter." Political scientist Richard Neustadt puts it this way:

[10]418 U.S. 683 (1974).

[11]Raoul Berger, *Impeachment: The Constitutional Problems* (Harvard University Press, 1973); Irving Brant, *Impeachment: Trial and Errors* (Knopf, 1972).

When it comes to action risking war, technology has modified the Constitution: the President, perforce, becomes the only such man in the system capable of exercising judgment under the extraordinary limits now imposed by secrecy, complexity, and time.[12]

The presidency has also become the pivotal office for regulating the economy and planning for full employment. Plainly, the president has become a key legislator as well as the nation's chief executive.

CUSTOMS AND USAGES

Customs and usages of the nation have rounded out our governmental system. Presidential nominating conventions and other party activities are examples of constitutional usages. Although no specific mention of these practices is in the Constitution, they are fundamental to an understanding of our constitutional system. In fact, it has been primarily through the development of national political parties and the extension of the suffrage within the states that our Constitution has become democratized. A broader electorate began to exercise control over the national government, and the presidential office was made more responsive to the people. In addition, the relationship between Congress and the president was altered, and through the growth of political parties, some of the Constitution's blocks to majority rule were overcome.

JUDICIAL INTERPRETATION

Judicial interpretation of the Constitution, especially by the Supreme Court, has played an important part in the continuous process of modernizing the constitutional system. The words of the Constitution are broad and ambiguous enough to allow many interpretations. As social and economic conditions have changed and new national demands have developed, the Supreme Court's interpretation of the Constitution has changed to reflect them. In the words of Woodrow Wilson, "The Supreme Court is a constitutional convention in continuous session."

Because the Constitution is so flexible and because it allows for easy adaptation to changing times, it does not require frequent formal amendment. The advantages of this flexibility may be appreciated when the national Constitution is compared with the rigid and often overly specific state constitutions. Many state constitutions, more like legal codes than basic charters, are so detailed that the hands of public officials are often tied. To adapt state governments to changing conditions, the constitutions must be amended frequently or replaced every generation or so.

A RIGID OR FLEXIBLE CONSTITUTION?

This picture of a constantly changing system disturbs many people. How, they argue, can you have a constitutional government when the Constitution is constantly being twisted by interpretation and changed by informal methods? This view fails to distinguish between two aspects of the Constitution. As an expression of *basic and timeless personal liberties*, the Constitution does not and should not change. For example, no government can destroy the right to free speech and remain a constitutional government. In this sense the Constitution *is* timeless and unchanging.

But when we consider the Constitution as an *instrument of government* and *a positive grant of power*, we realize that if it does not grow with the nation it serves, it will soon be pushed aside. The framers could not have

[12]Neustadt, *Presidential Power*, p. 280.

conceived of the problems that the government of more than 220 million citizens in an industrial nation would have to face in the 1980s. The general purposes of government remain the same—to establish liberty, promote justice, ensure domestic tranquillity, and provide for the common defense. But the powers of government adequate to accomplish these purposes in 1787 are simply inadequate in the 1980s.

"We the people"—the people of today and tomorrow, not just the people of 1787—ordain and establish the Constitution. "The Constitution," wrote Jefferson, "belongs to the living and not to the dead." So firmly did he believe this that he proposed a new constitution for every generation. But new constitutions have not been necessary, because in a less formal way each generation has taken part in the never-ending process of developing and changing the original Constitution.

Because of its remarkable adaptability, the Constitution has survived democratic and industrial revolutions, the turmoil of civil war, the tensions of major depressions, and the dislocations of world wars. The problem is, then, to preserve the Constitution as a protector of fundamental liberties, as a preserver of the essentials of justice and democracy upon which our system is based, and at the same time to permit government to operate in accordance with the wishes of the people and to adapt itself to new conditions.

Changing the letter of the constitution

The framers knew that future experience would call for changes in the text of the Constitution itself and that some means of formal amendment was necessary. Accordingly, they set up two ways to propose amendments to the Constitution and two ways to ratify them, and they saw to it that amendments could not be made by simple majorities.

PROPOSING AND RATIFYING

The first method of *proposing* amendments—the only one that has been used—is by a two-thirds vote of both houses of Congress. The second method is by a national convention called by Congress on receipt of petitions from the legislatures of two-thirds of the states. During the first hundred years of its existence, Congress received only ten such petitions, but since 1893 over three hundred have been filed.

The second method is full of imponderables. Who determines whether the necessary number of state legislatures have petitioned for a convention? If Congress called a convention, how would delegates be chosen and how many votes would each state have? Could the convention propose amendments on a variety of subjects, perhaps even an entirely new constitution? Who determines the method of ratification, Congress or the convention? Where would the convention assemble? Because we have not had a constitutional convention since the adoption of the present Constitution, we have no precedents. The general assumption is that these are political questions to be answered by Congress, either by a general law covering all such conventions or by Congress at the time it calls for a convention.

At the end of the 1960s, these questions ceased, at least for the moment, to be of only academic interest. Only one short of the required number of state legislatures had petitioned Congress to call a national constitutional convention. The purpose was to propose an amendment that would reverse the impact of Supreme Court rulings requiring both chambers of state legislatures to be apportioned on the basis of population.

Since state legislatures have now been reapportioned to reflect popula-

Pandora Project.

From *The Herblock Gallery*,
Simon and Schuster, 1968.

tion, new proposals for a constitutional convention to deal with this issue seem unlikely. Such a convention could well be called, however, on other topics—for example, abortion, capital punishment, and school busing. And the national concern about the constitutional crisis surrounding the Watergate affair added some political interest to proposals by a few academics for a basic reformation of our constitutional system. But Congress shows no signs of calling a convention. It seems probable that in the future, as in the past, whenever pressures develop for a constitutional change, Congress will propose the amendments to bring it about rather than call a convention to do so. (Perhaps Congress remembers the fate of its predecessor at the hands of the convention it called into being in 1787!)

After an amendment has been proposed, it must be *ratified* by the states. Again, two methods are provided—by approval of the legislatures in three-fourths of the states or by approval of specially called ratifying conventions in three-fourths of the states. Congress determines which method shall be used.

A state may change its mind and ratify an amendment after it has voted against ratification, but the weight of opinion is that once a state has approved a proposed amendment, it cannot change its mind and "unratify." (This question could come to the fore in the ratification battles over the Equal Rights Amendment.) A state must ratify proposed amendments within a reasonable time. Congress determines what a reasonable time is. The modern practice is for Congress to stipulate that an amendment is not to become part of the Constitution unless approved by the necessary number of states within seven years from the date of its submission.

The procedure of submitting amendments to legislatures instead of to ratifying conventions has been criticized, because it permits the Constitution to be changed without any clear expression of the voters' desires. State legislators who do the ratifying may even have been elected before

**Proponents and opponents of
the Equal Rights Amendment.**

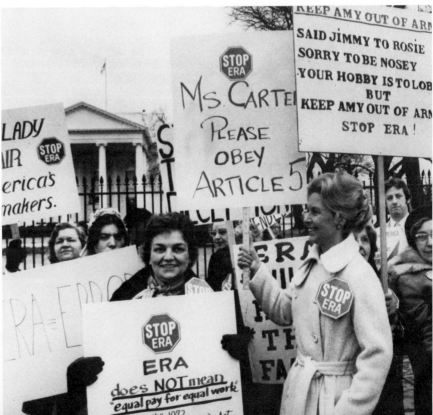

the proposed amendment was submitted to the states. In any event, state legislators are chosen because of their views on schools, taxation, bond issues, and other matters, or because of their personal popularity. They are almost never elected because of their stand on a proposed constitutional amendment.

Despite these objections to ratification by legislatures, the only amendment that has been submitted to ratifying conventions is the Twenty-first (to repeal the Eighteenth, or Prohibition amendment). The "wets" rightly believed that repeal had a better chance of success with conventions than with the rural-dominated state legislatures. This strategy, rather than any desire to submit the question to the electorate, was the important factor.[13]

The major obstacle to the adoption of constitutional amendments has not been ratification but getting Congress to propose amendments in the first place. Although dozens of resolutions proposing amendments are introduced in every session—over 6,000 since 1789—few make any headway. But what Congress proposes is usually ratified. Of thirty-two amendments proposed, twenty-six have been ratified. The proposed Equal Rights Amendment, the possible Twenty-seventh Amendment, is presently before the state legislatures (it must be ratified by March 27, 1979).

The president has no formal authority over constitutional amendments. His veto power does not extend to them, although his political influence in getting amendments through Congress is often crucial. Nor may governors veto approval of amendments by their respective legislatures, because the Constitution vests ratification in the legislatures alone.

The entire amending procedure has been criticized because neither a

---

[13]Philip J. Martin, "Convention Ratification of Federal Constitutional Amendments," *Political Science Quarterly* (March 1967), p. 61.

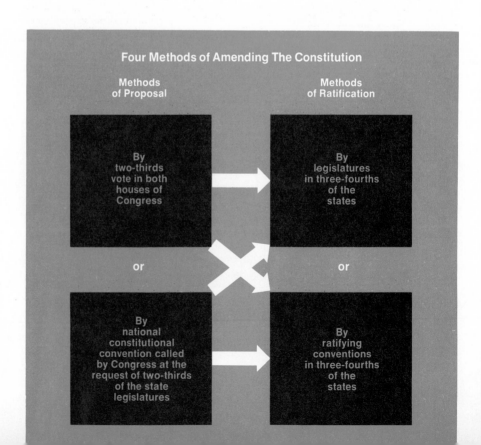

Four Methods of Amending The Constitution

Methods of Proposal

Methods of Ratification

By two-thirds vote in both houses of Congress

By legislatures in three-fourths of the states

or

or

By national constitutional convention called by Congress at the request of two-thirds of the state legislatures

By ratifying conventions in three-fourths of the states

majority of the voters at large nor even a majority of the voters in a majority of the states can formally alter the Constitution. But when a majority of the people are serious in their desire to bring about changes in our constitutional system, their wishes are usually carried out either by formal amendment or by the more subtle methods of interpretation and adaptation.

HOW THE AMENDMENT
PROCESS HAS BEEN USED

If we disregard the Bill of Rights, which for all practical purposes may be considered part of the original document, the Constitution has been amended only sixteen times, and two of these amendments, the Eighteenth and Twenty-first, involving prohibition, in effect cancel each other. The other sixteen amendments may be grouped into the following categories (see also the Constitution in the Appendix):

**Blacks registering to vote
for the first time in Tuskegee,
Alabama, in the early 1960s.**

1. *Those whose chief importance is to add to or subtract from the power of the national government.* The Eleventh Amendment took certain jurisdiction away from the national courts; the Thirteenth abolished slavery and authorized Congress to legislate against it; the Sixteenth made it possible for Congress to levy an income tax; the Eighteenth gave Congress authority to prohibit the manufacture, sale, or transportation of liquor; and the Twenty-first repealed the Eighteenth and gave to the states the authority to regulate liquor sales. Clearly, formal amendments have not been very important in adding to or subtracting from the power of the national government.

2. *Those whose main effect is to limit the power of the state governments.* The Fourteenth and Fifteenth Amendments, which along with the Thirteenth were adopted as a result of the Civil War, have had such a major impact on our political life that they will be dealt with at length in the chapters that follow. The Nineteenth deprived the states (and the national government) of the power to deny any citizen the right to vote because of sex; the Twenty-fourth forbade any state to impose a tax upon the right to vote; the Twenty-sixth denies states the power to interfere with the right of any citizen eighteen years of age or older to vote because of age.

3. *Those whose chief impact has been to add to or subtract from the power of the electorate.* The Seventeenth Amendment took from the state legislatures and gave to the electorate the right to select United States senators; the Twenty-second took from the electorate the right to elect any person to the office of President more than two full terms; the Twenty-third gave to citizens of the District of Columbia the right to vote for president and vice-president.

4. *Those making structural changes in our governmental machinery.* The Twelfth Amendment corrected deficiencies in the operation of the electoral college that were revealed by the development of a two-party national system (see Electoral College); the Twentieth altered the calendar for congressional sessions and shortened the time between the election of presidents and their assumption of office; the Twenty-fifth provided procedures to fill vacancies in the vice-presidency and to determine if presidents are unable to perform their duties because of illness.

Summary

1. Our Constitution both grants powers and limits them. The framers established a government to be operated by ordinary people, since they did not anticipate that Americans would be so special that they could be trusted to operate without checks and balances. The framers were suspicious of people, especially of those having political power, so they separated and distributed the powers of the newly created national government in a variety of ways.

2. At the same time that the framers separated power, they were also concerned that government be strong enough to act to solve public problems. They wanted the government to be responsive to the wishes of the people and to carry out those wishes—that is, the matured and refined wishes of the people. So they gave to the

national government substantial grants of power. But these grants were made with such broad strokes that it has been possible for the national government and the constitutional system to remain flexible and adapt to changing conditions.

3. In this chapter we have briefly looked at the operation of our separation of powers and checks and balances system and at the contrasting English system of concentrated responsibility. We have investigated the origins of judicial review in the great case of *Marbury* v. *Madison.*

4. We have seen how the system of checks and balances has been modified over time. We have described how the Constitution has been adapted to new conditions through congressional elaboration, modern presidential realities, customs and usages, and judicial interpretation. Finally, we have noted the procedures for formally amending the Constitution and how those procedures have been used.

5. The one principal feature of our constitutional system that remains to be examined is *federalism,* one of the most important "auxiliary precautions" against the abuse of power. The United States is not the only or even the oldest federal union, but it was the first successfully to operate a federal system on a continental scale. This has been one of America's major contributions to the science and art of government.

Chapter 3

American Federalism: Constitutional Dynamics

American federalism today is as different from that of two centuries ago as a stagecoach and a spaceship. Since 1787 our federal system has been molded by a dynamic society and altered by the thoughts and actions of millions of men and women. This chapter will explore the nature of American federalism and its constitutional structure.

A **federal system** is one in which a constitution divides governmental powers between the central, or national, government and the constituent governments (called states in the United States), giving substantial functions to each. Neither the central nor the constituent government receives its powers from the other; both derive them from a common source, a constitution. This constitutional distribution of powers cannot be changed by the ordinary process of legislation—for example, by an act of the national legislature or by acts of other constituent governments. Finally, both levels of government operate through their own agents and exercise power directly over individuals. Among the countries that have a federal system of government are the United States, Canada, Switzerland, Mexico, and Australia.[1]

A **unitary**, as opposed to a federal, system of government is one in which a constitution vests all governmental power in the central government. The central government, if it so chooses, may delegate authority to constituent units but what it delegates it may also take away. Britain, France, Israel, and the Philippines are examples of this unitary form of government. In the United States, the relation between states and their local governments, such as counties and cities, is ordinarily of this sort.

Some distinguish a **confederation** from a federation by defining the

[1]"Constitutional Law: Distribution of Powers," *International Encyclopedia of the Social Sciences,* Vol. III (Macmillan, 1968), p. 301. The description of federalism is based on Arthur W. MacMahon, *Administering Federalism in a Democracy* (Oxford University Press, 1972), pp. 3–5.

former as a government in which the constituent governments by constitutional compact create a central government but do not give it power to regulate the conduct of individuals. The central government makes regulations for the constituent governments but it exists and operates only at their direction. The thirteen states under the Articles of Confederation fit this definition.

Unfortunately for our understanding of federalism, the founders of our Constitution used the term *federal* to describe what we now would call a confederate form of government.[2] Today, *federal* is frequently used as a synonym for *national;* that is, people often refer to the government in Washington as "the federal government." In an exact sense, of course, the states *and* the national government make up our federal system.

As a way of distributing power, federalism raises key questions of representation and responsibility. What groups gain, what groups lose under the division of authority between national and state governments? To what extent does federalism advance or harm the welfare of the whole nation? To what extent does the fragmentation of power ("mild chaos") in the federal system prevent the effective solution of problems that cross jurisdictional lines? To what extent does dispersing power among one national, fifty state, and thousands of local governments help to open access to government? To what extent does it tend to support the charge of an actual *concentration* of power behind the appearance of dispersion?

Why federalism?

Why do we have a federal form of government? In part, because in 1787 there was no other practical choice. After confederation had been tried and found wanting, the only choice open to those who wanted a more closely knit union was federation. A unitary system was ruled out, because the leaders knew that most of the people were too deeply attached to the state governments to permit the states to be subordinated to central rule. Union of the states into a single unitary government was impossible short of military conquest by the more populous states.

The factors that led to the creation of our federal system in 1787 and that sustain it in the 1970s should not be confused with the arguments for and against federalism. (We retain federalism largely because our political and electoral structure is sufficiently decentralized to preserve the independence of the states in the face of the strong pressures that incline us to central controls.) But the arguments for federalism, whatever their merits, set the tone for our political debates. In the United States, public debate takes place within the context of *all* groups' insisting that their actions will "strengthen the federal system."

UNITY WITHOUT UNIFORMITY

Even if a unitary state had been possible in 1787, it probably would not have been chosen. Federalism was and still is regarded as the appropriate form of government for the people of the United States. It is thought to be ideally suited to the needs of a relatively heterogeneous people who are spread over a large continent, who are suspicious of concentrated power, and who desire unity but not uniformity.

Federalism embodies the American suspicion of concentrated power, for Americans tend to equate freedom and federalism. We often forget that

[2]Martin Diamond, "What the Framers Meant by Federalism," in Robert A. Goldwin, ed., *A Nation of States* (Rand McNally, 1963), pp. 24–41.

Confederation

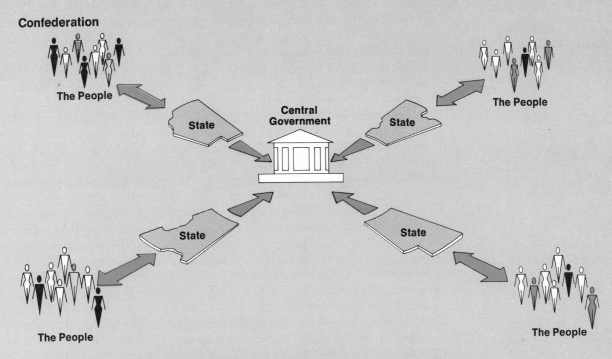

The Confederation was a union of states. The central government received power from the states and had no direct authority over the people.

—and Federation

The Federal Union is a union of people. The national government and state governments receive power from the people and exercise authority directly over them.

in the rest of the world federal forms have not been notably successful in preventing the rise of tyrannies, and that many unitary governments are democratic. The assumption that federalism is a major factor in preserving democracy is questionable, but federalism does lessen "the risk of a monopoly of political power by providing a number of independent points where the party that is nationally in the minority at the time can maintain itself while it formulates and partly demonstrates its policies and capabilities and develops new leadership."[3] Conversely, if, as Madison pointed out in *Federalist No. 10*, "factious leaders . . . kindle a flame within their particular states," national leaders can check the spread of the "conflagration into other states."

This diffusion of power, of course, has its own problems. It makes it difficult for a national majority to carry out a program of action, and it permits a majority in control of a state government to frustrate the consensus as expressed by national agencies of government. Whether this is an advantage or a disadvantage depends on one's political outlook. To the Founding Fathers it was an advantage. Federalism, they hoped, would make such a seizure of power by a national majority less probable, because national majorities could be checked by local majorities. Of course — and this is a point often overlooked — the size of the nation and the many interests within it are the greatest obstacles to the formation of single-interest majority. But if such a majority should be formed, the fact that it would have to work through a federal system would act as a check.

Under a federal system, local issues do not have to come into the national arena, thereby making it easier to develop a consensus on national problems. National politicians and parties do not have to iron out every difference on every issue in every state, because issues that might prove irreconcilable in Congress are disposed of in the state legislatures.

The size of the United States, with its many diverse cultures, makes it difficult to set national rules for local issues. Suppose, for example, that Congress had to establish a single uniform national policy on divorce, gun control, abortion, or dress codes for schools. Or take the issue of the regulation of alcoholic beverages. Many persons consider the moderate use of hard drink as one of the amenities of life and the prohibition of its sale as an infringment on personal liberty. Others are convinced that the unlimited sale of alcohol harms health and morals, causes social problems, and that its sale should be prohibited or closely regulated. Our federal system permits these battles to be fought in the state legislatures. There is no need to enforce a single national standard.

According to both the old and the new conventional wisdoms, federalism encourages experimentation. The old wisdom has it that the states serve as proving grounds. If they fail, new procedures are limited to a few states; if successful, they can be adopted by other states and the national government. Georgia was the first to permit eighteen-year-olds to vote. New York has shown the way in its assault on water pollution; California has pioneered air pollution control programs; New York, Massachusetts, Oregon, and Wisconsin established fair employment practice commissions before Congress got around to doing so. (By executive order, however,

[3]Arthur W. MacMahon, "The Problems of Federalism," *Federalism, Mature and Emergent* (Doubleday, 1955), p. 11.

Federal agents in a 1937 raid on a backwoods distillery in a then "dry" Georgia

Responses to environmental problems, such as water pollution and litter, are often provided by federal-state programs

President Franklin D. Roosevelt created such a commission before any state did.) Many states altered their abortion laws before the Supreme Court acted (whether this is progress or regression, like so many questions of politics, depends upon one's values).[4] Colorado has pioneered "sunset laws" that call for periodic reevaluation of agencies and programs to determine whether they are still needed.

The new wisdom puts more emphasis on the ability of the national government to encourage experimentation and is skeptical of the states' ability to do so. As Judge Wright of the United States Court of Appeals for the District of Columbia asserts, "Mr. Justice Brandeis' [one of the most famous Supreme Court justices, who sat on the Court from 1916 to 1939] wonderful laboratory theory for state government experimentation has been shipwrecked on the contemporary fact of industrial mobility. No state dares impose sweeping new regulations on industry, for their imposition would drive away business concerns whose presence in the state opens up employment opportunities and accounts for vital tax resources."[5] With its greater tax resources, the national government can sponsor research, provide demonstrations, and encourage national distribution of the results. National action gives industry no incentive to move from one state to another to avoid controls

We have to be cautious, however, about the widespread idea that the state and local governments are "closer to the people" than the national government.[6] Closer in what sense? Some people are more involved in local and state politics than with national affairs, but most people identify more often with national officials than with those of their own state. Voter participation in state elections is below that in national elections. Among schoolchildren "the state level is the last about which learning takes place."[7] The public believes that the federal government gives taxpayers more for their tax dollars than do state and local governments.[8] Never-

[4]Ira Sharkansky, *The Maligned States: Policy Accomplishments, Problems and Opportunities* (McGraw-Hill, 1972), p. 13; see also Jack L. Walker, "The Diffusion of Innovations Among the American States," *American Political Science Review* (September 1969), pp. 880–99.

[5]J. Skelly Wright, "The Federal Courts and the Nature and Quality of State Law," in S. I. Shuman, ed., *The Future of Federalism* (Wayne State University Press, 1968), pp. 75–76.

[6]Morton Grodzins, "Centralization and Decentralization in the American Federal System," in Goldwin, *A Nation of States*, pp. 9–15.

[7]Fred I. Greenstein, *Children and Politics* (Yale University Press, 1965), p. 155.

[8]Advisory Commission on Intergovernmental Relations, *Changing Public Attitudes on Governments and Taxes* (July 1976), p. 2.

3–1
The most popular level of government?

From which level of government do you feel you get the most for your money—federal, state, or local? (% U.S. public)

Level	1972	1973	1974	1975	1976
Federal	39%	35%	29%	38%	36%
Local	26	25	28	25	25
State	18	18	24	20	20
Don't know	17	22	19	17	19

SOURCE: Advisory Commission on Intergovernmental Relations, *Changing Public Attitudes on Governments and Taxes* (July 1976), p. 2.

theless, states and their local units remain very much a part of the political life of those involved in public matters. As Jennings and Zeigler conclude, "The states still loom large in the perspectives of the American public. Any attempted juggling of political units involving the states would probably confront a reservoir of mass attachments to the states as political entities."[9] Whatever the merits or demerits of federalism, it is a fact of our political life—and will remain so.

Constitutional structure of American federalism

The formal constitutional framework of our federal system may be stated simply: The national government has only those powers, with one important exception, delegated to it by the Constitution. The states have all the powers not delegated to the central government except those denied to them by the Constitution. But within the scope of its operations, the national government is supreme. Further, some powers are specifically denied to *both* the national and state governments; others are specifically denied *only* to the states; still others are denied *only* to the national government. Here is an outline of the constitutional structure of our federal system.

POWERS OF THE NATIONAL GOVERNMENT

The Constitution, chiefly in the first three articles, delegates legislative, executive, and judicial powers to the national government. In addition to these express powers, the Constitution delegates to Congress those implied powers that may be reasonably inferred from the express powers. The constitutional basis for the implied powers of Congress is the necessary and proper clause (Article I, Section 8), which gives Congress the right "to make all Laws which shall be necessary and proper for carrying into Execution the forgoing powers, and all other powers vested . . .in the Government of the United States."

In the field of foreign affairs, the national government has *inherent* powers that do not depend on specific constitutional grants but grow out of the very existence of a nation-state. The national government has the same authority in dealing with other nations as it would if it were a unitary government. For example, the government of the United States may acquire territory by discovery and occupation even though there is no specific clause in the Constitution allowing such acquisition. Even if the Constitution were silent about foreign affairs—which it is not—the national government would have the right to declare war, make treaties, and appoint and receive ambassadors.[10]

Federal tax dollars are often used to help state and local governments finance elementary school programs

National supremacy   Article VI states: "This Constitution, and the Laws of the United States which shall be made in Pursuance thereof; and all Treaties made . . . under the Authority of the United States, shall be the supreme Law of the Land; and the Judges in every state shall be bound thereby; any Thing in the Constitution or Laws of any State to the Contrary notwithstanding." All officials, state as well as national, are bound by constitutional oath to support the Constitution of the United States. States may not use their reserved powers to frustrate national policies (Local units of government are agents of the states. What states cannot

[9]M. Kent Jennings and Harmon Zeigler, "The Salience of American State Politics," *American Political Science Review* (June 1970), p. 535.

[10]*United States* v. *Curtiss-Wright Export Corporation*, 299 U. S. 304 (1936).

constitutionally do, local units cannot do. In our discussion of the constitutional structure of federalism, local units are included in all references to the states.)

POWERS OF THE STATES

The Constitution reserves to the states all powers not granted to the national government, subject only to the limitations of the Constitution. Powers that are not by provision of the Constitution or by judicial interpretation exclusively given to the national government may be *concurrently* exercised by the states as long as there is no conflict with national law. For example, the states have concurrent powers with the national government to levy taxes and to regulate commerce internal to each state.

These rather simple statements about the concurrent powers of the states and the national government conceal difficult constitutional questions. Take the power to tax: a state may levy a tax on the same item as does the national government—gasoline taxes are an example. But a state cannot by a tax "unduly burden" a function of the national government or interfere with the operation of a national law or abridge the terms of a treaty of the United States. Who decides whether a state tax is an "undue burden" on a national function? Ultimately, the Supreme Court.

Constitutional Distribution of Powers

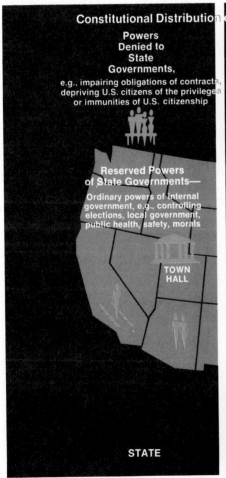

Powers Denied to State Governments, e.g., impairing obligations of contracts, depriving U.S. citizens of the privileges or immunities of U.S. citizenship

Reserved Powers of State Governments— Ordinary powers of internal government, e.g., controlling elections, local government, public health, safety, morals

TOWN HALL

STATE

Powers Denied All Governments, e.g., passing bills of attainder, depriving persons of life without due process

Concurrent Powers, e.g., taxation and spending for general welfare

PAY STATE TAXES HERE   PAY NATIONAL TAXES HERE

ROADS

STATE AND NATIONAL

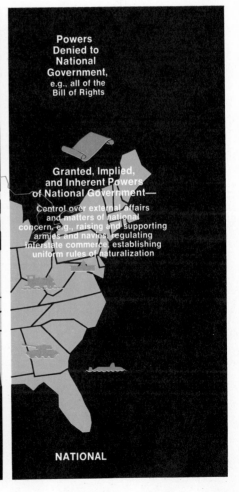

Powers Denied to National Government, e.g., all of the Bill of Rights

Granted, Implied, and Inherent Powers of National Government— Control over external affairs and matters of national concern, e.g., raising and supporting armies and navies, regulating interstate commerce, establishing uniform rules of naturalization

NATIONAL

What about commerce? Here the issues are even more complicated. The Supreme Court has ruled that when Congress has not acted, the states may regulate those local aspects of interstate commerce that do not require uniform national treatment. Who decides? If Congress is silent ultimately the Supreme Court decides. For example, the Court has upheld state laws imposing speed limits on trains within city limits and requiring the elimination of grade crossings, but it has invalidated laws requiring trains to stop at every crossing.[11]

What of state regulations designed to protect consumers from fraud, guard the public health, or collect a fair share of taxes from those who use state facilities? Again, if there is no clear congressional direction, the Supreme Court must decide whether such regulations are within the reserved powers of the state, whether they are overridden by, or come into conflict with, superior federal regulation, whether they unduly burden interstate commerce. For example, the Supreme Court has ruled that states and cities may not impose a curfew on jet takeoffs and landings at airports, but they can impose boarding charges on airline passengers to help defray the costs of airport construction and security (Congress later outlawed such charges).[12] Mississippi could not forbid the A&P to sell milk processed in Louisiana just because Louisiana would not sign an agreement to allow Mississippi milk producers to sell in Louisiana.[13]

In deciding these disputes, the Supreme Court has a difficult responsibility. The grant of power to Congress to regulate commerce among the

[11]*Erb* v. *Morasch*, 177 U.S. 584 (1900); *Erie R. Co.* v. *Public Util. Comrs.*, 254 U.S. 394 (1921); *Seaboard Air Line Ry. Co.* v. *Blackwell*, 244 U.S. 310 (1917); see also *Southern Pacific* v. *Arizona*, 325 U.S. 761 (1945) and cases mentioned therein.

[12]*City of Burbank* v. *Lockheed Air Terminal*, 411 U.S. 624 (1973); *United Airlines* v. *Mahin*, 410 U.S. 623 (1973); *Evansville-Vanderburgh Airport Authority District* v. *Delta Airlines*, 405 U.S. 707 (1972).

[13]*A & P. Tea Co.* v. *Cottrell*, 424 U.S. 366 (1976); *Complete Auto Transit Inc.* v. *Brady*, 430 U.S. 274 (1977).

Interstate highways and multi-state airports illustrate the need for federal coordination of state efforts.

states was designed to protect that commerce from discriminatory treatment and to prevent the creation of trade barriers at each state boundary. On the other hand, the commerce clause was not designed to permit business firms to hide behind it in order to avoid paying their share of taxes or to escape compliance with regulations state legislatures deem necessary to protect public health, welfare, safety, and morals. The Supreme Court remains the most important arbiter of these competing claims.

CONSTITUTIONAL LIMITS
AND OBLIGATIONS

The Constitution imposes certain restraints on the national and state governments. States are prohibited from making treaties with foreign nations, impairing the obligations of contracts, coining money, or (except with the consent of Congress) collecting duties on exports or imports or making compacts with other states.

The national government must not exercise its powers in such a way as to interfere substantially with the ability of the states to perform their responsibilities. For decades, and especially since 1937, it was easier to make this statement than to cite any specific examples of national action that unconstitutionally impaired the ability of the states to carry out their functions. The Supreme Court, relying on the principle of national supremacy, sustained every congressional enactment alleged to have prevented the states from carrying out their duties.

Then in 1976, in *National League of Cities* v. *Usery*, to the surprise of most observers, the Supreme Court held unconstitutional a 1974 amendment to the Fair Labor Standards Act that extended federal minimum wage and maximum hours provisions to all state and local government employees. Congress, said five members of the Court, by these provisions "impermissibly interfere(s) with the integral governmental functions" of state and local governments and has "sought to wield its power in a fashion that would impair the States' 'ability to function effectively within a federal system.' "[14] This decision leaves open many questions: What of federal minimum wage laws as applied to state and local employees engaged in commercial activities? What of federal laws requiring affirmative action to increase employment of blacks, women, native Americans, Latinos, disabled persons, and veterans? It is likely that these regulations, along with thousands of others, are going to survive challenges that they violate the right of a state to do its business without being subject to federal supervision. But the Usery decision does show that there is still life left in the doctrine that the national government must exercise restraint to ensure that its actions do not impair the states' ability to carry out their constitutionally granted powers.

More important than the constitutional limitations designed to preserve federalism are the limitations the Constitution imposes on both national and state governments to protect individual liberties. These restraints are set forth in Article I, Section 9; in the Bill of Rights; and in the Thirteenth, Fourteenth, Fifteenth, Nineteenth, and Twenty-sixth amendments.

The Constitution also requires the national government to guarantee to each state a republican form of government. The framers used the term to distinguish a republic from a monarchy on the one side and from a pure, direct democracy on the other. The enforcement of this guarantee is a congressional responsibility.[15] Congress determines that a state has a republi-

[14.]*National League of Cities* v. *Usery*, 426 U.S. 833 (1976).

[15.]*Pacific States Telephone and Telegraph Co.* v. *Oregon*, 223 U.S. 118 (1912).

can form of government if it permits the congressional representatives of the state to take their seats in Congress.

In addition to guaranteeing each state a republican form of government, the national government is obliged by the Constitution to protect the states against domestic insurrection. Congress has delegated authority to the president to send troops to put down insurrections on the request of the proper state authorities.[16]

HORIZONTAL FEDERALISM: INTERSTATE CONSTITUTIONAL RELATIONS

What obligations does the Constitution impose on the states in their dealings with one another? Three clauses, taken from the articles of Confederation, require the states to give full faith and credit to one another's public acts, records, and judicial proceedings; to extend to one another's citizens the privileges and immunities of their own citizens; and to return persons who are fleeing from justice to sister states.

Full faith and credit The full-faith-and-credit clause is one of the most technical provisions of the Constitution. In general, it requires each state to enforce civil judgments of other states and to accept their public record and acts as valid documents. (It does not require states to enforce the criminal laws of sister states; in most cases for one state to enforce the criminal laws of another would be unconstitutional.) The clause applies especially to noncriminal judicial proceedings. Suppose Smith obtains a $5,000 judgment against Jones from the Pennsylvania courts, but Jones moves to California and refuses to pay. Although California will not automatically enforce the judgment of the Pennsylvania courts, under the full-faith-and-credit clause Smith does not have to convince a California judge or jury that he is entitled to damages from Jones. In appropriate proceedings the California courts will give full faith and credit to the Pennsylvania judgment without inquiries into the merits of the legal dispute.[17]

Some idea of the complexity of the problems growing out of the full-faith-and-credit clause is suggested by the question of how much faith and credit a state must give to a divorce decree granted by another state. Clearly, a divorce granted by a state to two bona fide residents must be given full faith and credit by all the other states, even though they might not themselves have granted the divorce for the grounds alleged. On the other hand, what if Mrs. A, a citizen of North Carolina, goes to Reno, Nevada, in order to avoid the divorce laws of her own state, stays just the six weeks necessary to establish residence in Nevada, obtains a divorce in a proceeding in which Mr. A is not represented, and returns to North Carolina? Must North Carolina give full faith and credit to the divorce? Not necessarily, for the Supreme Court has held that under certain circumstances the courts of other states can rule that the divorce-granting state lacked jurisdiction over the parties. In our example, North Carolina would not be required by the Constitution to recognize Mrs. A's divorce, though in Nevada it would, of course, be unquestioned.

Interstate privileges and immunities States may not deny to citizens of other states the full protection of the laws, the right to engage in peaceful occupations, or access to the courts. States may not tax citizens of other

[16]*Luther* v. *Borden,* 7 How. 1 (1849).

[17]Harold W. Chase, "The Lawyers Need Help with 'the Lawyer's Clause,'" in Gottfried Dietze, ed., *Essays on the American Constitution* (Prentice-Hall, 1964), pp. 104–10.

states at a discriminatory rate or otherwise impose constraints on the use of their property within the states that are not imposed on their own citizens. In short, states must extend to citizens of other states the privileges and immunities they extend to their own citizens.

The interstate privileges and immunities clause of the Constitution does not, however, extend to *political* rights such as voting or serving on juries. Nor does the clause give those from outside the same rights as citizens of a state to attend publicly supported institutions such as schools or to be admitted to state-operated facilities such as hospitals. But the Supreme Court has started to set aside "durational residency" requirements that withhold certain benefits until a person has been a resident of the state for a certain period. These durational residency requirements may impose an unconstitutional burden on the right to travel and violate the equal protection clause of the Fourteenth Amendment.

Before the Supreme Court will sustain a state law that denies to newly arrived residents the same rights given to those who have lived in the state for some time, a state must show a "compelling interest" that requires it to impose the restraint. Thus, a state may not make new residents wait an unreasonable length of time before being eligible for welfare or for voting. A day seems to be about as long as the Supreme Court will tolerate for welfare payments; fifty days for eligibility to vote; and a year for the right to seek a divorce in state courts or to attend a state university.[18]

Extradition   The Constitution asserts that a state shall deliver to proper officials criminals who have fled from another state when requested to do so by the government of the state from which the criminals have fled. Congress has supplemented this constitutional provision for extradition by making the governor of the state to which fugitives have fled the responsible agent for returning them. Despite the use of the word *shall*, the federal courts will not order governors to surrender (extradite) persons wanted in other states. A governor of Michigan, stating that he was horrified at the conditions under which men lived in a prison farm, refused to hand over a fugitive to Arkansas officials. There was nothing that Arkansas could do about it. Normally, however, extradition is handled in a routine fashion. Furthermore, Congress has partially closed this gap by making it a federal crime to flee from one state to another for the purpose of avoiding prosecution for a felony.

Interstate compacts   In addition to these three obligations, the Constitution also requires the states to settle their disputes with one another without the use of force. States may carry their legal arguments to the Supreme Court or may negotiate interstate compacts, which may also be used to establish interstate agencies and to solve joint problems. Before interstate compacts become effective, the approval of Congress is required. After a compact has been signed and approved by Congress, it becomes binding on all signatory states, and its terms are enforceable by the Supreme Court. Not all agreements among states require congressional approval—only those, the Supreme Court held in 1893, "tending to increase the political power of the States, which may encroach upon or interfere with the just supremacy of the United States."[19] In practical terms the Supreme Court

[18]*Sosna* v. *Iowa* and cases cited therein, 419 U.S. 393 (1975).

[19]*Virginia* v. *Tennessee*, 148 U.S. 503 (1893).

meant to exclude from the requirement of congressional approval less formal agreements, for example, an agreement among two or more states to permit students to attend each other's colleges and universities without having to pay out-of-state fees.

This brief outline of the constitutional structure of federalism oversimplifies, and especially as related to the division of powers between the national government and the states, even misleads. For although the basic law setting up the system has not been changed, the ways in which it has come to be applied have.

As recently as the Great Depression of the 1930s, constitutional scholars and Supreme Court justices debated whether Congress had the authority to enact legislation dealing with agriculture, labor, education, housing, and welfare. Only a decade or so ago, there were constitutional questions about the authority of Congress to legislate against racial discrimination. And it remains technically correct to state that Congress lacks any *general* grant of authority to do whatever it thinks necessary and proper in order to promote the general welfare or to preserve domestic tranquillity. But as a result of the rise of a national economy, the growth of national demands on Washington, and the emergence of a world in which war could destroy us in a matter of minutes, our constitutional system has evolved to the point where the national government has authority to deal with any national or international program.

There may be a few subjects — for example, regulation of marriage, divorce, and minimum wages for state employees — about which the Supreme Court might raise objections to national legislation because of the principles of federalism, but it is now fairly accurate to say that Congress has power to do whatever it believes is necessary and proper to promote the general welfare.

Federalism, in short, no longer imposes serious constitutional restraints on the power of Congress, the president, or the federal courts. Today, restraints on national power stem from constitutional provisions that protect the liberties of the people rather than from those relating to the powers of the individual state governments. Still, despite the growth of national authority, states are vital and active governments backed by significant political forces. Federalism as a process remains a vital aspect of our political life.

Triumph of the nationalist interpretation

This summary of the constitutional construction of our federal system jumps over two hundred years of conflict and proclaims victory, at least for the moment, for the nationalist interpretation of that system. (The debate between those who favor national action as against those in favor of state and local levels continues, but it does so generally outside the framework of *constitutional* principles.) This victory for the nationalists is a recent one. Throughout most of our history, there have been powerful groups in favor of a states' rights interpretation.

The constitutional arguments revolving around federalism grew out of specific issues: whether the national government had the authority to outlaw slavery in the territories; whether states had the authority to operate racially segregated schools; whether Congress could regulate labor relations. The debates were frequently phrased in constitutional language and appeals were made to the great principles of federalism, but the struggles were practical ones to determine who was to get what, where, and how, and who was to do what to whom.

Among those who favored the states' rights interpretation were Thomas Jefferson, John C. Calhoun, the Supreme Court from the 1920s to 1937, and more recently Governor George Wallace of Alabama. Their position has been that the Constitution is an intergovernmental treaty among sovereign states which created the central government and gave it carefully limited authority. Because the national government is thus nothing more than an agent of the states, every one of its powers should be narrowly defined. In case of doubt whether the states had given a particular function to the central government or reserved it for themselves, the doubt should be resolved in favor of the states.

The states' righters hold that the national government should not be permitted to exercise its delegated powers in such a way as to interfere with activities reserved to the states. The Tenth Amendment, they claim, makes this clear: "The powers not delegated to the United States by the Constitution, nor prohibited by it to the States, are reserved to the States respectively, or to the people." They insist that the state governments are closer to the people and therefore that they reflect the people's wishes more accurately than the national government. They maintain further that the national government is inherently heavy-handed and bureaucratic and that in order to preserve our federal system and our liberties, the central authority must be kept under control.

The nationalist position, supported by Chief Justice John Marshall, Abraham Lincoln, Theodore Roosevelt, Franklin Roosevelt, and, throughout most of our history, the Supreme Court, rejects the whole concept of the Constitution as an interstate compact. Rather, the Constitution is a *supreme law* established by the people. The national government is an agent of the *people*, not of the states, for it was the people who drew up the Constitution and created the national government. The sovereign people gave the national government sufficient power to accomplish the great objectives listed in the Preamble. They intended that the central government's powers should be liberally defined and that it not be denied authority unless the Constitution so clearly states.

The nationalists contend that the national government is not a foreign entity but a government of all the people and that each state speaks for only some of the people. Of course the Tenth Amendment reserves powers to the states, but as Chief Justice Stone said, "The Tenth Amendment states but a truism that all is retained which has not been surrendered" (*United States* v. *Darby*, 1941).[20] The amendment does not deny the national government the right to exercise to the fullest extent all the powers given to it by the Constitution. The supremacy of the national government does, however, restrict the states, for a government representing part of the people cannot be allowed to interfere with a government representing all of them.

McCULLOCH V. MARYLAND

In 1819, in the famous case of McCulloch v. Maryland the Supreme Court had the first of many chances to choose between these two interpretations of our federal system.[21] Maryland had levied a tax against the Baltimore

[20]312 U.S. 100 (1941).

[21]4 *Wheaton* 316 (1819).

branch of the Bank of the United States, a semi-public agency which had been established in accordance with a law of Congress. McCulloch, the cashier of the bank, refused to pay on the ground that a state could not tax an instrument of the national government. Maryland's attorneys responded that in the first place the national government did not have the power to incorporate a bank, but even if it did, the state had the power to tax it.

Maryland was represented before the Court by some of the country's most distinguished lawyers, including Luther Martin, a delegate to the Constitutional Convention who had left early in the deliberations when it became apparent that a strong national government was in the making. Martin, basing his argument on the states' rights view of federalism, pointed out that the power to incorporate a bank is not one expressly delegated to the national government. He contended that Article I, Section 8, Clause 18, which gives Congress the right to choose whatever means are necessary and proper to carry out its delegated powers, gives Congress only the power to choose those means and to pass those laws absolutely essential to the execution of its expressly granted powers. Because a bank is not absolutely necessary to the exercise of any of its delegated powers, Congress has no authority to establish it.

What about Maryland's right to tax the bank? Martin's position was simply stated: The power to tax is one of the powers reserved to the states, which they may use as they see fit.

The national government was represented by equally distinguished men, chief of whom was Daniel Webster. Webster conceded that the power to create a bank is not one of the express powers of the national government. But the power to pass laws necessary and proper to carry out enumerated powers is expressly delegated to Congress, and this power should be interpreted to mean that Congress has authority to enact any legislation convenient and useful in carrying out delegated national powers. Therefore, Congress may incorporate a bank as an appropriate, convevient, and useful means of exercising the granted powers of collecting taxes, borrowing money, and caring for the property of the United States.

As to Maryland's attempt to tax the bank, Webster contended that though the power to tax is reserved to the states, states cannot use their reserved powers to interfere with the operations of the national government. The Constitution leaves no room for doubt: In case of conflict between the national and state governments, the former is supreme.

In 1819 the Supreme Court was presided over by Chief Justice John Marshall, a nationalist and an advocate of a broad interpretation of the central government's constitutional authority. Speaking for a unanimous Court, Marshall rejected every one of Maryland's contentions. In his usual forceful style, he wrote: "We must never forget that it is a *constitution* we are expounding. . . . [A] constitution intended to endure for ages to come, and consequently, to be adapted to the various crises of human affairs." "The government of the Union," he continued, "is emphatically and truly a government of the people. In form and substance it emanates from them, its powers are granted to them, and are to be exercised directly on them. . . . It can never be to their interest and cannot be presumed to have been their intention, to clog and embarrass its execution, by withholding the most appropriate means." Marshall summarized his views on how the powers of the national government should be broadly interpreted in these now-famous words: "Let the end be legitimate, let it be within the scope of the Constitution, and all means which are appropriate, which are plainly adapted to that end, which are not prohibited, but consist with the letter and spirit of the Constitution, are constitutional.''

Having thus established the doctrine of implied national powers, Marshall set forth the doctrine of national supremacy. No state, he said, can use its reserved taxing powers to tax a national instrument. ''The power to tax involves the power to destroy. . . . If the right of the states to tax the means employed by the general government be conceded, the declaration that the Constitution, and the laws made in pursuance thereof, shall be the supreme law of the land, is empty and unmeaning declamation.''

The long-range significance of *McCulloch* v. *Maryland* in providing support for the developing forces of nationalism can hardly be overstated. The arguments of the states' righters, if accepted, would have strapped the national government in a constitutional straitjacket and denied it powers needed to handle the problems of an expanding nation. In all probability, the Constitution would have been replaced many years ago as succeeding generations were forced, once again, to make the central government adequate to the needs of each new age.

Growth of the national government

The Constitution established a framework in which a national government could develop, but it was some time before a strong national community to support this national government actually existed. The nationalist interpretation of government finally triumphed at Appomattox Courthouse after the Civil War, but from the beginning of our history, events have supported this position. It has made no difference whether the party in power has been Federalist, Jeffersonian, Whig, Republican, or Democratic—the national government's sphere has constantly expanded.

CONSTITUTIONAL BASIS OF GROWTH

How has the expansion occurred? The formal constitutional powers of the national government are essentially the same today as they were in 1789. But the Supreme Court (building on Marshall's work in *McCulloch* v. *Maryland*), the Congress, the president, and the people have taken advantage of the Constitution's flexibility to permit the national government to use the powers needed to fight wars and depressions and to serve the needs of a modern industrial nation. All the central government's constitutional powers have been used to support this expansion of functions, but there are three major constitutional pillars on which the expansion has rested.

The war power   The national government is responsible for protecting the nation from external aggression and, when necessary, for waging war. In a world community that has known total war and that lives under the threat of total destruction, the power to provide for the common defense is of a scope never dreamed of in 1789. No longer does military strength depend solely on troops in the field; it also depends on the ability to mobilize the nation's industry and to apply its scientific knowledge to the tasks of defense. Everything from the physics courses taught in schools to the conservation of natural resources and the maintenance of a prosperous economy affects military strength. The national government has the power to wage war and to do what is necessary and proper to wage it successfully. In these times, this almost means the power to do anything that is not in direct conflict with constitutional guarantees.

The power to regulate interstate and foreign commerce Congressional authority extends to all commerce that affects more than one state and to all those activities, wherever they exist or whatever their nature, whose control is necessary and proper to regulate interstate and foreign commerce. The term *commerce* includes the production, buying, selling, and transporting of goods. The commerce clause packs a tremendous constitutional punch. In these few words the national government has been able to find justification for regulating a wide range of human activity and property. Today there are few aspects of our economy that do not affect commerce in more than one state.

The commerce clause can also be used to sustain legislation that goes beyond commercial matters. When the Supreme Court upheld the 1964 Civil Rights Act forbidding discrimination because of race, religion, or national origin in places of public accommodation, it said, "Congress' action in removing the disruptive effect which it found racial discrimination has on interstate travel is not invalidated because Congress was also legislating against what it considers to be moral wrongs." Discrimination restricts the flow of interstate commerce; interstate commerce was being used to support discrimination; therefore, Congress could legislate against the discrimination. Moreover, the law could be applied even to local places of public accommodation since these local incidents of discrimination have a substantial and harmful impact on interstate commerce. "If it is interstate commerce that feels the pinch, it does not matter how local the operation that applies the squeeze."[22]

Some have accused the Supreme Court of making strained interpretations of the commerce clause in order to justify national regulation. Although Justice Black did not question that Congress could bar racial discrimination under powers stemming from the Fourteenth Amendment, he felt the commerce clause should not be stretched "so far as to give the federal government complete control over every little remote country place of recreation in every nook and cranny of every precinct and county in every one of the fifty states."[23] But Justice Black was alone. Three justices have even gone so far as to contend that it is Congress and not the courts that should determine the extent of congressional power under the commerce clause. "The Constitution," they declared, "contemplates that restraints upon the exercise by Congress of its plenary commerce power lie in the political process and not in the judicial process."[24]

The Supreme Court has simply recognized the obvious integration of our economic and social life. Wheat planted in people's backyards does, as a matter of economic fact, affect the interstate price of wheat. A strike in Pittsburgh or West Virginia does affect commerce in California and New York. Discrimination by innkeepers and restaurant owners does make it difficult to travel in interstate commerce.

The power to tax and spend Congress lacks constitutional authority to pass laws solely on the ground that the laws will promote the general welfare, but it may raise taxes and spend money for this purpose. This dis-

[22]*Heart of Atlanta Motel* v. *United States,* 379 U.S. 241 (1964); see also *Perez* v. *United States,* 402 U.S. 146 (1971).

[23]Dissent in *Daniel* v. *Paul,* 395 U.S. 298 (1969).

[24]Justices Brennan, White, and Marshall, dissenting in *National League of Cities* v. *Usury.*

tinction between legislating and appropriating frequently makes little difference. For example, Congress lacks constitutional power to regulate education or agriculture directly, but it does have the power to appropriate money to support education or to pay farmers subsidies. By attaching conditions to its grants of money, Congress may regulate what it could not constitutionally control by law.

Because Congress puts up the money, it has a strong voice in determining how it shall be spent. By withholding or threatening to withhold funds, the national government can influence state operations or regulate individual conduct. For example, the 1964 Civil Rights Act provides that "No person in the United States shall, on the ground of race, color, or national origin, be excluded from participation in, be denied the benefits of, or be subjected to discrimination under any program or activity receiving Federal financial assistance." (Subsequent legislation extends these restraints on the use of most federal funds to cover discrimination because of sex or physical handicaps).

Until recently, the authority of Congress to appropriate money for whatever purpose it thought would promote the general welfare was almost beyond constitutional challenge.[25] Under a 1923 ruling, taxpayers could not raise the issue in a court of law. Neither could a state government. Then in 1968 the Supreme Court slightly modified the doctrine. It permitted a taxpayer to bring suit against the use of federal funds to buy books for public and private schools, including those operated by a church. Here the challenge was based on a specific constitutional prohibition, that against the establishment of a religion. However, since 1968 the Supreme Court has reaffirmed the more general principle that taxpayers cannot use the courts merely to air "generalized grievances about the conduct of government or the allocation of power in the Federal system."[26] Although taxpayer suits challenging federal appropriations are no longer flatly barred, the courts are not likely to hear them.

In addition to using its appropriating authority for regulatory purposes, Congress may levy taxes that have a regulatory impact. For example, Congress has so heavily taxed white phosphorus matches that it is no longer profitable to manufacture and sell these dangerous items. However, Congress may *not* use its taxing powers to deprive persons of specific rights secured by the Constitution; for example, to levy taxes in such a fashion that it compels persons to testify about criminal conduct. Congress may also use its taxing powers to persuade states to adopt certain kinds of programs. For example, Congress has levied a tax on employers but allows them to deduct from it the state taxes they pay to support state unemployment compensation. Because the employer has to pay this money anyhow, all the states have been persuaded to establish unemployment compensation programs.

These three constitutional powers—the war power, the power over interstate commerce, and the power to tax and spend for the general welfare—have made possible a tremendous expansion of federal functions. If all the laws Congress has passed under these powers were wiped off the

[25]*Frothingham* v. *Mellon*, 262 U.S. 447 (1923); *Massachusetts* v. *Mellon*, 262 U.S. 447 (1923); *Flast* v. *Cohen*, 392 U.S. 83 (1968).

[26]*United States* v. *Richardson*, 418 U.S. 166 (1974).

statute books, the size of the federal government and the scope of its functions would shrink drastically.

Umpiring the federal system

Although today there are few doubts about the national government's constitutional authority to deal with issues affecting the nation, whether civil rights, speed limits on highways, or the kinds of Christmas lights we may display, there are still constant conflicts between those who wish national action and those who believe that certain matters are better left to the states. Judges, and especially those on the Supreme Court, continue to play a vital role as one of the umpires of the federal system, along with Congress and state and local administrations.

THE ROLE OF THE SUPREME COURT

In many instances, judges must decide, when appropriate lawsuits are brought before them, whether state or local regulations will be permitted. Even when Congress acts, often there are questions about whether or not Congress intends to override state regulations. For example, do federal regulations on air and water pollution override or supplement state regulations? There are even still a few occasions on which the Supreme Court has had to face the issue of whether Congress has exceeded its authority and invaded the reserved powers of the state. The Supreme Court declared unconstitutional a provision of the Voting Rights Act of 1970 on the grounds that Congress lacked the authority to set the age requirement for voting for state officials.[27] (The Twenty-sixth Amendment resulted from that decision.) And as we have noted in *National League of Cities* v. *Usery*, the Supreme Court struck down provisions of the Fair Labor Standards Act that extended federal minimum wage and maximum hour provisions to state and local employees on the grounds that they interfered with state sovereignty.

The Supreme Court's role as the principal umpire of the federal system is not merely an exercise in legal interpretation. For as Robert H. Jackson wrote before he became a Supreme Court justice: "This political role of the Court has been obscure to laymen—even to most lawyers. It speaks only through the technical form of the lawsuit, which is not identified with politics in the popularly accepted sense. Yet these lawsuits are the chief instrument of power in our system. Struggles over power that in Europe call for regiments of troops, in America call out battalions of lawyers."[28]

The Supreme Court, itself a branch of the national government, has often been accused of bias. The states, it has been charged, have had to play against the umpire as well as against the national government itself. Over the years the Court's decisions have favored national powers, including its own powers vis-à-vis state courts. Especially in recent years, the Supreme Court has shown less of a tendency to favor local regulations than has Congress.

Those who control the state governments have often criticized the Court for its decisions curtailing their authority. But despite frequent criticism, few would deny the Court the power to review *state* actions. As Justice Holmes once remarked, "I do not think the United States would come to an end if we lost our power to declare an Act of Congress void. I do think the Union would be imperiled if we could not make that declaration as to

[27]*Oregon* v. *Mitchell*, 400 U.S. 112 (1970).

[28]*The Struggle for Judicial Supremacy* (Knopf, 1941), p. xi.

the laws of the several states."[29] Or, as Justice Story wrote many years earlier, a review by the Supreme Court of the constitutional decisions of state courts is necessary to maintain "uniformity of decisions throughout the whole United States, upon all subjects within the purview of the constitution. . . . Judges of equal learning and integrity, in different states might differently interpret a statute, or a treaty of the United States, or even the Constitution itself."[30]

OTHER UMPIRES (AND CONTESTANTS) OF THE FEDERAL SYSTEM

The Supreme Court is not the only umpire of the federal system; Congress has much to say about the distribution of functions and the extent to which federal or state standards will prevail. Through Congress, powerful local and state political interests are heard. Congress adopts laws imposing federal standards or supplementing state programs. After Congress acts, the president and federal administrators take over. They approve the guidelines for enforcing federal laws, decide which projects to approve, and have a considerable role in determining how federal standards shall be applied.

However, we should not be misled into thinking that it is a simple matter for federal authorities to impose their views on state and local communities. On a single issue, the dominant political power is not always on the side of those favoring national standards. A coalition of political forces may secure an act of Congress, but opposing pressures may be applied when it comes to enforcing that act.

The complexities of the political process are well illustrated by the Elementary and Secondary Education Act of 1965, in which Congress provided funds so that state and local school officials could develop special programs for the poor. Federal authorities have had great difficulty in influencing how the funds are used at the state and local levels. In the first place, federal authorities had no particular desire to engage in political battles with their counterparts in local school systems. But it was lack of political muscle that kept federal administrators from having an impact at the local level. They knew that in a crunch, Congress would be "sure to be more responsive to the wishes of state and local school officials than to the desires of bureaucrats in the executive branch."[31]

Umpiring the federal system is a complicated matter. "The feds" have increased their functions and have won many of the innings, but state and local officials are not politically powerless. Merely because Congress adopts a program and turns it over to federal bureaucrats for implementation does not insure that state and local officials — and the people they represent — will quietly conform to federal regulations. They might very well appeal to the courts or to Congress to get the "regs" (regulations) changed. In short, there are many umpires of the federal system and the battles over "who is in charge" take place in many different arenas.

Summary

1. Over the last two hundred years, our federal constitutional system has evolved into something that is only slightly different in form but significantly different in fact from the one we began with. Whether or not we ever had a system in which it was

---

[29]*Collected Legal Papers* (Harcourt, 1920), pp. 295–96.

[30]*Martin* v. *Hunter's Lessee*, 1 *Wheaton* 304 (1816).

[31]Jerome T. Murphy, "Title I of ESEA: The Politics of Implementing Federal Educational Reform," *Harvard Educational Review*, 41 (February 1971), p. 45.

possible to talk about neat divisions between the powers of the national and the state governments, it is certainly no longer accurate to do so today. Today the national government's authority is seldom restrained by constitutional principles flowing from the federal system.

2. To recognize that the national government has the constitutional authority to do whatever Congress thinks may be necessary and proper to do is not the same as saying that federalism is dead. The patterns of American politics are not simple and they make generalizations dangerous. The political tides do not all move in the same direction. Although during the last two centuries constitutional power has moved toward the national center, political power remains dispersed. Our federal system remains very much alive.

3. States remain active and significant political communities. Conflicts between national and state majorities continue to be active on our political agenda as do the issues of centralization versus decentralization. The spirit and rhetoric of federalism are heard in our electoral contests.

4. What has happened is that we no longer spend so much time debating the *law* of federalism. We have now moved to the *politics* of federalism. As now interpreted, the Constitution gives us the option to decide through the political process what we want to do , who is going to pay, and how we are going to get it done.

Chapter 4

American Federalism : Politics and Problems

The state and national governments are not hard, solid objects that collide with sharp impact. They *mesh* with one another, for they are made up of people who govern, and are governed by, other people. To talk of states' rights is a shorthand way of referring to the rights of people who live in states and to the authority of officials elected by them. Texans, not Texas, have rights.

National and state governments are arenas in which differing groups engage in political combat over public policies. Members of Congress and state legislators often respond to the same groups and express the same ideas, and we have "national-state cooperation." At other times, members of Congress and state legislators represent sharply different combinations of interests, and we have "national-state conflict." This conflict between the national and state officials is just one part of the continuing struggle among groups that makes up our political system: "Federalism does not involve a struggle between the nation and the states, but rather a struggle among interests which have favorable access to one of the two levels of government."[1]

The politics of federalism

From the day the colonists first set foot on the soil of the New World, Americans have been arguing about the "proper" division of powers between central and local governments. From time to time various governmental commissions and private study groups have tried to determine the proper balance, but the experts discovered, as did the Founding Fathers in 1787, that there are no objective, scientific standards to distinguish among functions.

[1] L. Harmon Zeigler and G. Wayne Peak, *Interest Groups in American Society*, 2nd ed. (Prentice-Hall, 1972), p. 48.

The questions are political in nature. At one time or another northerners, southerners, businesspeople, farmers, workers, Federalists, Democrats, Whigs, and Republicans have thought it improper to place a particular function in the national government. They have opposed "control by Washington" in the name of maintaining the federal system. But underlying the debates have been such issues as slavery, labor-management relations, government regulation of business, civil rights, and welfare.

With the advent of the New Deal in the 1930s and the growth of organized labor's influence at the national level, most business groups became supporters of states' rights. The national government came to be controlled by those in whom many businesspeople had little confidence and over whom they had less influence. They discovered that state legislatures and state courts were more likely than their national counterparts to make decisions favored by business. Labor leaders found national agencies more responsive to their claims. It is not surprising that while business groups have been quick to defend the states against what they call the "federal octopus," labor leaders have emphasized the need for national action and have charged the states with being dominated by "special interests."

Until recently, those who favor segregation dominated most governments in the South. They feared that national officials, responding to different political majorities, would support integration. Naturally, segregationists sang the virtues of local governments "close to the people"; they were quick to emphasize the dangers of overcentralization and argued that the regulation of civil rights was not a proper function of the national government. This appeal to states' rights in what was an attempt to secure the support of a national majority typifies the political technique of trying to give a political position an ideological wrapping in order to maximize support for it.

The debate continues. Those confident that the decisions made by Congress and federal administrators are more apt to reflect values they approve are likely to be skeptical about revenue-sharing or other procedures that give more leeway to state and local officials. Those who expect to have maximum influence at the state and local level tend to support arrangements that enhance the role of state and local authorities. Today, however, the politics of federalism have become more complicated than in the past: "Perhaps there was a time when it was possible to generalize casually about specific interests being satisfied by different planes of government. . . . Today it is simply no longer true about significant interests."[2] Take, for example, the business interests. By the 1960s, they were no longer so singlemindedly in favor of state as against national action. In 1966 the automobile industry changed its position against federal safety standards when it realized that by doing so it might be able to avoid the stricter regulations being imposed by California and New York, which control some 20 percent of the market.

Even in the area of civil rights, the issue of national versus state action has become more complicated. Although the ability of southern states to obstruct civil rights legislation naturally made most blacks look to Washington for protective legislation, by the time Congress passed open-housing legislation in 1968, "over 115 million Americans, including the over-

Drawing by Stevenson;
© 1958 The New Yorker Magazine, Inc.

[2]Daniel J. Elazar, *American Federalism: A View from the States*, 2nd ed. (Crowell, 1972), p. 213.

whelming majority of blacks living outside of the South, were living under state open-housing laws, some of many years standing."[3]

Conflicts between those favoring national action and those favoring states' rights seldom involve ideologically distinct interest groups lined up against each other. Conservative ideology continues to favor state and local action; liberal ideology tends to be more favorable to national action. But in recent years, these "solid" positions have begun to crumble. Participation by urban groups in school and local community affairs and increasing black control over the inner cities have led some liberals to rethink the values of local action, and some conservatives to appreciate the advantages of national standards. And much of the political talk from *all* political perspectives has become anti-Washington. Richard Nixon proclaimed: "Too many decisions that would better have been made in Seattle or St. Louis have wound up on the President's desk." Senator Robert Kennedy stated: "In the last analysis it should be in the cities and towns and villages where the decisions are made, not in Washington."[4] Radical groups have cried "power to the people." In the 1976 elections, candidates Carter and Ford both attacked the "feds" and proclaimed the virtues of government at the grass roots.

Nor do the political conflicts of federalism necessarily involve all the states on one side and the national government on the other. Different states take different sides on different issues. Plainly, the politics of federalism means something different to people in different parts of the system.[5] Now the Sunbelt states, which produce fuel and food — someone has called them our "OPEC states" — have budgetary surpluses, while the industrialized states of the Northeast and the Midwest find it difficult to support essential services. At the same time, these northern states are more and more disturbed by the fact that generally speaking they get less federal aid. The thinly populated western states have long received more federal help in per capita terms because of the importance of highway construction. As human resource programs have grown, the per capita figure is being somewhat more equalized. Still, the Northeast and the Midwest receive back fewer federal dollars per capita than they pay in federal taxes, whereas the southern states receive more.[6]

The battle is heating up. "We are going to have to fight like they (the South) did when they were poor," declared Senator Jacob Javits of New York.[7] It will be an interesting conflict for President Carter, who owes his election mainly to two regions, the South and the Northeast.

The politics of national growth

In Chapter 3 we discussed the constitutional bases for the expansion of the role of the national government. But why has this expansion of national functions occurred? "Big government" has come about because of deep-

[3]*Ibid.*, p. 212.

[4]Richard P. Nathan, *The Plot That Failed: Nixon and the Administrative Presidency* (Wiley, 1975), pp. 14–15.

[5]Charles D. Tarlton, "Symmetry and Asymmetry as Elements of Federalism: A Theoretical Speculation," *Journal of Politics* (November 1965), p. 861.

[6]*Speical Analysis: Budget of the United States Government, Fiscal Year 1978* (Government Printing Office, 1977), p. 272. "Where the Funds Flow," *The National Journal*, June 26, 1976, p. 882.

[7]*The Wall Street Journal*, January 17, 1977.

**The Interstate Commerce
Commission, shown here in
session, is a federal regulatory
agency having major impact on
intergovernmental relations.**

seated changes in our society and as the result of the pushing and hauling
of conflicting interest groups.

Since 1789 we have grown from a poor, sparsely populated agricultural
society to a rich, densely populated industrial nation. The United States
has grown from a weak, isolated debtor nation to a creditor that plays a
central role in the world community. Such great alterations in any society
would have a powerful impact on its government. People's attitudes toward the national government have changed, too. Whereas the government of the Confederation was viewed in the 1780s as a distant, even foreign government, today most people identify more closely with Washington than they do with their state governments.

The states and local governments have had to expand their functions,
but because many of our problems have become national in scope, great
responsibilities have come to the national government. The national government has gradually taken a larger role in business regulation, law enforcement, consumer protection, education, housing, civil rights, and welfare. Much that was local in 1789, or even in 1860, is now national. A state
could supervise the relations between a small merchant, who bought and
sold his products within the local market, and his few employees. But only
the national government can supervise the relations between a nationally
organized industry that buys and sells its materials all over the world and
its thousands of employees organized into national unions.

With the industrialization of the United States, there came concentration of economic power, first in the form of businesses and later in the
form of labor unions. These units, along with professional organizations,
are private governments exercising political as well as economic power. If
the unit of public government is not as powerful as the unit of private
government it is to supervise, the regulated often regulates the regulator.
The activities of the UAW or AT&T are too far-flung and their power is too
great for the states to provide the needed social control. General Motors
has twice the revenue of California and four times as many employees. Big
business, big agriculture, big labor all must add up to big government.

As industrialization progressed, various powerful interests began to
make demands on the national government. First the business groups
called on the government for aid in the form of tariffs; a national banking

system; a uniform and stable currency; and subsidies to railroads, airlines, and the merchant marine. Once the business groups obtained what they wanted and felt strong enough to take care of themselves, they began generally to oppose aid to other groups. But then farmers learned that the national government could give them more aid than could their states, and they too began to demand help. The farm groups used their power to secure such laws as regulation of the railroads, antitrust legislation, paper currency, parcel post, and finally, government support for farm prices. By the beginning of the present century, urban groups in general, and organized labor in particular, began to press their demands. Workers found that they could not organize unions with a hostile government issuing injunctions and calling out troops. They began to work for restrictions on injunctions and for friendly administrations. With increased industrialization and urbanization, city dwellers, including blacks who have migrated from the South to the northern central cities, began to make claims for federal funds to provide housing, welfare, education, mass transportation, and all the other things they consider necessary to make our big cities habitable.

Many of the problems affecting citizens most directly—housing, race relations, air pollution, energy, economic security—require resources available only to the national government. In the 1930s, states had neither the tax resources nor wide enough area jurisdiction to achieve recovery from the Great Depression; the national government was forced to act. In the 1970s, faced with financial crises in many cities and a few states, and an urgent need to improve life for the millions of Americans living in inner cities, the national government has had to move on a scale far beyond the capacity of individual states.

Faced with the urban crisis, the energy crisis, the pollution crisis, the unemployment crisis, the national government has become heavily involved in areas traditionally left to the states. One of the major ave-

A Pittsburgh family visits Washington to protest the inheritance tax.
In Boston, citizens grab for free fish, after a trawler owner decided to give the fish away rather than sell it for the regulated wholesale price.

nues for action has been grants-in-aid of various types. Let us first look at the general problem of grants-in-aid, and then focus on the national government's involvement with the urban crisis.

Federalism and federal grants

In Buffalo, long lines of job applicants await temporary jobs on emergency crews to clear snow during blizzards of 1977. A federal fund provided revenue to hire the workers, many of whom had become unemployed when local businesses shut down due to the heavy snows.

THE CATEGORICAL-FORMULA GRANT

The federal government can deal with most problems directly through its own agencies, as it does with social security insurance for the aged. But in many areas it has chosen to give the states and local governments dollars, stipulating some of the conditions under which they are to be spent, but leaving the actual responsibility for carrying out the policies to the state and local units. This form of federal action is called *grant-in-aid*, of which there are types varying from detailed, specific-purpose grants that leave state and local authorities very little discretion to general-purpose grants that decentralize decision making. Which type of grant-in-aid will be used depends upon practical political considerations and also on the purposes to be served by the grants. Among these purposes are the following:

1. To supply state and local governments with revenue.
2. To establish minimum national standards, for example in giving aid to the blind.
3. To equalize resources among the states, on the "Robin Hood principle" of taking through federal taxes money from people with high incomes and spending it through grants in states where the poor live.
4. To improve the operations and level of services of state and local governments.
5. To stimulate experimentation and new approaches.
6. To encourage the achievement of social objectives such as nondiscrimination.
7. To attack a major problem but minimize the growth of federal agencies.[8]

There are four general types of grants: the traditional categorical-formula grants, project grants, block grants, and revenue-sharing.

Prior to the Great Depression of the 1930s, Congress provided funds to the states for such clearly national functions as the building of post roads. During the Depression, fourteen programs were added to cover new services such as welfare, employment assistance, public and child health care, public housing, and school lunches. From the end of World War II to the 1960s, more programs were established: for example, airports, hospitals, urban renewal, and library services.

By the beginning of the Kennedy administration there were forty-four federal grant programs. In most instances the national government provided funds to the states by a formula, with so much going to each state. Grants of this kind were conditional: Each state that wanted to participate in a program had to put up some of its own funds to match the federal grant, agree to establish agencies to spend the funds, submit plans for advance approval, permit inspection by national officials of the completed work, and place the employees who administered the grant under a merit system. This was the traditional categorical-formula grant system. Although Congress determines for what purposes states receive federal funds, governors and state legislators have an active role in determining how the programs are carried out. Except for highways and welfare services, federal dollars were not then a sizable proportion of state and local spending.

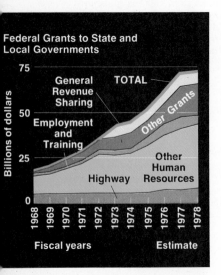

Federal Grants to State and Local Governments

[8]Adapted from Reagan, *The New Federalism*, pp. 66–72.

THE PROJECT GRANT

The 1960s brought an explosion of federal programs. Faced with demands from local communities, especially from big cities, Congress responded with billions to build houses, provide urban transportation, get rid of slums, fight crime, clean up air and water, and provide health insurance for the aged. Rural areas such as Appalachia were also given federal dollars. In the ten-year period of the 1960s, federal grants in dollar terms increased by 189 percent.

Most of the programs launched in these years do not distribute funds to states automatically according to a set formula. Rather, they establish project grants, an approach under which state or local agencies applying for federal assistance prepare applications and submit them to the nearest federal regional office.[9] Eligibility to receive a federal grant in some programs is extended to nongovernmental agencies, including individuals. And for many of the programs, the federal government supplies all the funds. The project grant approach permits Congress and the administration to decide where the money is most needed. They can bypass state governments and place the money directly "on the target."

THE BLOCK GRANT

The great growth of project grants brought major complaints. Governors complained that they did not have much of a voice in how federal funds were being spent within their states. Mayors, although not eager to see governors given greater involvement, pressed for a more coherent and better-funded program of federal assistance.

The Nixon administration and the Advisory Commission on Intergovernmental Relations and many scholars pressed for block grants. A block grant is a broad grant to a state or local general-purpose government in accord with a statutory formula to be used largely at the discretion of elected officials or general administrators for certain prescribed types of activities—for example, crime control.

Action has been slow in moving from or consolidating detailed categorical grants to block grants. Members of Congress, who control federal appropriations, and federal administrators, who administer them, are reluctant to see any changes made in the grant system. In this they have had the powerful support of the groups who benefit from existing arrangements. Consider the battle over libraries: "In 1969, the Administration proposed the consolidation of several narrow library grants. The Congress resisted, and the reason is simple. It can be expressed quantitatively: 99.99% of the public is not interested in library grant reform. Of the .01 percent who are interested, all are librarians and oppose it."[10]

But some progress has been made. Congress has consolidated some categorical grant programs in such areas as public health, manpower training, and vocational education into larger and more comprehensive blocks. An especially notable and controversial step was the Crime Control and Safe Streets Act of 1968, which provides block grants to states and cities to fight crime with relatively few federal strings. Block grants are likely to

"Its too bad you can't get federal matching funds, whatever they are."

Drawing by D. Fradon;
© 1969 The New Yorker Magazine, Inc.

[9]Advisory Commission on Intergovernmental Relations, *Eleventh Annual Report* (U.S. Government Printing Office, 1970), p. 2. See also Jeffrey L. Pressman, *Federal Programs and City Politics* (University of California Press, 1976).

[10]Richard P. Nathan, "Special Revenue Sharing: Simple, Neat, and Correct," unpublished manuscript.

grow. They are a politically acceptable compromise between "hardening of the categories" and the more general revenue sharing.[11]

In view of congressional reluctance to approve block grants and its earlier refusal to approve special revenue-sharing, many were surprised in the fall of 1972 when Congress did approve general revenue-sharing. Undoubtedly it did so because the State and Local Fiscal Assistance Act of 1972, while providing state and local governments with more dollars, by itself did not threaten any existing federal grant program but was an addition to the grant system.

In 1976 the act was renewed and extended to September 30, 1980. The amounts each unit of government receives are now pegged to the level of federal individual income tax collections. The more dollars the federal government receives from individual income taxes, the more money is available for revenue-sharing, although there is a "cap" that no more than $6.85 billion a year will be distributed. Many anticipate that when revenue-sharing is reconsidered by Congress in 1979, it will remove the cap, provided President Carter agrees. Revenue-sharing has meant that states and local governments have been receiving in excess of $6 billion each year from the federal government since 1972. Two-thirds of these dollars are going to 38,000 general-purpose local units of government—cities, counties, townships—and 332 Indian tribes and Alaskan native villages. The other third goes to the states.

States and local governments can use these funds almost any way they wish. The only limits are that none of the funds can be used to support a program that discriminates against any person because of race, color, national origin, sex, age, religion, or physical handicap. None of these federal dollars may be used to support any lobbying activity related to revenue-sharing. Before spending the money, each unit must hold a public hearing to allow citizens to express their views on how the funds should be used. Each unit must publicize these hearings in local newspapers and also inform the public after budgets have been adopted, "a provision that prompted a suggestion to rename the revenue-sharing act the 'State and Local Newspaper Relief Act of 1972.' "[12]

The 1976 amendments also strengthen the provisions designed to prevent revenue-shared dollars from being used in a discriminatory fashion. The secretary of the treasury and the attorney general have been given added powers to ensure compliance with the civil rights provisions. Private individuals now have authority to file civil suits alleging discrimination. Many argued that the money should not be given to state and local governments unless they first adopted certain procedural and structural reforms—for example, modern accounting practices, and consolidation of small units.[13] But the act contains no such conditions.

Like most debates over governmental structure, the arguments about revenue-sharing involve more than considerations of efficiency and economy. There are also basic differences about what is desirable public policy,

[11]Carl Stenberg, letter to authors, December 29, 1976.

[12]R. P. Nathan et al., *Monitoring Revenue Sharing* (The Brookings Institution, 1975), pp. 27–28.

[13]Advisory Commission on Intergovernmental Relations, *14th Annual Report, Striking a Better Balance: Federalism in 1972* (U.S. Government Printing Office, 1973), p. 6.

differing views about where power should be located, differing anticipations of who will gain or lose by the various procedures.

For those who believe in revenue-sharing, the major objective is to decentralize and to reverse the tendency for the "feds" to influence state policy through categorical grants. These supporters "would transfer not simply money, but power."[14] They hope to increase the role of state and local governments and to bring about greater public interest and participation in those governments that are closest to the people. Opponents of revenue-sharing, such as Michael D. Reagan, argue that Congress and federal administrators are more likely to put the money where it is most needed — that is, largely in the cities. He put it very directly: "State governments are structurally inadequate and politically weak even when they are not actually corrupt."[15] Vernon E. Jordan, Jr., executive director of the National Urban League, contends that revenue-sharing hurts blacks and other disadvantaged groups.[16] Proponents contend the record hardly shows that categorical programs are always effective in putting the dollars where the need is greatest: "Under the present project grant system, distributions appear to have been heavily influenced by skillful local administrators, powerful Congressmen, and the desire of federal administrators to spread funds broadly to build a base of political support for their program.[17] These things, rather than the amount of poverty in a city or some objective determination of need, seem to affect how the present system operates. Said another proponent of revenue-sharing: "Today there is simply no justification for thinking that the states and localities, either in principle or in practice, are less able to do the job than the federal government."[18]

Aaron Wildavsky predicts that a consequence of revenue-sharing will be to blur further the responsibility "for not solving our latest set of insoluble problems." He writes:

"All yours, boy."
© 1973 by Herblock in
The Washington Post

> Cities are now beginning to understand that they are getting a little money and a lot of trouble. Increasingly they become the center of demand and lack the capacity to respond. . . . The consequence, of course, need not be all bad: people with demands to make will find it more worthwhile to approach the cities and states because these will have more to give.[19]

Closely related to the debate over whether or not state and local governments can be trusted to spend federal dollars well is the concern over which state and local authorities are to be given the responsibility for deciding how the funds are to be spent. Those for revenue-sharing have promoted the idea that the funds should be given to the elected state and

---

[14]Nathan et al., *Monitoring Revenue Sharing*, p. 10.

[15]Reagan, *The New Federalism*, p. 111.

[16]Vernon E. Jordan, Jr., "Local Control Hurts Blacks," *The Wall Street Journal*, September 19, 1973, p. 13.

[17]Richard P. Nathan and Martha Derthick, "Local Control Helps Everyone," *The Wall Street Journal*, September 10, 1973, p. 12.

[18]Daniel J. Elazar, "The New Federalism: Can the States Be Trusted?" *Public Interest* (Spring 1974), p. 102.

[19]Aaron Wildavsky, "Government and the People," *Commentary*, (August 1973), p. 28.

local officials, especially the governors and the mayors, and the generalists who report to them, rather than to functional specialists such as health administrators, education officials, and welfare agents. For the arguments about the forms of grants involve much more than mere differences between national officials on one side and state and local officials on the other. More often the battles are between elected state and local officials who favor no-strings federal grants to themselves, and on the other side national, state, and local administrative specialists who favor federal grants only to programs controlled by professional specialists like themselves.

Specialists are likely to have more in common with one another, whether they work for the national government or a state or local agency, than with the elected officials of their respective governments. These specialists get together at professional meetings, read common journals, and jointly defend the independence of their programs from the attempts by elected officials to regulate them. They have powerful allies on citizen advisory committees and in other client groups who work to keep their particular programs "out of politics" — that is, not subject to control by governors, mayors, state legislators, or city councils. Their "independence" is well secured if there is a federal grant program providing funds directly to the specialists for spending only in their area.

These alliances among specialists, or "guilds," as Harold Seidman calls them, are a kind of fourth branch of government. It is a branch, Senator Edmund Muskie has charged, that "has no direct electorate, operates from no set perspective, is under no special control, and moves in no particular direction."[20] In contrast with governors and mayors, as Seidman points out, specialists have close contacts with key people in the federal executive departments and on congressional committees. These specialists have political power. They often can block or delay changes which they suspect may give governors and mayors more control over how the specialists spend federal grant money.

How have block grants and revenue-sharing worked? The results so far from the block grant programs have been mixed. Congress has started to recategorize them. It has provided for special programs in the areas of kidney diseases, cancer, and communicable disease control for migrant agricultural workers. The block grant system in public health has not worked, as hoped, to strengthen the role of governors. In many states, authority to administer the state health program was granted to an agency removed from the direct administrative supervision of the governor. The 1968 Safe Streets Act block grant has also been criticized. Congressional critics have accused the Law Enforcement Assistance Administration (LEAA), the federal agency created within the Department of Justice to administer the grant, of failing to monitor properly state programs. State officials have criticized LEAA for requiring elaborate reports, and for intruding into areas that are supposed to be left to the discretion of state officials. And various groups — those working to secure more help for juvenile programs, those wanting more dollars for the courts — have sought to amend the act to protect their special concerns.[21]

[20]Senate Committee on Government Operations, Subcommittee on Intergovernmental Relations, *The Federal System as Seen by State and Local Officials* (U.S. Government Printing Office, 1963), p. 2.

[21]Advisory Commission on Intergovernmental Relations, *The Block Grant: A Comparative Analysis* (1977), p. 41. See also the Advisory Commission's *Perspective*, "The Safe Street Act:

What of the impact of revenue-sharing? Many agencies have been monitoring it. What have they found? "It is a little like the elephant described by the blind man; it's a wholly different beast depending on where you grab hold of it."[22] Big-city mayors say that urban areas cannot survive without it. They like revenue-sharing "or whatever else the federal government is calling money this year."[23] Rural officials call it "the best thing since the milking machine."[24] Others have criticized the lack of attention to compliance with the nondiscriminatory features of the act and to the generally low level of citizen participation in determining how the funds are to be used.[25] For these reasons, the 1976 amendments strengthened the nondiscrimination, public participation, and reporting requirements.

Once enacted, revenue-sharing, like other federal aid programs, generates public support for its retention. Chairman George P. Mahon of the House Appropriations Committee said at the hearings of the 1975 budget, "We will stop the tides of the Passmoquoddy before we ever stop revenue-sharing."[26] It has become a permanent feature of our federal system.

It would be misleading to give too much emphasis to the *form* of federal financing of state and local programs. Those who look to revenue-sharing to solve all the problems of state and local governments and of better programming are likely to be disappointed. So will those who fear it will wreck the federally managed welfare state. The form of federal funding is simply not that important; organizational behavior, political climate, and bargaining among groups and political units are more likely to determine policy.[27]

ADMINISTRATION OF
FEDERAL GRANT PROGRAMS

Today state and local governments receive from the national government about a fourth of the money they spend. The national government is turning back to state and local communities about one in every six dollars it collects. Of the 72 billion federal dollars given to states and localities, 54 percent is being distributed through formula or project categorical grants, 35 percent in block grants, and 11 percent by revenue sharing. Twenty-one national departments and agencies administer over 600 separate grant programs for the benefit of 50 states and 78,000 local units of government. There are so many federal grant programs that some local governments

Seven Years Later" (Winter 1976). For an analysis of the passage and the controversy surrounding this 1968 act, see Thomas E. Cronin, "The War on Crime and Unsafe Streets, 1960–1976: Policy Making for a Just and Safe Society," in Allan P. Sindler, ed., *America in the Seventies* (Little, Brown, 1977), pp. 207–60.

[22]"Revenue Sharing: Report from the Grass Roots," *Carnegie Quarterly* (Winter 1976), p. 1.

[23]Calvin Trilling quoted by Richard P. Nathan, Advisory Commission on Intergovernmental Relations, *Block Grants: A Roundtable Discussion*, 1976), p. 20.

[24]*Ibid.*

[25]The National Project on Revenue-Sharing, The Center for National Policy Review, the Catholic University; Southern Government Monitoring Projects, Southern Regional Council, Inc.; Nathan et al., *Monitoring Revenue-Sharing*; Sarah Liebschutz, "General Revenue-Sharing as a Political Resource for Local Officials," in Charles O. Jones and Robert D. Thomas, eds., *Public Policy Making in a Federal System* (Russell Sage, 1976), p. 123.

[26]Quoted by Richard P. Nathan, "Methodology for Monitoring Revenue-Sharing," in Jones and Thomas, *Public Policy Making in a Federal System*, p. 77.

[27]Jerome T. Murphy, "Title V of ESEA: The Impact of Discretionary Funds on State Educational Bureaucracies," *Harvard Educational Review*, 43 (August 1973), 384–85.

have special personnel just to keep track of them. In fact, many governments do not even know the extent of the federal aid they receive.[28]

Every one of the last five presidents has created new machinery to deal with intergovernmental relations and to make the administration of grant programs more sensible. The responsibility for the function has shifted back and forth from the vice-president to other places in the executive office of the president. Terrence R. Duvernary, chief administrative officer of New Orleans, said: "Countless intergovernmental mechanisms are in place now. Nixon's executive orders were logically constructed. It was not the logic that failed but the commitment to make the system work." Perhaps under President Carter the commitment will be there. After all, Carter, the first governor to become president since Franklin D. Roosevelt, has said, "I will not preside over an administration which ignores the lessons of my own personal experiences."[29] On the other hand, people do change as they change responsibilities—or as someone once put it, "Where you stand depends on where you sit."

[28]*The National Journal*, January 29, 1977, p. 180.

[29]*The National Journal*, January 22, 1977, pp. 137 and 141; see also Advisory Commission on Intergovernmental Relations, *Improving Federal Grants Management* (1977).

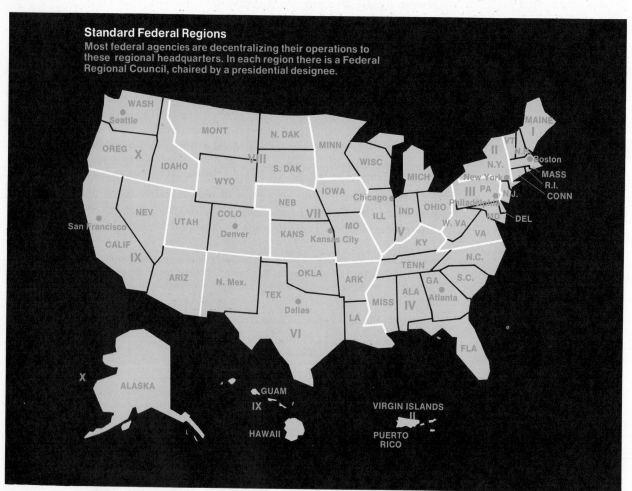

Standard Federal Regions
Most federal agencies are decentralizing their operations to these regional headquarters. In each region there is a Federal Regional Council, chaired by a presidential designee.

Federal grant programs: some questions

President Carter meets with Maynard Jackson, Mayor of Atlanta. Many urban problems require resources available only through the national government.

Is the flow of influence from the national government to state and local governments or vice versa? Murphy, for example, found that the fear of federal dominance of state educational programs has been caused by a misperception of power relationships in education: "If anything, research suggests that the states' problem is not federal control, but rather local autonomy."[30] Does the fact that states and local governments can get federal funds make them more or less responsive to particular constituents? Does the amount and kind of federal funding available alter the kinds of constituents to which state and local units will respond?

Does the federal grant system help to maintain and reinforce *regional pluralism* by enabling local majorities who control state and local governments to pursue their goals independently of the wishes of the national majorities? Or does it work the other way—that is, are federal grants used by the national majorities to bring state and local governments, and the groups to which they respond, under the control of national majorities? Certainly federal funds have been important in forcing states and cities and local school districts to adopt desegregation programs, in compelling universities and other federal contracting agencies to take affirmative action to hire and upgrade employment opportunities for women, blacks, and other victims of discrimination. On the other hand, the larger the number of dollars and the fewer the federal strings, the more local political processes determine how the funds will be used.

The choice, however, is not between giving the power to federal bureaucrats or to "the people." The "feds" are responsive to certain pressures, the local authorities to other pressures. Whatever the procedures for citizen participation, whether at national or local level, 90 percent of the input is likely to come from 1 percent of "the people." For example, in the distribution of Title XX social service block grant funds, the bulk of the money went to day care in the beginning. But as the grant began to be administered, the aged and the handicapped started to organize for a bigger share. What kind of politics, then, do we want? What mixes among national, state, and local political arenas are best for the maintenance of our democratic system? These questions and those raised above are not to be answered merely by analysis of evidence of what has happened and is likely to happen. They involve choices as to the kind of society we want and the kinds of procedures that are most likely to produce it.

Federalism and the urban crisis

Federal officials have dealt directly with city and county officials since the early nineteenth century. But not really until the urban crisis of the sixties and seventies did federal-city relations become significant in terms of either dollars or politics. As the urban crisis came to the forefront of domestic politics, the president and the Congress became increasingly responsive to urban values and demands. Today there are at least seventy programs that send some $12 billion—some of which go directly to local units, some of which are passed through the states—to the cities.

Many of the newer federal programs bypass the state governments. Because of the belief that "the poor and the black—especially the latter—would never get a fair shake from State governments, especially in the

[30]Murphy, "Title V of ESEA: The Impact of Discretionary Funds on State Educational Bureaucracies," p. 367.

South,"[31] some were framed to minimize state participation. Some have even attempted to circumvent City Hall and deal directly with agencies created to represent the poor:

> The expansion of direct federalism has given local governments unmistakable status as a third component of the system. The national government has become champion of the cities in attacking the tough urban problems produced by density and poverty. The states remain vital partners in the system, but their future is in question.[32]

Governors and state legislators, of course, do not like to see federal funds go directly to city officials. City officials favor such assistance — provided they have control over it. When Congress authorized federal grants to community action groups outside the structure of local governments in order to involve poor people in the administration of antipoverty programs, city officials complained loudly about being bypassed. Congress responded by returning antipoverty programs to local authorities.

Many large cities — actually city-states in many respects — have more influence within the circles of the national government than they do in their own state legislatures, which are dominated by rural and suburban representatives: "Today, for help in urban problems, committees of mayors are far more likely to journey to Washington than to their own state capitals."[33] The late Mayor Richard Daley of Chicago told a congressional committee, "I think a city the size of Chicago should be able to go directly to its Federal Government with its programs, because we find in many instances the greater responsiveness and greater understanding."[34] And former mayor Carl Stokes of Cleveland stated simply, "Why run to the federal government? Because that's where the money is."[35]

The Advisory Commission on Intergovernmental Relations, a federal agency in which state officials are involved, warned a few years ago: "The States are on verge of losing control over the metropolitan problem: if they lose this control they lose the major responsibility for domestic government in the United States and in turn surrender a vital role in the American Federal System."[36] The prediction that the states are doomed is not new. In 1933, Luther Gulick, seeing state governments helpless before the onslaught of the Great Depression, stated: "I do not predict that the States will go, but affirm that they have gone."[37] Thirty years later, Senator Ever-

---

[31]Advisory Commission on Intergovernmental Relations, *Metropolitan America: Challenge to Federalism* (U.S.Government Printing Office, 1966), p. 3.

[32]John M. DeGrove, "Help or Hindrance to State Action? The National Government," in Alan K. Campbell, ed., *The States and the Urban Crisis* (Prentice-Hall, 1970), p. 151.

[33]Address by the President at the 1957 Governors' Conference, *Report of the Joint Federal–State Action Committee* (U.S. Government Printing Office, 1957), p. 20.

[34]*Hearings on Federal–State–Local Relations before a Subcommittee of the House Committee on Government Operations*, 85th Cong., 1st Sess., 1957, p. 391.

[35]*Chicago Tribune*, March 4, 1968. See also his autobiography, *The Promises of Power* (Simon and Schuster, 1973).

[36]*Eighth Annual Report of the Advisory Commission on Intergovernmental Relations* (U.S. Government Printing Office, 1967), p. 9.

[37]"Reorganization of the States," *Civil Engineering* (August 1933), p. 421; quoted by Terry Sanford in *Storm over the States* (McGraw-Hill, 1967), p. 21.

ett Dirksen intoned that before too long, "The only people interested in state boundaries will be Rand-McNally."[38]

In many states reapportionment, which has been expected to increase the voice of the big cities, led instead to an alliance of the suburbs, rural areas, and small towns against those who live in the inner cities. As former mayor Stokes of Cleveland complained: "One man–one vote hasn't changed a thing so far as the central city is concerned. Instead of the farmer with his conservatism and detachment, you now have the man from suburbia, who is as conservative and detached, and sometimes as hostile to the city, as the rural member."[39] Suspicion and conflict are characteristic of the relations between many governors and the mayors of big cities.

The hard political realities are beginning to force a more active state role in the handling of urban problems. Pollution, crime, poverty, lack of jobs, and other "urban" problems are being felt in the suburbs too. Governors and state legislators are becoming more deeply immersed in these issues. More than half of the states, including all those with large cities, now have special agencies to deal with urban problems. States are increasing fiscal aid to cities. True, state aid continues to be concentrated in the traditional Big Four—education, highways, welfare, and health-hospitals—but the ten large industrial states (California, Connecticut, Illinois, Maryland, Michigan, New Jersey, New York, Ohio, Pennsylvania, and Wisconsin) provided substantial fiscal help for municipal-type programs (about 20 percent of the state help originates in the federal treasury).[40] New York state alone accounts for much of the fiscal help to its cities, something in a sense forced on it by New York City's financial emergency in 1975. It took the combined help of the state and the federal governments to head off bankruptcy by the city. This in turn has led to substantially greater state and federal control over the city's internal affairs.

The cities themselves are discovering that federal dollars alone are not sufficient. They also need help from their own statehouses. The nearly 280 metropolitan areas in the United States are governed on the average by ninety-one different governments, some by as many as a thousand. With authority so scattered among the central city and its suburbs and special-purpose districts, they must look to the states to reorganize their governmental systems.

Although Americans have strong attachments to their states, their concerns are with more immediate problems—clean air, equal rights, jobs, safety in the streets. They are willing to use whatever agencies or combinations of agencies they feel can best serve their needs and represent their interests. Federal-state-local relations, now as always, are undergoing change. As Tocqueville noticed nearly a hundred and fifty years ago, "I have never been more struck by the good sense and the practical judgment of the Americans than in the manner in which they elude the numberless difficulties resulting from the Federal Constitution."[41]

New York City Mayor Abraham Beame discusses the city's financial problems with Senator William Proxmire, chairperson of the Senate Banking Committee. In 1975, combined aid from state and federal government bailed the city out of bankruptcy.

[38]*The New York Times*, August 8, 1965, section IV, p. 2; quoted by Sanford, p. 37.

[39]Quoted by A. James Reichley, "The Political Containment of the Cities," in Campbell, *The States and the Urban Crisis*, p. 173.

[40]Advisory Commission on Intergovernmental Relations, *State Actions in 1976* (1976); see also *The States and Intergovernmental Aids* (1976).

[41]*Democracy in America*, Vol. I, ed. Phillips Bradley (Knopf, 1944), p. 167.

Summary

1. Ideological bias in favor of either national or state action is likely to reflect concrete political objectives, although in recent years the stand of conservatives in favor of states' rights and of liberals in favor of national action is no longer predictable. Shifting political issues have led in the past and continue today to lead to shifting allegiances among the various levels of government.

2. The politics of federalism are more complicated than conflicts between national government on the one side and all the states on the other, and in recent years conflicts among various regions of the nation over the distribution of federal dollars have begun to heat up.

3. The drift toward increasing federal action has been fueled more by underlying economic and social changes than by concerns about federalism in the abstract, but again we detect a vigorous trend toward the view that federalism as a political principle is worthy of being preserved.

4. The major instrument of federal intervention in recent decades has been the various kinds of grants-in-aid, of which the most prominent are categorical grants, project grants, block grants, and revenue-sharing.

5. Direct federal support to cities has become an important feature of our political scene, reflecting the acute problems of our urban areas. The state governments, especially of the more industrialized states, are also providing additional fiscal resources to the cities.

Part Two

Civil Liberties

A Problem Guide

HOW can we maintain the proper balance between liberty and order, between diversity and uniformity, between individual rights and collective needs? This is the main problem taken up in Part Two. To many Americans the safeguarding and broadening of individual freedom—of civil liberties and civil rights—is the most important task of a democratic society. These are the historic rights of the Western tradition—freedom of religion, freedom of speech, freedom of assembly, freedom of the press, equality under the law.

When we think of protecting the freedoms of the individual, we usually think of protecting them *against* government. But in a democracy the protection of the rights of the individual against the government is only part of the problem (though probably the major part). A person's freedom from governmental oppression is of little use, after all, except in a peaceful, orderly society. Hence citizens seek to achieve both peace and order, both liberty and equality, through government.

The problem, then, is how to balance individual rights against collective needs, remembering always that individual freedom and social order are necessary to each other. Chapter 5 describes how Americans have tried to achieve this balance in several important areas—freedom of religion and of speech and of the press, for example. Which goals—individual liberties or collective needs—should be the main goals if they come into conflict with each other? When and under what conditions should one or the other receive priority? Who should decide—judges, legislators, or someone else?

We have been talking about individual liberties, such as freedom of speech; there is also the matter of civil rights, such as the right to equal opportunity in education, jobs, housing, and the right to vote. Chapter 6 takes up the constitutional guarantees and political battles behind the idea that no person should suffer because of race, religion, national origin, or sex. In Chapter 7 we describe a different but equally important type of right—the right not to be arbitrarily deprived of life, liberty, and property. Both sets of rights—civil rights and procedural rights—pose the problem of the balance of individual rights against collective needs. Individual freedom may be threatened directly by other individuals as well as by government.

A person trying to speak from a soapbox may be knocked down by a mob and arrested by a police officer. Or the officer may protect him from the mob—a case of government guarding the liberty of one individual against other individuals. It is always advisable, when considering a problem of individual freedom, to ask the question *whose* civil liberties are to be protected, against *what*, by *whom*, and *how*?

Chapter 7 also deals with the rights of immigrants, aliens, and citizens. The Constitution does not guarantee the right of admission to the United States; aliens do not enjoy all the privileges of American citizens. But important issues of liberty are involved in our treatment of noncitizens.

Chapter 5

First Amendment Freedoms

"Congress shall make no law," declares the First Amendment, "respecting an establishment of religion, or prohibiting the free exercise thereof; or abridging the freedom of speech, or of the press; or the right of the people peaceably to assemble, and to petition the Government for a redress of grievances." Here are the fundamental supports of a free society—freedom of *conscience* and freedom of *expression*.

Although the framers drafted the Constitution, in a sense it was the people who drafted our basic charter of liberties. The Constitution drawn up at Philadelphia included no specific guarantee of the basic freedoms. The omission aroused suspicion and distrust among the people at large. In order to win ratification, the Federalists promised to correct this oversight. In the very first session of the new Congress they lived up to their promise. Congress proposed amendments that were ratified by the end of 1791 and became part of the Constitution. These ten amendments are known as the Bill of Rights.

Note that the Bill of Rights is addressed to the *national* government. As John Marshall held in *Barron* v. *Baltimore* (1833), the Bill of Rights limits the national but not the state governments.[1] Why not the states? In the 1790s the people were confident they could control their own state officials, and most of the state constitutions already had bills of rights. It was the new and distant central government that the people feared.

But as it turned out, those popular fears were largely misplaced. The national government, responsive to tens of millions of voters from a variety of races, creeds, religions, and economic groups, has shown less tendency to curtail civil liberties than have state and local governments. It was not long after the Bill of Rights was adopted that some people began to recog-

81   [1]7 Peters 243 (1833).

nize the mistake of exempting state governments from the prohibitions of the national Bill of Rights. Each state constitution also includes a bill of rights, but for the most part state judges have not been inclined to apply these bills of rights vigorously to protect civil liberties.

With the adoption of the Fourteenth Amendment in 1868, which *does* apply to the states, persons arguing before the Supreme Court tried to persuade the justices to interpret the due-process clause of this amendment to mean that the states are limited in the same way that the Bill of Rights limits the national government. They contended that freedom of speech at least should be understood to be included in the Fourteenth Amendment. For decades the Supreme Court refused to interpret the Fourteenth Amendment in this way. Then in 1925, in *Gitlow* v. *New York*, the Court announced: "For present purposes we may and do assume that freedom of speech and of press — which are protected by the 1st Amendment from abridgment by Congress — are among the fundamental personal rights and liberties protected by the due process clause of the 14th Amendment from impairment by the states."[2] *Gitlow* v. *New York* was a decision of major significance. Since that date, beginning in the 1940s and at a rapid rate in the 1960s, the Supreme Court has brought within the protection of the Fourteenth Amendment almost every applicable provision of the Bill of Rights.

Today virtually all Americans agree that governmental power should not be used to interfere with the freedoms of speech and conscience. Yet the country seems to be almost constantly involved in quarrels about specific applications of these restraints. It is all very well to respect our liberties in general. The trouble starts when we move from generalities to *specifics*. "All declare for liberty," wrote Justice Reed," and proceed to disagree among themselves as to its true meaning."[3] In few areas are the problems more difficult to resolve and the differences more intense than in that of religious freedoms.

A wall of separation

The very first words of the First Amendment are emphatic: "Congress shall make no law respecting an establishment of religion." The Fourteenth Amendment has been interpreted to impose the same restrictions on state and local governments.

Some have argued that this Establishment Clause does not forbid governmental support for religion but simply prohibits *favoritism* toward a particular religion. But the Supreme Court has consistently rejected this construction of the law. As Justice Powell said for the Court, "It is now firmly established that a law may be one 'respecting the establishment of religion' even though its consequence is not to be promote a 'state religion,' and even though it does not aid one religion more than another but merely benefits all religions alike." On the other hand, "It is equally well established . . . that not every law that confers an 'indirect,' 'remote,' or 'incidental' benefit upon religious institutions is, for that reason alone, constitutionally invalid."[4]

[2]*Gitlow* v. *New York* 268 U.S. 652 (1925).

[3]*Breard* v. *Alexandria*, 341 U.S. 622 (1951).

[4]*Committee for Public Education and Religious Liberty* v. *Nyquist*, 413 U.S. 756 (1973).

Sometimes the line between the permissible and the forbidden governmental involvement with religion can only be "dimly perceived." Jefferson's "wall of separation between church and state" has become "as winding as the famous serpentine wall" he designed for the University of Virginia.[5] The Supreme Court has put forward a three-part test to determine whether a statute violates the Establishment Clause: first, it must reflect a clear secular legislative purpose; second, its primary effect must neither advance nor inhibit religion; third, it must avoid "excessive government entanglement with religion." In other words, the Establishment Clause is designed to prevent three main evils: "sponsorship, financial support, and active involvement of the sovereign in religious activity."[6]

Because of the Establishment Clause, states may not introduce nondenominational devotional exercise into the public school curriculum or the devotional reading of the Bible or the recitation of the Lord's Prayer.[7] A state may not, as Arkansas tried to do, prohibit the teaching of evolution or the use of books discussing the Darwinian theory.[8] School authorities may not permit religious instructors to come into the public school buildings during the school day to provide religious instruction, even on a voluntary basis.[9] On the other hand, the Constitution does not prevent the study of the Bible or religion in public schools when presented as part of a *secular* program of education.

The Supreme Court has also approved Sunday closing laws. The Court majority conceded that these laws originally had a religious purpose and effect, but it reasoned that they have now taken on a secular purpose and effect of providing a day of rest, recreation, and family togetherness.[10] Tax exemption for church property, along with that for other kinds of nonprofit institutions, has also survived constitutional challenge.[11]

One of the more troublesome areas involves attempts by states to provide financial assistance to parochial schools.[12] During the last decade the Supreme Court has tried to draw a line between permissible public aid to *students* in sectarian schools and impermissible public aid to *religion*. Using this child-benefit justification and its three-part test, the Court has held that tax funds may be used to reimburse parents for bus fares to send children either to public schools or to church-operated schools. But such tax funds may not be used to pay for field trips from parochial schools.[13] The former kind of trip is aid to children; the latter, controlled by the

Owner of food store in New York State indicates his opposition to "blue laws," which would close supermarkets on Sundays.

[5]Justice Jackson concurring in *Illinois ex rel McCollum* v. *Board of Education*, 333 U.S. 203 (1948).

[6]*Walz* v. *Tax Commission*, 397 U.S. 664 (1970); *Lemon* v. *Kurtzman*, 403 U.S. 602 (1971).

[7]*Engel* v. *Vitale*, 370 U.S. 421 (1962); *Abington School District* v. *Schempp*, 374 U.S. 203 (1963).

[8]*Epperson* v. *Arkansas*, 393 U.S. 97 (1968).

[9]*Illinois ex rel McCollum* v. *Board of Education*.

[10]*McGowan* v. *Maryland*, 366 U.S. 420 (1961).

[11]*Walz* v. *Tax Commission*.

[12]Carnegie Commission on Higher Education, *The Capitol and the Campus* (McGraw-Hill, 1971), p. 93; and Norman C. Thomas, *Education in National Politics* (David McKay, 1975), pp. 43–45.

[13]*Everson* v. *Board of Education*, 330 U.S. 1 (1947); *Wolman* v. *Walter*, 53 L Ed 2d 714 (1977).

school and not the students, is "impermissible direct aid to sectarian education."

The Supreme Court has also approved the use of tax funds to furnish secular textbooks, standardized tests, and diagnostic speech and hearing services for pupils in parochial as well as in public schools,[14] except those private schools that exclude pupils because of race or religion.[15] Students at parochial schools may also receive tax supported guidance and remedial help, but at sites away from "the pervasively sectarian atmosphere of the church-related schools"—for example, in the public school building. In each of these instances the justices recognized that governmental action might indirectly benefit religion. But in each case a majority were persuaded that the programs had a secular purpose and effect of providing benefits for students, and that there was no excessive entanglement of government in religion.

On the other side of the ledger, the Court has ruled that tax funds may *not* be used to reimburse church-operated elementary and secondary schools for salaries of teachers; for instructional materials and equipment such as maps, globes, reading machines; and for the maintenance and repair of school facilities and equipment.[16] The Supreme Court has also declared unconstitutional attempts directly or indirectly to reimburse parents for tuition paid to send their children to parochial schools.[17]

Why the difference between public funds being used to pay for textbooks but not for teachers? Because, said the justices, "A textbook's content is ascertainable, but a teacher's handling of a subject is not."[18] When a state pays for teachers, there is a substantial risk of tax funds being used to provide religious instruction.[19] The Court has taken a somewhat different stand on state aid to religious colleges. At the college level, secular functions are more separable from religious activity than is true of elementary and high schools. Religious indoctrination is less likely to affect the entire program, and college students are less impressionable. At this level the Court has sustained grants of public funds to build buildings and even to provide annual subsidies, just so long as the dollars are not directly spent on buildings used for religious purposes or used to teach religious subjects.[20]

Each may worship in his or her own way

The Constitution not only forbids the establishment of religion, it forbids Congress and the states from passing any law "prohibiting the free exercise thereof." "Tensions inevitably exists between the Free Exercise and the Establishment Clause . . . and it may not be possible to promote the

---

[14]*Board of Education* v. *Allen*, 392 U.S. 236 (1968).

[15]*Norwood* v. *Harrison*, 413 U.S. 455 (1973).

[16]*Lemon* v. *Kurtzman; Committee for Public Education* v. *Nyquist; Levitt* v. *Committee for Public Education*, 413 U.S. 472 (1973).

[17]*Committee for Public Education* v. *Nyquist*, and *Sloan* v. *Lemon*, 412 U.S. 825 (1973).

[18]*Lemon* v. *Kurtzman*.

[19]Frank J. Sorauf, *The Wall of Separation: The Constitutional Politics of Church and State* (Princeton University Press, 1976), covers the activities of major groups involved in church-state litigation.

[20]*Tilton* v. *Richardson*, 403 U.S. 672 (1971); *Hunt* v. *McNair*, 413 U.S. 734 (1973); *Roemer* v. *Maryland Public Works Board*, 426 U.S. 736 (1976).

former without offending the latter.''[21] For example, a law that requires persons to do something that offends their religion might interfere with the free exercise of religion, but to exempt them from the law because of religious convictions might be to favor religion and offend the Establishment Clause. ''The Court has struggled to find a neutral course between the two Religion Clauses, both of which are cast in absolute terms, and either of which, if expanded to a logical extreme, would tend to clash with the other.''[22]

The right to hold any or no religious *belief* is one of the few absolute rights that exist in organized society. One's religious beliefs are inviolable, and no government has any authority whatsoever to compel the acceptance of or to censor any creed. A state may not compel a religious belief nor deny persons any right or privilege because of their beliefs or lack of them. Religious oaths as a condition of public employment or to run for public office are unconstitutional.[23] In fact, the only time the Constitution mentions the word ''religion'' is to state: ''No religious test shall ever be required as a Qualification to any Office or public Trust under the United States'' (Article VI).

The right to *advocate* one's religion, like the right to advocate anything else, may be curbed only when there is danger of immediate and substantial injury to the rights of others.

Although carefully protected, the right to *practice* one's religion has less protection than its advocacy or the right to hold particular beliefs: ''It was never intended that the First Amendment . . . could be invoked as protection against legislation for the punishment of acts inimical to the peace, good order, and morals of society.''[24] Religious convictions do not ordinarily mean one does not need to obey otherwise valid and nondiscriminatory laws designed to protect the public peace, health, safety, and morals. However, the Supreme Court will scrutinize laws that infringe on religious practices and insist upon some compelling public purpose. ''Only those interests of the highest order and those not otherwise served can overbalance legitimate claims to the free exercise of religion.''[25]

The Supreme Court has upheld laws forbidding the practice of polygamy as applied to Mormons; laws requiring vaccination of school children as applied to Christian Scientists; laws forbidding business activities on Sunday in order to promote health and rest as applied to Orthodox Jews.[26] On the other hand, the Court ruled a state may not require Jehovah's Witnesses (or for that matter anyone else) to participate in a public school flag salute ceremony or to display matters to which they object on official state license plates.[27] (New Hampshire tried to fine a Jehovah's Witness who covered up the state motto ''Live Free or Die'' on his license plate.) Similarly, parents have a constitutional right to send their children to church-

**Freedom of religion:
these members of a Colorado
religious community chant in
unison to the Gonhonza, a scroll
that represents to them an
individual's life.**

[21]*Committee for Public Education* v. *Nyquist.*

[22]*Walz* v. *Tax Commission.*

[23]*Torcaso* v. *Watkins*, 367 U.S. 488 (1961).

[24]*Reynolds* v. *United States*, 98 U.S. 145 (1879).

[25]*Wisconsin* v. *Yoder*, 406 U.S. 205 (1972).

[26]*McGowan* v. *Maryland.*

[27]*Board of Education* v. *Barnette*, 319 U.S. 624 (1943); *Wooley* v. *Maynard*, 51 L Ed 2d 752 (1977).

sponsored schools if they wish.[28] In the face of three centuries of established Amish religious practices, the Court ruled that Wisconsin could not compel the Amish to send their children to any kind of school beyond the eighth grade.[29]

What of those who have religious scruples against bearing arms? Such scruples do not give them a constitutional right to be exempt from draft laws (or from paying taxes), but Congress traditionally has chosen to exempt from the draft those who by reason of religious belief are conscientiously opposed to participating in war. Congress refused, however, to exempt those who were against participation on "political, sociological, or philosophical grounds." The Supreme Court, in part to avoid a clash between the Free Exercise and the Establishment Clauses, interpreted the word "religious" so broadly that any deeply held opposition to participate in *any* and *all* wars was included within the exemption.[30] Those who object just to a particular war, however, were not exempt. As a result, in World War II many Jehovah's Witnesses spent years in prison because they could not meet the test of opposition to all wars. They said they planned to fight in only one, on the day of the final clash between Grace and Reprobation at Armageddon. And in the Vietnam War many persons failed to win conscientious objector status because their opposition was not to fighting in all wars, but in that particular war.

Supreme Court rulings about the proper construction of the religion clauses always stir up sharp criticism. The cases arouse intense emotions. The problem of drawing the constitutional line is difficult. But in a world where many nations are sharply divided into religious factions, "the amicable accommodation of religious difference in America has been a significant achievement of our political experience."[31]

Free speech and free people

Government by the people is based on the individual's right to speak freely, to organize in groups, to question the decisions of the government, and to campaign openly against it. Only through free and uncensored expression of opinion can the government be kept responsive to the electorate and can governmental power be transferred peacefully. Elections, separation of powers, and constitutional guarantees are meaningless unless all have the right to speak frankly and to hear and judge for themselves the worth of what others have to say.

Despite the fundamental importance of free speech in a democracy, some people seem to believe that speech should be free only for those who agree with them. Once we leave the level of abstractions and move to the level of specific questions or conflicts, there is a discouragingly low level of support for free speech among the public.[32] One study, for example, reported that one out of two persons thought that newspapers should not be permitted, even in peacetime, to criticize the government.[33] Such peo-

---

[28]*Pierce* v. *Society of Sisters*, 268 U.S. 510 (1925).

[29]*Wisconsin* v. *Yoder*, 406 U.S. 205 (1972).

[30]*Gillette* v. *United States*, 401 U.S. 437 (1971).

[31]Alan P. Grimes, *Equality in America: Religion, Race, and the Urban Majority* (Oxford University Press, 1964), p. 41.

[32]Samuel Krislov, *The Supreme Court and Political Freedom* (Free Press, 1968), pp. 39 ff., summarizes and cites much of the relevant literature.

[33]CBS Poll, "60 Minutes," April 14, 1970.

THE BEST TEST OF TRUTH

The right to assemble and to protest is illustrated by anti-war participants in 1969 and 1970.

ple ask why evil or ignorant persons should be permitted to spread lies and confuse the minds of others. Why should they be allowed to utter dangerous ideas that stir up trouble among the people or subvert our democratic society?

Believers in democracy insist on free debate and the unlimited exchange of ideas because they feel that no group has a monopoly on truth. No group has the right to establish in the field of politics absolute standards of what is true and what is false. As Justice Holmes wrote: "The best test of truth is the power of thought to get itself accepted in the competition of the market." The insistence on free speech for others stems from the recognition that people are not infallible, that perhaps the other person is right or, at least, that "I might be wrong."

Free speech is not simply the personal right of individuals to have their say; it also the right of the rest of us to hear them. John Stuart Mill, whose *Essay on Liberty* is the classic defense of free speech, put it this way: "The peculiar evil of silencing the expression of opinion, is that it is robbing the human race. . . . If the opinion is right, they are deprived of the opportunity of exchanging error for truth; if wrong, they lose, what is almost as great a benefit, the clearer perception and livelier impression of truth, produced by its collision with error."

Freedom of speech is not merely freedom to express ideas that differ slightly from ours; it is, as the late Justice Jackson said, "freedom to differ on things that go to the heart of the matter." Some people say they believe in free speech, but they draw the line at ideas they consider dangerous. But what is a dangerous idea? Who decides? The dangerous ideas of yesterday are often the conventional beliefs of today. In the realm of political ideas, who can find an objective, eternally valid standard of right? The search for truth is an endless one. It involves the possibility—even the inevitability—of error. The search cannot go on unless it proceeds freely in the minds and speech of all. This means, in the words of Justice Holmes, not only freedom of expression for those who agree with us, "but freedom for the thought we hate."[34]

Despite the fact that the First Amendment denies the national government the power to pass any law abridging freedom of speech, the amendment has never been interpreted in such sweeping terms. Liberty of expression is important, but it is not absolute. Like almost all rights, the right to freedom of speech and press is limited by the fact that its free exercise "implies the existence of an organized society maintaining public order without which liberty itself would be lost in the excess of unrestrained abuses."[35] How is the line to be drawn between permissible and unconstitutional restraint on freedom of expression?

In discussing the constitutional power of government to regulate speech, it is useful to distinguish among belief, speech, and action. At one extreme is the right to *believe* as one wishes, a right about as absolute as any can be for people living in organized societies. Despite occasional deviations in practice, the traditional American view is that *thoughts* are inviolable. No government has the right to punish a person for beliefs or to interfere in any way with freedom of conscience.

[34]For a thoughtful statement of a somewhat contrary point of view, see Walter Berns, *The First Amendment and the Future of American Democracy* (New York: Basic Books, 1976).

[35]*Cox* v. *New Hampshire*, 312 U.S. 569 (1941).

At the other extreme from belief is *action*, which is constantly constrained. We may believe it perfectly all right to go sixty miles an hour through an intersection, but if we do so we may be punished. Because one man's action directly affects the liberty and property of others, "his right to swing his arm ends where the other fellow's nose begins."

Speech stands somewhere between belief and action. It is not an absolute, or almost absolute, right as is belief, but it is not so exposed to governmental restraint as is action. There are certain categories of expression—the obscene, the seditious, the libelous, fighting words—where the problem is one of definition in order to distinguish between what is protected by the First Amendment and what is not. We shall turn shortly to these problems. But what about speech outside these categories?

HISTORIC CONSTITUTIONAL TESTS

Although the Supreme Court seldom refers to the three great constitutional tests developed in this century to distinguish between protected and unprotected speech, these tests continue to reflect basic attitudes toward free speech issues. They are the dangerous tendency doctrine, the clear and present danger test, and the preferred position doctrine.

The dangerous tendency doctrine   This doctrine stems from the common law. It has not had the support of the Supreme Court since 1925 (*Gitlow* v. *New York*), but it appears to reflect the views of many Americans. According to its supporters, the legislatures and not the courts have the primary responsibility to determine what kinds of speech should be outlawed. The Constitution authorizes legislatures to outlaw speech that has a tendency to lead to illegal action. Moreover, "the legislature cannot reasonably be required to measure the danger from every . . . utterance in the nice balance of a jeweler's scale. . . . It may, in the exercise of its judgment, suppress the threatened danger in its incipiency."[36]

Let us take a hypothetical law and see how those who hold this interpretation of the First Amendment might respond. Suppose a legislature decides that utterances in public of abusive racial remarks are dangerous because such remarks often lead to violence. The legislature makes such remarks illegal. Those who believe in the bad tendency test would argue that this is not unreasonable, and that therefore the law is not unconstitutional. It may be applied if the evidence shows that persons did make the kind of comments the legislature has made illegal.

The clear and present danger test   Justice Holmes announced this celebrated test in *Schenck* v. *United States* when he wrote: "The question in every case is whether the words are used in circumstances and are of such a nature as to create a clear and present danger that they will bring about substantive evils" that Congress has a right to prevent.[37] Furthermore, "no danger flowing from speech can be deemed clear and present," wrote Justice Brandeis concurring in *Whitney* v. *California*, "unless the incidence of the evil is so imminent that it may befall before there is opportunity for full discussion."[38]

[36]*Gitlow* v. *New York.*

[37]*Schenck* v. *United States*, 249 U.S. 47 (1919).

[38]*Whitney* v. *California*, 274 U.S. 357 (1927).

Supporters of the clear and present danger doctrine agree that speech is not an absolute right. But they believe free speech to be so fundamental and important that no government should be allowed to restrict it, unless it can be demonstrated that there is such a close connection between a speech and illegal action that the speech itself takes on the character of the action. (To shout fire falsely in a crowded theater is Holmes' famous example.) A government should not be allowed to interfere with speech unless it proves that the particular speech in question presented an *immediate* danger of a major evil. For example, the speech clearly would have led to a riot, the destruction of property, the corruption of an election, or direct interference with recruiting of soldiers. Take our hypothetical law used as an example above. Advocates of the clear and present danger test would argue that even though the legislature had made it illegal to use abusive racial remarks in public, judges should not permit the law to be applied unless the government presents convincing evidence that the particular remarks made by a particular individual clearly and presently might have led to a riot or some other serious substantive evil.

The preferred position or absolutist doctrine   This was the official view of the Supreme Court for a brief time during the 1940s and is presently supported by a minority of the justices. Those who take this view come close to the position that freedom of expression, that is, the use of words, and maybe even pictures, must never, or almost never, be curtailed.

Those who hold the preferred position interpretation believe that the First Amendment freedoms have the highest priority in our constitutional hierarchy. Courts have a special responsibility to study laws trespassing on these freedoms. Legislative majorities are free to experiment and adopt various schemes regulating our economic lives. But when they tamper with freedom of speech, they close the channels of the political process by which error can be corrected. Any law that limits the First Amendment freedoms is presumed to be unconstitutional. Only if the government can show that limitations on speech are absolutely necessary to avoid imminent and serious substantive evils are such limitations to be allowed.

If the preferred position doctrine is applied to our example of a law against abusive racial remarks, the law would be declared unconstitutional. Restraints on such abusive speech are not absolutely necessary to prevent riots, according to this doctrine. Whatever danger may come from such remarks does not justify a restriction on free comment. Moreover, supporters of the preferred position doctrine contend that the law, on its face, and not merely its application violates the Constitution.

OTHER TESTS

These three doctrines are subject to many interpretations and applications. And they are not only formulas that the Supreme Court uses to measure the constitutionality of laws regulating speech. Among the other tests or doctrines or rules of thumb, perhaps the most important are the following: prior restraint, vagueness, overbreadth, and least means.

Prior restraint   Of all forms of governmental interference with expression, judges are most suspicious of those that impose restraints prior to publication; these include licensing requirements before a speech can be made, a motion picture shown, or a newspaper published. The Supreme Court has specifically refused to declare all forms of prior censorship unconstitutional, but "a prior restraint on expression comes to this court with a 'heavy presumption' against its constitutionality. . . . The Government thus carries a heavy burden of showing justification for the enforcement of such a restraint."[39]

In a celebrated case, *New York Times Company* v. *United States* (1971), the Supreme Court, by a six to three vote, held that the government had not met this burden. The attorney general had secured from a lower court an injunction against the publication by several newspapers of parts of the Pentagon Papers, a classified study of the government's decision-making process on Vietnam policy. Three justices — Black, Douglas, and Brennan — took the view that the First Amendment forbids a court to impose, however briefly and for whatever reason, any prior restraint on a newspaper. But the prevailing view was that in this particular instance the government had failed to show that the publication of these documents would cause immediate and specific damage to national security.[40]

Except as applied to motion pictures, the only example of the Court's approval of a prior restraint is its refusal to strike down a military regulation prohibiting the distribution of publications on a military base without the prior written approval of the adjutant general of the post. The regulations authorized the adjutant general to withhold approval only for the distribution of publications that present "a clear danger to the loyalty, discipline, or morale of troops at the installation."[41]

Vagueness Any law is unconstitutional if it "either forbids or requires the doing of an act in terms so vague that men of common intelligence must necessarily guess at its meaning and differ as to its application. . . ."[42] Laws touching First Amendment freedoms are required to meet an even more rigid standard. These laws must not allow those who administer them so much discretion that the administrators could discriminate against those whose views they disapprove. Also, the laws must not be so vague that people are afraid to exercise protected freedoms for fear of the law. The Supreme Court has struck down laws that condemn sacrilegious movies or publications of "criminal deeds or bloodshed or lust . . . so massed as to become vehicles for inciting violent and deprived crimes" because no one would know for sure what is or is not allowed.[43]

Overbreadth Closely related to the vagueness doctrine is the requirement that a statute relating to First Amendment freedoms cannot be so broad in scope that it sweeps within its prohibitions protected as well as nonprotected activities. For example, a loyalty oath that would endanger protected forms of association as well as illegal activities would be unconstitutional. A legislature must deal directly and precisely with the kinds of activities it has a right to prohibit. Since the very existence of an over-

Former Defense Department researcher Daniel Ellsberg, who leaked top-secret Pentagon Papers to the press, testifies before an unofficial House panel, which met to investigate this action.

[39]*Organization for a Better Austin* v. *Keefe*, 402 U.S. 415 (1971); *Nebraska Press Assoc.* v. *Stuart*, 427 U.S. 539 (1976).

[40]*New York Times Company* v. *United States*, 403 U.S. 713 (1971).

[41]*Greer* v. *Spock*, 424 U.S. 828 (1976).

[42]*Lanzetta* v. *New Jersey*, 306 U.S. 451 (1939).

[43]*Burstyn* v. *Wilson*, 343 U.S. 495 (1952); *Winters* v. *New York*, 333 U.S. 507 (1948).

broad statute can be used to repress freedom of speech and association, such a statute may be declared unconstitutional on its face.[44]

Least means Even for an important purpose, a legislature may not choose a law that impinges on First Amendment freedoms if there are other ways to handle the problem. For example, a state may protect the public from the improper practices of lawyers, but it may not do so by forbidding organizations to make legal services available to their members, or forbidding attorneys from advertising their fees for simple services. There are other ways to protect the public that do not impinge on the rights of free association or free speech.[45]

WHERE WE STAND TODAY

The Supreme Court, although not locked into any specific formula or doctrine, takes the position that whenever First Amendment rights are involved, the Court will look with suspicion upon the government regulation. It will not sustain a limitation on these rights unless the government demonstrates an overriding and compelling state interest.

But whatever the doctrines, doctrines do not decide cases—judges do. And judges are constantly searching and seeking and explaining. So the Supreme Court may undergo doctrinal changes, especially when it deals with issues on which there is no national consensus. Doctrines are judges' starting points; each case requires them to weigh a variety of factors. *What* was said? *Where* was it said? *How* was it said? What was the *intent* of the person who said it? What were the *circumstances* in which it was said? *Which* government is attempting to regulate the speech—the city council that speaks for a few people or the Congress that speaks for a wide variety of people? (Only a very few congressional enactments have ever been struck down because of conflict with the First Amendment.) *How* is the government attempting to regulate the speech? By prior censorship? By punishment after the speech? *Why* is the government attempting to regulate the speech? To protect the national security? To keep the streets clean? To protect the rights of unpopular religious minorities? To prevent criticism of those in power? These and scores of other considerations are involved. And there is the question of how much deference judges should show to the legislature's attempt to adjust these conflicting claims. In short, no test has been devised that will automatically weigh all the factors.

Freedom of the press

Today, information is seldom spread through streetcorner meetings or public assemblies. Rather, it is broadcast wholesale by the press, television, radio, movies, and other media of communication. The Supreme Court has been careful in guarding freedom of the press from governmental restriction. But how broad is this freedom?

Sometimes freedom of the press comes into conflict with another basic right—trial by an impartial judge and jury. When newspapers and other mass media report in vivid detail the facts of a crime and secure press releases from the prosecutor, it may be impossible to hold a trial in an atmosphere free from hysteria or to secure a jury that can decide in an impartial

[44]*Dombrowski* v. *Pfister*, 380 U.S. 479 (1965).

[45]*NAACP* v. *Button*, 371 U.S. 415 (1963); *Bates* v. *Arizona*, 53 L Ed 2d 810 (1977).

Clarence Darrow (left), one of the nation's most celebrated defense lawyers, at the trial of Leopold and Loeb, in Chicago, 1924, which was one of the country's most sensational murder trials. The two defendants were convicted of the killing of a young boy.

manner. In England the emphasis is on the side of the fair trial. British courts do not hesitate to hold in contempt newspapers that comment on pending criminal proceedings. In the United States the emphasis is on the side of free comment. The Court has sustained the right of the press to criticize judges, even to the point of allowing editors to threaten judges with political reprisals unless they deal with defendants in a certain fashion. As Justice Douglas put it, "Judges are supposed to be men of fortitude, able to thrive in a hardy climate."[46]

Juries, on the other hand, are more susceptible to prejudicial comments and events. "When the case is a 'sensational' one, tensions develop between the right of the accused to trial by an impartial jury and the rights guaranteed others by the First Amendment."[47] The trial judge has a responsibility to insulate the jurors from publicity. The Supreme Court, however, so far has refused to approve of "gag orders" prohibiting newspapers from publishing accounts relating to trials.[48] But although a judge may not be able to restrain the press because of First Amendment limitations, if pretrial publicity makes an impartial jury impossible, the judge is expected to provide a remedy such as trial in another area (known as change of venue), or postponement.[49] The Supreme Court has reversed convictions where prejudicial newspaper publicity, or an inflammatory prosecutor's statement to the press, or the televising of the accused reading a confession have so aroused a community that a jury selected from it could not be impartial.[50]

It is defendants who are entitled to public trials, not the media representatives. In fact, a defendant is deprived of due process if, over his objection, a judge allows television cameras into the courtroom. Four justices were of the view that the mere fact that the trial is televised is so likely to influence the behavior of the judge, witnesses, jury, and defendants that televising trials is a violation of due process. The other justices would ban television from a courtroom only if there is evidence that its impact on a particular judge, jury, or witness interferes with a fair trial.[51]

THE PRESS AND THE CAMPUS

Although lower federal courts have ruled that administrators of public universities, even if they function as the publishers, are restrained by the First Amendment in dealing with student newspapers, the Supreme Court has not yet ruled on this matter. The Court has held, however, that a publicly supported university may not expel a student for distributing what authorities considered to be an indecent newspaper.[52] The university may regulate the time, place, and manner of the distribution of printed matter on campus, but "the mere dissemination of ideas—no matter how offensive to good taste—on a state university campus may not be shut off in the name alone of 'conventional decency.'" The three dissenting jus-

---

[46]*Craig* v. *Harney*, 331 U.S. 367 (1947).

[47]*Nebraska Press Assoc.* v. *Stuart*, 427 U.S. 539 (1976).

[48]*Ibid.*, and *Oklahoma Publishing Co.* v. *District Court*, 51 L Ed 2d 355 (1977).

[49]Caren Dubnoff, "Pretrial Publicity and Due Process in Criminal Proceedings," *Political Science Quarterly* (Spring 1977), pp. 89–109.

[50]*Rideau* v. *Louisiana*, 372 U.S. 723 (1963), and cases cited therein.

[51]*Estes* v. *Texas*, 381 U.S. 532 (1965); and *Sheppard* v. *Maxwell*, 384 U.S. 333 (1966).

[52]*Papish* v. *University of Missouri Curators*, 410 U.S. 667 (1973).

tices felt that the materials were legally obscene, but that even if they would not justify a criminal conviction, the Constitution does not forbid a university from disciplining a student for distributing on campus publications "which are at the same time obscene and infantile." The dissenters also chided their colleagues for being unwilling to use in their opinion the four-letter words (the familiar "code abbreviations" were used) the majority felt were not of a nature to sustain disciplinary action against a student.

A RIGHT TO REPLY?

Some critics have charged that the "press lords" enjoy many opportunities to have their say, but that ordinary citizens find difficulty in getting their side of the issues presented. Especially when a newspaper levels an attack against a person, they argue, the editor should be required to give space for a reply to those who are criticized.

Whatever the merits of such arguments, the Supreme Court has shown little sympathy toward legislative attempts to force a right to reply. A unanimous Court ruled unconstitutional a Florida law requiring newspapers to provide free space for replies by candidates for public office criticized by a paper. Chief Justice Burger said that a newspaper involves a "crucial process" of editorial judgment that the state may not regulate. "A responsible press," he wrote, "is an undoubtedly desirable goal, but press responsibility is not mandated by the Constitution and like many other virtues it cannot be legislated."[53] A year before the Court had given a somewhat similar negative response to those who had argued that groups should be given a right of access to television. In fact, the only intrusion into the editorial judgments of newspapers and broadcasters that the Court has so far sustained involved classified advertisements.

CENSORSHIP AT THE SOURCE

Is there freedom of the press to *obtain* news as well as to print it? Recently reporters and others have charged that censorship at the source is undermining their ability to keep the people informed. Governments have always withheld information, especially during time of war, and it is generally agreed that some public business is best done in secret. But during the Cold War years, public officials began to classify more and more information as confidential, secret, or top secret, and made it a crime to divulge it.

Does the government have the authority to punish a reporter for publishing classified documents? In the *New York Times* case, some members of the Court hinted that although the government in that instance lacked authority to restrain the publication of the Pentagon Papers, they were not so sure that it could not punish the newspaper for publishing classified documents. Despite rumors that some newspapers were going to be prosecuted for doing so, no such action was taken against them.

The Pentagon Papers incident did revive interest in the use by the executive branch of its authority to classify documents and thereby keep them from the public. Justice Stewart in his opinion in the *New York Times* case pointed out, "[W]hen everything is classified, then nothing is classified, and the system becomes one to be disregarded by the cynical and careless and to be manipulated by those intent on self-protection or self-promotion." A good security system, he said, should provide "maximum possible disclosure, recognizing that secrecy can best be preserved when credi-

"This is awful—It's not one of ours"
© 1971 Herblock in *The Washington Post.*

---

[53]*Miami Herald Publishing Company* v. *Tornillo*, 418 U.S. 241 (1974).

bility is truly maintained." Justice Douglas, dissenting in another case, pointed out, ". . . [A]nyone who has ever been in the executive branch knows how convenient the 'Top Secret' or 'Secret' stamp is, how easy it is to use, and how it covers perhaps for decades the footprints of a nervous bureaucrat or wary executive."[54]

Congress has liberalized access to public records and presidents have issued executive orders designed to correct some of the abuses in the classification of documents. Most important is the Freedom of Information Act of 1966, as amended in 1974. The act makes all records of federal agencies public, subject to certain exceptions. For example, private financial transactions, personnel records, criminal investigation files, interoffice memoranda, and letters used in the decision-making process of the executive branches are excepted. The act also subjects to court review any decision by the president or his agents that certain documents are to be kept secret in the interest of national defense or foreign policy. It requires federal agencies to act promptly on requests for information, and gives persons a speedy hearing before a federal judge if they are denied the information they have requested. The burden is on the agency to explain its refusal to grant the materials. If the judge decides in favor of the plantiffs, the government has to pay the legal fees incurred.

Many states have passed so-called sunshine laws, and there are federal regulations requiring most public agencies to open their meetings to public and press. But there is no constitutional requirement that public agencies must deliberate in public. So far as the Constitution is concerned, a school board can hold its sessions in private or limit attendance to those having business before the board. If, however, a meeting is opened to the public, no groups may be denied their right to speak because of objections to the content of what they might say.[55]

A REPORTER'S RIGHT TO WITHHOLD INFORMATION

Most reporters contend they have a right to withhold information from grand juries, legislative committees, and other agencies of government. Without this right, they argue, they cannot assure their sources of confidentiality and will not be able to get the information they need to keep the public informed. But the Supreme Court ruled in *Branzburg* v. *Hayes* (1972) that reporters, and presumably scholars, have no constitutional right to withhold information from juries.[56] Justice White, speaking for the Court, quoted from Jeremy Bentham: "Were the Prince of Wales, the Archbishop of Canterbury, and the Lord High Chancellor, to be passing by in the same coach, while a chimney-sweeper and a barrow-woman were in dispute about a halfpennyworth of apples, and the chimney-sweeper or the barrow-woman were to think proper to call upon them for their evidence, could they refuse it? No, most certainly." The Court concluded: " 'The public has a right to every man's evidence,' except for those persons protected by a constitutional, common-law, or statutory privilege." If any privilege is to be given to newspeople, said the Court, it should be done by act of Congress and of the states. The dissenting justices argued: "when neither the reporter nor his source can rely on the shield of confidentiality

[54]*EPA* v. *Mink*, 410 U.S. 73 (1973).

[55]*Madison School District* v. *Wisconsin Employment Commission*, 429 U.S. 167 (1976).

[56]408 U.S. 665 (1972).

against unrestrained use of the grand jury's subpoena power, valuable information will not be published and the public dialogue will inevitably be impoverished."

Congress has not yet responded to the Supreme Court's suggestion that since it is in the better position to weigh conflicting claims, it should adopt a shield law, a law establishing the conditions under which newspaper people would be protected from having to respond to federal investigatory and judicial agencies. In the meantime, the attorney-general has issued guidelines limiting federal prosecutors' discretion in the issuance of subpoenas to newspersons. Twenty states have shield laws limiting state officials, and others are considering their adoption.

EXECUTIVE PRIVILEGE

President Nixon and his predecessors have claimed a constitutional right to withhold information even from Congress and the courts if its release would jeopardize national security or interfere with the confidentiality of advice given to the president. In the celebrated case of *United States* v. *Nixon* (1974), the Supreme Court ruled that a president does not have an absolute executive privilege to withhold information. He is subject to a subpoena for material relevant to a criminal prosecution.[57]

This historic decision—historic in more than one sense, for it was the first time the Supreme Court has decided a matter directly involving the president as a party to a case, in contrast to his agents—rightly focused attention on the Supreme Court's rejection of the president's claim that he has an absolute executive privilege, and that he, rather than the courts, has the final say about what information to release and what to withhold. But initially overlooked was the fact that the Court fully recognized that a president does have a *limited* executive privilege.[58]

In the first place, if a president claims the privilege because disclosure would reveal military or diplomatic secrets, the courts should show "utmost deference" to his decision. And even outside these areas, his "singularly unique" role requires that great efforts be made to ensure that his communications are kept confidential. The trial judge was instructed to look at the subpoenaed materials in secret, release to the prosecutor and thus to the public only the information the judge thought related to the trial, and return the other material to the president "restored to its privileged status." He is also to be protected against "vexatious and unnecessary subpoenas."

LIBEL

Libel prosecutions used to be a favorite weapon to suppress criticism of government officials. But through a progressive raising of the constitutional standards, the danger of civil damages or criminal prosecution for libel no longer constitutes a serious threat to free communication. As far as public officials and public figures are concerned, no person may be made to pay damages or be punished for any comments he or she makes about such a person unless it can be proved that the comments were maliciously made with a knowledge of their falsity or with reckless disregard

[57]418 U.S. 683 (1974).

[58]See the symposium on *United States* v. *Nixon* in the *UCLA Law Review* (October 1974), pp. 4–140. See also Howard Simon and Joseph A. Califano, Jr. (eds.), *The Media and the Law* (Praeger, 1976).

for whether they are true or false.[59] The mere fact that a statement is wrong or even defamatory is not sufficient to sustain a charge of libel.

The constitutional standards for libel actions brought against private individuals is not so rigid. States may allow damage awards to private citizens for defamatory falsehoods if there is evidence of negligence. However, if this less rigid standard is used, damages must be limited to compensation for actual injury to the plaintiff and his or her reputation.[60]

OBSCENITY

Obscene publications are not entitled to constitutional protection, but the members of the Supreme Court, like everybody else, have had great difficulty in determining how obscenity is to be constitutionally defined. As Justice Harlan pointed out, "The subject of obscenity has produced a variety of views among the members of the Court unmatched in any course of constitutional adjudication."[61] And as Justice Brennan has written, "No other aspect of the First Amendment has, in recent years, commanded so substantial a commitment of our time, generated such disharmony of views, and remained so resistant to the formulation of stable and manageable standards."[62] Since the Supreme Court entered the field in 1957, there have been over eighty-five separate opinions written by the justices.

In *Miller* v. *California* (1973), Chief Justice Burger, speaking for only five members of the Court, once again tried to clarify and redefine the constitutional standards: A work may be considered legally obscene provided: (1) the average person, applying contemporary standards of the particular community, would find that the work, taken as a whole, appeals to a prurient interest in sex; (2) it depicts or describes in a patently offensive way sexual conduct specifically defined by the applicable law or authoritatively construed; and (3) the work, taken as a whole, lacks serious literary, artistic, political, or scientific value.[63] The Chief Justice specifically rejected part of the previous test—the so-called *Memoirs* v. *Massachusetts* (1966) formula—that had been applied by the Supreme Court: No work should be judged obscene unless it is "utterly without redeeming social value."[64] The Chief Justice argued such a test made it impossible for a state to outlaw hard-core pornography.

Under the current test, the jury is to determine whether or not a work appeals to prurient interests and is patently offensive. It is to apply the standards of the community from which the prosecution comes, leaving open the possibility that a particular book or movie might be legally obscene in one community but not in another. The literary, artistic, political, or scientific value part of the test, on the other hand, is not limited by the values of the community and is a determination especially open to review by judges.[65]

"Correctly numbered pages are not a redeeming social value."

Drawing by Savage. ©1969 by The New York Times Company.

[59]*New York Times* v. *Sullivan* (1964); *Curtis Publishing Co.* v. *Butts* (1967); *Rosenbloom* v. *Metramedia, Inc.* (1971), and cases cited therein.

[60]*Gertz* v. *Robert Welch, Inc.*, 418 U.S. 323 (1974).

[61]*Interstate Circuit, Inc.* v. *City of Dallas*, 390 U.S. 676 (1968).

[62]*Paris Adult Theatre I* v. *Slaton*, 413 U.S. 49 (1973).

[63]*Miller* v. *California*, 413 U.S. 15 (1973).

[64]*Memoirs* v. *Massachusetts*, 383 U.S. 413 (1966).

[65]*Smith* v. *United States*, 431 U.S. 291 (1977).

Did the Miller decision mean that henceforth local communities could ban whatever a prosecutor could persuade a jury was obscene? There were many who hoped so; there were many who feared so. They read Miller to mean that the Supreme Court would no longer review each book or movie in order to second-guess the decision of local authorities. But how far could the local community go? What if it decided to ban "Little Red Riding Hood"? After all, who really knows what went on in that bedroom?

A year after the Miller decision, the Supreme Court warned: "It would be a serious misreading of Miller to conclude that juries have unbridled discretion in determining what is patently offensive." Appellate courts, said Justice Rehnquist speaking for the majority, should closely review jury determinations to ensure compliance with constitutional standards. And the Supreme Court itself, after such a review, ruled that the movie *Carnal Knowledge* was not patently offensive, contrary to the conclusion of a jury in Albany, Georgia.[66]

Four members of the Supreme Court would go even further. They include Justice Stewart, who once said that although he could not define hard-core pornography, "I know it when I see it."[67] But after struggling to develop a constitutional definition, he joined Justices Brennan and Marshall in finally coming to the conclusion that it is impossible to do so without endangering protected speech and miring the court in a "case-by-case determination of obscenity." These justices would let adults see or read whatever they wish. But for minors, the justices are in greater agreement. They would permit considerable governmental regulation aimed at preventing the distribution and sale of pornography to minors.

Obscenity, then, is not entitled to constitutional protection. But governments must proceed under laws that define specifically the kinds of sexual conduct forbidden in word or picture. Moreover, it cannot be made a crime for booksellers to offer an obscene book for sale: it must be shown that they did so knowingly.[68] Otherwise booksellers would tend to avoid placing on their shelves materials that some police officer or prosecutor might consider objectionable and the public would be deprived of an opportunity to purchase and read anything except the "safe and sanitary."

The mere private possession of obscene materials also cannot be made a crime.[69] But persons may be convicted for transporting such literature in interstate commerce or importing it from abroad even if it is for their own use.[70] These limitations on the right to read privately led Justice Douglas to observe in dissent that "a person can read whatever he desires . . . only if one wrote or designed a tract in his attic, printed or processed it in his basement, so as to be able to read it in his study."[71]

Recently five members of the Court concluded that non-obscene but "erotic" literature and movies, although constitutionally protected, are entitled to less protection than a political speech. The Court upheld a zon-

[66]*Jenkins* v. *Georgia*, 418 U.S. 153 (1974).

[67]*Jacobellis* v. *Ohio*, 378 U.S. 184 (1964).

[68]*Smith* v. *California*, 361 U.S. 147 (1959).

[69]*Stanley* v. *Georgia*, 394 U.S. 557 (1969).

[70]*Stanley* v. *Georgia.*

[71]*United States* v. *12,00-ft Reels of Super 8 MM Film*, 418 U.S. 123 (1973); and *Hamling* v. *United States*, 418 U.S. 87 (1974), and cases cited therein.

ing ordinance forbidding "adult motion picture theaters" from being located within 1,000 feet of two other such theaters. Justice Stevens wrote for the majority: "It is manifest that society's interest in protecting this type of expression is of a wholly different, and lesser, magnitude than the interest in untrammeled political debate. . . . The state may legitimately use the content of these materials as a basis for placing them in a different classification from other motion pictures."[72]

States are primarily responsible for regulating obscene literature. But ever since Anthony Comstock started a national crusade against "smut" in the 1880s, Congress has been concerned with the subject. Congress has adopted, and the Supreme Court has upheld, laws forbidding importing into the United States pornographic materials or the sending of such materials through the mails or interstate commerce, even to willing adults, even transported by a person in a briefcase on an airline for private use.[73]

The Supreme Court, however, declared unconstitutional laws authorizing postal authorites to exclude from the mails matter they consider obscene and to cut off all incoming mail to the alleged pornographers. This is prior censorship without any judicial review.[74] On the other hand, the Court has upheld a law giving householders unlimited power to ask the postmaster to order mailers to delete their names from mailing lists and refrain from sending any advertising material they believe to be "erotically arousing or sexually provocative." It does not make any difference if a householder includes in such a category a "dry-goods catalogue." This is not governmental censorship: "The mailer's right to communicate must stop at the mailbox of an unreceptive addressee."[75]

Censorship of films and books may be imposed by a variety of means other than formal action. In some cities a local group such as the Legion of Decency may put pressure on the authorities. Local police have been known to threaten an exhibitor or a bookseller with criminal prosecution if he persists in showing films or selling books of which some local people disapprove. Such a threat is often enough to compel exhibitors to stop showing the films or selling the books. Of course any group is free to stay away from pictures or books that it dislikes, even to try to persuade others to stay away. What the Constitution forbids is the use of the coercive powers of government.

Today, fears about obscenity appear to have replaced the seventeenth-century fears about heresy and the 1950s fears about sedition. Conflicts over how it should or should not be regulated will remain lively parts of our political debates, especially at the community level.[76]

"And that's the opinion of the management of this station."

Drawing by Levin. © 1976 The New Yorker Magazine, Inc.

FIGHTING WORDS

There are certain well-defined and narrowly limited classes of speech "which by their very utterance inflict injury or tend to incite an immediate breach of peace" that governments may constitutionally punish.[77] The

[72]*Young* v. *American Mini Theatres*, 427 U.S. 51 (1976).

[73]*United States* v. *Orito*, 413 U.S. 139 (1973).

[74]*Blount* v. *Rizzi*, 400 U.S. 410 (1971).

[75]*Rowan* v. *Post Office Department*, 397 U.S. 728 (1970).

[76]For a review of the interbranch involvement at the national level, see Lane V. Sunderland, *Obscenity: The Court, the Congress and the Presidential Commission* (American Enterprise Institute for Public Policy Research, 1975).

[77]*Chaplinsky* v. *New Hampshire*, 315 U.S. 568 (1942).

state must treat these fighting words by narrowly drawn statutes that cannot be applied to protected expression. And the category of what will be considered fighting words is very narrow. For example, a four-letter word used in relation to the draft and worn on a sweater is not a fighting word, at least when not directed to any specific person.[78]

COMMERCIAL SPEECH

Prior to 1975, advertising was not entitled to constitutional protection, but in that year the Court held that a state cannot forbid advertisements about where to obtain abortions.[79] Since then it has ruled that a state cannot forbid pharmacists to advertise the price of prescription drugs,[80] or lawyers the price of routine services, such as an uncontested divorce or a simple adoption.[81] (The latter decision was five to four, with the majority hinting that ads by a lawyer such as ''best services in town'' or via radio and television are subject to regulation to prevent deception.) Nor may a city, as a means of combatting panic selling because of racial fears, forbid people from placing for sale signs in front of their homes.[82] (The Court left open the possibility that a city might ban all signs or regulate their size in order to promote esthetic values or any other value ''unrelated to the suppression of free expression.'')

Although commercial speech is protected by the First Amendment, it is subject to more regulation than would be allowed for noncommercial speech. A state, for example, may forbid false and deceptive advertising, but a law forbidding false and deceptive political comment would clearly be unconstitutional. It can be determined, for example, whether a particular item will or will not be sold for $1.98. But who is to say which political doctrines are true or false?

Of course, drawing the line between permissible and impermissible government regulation of commercial speech is not easy. Federal regulatory agencies have been allowed, for example, to ban the advertising of tobacco on television. And the Supreme Court sustained a regulation forbidding newspapers to list help wanted advertisements classified by sex. But the vote was close.[83] Justice Powell, speaking for a five-man majority, distinguished such advertisements from advertisements advocating sexism, which could not be banned. The latter would be communication of ideas. The former, like advertising the sale of narcotics or soliciting for prostitution, was advertising for illegal acts. Since hiring on the basis of sex is illegal, Justice Powell argued, advertising a particular job on this basis could also be banned.

OTHER MEANS OF COMMUNICATION

Motion pictures Films may be treated differently from books or newspapers. Prior censorship of films is not necessarily unconstitutional under all circumstances.[84] However, laws calling for submission of all

[78]*Lewis* v. *New Orleans*, 408 U.S. 913, and cases cited therein; *Cohen* v. *California*, 403 U.S. 15 (1971).

[79]*Bigelow* v. *Virginia*, 421 U.S. 808 (1975).

[80]*Virginia State Board of Pharmacy* v. *Virginia Citizens Consumer Council, Inc.*, 425 U.S. 748 (1976).

[81]*Bates* v. *Arizona*, 53 L Ed 2nd 810 (1977).

[82]*Linmark Associates, Inc.* v. *Willingboro*, 431 U.S. 85 (1977).

[83]*Pittsburgh Press Co.* v. *Pittsburgh Commission on Human Relations*, 413 U.S. 376 (1973).

[84]*Times Film Company* v. *City of Chicago*, 365 U.S. 43 (1961).

films to a review board are constitutional only if the review board is required promptly to grant a license or promptly go to court for a judicial hearing and a determination that the film in question is obscene. And the burden is on the board to prove to the court that the film is in fact obscene under standards set by the Supreme Court.[85]

Radio and television Radio and especially television have increasingly become the most important means for the distribution of news to the public as well as the primary forum used by candidates to appeal for votes. The Supreme Court has had to deal with the difficult problem of applying to television the First Amendment, whose principles were first developed when the town meeting, the handbill, and the street speaker served as the chief marketplace for ideas.

Congress has established a system of private broadcasting, recently supplemented by the Public Broadcasting System, subject to general regulation by the Federal Communications Commission. Broadcasters use publicly owned airwaves, and no one has a constitutional right to use these facilities without a license. The FCC grants these licenses for limited periods and makes regulations consistent with the "public convenience, interest, or necessity." Congress has specifically denied the commission the authority to censor what is transmitted or to interfere with the right of free speech. The First Amendment would prevent such censorship if the FCC tried to impose it. But the First Amendment does not prevent the FCC from refusing to renew a license if in its opinion a broadcaster has not served the public interest or from imposing regulations designed to ensure fair coverage of events.

Congress and the FCC have adopted the fairness doctrine, which imposes on licensees the obligation to see that issues of public significance are covered adequately and reflect differing viewpoints. If a paid sponsor is unavailable to present an opposing view, the broadcaster must provide free time. He must present programming on public issues if no one seeks to do so. In the case of persons subjected to personal attack, a licensee has an obligation to notify those attacked and give them an opportunity to respond. If licensees make editorial statements or endorse candidates, they must give opponents an opportunity to respond. In the case of candidates for public office, Congress has imposed an equal-time requirement.[86]

Does a group, like a political party, a candidate, or those who organize to promote particular political views, have a constitutional or legal right to access to radio or television time if it is willing to pay for it? Or does a licensee have a constitutional and legal right to refuse to accept paid political announcements if in its journalistic judgment it would be wise to do so? As we have noted, a unanimous Supreme Court concluded that so far as newspapers are concerned there is no constitutional right to reply, and a state may not interfere with a journalist's decision about what to print. But for broadcasters, civil libertarians have a more difficult time answering these questions. It is hard to tell the good guys from the bad guys.[87]

---

[85]*Teitel Film Corp.* v. *Cusack*, 390 U.S. 139 (1968).

[86]*Red Lion Broadcasting Co.* v. *Federal Communications Commission*, 395 U.S. 367 (1969). See also Fred W. Friendly, *The Good Guys, the Bad Guys, and the First Amendment* (Random House 1976), for a detailed discussion of the fairness doctrine, its evolution, and application; and Eric Sevareid, "Why a Second-Class First Amendment for Broadcasting?" Address to National Association of Broadcasters' Convention, Washington, D.C., March 28, 1977.

[87]See comments of Judge J. Skelly Wright in Friendly, *The Good Guys*, p. x.

The Supreme Court has had the same difficulty. It could not muster a majority who could agree on the reasons, but seven justices concluded that neither the Federal Communications Act nor the First Amendment requires broadcasters to accept paid editorial advertisements. The opinion of Chief Justice Burger, for the plurality, after observing that if broadcasters had to accept all paid editorials there would be a substantial risk that those with the most money could monopolize the airwaves, concluded that the First Amendment did not require broadcasters to accept such paid announcements. But neither does it forbid the FCC and Congress to impose some kinds of access requirements if they wish. Justice Douglas was with the majority in this case, but he was of the view that the First Amendment forbids Congress or the FCC from imposing any such restraints on the journalistic judgments of the licensees. On the other side, Justices Brennan and Marshall argued that a ban by broadcasters, agreed to by the FCC, violates the First Amendment rights of those who wish to buy time.[88]

The coming of cable television is likely to ease the access problems somewhat since it will provide more channels for more groups. It is undoubtedly going to raise new problems of applying the principles of free speech to new technologies.

Handbills The distribution of religious and political pamphlets, leaflets, and handbills to the public—a historic weapon in the defense of liberty—is constitutionally protected. Of course, cities may prosecute those who engage in fraud or libel or who deliberately litter the streets. But keeping the streets clean does not justify interference with the right to pass out political or religious literature. When Los Angeles tried to outlaw the distribution of anonymous handbills, the Supreme Court ruled that the city's interest in identifying those who might be responsible for fraud, false advertising, or libel was not substantial enough to justify a ban on all anonymous handbills.[89]

Picketing A state law forbidding all peaceful picketing carried on for any purpose would be an unconstitutional invasion of freedom of speech.[90] However, "picketing involves elements of both speech and conduct, i.e., patrolling," and "because of this intermingling of protected and unprotected elements, picketing can be subjected to controls that would not be constitutionally permissible in the case of pure speech."[91] Even peaceful picketing can be restricted by a state if it is conducted for an illegal purpose.[92] As far as trade-union picketing is concerned, federal regulations are so comprehensive that the power of states to interfere with such picketing is much narrower than it might appear if one looked only at decisions relating to freedom of speech.

Symbolic speech "We cannot accept the view," wrote Chief Justice Warren, "that an apparently limitless variety of conduct can be labeled

[88]*Columbia Broadcasting System, Inc.* v. *Democratic National Committee*, 412 U.S. 94 (1973).

[89]*Talley* v. *California*, 362 U.S. 60 (1960).

[90]*Thornhill* v. *Alabama*, 310 U.S. 88 (1940).

[91]*Amalgamated Food Employees Local 590* v. *Logan Valley Plaza, Inc.*, 391 U.S. 308 (1968).

[92]*Teamsters Union* v. *Vogt*, 354 U.S. 284 (1957).

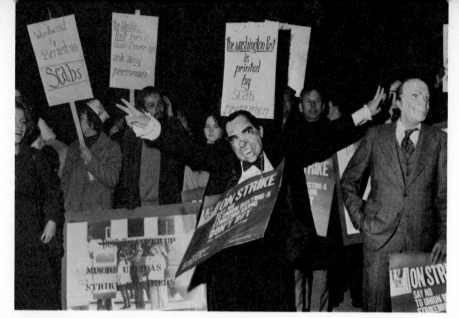

Striking pressmen of the *Washington Post*, wearing Richard Nixon and Gerald Ford masks, picket the premier of film "All the President's Men." Because picketing involves elements of both speech and conduct, it is subject to controls that would be unconstitutional if only pure speech were involved.

speech whenever the person engaged in the conduct intends thereby to express an idea."[93] Or as Chief Justice Burger wrote, "Conduct that the State police power can prohibit on a public street does not become automatically protected by the Constitution merely because the conduct is moved to . . . a 'live theatre' stage, any more than a 'live' performance of a man and woman locked in a sexual embrace at high noon in Times Square is protected by the Constitution merely because they simultaneously engaged in a political dialogue."[94]

Of course, the line between speech and conduct is not always clear. Deliberately burning a draft card in violation of a congressional regulation that makes it a crime to do so knowingly is not a constitutionally protected form of speech.[95] Municipal police officers have no constitutional right to have long hair while serving on the police force.[96] But on the other side of the constitutional line, although public school authorities can impose a reasonable dress code, they cannot forbid students to wear black armbands to school to protest political events such as the war in Vietnam.[97]

Right of the people peaceably to assemble, and to petition the government

The right to assemble peaceably applies not only to meetings in private homes and meeting halls, but to gatherings held in public streets and parks, which, the Supreme Court has said, since ". . . time out of mind have been used for purposes of assembly . . . and discussing public questions."[98] But people are not free to incite riots, to block traffic, to take over a school, to seize and hold the office of a mayor (or a university chancellor), to hold parades, or to make speeches in the public streets during rush hours. The government may make reasonable regulations over time, place, and manner in order to preserve order.

[93]*United States* v. *O'Brien*, 391 U.S. 367 (1968).

[94]*Paris Adult Theatre I* v. *Sullivan*, 413 U.S. 49 (1973).

[95]*United States* v. *O'Brien*.

[96]*Kelley* v. *Johnson*, 425 U.S. 238 (1976).

[97]*Tinker* v. *Des Moines School District*, 393 U.S. 503 (1969).

[98]*Hague* v. *C.I.O.*, 307 U.S. 496 (1939).

The courts will look carefully at regulations and police actions that obstruct the right of public assembly, especially in circumstances that raise a suspicion that a law is not being applied evenhandedly. The Supreme Court is unwilling to approve regulations that let public authorities determine which groups will be allowed to hold public meetings, or laws that are so vague that they give the police broad discretion to determine whom to arrest and courts latitude to decide whom to convict.

Governments may regulate the use of the streets, but they must do so by precisely drawn and fairly administered statutes that are neutral concerning differing points of view. The Supreme Court, for example, sustained a Louisiana law that made it an offense to picket or parade in or near a courthouse with the intent to influence a judge, juror, witness, or to impede the administration of justice.[99]

What of public facilities, such as libraries, courthouses, schools, and swimming pools, that are designed to serve purposes other than demonstrations? As long as persons assemble to use such facilities within the normal bounds of conduct, they may not be constitutionally restrained from doing so. However, if they attempt by demonstrations to interfere with programs or try to appropriate facilities for their own use, a state has the constitutional authority to punish such activities. Of course, the discretion accorded to those enforcing the law must be properly limited and discriminatory application of the laws should not take place. What of private property and the right to protest? The right to assemble and to petition does not include the right to trespass on privately owned property. The state may protect owners against those who attempt to convert property to their own use even if they are doing so to express ideas.

Does the right of peaceful assembly and petition include the right nonviolently but deliberately to violate a law? Again we have no definite answer. But speaking in general terms, civil disobedience, even if peacefully engaged in, is not a protected right. When Dr. Martin Luther King and his followers refused to comply with a state court's injunction that forbade them to parade in Birmingham without first securing a permit, the Supreme Court sustained their conviction even though there was a serious doubt about the constitutionality of the injunction and the ordinance on which it was based. Justice Stewart, speaking for the five-man majority, said, "No man can be judge in his own case, however exalted his station, however righteous his motives, and irrespective of his race, color, politics, or religion." Persons are not "constitutionally free to ignore all the procedures of the law and carry their battles to the streets."[100] The four dissenting justices emphasized that one does have a right to defy peacefully an obviously unconstitutional statute or injunction.

FREEDOM OF ASSOCIATION

The right to organize for the peaceful promotion of political and other causes is not mentioned in the Constitution. But as the Supreme Court has said, "It is beyond debate that freedom to engage in association for the advancement of beliefs and ideas is an inseparable aspect of the 'liberty' protected by the Constitution."[101] Of course, the right of association, like other constitutional rights, may be regulated under certain conditions. For

[99]*Cox* v. *Louisiana*, 379 U.S. 559 (1965).

[100]*Walker* v. *Birmingham*, 388 U.S. 307 (1967).

[101]*NAACP* v. *Alabama*, 356 U.S. 449 (1958).

example, anti-Klan laws that make it a crime to parade on public streets with faces masked have been sustained.[102] But laws affecting rights to associate are subject to close judicial scrutiny.

Subversive conduct and seditious speech

"If there is any fixed star in our constitutional constellation," Justice Jackson said, "it is that no official, high or petty, can prescribe what shall be orthodox in politics, nationalism, religion, or other matters of opinion. . . ."[103] Any group can champion whatever position it wishes: vegetarianism, feminism, sexism, communism, fascism, black nationalism, white supremacy, Zionism, anti-Semitism, Americanism. But what of those who are unwilling to abide by democratic methods and attempt through force or violence to impose their views on others? Here is a problem for a democratic government: How to protect itself against antidemocrats who are working to destroy the democratic system, but at the same time to preserve constitutional freedoms and democratic procedures.

TRAITORS, SPIES, SABOTEURS, REVOLUTIONARIES

Laws aimed at acts of violence, espionage, sabotage, or treason in themselves raise no constitutional questions, nor do they infringe on protected constitutional liberties. However, they can be used to intimidate if they are loosely drawn or indiscriminately administered. The framers of the Constitution—themselves considered traitors by the English government—knew the dangers of loose definitions of treason. Accordingly, they carefully inserted a constitutional definition by stating that treason consists only of the overt acts of giving aid and comfort to the enemies of the United States or levying war against it. Furthermore, in order to convict a person of treason, the Constitution requires the testimony of two witnesses to the overt treasonable acts or the defendant's confession in open court.

But treason does not exhaust the limits of the constitutional power of the national government to move against conduct designed to subvert the democratic system. Congress, for example, has made it a crime to engage in espionage or sabotage; to cross interstate boundaries or use the mails or interstate facilities to bomb buildings and schools. (This law was passed in 1960 and aimed at the white segregationists who were alleged to have blown up black churches and used force to intimidate black leaders and

[102]*Bryant* v. *Zimmerman*, 278 U.S. 63 (1928).

[103]*West Virginia State Board of Education* v. *Barnette*, 319 U.S. 624 (1943).

Demonstrators picket in front of the White House while awaiting the Supreme Court decision in the case of convicted atom spies Julius and Ethel Rosenberg. Persons at left and right carry signs on behalf of the Rosenbergs; to the left of the policeman are people carrying signs with opposite views.

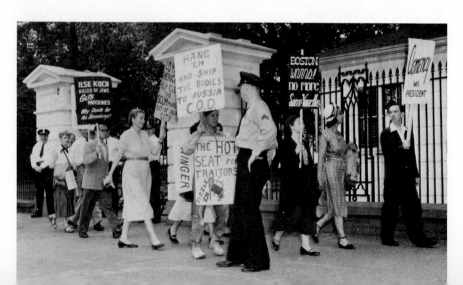

their white allies.) It is also a crime to cross state lines or use interstate facilities with the intent to incite a riot (the so-called Rap Brown law passed in 1968 aimed at black militants who were alleged to foment riots); or to conspire to do any of the above.

More often than not, when the government prosecutes under such laws the charge is conspiracy. It is easier to prove conspiracy than to get evidence to sustain a charge against a named defendant that he or she has thrown a brick, planted a bomb, engaged in a riot, or committed an act of violence. But conspiracy charges, although long known to Anglo-American jurisprudence, are especially dangerous to civil liberties; they can be abused by prosecutors to intimidate the politically unpopular.

For the most part, the highly charged prosecutions of the late 1960s and the early 1970s against political radicals and black militants for allegedly engaging in, or conspiring to engage in, violent acts led either to verdicts of not guilty or reversals on appeal. To some, this is evidence that our court system is strong and can be counted on to protect the innocent. To others it is evidence of the inability of the government to bring to justice those who should have been punished for their deeds. To still others it is evidence of how governments can use legal procedures to intimidate adherents of unpopular causes. For even if defendants are finally acquitted, the effort and expense of defending themselves in court has an intimidating impact on political dissenters. Historians, journalists, political scientists, and others will be debating the lessons of these trials for many years.

SEDITIOUS SPEECH

It is one thing to punish persons for what they do; it is quite another to punish them for what they say. The story of the development of free government is in large measure the story of making clear this distinction. Until recent centuries, seditious speech was so broadly defined that all criticism of those in power was considered criminal. As late as the eighteenth century in England, seditious speech was defined as covering any publication intended to incite disaffection against the king or the government or to raise discontent among the people or to promote feelings of ill will between different classes.[104] And it did not make any difference if what was said was true. On the contrary, "the greater the truth the greater the libel." For if one charged the king's ministers with being corrupt and in fact they were corrupt, such a charge would more likely cause discontent among the people than if it were false.

The adoption of the Constitution and the Bill of Rights did not result in a quick, easy victory for those who wished to establish free speech in the United States.[105] In 1798, only seven years after the First Amendment had been ratified, Congress passed the first national sedition law. Those were perilous times for the young republic, for war with France seemed imminent. The Federalists, in control of both Congress and the presidency, persuaded themselves that national safety required a little suppression of speech. The Sedition Act made it a crime to utter false, scandalous, or malicious statements intended to bring the government or any of its officers

[104]Zechariah Chafee, Jr., "The Great Liberty: Freedom of Speech and Press," in Alfred H. Kelly, ed., *Foundations of Freedom in the American Constitution* (Harper & Row, 1958), p. 79.

[105]Leonard Levy, *Legacy of Suppression* (Harvard University Press, 1960), and *Freedom of the Press from Zenger to Jefferson* (Bobbs-Merrill, 1966).

into disrepute or "to incite against them the hatred of the good people of the United States."[106]

The popular reaction to the Sedition Act helped defeat the Federalists in the elections of 1800. They had failed to grasp the core of the democratic idea that a person may criticize the government of the day, may work for its downfall, and may oppose its policies, but still be loyal to the nation.

THE SMITH ACT OF 1940

During World War I and the "Red scare" that followed it, there was a flurry of legislation and prosecutions aimed at seditious speech. Hundreds of people who expressed mildly radical ideas found themselves in trouble. Some went to jail.[107] But the first peacetime sedition law since the Sedition Act of 1798 was the Smith Act of 1940. The Smith Act forbids persons to advocate forceful overthrow of the government with the intent to bring it about; to distribute, with disloyal intent, matter teaching or advising the overthrow of government by violence; and to organize knowingly or to help organize any group having such purposes.

In *Dennis v. United States* (1951) the Court agreed that the Smith Act could be applied to the leaders of the Communist Party, who had been charged with conspiring to advocate the violent overthrow of the government.[108] But when the Department of Justice, and in many states local prosecutors, began to go after the second-string Communist leaders, the Supreme Court modified its earlier decision. First it ruled that the Smith Act precludes state prosecutions for seditious advocacy against the national government.[109] Then it held that the Dennis decision had been misunderstood. Congress did not and may not outlaw the mere advocacy of the abstract doctrine of violent overthrow. Justice Harlan explained: "The essential distinction is that those to whom the advocacy is addressed must be urged *to do* something now or in the future, rather than merely *to believe* in something."[110] More recently, the Supreme Court narrowed Dennis even further: Advocacy of the use of force may not be forbidden "except where such advocacy is directed to inciting or producing *imminent* lawless action and is likely to incite or produce such action."[111]

Seditious speech, if narrowly defined to cover only the advocacy of *immediate* and *concrete* acts of violence, is not constitutionally protected. But such narrow interpretation of antisedition laws means people are free to work for their political objectives so long as they abandon the use of force as a means of bringing it about or its specific and immediate advocacy.

Summary

1. First Amendment freedoms—freedom of religion, freedom from the establishment of religion, freedom of speech, freedom of press, freedom of assembly and petition, and freedom of association—are at the very heart of the democratic process.

[106]See James Morton Smith, *Freedom's Fetters: The Alien and Sedition Laws and American Civil Liberties* (Cornell University Press, 1956).

[107]The classic coverage of this episode is Zechariah Chafee, Jr., *Free Speech in the United States* (Harvard University Press, 1941). See also John P. Roche, *The Quest for the Dream* (Macmillan, 1963).

[108]341 U.S. 494.

[109]*Pennsylvania* v. *Nelson*, 350 U.S. 497 (1956).

[110]*Yates* v. *United States*, 354 U.S. 298 (1957).

[111]*Brandenburg* v. *Ohio*, 395 U.S. 444 (1969); *Hess* v. *Indiana*, 414 U.S. 105(1973).

2. Roughly since World War I, the Supreme Court has become the primary agency for giving meaning to these constitutional restraints. And since 1925 these constitutional limits have been applied not only to Congress but to all governmental agencies, national, state, and local.

3. Clashes about First Amendment freedoms are not profitably thought of as battles between the "good guys" and the "bad guys," or as dramas in which the judges at the last moment rush to the rescue of liberty threatened by tyrannical congressmen or backward city councilmen. Rather, these are arguments over conflicting notions of what is good, between conflicting rights. Those who argue for restraint do so in the name of virtue, to protect the true faith, to preserve morality, to prevent the rich from having too much influence in elections and so on.

4. The Supreme Court, over the years, has taken a practical approach to First Amendment freedoms. It has refused to make them absolute rights above any kind of governmental regulation, direct or indirect, or to say that they must be preserved at whatever price. But the justices have recognized that a democratic society tampers with these freedoms at great peril. It has insisted upon compelling justification before permitting these rights to be limited. How compelling the justification is, and in a free society always will remain, an open question.

Chapter 6

Equality under the Law

Consider again the ringing words of the Declaration of Independence: "We hold these truths to be self-evident, that all men are created equal, that they are endowed by their Creator with certain unalienable Rights, that among these are Life, Liberty, and the pursuit of Happiness. . . ." The Declaration does not talk about the equality of white, Christian, or Anglo-Saxon men but of *all* men. (Undoubtedly if the framers of the Declaration were to revise it today, they would speak of persons rather than men.) This creed of individual dignity and equality is older than our Declaration of Independence; its roots go back at least as far as the teachings of Judaism and Christianity. To act by this creed, to bring practice into conformity with principles, has long been a central preoccupation of Americans. Establishing civil rights is implementing the Constitution. For when we talk about civil rights, we are talking about the question of whether black, brown, or red Americans or women are to be given the rights and opportunities to take full part in the political system created by the American Constitution.

Certain liberties are essential to the operation of democratic government. But these liberties are not merely *means* of attaining self-government; they are *ends* in themselves. They do not exist to protect the government; the government exists to protect them. Long ago they were called natural rights—today we speak of *human* rights—but the belief is still the same: the moral primacy of people over government and the dignity and worth of each individual.

Today no problem is more compelling than that of ensuring all Americans their basic civil rights—rights to enjoy life and liberty and to pursue happiness—without discrimination because of race, religion, national origin, or sex. American democracy, despite its many triumphs, has not extended civil rights to all people. From the time they are born until they die minorities and women suffer handicaps other Americans do not face; they are victims of history. These injustices are injuries Americans live with daily.

What should we do to protect civil rights and to extend opportunities for those who have been discriminated against? These questions have been important in presidential elections; they give rise to battles in Congress and to debates before judges, in state legislatures, city councils, and school boards. And what we do, or fail to do, has significance beyond our national borders. Peoples everywhere follow the treatment of our minorities with more than casual interest.

Denial of equal rights not only negates the equality that the Declaration of Independence asserts, it is also contrary to the guarantees of the Constitution. The Constitution provides two ways of protecting civil rights: first, by seeing to it that government itself imposes no discriminatory barriers; second, by granting the national and state governments authority to protect civil rights against interference by private individuals. In this chapter we will be concerned with both aspects—government as a *threat* to civil rights and government as the *protector* of civil rights.

To secure racial justice—an overview

In order to put into context the court decisions, laws, and other kinds of governmental action relating to civil rights for blacks, and more recently, Latinos and other minorities, it is useful to review the accelerating drive to make real the promises of the Declaration of Independence and the Constitution. For the human rights crusade is not just a series of legal decisions and statutes, as important as they may be; it is an involvement of the entire social, economic, and political system of the United States. Governmental action and reaction is as much the result as the cause of the civil rights movement.

Resolving racial tensions is not unique to this nation. Racial tensions are probably the most divisive internal issues faced by any society, but they are not the only causes of internal division. There are, for example, the white-against-white religious battles in Northern Ireland, the black-against-black conflicts in Nigeria. But Americans have had a special confrontation with the problem of race—before, during, and after the Civil War. Because the North won that war, the Thirteenth, Fourteenth, and Fifteenth Amendments—to abolish slavery and all badges of servitude, and grant to blacks all rights enjoyed by every other American—became part of the Constitution. Congress enacted a series of civil rights laws to enforce these promises and established special programs, such as the Freedmen's Bureau, to provide educational and social services to the recently freed slaves.

But before these programs had a significant impact, the political community of white Americans became reunited. By 1877, northern political leaders abandoned blacks to their fate at the hands of their former white masters. The president no longer concerned himself with the enforcement of civil rights laws. Congress ceased to enact new ones, and the Supreme Court either declared civil rights acts unconstitutional or so narrowly interpreted them that they were ineffective. The Court also gave such limited construction to the Thirteenth, Fourteenth, and Fifteenth Amendments as protections against racial discrimination that there ceased to be any effective limitation on the authority of the dominant white groups.

By the end of the century, white supremacy reigned unchallenged in the

Ku Klux Klan members marched in silent protest against Civil Rights Act of 1964.

South, where most blacks lived at the time. Despite the Constitution, blacks were kept from voting, forced to accept menial jobs, and denied educational opportunities. In 1896 the Supreme Court, by an eight to one vote, gave constitutional sanction to governmentally imposed racial segregation. Even if the Court had declared segregation unconstitutional, a decision so contrary to popular feeling and political realities would have had little impact. Blacks were considered by many whites, North and South, to be childlike. Southern political leaders openly espoused white supremacy. In 1896 blacks were lynched at an average of one every four days, and few citizens raised a voice in protest.

During World War I blacks began to migrate to northern cities, and by then there were small beginnings toward educational opportunities and jobs. These trends were accelerated by the New Deal and World War II. And the South, through urbanization and industrialization, became more like the rest of the nation. As the migration of blacks out of the rural South into southern and northern cities shifted the racial composition of cities, the votes of blacks became important in national elections. There was continuing discrimination, but also more jobs, more social gains. And above all, these changes created a black middle class to which segregation as a symbol of servitude and a cause of inequality became a primary target. By the middle of the twentieth century urban blacks were active and politically powerful citizens. There was a growing, persistent, and insistent demand for the abolition of color barriers.

GOVERNMENT BEGINS TO RESPOND

The first branch of the national government to become sensitized to these growing pressures was the presidency. Because of the special nature of the electoral college and the pattern of our political system, by the 1930s no person in the White House, or hoping to live there, could afford to ignore the aspirations of blacks. The commitment of our presidents to the cause of equal protection under the laws became translated into the appointment of federal judges more sympathetic to a broader construction of the Thirteenth, Fourteenth, and Fifteenth Amendments.

In the 1930s blacks started to resort to law to secure their rights. They did so especially to challenge the doctrine of segregation as a device to impose discrimination. They emphasized litigation because at the time they had no alternative; they lacked the political power to make their demands effective before either the state legislatures or Congress.

By the 1950s civil rights litigation began to have its impact. Under the leadership of the Supreme Court, federal judges started to use the Fourteenth Amendment to reverse earlier decisions that rendered it and federal legislation ineffective. The Court outlawed all forms of governmentally imposed racial segregation and struck down most of the devices that had been used by state and local authorities to keep blacks from voting.[1] Presidents, too, were using their executive authority to fight segregation in the armed services and the federal bureaucracy. They were directing more of the resources of the Department of Justice to enforce whatever civil rights laws were available.

---

[1] For a general history of Supreme Court decisions affecting the constitutional rights of blacks, see Loren Miller, *The Petitioners* (Meridian Books, 1967); for history of the political role of blacks, see Robert P. Turner, *Up to the Front Line: Blacks in the American Political System* (Kennikat Press, 1975).

As the 1950s came to a close, the emerging national consensus in favor of governmental action to protect civil rights and the growing political voice of blacks began to have their impact on Congress. In 1957, Congress overrode a southern filibuster in the Senate and enacted the first federal civil rights laws since Reconstruction. During the 1960s came additional and significant civil rights legislation, but the issues and battles changed. During the 1950s, the conflict was seen primarily as an attempt by the national government to compel southern state governments to stop segregating blacks into inferior schools, parks, libraries, houses, and jobs. The major effort had been to put down determined southern resistance to the Supreme Court's frontal attack on segregation, especially in the schools. Then came 1963.

1963: A TURNING POINT

A decade after the Supreme Court declared public school segregation to be unconstitutional, most black children in the South still attended segregated schools. In the North, segregation in housing and education remained the established pattern in the cities. Congress had enacted laws, judges has issued injunctions, presidents had proclaimed executive orders and appointed commissions. Most legal barriers in the path of equal rights had fallen. But black Americans still could not buy a house where they wanted, secure the job they needed, find educational opportunities for their children, or walk secure in the knowledge that they would not be subjected to insults. And what had once been thought of as a southern problem was recognized as a national problem. By 1963 the struggles in the courtrooms were being supplemented by a massive social, economic, and political movement. What had been largely a conflict arousing the emotions and commitments of the more highly educated and economically secure blacks gripped the feelings of thousands of men and women, from the domestic servant to the Nobel Prize winner.

The black revolt of 1963 did not come unannounced, and its immediate background was not the struggle to desegregate the schools. In one sense it began when the first black slave was educated three hundred years ago. Its more immediate origin was in 1955 in Montgomery, Alabama, when the black community boycotted city buses to protest segregation on them. The boycott worked. Montgomery produced the first charismatic civil rights leader—the Reverend Martin Luther King. Through his Southern Christian Leadership Conference and his doctrine of nonviolent resistance, he gave a new dimension to the struggle for civil rights. By the early 1960s, new organizational resources to support and sponsor sit-ins, freedom rides, live-ins, and mass demonstrations came into existence in almost every city.

In the summer of 1963 the forces of social discontent created a national crisis. It started with a demonstration in Birmingham, Alabama, which was countered by the use of fire hoses, police dogs, and mass arrests. It ended in a march in Washington, D.C., where over 200,000 people heard King speak of his dream of the day when children "will live in a nation where they will not be judged by the color of their skin, but by the content of their character." By the time the summer was over there was hardly a city that had not had a demonstration, protest, or sit-in; in many, there were riots. This direct action had some effect: civil rights ordinances were enacted in many cities and existing legislation broadened; more schools were desegregated that fall than in any year since 1956. At the national level, President Kennedy urged Congress to enact a comprehensive civil rights bill. But Congress did not act.

Late in 1963, the nation's grief over the assassination of John Kennedy, who had become identified with civil rights goals, added political fuel to the drive for federal action.[2] President Johnson gave the adoption of civil rights legislation the highest priority of his program. On July 2, 1964, after months of debate, President Johnson signed the Civil Rights Act of 1964 into law.

BLACK MILITANCY, BLACK AWARENESS, AND BLACK POWER

At the close of the 1960s, the legal phases of the civil rights movement had about come to a close. But as "things got better," discontent became more intense. Once the chains of slavery began to be withdrawn, the stings that remained hurt more. When blacks had been completely subjugated, they had lacked resources to defend themselves. But, as is true of almost all social revolutions, as conditions began to improve, demands became more and more insistent. Millions of impoverished black Americans, like the white Americans who came before them, have demonstrated growing impatience with the discrimination that remains. These are the same frustrations now heard from the dispossessed around the world.

It is not surprising that this volatile situation should give way to racial violence and disorders. By 1965, the year of the Watts riots in Los Angeles, it was all too clear that disorders were becoming a part of the American scene. In 1966 and 1967 these disorders increased in scope and intensity; the Detroit riot in July 1967 was the worst race riot in modern American history. In July 1967 President Johnson said, "Not even the sternest police action nor the most effective federal troops can ever create lasting peace in our cities." And he appointed a special Advisory Commission on Civil Disorders to investigate the origins of the disorders and to recommend measures to prevent or contain such disasters in the future.

TWO SOCIETIES?

When the Commission, known as the Kerner Commission after its chairman, then Governor Otto Kerner of Illinois, issued its report, it said in stark, clear language: "What white Americans have never fully understood — but what the Negro can never forget — is that white society is deeply implicated in the ghetto. *White institutions created it, white institutions maintain it, and white society condones it.*"

The basic conclusion of the commission was that "our nation is moving toward two societies, one black, one white — separate and unequal" and that "only a commitment to national action on an unprecedented scale" could change this trend. National action, said the commission, should be based on these objectives:

Opening up opportunities to those who are restricted by racial segregation and discrimination, and eliminating all barriers to their choice of jobs, education and housing.

Removing the frustration of powerlessness among the disadvantaged by explicitly helping them to deal with the problems that affect their

---

[2]For treatments of John F. Kennedy and civil rights policy, see Carl M. Brauer, *John F. Kennedy and The Second Reconstruction* (Columbia University Press, 1977); and Bruce Miroff, *Pragmatic Illusions: The Presidential Politics of John F. Kennedy* (McKay, 1976). See also Joel D. Aberbach and Jack L. Walker, "The Meanings of Black Power," *American Political Science Review* (June 1970), pp. 367–88.

own lives and by increasing the capacity of our public and private institutions to respond to these problems.

Increasing communication across racial lines to destroy stereotypes, halt polarization, end distrust and hostility, and create common grounds for efforts toward public order and social justice.[3]

To fulfill these objectives, the commission made sweeping recommendations concerning employment, education, housing, and the welfare system. Although the Vietnam War, the Nixon resignation, and the partial calming down of racial tensions have diverted attention momentarily away from questions about how the two nations can live together in peace and with justice, this remains our most important internal issue.

Where do we stand? Legal barriers have been lowered by civil rights legislation and judicial decisions. The remaining restraints appear to be primarily economic and social. Not that there is complete compliance with the legislation; ways are still found to thwart, circumvent, or obstruct the force of these laws, especially those that apply to housing. But what now appears to stand in the way of faster advancement by the impoverished blacks of our cities and rural countryside is lack of modern job skills, poor education, and inadequate housing and income. Future legislation is more likely to be aimed at creating programs to overcome these handicaps than was the civil rights legislation of the 1960s.

There will be continuing friction among black Americans (and white Americans) not only over the means of achieving the goals of equality, but over ends as well. A few black Americans see violent action as the only way to get "the system" to respond; more believe that changes can be brought about through peaceful direct action. But most apparently still favor the traditional electoral and political methods of bargaining, negotiation, and building coalitions with other political interests.[4] Black Americans also differ over where such strategies should lead. Some see integration of the races as the end; others—such as the black nationalists—see separation of the races as the only realistic solution. Still others see cultural pluralism as the answer: a society in which there will remain identifiable black and white communities, but communities that individuals are free to move into and out of, neighborhoods of choice rather than of compulsion.

THREE SOCIETIES OR MORE?

The rise of black militancy and the struggle for racial justice stimulated other minorities, especially Latinos and American Indians, to organize and to insist that they too be accorded the rights promised by the Declaration of Independence and secured by the Constitution. To black power has been added brown power, sometimes as an ally, sometimes as an opponent, but all part of the rising political activity of what have come to be called "disadvantaged groups." As the 1960s came to a close, these forces

---

[3]*Report of the National Advisory Commission on Civil Disorders* (U.S. Government Printing Office, 1968).

[4]See Matthew Holden, Jr., *The Divisible Republic: Part I, The Politics of the Black Nation* (Aelard-Schuman, 1973), esp. pp. 42–131; see also Lucius J. Barker and Jesse J. McCorry, Jr., *Black Americans and the Political Systems* (Winthrop, 1976), esp. pp. 332–53; Harrell R. Rodgers, Jr., ed., *Racism and Inequality: The Policy Alternatives* (W. H. Freeman, 1975); Louis B. Moreland, *White Racism and the Law* (Charles E. Merrill, 1970).

of discontent were dramatically augmented by a revival of the long-smoldering feminist movement, now called women's liberation. Although the Nineteenth Amendment had ended discrimination against women as voters, it had not brought to an end the discrimination they suffered in employment, schooling, and freedom to manage property.

Finally, as the 1970s opened, there was also a revival of concern about the "ethnics"—that is, white Americans not of Anglo-Saxon heritage. In the past the American model was supposedly the melting pot in which all persons regardless of background would become more and more alike. But in part as a reaction to the rise of the blacks and browns, in part as a statement in defense of ethnic neighborhoods, but also in part as a recognition of the values of cultural pluralism, we now also hear about Polish power and Irish power.

More than 220 million Americans of all colors and ethnic backgrounds have managed, not always wisely or fairly, to operate within the framework of a single society and government. The challenge is to move from survival as a nation to give reality to the promise of equal justice for all.

These are the social and political realities of the struggle for justice. But what have been the governmental response and initiatives in the areas of segregation, voting, criminal justice, housing, employment, and public accommodations? Before we examine them, it is valuable to review the constitutional standards that relate most directly to the question of equal justice under the law.

Equal protection under the laws—what does it mean?

The Fourteenth Amendment declares, "No state [including any subdivision thereof] shall . . . deny to any person within its jurisdiction the equal protection of the laws." Although there is no equal-protection clause limiting the national government, the Fifth Amendment's due process clause has been understood to impose the same restraints on the national government.

The Constitution does not forbid the government from making distinctions among people, for it could not legislate without doing so. What the Constitution forbids is *unreasonable* classifications. In general, a classification is unreasonable when there is no relation between the classes it creates and permissible governmental goals. For example, a law prohibiting redheads from voting would be unreasonable, because there is no relation between having red hair and the ability to vote. On the other hand, laws denying to persons under eighteen the right to vote, to marry without the permission of their parents, or a license to drive a car are reasonable because there seems to be (at least to most persons over eighteen) a relationship between chronological age and the ability to vote sensibly, marry wisely, and drive safely. Similarly, the Supreme Court has held that it is reasonable to treat the rich differently from the poor for the purpose of levying taxes (but not for voting), and to classify property according to its use for zoning purposes.

THE RATIONAL BASIS TEST

The traditional test to determine whether a law complies with the equal protection requirement places the burden of proof on those attacking it. If any facts justify a classification, it will be sustained. "It's enough that the State action be rationally based and free from invidious discrimination. . . . It does not offend the Constitution because the classification is not made with mathematical nicety or because in practice it results in some inequality."[5] To illustrate: Illinois' exemption of individuals from paying personal property taxes while at the same time imposing such taxes on corporations was sustained. Said Justice Douglas for the Court: "Where taxation is concerned, and no specific federal right apart from equal protection is imperiled, the states have large leeway in making classifications and drawing lines which in their judgment produce reasonable systems of taxation."[6] And Ohio was permitted to deny unemployment benefits to those laid off because of strikes in other companies. The statute, thought the Court, did not involve any fundamental rights or "apply to any particularly protected class and the test therefore is whether the statute has a rational relation to legitimate state interests."[7]

But the Supreme Court's deference to the judgment of the legislatures and its use of the less exacting, more relaxed "rational basis" test does not hold in three situations: first, when a suspect classification is involved; second, when an almost-suspect classification is involved; and third, when a fundamental right is involved.

SUSPECT CLASSIFICATIONS

There are certain classifications that are "odious to our system," "constitutionally suspect," "subject to the most rigid scrutiny," and in most instances irrelevant. The traditional tests of suspectness are: 1) A class saddled by history with disabilities or, 2) Subjected by history to purposeful unequal treatment, or 3) Relegated by our society to a position of such political powerlessness as to require extraordinary judicial protection.[8]

Race and *national origins* are clearly suspect classifications.[9] So probably is religion, although there is no specific Supreme Court decision to this effect, probably because states have seldom tried to classify persons on the basis of religion. *Alienage* (the condition of being an alien) is a suspect classification so far as *states* are concerned. But Congress under its power to regulate immigration and naturalization may subject aliens to restrictions not permissible for states.[10] Thus, when a law comes before the Court involving race, national origin, or aliens (if it is a state law), the normal presumption of constitutionality is *reversed.* It is not sufficient that the law merely be a reasonable and rational means for handling a particular problem. The Supreme Court must be persuaded that there is some "compelling public interest" to justify the law. The state must also demonstrate that there is no alternative way less restrictive in its impact on the suspect classification to accomplish the compelling public purpose.

RACE—A SUSPECT OR AN OUTLAWED CLASSIFICATION? —THE BAKKE CASE

Of all suspect classifications, the most suspect are those based on race. Plainly, racial classifications that impose a disability on a racial minority are unconstitutional. And it is also clear that the equal protection clause protects not just blacks, but any person being denied rights because of race or color. What if the government "takes race into account when it

[5]*Dandridge* v. *Williams* 397 U.S. 471 (1970); *Jefferson* v. *Hackney,* 406 U.S. 535 (1972); *Kahn* v. *Shevin,* 416 U.S. 351 (1974).

[6]*Lehnhausen* v. *Lake Shore Auto Parts Co.,* 410 U.S. 356 (1976).

[7]*Ohio Bureau of Employment Services v. Hodory.*

[8]*San Antonio School District* v. *Rodriguez,* 411 U.S. 1 (1973).

[9]*Ibid.*

[10]*Fiallo v. Bell,* 430 U.S. 787 (1977); *Nyquist v. Mauclet,* 432 U.S. 1(1977).

acts not to demean or insult any racial group, but to remedy disadvantages cast on minorities by past racial prejudice?[11] There has been no more hotly debated constitutional question than this one.[12]

The issue came to the fore when Allan Bakke, a white male, argued that the denial of his admission to the Medical College of the University of California at Davis, while less well qualified blacks were admitted under a special admission procedure, had deprived him of his rights under the equal protection clause as well as rights secured to him by Title VI of the Civil Rights Act.

On June 28, 1978, the Supreme Court rendered its judgment. Justice Powell spoke for the Court, but in an opinion in which no other justice completely joined. He ruled that Davis's dual admission program which "focused solely on race" was unconstitutional and that Bakke was entitled to admission. But for the Court he reversed the judgment of the Supreme Court of California that any consideration of race in the admissions process is unconstitutional.

Justice Powell took the view that race is just as suspect a classification when it works to the disadvantage of whites as when it works to the disadvantage of blacks. He denied that the University's purpose of aiding a victimized group gain access to the medical profession or medical school was a legitimate goal of a university. However, Justice Powell concluded that the University of California did have a legitimate educational purpose in trying to obtain a diverse student body and that for this compelling and legitimate purpose it could take race into account as "one element in a range of factors."[13]

Justices Brennan, White, Marshall, and Blackmun agreed that race could be taken into account, but they would go further than Justice Powell. They argued that the Davis program was constitutional. They emphasized that education is not a fundamental right and that whites as a class, unlike blacks, have not any of the "traditional indicia of suspectness." They agreed that where race is used for a benign and not stigmatizing purpose, it should nonetheless be subject to a strict scrutiny, but not "strict in theory and fatal fact." Brennan proposed a two-pronged test to review benign racial classifications: "(1) an important articulated purpose for its use must be shown, and (2) it must not stigmatize any group or single out those least well represented in the political purpose to bear the brunt of a benign program."[14]

"It cannot be questioned," said Justice Brennan, "that in the absence of the special admissions program, access of minority students to the Medical School would be severely limited." As to the second part of the test, there is no evidence that the Davis program was merely "a cover to discriminate against any minority group."[15] True, whites are excluded from participation in the special admissions program, but the use of racial preferences for remedial purposes does not inflict a pervasive injury upon individual

[11]Justice Brennan in *Regents of the University of California v. Bakke*, 57 L Ed 2d 750 (1978).

[12]See Robert M. O'Neil, *Discrimination Against Discrimination* (Indiana University Press, 1975) in favor of such programs and Nathan Glazer, *Affirmative Discrimination* (Basic Books, 1976) against.

[13]*Regents of the University of California* v. *Baake.*

[14]*Ibid.*

[15]*Ibid.*

whites in the sense that wherever they go or whatever they do there is a significant likelihood that they will be treated as second-class citizens because of their color.

Justice Marshall in a separate opinion stressed the fact that the very purpose of the Fourteenth Amendment was to protect blacks, but that it had not been so used until very recently. "While I applaud the judgment," he wrote, "of the Court that a university may consider race in its admissions process, it is more than a little ironic that, after several hundred years of class-based discrimination against Negroes, the Court is unwilling to hold that a class-based remedy for that discrimination is permissible."[16]

Justice Stevens, the Chief Justice, Justice Stewart, and Justice Rehnquist, concluded that it was unnecessary to decide the constitutional questions because, "Under Title VI it is not permissible to say 'yes' to one person, but to say 'no' to another person, only because of the color of their skin." (The other members of the Court had argued that Title VI does not go beyond constitutional standards in imposing "color-blindness" in the administration of federally supported programs.)

Well, what does it all mean? Bakke will be interpreted for years. Even in the opinions in the Bakke decision itself the justices argue with one another about what they have decided. There will be other cases questioning and testing various programs designed to overcome for blacks, for ethnic minorities, and for women the impact of past social discrimination. But this much seems clear: Race remains a suspect classification, but not an outlawed one. Programs that classify by race, even those that have a benign purpose, will be subject to close judicial scrutiny. And specifically, so far as college and university admissions are concerned, race may be taken into account as one factor to achieve a diversified student body, but no person can be denied consideration for admission to a program solely because of race.

ALMOST SUSPECT CLASSIFICATIONS: SEX AND ILLEGITIMACY

Recently the Supreme Court distinguished another category—classifications not subject to such stringent tests of constitutionality as those of a suspect classification, but subject to considerably more stringent tests than the rational basis category. These are the classifications of illegitimacy and sex. "Illegitimacy is analogous in many respects," said Justice Powell for the Court, " 'to the personal characteristics that have been held to be suspect. . . . We nevertheless conclude that the analogy is not sufficient to require our most exacting scrutiny.' "[17] Yet in reviewing laws imposing disabilities on illegitimates, the Court has held most of them to be unconstitutional, making it clear that the scrutiny of such laws "is not a toothless one."[18]

What of classifications based on sex? It was as late as 1971 before any classification based on sex was declared unconstitutional. Prior to that time, many laws that purported to provide special protection for women, such as one in Ohio forbidding any women other than the wife or daughter of an owner of a tavern to serve as barmaids, were upheld.[19] As Justice

[16]*Ibid.*

[17]*Trimble* v. *Gordon*, 430 U.S. 762 (1977); *Mathews* v. *Lucas*, 427 U.S. 495 (1976).

[18]*Ibid.*

[19]*Goesaert* v. *Cleary*, 335 U.S. 464 (1948).

Brennan wrote for the Court in 1973, "There can be no doubt that our nation has had a long and unfortunate history of sex discrimination. Traditionally such discrimination was rationalized by an attitude of 'romantic paternalism' which, in practical effect put women, not on a pedestal, but in a cage."[20]

Some members of the Court would treat sex like race, that is, as a suspect classification. But so far a majority has not taken this position. The majority view is that classifications by sex, although not subject to as severe scrutiny as those based on race, are subject to more stringent testing than those relating to economic regulation. To sustain a classification based on sex, the burden is on the government to show that it serves "important governmental objectives" and is substantially related to the achievement of these objectives. Treatment of women differently from men (or vice versa) is forbidden by the Constitution when supported by no more substantial justification than "archaic and overbroad generalizations," "old notions," and "the role-typing society has long imposed upon women."[21]

Applying these tests, the following have been declared unconstitutional: a preference for fathers over mothers in the administration of their children's estates;[22] a federal law providing for dependency benefits for the wives of male military officers but only for such husbands of female officers who were dependent on their wives for over one-half of their support;[23] provisions of social security laws giving widows more benefits than widowers;[24] a state law giving sons child support from their fathers until they were twenty-one but daughters only until they were eighteen;[25] a state law prohibiting the sale of beer to males under twenty-one but to females under eighteen.[26]

On the other side, the Supreme Court has sustained some laws treating women differently from men, especially those that favor women over men. For example, the Court upheld a law granting to widows but not to widowers an annual property tax exemption.[27] The Court majority thought that a state could reasonably conclude a lone women is more likely to face financial difficulties than a lone man. The dissenting justices argued that if the state was anxious to help poor widows, it should have limited its exemption to those who are poor, whether male or female. They pointed out there are such things as rich widows and poor widowers. Nor does the Constitution preclude a naval regulation that gives women thirteen years either to be promoted or to be discharged, but gives male officers only nine years.[28] The Court majority contended that the difference was rational, since women have fewer chances for promotion within the Navy than do men. Along the same lines, the Court held that Congress could give

Chris Wenzel, foreperson of diesel maintenance shop in Minneapolis, operates electric hoist, which moves a two-ton set of locomotive drive wheels onto tracks. Other formerly all-male jobs now being held by women include locomotive engineer, yardmaster, track worker, and brake operator.

[20]*Frontiero* v. *Richardson*, 411 U.S. 677 (1973).

[21]*Califano* v. *Webster*, 430 U.S. 313 (1977).

[22]*Reed* v. *Reed*, 404 U.S. 71 (1971).

[23]*Frontiero* v. *Richardson*.

[24]*Califano* v. *Goldfarb*, 430 U.S. 199 (1977).

[25]*Stanton* v. *Stanton*, 421 U.S. 7 (1976).

[26]*Craig* v. *Boren*, 429 U.S. 190 (1976).

[27]*Kahn* v. *Shevin*, 416 U.S. 251 (1974).

[28]*Schelisinger* v. *Ballard*, 419 U.S. 488 (1975).

Anti-ERA protesters picket outside the White House (left), Bella Abzug of New York addresses ERA supporters (right).

women greater social security retirement benefits than men "to compensate women for past economic discrimination . . . whether from overt discrimination or from the socialization process of a male-dominated culture, the job market is inhospitable to the women seeking any but the lowest paid jobs."[29]

Thus, in recent years the Supreme Court has struck down almost every law brought before it alleged to have discriminated against women, but has sustained a few despite the charge that they discriminated in favor of women. About the only decisions in the other direction are those in which the Court has held that state and private disability insurance programs which exclude disabilities resulting from normal pregnancy do not violate either the equal protection clause or the Civil Rights Act of 1964.[30] (Congress is likely to reverse the impact of these decisions.) And the Supreme Court has ruled that women are not denied equal protection when disqualified from serving as penal guards in maximum security male penitentiaries.[31]

Unless the Equal Rights Amendment, which would make sex classifications imposed by or sanctioned by governments totally unacceptable, is adopted, such classifications, although not suspect, require considerable justification. And in view of recent decisions, it could be that the immediate beneficiaries of ERA are likely to be men as well as women. Nor will the adoption of ERA end all constitutional debates flowing from sex classifications: For example, may a state for some purposes treat mothers differently from fathers?

FUNDAMENTAL RIGHTS

The Supreme Court also subjects state regulations to especially stringent scrutiny when the laws impinge on "fundamental rights." The justices are not too clear what makes a right fundamental. But Justice Powell, speaking for a five-man majority in *San Antonio School District* v. *Rodriguez* (1973), explained that it is not the social importance of the right nor the justices' conclusions about the significance of the right that determines whether or not it is fundamental, but whether *it is explicitly or implicitly guaranteed by the Constitution.* Under this test, the right to travel has been held to be fun-

[29]*Califano* v. *Webster*, 430 U.S. 313 (1977).

[30]*Geduldig* v. *Aiello*, 417 U.S. 484 (1974); *General Electric* v. *Gilbert*, 429 U.S. 125 (1976).

[31]*Dothard* v. *Rawlinson*, United States Law Week, 53 L Ed 2d 786 (1977).

119

damental, along with the right to vote and First Amendment rights, but not the right to an education or to housing or welfare benefits. Important as are these latter rights, there is nothing in the Constitution guaranteeing to any person that the government will provide an education, a house, or welfare benefits. Nor are there any specific constitutional provisions protecting these rights from governmental regulation.[32]

Once the Court decides that a right is fundamental, laws restricting it, like those that have an impact on a suspect classification, must meet the more stringent constitutional test: The state must demonstrate a compelling public need and persuade the Court that it has acted by procedures which place the least possible restraint on the fundamental right in question.

The new equal protection

If the Supreme Court decides that a law does not deal with a fundamental right or a suspect or almost-suspect classification, it almost never finds the law unconstitutional. On the other hand, if it decides that the law does deal with a fundamental right or a suspect or almost-suspect classification, it almost never finds it constitutional. Critics of this new and more rigid equal protection test contend that all that it amounts to is that the judges are substituting their own policy judgments for those of the legislators. Justice Rehnquist, for example, has written in dissent: ". . . this Court seems to regard the Equal Protection Clause as a cat-of-nine-tails to be kept in the judicial closet as a threat to legislatures which may, in the view of the judiciary, get out of hand and pass 'arbitrary,' 'illogical,' or 'unreasonable' laws. Except in the area of the law in which the Framers obviously meant it to apply—classifications based on race or on national origin, the first cousin of race, the Court's decisions can fairly be described as an endless tinkering with legislative judgments, a series of conclusions unsupported by any central guiding principle."[33]

PROVING DISCRIMINATION

Discrimination by governmental agencies based on race, national origin, sex, or alienage is almost always unconstitutional. But how is discrimination to be proved? Does the fact that a law or a regulation has a differential impact on persons of different races by itself establish that it is unconstitutional?

In one of its more important decisions of recent years, *Washington* v. *Davis* (1976), the Supreme Court stated: "The invidious quality of a law claimed to be racially discriminatory must ultimately be traced to a racially discriminatory *purpose*. Disproportionate impact is not irrelevant, but it is not the sole touchstone of an invidious racial discrimination forbidden by the Constitution. Standing alone, it does not trigger the rule that racial classifications are to be subjected to the strictest scrutiny and are justified only by the weightiest of considerations. . . ."[34]

What in practical terms does this mean? Suppose a city gives a test as a condition for being a police officer, which test one race passes in larger ratio than another. By itself this does not establish that the test is unconstitutional. Or if a city has a zoning regulation that permits only single-family residences and thus makes low-cost housing projects difficult, this fact

"You mean these apply to the riffraff too?"

The Herblock Gallery (Simon & Schuster, 1968)

[32]*San Antonio School District* v. *Rodriguez* (1973), and cases cited therein.

[33]*Trimble* v. *Gordon.*

[34]*Washington* v. *Davis*, 426 U.S. 229 (1976).

alone does not establish unconstitutional discrimination either against the poor or against blacks.[35] Unless there is evidence that a discriminatory *purpose* was a motivating factor in a zoning regulation, a city may adopt regulations that affect persons of different races in different ways.

However, the racially differential impact is not irrelevant. For example, if in a community where there are a large number of blacks or Latinos relatively few such persons are called for jury duty, this creates a suspicion that juries are being selected with a discriminatory purpose. Under these circumstances, the burden of proof shifts to the state to demonstrate that it has not engaged in unconstitutional discriminatory conduct.[36]

In addition, Congress and the states, if they wish, may make illegal what is not unconstitutional. Thus some civil rights legislation forbids the use of certain tests even when the purpose is not to discriminate. Congress, in its wisdom, has outlawed the use of tests unrelated to job performance if such tests screen out the members of one race or sex to a greater extent than another.[37]

The life and death of Jim Crow

This review of the Supreme Court's interpretation of the equal-protection clause gets us considerably ahead of our story. We must return to the last century.

Laws requiring the segregation of blacks and whites date only from the end of the nineteenth century.[38] Prior to that time it was social custom and economic status, rather than law, that kept the two races apart. But segregationists began to insist that laws were needed to maintain racial segregation. Before long, southern states and cities had made it a crime for whites and blacks to ride in the same car on a train, attend the same theater, or go to the same school. Jim Crow laws, as they came to be called, soon blanketed southern life. How could these laws be adopted and enforced in the face of the equal-protection clause?

IS SEGREGATION DISCRIMINATION?: *PLESSY* V. *FERGUSON*

In 1896 the Supreme Court, in *Plessy* v. *Ferguson*, endorsed the view that racial segregation did not constitute discrimination and that states could require the separation of races as long as equal accommodations were provided for all.[39] Even equal accommodations were not required except for services provided by public funds or for a limited category of public utilities, such as trains and buses. Under this *separate-but-equal* formula, several states, most of which were in the South, enforced segregation in transportation, places of public accommodation, and education.

The Plessy decision was forward-looking for its time, because it did require equality as the price for a state to adopt a program of compulsory segregation. But for many years the "equal" part of the formula was meaningless. States segregated blacks into unequal facilities, and blacks lacked a political voice to protest. The Supreme Court did not help. In 1899, for example, the Court found no denial of equal protection in the fact that a county provided a high school for white citizens but none for the sixty

[35]*Arlington Heights* v. *Metro Housing Corp.*, 429 U.S. 252 (1977).

[36]*Castaneda* v. *Partida*, 430 U.S. 482 (1977).

[37]*Griggs* v. *Duke Power Co.*, 401 U.S. 424 (1971); *Dothard* v. *Rawlinson*, 53L Ed 2d 786 (1977).

[38]C. Vann Woodward, *The Strange Career of Jim Crow*, rev. ed. (Oxford University Press, 1968).

[39]163 U.S. 537.

black children in the district.[40] The passage of time did not lessen the inequality. In 1950, in all the segregated states, there were fourteen medical schools for whites, none for blacks; sixteen law schools for whites, five for blacks; fifteen engineering schools for whites, none for blacks; five dentistry schools for whites, none for blacks.

Beginning in the late 1930s, blacks started to file lawsuits challenging the doctrine. They cited facts to show that in practice separate-but-equal always resulted in discrimination against blacks. However, the Supreme Court was not yet willing to upset the doctrine directly. Rather, it began to undermine it. The Court scrutinized each situation and in case after case ordered facilities to be equalized.

THE END OF SEPARATE-BUT-EQUAL: *BROWN* V. *BOARD OF EDUCATION*

Finally, in the spring of 1954 in *Brown* v. *Board of Education*, the Supreme Court reversed its 1896 holding as applied to public schools and ruled that "separate but equal" is a contradiction in terms and that segregation is itself discrimination.[41] A year later, the Court ordered school boards to proceed with all deliberate speed to desegregate public schools at the earliest practicable date.[42]

It was one thing for the Supreme Court to declare unconstitutional racial segregation in the public schools. It was another to abolish such segregation. In the South, some school officials tried to circumvent desegregation orders by assigning pupils to segregated schools for reasons other than race, closing schools to which blacks had been assigned, and using the pretext of violence as justification for delaying action. In the North, racial segregation in housing resulted in de facto segregation, with black children often being crowded into the worst schools with least resources.

In the years following the Brown decisions, federal judges struck down a whole battery of evasive schemes. In the Little Rock, Arkansas, case (*Cooper* v. *Aaron*, 1958), in an opinion signed by all members of the Court individually—an unprecedented move to indicate their unanimity and strength of conviction—the Court stated: "The constitutional rights of children not to be discriminated against in school admission on grounds of race or color . . . can neither be nullified openly and directly by state legislators or state executives or judicial officers, nor nullified indirectly by them through evasive schemes for segregation whether attempted ingeniously or ingenuously." Community opposition, even violent protests, said the Court, could not justify delay: "Law and order are not . . . to be preserved by depriving the Negro children of their constitutional rights."[43]

Beginning in 1963, the Supreme Court gradually reversed its second Brown decision granting school districts time to prepare for desegregation. In 1969 the Court stated unequivocally: "Continued operation of ra-

---

[40]*Cumming* v. *County Board of Education*, 175 U.S. 528 (1899).

[41]*Brown* v. *Board of Education*, 347 U.S. 483 (1954). See also J. W. Peltason, *Fifty-Eight Lonely Men: Southern Federal Judges and School Desegregation* (University of Illinois Press, 1971), p. 248.

[42]*Brown* v. *Board of Education*, 349 U.S. 294 (1955). For a comprehensive and fascinating history of the events leading up to *Brown* v. *Board of Education*, see Richard Kluger, *Simple Justice* (Knopf, 1976); Earl Black, *Southern Governors and Civil Rights: Racial Segregation as a Campaign Issue in the Second Reconstruction* (Harvard University Press, 1977) shows response, reaction, and eventually neutralization of race as a political issue following the Brown decision.

[43]358 U.S. 1 (1958).

cially segregated schools under the standard of 'all deliberate speed' is no longer constitutionally permissible. School districts must immediately terminate dual school systems based on race and operate only unitary school systems."[44]

Congress and the presidency gradually increased their involvement in bringing about desegregation. The 1964 Civil Rights Act authorizes the attorney general to begin desegregation suits. But of even greater significance, Title VI of the act stipulates that federal dollars—of major importance since the passage of the Elementary and Secondary Education Act of 1965—must be withdrawn from any school district or public institution of higher education that discriminates "on the ground of race, color, or national origin in any program or activity receiving federal financial assistance."[45] (The Education Act of 1972 adds sex to the list; other acts have added handicapped, the aged, veterans of the Vietnam era, and disabled veterans to the protected categories.) Not only does Title VI forbid discrimination, it also imposes on schools the responsibility for taking affirmative action to ensure that protected categories are not denied access to any federally supported program or activity. (It was under the Civil Rights Act and HEW regulations, for example, that the San Francisco school system was told that it had an obligation to provide English language instruction for the more than 1,800 students of Chinese ancestry who do not speak English.)[46] The act, in addition, makes federal funds available to help school districts desegregate. During the fifteen years following adoption of the Civil Rights Act the Justice Department has initiated legal actions against more than 500 school districts; HEW threatened to suspend federal aid in 600 cases.

BUSING

One of the most hotly debated issues of our times is whether school officials can and should be required to bus pupils from one neighborhood to another in order to achieve racial integration. If Congress is a reflection of popular opinion, most people oppose such busing. Each year, Congress has adopted stronger and stronger antibusing provisions designed to forbid the Department of HEW to require school districts to bus children past the school nearest their homes.

The Supreme Court, however, has endorsed busing as one of the tools a court may use to remedy officially sanctioned school segregation. In the Charlotte-Mecklenburg Board of Education case, Chief Justice Burger said: "All things being equal with no history of discrimination, it might well be desirable to assign pupils to schools nearest their homes." But where it is established that districts have operated segregated systems, "desegregation plans cannot be limited to walk-in schools."[47]

The Supreme Court has carefully limited its endorsement of busing to school districts where a judge has found that school authorities have *intentionally* discriminated against minorities, and where the busing required is limited to that necessary to eliminate the effects of past official acts or omissions designed to segregate. Where official misconduct is found, not

[44]*Alexander* v. *Board of Education*, 396 U.S. 19(1969).

[45]Gary Orfield, *The Reconstruction of Southern Education: The Schools and the 1964 Civil Rights Act* (Wiley, 1969), p. 355.

[46]*Lau* v. *Nichols*, 414 U.S. 563 (1974).

[47]402 U.S. 1 (1971). See also James Bolner and Robert Shanley, *Busing: The Political and Judicial Process* (Praeger, 1974).

only may judges order busing, but they may do whatever else is necessary to overcome the consequences of *de jure* (by law) segregation. For example, they may order the school and the state to spend funds for remedial courses for blacks who have been the victims of past discrimination.[48]

Limits to the authority of a federal court are illustrated by the Supreme Court's decision in the Detroit school case. A federal district judge had concluded that Detroit school authorities and Michigan state officials had acted to bring about segregation in the Detroit schools. He also found that the Detroit schools could not be desegregated effectively if considered in isolation. Therefore, he ordered the assigning and busing of pupils throughout the city and fifty-four adjacent school districts on a consolidated basis. But the Supreme Court (*Milliken* v. *Bradley*, 1974) by a five-to-four vote reversed this decision. The majority, speaking through Chief Justice Burger, ruled that where it was not shown that the school district lines had been drawn for the purpose of maintaining segregation, and where there was no evidence that the suburban districts were being operated in a racially discriminatory fashion, a judge should not order cross-district busing. To do so, the Chief Justice commented, would make the judge in effect the superintendent of schools for the entire metropolitan area, a task "which few, if any, judges are qualified to perform and one which would deprive the people of control of schools through their elected representatives."[49]

The dissenting justices were especially biting in their comments. Justice Douglas called the decision a dramatic retreat from *Brown* v. *Board* because the black children of Detroit were not only to be kept in separate schools, but the schools are not even to be equal to those of the white children in the suburbs. Justice White said the majority had ignored the role of the state and had left the people of Detroit with no effective remedy to overcome school segregation. Justice Marshall commented that "unless our children begin to learn together, there is little hope that our people will ever learn to live together."

Obviously the Court's decision in this and the other busing cases does not end the matter. The highly charged nature of busing is such that Congress, the president and the entire electorate are also participating in its resolution.

WHERE DO WE STAND?

De jure segregation, that is segregation required by law, has disappeared, even in the Deep South.[50] De facto segregation, however, is still very much with us. More children attend de facto segregated schools in the North than in the South.

Some blacks have become disillusioned about securing integrated schools or even about the desirability of integration. The general counsel of the New York City Commission on Human Rights told a Senate committee: "You are simply not going to integrate most of the children now trapped inside the sprawling ghettos of Chicago, Detroit, Philadelphia, St. Louis, New Orleans, Houston, and many other cities. . . . And to pre-

[48]*Austin Independent School District* v. *United States*, 429 U.S. 990 (1976); *Milliken* v. *Bradley*, 53 L Ed 2d 745 (1977).

[49]*Milliken* v. *Bradley*. 418 U.S. 717, (1974).

[50]Robert L. Green, *Northern School Desegregation: Educational, Legal, and Political Issues* (National Society for the Study of Education, 1974); Harrell R. Rodgers, Jr., and Charles S. Bullock III, "School Desegregation," *American Politics Quarterly* (April 1976), pp. 172ff.

tend that it might be done is to play a cruel hoax on those black communities searching desperately for better education."[51] Many black children are still denied an adequate education. Nonetheless, "Even though the re-ordering of race relations in Southern (and Northern) schools was halting and incomplete . . . no nation has accomplished, without war or revolution, a social transformation as profound and as rapid as that implied by the partial integration of the schools of the South."[52]

Barriers to voting

The Constitution leaves to the states the power to determine suffrage qualifications for all elections, but the states are subject to a variety of constitutional restraints in exercising this power. Under Article I, Section 4, Congress has power to supersede state regulations as to the "times, places, and manner of elections for federal officers." Congress has used this authority to set age qualifications for congressional and presidential elections, to set residency requirements to vote for presidential electors, to set a uniform day for all states to elect congressmen and presidential electors, and to give American citizens who reside outside of the United States the right to vote in federal elections in the state in which they previously lived.

The main thrust of constitutional restraints on state power over elections, however, is to prevent interference with the right to vote because of race or sex or because a person is just eighteen years of age. But these are not the only limitations. In addition, the Fourteenth Amendment has been interpreted to forbid states from setting "unreasonable" requirements. For example, a state cannot exclude nonparents or nontaxpayers from voting for members of school boards[53] or prohibit members of the armed forces from voting. "The uniform of our country . . . must not be the badge of disfranchisement for the man or woman who wears it," the Court declared.[54] But the major impact of the Fourteenth Amendment on voting is to prevent states from imposing any racial qualifications. And what the Fourteenth Amendment does implicitly, the Fifteenth does explicitly: "The right of citizens of the United States to vote shall not be denied or abridged by the United States or by any State on account of race, color, or previous condition of servitude." The Fifteenth Amendment also empowers Congress to enact any law necessary and proper to enforce the prohibitions of the amendment.

For over a decade after the Civil War, the provisions of the Fourteenth and Fifteenth Amendments were backed up by federal troops. Blacks, in alliance with northern radical Republicans (carpetbaggers) and certain white southerners (scalawags), assumed control of some state governments. The new regimes passed good laws as well as bad, but they were hated by "patriotic" white southerners. Then came the counterrevolution. Even before federal troops were withdrawn from the South in 1877, white Democrats had begun to regain power. Organizing secret societies such as the Knights of the White Camellia and the Ku Klux Klan, the aroused Southerners set out to restore southern government to white rule. Often they resorted to threats, force, and fraud, to midnight shootings, burnings, and whippings. Many blacks concluded that it would be healthier to stay

[51] As reported in *Congressional Quarterly Weekly Report* (September 1970), p. 2177.

[52] Orfield, *Reconstruction of Southern Education*, p. 355.

[53] *Phoenix* v. *Kolodziejski*, 399 U.S. 204 (1970); *Kramer* v. *Union Free School District*, 395 U.S. 621 (1969).

[54] *Carrington* v. *Rash*, 380 U.S. 89 (1965).

away from the polls than to insist on their vote, and the carpetbaggers began to retreat north.

Once they had regained control of state governments, southern Democrats resolved to continue to keep the blacks from voting. At first they continued to rely on social pressures and threats of violence. But toward the end of the nineteenth century, for the first time since the Civil War, there were two strong political parties—the Democrats and the Populists—in many parts of the South. White supremacists were fearful that the parties might compete for the black vote and that the blacks might come to have a balance-of-power role. To continue to rely on extralegal and illegal means to disfranchise blacks had disadvantages: It undermined the moral fabric of the society, and a too flagrant use of force and fraud might cause the president and Congress to intervene. So white supremacists searched for "legal" means.

Southern leaders reasoned that if they could pass laws that deprived blacks of the vote on grounds other than race, blacks would find it difficult to challenge the laws in the courts. Some whites protested that such laws could be used against whites as well as blacks. But keeping poor whites from voting did not disturb the conservative leaders of the Democratic party who were in control of some southern states, for they were often just as anxious to undermine white support for the Populist party as they were to disfranchise blacks. Leaders in the states where blacks constituted a large minority and sometimes even a majority skillfully played on memories of black rule and northern intervention. "The disfranchisement movement of the 'nineties' gave the Southern states the most impressive systems of obstacles between the voter and the ballot box known to the democratic world."[55]

In the 1940s the Supreme Court began to strike down one after another of the devices used to keep blacks from voting. In 1944 *(Smith* v. *Allwright)* the Court declared the "white primary" unconstitutional.[56] In 1957 it held that racial gerrymandering was contrary to the Fifteenth Amendment.[57] The Twenty-fourth Amendment got rid of the poll tax in federal elections, and in 1966 the Court held that the Fourteenth Amendment forbade the tax as a condition in any election.[58]

As the white primary, poll taxes, racial gerrymandering, and other laws were struck down, those wishing to deny blacks the right to vote relied on registration requirements. On the surface, these requirements appeared to be perfectly proper. It was the manner in which they were administered that kept blacks from the polls, for they were often applied by white election officers while white policemen stood guard, with white judges hearing appeals from decisions of registration officials.

Registration officials often seized on the smallest error in an application blank as an excuse to disqualify a voter. In one parish in the state of Louisiana, after four white voters filed affidavits in which they challenged the legality of the registration of black voters on the grounds that these voters

---

[55]V. O. Key, Jr., *Southern Politics* (Knopf, 1949), p. 555. For a history of the rise and fall of the black disfranchisement, see Steven F. Lawson, *Black Ballots: Voting Rights in the South, 1944–1969* (Columbia University Press, 1976).

[56]321 U.S. 649 (1944).

[57]*Gomillion* v. *Lightfoot*, 364 U.S. 339 (1960).

[58]*Harper* v. *Virginia*, 383 U.S. 663 (1966).

had made an "error in spilling" *(sic)* in their applications, registration officials struck 1,300 out of approximately 1,500 black voters from the polls.[59] In other instances, blacks were denied the right to register because when they stated their ages, they did not stipulate precisely to the day: "I am twenty-one years, six months, and five days old."

In many southern areas literacy tests were administered by registration officials to discriminate against blacks. Some southern states, either as an additional requirement or as a substitute for literacy tests, required an applicants to demonstrate to the satisfaction of election officials that they understood the national and state constitutions and, further, that they were persons of good character. Whites were often asked simple questions; blacks were asked questions that would baffle a Supreme Court justice. In Louisiana, 49,603 illiterate white voters were able to persuade election officials they could understand the Constitution, but only two black voters were able to do so.

ACTION BY THE NATIONAL GOVERNMENT

For over twenty years federal courts under the leadership of the Supreme Court, carefully scrutinized voting laws and procedures in cases brought before them. But this case-by-case approach did not open the voting booth to millions of blacks, especially those living in rural areas of the Deep South. As the United States Civil Rights Commission reported, "Suits must proceed in a single court at a time, and they are time consuming, expensive, and difficult. After one law or procedure is enjoined, the state or county would adopt another."[60]

Finally Congress began to act. At first, as in the Civil Rights Acts of 1957, 1960, and 1964, the major responsibility was left with the courts: Civil rights statutes protecting the right to vote were strengthened, and the Department of Justice was authorized to seek injunctions. The Civil Rights Act of 1964 had hardly been enacted when events in Selma, Alabama, dramatized the inadequacy of depending on the courts to prevent racial barriers in polling places. A voter registration drive in that city lead by Martin Luther King produced police arrests, marches on the state capitol, and the murder of two civil rights workers. But there was no major dent in the color bar at the polls. President Johnson, responding to events in Selma, made a dramatic address to the nation and to Congress calling for federal action to ensure that no person would be deprived of the right to vote in any election for any office because of color or race. Congress responded with the Voting Rights Act of 1965.

THE VOTING RIGHTS ACT OF 1965

The Voting Rights Act of 1965 marks a major departure from prior civil rights acts. Instead of depending on lawsuits and on local officials to carry it out, it authorizes direct action by federal officials to register voters, see to it that they are allowed to vote, and that their ballots are honestly counted. The act, whose constitutionality was upheld in *South Carolina* v. *Katzenbach* (1966),[61] has been twice extended and strengthened by Congress, once in 1970 and again in 1975. It is presently scheduled to remain in effect until 1982.

[59]*Report of the United States Commission on Civil Rights* (U.S. Government Printing Office, 1959), pp. 103–4.

[60]*Ibid.*, and United States Commission on Civil Rights, *Civil Rights: Excerpts* (U.S. Government Printing Office, 1961), p. 18.

[61]*South Carolina* v. *Katzenbach*, 383 U.S. 301 (1966).

As first adopted, the act concentrated on the one hundred rural southern counties which had a long history of discrimination against blacks. Since then it has been amended to cover other areas, including those that contain more than 10 percent of voting-age citizens of language minorities — persons of Spanish heritage, Asian Americans, American Indians, and Alaskan natives. As a result, the covered area now includes all of Alabama, Georgia, Louisiana, Mississippi, North Carolina, South Carolina, Virginia, Texas, and Alaska, and scattered counties and townships in Arizona, California, Connecticut, Hawaii, Idaho, New Hampshire, New York, Maine, Massachusetts, Wyoming, Colorado, Florida, New Mexico, Oklahoma, South Dakota, and Utah.

Here is how the law works: Literacy tests are set aside everywhere. In areas covered by the law, except those that are included only because of the presence of language minorities, the attorney general may, without any court action, call upon the Civil Service Commission to appoint federal examiners to go into election districts and register voters. Then if local election officials turn away any voter the federal examiners have determined is entitled to vote, the examiners go into a federal district court and secure an order impounding all the ballots in that election district until all persons entitled to vote are allowed to do so. The attorney general may also appoint poll watchers to ensure that the votes of all qualified persons are properly counted. In areas covered because of the presence of language minorities, bilingual election materials must be provided.

To keep states from changing requirements or otherwise minimizing the impact of the voting power of blacks, the law has another safeguard. New voting laws, including legislative reapportionments, must be approved by the attorney general of a three-judge district court for the District of Columbia. The burden of proof is on the state to show that the proposed changes are free of a racially discriminatory effect.

THE RESULTS

It is too soon to determine what the impact of the more recent amendments will be with respect to voting by language minorities. But so far as blacks are concerned, the Voting Rights Act has been one of the most effective laws ever adopted. Although it was necessary in some areas to appoint federal examiners, in most areas the mere threat of their being sent in was enough. For the first time blacks find no legal obstacle to registering and voting in every district in the United States.

Since its adoption, more than 4 million blacks have registered to vote in the eleven southern states. More than 1,000 blacks are holding state, local, or party offices in the South — mostly, however, in relatively minor offices. Clearly blacks have become an important factor in southern political life. The black vote can no longer be ignored by those running for public office. It is especially important where the political situation does not become polarized around race: that is, where voters do not find race such an important issue that all whites vote only for white candidates and all blacks vote only for black candidates. Except in local areas where blacks outnumber whites, the black minority is most likely to have the largest political impact where its votes can provide the margin of victory. In a growing number of areas and election contests, public officials no longer find it politically profitable to be identified with the more extreme white supremacists.

In the North, black voting power is beginning to assert itself in practical politics. The election of black mayors in cities such as Cleveland, Los Angeles, Detroit, Atlanta, and Washington, D. C., and the increase of blacks in elective and appointive positions at the state and local levels generally are evidence of the growing influence of black Americans in the American political process.[62]

Barriers to homes, jobs, and public accommodations

Until recently, those who wanted to keep blacks or Jews or Latinos or Indians or any other kind of person from buying homes in their neighborhood or eating lunches at the same counters or working in the same plants could use the power of government to enforce these discriminatory practices. Not so today. Laws and regulations that interfere with equal access to homes, jobs, or public accommodations are now unconstitutional.

Private discrimination, however, does not violate the Fourteenth Amendment: "Where the impetus for the discrimination is private, the State must have "significantly involved itself with invidious discriminations in order for the discriminatory action to fall within the ambit of constitutional prohibition."[63] There must be "state action" to bring the Fourteenth Amendment into play.

The Supreme Court has developed an elaborate set of rules in trying to draw the line between what is and what is not state action. And the judges inspect any conduct where there is suspicion of state involvement in discrimination. Trade unions may not discriminate, since they get their rights to engage in collective bargaining from federal and state laws.[64] A restaurant leasing space in a public parking garage thereby becomes subject to the equal protection clause.[65] However, merely receiving a liquor license from a state does not by itself make the discriminatory conduct of a private club the action of the state.[66]

The Supreme Court found state involvement sufficient to declare unconstitutional an amendment to the California constitution that in effect rendered unenforceable previous legislation forbidding racial discrimination in the sale of real estate. The people of California, in amending their constitution, had made it more difficult for blacks than for whites to buy houses.[67] Similarly, Akron, Ohio's action was unconstitutional when it adopted a charter amendment requiring only open housing ordinances to be submitted to popular approval. Here again the power of government was being used to make it more difficult for those who favored open housing legislation to secure its enactment than for those who favor other kinds of legislation.[68]

The Supreme Court refused, however, to extend the Akron precedent to a California constitutional provision requiring approval by a majority of the voters before any city or county public housing authority could be developed or a low-rent housing project acquired. On its face, the provision was racially neutral.[69]

[62]Leonard A. Cole, *Blacks in Power: A Comparative Study of Black and White Elected Officials* (Princeton University Press, 1976).

[63]*Moose Lodge No. 107* v. *Irvis*, 407 U.S. 163 (1972).

[64]*Conley* v. *Gibson*, 365 U.S. 41 (1957).

[65]*Burton* v. *Wilmington Parking Authority*, 365 U.S. 715 (1961).

[66]*Moose Lodge No. 107* v. *Irvis*.

[67]*Reitman* v. *Mulkey*, 387 U.S. 369 (1967).

[68]*Hunter* v. *Erickson*, 393 U.S. 385 (1969).

[69]*James* v. *Valtierra*, 402 U.S. 137 (1971).

Although discriminatory action by a private individual unsupported by government does not violate the Fourteenth Amendment, these days such conduct is likely to violate a state or federal law. True, the Constitution creates "a zone of privacy which precludes government from interfering with private clubs or groups. The associational rights which our system honors permit all white, all black, all brown and all yellow clubs to be established. They also permit all Catholic, all Jewish, or all agnostic clubs. . . . Government may not tell a man or a woman who his or her associates must be. The individual may be as selective as he desires."[70] But, "the Constitution places no value on discrimination" and it has never "been accorded affirmative constitutional protection."[71]

When individuals act outside their own homes, clubs, or close social circles and offer services to the general public, however, governments have the constitutional authority to prevent them from discriminating. Today in many states there are laws making illegal racial, religious, national origin, or sex discrimination in a wide variety of areas. Employment, places of public recreation and accommodation, housing, and education are those most commonly covered.

It was the hope of some of the members of Congress who proposed the Fourteenth Amendment over a hundred years ago that its ratification would authorize federal action against nongovernmental discrimination. And Section 5 of that amendment states: "The Congress shall have power to enforce, by appropriate legislation, the provisions of this article." So in 1875 Congress made it a federal offense for any owner or operator of a public conveyance, hotel, or theater to deny accommodations to any person because of race or color. But in the *Civil Rights Cases* (1883), the Supreme Court invalidated this law on the ground that the Fourteenth Amendment applies only to state action and does not give Congress authority to forbid discrimination by private individuals.[72]

What of the Thirteenth Amendment? Unlike the Fourteenth, this amendment applies to all persons. It outlaws all forms of involuntary servitude. It also empowers Congress to pass whatever laws are necessary and proper to prevent slavery or involuntary servitude. For a hundred years some people, including the first Justice Harlan, argued that the Thirteenth Amendment gives Congress authority to legislate against all the badges of slavery—that is, against racial discrimination in all its forms, regardless of its source. But the Supreme Court interpreted the Thirteenth Amendment so narrowly that slavery meant only physical compulsion or peonage (a condition of compulsory servitude based on indebtedness of the worker to the employer). Thus it was held that Congress received no power from the Thirteenth Amendment to legislate against racial discrimination.

Then, in *Jones* v. *Mayer Co.* (1968), Justice Stewart, speaking for a seven-man majority, adopted the view of the first Justice Harlan (his grandson, the second Justice Harlan, dissented). The immediate question before the Court was the meaning and constitutionality of an 1866 act relating to the purchase of property. Justice Stewart stated that the Thirteenth Amend-

[70]Justice Douglas dissenting in *Moose Lodge No. 107* v *Irvis.*

[71]*Norwood* v. *Harrison*, 413 U.S. 455 (1973).

[72]109 U.S. 3.

ment became part of the Constitution so that Congress could have the power to remove the "badges of slavery" from the nation. "When racial discrimination," he wrote, "herds men into ghettos and makes their ability to buy property turn on the color of their skin, then it too is a relic of slavery. . . . At the very least, the freedom that Congress is empowered to secure under the Thirteenth Amendment includes the freedom to buy whatever a white man can buy, the right to live wherever a white man can live. If Congress cannot say that being a free man means at least this much, then the Thirteenth Amendment made a promise that the Nation cannot keep."[73]

The Supreme Court has not only reaffirmed *Jones* v. *Mayer*, it has extended it. It has ruled that the Civil Rights Act of 1866, which prohibits racial discrimination in the making and enforcing of contracts, prevents employers from discriminating against persons either because they are black or because they are white.[74] The same law also makes discrimination by private schools illegal if the schools have extended a public offer open on its face to any child meeting the minimum qualifications.[75] There is no longer any doubt about the constitutional authority of Congress under the Thirteenth Amendment to enact whatever legislation it thinks necessary to protect persons against disabilities because of race, whether the disabilities are imposed by private or state action. And without waiting for Congress to implement the Thirteenth Amendment, the Supreme Court has reinterpreted the civil rights laws of the Reconstruction era to prohibit discriminatory action by private individuals. Before these more recent liberal constructions, Congress had to rely on its power to regulate commerce among the states in order to extend federal protection against discriminatory acts. This is what it did in 1964 when it adopted a sweeping Civil Rights Act to protect persons against discrimination in places of public accommodation and employment.

THE CIVIL RIGHTS ACT OF 1964—TITLE II: PLACES OF PUBLIC ACCOMMODATION

For the first time since Reconstruction, Congress authorized the massive use of federal authority to combat privately imposed racial discrimination. Title II forbids discrimination in places of accommodation and makes it a federal offense to discriminate against any customer or patron because of race, color, religion, or national origin. It applies to any inn, hotel, motel, or lodging establishment (except establishments with fewer than five rooms and occupied by the proprietor—in other words, small boarding houses); to any restaurant or gasoline station that offers to serve interstate travelers or serves food or products of which a substantial portion have moved in interstate commerce; and to any motion picture house, theater, concert hall, sports arena, or other place of entertainment that customarily presents films, performances, athletic teams, or other sources of entertainment that are moved in interstate commerce. Title II also applies to any establishment that attempts to discriminate or segregate in response to state law or order of any public official.

The attorney general may initiate proceedings as well as intervene in cases initiated by individuals. States with laws against discrimination in places of public accommodation are given thirty days to see if they can

[73]392 U.S. 409.

[74]*McDonald* v. *Santa Fe Trail Transportation Co.*, 427 U.S. 273 (1976).

[75]*Runyon* v. *McCrary*, 427 U.S. 160 (1976).

bring compliance. Federal judges may refer complaints to the Community Relations Service in the Department of Justice in order to seek voluntary compliance. But if these procedures fail, judges are to provide prompt hearings with direct appeals to the Supreme Court whenever the attorney general believes the case is of general public importance.

Within a few months of the enactment of Title II, the Supreme Court unanimously sustained its constitutionality in *Heart of Atlanta Motel* v. *United States*, 1964.[76] The adoption of Title II brought an organized program of testing by blacks to publicize lack of compliance. The Department of Justice filed more than four hundred lawsuits. Faced with these actions, most large establishments in cities, including those in the South, opened their doors to all customers. Today, Title II has effectively opened places of public accommodation.

TITLE VII: EMPLOYMENT

Title VII with its amendments, supplemented by other acts, now makes it an unfair employment practice for any employer, including state and local agencies such as schools and universities, or trade unions in any industry affecting interstate commerce that have fifteen or more employees or members, to discriminate in any fashion against any person because of race, color, religion, national origin, physical handicap, or being a disabled veteran or a veteran of the Vietnam era, or age for those between forty and sixty-five. Religious institutions such as parochial schools may use religious standards. The law permits exceptions to the ban against discrimination because of age, sex, or handicap where there are bona fide occupational qualifications reasonably necessary to the normal operation of a particular business or enterprise.

The bona fide occupational qualification exception has been interpreted to permit a state to deny women the right to serve as guards in maximum security prisons for males, but not to permit a state to establish a minimum general weight requirement of 120 pounds and height requirement of 5 feet 2 inches for prison guards because of the adverse impact on women. An airline may not specify that one must be female to serve as a stewardess or fire a stewardess for getting married.[77] Since persons denied jobs because of race, sex, or any other improper reasons often have neither the knowledge nor the money to file lawsuits, Congress, in the Civil Rights Act of 1964, created an Equal Employment Opportunity Commission. The commission, consisting of five members appointed by the president with the consent of the Senate, works with state authorities and uses conciliation wherever possible to bring about compliance with Title VII. If this fails, EEOC has authority to seek court orders. It is entitled to a quick court hearing on its complaints.

EEOC has had difficulty in handling its responsibilities. By 1976 there was a backlog of 126,000 job discrimination charges, of which only 10 percent had progressed beyond the investigative stage.[78] EEOC has announced a variety of new procedures designed to speed action, but there are some who believe it needs to be given additional funds for more

"Thanks for coming in. It's such a relief to be able to deny someone a loan when there's no possibility of being charged with sex, race, age, or ethnic bias."

Drawing by Ed Fisher; © 1976 The New Yorker Magazine, Inc.

[76]379 U.S. 421 (1964).

[77]*Dothard* v. *Rawlinson*, 53 L Ed 2d 786 (1977).

[78]For a critical report, see U.S. General Accounting Office, *The Equal Employment Opportunity Commission Has Made Limited Progress in Elimination of Discrimination* (Government Printing Office, 1976).

Specific nondiscrimination law	Coverage	Federal enforcement agency	Enforcement action
*Title VI – Civil Rights Act of 1964	Discrimination on basis of race, color, religion, national origin prohibited in programs receiving federal funds.	Equal Employment Opportunity Commission, delegated to Office for Civil Rights, HEW for education institutions.	Withholding of federal grants and/or contracts.
Title VII – Civil Rights Act of 1964	Forbids all discrimination in employment because of race, color, religion, sex or national origin.	Equal Employment Opportunity Commission delegated to Office of Civil Rights, HEW for educational institutions.	U.S. Attorney General may file suit on behalf of complainant. EEOC generally attempts conciliation and voluntary compliance. EEOC also issues "right to sue" letters for private action in federal district court.
*Executive Order 11246, amended by 11375 (to include sex)	Discrimination in employment (hiring, salaries, fringe benefits, etc.) on basis of race, color, religion, national origin, sex prohibited.	Office of Federal Contract Compliance, delegated to Office for Civil Rights of HEW for educational institutions.	Debarment from federal contracts and grants, withdrawal of current federal funds.
Age Discrimination in Employment Act of 1967	Same as Title VII for those persons over 40 and under 65 years of age.	Department of Labor, Wage and Hour Division.	Provides for a civil suit after complainant has filed with Department of Labor
*Vocational Rehabilitation Act of 1973, amended December, 1974	Forbids discrimination against the handicapped under any program or activity receiving federal funds.	Department of HEW.	May result in suspension, termination or refusal to grant federal funds. Referred to Department of Justice for recommendation for appropriate proceedings in case of a violation or to any applicable state or local law.
*Vietnam Era Veterans Readjustment Act of 1974 (Section 2012)	Affirmative Action in employment for Veterans of the Vietnam Era and Disabled Veterans required by all contractors holding contracts in the amount of $10,000 or more.	Department of Labor, Veterans' Employment Service.	Department of Labor may file suit. Debarment from new grants and contracts and cancellation of current funds and withholding of funds is possible under this act.
*Title IX of the Education Amendments of 1972	Forbids discrimination against students, employees, etc. in educational institutions.	HEW, Office of Civil Rights.	Debarment from new awards, cancellation and termination of new, pending, or current federal funds. Also, Department of Justice can sue at HEW's request.

*Those laws which carry withholding of federal funds or debarment from federal grants in contracts as an enforcement action.

enforcement officials. Perhaps it should be given power to issue cease and desist orders on its own, and not have to go to court to seek enforcement.

In the area of employment, the problem appears to be primarily practices that work to the disadvantage of blacks, women, Latinos and other disadvantaged groups rather than open discrimination. Title VII prohibits such practices unless they can be shown to be related to on-the-job performance. It goes beyond constitutional standards. It forbids a company, for example, from requiring prospective employees to take tests, even if the tests are racially neutral, if the tests cannot be shown to be job related and if they exclude disproportionately persons of a particular race or sex who are capable of performing in the desired position.[79]

Discriminatory employment practices are not only outlawed by Title VII. Presidential executive orders require all contractors of the federal government, including universities, to adopt and implement affirmative action programs to ensure a properly balanced labor force.[80] Federal officials deny that these plans call for quotas, but they do call on contractors to establish timetables and goals; to follow open recruitment procedures; to keep records of applicants by race, sex, and national origin; and to explain why their labor force does not reflect the same proportion of persons in the covered categories as are within the appropriate labor market pools. These executive orders and laws supplementing these orders now cover race, sex, Latinos, Asian Americans, native Americans, the physically and mentally handicapped, the aged, veterans of the Vietnam war, and disabled veterans. Failure of a contractor to file and to implement an approved affirmative action plan may lead to loss of federal contracts or federal grants.

HOUSING: THE CIVIL RIGHTS ACTS OF 1866 AND 1968

We have made considerable progress in cutting down open discrimination in places of public accommodation and employment. Discrimination in housing, however, remains one of the most difficult of our social problems. In turn, it has had an impact on school desegregation and the isolation of black Americans from the suburbs. Residential segregation results from the refusal of lending agencies, brokerage agencies, and owners and operators of houses and apartments to allow blacks to rent or buy homes for their families except within certain restricted areas.

In 1948, the Supreme Court (*Shelley* v. *Kraemer*) held that judges would no longer enforce racially restrictive covenants (a provision in a deed to real property restricting its sale).[81] In 1962 President Kennedy ordered the Federal Housing Administration, the Veterans Administration, and other federal housing authorities to cease making federal funds or help available to any project that was operated on a segregated basis. Yet most of the nation's housing was still denied to black Americans, and they had to pay more for what was available. Then Congress enacted the Civil Rights Act of 1968. The act covers 80 percent of all housing for rent or sale, exempting from its coverage only private individuals owning not more than three

"Well, I'll be darned! It was already unlocked."

Copyright © 1968 The Chicago Sun-Times; reproduced by courtesy of Wil-Jo Associates, Inc., and Bill Mauldin.

[79]*Griggs* v. *Duke Power Co.*, 401 U.S. 24 (1971); *Albermarle Paper Co.* v. *Moode*, 422 U.S. 405 (1975).

[80]Richard P. Nathan, *Jobs and Civil Rights: The Role of the Federal Government in Promoting Equal Opportunity and Employment and Training.* Report prepared for the U.S. Civil Rights Commission by the Brookings Institution, 1969.

[81]334 U.S. 1.

houses who sell or rent their houses without the services of a real estate agent and who do not indicate any preference or discrimination in their advertising; dwellings that have no more than four separate living units in which the owner maintains a residence (the so-called Mrs. Murphy boarding houses); and religious organizations and private clubs housing their own members on a noncommercial basis. For all other housing, the Civil Rights Act forbids refusal to sell or rent to any person because of race, color, religion, or national origin. No discriminatory advertising is to be permitted. So-called blockbusting techniques—that is, attempts to persuade persons to sell or rent a dwelling by representing that blacks or any other racial or religious group are about to come into the neighborhood—are outlawed. Real estate brokers and lending institutions are also prohibited from discriminatory practices.

Although the attorney general may initiate action under the Civil Rights Act of 1968 whenever he finds a pattern of discrimination, the act depends for enforcement upon "private attorneys general"—that is, on the persons injured by the discriminatory conduct. The injured party does not necessarily have to be black. A white person denied the opportunity to live in an integrated community also has been injured and has standing to sue.[82] The person first must file a complaint with the Secretary of the Department of Housing and Urban Development. If this fails to bring relief, he or she may file a suit in any court for injunctive relief and for damages. (In a suit for damages, the defendant has a constitutional right to demand a jury trial.)[83]

The Civil Rights Act of 1968 had not even had time to become effective when the Supreme Court announced its decision in *Jones* v. *Mayer Co.* (1968). Mr. and Mrs. Jones had filed a complaint three years before against a housing development in St. Louis that had refused to sell them a home because Mr. Jones was black. At that time few people thought they had much chance to win their case. Congress had enacted no civil rights laws to cover housing since the moribund act of 1866. Even if it did, there was some doubt about its power to make discrimination by private persons a federal offense. Even if the Joneses won, it was assumed the Supreme Court would base its decision on state involvement in the discrimination because of the financial support the state had given the developer.

The Joneses cited the Civil Rights Act of 1866, which reads: "All citizens of the United States shall have the same right, in every state and territory, as is enjoyed by white citizens thereof to inherit, purchase, lease, sell, hold, and convey real and personal property." Because of the Supreme Court's long-standing requirement of state action to bring the Fourteenth Amendment into play and its narrow construction of the Thirteenth, the 1866 act had been more or less forgotten. But the Supreme Court sustained the Jones' petition and ruled that the Congress of 1866 meant what it had said and that the Thirteenth Amendment gave Congress ample authority to enact the law.

But progress in securing open housing has been very, very slow. The Fair Housing Act of 1968 has seldom been used. Although the Justice Department filed or joined in some two hundred cases during the first six years, especially those involving large apartment complexes, "this effort

[82]*Trafficante* v. *Metropolitan Life Insurance Co.*, 405 U.S. 205 (1972).

[83]*Curtis* v. *Loether*, 415 U.S. 189 (1974).

was as the dropping a single vial of purifier into the Mississippi River."[84] "No serious effort was being made . . . to apply the housing act or dramatize its scope, and most people in America were unaware that any such federal law existed."[85] Still, some progress has been made. Between 1970 and 1977 blacks increased their share of the suburban population from 4.5 to 5.1 percent. Four million blacks now live in the suburbs. And in many smaller communities, middle-class blacks have been able to move out of the ghetto. But the basic fact of residential segregation remains: Most blacks in the North are concentrated in the central core areas of our cities.

AGE DISCRIMINATION

The Age Discrimination in Employment Act of 1967 added old age to Title VI of the Civil Rights Act as one of the forbidden reasons for refusing employment, except for persons 65 or over and where old age would prevent a person from proper performance. A state may compel its police officers to retire at age 50, a theatrical company refuse to hire a 60-year-old person to play a youthful part, and Greyhound can refuse to hire new bus drivers older than 35.[86]

In the Older Americans Act of 1975, Congress has taken additional steps to prevent "unreasonable discrimination" based on age. It has stipulated that no federal funds are to be given to any program or activity that denies to any person because of old age the benefits of the program or subjects such a person to unreasonable discrimination. The U.S. Commission on Civil Rights is to identify such discrimination and make a report to the secretary of HEW. The secretary is then to issue detailed regulations to take effect on January 1, 1979, to implement the ban on unreasonable age discrimination.

Congress took this somewhat roundabout way to ban age discrimination, Senator Eagleton explained, "because unlike race discrimination, age discrimination is not per se arbitrary. Our laws commonly make distinctions among individuals based on their age."[87] But rather than a case-by-case court determination of what is or is not unreasonable age discrimination, HEW is to deal with the matter by regulation. Presumably, Congress will be given time to review the regulations before they go into effect.

Summary

1. Progress in civil rights was a long time in coming. After the Civil War the federal government tried briefly to secure for the freed slaves some measure of protection. But blacks were largely uneducated, illiterate, and completely dependent on the white community. Moreover, they were an insignificant political force. In 1877 the federal government withdrew from the field and left blacks to their own resources.

2. At the end of World War II, a national debate began over civil rights. Black leaders and others urged Congress to adopt federal laws to protect civil rights. But white southerners and many others contended that federal civil rights laws would upset the federal system and lead to a dangerous centralization of power. They insisted that national legislation would create more problems than it solved. Let the states do the job, for they could protect civil rights by laws adapted to the attitudes of the local citizenry. Anyway, they added, "you can't legislate morality."

[84.]Ford Foundation letter, October 1, 1976.

[85.]Richard Kluger, *Simple Justice* (Knopf, 1976), p. 761.

[86]Morton C. Paulson, "How to Protect Your Job If the Boss Says You're Too Old," *The National Observer*, July 4, 1977.

[87]*Congressional Quarterly*, November 29, 1974, p. 2595.

3. Champions of national action argued that states had failed to protect civil rights and that, in fact, in many areas state governments themselves were the major instruments of discrimination. Furthermore, the denial of civil rights is not merely a local matter, for it has national implications. The Constitution promises to every person who lives in the United States equal treatment before the law without respect to race, religion, or national origin. It is up to the national government to see that this promise is kept. Whatever the merits of local rather than national action, as a matter of practical political fact, civil rights could be extended only by the national majority using the power of the national government. By the end of the 1950s, the debate over whether the national government had a responsibility to protect civil rights was over. The question became, what should it do?

4. As we enter the 1980s, some minorities demand recognition less for their individual rights than for their rights as a group—as blacks, as Indians, as Latinos. Some contend that equality is not enough—what they want is reverse discrimination. They want laws to be passed and enforced deliberately for their benefit; they want a social and economic "handicap" much like the handicap that favors the weaker golfer.

5. Each year more and more blacks, Latinos, and Indians exercise their voting power. Increasingly, they understand the connection between voting and better schools, houses, and jobs. And with these advances, more and more blacks and Latinos and Indians are coming to insist on full participation in the political, economic, and social life of the country. The impact of their political power, when combined with that of increasingly assertive women, is being felt long before every member of each group has become politically self-conscious. There is no stopping place between the granting of a few rights and full citizenship. Blacks, Latinos, American Indians, and women are demanding the same rights as other citizens. No Americans have asked for more than this—or settled long for less.

Chapter 7

Rights to Life, Liberty, and Property

Public officials have great power. Under certain conditions, they can seize our property, throw us into jail, and in extreme circumstances, even take our lives. It is necessary to give great power to those who govern; it is also dangerous. It is so dangerous that to keep officials from becoming tyrants we are unwilling to depend on the ballot box alone. For we know that political controls mean little when a majority uses that power to deprive unpopular minorities of their rights.

Because public power can be dangerous, we parcel it out in small chunks and surround it with restraints. No single official can decide to take our life, liberty, or property. And officials must act according to the rules. If they act outside the scope of their authority or contrary to the law, they have no claim to our obedience.

The Constitution also protects our right to become and to remain a citizen. All nations have rules that determine nationality—the condition of membership in, owing allegiance to, and being the subject of a nation-state. But in democratic theory citizenship is something more than nationality, something more than merely being a subject. *Citizenship* in a democracy is an office and, like other offices, carries with it certain powers and responsibilities.

The constitution protects citizenship

It was not until 1868, with the adoption of the Fourteenth Amendment, that this basic right of membership in the body politic was given constitutional protection. This amendment makes "all persons *born or naturalized* in the United States and subject to the jurisdiction thereof . . . citizens of the United States and of the State wherein they reside." All persons born in the United States, with the exception of children born to foreign ambassadors and ministers, are citizens of this country regardless of the citizenship of their parents. (Congress has defined the United States to include Puerto Rico, Guam, the Northern Marianas, and the Virgin Islands.)

138

The Fourteenth Amendment alone does not make members of Indian tribes citizens of the United States or of the state in which they live. But Indians are American citizens by act of Congress. They have the right to vote and to use state courts. When they leave Indian reservations, they can exercise all the rights and obligations of any other citizen. Indians living on reservations are subject to preemptive regulation by the national government. The relations of Indian tribes with the United States are complex: They are regarded not as states, not as nations, but as a separate people, with the power of regulating their own internal relations.[1]

The Fourteenth Amendment confers citizenship according to the principle of jus soli—by place of birth. In addition, Congress has granted, under certain conditions, citizenship at birth according to the principle of jus sanguinis—by blood. A child born of an American parent living abroad becomes an American citizen at birth as long as one citizen parent has been physically present in the United States before the child's birth. In order to retain citizenship derived through only one citizen parent, a person must come to the United States and live here for at least five years between his or her fourteenth and twenty-eighth birthdays.

Citizenship may also be acquired by naturalization. The granting of citizenship to the Northern Marianas in 1977 by an act of Congress is an example of collective naturalization. Individual naturalization requirements are determined by Congress.

Today, with minor exceptions, nonenemy aliens over eighteen who have been lawfully admitted for permanent residence and who have resided in the United States for at least five years and in a state for at least six months are eligible for naturalization. The requirements for citizenship are as follows:

1. To file a petition of naturalization with a clerk of a court of record, federal or state, verified by two witnesses.
2. To be able to read, write, and speak English.
3. To be of good moral character.
4. To understand and demonstrate attachment to the history, principles, and form of government of the United States.
5. To demonstrate that one is well disposed toward the good order and happiness of the country.
6. To demonstrate that one does not now, nor within the last ten years has ever, believe in, advocate, or belong to an organization that supports opposition to organized government, overthrow of government by violence, or the doctrines of world communism, or any other form of totalitarianism.

The Immigration and Naturalization Service makes the necessary investigations. The examiner makes a report to the judge. The final step is a hearing in open court. If the judge is satisfied, the applicant renounces all allegiance to his or her former country and swears to support and defend the Constitution and laws of the United States against all enemies and to bear arms in behalf of the United States when required by law. (Those with religious beliefs against the bearing of arms are allowed to take an oath to serve in the armed forces as noncombatants or to perform work of national importance under civilian direction.) Then the court grants a certificate of naturalization.

[1]*McClanahan* v. *Arizona State Tax Commission*, 411 U. S. 164 (1973).

Naturalized citizenship may be revoked by court order if the government can prove that it was won by deception. In addition, citizenship, however acquired, may under certain circumstances be voluntarily renounced.

Congress believes it has the power to take away a person's citizenship as a penalty for committing certain crimes and for certain kinds of conduct. The Supreme Court thinks otherwise. The justices have had difficulty developing a coherent and consistent majority position, but in essence the Court has ruled that what the Constitution gives, Congress may not take away. Justice Black, speaking for a five-man majority, states: "Congress has no power under the Constitution to divest a person of his United States citizenship absent his voluntary renunciation thereof."[2]

Five of the types of conduct Congress has considered expatriating acts have been challenged in the courts. By a divided vote, the Supreme Court has declared four unconstitutional, and one constitutional. The four unconstitutional acts would have deprived persons of citizenship for: (1) voting in a foreign election; (2) conviction by a court-martial or desertion during time of war; (3) departing from or remaining outside the United States in time of war or national emergency to avoid military service; (4) residence by a naturalized citizen in the country of national origin for more than three years.[3] The one upheld denies citizenship to persons born outside the United States to one citizen parent only if such persons do not return to the United States for five years between the ages of fourteen and twenty-eight. The Fourteenth Amendment, said the Court majority, does not apply except to persons born or naturalized in the United States.[4]

RIGHTS OF AMERICAN CITIZENSHIP

American citizenship confers some special rights. First, an American citizen obtains state citizenship merely by residing in a state. (*Resident*, as used in the Fourteenth Amendment, means domicile, the place one calls home. The legal status of *domicile* should not be confused with the fact of physical presence. A person may be living in Washington, D.C., but be a citizen of California—that is, he may consider California home. Residence is a question primarily of intent.) It is from state citizenship that many of our most important rights flow. For example, states determine—subject to constitutional limitations—who shall vote. Although states could confer the right to vote on aliens, no state today does so.

Do American citizens have rights other than the right to become a citizen of the state in which they reside? The Supreme Court in the *Slaughter House Cases* (1873) carefully distinguished between privileges of United States citizens and of state citizens. It held that the only privileges attaching to national citizenship are those that "owe their existence to the Federal Government, its National Character, its Constitution, or its laws."[5] These privileges of United States citizenship have never been completely specified, but they include the right to use the navigable waters of the United States; to assemble peacefully; to petition the national government for redress of grievances; to be protected by the national government on

A large group of persons become new United States citizens during naturalization ceremonies in Miami Beach, Florida.

[2]*Afroyim* v. *Rusk*, 387 U.S. 253 (1967).

[3]*Trop* v. *Dulles*, 356 U.S. 86 (1958); *Schneider* v. *Rusk*, 377 U.S. 163 (1964); and cases cited therein.

[4]*Rogers* v. *Bellei*, 401 U.S. 815 (1971).

[5]16 *Wallace* 36 (1873).

the high seas; to vote, if qualified to do so under state laws, and to have one's vote counted properly; and to travel throughout the United States.

The right to travel abroad   This right is also constitutionally protected. Under present law, though there is some confusion about it, it is unlawful (except as otherwise provided by the president as he has for travel to Mexico and Canada) for citizens to leave or enter the United States unless they have a valid passport. The Department of State says it may deny passports to those whose travel abroad may "be prejudicial to the orderly conduct of the foreign relations of the United States or otherwise be prejudicial to the interests of the United States." The Supreme Court has never ruled directly on this contention or on Congress' power to require passports for foreign travel. The Court has declared unconstitutional a law that made it a crime for a member of a registered communist organization to apply for a passport.[6] But it avoided a ruling on the constitutionality of area restrictions whenever and wherever the State Department feels that travel to certain nations by American citizens is not in the best interest of the United States. The Court interpreted these limitations merely as announcements that if people go to such countries, they cannot be assured of the protection of the United States, but that to go is not criminal conduct.[7]

The right to live in the United States   This right of American citizens is not subject to any congressional limitation. Aliens have no such right.

RIGHTS OF ALIENS

Congress has the power to decide which aliens shall be admitted to the United States and under what conditions. By 1875, it had begun to restrict the entry of certain types of "undesirables" such as prostitutes and revolutionaries. During World War I and in the 1924 Immigration Act, Congress set limits on the number of those who could be admitted. It also created a national origin system that discriminated against immigrants from southern and southeastern Europe and Asia.

In 1965, after years of debate, a new immigration law was adopted. As amended in 1976, this law sets a ceiling of 170,000 immigrants a year for all countries outside the Western Hemisphere; a ceiling of 120,000 a year for nationals within this hemisphere; and no more than 20,000 a year from any country in any one year. Within these overall ceilings, there is a seven-point preference system. First preference is given to unmarried sons and daughters of American citizens under twenty-one; seventh preference is given to refugees driven from their homes by political or racial persecution.

"Over no conceivable subject is the legislative power of Congress more complete than it is over the admission of aliens."[8] It may even go so far, and it has done so, as to give the attorney general the discretion to exclude aliens merely because they have advocated or published Communist doctrines.

Once here, aliens remain so long as the national government allows them to. Aliens who enter illegally may be rather easily expelled. Deporta-

During World War II, thousands of people, both Japanese aliens and Americans of Japanese descent, were taken from their homes on the West Coast and sent to relocation centers. This small evacuee was one of them.

[6]*Aptheker* v. *Secretary of State*, 378 U.S. 500 (1964).

[7]*Zemel* v. *Rusk*, 381 U.S. 1 (1965); *United States* v. *Laub*, 385 U.S. 475 (1967).

[8]*Kleindienst* v. *Mandel*, 408 U.S. 753 (1972); *Fiallo* v. *Bell*, 52 L Ed 2d 50 (1977).

tion, despite its drastic consequences, is a civil rather than a criminal proceeding, so the normal constitutional safeguards that protect those accused of crimes do not apply. Aliens may be deported for acts that were not grounds for banishment when they were performed or for such things as convictions for two crimes involving moral turpitude, joining an organization that advocates revolution, or engaging in activities that the attorney general believes are "subversive to the national security."

Yet while living within the United States aliens are not without constitutional protection. Most of the provisions of the Constitution speak of rights of persons, not just of citizens. Congress and the states, for example, have no greater authority to interfere with an alien's freedom of religion than with that of citizens.

States have much less authority to make distinctions between aliens and citizens than does the national government. In fact, state and local regulations are considered to affect a suspect classification and are subject to the closest judicial scrutiny. Recently almost every state regulation against aliens to come before the Supreme Court has been declared unconstitutional: a state may not deny aliens admitted for permanent residence the right to be admitted to the bar, or to be engineers; nor may a state impose a flat ban on aliens working for the state or receiving state financial assistance in order to go to college.[9] A state may, however, deny aliens the right to vote or hold elected public office or appointment to policy-making public offices.

Constitutional protection of property

By *property rights* we mean the rights of an individual to own, use, rent, invest, or contract for property. From Aristotle to the founding fathers, there has run a persistent emphasis on the close connection between liberty and ownership of property, between property and power. This emphasis has been reflected in American political thinking and American political institutions. A major purpose of the framers of our Constitution was to establish a government strong enough to protect each person's right to use and enjoy his property. At the same time, they wanted a government so limited that it could not endanger that right. The framers were disturbed by the efforts of some state legislatures in behalf of debtors at the expense of creditors. So in the Constitution they forbade states to make anything except gold or silver legal tender for the payment of debts or to pass any law "impairing the obligation of contracts."

THE CONTRACT CLAUSE

The obligation of contracts clause of the Constitution was designed to prevent states from enacting legislation to extend the period during which debtors could meet their payments or otherwise relieve themselves of their contractual obligations. The framers had in mind an ordinary contract between private persons. But beginning with Chief Justice John Marshall, the Supreme Court expanded the coverage of the clause to prevent states from altering in any way privileges previously conferred on a corporation.[10]

In effect, the contract clause was being used to protect vested property at the expenses of the power of the states to guard the public welfare. Gradu-

[9]*Sugarman* v. *Dougall*, 413 U.S. 634 (1973); *In Re Griffiths*, 413 U.S. 717 (1973); *Examining Board* v. *Flores de Otero*, 426 U.S. 572 (1976).

[10]*Fletcher* v. *Peck*, 6 Cranch 87 (1810).

ally, however, the Court began in the 1880s to restrict the coverage of the contract clause and to subject contracts, like other forms of property, to the states' power to protect the public health, safety, welfare, or morals. In 1934 the Supreme Court went so far as to hold that even contracts between individuals—the very ones the contract clause was intended to protect—could be modified by state law in order to avert social and economic catastrophe.[11]

The contract clause is not dead; in 1977 it was used by the Court to strike down New Jersey's repeal of a 1962 promise not to use certain reserves except to pay off designated bonds.[12] Yet this action is most unusual.

DUE PROCESS OF LAW

Perhaps the most difficult parts of the Constitution to understand are the clauses in the Fifth and Fourteenth Amendments that forbid national and state governments to deny any person life, liberty, or property without due process of law. These due process clauses have resulted in more Supreme Court decisions than any others in the Constitution, although the equal protection clause is about to catch up. Even so, it is impossible to give due process any exact explanation. The Supreme Court itself has refused to give it a precise definition.

There are two kinds of due process—procedural and substantive. Procedural due process refers to the methods by which a law is enforced, but there are several ways in which a law itself, as enacted, may violate the procedural due process requirement.

First, the statute may be vague: "A statute which either forbids or requires the doing of an act in terms so vague that men of common intelligence must necessarily guess at its meaning and differ as to its application, violates the first essential of due process of law."[13] A vague statute fails to provide adequate warning, and does not contain sufficient guidelines for law enforcement officials, juries, and courts. Here are some examples of laws struck down for vagueness: a statute making it a crime "to treat contemptuously the flag,"[14] a "suspicious persons ordinance" that made it illegal for any person to be found on a street at late or unusual hours without any visible or lawful business and who could not give a satisfactory account of himself;[15] a vagrancy ordinance that declared to be vagrants a wide variety of people such as "rogues and vagabonds," "dissolute persons who go about begging," "common night walkers," and so on.[16]

A second way in which a law itself may deny a person procedural due process is by creating a presumption of guilt "where there is no rational connection between the facts proved and the facts presumed." For example, the Court has declared unconstitutional laws which created a presumption that a firearm in the possession of a person convicted of a crime of violence has been transported or received in violation of a law.[17] Anoth-

"What's so great about due process? Due process got me ten years."

Drawing by Handelsman; © 1970 The New Yorker Magazine, Inc.

[11]*Home Building and Loan Association* v. *Blaisdell,* 290 U.S. 398 (1934).

[12]*United States Trust Co.* v. *New Jersey,* 431 U.S. 1 (1977).

[13]*Connally* v. *General Constr. Co.,* 269 U.S. 385 (1976).

[14]*Smith* v. *Goguen,* 415 U.S. 566 (1974).

[15]*Palmer* v. *City of Euclid, Ohio,* 402 U.S. 544 (1971).

[16]*Paparchristou* v. *City of Jacksonville,* 405 U.S. 156 (1972).

[17]*Tot* v. *United States,* 319 U.S. 463 (1943).

er law declared unconstitutional was written so that possession of marijuana or cocaine creates the presumption that the drugs were obtained illegally.[18] (The constitutionality of such a presumption in the case of heroin has been sustained, since little if any heroin is made in this country and virtually all of it is illegally imported.)[19]

Traditionally, however, procedural due process refers to the *procedures* by which a law is applied. It requires, to paraphrase Daniel Webster's famous definition, a procedure that "hears before it condemns, proceeds upon inquiry, and renders judgment only after a trial." Originally procedural due process was limited to criminal prosecutions. It now applies to many different kinds of governmental proceedings. For instance, it is required in juvenile hearings, disbarment proceedings, proceedings to determine eligibility for welfare payments or terminations of them, parole revocations, revocation of drivers' licenses, and disciplinary proceedings in state universities and in public schools.[20]

Procedural due process has taken on new importance because the Supreme Court has expanded the meanings of "liberty," and "property." In recent years, it has set aside the distinction between a privilege and a right. The liberty that is protected is more than freedom from being thrown into jail, and the property that is secured goes beyond mere ownership of real estate, things, or money. The liberty protected by the Constitution includes "the right of the individual to contract, to engage in any of the common occupations of life, to acquire useful knowledge, to marry, to establish a home and bring up children, to worship God according to the dictates of his own conscience, and generally to enjoy those common law privileges long recognized as essential to the orderly pursuit of happiness by free men."[21] The blurring of the distinction between rights and privileges means that public welfare, housing, education, employment, professional licenses, and so on are now more and more matters of entitlement. To deprive someone of them calls into play some form of due process.[22]

But "the range of interests protected by procedural due process is not indefinite."[23] For example, a university does not have to give a nontenured faculty member a hearing before it decides not to renew an appointment. True, faculty members are entitled to freedom of speech, along with everybody else, but "the interest in holding a teaching job at a state university . . . is not itself a free speech interest."

Recently the Supreme Court has retreated somewhat from this idea of entitlement. It has ruled that a state may, if it wishes, have its employees serve at pleasure, which means they are not entitled to due process hear-

---

[18]*Leary* v. *United States*, 395 U.S. 6 (1969).

[19]*Turner* v. *United States*, 396 U.S. 398 (1970).

[20]*Groppi* v. *Leslie*, 404 U.S. 496 (1972); *Bell* v. *Burson*, 402 U.S. 535 (1971); *Goss* v. *Lopez*, 419 U.S. 565 (1975); *Dixon* v. *Love*, 431 U.S. 105 (1977) and cases cited therein; and *UGSA* v. *Peltason*, Federal District Court for Eastern Illinois, May 1974.

[21]*Meyer* v. *Nebraska*, 262 U.S. 390 (1923).

[22]J. Harvie Wilkinson III, "*Goss* v. *Lopez*: The Supreme Court as School Superintendent," in Philip B. Kurland ed., *The Supreme Court Review 1975* (University of Chicago Press, 1976), p. 37. See also in the same volume Mark Tushnet, "The Newer Property: Suggestion for the Revival of Substantive Due Process," pp. 261ff.

[23]*Board of Regents* v. *Roth*, 408 U.S. 564 (1972).

ings before being fired. That is, they have no property right or entitlement to a state job. Wrote Justice Stevens: "In the absence of any claim that the public employer was motivated by a desire to curtail . . . the exercise of an employee's constitutional rights . . . the federal court is not the appropriate forum in which to review the multitude of personnel decisions that are made daily by public agencies. . . . The Due Process Clause . . . is not a guarantee against incorrect or ill-advised personnel decisions."[24] And after holding that prisoners are entitled to a hearing before being deprived of "good time credits" or disciplined for violating prison rules, the Court decided that a prisoner is not entitled to a hearing prior to being transferred from one penitentiary to another. Not every "grievous loss visited upon a person by the State is sufficient to invoke the procedural protections of the Due Process Clause," said the Court. "The determining factor is the nature of the interest involved rather than its weight."[25]

"Once it is determined that due process applies, the question remains what process is due."[26] What is due varies with the kind of interest involved. As applied in a federal courtroom, due process requires the careful observance of the provisions of the Bill of Rights as outlined in amendments 4 through 8. For other kinds of proceedings, the question in each instance is what must be done to ensure *fundamental fairness*. It is hard to generalize because of the many kinds of proceedings involved. But at a minimum there must be *adequate notice* and an *opportunity to be heard*. The hearing required must be appropriate to the interest involved. For example, juveniles cannot be declared delinquent without a hearing in which they are given the right to confront hostile witnesses and to cross-examine them, to present oral evidence, and to be represented by counsel. The level of proof must show delinquency beyond any reasonable doubt, but they are not entitled to have the decision made by a jury.[27] Prisoners facing disciplinary proceedings should be given written notice of the reasons for the action, but they are not entitled to confront their accusers, to cross-examine adverse witnesses, or to have legal counsel.[28] School pupils may be punished after a conference: that is all the process they are due.[29] And even suspension requires no more than a chance to tell the principal their side of the story. For long-term expulsion, the procedures must be a little more formal.[30]

SUBSTANTIVE DUE PROCESS

Procedural due process places limits on *how* governmental power may be exercised; substantive due process places limits on *why* that power may be exercised. Procedural due process has to do with the *procedures* of the law; substantive due process has to do with the *content* of the law. Procedural due process mainly limits the executive and judicial branches; substantive due process mainly limits the legislative branch. Substantive due

[24]*Bishop* v. *Wood*, 426 U.S. 341 (1976).

[25]*Meachum* v. *Fano*, 427 U.S. 215 (1976).

[26]*Morrissey* v. *Brewer*, 408 U.S. 471 (1972).

[27]*In Re Gault*, 387 U.S. 1 (1967); *McKeiver* v. *Pennsylvania*, 403 U.S. 528 (1971).

[28]*Wolff* v. *McDonnell*, 418 U.S. 539 (1974).

[29]*Goss* v. *Lopez*.

[30]Judge H. J. Friendly, "Some Kind of Hearing," *University of Pennsylvania Law Review*, 123 (1975), p. 1267.

In *Moore vs. City of East Cleveland*, the Supreme Court upheld Mrs. Inez Moore's right to live with her grandchildren despite an East Cleveland zoning regulation that limits dwellings to single families. The Court ruled that it is unreasonable to define "family" in such a way as to preclude a grandmother from inviting to live with her in her home all of her children.

process means that an unreasonable law, even if properly passed and being properly applied, is unconstitutional.

Here are some examples of the recent application of substantive due process: School board regulations requiring teachers to cease teaching past the fourth month of pregnancy and barring them from returning to the classroom until three months after the birth of a child are unreasonable interferences with the liberty of women teachers to bear children.[31] To confine against their wishes nondangerous mentally ill persons is an unreasonable deprivation of their liberty.[32] A city may adopt zoning regulations to limit dwellings to single families, but it is unreasonable to define "family" in such a way as to prevent a grandmother from inviting all her grandchildren to live with her in her home.[33]

Before 1937, substantive due process was used primarily to protect "liberty of contract," that is, business liberty. Indeed, the adoption of the doctrine of substantive due process and the simultaneous expansion of the meaning of liberty and property made the Supreme Court, for a time, the final judge of our economic and industrial life. During this period, the Supreme Court was dominated by conservative jurists who considered almost all social welfare legislation unreasonable. They used the due process clause to strike down laws regulating hours of labor, establishing minimum wages, regulating prices, and forbidding employers to fire workers for union membership. The Supreme Court vetoed laws adversely affecting property rights unless the judges could be persuaded that such laws were necessary to protect the public health or safety.

But what is "unreasonable"? The trouble with the substantive interpretation of due process is that the reasonableness of a law depends on one's economic, social, and political views. In democracies, elected officials are supposed to accommodate opposing notions of reasonableness and to decide what regulations of liberty and property are needed to promote the

[31]*Cleveland Board of Education* v. *LaFleur*, 414 U.S. 632 (1974).

[32]*O'Connor* v. *Donaldson*, 422 U.S. 563 (1975).

[33]*Moore* v. *City of East Cleveland*, 52 L Ed 2d 531 (1977).

public welfare. When the Supreme Court substitutes its own ideas of reasonableness for the legislature's, it acts like a superlegislature. But how competent are judges to say what the nation's economic policies should be? Or other kinds of policies?

Because of this criticism, the Supreme Court since 1937 has largely abandoned the doctrine of "liberty of contract" and in general has refused to apply the doctrine of substantive due process to laws regulating the economy. The Court now consists of justices who believe that deciding which are reasonable regulations of the uses of property is a legislative and not a judicial responsibility. As long as the justices see some connection between such a law and the promotion of the public welfare, the Supreme Court will not interfere.

The abandonment of the doctrine of substantive due process as a limit on the government's power to regulate property rights has not meant a return to the old narrow conception of liberty or the abandonment of substantive due process. Quite the contrary. Since 1937 the word "liberty" in the Fifth and Fourteenth Amendments has been expanded to include the basic civil liberties; substantive due process has been given new life as a limitation on governmental power in the field of these liberties.

Further, as we have noted, since the 1960s the Supreme Court has developed a substantive interpretation of the equal-protection clause to supplement the substantive interpretation of due process. And just as prior to 1937, liberal justices in dissents, and liberal commentators, used to chide conservative justices in the majority for using substantive due process to impose their own ideas of what was a reasonable regulation of the economy upon the nation, so today conservative judges, now in the minority, are contending that once again the Supreme Court justices in the majority are going beyond the bounds of their responsibilities. Justice Rehnquist, for example, the Court's most outspoken conservative, has chided his colleagues for acting like legislators rather than judges. Judges, he argues, are to decide what the Constitution means, not to impose their own view of "reasonableness" upon the country. He has been especially critical of what he thinks to be the imposition of the justices' own policy preferences for state regulation of abortions when the Court majority ruled: (1) It is unreasonable for states to forbid abortions during the first three months of pregnancy; (2) it is reasonable to forbid abortions except when necessary to protect the health of the mother and fetus during the second three months; (3) it is reasonable to forbid abortions altogether during the last three months of pregnancy; (4) it is not constitutionally unreasonable, and therefore permissible, for a state, if it wishes, to refuse to pay for voluntary abortions for women unable to afford them.[34]

Justices who support the majority position, of course, deny that they are substituting their own values for those of the legislature. They argue that there is a fundamental difference between what they are doing in protecting civil liberties and what the conservative pre-1937 justices did to protect property rights. The earlier justices were writing into the Constitution the principles of laissez-faire economics, whereas they are extracting from the Constitution its principles of civil liberties. Justice Powell, in behalf of the Court, conceded:

The controversy over the Supreme Court's ruling on abortions is demonstrated by these two groups of marchers.

[34]*Roe* v. *Wade*, 410 U.S. 113 (1973); *Maher* v. *Roe*, 53 L Ed 2d (1977).

Substantive due process has at times been a treacherous field for this Court. There are risks when the judicial branch gives enhanced protection to certain substantive liberties without the guidance of the more specific provisions of the Bill of Rights. . . . There is reason for concern lest the only limits to such judicial intervention become the predilections of those who happen at the time to be Members of this Court. . . . That history counsels caution and restraint. But it does not counsel abandonment [of substantive due process].[35]

The notion that laws must be reasonable has deep roots in natural law concepts and a long history in the American constitutional tradition. For most Americans most of the time, it is not enough merely to say that a law reflects the wishes of the popular or legislative majority.[36] We also want our laws to be just. And we continue to rely heavily on judges to decide what is just. These tensions between democratic procedures and judicial guardians are ones to which we shall return when we discuss the role of judges in Chapter 15.

EMINENT DOMAIN

Many government regulations affect the value of the property we own. For example, a zoning law restricting a particular area to residential uses may lower the immediate value of a particular property. (Maybe the owner was planning to use that land for a gas station.) The government does not have to pay the owner for such losses; she or he loses money—but the rest of the community gains.

What if the government goes beyond reasonable regulation and takes property? Both the national and state governments have a constitutional right to do so. They can exercise what is known as the power of eminent domain. But the Constitution requires that property be taken only for public purposes and that the owner be paid a fair price. If there is any dispute about what price is fair, the final decision is made by the courts.

Freedom from arbitrary arrest, questioning, and imprisonment

James Otis's address in 1761 protesting arbitrary searches and seizures by English customs officials was the signal for the American Revolution; as John Adams later said, "American independence was then and there born." The Fourth Amendment states: "The right of the people to be secure in their persons, houses, papers, and effects, against unreasonable searches and seizures, shall not be violated, and no Warrants shall issue, but upon probable cause, supported by Oath or affirmation, and particularly describing the place to be searched, and the persons or things to be seized."

WHAT IS UNREASONABLE SEARCH AND SEIZURE?

Despite what we see in television police dramas and sometimes read about in the news, law enforcement officers have no general right to invade homes and break down doors. They are not supposed to search people except under certain conditions; and they have no right to arrest except under certain circumstances. This is a highly technical area in which the Supreme Court itself has had difficulty in determining what the Constitution means. As Justice Powell has written, "Searches and seizures are an

[35]*Moore* v. *City of East Cleveland.*

[36]For a review of the issues, see Jacob Landynski, "Due Process and the Concept of Ordered Liberty," *Hofstra Law Review* (Winter 1974), pp. 1ff.

opaque area of the law; flagrant Fourth Amendment abuses will rarely escape detection but there is a vast twilight zone with respect to which our own decisions . . . are hardly noted for their predictability."[37] And the law in this area is constantly changing. It is on the reasonableness of searches and seizures that the Burger Court has been especially likely to move away from the more restrictive decisions of the Warren Court.

The Constitution does not forbid searches and seizures, only "unreasonable" ones. The more serious restraint, an arrest, is subject to less protection than are searches. Police may make warrantless arrests, at least in public places, whenever they have probable cause to believe that a person has committed or is about to commit a crime. When in hot pursuit, police may follow persons into their homes and place them under arrest even without a warrant. Immediately following an arrest, however, the Fourth Amendment requires the police to take a person before a magistrate for a hearing. The magistrate, and not just the police, may determine whether probable cause did exist to justify the arrest.[38]

What of searches? In general, except in carefully defined cases, a search without proper consent is constitutionally unreasonable unless it has been authorized by a valid search warrant issued by a magistrate.[39] The exceptions, and under the Burger Court the listing is growing, are as follows:

1. Searches of automobiles that the police have probable cause to believe contain evidence of crimes or are being used to commit crimes.[40] The Court refused to expand this exception to cover a footlocker found in the trunk of an automobile: "A person's expectations of privacy in personal luggage are substantially greater than in an automobile."[41]

2. Officers may stop and search suspects if they have reason to believe they are dealing with armed and dangerous persons, regardless of whether or not they have probable cause to make an arrest. Such searches must be confined to looking for weapons that might be used to assault the arresting officer.[42]

3. When making a lawful arrest, either with an arrest warrant or because of probable cause, police may make a warrantless, full search of the persons, the areas under their immediate control, and the possessions they take with them to the place of detention.[43]

4. If an officer, under exception 2, stops and frisks a suspect to look for weapons, but instead finds criminal evidence that justifies an arrest, then under exception 3 he can make a full search. To illustrate: An officer, acting on an informer's tip, approached a man sitting in a car. The officer ordered the suspect to get out of the car, but he merely rolled down the window. The officer saw a weapon on the suspect's waistband. He arrested him—although the mere possession of the weapon in that state is not a crime—and made a search and found heroin. Justice Rehnquist,

---

[37]Concurring in *Schneckloth* v. *Bustamonte*, 412 U.S. 218 (1973); and quoting from Justice Harlan in *Ker* v. *California*, 374 U.S. 23 (1963).

[38]*Gerstein* v. *Pugh*, 420 U.S. 103 (1974). Jacob Landynski, "Search and Seizure," in Stuart S. Nagel, ed; *The Rights of the Accused* (Sage Publications, 1972). David Fellman, *The Defendant's Rights Today* (University of Wisconsin Press, 1976), provides a comprehensive explanation from arrest to conviction.

[39]*A.G.M. Leasing Corp.* v. *United States*, 429 U.S. 338 (1977).

[40]*Carroll* v. *United States*, 267 U.S. 132 (1925); *Texas* v. *White*, 423 U.S. 67 (1975).

[41]*United States* v. *Chadwick*, 53 L Ed 2d 538 (1977).

[42]*Terry* v. *Ohio*, 392 U.S. 1 (1968).

[43]*Chimel* v. *California*, 395 U.S. 752 (1969); *United States* v. *Edwards*, 415 U.S. 800 (1974).

speaking for the Court, said: "The Fourth Amendment does not require a policeman who lacks the precise level of information necessary for probable cause to arrest to simply shrug his shoulders and allow a crime to occur or a criminal to escape." The dissenting justices argued that the majority had ignored the fact that the stop-and-frisk exception to the warrant requirement had been "begrudgingly" granted only to protect the safety of officers of the law.[44]

5. When there is probable cause to make an arrest, even if one is not made, limited searches necessary to preserve easily disposed of evidence such as scrapings under fingernails are permitted.[45]

6. Searches based on consent voluntarily given, even if the persons who give the consent are not told that they have a right to refuse to grant permission, are allowed.[46]

7. Searches at border crossings of persons and the goods they bring with them are permissible.[47] The border search exception also permits officials to open mail entering the country if they have a "reasonable cause" to suspect it contains merchandise imported contrary to the law.[48]

8. Seizures of incriminating evidence in plain view, as for example on the outside of an automobile.[49]

9. Under "exigent circumstances," that is, when officers do not have time to secure a warrant because evidence is about to be destroyed or otherwise be moved to escape detection.[50]

With these exceptions, before engaging in a search police are to appear before a magistrate and under oath indicate they have "probable cause" to believe that the search will produce criminal evidence. The magistrate need not be a legally trained judge, but a prosecutor or a state's attorney will not do; nor will a justice of the peace who receives a fee if he issues a warrant but nothing if he refuses to do so.[51] The magistrate must "perform his 'neutral and detached' function and not serve merely as a rubber stamp for the police."[52] The warrant must describe what places are to be searched and what things are to be seized. A blanket authorization to search indiscriminately is a general search warrant and violates the Constitution. The premises protected against warrantless searches include any place a person has a legitimate right to be, including hotel rooms, rented homes, apartments of friends, or even telephone booths. As the Court has said, "the Fourth Amendment 'protects people, not places'; more particularly, it protects people from unreasonable government intrusions into their legitimate expectations of privacy."[53]

The inventions of science have confronted judges with new problems in applying the prohibition against unreasonable searches and seizures.

[44]*Adams* v. *Williams*, 407 U.S. 143 (1972).

[45]*Cupp* v. *Murphy*, 412 U.S. 291 (1973).

[46]*Schneckloth* v. *Bustamonte; United States* v. *Matlock*, 415 U.S. 164 (1974).

[47]*Almeida-Sancez* v. *United States*, 413 U.S. 266 (1973); *United States* v. *Ortiz*, 422 U.S. 873 (1975).

[48]*United States* v. *Ramsey*, 52 L Ed 2d 617 (1977).

[49]*Cardwell* v. *Lewis*, 417 U.S. 583 (1974).

[50]*United States* v. *Watson*, 423 U.S. 411 (1976).

[51]*Shadwick* v. *City of Tampa*, 407 U.S. 345 (1972); *Coolidge* v. *New Hampshire*, 403 U.S. 433 (1971); *Connally* v. *Georgia*, 429 U.S. 245 (1977).

[52]*Aguilar* v. *Texas*, 378 U.S. 108 (1964).

[53]*United States* v. *Chadwick; quoting Katz* v. *United States*, 389 U.S. 347 (1967).

Obviously, the framers of the Fourth Amendment had in mind physical objects such as books, papers, letters, and other kinds of documents they felt should not be seized by police except on the basis of limited search warrants issued by magistrates. But what of tapping phone wires or using electronic devices to eavesdrop?[54] In *Olmstead* v. *United States*, decided in 1928, a bare majority of the Supreme Court held that there was no unconstitutional search unless there was seizure of physical objects or an actual physical entry into a premise. Justices Holmes and Brandeis, in dissent argued that the Constitution should be kept up with the times; the "dirty business" of wiretapping produced the same evil invasions of privacy that the framers had in mind when they wrote the Fourteenth Amendment.[55]

Forty years later, in *Katz* v. *United States* (1967), the Supreme Court adopted the Holmes-Brandeis position: "The Fourth Amendment protects people—and not simply 'areas'—against unreasonable searches and seizures." The use by police officers of electronic devices to overhear a conversation in a public telephone booth is a search and seizure within the meaning of the Constitution. "Wherever a man may be, he is entitled to know that he will remain free from unreasonable searches and seizures."[56]

Since conversations are now constitutionally protected against unreasonable searches and seizures, legislatures and judges have had to develop rules to determine the conditions under which conversations may be intercepted. The basic federal legislation is contained in the Crime Control and Safe Streets Act of 1968, which Congress adopted over President Johnson's objection. He felt that it would lead to a "nation of snoopers bending through the keyholes of the homes and offices of America, spying on our neighbors." The 1968 act made it a crime for any unauthorized person to tap telephone wires or use or sell in interstate commerce, electronic bugging devices. But it authorizes the attorney general to secure permission for federal agents to engage in bugging by applying for a warrant from a federal judge for a whole range of specified federal offenses. The attorney general must authorize the wiretapping personally or through an assistant specifically designated by him for that purpose. This authority may not be further delegated.[57]

At the state level, the act authorizes the principal prosecuting attorney of any state or political subdivision to apply to a state judge for a warrant approving wiretapping or oral intercepts for felonies. Judges are to issue warrants only if they decide that probable cause exists that a crime is being, has been, or is about to be committed and that information relating to that crime may be obtained only by the intercept. In addition to these intercepts under warrant, the act permits police officers to act without a warrant for forty-eight hours in "an emergency situation relating to conspiratorial activities threatening the national security" or involving organized crime.

In the few cases that have come before it under the act, the Supreme Court has interpreted it as narrowly as possible. The president's authority

"The Court finds itself on the horns of a dilemma. On the one hand, wiretap evidence is inadmissible, and on the other hand I'm dying to hear it."

Drawing by J. B. Handelsman; © 1972 The New Yorker Magazine, Inc.

[54]See Walter F. Murphy, *Wiretapping on Trial: A Case Study in the Judicial Process* (Random House, 1965).

[55]277 U.S. 438 (1928).

[56]389 U.S. 347 (1967).

[57]*United States* v. *Giordano*, 416 U.S. 505 (1974).

to protect the nation against foreign attack and violent overthrow does not include the right to authorize electronic surveillance of persons suspect of domestic subversion. Justice Powell, speaking for the Court (*United States v. United States District Court, 1972*), said, ''The danger to political dissent is acute where the Government attempts to act under so vague a concept as the power to protect 'domestic security.'''[58] The Court did not rule on the constitutionality of authorizing surveillance over the activities of agents of foreign powers, within and without the country. However, the Court in no way has ever hinted that a president has any constitutional authority to authorize breaking and entry for surveillance purposes.

THE EXCLUSIONARY RULE

Combining the Fourth Amendment prohibition against unreasonable searches and seizures with the Fifth Amendment injunction that no person shall be compelled to be a witness against himself—and using the Fourteenth Amendment (*Mapp* v. *Ohio*, 1961) to make its ruling applicable to the state and local courts—the Supreme Court has ruled that evidence unconstitutionally obtained cannot be used in a criminal trial against persons from whom it was seized.[59] The exclusionary rule however, does not extend to grand jury proceedings. Grand juries may consider evidence even if it has been obtained improperly.[60]

The exclusionary rule was adopted in large part to prevent police misconduct. The police are seldom prosecuted for making illegal searches, nor are they made to pay civil damages. The exclusionary rule is about the only sanction available to judges to enforce the Fourth Amendment. There are critics of the rule, including some justices of the Supreme Court. Why let criminals go free, they argue, because of the misconduct of the police? Moreover, they say, the rule is not effective, especially in circumstances where the police are not particularly interested in using evidence to prosecute, but merely to harass. So far the arguments against the exclusionary rule have not prevailed, although the Supreme Court has started to limit its application.

THE RIGHT TO REMAIN SILENT

During the seventeenth century, certain special courts in England forced confessions of heresy and sedition from religious dissenters. It was in response to these practices that the British privilege against self-incrimination developed. The framers of our Bill of Rights were familiar with this history and so they included in the Fifth Amendment the provision that persons shall not be compelled to testify against themselves in criminal prosecutions. The protection against self-incrimination is designed to strengthen a fundamental principle of Anglo-American justice—that no person has an obligation to prove innocence. Rather, the burden is on the government to prove guilt.

The privilege against self-incrimination applies literally only in criminal prosecutions, but it has always been interpreted to protect any person subject to questioning by any agency of government. A witness before a congressional committee, for example, may refuse to answer incriminating questions. But to invoke the privilege it is not enough that the witness' answers might be embarrassing or incriminate others; there must be a

[58]407 U.S. 297 (1972).

[59]367 U.S. 643 (1961).

[60]*United States* v. *Calandra*, 414 U.S. 338 (1974).

reasonable fear that the answers might support a criminal prosecution or "furnish a link in the chain of evidence needed to prosecute" a crime.[61] If defendants refuse to take the stand in their own defense, the judge must warn the jury not to be prejudiced by their silence. If defendants do choose to take the stand, they cannot claim the privilege against self-incrimination to prevent cross-examination by the prosecution.

Sometimes authorities would rather have answers from a witness than prosecute. Congress has established procedures so that prosecutors and congressional committees may secure from a federal judge a grant of immunity for a witness. After the immunity has been granted, a witness may no longer claim a right to refuse to testify, even though the immunity that Congress presently provides is only that the government cannot use the information derived from the compelled testimony.[62]

THE THIRD DEGREE

The questioning of suspects by the police is a key procedure for solving crimes. It is also one that can easily be abused. Police officers sometimes forget or ignore the constitutional rights of suspects, especially of those who are frightened and ignorant. Torture, detention, and sustained interrogation to wring confessions from suspects are common practices in police states, and are not unknown in the United States. What is the good of constitutional protections at the time of a trial, or the guarantee of the right to assistance of counsel at the trial, or the presumption of innocence if, long before an accused is brought before the court, he is detained and forced to prove his innocence to the police? What happens in the police station can reduce the courtroom proceedings to a mere formality.

Judges, especially those on the Supreme Court, have done much to stamp out police brutality. The Supreme Court has ruled that even though there may be sufficient evidence to support a conviction apart from a confession, the admission into evidence of a coerced confession violates the self-incrimination clause, deprives a person of the assistance of counsel guaranteed by the Sixth and Fourteenth Amendments, deprives a person of due process, and undermines the entire proceeding.[63]

"Why, this is a revelation! I never dreamed I had so many rights."

Drawing by J. Mirachi; © 1970 The New Yorker Magazine, Inc.

The federal rules of criminal procedure and the laws of all our states require officers to take those whom they have arrested before a magistrate promptly. The magistrate is to inform persons in custody of their constitutional rights and allow them to get in touch with friends and to seek legal advice. The police have no right to hold persons for questioning prior to a hearing before the magistrate, but they are often tempted to question first. Sometimes they lack the evidence to make an arrest stick but feel that if they can quiz suspects before they know their constitutional rights to remain silent, they can get them to confess.

Beginning in 1957, the Supreme Court handed down a series of decisions based on the self-incrimination clause of the Fifth Amendment, the right-to-counsel clause of the Sixth, and the due process clause of the Fifth and Fourteenth that began to cast doubt on the constitutional validity of any private questioning of persons suspected of crime by federal or state police.

Then, in *Miranda* v. *Arizona* in 1966, by a five-to-four vote the Supreme

[61]*Blau* v. *United States*, 340 U.S. 332 (1951).

[62]*Kastigar* v. *United States*, 406 U.S. 441 (1972).

[63]*Payne* v. *Arkansas*, 356 U.S. 560 (1958).

Court announced that no conviction—federal or state—could stand if evidence introduced at the trial had been obtained by the police as the result of "custodial interrogation," unless the following conditions were met. Suspects must have been (1) notified that they are free to remain silent; (2) warned that what they say may be used against them in court; (3) told that they have a right to have an attorney present during the questioning; (4) informed that if they cannot afford to hire their own lawyer, an attorney will be provided for them; and (5) permitted at any stage of the police interrogation to terminate it. If suspects answer questions in the absence of an attorney, the prosecution must be prepared to demonstrate that suspects knowingly and intelligently gave up their rights to remain silent and to have their own lawyer present. Failure to comply with these requirements will lead to reversal of a conviction even if other evidence would be enough to establish guilt.[64]

There are many critics of the Miranda decision who argue that the Court has unnecessarily and severely limited the ability of the police to bring criminals to justice. (The importance of pretrial interrogations is underscored by the fact that roughly 90 percent of all criminal convictions result from pleas of guilty and never reach the full trial stage.)[65] Persuaded by these critics, Congress in 1966 adopted rules for federal trials that may be in conflict with some parts of the Miranda ruling.[66] But the Supreme Court has stuck with Miranda, although it has modified it to some extent: Evidence obtained contrary to the Miranda guidelines is now allowed to be used for limited purposes—for example, attacking defendants' statements if they take the stand and make statements inconsistent with what they previously told the police.[67]

Miranda applies only to "custodial interrogations." Officials are not required to give Miranda warnings to everyone they question, but only to persons "taken into custody or otherwise deprived of their freedom of action."[68] And Miranda warnings are not necessary for persons called to testify before a grand jury.[69]

THE RIGHT OF PRIVACY

There is no mention of the right of privacy in the Constitution, and the Supreme Court has said "there is no general constitutional right to privacy."[70] But after reading the Court decisions of the last decade, it is fair to conclude that the Supreme Court has come to recognize that personal privacy is one of the rights protected by the Constitution. The Court has done this by putting together some elements of the Fourth and Fifth Amendments; the First Amendment's protection for intellect, tastes, and beliefs; the liberty protected by the due process clauses of the Fifth and Fourteenth

[64]*Miranda* v. *Arizona*, 384 U.S. 436 (1966).

[65]Donald J. Newman, *Conviction: The Determination of Guilt or Innocence without Trial* (Little, Brown, 1966), p. 3.

[66]Adam Caryle Breckenridge, *Congress Against the Court* (University of Nebraska Press, 1970), p. 95.

[67]*Harris* v. *New York*, 401 U.S. 222 (1971).

[68]*Beckwith* v. *United States*, 425 U.S. 341 (1976); *Oregon* v. *Mathiason*, 429 U.S. 492 (1977).

[69]*United States* v. *Mandujano*, 425 U.S. 564 (1976).

[70]*Katz* v. *United States*, as quoted by Justice Stewart concurring in *Whalen* v. *Roe*, 429 U.S. 589 (1977).

Amendments; and the rights reserved to the people by the Ninth Amendment. The concept still remains largely undefined, but there appear to be three aspects of the right: (1) to be free from governmental surveillance and intrusion; (2) not to have private affairs made public by the government; (3) to be free in action, thought, and belief from governmental compulsion.[71]

Congress has begun to show concern about privacy with the adoption of the Family Educational Rights Act of 1974 and the Privacy Act of 1974. These new laws limit the recordkeeping and record-disclosing activities of schools and universities that receive federal funds; place restraints on files kept by federal agencies; and under certain conditions permit individuals access to government files in order to correct information about them. The Privacy Act also created a commission to look into recordkeeping by banks, insurance companies, credit card operators, and other businesses and it has recommended to Congress additional legislation. But privacy, although highly valued in the abstract, has often run afoul of other rights—for example, the right of the press. And when in conflict with these other rights, it has not fared well either before Congress or the Courts. The exception is the Supreme Court's protection of "marital privacy" from state regulation.

THE WRIT OF HABEAS CORPUS

Even though the framers did not think a Bill of Rights necessary, they considered certain rights important enough to be included in the original Constitution. Foremost is the guarantee that the writ of habeas corpus will be available unless suspended in time of rebellion or invasion. Permission to suspend the writ is found in the article setting forth the powers of Congress, so presumably only Congress has the right to suspend it.

As originally used, the writ was merely an inquiry by a court to determine whether or not a person was being held in custody as the result of an act of a court with proper jurisdiction. But over the years it has developed into a remedy "available to effect discharge from any confinement contrary to the Constitution or fundamental law."[72] Simply stated, the writ is a court order to any person having another in his custody directing the official to produce the prisoner in court and explain to the judge why the prisoner is being held. Those held in custody or subject to restraint apply under oath, usually through their attorney, and state why they believe they are being unlawfully held. The judge then orders the jailer to show cause why the writ should not be issued. If the judge finds that the petitioner is being unlawfully detained, he may order the prisoner's immediate release.

The case of Duncan and White is a good example of one use of the writ. Duncan and White were civilians who had been convicted by military tribunals and were being held by military authorities in Hawaii during World War II. They filed petitions for writs of habeas corpus in the district court of Hawaii, citing both statutory and constitutional reasons to prove

---

[71]Philip B. Kurland, "Some Reflections on Privacy and the Constitution" (The University of Chicago, Center for Policy Study, 1976), p. 9. A classic and influential article first raising the question is S. D. Warren and L. D. Brandeis, "The Right to Privacy," *Harvard Law Review*, 4 (December 15, 1890), pp. 193–220. A useful contemporary review of an important aspect of the right is E. J. Bloustein, "Group Privacy: The Right to Huddle," *Camden Law Journal* (Winter 1977), pp. 219–283. William Prosser, "Privacy," *California Law Review* (1960); pp. 383ff is an influential article.

[72]*Preiser* v. *Rodriguez* 411 U.S. 475 (1973).

that the military had no right to keep them in prison. The court then asked the military to show cause why the petition should not be granted. The military replied that Hawaii had become part of an active theater of war; that the writ of habeas corpus had been suspended; that martial law had been established; and that consequently the district court had no jurisdiction to issue the writs. Moreover, the writ of habeas corpus should not be issued in this case because the military trials of Duncan and White were valid. After hearing both sides, the district court, in an action eventually approved by the Supreme Court, agreed with Duncan and White and issued writs ordering their release.[73]

Under our federal system, state courts may not issue writs to inquire why a person is being held by national authorities. But federal judges may inquire about those restrained by state authorities, provided the petitioner has first sought and been denied relief in the state courts. The expansion in recent decades of the federal court's habeas corpus jurisdiction to permit more postconviction review by federal district judges of the judgments of state courts in criminal cases is a major point of dispute between state and federal judges. As a state judge wrote, "The . . . assumption . . . that federal court protection is needed in addition to state court protection which cannot be trusted with the task . . . has raised the hackles or blood pressure of many of my state court colleagues."[74]

It is not likely that many state judges were pleased by Justice Brennan's comments in a 1976 decision: "State judges popularly elected may have difficulty resisting popular pressures not experienced by federal judges given lifetime tenure designed to immunize them from such influences, and the federal habeas statutes reflect the Congressional judgment that such detached federal review is a salutary safeguard against *any* detention of an individual 'in violation of the Constitution or laws of the United States.'"[75] But these words were written in dissent. The majority of the Court, perhaps as a result of the criticism by state judges but also because of concern about overloading federal courts, has begun to restrict the use of habeas corpus by federal judges. For example, where a state has provided an opportunity for litigation of a Fourth Amendment search claim, a state prisoner is not to be granted another hearing by a habeas corpus writ in a federal court.[76]

EX POST FACTO LAWS AND BILLS OF ATTAINDER

The Constitution forbids both the national and state governments to pass ex post facto laws or enact bills of attainder (Article I, Sections 9 and 10).

An **ex post facto law** is a retroactive criminal law that works to the disadvantage of an individual. For example, it can be a law making a particular act a crime that was not a crime when committed. Or it can be a law that increases the punishment for a crime after it was committed or that changes the proof necessary to convict for a crime after it was committed.[77] The prohibition does not prevent the passage of retroactive penal laws that work to the benefit of an accused—for example, a law decreasing pun-

[73]*Duncan* v. *Kahanamoku*, 327 U.S. 304 (1946).

[74]Charles S. Desmond, "The Federal Courts and the Nature and Quality of State Law," in S. I. Shuman, ed., *The Future of Federalism* (Wayne State University Press, 1968), p. 97.

[75]*Stone* v. *Powell*, 428 U.S. 465 (1976).

[76]*Ibid.*

[77]*Dobbert* v. *Florida*, 53 L Ed 2d (1977).

ishment. And not every procedural change is necessarily forbidden. The Supreme Court, for example, recently ruled that there had been no violation of the ex post facto clause when a person was tried for murder under a death penalty law passed after the crime had been committed, and after an earlier death penalty statute had been declared unconstitutional. The newer law provided procedures to comply with Supreme Court rulings that made the imposition of the death penalty more difficult.[78] The prohibition against ex post facto laws does not prevent the passage of retroactive civil laws. For example, income tax rates as applied to income already earned may be increased.

A bill of attainder is a legislative act inflicting punishment without judicial trial on named individuals or members of a specified group. Although the fact that a law works to the disadvantage of an individual does not make it a bill of attainder, such bills are not limited to those that impose criminal sanctions; they include deprivations of property or loss of jobs. Bills of attainder have been rare in American history, but Congress has enacted two in the last three decades, and it was alleged by former president Nixon to have enacted a third.[79]

In 1974, four months after Nixon resigned and after he had signed an agreement with the administrator of the General Services Administration relating to the disposition of his presidential papers and tapes, Congress directed the administrator to take custody of the materials. The act instructed the administrator to issue regulations that would eventually return to Nixon his personal and private papers, but would preserve in government custody, and eventually make public, those papers having historical value. Since every previous president had been given custody of his own papers, Nixon alleged that Congress had singled him out for punishment. The Supreme Court majority agreed that legislation that subjects a named individual to this humiliating treatment raises serious questions under the bill of attainder clause. But seven members held that Nixon was a "legitimate class of one," and that Congress was not motivated by a desire to punish. Pending study as to the disposition of future presidential papers, Congress could act to preserve the Nixon papers while accepting the fact that other presidential papers were already housed in special libraries under terms set by former presidents.[80]

Rights of persons accused of crime

Some feel that the rights of persons accused of crime are less important than other civil liberties, but as Justice Frankfurter observed, "The history of liberty has largely been the history of observance of procedural safeguards." These safeguards, moreover, have frequently "been forged in controversies involving not very nice people." Their purpose is not "to convenience the guilty but to protect the innocent."

THE FEDERAL COURTS

The rights of persons accused of crime by the national government can be found in the Fourth, Fifth, Sixth, and Eighth Amendments. In order to gain some idea of the application of these constitutional safeguards, we shall follow the fortunes and misfortunes of John T. Crook (a fictitious name).

[78]*Ibid.*

[79]*United States* v. *Lovett,* 328 U.S. 303 (1946); *United States* v. *Brown,* 381 U.S. 437 (1965).

[80] *Nixon* v. *Administrator of General Services, James M. Burns, et al.,* 53 L Ed 2d. (1977).

Crook sent circulars through the mails soliciting purchases of stock in a nonexistent gold mine, an action contrary to at least three federal laws. When postal officers uncovered these activities, they went to the district court and secured from a United States magistrate warrants for the arrest of Crook and to search his home for copies of the circulars. They found Crook at home, read the Miranda warning to him, emphasizing especially his right to remain silent and to have the assistance of counsel. They showed him the warrants, arrested him for using the mails to defraud, and found and seized some of the circulars mentioned in the search warrant.

Crook was promptly brought before a federal district judge who again emphasized to Crook that he had the constitutional right to the assistance of counsel. What was once merely a right to be represented by an attorney during a trial if a defendant wanted and could afford such help is now a positive obligation in federal trials (*Johnson* v. *Zerbst*, 1938)[81] and since 1963 also in state trials(*Gideon* v. *Wainwright*, 1963) to see to it that all persons subject to any kind of custodial interrogation are represented by a lawyer.[82]

Unless the record clearly shows that the accused were fully aware of what they were doing and gave up the right to counsel or intelligently exercised the right to represent themselves, the absence of such counsel will render criminal proceedings unconstitutional.[83] The right extends to all trials, for all offenses for which an accused may be deprived of liberty, whether or not a jury trial is required. Trials in which fines are the only penalty are exempt from the assistance of counsel requirement.[84] This assistance is required at every stage of a criminal proceeding—preliminary hearings, bail hearings, trial, sentence, and appeal. The Supreme Court has gone far to insist on the assistance of counsel. Over the bitter dissent of four members, it reversed a conviction based on a confession made to a police officer after a prisoner had been arrested but while he was being driven to jail. His attorney had warned him not to talk and the police had promised not to question him on the ride. But the defendant showed the police where the body of the little girl he had been accused of murdering was located after the officer had asked him to do so "because her parents were entitled to a Christian burial for the girl."[85]

To return to Crook: when Crook told the judge he could not afford to hire his own counsel, the judge appointed an attorney to represent him paid for by the federal government. The judge set bail at $1,500, and Crook was held over until the convening of the next federal grand jury. After posting bond, Crook was permitted his freedom as long as he remained within the judicial district. The Eighth Amendment forbids imposition of excessive bail, for it is a basic principle of American justice that no person is guilty until pronounced so after a fair trial. To set bail higher than necessary to assure the presence of a defendant at his trial is "excessive." The Bail Reform Act of 1966 allows federal judges to release persons without bail if, after taking into account such factors as past record or family and community ties, bail seems unnecessary. For capital crimes, judges may

[81]*Johnson* v. *Zerbst*, 304 U.S. 458 (1938).

[82]*Gideon* v. *Wainwright*, 372 U.S. 335 (1963).

[83]*Faretta* v. *California*, 422 U.S. 800 (1975).

[84]*Argesinger* v. *Hamilton*, 407 U.S. 25 (1972).

[85]*Brewer* v. *Williams*, 430 U.S. 387 (1977).

refuse to release a person on bail; no amount of money may be sufficient to ensure that one who stands in jeopardy of losing his life will be around for his trial.

When the next grand jury was convened, the United States district attorney brought before the twenty-three jurors evidence to indicate that Crook had committed a federal crime. Grand jurors are concerned not with a person's guilt or innocence, but merely with whether there is enough evidence to warrant a trial. No person has a right to appear before a grand jury, but may be invited or ordered to do so. If a majority of the grand jurors agree that a trial is justified, they return what is known as a *true bill*, or indictment. Except in cases arising in the military forces involving service-connected crimes,[86] the national government cannot force any person to stand trial for any serious crime except on grand jury indictment. In our particular case, the grand jury was in agreement with the United States district attorney and returned a true bill against Crook.

After a copy of the indictment was served on Crook, he was again ordered to appear before a federal district judge. The Constitution guarantees the accused the right to be informed of the nature and cause of the accusation so that he can prepare his defense. Consequently, the federal prosecutor had seen to it that the indictment clearly stated the nature of the offense and that copies had been properly served on Crook and his lawyer.

Actually, Crook's attorney, prior to his hearing, had discussed with the United States Attorney's office the possibility of Crook pleading guilty to a lesser offense. This kind of "plea bargaining" is often used. Prosecutors, faced with more charges than they can handle, often prefer to accept a guilty plea to a reduced charge rather than to prosecute for the more serious offense. And defendants are often willing to "cop a plea" to a lesser offense to avoid the risk of more serious punishment.

But when a defendant pleads guilty to a lesser offense, he gives up his constitutional rights and under most circumstances is forever prevented from raising objections to his conviction—for example, that the grand jury that indicted him had been improperly empaneled.[87] This is why a judge before accepting a guilty plea ordinarily will question the defendant to be sure that his attorney has explained the alternatives to him and that he knows what he is doing. It never came to this in Crook's case, however. After discussing the matter with his attorney, he elected to stand trial on the charge and entered a plea of not guilty.

After indictment, Crook's bail was raised to $3,000. Now the federal government was obliged to give him a speedy and a public trial. The word "speedy," however, should not be taken too literally. Crook had to be given time to prepare his defense. And defendants often ask for delays, since these work to their advantage. Crowded court dockets often lead to delay, although federal courts have recently adopted a rule of procedure that requires them to state in advance the time limits in which the case must be brought to a hearing. For if the government denies the accused a speedy trial in a constitutional sense, the remedy is drastic. It is not merely that the conviction may be reversed, but the case must be dismissed outright.[88]

---

[86]*O'Callahan* v. *Parker*, 395 U.S. 258 (1969); *Relford* v. *Commandant*, 401 U.S. 355 (1971).

[87]*Tollet* v. *Henderson*, 411 U.S. 258 (1973).

[88]*Strunk* v. *United States*, 412 U.S. 434 (1973).

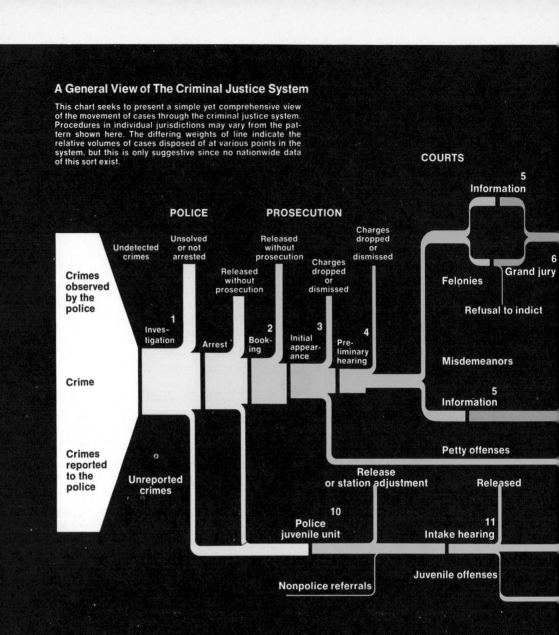

A General View of The Criminal Justice System

This chart seeks to present a simple yet comprehensive view of the movement of cases through the criminal justice system. Procedures in individual jurisdictions may vary from the pattern shown here. The differing weights of line indicate the relative volumes of cases disposed of at various points in the system, but this is only suggestive since no nationwide data of this sort exist.

COURTS

POLICE

PROSECUTION

5
Information

Crimes observed by the police

Undetected crimes

Unsolved or not arrested

Released without prosecution

Charges dropped or dismissed

6
Grand jury

Released without prosecution

Charges dropped or dismissed

Felonies

1
Investigation

Arrest

2
Booking

3
Initial appearance

4
Preliminary hearing

Refusal to indict

Crime

Misdemeanors

5
Information

Crimes reported to the police

Unreported crimes

Petty offenses

Release or station adjustment

Released

10
Police juvenile unit

11
Intake hearing

Nonpolice referrals

Juvenile offenses

1 May continue until trial.
2 Administrative record of arrest. First step at which temporary release on bail may be available.
3 Before magistrate, commissioner, or justice of peace. Formal notice of charge, advice of rights. Bail set. Summary trials for petty offenses usually conducted here without further processing.
4 Preliminary testing of evidence against defendant. Charge may be reduced. No separate preliminary hearing for misdemeanors in some systems.
5 Charge filed by prosecutor on basis of information submitted by police or citiz Alternative to grand jury indictment; of used in felonies, almost always in misdemeanors.
6 Reviews whether government evidence sufficient to justify trial. Some states ha grand jury system; others seldom use it

The Challenge of Crime in a Free Society: Report by the President's Commission on Law Enforcement and Administration of Justice (Government Printing Office, 1967), pp. 8-9

Crook's lawyer pointed out that under the Sixth Amendment, he had a right to trial before an impartial jury selected from the state and district where the alleged crime was committed. For he was being tried for a serious crime—that is, one defined by the court as being punishable by more

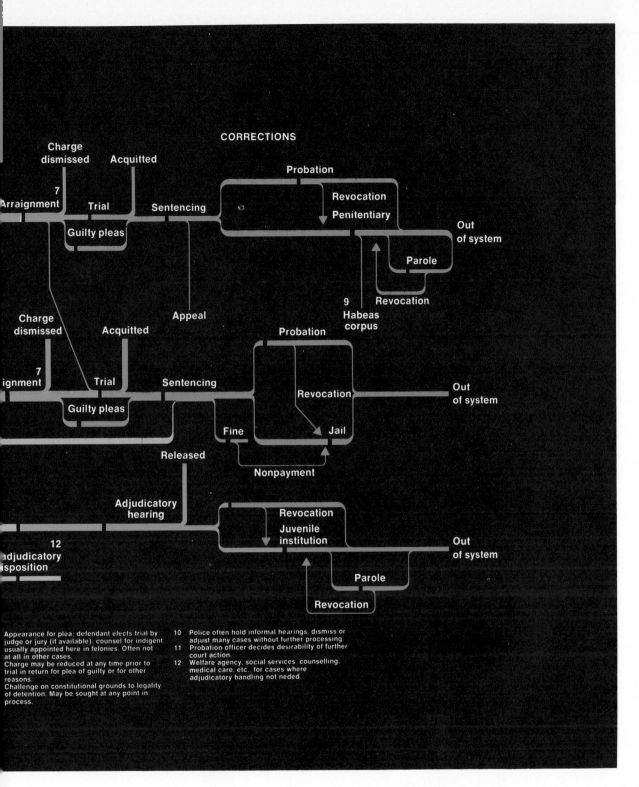

CORRECTIONS

Charge dismissed

Acquitted

Probation

7

Arraignment

Trial

Sentencing

Revocation

Penitentiary

Guilty pleas

Out of system

Parole

Appeal

9 Revocation

Habeas corpus

Charge dismissed

Acquitted

Probation

7

ignment

Trial

Sentencing

Revocation

Out of system

Guilty pleas

Fine

Jail

Released

Nonpayment

Adjudicatory hearing

Revocation

Juvenile institution

Out of system

12

adjudicatory isposition

Parole

Revocation

Appearance for plea: defendant elects trial by judge or jury (if available), counsel for indigent usually appointed here in felonies. Often not at all in other cases.
Charge may be reduced at any time prior to trial in return for plea of guilty or for other reasons.
Challenge on constitutional grounds to legality of detention. May be sought at any point in process.

10 Police often hold informal hearings, dismiss or adjust many cases without further processing.
11 Probation officer decides desirability of further court action.
12 Welfare agency, social services counselling, medical care, etc., for cases where adjudicatory handling not neded.

than six months in prison or a $500 fine.[89] Federal law provides for juries of twelve in criminal courts; but if Congress wished, it could provide for

[89]*Dyke* v. *Taylor Implement Manufacturing Co.*, 391 U.S. 216 (1968).

juries of other sizes, the Supreme Court has held (*Williams* v. *Florida*, 1970).[90] The Sixth Amendment apparently still requires federal juries to convict by a unanimous vote. The Supreme Court gave its approval to nonunanimous verdicts in state courts, with four justices explicitly stating that in their view such verdicts do not violate the Sixth Amendment (*Apodaca* v. *Oregon*, 1972).[91]

An impartial jury, and one that meets the requirements of due process and equal protection, consists of persons who represent an unbiased cross-section of the community. Although blacks, for example, are not entitled to a jury on which there are blacks, they are entitled to a jury from which persons have not been excluded because of race. So, by the way, are whites—that is, a white or a black is deprived of his or her constitutional rights if tried by a jury from which whites or blacks have been excluded because of race.[92] Such actions would also violate the civil rights of those denied the opportunity to serve on juries.[93] And in those categories to which the Constitution gives special protection—race, religion, national origin, alienage, and probably sex—a defendant's attorney has a right to question potential jurors about their attitudes toward those of the defendant's particular category. The Supreme Court, however, refused to make it a matter of constitutional right for bearded defendants to interrogate jurors about their possible prejudice against persons with beards; the Court left this to the discretion of the trial judge.[94]

In preparation of his defense, Crook told his lawyer that he had dinner with George Witness on the night on which he was charged with sending the damaging circulars. The attorney took advantage of Crook's constitutional right to obtain witnesses in his favor and had the judge subpoena Witness to appear at the trial and testify. Witness could have refused to testify on the grounds that his testimony would tend to incriminate him, but he agreed to do so. Crook himself, however, chose to use his constitutional right not to be a witness against himself and refused to take the stand. He knew that if he did so, the prosecution would have a right to cross-examination, and he was fearful of what might be uncovered. The federal judge conducting the trial cautioned the jury against drawing any conclusions from Crook's reluctance to testify. All prosecution witnesses appeared in court and were available to defense cross-examination, because the Constitution insists that the accused has the right to be confronted with the witnesses against him.

At the conclusion of the trial, the jury brought in a verdict of guilty. The judge then raised Crook's bail to $5,000 and announced that he would hand down a sentence on the following Monday. The Eighth Amendment forbids the levying of excessive fines and the inflicting of cruel and unusual punishments. When the judge, in accord with the law, gave Crook the maximum punishment of $5,000 and five years in the penitentiary, the punishment could not be considered cruel and unusual.

The ban against cruel and unusual punishments limits government in

[90]399 U.S. 78 (1970).

[91]406 U.S. 404 (1972).

[92]*Peters* v. *Kiff*, 407 U.S. 493 (1972); *Taylor* v. *Louisiana*, 419 U.S. 522 (1972).

[93]*Carter* v. *Jury Commissioners*, 396 U.S. 320 (1970).

[94]*Ham* v. *South Carolina*, 409 U.S. 524 (1973).

three ways:[95] (1) It limits the kinds of punishments that can be imposed, for example, torture or intentionally denying to prisoners needed medical care.[96] (2) It prohibits punishment out of proportion to the severity of the crime—the death penalty for the rape of an adult woman for example.[97] (3) It limits what can be made a criminal offense; for example, the mere act of being a chronic alcoholic may not be made a crime, although being drunk in public *may* be made an offense.[98] The ban applies only to persons convicted of crimes: by a five to four vote the Supreme Court held that it does not protect public school students from corporal punishment by their teachers or principals.[99]

What of capital punishment? After much soul searching and a whole series of cases, the Supreme Court has ruled that the death penalty is not cruel and unusual punishment for the crime of murder. But the state must ensure that whoever imposes the penalty—judge or jury—does so only after careful consideration of the character and record of the person and the circumstances of the particular crime.[100] The automatic use of the death sentence for every person convicted of a specified capital offense will not do: "It is essential that the capital sentencing decision allow for consideration of whatever mitigating circumstances may be relevant to either the particular offender or the particular offense."[101] The Court has suggested that the best procedure is first to have a jury determine guilt, and then in a subsequent proceeding focus attention on whether the circumstances justify the death penalty. Although it has never ruled on crimes other than murder or rape, the Court implied that "the death penalty may be properly imposed only as to crimes resulting in the death of the victim."[102]

THE NATIONALIZATION OF THE BILL OF RIGHTS

While still in the federal penitentiary, Crook was taken by federal authorities before the state courts to answer charges that he had also committed a state crime. Since Crook was entitled to a speedy trial on these state charges, the state could not wait until he had been released by federal authorities before bringing him to justice.[103]

Crook, through his state-appointed attorney, protested that he had already been tried by the federal government for using the mails to defraud; he pointed to the Fifth Amendment provision that no person shall be "subject for the same offense to be twice put in jeopardy of life or limb." This double jeopardy limitation, Crook's attorney pointed out, has been interpreted by the Supreme Court (*Benton* v. *Maryland*) to be part of the Fourteenth Amendment and therefore a limit on the power of a state.[104]

[95]See Larry Charles Berkson, *The Concept of Cruel and Unusual Punishment* (Lexington Books, 1975), for a broad historical overview.

[96]*Estelle* v. *Gamble*, 429 U.S. 97 (1972).

[97]*Coker* v. *Georgia*, 53 L Ed 2d 982 (1977).

[98]*Robinson* v. *California*, 370 U.S. 660 (1972); *Powell* v. *Texas*, 392 U.S. 514 (1969).

[99]*Ingraham* v. *Wright*, 430 U.S. 651 (1977).

[100]*Woodson* v. *North Carolina*, 428 U.S. 289 (1976); *Gregg* v. *Georgia*, 428 U.S. 153 (1976).

[101]*Roberts* v. *Louisiana*, 52 L Ed 2d 637 (1977).

[102] Justice Stevens concurring in *Coker* v. *Georgia*.

[103]*Dickey* v. *Florida*, 398 U.S. 30 (1970).

[104]395 U.S. 784 (1969).

The judge answered: "The Supreme Court has said that double jeopardy prevents two criminal trials by the *same* government for the same criminal offense."[105] (Trial by a state and one of its municipalities is trial by the same government;[106] trial in a juvenile proceeding precludes another trial for the same offense by the state in its regular courts.[107]) It does not prevent punishment by the state and the national governments for the same offense. He pointed to a 1959 Supreme Court decision, somewhat undermined by more recent decisions but still not reversed, that sustained a state conviction of a man for robbing a bank after he had previously been acquitted of the same offense by a federal court.[108]

What constitutional rights can Crook claim in the state courts? In the first place, every state constitution contains a bill of rights listing practically the same guarantees as the Bill of Rights in the national Constitution. But, state judges have been less inclined than federal judges to interpret constitutional guarantees of their own state constitutions liberally in favor of those accused of crime.

To what extent does the national Constitution protect courtroom procedures from state actions? The Bill of Rights does not apply to the states, but the Fourteenth Amendment does. As we have noted, the equal protection clause forbids discriminatory conduct in courtroom procedures. And for some time a persistent minority of the Supreme Court justices has argued that the due process clause of the Fourteenth Amendment should be interpreted to impose on the states exactly the same limitations that the Bill of Rights imposes on the national government. The Supreme Court still has not gone so far as to make the due process clause of the Fourteenth Amendment a mirror image of the Bill of Rights. It has not adopted the doctrine of "total incorporation," or as it is sometimes called, "absorption." But it has come very close to this position.

Until recently the official doctrine of the Court was that only those rights "implicit in the concept of ordered liberty" that are so important that neither "liberty nor justice would exist if they were sacrificed" are automatically included within the Fourteenth Amendment. Outside the scope of these rights, the test in each case was whether the procedures adopted by a state were fundamentally fair—not whether the procedures were those required of the national government by the Bill of Rights.

This formula, known as the Palko test or the doctrine of selective incorporation, was formulated by Justice Cardozo.[109] Using it, the Court distinguished between such rights as First Amendment freedoms, which are so fundamental there can be no liberty or justice if they are lost, and indictment by grand jury or trial before a jury in civil cases. Replacement of these latter rights by other procedures would not necessarily be a denial of justice or liberty.

Beginning in the 1930s and accelerating after 1964, the Supreme Court has selectively incorporated provision after provision of the Bill of Rights into the requirements of the due process clause of the Fourteenth Amend-

[105]*One Lot of Emerald Cut Stones* v. *United States*, 409 U.S. 233 (1972).

[106]*Waller* v. *Florida*, 397 U.S. 387 (1970).

[107]*Breed* v. *Jones*, 421 U.S. 519 (1974).

[108]*Bartkus* v. *Illinois*, 359 U.S. 121 (1959).

[109]*Palko* v. *Connecticut*, 302 U.S. 319 (1937).

ment. It has also revised the Palko test. Instead of asking if a particular safeguard is necessary for a civilized society, the Court now asks if such a safeguard is fundamental to an Anglo-American regime of ordered liberty.

Today, the Fourteenth Amendment imposes on the states all the requirements of the Bill of Rights except those of the Second, Third, Seventh, and Tenth Amendments. The Supreme Court, however, may not accept the doctrine of total incorporation in order to allow the states to use such procedures as indictment by information. Twenty-eight states, for example, allow the prosecuting attorney to dispense with grand jury indictments for all but the most serious crimes. The prosecutor files an information affidavit that he has evidence in his possession to justify a trial.

Now that the Bill of Rights has been almost incorporated into the Fourteenth Amendment, future constitutional battles are likely to develop. There are those who argue, like the late Justice Black, that "the first section of the Fourteenth Amendment not only incorporates the specifics of the first eight amendments, but it is *confined to them.*"[110] There are also those who believe, like former Justice Douglas, that in addition to incorporating all the specific provisions of the Bill of Rights, the due process clause protects other fundamental rights too—for example, the right to privacy. Justice Douglas saw the Supreme Court as the champion of the poor and oppressed and quoted the views of the late Edmond Cahn: "Be not reasonable with inquisitions, anonymous informers, and secret files that mock American justice. . . . Exercise the full judicial power of the United States; nullify them, forbid them, and make us proud again." Justice Black, long a champion of total incorporation and vigorous enforcement of the Bill of Rights, would not allow members of the Court to impose on the country their own notions of fundamental rights except those specified in the Constitution. He quoted approvingly from Judge Learned Hand: "For myself it would be most irksome to be ruled by a bevy of Platonic Guardians, even if I knew how to choose them, which I assuredly do not."[111]

How just is our system of justice?

What are the major criticisms of the American system of justice? How have they been answered?

TOO MANY LOOPHOLES

It is argued that to protect the innocent and place the burden of proof on the government, we have established so many elaborate procedures that justice is delayed, disrespect for the law is encouraged, and guilty persons go unpunished. Justice should be swift and sure without being arbitrary. But under our procedures criminals may go unpunished because (1) the police decide not to arrest them; (2) the judge decides not to hold them; (3) the prosecutor decides not to prosecute them; (4) the grand jury decides not to indict them; (5) the jury decides not to convict them; (6) the judge decides not to sentence them; (7) an appeals court decides to reverse the conviction; (8) a federal judge decides to release them on a habeas corpus writ; (9) if retried and convicted, the executive decides to pardon, reprieve, or parole them. As a result, the public never knows whom to hold responsible when laws are not enforced. The police can blame the prosecutor, the prosecutor can blame the police, and they can all blame the judges.

[110]Henry J. Abraham, *Freedom and the Court: Civil Rights and Liberties in the United States* (Oxford University Press, 1967), p. 75.

[111]*Griswold* v. *Connecticut,* 381 U.S. 479 (1965).

Some argue that in our impossible pursuit of perfect justice, we are not achieving effective justice.[112] Many critics blame the Supreme Court for imposing its own notions of justice on the country and placing so many disabilities on police and prosecutors that they are finding it increasingly difficult ever to bring any cases to conclusion.

Others take a different view. They doubt that the decisions of the Supreme Court have had that much impact on actual police and prosecutors. And they point out that there is more to justice than simply securing convictions. All the steps in the administration of criminal laws have been developed out of centuries of trial and error, and each has been constructed to provide protection against particular abuses. History warns against entrusting the instruments of criminal law enforcement to a single officer. For this reason, responsibility is vested in many officials.

TOO UNRELIABLE

Critics who complain that our system of justice is unreliable often point to trial by jury as the chief source of trouble. Trial by jury, they argue, leads to a theatrical combat between lawyers who base their appeals on the prejudice and sentiments of the jurors. "Mr. Prejudice and Miss Sympathy are the names of witnesses whose testimony is never recorded, but must nevertheless be reckoned with in trials by jury."[113] Too often, verdicts are influenced by the jurors' dislike of an attorney's personality or a defendant's appearance. Juries lack the training to distinguish between fact and fiction. No other country relies so much on trial by jury as the United States. And jury trials are time-consuming and costly.

Defenders of the system reply that trial by jury provides a check by nonprofessionals on the actions of judges and prosecutors. As to the charge that juries are unreliable, there is no evidence to support it. On the contrary, decisions of juries do not systematically differ from those of judges.[114] The jury system, moreover, helps to educate citizens and enables them to participate in the application of their own law.

Another instrument that many critics believe contributes to the unreliability of our criminal justice system is the grand jury, provided for by one of the few provisions of the Bill of Rights that has not been incorporated into the Fourteenth Amendment. In theory the grand jury has two functions: to protect the innocent from having to stand trial by requiring the prosecutor to demonstrate behind closed doors that he has evidence to justify trial; and to provide an independent agency to investigate wrongdoing that is uncontrolled by those in power. Critics charge, however, that the grand jury has become a tool of the prosecutor. Said Justice Douglas, "It is, indeed, common knowledge that the grand jury, having been conceived as a bulwark between the citizen and the Government, is now a tool of the Executive."[115]

During the early 1970s, critics from the left side of the political spectrum

[112]Macklin Fleming, *The Price of Perfect Justice* (Basic Books, 1974).

[113]Jerome Frank, *Courts on Trial* (Princeton University Press, 1949), p. 122. See Harry Kalven, Jr., and Hans Zeisel's *The American Jury* (University of Chicago Press, 1971) for findings of the University of Chicago's massive study of the jury system; Rita James Simon, ed., *The Jury System in America: A Critical Overview* (Sage Publications, 1975), is especially good for bibliography essays.

[114]Kalven and Zeisel, *The American Jury*, pp. 57ff.

[115]*United States* v. *Mara*, dissenting, 410 U.S. 19 (1973).

charged that grand juries had become instruments to intimidate radicals, blacks, and antiwar militants. By 1973 grand juries were being used to investigate the executive branch. It was through the use of the grand jury that the special prosecutor was able to get before the courts his contention that the president had no constitutional right to withold information about wrongdoing. As the editors of the *Congressional Quarterly* have pointed out, "liberals can applaud grand juries for investigating Watergate and denounce them for intimidating militants. Conservatives might just as easily reprove them for the former and commend them for the latter. The important question about grand juries is whether they are an effective instrument for protecting the innocent and bringing the guilty to trial. . . . On these questions, the jury is still out."[116]

DISCRIMINATION

Perhaps on no problem has the Supreme Court worked harder during the last several decades than to give reality to the ideal of equal justice under the law. At the trial level, persons accused of crime who cannot afford an attorney must be furnished one at state expense. If a state requires transcripts for appeals, it must see that such transcripts are made available to those who cannot afford to purchase them.[117] If the state provides for appeals as a matter of right, it must provide the poor with legal assistance. That is as far, however, as a state's constitutional obligation to provide legal counsel goes. It has no duty to continue to furnish legal counsel at state expense for those who wish to continue their legal appeals at the state or federal levels—for example, by asking for a review of the state decision by the Supreme Court of the United States.[118] Once a poor person is sentenced, a state may not keep that person in jail beyond the term of the sentence because the person cannot afford to pay a fine, or imprison him or her for inability to do so.[119] The Supreme Court has also started to move against fee systems that keep the poor from pursuing civil justice—for example, divorce proceedings.[120]

Congress, too, has acted. Each United States district court must now have a plan to provide counsel and investigative, expert, and other services necessary for an adequate defense for those unable to afford such help. Each district must provide for private attorneys (paid from the federal treasury) to serve the poor, but it may in addition establish a federal public defender system with a full-time, publicly paid staff. If it prefers, it can create a community defender organization through the help of a federal grant to provide defense counsel.

The major area of difficulty arises outside the courtroom, for one of the most acute problems of our society is the tension between the police officer and the black community congregated in the ghettos of our large cities: "Most Negro citizens do not believe that we have equal law enforcement in any city in this country. Whether the stated belief is well founded or not

[116]"The Supreme Court: Justice and the Law," *Congressional Quarterly* (1973), p. 93. Leroy D. Clark, *The Grand Jury: The Use and Abuse of Political Power* (Quadrangle, 1975), is a critical account calling for reform of the grand jury.

[117]*Griffin* v. *Illinois*, 351 U.S. 12 (1956); *Douglas* v. *California*, 372 U.S. 535 (1963); *United States* v. *MacCollom*, 426 U.S. 317 (1976).

[118]*Ross* v. *Moffit* 417 U.S. 600 (1974).

[119]*Williams* v. *Illinois*, 399 U.S. 235 (1970); *Tate* v. *Short* 401 U.S. 395 (1971).

[120]*Boddie* v. *Connecticut*, 401 U.S. 371 (1971); *United States* v. *Kras*, 409 U.S. 434 (1973).

is at least partly beside the point. The existence of the belief is damaging enough."[121] Blacks see the police as enforcers of white law. Studies of prejudice on the part of some white police officers and the examples of undignified, if not brutal, police treatment of blacks are ample.

Yet it would be as wrong of us to overgeneralize about the behavior of the police officer as it is of some police to overgeneralize about those who live within slum areas. The issue is the conditions that produce both kinds of behavior; there is too much at stake to content oneself with charges of police brutality. For "the policeman," wrote former Attorney General Ramsey Clark, "is the most important American. . . . He works in a highly flammable environment. A spark can cause an explosion. He must maintain order without provocation which will cause combustion."[122] The police officer has a vital role in preserving (or restricting) civil liberties. He determines who shall be arrested; he gives daily reality to the protections of our Constitution; and, as in the 1960s, events in our large cities made clear, he has much to do with preventing or causing riots. Yet this person on whom we depend for so much, the only one in our civil society whom we arm with deadly weapons, is grossly underpaid. In performing his tasks, he often discovers that the public is indifferent, even hostile. Little wonder he is sometimes impatient with reformers and academics who talk about the complexities of the cycle of poverty or the refinements of the law governing search and seizure, for it is the police officer and not the scholar who at 2 A.M. must go into an area of high crime in the middle of a hostile population to search a dark alley in response to a call about a prowler.

Until recently the role of the police officer was generally ignored. But in the late 1960s, for a variety of reasons, a sustained drive was begun to improve the quality of police services and to understand the problems the police face. In the larger cities steps have been taken to improve police training, to provide them with more opportunity to understand social problems, and to establish community relations programs. This is a beginning, but much remains to be done.

Courts and police are composed of people who reflect the prejudices and values of the society of which they are a part. When poverty and prejudice exist in the community, they will affect all its institutions. And yet there are few agencies that do as much as the courts to isolate prejudice and to compensate for poverty. As the Commission on Civil Rights states, "There is much to be proud of in the American system of criminal justice. For it is administered largely without regard to the race, creed, or color of the persons involved. . . ."[123]

The Supreme Court and civil liberties

It is clear that the judges, especially those on the Supreme Court, play a major role in enforcing constitutional guarantees. In fact, this combination of judicial enforcement and written guarantees of enumerated liberties is one of the basic features of the American system of government. As Justice Jackson wrote: "The very purpose of a Bill of Rights was to withdraw cer-

[121]George Edwards, *The Police on the Urban Frontier* (Institute of Human Relations Press, The American Jewish Committee, 1968), p. 28. See also Arthur Niederhoffer, *Behind the Shield: The Police in Urban Society* (Doubleday, 1967).

[122]Foreword to Edwards, *The Police on the Urban Frontier*, p. viii.

[123]United States Commission on Civil Rights, *Report on Justice* (U.S. Government Printing Office, 1961), pp. 26 ff.

tain subjects from the vicissitudes of political controversy, to place them beyond the reach of majorities and officials and to establish them as legal principles to be applied by the courts. One's right to life, liberty, and property, to free speech, a free press, freedom of worship and assembly, and other fundamental rights may not be submitted to vote: they depend on the outcome of no elections."[124] Or as Samuel Krislov has pointed out: "One is reminded of Godfrey Cambridge's nightmare: A telephone rings and a voice announces: 'We've had a referendum on slavery in California and you lost. Report to the auction block in four hours.'"[125]

This emphasis on constitutional limitations and judicial enforcement is an example of the "auxiliary precautions" James Madison felt were necessary to prevent arbitrary governmental action. Other free nations rely more on elections and political checks to protect their rights; in the United States we look to judges to hear appeals from people who feel their freedoms are in danger. All judges, not only those on the Supreme Court, have taken an oath to measure the actions of public officials against the appropriate constitutional, as well as legislative, provisions.

British judges have authority to restrain executive officials from depriving people of their legal rights, but they do not have the power to declare legislative acts unconstitutional. Moreover, the English place primary reliance on an alert and aroused public opinion, operating through elected officials, to safeguard their liberty. Justice Jackson once commented:

> I have been repeatedly impressed with the speed and certainty with which the slightest invasion of British individual freedom or minority rights by officials of the government is picked up in Parliament, not merely by the opposition but by the party in power, and made the subject of persistent questioning, criticism, and sometimes rebuke. There is no waiting on the theory that the judges will take care of it. . . . In Great Britain, to observe civil liberties is good politics and to transgress the rights of the individual or minority is bad politics. In the United States, I cannot say this is so.[126]

In the United States, our emphasis on judicial protection of civil liberties focuses attention on the Supreme Court. But only a small number of controversies are carried to the Court, and a Supreme Court decision is not the end of the policy-making process. Compliance with its rulings "does not necessarily, universally, or automatically follow their enunciation."[127] It is the judges of lower courts, the police, the superintendents of schools, and the local prosecutors who translate the doctrines enunciated by the Court and who do or do not apply them.

[124]*West Virginia State Board of Education* v. *Barnette*, 319 U.S. 624 (1943).

[125]*The Supreme Court and Political Freedom* (Free Press, 1968), p. 35.

[126]Robert H. Jackson, *The Supreme Court in the American System of Government* (Harvard University Press, 1955), pp. 81–82; Jonathan D. Casper, *The Politics of Civil Liberties* (Harper & Row, 1973).

[127]See Richard M. Johnson, *The Dynamics of Compliance: Supreme Court Decision-Making from a New Perspective* (Northwestern University Press, 1967), p. 3; "Interrogations in New Haven: The Impact of *Miranda*," *Yale Law Journal* (July 1967), pp. 1519–1648; Stephen L. Wasby, *The Impact of the United States Supreme Court: Some Perspectives* (Dorsey Press, 1970), Part II; Stephen L. Wasby, *Small Town Police and the Supreme Court* (D. C. Heath; 1976).

And the Supreme Court can do little unless its decisions reflect a national consensus. The judges by themselves cannot guarantee anything. Neither can the First Amendment. As Justice Jackson once asked: "Must we first maintain a system of free political government to assure a free judiciary, or can we rely on an aggressive, activist judiciary to guarantee free government? . . . [It] is my belief that the attitude of a society and of its organized political forces, rather than its legal machinery, is the controlling force in the character of free institutions. . . . [Any] court which undertakes by its legal processes to enforce civil liberties needs the support of an enlightened and vigorous public opinion. . . ."[128] In short, only so long as we desire liberty for ourselves and are willing to restrict our own actions in order to preserve the liberty of others can freedom be maintained.

Summary

1. One of the basic distinctions between a free society and a police state is that there are *effective restraints* in a free society on the way public officials, especially law enforcement officials, perform their duties. In the United States these constitutional restraints are judicially enforceable.

2. The Constitution protects the acquisition and retention of citizenship. It protects the basic liberties of aliens as well as of citizens. It protects our property from arbitrary governmental interference, although debates as to which interferences are reasonable and which are arbitrary are not easily settled.

3. The Constitution imposes limits not only on the procedures government must follow, but also on the *ends* it may pursue. Some things are out of bounds no matter what procedures are followed. In this determination of what is reasonable and what is unreasonable, legislatures have the primary role. But the Supreme Court continues to exercise its own independent and final review of legislative determinations of reasonableness, especially on matters affecting civil liberties and civil rights.

4. The founding fathers knew from their own experiences that in their zeal to maintain power and to enforce the laws, public officials are often tempted to infringe on the rights of those accused of crimes. To prevent such abuse, the Constitution imposes detailed *procedures* national officials must follow in order to make searches and arrests, and to bring people to trial.

5. Recently the Supreme Court has interpreted the Constitution, especially the Fourteenth Amendment, to impose on state and local governments about the same restraints in the administration of justice imposed on the national government.

6. The Supreme Court continues to play a prominent role in the development of public policy designed to protect the *rights of the accused* and to ensure that the innocent are not punished, and to ensure that the *public is protected* against those who break the laws. The Court's decisions influence what the public believes and how police officers and others involved in the administration of justice behave. But the Court cannot—and should not—do it alone.

---

[128]Jackson, *The Supreme Court*, p. 82.

Part Three

The People in Politics

A Problem Guide

A central problem in realizing government by the people in a mass society is popular representation. Part Three raises these crucial questions: Who really governs in a democratic society? Do all people take part? Do elite groups have more political influence than others? How do people express themselves politically—through mass media, political parties, demonstrations, violence? How are the people organized to take part in government? And how do these different types of political organization and forms of representation fit with the ideals of democratic government?

The basic inquiry in Chapter 8 concerns the formation and expression of political attitudes. What is the nature and role of public opinion? Who are the shapers of opinion? TV news commentators, newspaper editors and columnists, politicians? How much influence do they have over our political behavior? Do they really represent popular political opinion?

Chapter 9 develops the problem of popular representation in its major forms: voting and interest group activity. A key issue is the extent of representation. Some Americans do not vote because they are kept from the polls; millions of others do not vote because it does not seem worth the trouble. How well do candidates understand the needs and attitudes of those they want to represent? How much equality of influence do we have in our society?

Chapter 10 on political parties deals with the same problem of fair representation, but in connection with another part of our political system. Under a two-party system, in theory at least, the party that wins the most votes proceeds to represent the interests of that popular majority in government. How effectively does the winning party speak for those who elected it? That raises another question: Can the parties be made stronger so that they may better represent their supporters? And what about the role of third parties? Can the minority party do the job of opposing the majority as well as it should?

A final problem of Part Three is the fairness and efficiency of the electoral system. We might think electoral machinery is neutral, but in point of fact it is not. Some election arrangements make it difficult for people to vote. Others—for example, the electoral college—give some voters more weight than others in an election. How fair is our system of nominating political candidates—especially the president? Chapter 11 raises such problems, which all relate to the basic question in Part Three—the question of equality of political influence for the sake of fair representation in government. Some of the problems raised in Chapter 11 are addressed again in Chapter 17, a summary and analysis chapter at the end of the next part.

Chapter 8

"We the People":
Public Opinion

The crowds along Pennsylvania Avenue were electrified when Jimmy Carter jumped out of his limousine on his way back from the Inaugural and marched hand in hand with his wife and daughter to the White House. It reminds us of Thomas Jefferson 166 years earlier walking to his first Inaugural and then back to his boarding house, where the dining room was full and he quietly waited until he could find a place. Soon President Carter was cutting down on White House ceremonies, banning dozens of White House limousines, taking telephone calls from average citizens on a toll-free "hot line." As a "populist" candidate, he had promised to bring the people into government and government closer to the people. Most Americans approved. But just what did it all mean?

"We the People." The Constitution begins with these words. "Government by the people" was a favorite phrase of Abraham Lincoln's. Government by the people is supposed to be government in accordance with the will of the people. But is there one popular will—one voice of the people? Or are there many wills, many voices—of many people, of many groups of people, of countless interests? What does government do when people disagree? Should government itself try to influence public opinion?

And if government *can* represent people in all their variety, *should* it? Think for a moment of how senators in Washington face these questions about "We the People." They usually wish to do what the voters back home want them to do, if only so they can stay in office. But they are not sure *what* the voters want. They cannot really tell from the mail. Public opinion polls have their limitations. Senators are not sure what issues they were elected on, if any. They listen for the voice of the people—but the people speak with many voices. Or they may not speak at all.

Not far from Pennsylvania Avenue one of the authors earlier had talked with a bus driver. "I never vote," said the driver. "I don't want to get in-

173

volved. I'm a Democrat but I just don't have the time to vote and really don't have time to follow what's going on. If I don't really know everything that's going on I don't think I should vote. . . . My sister went to California and has become a Republican and she is all involved . . . but I just don't understand her. I just want to be left alone and that goes for our union here too. . . . To stay on the job you have to be careful not to bother either the managers and big bosses or the union leaders. . . . No, I have finally decided just to do your job and they can't get you, stay away from union politics and I don't have time for any of the other politics either. . . ." How can representatives represent this kind of person?

How are people's attitudes shaped? What is the influence of the mass media? Is that influence too great? How is political opinion measured? Can and should political leaders influence it? And what is the implication of these questions for "government by the people?" In this chapter we will focus mainly on people's opinions as they relate to government. In the next chapter we will note how people with such opinions behave politically. We will then turn to political parties as an especially important aspect of that behavior, and in the following chapter (Chapter 11), we will note how all these forces come to a climax in elections—the outcome of which may or may not truly represent the opinions of "We the People."

Public opinion: colorful and complex

There is no one public opinion. This might seem rather obvious, but how often have you heard a politician claim that "the public" wants such and such, or a columnist that "the people" reacted in a certain way?

Suppose a group of students invites a notorious criminal to speak on crime and punishment. Think of this incident in terms of the "public opinion" it creates. The public is actually made up of a number of publics—the rest of the student body (itself divided into subpublics), the administration, the faculty, the local townspeople, parents, taxpayers. And all react in different ways. Some don't react at all; others shake their heads and promptly forget about it; others write to the governor or their state legislator. Many approve the invitation, but for conflicting reasons.

Translate the student episode into a national issue. When the president makes a speech about labor legislation, his words fall differently on the ears of union leaders and members, businesspeople, farmers, Democrats, Republicans, and so on. When a senator calls for the end of government "handouts," many businesspeople applaud because they want lower taxes, but some business people *receiving* subsidies—ship operators, for example—are critical. Most likely they cry out that "the American public" wants a strong merchant marine. Instead of one public opinion, we must think in terms of the diversity of opinion within a particular population. We must ask: What portion of the people is on one side of an issue, what portion on the other? Who feel strongly, who do not? What, in short, makes up the fabric of public opinion?

Stability Certain kinds of opinions change very little; they are part of our personality. We may hang onto them all our lives. Other opinions may change slowly, even though the world is changing rapidly. This is especially true of loyalty toward one's own group and hostility toward competing groups. In general, people who remain in the same locality, in the same occupation, in the same income group throughout their lives are likely to have more stable opinions. But people can carry their attitudes with them. Families moving from cities to suburbs often retain their old big-city attitudes long after they have made their move.

Fluidity   Certain kinds of public opinions, on the other hand, can change dramatically, and almost overnight. Thus opposition to Roosevelt's foreign policies in 1941 practically disappeared following Japan's attack on Pearl Harbor. Change often comes about as a result of *events*—a depression, the nomination by a major party of a southerner for the first time in over a hundred years, a sharp increase in the crime rate, a natural event like a long drought in the Southwest.

Sometimes even the strongest and most stable attitudes are subject to change. One of the "sacred cows" of American politics ten years ago was nonrecognition of the People's Republic of China. A powerful lobby, composed of leaders of both major parties, carried on a militant campaign against admitting "mainland China" to the United Nations. Then President Nixon, who had earlier been a "hardliner" against the recognition of Peking, made his dramatic trip to the People's Republic. Soon he was following a policy of detente toward Peking. Many Americans, responding to Nixon's leadership, shifted their own position. Most interesting of all, adherents of the Republican party, previously most hostile to the Chinese regime, were now more likely to support friendlier relations with Peking.

Intensity   This factor produces the brightest and deepest hues in the fabric of public opinion. People vary greatly in the fervency of their beliefs. Some are mildly in favor, for example, of gun-control legislation; others are mildly opposed; still others are fanatically for or against. Some people may have no interest in the matter at all and may not even have heard of the issue. It is, of course, easier to change the attitudes of the mildly involved than of the intensely involved. And the latter are the ones that can be most easily aroused to action—to organize, to campaign, to try to influence others.

Latency   Political attitudes may exist merely as a *potential*. They may not have crystallized. But they still can be very important, for they can be evoked by leaders and converted into action. Latent opinions set rough boundaries for leaders, who know that if they take certain actions, the opposition or support of millions of persons will be triggered. But latent opinions are also a great opportunity for leaders. If they have some understanding of people's real wants and needs and hopes, they will know how to activate those motives, mobilize people in groups or parties, and draw them to the polls on election day.

Relevance   What causes opinions to be stable or fluid, intense or latent? A major factor is relevance. Some people are deeply involved in certain issues and care little or nothing about others. By "relevant" we mean that people feel that the issue relates to their own lives; it *connects* with them.[1] Your next-door neighbor may feel intensely about abortion or gun control, whereas you get excited about inflation or unemployment. Most persons are more concerned about personal issues like health and jobs and families

---

[1]The technical term for this quality is salience. See Alan D. Monroe, *Public Opinion in America* (Dodd, Mead, 1975), pp. 56–57.

than about national issues. But connect their personal concerns with national issues and relevance rises sharply.

Relevance may change over time. During the depression of the 1930s, Americans were mainly concerned about jobs and wages and economic security. In the late thirties and early forties, foreign and war issues came to the fore. In the sixties, problems of race, poverty, and drugs aroused intense feeling, followed by the agony of Vietnam and then of Watergate. Recently, jobs and prices have seemed to top the agenda of popular attention.[2]

How we learn our political opinions

We hear a person called a "born Democrat" or a "born conservative," but no one is *born* with political opinions. We *learn* them, and we have many teachers, intentional or not. Children in the United States typically will show political interest by the age of ten, and by the early teens that interest is fairly high. Religious opinions usually develop even earlier, and these may have important political implications. These learning experiences slowly harden into the opinions of adults. What most influences the early forming of opinions in the United States? The family and the school.

THE INFLUENCE OF THE FAMILY

We begin to form our picture of the world listening to our parents talk at breakfast or to the tales our older brothers and sisters bring home from school. What we learn in the family at the start are not so much specific political opinions, but the basic attitudes that will shape our future opinions—attitudes toward our neighbors, toward other classes or types of people, toward society in general. Some of us may rebel against the ways of the close little group in which we live, but most of us conform. The family is a sort of link between the past and the present. It translates the world to us, but it does so on its own terms.

Studies of high school students, for example, indicate a high correlation between parents and children in the political party they support. And this relatively high degree of correspondence continues throughout life. Such a finding raises an interesting question: Is it the *direct* influence of parents on their children's political attitudes that creates that correspondence? Or is it the fact that most children grow up in the *same social situation* their

Lyndon Johnson takes the oath of office as vice-president shortly before John Kennedy is sworn in.
(1) Adlai Stevenson;
(2) Dwight D. Eisenhower;
(3) Earl Warren; (4) Dean Rusk;
(5) John F. Kennedy;
(6) Sam Rayburn; (7) Frank Dryden;
(8) Lyndon B. Johnson;
(9) Richard M. Nixon.

[2]On issue change and its many implications, see Norman H. Nie, Sidney Verba, and John R. Petrocik, *The Changing American Voter* (Harvard University Press, 1976), esp. chaps. 6 and 12; Warren E. Miller and Teresa E. Levitin, *Leadership and Change* (Winthrop, 1976), esp. chap. 2. For a study of how families in one southern California community responded to changing political issues in the early 1970s, including Vietnam, protests, Watergate, and Nixon, see Karl A. Lamb, *As Orange Goes: Twelve California Families and the Future of American Politics* (Norton, 1974).

parents did and that parents and children are equally influenced by their environment? The answer is *both*—and one influence often strengthens the other. Thus a daughter of Democratic parents growing up in a small southern town of strong Democratic leanings will be affected by friends, by other parents, and perhaps by youngsters in a Sunday school group, all of whom may reinforce the attitudes of her parents.

Who has the greater influence, the mother or the father, over children's political opinions? It used to be assumed that the father had the dominant impact, perhaps because it was also assumed that "politics is a man's business." But the balance of influence between the two parents seems to be surprisingly level; it may even be tipped in the mother's favor.[3] What happens when mother and father disagree politically? The child is likely to favor the party of the parent with whom he or she has had closer ties.[4]

Still, older children sometimes do not share the views of their parents. What other forces are at work?

POLITICAL IMPACT OF
THE SCHOOLS

Schools are also opinion shapers, and perhaps the most important of all. At an early age schoolchildren begin to pick up specific political values and to acquire basic attitudes toward our system of government. Even very small schoolchildren know the name of the president and his party affiliation and have strong attitudes toward him. Children as young as nine or ten begin to have a fairly precise knowledge of what a president stands for, though this will vary with the personality of the president. For example, one researcher found that "the Kennedy image was rich, specific, and considerably more politicized than we had anticipated. He was particularly well remembered for his efforts on behalf of peace and civil rights."[5]

Do school influences tend to give young people a greater faith in existing political institutions? Probably yes: "The thrust of school experience is undoubtedly on the side of developing trust in the political system in general," according to one study. In one school that stressed our traditional democratic creed—equality, tolerance, civic participation—there was a decided increase of support for that creed among students. But schools in working-class areas are less likely to encourage civic education and political participation than schools in middle- or upper-class areas.[6]

In short, scholars are confirming what every high school student knows—that schools have a certain, usually rather Establishment, point of view. But here again the political scientist must look more closely at what

Basic attitudes that shape future
opinions often originate in
the family setting.

[3]Richard G. Niemi, "Political Socialization," in Jeanne N. Knutson, ed., *Handbook of Political Psychology* (Jossey-Bass, 1973), p. 128. This book covers comprehensively psychological, social, and other factors influencing political attitudes and behavior.

[4]M. Kent Jennings and Kenneth P. Langton, "Mothers versus Fathers: The Formation of Political Orientations among Young Americans," *Journal of Politics* (May 1969), p. 357.

[5]Roberta S. Sigel, "Image of a President: Some Insights into the Political Views of School Children," *American Political Science Review* (March 1968), pp. 216–26. See also F. Christopher Arterton, "The Impact of Watergate on Children's Attitudes Toward Political Authority," *Political Science Quarterly* (June 1974), pp. 269–88.

[6]Edgar Litt, "Civic Education, Community Norms, and Political Indoctrination," *American Sociological Review* (February 1962), pp. 69–75. See also Elizabeth Léonie Simpson, *Democracy's Stepchildren* (Jossey-Bass, 1971); M. Kent Jennings and Richard G. Niemi, *The Political Character of Adolescence* (Princeton University Press, 1974); and Stanley Allen Renshon, "Personality and Family Dynamics in the Political Socialization Process," *American Journal of Political Science* (February 1975), pp. 63–80.

shapes attitudes. Is it the teachers, the other students, the classes, or the fact that both teachers and students are subject to common stimuli? These are difficult factors to untangle. One study found no evidence that the civics curriculum has a significant effect on the political orientations of the great majority of American high school students. Of course students differed in their interest in politics, but this resulted not from taking (or not taking) civics or government courses, but from the students' backgrounds and life plans.

What about the influence of *college* on political opinions? One study suggested that students planning to attend college were more likely to be knowledgeable about politics, to be more interested in politics, to be more in favor of free speech, and to talk and read about politics.[7] College students *in general* tend to become more tolerant and unprejudiced the longer they stay in college. Is this the influence of their professors, of the curriculum, or of other students? It is difficult to generalize. Parents sometimes fear that the "professoriat" has too much influence on their offspring in school; the professors are likely to be skeptical about this. But why talk in generalities when students reading this book can make their own judgments? What has influenced *you* most— a teacher, a book (possibly even a *textbook?*), a particular course, bull sessions with other students, or something else? And *how* have you been influenced?

Finally, are adults simply the sum of all these early influencing experiences? Usually not. Analysts are becoming more and more interested in ways in which adults keep on modifying their views after school or college. A crucial factor here is *experience;* it is quite true that experience is a powerful teacher. The shock of major events, like a war or a depression, on accepted ideas can be shattering. And this influence can start early in life. An interesting example is the influence of Watergate on children's attitudes toward the president. As noted above, most children have tended to look on presidents as benign figures. But the scandal of Watergate may

---

[7]Kenneth P. Langton and M. Kent Jennings, "Political Socialization and the High School Civics Curriculum in the United States," *American Political Science Review* (September 1968), pp. 852–67.

Public hearings and local town meetings serve as forums for public opinion.

"You're wasting your time! . . .
My mind is totally controlled by
what the mass media feeds
into it."

By Lichty;
© Field Enterprises, Inc., 1973.

have deeply affected that attitude. Here is a portion of a mid-1970s interview with a seventh-grader:

Interviewer: Suppose a foreign child asked you, "What is the President?"
Seventh-grader: Richard M. Nixon.
Interviewer: What does he do?
Seventh-grader: He's the President. He signs papers and, like, helps turn out the laws, and stuff like that.
Interviewer: Anything else?
Seventh-grader: Well . . . he gets in trouble a lot.
Interviewer: What kind of trouble?
Seventh-grader: I don't know. The Watergate and everything like that now.[8]

Thus events—especially *political* events—can reshape political attitudes. And we "see" those events largely through the eyes of the mass media.

The politics of the mass media

During the presidential election of 1976 there was the usual debate over "bias" in the press. Republicans charged that the "Eastern-dominated" media was unfair to Gerald Ford; Democrats contended that the "Republican-controlled" press was just as unfair to Jimmy Carter. The debate over the role of the press continued after the election. There was criticism of the "boys on the bus"—the reporters who covered the presidential candidates—and their tendency to indulge in "pack journalism"; that is, ganging up on a candidate whenever he made a mistake. And there was continued worry about "monopoly" in the media. "We don't have a free-wheeling, competitive, diverse, unrestricted free press as was contemplated by the First Amendment, but a Government-regulated monopoly," wrote the editor of *Rolling Stone.* "We have a Big Three in New York just like we have a Big Three in Detroit. And what has happened to news is no different from what has happened to cars: We are offered products that are essentially similar, inefficient, and unresponsive to the public interest."[9]

The criticism is basically threefold: The press (newspapers, radio, television) has an undue influence on our political opinions. Free and full competition does not exist within the media. And the press is biased and partisan. Let us consider these questions in turn.

AN IRRESISTIBLE FORCE?

The influence of the media on political opinion would indeed seem to be immense. It is estimated that 55–58 million Americans watch some part of the weekday early evening news programs on the three networks. Ameri-

[8]Fred I. Greenstein, "The Benevolent Leader Revisited: Children's Images of Political Leaders in Three Democracies," *American Political Science Review* (December 1975), p. 1393. See also John L. Sullivan and Daniel Richard Minns, " 'The Benevolent Leader Revisited': Substantive Finding or Methodological Artifact?" *American Journal of Political Science* (November 1976), pp. 763–72. One study concluded that Watergate neither destroyed children's faith in the presidency, as was feared, nor provided them with a lasting lesson in civic education, as was hoped. See Michael Lupfer and Charles Kenny, "The Impact of Watergate on Youths' Views of the Presidency," *Public Affairs Forum*, Institute of Governmental Studies and Research, Memphis State University, V, 6 (April 1976), 1–8.

[9]Jann S. Wenner, "Worry about the Quality of News Reporting," *The New York Times*, December 19, 1976. See also John B. Connally, "Advice to the Press," *The New York Times*, May 2, 1977.

cans buy about 65 million newspapers a day, and there are countless foreign-language newspapers, thousands of weeklies, and a free-wheeling underground press. Walter Lippmann called the newspaper the "bible of democracy, the book out of which a people determines its conduct." And radio continues to reach tens of millions of persons, though its political impact is somewhat less than that of the other media. Yet political scientists and other opinion analysts are not certain that the mass media have the powerful effect on public opinion that many have assumed. Attitudes built into the slowly developing person through a long process of socialization are too strong to be easily overcome. The influence of family and school and church hangs on for many years and resists easy conquest. Three forces are especially important:

1. *Selective perception.* People are not empty vessels to be filled up by torrents of television talk or acres of newsprint. Attention and perception are always selective. Out of all the speeches, articles, news stories, and political pamphlets, many voters pay attention to very few. We all tend to focus on those speeches and those news stories and subscribe to those magazines that support our own biases. We have an enormous capacity to perceive things in ways that stem from our own social and attitudinal development; that is, the "facts" we see are filtered through spectacles that distort in an infinite variety of ways. This is **selective perception.** An accurate estimate of the impact of mass media requires paying attention to what the communicators said, what the audience saw or heard, and how the audience was affected.[10] The difference between *exposure* and *effect* can be enormous.

2. *Popular suspicion of the media.* Most Americans, according to a recent survey, seemed satisfied with the amount of news they were getting from the media, but more than half the people polled felt that some events were not being adequately reported. This credibility gap broadened when it came to comparing news stories with events people had directly witnessed or participated in. Popular skepticism of the accuracy of reporters and of the objectivity of editors is of course an old story in

[10]Kurt Lang and Gladys Engel Lang, *Television and Politics* (Quadrangle, 1968).

8–1
Where people get their information and how they rate media credibility, 1959–76

Major source of news?

Source of most news*	1959	1963	1967	1971	1974	1976
Television	51%	55%	64%	60%	65%	64%
Newspapers	57	53	55	48	47	49
Radio	34	29	28	23	21	19
Magazines	8	6	7	5	4	7
Don't know, etc.	1	3	2	1	—	—

In case of conflicting news accounts, which is most believed?

Most believable	1959	1963	1967	1971	1974	1976
Television	29%	36%	41%	49%	51%	51%
Newspapers	32	24	24	20	20	22
Radio	12	12	7	10	8	7
Magazines	10	10	8	9	8	9
Don't know, etc.	17	18	20	12	13	11

SOURCE: Burns W. Roper, *"Trends in Attitudes toward Television and other Media: An Eighteen-year Review,"* A Report by the Roper Organization, Inc. (May, 1977), pp. 3–4.
*Figures add to more than 100 percent because of multiple responses.

the United States. To a degree, that skepticism is doubtless a good thing in a re-public. But intense suspicion of the press could endanger the maintenance of faith in the free, fair, and open exchange of information and ideas in a democracy.

3. *Primary groups as filters.* The family and other primary groups that heavily in-fluence the growing child also screen adults from the full and direct impact of the media. It is direct, face-to-face contacts that reach people, whether in families, neighborhoods, or small groups. The more *personal* the means of communication, according to many studies, the more effective it is in influencing opinions. Thus the average face-to-face conversation probably has more effect than a television speech, and a television speech has more influence than a newspaper story.

Does this mean that personal methods of communication have more ef-fect on opinions than organized methods such as newspapers? Possibly, but the situation is not that simple. For the local opinion leaders—the law-yer next door, the bartender, the campus politician, the ward leader, the head of the local League of Women Voters—may have received some of their ideas from a newspaper or magazine. If a friend drops in and sells me on the need for a sales tax, and if he in turn got the idea from a popular magazine, what is the source of the influence on me? *Opinions are the prod-uct of the interplay of many forces.*

A FREE MARKETPLACE
FOR IDEAS?

Kansas City: The famous Kansas City *Star* sells out to a conglomerate that publishes, among other things, *Women's Wear Daily*.

Michigan: A family-owned enterprise that publishes eight dailies in cit-ies throughout the state is acquired by Samuel Newhouse, who already owns twenty-two newspapers, ten television and radio stations, and five magazines.

New York City: An Australian "newspaper baron" buys the *New York Post*, one of the oldest newspapers in the country, and adds it to his inter-national collection.

Reports like these worry some people who fear that political influence over voters' opinions is so concentrated in the press that democracy itself may be threatened. The critics remind us too that this century has been one of "dying dailies" and that most cities have become one-newspaper towns. They echo Justice Oliver Wendell Holmes's classic dictum that "the best test of truth is the power of the thought to get itself accepted in the competition of the market." What kind of competition is possible, critics demand, when three networks dominate the television news and a few newspapers or newspaper chains dominate the press? Finally, the critics attack the sheer commercialism of the press, charging that it panders to the lowest tastes of its readers or viewers just to sell more copies and more advertising.

Others believe that these charges are overdrawn. A newspaper is a busi-ness, they point out, and must depend on selling advertisements and copies. If readers like screaming headlines, sex, comics, scandal, and crime at the expense of full and balanced news coverage and editorial comment, a newspaper can hardly hold out against the customers. Advertisers might have controlled editorial policy in the past, but this is most unusual today. As for "monopoly," the decline in competition among newspapers has been more than matched by the rise of competing media—first radio and then television. The city that lacks competing dailies is likely to have at least one television station and probably several radio stations. Editors in one-newspaper cities often make a point of offering columns and news features that take opposing political viewpoints. The critics respond that it is not direct business control over the press that they fear, but the fact that newspaper publishers and television station owners are businesspeople, associate with businesspeople, and share the conservative attitudes of businesspeople.

A PARTISAN PRESS?

"Basically, they're ultra-liberal and I am conservative. . . . The reasons for their attitudes toward the President go back many years, but they're basically ideological, and I respect that. If I would pander to their liberal views, I could be infinitely popular with some of our friends out there, and a lot of the heat would go out of Watergate. . . ." So spoke Richard Nixon, as the coils of Watergate tightened around him. But he long had battled with the press, and a year after entering the White House he had launched a campaign against the television networks which, he felt, had treated him unfairly. His vice-president, Spiro Agnew, spearheaded the campaign. "Nowhere in our system are there fewer checks on vast power," Agnew said of the television networks. This was by no means the first time that politicians had attacked the news media, or at least tried to turn it to their own uses. Jefferson was so upset by the influence of the Federalist press that he founded a Republican newspaper. During the nineteenth century, most newspapers were proudly and openly partisan. In recent decades, liberals have contended that the newspapers were overwhelmingly biased toward conservative policies and candidates. Finding the press in mainly Republican hands, Franklin Roosevelt turned to radio and made skillful use of it, as John Kennedy did of televised news conferences.

It is true that in recent decades newspapers have tended, sometimes by overwhelming margins, to endorse Republican over Democratic presidential candidates. Nixon had 83 percent of the daily circulation with him in 1960 and 78 percent in 1968 (though Goldwater in 1964 and Gerald Ford in 1976 had less support.) But the issue today is not so much *partisanship* (few newspapers support a party as such) but ideology or general point of view. President Lyndon B. Johnson believed that the "big" media were controlled by a handful of persons in the Northeast who hated him because he was a Texan and an outlander. Moderates and conservatives like Irving Kristol and Kevin Phillips fear that the big newspapers, television networks, wire services, and many magazines are controlled by members of the "liberal establishment." Daniel P. Moynihan, long before he became senator from New York, saw a growing tendency for journalists to be recruited among college graduates, and especially those graduates who hold hostile attitudes toward middle-class Americans.[11] Others contend that although reporters may tend to be liberal, this is offset by the publishers who take conservative positions because, like other businesspeople, they worry about labor demands, sales, taxes, dividends, and profits.

Certain newspapers, such as *The New York Times* and the *Washington Post*, have special influence because of the leaders they reach at home and abroad. They even serve as communications links among such leaders. Readers of these newspapers tend to be more affluent and more liberal than the rest of the nation. Moynihan contends that both as a result and a cause of this liberal audience, our most influential newspapers tend "to set a tone of pervasive dissatisfaction with the performance of the national

---

[11]"The Presidency and the Press," *Commentary* (March 1971), p. 43.

government, whoever the presidential incumbent may be and whatever the substance of the policies."[12]

It has long been said that the editorial columns of newspapers do not affect opinion very much because editors think one way and people vote the opposite. Franklin D. Roosevelt's four presidential victories in a row, against heavy editorial opposition, are cases in point; so, to a lesser degree, is Kennedy's victory in 1960. Although it is significant that Roosevelt or Kennedy won despite heavy press opposition, the central question is the extent to which they had to modify their political views in order to minimize the effect of that opposition.

The real question is not only whether editorials directly influence our political attitudes and voting decisions; it is whether the press (and the media as a whole) shapes our political opinions through its overall news and editorial posture. The newspaper—in its front-page makeup, its headlines, its use of pictures, its playing up of some items, its distortion of important information, its lack of attention to problems that may be evolving into crises—influences the "picture in our heads," the very basic attitudes that predispose us to interpret news one way or another. The press has a long-run, continuous influence on opinions that may not be obvious in a particular election.

Criticism of newspapers has been abundant; practical remedies have been few. Some have suggested that newspaper chains be broken up through antimonopoly legislation. Others have proposed that the government subsidize competing newspapers—a kind of "T.V.A. yardstick" for the opinion industry. Such proposals have received little support because many Americans oppose any action that might, in their view, threaten the freedom of the press under the First Amendment. Better a biased, uncompetitive, commercially oriented press, they feel, than a government-controlled one. So the problem of dealing with press bias has been left to self-policing.

TELEVISION NEWS:
BIG BROTHER?

Some observers believe that television in general, and TV news in particular, is a much greater threat to popular government than has been recognized. Television, they contend, is not just another medium. Its influence is far more pervasive than that of the other media. Numerous newspapers that cross state lines provide considerable choice for the reader, they note, but only three networks dominate the American television scene, each with about 200 local affiliates. And people seem exceptionally vulnerable to the tube. They *trust* television far more than they do their newspapers; hence they are more vulnerable to it. They get far more of their political campaign information from television than from newspapers. Television news exposure cuts across age groups, educational levels, social classes, and races to an astonishing degree. The TV audience is often a captive one, compared to newspaper subscribers who can read selectively. And video, with all its concreteness, vividness, and drama, has an emotional impact that print cannot hope to match.[13]

---

[12]*Ibid.*, p. 44.

[13]Gary L. Wamsley and Richard A. Pride, "Television Network News: Re-Thinking the Iceberg Problem," *Western Political Quarterly* (September 1972), pp. 434–50; see also Edward C. Dreyer, "Media Use and Electoral Choices: Some Political Consequences of Information Exposure," *Public Opinion Quarterly* (Winter 1971–72), pp. 544–53.

The great fear of television as "big brother" is that it may become allied with "big government"—indeed, some people fear that this is already happening in the relationship between the president and television. The chief executive can command the television networks at prime time, as he wishes. He can speak directly to the nation. He does not need to answer questions, except in a televised press conference, and he can minimize his press conferences, as Nixon did. As a result of its linkage with executive power, according to one study, television has been converted into an "electronic throne":

> No mighty king, no ambitious emperor, no pope, or prophet ever dreamt of such an awesome pulpit. . . . At best the wizardry of radio had been an artery of audio communication which sent a voice into the living room. Television was a comprehensive transportation which carried the viewer to the convention floor, to the Vietnam battlefield, to the face of the moon, and to the White House, wherever the camera was directed. The president, in his ability to command the national attention, diminished the power of all other politicians and, in the case of Richard Nixon, fostered a distortion of our systems of safeguards.[14]

Still, television was not able to save Nixon from Watergate.

Taking the pulse of the people

"What I want," Abraham Lincoln once said, "is to get done what the people desire to have done, and the question for me is how to find that out exactly." This perplexing question faces every politician, in office or out. Another president, Woodrow Wilson, once complained to newspapermen that they had no business to say, as they often did, that all the people out their way thought so and so: "You do not know, and the worst of it is, since the responsibility is mine, I do not know, what they are thinking about. I have the most imperfect means of finding out, and yet I have got to act as if I knew. . . ."

How can the politician find out what the people are thinking? The usual way, of course, is to look at the election results. If John Brown wins over James Smith, presumably the people want what John Brown stands for. If Brown is an advocate of gun regulation and Smith is 100 percent against any form of control, evidently the majority of the people support some kind of firearms regulation. But we know that in practice things do not work this way. Elections are rarely fought on single issues, and candidates rarely take clear-cut stands. It is impossible, moreover, to separate issues from candidates. Did Nixon win in 1972 because of Vietnam, crime, taxes, his personality, or shifts in party support? The answer is that he won for some of these reasons and for many others. Which brings us back to the question—what do the people want?

This is where straw votes and public opinion polls come in. In this country public opinion polls are over a century old, but their main development has taken place in the last three decades. Some of the techniques were originally worked out by market research analysts hired by

---

[14]Newton M. Minow, John Bartlow Martin, Lee M. Mitchell, *Presidential Television* (Basic Books, 1973), pp. vii–viii; see also Harold Mendelsohn and Irving Crespi, *Polls, Television, and the New Politics* (Chandler, 1970); James Aronson, *Deadline for the Media: Today's Challenges to the Press, TV, and Radio* (Bobbs-Merrill, 1974).

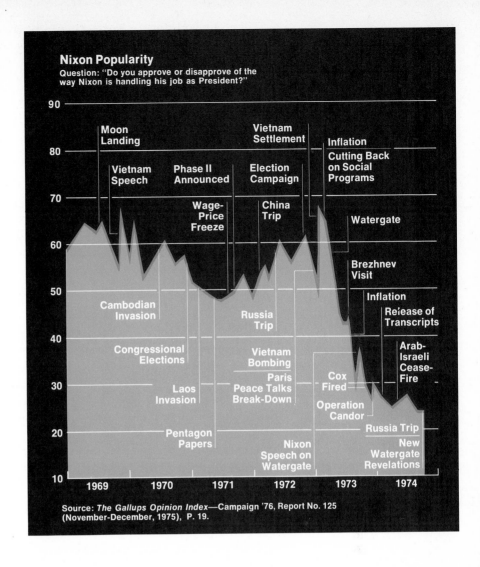

Nixon Popularity

Question: "Do you approve or disapprove of the
way Nixon is handling his job as President?"

Moon
Landing

Vietnam
Settlement

Inflation
Cutting Back
on Social
Programs

Vietnam
Speech

Phase II
Announced

Election
Campaign

Wage-
Price
Freeze

China
Trip

Watergate

Brezhnev
Visit

Cambodian
Invasion

Russia
Trip

Inflation

Release of
Transcripts

Congressional
Elections

Vietnam
Bombing

Arab-
Israeli
Cease-
Fire

Laos
Invasion

Paris
Peace Talks
Break-Down

Cox
Fired

Operation
Candor

Russia Trip

Pentagon
Papers

Nixon
Speech on
Watergate

New
Watergate
Revelations

1969   1970   1971   1972   1973   1974

Source: *The Gallups Opinion Index*—Campaign '76, Report No. 125
(November-December, 1975), P. 19.

business to estimate potential sales for products and then were adapted to
measuring opinions on general issues. Today there are over a thousand
polling organizations. Perhaps the best known is the Gallup Poll. We are
especially aware of their frequently published reports on the degree to
which we approve our presidents.

SAMPLING METHODS

Everybody conducts polls, or more precisely, most of our judgments are
based on samples of evidence. The choice is not between polling (sampling) and not polling, but between biased and representative sampling.
Most of us, in a majority of cases, draw conclusions from biased samples.
For example: The congressman who reports that he is opposed to H.R. 506
and who is sure that the voters are too because his mail has been running
six to one against the bill; the reporter who writes that students are becoming less radical, based on interviews with a dozen students on the Yale
campus; the undergraduate who predicted that Ford would win, based on
her discussions with several of her classmates. We can have little confidence in such assessments.

If a politician or a social scientist wants to measure opinion more pre-

The nationally televised Nixon-Kennedy debate in 1960 was helpful to Kennedy but hurt Nixon. The Carter-Ford debates of 1976 were declared a "draw"—but, overall, tended to help Carter.

cisely, the first thing he must determine is the **universe,** that is, the whole group whose opinion he is interested in—every adult, all students on this campus, all students in the United States, voters in city X. If the universe consists of only thirty units—all students in a particular class—the most precise way to find out what they think on a particular issue would be to poll every one of them. But for most politically significant problems this is impossible, so pollsters *sample* the universe they are interested in. The accuracy of the results of the poll turns largely on securing a sample **representative** of the total universe. If drawn properly so that each unit in a universe has an equal chance to be included, a relatively small sample can provide accurate results. Beyond a certain point, an increase in the size of the sample reduces only slightly the **sampling error**—that is, the range between the divisions found in the sample and those of the universe.

One way to develop a representative sample would be to draw the sample completely at random. But this type of **random sampling** is impossible for most political surveys. Instead we use census tracts (where these are available) which give the number of residences and their locations. By shuffling census tracts, drawing out at random the required number, and then sending interviewers to every fifth or tenth or twentieth house, we get a random sample. A less complicated, but less reliable, sample is **quota sampling.** Here an attempt is made to secure a sample which reflects those variables among the population that might affect opinion. One polling organization, in testing opinion that is thought to be affected by income status (for example, views on the income tax), makes up a sample based on two wealthy persons, fourteen members of the upper-income class, fifty-two from the middle-income groups, and thirty-two from the poor. Interviewers are instructed to interview people in each group until they have reached the quota for that group.

People are often suspicious of results based on what appears to be a small sample. Is it really possible, they wonder, to generalize about the opinions of 220 million persons on the basis of a few thousand interviews? Can such a small sample be truly representative? The answer is yes. In comparisons of demographic characteristics based on census results and those based on a carefully drawn sample, the differences were very small. The census reported that 18.8 percent of the population was between the ages of 21 and 29, 23.5 percent was between 30 and 39, and 20.9 percent

186

was between 40 and 49. The sample results were 18.4, 23.8, and 21.5, respectively.[15] Social scientists assume that if a sample chosen by modern techniques reproduces such characteristics of the population so precisely, it will reproduce the attitudes and opinions of the total population equally well.

ASKING THE RIGHT QUESTIONS IN THE RIGHT WAY

What questions should pollsters ask? The answer might seem obvious, but in fact pollsters have a lot of leeway in choosing the questions. The average man or woman may be concerned about problems that pollsters and political leaders hardly know of, or have trouble defining. Another major difficulty in securing accurate results from a survey is in phrasing the questions. If you ask a question in a certain way, you can get the answer you want. Ask a man if he favors labor unions and he may say No. Ask him if he favors organized efforts by workers to improve their well-being, and chances are he will answer Yes. Also, trouble may arise in the alternatives that a question presents. Clearly, asking a person "Do you favor the United States entering a world government, or do you prefer our traditional independence in determining our own affairs?" is loading the dice. Polling organizations go to great efforts to make their questions fair; some of them conduct trial runs with differently worded questions.

One way to avoid this difficulty is to ask a multiple-choice question. For example, a Gallup poll asked, "How far do you, yourself, think the federal government should go in requiring employers to hire people without regard to race, religion, color, or nationality?" The respondent could answer: All the way; None of the way; Depends on type of work; Should be left to state governments; or Don't know. A variation of this type—the open-ended question—allows the respondent to supply his own answer. He may be asked simply, "How do you think we should deal with the problem of air pollution by automobiles?" (The answers to this type of question are, of course, hard to tabulate accurately.)

Interviewing itself is a delicate task. The interviewer's appearance, clothes, language, and way of asking questions may influence the replies. Inaccurate findings may result from the bias of the interviewer or from his failure to do his job fully and carefully. And the persons interviewed may be the source of error. Respondents suspicious of the interviewer's motives may give false or confused answers. Their memories may be poor. To cover up ignorance they may give neutral answers or appear undecided. Or they may give the answers they think the interviewer would like them to give.

Polls may give a false impression of the firmness and intensity of opinion; as we have seen, opinions may be volatile and fleeting. Moreover, polls do not differentiate among people—they give equal weight to a follower and to an opinion leader who may in the end influence other voters. Studies at the Survey Research Center at Michigan suggest that public opinion is not like an iceberg, where the movement of the top indicates the movement of the great mass under the water. The visible opinion at the top may be moving in a different direction—indeed it may even be differently located—from that of the great mass of opinion that is far less visible. In short, it is far easier to measure the surface of public opinion than its depth and intensity.

"That's the worst set of opinions I've heard in my entire life."

Drawing by Weber; © The New Yorker Magazine, Inc., 1975.

[15]Samuel A. Stouffer, *Communism, Conformity, and Civil Liberties* (Doubleday, 1955), p. 238.

To the average American, election forecasting is the most intriguing use of a survey, for everyone likes to know in advance how an election will turn out. During the campaign, pollsters submit regular "returns" on the position of the candidates. On the whole, the record of the leading forecasters in "day-before" polling has been good, as Table 8–2 shows. The most sensational slip came in 1948, during the presidential battle between President Truman and Governor Dewey. The polls repeatedly indicated that Mr. Truman was running far behind. The president denounced the polls as unreliable, but the pollsters stood pat on their statistics. Early in September one of them actually announced that the race was over. Gallup gave the president 44.5 percent of the popular vote in his final forecast, and Roper's prediction was 37.1 percent. Mr. Truman won 49.4 percent of the popular vote, and the pollsters were subjected to general ridicule. Since then they have been more cautious in making predictions from their data, and more careful in their methods.[16]

Political polls have taken on increasingly significant functions in our political system. Candidates use polls to determine where to campaign, how to campaign, and even whether to campaign. In the years and months preceding a national convention, politicians watch the polls to determine who among the hopefuls has political appeal. Jimmy Carter used polls systematically in both his preconvention and election campaigns, as do most presidential candidates. Questions have been raised about this use of polls. Should candidates run for office only when it seems safe to do so? If a candidate believes in a cause, should he not defend it publicly in order to present a meaningful choice to the voters?[17]

Surely the polls at best are no substitute for elections. Faced with a ballot, voters must translate opinions into concrete decisions between personalities and parties. They must decide what is important and what is not. Then, out of the welter of views of all the voters, a decision emerges for some candidate who will act in terms of some program (however vague), and who will have the people's trust (again vague) to act on future

[16]See Mendelsohn and Crespi, *Polls, Television, and the New Politics*, Chap. 2.

[17]Critical analyses of public opinion polling are C. W. Roll, Jr., and A. H. Cantril, *Polls: Their Use and Misuse in Politics* (Basic Books, 1972); and Leo Bogart, *Silent Politics: Polls and the Awareness of Public Opinion* (Wiley, 1972).

8–2

Some recent presidential forecasts by the pollsters (by percentage)

Year	Actual Dem. vote	Roper Poll	Gallup Poll	Harris Poll
1936	60.2	61.7	53.8	—
1940	54.7	55.2	55.0	—
1944	53.8	53.6	53.3	—
1948	49.4	37.1	44.5	—
1952	45.+	43.0	46.0	—
1956	42.0	40.0	40.5	—
1960	49.4	47.0	49.0	—
1964	61.4	—	61.0	—
1968	42.7	—	40.0	43.0
1972	37.7	—	35.0	34.8
1976	51.0	51.0	46.0*	46.0*

In 1976 both Gallup and Harris said it was a "toss up" and refused to make a prediction. They also reported that more people than was usual had not made up their minds.

problems. For democracy is more than the expression of views, more than a simple mirror of opinion. It is also the *choosing* among leaders taking sides on certain issues, and among the governmental actions that may follow. Democracy is the thoughtful participation of people in the political process; it means using heads as well as counting them. Elections, with all their failings, at least establish the link between the many voices of "We the People" and the decisions of their leaders.

Summary

We can summarize this chapter by answering the leading questions posed:

1. Public opinion is not one solid opinion or voice but a complex combination of opinions or voices. It takes on various qualities of stability, fluidity, intensity, and latency, all affected by the person's feeling about the relevance of opinions to themselves. Leaders in government try to combine groups of voters in support of leaders' positions. Whether or not government *should* try to influence public opinion, it inevitably will do so. (These last two questions will be further considered in subsequent chapters.)

2. People's attitudes are shaped by family, school, and later learning and experience. Despite assertions that some single force, such as mother or father, early schooling, college, television has the dominant role in molding opinion, people actually seem to be influenced by many forces that interact with one another.

3. The influence of the mass media is significant but not overwhelming. People may or may not pay attention to newspapers or television. They may be critical or suspicious of the media and hence resistant to it. They live in groups that reject or "filter" opinions coming in from "outside" and they may respond more to other persons on a face-to-face basis than to the media.

4. In the diffusion of ideas and opinions we do not have a wholly free market. In the press and other mass media, we find tendencies toward concentration, commercialism, and conservatism partly offset by the liberalism of many journalists and of some of the most prominent newspapers.

5. We have fairly reliable methods for roughly measuring people's opinions at a given time, provided the polling is done carefully and responsibly, using tested procedures and safeguards.

Chapter 9

Political Behavior: The American Voter

In the mid-1970s it became evident to analysts of political behavior that American voters were going through profound changes. These changes were not as dramatic as the civil rights struggles of the mid-1960s that erupted in riots and burning cities, or the elections that later brought many more blacks to office. Nor were the changes as searing as was the tumult over Vietnam in the late sixties and early seventies—tumult that brought, among other things, the closing down of scores of colleges and universities by students. The changes uncovered in the mid-1970s were much quieter, but in the long run they might have greater effect on American politics than the earlier dramas. And the chances are more than even that the student reading this book is part of those changes!

In this chapter we will deal with those changes as part of both old and emerging patterns in American politics. We will focus mainly on *voting patterns*, but keep in mind that voting is only one of many types of political participation. Some Americans campaign for office or help other candidates. Some are active in their party, others in an interest group such as a veteran's organization or farm group, still others in their community. Some merely give money to a candidate or party; others attend a meeting. So-called extremists hold protest meetings, confront authorities, demonstrate, picket, perhaps resort to violence. A few Americans participate in all these ways; some in none of them; many others in some but not other ways—and they may change their "mix" of political activities from election to election.

Of all these ways of taking part in American politics, why do we concentrate mainly on *voting?* Because the most common kind of political participation is casting a ballot (usually by pulling a lever). Because political scientists armed with voting statistics and computers have done some of the most exciting work in their discipline. Because many of the other forms of political participation, such as helping a candidate or giving to a party, are focused on the election itself, so voting becomes a guide to political behavior generally. And—most important—because elections empower certain politicians to govern and send others out into the political cold, so that voting is the crucial factor in what government does and fails to do. The ballot is the payoff.

Who votes? who does not vote?

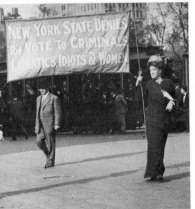

The great struggle for voting rights for women (top) was finally rewarded with passage of the Nineteenth Amendment. The women (bottom) are voting for the first time.

The history of *suffrage*—the right to vote—in the United States has been a long battle to extend that right from a small group of property-owning males—perhaps one person out of every twenty or thirty—to the great mass of the people.

Three great struggles have been fought over this issue. The first was against *property tests* for voting. Conservatives argued that universal male suffrage would jeopardize the rights of property, that if poor people gained the right to vote they would sell their votes to the rich. The democratic, egalitarian mood of America, eastern immigration and the western frontier, and the eagerness of politicians to lower voting barriers so they could pick up votes all led to the end of property (and taxpaying) restrictions by the middle of the nineteenth century.

The second great struggle was for *women's voting rights*. Husbands and fathers once argued that women had no place at the polling booth, that husbands could vote for the interests of the whole family—but these arguments had a hollow ring. The aroused women conducted noisy parades, drew up petitions, organized a Washington lobby, picketed the White House, got arrested, went on hunger strikes in jail. They won the vote in some states and finally achieved a breakthrough with the passage of the Nineteenth Amendment in 1920.

The third great struggle—for the right of black Americans to vote—has been mainly won (see Chapter 6). The most recent major extension of the right to vote has been to youths eighteen to twenty years old. Unlike the earlier expansions of the suffrage, this was hardly the result of a struggle by young people. It was in part a recognition by those twenty-one and older that younger persons were being educated to a point where they could vote intelligently. It was also a response to the widespread student protests during the 1960s, and the view that if you were old enough to fight in wars for your country, you were old enough to help select its leaders.

By the mid-seventies the overwhelming number of Americans, including women, blacks, and the young, possessed the right to vote. What do they do with it?

THE NONVOTER: MILLIONS OF "NO-SHOWS"

One of the big questions before the 1976 election was how many persons would show up at the polls to vote. Prospects for a good turnout seemed higher than in the recent past. To be sure, the number of Americans registering to vote had been falling, and the number of those registered actually voting had been dropping too. But observers felt that the dropoff might have been due to the absence of a real race in the lopsided battle between George McGovern and Richard Nixon in 1972. Or perhaps voters had been turned off by both candidates, in that election and earlier ones. 1976 looked more promising. Jimmy Carter was a fresh face on the political scene, and the voters seemed to have a meaningful choice between him and President Ford. And as November 2 approached, it truly did look like a horse race.

A horse race it was, but in a sense neither Ford nor Carter really "won" the election. The millions of "no-shows" almost outvoted the Ford and Carter voters combined. Turnout, which had fallen from 60.7 percent in 1968 to 55.4 percent in 1972, dropped to below 54 percent in 1976. This near-victory of the no-shows led to editorials about the "apathy" of American voters. Columnists noted that turnout had been much higher in this country in the nineteenth and early twentieth centuries. They pointed to the much greater turnout in European democracies — as much as 80 percent and even 90 percent in election after election. Some years ago over 100 nations were ranked on voter turnout. The United States ranked twelfth from the *bottom* — a little above Barbados!

How serious a problem is this low voting turnout? Certain factors should be noted. Americans conduct far many more elections and *types* of elections than Europeans do, so voters in this country can express their wishes in state and local elections, for example, if they are not interested in the national. The student of voting behavior must be careful, too, to note whether turnout figures are based on the percentage of voters in the *total population*, which inflates the size of the "universe" by including aliens, criminals, and lunatics, as opposed to those eligible to vote.[1] And Americans, of course, have an absolute right *not* to vote. Still, we would expect a higher turnout, as a matter both of "civic virtue" and of defense of one's own self-interest.

WHY IS TURNOUT SO LOW?

The easiest answer to this question is: Apathy. It is easy to denounce those who are just "too lazy" to vote. If people don't want to vote, a columnist wrote, "to hell with them — serves them right." The problem really is not that simple. Of course there are some people who just don't care. They will not vote no matter what. They would not go to the polls if King Kong were running against Snow White. But these persons are in a small minority. The main reasons for nonvoting are *institutional* and *political*. Let us consider both.

The institutional block is mainly registration and absentee ballot requirements. People may forget to register in time (especially if the cutoff date is set far in advance of the election, as it often used to be). They may be bedridden or away on long trips. Registration in itself can be bothersome and time-consuming. Getting an absentee ballot also can be difficult, as many a student has discovered. Residence requirements used to be strict. In recent years, the Supreme Court has ruled that states may not impose residency requirements of longer than fifty days. Disturbed by the low turnout, Congress in 1970 established for presidential elections a uniform thirty-day residency requirement and set simpler procedures for absentee voting.

The prime reasons for nonvoting, however, are not institutional but political, in the broadest sense. Millions of Americans fail to show up at the polls because they feel it is not worth the trouble. Often this is a deliberate decision. They stay home on election day not because they lack interest but because their real interest, they feel, is not reflected in the "system." They feel that there is no real choice between candidates or parties. They believe that politicians make promises they fail to carry out. They feel that the government does not respond to their real needs and hopes. A few

[1]Austin Ranney, "Participation in American Presidential Nominations — 1976" (American Enterprise Institute, 1977).

charge that the same "elites" run the government, no matter who wins the elections. Some are simply "disgusted" by politics. They are not apathetic toward politics, they contend—American politics is apathetic toward *them.*

College students in particular have seemed to feel this way toward politics in recent years. When students mobilized for action after President Nixon's Cambodia invasion of 1970, it was estimated that half a million of them would take part in the congressional elections of that year. In fact, only a small minority showed up at the polls. The vast majority of *interested* students did more talking than electioneering. In general, of all major categories of voters, the lowest percentage of voter turnout is among the eighteen- to twenty-year-olds.[2]

WHO FAILS TO VOTE?

Nonvoting might not be a serious problem if those who *do* vote were a cross section of those who do not. But this is not the case. The extent of voting varies widely among different types of *voters*, different *areas*, and different *elections.*

The most serious difference lies between persons with high and low incomes. In 1972 about 70 percent of persons in families making over $15,000 a year showed up at the polls. Participation dropped to about half in families with incomes of $7,500 to $10,000, and to less than half for families with incomes under $7,500. Turnout is high among white-collar professionals, is less among white-collar sales and clerical workers, and even less among skilled blue-collar workers. Education is a related factor. The less schooling persons have, the less likely they are to vote. Other differences in turnout are equally interesting though perhaps less significant. The older you are (unless you are *very* old and perhaps infirm), the more likely you are to vote. People under thirty-five, and especially under twenty-five, have a poorer turnout record. Those who are active in their political party or in organized groups are far more likely to vote than those who are not. One long-time difference in turnout, that between men and women, has virtually disappeared.

Summing up, if you are young, less educated, low-paid, and not active in organizations, you are far less likely to turn out even for an exciting presidential election than if you are older, better paid and educated, and a member of a union or party or other associations. Since a key function of government is redistributing income, the most important of these voter-nonvoter differences is income. Why do low-income people vote in fewer numbers than the wealthy, especially when the poor would seem to have such a stake in government? For several reasons: they have less sense of involvement and confidence; they feel less of a sense of control over their political environment; they feel at a disadvantage in social contacts; their social norms tend to deemphasize politics (compared, say, with sports). Thus nonvoting is not accidental; it is part of a larger political and psychological environment that discourages political activity.[3]

[2]Walter T. Murphy, Jr., "Student Power in the 1970 Elections: A Preliminary Assessment," *Political Science* (Winter 1971), pp. 27–32. See also Sidney Hyman, *Youth in Politics* (Basic Books, 1972).

[3]See Angus Campbell, Philip E. Converse, Warren E. Miller, and Donald E. Stokes, *The American Voter* (Wiley, 1960). This volume remains a foundation of modern voting analysis despite much new evidence and reinterpretation. See also Norman H. Nie, Sidney Verba, and John R. Petrocik, *The Changing American Voter* (Harvard University Press, 1976) and Warren E. Miller and Teresa E. Levitin, *Leadership and Change* (Winthrop, 1976).

Many voters feel elections do not offer them a real choice between candidates and parties. They respond to this situation by not voting at all.

Voting Turnout for President and U.S. House of Representatives, 1948-1972

For President

For U.S. Representatives

Percentage of age-eligible voters voting

70
65
60
55
50
45
40
35

1952 1954 1956 1958 1960 1962 1964 1966 1968 1970 1972 1974 1976

Years

Political institutions have an impact on nonvoting. You might think that the smaller the election district, the more closely involved people would feel with their elected officials, and hence the higher the voting turnout. You might also assume that people would tend to vote more heavily in elections for legislators than for executives, since the former are usually chosen in smaller districts. But note:

1. *National* elections bring out more voters than state or local campaigns. *Presidential* elections attract the greatest number of voters. Off-year congressional elections draw fewer persons to the polls. City and other local elections tend to attract an even smaller number. And participation is lowest in *party primaries*. Even when voters are marking a ballot that offers a variety of national and local contests, some voters will check their presidential choice but not bother with others.
2. Elections for *chief executives* attract more voters than elections for legislators. Turnout for representatives is considerably higher in years when a president is elected than in off-presidential years, as the chart indicates. A somewhat similar difference exists at the state level between gubernatorial and legislative elections. The difference in executive and legislative turnout has major implications for governmental policy.
3. Voting is *lowest* in areas where there is little two-party competition. Thus, the lowest voting figures are likely to be found in states such as Mississippi, Alabama, and South Carolina, although recently there has been a marked upswing of voting in the South.

How serious is the low rate of voting? Does it indicate that our democratic system is in danger? Should we encourage—perhaps even force—everyone to vote? No, answer some authorities. It is not a low rate of voting that signals danger to a democracy, but a high rate. They see nonvoting as a sign of some satisfaction with the state of affairs. Others strongly disagree. The decreased voting turnout in the presidential elections from 1964 through 1976, they say, hardly indicates increased satisfaction with the American political situation. Rather, it suggests that people were disgusted, cynical, increasingly "turned off" and "tuned out" of the political system.

An acute dilemma for democrats emerges from the problem of voting turnout. Nothing would be gained from forcing to the polls people who had little knowledge about, or interest in, an election. And sudden increases in voting triggered by a social crisis or the appeal of an authoritarian leader may be a danger sign, since those hostile to democratic values would be mobilized. For there is some evidence that persons with low levels of political sophistication tend to take a simplified view of politics, fail to show tolerance toward people who disagree with them, and find it hard to grasp democratic norms. On the other hand, persons low in income and social status are precisely the ones who should be involved in voting and other political activity. They need to have more influence over government for their own welfare, and a central idea of democracy is to include all citizens in its processes. How to integrate persons with low information and interest and limited democratic values into a system of self-government in a manner that will both advance their interests *and* strengthen the whole system remains one of the major challenges to a government by the people.

One answer may be to increase voting gradually but systematically, especially in the low socioeconomic levels. How to do this? Preaching about the duties of citizenship fails to reach its chief target. Increased educational opportunity may help, though the expansion of education during this century hardly seems to have brought increased voting. Something could be accomplished through *political* changes. Shorten the ballot by cutting down the number of unimportant elective positions. Simplify residence and registration requirements (permanent registration, or registration by postcard, are possibilities here). Make absentee voting easier. Make election day a big holiday and dramatize the importance of voting. Above all, make the parties more competitive in state and local as well as national elections, so that nonvoters would begin to see that they have a significant choice at the polls.

So much for the nonvoter. What about the people who *do* vote?

How we vote

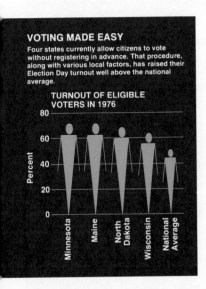

VOTING MADE EASY

Four states currently allow citizens to vote without registering in advance. That procedure, along with various local factors, has raised their Election Day turnout well above the national average.

**TURNOUT OF ELIGIBLE
VOTERS IN 1976**

(bar chart with Percent on vertical axis, scale 0 to 80; bars for Minnesota, Maine, North Dakota, Wisconsin, National Average)

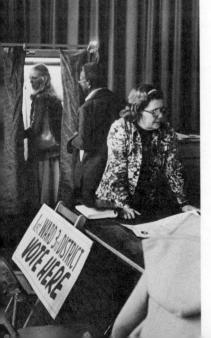

**Election-day scene:
first ward, third district, USA.**

1st WARD 3 DISTRICT
VOTE HERE

Sometimes Americans are called fickle voters who switch from party to party. Actually, the great majority of Americans stay with one party year after year, and their sons and grandsons vote for the same party long after that. Politically, these voters are "set in their ways." Both parties count on the support of a certain minimum of voters who will go Republican or Democratic almost by habit.

Of course, there are still millions of so-called independent voters. They help make our elections the unpredictable and breathless affairs that they so often are. Still, even in the variations from year to year there are certain persistent elements. Looking closely at the complex mosaic of American politics, we can see patterns of voting habits that help us understand how we vote and a little about why we vote as we do.

1. A pattern of *sectional voting*. The South is the most famous example. The Democratic solidarity of the states that formed the Confederacy lasted over eighty years in presidential elections, and continues today in congressional elections. Republican sectionalism was not so clearcut, but northern New England and parts of the Midwest have been dependable areas for the GOP. Thus Vermont has given its electoral votes to the Democrats only once since the Civil War, and Maine only twice since 1912. More recently, the South has become more Republican and the Northeast more Democratic, but Jimmy Carter partially reversed that Republican "trend" in the South in 1976.[4]

Sectional patterns may be fuzzy and brief. There was much talk before the 1976 election of the "Sunbelt" politics of the area stretching from the southeastern states across the nation to California. This region was seen as the base of a rising American conservatism. In 1976, however, the sunbelt split, with the whole eastern tier going to Carter. The western half of the nation, including the plains states, has shown a strong Republican trend in the last three presidential elections, but this pattern may not last long. Sectional patterns often reflect very close election results *within* states, and those patterns can easily be changed by other influences.

2. A pattern of *national* voting. These traditional sectional alignments also give way to national trends. One of the striking aspects of a great national swing is the way in which virtually all areas are part of that movement. The Franklin Roosevelt administration, for example, ushered in a new age of Democratic party popularity that affected even the most

[4]Important recent works on southern politics are Jack Bass and Walter DeVries, *The Transformation of Southern Politics* (Basic Books, 1976); Louis Seagull, *Southern Republicanism* (Wiley, 1975). A provocative sectional theme is found in Kirkpatrick Sale, *Power Shift: The Rise of the Southern Rim and Its Challenge to the Eastern Establishment* (Vintage, 1976).

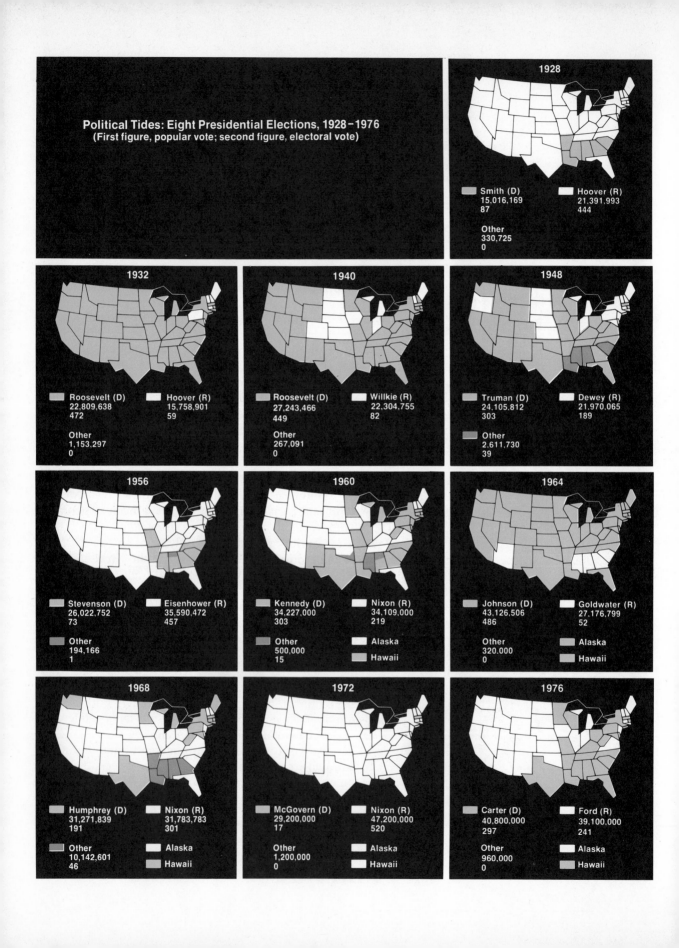

Political Tides: Eight Presidential Elections, 1928–1976
(First figure, popular vote; second figure, electoral vote)

1928

Smith (D)
15,016,169
87

Hoover (R)
21,391,993
444

Other
330,725
0

1932

Roosevelt (D)
22,809,638
472

Hoover (R)
15,758,901
59

Other
1,153,297
0

1940

Roosevelt (D)
27,243,466
449

Willkie (R)
22,304,755
82

Other
267,091
0

1948

Truman (D)
24,105,812
303

Dewey (R)
21,970,065
189

Other
2,611,730
39

1956

Stevenson (D)
26,022,752
73

Eisenhower (R)
35,590,472
457

Other
194,166
1

1960

Kennedy (D)
34,227,000
303

Nixon (R)
34,109,000
219

Other
500,000
15

Alaska

Hawaii

1964

Johnson (D)
43,126,506
486

Goldwater (R)
27,176,799
52

Other
320,000
0

Alaska

Hawaii

1968

Humphrey (D)
31,271,839
191

Nixon (R)
31,783,783
301

Other
10,142,601
46

Alaska

Hawaii

1972

McGovern (D)
29,200,000
17

Nixon (R)
47,200,000
520

Other
1,200,000
0

Alaska

Hawaii

1976

Carter (D)
40,800,000
297

Ford (R)
39,100,000
241

Other
960,000
0

Alaska

Hawaii

traditionally Republican areas. States and sections are subject to a variety of local influences but they cannot resist the great political tides that sweep the nation. There has not been such a tide in the four decades since FDR's reelection triumph of 1936. (In 1972 Nixon carried every state except Massachusetts and the District of Columbia, but other Republicans did not do so well.)

3. A pattern of *similar* voting for *different* offices. Sectional and national forces affect voting for different candidates and offices in the same election. Well over half the voters usually vote a straight ticket—that is, they throw their support to every one of their party's candidates. If one candidate is an especially able votegetter, the party's whole slate may gain. This is the famous coattail effect, whose precise nature is one of the challenging problems in the study of political behavior. Evidently popular presidential candidates like Roosevelt or Johnson have long coattails that help elect many other candidates on their party tickets. But congressional and state candidates may have helpful coattails too, and it is not easy to tell which candidates ride on whose coattails or just how important the relation is.[5] This pattern recently seems to have changed, with a sharp increase in split-ticket voting continuing into 1976. Thus Nixon won overwhelmingly in 1972, but Congress remained decisively in Democratic hands, and Republican candidates fared poorly in many states. Carter rode more on the coattails of congressional and state candidates than the reverse.

4. A pattern of voting over *time*. Great political tides seem to flow back and forth across the generations. Most presidential elections are maintaining elections; the pattern of partisan support of the preceding period persists. Long periods of maintaining elections are occasionally interrupted by deviating elections, which the "out" party wins because it has an especially attractive presidential candidate or because the existing administration has lost the nation's confidence. In these elections the underlying division of party support is not long disturbed. Wilson's victories in 1912 and 1916 are cases in point. Very occasionally, however, there occurs a realigning election that brings a basic and long-lasting transformation of party loyalties. A whole new balance of parties comes into being, as it did in the 1930s.[6] Some have predicted that we are on the eve of another series of realigning elections and a historic realignment of the parties. Others see mainly a pattern of confusion and dislocation today—a pattern that defies easy categorization. We will return to this question in Chapter 10.

Why we vote as we do

What causes the political tides to rise and fall? Why do some voters stick with one party while others shift back and forth from election to election, and still others vote a split-party ticket in every election? In recent decades, a vast amount of effort has been devoted to answering questions such as these.

[5]For an example of some of the complex factors at work, see Barbara Hinckley, "Incumbency and the Presidential Vote in Senate Elections: Defining Parameters of Subpresidential Voting," *American Political Science Review* (September 1970), pp. 836–42. See also William B. Moreland, "Angels, Pinpoints, and Voters: The Pattern for a Coattail," *American Journal of Political Science* (February 1973), pp. 170–76; Gary C. Jacobson, "Presidential Coattails in 1972," *Public Opinion Quarterly* (Summer 1976), pp. 194–200.

[6]These three types of elections are defined and discussed in Angus Campbell, Philip E. Converse, Warren E. Miller, and Donald E. Stokes, *Elections and the Political Order* (Wiley, 1966); see also Walter Dean Burnham, *Critical Elections and the Mainsprings of American Politics* (Norton, 1970).

Campaign buttons from years past reflect the changing patterns in American politics.

A traditional explanation for the great political tides has been economic. A drop in business activity has often preceded a loss of congressional seats and then a presidential defeat for the party in power. But we cannot be sure that business cycles *cause* political cycles. Sometimes the two cycles diverge. Psychological, political, traditional, sectional, international, and other forces may muddle the effect of economic factors. It was not primarily economic issues but the sharply rising concern over slavery that precipitated the breakup of the Democratic-Whig party system in the 1850s. On the other hand, the Great Depression in the early 1930s doubtless was the main reason the GOP was toppled after its long period of supremacy.

So if there are patterns in American politics, these patterns are rough and are often blurred by unexplained variations. Indeed, the patterns may exist for years and then disappear. Before the 1948 election, a change in party control of Congress in an off-year election had regularly preceded a change in party fortunes in the following presidential election. But the Democrats, who lost control of Congress in 1946, won both houses of Congress and—to the surprise of everyone especially of Thomas Dewey and perhaps even Harry Truman—the presidency in 1948. And despite a 1954 congressional victory for the Democrats, the GOP won the presidential election of 1956. So we have heard less of this "pattern" since then.

VOTING PATTERNS

Still, despite the murkiness of voting tendencies, analysis of massive amounts of voting data has uncovered some basic patterns.

1. Voting as members of *groups*. Most Americans vote the same way that their families or friends or workmates vote. On election day they mark their ballots or check off their voting machine levers in private, but voting is largely a group experience. The most homogeneous of all groups in molding political opinions and ultimately the voting behavior of its members is doubtless the family. Members of the family shape one another's attitudes (often unintentionally); and members of the same family are naturally exposed to similar economic, religious, class, and geographical influences.[7]

As young adults move away from their families they may become members of many different groups. Some of their group memberships may mutually *reinforce* their voting decisions. Thus a young engineer who has grown up in a Democratically inclined family may marry a more conservatively inclined woman, associate on his job with Republican executives, socialize a good deal with fellow members of a country club, and join a taxpayer's organization. The engineer will probably become a Republican, though he will long feel a Democratic tug from his family years. Or group memberships may have conflicting impacts on a person's vote. Thus a woman factory worker may associate with Democrats in her local union but with Republicans in her social group or ethnic organization. Such persons are said to be "cross-pressured" and sometimes take the easiest way out by not voting at all!

Group influences on voting may change over time. The blue-collar worker, the black, and the urban ethnic tended to rally round FDR and the New Deal in the 1930s in part because they felt that the Republican party had failed them, in part because the New Deal Democrats recognized them and gave them concrete social and economic benefits. Business and professional men and women tended to be members of group interests opposed to New Deal "experimentation" and "waste." In the 1960s and 1970s newer issues—Vietnam, race, law and order, Watergate—cut across group alignments, created new group allegiances to Republican candidates, and caused severe splits within the Democratic party coalition.

2. Voting as members of *parties*. In this century most voters have identified with one or the other major parties. Many support their party almost automatically, no matter who the candidate or what the issues. Party iden-

[7]See generally Richard E. Dawson and Kenneth Prewitt, *Political Socialization;* and for a specific example of an intrafamily relationship, M. Kent Jennings and Richard G. Niemi, "The Division of Political Labor Between Mothers and Fathers," *American Political Science Review* (March 1971), pp. 69–82.

tification was relatively stable during the 1950s and 1960s.[8] This traditional allegiance is not necessarily blind or irrational. A person may vote for the same party over the years because he has thoughtfully concluded that that party serves his interests best.

Is party loyalty declining? A large number of Democrats ignored their long-time party identification in 1972, as did many Republicans in 1976. Democratic and Republican party self-identifiers (that is, persons who state that they are to some degree "Democrats" or "Republicans" when asked by pollsters) have dropped sharply in recent years. Many voters identify with one of the major parties but vote for the opposition candidate. People usually do not openly and suddenly give up their party membership; rather they talk more about voting "for the person and not the party." Whether the drop in party identification is a short-run or long-run development remains to be seen. We will return to this question in Chapter 10.

3. Voting in terms of *class, occupation, income.* Most studies of voting behavior confirm what everyday observation has already indicated. The highest proportion of persons who prefer the Republican party are in the upper income brackets, especially with incomes over $25,000 a year. But we cannot make too much of this factor, or indeed of any single factor. The relation of social class to party choice has declined over the whole span of post-World War II years. Older voters, with their memories of the Depression, still tend to vote on the basis of socioeconomic status, but younger voters are much less influenced by social and economic factors.[9]

[8]The Center for Political Studies, University of Michigan, periodically measures dimensions of party support. See also Judson L. James, *American Political Parties in Transition* (Harper & Row, 1974), pp. 126–30; and William R. Shaffer, "Partisan Loyalty and the Perceptions of Party, Candidates, and Issues," *Western Political Quarterly* (September 1972), pp. 424–33.

[9]On economic and social factors in voting in general, in the United States and elsewhere, see

9–1

The demography of the vote in recent presidential elections

Demographic Characteristic	1948		1956		1960	
	Dem.	Rep.	Dem.	Rep.	Dem.	Rep.
Religion						
Protestant	47†	53†	37	63	38	62
Catholic	66†	34†	51	49	78	22
Jewish			75	25	81	19
Race						
White	53†	47†	41	59	49	51
Black	81†	19†	61	39	68	32
Union labor families	74‡	26	57	43	65	35
Young voters (age 21–29 yr.)	62‡	38	43	57	54	46
Sex						
Women	53†	47†	39	61	49	51
Men	56†	44†	45	55	52	48

*The American Independent party, headed by George Wallace.
†Figures accompanied by a dagger are taken from Angus Campbell et al., *The Voter Decides* (New York: Harper & Row Publishers, 1954), pp. 70–71. Data given there were converted from a percentage of the total sample to a percentage of those voting, ignoring the "Other" column. Other data are taken from releases of the American Institute of Public Opinion (the Gallup Poll), and from NBC and CBS samples as reported in *Congressional Quarterly Weekly Reports*, November 11, 1972, p. 2949. 1976 data from *The New York Times*, November 4, 1976, p. 25.
‡Includes Democratic, Progressive, and States' Rights votes.

4. Voting by *religion* and *race*. Analysis of the 1960s show that "religion remained a potent source of political cleavage in the United States. . . . The detailed coding of the religious variable revealed that it was the single most important of four predictors of political party identification, and was comparable to, if not more important than the *combined* effects of education, occupation, and income."[10] John Kennedy's campaign for the presidency tended to align Catholics even more with the Democrats, and Protestants with the GOP. The influence of religion declined in the next two elections, and there is some evidence that "religious cleavages in American politics continue on a downward trend from past polarization."[11]

Racial voting has been a polarizing force. During the late nineteenth century northern blacks voted heavily Republican and southern whites almost exclusively Democratic—a carryover from the Civil War. During Roosevelt's New Deal and Truman's Fair Deal, blacks began shifting over to the Democratic party and to the civil rights policies that party was supporting. For the same reason, southern whites began to move toward the Republican party. Blacks today are probably the most strongly Democratic of all socioeconomic groups. Blacks stuck with George McGovern in 1972 when other groups deserted him, and they were crucial to Carter's victory in 1976.

Robert R. Alford, *Party and Society* (Rand McNally, 1963); on generational aspects see Paul R. Abramson, "Generational Change in American Electoral Behavior," *American Political Science Review* (March 1974), pp. 93–105; Gerald Finch, "Physical Change and Partisan Change: The Emergence of a New American Electorate, 1952–1972," in Louis Maisel and Paul Sacks, eds., *The Future of Political Parties* (Russell Sage, 1975).

[10]David Knoke, "Religion, Stratification and Politics: American in the 1960s," *American Journal of Political Science* (May 1974), p. 344.

[11]*Ibid.*

| 1964 | | 1968 | | | 1972 | | 1976 | |
Dem.	Rep.	Dem.	Rep.	AIP*	Dem.	Rep	Dem.	Rep.
55	45	35	49	16	30	70	46	54
75	25	59	33	8	48	52	55	45
90	10	83	17	—	61	39	68	32
59	41	38	47	15	32	68	48	52
94	6	85	12	3	87	13	83	17
—	—	—	—	—	46	54	62	38
64	36	47	38	15	48	52	56	44
62	38	45	43	12	38	62	52	48
60	40	41	43	16	37	63	52	48

To identify the political preferences of sociological groups may give a misleading picture of voting behavior, for over time these distinctions change, and they fail to take into account the impact of national and international developments and the personality factors of individual voters and the way they respond to candidates. "Events, communications, and attitudes—may all be more or less independent of group memberships and social classifications," points out Warren Miller. They all make important contributions to the individual's political behavior. But their importance is minimized in group-oriented descriptions of electoral behavior. To know someone's party affiliation does not tell us for sure how he or she will behave politically.

Is it a healthy sign that our political parties do not reflect too accurately basic social, economic, geographical, and religious differences? Or does this lead to a blurring of party lines, and in turn to fuzzy programs and a failure of American government to deal with crises and problems? The fact that many Jews are Republicans, that some wealthy people are Democrats, that neither party can claim a monopoly of any group, keeps the parties from reinforcing and exaggerating differences. Lipset observes, "Where parties are cut off from gaining support among a major stratum, they lose a major reason for compromise."[12] Some party activists disagree. Parties with more clear-cut electoral support, they say, might supply national leaders with the kind of mandate they need to offer a firmer sense of direction to the American people and to put across the program the winning party has promised.

WHO ARE THE INDEPENDENTS?

"Me, I vote the man, not the party. Hoover, Landon, Dewey, Eisenhower, Goldwater, Nixon, Ford . . ."

© 1956 Crowell, Collier Publishing Company; reproduced by courtesy of Bill Mauldin.

Roughly a quarter to a third of the voters can be classified as independents—but "independent" is a tricky term. Some persons are called independent because they are party-switchers; they cross and recross party lines from election to election. Some are ticket-splitters; at the same election they vote for candidates of different parties.[13] Some are independents because they *feel* independent. Some call themselves independents because they think it is socially more respectable, but actually they vote with the same degree of regularity for one party as do others who are not so hesitant to admit party loyalty. A study indicates that younger voters with above-average incomes and college educations tend to be more independent than other groups but that the independent vote is rather evenly distributed throughout the population. And the number of independents, whether switchers or splitters, has sharply increased in recent years.

Is the independent voter the more informed voter? There has been heated debate over this question, but much of it is fruitless because everything depends on what kind of independent we are talking about. If independents are defined as those who fail to express a preference between parties, the independent voter tends to be less well informed than the partisan voter, for such independents include chronic nonvoters, apathetic people, and the like. But if we mean those who switch parties between elections, we find some who are highly informed and who carefully pick and choose at the polls. Oddly, perhaps, the independent is really not all that different from the partisan. Independents seem to be neither more nor

[12]S. M. Lipset, *Political Man* (Doubleday, 1960), p. 31.

[13]Walter De Vries and V. Lance Tarrance, *The Ticket-Splitter: A New Force in American Politics* (Erdmans, 1972).

less cynical about the "system" than party supporters are. Most independents seem to vote as regularly for one or the other party as do those who identify with a party. Still, in a nation where parties seem to be losing many of their oldtime supporters, candidates will seek to appeal to the "independent" voter, however defined.[14]

Apathetics, participants, leaders

© 1961 United Feature Syndicate

Students interviewing a cross section of a population are often surprised to find people who seem to know nothing about the questions they are asked. The newspapers may be full of headlines and discussion about a Howard Baker or a Jerry Brown, but some citizens can place the names only vaguely in politics. "The first noteworthy fact about citizen participation in a democracy is that it is thin. Most citizens are little interested in playing even a small policy-making role; fully a third of American citizens neither vote, join interest groups, do party work, communicate with their representatives, nor talk politics with their friends except occasionally in a vague and uninformed way."[15] The completely uninvolved are called isolates, apathetics, or even "chronic know-nothings."

On the other hand, some citizens are influential enough to manipulate other people's political behavior. City bosses, student leaders, local newspaper editors, and national columnists sometimes have this kind of power imputed to them. The classic statement of political influence is one attributed to Boss Plunkitt, a Tammany district leader, years ago:

There's only one way to hold a district; you must study human nature and act accordin'. You can't study human nature in books. Books is a hindrance more than anything else. If you have been to college, so much the worse for you. You'll have to unlearn all you learned before you can get right down to human nature, and unlearnin' takes a lot of time. Some men can never forget what they learned at college. Such men may get to be district leaders by a fluke, but they never last.

To learn real human nature you have to go among the people, see them and be seen. I know every man, woman, and child in the Fifteenth District, except them that's been born this summer—and I know some of them, too. I know what they like and what they don't like, what they are strong at and what they are weak in, and I reach them by approachin' at the right side.

For instance, here's how I gather in the young men. I hear of a young feller that's proud of his voice, thinks that he can sing fine. I ask him to come around to Washington Hall and join our Glee Club. He comes and sings, and he's a follower of Plunkitt for life. Another young feller gains a reputation as a baseball player in a vacant lot. I bring him into our baseball club. That fixes him. . . . I don't trouble them with political arguments. I just study human nature and act accordin'. . . .

As to the older voters, I reach them, too. No, I don't send campaign literature. That's rot. People can get all the political stuff they want to read—and a good deal more, too—in the papers. Who reads speeches, nowadays, anyhow? It's bad enough to listen to them.[16]

[14]On independent-partisan similarities and differences, see Bruce Keith, David Magebly, Candice Nelson, Elizabeth Orr, Mark Westlye, and Raymond E. Wolfinger, *The Independent Phenomenon* (forthcoming).

[15]Charles E. Lindblom, *The Policy-Making Process* (Prentice-Hall, 1968), p. 44.

[16]W. L. Riordon, *Plunkitt of Tammany Hall* (McClure, Phillips, 1905), pp. 33–34.

In between the highly influential—the leaders—and the apathetics are the participants who follow politics, talk about issues, and vote. But even these three groupings are oversimplified. Actually we find a *range* or *spectrum* of political participation, as Table 9−2 suggests.

A range of activity (or inactivity) is also found among apathetics. Some literally never vote or talk politics. Others might vote occasionally and, if not talk politics, influence the talkers by their responsiveness or indifference. Apathy and participation also vary over time. A person may ignore one national election and become intensely involved in the next; he or she may vote in fall elections but ignore the primaries. And a person might be highly active in town or city elections and uninterested in state or national elections.

In general, to be sure, people active at one level of politics tend to be active at other levels. But we must be careful about generalizations concerning political apathy, such as "the poor don't take part in politics." As analysts we must think in terms of specific elections, types of individuals, and political situations, as well as broad patterns.

WHY PEOPLE PARTICIPATE
IN POLITICS

A vast amount of study has gone into the questions of how and why people get involved in politics. Participation is widely seen as a function of the following factors:[17]

1. *Political stimuli.* Citizens contacted personally are more likely to vote and show interest in the campaign. Those lacking education and understanding about politics tend to shut out political stimuli. Middle-class persons, men, and urban dwellers are exposed to more stimuli about politics than, respectively, working-class persons, women, and country dwellers. Children growing up in a politically involved home are more likely to maintain a high level of exposure to stimuli about politics when they become adults.

2. *Personal factors.* Those psychologically involved in politics are more likely to feel effective in political action. Persons of higher income and social status are more likely to become highly involved psychologically in politics than persons of lower status.

[17]The leading work on participation in the United States is Sidney Verba and Norman H. Nie, *Participation in America: Political Democracy and Social Equality* (Harper & Row, 1972); see also a major review of this work, Jerrold G. Rusk, "Political Participation in America: A Review Essay," *American Political Science Review* (June 1976), pp. 583−91, and sources cited therein.

9−2
Approximate
percentage of
American citizens
participating in
various forms of
political activity

Holding public and party office ⎤	**Less**
Being a candidate for office ⎬	**than**
Soliciting political funds ⎦	**1**
Attending a caucus or a strategy meeting ⎤	
Becoming an active member of a political party ⎦	**4−5**
Contributing time in a political campaign	
Attending a political meeting or rally	
Making a monetary contribution to a party or candidate	**10**
Contacting a public official or a political leader	**13**
Wearing a button or putting a sticker on the car	**15**
Attempting to talk another into voting a certain way	**25−30**
Initiating a political discussion ⎤	
Voting ⎬	
Exposing oneself to political stimuli ⎦	**40−70**

SOURCE: Charles E. Lindblom, *The Policy-Making Process* (Prentice-Hall, 1968), p. 45.

3. *Political setting.* Persons contacted by party workers are more likely to participate in political activity. The relation works the other way too: those who are more
interested in politics are more likely to know party workers. Again, there is an *effectiveness* factor. Those who see themselves or their group as having an impact on
public policy are more likely to inform public officials of their views than are those
who feel ineffective.

4. *Class status.* A major conclusion of a recent intensive study of participation is
that "class" relates strongly to participation rates: "Indeed—and we think these data
are quite surprising—social status has a closer relationship to political participation in the United States" than in eight other leading democracies. This is true of political participation in its many different forms; voting alone, according to this study,
tends to be less class oriented.[18]

In general, those who feel nearer the center of society are more likely to
participate in politics than those who feel near the periphery. Union members are more likely to participate in some form than nonunion workers.
Those who feel most insecure, vulnerable, and fearful of some kind of retali-
ation are the least likely to be politically involved or even to vote.[19] Many of
these generalizations are obvious or a matter of common sense. And they
do not necessarily explain the deeper causes of interest or lack of interest
in political activity. But these correlations and interrelationships do help
us understand how to get to the deeper causes. Paralleling as they do our
earlier generalizations about voting and nonvoting, they indicate the complex factors affecting participation and so help us to avoid stereotypes.

Noting the *range* of activity—from completely uninvolved persons to
heavily "politicized" persons—helps also to deal with a central issue between those who say elites run everything and those who argue that our
political system is reasonably democratic and open. Some believe that
American society is divided between an elite or a few elites, who dominate political activity, and the "masses," who are virtually detached from
the political process. In fact, Americans are active in a multitude of ways
and in many different degrees. A minority are completely apathetic or inactive, just as a minority are completely involved; in between is the great
number of Americans who are involved in various ways, becoming more
or less active as elections come and go. It may be that not enough Americans are sufficiently interested, but this is quite a different argument from
the claim that the opinions of the great mass of Americans simply don't
matter.

From stability to change?

Our review of political behavior has shown large areas of both stability
and change. The pattern of participation has remained essentially the
same over the years. Influences on voting, such as region, religion, and
class, change only slowly. The relationship among turnouts for elections
for different offices remains fairly stable over the years. But change—especially in recent decades—is also apparent. Support for the two major
parties has been ebbing. Independent voters have been on the increase.
Most important, the capacity of Americans to vote "rationally"—to vote on
the basis of knowledge, group interest, and self-protection—apparently

[18]Verba and Nie, *Participation in America*, pp. 339–40.

[19]Lester M. Salamon and Stephen Van Evera, "Fear, Apathy, and Discrimination: A Test of
Three Explanations of Political Participation," *American Political Science Review* (December
1973), pp. 1288–1306.

has been rising. We will conclude this chapter by looking at this last question of voter rationality in more detail.

ARE VOTERS FOOLS?

This might seem to be a foolish question in itself. But it was a question that emerged from the first broad, in-depth investigations of American voters a quarter of a century ago. The questions actually were several: Is the great mass of American voters like sheep, led by propagandists and other manipulators? Are they so affected by a candidate's face or television style that they forget their "real" interests and vote for the most engaging personality? Are they so bored by politics or otherwise withdrawn from it that they leave the crucial decision-making to the few who *are* interested in politics—even just to the elites? Are they so "locked into" their family, school, party, group, and other "cells" of their social background that they cannot view parties, candidates, and issues realistically and self-protectively?

In posing this question of *voting rationality*, note the questions that are *not* at issue. A number of Americans—too large a number—*are* passive, withdrawn, ignorant, emotional, locked in, manipulated. The question is whether *most* Americans are, and to what degree, and whether this degree affects the distribution of power in a government by the people. We cannot evaluate the voting behavior of Americans in terms of some utopian

Scenes from the 1976 Democratic Convention in New York City.

model of angelic citizenry—or even a citizenry that agrees with us. For the great advantage of the democratic process is that it does not require a nation of angels for successful operation. All we can ask, probably, is whether most Americans bring to politics a fair degree of knowledge of issues and candidates, an ability to make choices between alternatives at the polls, a capacity to learn whether the leadership they supported actually performed as they wished—in short, an ability to figure out their own interests in relation to politics.

Doubt about the capacity of Americans to govern themselves rationally was intensified as a result of voting studies conducted in the 1950s, a period of increasing sophistication and broadening activity in the field of voting and public opinion research. People seemed to know little about candidates, especially candidates for Congress. Less than half knew which party controlled Congress. Above all, voters were ill-informed on the issues. They did not know where the candidates stood, and often they did not know where they themselves stood because they were foggy about the nature of the issue, where the parties stood on the issue, and how the issue related to them personally. When people bothered to vote at all, they were more influenced by candidate images or by their traditional party affiliation than by the positions candidates or parties took on the issue. Truly the voters seemed locked-in to their parties, groups, occupations, religion.[20]

RATIONAL POLITICAL MAN?

More recent studies have modified this portrait of the American voter. In the mid-1960s V. O. Key, Jr., perhaps the leading political scientist of his day, began to go through public opinion and voting data with these questions in mind. He did not pretend to come to definitive findings; indeed, he died before finishing the book. But Key did conclude that the picture of an ignorant, apathetic, manipulated, and locked-in electorate had been greatly exaggerated. He looked especially at standpatters—those who clung to the same party year after year—and at switchers. Both types of voters had been often viewed as *irrational*—the former because they stuck to the same old party or candidate no matter how much conditions might have changed, and the latter because they seemed to move unthinkingly back and forth between parties and candidates.

Key found that standpatters often stood pat for a very good reason. They understood the policies of a particular party, felt that those policies favored their own interest, and stuck with their proven friends in office. Nor were most switchers irrational. They were people of more than average education, information, and interest. Election outcomes were also influenced by a third factor—the entrance or reentrance of millions of new voters into the political arena—but new voters too showed a capacity to deal with candidates in relation to issues that had meaning for them.[21]

The most recent research tends to support Key's view. Analysis of voting studies, mainly in the 1960s, indicated a significant shift in the voters' ability to comprehend issues and the stands of the major parties on these issues. Thus, voters seemed to be becoming increasingly aware that the

[20]See generally Angus Campbell et al., *The American Voter* (Wiley, 1960).

[21]V. O. Key, Jr., *The Responsible Electorate* (Harvard University Press, 1966); see also Michael J. Shapiro, "Rational Political Man: A Synthesis of Economic and Social-Psychological Perspectives," *American Political Science Review* (December 1969), pp. 1106–19.

Democratic party was more favorable, and the Republican less favorable, to federal government activism. Why the change? The answer did not seem to lie in educational or other social or economic developments, according to one study. The change was more likely to be caused by the coming of several presidential campaigns—especially 1964 and presumably 1972 as well—in which the candidates and parties seemed to offer a real and compelling choice to the voters.[22]

How lasting will this change be? Another study indicated that the importance of issues varies from election to election. Issues were highly related to voting decisions in 1968 because people were aroused about Vietnam, law and order, urban problems, Johnson's personality, and his performance as president. The importance of issues also varied with the nature of the issues themselves. Some issues like inflation are close to the voters. They perceive the relation between the issues, the positions of candidates and parties, and what government finally does. On other issues that interrelation seems very hazy.[23] Finally, different types of political participation may stimulate different degrees of rationality. A person might be somewhat irrational in voting but fairly intelligent and effective in, say, contacting his congressman about a personal need or helping some candidate in the campaign.[24]

THE 1970s: ACCELERATING CHANGE

The most recent voting studies paint a picture of millions of voters undergoing accelerating political change. Investigators are struck by the shifts during the last twenty years, and especially by those in the 1970s.[25]

Let us look a generation back. In the 1950s the voters as a whole strongly supported the two major parties. But they were only moderately interested in politics; they had only a hazy grasp of policy issues; and they pretty much accepted the political system as it was. For people as a whole, politics was not central to their day-to-day concerns. Most people did little more than vote, if that. Especially significant—because of its significance for party unity and party platforms—was voters' small sense of the *interrelation* of different public policy issues. They often seemed to see little logical relationship among various domestic policies, or between domestic and foreign policies. One of the authors remembers talking to a small restaurant owner who grumbled about bureaucracy. He said he would like to go to the state capital and "shoot all the bureaucrats." He then was asked, "What would you like *from* government?" "Socialized medicine," he promptly replied, as though that program would not mean a large increase in the very bureaucracy he deplored.

Twenty years seem to have brought basic changes on these scores. Party support has dropped sharply. Trust in our political system after Watergate

[22]Gerald M. Pomper, "From Confusion to Clarity: Issues and American Voters, 1956–1968," *American Political Science Review* (June 1972), pp. 415–28. See also Gerald Pomper and colleagues, *The Election of 1976* (David McKay, 1977), Chaps. 2, 3.

[23]Richard W. Boyd, "Popular Control of Public Policy: A Normal Vote Analysis of the 1968 Election," *American Political Science Review* (June 1972), pp. 429–49. See also comments on the Pomper and Boyd articles by Richard A. Brody and Benjamin I. Page, and by John H. Kessel, and rejoinders by the two authors., *ibid.*, pp. 450–70.

[24]Verba and Nie, *Participation in America*, chap. 7.

[25]The comparison of the 1950s and 1970s is drawn largely from Nie, Verba, and Petrocik, *The Changing American Voter*, and from Miller and Levitin, *Leadership and Change*.

and other scandals has declined. But the average American has become much more politically aware. Americans have a better grasp than before of the nature of the issues facing government. They have a better sense of the *interrelationship* of issues; that is, persons who hold conservative views on certain issues are likely to hold similar views on others. People are able to *conceptualize* better and to think in more logical and comprehensive terms. They relate parties and candidates more closely to issues. This does not mean that the United States has suddenly become a nation of philosophers. But politically the voters are "putting two and two together" more than they used to.

Why the change? In part because of the dramatic and momentous events of the intervening decade, the 1960s: race conflict, urban disorder, Vietnam, student tumult. In part because leaders arose who embodied new ideas, hopes, and conflicts: John Kennedy, Barry Goldwater, Eugene McCarthy, Martin Luther King, Robert Kennedy. These events not only had profound impact on public attitudes, as Nie, Verba, and Petrocik have noted, but "are issues that cut across the old alliance pattern of American politics."[26] Leaders are great issue clarifiers and issue dramatizers, so in the continuing interplay of issues, events, party affiliation, and leadership, it is leadership that has the decisive role. The ability to dramatize new issues by political leaders, according to Miller and Levitin, "is the major new component in American politics that distinguishes the politics of the 1970s from the politics of the 1950s."[27] Striking issue leadership has continued in the 1970s, as exemplified by George McGovern, Ronald Reagan, John B. Connally, Edward Kennedy, and perhaps Jimmy Carter.

The outcome today, in the late 1970s, is what Miller and Levitin have called the New Politics. The most visible participants in the New Politics are the New Liberals, who support its liberal thrust, and the Silent Minority, who oppose it. These two groups are almost polar opposites on key issues. They have a polarizing influence on people's attitudes and on national politics. By the early 1970s the New Liberals—those who took a liberal position (a pro-attitude) on abortion, gun control, civil liberties, women's rights—were the dominant group in the electorate. The Silent Minority, who take opposite stands on such issues, are smaller in numbers but strong in the intensity of their views and political activism. Democrat George McGovern led the New Liberals in 1972 but was unable to muster enough supporters at the polls. Republican Ronald Reagan aroused such phenomenal support from the Silent Minority that he almost succeeded in bringing off the feat—unprecedented in this century—of defeating the incumbent president, Gerald Ford, in the nomination race in 1976.

Young voters have had a major role in these critical changes. There had been much loose talk about the millions of young voters "taking over American politics" after the eighteen- and twenty-year-olds won the right to vote. In fact, the proportion of young persons voting continues to be relatively low. And they have shown little interest in supporting either of the two parties. But they have influenced the *quality* and *direction* of American politics. They are somewhat more changeable than other voters, and hence they are "up for grabs" by candidates. And many of them are deeply engaged in the New Politics.

"I'll tell you what's wrong with the country! The women are polarized, the kids are polarized, the minorities are polarized, the hardhats are polarized and nobody knows what polarized means!"

Drawing by Sanzo. © 1976 by the *Saturday Review*

[26]Nie, Verba, and Petrocik, *The Changing American Voter*, p. 1.

[27]Miller and Levitin, *Leadership and Change*, p. 7.

Summary

1. Voting is the most important and most measurable element of political behavior.

2. Persons with little money or property, women, blacks, and young people have each entered the voting arena in turn.

3. Higher-income, better-educated, older, and more group- or party-involved persons are more likely to vote than are their opposites.

4. Voting tends to be higher for national elections than for state and local ones, and higher for executive elections than for legislative.

5. How Americans vote is influenced by national, regional, party, interest-group, ethnic, and class (income-level) factors, as well as by key events and leaders.

6. Some Americans are completely involved in politics; some are completely apathetic; others may listen to a campaign talk, wear a candidate's button, or give money to a campaigner.

7. Stable party membership has given way in recent years to declining party support, better grasp of the issues, a polarization of the electorate between new liberals and new conservatives, and less faith in the American political system.

8. Obviously our knowledge of these complex matters is still limited. Political scientists and other scholars stand on a research frontier. We must know much more than we do about the workings of the average voter's "political mind" and we must test our findings on a large scale. Even more important—for political scientists, at least—we must see how the voters' thinking is influenced by political phenomena and institutions—by parties, registration laws, the media, the nature of the opposition to the existing government, and the issues facing the people.

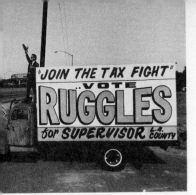

Chapter 10

The Declining Parties: Do We Care?

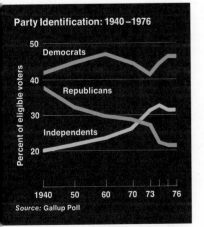

Party Identification: 1940–1976

Percent of eligible voters

Democrats

Republicans

Independents

1940 50 60 70 73 76

Source: Gallup Poll

Our two main political parties seem to be in trouble. For twenty years or so they have been declining in popular support and organizational strength. "Strong" Republicans and "strong" Democrats have dropped by about a third in each party in the past quarter century. The number of independents has grown rapidly during the same period. Party organization is feeble in most states. Where the party is strong locally, it is often ruled by a small group of "old timers." Americans have been losing faith in parties as they have in most other institutions.[1]

The fight for the presidency in 1976 dramatized the weakness of the parties. Jimmy Carter had had few connections with the national Democratic party; yet he easily seized the nomination from the regulars. Ronald Reagan took on a sitting president, long a leader in the GOP, [Republican Party] and almost beat him in the primaries and convention.

Few Americans would shed many tears for our parties. Critics charge that the parties evade the issues; that they fail to deliver on their promises; have no new ideas; follow public opinion rather than lead it. They are also sources of corruption and misgovernment. Other Americans favor our party system and take part in it. Most Americans have mixed feelings about the parties. They believe that parties are necessary in a democracy, but they refuse to give money to a party or be active in one. They believe in party conflict—but not too much conflict. They believe in voting for individual candidates regardless of party label, but they want party labels on the ballot.[2]

[1] On popular attitudes toward our parties, see Jack Dennis, "Trends in Public Support for the American Party System," *British Journal of Political Science* (April 1975), pp. 187–230.

[2] These mixed attitudes toward parties are summarized in Austin Ranney, *Curing the Mischiefs of Faction* (University of California Press, 1975), pp. 53–56.

Watergate revealed both the weakness of parties and the mixed attitudes toward them. The president is expected to be the leader of his party. In 1972, however, President Nixon largely bypassed the Republican party and depended on his personal organization, the Committee for the Reelection of the President—the famous CREEP. Much of Watergate grew out of the excesses of CREEP—its illegal actions, its secrecy, its financing, and its personal loyalty to Mr. Nixon. Some Republicans point out that recent Democratic presidents have also often favored their personal organization over the needs of the Democratic party.

So our political parties are in crisis. Does it matter? What are the functions of parties? How well do they perform them? Are parties relevant to a "government by the people"? Why not let them die?

Parties: their rise and their role

Our two major parties are so big that they remind us of the blind men and the elephant: Each man felt a different part of the elephant and pictured the whole animal in a different way. By parties we do *not* mean two solid organizations confronting each other in a kind of continuous town meeting. We define party as (1) a structure of national, state, and local organizations; (2) inner circles of leaders holding or seeking public office; (3) networks of leaders (sometimes called "bosses") who tend the organizational machinery around the clock, around the year; (4) party activists (usually called "party regulars") who give money, time, and enthusiasm to the party's candidates; and (5) voters who identify with the party, almost always support its candidates, and break away from the party only as a result of major events, such as depression, an unpopular war, or a scandal like Watergate.

THE RISE OF THE GRAND COALITIONS

One way to look at parties is historically. We can see them as a series of grand coalitions of groups and leaders and interests that slowly shift allegiance over time. First was the Federalist grouping under Washington and Hamilton. This group was dominated by bankers, traders, big landowners, and small manufacturers. A narrow coalition, it was challenged by the first Republican party, under the leadership of Jefferson and Madison, and later Jackson. (The present Republican party is a different organization.) The Republicans included farmers, laborers, and slaveowners who had their base in the southern and central states. This coalition was dominant in American politics for two generations, as the Republicans were slowly transformed into the Democratic party.

Another party, the Whigs, rose to challenge the Democratic party. But the Democrats, using their Jeffersonian symbols and holding on to their coalition, were able to overcome the Whig opposition in most elections. Neither party, however, was able to deal effectively with the explosive issue of slavery. Out of the Civil War came a new major party, the second Republican party. As the "party of the Union," the Republicans won the support not only of financiers, industrialists, and merchants, but also of large numbers of workers, farmers, and newly freed blacks. For fifty years after 1860, this Republican coalition was to win every presidential race, except for Grover Cleveland's victories in 1884 and 1892.

The Democratic party survived with its durable base in the South. For all their noisy battles during the century, both parties remained true to the rule that under a two-party system neither side can afford to be extremist. Both parties contained liberal and conservative elements and both appealed for support from all major interests, including business and labor.

President Dwight Eisenhower is presented with key to the city of Denison, Texas. During the 1950s, Eisenhower's popularity helped to build a strong coalition of voters for the Republican party.

Would the Republicans rule forever? The Democrats were unable to build a durable winning coalition against the "Grand Old Party" until the early 1930s, when the Hoover administration was overwhelmed by the Great Depression. Franklin Roosevelt strengthened the farm-labor-southern alliance that Woodrow Wilson had begun to build. He also put together a "grand coalition" of these groups plus unemployed middle-class persons, and national and racial minorities. This coalition reelected Roosevelt three times and brought presidential victories to the Democrats (except when Eisenhower ran) for two decades after Roosevelt died.

Still, the "Roosevelt coalition" was vulnerable to Dwight Eisenhower's personal popularity and to Richard Nixon's own coalition-building. In 1968 Nixon brought together a coalition of middle-class voters, "hardhat" workers, southern conservatives, suburbanites, and business elements. Neither Hubert Humphrey in 1968 nor George McGovern in 1972 was able to overcome the Nixon organization, though the Democrats retained large majorities in Congress. In 1976 Jimmy Carter brought together just enough of the "old coalition" of union members, blacks, party regulars and New Liberals to produce a razor-thin majority at the polls.[3] Whether he could convert that *electoral* coalition into a *governing* coalition was still an open question half way through his term.

NEW WINE IN OLD BOTTLES?

Both major parties are middle-aged: The Republicans have celebrated their centennial and the Democrats will soon mark their bicentennial. (They contend that the Democratic party grew directly out of the first Republican party, which was born when Thomas Jefferson departed from Washington's administration). The longevity of the two parties is remarkable, considering the depressions, wars, social changes, and political crises they have survived. But if the names and the symbols have stayed the same, what they represent has changed markedly. There have been extensive shifts in the policy positions of the major parties and in their social bases and electoral support.

Most party programs and policies have been moderate ones. Successful party leaders must be group diplomats; they must find a middle ground among more or less hostile groups so that agreement can be reached on general principles. Moreover, each party assumes that voters are distributed across an ideological spectrum from Left to Right. It takes its extremist supporters more or less for granted and seeks out the voters in the middle. This is one reason college students on the far Left or far Right are impatient with the major political parties. Both parties seem to such students to operate in the center—and in fact they do.

NO PLACE FOR THIRD PARTIES?

Another pattern in American party politics has been the absence of strong third parties. To be sure, third parties have had a place. They have drawn attention to controversial issues that the major parties wished to evade. They have organized special interest or "cause" groups such as antislavery, prohibitionists, and southerners opposing the national thrust toward integration. But they have never beaten both major parties in a presidential election, and they have never shaped national policy from inside the government.

[3]Warren E. Miller and Teresa E. Levitin, *Leadership and Change*, 2nd ed. (Winthrop, 1977), Chap. 7, "The Election of 1976." See also Gerald M. Pomper et al., *The Election of 1976* (McKay, 1977).

Third parties have taken two different forms. One type has been the *doctrinal* party, such as the small labor and socialist parties on the Left and the even smaller conservative movements on the Right. Most of these parties, such as the American Socialist party, have lived on for decades publicizing their ideas but not expecting to win elections. The other type is the third party that arises over a particular issue and then dies as the issue is resolved or fades away. Several such third parties, such as the Free Soilers, rose and fell before the Civil War. The Progressive parties of Theodore Roosevelt in 1912 and of Robert La Follette in 1924 challenged the political power of big business. Most recently George Wallace's American Independent Party won about 13 million votes in 1968 over desegregation and other race issues. But the AIP was evidently fading even before Wallace was badly wounded in an assassination attempt in May 1972.[4]

Why this pattern of failure? Why do we stick to a two-party system when most democracies have multiparty systems? In part, because the American people, despite their many divisions over religion, race, and the like, have been united enough that the two big parties could adequately represent them. In part it is also because of the nature of our election system. Most of our election districts have a single incumbent, and the candidate with the most votes wins. Because only one candidate can win, the largest and second-largest parties have a near-monopoly of office. The system of electing the president operates in this way on a national scale. The presidency is the supreme prize in American politics: a party that cannot attain it, or show promise of attaining it, simply does not operate in the political "major leagues."

Party tasks: the heavy burden

Our major parties are expected to take on many heavy tasks—so many tasks that the parties might be excused for not carrying all of them out very well. Historically, one of the key functions of our two-party system has been to unify the electorate and bring together groups, sections, and ideologies. The parties failed to bring the sections together in 1860 and broke up under the pressure of the North-South rupture. For over a century since that great break, however, the parties have managed to please various power groups—South and North, labor and capital, producer and consumer—and thus to continue in operation.

The functions of the parties have also changed over time. Party activity used to be an important source of public welfare. To win votes, local party organizations gave the needy jobs, loans, free coal, picnics, and recreation; they helped those in trouble over pensions, taxes, and licenses. The boss of the Republican machine in Philadelphia bragged that his organization was "one of the greatest welfare organizations in the United States . . . without red tape, without class, religion, or color distinction." The takeover of welfare by the government during the New Deal drained this function away from most city organizations, but not entirely. In Kansas City, for example, Boss Pendergast got control of New Deal agency patronage and greatly increased his power.[5] Today this kind of takeover has become less likely, for the Supreme Court has ruled that to dismiss public employees for partisan political reasons is unconstitutional.

The late Mayor Daley of Chicago, shown here at the 1976 Democratic Convention, was often a powerful voice in his party.

[4]Daniel A. Mazmanian, *Third Parties in Presidential Elections* (Brookings, 1974), pp. 5ff; see also Murray S. Stedman and Susan W. Stedman, *Discontent at the Polls* (Columbia University Press, 1950), for a comprehensive treatment.

[5]Lyle W. Dorsett, *The Pendergast Machine* (Oxford University Press, 1968).

PARTY FUNCTIONS TODAY

To gain votes, parties simplify the people's choices. Usually they present the voters with two relatively different alternatives. Hence they allow voters to choose between a few options instead of a bewildering variety of them. But some people argue that parties confuse rather than simplify alternatives—again for vote-getting purposes.[6] On a popular issue, the parties may try to appeal to such a wide electorate that there seems to be no difference between them. Parties also help to stimulate interest in public affairs. An election contest is exciting. It makes politics look like a big prize-fight, or world series, and draws millions of people into controversy. And after a polite interval following the election, the opposition party begins to criticize the party in power. But the opposition often fails to perform this role very effectively. It tends to break up into opposing factions that take potshots at the government from all directions, or to mute its

[6]See Donald E. Stokes, "Spatial Models of Party Competition," in Angus Campbell et al., *Elections and the Political Order* (Wiley, 1966), especially pp. 170–71.

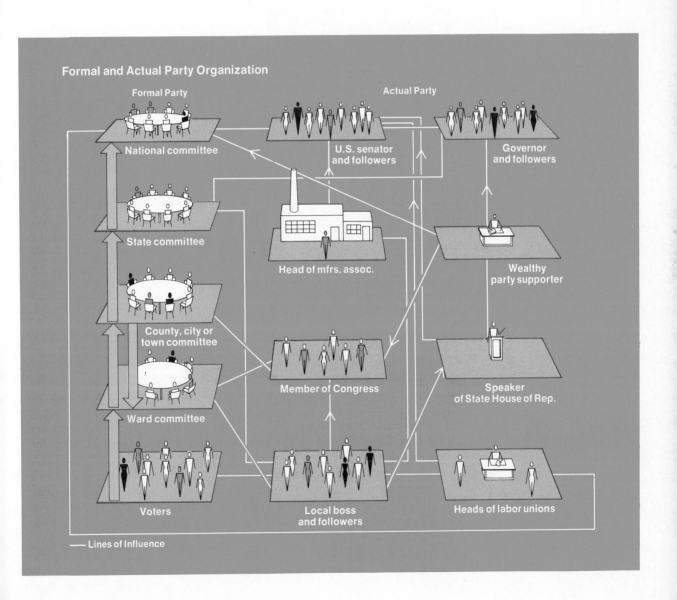

Formal and Actual Party Organization

criticism on the grounds that some issues—foreign policy, religion, education and so on—should be "above" politics.

Parties recruit political leaders. In the past, they were important channels of upward mobility for integrating those "on the outside" into American public life. Irish-Americans and Italian-Americans are good examples. Some blacks rose to leadership positions in the Republican party during the last century; in this century numerous blacks have found the Democratic party a "ladder of opportunity."

Parties, under most conditions, are key instruments for uniting persons of differing races, religions, and classes. Parties have a vested interest in playing down conflicts. Despite the fact that most Americans are white Protestants, party leaders and candidates for public office seek to please Catholics, blacks, and Jews, if only because they represent a large number of votes. Of course, parties at times are divisive, as when Democrats play up issues that divide the country, such as civil rights or social welfare, in order to win support. Just when parties should unite people and when they should divide them is a major tactical, strategic, and moral question for party leaders.

Parties can serve as the link between the wishes of the people and what government finally does. By choosing candidates in an open and democratic way, parties help legitimize our elected policy makers. They help organize the machinery of government and influence the men and women they have helped put into office. The president serves as party leader; Congress is organized on party lines; even bureaucrats are supposed to respond to new party leadership. Thus, parties partly bridge the separation of powers and prevent the constitutional checks and balances from fragmenting government. But the parties have only limited success in this role.

Of all these functions, the average citizen probably feels that confronting, posing, and clarifying issues is among the most important. Many citizens have been skeptical of the ability of parties to state issues clearly and offer concrete alternatives. Scholarly studies of voting during the "bland" Eisenhower era have added to this skepticism. More recently, however, researchers have found a marked increase in the relation between party identification and opinion on a number of major issues such as social welfare and foreign aid.[7] "Contrary to what has been found in the past," one study concludes, "there is indeed considerable party-relatedness of vote based on specific issues."[8]

CHOOSING CANDIDATES

Certainly the function that takes most of the party's energy is the recruiting and selecting of candidates for office. From the very beginning, parties have been the mechanism by which candidates for public office are selected. The earliest method was the caucus, a closed meeting of party leaders. It was the method used in Massachusetts only a few years after the *Mayflower* landed, and it played an important part in pre-Revolutionary politics. After the Union was established, for several decades party groups in the national and state legislatures served as the caucus. The legislators in

[7]Gerald M. Pomper, "From Confusion to Clarity: Issues and American Voters, 1956–1968," *American Political Science Review* (June 1972), pp. 415–28.

[8]David E. RePass, "Issue Salience and Party Choice," *American Political Science Review* (June 1971), p. 400.

each party simply met separately to nominate candidates. Our first presidential candidates were chosen by senators and representatives meeting as party delegates.

But the legislative caucus brought to mind secret deals and smoke-filled rooms. Moreover, it could not be representative of the people in areas where a party was in a minority, because only officeholders were members. There were efforts to make the caucus more representative: for example, the mixed caucus brought in delegates from districts where the party had no elected legislators. Gradually during the 1830s and 1840s, however, a system of party conventions took its place. The conventions were made up of delegates, usually chosen directly by party members in towns and cities, and served several purposes. They chose the party standardbearers. They debated and adopted a platform. And they provided a chance to whip up party spirit and perhaps to celebrate a bit. But the convention method in turn came under criticism. It was charged that the convention was subject to control by the party bosses and their machines. At times, delegates were freely bought and sold, instructions from rank-and-file party members were ignored, and meetings got completely out of control.

To make party selections fairer and more democratic, and to cut down the power of party "bosses," the direct primary was used by Wisconsin on a statewide basis in 1903. It was adopted by state after state during the next fifteen years. This system gives every member of a party the right to vote on candidates in a primary election. The state supplies the ballots and supervises the election, which takes place some time before the general election in November. The direct primary was hailed by some as a major cure for party corruption. But it did not cure all the evils, and it led to some new ones. The rise of primaries has been an important development in American politics; we will return to this subject in the next chapter.

Today the primary is the main method of picking party candidates, but the nominating convention is available in one form or another in a few of the states. The convention has also been retained nationally for picking presidential candidates. In either case, the party carries the main burden, although many of its electoral activities are closely regulated by law. In the general election, too, the party has a role. It campaigns for its candidates, mobilizes its machinery in their behalf, and helps finance them. On election day, it produces cars, advice to voters, and workers at the polls to watch the counting of the ballots.

The clanking party machinery

If you look at an organization chart of the Democratic or Republican parties, everything seems neat and tidy. At the top is the presidential convention, which meets every four years and sets policy for the party. Below it is the national committee, and then the pyramid widens out to state committees, hundreds of county and city committees, and thousands of ward, town, and precinct committees. But the organization chart is deceptive. In fact, the national organizations have limited power over the state and local ones; power typically flows up rather than down. Our parties have been essentially loose coalitions of state and local committees, with little national machinery, cohesion, or discipline.

Why have our parties been so decentralized? The main reason is the *federal* basis of our government. The Constitution has shaped our political system, just as the political system shaped governmental structure. Parties are a prime example of this circular relation. They tend to be structured around elections and officeholders. Because our federal system sets up elections and offices on a national-state-local basis, our parties are organized on a similar basis. Thus, the Constitution has given us federalism in our parties as well as in our government.

In both major parties the supreme authority is the national presidental convention. The convention meets every four years to nominate candidates for president and vice-president, to ratify the party platform, and to elect officers and adopt rules. But the convention in fact has limited power. The delegates have only three or four days to accomplish their business, and many key decisions have been made ahead of time. The convention is usually dominated by officeholders and seekers rather than by the mass of rank-and-file delegates.

More directly in charge of the national party—at least on paper—is the national committee. In the past, the national committee was "impotent and invisible." The committee gave large states only a little more representation than small ones. Committee members were usually influential in their states but had little national standing, and the committees rarely met. The Republicans recently made their national committee more representative. The Democrats, largely as a result of the reform spirit of 1968, enlarged their national committee to make it more responsive to areas that tended to be more populous and more Democratic. More representative committees, however, will not necessarily bring stronger leadership.

The main job of the national party committee chairperson is to manage the presidential campaign. Although this top officer is elected by the national committee, actually he or she is chosen by the party's presidential candidate at the close of the convention. Once that candidate enters the White House, the power of the chairperson dwindles. He or she is often described as a mere errand-runner and party liaison person for the White House. Usually the national chairperson serves at the pleasure of the president. A *defeated* presidential candidate, on the other hand, may have little control over the national chairperson, or the national committee may elect a new head who responds to the balance of forces within the committee. The basic tasks have been well summarized as image-maker, fund raiser, campaign manager, administrator, and hell-raiser.[9]

It is the national chairperson, backed by the president, who gives the party a little measure of unity and direction when it is in power. When the party loses a presidential race, it often has no real central leadership. The defeated nominee is the titular leader, but he usually has little power over the organization. He has no jobs or other rewards to hand out. As a result, the party out of power in the White House has no one who can really compete with congressional leaders in calling signals for their party.

Who should speak for the "loyal opposition"—the party's leaders in the House and Senate, or the national chairpersons? There is no agreement about this within either party. Congressional leaders have never been willing to take a back seat to the party chairperson. At times, party leaders have tried to assert themselves. William Brock was one of the more ag-

Democratic National Party Committee Chairperson Kenneth Curtis, left, appears with former Chairperson Robert Strauss (top). Republican National Party Committee Chairperson William Brock, left, confers with the Committee's General Counsel William C. Cramer (bottom).

[9]Cornelius P. Cotter and Bernard C. Hennessy, *Politics Without Power: The National Party Committees* (Atherton Press, 1964), p. 67.

gressive leaders of the Republican party when he took charge during Carter's first term. But other Republican leaders on Capitol Hill, such as Howard Baker, also competed for the limelight.

Even when the party heads are given some room to manuever by their own party followers, they are no match for the president. Nixon, through his ready access to television and other media, dominated the air waves no matter how hard Democratic party chairman Lawrence O'Brien tried to speak out for his party. O'Brien was granted a half-hour of prime time on ABC, and CBS offered him time for a four-part series. CBS took such a beating from a variety of sources, including the White House, that the second segment was postponed until *after* the November 1970 congressional elections. Appeals to the Federal Communications Commission, which was headed by a Nixon appointee, proved fruitless.[10] During the Carter administration Republican party chiefs face a similar problem of access to the media in order to carry on a strong opposition campaign.

The congressional and senatorial campaign committees aid members of Congress in their reelection campaigns. Today, both the Republican and Democratic senatorial campaign committees are composed of senators chosen for two-year terms by party members in the Senate. The two House of Representatives' campaign committees are chosen in the same way. After candidates have been nominated, the committees send them money, provide speakers, and supply campaign material. During presidential election years, the activities of the national committee tend to overshadow the work of the congressional and senatorial campaign committees. But during off-year elections, these committees often provide the only nationally directed campaign.

Both a cause and a result of party disorganization is the manner in which candidates are *nominated*. Ordinarily, politicians seeking nomination run on their own; the party remains, outwardly at least, neutral. Lacking organized party support, each candidate builds a personal organization. Thus, because many candidates are usually running for a dozen or more offices, from governor to local jobs, the party becomes a confused arena. Candidates campaign on their own, raising their own money and putting out their own publicity. Primary campaigns often develop sharp rivalries between Democrats or between Republicans. These rivalries may carry over into the general election, even though the party should be unified in order to put up a strong fight. When a heated primary contest does take place, it may seem democratic. But it can also be damaging to party unity.[11]

PARTIES AT THE GRASS ROOTS

At the next lower level in the hierarchy are the state committees, which are like the national committees but are filled by members chosen locally in counties or other areas. Most state committees are not powerful. They are often dominated by the governor, a senator, or a coalition of strong local leaders, just as the president dominates his party's national committee. The state chairperson is sometimes chosen by the governor or senator; occasionally, however, he or she is really the party's boss on the state level and is able to influence the nomination of governors, senators, and other

[10]For O'Brien's version of these events, see Lawrence F. O'Brien, *No Final Victories* (Doubleday, 1974), esp. pp. 276–80.

[11]Robert A. Bernstein, "Divisive Primaries Do Hurt," *American Political Science Review* (June 1977), pp. 540–45.

key officials. Many state parties are as undisciplined and decentralized as the national party.

Below the state committees, each party hierarchy broadens out into district and county committees. These too vary tremendously in functions and power. Some county chairmen (they are almost all men) are powerful bosses, as the late Mayor Richard J. Daley was in Cook County.[12] Many county chairmen make up the party slates for offices such as county commissioner, sheriff, and treasurer. Some, however, are just figureheads.

It is at the base of the party pyramid—at the city, town, ward, and precinct level—that we find the grass roots of the party in all their richness and variety. In a few places, party politics is a round-the-clock, round-the-year occupation. The local ward and precinct leaders do countless favors for constituents, from fixing parking tickets to organizing clambakes. But such strong local organization is rare. Most local committees are small, poorly financed, and inactive except during the few weeks before election day. Party activities are amateurish.[13]

Our party systems are very complex. For example, a state party organization may include a state committee, congressional district committees, county committees, state senatorial district committees, state judicial district committees, and precinct committees. Why such complexity? Partly because contemporary politics tends to be individualistic and personalized; it would be more nearly correct to say that we have *candidate* or *officeholder* politics rather than party politics. Also, our constitutional arrangements provide for many officeholders at many levels of government. And the diversity of our country and the absence of strong national direction and control mean that party systems vary a good deal from state to state.

This situation opens a great gulf between national party headquarters and state and local parties. Deepening this gulf is the fact that elections—the main activity of parties—are actually regulated and run by the *states*, not by the national government. Some states hold their state and local elections in different years from national elections (mostly in an effort to insulate state politics from national). New York State, for example, elects its governors for four-year terms in even-numbered years between presidential elections, and New York City elects its mayors every four years in odd-numbered years.

Are the parties worth saving?

Clearly there is a big gap between what American parties *might* do and what they *actually* do. Ideally, parties build a bridge between the people and their government. They strengthen national unity by bringing conflicting groups together. They soften the impact of extremists at both ends of the political spectrum. They stimulate and channel public discussion. They find candidates for the voters and voters for the candidates. They help run elections. They both stimulate and moderate conflict. In short, parties do much of the hard, day-to-day work of democracy. But in fact parties do not perform these tasks very well.

People Who Join a Political Party

Leaders

Strongly Partisan

Mildly Partisan

Independents
(those who vote for a party in one election, but have little loyalty to that party)

[12]For a fascinating account of Daley's chairmanship in Cook County, Illinois, see Milton Rakove, *Don't Make No Waves, Don't Back No Losers* (Indiana University Press, 1975).

[13]Local party effort is hard to measure, but it probably has significant influence; see Phillips Cutright, "Measuring the Impact of Local Party Activity on the General Election Vote," *Public Opinion Quarterly* (Fall 1963), pp. 372–86; Raymond E. Wolfinger, "The Influence of Precinct Work on Voting Behavior," *ibid.*, pp. 387–98; William J. Crotty, "Party Effort and Its Impact on the Vote," *American Political Science Review* (June 1971), pp. 439–50.

There are two main charges against the American party system: (1) The parties do not take meaningful and contrasting positions on issues, especially the issues of the 1970s. (2) Organizationally, they are in such a mess that they could not achieve their goals even if they wanted to. Hence parties are not vehicles for popular expression and social progress. How valid are these charges?

TWEEDLEDUM AND TWEEDLEDEE?

The typical party platform, it is said, seems designed to pick up every stray vote rather than speak out in a convincing manner on the vital questions of the day. Pity the poor voters! Platforms are so vague, and candidates' statements so ambiguous, that they have no basis on which to choose. According to an old saying, party platforms are like train platforms—something to get in on, not to stand on.

This charge may once have been valid, but recent scholarship indicates that it overstates the problem. By the 1960s, at least, many voters *saw* their own party or the opposition party as standing for something. Their ideas of party position may be rather crude, but they seem to make sense. Thus most business and professional people see the Republican party as the party that best serves their interests. Workers tend to look on the Democrats as the party most helpful to them. It is likely that this proportion seeing important differences increased sharply from 1964 to 1972, when parties seemed to become more polarized. Of course there may be some *mis*perception involved. People who are strong Democrats or Republicans tend to look at events through the eyes of their party. This tendency is called selective perception or perceptual distortion: the more partisan people are, the more they may selectively perceive and distort their own and the other party's positions. Of course parties share much in common, if only because both compete for voters who are agreed on many issues.

One scholar took the trouble to study recent party platforms to see how similar they were. "Democrats and Republicans are not 'Tweedledee' and 'Tweedledum,'" Pomper concluded.[14] The difference between the two parties is not sharp, but it is significant. Even in 1972, when the two major parties seemed so polarized, a major study found a good deal of agreement *between* the parties as well as within them.[15] Parties share a consensus on many matters, but their platforms and supporters are hardly identical. And although senators and representatives often vote with the opposition, party lines do generally hold in Congress on votes relating to the platform.

PARTIES IN DISARRAY?

The second general charge is that our national parties are badly led at the top, weakly structured in the middle, and disorganized at the foundations. Some critics believe that the root of all this trouble lies at the base of the parties in the absence of big, solid, rank-and-file memberships. They note that any person eighteen or over can "join" a party simply by registering as a party member or (in some states) by voting in a primary and asking for the ballot of a particular party (which automatically registers them in that party). Critics point out that these party "members" pay no dues, do no work for the party, and rarely take part in party discussions or activi-

[14]Gerald M. Pomper, *Elections in America* (Dodd, Mead, 1968), p. 200. See also Dan D. Nimmo and Robert L. Savage, *Candidates and Their Images* (Goodyear, 1976).

[15]Jeane Kirkpatrick, *The New Presidential Elite* (Russell Sage Foundation and the Twentieth Century Fund, 1976), pp. 274–75.

ties. Such people are usually more active in their favorite social club than in the organization that assumes responsibility for governing the nation, the states, and most of the big cities.

Some local party organizations do have active memberships. The motive for joining and participating in parties varies widely. Some active workers are in the party mainly for personal and material reasons—jobs, favors, access to government officials. Others belong mainly for social reasons—the local committee or club gives them a chance to meet other people. Others use the party to advance public policies or candidates they support. The former types are the "professionals" or "regulars"; they stick with their party through thick and thin, support all its candidates, and keep the organization going between elections. The latter are the "volunteers" or "amateurs," who see party activity not as just an end in itself, like getting a political job, but as a *means* to a greater good, such as governmental policies or social programs.

Tension and hostility sometimes develop between the two types of party members. The party "pros" often come from low-income backgrounds. The amateurs may be better educated and more ideological. Over a period of time, however, amateurs may gradually assume the political style and motive patterns of the professionals, with the result that the party becomes less concerned with ideology and programs. Some fear that the "defection" of the amateurs to the professional style may make the party less active as an agent of the "masses," but this view assumes that the well-educated, issue-oriented amateur is more representative of the general population than the professional.[16]

Others fear that if both parties are taken over by amateurs, intense social conflict would mean danger for the democratic system. Certainly the involvement of amateurs has had unintended consequences. In 1964, for example, Goldwater Republicans were so convinced of the rightness of their cause, so anxious to provide the country with "a choice, not an echo," that they antagonized more moderate Republicans.[17] In 1972 McGovern Democrats, thousands of persons embittered by the Vietnam war and furious in general with the "Establishment," antagonized large numbers of professionals, including leaders of labor and ethnic groups. In both cases the opposition candidate—Johnson in 1964 and Nixon in 1972—won in a landslide. Jimmy Carter, however, managed to recruit large numbers of amateurs without antagonizing crucial groups in the party, and without losing the election.

All this reminds us that there are different kinds of party membership. The professional and the amateur each offer certain strengths and weaknesses. The party base will have splits in it as long as the party appeals to a great range of people with very different motives. But different kinds of membership may also provide the parties with greater strength and durability.

"I'm not worried. The Democrats are always in disarray."

Drawing by Lorenz. © 1975
The New Yorker Magazine, Inc.

[16]For further data on distinctions between amateurs and professionals, see Kirkpatrick, *The New Presidential Elite*, Chap. 10.

[17]See also David Nexon, "Asymmetry in the Political System: Occasional Activists in the Republican and Democratic Parties, 1956–1964," *American Political Science Review* (September 1971), pp. 716–30; Arthur H. Miller, Warren E. Miller, Alden S. Raine, and Thad A. Brown, "A Majority Party in Disarray: Policy Polarization in the 1972 Election," *American Political Science Review* (September, 1976), pp. 753–78.

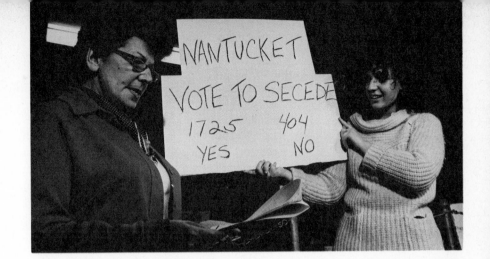

Nantucket, Massachusetts citizens voted, in a nonbinding election, to secede from Massachusetts.

PARTIES VERSUS PROGRESS?

American parties, some charge, are not vehicles for social reform. The fact that both major parties must be such inclusive and moderate organizations means that neither one can act boldly for the great mass of lower-class, low-income, and politically vulnerable people. Hence the parties use up social and political energies that might be better used in other strategies of change. Much, of course, depends on the times. Over the course of American history, Ladd says, this "party passiveness before social change" has probably had a good effect, helping the parties to perform a peacemaking or reconciling function. But in a period of exceptionally rapid and extensive change it also has the bad effect of dulling and slowing down the political system.[18] Since rapid social change seems continuous these days, it can be argued that parties were useful only in the past and are now outdated and should be scrapped.

The argument of those who hold this view is that weak parties simply end up strengthening the status quo. The rich and powerful have plenty of political weapons of their own, such as lobbyists, money, and influence over the media; the political party is peculiarly the vehicle of collective popular action. It is the "people's lobby." If the party is insipid in doctrine, ineffective both when in power and when in opposition, and disorganized from top to bottom, it blights the people's hopes instead of realizing them. Others contend that parties are more effective than critics admit. Voters can always turn to popular candidates—men like Franklin or Theodore Roosevelt, John Kennedy, Dwight Eisenhower—if parties fail them. And pluralistic, decentralized parties are appropriate for a pluralistic, individualistic people. Why, they ask, try to "Europeanize" or "Anglicize" parties that have their roots in the American tradition and cannot and need not change?

The argument has not been left there. Parties, no matter how flabby or sluggish, are nevertheless growing and living institutions.

Can the parties be saved?

To some, the Democratic party in 1968 seemed to be falling apart. President Johnson, stalemated militarily and politically by Vietnam, had an-

---

[18]Everett Carll Ladd, Jr., *American Political Parties: Social Change and Political Response* (Norton, 1970), pp. 307–08. For the contention that mass-membership organizations impede rather than facilitate political action by the poor, see Frances Fox Piven and Richard A. Cloward, *Poor People's Movements* (Pantheon Books, 1977).

nounced he would quit at the end of his first full term. Robert F. Kennedy had been shot down in a Los Angeles hotel. Eugene McCarthy and his followers had polarized the party. The Republicans, in contrast, seemed united behind Richard Nixon.

Passions exploded when the Democrats met for their party convention in Chicago. Out of this same convention, however, came a strong push to reform. A group of delegates led by Senator McCarthy and others won passage of a resolution to make the election of delegates to the 1972 convention a more open process. In the following years a series of Democratic party commissions proposed basic changes for the party. These proposals were of four basic types:[19]

1. *Procedural reforms.* It was found that state and local parties occasionally ignored the requirements of fair play. State parties were instructed to forbid proxy voting; to ban the use of the unit rule (under which the vote of a whole delegation was cast as the majority voted, no matter how strongly the minority differed); to ensure that party meetings were held with proper advance notice, in public places, and at set times; to require proper quorums, and other reforms.

2. *Reforms to broaden participation.* Here the commissions proposed two basic changes. One was not controversial—ensuring that party rules specified no discrimination on the basis of race, color, creed, sex, or national origin. Another was a bit controversial—allowing and encouraging all those eighteen years or older to take part in all party affairs. Another was *very* controversial—taking specific steps to encourage representation in party affairs (and especially nomination decisions) of young people, women, and minority groups "in reasonable relationship to their presence in the state's population." The quoted words seemed to require *quotas* imposed from above, and the critics flatly opposed such a requirement.

3. *Reforms to alter the delegate selection process.* These proposals will be discussed in Chapter 11.

4. *Party modernization.* The emphasis here was on turning the Democratic party into a more activist, policy-oriented organization. This feeling came to a head in a movement to call a "charter conference"—virtually a constitutional convention—of the Democratic party to reorganize the party structure and to consider a proposal to set up national policy conferences between presidential conventions. Such conferences would bring the party platform up to date, select new party officers if necessary, modernize the party rules, and in general do everything presidential conventions do except nominate candidates. It was hoped that such conferences could be a "shot in the arm" for Democrats, many of whom felt frustrated and helpless during the long period between national conventions.

These proposals were hotly opposed by some Democrats. Although they favored broadening the party, the centrists feared that too much effort would be made to bring in young people and women but not working-class people, labor unionists, the elderly, and others. The emphasis on a "participatory" rank-and-file party, they declared, was really undemocratic: Those who would attend open grass-roots caucuses were the more educated and affluent who had the time and the stamina and interest to debate all night. Working and poor people lacked the leisure, energy, or self-confidence to express their interests at meetings or even to attend them. Critics especially opposed the quota system—"democracy by

[19]These proposals are drawn mainly from the report of the McGovern Commission: *Mandate for Reform: A Report of the Commission on Party Structure and Delegate Selection to the Democratic National Committee* (Commission on Party Structure and Delegate Selection, Democratic National Committee, 1970).

demography"—as arbitrary and basically unrepresentative.[20] So heavy was the opposition to the quota system that its revival became unlikely.

These opposing ideas came into direct confrontation in 1974 in Kansas City at an unprecedented meeting—a Democratic party "charter conference" to draw up a constitution for the party. The two thousand delegates approved a number of changes that will be discussed in the next chapter. The conference in its new constitution and in other measures acted also to strengthen and centralize the party's national structure. Some of these steps included the following:

1. Recognizing the national convention as the supreme governing body of the party and requiring state parties to adapt their rules and practices to national party standards.
2. Enlarging the Democratic National Committee to make it stronger and more representative.
3. Strengthening national financial and educational agencies in the party.
4. Authorizing midterm national party conferences for the discussion of issues at a point half way through the presidential term.

The midterm conference was considered the most important of these steps, even though the national committee was given the power to decide whether or not to convene it.[21] The fact that the party in 1976 decided on a midterm issues conference to be held in 1978 suggests that the conference may become a permanent feature of the national party structure.

The strengthening of the national Democratic party at the top did not necessarily mean the weakening of state and local parties. To meet national standards for participation and organization, some state parties may find it necessary to reform their own organizations. The national "charter conference" of 1974 and the midterm conference of 1978 may also serve as a model for state parties. Thus, in 1977 Massachusetts Democrats at a statewide convention agreed to draw up a new state party constitution in 1978. This was a notable step for a state party that had long been considered one of the weakest in the nation.

Republicans, concerned about the health of their own party, were not idle during this period of renewal among the Democrats. The GOP, however, faced somewhat different problems. The national Republican party had long been better organized and funded than the Democrats, with a larger, more professional staff in Washington. At the same time, Republicans had long believed in a decentralized system and had no strong wish to "nationalize" the party. As a result, they have followed a middle road in efforts at reform and renewal. Committees have proposed giving the national committee more control over presidential campaigns in an effort to avoid Watergate-type excesses. State parties have been urged to encourage broader participation by all groups, including women, minorities, youth,

"The trouble with centrists is they're too damn far to the left."

Copyright © 1976 by James Stevenson.

[20]Coalition for a Democratic Majority, Task Force on Democratic Party Rules and Structure, "Toward Fairness and Unity for '76," mimeographed (1974).

[21]William J. Crotty, *Political Reform and the American Experiment* (Crowell, 1977), pp. 252–55, offers a full listing of the resolutions of the Democratic Charter conference. See, in general, Austin Ranney, *Curing the Mischiefs of Faction* (University of California Press, 1975). John S. Saloma III and Frederick H. Sontag, *Parties: The Real Opportunity for Effective Citizen Politics* (Knopf, 1972); and David S. Broder, *The Party's Over* (Harper & Row, 1971) present the case for reformed and reorganized parties.

and the poor. The party took a notable step in choosing the first national party chairwoman, Mary Louise Smith, in its history. And former president Gerald Ford created a stir by submitting a plan for creating a new Republican coordinating committee that would establish a "shadow cabinet" to make the GOP a real "loyal opposition."

Summary

1. Americans have long been critical and suspicious of political parties, especially strong parties. The two major parties have served as unifying and modifying forces over the decades, but not always with success. Third parties, whether doctrinal parties or parties forming around issues, have been notably unsuccessful in the American political environment.

2. The two major parties have been weak at the top, poorly organized in the middle at the state party level, and lack rank-and-file organized strength at the base. The parties have a variety of functions: winning votes, stimulating interest in public affairs, recruiting political leaders, uniting different regions, religious and racial groups, and minorities, and serving as a link between the people and their government.

3. The parties are not instruments of major social change. They are declining in strength and seem to be in organizational disarray. But many Americans believe the parties must survive, because they do offer real choices to the voters, usually live up to most of their promises, and are making an effort to reform and revitalize themselves.[22]

[22]For recent general treatments of American parties, see Joyce Gelb and Marian Lief Palley, *Tradition and Change in American Party Politics* (Crowell, 1975); Frank J. Sorauf, *Party Politics in America*, 3rd ed. (Little, Brown, 1976); William J. Keefe, *Parties, Politics, and Public Policy in America*, 2nd ed. (Dryden, 1976); and Everett Ladd with Charles Hadley, *Transformations of the American Party System* (Norton, 1975).

Chapter 11

Elections: Rule by the People?

MANY TEEN-AGERS ARE IGNORANT ABOUT GOVERNMENT, SURVEY FINDS, a *New York Times* headline proclaimed not long ago.[1] A survey of students 13 and 17 years old had revealed that:

About one-fifth of the 17-year-olds thought the United States was the only country that had political parties.

Half the 13-year-olds thought it was against the law to start a new political party.

About half the students of either age believed that the president can appoint members of Congress.

More than 10 percent of all the students felt that "some people should not be allowed to vote in elections because these people are not smart enough."

We assume that the readers of this book are reasonably well informed about our political system. In this chapter we will deal with certain aspects of elections that raise important questions about government by the people. In studying elections, and also in taking part in them, it is useful to know about election procedures familiar to the "old pros" who often run the day-to-day business of election politics. Examples: how you qualify to vote; when and where to vote; how you go about getting on the ballot; the importance of where a candidate's name is placed on the ballot (or voting machine); the use of stickers and write-ins; how to conduct a recount. Consider ballot placement, for example. As a candidate you will probably pick up extra votes if you are at the top of a list. Or take the question of whether candidates are listed by party (the party-column, or Indiana ballot) or by office (the office-group, or Massachusetts ballot). These things can affect election outcomes.

Election arrangements vary so widely from state to state that they cannot

[1]*The New York Times*, January 2, 1977.

Candidates for political office utilize different campaign strategies to gain votes. Top, Massachusetts Senate candidates debate the issues. Edmund G. Brown meets with a constituent while visiting a San Francisco housing project during his race for governor of California. Bottom, Illinois Republican gubernatorial candidate James Thompson speaks at Republican Committee luncheon.

be summarized here. Two aspects of elections in all states, however, confuse nearly everyone. One of these is registration; the other is the party primary for choosing candidates.

"You must register if you want to vote." How many of us hear this warning, but find that we cannot vote on election day because we're not on the voting list. About 45 million citizens of voting age failed to register for the 1976 elections. Regulated mainly by state law, registration requirements vary from state to state. But the Supreme Court has ruled that states may not impose "unreasonable" requirements as to how far in advance of an election a voter must register. In the Voting Rights Act of 1965 Congress set up procedures for registration in areas that had a record of using such procedures to discriminate against blacks. The act also changed residence requirements for voting in presidential elections; it was made easier for those moving from one place to another around election time to vote either in their old home district or in their new one. But registration remained low.

Two months after taking office, President Carter called for a major reform: election-day registration. He noted that the United States ranked behind at least twenty other democracies in level of voter participation. The president proposed that "citizens qualified to vote under state laws could go to their polling places on the day of a Federal election and register there after proving their eligibility. The states would be encouraged to adopt a similar system of registration for state and local elections." Several states that do allow people to register on election day have had high rates of voting.[2]

Carter's proposal on registration brought a mixed response. Most Democrats calculated that, since low-income and minority persons make up a large proportion of the unregistered, election-day registration might bring many potential Democrats to the polls. Republicans feared this same possibility; they were also concerned that the Carter proposal might increase the opportunities for election fraud—especially the possibility of falsely identifying or registering voters. Carter's proposal failed to pass during his first year in office, in part because many Democrats from the big cities feared that "instant registration" might weaken their control over election outcomes in their cities.

Almost all elected officeholders in the United States—except for the president and vice-president and some local officials—were first *nominated* in party primaries. The party primary is an almost uniquely American institution; in other democracies, nominees for national parliaments are chosen by relatively small numbers of party leaders and members meeting in their own party conferences, with practically no governmental supervision. In the United States party primaries are financed by the public treasury, run by regular election officials, and held in the same polling places as the November election. Moreover, the voters are protected by the same legal safeguards. Officeseekers do not even need to be very active in the party to get on the primary ballot; they usually need only file a petition signed by a required number of voters (who also do not need to be active party members). In practice this means that almost anyone can get on the ballot if he or she does enough legwork. The result is that the voter may have to choose among five or ten or even more aspirants.

Who can vote in a party primary? The answer depends on whether it is an *open* or *closed* primary. In the closed primary, which is more common, voters must publicly acknowledge membership in a party in order to help pick that party's nominee. They can do this by making a pledge of support of the party or simply by allowing themselves to be listed as a party member after taking part in the primary. But party membership is a rather vague thing in the United States, so these requirements are not very restrictive. The open primary does not even require that much party loyalty: Qualified voters can participate in any party primary without having to take a party pledge or reveal party affiliation. Thus a voter can participate in one party primary one year, the other party primary the next year. Open primaries allow "one-day" Democrats or Republicans to "raid" the opposition party by entering its primary and voting for the weakest candidate.

[2]Press release, The White House, March 22, 1977.

Party primaries were urged by reformers around the turn of the century as a means of overcoming the bossism and corruption associated with the other main way of nominating candidates, the convention system. The primaries did help "purify" politics; but they have also tended to erode party unity and organization. Whether parties should be allowed or encouraged to regain control of the nomination process through the reestablishment of strong party conventions is a leading question confronting those who believe in government by the people.[3]

Political money

For many years Americans have worried about the use of money to buy influence in politics. Watergate, the resignations of President Nixon and Vice-President Agnew, "laundering" of money, secret campaign donations, and secret use of money by South Korea have sharpened these worries. But the world of political money still remains shadowy. How much does election campaigning cost and should it cost that much? Who gives? Why? Where does the money go? Is political money a serious problem? If so, what has been done about it? What *can* be done about it?

Big round figures suggest that political campaigns do indeed cost too much. In 1976 about $114 million was spent on the presidential campaign alone. Some individual campaigns seem extremely costly. A wealthy young Democrat spent about $4.5 million in an unsuccessful effort to win a seat in the United States Senate. A wealthy young Republican spent about the same to win a United States Senate seat in Pennsylvania in 1976. One of Nelson Rockefeller's campaigns for governor was *officially* reported at $7.5 million.

Yet if we put the question of campaign finance in broader perspective, the problem dwindles a bit. The $177 million spent on national races in 1976 was but a fraction of a percent of the total cost of government. One Trident submarine costs hundreds of millions. Government *must* spend a great deal of money to recruit leaders and to inform voters as to what leaders stand for. Or compare the cost of political campaigns with the money spent on commercial advertising. One big soap company will budget in 1980 almost as much as the cost of all campaigning for that presidential year. Or compare political expenditure per voter in the United States with the same in other countries. Americans spent $1.12 per capita in a recent year, much less than most countries and far less than the cost for Israelis of $21.20 per voter.[4]

The peculiar nature of American elections also raises the cost of campaigns. There are really two campaigns, one for nomination and one for election, and each of them lasts months. A presidential aspirant may campaign for at least a year before the elections, as Goldwater did in 1964, McGovern in 1972, and Carter in 1976. Another reason for the high cost of getting elected (or defeated) is the growing use of professional campaign

[3]For more general treatments of parties and the nominating process, see Frank J. Sorauf, *Party Politics in America*, 3rd ed. (Little, Brown, 1976); Thomas W. Madron and Carl P. Chelf, *Political Parties in the United States* (Holbrook, 1974); and, with emphasis on the role of state party chairpersons, Robert J. Huckshorn, *Party Leadership in the States* (University of Massachusetts Press, 1976).

[4]These examples are from Herbert E. Alexander, *Political Financing* (Burgess, 1972), pp. 1–4, 38–39; see also David W. Adamany, *Campaign Finance in America* (Wadsworth, 1972), Chaps. 2, 3. The $177 million spent on national races in 1976 covered all Senate, House, and presidential campaigns.

A $300,000 Budget for a Recent Congressional Campaign			
Entertainment	$ 5,381.57	Stamps	$ 4,228.00
Travel	8,656.00	Telephone Charges	9,783.71
Advances for Expenses	4,732.00	Telephone Deposits	17,100.00
Hotels	538.50	Tickets for Dinners, etc.	5,376.00
Hq. Equipment, Furniture	7,626.00	Staff Payroll	54,955.00
Rents	9,025.00	Direct Mail Campaign	49,521.00
Media Consultant	19,326.00	Advertising	17,102.00
Printing	33,013.00	Polls	11,600.00
Research	1,122.00	Voter Surveys	15,000.00
New York State Income Tax	8,630.00	Mail & Vote List Computerizing	8,200.00
Soc. Security & Federal Taxes	17,592.38	Video-Tape Machines	1,267.95

managers. Years ago, a candidate used an old-fashioned party organization staffed by hundreds of persons eager to get jobs or favors. Today, partly as a result of the key role of television in many campaigns, candidates are using merchandising techniques. "Big-time" candidates may hire a professional campaign firm, a computer expert, a polling organization, an advertising agency, a specialist in film-making, an expert in direct-mail campaigns. Television is enormously expensive; and the United States, almost alone among democratic nations, does not provide candidates free access to television (or radio).

The problem is not so much the amount of money; politics will always be expensive. The problem in a democracy is *inequality* — whether the doctrine of one person, one vote becomes meaningless when one person can give tens of thousands of dollars and another can give nothing. How does this inequality square with the doctrine of government by the people?

WHO GIVES AND WHY?

Broadly speaking, those who give most are those who have the most. Ideally in a democracy, millions of average citizens might give something to their candidates and parties, but this has not been the tradition in the United States. A number of experiments in mass fund raising have been tried, but they have not been very successful. However, presidential candidates with many involved and loyal supporters have succeeded in gathering most of their money from small contributions. During a nine-month period in 1968, George Wallace collected over $6 million, of which more than 75 percent was made up of contributions of less than $100. A record was set by George McGovern, who raised a total of $33 million, almost two-thirds of which came in donations of $100 or less.[5]

But the great bulk of the money comes from business and professional people and from labor unions. Most of the money comes in large donations. The size and number of the gifts have been escalating: between 1952 and 1968 the number of contributors giving over $10,000 quadrupled. Federal law prohibits both unions and corporations from making contributions or expenditures in connection with candidacy for federal office, so

[5]Stephen Schlesinger, "Running for Office: All You Need Is an Issue," *Washington Monthly* (October 1972), pp. 45–48.

donations are made by "individuals" even though they may come indirectly from corporations and unions. In 1972 some corporations did give money directly to the Nixon campaign, and more than a dozen executives were prosecuted and fined. Some individuals and families made huge donations, and these were legal.

The money, whether legal or not, is not always given openly, of course. Watergate made us familiar with the obscure channels through which political money flows: the use of "fronts" and "drops," the "laundering" of money to hide its real origin, and other devices. A far more common—and legal—device is the $100 or $1,000 a plate dinner, for which large contributors buy whole tables or blocks of tables—and perhaps buy an expensive ad in a dinner "program" to boot. Party dinners tend to be a bit more ordinary. The Democrats run a series of Jackson Day dinners throughout the country, charging as low as $5 or $10 a plate; the Republicans have Lincoln Day dinners, also for a wider group. The Democrats in recent years have had considerable success with day-long "telethons" featuring party leaders and Hollywood actresses.

The reasons for giving political money are many. Most givers want something specific. Business, labor, and other groups want certain laws passed or repealed, certain funds appropriated, certain administrative decisions rendered. Those holding government jobs want to stay in office (and in certain cities pay the party an assessment to do so). Some big donors want ambassadorships or other important posts. Some want recognition—an invitation to a White House dinner, a low license plate number, an honorific appointment. Others simply want *access* to officeholders. They neither expect nor get specific government rewards for their "cash on the barrelhead;" what they *do* expect and usually get is the opportunity to see the officeholder after the election and present their case.

Many givers are moved by somewhat higher motives. They believe that their candidate or party will govern best for them and their country. Their motives range from the vaguest idealism to hardheaded calculation that certain candidates, parties, or government actions would be best for the nation. Reagan, McGovern, Wallace and others have demonstrated how powerful this appeal can be when sounded by candidates who are seen as genuinely committed to the doctrines they preach.

Is giving worthwhile? Is there a payoff? This question is unanswerable because the relation between giving money and the passage of an act, for example, is extremely obscure. Too many other factors are involved (including the giving of money by people on the other side of an issue). Perhaps it is enough to say that most politicians and most donors *think* that giving money brings results.

REFORM OF POLITICAL MONEY

For many years the national and state governments have been trying to "sanitize" campaign finance, with very mixed results. The reformers have assumed that big donors were able to buy political influence. In any event, the image of "fat cats" gaining political power was an affront to American notions of equality and justice. Concern has risen in recent years along with the inflation of political money. One scholar contends that money has become so important that candidates must conduct *three* campaigns: for a party nomination, for the election, and for campaign finance. This third campaign begins before the candidate starts running, and continues all through the primary and the election contests. It is revived at the end of the campaign when the winners and losers add up their campaign debts.[6]

Reformers have tried three basic strategies in trying to prevent abuse: limitations on the giving, receiving, and spending of political money; disclosure of the sources and uses of political money; governmental subsidies of campaigns, including incentive arrangements. Recent campaign finance laws have tended to use all three in attempts to deal with a problem that sometimes seems insoluble.

Limiting campaign spending is one of the older methods. Under the 1925 Corrupt Practices Act, a candidate for the United States House of Representatives could not spend more than $2,500, a candidate for senator not more than $10,000. Higher amounts were allowed for larger states or districts, but the act was utterly unrealistic and easily evaded. Reporting was inadequate; often reports were filed after the election was over. Policing was almost nonexistent. Much of the corrupt practice legislation did not cover primary elections. President Johnson called the 1925 act "more loophole than law."

In 1971, Congress decided on a different emphasis: *disclosure*. All political committees that anticipated receiving or spending more than $1,000 on behalf of federal candidates in any year were required to register with the government; periodic reports had to be filed including full data on all major contributions and expenditures; one person was not allowed to contribute in the name of another person. In contrast to earlier laws, ceilings on political contributions were abolished (except for candidates, or their immediate families, contributing to their own campaigns). Candidates for federal office were also limited in the amounts they could spend on campaign advertising (television, radio, billboards) to 10 cents per voting-age person. The main thrust of the act was to throw the "pitiless light" of full publicity onto the sources and uses of political money. Its impact to date seems to be limited.

In another act of 1971, Congress turned to a different strategy: *subsidy tax incentives*. The purpose was to draw into politics more money with no strings attached. The law provided that political donors might claim a tax credit against federal income tax for 50 percent of their contributions, up to a maximum of $12.50 on a single return or $25 on a joint return; or they might claim a deduction on the full amount of the contributions, but not more than $50 on a single return or $100 on a joint return. The 1971 law also provided a *tax checkoff* that allowed taxpayers to designate $1 of their tax obligation for a fund to subsidize presidential campaigns.

Watergate gave a sharp push to further regulation of political money. Late in 1974, after prolonged debate, Congress passed and President Ford signed the most sweeping campaign reform measure in American history. The new act established more realistic limits on contributions and spending. For example, there would be a spending limit of $20 million for each presidential candidate in the general election, and $700,000 for each congressional candidate. It tightened disclosure, reporting, and accountability and created a new full-time bipartisan elections commission to administer the act. But what made the new measure a breakthrough was a new set of provisions for *public financing* of presidential campaigns. Major party candidates automatically qualified for full funding before the campaign. Pub-

---

[6]Delmer D. Dunn, "Contributors in the American Electoral Process," *American Politics Quarterly* (April 1974), pp. 221–29.

lic funding would also be available to national parties for their presidential nominating conventions. Matching public funds of up to $5 million would be available to each candidate in presidential primaries.

The new law was promptly challenged in the courts. A group of conservatives and liberals contended that the act violated their First Amendment rights. In January 1976 the Supreme Court made its ruling.[7] Seven members of the Court ruled unconstitutional the limitation on the amount of money a person could spend to promote a political cause or the candidacy of another person; six members ruled unconstitutional the limitations on the amount of one's own money that could be spent to promote one's own election. Under the First Amendment, persons have a constitutional right to spend their money in any lawful way in order to get across to the voters their own views in behalf of any candidate or cause of their choice.

On the other hand, six members of the Court distinguished between the act of *spending* money and the act of *giving* it. They ruled that Congress may limit the amount of money a person can contribute to a candidate or party, in order to limit the influence of the rich and to prevent the appearance of buying political favors. The court majority also held that, although candidates had a right to spend as much of their own money as they could collect, if a party or candidate took public funds, that party or candidate could be required to limit what they spent on the campaign.[8]

How has the 1974 law worked out? It had a marked effect on the 1976 election. Reversing past trends, the overall cost of the presidential primaries and general election dropped between 1972 and 1976. About $114 million was spent on the 1976 presidential campaign. For the first time in American political history, about 60 percent of that was covered by public subsidies. The amount of private money invested in the national election dropped from $127 million in 1972 to less than half of that.[9] The "fat cats" and private interests, said some, had had their day.

Others were more critical of the new law. The public funds were coming out of the taxpayers' pockets, even though the checkoff was voluntary. Subsidies went only to candidates, not parties. The result might be an even more fragmented, personalistic, and individualistic politics than already exists. But if campaigns were publicly funded through political parties, the national parties, at least, might become more organized and responsible. This would be especially likely if the parties had to match public funds with their own. A major criticism of the new act was that it affected presidential but not congressional campaigns, even though the influence of money was seen as even more serious in the legislative branch than the executive.

President Carter agreed with this last criticism. In March 1977 he urged Congress to extend public financing to campaigns for both the House and Senate:

[7]*Buckley* v. *Valeo*, 424 U.S. 1 (1976).

[8]For a full summary of the 1974 law (technically the Federal Election Campaign Act Amendments of 1974), see Herbert E. Alexander, *Financing Politics* (Congressional Quarterly Press, 1976), appendix.

[9]Report of the Federal Election Commission, June 4, 1977, *The New York Times* (June 5, 1977), p. 25.

The record of the first publicly financed Presidential campaign has demonstrated that public financing is workable and widely accepted by the American people. Public financing of candidates not only minimizes even the appearance of obligation to special interest contributors, but also provides an opportunity for qualified persons who lack funds to seek public office. It would be a tragic irony if the 1974 law, which reduced the pressure special interests could place on Presidential candidates, increased the pressures on candidates for Congress as the large contributors look for new means of gaining influence with their political funds.[10]

He urged that public funding apply to congressional primaries as well as elections.

Many were skeptical that Congress would reform itself. They pointed out that Congress would fear a subsidy program might encourage people to run against incumbent senators or representatives. On the other hand, if challengers for the seats had to accept ceilings on campaign spending (as they would have to do if they accepted public funds), the proposed extension might freeze present members of Congress in place and prevent necessary turnover. The president's proposal led to a stiff battle in House and Senate. The proposal was defeated by a Senate filibuster in 1977, but was expected to come before Congress again in subsequent sessions.

Running for congress

How you run for Congress obviously depends largely on the nature of your district or state. Much also depends on who you are: a freshman senator or congressman running for reelection for the first time, a veteran with a strong personal organization, or a novice who has never run for Congress before. But we can note certain similarities between and among Senate and House elections.

One is the typical lack of competitiveness in elections to the House of Representatives. Competitiveness (usually defined as neither candidate getting more than 55 percent of the two-party vote split) has declined sharply over the last twenty years. Competition in party primaries does not seem to make up for the lack of competition in the November elections.[11] The existence of such a large number of safe seats in the House affects the number and kind of persons willing to compete, and also the policy-making process and output of the House. Many Senate seats tend to be noncompetitive, but less so than in the House. The population of a whole state is much more diverse than that of the usual congressional district.

The second similarity is the influence of presidential elections on congressional elections. We have noted the coattail influence: strong presidential candidates attract voters to the polls and affect their attitudes in ways that help determine who wins congressional races as well. But there is some evidence that presidents affect congressional district races even in the midterm elections. To some degree the votes cast in these elections

[10]Press Statement, Office of the Vice President, The White House, March 22, 1977.

[11]Harvey L. Schantz, "Julius Turner Revisited: Primary Elections as the Alternative to Party Competition in 'Safe' Districts," *American Political Science Review* (June 1976), pp. 541–45. For the view that incumbents' main motivation is simply staying in office, see David R. Mayhew, *Congress: The Electoral Connection* (Yale University Press, 1974).

seem to be a judgment or referendum on the performance of the president and especially his management of the economy. "Although the in-party's share of the nationwide congressional vote almost invariably declines in the midterm compared to the previous on-year election," according to a recent study, "the *magnitude* of that loss is substantially smaller if the President has a high level of popular approval, or if the economy is performing well, or both."[12] The outcome of the 1978 House elections is an interesting test of this finding.

Most campaigns for House and Senate have been much influenced by the new technology of politics: campaign managers for hire, campaign agencies, opinion polling, consultants, heavy use of the media, "political packaging," basic information systems, and all the rest.[13] There has been some fear that this new technology would so emphasize *personality* that issues would come to be ignored. However, the entrance into politics of more issue-minded groups in recent years suggests that campaign technology may assist candidates in presenting issues more clearly.

CAMPAIGNING FOR THE HOUSE   There are other patterns and rules of thumb, especially in campaigning for a seat in the House.[14] For a person with some political experience and contacts throughout the district, the first question is one of timing. Does the year look good for the candidate and his or her party? Is there any kind of groundswell against incumbents? If it is a presidential election year, will the party's ticket be headed by attractive national or state candidates; if so, can he or she get a firm hold on their coattails? Would it be better to wait two or four years until the candidate has broadened his own range of acquaintances? Or will it be too late by then?

If he or she decides to go, the candidate must first plan a primary race, unless there happens to be no opponents for the party's nomination. (This piece of luck is more likely when a party has little chance of carrying the district.) The first step is to build a personal organization, because the party organization is supposed to stay neutral until the nomination is decided. A candidate can build an organization as a holder of a lesser office such as state representative, or by deliberately getting to know people, serving in civic causes, helping other candidates, and being conspicuous without being overly controversial. The next step is to raise funds to hire campaign managers and technicians, to buy television and other advertising, to conduct polls, and so on.

Once nominated, candidates come into a rich inheritance—the large

[12]Edward R. Tufte, "Determinants of the Outcomes of Midterm Congressional Elections," *American Political Science Review* (September 1975), pp. 812–26, p. 824 (emphasis added).

[13]For a general treatment, see Robert Agranoff, *The Management of Election Campaigns* (Holbrook, 1976); on developing campaign technology, see Dan Nimmo, *The Political Persuaders* (Prentice-Hall, 1970).

[14]These generalizations are drawn in part from David A. Leuthold, *Electioneering in a Democracy: Campaigns for Congress* (Wiley, 1968); the illuminating studies of primary and election campaigns, *Eagleton Institute Cases in Practical Politics*, sponsored by the Eagleton Foundation Advisory Board at Rutgers University (McGraw-Hill); Lewis A. Froman, Jr., "A Realistic Approach to Campaign Strategies and Tactics," in David W. Abbott and Edward T. Rogowsky, eds., *Political Parties: Leadership, Organization, Linkage* (Rand McNally, 1971), pp. 280–98; and Donald G. Herzberg and J. W. Peltason, *A Student Guide to Campaign Politics* (McGraw-Hill, 1970).

bloc of votes of the party faithful who will almost automatically support their party's nominee. They will also get considerable recognition from the press and from state and national party leaders. But the candidates for Congress usually have some troubles. The party will provide them with far less financial support than needed. Except in a few places such as Chicago, the party organization is either feeble or strained to the limit in trying to help all its candidates. So candidates find they must depend on a personal organization. But the main problem usually is one of *visibility.* In a large metropolitan area, it is hard to get attention in the press and on television, both of which are paying attention to the major candidates. And in rural areas the press may play down political news.

As a result, congressional candidates often stress advertising and promotion. This must be supplemented by personal contact—shaking hands, canvassing homes, emphasizing local problems. A congressional election is usually a combination of national policy and local politics.

Running for the senate

Because states vary in population so widely, generalizing about Senate campaigns is difficult. But running for the Senate is big-time politics. The six-year term and the national exposure make a Senate seat a glittering prize, so competition is likely to be intense. The race may easily cost several hundred thousand dollars, whereas congressional campaigns typically cost considerably less. Candidates for the Senate are far more visible. They find it more important to take positions on national problems, and cannot duck tough issues very easily.

Otherwise, Senate races tend to be much like those for the House. The essential tactics, as Froman has summed it up, are to get others involved, use as much personal contact as possible, be brief in statements to the public, not to publicize the opposition if you can help it, and have a simple campaign theme. Persuade people through the basic methods of *reinforcement* of present feelings, *activation* of latent attitudes, and *conversion* of opposing views to the extent possible. Remember that facts do not speak for themselves—an intellectual and psychological framework must be provided.[15] And Senate races usually call for even more campaign technology than those for the House.

All other things being equal, incumbency weighs heavily in Senate elections. The reason is not wholly clear. "It may simply be," says Barbara Hinckley, "that an incumbent is more widely known than his opponent—due to the publicity available as a member of the Senate, the franking privilege, etc.—and that with generally low levels of voter interest and information about Congress, voters will tend to vote for the more familiar (less unfamiliar) name."[16] But incumbents are not unbeatable. In 1974, for example, Senator William Fulbright, a national figure, a thirty-year veteran of the Senate, and probably its most distinguished spokesman on foreign policy, was beaten in the primary in Arkansas by a young, vigorous, and popular governor, Dale Bumpers.

[15]Lewis A. Froman, Jr., *A Realistic Approach to Campaign Strategies.* See also John W. Kingdon, *Candidates for Office: Beliefs and Strategies* (Random House, 1968).

[16]Barbara Hinckley, "Incumbency and the Presidential Vote in Senate Elections: Defining Parameters of Subpresidential Voting," *American Political Science Review* (September 1970), pp. 841–42.

Democratic Senator James Allen of Alabama, left, greets Senator Dale Bumpers of Arkansas, right, and former Senator Joseph Montoya of New Mexico at a party policy session. In 1974 Bumpers proved that incumbents are not always unbeatable, when he won the race for Senate—his opponent was William Fulbright, a thirty-year veteran of Congress.

Is there any place for rational planning in all this? Or is it simply a matter of following a few obvious rules of thumb like those listed above? Most politicians would argue that victory is nine-tenths perspiration and one-tenth inspiration. But careful calculation may pay off, especially in the tricky business of picking a good year to run, and a good presidential candidate to run with or against.

In 1964 Republican candidates faced the difficult decision of whether to cling to the coattails of Barry Goldwater or conduct independent campaigns. Those who thought Goldwater a sure winner and climbed aboard his bandwagon fared worse at the polls than those who ran a somewhat separate campaign. A decade later, Republican candidates in most districts did their best to separate themselves from President Nixon, Watergate, and inflation. But the results in most elections are also affected by factors over which candidates have little control. Some of these are ballots that emphasize the link between presidential and congressional candidates, national trends, as well as party registration and the influence of local candidates.[17]

We may be entering a period in which campaigns will become more significant in determining election outcomes. This may happen not merely because of the greater effectiveness of new political techniques, but also because of the growing number of young voters who are not loyal to any one party. They enter the campaign periods ready to be persuaded. Although party loyalties will probably not disappear altogether, there are

[17]Robert A. Schoenberger, "Campaign Strategy and Party Loyalty: The Electoral Relevance of Candidate Decision-Making in the 1964 Congressional Elections," *American Political Science Review* (June 1969), pp. 515–20. See also Robert J. Huckshorn and Robert C. Spencer, *The Politics of Defeat* (University of Massachusetts Press, 1971), which emphasizes the difficulty of challenging incumbents in noncompetitive districts.

likely to be fewer voters to whom candidates can appeal in terms of party loyalty alone.[18]

Running for the presidency

To attain the presidency candidates have to run three races and win them all. First they must win delegate support in the state contests; then they must be nominated at their party's national convention. Then they must get a majority of the nation's electoral votes.

NOMINATING A PRESIDENT

Probably the first convention was held in 1808, when a few Federalist leaders met secretly in New York to nominate candidates for president and vice-president. In 1831, under Jackson's leadership, the first real national convention was held by a major party. Today the national convention is a famous and unique political institution. Every four years each party enjoys world attention; covered by batteries of cameras and by battalions of newsmen, every incident in the great convention hall is carried to millions in this country and abroad.

The preconvention campaign usually starts at least a year before the convention itself. Early in 1975, candidates for nomination by the 1976 party conventions were already hard at work. Candidates must choose among several preconvention strategies: announcing early and going "all out;" keeping silent in order not to show strength (or weakness) too early; quietly trying to win over party leaders within the states—leaders who may be able to deliver solid delegate support at the crucial moment in the convention battle. In recent years the candidate's main effort has been winning personal support that could be translated into voting support in primaries across the nation. Some observers believe that winning national and local attention for *one or two years before election year* has become so important that the nomination is just about decided before the first primary is held.[19]

All these tactics, however, are dominated by the rules of the presidential nomination game. In each national convention the object is simple: to win a straight majority of the votes cast on the first or any other ballot. Delegates arrive at the convention in all stages of commitment, noncommitment, or semicommitment to a candidate. Some delegates will be pledged to a candidate only on the first ballot; others pledge themselves (or are pledged by their election) to one person for all ballots; others have mixed and divided commitments to candidates.

CHOOSING DELEGATES

The key factor in the national convention is the makeup of the state delegations. Each party convention represents the states roughly in proportion to the number of voters in the state. At the same time, there is a bonus for states where the party is strong. The two parties have often changed their rules for dividing the votes among the states in an attempt to satisfy both requirements. Democrats grant some delegates only half a vote, whereas Republicans favor arrangements that give delegates a single vote. Democratic conventions therefore have more delegates.

The method of selecting delegates is set by state law and party rules and varies from state to state. In most of the states, including most of the popu-

[18]Warren E. Miller and Teresa E. Levitin, *Leadership and Change*, 2nd ed. (Winthrop, 1977).

[19]See, for example, Arthur T. Hadley, *The Invisible Primary* (Prentice-Hall, 1976). See also William R. Keech and Donald R. Matthews, *The Party's Choice* (Brookings Institution, 1976).

Today the national convention, is brought into the homes of millions of people by extensive newspaper and television coverage.

lous ones, delegates are picked in state presidential primaries. These primaries have become the most important way of choosing delegates to presidential conventions. In 1980 well over two-thirds of the delegates will be chosen or bound by them, compared to less than half only ten years ago.

In about one third (or less) of the states, delegates will be chosen in 1980 by state conventions, committees, and/or caucuses. This system often allows the party leaders to select the delegates. It may be no problem where the party leadership is representative, but that is sometimes not the case. In the past, most Republican party organizations in the South, for example, were controlled by a few officeholders in Washington with the help of patronage. In such situations the question of who speaks for the ordinary party member becomes very obscure. This problem was the cause of a fierce fight between the Taft and Eisenhower supporters in the 1952 Republican convention. It ended in the unseating of the Taft delegations from Georgia, Louisiana, and Texas and the seating of the Eisenhower forces. Since that time, the Republican party has broadened its base in the South. In some states, such as Minnesota, open and participatory party caucuses dominate the early stages of the delegate-choosing process.

The *presidential primaries* provide most of the excitement and conflict of preconvention politics; these are the election contests that are so dra-

matically covered by television. The battles of Robert Kennedy and Eugene McCarthy in the 1968 presidential primaries and Jimmy Carter's string of victories in the early 1976 primaries will long be remembered in the Democratic party. So will Barry Goldwater's victories in 1964 and Ronald Reagan's determined effort in 1976 among Republicans. With greater use of presidential primaries, moreover, they seem more and more important in forecasting—and perhaps influencing—the outcome of the convention voting.

PRESIDENTIAL PRIMARIES

Presidential primaries come in many different forms in different states. The voters must learn the specific arrangements in their own states—*and the significance of those arrangements for political outcomes*. Here are the key variations to look for:

1. *Direct election of delegates.* Under this alternative, voters choose from a list (or slate) of candidates for delegates to the national convention. Voters do not necessarily know what presidential candidates those delegate candidates favor. In effect the voter says: "I will vote for you to go as a delegate to the national convention and I will depend on you to choose a good presidential candidate for me."

2. *Voting one's presidential preference.* In this kind of presidential primary, voters can indicate their choice among the party's presidential candidates. The ballot will list those candidates and the voter simply pulls the lever for the person he favors. Much depends on whether the outcome of these presidential votes is binding on the delegates to the national convention. It may or not be binding in a particular state. If it is, the delegates must vote for the preferred candidate on at least the first ballot at the convention. If it is not, the preference vote becomes a popularity contest. But it is one that may influence the candidate's national standing with press and public.

"Sure it's cockeyed, but it's the only roulette wheel in town."

© 1976 Herblock

These two basic elements are found in primaries in different combinations; *how* they are combined can be crucial. Some states closely link delegate election and presidential preference. By a single X at the top of the column headed, say, "Delegates preferring Jimmy Carter," voters can indicate both the person they want *and* vote for a delegate (or delegate slate) pledged to that candidate at the convention. But other states separate the two processes. Voters indicate their presidential preference in one part of the ballot and their delegate selection in another. And there may be no relation between the two. Whether these processes are linked or separate has great importance for both practical presidential politics and theories of representation.

The variety of methods of choosing delegates, along with the variety of power patterns in state parties, makes it impossible to generalize about the nature of the delegations. Some may be under the thumb of influential state, county, or city leaders; some may operate as a unit to support a favorite son or to maximize their bargaining power; others may be split wide open. Most state delegations reflect the factions in the state party. But sometimes a strong and well-organized faction will gain control of the whole delegation. A major effect of recent party reforms has been to encourage factionalism in state delegations as small blocs form around various presidential hopefuls. (This and related questions are taken up in Chapter 17.)[20]

[20]For an analytical study of the effect of presidential primaries, including recent reforms, on the political and social process, see James I. Lengle and Byron Shafer, "Primary Rules, Political Power, and Social Change," *American Political Science Review* (March 1976), pp. 25–40.

The convention adjourns immediately after the presidential and vice-presidential candidates deliver their acceptance speeches to the delegates. The presidential nominee may choose a new party chairman, who usually serves as his campaign manager. After a rest, the candidate spends the final days of the summer binding up party wounds, gearing the party for action, and planning campaign strategy. By early fall the presidential race is on.

Strategy differs from one election to another, but politicians, pollsters, and political scientists have collected enough information in recent decades to agree broadly that a number of basic factors affect it. The great bulk of the electorate votes on the basis of party, candidate appeal, and issues. Much depends on voter turnout as well as on party disposition. Nationally the Democrats have a great advantage in party registration and support. But the Republicans have an advantage because their partisans are more likely to turn out on election day, and they have better access to money and usually a somewhat more favorable press. Pledges on policy and program may not arouse the mass of the electorate, but they do help activate interest groups and party organizations, which in turn help get out a favorable vote.

The course of the presidential campaign has become familiar over time. First there is a postconvention breathing spell while the candidates and their entourages plan strategy. One crucial question is where to stump, with the electoral college influencing the decision. Building group support calls for a major effort. Each candidate sets up hosts of veterans, farmers, and other campaign groups to operate within the big interest-group organizations such as the American Legion, the AFL-CIO, and the organized doctors. The question of offensive or defensive tactics plagues the tacticians: Do Americans vote for or against candidates? Should the opposition be attacked or ignored? Should the candidate campaign aggressively or seem to stay above the battle? And always there is the need to work on the image of the candidate. This was a major, and evidently highly effective, effort of the 1968 Nixon campaigners. They knew that the Republican nominee must shed his old image of divisive campaigning and, indeed, of failure as a campaigner.[21]

No one has captured the spirit of presidential campaigning better than Adlai E. Stevenson, the unsuccessful Democratic candidate in 1952 and 1956:

> You must emerge, bright and bubbling with wisdom and well-being, every morning at 8 o'clock, just in time for a charming and profound breakfast talk, shake hands with hundreds, often literally thousands, of people, make several inspiring, "newsworthy" speeches during the day, confer with political leaders along the way and with your staff all the time, write at every chance, think if possible, read mail and newspapers, talk on the telephone, talk to everybody, dictate, receive delegations, eat, with decorum — and discretion! — and ride through city after city on the back of an open car, smiling until your mouth is dehydrated by the wind, waving until the blood runs out of your arm, and then bounce gaily, confidently, masterfully into great howling halls, shaved and all

---

[21]On the key factor of personality in presidential campaigning, see Richard W. Boyd, "Presidential Elections: An Explanation of Voting Defection," *American Political Science Review* (June 1969), pp. 498–514.

made up for television with the right color shirt and tie—I always forgot—and a manuscript so defaced with chicken tracks and last-minute jottings that you couldn't follow it, even if the spotlights weren't blinding and even if the still photographers didn't shoot you in the eye every time you looked at them. (I've often wondered what happened to all those pictures!) Then all you have to do is make a great, imperishable speech, get out through the pressing crowds with a few score autographs, your clothes intact, your hands bruised, and back to the hotel—in time to see a few important people.

But the real work has just commenced—two or three, sometimes four hours of frenzied writing and editing of the next day's immortal mouthings so you can get something to the stenographers, so they can get something to the mimeograph machines, so they can get something to the reporters, so they can get something to their papers by deadline time. (And I quickly concluded that all deadlines were yesterday!) Finally sleep, sweet sleep, steals you away, unless you worry—which I do. . . .[22]

In recent years presidential debates have enlivened—or at least focused—the campaigns. In 1960 John Kennedy and Richard Nixon challenged each other to a series of debates. Kennedy's apparent "victory" in the first debate gave his campaign a sharp impetus. In the following elections incumbent presidents Johnson and Nixon did not deign to give their opponents equal billing in debates, but in 1976 President Ford had the courage to do so. He and Carter squared off in three debates sponsored by the League of Women Voters. Both contenders debated well, and the outcome was widely viewed as a standoff. A new feature in the 1976 campaign was a debate between the vice-presidential candidates. Again, both showed their debating skills, but Walter Mondale, according to many observers, gained some votes for his national ticket.

Even more enlivening are the inevitable mistakes that occur in presidential campaigns. In speaking for the "absolute and total separation of church and state," Jimmy Carter warned in a *Playboy* interview against the sin of pride; to illustrate his point he went on, "I've looked on a lot of women with lust. I've committed adultery in my heart many times." This comment became a "nine-days' wonder" at the height of the campaign. President Ford matched this blunder by stating, in defending his record of negotiating with Russia over Eastern Europe, that each of these countries "is independent, autonomous, it has its own territorial integrity," and none was under Soviet domination. The Democrats exploited this for a full week.[23] Such blunders probably have little effect on the final vote. The major influences on the election outcome are party affiliation, interest group membership, attitudes on issues, candidate personality, and how the nominees exploit these various factors.

One standard feature of presidential campaigns almost disappeared in

[22]Adlai E. Stevenson, *Major Campaign Speeches*, 1952 (Random House, 1953), pp. xi–xii. Copyright 1953 by Random House, Inc.

[23]Gerald Pomper et al., *The Election of 1976* (David McKay, 1977) deals with this and many other aspects of the Carter-Ford contest, the congressional, state, and local elections, of 1976, and implications for the future. See also Jules Witcover, *Marathon, 1972–1976* (Viking, 1977).

1976—the desperate search for money. Harry Truman ran so short in 1948 that funds had to be raised from day to day to keep the campaign train moving. Presidential candidates have found the task of raising money a demeaning business, aside from the ever-present worry that donors are trying to buy special influence, or at least access. In 1976, for the first time, government funding was available for the fall campaign. Ford and Carter each received a flat grant of almost $22 million. In accepting these funds, they became ineligible to receive private donations. Each major party was allowed to raise for election expenses about $3 million more, from private donations.[24] Aside from the federal grants to the parties for their conventions, the big subsidies went directly to the candidates, not to their parties.

THE ELECTORAL COLLEGE SYSTEM: MECHANICS

To win the presidency, a candidate must put together a combination of electoral votes that will give him a majority in the electoral college. This unique institution never meets and serves only a limited electoral function. Yet it has an importance of its own. The framers of the Constitution devised the electoral college system because they wanted the president chosen by electors exercising independent judgment. Subsequent political changes have transformed the electors into straight party representatives who simply register the electorate's decision.

The system today works as follows: In making his presidential choice on election day, the voter technically does not vote directly for a candidate but chooses between slates of presidential electors. Each slate is made up of persons selected by the state party (in most states in party conventions) to serve in this essentially honorary role. The slate that wins the most popular votes throughout the state gets to cast all the electoral votes for the state (a state has one electoral vote for every senator and representative).

The electors on the winning slate travel to their state capital the first Monday after the second Wednesday in December; go through the ceremony of casting their ballots for their party's candidates; perhaps hear some speeches; and go home. The ballots are sent from the state capitals to Washington, where early in January they are formally counted by the House and Senate and the name of the next president is announced.

The House and Senate also must act when no candidate secures a majority of the electoral votes. This is not likely so long as there are only two serious contending parties, but it has happened twice in the case of president and once in the case of vice-president. When the situation occurs, the House chooses the president from among the top three candidates. Each *state delegation has one vote*, and a majority is necessary for election. If no person receives a majority of the electoral vote in the vice-presidential contest, the Senate picks from among the top two candidates. Each senator has one vote, and again a majority is required.

THE ELECTORAL COLLEGE SYSTEM: POLITICS

The operation of the electoral college, with its statewide electoral slates, sharply influences the presidency and presidential politics. In order to win a presidential election, a candidate must appeal successfully to urban and suburban groups in states such as New York, California, Pennsylvania, and Illinois. Under the electoral college system, as we have seen, a candi-

---

[24]Alexander, *Financing Politics*, pp. 243–45.

"**You have yourself a deal—you explain cricket and I'll explain the American electoral system.**"

© Copyright 1976 by David Langdon

date wins either *all* a state's electoral votes or *none*. Hence the presidential candidate ordinarily will not waste his time campaigning in states unless he has at least a fighting chance of carrying them; nor will he waste time in states that are on his side. The fight usually narrows down to the medium-sized and big states where the balance between the parties tends to be fairly even.[25]

Obviously the presidential candidate must win over masses of voters in industrial centers. He must show sensitivity to their problems—inflation, housing, wages, social security, and relations with foreign nations, especially nations whose sons and daughters have come by the million to our shores. Moreover, the candidate's appeals must also transcend local matters and dramatize the great national issues. The candidate, in short, strikes out for a national majority rooted in the largest states and sacrifices many narrow issues in order to exploit the broader ones. Candidates for Congress, on the other hand, often win votes by pressing local and sectional claims against those of the rest of the nation.

Both the mechanics and politics of the electoral college can be unpredictable. In 1976 an elector in the state of Washington chosen on the Republican ticket refused to cast his vote for Ford and gave it to Ronald Reagan. Such departures from custom are rare and have never affected the outcomes of an election. But many people agree it is dangerous to have a system that allows individual electors to vote for whomever they wish despite the results of the popular vote in their state. In a close election a small group of persons could go against the wishes of the majority. Although under the present system some states attempt by law to bind electors to vote for the presidential and vice-presidential candidates of their party, these laws may not be enforceable.

All states except Maine now provide for the selection of electors on a general, statewide, winner-take-all, straight-ticket basis. This makes it possible for a person to receive a majority of the national popular vote without receiving a majority of the electoral vote. This happened in 1824 when Andrew Jackson won 12 percent more of the vote than John Quincy Adams; in 1876 when Samuel Tilden received more popular votes but lost the electoral vote to Hayes; and again in 1888 when Grover Cleveland, despite his larger popular vote, got fewer electoral votes than Harrison.

Summary

1. Election processes—registration, party primaries, election procedures, etc.—can affect election outcomes. Because present registration requirements are thought to discourage voting, President Carter has endorsed election-day registration.

2. Because large campaign contributions are suspected of improperly influencing government officials, Congress has long sought to regulate political money. The main methods of curbing political money are: (1) limitations on receiving or spending it; (2) disclosure of the sources and uses of political money; (3) government subsidy of candidates, campaigns, or parties. President Carter has favored extending public financing of campaigns to congressional general elections.

[25]That the electoral college makes the large states the key target of presidential candidates, *even out of proportion to their size*, is demonstrated in Steven J. Brams and Morton D. Davis, "The 3/2's Rule in Presidential Campaigning," *American Political Science Review* (March 1974), pp. 113–34. See also Wallace S. Sayre and Judith H. Parris, *Voting for President: The Electoral College and the American Political System* (Brookings, 1970), p. 41.

3. How to run for Congress varies widely from state to state and district to district. Many factors influence the outcome, but perhaps the crucial ones are localism, personality, and incumbency.

4. Running for president usually requires candidates to "go all out" at an early point, for presidential hopefuls must get delegate support in scores of national and local situations.

5. The electoral college introduces a bias into our electoral system by giving undue importance to the large states. We will return to the question of reforming some of our failing or biased election processes in Chapter 17.

Part Four

The Policy-Makers

A Problem Guide

THE main problem posed by Part Four is responsible leadership. By *leadership* we mean the readiness and ability of policy makers to act effectively in meeting public problems. By *responsible* we mean the ability of voters sooner or later to hold those policy makers accountable for their actions, and the obligation of officials to safeguard both the processes and the substance of democracy.

Our assessment of responsible leadership begins with the treatment of Congress in Chapter 12. How quickly and effectively can Congress take the lead in meeting contemporary problems? What are the obstacles to a revitalized Congress? To whom is Congress responsible? Mainly to the voters, of course. But to which voters? Should Congress respond to a broader interest, such as a majority of the national electorate?

The presidency, discussed in Chapter 13, clearly poses the problem of accountable leadership. The powers of the office, combined with the fixed four-year term, generally give the president enormous resources. Most strong presidents have used these tools well. Yet, as we now know, the great political resources of the modern presidency can be abused and misused, just as they can be underused. What is the proper balance that would ensure both imaginative, progressive leadership and responsible use of power?

What about congressional-presidential relations? We have heard much talk in the late 1970s about a revitalized Congress. Why did it need reform? What has it been able to accomplish? These are many of the central concerns in Chapter 14, which examines the "imperial presidency" argument and outlines how Congress has tried to regain lost powers or make better use of the powers it already has. The struggle between these two major policy-making branches will obviously continue well into the future. But this is an excellent time to reconsider their relationship: We must ask both to whom are they accountable, and to whom are they responsive.

Chapter 15 treats federal judges and the judicial process. Judges, although not directly chosen by the voters, frequently make policy. Yet to whom are they responsible? To the president? To Congress? To the voters? To the Constitution? To their own professional standards or consciences? To all these, of course. But what if they must choose between different kinds of responsibilities?

What about civil servants and the federal bureaucracy? To whom are they responsible? To the president? To Congress? To the law? To their own perspectives and judgments? Bureaucrats are not usually expected to lead. In fact, however, government administrators are constantly making policy as they carry out the directives of president and Congress. Chapter 16 examines the growing importance of the bureaucrats and the factors or forces that help to keep them accountable and within the Constitution.

How can we make the various participants in national policy making responsible to the majority of voters? Because most of our policy makers win power through political parties seeking majority support, this problem raises again the question of how strongly, if at all, the winning party should control the people in office. Should we make legislative and executive branch officials more responsible to the majority of the people? If so, how? Or do we want a looser, more decentralized system that gives more power to shifting coalitions of minority groups, working through and around parties?

In studying the question of responsibility in the context of national policy making, we are trying to discover to which voters and which interests the leaders are responsible and just how they exercise that responsibility.

Chapter 17 serves as a summary for this and earlier parts of the book. We again pose the central questions and themes of the book and offer an appraisal of political developments that are currently affecting the American political system.

Chapter 12

Congress: The People's Branch?

Despite vigorous efforts in the 1970s to democratize its operations and reform its procedures, Congress is still often in the nation's doghouse. Newspaper editors, television commentators, and plain citizens never tire of berating individual legislators or Congress as a whole. Cartoonists delight in portraying members of Congress as lazy, timid, ignorant, greedy, and narrow-minded. Polls indicate that the public seldom has much confidence in its national legislature.

Much of this ridicule is unjustified. Critics usually forget that our national legislature is particularly exposed. In the first place, Congress does nearly all its work directly in the public eye. Unfortunate incidents—quarrels, name-calling, evasive actions, inaccurate statements—that might be hushed up in the executive or judicial branches are almost always observed by journalists. In the second place, Congress by its nature is controversial and argumentative. Its members are found on both sides, sometimes on half a dozen sides, of every important question, and the average citizen holding one opinion is likely to be intolerant of other views and the legislators holding them. Also there is a considerable difference between merely holding an opinion and writing legislation.

Some of the disappointment, moreover, stems from confusion *about* Congress as well as confusion *in* Congress. There is lack of agreement as to what the primary function of Congress should be. Should it concentrate on making policies, debating them, investigating administrative problems, curbing the president and the national bureaucracy—or something else? In fact, Congress can and does do all these things, and more. Confusion *in* Congress arises from the many different jobs it does, the complexity of its procedures, the sheer number (535) of legislators, the diversity of viewpoints, the maze of party and group conflicts, and its highly decentralized power arrangements. At a baseball game almost anyone can understand the duel between pitcher and batter because attention is concentrated on that one spot in the field. In Congress, however, dozens of pitchers throw balls to dozens of batters, so it is impossible to keep your eye on where the action is. This confusion is not the fault of the Congress so much as it is the result of a constitutional system that divides up authority and checks power with power.

The chief public complaints about Congress are that it is inefficient, unrepresentative, and not accountable enough. Some critics contend that Congress is two "Houses of Misrepresentatives," with many of its members beholden to "special interests." Legislators are described as too obsessed with staying elected and as either indifferent or ineffective in dealing with the critical issues of energy, defense systems, inflation, and so on. Another complaint is that Congress confuses rather than clarifies foreign policy.

Senators and representatives themselves sometimes complain about how Congress goes about its business. Former Congresswoman Bella Abzug (D., N.Y.) says she loved Congress, but that its members "don't really represent America . . . Most of the people there are from one group: white, middle-aged men—lawyers and businessmen. Congress needs more women, some trade unionists, city planners, younger people, and minority members."[1] House Republican leader John J. Rhodes (Arizona) argues that "The majority of congressional actions are aimed not at producing results for the American people as much as at perpetuating the longevity and comfort of the men who run Congress. It is a rip-off of the American taxpayer, injurious to the national interest and an insult to the dignity of the legislative branch envisioned by the founding fathers."[2] A congressman from Ohio observed that the more informed Congress becomes, "the more divided we are." He attributed this to the existence of countless little committee "empires," an absence of party discipline, a lack of congressional leadership, and a "profound historic strain of Know Nothingism," or distrust of expert evidence. "Congress reflects the public's demand for simple answers," he said. "But these aren't the kind of answers you get from scientific inquiry."[3]

Cartoon by Jack Moore. © 1976 by Universal Press Syndicate.

Who are the legislators?

All members of Congress are successful politicians, men and women, mostly between the ages of thirty-five and seventy, who have risen to national politics through local processes in their home communities and states. The entire membership of the House of Representatives (435) is elected every second year. Elections for the six-year Senate terms are staggered, so that one-third of the Senate's 100 members are chosen every two years.

"From log cabin to White House" is one of the most pervasive ideals in American politics. The Constitution, at least, sets up no major barriers

---

[1]Bella Abzug, quoted in *The New York Times*, September 16, 1976, p. 35.

[2]John J. Rhodes, *The Futile System* (EPM Publications, 1976), p. 15. Normally a conservative person, Rhodes has written an almost radical study of Congress's faults and how it should be reformed. For political scientists' views, see Leroy N. Rieselbach, *Congressional Reform in the Seventies* (General Learning Press, 1977), and Morris P. Fiorina, *Congress—Keystone of the Washington Establishment* (Yale University Press, 1977).

[3]Charles A. Mosher, quoted in Luther Carter, "Somber Reflections on Congress by a Retiring Member," *Science* (December 26, 1975), p. 1276.

Representative Millicent Fenwick of New Jersey.

except age. Members of the House of Representatives must be twenty-five years old and have been U.S. citizens for seven years. Senators must be at least thirty and have been citizens for nine. Despite this lack of requirements, the composition of Congress does not reflect the socioeconomic makeup of the people as a whole. The overwhelming number of national legislators are male, well educated, middle-aged, and from middle or upper-middle income backgrounds. Until recently, members were also mainly WASPS—white Anglo-Saxon Protestants. The greater numbers of Roman Catholics and Jews in recent Congresses—about 120 Catholics and nearly twenty-five Jews—now bring the religious makeup of the Congress closer in line with that of the general population. But there are fewer blacks and women in Congress than in the general public (see Table 12–1). In the 95th Congress (1977–79) there are also five members of Oriental descent and four with Spanish surnames. About 90 percent of the members are married—two of them to each other (Representative Martha Keys of Kansas married Representative Andrew Jacobs of Indiana in 1976; they both won reelection).

Well over 50 percent of the legislators are lawyers. The 95th Congress also includes one veterinarian, two astronauts, three former professional athletes, six clergymen, about two dozen farmers, and a large number of teachers, professors, and businesspeople. Plainly, Congress occupationally does not mirror the nation as a whole. Rarely does a member of Congress emerge out of trade unions or the so-called blue collar occupations, although fourteen members of the House of Representatives have formed a "blue-collar caucus" composed of members with working-class back-

12–1 Background statistics of the 95th's members (1977–79)*

	House	Senate
PARTY		
Democrat	290	61
Republican	145	38
Independent	0	1
SEX		
Men	417	100
Women	18	0
AGE		
Youngest	28	35
Oldest	78	82
Average	49	54
MINORITIES		
Black	16	1
Oriental	2	3
Spanish	4	0
RELIGION		
Protestant	254	69
Roman Catholic	108	12
Jewish	18	5
Mormon	51	3
Other	4	11
PROFESSION *(Includes some lawmakers who list themselves in more than 1 category)*		
Lawyers	223	68
Businessmen and Bankers	119	24
Educators	70	13
Farmers	16	9
Journalists	27	6

*Statistics as of 1978.

grounds. Among these are a former longshoreman, a pipefitter, a ware-house worker, and an ex-riverboat captain. How important is this "mis-representation"? Critics say that it offers just one more instance of government of the elite by the elite and for the elite. Defenders point out that we would hardly expect to find the national percentage of high school drop-outs mirrored in Congress. Whatever its makeup, however, the more important question is whether a Congress composed of legislators drawn from a restricted segment of the population is biased in favor of certain points of view.

SAFE DISTRICTS
AND CAREERISM

Congress has left almost complete control over the drawing of congressional districts to the state legislatures. Senators, of course, represent entire states, but House seats are distributed among the states according to population, with each state receiving at least one.

In many states the party in control of the state legislature openly engages in gerrymandering—that is, it tries to draw district boundaries in such a way as to secure for its party as many representatives as possible. This is why congressional districts take on a variety of weird shapes. The once rural-dominated legislatures used to arrange the districts so as to overrepresent rural areas. But this was ended both by the population shift to the cities and suburbs and by a notable Supreme Court decision, *Wesberry v. Sanders* (1964)[4] In this case, the Court ruled that the Constitution requires that all congressional districts in a state have the same number of people (as nearly as possible), so that one person's vote would be equal to that of every other person. How much difference did this and subsequent Supreme Court rulings make? Population inequalities have ended. The voice of suburban populations has been strengthened. Gerrymandering, however, continues as state politicians still draw boundary lines to protect incumbents.

Some analysts believe that these redistricting policies have had the effect of creating more safe seats and encouraging careerism. In election after election in recent years, the vast majority of representatives as well as senators are returned to office. Usually, about 80 percent of Senate incumbents and about 90 percent of House members who run again are re-elected. Most House seats are "safe" in the sense that incumbents win by such sweeping majorities that the chances of challengers defeating them are minimal.

Some critics of Congress point to this apparently increasing lack of competition as one of the causes of congressional conservatism. The whole election system, they say, guarantees that Congress will be more tied to the status quo than will a president. As long as the members can keep "the folks and the interests back home" happy, they can remain reasonably independent from the president and their party leadership. Of course, an incumbent can be voted out of office, especially if a legislator loses touch with constituents or national needs. But how would the voters know if this was the case? Few people know the name of their representative or senator. Still fewer evaluate legislators on their stands or votes on issues. Unhappily (or happily, depending on your view) the members of Congress are judged on service to their constituents, their communications with the district, their attendance records, "small favors done over the years," and

[4]376 U.S. 1 (1964)

other such nonlegislative matters. Not surprisingly, most members of Congress pursue policies and assignments, and allocate their time and energy, in ways they feel will enhance their prospects for reelection. A safe seat, on the other hand, permits a legislator to serve as a national leader without having to worry too much about constantly returning home. Senator Frank Church, for example, as long as he does not take issue with sensitive domestic concerns of the people of Idaho, can count on a base from which he has become a national spokesman for certain foreign policy attitudes and for greater congressional control of the Central Intelligence Agency. Representatives from competitive states or districts, on the other hand, find it more difficult to ignore local concerns, and tend to concentrate their time and energies on narrower issues.[5]

The powers of the congress

The Constitution is generous in its grant of congressional powers. In the very first article, the founding fathers outlined the structure, powers, and responsibilities of Congress, giving it "all legislative powers herein granted." Among these legislative powers are the power to spend and tax in order to "provide for the common defense and general welfare of the United States"; the power to borrow money; to regulate commerce with foreign nations and among the states; to declare war, raise and support armies, provide and maintain a navy; to establish post offices and postroads; to set up the federal courts under the Supreme Court. As a final catch-all, the Constitution gave the Congress the right "to make all laws which shall be necessary and proper for carrying into execution" the powers set out. Several nonlegislative functions were also granted, such as participating in the process of constitutional amendment and impeachment given to the House, and trying an impeached federal officer given to the Senate.

The Constitution confers special additional responsibilities on the Senate. The Senate has the power to confirm presidential nominations, including between 200 to 400 key executive and judicial nominees each year (we shall discuss how the Senate meets this responsibility in Chapter 14). The Senate also has the responsibility of giving consent, by a two-thirds vote of the senators present, before a president may ratify a treaty. This gives the Senate a special role in the conduct of foreign policy.

The House also has some special responsibilities, but these have not proved to be as important as have those given to the Senate. For example, all revenue bills must originate in the House. In fact, this has made little practical difference, since the Senate has freely amended the bills that originate in the House, and changed everything except the title.

The framers had, of course, no intention of making Congress all-powerful. As we have seen, they reserved certain authority to the states and gave other powers to the executive and judicial branches of government. As time passed, Congress gained power in some respects and lost it in others. The power of Congress also changes depending on the times and on who

---

[5]See Roger H. Davidson, *The Role of the Congressman* (Pegasus, 1969), esp. chap. 4. For additional discussion of factors that contribute to safe seats, see Albert D. Cover and David Mayhew, "Congressional Dynamics and the Decline of Competitive Congressional Elections," in Larry Dodd and Bruce Oppenheimer, eds., *Congress Reconsidered* (Praeger, 1977), pp. 54–72. On the importance of the "electoral connection" in motivating congressional behavior, see David R. Mayhew, *Congress: The Electoral Connection* (Yale University Press, 1974). See also Fiorina, *Congress: The Keystone to the Washington Establishment* (Yale University Press, 1977).

is president. As the role and authority of the national government have expanded, so have the policy making and oversight responsibilities of Congress. Many analysts feel, however, that Congress has not kept pace with its great rival, the presidency, which in many respects today holds the place in our national government that most of the founding fathers apparently wanted Congress to have. This may be part of a worldwide trend. Legislative bodies have almost everywhere become subordinate to the executive at all levels of government.

Despite its secondary role in recent decades, Congress still performs at least these six important functions: *representation, lawmaking, consensus-building, overseeing, policy-clarification,* and *legitimizing*. Representation is expressing the diversity and conflicting views of the economic, social, racial, religious, and other interests making up the United States. Lawmaking is enacting measures to help solve substantive problems. Consensus-building is the bargaining process by which these interests are reconciled. Policy-clarification, or "policy-incubation," as it is sometimes called, is the identification and publicizing of issues. Legitimizing is the formal ratification of policies by what are accepted as proper channels.

The job of the legislator

National legislators lead a hectic life. Congress now meets year round, whereas a hundred years ago it often met for just a few months each year. There is never enough time to digest all the information, letters, complaints, reports, and advice that pour in. Staying elected is a chief priority; some members seem to have few other interests. But for most, there are the constantly demanding secondary tasks of keeping on top of their committee responsibilities, staying in touch with key leaders and activists back home, and striving to understand national problems. Most legislators are extremely hard-working: They drive themselves at a pace far harder than that of the typical professional or business person. Their travel commitments are almost as demanding as those of airline pilots and cross-country truck drivers. The average member stays elected about eleven or twelve years. Depending on the kind of district, the personality of the member, and the issues of the day, he or she may emphasize representation, lawmaking and committee work, or reelection tasks.

LEGISLATORS AS REPRESENTATIVES

For whom does the representative speak? The geographical district and its immediate interests? the party? the nation? some special clientele? his or her conscience? How legislators define their representative roles has been one of the major questions in political science—and for good reason. Congress was intended to serve as a forum for registering the interests and values that make up the nation. It was never intended that the legislative branch should represent views identical with those of the executive. But to whom does the individual representative listen?

Certain patterns are evident, but their meaning is far from clear. For one thing, members of Congress perceive their roles differently. Some believe they should serve as **delegates** from their districts; they should find out what the "folks back home" need or want and serve those needs as effectively as possible. In a sense they would simply *re-present* the voters who sent them to Washington. This orientation, studies show, is often assumed by Republicans, nonleaders, non-southerners, and members with low seniority.[6]

---

[6]*Ibid.,* p. 140.

The Capitol

Congress is the seat of legislative authority, the center of public debate, a carry-over of folksy political traditions from earlier days—and a collection of several hundred relatively independent politicians with separate but overlapping constituencies. The architecture of the Capitol bespeaks its ways—two chambers, endless corridors, ornate rotundas and galleries, and a rabbit warren of grand rooms, tiny offices, winding passageways. There is no culminating point of authority but a multiplicity of decision centers.

PUBLIC AREAS

18 Statuary Hall
19 Rotunda
20 Senate Rotunda
21 Old Senate Chamber
    *(being restored as old
     Senate Chamber)

SENATE
Washington, D.C. 20510

22 Senators' Offices
23 Executive Clerk
24 Senate Conference Room
25 Senate Disbursing Office
26 Minority Leader
27 Majority Leader
28 Office of the Vice President
29 Senators' Reception Room

30 Cloakrooms
31 Senate Chamber
32 Marble Room
33 President's Room
34 Office of the Secretary
35 Chief Clerk
36 Bill Clerk and Journal Clerk
37 Official Reporters of Debates

HOUSE OF REPRESENTATIVES
Washington, D.C. 20515

1 Speaker's Office
2 Committee on Ways and Means
3 Parliamentarian
4 House Floor Library
5 Cloakrooms
6 Members' Retiring Room
and Lobby
7 House Chamber
8 Committee on Appropriations

9 Minority Whip
10 House Reception Room
11 House Minority Conference Room
12 House Majority Conference Room
13 House Document Room
14 Subcommittee on Foreign Affairs
15 Representatives' Offices
16 Prayer Room
17 Minority Leader

ON CONGRESSIONAL PAY AND PERQUISITES

Not a bad lot

For the conscientious member of Congress, the job is one of the most demanding in public life. Yet no congressional seat has ever gone vacant because no one wanted it. One reason is that the pay, now $57,500, is good. And so are the fringe benefits. Among the compensating comforts are:

■ A $7,000 personal expense allowance for each member.

■ Thirty-three round-trips home each year at public expense, plus a minimum of $2,250 or 10% of the total cost.

■ A stationery allowance—which can no longer be pocketed—of $6,500 a year.

■ Almost unlimited franking privileges to mail official nonpolitical material to constituents.

■ Extra postage, called a "constituent communication allowance" of $5,000 a year.

■ A telephone and telegraph allowance of at least $6,000 a year.

■ Unlimited U.S. telephone calls between 5 p.m. and 9 a.m. weekdays and all day on weekends and holidays for payment of a single small fee.

■ An allowance of $255,144 a year to hire staff in Washington and in the home district.

■ Free furnished office space in Washington. Free plants and flowers from the Botanic Garden.

■ Reimbursed rental for 1,500 sq ft. of home district office space at the highest local rate, and a $27,000 allowance for furniture and equipment, which belongs to the government.

■ Free medical care and drugs provided by the Capitol physician. Low rates at Bethesda Naval Hospital.

■ Cut-rate life insurance.

■ Special low rates for photographers; use of a professionally staffed radio and television recording studio; $2 haircuts.

■ Free use of the research staff of the Library of Congress.

■ Generous retirement pay, now being recomputed under the raised salary. Previously as high as $35,680 after 32 years' service, it will be increased.

■ Travel gear: one free trunk per session—a holdover from the pioneer past.

TIME, March 14, 1977

Too Nice a Deal?

Washington—No one, absolutely no one, should be paid $57,500 a year, a Washington cab driver was saying when—fortunately for his passenger—the end of the trip ended the harangue.

Unlike their chatty New York counterparts, cabbies in the capital are disposed to sulk silently, but the subject of new congressional salaries unleashes a tirade of bitter words from even the most closed-mouth drivers.

However, a look at the schedule of Rep. Richard Bolling of Missouri makes it seem possible that at least a few members of Congress may come as close to earning the $57,500 as anyone can.

Tuesday, a day only slightly busier than usual for Bolling, the Kansas City Democrat, began by sitting as chairman of the House-Senate Joint Economic Committee, the British chancellor of the exchequer was on hand to talk about international trade and monetary policies.

An hour later Bolling was sitting as the ranking Democrat on the House Rules Committee to clear strip-mining legislation for floor debate. At noon he was on the House floor handling a rule on the first budget recommendations for fiscal 1978.

His afternoon began with a session of the House Democratic Steering Committee where strategy was planned for the strip-mining debate. In midafternoon Bolling was meeting with the House Ethics Committee to draw the line on gifts representatives may receive.

At 4 p.m. the new House Energy Committee held its first meeting to prepare for the President's massive energy proposal. For the fourth time that day Bolling was sitting as the ranking Democrat on a committee—first in line behind the chairman.

As the day stretched into late afternoon, Bolling canceled an appearance at a dinner where honored guests included the Rev. Maurice Van Ackeren, president of Rockhurst College in Kansas City. Pacing himself turned out to be the right decision—the House session Wednesday was to run past 1 a.m.

Bolling's schedule is the penalty he pays for hanging around a seniority-conscious Congress 30 years. At the end of a legislative day he has little enthusiasm for social events preferring to stay at home, where a room was enlarged recently for leisure activities.

Along with his assignments come the privileges of power. On Bolling's schedule this week are two White House sessions with the President, one today on an unannounced subject and another Wednesday with the House Energy Committee.

Is the veteran lawmaker earning his $57,500? Or half of it? After all, Missouri's 5th district gets two for the price of one. Bolling's wife, Jim, makes the daily trip to the capital from Maryland with her husband and as an unpaid aide keeps substantially the same hours.

From the Kansas City Times, Capitol Hill (by Henry Clay Gold) May 2, 1977. Reprinted in the Congressional Record PE2814, May 6, 1977.

Others see their proper role as a trustee; their constituents, they argue, did not send them to Congress to serve as agents. They are to vote independently, on the basis of their own better information and greater experience, for the welfare of the whole nation. This view echoes the stand once championed by the famed English legislator Edmund Burke, who said his judgment and conscience ought not to be sacrificed to the opinions of others.[7] In his view, a legislature was a place for deliberation and learning. It was not a mere gathering of ambassadors from localities. Interviews with members of the House of Representatives suggest that the trustee, or national, focus is more common among Democrats, House leaders, southerners, and high-seniority members.

Although the question of delegate versus trustee is an old one, it is somewhat misleading. Representatives cannot follow detailed instructions from their constituents because such instructions seldom exist. On many important policy questions, members hear nothing from their constituents. And they hear most often from those who agree with them. On the other hand, it is rather unrealistic to expect a legislator to define the national interest if this means understanding the needs and aspirations of millions of people. Most legislators shift back and forth in their representative role, depending on their perception of the public interest, the electoral facts of life, and the pressures of the moment.

LEGISLATORS AS LAWMAKERS

The major role of both senators and representatives is that of *lawmaker*. How the members of Congress perceive the nation's key problems and what can be done about them; how they respond to the interests of their constituents; the extent to which they follow cues from (and give cues to) the president, from colleagues within the Congress, and from lobbies all influence drafting and voting decisions in both houses.

The influence of the voters Most of the time, however, the main single influence on legislators is their perception of how their constituents feel about the matter. Party and executive branch pressures also play a role, but when all is said and done, the members' political future depends on how a majority of voters feel about their performance. It is the rare person who consistently and deliberately votes against the wishes of the people back home. If too many did so, it would break the major democratic link between the electorate and the decision makers.

This commonsense observation is supported by several studies. On domestic issues such as social welfare and civil rights, there usually is a great deal of agreement between legislators and their districts. Junior members from competitive seats, in particular, vote their constituencies' attitudes, as they perceive them. But even members who win by a substantial margin are not necessarily free to ignore the concerns of the voters. They may, in fact, have won easily just because people know they will follow their wishes on issues important to them.[8] Of course, the extent

[7]See Heinz Eulau, et al., "The Role of the Representative: Some Empirical Observations on the Theory of Edmund Burke," *American Political Science Review* (Sept. 1959), pp. 742–56.

[8]John W. Kingdon, *Congressmen's Voting Decisions* (Harper & Row, 1973), p. 31. His interviews with a sample of members of the 91st Congress (1969) indicated that fellow congressmen and constituency factors were the most important influences on voting decisions, followed in importance by interest group, staff, and executive branch and party leadership factors. For a short case study of how an activist senator operates his office and seeks advice, see James MacGregor Burns, *Edward Kennedy and the Camelot Legacy* (Norton, 1976), chap. 7.

to which members try to respond to their constituents' views also depends on the measure under consideration. Legislators might pay more attention to voter attitudes on social and economic matters than on policies on which mass opinion is not so well informed.

Something of a paradox is evident here. Members of Congress feel that their individual lawmaking actions may have considerable impact on voters. Yet the voters' ignorance of members' actions implies that the impact can be small. Members may think the folks back home like (or dislike) what they are doing, when actually the voters have little idea of what is going on in Congress. This is explained in part by the tendency of legislators to overestimate their visibility. Partly, too, members must constantly be concerned about how they will explain their votes, especially if they fear those votes may be unpopular with influential citizens back home. Also, on election day, members are dealing in increments and margins. Even if only a few voters are aware of their stand on a given issue, they fear that disappointing this group might make the difference between victory and defeat.

"So far, my mail is running three to one in favor of my position."

Drawing by Robert Day;
© 1970 The New Yorker Magazine, Inc.

The influence of colleagues Voting decisions are also affected by the advice members obtain from other representatives. Severe time limitations and the frequent necessity to make decisions with only a few hours' or even minutes' notice force legislators to depend on others. Most members develop friendships with people who think as they do. They often ask one another what they think of a piece of pending legislation. In particular, they ask respected members of the committee working on the bill.[9]

Unlike most of the voters back home, other members usually have detailed knowledge about many of the issues before Congress. Their views are often public. They may have voted on the matter in previous sessions, or in committee, and their public statements may have been placed in the *Congressional Record.* Sometimes members are influenced to vote one way merely because they know a colleague is on the other side of the issue. More often, legislators find out how their friends stand on an issue, listens to the party leadership's advice, and take into account the various committee reports. If they are still in doubt, they consult additional friends and staff.

The members most often consulted by their colleagues are those who represent similar districts or the same region or state, or likeminded members of the same party or faction. If these advisors are respected and known to be well informed on the legislation, this factor alone sometimes sways members. They may vote against their party, and sometimes even against what they think is the mood of their constituency.

The influence of the party Another important source of influence on legislative behavior is the *political party*. Friendships tend to develop within the party; and party leaders in both the executive and legislative branches apply rewards and penalties. Of course, there is a fair amount of natural agreement among party colleagues. On some issues, the pressure for conformity to a party position is immediate and direct. There is often pressure to go along with the party even when a member does not believe in the party position.

[9]Donald R. Matthews and James A. Stimson, *Yeas and Nays: Normal Decision-Making in the U.S. House of Representatives* (Wiley, 1975).

The result of party pressures is a tendency, on major bills, for *most* Democrats to be arrayed against *most* Republicans. In party-line votes, members of Congress typically vote with their party majority about two-thirds of the time. However, senators are slightly more independent than representatives. Party influence also varies over time. It was stronger during the nineteenth century than it has been in this century, and it has been stronger in the mid-1970s than in the post-World War II era. Party influence varies by issue. Party differences have been stronger over domestic, regulatory, and welfare measures than over foreign policy and civil liberty issues.[10] Much depends, of course, on what we mean by party—the presidentially led party outside Congress, state or local parties, or the party leadership within Congress.

Other influences   Many forces—regional, local, ideological—can override party influence. One voting pattern in Congress reflects a conservative coalition of Republicans and southern Democrats. In the 1950s and 1960s, a majority of southern Democrats and a majority of Republicans voted against the majority of northern Democrats on about a quarter of the important roll call votes.[11] This is less the case in the mid and late 1970s. This conservative coalition is most likely to appear on domestic issues, especially social welfare legislation. But its strength in Congress cannot be measured by voting decisions alone, because the many committee chairmen who are members of this group are often able to prevent legislation they oppose from ever being voted on. The pattern is now changing, as Democrats elected from the South in recent years are more "national" than "sectional" in their voting patterns and the Democrats, especially in the House, have strengthened party discipline.

Senate Majority Leader Robert Byrd (left) and Senate Minority Leader Howard Baker.

Presidents and the executive branch can also influence how legislators vote. Some critics say Congress has yielded exclusive policy initiation and budgetary planning to the administrative branch: "No matter how hard the Congress may struggle on one issue, it is overwhelmed by the vastly greater forces of the presidency. Whether Congress wins or loses, the president ends up on top."[12] Even a fair number of congressmen complain today, as they have throughout our history, that as now organized and staffed, Congress cannot really come to grips with the enormously complex questions involved in making national policy.

Complexity of issues and increasingly demanding schedules have led to an explosion in congressional staffs. Approximately 25,000 staff members, researchers, budget analysts, and others now work for Congress. This number has grown at least fourfold in the last twenty-five years. But numbers only begin to tell the story of staff influence. Members of Congress have become willing or have had to delegate all kinds of tasks to their personal and committee staffs. It has reached the point where some members now ask whether they or their staffs are in charge. Much of the growth in congressional staffs occurred during the period when Congress believed the executive branch was failing to share needed information and studies. Moreover, as one writer has noted, Congress is the only legislature in the

[10]See, for example, Aage R. Clausen, *How Congressmen Decide* (St. Martin's, 1973).

[11]See John F. Manley, "The Conservative Coalition in Congress," *American Behavioral Scientist* (December 1973), pp. 223–47.

[12]Mark J. Green, James M. Fallows, David R. Zwick, *Who Runs Congress?* (Bantam, 1972), p. 94.

world with much of a staff and this is one of its chief sources of power, for without its staff Congress would doubtless become too much the prisoner of the executive branch and interest groups.[13]

Even if Congress were better organized or its members more expert, the growing significance of foreign policy and complicated economic issues means that the role of the president must be enhanced. The president has the tools of foreign policymaking in his hands, and even those he shares with Congress, such as the treaty-making power, have become less significant.

Although a president, through the full use of his emergency, constitutional, and political powers, has become a major partner in legislation, members of Congress are reluctant to admit that they are influenced by pressures from the White House. Studies suggest, moreover, that presidential influence on congressional voting decisions may not be as significant as most observers believe. A president has more impact on votes in the area of international politics. On key domestic issues, legislators are more likely to be influenced by what the voters want (or what they think the voters want) and by party considerations than by what the White House wants.

The legislative obstacle course

From the very beginning, Congress has been a system of multiple vetoes. This was in part the intent of the framers, who wanted to disperse powers so they could not be assembled by any would-be tyrant. In addition, to cope with its duties, Congress has developed an even more elaborate system that distributes political influence in different ways to different people. To follow a bill through Congress is to see this *dispersion of power*. Procedures and rules in the two houses are somewhat different, but the basic distribution of power, in its effect on the shaping of legislation, is roughly the same. Every bill, including those drawn up in the executive branch, must be introduced in either house by a member of that body. The vast majority of the 20,000 or so bills introduced every two years die in a subcommittee for lack of support. On major legislation that has significant backing, the committee or one of its subcommittees will hold hearings to receive opinions. It then meets to "mark up" (discuss and revise) and vote on the bill. If the subcommittee and then the parent committee vote in favor of the bill, it is reported—or sent—to the full house, where it is debated and voted on. If passed, it then goes to the other house, where the whole process is repeated. If there are differences between the bills as passed by House and Senate—and there often are—the two versions must go to a conference committee for reconciliation.

In 1789–90, 142 bills were introduced in the House of Representatives and only 85 reports were filed from committees. By the late 1970s, about 20,000 bills were introduced in every two-year session and at least 2,000 committee reports prepared by every new Congress. An indication of the contemporary workload of the House is shown in Table 12–2.

[13]Michael J. Malbin, "Congressional Committee Staffs: Who's in Charge?" *Public Interest* (Spring 1977), p. 19. See also Michael A. Scully, "Reflections of a Senate Aide," *Public Interest* (Spring 1977), p. 41; Allen Schick, "The Supply and Demand for Analysis on Capitol Hill," *Policy Analysis* (Spring 1976), pp. 215–34; and Harrison W. Fox, Jr., and Susan Webb Hammond, "The Growth of Congressional Staffs," in Harvey C. Mansfield, Sr., ed., *Congress Against the President* (Proceedings of the Academy of Political Science, 1975), pp. 112–24.

12—2
The average house legislative workload 80th through 92nd and 94th Congress (1946—72; 1975—77)

Category	Average per Congress 1946–72	94th Congress 1975–77
Bills introduced	13,711	19,371[2]
Committee reports	2,456	1,495[3]
Public laws passed	790	588[4]
Private laws passed	618	141
Total laws and resolutions	1,408	1,624
Presidential messages to Congress	185[1]	251
Presidential messages referred to committee	167	238
Executive branch communications	2,372	4,129

[1]Figures for 89th through 92nd Congress only (1965–72).
[2]Figure includes all bills and resolutions.
[3]Figure includes reports on bills and resolutions only.
[4]In addition, 711 resolutions were passed by Congress.

SOURCE: Final House Calendars. Reprinted from *Report of the Select Committee on Committees,* U.S. House of Representatives, to Accompany H. Res. 988, 93rd Congress (March 21, 1974). Also, *Congressional Record*—Daily Digest, October 26, 1976 and Office of the Bill Clerk, House of Representatives.

MULTIPLE OPPORTUNITIES FOR DELAY

The complexity of the congressional system provides a tremendous built-in advantage for the opponents of any measure. Those who sponsor a bill must win at every step; opponents need to win only once. Multiple opportunities for vetoes exist because of the dispersion of influence and because at a dozen points in committee or in the house a bill may be killed or allowed to die. Whether good or bad, a proposal can be delayed by any one of the following: (1) the chairperson of the House substantive

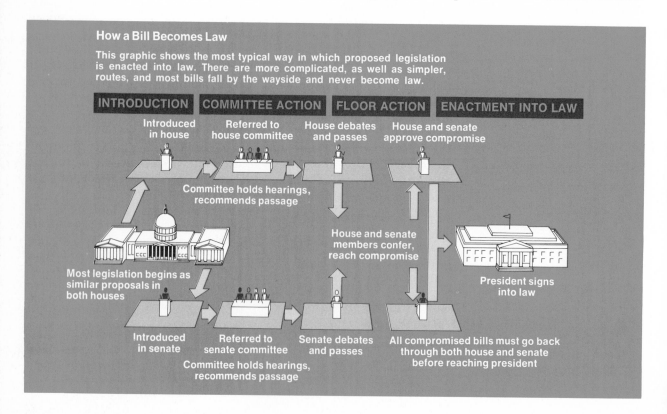

How a Bill Becomes Law

This graphic shows the most typical way in which proposed legislation is enacted into law. There are more complicated, as well as simpler, routes, and most bills fall by the wayside and never become law.

INTRODUCTION | **COMMITTEE ACTION** | **FLOOR ACTION** | **ENACTMENT INTO LAW**

Introduced in house — Referred to house committee — House debates and passes — House and senate approve compromise

Committee holds hearings, recommends passage

Most legislation begins as similar proposals in both houses

House and senate members confer, reach compromise

President signs into law

Introduced in senate — Referred to senate committee — Senate debates and passes — All compromised bills must go back through both house and senate before reaching president

Committee holds hearings, recommends passage

subcommittee, (2) the House substantive committee, (3) the House rules committee, (4) the House, (5) the chairperson of the Senate subcommittee, (6) the Senate committee, (7) the majority of the Senate, (8) forty-one members of the Senate in the event of a filibuster, (9) the House-Senate conference committee if the chambers disagree, and (10) the president. If the agreement of still other committees is required—appropriations, for example—the points of possible veto are multiplied.

Clearly, a controversial bill cannot get through without good legislative leadership. One tactical question at the start is whether to push for initial action in the Senate or the House. If a bill is expected to face rough sledding in the Senate, for example, its sponsors may seek passage in the House and hope that a sizable victory will spur the Senate into action. Another question is what committee the bill should be assigned to for favorable action. Normally, referral to a committee is automatic. Sometimes, however, a bill cuts across more than one jurisdiction, so it can be written in such a way that it is bound to go to one committee rather than another.

Getting a bill through Congress requires more than a majority at any one time or place. Majorities must be mobilized over and over again, in subcommittee, in committee, and in chamber. These are shifting and changing majorities, involving different legislators in different situations at different points in time. New coalitions must be built again and again.

These days, almost everything Congress wants to do by legislation requires dollars. So even if a bill passes, it must go through the process again to secure the appropriations. Congress may go through the entire process of authorizing a program, and then fail to appropriate money to implement it, or appropriate so little money that what was authorized cannot be carried out.

The houses of congress

The single most important fact about Congress is the dispersion of power between its two houses. The Senate and the House each have an absolute veto over the lawmaking of the other. Each house runs it own affairs, sets its own rules, and conducts its own investigations. The lawmaking role, however, is shared. Each house must be seen as a separate institution, even though it reflects somewhat similar political forces and shares organizational patterns as the other.

THE HOUSE OF REPRESENTATIVES

Organization and procedure in the House are somewhat different from that in the Senate, if only because the House is over four times as large as the Senate. In recent years, these two bodies have grown more similar. Still, *how* things are done usually affects *what* is done. The House assigns different types of bills to different calendars. For example, finance mea-

Mexican President Jose Lopez Portillo addresses members of the U.S. Congress.

sures—tax or appropriations bills—are put on a special calendar for quicker action. The House has worked out other ways of speeding up law-making, including an electronic voting device. Ordinary rules may be suspended by a two-thirds vote, or immediate action may be taken by unanimous consent of the members on the floor. By sitting as the committee of the whole, the House is able to operate more informally and more quickly than under its regular rules. A quorum in this committee is only 100 rather than a majority of the whole chamber, and voting is quicker and simpler. Members are limited in how long they can speak. In contrast to the Senate, debate may be cut off simply by majority vote.

The speaker   The speaker is the presiding officer in the House of Representatives. He is formally elected by the House, but actually selected by the majority party. Throughout most of this century, House members were unwilling to vest power in their party leaders. Revolts in 1910 by the rank-and-file Progressives stripped the speaker of most of his authority, which included control over who served on congressional committees. In the mid-1970s, however, several "reforms" have strengthened the speakership. (We put the word reforms in quotes because the 1910 changes to reduce the power of the speaker were introduced as progressive reforms. Sixty years later, progressive reforms were to give back to the speaker some of the powers previously taken away from him.)

The routine powers of the speaker include recognition of members who wish to speak, ruling on questions of parliamentary procedure, and appointment of members to select and conference—that is, temporary—but not standing committees. In general, the speaker directs the business on the floor of the House. More significant, of course, is a speaker's political and behind-the-scenes influence. As a result of the changes in the 1970s, the speaker now enjoys some additional leeway in influencing certain committee appointments. He also chairs the influential Democratic Steering and Policy Committee created in 1973. This new committee consists of about twenty-four members: the speaker's lieutenants, four others appointed by him, and twelve elected by regional caucuses within the House Democratic party. It devises and directs party strategy. In 1975, the speaker was given the authority to refer legislation to what he deems the relevant committee and to select most members and the chair of the House Rules Committee.

The job of speaker usually goes to a member of the majority party with substantial seniority. Speaker Thomas "Tip" O'Neill, elected in January 1977, for example, had served in the House since 1953.[14] The speaker is assisted by a majority floor leader who helps plan party strategy, confers with other party leaders, and tries to keep members of his party in line. The minority party elects a minority floor leader, who usually steps into the speakership when his party gains a majority in the House. Assisting each floor leader are the party whips (the term comes from the whipper-in, who in fox hunts keeps the hounds bunched in the pack). The whips serve as liaison between the House leadership of each party and the rank-and-file. They inform members when important bills will come up for a vote and prepare summaries of the bill's content, exert mild pressure on them

---

[14]For an analysis of how congressional leaders get selected, see Robert L. Peabody, *Leadership in Congress: Stability, Succession and Change* (Little, Brown, 1976).

to support the leadership, and try to ensure maximum attendance on the floor for critical votes.

At the beginning of the session and occasionally afterward, each party holds a caucus (or conference, as the Republicans call it). The caucus, composed of all the party's members in the House, meets to elect party officers, approve committee assignments, elect committee chairmen, discuss important legislation, and perhaps try to agree on party policy.

The House rules committee One way in which the House differs from the Senate is the procedure for deciding the flow of business. In the House this power is vested in the Rules Committee, one of the regular House standing committees. In the normal course of events, a bill does not come up for action on the floor without a rule from the Rules Committee. By failing to act or refusing to grant a rule, the committee can veto a bill. Furthermore, the rule granted gives the conditions under which the bill will be discussed, and these conditions may seriously affect the chance of passage. The Rules Committee may grant a rule that makes it easy for a bill to be amended to death on the floor. A special rule may prohibit amendments altogether or provide that only members of the committee reporting the bill may offer amendments. The rule also sets the length of debate.

Up to about the mid-1960s, the Rules Committee was dominated by a coalition of conservative Republicans and Democrats. Liberals denounced it as being unrepresentative, unfair, and dictatorial. Today it seldom blocks legislation unless the House leadership prefers measures to be held up. Meanwhile, the Rules Committee membership—due to deaths and new appointments—has come to reflect the views of the total membership of the majority party. Because the speaker can control its membership, the Rules Committee today is usually an arm of the leadership. And rather than blocking legislation, it offers what one analyst calls a "dress rehearsal" opportunity to those who are trying to press for new legislation. It

> gives the proponents and opponents a chance to test their presentations on a committee that is broadly representative of the entire body. This not only provides them with important feedback and makes them aware of problems they will face on the floor, but also supplies an important opportunity to publicize their positions and to set the boundaries for debate by the entire body . . . .
>
> But more important, by serving as critics at the dress rehearsal, the Rules members serve the House. It is impossible for the House members to keep track of the legislation forthcoming from all the committees and subcommittees of which they are not members. They need someone whose judgment they can trust, who is not intimately involved in the writing of the legislation, just like the theatergoer needs a good critic to sort through the many available entertainment offerings. From the Rules critic the House members can learn whether the committee producing the legislation has done its job well. What strengths and weaknesses exist? Has consensus been built? Is it likely to pass? Have his interests been protected? When is it scheduled for the floor?[15]

[15]Bruce I. Oppenheimer, "The Rules Committee: New Arm of Leadership in a Decentralized House," in Dodd and Oppenheimer, eds., *Congress Reconsidered*, p. 113. For a perceptive analysis of the House rules committee since 1961, see Spark M. Matsunaga and Ping Chen, *Rulemakers of the House* (University of Illinois Press, 1976).

In many respects, the Senate resembles the House. There is the same basic committee structure, the elected party leadership, the same dispersion of power. But because the Senate is a smaller body, its procedures are considerably more informal and it has more time for debate.

The president of the Senate (the vice-president of the United States) has little influence. He can vote only in case of a tie and is seldom consulted when important decisions are made. The Senate also elects from among the majority party a president pro tempore, who is the official chairman in the absence of the vice-president. But presiding over the Senate is a thankless task and is generally carried out by a junior member of the chamber.

Party machinery in the Senate is somewhat similar to that of the House. There are party conferences (caucuses), majority and minority floor leaders, and party whips. Each party has a *policy committee*, composed of the leaders of the party, which is theoretically responsible for the party's overall legislative program. (In the Senate the party steering committees handle only committee assignments.) Unlike the House steering committees, the Senate's policy committees are formally provided for by law, and each has a regular staff and a budget. Although the Senate policy committees have some influence on legislation, they have not asserted strong legislative leadership or managed to coordinate party policy.

The majority leader, however, is usually a person of influence within the Senate and sometimes nationally. He has the right to be the first senator heard on the floor. In consultation with the minority floor leader, he determines the Senate's agenda. He has much to say about committee assignments for members of his own party. But the position confers somewhat less authority than the speakership in the House, and its influence depends on the person's political and parliamentary skills and the national political situation.

Political environment   Senators are a somewhat different breed of political animal from the average member of the House, and some people feel the Senate has a character all its own. If only because of the six-year term, senators have more political elbow room than representatives. In addition, senators are more likely to wield political power in their state parties. Average senators become visible and politically significant earlier in their careers. Part of this is due to the relative smallness of the Senate and easier access to the media; part also is due, no doubt, to larger staffs.

To a degree, the Senate is a mutual protection society. Members tend to guard the rights and privileges of fellow senators — so that their own rights and privileges will be protected in turn. Members learn to live together. Two senators may attack each other rather sharply on the floor, only to be seen a short time later strolling together in the corridors. Like many close-knit social or professional groups, the Senate has developed a set of informal folkways — standards of behavior to which new members are expected to conform. Courtesy in debate is a cardinal rule, for example, and debate takes place in the third person. By far the most important folkway is *reciprocity*. A senator requests and receives many favors and courtesies from fellow senators always with the understanding that he will repay the kindness in some form. A senator may be out of town and request that the vote on a particular bill be delayed. A senator asks a committee chairman how a given bill will affect constituents, and relies on the colleague's judgment. Reciprocity may involve trivial pleas-antries—or millions of dollars in traded votes for public works ap-propriations.

In the mid-1950s, liberal senators and freshmen used to complain of a conservative "Establishment" or "club" that dominated the Senate through the power of these folkways and through control of key commit-tees and processes. But the Senate has changed. An activist and attrac-tive senator, especially one representing a large state, often becomes a national political figure and is sometimes even talked about as a possible candidate for the presidency. The key aspect of the Senate today is not so much the concentration of power in some Old Guard or Establishment as the dispersion of power among party leaders, a dozen or more committee chairmen, several key subcommittee chairmen, senators from the larger states, and young activists. The contemporary Senate is individualistic. Committee chairmen have more power than nonchairmen, but with the expanding role of subcommittee chairmanships and expanding staff, their influence has lessened. More and more key decisions are made on the Senate floor and the Senate is a more open and fluid and more decentral-ized body now than it was in the 1950s or early 1960s.[16] It also has a con-siderably increased workload (see Table 12–3).

The filibuster rule One major difference between the Senate and the House is that debate is almost unlimited in the Senate. Once a senator gains the floor, he has the right to go on talking until he relinquishes it voluntarily or through exhaustion. This right to unlimited debate may be used by a small group of senators to filibuster—to delay the proceedings of the Senate in order to prevent a vote.

At one time, the filibuster was the favorite weapon of southern senators to block civil rights legislation. More recently, the filibuster has been used less frequently. But at the end of any Senate session, when there is a fixed date for adjournment, threat of filibuster is a real danger for controversial legislation. The knowledge that a bill might be subject to a filibuster is of-ten just enough to force a compromise satisfactory to its opponents. Of

[16]Norman Ornstein, Robert Peabody, and David Rohde, "The Changing Senate: From the 1950's to the 1970's," in Dodd and Oppenheimer, eds., *Congress Reconsidered*, p. 16. See also Randall Ripley, *Power in the Senate* (St. Martin's, 1969).

**12-3
More issues:
less time**

Year	Senate days in session	Total roll call votes	Average record votes per day	Study hours available to each senator per vote[1]
1955	103	85	.82	12.0
1960	140	215	1.53	5.5
1965	177	259	1.46	5.7
1970	208	422	2.02	4.2
1975	178	611	3.43	2.7

[1]Assuming no other activity whatsoever. Available hours calculated using 8 hour day and number of days in standard in-session Senate work year. The workload in the House is at least as bad and probably even worse.

SOURCE: *Congressional Record*, August 4, 1976, P. S13463.

course, if there are enough votes the objections can be overcome, if there is enough time. But at the end of a session, with senators anxious to go home and campaign, sometimes there is no time. And sometimes the Senate leadership, knowing that a filibuster would tie up the Senate and keep it from enacting other needed legislation, does not bother to bring a bill to the floor.

How may a filibuster be defeated? The majority can keep the Senate in continuous session so that the filibustering senator or senators will have to give up the floor. But if two or more senators cooperate, they can keep on talking almost indefinitely. They merely ask one another long questions that permit their partners to take lengthy rests. As long as the senator who is doing the talking stays on his feet, debate can be shut off only by a cloture vote. Under the rule of cloture, if sixteen members sign a petition, two days later the question of curtailing debate is put to a vote. If three-fifths of the total number of elected senators vote for cloture, no senator may speak for more than one hour. Then the motion before the Senate must be brought to a vote.

Until early 1975, it took a two-thirds vote of the senators present to close off debate. But in that year, the Senate voted to modify its cloture rule to make it slightly easier to end debate. Most liberals argued for a simple majority of those present and voting to force an end to a filibuster. Most conservatives wanted to retain the two-thirds requirement. The three-fifths of the entire membership (or 60 votes if there are no vacancies) was a compromise decision. Filibusters are rare. Still, the filibuster, *and the threat of it*, remains a delaying device available to Senate minorities. But, a determined majority can now overcome the filibuster, either by wearing the speakers down or by mobilizing the necessary votes for cloture.

Committees: The little legislatures

Chairperson Al Ullman of the House Ways and Means Committee (center) speaks with Labor Secretary F. Ray Marshall (left) and Treasury Secretary W. Michael Blumenthal about President Carter's proposed economic measures to stimulate the economy.

It is sometimes said that Congress is a collection of committees that come together in a chamber every once in a while to approve one another's actions. There is much truth in this. The main struggle over legislation takes place in committees and especially in subcommittees, for this is where the basic work of Congress is done. Deluged by several thousand bills a year, Congress could not do its job unless it delegated work to these "little legislatures." The House of Representatives has more than 30 committees with an average membership of about thirty. These are divided into more than 150 subcommittees. The committees are, as Speaker Thomas B. Reed once said, "the eye, the ear, the hand, and very often the brain of the House."

Standing committees have great power, for all bills introduced in the House are referred to them. They can defeat bills, pigeonhole them for weeks, amend them beyond recognition, or speed them on their way. A committee reports out favorably only a small fraction of all the bills that come to it. Although a bill can be forced to the floor of the House through a discharge petition signed by a majority of the membership, legislators are reluctant to bypass committees. For one thing, they regard committee members as experts in their field. Sometimes, too, they are reluctant to risk the anger of committee leaders. And there is a strong sense of reciprocity—"you respect my committee's jurisdiction and I will respect yours." It is not surprising that few discharge petitions gain the necessary number of signatures.

The Senate has twenty-one standing committees, each composed of seven to twenty-seven members. Whereas members of the House hold relatively few committee assignments, each senator normally serves on three committees and often on as many as eight subcommittees. Among the most important Senate committees are foreign relations, finance, and appropriations. Senate committees have the same powers over the framing of legislation as do those of the House, but they do not have the same power to keep bills from reaching the floor.

CHOOSING COMMITTEE MEMBERS

Partisanship shapes the control and staffing of standing committees. The chairman and a majority of the members are elected from the majority party. The minority party is represented roughly in relation to the proportion of its members in the entire chamber. Getting on a politically advantageous committee is important to members of Congress. A representative from Kansas, for example, would usually much rather serve on the agriculture committee than on the merchant marine and fisheries committee. Members usually stay on the same committee from one Congress to the next, although new members who have had undesirable assignments often bid for a better committee when places become available.

How are committee members chosen? In the House of Representatives, a committee on committees of the Republican membership allots places to new Republican members. This committee is composed of one member from each state having Republican representation in the House; this member is almost always the senior member of the state's delegation. Because each member has as many votes in the committee as there are Republicans in the delegation, the group is dominated by senior members from the large-state delegations. On the Democratic side, assignment to committees is handled by the steering committee of the Democratic caucus (which includes the speaker and majority leader as key members) in negotiation with senior Democrats from the state delegations. In the Senate, veterans also dominate the committee-assignment process, with each party having a small steering committee for the purpose. In making assignments, leaders are guided by various considerations: their estimates of a member's talents and cooperativeness, whether his state or region is already well represented on a committee, and whether the assignment will aid in reelection. In general, leaders like to comply with members' preferences. About three-fourths of the freshmen are granted some committee they requested.[17]

One reason Congress can cope effectively with its huge workload is that its committees and subcommittees are organized around subject-matter specialties. This allows members to develop technical expertise in specific areas and to recruit skilled staffs, so that Congress is often able to criticize and challenge experts from the bureaucracy. Interest groups and lobbyists realize the great power a specific committee has in certain areas and focus their attention on its members. Similarly, members of executive departments are careful to cultivate the committee and subcommittee chairs and members of "their" committees. One powerful Senate committee chairman reminded his constituents of the amount of federal tax money being spent in their state: "This does not happen by accident," the senator's campaign folder says. "It takes power and influence in Congress."

COMMITTEE DIVERSITY AND PERSISTENCE

Most committees are separate little centers of power, with rules, patterns of action, and internal processes of their own. Analyzing the House appropriations committee, Fenno discovered that it is characterized by a remarkable agreement among its members on key issues and the role the

---

[17]David W. Rohde and Kenneth A. Shepsle, "Democratic Committee Assignments in the House of Representatives," *American Political Science Review* (September 1973), pp. 889–905.

committee should play. Leadership is stable, and members tend to remain a long time. They have worked out a way of life emphasizing conformity, give-and-take, and hard work. The subcommittee chairmen of the House appropriations committee become specialists on the budgets and programs of the agencies within their jurisdiction and often exercise more influence over administrative policy than any other single representative. For example, the chairman of the subcommittee on foreign aid has more influence over that program than the chairman of the House committee on foreign affairs. The various appropriations subcommittees defer to one another's recommendations and back up the decisions of the parent committee.[18]

Committees, however, differ. Some are powerful, others are much less important. Because of the Senate's special role in foreign policy, for example, the Senate Foreign Relations Committee is usually far more influential than the House committee on International Relations. For the two appropriations committees, however, the reverse is true. The House committee sometimes plays a more significant role than the Senate committee. However, these differences are less than they used to be. Committees differ not only for institutional reasons, but also according to the goals and abilities of their members. As one student of the committee process observed: "I suspect that our current interest in exhorting all committees to acquire more information with which to combat the executive may be misplaced. Information is relatively easy to come by — and some committees have a lot of it. What is hard to come by is the incentive to use it, not to mention the time and the trust necessary to make it useful."[19]

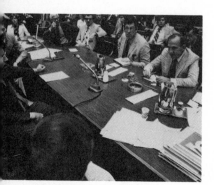

A meeting of the ad hoc House Energy Committee.

Bloom of National Journal

How Congress uses committees is critical in its role as a partner in national policy making. Much progress has been made in recent years to open hearings to the public and to improve the quality of committee staffs. But efforts to modernize jurisdictions were dealt a setback in 1974. Missouri's Richard Bolling and nine other congressmen had been working at a bipartisan effort to overhaul the House committee system, which had not been changed significantly since 1946. Jurisdictional overlap is common. For example, eighteen different committees deal with educational programs. And until Spring 1977, no committee had primary responsibility for energy policy. (In April 1977, the House created an ad hoc committee on energy.) Bolling's House Select Committee on Committees (1973–74) called for reassigning jurisdiction of several key committees, abolishing two longtime standing committees, and splitting another in two. But House Democrats meeting in caucus sent the plan to another committee for "further study." This effectively killed its chances. Only a few changes were eventually made. What started out as an effort to make the House committee system more rational was soon seen as a threat to the delicate balance of power within the House.[20] In early 1977, the Senate streamlined its committee structure. The new system limits any senator from chairing

[18]See Richard F. Fenno, Jr., *The Power of the Purse: Appropriations Politics in Congress* (Little, Brown, 1966).

[19]Richard F. Fenno, Jr., "If, as Ralph Nader Says, Congress is 'The Broken Branch,' How Come We Love Our Congressmen So Much?" (Paper delivered in Boston, Massachusetts, December 12, 1972). See also his comprehensive comparative study of congressional committees, *Congressmen in Committees* (Little, Brown, 1972).

[20]The definitive study of this 1974 attempt to reform the House committee structure is Roger Davidson and Walter Oleszek, *Congress Against Itself* (Indiana University Press, 1977).

more than three committees and subcommittees, reduces the number of Senate committees, provides for somewhat more coherent committee jurisdiction, and establishes a computer system to schedule the meetings of committees and subcommittees to avoid conflicts.

THE IMPORTANCE OF CHAIRMANSHIPS

Committee and subcommittee chairmen play a crucial role in protecting the power of congressional committees and in widening the dispersion of power in the whole Congress. They still exercise considerable power over both the operations of their committees and the final output of Congress. Until the mid-1970s, chairmen determined the total workload of their committees; hired and fired staff; and formed subcommittees and assigned them jurisdictions, members, and aides. Chairmen also managed the most important bills assigned to their committees.[21]

The relationship between committees and subcommittees has come in for increasing attention both by members and by students of Congress. In recent years, as more activists and younger members have been elected, they have insisted that they be given more authority and have been impatient with their seniors. There has been a tendency to give subcommittee chairmen more independence from the parent committee. It is not uncommon these days for a congressman of only one or two terms to be the chairman of the important subcommittee, and indeed this is the tradition in the Senate.

Chairmanships are still usually awarded on the basis of seniority. The member of the majority party who has had the longest continuous service on the committee ordinarily becomes its head. The chairman may be at odds with other members of his party, may oppose his party's national program, and may even be incompetent—still, he usually wins the chairmanship because of seniority.

MODERATING SENIORITY

Committee chairmanships as well as assignments are the responsibility of the party caucuses in both chambers. The custom of seniority still prevails, but it is not a written rule and other factors are beginning to be taken into account. In 1971, for example, the House Republican conference decided that ranking Republicans on committees henceforth would be elected by the conference by a secret ballot. In the same year, House Democrats agreed that any ten members of a committee could force a record vote in the Democratic caucus on the chairmanship. In 1973 they authorized a secret ballot vote on chairmanships if 20 percent of the caucus demanded it. In 1975, rank-and-file House Democrats, their ranks swollen and resolve stiffened by 75 mostly liberal newcomers, removed, from their membership, three elderly committee chairmen.

At the present time in the Senate the Republican members of standing committees choose the person who becomes the ranking minority member when the Republicans are in a minority but who would become the chair if the Republicans were to have a majority of the Senate. In fact, however, Republican members almost always elect the senior member to serve as their leader on the committee.

The Senate Democrats choose their nominees for chair by a secret ballot of the Democratic Conference whenever requested to do so by 20 percent

[21]Nelson W. Polsby, Miriam Gallagher, and Barry Spencer Rundquist, "The Growth of the Seniority System in the U.S. House of Representatives," *American Political Science Review* (September 1969), p. 789.

of the Senate Democratic membership. (Nomination by the Democratic Conference guarantees election by the Senate as chair whenever the Democrats control the Senate.) In fact, the Democrats almost always do elect the senior Democratic member of the Committee to serve as chair, but the fact that the Democratic Conference could by secret ballot do otherwise has forced senior members to make concessions to insure their re-election.

Many people feel the seniority practice tends to give the most influence in Congress to those constituencies that are politically stable or even stagnant. These are the areas where party competition is low or where a particular interest group or machine predominates. It stacks the cards against areas where the two parties are more evenly matched, where interest in politics is high, where the number of votes is large, and where competition is keen. These are the very areas most likely to reflect the political tides that are sweeping the nation.[22]

Seniority has its friends. It is defended on the grounds that elevating the most experienced members to leadership positions is automatic and impersonal and prevents disputes. Basically, the argument over seniority is about self-interest. Rural interests tend to favor the system. It is opposed by such groups as organized labor, advocates of civil rights legislation, and other urban-based interests who feel it gives rural interests and their conservative representatives too much power in Congress. Yet liberal groups also profit from the system when it is within their power to do so. If reapportionment and the passage of time cause the seniority custom to increase the influence of suburban and urban-based northern interests, we may see those defending and those opposing seniority switch sides.

The seniority practice remains because it supports the interests of congressional leaders. Many legislators have concluded "the longer I'm here, the better I like the system." Further, those who are most anxious to change the system have the least power to produce such changes. Most liberals quarrel with the seniority system because they have been less able to control seniority posts. As liberals have come to dominate Democratic caucuses on both sides of Capitol Hill, they have sought to limit committee chairmen's powers and enhance those of *sub*committee chairmen. The latter positions are controlled by members with less seniority who are more likely to represent liberals than the committee chairmen. In the Senate, all but a handful of Democrats chair their own subcommittee; in the House, more than 100 Democrats are subcommittee chairs. This provides staff privileges and gives the members added leverage against committee chairmen. At the same time, there have been moves to strengthen the powers of the party leaders and caucuses—again at the expense of the committee chairmen.

COMMITTEE INVESTIGATIONS

One of the controversial activities of Congress has been the committee investigation, especially such well-publicized open hearings as those of the Senate Foreign Relations Committee during the Vietnam war. Why does Congress investigate? Hearings by standing committees, their subcommittees, or special select committees are an important source of information and opinion. They provide an arena in which experts can submit

[22]For the view that the "bias" in chairmanships largely reflects a more basic bias in congressional membership itself toward certain regions, see Barbara Hinckley, "Seniority in the Committee Leadership Selection of Congress," *Midwest Journal of Political Science* (November 1969), pp. 613–30.

their views, statements and statistics can be entered in the record, and congressmen can question a variety of witnesses.

But committee investigations serve other functions as well. Public hearings are an important channel of communication and influence. A committee or its chairman may use a hearing to address the Congress. Thus Senator Frank Church's hearings on the CIA and FBI in 1976 were one way of impressing upon Congress the need for legislation to prevent the abuse of power in the intelligence agencies. Committee hearings may also be used to communicate with the public at large. Senator Ervin's Watergate committee's televised investigations into election practices and campaign finance abuses in 1973 were not intended merely to obtain new information. The senators involved were attempting to arouse citizens and to promote public support for election reforms, among other things.[23] Some investigations by regular committees involve the overseeing of administration. A committee can summon administration officials to testify in hearings. Some officials fear these inquiries; they dread the loaded questions of hostile congressmen and the likelihood that some administrative error in their agency may be uncovered and publicized.[24] Former Senator Sam Ervin sums up the assets and the liabilities of congressional investigations:

> A legislative inquiry can serve as the tool to pry open the barriers that hide corruption. It can be the catalyst that spurs Congress and the public to support vital reforms in our nation's laws. Or it can debase our principles, invade the privacy of our citizens, and afford a platform for demagogues and the rankest partisans.[25]

Are there any constitutional limits to Congress's power to compel private citizens to answer questions? The Supreme Court in 1957 in Watkins v. United States cautioned Congress that the First Amendment limits its power to investigate, that no committee has the power "to expose for the sake of exposure," that Congress and its committees are not courts to try and punish individuals, and that "no inquiry is an end in itself; it must be related to, and in furtherance of, a legitimate task of Congress." But only a minority of the Supreme Court has shown any inclination to set up a judicial check on legislative investigations in behalf of First amendment rights.[26] The judicial checks used so far are only two: The Fifth Amendment protection against self-incrimination has been construed broadly to protect witnesses who are willing to risk public censure by invoking the amendment to refuse to answer questions. The Supreme Court has also narrowly construed the crime of contempt of Congress in order to avoid punishment of witnesses for refusing to answer questions unless these questions are clearly important to the functions of an authorized committee.

[23]For a study of the role of congressional investigations, see James Hamilton, *The Power to Probe: A Study of Congressional Investigations* (Vintage, 1976).

[24]See Morris S. Ogul, *Congress Oversees the Bureaucracy* (University of Pittsburgh Press, 1976).

[25]Sam J. Ervin, Jr., introduction to Hamilton, *The Power to Probe*, p. xii.

[26]354 U.S. 178(1957); *Barenblatt* v. *United States* 360 U.S. 109(1959); *Wilkinson* v. *United States* 365 U.S. 399(1961); *Braden* v. *United States* 365 U.S. 341(1961). For an excellent discussion of this issue, see Martin Shapiro, *Law and Politics in the Supreme Court* (Free Press, 1964), Chap. 2.

The house versus the senate

When the framers created a two-house national legislature, they anticipated that the two chambers would represent sharply different interests. The Senate was to be a small chamber of men elected indirectly by the people and holding long, overlapping terms. As noted, it would have the sole power to confirm nominations. Proposed treaties required the approval of a two-thirds vote in the Senate. The Senate was to be a chamber of scrutiny, a gathering of "wise men" who would counsel and sanction a president—whether that president liked it or not.

The House of Representatives, elected anew every two years, was to be the direct instrument of the people. The Senate was a conservative check on the House, especially in the late nineteenth and early twentieth centuries, when it was extremely conservative and something of a rich man's club. But some factors, chiefly political, have altered the character of the House and Senate. Sometimes now the House serves as a conservative check on the Senate. Executive departments and agencies often see the Senate as a court of appeals for appropriations that have been shot down by the House.

How has this come about? One reason is that, at least until recently, the number of safe, noncompetitive House districts has been increasing, and the number of safe, noncompetitive Senate seats has been decreasing. The urbanization of the nation has left most states with large and growing metropolitan areas. Hence a senator's constituency nearly always consists of a wider variety of interests than does that of a member of the House. But the Senate's behavior is also partly a result of the appropriation process and institutionalized rules. As Richard Fenno has noted:

> The House Committee follows a decision pattern that regularly anticipates Senate Committee action; Senate Committee decisions regularly take the form of reactions to prior House decisions. Their self-prescribed goals, as budget cutter or appeals court, take into account the order in which they act relative to one another.[27]

Given the differences between House and Senate, it is not surprising that the version of a bill passed by one chamber may differ substantially from the version passed by the other. Only if both houses pass an absolutely identical measure can it become law. As a general rule, one house accepts the language of the other, but about 10 percent of all bills passed (usually major ones) must be referred to a conference committee.

If neither house will accept the other's bill, a conference committee—a special committee of members from each chamber—settles the differences. Both parties are represented, with the majority party having more members. The proceedings of this committee are usually an elaborate bargaining process. When it is brought back to the houses, the conference report can be accepted or rejected (often with further negotiations ordered), but it cannot be amended. Each set of conference members must convince its colleagues that any concessions made to the other house were on unimportant points and that nothing basic in their own version of the bill was surrendered.

How much leeway does a conference committee have? Ordinarily the members are expected to stay somewhere between the alternatives set by

[27]Fenno, *The Power of the Purse*, pp. 690–91.

the different versions. On matters where there is no clear middle ground, members are sometimes accused of exceeding their instructions and producing a new bill. The conference committee has even been called a "third house" of Congress, one that arbitrarily revises policy. Conference committees are also criticized on the ground that they are not representative, even of the committees approving the bill, and that they disproportionately represent senior committee leaders. Critics also complain that little can be done about biases that may creep into the bill in the conference committee, since the houses are usually confronted with a take-it-or-leave-it situation.[28] Despite such criticism, some kind of conference committee is needed for a two-house legislature to work. Conference committees integrate the houses, help resolve disputes, and get compromises made.

Congressional reform

There is so much criticism of Congress that here we can only briefly review the main charges against it.

1. Congress is *inefficient*. The House and Senate are simply not suited to the needs of an industrial nation. Bills require an endless amount of time to get through the complicated legislative process and are often blocked in the middle. Members are not as well informed as they should be. The dispersion of power guarantees slowness, if not inertia.

Much of this criticism is exaggerated. An evaluation of procedure and structure is difficult to separate from views about how they affect specific policies. It is often a matter of whose ox is being gored. For example, from the White House vantage point, Congress is inefficient when it does not process the president's bills quickly.

[28]David J. Vogler, *The Third House: Conference Committees in the United States Congress* (Northwestern University Press, 1971). But see also Gerald S. Strom and Barry S. Rundquist, "A Revised Theory of Winning in House and Senate Conferences," *American Political Science Review* (June 1977), pp. 448–53 for an explanation of why the Senate usually wins.

---

15 Ideas to improve congress

A sampling of the variety of ideas suggested by lawmakers for making Congress more effective, according to a *U.S. News & World Report* survey—(1976)

- Do away with the seniority system.
- Make better use of computers and other electronic aids.
- Reduce the number of recesses.
- Cut down on quorum calls and time spent on parliamentary haggling.
- Realign committee jurisdictions to avoid overlapping responsibilities.
- Require better attendance for floor debates.
- Permit television coverage of floor action.
- Open up all legislative drafting sessions and conference-committee meetings to the public.
- Require all lobbyists to register and report their activities.
- Set aside more time for long-range planning.
- Authorize appropriations for several years at a time, instead of annually.
- Have extensive orientation periods for new members and their key staff aides.
- Bring in outside consultants to point out Congress's weaknesses.
- Beef up oversight of executive agencies and departments.
- Provide committee-staff aides to assist junior Congressmen, as well as older members.

SOURCE: A survey by *US News & World Report* (1976) of several dozens of members of Congress.

Measured simply in terms of workload, Congress deals with an enormous number of complex measures. Many procedures in both houses expedite handling of bills. The committee and subcommittee system is about the most reasonable device for hearing arguments and compiling information. Still, the question of efficiency remains. Many members themselves feel defeated by the system. "I am appalled," one said, "at how much congressmen are expected to do for the nation. . . . We just don't have the time to keep informed properly."[29] Study groups inside and outside Congress have urged the houses to reduce the number of committee assignments, establish better information systems, acquire better staffs, and strengthen majority rule.

2. Congress is *unrepresentative*. The complaint is often made that Congress represents local interests over the national interest. Thus it is said that the committee system responds to organized regional and minority interests. The seniority system, even with its modifications, biases both houses toward conservatism. Defenders of Congress contend that there should be a strong institution to guarantee minority rights and to act as a check on mindless majority rule. Critics answer by arguing that minorities should have a right to publicize and delay what the majority proposes to do, but not to defeat it.

Both houses, critics hold, overrepresent well-organized economic power structures at the expense of the Joe Sixpacks and Aunt Nellies. Can the members of Congress, who are so much the products of upper or upper-middle class backgrounds really speak for the needs of low-income groups? Can a Congress that has only a 2 percent black membership truly represent our black population?

Yet most of the recent changes in Congress have been efforts to strengthen its representative character. Richard Fenno contends: "Congress, not the president, is most closely in touch with the people who live beyond the nation's capital. Our recent experience—with two presidents [Johnson and Nixon] who lost their constituencies and a third who cannot find one [Ford]—helps remind us that Congress remains our most representative institution."[30]

In fact we have a system of dual representation in which both Congress and president can and do claim to speak for the people. But since "the people" seldom if ever speak with a single voice, the structure and character of the two systems tend to give us a Congress that speaks for one majority and a president who often speaks for another. Between the two, we sometimes get a kind of balance, and sometimes a deadlock.

3. Congress is *unethical*. Many critics complain that some members of Congress are too tied to the economic interests they are asked to regulate. There is also the charge that members of Congress get too many personal privileges and that there have been too many abuses of these so-called fringe benefits. To be sure, the misbehavior of congressmen is more frequently played up in the press than the misbehavior of others. Thus, the Elizabeth Ray sex scandal (she was the typist who could not type), the South Korean government's favors and contributions to several influential

---

[29]Donald R. Matthews, *U.S. Senators and Their World* (University of North Carolina Press, 1960), p. 89. See also Donald Riegle, *O Congress* (Doubleday, 1972).

[30]Richard F. Fenno, Jr. "Strengthening a Congressional Strength," in Dodd and Oppenheimer, eds., *Congress Reconsidered*, p. 262.

legislators, and similar affairs become public matters, as indeed they should.

In response to these and other scandals, both houses passed reasonably strong ethics codes during the 95th Congress. These changes require full public disclosure of income and property holdings by legislators, key aides, and spouses. They also bar gifts of over $100 to a legislator, his staff, or his family from a registered lobbyist, an organization with a political action committee, a foreign government, or a business with an interest in legislation before Congress. Both houses acted in the hope that these changes will lessen conflicts of interest and reestablish trust in an institution that affects all our lives.

4. Congress is *irresponsible*. The main problem in Congress is the dispersion of power among committee and subcommittee leaders, elected party officials, factional leaders, and other legislators. No one is in control. This dispersion of power means that to get things done, congressional leaders must bargain and negotiate. The result of this "brokerage" system is that laws may be watered down, defeated, or delayed. Too much leeway, according to some critics, is given to unknown bureaucrats. Accountability is confused, responsibility is eroded, and well-organized special interests who know how to work the system are given an unfair advantage.

Those charging irresponsibility fear not that Congress is the tool of a single interest but that it responds to so many minorities that it cannot speak for the great majority or for the nation as a whole. It cannot anticipate problems, plan ahead, and mobilize legislative power to deal with major social problems. Those concerned about congressional irresponsibility do not blame a few conservative interests or elite elements. They recognize that brokerage is mainly the result of a constitutional system which divides authority, checks power with power, and disperses political leadership.

5. Congress *delegates too much to the executive branch*. Still an additional charge is that Congress fails to do its job, and tends to delegate too much authority to the executive branch. Because of the complexity of modern problems and an inability to work out coalitions and compromises, there is a tendency to merely say, for example, "do something" about affirmative action, or "do something" about consumer product safety. Congress turns the matter over to an administrative agency, with the result that the rules and regulations issued by the administrators are actually legislation. So it is charged that Congress is failing to carry out its legislative responsibilities.

Those making these charges often disagree with the policy initiatives in question. Still, the complaint is valid, for we expect our *elected* officials to hammer out public policies. Congress is aware of this criticism, but sometimes the escape from responsibility outweighs its willingness to prepare specific legislation. Such laws would cause affected persons or groups to blame Congress rather than the administrative agencies—and perhaps even particular members of Congress, who then might lose their seats.

Washington Star Syndicates Inc.

Summary

1. Senators and representatives come primarily from upper- and middle-class backgrounds. They are far better educated than Americans as a whole. The typical member of Congress is a middle-aged, white, male lawyer.

2. Most of the work in the Congress gets done in committees and subcommittees. Congress has attempted in recent years to streamline its committee system and

modify its methods of selecting committee chairmen. Seniority practices are still generally followed, but the threat of removal forces committee chairs to consult with younger members of the majority party. Subcommittees are now more important in an increasingly decentralized Congress.

3. Congress performs these functions: representation, lawmaking, consensus-building, overseeing, policy-clarification, and legitimizing.

4. The workload for Congress has never been greater. There obviously is much that could be done to make our national legislature perform its functions more effectively. Some things have been done in recent years: Redistricting and reapportionment have shaped a Congress that more accurately reflects the population. The filibuster in the Senate and the Rules Committee in the House are less obstructive than they once were. The role of the speaker and the party steering committee have been enhanced, and the Congress is better staffed.

5. The critical image of Congress as a ponderous or sluggish institution is still common. Its greatest strengths—its diversity and deliberative character—also serve to weaken its capacity and will to be a match for the executive branch. Its members will rarely be fast on their 1,070 feet. The 535 members divided into two houses, two parties, dozens of committees, and hundreds of subcommittees will always have a difficult time arriving at a common strategy to combat a president determined to use his powers to the full. How effectively can Congress reassert itself? We shall return to a consideration of this vital question in Chapter 14, after we have had a chance to examine the modern presidency and its responsibilities.

Chapter 13

The Presidency: Leadership Branch?

In the 1976 Presidential campaign, Jimmy Carter sensed Americans were looking for a revival of trust in government, a trust that had been shattered by the social upheavals and misuses of power of previous years. His top advisers encouraged him to devise a strategy based around three major themes: open government, competent government, and efficient government. Charles Kirbo, his senior political counselor, said: "I told [Jimmy] not to run his campaign on an intellectual approach to issues, but on a restoration of confidence in government. I thought people would buy that. They were worn out on the issues."[1]

Critics called it a no-issues campaign, one in which the basic appeal was a vague call for something better. "I want you to help me overcome two handicaps I have in my race for President," Carter shouted at rallies, "I am not a lawyer and I don't come from Washington."[2] Perhaps he correctly perceived the nation's mood. Having *no* Washington experience became an asset.

People evidently liked the image of the "outsider," but Carter the person remained a mystery to most people. An exasperated Morris Udall, running against Carter in the Democratic primaries put it this way:

> Who is he and what does he stand for? The *New York Times* told liberals he was a liberal, the conservatives thought he was conservative, and the moderates thought he was moderate. In Iowa he had the abortion vote and the anti-abortion vote, he had labor and anti-labor. He had opposites on all sides. In politics you can't do that but [Carter's] done it.[3]

[1]Kandy Stroud, *How Jimmy Won* (Morrow, 1977), p. 202.

[2]Arthur Hadley, *The Invisible Primary* (Prentice-Hall, 1976), p. 240.

[3]Stroud, *How Jimmy Won*, p. 258. See also Jules Witcover, *Marathon, 1972–1976: The Pursuit of the Presidency*. (Viking, 1977); and Gerald Pomper, et al., *The Election of 1976* (David McKay, 1977). On the role of personality and issues in presidential elections, see William R. Keech, "Selecting and Electing Presidents," in Thomas E. Cronin and Rexford G. Tugwell, eds., *The Presidency Reappraised*, 2nd ed. (Praeger, 1977), p. 98; and James David Barber, *The Presidential Character*, 2nd ed. (Prentice-Hall, 1977).

Some critics deplore the role personality played in the 1976 campaign and the fact that issues did not seem to count for much. But personality or the character of presidential hopefuls has always been important. This is not as irrational as it is sometimes made to appear. After all, presidents have enormous power, especially in emergencies. It is important to assess their characters and to know about them as individuals — how they are likely to cope with crises and with issues, to handle Congress, the press, advisers, and critics. And even though issues are not on the ballot, voters do get some general idea of the candidate's thinking. Carter's views on busing, the military budget, aid to the cities, environmental protection, and energy conservation came to the fore, much as he may have tried to downplay them.

Patrick H. Caddell, Carter's pollster, evidently urged a stress on personality and style rather than programs: "Too many good people," Caddell wrote, "have been beaten because they tried to substitute substance for style."[4] Opinion polls nearly always indicate that the American people want an honest person in the White House. This is not a surprising finding, but what is significant is that the voters time and again place more emphasis on their judgment about a candidate's character than they do on a candidate's policy preferences. We have to be a little cautious here, because people tend to like the character of those with whom they agree, and if they like the personality, they are likely to judge that the person's policy ideas are similar to their own.

The public just as strongly wants toughness, decisiveness, and competence in presidents. Voters recognize the need, even in a democracy, for strong leadership. People yearn for a leader with foresight and personal strength. In short, people want someone who will personalize government and authority, who will simplify politics, who will symbolize the protective role of the state, who will seem to be concerned with *them*. Some people believe the human heart ceaselessly reinvents royalty. Has this tendency to turn to the president reached an undesirable state of dependency on the executive?

Former President Ford visits with President Carter at White House after election victory.

Americans applaud presidents when things go well. But we blame them and treat them harshly when things go wrong. Disasters as well as triumphs are credited to presidents — Wilson's League of Nations, Hoover's Depression, Roosevelt's New Deal, Johnson's Vietnam War, Nixon's Watergate. An exaggerated sense of presidential wisdom and power has caused us to forget that there are limits to what presidents can accomplish. The tragedies of U.S. involvement in Vietnam and of presidential involvement in the Watergate scandals deglamorized the presidency. Still the vitality of our democracy depends in large measure on creative presidential leadership. Carefully planned change is difficult without leadership.

The strong presidency reappraised

Some critics see the presidency as fast becoming inconsistent with democratic ideals. They view it as an often remote, autocratic institution, the citadel of the status quo, the center of the industrial-military-political complex, the very heart of the Establishment. They charge:

> Presidents have become almost like absolute monarchs on issues of war and diplomacy.

[4]Patrick H. Caddell, quoted in James T. Wooten, "Pre-Inaugural Memo Urged Carter To Stress Style Over Substance," *The New York Times* (May 4, 1977), p. 1.

Presidents too often serve elite interests or become pawns of strategic business and professional elites.

Presidents are less accountable today than ever before. They are able to get around the formal checks and balances designed by the framers.

Presidents now manipulate the public's sense of reality by relying on secrecy, emergency powers, and the "electronic throne" of television.

Presidents undermine partisan debate and dissent by personalizing their office and proclaiming consensus or bipartisan politics.

Some critics care less about the extent of presidential authority than the *purposes* for which it is used. If the president acts in behalf of what they consider to be improper interests or for what they describe as personal power, then they argue his power should be curbed. If, on the other hand, the president appears to represent interests that they approve, then they argue his power should be left unchecked.

Other critics are more concerned about *process*. If the president's actions reflect the wishes of the majority of the people most of the time, then they contend the process is working properly. If he acts in a fashion contrary to the wishes of most of the people most of the time, then the process is not working and his power should be checked.

Most liberals in both parties look to the president as the potential spokesman of popular majorities. Throughout our history, active presidents have tended to act in behalf of changes pleasing to the liberal-progressive forces. There is no guarantee, of course, that a strong president will be liberal or pleasing to the liberal critics. Vietnam provides a classic example to the contrary.

Many historians contend that the great presidents have been the strong presidents who have moved outside elite power structures to reach the masses. That was how Jefferson and Jackson overcame the Adamses of their day; that is how the two Roosevelts overcame the "economic royalists" of their day. To be sure, they say presidents often have to compromise with existing elites. But presidents know that a president sometimes has the power to defy minority interests. They like to quote Franklin Roosevelt who, after some businessmen had cursed him for his "radical" New Deal policies, cried out at the height of his 1936 reelection campaign: "I should like to have it said of my first Administration that in it the forces of selfishness and of lust for power met their match. I should like to have it said of my second Administration that in it these forces met their master!"

But if it is clear that presidents must be granted broad power to govern, so it is clear that no president can be blindly trusted with power. The potential for abuse is there. Watergate taught us that new checks and balances may be needed as the presidency becomes an even more centralized and dominant political influence.

The president's constitutional position

The framers of the Constitution created a presidency of limited powers. They wanted a presidential office that would stay clear of parties and factions, enforce the laws passed by Congress, deal with foreign governments, and help the states put down disorders. They seemed to have in mind — and that is the way President Washington acted — that the president should be an elected king with substantial personal power, acting above parties.

The delegates rejected a *plural* or *collegial* executive. They also rejected an *unlimited* term. The term would be for four years, with presidents eligible for reelection. Independent from the legislature, presidents would still share considerable power with Congress. The essence of the arrangement would be an *intermingling* of powers. To achieve change, the separate branches would have to work in cooperation and consultation with one another. A president's major appointments had to be approved by the Senate; Congress could override his veto by a two-thirds vote of each chamber; he could make treaties only with the advice and consent of two-thirds of the senators. And, of course, all appropriations would be determined by Congress, not the president. Even a presidency with such limited powers, hemmed in by the system of checks and balances, worried some Americans in 1787. But they were reassured by the fact that George Washington was to be the first chief executive.

THE SWELLING OF THE PRESIDENCY

For decades, American presidents have been extending the limits of executive powers, and Congress and the courts usually have been willing partners. Whenever emergencies occur, Congress rushes to delegate rule-making discretion to the executive branch. Congress sometimes seems incapable of dealing with matters that are highly technical, or that require constant management or consistent judgment. Some people feel that what Congress lacks most is the will to use the powers it already has. But this hardly seems to be a satisfactory explanation. For Congress is not unique, among legislative bodies, in this respect. During the last two centuries in all democracies, and at all levels, power has drifted away from legislators to executives. The English prime minister, the French president, the governors of our states, the mayors of our cities are all playing a more dominant role than was true, generally speaking, one hundred years ago. There are strong forces at work that help to explain this beyond the mere lack of will in Congress.

The danger of war plainly increases a president's impact on the nation's affairs. The Cold War shattered any remaining nostalgia for once-cherished traditions against standing armies and entangling alliances. The combination of an enormous standing army, nuclear weapons, and the nation's Cold War commitments (to quote President Kennedy) "to pay any price, bear any burden, meet any hardship, support any friend, oppose any foe . . ." invited presidential dominance in national security matters.

Television also contributes immeasurably to the growth of presidential influence. With access to coverage nearly any time he wants it, a president can take his case directly to the people. The invitation to bypass and thus ignore Congress, the Washington press, and even his own party leaders weakens the checks once posed by the necessity of securing cooperation from other political leaders in order to get a message to the voters.

The great growth of the federal role in domestic and economic matters has enlarged presidential responsibility. It has also contributed to the swollen presidential establishment. Problems that are not easily delegated to any one department often get pulled into the White House. When new federal programs concern several federal agencies, someone near the president seems to be required to fashion a consistent policy and reconcile conflicts. White House aides, with some justification, claim the presidency is the only place in government where it is possible to set and coordinate national priorities. And presidents constantly set up central review and coordination units. These help formulate new policies, settle jurisdictional disputes among departments, and provide access for the well-organized interest groups who want their views to be given weight in decision-making.

The swelling of the presidency has been encouraged as well by the public's expectations. Although we may dislike or condemn individual presidents, especially late in their terms, popular attitudes toward the institution of the presidency border on worship. We want very much to believe in and trust our presidents. Perhaps it is because we have no royal family, no established church, or no common ceremonial leadership divorced from executive responsibilities. In an effort to live up to unrealistic expectations, some presidents overextend themselves; maintaining the presidential image requires them to expand their power, and so a circle of rising expectations is at work.

"WHAT IS GOOD FOR THE PRESIDENCY . . ."

Circumstances usually dictate that a president can break new ground in only a few policy areas. If the delegated powers and institutionalized trappings of authority have increased dramatically, it does not automatically follow that a president's powers are a match for his responsibilities. Nor is there any guarantee that the increased powers are used for ends desired by the majority of the people. So although strengthening the presidency is an old practice, many Americans now question the blind assumption that what is good for the presidency is good for the nation.

The president is under the law. Of course, the special nature of his responsibilities and the fact that he is the elected representative of all the people means that the law often applies to the president in a different way than it does to an ordinary citizen. But the president has no authority to deprive persons of their constitutional rights and certainly not to try to stifle the guarantees of freedom of speech or to try to retain his power by interfering with elections. Lincoln in the midst of the Civil War did suspend the writ of habeas corpus and justified it on the grounds that it was necessary to bend the Constitution in order to save the Union. But even in the midst of the Civil War he made no attempt to prevent the holding of a free and open election.[5]

Is it possible to create a strong presidency that is leaner, more open, and more responsive to the voters than it is at present? And how much of the needed leadership in the nation should we expect solely from a president?

People often do not know at the time that they stand at turning points in history. Perhaps we live at a time when the political and constitutional currents are flowing away from the White House. Some people say we are in a period of diminished presidential leadership, at least in domestic affairs. For one of the aftermaths of Watergate is a lingering suspicion of the presidency. And while presidents have grown in power and influence over the last several decades, a critical skepticism toward them has also grown.

Again, historical trends do not move all in the same direction. Who knows? A few years from now political scientists may be writing books about the lack of initiative in Washington because of the imperiled presidency. We will return to these questions in the following chapter after we have looked at the functions we expect a president to perform today.

[5]See the useful expert opinions and discussion that refute Nixon's claim that a president could be above the law, *U.S. News and World Report*, May 30, 1977, p. 66. For added perspective see Clinton Rossiter, *The Supreme Court and the Commander in Chief*, expanded edition with notes and additional text by Richard P. Longaker (Cornell University Press, 1976).

Symbolic leadership

A president is the nation's number-one celebrity, and almost anything he does is news. Merely by going to church or to a sports event a president commands attention. A cult of personality often develops. By his actions, a president can arouse a sense of hope or despair, honor or dishonor.

The Founding Fathers did not fully anticipate the symbolic functions a president must perform. Certain magisterial functions such as the granting of pardons were conferred. But the presidency over time has acquired enormous symbolic significance. No matter how enlightened or rational we consider ourselves to be, all of us respond in some way to symbols and rituals. The president often affects our images of authority, legitimacy, and confidence in our political system.

THE POPULAR NEED FOR LEADERSHIP

A president's personal conduct affects how millions of Americans view their political loyalties and civic responsibilities. Of course the symbolic influence of presidents is not always evoked in favor of worthy causes, and sometimes presidents do not live up to our expectations of moral leadership. But even in this nation of hard-nosed pragmatists, we yearn for a sense of purpose, a vision of where the nation is going. "The Presidency is the focus for the most intense and persistent emotions. . . . The President is . . . , the one figure who draws together the people's hopes and fears for the political future. On top of all his routine duties, he has to carry that off — or fail.[6]

It would be much easier for everyone, says Michael Novak, if our president were a prime minister, called on merely to manage the affairs of government in as efficient and practical a way as possible. But this is not the case. We have not found a way to separate the function of symbolizing the hopes and aspirations of the nation from the office of exercising executive power.[7] Of course, nearly everybody in positions of authority makes

[6]Barber, *The Presidential Character*, p. 4.

[7]For a more extensive treatment of the symbolic implications of the presidency, see Michael Novak, *Choosing Our King* (Macmillan, 1974).

Woodrow Wilson (right) was one of the first presidents to set trends in national policy-making. Here he discusses the League of Nations and its goal of world peace with (from left) Lloyd George of England, Orlando of Italy, and Clemenceau of France.

promises for a brighter, better tomorrow. Indeed, it can be argued that an important part of leadership is to offer hope.

Presidential head-of-state duties often seem trivial and unimportant. For example, pitching out the first baseball of the season, buying Christmas or Easter seals, pressing buttons that start big power projects, and visiting the scene of national disasters do not require executive talents. Yet our president is asked continuously to champion our common heritage, to help unify the nation, and also to create an improved climate within which the diverse interests of the nation can work together. He is expected also to see that the nation lives up to the idealistic values it presents to other countries.

A PRESIDENTIAL DILEMMA

Under ordinary conditions, the presidential claim to be the "leader of *all* the people," or symbolic leader of the nation, keeps running headlong into the president who tries to act for *part* of the people. Some presidential functions are fundamentally inconsistent with one another. On the one hand he is *party* leader, the spokesman and representative of a segment of the population—usually not even a popular majority these days—that is more or less organized in the party he heads. As party chief he not only directs the national party organization; he also uses his powers as chief legislator to affect the party's program. On the other hand, as *symbolic* leader and *chief of state*, he attempts to act for all the people. As chief executive he must faithfully administer the laws, whether these laws were passed by Democratic or Republican majorities in Congress. Yet in choosing his subordinates and in applying the law, he understandably often thinks first of the interests of his popular majority.

**President Carter hosts
King Hussein at the White House.**

The relationship between these diverse presidential roles is uneasy. For example, the president may wish to address the nation on a problem. As president he is entitled to free time on radio and TV. But if an election is in the offing, the opposition often charges that the president is really acting in his capacity as party chief and that his party should pay for the radio or TV time. The same question comes up in connection with a president's inspection trips, especially when he uses them as occasions for political talks and general politicking.

Most of the time, presidents manage to combine their roles of chief of state and party leader without too much difficulty. The people expect him to hold both roles, and he moves from one to the other as conditions demand. There is nothing wrong with the symbolic powers that come with the office. They become a problem only when they leave the public believing ceremony equals accomplishment or when ceremonial and symbolic responsibilities keep presidents from performing their more demanding duties.

Priority-setting and policy formulation

Presidents, by custom, have become responsible for proposing new initiatives in the areas of foreign policy, economic growth and stability, and the quality of life in America. This was not always the case. But beginning with Woodrow Wilson and especially since the New Deal, a president is expected to promote peace, prevent depressions, and propose reforms to ensure domestic progress. The trend in national policy-making is toward greater centralization: "Increasingly, federal programs are conceived by the President in his search for campaign issues or legislative program material, and they are planned by his Executive Office or special task forces and commissions that he has appointed."[8]

NATIONAL SECURITY POLICY

Presidents have more leeway in foreign and military affairs than they have in domestic matters. This is partly due to grants of authority stipulated in the Constitution, and partly due to the character of diplomatic and military activity. The framers foresaw a special need for speed and unity in our dealings with other nations. And the Constitution vests in a president command of the two major instruments of foreign policy—the diplomatic corps and the armed services. It also gives him responsibility for negotiating treaties and commitments with other nations.

Congress has granted presidents wide discretion in initiating foreign policies, for diplomacy frequently requires quick action. A president can act swiftly; Congress usually does not. Congress thus has given up a considerable amount of its powers over foreign policy to the president.

The Supreme Court has repeatedly upheld strong presidential authority in this area. In the Curtiss-Wright case in 1936, the Court referred to the "exclusive power of the President as the sole organ of the Federal Government in the field of international relations—a power which does not require as a basis for its exercise an act of Congress, but which, of course, like every other governmental power, must be exercised in subordination to the applicable provisions of the Constitution."[9] These are sweeping words. Yet a determined Congress *that knows what it wants to do*, and can agree on it, does not lack power in foreign relations. It must authorize and appropriate the funds that back up our policies abroad. It is a forum of debate and criticism. And, as it at least tried to do after the Vietnam War, it can specify the conditions of war-making (more on this in the next chapter).

ECONOMIC POLICY

Ever since the New Deal, presidents have been expected to initiate action to prevent unemployment, to fight inflation, to keep taxes down, to ensure economic growth and prosperity, and to do whatever they think necessary and proper to prevent depressions. The Constitution does not place these duties on the White House, but a president knows that if he fails to act he will suffer the fate of Herbert Hoover, who was denounced for years by the Democrats for his alleged inaction during the Great Depression. Ford's defeat in 1976 was linked at least in part to his apparent inability to handle the economy.

The chief advisers to the president on economic policy are the three members of the Council of Economic Advisers, the Secretary of the Treasury and the Director of Office of Management and Budget. Presidents often get their economic advice elsewhere, but these persons advise the president as to what actions he should take or propose to the Congress, to increase employment opportunities and stabilize the economy.

The growth and complexity of economic problems have placed even more initiative in the hands of the president. Clearly, the delicate balancing required to keep a modern economy operating means that the presidency plays a central role.

[8]Martha Derthick, *New Towns In-Town* (The Urban Institute, 1972), p. 96. See also Thomas E. Cronin, *The State of the Presidency* (Little, Brown, 1975).

286

[9]*United States* v. *Curtiss-Wright Export Corp.*, 299 U.S. 304 (1936).

A leader is one who knows where the followers are. Lincoln did not invent the antislavery movement; Roosevelt hardly started the Depression. Kennedy and Johnson did not begin or lead the civil rights movement. But they all, in their respective times, became embroiled in these controversies, for a president cannot ignore for long what divides the nation.

The essence of the modern presidency lies in its institutional capability to resolve societal conflicts. To be sure, a president much of the time will avoid conflict where possible, seeking instead to defer, delegate, or otherwise delay controversial decisions. The effective president, however, will clarify the major issues of the day, define what is possible, and organize the governmental structure so that important goals can be realized.

A president—with the cooperation of Congress—can set national goals and propose legislation. Close inspection indicates, however, that in most instances a president's "new initiatives" in domestic policy are measures that have been under consideration in previous sessions of Congress. Just as the celebrated New Deal legislation had a fairly well-defined history extending back several years before its embrace by Franklin Roosevelt, so also most New Frontier and Great Society legislative programs were the fruits of long campaigns by congressional activists and special-interests.[10] And many of Carter's domestic policy initiatives are new attempts at old compromises or revivals of previously unsuccessful measures.

The Constitution says that the president "shall from time to time give to the Congress information on the State of the Union, and recommend to their Consideration such Measures as he shall judge necessary and expedient." From the start, strong presidents have exploited this power. Washington and Adams came in person to Congress to deliver information and recommendations. Jefferson and many presidents after him sent written messages, but Wilson restored the practice of delivering a personal, and often dramatic, message. Franklin Roosevelt used personal appearances (as have most presidents since then) to draw the attention of the whole nation to his program. Carter went to Congress to unveil his energy program.

Less obvious, but perhaps equally important, are the frequent written messages dispatched from the White House to Capitol Hill on a vast range of public problems. These messages may not create much stir at the moment, but they are important in defining the administration's position and giving a lead to friendly legislators. Moreover, these messages are often accompanied by detailed drafts of legislation that may be put into the hopper with hardly a change. These administration bills, the products of bill-drafting experts on the president's own staff or in the departments and agencies, may be strengthened or diluted by Congress, but many of the original provisions may survive.

"Blessed is the small car owner, for he shall get 30 miles to the gallon. Blessed is the homeowner, for he shall be forced to insulate. Blessed are the middle class, for they shall pay through the nose,".

Courtesy of the *Boston Globe*.

Crisis management

Nearly two centuries of national expansion and recurrent crises have increased the powers of the president over those specified by the Constitution.[11] The complexity of Congress's decision-making procedures, its unwieldy numbers, and its constitutional tasks of debate, discussion, and

[10]Lawrence H. Chamberlain, *The President, Congress and Legislation* (Columbia University Press, 1946); and James L. Sundquist, *Politics and Policy* (Brookings Institution, 1968).

[11]See Arthur M. Schlesinger, Jr., *The Imperial Presidency* (Houghton Mifflin, 1973), esp. chaps. 1–7. Also see Louis Fisher, *Presidential Spending Discretion* (Princeton University Press, 1975).

YOU CAN CALL UP PRESIDENT CARTER FREE THIS SATURDAY, MARCH 5.

(900) 242-1611

Talk to the President of the United States about what's on your mind. He'll take as many calls as time permits from all over the country in the first Presidential phone-in.

In March 1977, President Carter conducted the first presidential "phone-in."

authorization make Congress a more public, deliberative, and divided organization. When major crises occur, Congress traditionally holds debates but just as predictably delegates vast authority to a president, charging him to take whatever actions are necessary to restore order or regain control over the situation.

"The President shall be Commander in Chief of the Army and the Navy of the United States," reads Section 2 of Article II of the Constitution. Even though this is the first of the president's powers listed in the Constitution, the framers intended that his military role be a limited one. His *powers* were to be far less than a king's. It was as if he would be a sort of first general and first admiral. As it turns out, his military role has become much more important. He has his finger on the nuclear button and appears to have sole authority over limited wars as well.

The primary factor underlying this transformation in the president's function as commander in chief has been the changed role of the United States in the world, especially since World War II. In the postwar years we rapidly became the spokesman for preserving the "free world" from communism. Every president argued for and won widespread support for the position that military strength, especially military superiority over the Soviet Union, was the primary route to national security. Nations willingly grew dependent on our assistance, which rapidly became translated into a multitude of treaties, pacts, and executive agreements. From then on, nearly every threat to the political stability of our far-flung network of allies became a test of whether we would honor our commitments in good

The White House
1600 Pennsylvania Ave., N.W.
Washington, D.C. 20500

EAST WING

WEST WING

MANSION

The White House is an executive office, a ceremonial mansion, and a home. Several presidents have viewed it almost as a jail, preferring to spend as much time as possible at other presidential retreats outside of Washington. But most Americans view the rather elegant White House as the center of political and social activity in the nation's capital. It is also something of a national shrine as millions of people from America as well as around the world visit and inspect it each year.

EAST WING

1   Theater
2   Tour Entrance
3   Official Visitors' Lobby
4   President's Military Aide
5   First Lady's Press Secretary
6   Social Correspondence
7   Congressional Relations Staff

Second Floor

First Floor

Third Floor

Second Floor

First Floor

MANSION

Ground Floor
1 Housekeeper
2 Secret Service
3 Doctor's Office
4 Diplomatic Reception Room
5 China Room
6 Gold Room
7 Kitchen
8 White House Curator
9 Library
10 Vaulted Arch Hallway

First Floor
11 State Dining Room
12 Red Room
13 Blue Room
14 Green Room
15 Private Dining Room
16 Main Lobby
17 Cross Hall
18 East Room

Second Floor
19 Yellow Oval Room
20 Treaty Room (Monroe Room)
21 Lincoln Bedroom
22 Lincoln Sitting Room
23 Presidential Family Living Quarters
24 Queen's Room (Rose Room)
25 Queen's Sitting Room

Third Floor
26 Staff Living Quarters

Ground Floor

WEST WING

1 Situation Room
2 National Security Council Staff
3 Oval Office
4 Cabinet Room
5 West Lobby
6 Roosevelt Room (conference room)
7 Assistants to the President
8 Presidential Press Secretary
9 Press Room
10 Vice President's Office

Second Floor

Main Floor

Basement

faith. These commitments plus the fear of nuclear war and the importance of deterrence all prompted Congress to give a lot of leeway to presidents in this area.

The Constitution delegates to Congress the authority to *declare* the legal state of war (with the consent of the president), but in practice the commander in chief often starts or initiates war (or actions that lead to war). This power of making war has been used by the chief executive time and time again. Polk in 1846 ordered American forces to advance into disputed territory; when Mexico resisted, Polk informed Congress that war existed by act of Mexico, and a formal declaration of war was soon forthcoming. McKinley's dispatch of a battleship to Havana, where it was blown up, helped precipitate war with Spain in 1898. The United States was not formally at war with Germany until late 1941, but prior to Pearl Harbor Roosevelt ordered the Navy to guard convoys to Great Britain and to open fire on submarines threatening the convoys. Truman had no specific authorization from Congress in 1950 when he ordered American forces to resist aggression in Korea. Nor did President Kennedy when he ordered a troop buildup during the Berlin crisis of 1961, when he sent forces into Southeast Asia in the spring of 1962, and when he ordered a naval quarantine of Cuba in the fall of 1962. Nor did President Johnson when he bolstered American forces in Vietnam from 1965 to 1968. Nor did Nixon in his invasion of Cambodia in 1970, or in his support for Saigon's invasion of Laos in 1971. In the following chapter we shall examine the attempt by Congress in the 1970s to reassert itself in this controversial area.

Coalition-building

An effective president is an effective politician—the most visible and potentially the strongest mobilizer of influence in the American system of power. *Politician* is a nasty word to many Americans; it denotes a scheming, evasive person out for his own self-interest. Little wonder many politicians claim they are "above politics."

There is, however, a more constructive definition of *politician:* one who helps manage conflict, one who knows how to negotiate, bargain, and fashion compromises required in making the difficult and desirable become a reality. A president cannot escape these tasks. As a candidate he has made promises to the people. To get things done he must work with many people who have differing loyalties and responsibilities. Inevitably, the president is embroiled in legislative politics, judicial politics, bureaucratic politics.

Despite his tremendous powers, a president can rarely command: he spends most of his time persuading people. Potentially he has great persuasive power, but in the long run people think of their own interests and obligations. In a government of separated institutions that share powers,[12] some congressional and bureaucratic leaders are beyond the political reach of the president. They have their own constituencies—a House committee, for example, or a powerful interest group. Presidents cannot simply give orders like a first sergeant. Before Eisenhower became president, Harry Truman said of him: "He'll sit here, and he'll say, 'Do this! Do that!' And nothing will happen. Poor Ike—it won't be a bit like the Army. He'll find it very frustrating."[13] *All* presidents have found it frustrating.

[12]Richard E. Neustadt, *Presidential Power* (Wiley, 1976), p. 101.

[13]Quoted in *ibid.*, p. 77.

But a president is not without resources. Besides the authority and trappings of his office, the president has two other special sources of political influence — his influence over public opinion and his role as party chief.

No other politician (and few television or film stars) can achieve a closer contact with the people than does the president. Typically, he has been a prominent senator, a vice-president, or a governor, and has built up a host of followers. He has won a nomination and an election and hence has been under the public gaze for years. But the White House is the finest platform of all. The president has his television studio, which he can use to appeal directly to the people. He can summon the press when he wishes, arrange fireside chats or radio call-in shows, choose a sympathetic audience, undertake a "nonpolitical" speaking tour. And he can time all these moves for maximum advantage.[14]

The press conference is an example of how systematically the president can employ the machinery of communication. Years ago the conferences were rather casual affairs. Franklin Roosevelt ran his informally and was a master at withholding information as well as giving it. Under Truman, the conference became "an increasingly routinized, institutionalized part of the presidential communications apparatus. Preparation became elaborately formalized, as did the conduct of the meetings themselves."[15] Kennedy authorized the first live telecast of a press conference and used it frequently for direct communication with the people. That Nixon held big televised conferences less frequently led to much grumbling by the Washington correspondents. Carter's frequent press conferences and openness with the press did much to explain his early popular support.

Presidents commission private polls to gauge public opinion on public controversies. Every president, says a former White House aide, must be a "keen judge of public opinion. He must be able to distinguish its petty whims, to estimate its endurance, to respond to its impatience, and to respect its potential power."

Despite these advantages, the president finds difficulties in both gauging and shaping public opinion. A president must know not only what to do but *when* to do it. Public opinion can be unstable and hence somewhat unpredictable. President Johnson recognized that his wide popular support of the mid-1960s had melted away by 1968 when he decided not to run again. President Nixon's dramatic drop of nearly 45 percentage points in public opinion polls, a result of the Watergate scandals, helped force his resignation. And nearly every president loses support the longer he is in office. Dissatisfaction sets in; interest groups grow impatient; and promises seem to be unkept. The presidency gets blamed for whatever goes wrong.

A second main source of influence for the president is his political party. Most presidents since Jefferson have been party leaders, and generally the more effective the president, the more use he has made of party support. Men such as Wilson and the two Roosevelts fortified their executive and

[14]See Newton W. Minow, John B. Martin, and Lee M. Mitchell, *Presidential Television* (Basic Books, 1973).

[15]Elmer E. Cornwell, Jr. *Presidential Leadership of Public Opinion* (Indiana University Press, 1965), p. 175.

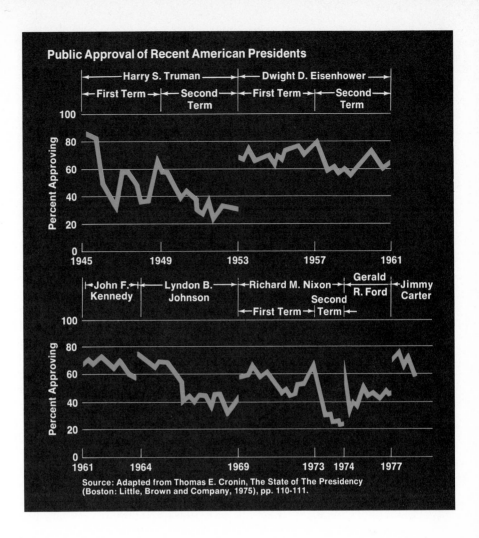

Public Approval of Recent American Presidents

Source: Adapted from Thomas E. Cronin, The State of The Presidency
(Boston: Little, Brown and Company, 1975), pp. 110-111.

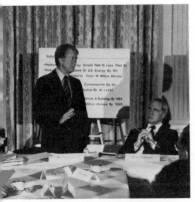

**President Carter, flanked by
Energy Chief James Schlesinger
(right) and Rep. Thomas Ashley,
discusses energy plan with ad
hoc House Energy Commission.**

legislative influence by mobilizing support within their party. Yet no president has fully led his party, and the history of all presidents includes party failures as well as triumphs.

The president has no formal position in the party structure, but his vast influence over national policies and over thousands of appointments commands respect from party leaders. Both president and party need each other. He needs the party's backing throughout the government in order to enact his program. The party needs his direction, his prestige, and the political "gravy" that flows from the White House.

The strings of the national organization all lie in a president's hands. Formally, the national party committee picks the national party chairman; actually, the president lets the committee know whom he wants—and they choose that person. Today the president can hire or fire national party chairmen much as he shifts department heads or even his own staff. His pronouncements on national party policy are more authoritative than any party committee's, even more significant than the party platform itself.[16] He can give a candidate a good deal of recognition and publicity in Wash-

[16]David Broder, *The Party's Over* (Harper & Row, 1971).

ington. He can grant—or deny—campaign assistance and even financial assistance.

Yet the president's practical power over his party is sharply limited and often comes to an end precisely when he needs it most. He rarely has influence over the selection of party candidates for Congress and for state and local office. In part the reason is his limited control of state and local organizations. Even more, it is that party organizations themselves do not control their candidates in office. They do not control them because most candidates win office less through the efforts of the organized party than through their own individual campaigning. Of course, the situation varies from place to place, but in most instances *a personalized politics* emphasizing the candidate triumphs over *a programmatic politics* emphasizing party and issues.

Franklin Roosevelt's "purge" of 1938 is a dramatic example of the limits of the president's power. Despite his own sweeping victory in the 1936 election and the lopsided Democratic majorities in Congress, Roosevelt ran into heavy opposition from many Democratic senators and representatives in 1937 and 1938. Angered by this opposition within the party Roosevelt decided to use his influence to bar the nomination of anti-New Deal candidates in the 1938 congressional primaries. He announced that not as president but as "head of the Democratic party, charged with the responsibility of carrying out the definitely liberal" 1936 Democratic party platform, he would intervene where party principles were clearly at stake. Roosevelt won a significant victory in New York City when he repudiated the anti-New Deal chairman of the House Rules Committee and he helped a pro-administration Democrat win nomination. But elsewhere—mainly in the South—he was defeated.

A president must *bargain* and *negotiate* with party leaders as he does with other independent power centers. Lacking full support from the whole party, the president usually falls back on the personal organization that originally enabled him to gain the presidential nomination.

Administration and organization: the presidential establishment

The Constitution charges the president to "take care that the laws be faithfully executed." A president, however, can be only a part-time administrator, for other responsibilities demand most of his attention. He is, then, dependent on his dependents. Theoretically, at least, orders flow down an administrative *line*, from president to department heads, to bureau chiefs, and down to smaller offices. The president, like all top executives, is assisted by a *staff*, who advise him from *his* point of view. This line and staff organization is inherent in any large administrative entity, whether the Army, General Motors, or the United Nations.

Presidents have come to rely heavily on their personal staffs. Nowhere else—not in Congress, not in his cabinet, not in his party—can he find the loyalty, the single-mindedness, and the team spirit that he can build among his closest aides. Moreover, presidents come to view most cabinet heads as advocates, peddling ideas that would benefit the particular clientele or programs of their department. Presidents apparently feel their own aides will provide them with more neutral and objective advice. But there are substantial costs to listening only to one's closest aides. George Reedy, a former press secretary to President Johnson, depicts the White House as a palace court with strong presidents creating an environment in which any assistant who persists in presenting irritating thoughts is weeded out. "Palace-guard survivors learn early to camouflage themselves with a coating of battleship grey. . . . Inevitably in a battle between courtiers and advisers, the courtiers will win out. This represents the greatest of all barriers to presidential access to reality. . . ."[17] And an astute British writer notes: ". . . if a president needs to be protected by his White House staff against the departments, he also needs to be kept on guard by the departments against his White House staff, who may all too easily begin to think only they know the purposes and the needs and the mind of their president, until *he* becomes *their* creature and believes that his interests are safe with them."[18]

The number of employees in the presidential entourage grew steadily since the early 1900s, when only a few dozen people served a president at a cost of less than a few hundred thousand dollars annually. The Executive Office of the President, approved by Congress in 1939, was the recommendation of President Roosevelt's Committee on Administrative Management. The Executive Office was to provide the president help he obviously needed in carrying out the growing responsibilities imposed by the Depression, and the enlarged role of government. Carter has succeeded in cutting the size of both the White House staff and the Executive Office — but future emergencies could once again reverse this new trend.

THE EXECUTIVE OFFICE OF THE PRESIDENT

The Executive Office of the President consists of the Office of Management and Budget, the Council of Economic Advisers, and several other staff units. The most prominent and controversial presidential staff, of course, is the White House Office. A president's immediate staff, working out of the White House itself, does not have fixed form; indeed, part of its value lies in its flexibility and adaptability. Most presidents, however, have an appointments secretary, a press secretary, a correspondence secretary, a legal counsel, a national security advisor, military aides, and several other legislative, administrative, and political assistants. The staff of the White House office can be categorized by functions: (1) domestic policy, (2) economic policy, (3) national security or foreign policy, (4) administration and personnel matters (as well as personal paper work and scheduling for the president), (5) congressional relations, and (6) public relations.

Vice-President Mondale participates with John Denver at a party fund-raising event.

Presidential aides sometimes insist that they are simply the eyes and ears of the president, that they make few important decisions, and that they never insert themselves between the chief executive and the heads of departments. But the burgeoning White House staff has made this traditional picture nearly obsolete. Some White House aides, impatient with what they viewed as bureaucratic and congressional slowdowns and even sabotage, come to view the presidency as if it alone was *the* government. Separation of powers has meant little to them. They may have lost sight of their location within the larger constitutional system. Listen to Nixon's John Ehrlichman: "There shouldn't be a lot of leeway in following the President's policies. It should be like a corporation, where the executive

[17]George Reedy, *The Twilight of the Presidency* (World, 1970), p. 98.

[18]Henry Fairlie, *The Kennedy Promise* (Doubleday, 1973), pp. 167–68. See also Stephen Hess, *Organizing the Presidency* (Brookings Institution, 1976); and Edward Weisband and Thomas M. Frank, *Resignation as Protest* (Penguin, 1975).

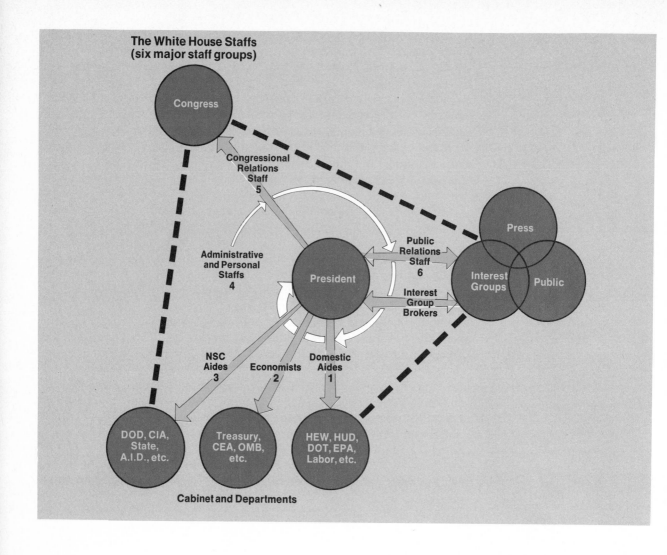

The White House Staffs (six major staff groups)

Congress

Congressional Relations Staff 5

Administrative and Personal Staffs 4

President

Public Relations Staff 6

Press

Interest Groups

Public

Interest Group Brokers

NSC Aides 3

Economists 2

Domestic Aides 1

DOD, CIA, State, A.I.D., etc.

Treasury, CEA, OMB, etc.

HEW, HUD, DOT, EPA, Labor, etc.

Cabinet and Departments

vice-presidents [the cabinet officers] are tied closely to the Chief Executive, or to put it in extreme terms, when he says jump, they only ask how high."[19] And a Carter aide told one of your authors in the summer of 1977 that giving so much power to the cabinet members "was probably President Carter's biggest mistake in 1977."

The office of the vice president provides various support functions for the vice president. It has expanded in recent years as the job of the vice president has become more of an executive than a congressional officer, although vice presidents still serve as President of the United States Senate.

The Office of Management and Budget continues to be the central presidential staff agency. Its director advises the president in detail about the hundreds of government agencies—how much money they should be allotted in the budget and what kind of job they are doing. OMB seeks to improve the planning, management, and statistical work of the agencies.

[19]John Ehrlichman, interview published in *The Washington Post* (August 24, 1972). See also Jeb Stuart Magruder's account of White House life in the Nixon administration, *An American Life: One Man's Road to Watergate* (Atheneum, 1974); and John Dean, *Blind Ambition* (Simon and Schuster, 1976).

The OMB makes a special effort to see that each agency conforms to presidential policies in its dealings with Congress by requiring clearance for policy recommendations to the legislature.

A budget is not just a financial plan, for it deals with the purposes of people in a political environment. It is a reflection of the outcomes of power struggles, an indication of policy directions, and sometimes wishful thinking.[20] But to a president the budget is usually a means of control over administrators trying to join ranks with politicians or interest groups to thwart presidential priorities. Through the long budget-preparing process the president uses the Office of Mangement and Budget as a way to conserve and centralize his own influence.

In July of 1977, President Carter, through the use of a Reorganization Plan, streamlined the Executive Office of the President by eliminating seven of the older units of the office. These units were either discontinued altogether or their functions were transferred to appropriate cabinet departments. Carter said that wherever possible the functions of the Executive Office should bear a close relationship to the work of the president. If they did not, they should be decentralized to some other level within the executive branch. In general the Carter plan held that the major functions for the Executive Office staffs were these:

Provide day-today operational support (e.g. scheduling, appointments) and help the president communicate with the public, the Congress, and the press.

Manage the budget and coordinate Administration positions on matters before the Congress.

Manage the presidential decisionmaking processes efficiently and fairly, and bring the president the widest possible range of opinions.

Help the president: plan and set priorities; monitor and evaluate progress toward achieving the president's objectives; understand and resolve major conflicts among line subordinates; manage crises, especially in national security matters.

The organizational lineup of Executive Office units *before* and *after* this 1977 reorganization was as follows:

Executive Office of the President *Before July, 1977*	Executive Office of the President *After July, 1977*
White House Office	White House Office
Office of the Vice President	Office of the Vice President
Office of Management and Budget	Office of Management and Budget
National Security Council	Council of Environmental Quality
Domestic Council	Council of Economic Advisers
Council on International Economic Policy	Office of Science and Technology Policy
Council of Economic Advisers	Office of the Special Representative for Trade Negotiations
Council on Wage and Price Stability	National Security Council
Office of the Special Representative for Trade Negotiations	Intelligence Oversight Board
Council on Environmental Quality	Council on Wage and Price Stability
Office of Science and Technology Policy	
Office of Drug Abuse Policy	
Office of Telecommunications Policy	
Intelligence Oversight Board	
Federal Property Council	
Energy Resources Council	
Economic Opportunity Council	

[20]Aaron Wildavsky, *The Politics of the Budgetary Process*, rev. ed. (Little, Brown, 1974).

Carter promised that these staff reductions would mean a 28 percent cut of staff from his own immediate White House office and an overall reduction of about 250 persons from the payroll of the Executive Office with a saving, he said, of at least $6 million. Supporters of the Carter reorganization praised the move to weed out unnecessary jobs that bloated the Executive Office and interfered with direct president-to-cabinet relations. Critics claim that Carter's reorganization of his Executive Office really did not change things very much and that the staff size will probably grow anyway, especially when Carter faces some tough crises where he will need to rely on more staff and more government workers "on loan" from other departments.

THE CABINET

It is hard to find a more unusual institution than the cabinet. It is not mentioned by name in the Constitution. Yet, since George Washington's administration, every president has had a cabinet. Washington's consisted of his secretaries of state, treasury, and war plus his attorney general. Today the cabinet consists of the president, the vice-president, the officers who head the twelve executive departments, and a few others. The cabinet has always been a loosely designated body, and it is not always clear who belongs to it. In recent years, for example, certain executive branch administrators and White House counselors have been accorded cabinet rank as well.

Cabinet government as practiced in parliamentary systems simply does not exist in America. In fact, a president is not required by law to form a cabinet or hold regular meetings. Kennedy, Johnson, and Nixon all preferred smaller conferences with those specifically involved in a problem to formal cabinet meetings. Kennedy saw no reason to discuss defense department matters with his secretaries of agriculture and labor present. He thought cabinet meetings were wasting valuable time for too many already busy people. Crucial decisions were more often reached in informal conferences between the president, the heads of two or three major departments, and staff members.

Presidents seldom turn to the cabinet as a collective board of directors

1901

1923

Vice-presidents who moved into the White House, from top: Theodore Roosevelt, Calvin Coolidge, Harry Truman, Lyndon Johnson, Richard Nixon, and Gerald Ford. In this century, the U.S. has had fifteen presidents, starting with McKinley, and eighteen vice-presidents. Six of those vice-presidents subsequently became Chief Executive.

1945

1963

1969

1974

for advice. Votes are rarely taken, and a president sometimes ignores cabinet sentiment. Lincoln, finding the whole cabinet opposed to him on one occasion, could say, "Seven nays, one aye—the ayes have it." Nixon went ahead and proposed his Family Assistance Plan in 1969 despite opposition or indifference to it from at least half his cabinet.

The cabinet as a collectivity often seemed nonexistent. Personal presidential advisers and the heads of various central review units such as OMB, the National Security Council, and others have gained superior status over most of the department heads. This has happened in part because presidents feel many of their department heads adopt narrow advocate views. Good relations between presidents and these cabinet members weaken, as presidents, in frustration, turn more and more to their close, trusted staffs to settle conflicts. Tension especially builds up between senior White House domestic staff aides and domestic cabinet members.

The head of a large domestic department under both Kennedy and Johnson said:

> There is a tendency on the inside to guard the president too much—they [White House aides] develop considerable power by tightening up the ring around the president. They all play on the fact that he hasn't any time for this or that, etc. But a good cabinet member—one who isn't filling some political niche—can be a very excellent corrective to the White House "hot house" staff who are confined there and are virtually locked up fourteen hours a day. . . . The president needs to hear from his cabinet. . . . A president should occasionally sit down in a leisurely way with his cabinet members and listen and ask that important question: "What do you think?" But this occurred very rarely.

The cabinet may someday become a team that both sustains the president and renders him more responsible to the people. But at present the American cabinet bears little resemblance to the cabinet described by Harold J. Laski as "a place where the large outlines of policy can be hammered out in common, where the essential strategy is decided upon, where the president knows that he will hear, both in affirmation and in doubt, even in negation, most of what can be said about the direction he proposes to follow."

The vice-presidency

Though the vice-presidency is now very much a part of the presidential establishment, it has not been so for long. Most vice-presidents served mainly as president of the Senate. In most administrations the vice-president was at best a kind of fifth wheel and at worst a political rival who sometimes connived against the president. The office was often dismissed as a joke. The main reason for the vice-president's posture as outsider was that presidential nominees usually chose as running mates men who were geographically, ideologically, and in other ways likely to "balance the ticket."

In recent decades, however, presidential candidates have selected more like-minded men for their running mates and have made more use of them. Eisenhower gave Nixon a fairly prominent role in his administration, as did Kennedy to Johnson, and Johnson to Humphrey. Spiro Agnew, Gerald Ford, and Nelson Rockefeller, in their different ways, were used chiefly to rally the party faithful. President Carter, however, has given more responsibilities to Vice President Walter Mondale than any other president. Mondale appears to be a senior adviser on a wide range of policy and political issues.

Ideally a vice-president serves several roles in addition to the largely ceremonial functions of acting as president of the Senate. Because he succeeds to the president's job should the president die, resign, or become incapacitated, a vice-president works as an understudy. He can assume some of the president's party and ceremonial duties, thereby easing some of the president's burden. A vice-president can also perform several specialized assignments, for example, chair advisory councils, cabinet-level committees, or a White House conference, or undertake goodwill missions abroad.

Tensions usually develop between top presidential aides and the vice-president and his staff. Part of the problem arises because presidents prefer not to give up any ceremonial duties for which they themselves can win credit or favor. Neither do cabinet members like to share their responsibilities with vice-presidents, which makes it very hard for vice-presidents to gain administrative experience. Then too, presidents often delegate unpleasant political chores to a vice-president.

The search for a better way to select and use vice-presidents is made more urgent by the fact that eight presidents have died in office, four by assassination, four by natural death, and one president has resigned. One-third of our presidents were once vice-presidents, including four of our last seven presidents.

Some feel that a vice-presidency is no longer needed. They recommend that some officer, like the secretary of state or the speaker of the House of Representatives, serve as acting president in the event the office becomes vacant until 90 days later, when a special election for a president could be held. The intent of such proposals is that the president must, except for the briefest periods, be a person elected to that office by the people.

If most people feel the office should be continued, this does not mean they are wholly satisfied with it. There is substantial support for devising better ways to pick vice-presidential nominees as well as for making the vice-presidency a less insignificant office. Both major parties have considered practical means of making the selection procedure for the vice-presidency more democratic. Under the existing system, presidential nominees have a free hand in choosing their running mates. Although there are some notable advantages to the present system—especially the possibility that the ticket will be ideologically compatible—drawbacks are also clearly present. For example: ". . . the pressure of time (which contributed to the abortive choice of Senator Thomas F. Eagleton by George McGovern in 1972), the lack of formalized consultation within the party, the rubber-stamp role for convention delegates, and the absence of public scrutiny and judgment of prospective vice-presidential candidates before the nomination."[21]

The vice-presidency has been significantly affected by two post-World War II constitutional amendments. The Twenty-second Amendment, by imposing a two-term limit on the incumbent, means vice-presidents

"It's easy, but . . ."—former Vice-President Nelson Rockefeller explains some of the problems of being vice-president to Walter Mondale.

[21]John Etridge, "Nation's No. 2: Is He Always the Second Best?" *Los Angeles Times* (October 28, 1973), Part VII. See also Arthur Schlesinger, Jr., "Is the Vice-Presidency Necessary?" *Atlantic Monthly* (May 1974), pp. 37–44.

should have a better chance to move up to the presidency. The Twenty-fifth Amendment, ratified in 1967, confirms prior practice that on the death of a president, the vice-president becomes not acting president but president. Of greater significance, this amendment provides a procedure to determine whether an incumbent president is unable to discharge the powers and duties of his office, and it establishes procedures to fill a vacancy in the vice-presidency. In the event of a vacancy in the office of the vice-president, the president nominates a vice-president who takes office upon confirmation by a majority vote of both houses of Congress. This procedure ensures the appointment of a vice-president in whom the president has confidence. If the vice-president, under these circumstances, has to take over the presidency, he can be expected to reflect most of the policies of the person the people had originally elected to office. President Nixon selected Gerald Ford, and President Ford selected Nelson Rockefeller according to these new methods.[22]

What is likely to happen to the vice-presidency? The office will doubtless remain attractive to aspiring politicians if only because it is one of the major paths to the presidency. The Mondale experience may increase its prestige as a position of influence. However, the tensions between a president and a vice-president (after all everybody else who works closely with a president can be fired by him) are natural. It will be interesting to see if Carter and Mondale can overcome these tensions and make it work. Even if they do, it is almost certain the vice-president will continue to have an undefined role, subject more to the good will and moods of the president than to any fixed job description.

Making the presidency safe for democracy

The startling series of events in the Watergate scandals sharpened the old question: How much executive power can a democracy afford? New questions also were raised: Was the swelling of the presidency due to effective presidential leadership or an attempt to compensate for institutional weaknesses? Was a bigger presidency necessarily better? Did presidential powers grow because they were usurped by presidents or handed over by Congress?

Specific complaints against the presidency in the mid-1970s were many: impoundment of billions of congressionally approved funds, alleged obstruction of justice, abuse of the doctrine of executive privilege, White House lying about the conduct of the Vietnam War, and excessive secrecy. Trust in the president plunged. People lost confidence first in Johnson's and then in Nixon's brand of leadership. The very legitimacy of the presidency was being tested.

How much formal authority does and should a president have? The Constitution is vague in the matter. It seems to grant broad executive authority without defining boundaries. Some scholars hold that in emergencies the president has wide powers to protect the public interest without specific legal authority and even at the cost of overriding existing laws. There seems to be a kind of *inherent* power in the presidency, vast but undefined, that an aggressive president can exploit in times of crisis. The problem is that crisis is now the rule rather than the exception.

[22]The best analysis of the Twenty-fifth Amendment and the problem of presidential succession and vice-presidential selection is found in Allan P. Sindler, *Unchosen Presidents: The Vice President and Other Frustrations of Presidential Succession* (University of California Press, 1976).

Franklin Roosevelt's conception of his powers—sometimes called the *prerogative theory*—was that, in the face of emergencies, a president had the same power John Locke once argued kings had—the power, in Locke's words, "to act according to discretion for the public good, without the prescription of the law and sometimes even against it."[23] The World War II destroyer-bases agreement, for example, in which the president on his own initiative traded naval destroyers to England in return for some military bases, conflicted with several laws.

PRESIDENTIAL CHARACTER

What about presidential personality? If the presidency has too much power for the safety of the country (and the world) and yet not enough to solve some of the nation's toughest problems, what kind of person do we need in this highest office? Political scientist James David Barber writes that because the issues are always changing, we should be concerned somewhat less with the stands a candidate takes than with the candidate's *character*. The character, Barber claims, will stay pretty much the same.[24]

Barber contends that we can classify presidents and would-be presidents according to their *activism* on the one hand and their *enjoyment* of politics and public service on the other. With these two dimensions, he says, we can pretty well predict presidential performance. Table 13–1 shows his classification scheme and how he assesses most twentieth-century presidents. Barber holds that the people best suited for the presidency are politicians who creatively shape their environment and savor the give and take exchanges in political life. He calls them "active-positives." Beware, he tells us, of the active-negative types. They are the driven personalities, compelled to feverish activity, yet doomed by rigidity and personal frustration in the way they approach their jobs. Wilson, Hoover, Johnson, and Nixon are illustrative cases.

Our understanding of personality and character, however, is not yet developed to the stage where accurate predictions can be made about

[23]E. S. Corwin, *The Constitution and What It Means Today*, 10th ed. (Princeton University Press, 1948), p. 85. See also Clinton Rossiter, *Constitutional Dictatorship* (Harcourt Brace Jovanovich, 1948).

[24]Barber, *The Presidential Character*. See evaluations of this study by Alexander L. George, "Assessing Presidential Character," *World Politics* (January 1974), pp. 234–82, and by Alan C. Elms, *Personality in Politics* (Harcourt, Brace, Jovanovich, 1976), Chap. 4. See also the exchange between a Barber critic and Barber in *The American Political Science Review* (March 1977), pp. 182–225.

13–1 Barber's classification of American presidents

		Energy Level in Their Political Job	
		Active	Passive
Emotional Attitude toward Politics and the Job of the Presidency	Positive:	Franklin Roosevelt Harry Truman John F. Kennedy Gerald Ford Jimmy Carter	William H. Taft Warren Harding
	Negative:	Richard Nixon Lyndon Johnson Herbert Hoover Woodrow Wilson	Dwight Eisenhower Calvin Coolidge

suitable presidential candidates. Moreover, some critics doubt that Barber's generalizations are based on sufficient evidence. Still others, who are persuaded by Barber's analysis, doubt that we can really put it to work during most elections. Using strict character criteria to screen candidates, for example, probably would have prevented the moody and often depressed Abraham Lincoln from winning office. Nor can we be sure that a president's character will stay the same through his term or even over the life span of an issue. And just as we need to learn more about a presidential candidate's character, we need more clearly defined issues. It would also help to know the kind of people a candidate seeks out as advisers.

NEW CHECKS AND BALANCES

Presidential power is doubtless greater today than ever before. It is misleading, however, to infer from a president's capacity to drop an H bomb that he is similarly powerful in most other policy-making areas.

The more analysts study policy developments over time and engage in revisionist treatments of past presidents, the more it is clear that presidents, in fact, are seldom free agents in effecting basic social change. We have seen that as priority-setter, politician, and executive a president must share power with members of Congress, bureaucrats, and interest-group elites, among others. The ability to set priorities and even to pass laws is not the same as being able to enforce and administer them properly. A president who wants to be effective in implementing policy changes must know what he wants to achieve, and how to motivate and strengthen the bureaucracy to that end.

"Remember how we all grew up wanting to be President?"

Copyright © 1974. Reprinted by permission of *Saturday Review/World* and Herbert Goldberg.

This is a tough assignment in a political system held together in such large measure by compromise and contradictory goals. Not only must a president deal with key congressional leaders, cabinet members, important bureaucrats, a vice-president, party chiefs, and even leaders of the opposition party, he must also cope with the political forces operating around the White House—public opinion, pressures from organized interests, demands from his own party. He must negotiate endlessly among individuals and among interests. He will constantly be in battle with investigative reporters and the muckrakers. And he must respond to public sentiment at the time that he educates it. The fierce light of public opinion, magnified by the press and the electronic media, always beats down upon the White House.

A NEW ATTITUDE TOWARD THE PRESIDENCY?

In one sense, the best safeguard and restraint on the most dangerous of presidential powers rests with the attitudes of the American people. Citizens have far more power than they generally realize. Presidents usually hear them when they are "sending a message." Citizens can also "vote" between elections in innumerable ways—by changing parties, by organizing protests, by their votes in off-year special elections.

Unrealistic expectations of the presidency have helped to weaken it. Part of the reason presidents turn to secrecy, to subordinating substance to style, has been the overburdening of the office with exaggerated expectations. We elect a politician and then insist on a superhuman performance. As currently designed, the presidency is an institution that manipulates its occupants, and accentuates their *shortcomings* as well as their virtues.[25]

---

[25]See Magruder, *An American Life;* and Carl Bernstein and Bob Woodward, *All the President's Men* (Simon and Schuster, 1974).

It seems cruel to put someone in a position where it is nearly certain he will fail and then condemn him for not succeeding, but this is what we usually do.

We need a healthy skepticism toward presidential decisions, but there is every reason to believe that the American public will expect presidents to do more, not less, than at present. Circumstances are such that our presidents will probably be more important and yet less popular than they have been in the past. A major lesson learned from the Watergate period, most scholars agree, is not that the powers of the presidency should be lessened but that other institutions—parties, Congress, the courts—should grow in stature. Unless we can find ways to revitalize our political parties, to achieve some measure of responsiveness to the electorate and party control over public policy, we may well be destined to continue the march toward an American version of the De Gaulle model of leadership in France.

One of the persisting paradoxes of the American presidency is that it is on the one hand always too powerful and on the other hand too weak. That is, it is always too strong because in so many ways it is contrary to our ideals of government by the people and decentralization of power. Yet the office seems to have inadequate powers because presidents seldom seem able to keep the promises they make. Of course, the presidency is always too strong when we dislike the incumbent. And the limitations of the office are criticized when we believe a president is striving to serve the public interest as we define it. For many people, the presidency of Lyndon Johnson illustrates this paradox: Many of those who felt he was too strong in his handling of the Vietnam War also felt he was too weakly equipped to wage his War on Poverty. The ultimate dilemma for concerned Americans is that curbing the powers of a president who abuses the public trust will usually undermine the capacity of a fair-minded president who would dedicate himself to serving the public interest. In the nearly two centuries since Washington took office, we have multiplied the requirements for presidential leadership and yet made it increasingly difficult to lead.

The presidency will surely remain one of our nation's best sources for creative policy change. It will almost certainly also continue to be a hard-pressed office, laden down with the cumulative weight of contradictory expectations. Americans' mixed views of the job of the president often put our presidents in "no-win" situations.[26] Thus, we want our president to be

1. Gentle and decent *but* also forceful and decisive
2. A common man who can give an uncommon performance
3. Above politics yet a skilled political coalition builder
4. An inspirational leader who never promises more than can be achieved
5. A programmatic but also pragmatic and flexible leader
6. Innovative and inventive, ahead of the times, yet always responsive to popular majorities
7. A moral leader yet not too preachy or moralizing
8. A leader of all the people, but also a leader of one political party

---

[26]These and related paradoxes are discussed in Thomas E. Cronin's essay "The Presidency and Its Paradoxes," in Cronin and Tugwell, eds., *The Presidency Reappraised*, Chap. 4.

Perhaps it is a characteristic of the American mind to hold contradictory ideas simultaneously without bothering to resolve the potential conflict between them. Perhaps too, some of these paradoxes are best left unresolved, especially as ours is an imperfect world and our political system is held together by a variety of compromises. A better rigorous understanding of some of these paradoxes, however, should promote more sensitivity to the limits of what a president can do. Exaggerated or hopelessly contradictory public expectations tend to encourage presidents to attempt more than they can accomplish, to overpromise and to overextend themselves. We seem to want so much so fast that any president gets condemned as ineffectual. Hence, while demanding that our presidents give us their best, we should guard against asking them to deliver more than the presidency—or any single institution—has to give.

History suggests there is no foolproof way to guarantee that our presidents will possess the appropriate functional skills as well as the moral character the office requires. Voters have selected both wisely and mistakenly in the past. James Madison's advice remains useful: "A dependence on the people is, no doubt, the primary control on the government; but experience has taught mankind the necessity of auxiliary precautions."[27] With Watergate in our past and "1984" in our future, we must move to enhance and maintain the effectiveness of these "auxiliary precautions"—Congress, parties, the courts, the press, and concerned citizens' groups—if we are to ensure a properly balanced and constitutional presidency.

Summary

1. Presidents must act alternately, and often simultaneously, as symbolic, priority-setting, crisis-managing, coalition-building, and managerial leaders. No president can divide his job into tidy compartments. Ultimately, all his responsibilities mix with one another. Being president is often like being a juggler already juggling too many balls who, at the most critical moments, is forever having more balls tossed at him.

2. The presidency is a combination of the huge presidential establishment, a president's personality and character, and the heavy demands and expectations on the chief executive. It is still being reshaped as new presidents like Jimmy Carter with ideas of their own and a style of their own move into the White House.

3. The expansion of presidential powers has been a continuous development during the past several decades. Crises, both foreign and economic, have enlarged the powers of the president. When there is a need for decisive action, presidents are asked to supply it. Congress, of course, is traditionally expected to share in the formulation of national policy. Yet Congress is often so fragmented that it has been a willing partner in the growth of the presidency, at the same time that it is constantly setting boundaries on how far a president can extend his influence. Every president must learn anew that he has to work closely with the members of Congress and enlist their support before any major policy changes can be made.

4. The overriding task of American citizens is to bind a president to the majority will without shackling him as a source of creative policy leadership. To expect too much of our presidents may be to weaken them in the leadership tasks we need them to perform. To require immediate accountability might paralyze the presidency. Presidential leadership, properly defined, must be more than the power to persuade and less than the power to coerce: it must be the power to achieve by democratic means results acceptable to the people.

[27]James Madison, *Federalist*, No. 51 (Modern Library, 1937), p. 337.

Chapter 14

Congress vs. President: Can Congress Reassert Itself?

"We want a strong and intelligent President, but he has to bear one thing in mind—we got elected too,"[1] said John Brademas, House of Representatives majority whip, reflecting the post-Watergate suspicion in Congress toward Jimmy Carter and toward presidents in general. Responsible members of Congress recognize the need for strong, effective executive leadership. But, especially since Watergate, they also feel their most important mandate is to exercise their own separate and distinct constitutional role in the operation of the federal government.

The United States is unique among major world powers because it is neither a parliamentary democracy nor an exclusively executive-dominated government. Our Constitution invites both Congress and president to set policy and govern the nation. Much of the time during our nation's history, the main role of Congress has been to respond to presidential leadership. But today Congress spends a good deal of its time undoing presidential initiatives and curbing or redefining presidential powers. This struggle for control of the government sometimes makes it difficult to follow just what is going on in Washington.

Checks and balances: old model, new tests

Article I of the Constitution grants to Congress "all legislative powers" but limits them to those "herein granted." It then sets forth in some detail the powers vested in Congress. Article II, in contrast, grants to the president "the executive power," but describes these powers only in vague terms. Is there any significance to this difference? Some scholars and most presidents have argued that a president has an undefined power to act to promote the well-being of the United States. Therefore, they contend, a president is not limited to the powers spelled out in the Constitution, as is Congress. Other scholars and most members of Congress have argued

304

[1]Rep. Brademas quoted in Stanley Karnow, "President-Congress Tension: It's Healthy," *Boston Globe*, June 20, 1977, p. 14.

that the president has no such inherent power: the language of Article II merely gives the title of the officer who has the executive powers listed thereafter.

Whatever the language of the Constitution, powers not expressly defined in it have often been exercised by the president. As political scientist Louis Fisher writes:

> These extraconstitutional powers have a variety of names: implied, inherent, inferable, incident, residual, moral, aggregate, and emergency. . . . While implied powers are often considered to be more restricted in scope than that of inherent or emergency powers, such distinctions are hard to establish. For instance, the President has the power to remove executive officials. Is that an implied power or an inherent power? It is possible to argue the case either way. When the President intervenes in Cambodia and Laos, for the announced purpose of protecting American lives, is that an inherent power or is it implied in the constitutional role of Commander-in-Chief? When the Constitution was threatened by the secession of the South, Lincoln justified his wartime initiatives partly on his oath to preserve, protect, and defend the Constitution. In this case the exercise of emergency power was based on a broadly conceived implied power.[2]

The founding fathers never intended the president to be the dominant agent in national policy making. They probably did expect presidents to be a major influence in the field of foreign affairs. In the eighteenth century, foreign affairs were generally thought to be an executive matter, but our framers did not want the president to be the only agent. Indeed, many of the powers specified in the Constitution as being vested in Congress were designed to bring Congress into foreign policy.

For much of the twentieth century, however, scholars held that we needed a strong, dynamic presidency to overcome the tremendous fragmentation of power in America. The creaky machinery of our government could be made to work only if we gave a president the proper amount of help and authority. The American people generally favored the expansion of presidential powers. With the development of radio and television, the visibility of the president increased. Indeed, considering the publicity given presidents, it is hardly surprising that citizens look to them to solve the nation's problems. One student of public opinion in the 1960s found that Americans wanted "a man who is strong, who has ideas of his own on how to solve problems, and who will make his ideas prevail even if Congress or the public should oppose him."[3]

Until Vietnam and Watergate, both citizens and scholars held that the presidency was "the great engine of democracy," the "American people's one authentic trumpet," "the central instrument of democracy." A president was "a kind of magnificent lion who can roam widely and do great deeds." What was good for the presidency was good for the country.[4]

[2]Louis Fisher, *President and Congress* (Free Press, 1972), pp. 31–32. See also his *The Constitution Between Friends: Law and Politics in America* (St. Martins Press, 1978).

[3]Roberta S. Sigel, "Image of the American Presidency," *Midwest Journal of Political Science* (February 1966), pp. 123–37.

[4]See a critical discussion of the romanticized view of the presidency in Thomas E. Cronin, *The State of the Presidency* (Little, Brown, 1975), esp. chapter 2.

In the early seventies, however, a feud broke out between Congress and the president for control of national policy and it continues today. Reaction to Watergate and Vietnam took at least two forms. Critics said here was real evidence that the presidency was isolated, autocratic, and imperial. They charged that the deceptions during Vietnam and the corruptions of Watergate occurred because our checks and balances did not work. Too much power had been given to the presidency.

Other observers argued that Vietnam and Watergate were not so much examples of the *excess* of power as of the *abuse* of power. Moreover, supporters of our system of dispersed powers saw at least some evidence that the system was working; that is, they felt the courts, the press, and even Congress did assert themselves when put to a test.

Watergate and the first forced resignation of a president in our history aroused public concern about the role of Congress. Most of the people appeared to want Congress to become a more coequal branch of government, more assertive and alert, more jealous of its own powers. The change in public attitudes is documented by polls taken before and after Vietnam and Watergate. In 1959, pollers asked: "Some people say the president is in the best position to see what the country needs. Other people think the president may have good ideas about what the country needs, but it is up to the Congress to decide what ought to be done. How do you feel about this?" Sixty-one percent chose the president and 17 percent chose Congress (the remainder said about equal, or were undecided). In 1977, *The New York Times* asked virtually the same question: "In general, who do you think *should* have the most to say in the way our government is run, the Congress or the President?" This time, 58 percent chose Congress and only 26 percent the president (the remainder said about equal or were undecided).[5]

What form has congressional reassertion taken? Has Congress really taken up the charges made against the "imperial presidency"? Could a vast new array of checks and balances cripple the presidency and undermine its potential for creative leadership? Is there a danger in overreacting to Vietnam and Watergate? This chapter examines these questions and how Congress tried in the 1970s to reclaim its policy-making powers.

"Ouch!"
Copyright 1975 by Herblock
in The Washington Post

The imperial presidency

In this section we examine the charge that the presidency has become too powerful and dangerous to our democracy. In later sections we will evaluate the merits of this argument. We will also look into the actions taken by Congress and the courts to bring the branches of government into balance again.

Many critics held that during the 1960s and early 1970s the presidency became an imperial institution. This steady growth of the power of the White House came about because of abuse of power by presidents, especially abuse of the war powers and secrecy. For example, in his book *The Imperial Presidency*, historian and former Kennedy adviser Arthur M. Schlesinger, Jr., argues that presidential power was so expanded and misused by 1972 that it threatened our constitutional system.[6] The claim is that an imperial presidency was created as a result of America's wartime experiences, particularly Vietnam.

[5] Sigel, "Image of the American Presidency." The 1977 data are adapted from *The New York Times*/CBS poll of April 1977.

[6] Arthur M. Schlesinger, Jr., *The Imperial Presidency* (Houghton Mifflin, 1973).

The imperial presidency theorists argue that the difficulty stems in part from ambiguity in the president's power as commander-in-chief: it is an undefined *office*, not a *function*. Schlesinger and others acknowledged that Nixon and Johnson did not create the imperial presidency; they merely built on some of the more questionable practices of their predecessors. But observers contend there is a distinction between the *abuse* and the *usurpation* of power. Abraham Lincoln, FDR, and Harry Truman temporarily usurped power in wartime. Johnson and Nixon abused power, even in peacetime, by claiming absolute power to be a part of their office.

On the use of secrecy to protect and preserve a president's national security power, it is argued that Nixon pushed the doctrine beyond acceptable limits. Before Eisenhower, the presumption was that Congress would get the information it sought from the executive branch. Instances of secrecy and executive privilege were the rare exceptions. Since then, they have become the rule. And a Congress that knows only what the president wants it to know is not an independent body.[7]

Those who are critical of Nixon contend that under him the presidency became not only fully imperial, but also revolutionary. In authorizing the "plumbers" group, for instance, Nixon became the first president in our history to establish an extralegal investigative force, paid for by the taxpayers but unknown to Congress and accountable to no one but himself. Other misuses of intelligence agencies and authorized breaking and entering meant that Nixon became the only American president who had ever supervised lawless actions in peacetime.

Schlesinger's book is a useful point of departure for a discussion of the general charges of a too-powerful presidency. These were his chief complaints: presidential war-making, too many emergency powers, diplomacy by executive agreement, secrecy and executive privilege, impoundment, government by veto.

PRESIDENTIAL WAR-MAKING

The Constitution gives Congress the power to declare war. But the actual fighting has always been the decision of the president. From Washington's time on, by ordering the troops into battle the president has decided when Americans will fight and when they will not. When the cause has had political support, the president's use of this authority has been approved. Abraham Lincoln called up troops, spent money, set up a blockade, and fought the first few months of the Civil War without even calling Congress into session. Over the years, it had become obvious that the presidency needed the power to respond to sudden attacks and to protect the rights and property of American citizens. In a 1966 legal memorandum, the State Department described this enlarged mandate this way:

> In the twentieth century the world has grown much smaller. An attack on a country far from its shores can impinge directly on the nation's security . . . . The Constitution leaves to the President the judgment to determine whether the circumstances of a particular armed attack are so urgent and the potential consequences so threatening to the security of the U.S. that he should act without formally consulting the Congress.[8]

---

[7]*Ibid.*, Chapter 10. See also Louis Henkin, *Foreign Affairs and the Constitution* (Norton, 1975).

[8]Leonard C. Meeker, "The Legality of U.S. Participation in the Defense of Vietnam," *Department of State Bulletin* (March 28, 1966), pp. 484–85.

President Franklin D. Roosevelt, surrounded by Congressional leaders, signs Declaration of War against Japan on December 8, 1941.

But Congress was upset because President Johnson in 1964 got the Gulf of Tonkin Resolution passed on misleading information. (Congress in the early 1970s repealed this resolution.) A secret air war was waged in Cambodia in 1969 and 1970 with no formal congressional knowledge or authorization. The military also operated in Laos without formally notifying Congress. It was to prevent just such acts as these that the framers of the Constitution gave Congress the power to declare war. They sought to create a permanent institutional safeguard against presidential warmaking. Most members of Congress believe that what happened in Indochina was the result of the White House ignoring the Constitution. But they also agree that presidential excesses came about because Congress either agreed with the president or did nothing to stop him.

What the Johnson and Nixon war experiences also show is that at the beginning of hostilities, the country and Congress rally behind a president. As casualties mount and the fighting continues, support usually falls off. In both Korea and Vietnam, presidential failure to end the use of American ground forces led to trouble. Eisenhower swept into power in 1952 on the promise to bring the boys home; Nixon won in 1968 when Johnson was forced out over Vietnam.

Congress should not be allowed off the hook entirely on the Gulf of Tonkin Resolution. Perhaps it was misled. But Congress enthusiastically supported the president at the time and went along with his actions. Then when the war turned sour, senators and representatives charged that they were misled. Why then were they so easily talked into endorsing the Vietnam war? They continued to pass appropriations for it right up to April 1975. The more general lesson appears to be that the country and Congress tend to go along with a president's judgments about military action overseas.

There are additional reasons why there have been no formal declarations of war. These include: The president assumes, during the state of war certain legal prerogatives that Congress might not always be willing to grant, nor for that matter would the president always be willing to assume them. There are, too, certain international legal consequences of a formal declaration of war regarding foreign assets, the rights of neutrals, and so on, which our allies would not always be willing to recognize and would be difficult to insist upon. Moreover, there is the psychological consequence of declaring war which is compounded by the fact that, according to Article 2, Section 2 of the United Nations Charter, war is illegal except as self-defense.

TOO MANY EMERGENCY POWERS

Since the early 1930s Congress has passed about 500 federal statutes that collectively give a president extraordinary powers. Once a state of emergency is declared, for example, a president may have these powers: He may seize property, organize and control the means of production, seize commodities, assign military forces abroad, declare martial law, and control all transportation and communications. He may, in fact, control almost all aspects of citizens' lives. Abuses of presidential power under these emergency laws include the detention of Japanese aliens during World War II, the coverup of the bombings in Cambodia, and the directives to the FBI for illegal domestic surveillance and intelligence work.[9]

[9]For a discussion of abuses of power in U.S. intelligence agencies during the Cold War years, see Morton H. Halperin, Jerry J. Berman, Robert L. Borosage, and Christine M. Marwick, *The Lawless State* (Penguin, 1976); and David Wise, *The American Police State: The Government Against the People* (Random House, 1976).

"If the President were to make use of all of the power available to him under the emergency statutes on the books, he could conduct a government without reference to usual constitutional processes," declared Senator Frank Church (D-Idaho). "These powers taken together could form a basis for one-man rule."[10] In 1972, Congress launched a drive to terminate and rewrite emergency law procedures.

TOO MUCH DIPLOMACY BY EXECUTIVE AGREEMENT

As indicated in Table 14–1, the growing use of executive agreements shows their popularity with recent presidents. Treaty ratification procedures provide that diplomatic agreements must receive the consent of the Senate. But executive agreements permit a president to enter into formal arrangements with a foreign nation without senatorial approval. These agreements have been recognized as distinct from treaties since George Washington's day. And their use by the executive has been upheld by the courts.

What irked Congress in the 1960s and 1970s was that the Senate was being asked to ratify international accords only on trivial matters. Critically important mutual aid and military base agreements were being arranged by the White House without even informing Congress. Many members of Congress therefore feel that the subversion of the treaty ratification process has been an important aspect of the imperial presidency.

For example, while the Senate was ratifying treaties on such questions as the preservation of archeological artifacts in Mexico and maintenance of certain lights in the Red Sea, the president by executive agreement was making vital decisions about the United States presence in Vietnam, Laos, Korea, and Thailand.[11] Walter F. Mondale, then a senator, and others argued that these practices were a violation of the Constitution's intent that Congress share in making foreign policy. These agreements, said Senator Lloyd Bentsen (D-Texas), "reflect our national priorities" and "lie at the very heart of the foreign policy process."[12] And so the members of Congress began to look for ways to limit a president's executive agreement authority.

Ironically, conservative members of the Congress had made efforts during the 1930s and 1940s to check a president's power to make executive

[10]Church, quoted in "The President Versus Congress: The Score Since Watergate," *National Journal*, May 29, 1976, p. 736.

[11]Walter F. Mondale, *The Accountability of Power* (David McKay, 1975), pp. 114–15.

[12]Lloyd Bentsen, testimony, *Congressional Oversight of Executive Agreements—1975, Hearings Before the Subcommittee on Separation of Powers of the Committee on the Judiciary*, United States Senate, 94th Congress (U.S. Government Printing Office, 1975), p. 79.

14–1
Treaties and executive agreements (1789–1973)

Period	Treaties	Executive Agreements	Totals
1799–1839	60	27	87
1839–1889	215	238	453
1889–1939	524	917	1441
1940–1973	364	6395	6759
	1163	7577	8740

Louis Fisher, *President and Congress* (Free Press, 1972), p. 45, and David Sale, *Executive Agreements* (Congressional Research Service, 1975), p. 4.

agreements. Senator John Bricker (R-Ohio) introduced a constitutional amendment in the 1930s that would have required Congress to approve all executive agreements. He was opposed by liberals, especially liberal political scientists and historians. Advocates of an activist and internationalist foreign policy, they feared the Bricker amendment would reintroduce a mindless isolationism. In the wake of Vietnam and especially during the Nixon administration, the shoe was on the other foot.

SECRECY AND EXECUTIVE PRIVILEGE

The founding fathers did not intend that the president should decide what information Congress and the American people should have. They were aware of the maxim that he who controls the flow of information rules our destinies. Without information, Congress cannot oversee the execution of its laws; if it cannot do that, it is scarcely in a position to legislate at all. The difficulty arises because constitutional scholars, the courts, and Congress agree that a president does have the right to withhold information vital to national security. Thus, during World War II, the time and place of the Normandy Beach invasion were properly kept secret.

Recently presidents have invoked the doctrine of executive privilege to claim that a president may withhold information, even from Congress, whenever he thinks it is necessary to protect the public interest. It was not until the Watergate events, however, that the doctrine became highly controversial. President Nixon and his lawyers claimed that the president's decision to invoke executive privilege was not subject to review either by Congress or the courts. Thus on these grounds Nixon refused to turn over to congressional committees documents and tapes they had requested.

Raoul Berger, a legal historian, argued that executive privilege is "a myth, without constitutional basis,"[13] but most people felt that the truth is somewhere between the Nixon and the Raoul Berger points of view. As we noted in Chapter 5, the Supreme Court ruled in 1974 that a president does have a limited power of executive privilege, but it is subject to judicial scrutiny.

PRESIDENTIAL POLICY: IMPOUNDMENT

Some members of Congress used to joke during the Nixon period that ours was a system of checks and balances all right: Congress wrote the checks and the White House kept the balance. They were referring to President Nixon's frequent use of the power to impound funds appropriated by Congress.

Impoundment refers to an order of a president forbidding agencies to spend funds even though they have been appropriated by Congress. *Impoundment* is a complicated practice because it can take and has taken so many forms. Refusals to spend have meant savings in the past because of a change in events (a war ends) or for managerial reasons (a project can be carried out more efficiently). Before Nixon, impoundments were infrequent, usually temporary, and generally involved small amounts of money. Still, the precedent was set. Nixon stretched the use of impoundment to new limits. Altogether he impounded about $18 billion of funds appropriated by Congress. (Nixon's defense was that an undisciplined "credit card" Congress controlled by the Democrats was spending too much and causing huge deficits.) What bothered Congress about Nixon's

---

[13]Raoul Berger, "The Grand Inquest of the Nation," *Harper's* (October 1973) p. 12. See also his *Executive Privilege: A Constitutional Myth* (Harvard University Press, 1974).

impoundments of water pollution control funds, urban aid funds, and other programs was that he used impoundment to set policy. Congress felt it was one thing for a president to delay funds for purposes of efficiency; it was quite another for him to use impoundment for extensive policy making or priority setting.

Congress responded to Nixon's impoundments in a relatively united manner. A clause in the Constitution reads: "No money shall be drawn from the Treasury, but in consequence of appropriations made by law." Congress took this to mean it had the final say in fiscal policy making. By refusing to spend appropriated funds, the executive was in effect exercising an *item veto*. He was destroying or delaying a program while avoiding a public veto message and the risk of a congressional override. It was a question of which branch should decide how to allocate the public funds.[14]

GOVERNMENT BY PRESIDENTIAL VETO?

A president can veto a bill by returning it with his objections to the house in which it originated. Congress, by a two-thirds vote in each chamber, may then pass it over his veto. If the president does not sign or veto the bill within ten weekdays after he receives it, it becomes law without his signature. If Congress adjourns within the ten weekdays, however, the president, by taking no action, can kill the bill. This is known as the *pocket veto*.

The veto's strength lies in the ordinary failure of Congress to get a two-thirds majority of both houses. Historically, Congress has overridden only about 3 percent of the president's vetoes.[15] Yet a Congress that can repeatedly mobilize such a majority against a president can almost take command of the government. Such was the fate of President Andrew Johnson.

In ordinary times, Congress can manipulate legislation to reduce the chance of a presidential veto. For example, it can attach irrelevant but controversial provisions, called *riders*, to vitally needed legislation. The president must either accept or reject the whole bill, for he does not have the power to delete individual items; that is, he does not have the item veto. Appropriations are a special case in point. In one appropriations bill, lawmakers may combine badly needed funds for the armed forces with costly pork-barrel items. The president must take the bill as it is or not at all.

For his part, the president can also use the veto power in a positive way. He can announce that a bill under consideration by Congress will be turned back unless certain changes are made. He can use the threat of a veto against some bill Congress wants badly in exchange for another bill that he wants. But the veto is essentially a negative weapon of limited use to a president who has a positive program. For it is the *president* who usually is pressing for action.

Controversy over the presidential veto power has been less heated than over the other charges we have discussed. Still Nixon's 43 and Ford's

Drawing by Brickman. Washington Star Syndicate.

[14]The best source on impoundment and related questionable financial strategies used by presidents in modern times is Louis Fisher, *Presidential Spending Power* (Princeton University Press, 1975). See also Fisher's case study, "Impoundment of Clean-Water Funds: The Limits of Discretion," in Robert L. Peabody, ed., *Cases In American Politics* (Praeger, 1976), pp. 44–70.

[15]Carlton Jackson, *Presidential Vetoes: 1792–1945* (University of Georgia Press, 1967); and Jong R. Lee, "Presidential Vetoes from Washington to Nixon," *Journal of Politics* (May 1975), pp. 522–46.

69 vetoes and the occasional use of the pocket veto did stir criticism, most especially from their partisan foes. Congressman Bob Eckhardt (D-Texas) complained, "Certainly, the Founding Fathers envisoned a more limited use of the veto . . .."[16] Other members of Congress, led by Senator Edward Kennedy objected to Nixon's use of the pocket veto during short holiday congressional recesses. Kennedy went to court to contend that the pocket veto did not apply while Congress was in recess, but only when it had adjourned. The courts upheld his contention.

In fact, there is little that Congress can do when confronted with a presidential veto. It must either get enough votes to override the veto or modify the legislation and try again. However, Congress may be retaliating for presidential vetoes by its own increasing use of the so-called legislative or congressional veto, which will be discussed later in this chapter.

Congress reasserts itself

The end of the war in Vietnam, the 1974 impeachment hearings, and the resignation of President Nixon seemed to give Congress new life. It set about to recover lost authority and discover new ways to participate more fully in national policy making. Some of the more notable efforts to reassert itself are outlined below.

THE WAR OVER THE WAR POWERS

In 1973 Congress took an unprecedented step, even overriding a presidential veto, and enacted the War Powers Resolution. Nixon called it an unconstitutional intrusion into the president's constitutional authority; it was an "action that seriously undermines this nation's ability to act decisively and convincingly in times of international crisis." Nevertheless, Congress declared that henceforth the president can commit the armed forces of the United States (1) only after a declaration of war by Congress, (2) by specific statutory authorization, or (3) in a national emergency created by an attack on the United States or its armed forces. After committing the armed forces under the third condition, the president is supposed to report immediately to Congress. Within sixty days, unless Congress has declared war, the troop commitment is to be ended. The president is allowed another thirty days if he asserts that the safety of U.S. forces requires their continued use. After ninety days, this resolution permits Congress, by concurrent resolution *not subject to presidential veto*, to direct the president to disengage such troops. A president is also obligated by this resolution to consult Congress "in every possible instance" before committing troops to battle.

The S S Mayaguez was seized by Cambodia in 1975, whereupon President Gerald Ford ordered marines to free the vessel.

Not everyone was pleased by the passage of the War Powers Resolution. Some supported President Nixon's stand. Others felt this resolution granted a president more power than he already had, and even encouraged short-term interventions.[17] Whether or not this act will make any difference, it does reflect a new determination in Congress. The legislature will try to control the president's discretion to decide how American troops will be used. Any future president will know that commitment of American troops is subject to the approval of Congress. He will have to

[16]Bob Eckhardt, "President Ford and the Veto Power," *Congressional Record* (October 1, 1976), p. E5616.

[17]See, for example, Thomas F. Eagleton, *War and Presidential Power: A Chronicle of Congressional Surrender* (Liveright, 1974).

persuade the nation that his actions are justified by the gravest of national emergencies.[18] Since its adoption in 1973 the process spelled out in the War Powers Resolution has been used four times; the most dramatic was when Marines were sent to free the merchant cargo ship *Mayaquez* which had been captured by the Cambodians. Although many felt President Ford had the constitutional authority to take such action anyway, he did send a report to Congress within the forty-eight-hour period. Others criticized him for failing to consult Congress before committing the troops. (The president had just informed congressional leaders of what he intended to do.)

Whether the intensity of the reaction against the use of presidential authority to send the armed forces into combat will last longer than the disenchantment over Indochina remains an open question. Congress has the constitutional authority to intervene whenever it has the will to do so. But past experiences suggest that at the beginning of a crisis, a president will have most of the country and Congress behind him. And certainly within sixty days a president can maneuver the armed forces into a situation in which it is unlikely the Congress will oppose him. Only after the initiative is shown "not to work," and most especially if there are extensive combat casualties and sacrifices at home do people get "turned off." The Congress begins to reflect the new popular feelings.

CURBING THE EMERGENCY POWERS

A law enacted in 1976 terminated (as of September 1978) the congressional delegation of emergency powers to the president, which had dated back to the 1930s. The new law establishes procedures for presidential declaration of future emergencies and his use of emergency powers, but in a manner that is designed to define more clearly these emergency powers and to provide for regular congressional review.

Under the new law, a president must inform Congress in advance of which laws that have emergency provisions he intends to use when he declares that an emergency exists. The use of these emergency powers is to terminate after six months, although a president may then declare he intends to use these emergency powers for another six months. Congress, however, by a majority vote in both the Senate and House could deny to the president the use of emergency powers.[19] What emergency powers Congress delegates to the president, it can clearly withold. More controversial, however, is the question of whether Congress can deny to a president the use of emergency powers he might claim are given to him directly by the Constitution.

CONGRESS AND THE INTELLIGENCE AGENCIES

Abuse of the intelligence and spying agencies was another charge against the imperial presidency. The Central Intelligence Agency (CIA) was established in 1947, when the threat of "world communism" led to a vast number of national security efforts. When the CIA was established,

---

[18]For useful discussions of the likely consequences of the War Powers Resolution, see Graham T. Allison, "Making War: The President and Congress, " in Thomas E. Cronin and Rexford G. Tugwell, eds., *The Presidency Reappraised*, 2nd ed. (Praeger, 1977), pp. 228–47; and James A. Nathan and James K. Oliver, *United States Foreign Policy and World Order* (Little, Brown, 1976), pp. 527–34.

[19]*National Emergencies Act, Report of the Committee on Government Operations, United States Senate* (U.S. Government Printing Office, 1976), p. 2.

Senate Intelligence Committee Chairman Frank Church (far left) faces CIA Director William Colby prior to hearings to investigate alleged "murder plots" developed by the CIA.

Congress recognized the dangers to a free society inherent in such a secret organization. Hence it was stipulated that the CIA *was not to engage in any police work or to perform operations within the United States.*

From 1947 to the mid-1970s, no area of national policy making was more removed from Congress than CIA operations. In many instances Congress acted as if it really didn't want to know what was going on. Said one senator: "It is not a question of reluctance on the part of CIA officials to speak to us. Instead it is a question of our reluctance, if you will, to seek information and knowledge on subjects which I personally, as a Member of Congress and as a citizen, would rather not have."[20] There is much evidence that Congress as well as the White House was lax in supervising intelligence activities.

In recent years, Congress has tried to change this. In 1975 the Senate established a temporary committee of inquiry chaired by Senator Frank Church (D-Idaho). It found widespread abuses of power and violations of citizens' rights in foreign and domestic intelligence operations. The Church committee recommended that Congress bring all intelligence operations under tighter congressional supervision.[21]

The Senate created, in 1976, a permanent Select Committee on Intelligence. This Committee has legislative and budgetary authority over the CIA and other intelligence agencies. A year later, in mid-1977, the House established a similar committee. Since we now know that even presidents have had difficulty getting a handle on the CIA, there is some doubt about whether these committees will have any better luck. Yet in an unprecedented exercise of its power, Congress in 1976 amended the defense appropriations bill to end covert American intervention in Angola: "The inevitable public disclosure of a secret operation served, in this instance, the will of Congress; and in the short run the Angola controversy was a warning that the executive should proceed with caution."[22]

How likely is it that Congress will actually regulate the CIA? Some people say the Senate and House committees should spell out a charter.

[20]Statement of Senator Leverett Saltonstall (R-Mass.) quoted in Henry Howe Ransom, *The Intelligence Establishment* (Harvard University Press, 1970), p. 169.

[21]Useful discussions of these efforts by Congress are found in Harry Howe Ransom, "Congress and the Intelligence Agencies," in Harvey C. Mansfield, Sr., ed., *Congress Against the President* (Academy of Political Science, 1975), pp. 153–66; and John T. Elliff, "Congress and the Intelligence Community," in Larry Dodd and Bruce Oppenheimer, eds., *Congress Reconsidered* (Praeger, 1977), pp. 193–206.

[22]Elliff, "Congress and the Intelligence Community," p. 204.

The charter should limit the CIA to foreign operations, severely restrict and control all covert activities, and require written approval for any major field operations. The political intelligence work of the FBI should be stopped. Others feel full disclosure of the intelligence community's budget is necessary. Still others admit that the intensity and direction of congressional interest in this area depend on larger political forces. When a national consensus supports a president and his foreign policy initiatives as it did in the early part of the Cold War, Congress is likely to go along. But without such a consensus, a more assertive Congress may act. It may, for example, try to find a more realistic system of accountability for intelligence agencies.

THE BUDGET AND IMPOUNDMENT CONTROL ACT OF 1974

"Congress has seen its control over the federal purse-strings ebb away over the past 50 years because of its inability to get a grip on the overall budget, while the Office of Management and Budget in the executive branch has increased its power and influence," said Senator Edmund S. Muskie (D-Maine) in 1974.[23] Congress became dependent on the president's budget proposals. It had no budget system of its own—only many separate actions and decisions coming at various intervals throughout the year.

Muskie was one of the chief authors of the 1974 Congressional Budget and Impoundment Control Act. This was designed to encourage Congress to evaluate the nation's fiscal situation and spending priorities in a comprehensive way. It was also hoped that in a period of high inflation Congress could help put a lid on unnecessary spending. The act creates a permanent budget committee for each chamber. In the House, it is a twenty-five-member committee: five members from the Ways and Means Committee, five from the Appropriations Committee, thirteen from remaining legislative committees, and one member each from the majority and minority leadership. The Senate committee is a sixteen-member committee picked in the regular fashion.

Under this law, Congress also established a Congressional Budget Office (CBO). It provides budgetary and fiscal experts and computer services and gives Congress technical assistance on the president's proposals. Some members of Congress hoped the CBO would provide hard, practical data to guide the drafting of spending legislation. Others saw it as a potential "think tank" that might propose standards for spending and national priorities. In fact, CBO is most frequently used to provide routine cost estimates of spending and tax bills and to keep track of the overall budget level.

Optimists feel the budget reform act will force Congress into more systematic and timely action on budgetary legislation. It may tie separate spending decisions in with fiscal policy objectives. The new budgetary timetable gives Congress three additional months to consider the president's recommendations (see Table 14–2). By May 15 of each year, Congress adopts a tentative budget that sets target totals for spending and taxes. This target serves as a guide for the committees considering detailed appropriation measures. By September 15, Congress adopts a second resolution that either affirms or revises the earlier targets. If necessary to meet the final budget totals, this resolution must also dictate any changes in expenditures and revenues.

[23]Quoted in *National Journal*, May 29, 1976, p. 742.

How has it worked so far? The new budget process clearly has meant more congressional participation in fiscal policy making. The budget resolutions provide a vehicle for debate on key economic issues; the newly created budget committees can challenge the president's monopoly on fiscal policy proposals. The long-term success of this experiment will depend very much on the new budget committees. They must become powerful enough to assume leadership in Congress and get cooperation with their target and ceiling resolutions.[24]

The impoundment control provisions of this new law have not worked out as well; but here again, Congress has put the executive branch on the defensive. If a president withholds funds temporarily, he reports to Congress; his action can be overturned by a resolution of either chamber. But if a president impounds funds for some project permanently, his action is ineffective unless both houses approve within forty-five days. If the comptroller general (in the General Accounting Office) finds that impoundments have been made without proper reports to Congress, he may report them himself. Congress may then act to force release of the funds. Should a president fail to comply with action overruling an impoundment, Congress may ask for a court order requiring the funds to be spent.[25]

There have been complaints that the new impoundment law creates a vast amount of paperwork. Reports need to be sent to Congress even when a few thousand dollars are not spent for simple managerial and efficiency purposes. Other complaints stem from the vagueness of the law's provisions. There will doubtless be further changes in the law to correct these problems.

CONFIRMATION POLITICS

The Senate and the president often struggle over control of top personnel in the executive and judicial branches. The Constitution leaves the question somewhat ambiguous: "The President . . . shall nominate, and by and with the advice and consent of the Senate, shall appoint Ambassadors, other public Ministers and Consuls, Judges of the Supreme Court, all other officers of the United States. . . ." Presidents, however, have never enjoyed exclusive control over hiring and firing in the executive branch. The Senate jealously guards its right to confirm or reject major appointments; during the period of congressional government after the Civil War, presidents had to struggle to keep their power to appoint and dismiss. But for most of the twentieth century presidents have gained a reasonable amount of control over top appointments. This has happened in part because public administration experts warned that a chief executive cannot otherwise be held accountable.

Since Watergate, and the Bert Lance affair in 1977, the Senate has taken a much tougher stand on presidential appointments. The Senate is trying to take seriously its powers to provide "advice and consent" to the president. Senators are especially concerned about potential conflicts of interest. "Our tolerance for mediocrity and lack of independence from economic interests is rapidly coming to an end," said one senator. Another summed it up this way: "Surely, we have learned that one item the gov-

Theodore Sorensen, a Carter nominee for CIA director, announces to a 1977 senate hearing that he is withdrawing his name from consideration, after strong opposition to the appointment developed.

[24]See James A. Thurber, "Congressional Budget Reform and New Demands for Policy Analysis," *Policy Analysis* (Spring 1976), pp. 197–214; Louis Fisher, "Congressional Budget Reform: The First Two Years" *Harvard Journal on Legislation*, Vol. 14 (April, 1977), 413–57.

[25]See "Powers of the Congress," *Congressional Quarterly* (1976), p. 43.

14–2 Congressional budget timetable

Between October and December:	**Congressional Budget Office (CBO) submits a five-year projection of current spending.**
By November 10:	**President submits the current services budget.**
Fifteen days after Congress meets:	**President submits his budget.**
Between January and March:	**Budget committees hold hearings and start work on the first budget resolution.**
By March 15:	**Legislative committees submit reports to the budget committees.**
By April 15:	**Budget committees report the first concurrent resolution on the budget to their respective chamber.**
By May 15:	**Appropriate committees report bills and resolutions authorizing new budget authority, and Congress completes all action on the first concurrent budget resolution.**
By August:	**Budget committees prepare the second concurrent budget resolution and report to their Houses.**
By September 15:	**Congress completes all action on the second concurrent budget resolution.**
By September 25:	**Congress completes action on a reconciliation bill or resolution containing provisions necessary to accomplish any change in budget authority, revenues, or the public debt directed by the second budget resolution.**
October 1:	**The fiscal year begins.**

ernment is short on is credibility." Screening is much tighter now. President Ford, for example, had several high-level appointees turned down. And one of President Carter's first difficulties with Congress was resolved only when Theodore Sorensen, his nominee to head the CIA, voluntarily withdrew. Carter's arms control negotiator, Paul Warnke, had to endure close scrutiny from the Senate and only won confirmation by a narrow margin.

Plainly, the Senate is not bashful in its use of this prerogative. A notable blow to presidential authority to appoint came when Congress, over President Nixon's objection, required Senate confirmation for directors and deputy directors of the Office of Management and Budget. These appointments previously were made solely by the president.

It is difficult to tell to what extent this trend toward greater congressional activity was the result of normal antagonism when one party controls Congress and the other the White House. Partisan factors must have contributed to this development in the 1969–77 period. But the scandal of Watergate, in which so many appointees were indicted and convicted, also contributed. The test will come when we look back at the Carter years and see whether the Senate has continued its tougher standards.[26]

There is one area, however, where the Senate is likely to remain very

[26]Helpful studies in this area include Ronald C. Moe, "Senate Confirmation of Executive Appointments: The Nixon Era," in Mansfield, *Congress Against the President*, pp. 141–52; Judith H. Parris, "The Senate's Power to Confirm Nominations as a Constraint on Presidential Government," paper delivered at a conference on the presidency at American University, April 20, 1976 (unpublished).

much involved. When the president appoints someone to a federal position in a *state* (a U.S. attorney for example), he needs the approval of the senators from the state, most especially if they are members of his party and his party controls the Senate. He needs that approval because of a practice known as *senatorial courtesy*: the willingness of the Senate to confirm presidential appointments only if they are not "personally obnoxious," that is, politically objectionable to the senators from that state. The practice is strongest when the senators belong to the same party as the president and that party controls the Senate, but presidents also find it wise to get the clearance for their nominees even from senators of the other party. Thus for nearly all district court judgeships, many appellate court judgeships, and a variety of other positions, senators exercise what is in fact a veto. It can be overriden only with the greatest difficulty, is usually exercised in secret, and is subject to little accountability. But the patronage is so important to the senators that senatorial courtesy is likely to continue.

THE CONGRESSIONAL VETO

Within recent years Congress has turned the so-called congressional veto into a major instrument of policy making. The Constitution stipulates that every bill or resolution or vote to which the concurrence of the Senate and House may be necessary shall be presented to the president for his approval or veto. But "concurrent resolutions," in contrast to "joint resolutions," do not have to be submitted to the president. In the past this made little difference, since concurrent resolutions were used to express congressional opinion and had no force of law.

Then in 1932 Congress passed a joint resolution allowing President Hoover limited authority to reorganize the executive agencies. But it stipulated that the president's proposals would not be put into effect for ninety days, during which time either house by a simple resolution could veto the proposal. Since then, the congressional veto, as it has come to be called, has come to be a standard practice. The types of such veto vary. In some instances a proposed measure becomes effective after certain days unless one or both houses of Congress disapprove. In other instances a proposed measure does not become effective unless both houses approve. Whatever the variant, the use of a congressional veto allows Congress to delegate power and then take it away without having to secure presidential approval.

Since 1932 more than 300 pieces of legislation have carried some form of congressional veto. About half of them have been enacted since 1972. Significant statutes with legislative veto provisions include the Budget and Impoundment Control Act of 1974, the Trade Act of 1974, and the Energy Policy and Conservation Act of 1975.

In 1976 the House of Representatives was only two votes short of passing a bill that would have required federal agencies to submit all new regulations to Congress for sixty legislative days and such regulations would be subject to veto by either chamber.

Most members of Congress favor the use of the congressional veto; they contend it is an effective device to ensure that bureaucrats issue regulations that conform to congressional intentions, a very important matter since regulations are quickly overtaking statutes. In 1974, for example, Congress passed 404 public laws. Sixty-seven executive agencies adopted 7,496 regulations.[27]

Many White House aides and supporters of the presidency consider the congressional veto a violation of the doctrine of separation of powers. They also argue that it gives lobbyists more of a chance to influence the work of government. The congressional veto

> eliminates the president from the lawmaking function by not presenting him with "legislation" that he can veto. It allows Congress to change its mind an unlimited number of times about what a statute is intended to do after passage of the statute — in effect, amending the statute. . . . The President's administrative authority — his duty to "take care that the laws be faithfully executed" — is impinged because he is prevented from implementing regulations he deems suitable and consistent with the enabling legislation.[28]

Whatever its merits, Congress has surely used the congressional veto to reassert itself; it has become a new, significant feature of our constitutional system. During coming years, the question of its constitutionality is likely to be tested in the courts.

OTHER ACTIONS

The maintenance of democratic control over foreign and military policy has become increasingly difficult in the nuclear age. Secrecy has been at the heart of the problem. President Nixon argued: "You cannot in today's world have successful diplomacy without secrecy. It is impossible. . . . And it is particularly impossible when you are dealing not with your friends, but with your adversaries."

But executive secrecy is subject to abuses, as Watergate illustrated. People could understand the use of secrecy in negotiations with China or diplomatic initiatives in the Middle East. But most people found it difficult to understand the use of secrecy in dealing with congressional leaders. The tapping of telephones to prevent security leaks, the breaking into offices: these are the tactics not of politics, but of *war*. They may be appropriate ways to deal with enemies, but they are not appropriate ways to deal with domestic political opponents.

How can we prevent what may be a necessary evil — secrecy for diplomatic purposes — from becoming secrecy to cover up obstruction of justice? Many Americans felt that even at the risk of a less effective foreign policy, what was needed was greater power-sharing with Congress.

Congress has also become more involved in general foreign policy making. Shaking off years of inertia, Congress imposed a cutoff of aid to Vietnam and a bombing halt in Cambodia. As of 1972 it requires the Secretary of State to submit to Congress the final texts of executive agreements. It restrained the Ford administration from getting involved in Portugal and Angola. Led by Senator Henry Jackson (D-Wash.), Congress refused

[27]Quoted in Mary Russell, "Bill to Give Congress Veto Power Is Defeated," *The Washington Post*, September 22, 1976.

[28]John R. Bolton, *The Legislative Veto: Unseparating the Powers* (American Enterprise Institute, 1977), pp. 31–32. But see the different views in *Congressional Review of Administrative Rulemaking*, Hearings before the House Committee on the Judiciary (U.S. Government Printing Office, 1975).

to permit the White House to grant the Soviet Union the "most-favored nation" treatment allowed for in the Trade Reform Act of 1974. This was clearly a case of Congress imposing its goals on the executive. Congress has also demanded and won a greater role in arms sales abroad and in determining U.S. aid to Turkey.

Some congressional reassertion proposals have not succeeded. These include former Senator Sam Ervin's proposal to remove the Department of Justice from the executive branch. He felt that this was necessary to separate the justice and prosecution functions from partisan politics and White House influence. He failed, however, to persuade most members of Congress. Representative Henry Reuss (D-Wisc.) proposed a vote of no-confidence measure that would permit Congress to call for new elections when it believed a president had become incompetent or lost the support needed to govern effectively. His reform would have required a new constitutional amendment to be passed and it doubtless would have profoundly altered our system of government. It did not receive favorable treatment in Congress.[29] Still others proposed a constitutional amendment to create a single six-year presidential term, but the motion never went beyond committee hearings.[30]

Another proposal is the notion of an American "question hour." Cabinet members or even the president would regularly go before Congress to answer questions on major policy decisions.[31] Finally, some members of Congress want to establish ceilings on how many White House aides there should be; they also want to involve Congress in overseeing the policy made by the White House staff. This measure always fails, in part because of the president's claim of separation of powers. It also fails because congressional staffs have grown so much in recent years that Congress really cannot point fingers in this case.

Restoring the balance or overreaction?

The 1970s have been a decade of redressing the constitutional balance. As the decade comes to an end, however, politicians and political analysts differ about the results of congressional assertion. Has Congress overreacted to Nixon and endangered the effectiveness of the presidency? Some experts think so. Some rebalancing may have been needed, but Congress has been carried away, they contend. Others, however, think reassertion was not only much needed, but has been achieved with due respect for an effective presidency. Still others are skeptical of Congress's ability to match the advantages of the presidency and become a truly coequal branch.

THE DANGER OF AN IMPAIRED PRESIDENCY

Many observers fear that in the 1970s we overreacted to what was wrongly perceived as an excess of presidential power. They say that presidential powers were not necessarily too strong, but that Watergate and Vietnam were illustrations of the abuse or misuse of those powers.

[29]See "Symposium on the Reuss Resolution: A Vote of No Confidence in the President," *The George Washington Law Review* (January 1975), pp. 333–500.

[30]The six-year term is discussed in Cronin, *The State of the Presidency*, pp. 298–306.

[31]This was advocated by Jimmy Carter in *Why Not the Best?* (Bantam Books, 1976), pp. 144–45 and p. 170; and by Walter F. Mondale in *The Accountability of Power*, pp. 148–51, and p. 216. See also the discussion by Philippa Strum, "A Symbolic Attack on the Imperial Presidency: An American Question Time," in Cronin and Tugwell, eds., *The Presidency Reappraised*, pp. 248–64.

Those who hold this "overreaction" view say the White House today is so crippled by regulations and constraints that even a Franklin Roosevelt could not provide leadership. They contend that given the necessary role of the United States in the world today, a serious reduction of the executive power could be a disaster. Our presidents must possess the strength and administrative flexibility to provide us with responsible leadership. "We have survived caretaker Presidents in the past, but the price of those deceptively quiet periods in our history has always had to be paid later."[32]

"Probably no development in the 1960s and 1970s," writes Samuel Huntington of Harvard, "has greater import for the future of American politics than the decline in the authority, status, influence, and effectiveness of the Presidency."[33] Huntington suggests that the only really national government the United States ever has is provided by presidents. He thinks we have almost returned to the relations between Congress and president that prevailed during the congressional caucus period early in the nineteenth century. Others, like former Attorney General Edward Levi, have warned that we are close to returning to the period of congressional government that followed the Civil War.

In the wake of a diminished or imperiled presidency, can Congress furnish the leadership necessary to govern the country? Former President Gerald Ford does not think so: "When a crisis breaks, it is impossible to draw the Congress into the decision-making process in an effective way." Speaking in behalf of the repeal of the War Powers Resolution of 1973, Ford cited these reasons:[34]

Legislators have too many other concerns to be abreast of foreign policy situations.

It is impossible to wait for a consensus among scattered and perhaps disagreeing congressional leaders.

Sensitive information supplied to legislators, particularly via the telephone, might be disclosed.

Waiting for consultation could risk penalities for the president "as severe as impeachment."

Consultations with congressional leaders might not bind the rank and file, particularly independent younger members.

Supporters of a strong, powerful presidency also worry about the effect of congressional assertion. They believe a president has always had too little power to tackle economic and energy resource problems effectively. For example, he has little influence over the Federal Reserve Board's policies on credit and money. He has few tools for effective, long-range economic planning. And, as President Carter learned in his first year of office, his authority over government reorganization is seriously limited.

Supporters of the overreaction thesis also claim that the history of American political reform shows that good intentions often lead to bad

[32]Theodore C. Sorensen, *Watchmen in The Night: Presidential Accountability after Watergate* (MIT Press, 1975), p. 70.

[33]Samuel P. Huntington, "The Democratic Distemper," in Nathan Glazer and Irving Kristol, eds., *The American Commonwealth* (Basic Books, 1976), p. 24.

[34]Ford, quoted in Don Oberdorfer, "Ford: War Powers Act Not Practical," *The Washington Post*, April 12, 1977, p. 8.

policies. As the attack on the presidency gained momentum, comments like the following were often heard:

> The frustrations and anxieties of the moment are sometimes confused with more enduring values. When an institution is unresponsive to our wishes, it is only human to want to reduce its power in order to give freer play to more receptive institutions. We tend to forget that the time may come when the institution that now favors us may be on the other side, and that the one we now condemn may be our champion—if enough of it survives to perform that function. We tend to forget that when two sides manipulate the rules of their relationship for short-run advantage, the game itself may be destroyed. We tend to forget the law enunciated by the late Professor Wallace S. Sayre of Columbia: "The benefits of reform are immediate, but the costs are cumulative."[35]

Further, these people say, fears of presidential dictatorship are exaggerated. They contend it is unfortunate people dwell so much on Richard Nixon and his practices. The Nixon presidency, they argue, was one of a kind and was dealt with effectively by the impeachment provisions of the Constitution.

Their argument rests also on longer-run considerations. The president's importance has been founded in the necessities of our political system. Today, the federal government is committed to burdens that demand vigorous, positive leadership. We live in a continuous state of emergency. Nuclear warfare could destroy the country in a matter of minutes. Global competition of almost every sort highlights the need for swiftness, efficiency, and unity in our government. Furthermore, today's problems of urban financial distress, racial stress, and severe energy needs require presidential leadership. A weakening of the presidency means a strengthening of the bureaucracy more than a strengthening of Congress. Any reduction in the powers of the president might leave us naked to our enemies—to the forces of inflation and depression at home, and to the forces of unrest and aggression abroad.[36] Finally, they contend, Congress is not designed to govern; it is designed to obstruct, "a worthy function, which it performs with its own skills."

THE CASE FOR AN EVEN MORE ASSERTIVE CONGRESS

Many, however, insist that congressional reassertion has been a much needed corrective. As former Senator Mike Mansfield put it, "Of course we have to be sure the pendulum doesn't swing too far in the other direction. But the President will not continue to accumulate more power at the expense of Congress. There will be no more Vietnams."[37]

While still a U.S. Senator, Vice President Walter Mondale advocated more congressional reassertion.

> The cause for concern was—and still is—a real one. Over a period of decades, the power of the Congress—intended to be both a force for

[35]Herbert Kaufman, "In Defense of the Presidency," *The Brookings Bulletin* (Winter 1974), p. 9.

[36]Clinton Rossiter, *The American Presidency* (Mentor, 1956); and Clinton Rossiter, *Constitutional Dictatorship: Crisis Government in the Modern Democracies* (Princeton University Press, 1948).

[37]Mansfield, quoted in Philip Shabecoff, "Presidency Is Found Weaker Under Ford," *The New York Times,* March 28, 1976, p. 44.

positive government and the principal check against executive branch tyranny—had been systematically eroded and weakened. A potent combination of Presidential action and Congressional inaction had shifted the balance of power, particularly in foreign affairs, undercutting much of Congress's role as a restraint against arbitrary exercise of Presidential power.[38]

Has Congress truly reestablished itself as an equal partner with the president? Some supporters of a stronger Congress do not think so. They question the depth, sincerity, and staying power of congressional assertiveness. They point to President Ford's alleged failure to comply with the War Powers Resolution of 1973 when he ordered military action in connection with the rescue of the *Mayaguez*. They note that the Defense Department's budgets continue to grow and to pass through Congress with few changes. They point to President Carter's habit of surprising Congress or bypassing it with appeals to the public. They contend too that despite all the talk about better and more program oversight, most members of Congress find this type of work the least appealing, especially in terms of winning reelection. Hence they wonder whether Congress will really stay involved.

CONGRESS AND PRESIDENT: INTO THE 1980s

Our system is designed to encourage tension between the Congress and the president. They are supposed to share powers and to represent different constituencies. A certain amount of haggling is desirable. Sometimes they may be deadlocked, but far more often the relationship is marked by compromise and cooperation, by give and take and mutual adjustment.[39] That's the way it should be.

The process is uniquely American. It was, as the courts sometimes remind us, not designed to promote efficiency as much as to prevent autocratic rule and encourage the politics of consultation. There is always a good deal of wrangling and bargaining in the relationship. But it has worked remarkably well for some 190 years, or so most people feel.

There is fortunately a new emphasis on accountable and responsible leadership. We now know that a strong presidency may not be an accountable one. We now know that a strong and responsible president does not hold himself above the law, disregard the Constitution, misuse the intelligence agencies, and intimidate the press. Strength in the White House these days is judged more on the quality of ideas, strength of character, and negotiating skills. It is also judged on the basis of the team a president can attract to help run the government.

The American public may have lost confidence in certain of our recent presidents, but it has not lost confidence in the efficacy of strong presidential leadership linked with purpose. Many people still believe that great power makes great leadership possible. Despite Watergate and Vietnam, many Americans long for dynamic, reassuring and aggressive presidential leadership. It is still the Jeffersons, Jacksons, Lincolns and Roosevelts that get placed on the top of the lists of the great presidents. We still

[38] Quoted in Cronin and Tugwell, eds., *The Presidency Reappraised*, p. 26.

[39] Three of the best studies examining bargaining between Congress and the White House are: Abraham Holtzman, *Legislative Liaison* (Rand McNally, 1970); Lawrence F. O'Brien, *No Final Victories* (Doubleday, 1975); and Morris S. Ogul, *Congress Oversees the Bureaucracy* (University of Pittsburgh Press, 1976).

applaud those presidents who stretch their office and leave it larger than when they came to it. The day of the strong presidents is here to stay. Most people want it that way. And almost all of the great presidents — the men who built the presidency — made a practice of sharply opposing Congress. This may not be the textbook ideal, but it is realistically what the situation is. Hence, even as the presidency was criticized for the abuse of power in the 1970s, we are likely to hear repeated calls in the 1980s for strong presidential leadership.

Congress has the constitutional tools it needs to become a reasonably effective partner in the shaping of national policy. The reassertion most needed in Washington is one of Congress emphasizing its traditional powers: the power of the purse, the power to confirm, the power to investigate and oversee national programs. Congress will probably achieve far less by passing symbolic reform measures such as the War Powers Resolution or by writing detailed legislation with veto provisions that make the implementation of laws an administrative nightmare. In the end, both Congress and president have to recognize they are not two sides out to "win" but two parts of the same government, both elected to pursue together the common interests of the American people. Too much was made by too many presidents and scholars of that partial truth that *only the president* is the representative of *all the people*. Members of Congress may not represent them exactly as he does, but its two houses collectively represent them in ways a president does not.

Summary

1. Congressional-presidential relations are not merely *constitutional* questions, but also *political* struggles for the support of public opinion. People may be far more attentive to presidents than to the operations of the Congress, yet most Americans today believe that Congress should also have a major role in forming public policy.

2. The 1970s have witnessed notable efforts by the Congress to reassert itself as a coequal policy-making branch. There has been an increase in congressional self-confidence as it has reformed many of its own practices and redefined certain presidential practices. Whether or not Congress can sustain its more aggressive stance toward the executive branch is an open question.

3. We have a policy-making system of checks and balances that, even as conditions change, is designed to be strong enough for effective leadership, but in which power is dispersed enough to assure liberty. This, of course, is a delicate balance; rebalancing efforts — such as the congressional reassertion of the 1970s — in one form or another are nearly always taking place.

4. A cycle theory of congressional-presidential relations has long been fashionable. This holds that there will be periods of presidential ascendancy followed by periods of congressional reaction and reassertiveness. Usually these have been periods of a decade or more and often a generation in length. A moderate congressional reassertion has taken place in the immediate post-Watergate years. But the responsibilities of the presidency today coupled with the complexities of foreign and economic policy do not really permit any serious weakening of the presidency and this the Congress has not done. Congress has its work cut out for itself just strengthening and organizing itself to stay involved in national policy making.

Chapter 15

Judges and the Courts

Foreigners are often amazed at the great power Americans give their judges, especially federal judges. In 1848, after his visit to America, the French aristocrat Alexis de Tocqueville wrote, "If I were asked where I place the American aristocracy, I should reply without hesitation . . . that it occupies the judicial bench and bar. . . . Scarcely any political question arises in the United States that is not resolved, sooner or later, into a judicial question."[1] A century later the English laborite Harold Laski observed, "The respect in which federal courts and, above all, the Supreme Court are held is hardly surpassed by the influence they exert on the life of the United States."[2]

Perhaps Tocqueville and Laski exaggerated. Over time, the Supreme Court does not appear to command significantly more respect among either the public or the elite than do the other two branches of government.[3] Still, the Supreme Court remains one of the most important arenas for the making of public policy. In no other governmental system do judges have such a vital part in the political life of the nation.

Should our judges play such a central role in our political life is a question to which we shall return. A prior question is: *Why* do they have such great influence? One reason is the power of judicial review—that is, their

[1]*Democracy in America*, ed. Phillips Bradley (Knopf, 1944), I, pp. 278–80.

[2]*The American Democracy* (Viking, 1948), p. 110.

[3]See the research of such scholars as Murphy and Tanenhaus, Dolbeare and Hammond, Richard Johnson, findings of Gallup Polls and Harris Surveys as reported and cited in David Adamany, "Legitimacy, Realigning Elections, and the Supreme Court," *Wisconsin Law Review* (1973), pp. 808–20; Sheldon Goldman and Thomas P. Jahnige, eds., *The Federal Courts as a Political System* (Harper & Row, 1976), pp. 136–54 contains a comprehensive review of the literature and an analysis of support for the Supreme Court. It also provides excellent coverage of the materials in this chapter in greater detail than can be provided here.

power to make the authoritative interpretation of the Constitution. Only a constitutional amendment (and the judges would interpret the amendment) or a later High Court itself can modify the Court's doctrine. Justice Frankfurter once put it tersely: "The Supreme Court is the Constitution." Even without judicial review, however, judges would be influential members of the policy-making elite. Indeed, constitutional questions are not involved in many of the cases that come before them. But when judges interpret statutes and resolve conflicts, they often make rules that affect the conduct of millions of people.

The law

The Constitution does not require judges to be lawyers. Yet all Supreme Court justices, as well as other federal judges, have been members of the bar. The reason for this is obvious: The business of courts is law, and law is a professional discipline, a technical subject that requires specialized training. What kind of law do federal judges apply?

TYPES OF LAW

In many instances, a judicial decision is based on statutory law. This is law formulated by the legislature, although it also includes treaties and executive orders. It is law that comes from authoritative and specific law-making sources. If there is no statutory law governing a case that comes before a court, the judges must apply the common law. Common law is

Members of the Supreme Court: (from left) Associate Justices Stevens, Powell, Blackmun, Rehnquist, Marshall, Brennan, Chief Justice Burger, Associate Justices Stewart and White.

judge-made law. It reaches back through centuries of judicial decisions and originated in England in the twelfth century, when royal judges began traveling around the country settling disputes in each locality according to prevailing custom. Gradually these customs became the same for the entire nation. The common law continues to develop according to the rule of stare decisis, which means "let the decision stand." This is the rule of precedent, which requires that once a rule has been established by a court, it shall be followed in all similar cases.

The American common law began to branch off from the English system in the seventeenth century. (In Louisiana, the legal system is based on the other great Western legal tradition, the *civil law*. The civil law gives more emphasis to codes of lawgivers and less to past judicial decisions. In Louisiana the civil law has been influenced by and intermingled with the common law.) Whenever federal judges have to decide disputes between citizens of two states and there is no applicable state statute, they apply the common law as interpreted by the state courts. Only if there is no state interpretation do federal judges strike out for themselves.

Federal judges also apply equity. Like common law, equity is a system of judge-made law that had its origins in England. Early in the development of the common law, it was discovered that in certain circumstances it did not ensure justice. For example, under the common law, a person whose property rights are about to be injured has no choice but to wait until the injury has taken place and then to seek money damages. But the injury may do irreparable harm for which money damages cannot provide adequate compensation. Accordingly, another set of rules was worked out to be used where the law was inadequate. Under equity, a person may go to a judge, show why the common law remedy is inadequate, and ask for equitable relief—an injunction, for example, to prevent an act that threatens irreparable harm. If the wrongdoer persists, he may be punished for contempt of court.

Sometimes judges apply *constitutional law*. Because the Constitution contains only 7,500 words or so and can be read in a half-hour, it might be assumed that any person could learn constitutional law after a little study. But constitutional law consists of doctrines and rules that are not to be found in the written words of the Constitution. They come from the decisions of the Supreme Court. Constitutional law, in other words, consists of statements about the interpretation of the Constitution that have been given Supreme Court sanction.

Admiralty and maritime law is also applied by federal judges. This is a complex and technical body of rules applicable to cases arising in connection with shipping and water-borne commerce on the high seas and, by decision of the Supreme Court,[4] on the navigable waters of the United States.

A kind of law that has become increasingly prominent in the decisions of federal judges is administrative law. Within the past several decades, Congress has delegated to administrators and administrative agencies so much rule-making authority that today there is, in volume, more administrative than statutory law. The rules and decisions of administrators may be reviewed by federal judges, and judges are often called on to determine whether the administrators have acted properly and within their authority.

---

[4]*The Genesee Chief,* 12 Howard 443 (1852).

Law may also be classified as criminal or civil. *Criminal law*, which is almost entirely statutory, defines crimes against the public order and provides for punishment. Government has the primary responsibility for enforcing this type of law. The great body of criminal law is enacted by states and is enforced by state officials in the state courts, but the criminal business of federal judges is growing.

Civil law governs the relations between individuals and defines their legal rights. For example, Jones, who has a trademark for Atomic Pills, discovers that Smith is advertising Atomic Tablets in national magazines. If Jones wishes to protect his trademark, he may proceed against Smith before a federal judge. But the government can also be a party to a civil action. Under the Sherman Antitrust Act, for example, the federal government may initiate civil as well as criminal action to prevent violations of the law.

THE SCOPE OF JUDICIAL
POWER: THE FIGHT THEORY

The American judicial process is based on the *adversary system*. A court of law is a neutral arena in which two parties argue their differences before an impartial arbiter. The basis of the adversary system is that the best way for the court to discover the truth is for each side to strive as hard as it can to present its point of view. Whether or not the fight theory is an adequate way of arriving at the truth, the fact that it lies at the basis of our judicial system is crucial. First, the logic of the adversary system imposes formal restraints on the scope of judicial power; second, the rhetoric of the adversary system leads us to conceive the role of the judge in a very special way.

Judicial power is essentially *passive*—that is, courts cannot act until someone comes to them. The judiciary is said to lack a self-starter.[5] Furthermore, not all disputes are within the scope of judicial power. Judges decide only *justiciable disputes*—those that grow out of actual cases and are capable of settlement by legal methods. Not all governmental questions or constitutional problems are justiciable. Some claims of unconstitutionality raise political, not justiciable questions. What is meant by "political"? It means an issue that requires knowledge of a nonlegal character, that requires the use of techniques not suitable for a court, or that the Constitution addresses to the political branch of government. Examples of political questions are these: Which of two competing state governments is the proper one? What is a republican form of state government?[6]

Judges are not supposed to use their power unless the controversy is a real one. Two people cannot make up a suit merely to contest legislation. For example, in 1889 a man named Wellman tried to purchase a railway ticket the day after the Michigan legislature had fixed the rates. The ticket agent refused to sell a ticket at the new rate, and Wellman brought suit. During the trial Wellman did not challenge the railway company's testimony. It became clear that Wellman wanted the railway company to win; he made no attempt to present all the facts in the case. The Supreme Court refused to allow federal courts to decide the case, saying, "It was never thought that, by means of a friendly suit, a party beaten in the legislature could transfer to the courts an inquiry as to the constitutionality of a legislative act."[7] (This, of course, is exactly what is done in a nonfriendly suit.

[5]Walter F. Murphy, Jr., *Elements of Judicial Strategy* (University of Chicago Press, 1964), p. 21.

[6]*Luther v. Borden*, 7 Howard 1 (1849); *Coleman v. Miller* 307 U.S. 433 (1939).

[7]*Chicago & Grand Trunk Railway Co.* v. *Wellman*, 143 U.S. 226 (1897).

In such cases, however, the two parties have an interest in getting the full facts before the court.)

May anybody challenge a law? No. They must have "standing to sue" — that is, they must have "sustained or [be] immediately in danger of sustaining a direct injury. It is not sufficient that [they have] merely a general interest common to all members of the public."[8] Furthermore, the injury must be substantial.

In recent years the Supreme Court and Congress have liberalized the doctrine of "standing" in order to permit a wider range of persons to use the courts to challenge the actions of the government or to attack corporate practices.[9] Yet the Supreme Court has not gone as far as former Justice Douglas wanted. He would give standing to sue to trees and other inanimate objects "about to be despoiled, defaced, or invaded by roads and bulldozers."[10] Nor will federal judges, as do some state judges, give advisory opinions to Congress or the president about whether a particular act or law may or may not be constitutional.

The logic of the adversary system requires that judges decide only what is necessary to dispose of the case before them. Justice Brandeis wrote,

> It is not the habit of the court to decide questions of a constitutional nature unless absolutely necessary to a decision of the case. . . . The Court will not "formulate a rule of constitutional law broader than is required by the precise facts to which it is applied. . . ." The Court will not pass upon a constitutional question although properly presented by the record, if there is also present some other ground upon which the case may be disposed of. . . . [It] is a cardinal principal that this Court will first ascertain whether a construction of the statute is fairly possible by which the question [of constitutionality] may be avoided.[11]

These guidelines give the Supreme Court considerable latitude. The first Justice Harlan made this quite clear: "The courts have rarely, if ever, felt themselves so restrained by technical rules, that they could not find some remedy, consistent with the law, for acts. . . that violated natural justice. . . ."[12]

DO JUDGES MAKE LAW?

"Do judges make law? Course they do. Made some myself," remarked Jeremiah Smith, former judge of the New Hampshire Supreme Court.[13] Although such statements are now quite common, they are somehow disquieting; they do not conform to our notion of the proper judge. Why should this be? Why is it that so many still cling to the notion that judges do not make law?

The conception many people have of the role of a judge is that it is similar to that of a referee in a prizefight. What do we expect of the referee? He must be impartial; he must be disinterested; he must treat both parties as

---

[8]*Ex parte Levitt*, 302 U.S. 663 (1937); *Schlesinger* v. *Reservists Committee* 1418 U.S. 208 (1974).

[9]Karen Orren, "Standing to Sue, Interest Group Conflict in the Federal Courts," *The American Political Science Review* (September 1976), pp. 723–41.

[10]*Sierra Club* v. *Morton* 405 U.S. 727 (1972).

[11]Concurring opinion in *Ashwander* v. *T.V.A.* 297 U.S. 288 (1936).

[12]Quoted by Murphy, *Elements of Judicial Strategy*, p. 30.

[13]Quoted in Paul A. Freund, *On Understanding the Supreme Court* (Little, Brown, 1949), p. 3.

Judge Learned Hand.

equals. Referees do not make rules; they apply the rules the boxing commission has established. Insofar as the function of a judge is like that of a referee, these same expectations may be applied. But the analogy must not be pushed too far. The referee need do nothing more than apply the boxing commission's rules, because the boxing commission has anticipated practically every conceivable situation in the ring. But the situations with which the legislature must deal are infinitely more complex.

Herein lies the answer to the question: Do judges make law? Not only do they, but they must. Legislatures make law by enacting statutes, but judges apply the statutes to concrete situations. Inevitably, discretion is involved. There will be some cases to which general expressions are clearly applicable: "If anything is a vehicle, a motor-car is one."[14] But does the word *vehicle* in a statute include bicycles, airplanes, and roller skates? A judge is constantly faced with situations that possess some of the features of the similar cases—but lack others. "Uncertainty at the borderline is the price to be paid for the use of general classifying terms." Statutes are drawn in broad terms: Drivers shall act with "reasonable care;" no one may make "excessive noise" in the vicinity of a hospital; employers must maintain "safe working conditions." The reason broad terms must be used is that legislators cannot know all the possible combinations of circumstances the future may bring. Thus, a statute does not settle many questions, because it could not have been anticipated that they would be raised. "In every legal system a large and important field is left open for the exercise of discretion by courts and other officials in rendering initially vague standards determinate, in resolving the uncertainties of statutes, or in developing and qualifying rules only broadly communicated by. . . precedents."[15]

These problems are made greater when judges are asked—as American judges are—to apply the Constitution, written nearly 200 years ago. If Congress passed a law extending the terms of senators beyond six years, its unconstitutionality would be apparent to everyone. But the Constitution is full of generalizations: "due procees of law," "equal protection of the laws," "unreasonable searches and seizures," "commerce among the several states." It is not likely that recourse to the intent of the framers will help judges faced with cases involving electronic wiretaps, General Motors, or birth-control pills. Because the rules by which society is governed cannot interpret themselves, judges cannot avoid making law.

STARE DECISIS

The rule of precedent, or stare decisis, pervades our judicial system. A judge is expected to abide by all previous decisions of his own court and all rulings of superior courts. Although the rule of precedent imposes regularity on the legal system, it is not nearly so restrictive as some people think.[16]

Consider, for example, the father who, removing his hat as he enters a church, says to his son, "This is the way to behave on such occasions. Do as I do."[17] The son, like the judge trying to follow a precedent, has a wide

[14]This discussion is based on H. L. A. Hart, *The Concept of Law* (Oxford University Press, 1961), Chap. 7.

[15]*Ibid.*, pp. 125, 132.

[16]Benjamin Cardozo, *The Nature of the Judicial Process* (Yale University Press, 1921).

[17]This discussion is based on Hart, *Concept of Law*, pp. 121, 122.

range of possibilities open to him: How much of the performance must be imitated? Does it matter if the left hand is used, instead of the right, to remove the hat? That it is done slowly or quickly? That the hat is put under the seat? That it is not replaced on the head inside the church? The judge can *distinguish* precedents by stating that a previous case does not control the immediate one because of differences in context. In addition, in many areas of law, there are conflicting precedents, one of which can be chosen to support a decision for either party.

The doctrine of *stare decisis* is even less controlling in the field of constitutional law. Because the Constitution, rather than any one interpretation of it, is binding, the Court can reverse a previous decision it no longer wishes to follow. Supreme Court justices are therefore not seriously restricted by the doctrine of *stare decisis*. As the first Justice Harlan told a group of law students: "I want to say to you young gentlemen that if we don't like an act of Congress, we don't have too much trouble to find grounds for declaring it unconstitutional."[18]

Federal justice

The Constitution in Article III says, "The judicial Power of the United States, shall be vested in one supreme Court, and in such inferior Courts as the Congress may from time to time ordain and establish." Courts created to carry out this judicial power are called Article III or constitutional courts. In addition Congress may also establish legislative, or Article I, Courts to carry out the legislative powers the Constitution has granted to Congress. The main difference between a legislative and a constitutional court is that the judges of the former need not be appointed "during good behavior" and may be assigned other than purely judicial duties.

A Supreme Court is a necessity if the national government is to have the power to frame and enforce laws superior to those of the states. The lack of such an agency to maintain national supremacy, to ensure uniform interpretation of national legislation, and to resolve conflicts among the states was one of the glaring deficiencies of the central government under the Articles of Confederation.

It is up to Congress to decide whether there shall be federal courts in addition to the one Supreme Court ordained by the Constitution. (The Constitution also allows Congress to determine the size of the Supreme Court.) The First Congress divided the nation into districts and created lower national courts for each district. That decision, though often supplemented, has never been seriously questioned. Today the hierarchy of national courts of general jurisdiction consists of *district courts*, *courts of appeals*, and one *Supreme Court*.

FEDERAL COURTS OF GENERAL JURISDICTION

The workhorses of the federal judiciary are the eighty-nine district courts within the states, one in the District of Columbia, and one in Puerto Rico. Each state has at least one district court; the larger states have as many as the demands of judicial business and the pressure of politics require (though no state has more than four). Each district court is composed of at least one judge, but there may be as many as twenty-seven. District judges normally sit separately and hold court by themselves. There are 403 permanent district judgeships, all filled by the president with the consent of the Senate. All district judges hold office for life.

[18]Quoted by E. S. Corwin, *Constitutional Revolution* (Claremont and Associated Colleges, 1941), p. 38.

District courts are trial courts of *original jurisdiction*. They are the only federal courts that regularly employ *grand* (indicting) and *petit* (trial) juries. Many of the cases tried before district judges involve citizens of different states, and the judges apply the appropriate state laws. Otherwise, district judges are concerned with federal laws. For example, they hear and decide cases involving crimes against the United States—suits under the national revenue, postal, patent, copyright, trademark, bankruptcy, and civil rights laws.[19]

District judges are assisted by clerks, bailiffs, stenographers, law clerks, court reporters, probation officers, and United States magistrates. All these persons are appointed by the judges. The magistrates, who serve

[19]Glendon A. Schubert, *Judicial Policy-Making*, rev. ed. (Scott, Foresman, 1974).

Organization of Federal Courts

U.S. Supreme Court

Original jurisdiction:
1. Cases involving ambassadors, ministers, and consuls
2. Cases in which a state is a party

Appellate jurisdiction:
1. From the lower federal courts
2. From state courts of last resort if a federal question is involved "under such regulations as the Congress shall make"

Court of Claims

1. Claims against the U.S. other than tort actions (many cases involving claims arising out of public contracts)
2. Limited appellate review of tort actions against the U.S.

Court of Military Appeals

Review of courts martial

Courts of Appeals in Numbered Judicial Circuits and for the District of Columbia

1. Appellate jurisdiction from district courts
2. Review and enforcement of actions of certain quasi-judicial agencies

4 District Courts in Territories

Mixed federal and local jurisdiction

89 District Courts in 50 States and the District of Columbia

1. General original jurisdiction over:
   (a) Federal crimes
   (b) Federal-question cases where the amount in controversy exceeds $10,000 (jurisdictional amount waived in cases brought by the U.S. or against the U.S. or involving admiralty, bankruptcy, commerce, patent, copyright, postal, internal revenue, civil rights law)
   (c) Suits between citizens of different states, where amount in controversy exceeds $10,000
   (d) Suits between citizens of one of the 50 states and foreign states, or their citizens or subjects, or the District of Columbia, where amount in controversy exceeds $10,000
2. Review and/or enforcement of actions of certain quasi-judicial agencies
3. Tort claims against the U.S.
4. Concurrent jurisdiction with Court of Claims to hear claims up to $10,000 against the U.S. other than tort actions, e.g., to recover for overpayment of taxes or for breach of contract on the part of the U.S.

Three-judge courts
Certain types of cases specifically mandated by Congress, for example, challenges to legislative reappointment

eight-year terms, handle some of the preliminaries. They issue warrants for arrest and often hear the evidence to determine whether an arrested person should be held for action by the grand jury. If so, the magistrate may set the bail. Magistrates may even conduct trials for petty offenses. A United States marshal, appointed by the president, is assigned to each district court. Although marshals no longer exercise general police jurisdiction, they maintain order in the courtroom, guard prisoners, make arrests, and carry out court orders, such as serving summonses for witnesses.[20] At times, they carry out orders of a federal court even in the face of violence.

Although a few kinds of district court decisions may be appealed di-

[20]Rita W. Cooley, "The Office of United States Marshal," *Western Political Quarterly* (March 1959), pp. 123–40.

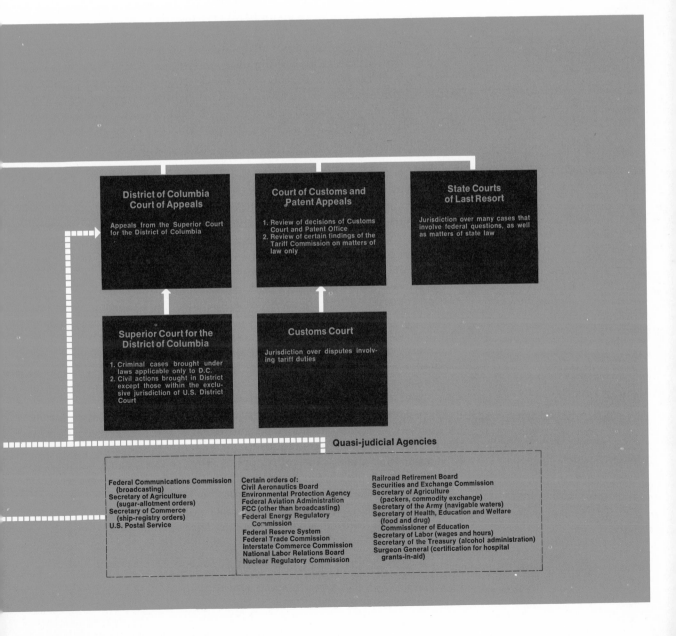

District of Columbia Court of Appeals

Appeals from the Superior Court for the District of Columbia

Court of Customs and Patent Appeals

1. Review of decisions of Customs Court and Patent Office
2. Review of certain findings of the Tariff Commission on matters of law only

State Courts of Last Resort

Jurisdiction over many cases that involve federal questions, as well as matters of state law

Superior Court for the District of Columbia

1. Criminal cases brought under laws applicable only to D.C.
2. Civil actions brought in District except those within the exclusive jurisdiction of U.S. District Court

Customs Court

Jurisdiction over disputes involving tariff duties

Quasi-judicial Agencies

Federal Communications Commission (broadcasting)	Certain orders of: Civil Aeronautics Board	Railroad Retirement Board
Secretary of Agriculture (sugar-allotment orders)	Environmental Protection Agency Federal Aviation Administration	Securities and Exchange Commission Secretary of Agriculture
Secretary of Commerce (ship-registry orders)	FCC (other than broadcasting) Federal Energy Regulatory	(packers, commodity exchange) Secretary of the Army (navigable waters)
U.S. Postal Service	Commission	Secretary of Health, Education and Welfare (food and drug)
	Federal Reserve System Federal Trade Commission	Commissioner of Education
	Interstate Commerce Commission National Labor Relations Board	Secretary of Labor (wages and hours) Secretary of the Treasury (alcohol administration)
	Nuclear Regulatory Commission	Surgeon General (certification for hospital grants-in-aid)

rectly to the Supreme Court, especially those that still must be heard by three judges, most decisions must first be appealed to a United States court of appeals. In fact, the majority of district court decisions are not appealed. Of those that are, the court of appeals is for the vast majority the court of last resort.

The United States courts of appeals are most important judicial policy makers.[21] The United States is divided into eleven judicial circuits, including the District of Columbia as one. Each has a court of appeals consisting of three to fifteen permanent circuit judges, ninety-seven in all. Congress is presently considering a revision of the boundaries of the circuits, especially the possibility of dividing into two circuits the Fifth Circuit—the Deep South—which Chief Justice Burger has labeled "an unmanageable administrative monstrosity." The Far West Ninth Circuit, which includes Alaska and Hawaii as well as the mainland western states, is also a candidate for change.

Circuit judges are appointed for life by the president with the consent of the Senate. The United States courts of appeals have only *appellate* jurisdiction. They review decisions of the district courts within their circuit and also some of the actions of the independent regulatory agencies such as the Federal Trade Commission. Each court of appeals normally utilizes panels of three judges to hear cases, although in the event of especially important and controversial cases the whole court may sit. One Supreme Court justice is assigned to each circuit, but his duties as circuit justice are only nominal.

SPECIAL COURTS

In addition to Article III courts of general jurisdiction, Congress has created constitutional courts with special jurisdiction: the Court of Claims, the Customs Court, and the Court of Customs and Patent Appeals.

The Court of Claims consists of a chief and six associate judges, with jurisdiction over all property and contract damage suits against the United States. The court sits in Washington, but commissioners of the court travel throughout the United States taking evidence.

The United States Customs Court, consisting of nine judges, has jurisdiction to review rulings of collectors of the customs. Its decisions in turn may be appealed to the Court of Customs and Patent Appeals, a five-member court. This court also reviews decisions of the Patent Office and, on a more restricted scale, certain rulings of the United States Tariff Commission.

ARTICLE I OR LEGISLATIVE COURTS

One of the more important legislative courts is the United States Court of Military Appeals, created by Congress under its grant of authority to make the rules and regulations for "land and naval Forces." It is composed of three civilian judges appointed for fifteen years by the president with the consent of the Senate. This court applies military law, which is separate from the body of law that governs the rest of the federal court system.

The Constitution specifically exempts the Fifth Amendment requirement of indictment by Grand Jury for "cases arising from the land or naval forces, or in the Militia, when in actual service in time of War or public danger." As to the other provisions of the Bill of Rights, the Supreme Court has sidestepped the question of whether they are all applicable in

---

[21]Sheldon Goldman, "Voting Behavior on the U.S. Courts of Appeals Revisited," *The American Political Science Review* (June 1975) pp. 491–506.

military trials in the same fashion as they are in civilian trials.[22] The weight of informed opinion, though there is dissent, is that they are not. But whether required or not by the Constitution, Congress by law has imposed on military courts most of the procedural safeguards the Constitution imposes on the regular civilian courts.

Perhaps of even more significance, the Supreme Court has narrowly construed the phrase "arising in the military forces" in order to limit the jurisdiction of the military courts. Even members of the armed forces, at least during time of peace and while serving within the United States, must be tried in civilian Article III, not military Article I, courts for crimes not connected with the military services.[23]

STATE AND FEDERAL COURTS

In addition to this complex structure of federal courts, each of the fifty states maintains a complete judicial system of its own. (And many of the large municipalities have judicial systems as complex as those of the states.) This dual system of courts is not common, even among nations with federal systems. "The usual pattern in such countries is to entrust the enforcement of the federal law to the state courts. At the time of the adoption of our Constitution, however, the states and the federal government were too jealous of each other to accept a unitary judicial system."[24] The framers gave the national courts the power to hear and decide cases in law and equity if:

1. The cases arise under the Constitution, a federal law, or a treaty.
2. The cases arise under admiralty and maritime laws.
3. The cases arise because of a dispute involving land claimed under titles granted by two or more states.
4. The United States is a party to the case.
5. A state is a party to the case (but not including suits begun or prosecuted against a state by an individual or a foreign nation).
6. The cases are between citizens of different states.
7. The cases affect the accredited representatives of a foreign nation.

What is the relation between the federal and state courts? The common impression that all federal courts are superior to any state court is wrong. The two court systems are related, but they do not exist in a superior-inferior relationship. Over some kinds of cases only the state courts have jurisdiction; over other kinds both court systems have jurisdiction; and over others only the federal courts have jurisdiction. Moreover, except for the limited habeas corpus jurisdiction of the district courts, the Supreme Court is the only federal court that may review state-court decisions, and it may do so only under special conditions.

State courts have sole jurisdiction to try all cases not within the judicial power granted by the Constitution to the national government. Congress determines whether the judicial power granted to the national government shall be exclusively exercised by national courts, concurrently exercised by both national and state courts, or denied to either or both national and state courts. For example, Congress has stipulated that prosecutions

[22]*Middendorf* v. *Henry*, 425 U.S. 25 (1976).

[23]*O'Callahan* v. *Parker*, 394 U.S. 258 (1969); *Relford* v. *Commandant*, 401 U.S. 355 (1971).

[24]Milton D. Green, "The Business of the Trial Courts," in Harry W. Jones, ed., *The Courts, the Public, and the Law Explosion* (Prentice-Hall, 1965), pp. 8–9.

for violations of federal criminal laws, suits for penalties authorized by federal laws, and cases involving foreign ambassadors are within the exclusive jurisdiction of national courts. On the other hand, legal disputes between citizens of different states involving more than $10,000 may be tried in either national or state courts. If the amount is less, the case can be tried only in state courts. (Of course, federal courts may have jurisdiction over suits between citizens of different states for some other reason, for instance if the dispute arises under national law.)

Administering and reforming the federal system

Chief Justice Burger has challenged bench, bar, nation, and Congress to modernize the federal court system so that the judges may better handle the constantly expanding volume of litigation. During the last quarter century, we have almost doubled the number of federal judges, but cases may still take months to be disposed of. More than 80,000 cases are pending in the federal system, and one-fourth of them are more than two years old.[25] Although the adoption of Rule 50 (b), the so-called speedy trial rule, requiring district courts to specify a time limit within which defendants must be tried, has advanced the processing of criminal trials, thousands of persons still wait endlessly for their day in court.[26] (Even more thousands maneuver to delay their day in court, for this is a tactic that often works to the advantage of the accused.)

We do not have a ministry of justice with overall responsibility for the operation of our courts; such a centralized system is contrary to our traditions. Rather, each federal judge, appointed to hold office during "good behavior," is an independent person over whom no one has administrative authority. What happens if a judge fails to decide cases promptly or if in one district the judges are overworked while in another they have too little to do? Who proposes changes to make judicial business flow more smoothly?

In recent decades Congress had introduced an administrative structure to the federal judicial system while still leaving considerable district and circuit court autonomy. With the help of a recently created position of administrative assistant, the chief justice now spends a third of his time on administrative duties. He presides over the Judicial Conference of the United States, which consists of the chief judge of each of the courts of appeals and one district judge from each circuit.[27] The conference, through its many committees, makes recommendations for the general procedural rules to be followed by the federal courts. The Supreme Court transmits these recommendations to Congress, and the rules become effective unless vetoed by either house within a certain time.

The conference is assisted by the Administrative Office of the United States Courts, whose director prepares budgets, develops reports, and

[25]James O. Monroe, Jr., "The Urgent Case for American Law Reform: A Judge's Response to a Lawyer's Pleas," *DePauw Law Review* (Spring 1970), pp. 466–89; see also Commission on Revision of the Federal Court Appellate System, *The Geographical Boundaries of the Several Judicial Circuits: Recommendations for Change* (Washington, D.C., 1973).

[26]Mark W. Cannon, "Administrative Change and the Supreme Court," *Judicature* (March 1974), p. 341. Mr. Cannon is the administrative assistant to the chief justice of the United States, the first person to hold this new post.

[27]Peter Graham Fish, *The Politics of Federal Judicial Administration* (Princeton University Press, 1973), pp. 379–426; Russell Wheeler and Howard R. Whitcomb, *Perspectives on Judicial Administration* (Prentice-Hall, 1976).

handles financial transactions. The chief justice also supervises the Federal Judicial Center, the research arm of the federal courts, designed in the words of President Johnson "to enable the courts to begin the kind of self-analysis, research, and planning necessary for a more effective judicial system."

For each circuit there is a judicial council consisting of all the judges of the court of appeals. The council may assign work among the several district courts; it may determine whether a judge is sufficiently disabled so that he cannot perform his duties (in which case the president may appoint an additional judge). One council has even gone so far as to order that no additional cases be assigned to a particular district judge because of doubts about his continuing to hear cases. (The Supreme Court sidestepped the question of whether such action conflicts with the constitutional requirement that judges be allowed to serve "during good behavior."[28])

What of the Supreme Court? Most observers are concerned that the Court lacks the time to be properly reflective and meticulous in its work. In the 1978 term the Supreme Court reviewed more than three times as many cases as it did twenty years before. Its written output is more than twice as many pages as a decade ago, and more than 50 percent additional opinions. The work has become more complicated; the number of constitutional cases has doubled in a decade. If the growth rate should increase in the next decade at the same rate as the last one, each justice will have to consider more than 7,500 cases.[29]

What can be done? An additional law clerk has already been assigned to each justice, a legal officer has been appointed to the staff of the Court, and in 1976 Congress eliminated the need for three-judge courts with the direct appeal to the Supreme Court in a number of situations. Among other suggestions being considered—not just for the benefit of the Supreme Court but to lighten the load of all federal courts—are these:

1. Eliminate the remaining requirement for three-judge courts with direct appeals to the Supreme Court.
2. Abolish diversity jurisdiction (cases between citizens of different states), thereby eliminating about 25 percent of the civil work caseload of the federal courts.
3. Reform the system of workmen's compensation for railroad workers, longshoremen, and seamen and thus eliminate another 7 percent of the civil case load.
4. Create an additional court of special jurisdiction to handle technical issues like antitrust, tax, and patent questions.
5. Make greater use of computers for processing data.
6. Assign more administrators to take from the judges the burdens of courtroom administration so that they can spend more of their time judging.
7. Reduce the size of juries.[30]

Chief Justice Burger has even suggested that the bar associations might concentrate on improving the caliber and capacities of lawyers, perhaps along the lines of the English system. There, specialists known as barris-

"It's nothing personal, Prescott. It's just that a higher court gets a kick out of overruling a lower court."

[28]*Chandler* v. *Judicial Council*, 398 U.S. 74 (1970).

[29]Mark W. Cannon, "Administrative Change," pp. 338–39.

[30]See Henry J. Friendly, *Federal Jurisdiction: A General View* (Columbia University Press, 1973), for a federal judge's recommendations.

ters argue cases while the rest of the lawyers, known as solicitors, take care of legal work outside the courtroom.

The most controversial of all the proposals is the recommendation of the so-called Freund Study Group (appointed by the chief justice and named after its chairman, a distinguished Harvard law professor, but then all Harvard professors are distinguished) that a national court of appeals be established. The new national court of appeals would consist of a rotating membership drawn from the judges of the courts of appeals. It would screen cases and allow only the most important ones to be sent on to the Supreme Court. There are variants of this proposal, depending on how far the proposers would go in allowing such a court to dispose of matters presently being handled by the Supreme Court.

Once again, as we have so often noted, although everybody may agree in the abstract that it would be desirable to modernize the federal court system and to provide for faster processing of cases, actual changes will involve policy choices about which there are considerable differences of opinion. Judicial reform is likely to be a slow and cautious effort.

Prosecution and defense: federal lawyers

Judges decide cases; they do not prosecute persons. That job, on the federal level, falls to the Department of Justice: to the attorney general, the solicitor general, the 94 United States attorneys, and the 1,200 assistant attorneys. The president, with consent of the Senate, appoints a United States attorney for each district court. He serves a four-year term, but may be dismissed by the president at any time. These appointments are of great interest to senators, who, through senatorial courtesy, exercise significant influence over their selection. The U.S. attorneys are almost always members of the president's political party, and it is customary for them to resign when the opposition party wins the White House.

The attorney general, in consultation with the U.S. attorney in each district, appoints assistant attorneys. In some districts there is only one. In the largest, the Southern District of New York, there are over sixty-five. Working with the U.S. attorney, assisted by the Federal Bureau of Investigation and other federal law enforcement agencies, these attorneys begin proceedings against those alleged to have broken federal laws. They also represent the United States in civil suits. In criminal cases, the United States attorney or one of the assistants presents evidence to a grand jury that a national law has been violated by a particular person. If the grand jury agrees it indicts, and the U.S. attorney's office prosecutes.

THE KEY ROLE OF PROSECUTORS

Prosecutors decide whether to charge an offense and which offense to charge. They negotiate with defendants (usually through their lawyers) and work out plea bargains in which defendants often agree to plead guilty to one offense to avoid having to stand trial for a more serious one. Prosecutors make recommendations to judges about what sentence to recommend.[31]

Although judges are the most thoroughly studied part of the federal system, the role of the Department of Justice should not be underestimated. Attorneys from the Department and from other federal agencies participate in well over half the cases on the Supreme Court's docket. Within the Department of Justice special divisions—such as the criminal division,

[31]Herbert Jacob, *Justice in America: Courts, Lawyers, and the Judicial Process* (Little, Brown, 1965), p. 161.

civil division, antitrust division, and civil rights division—coordinate the work of the attorneys in the field, develop cases, and send out specialists to assist the attorneys. Of special importance is the solicitor general, who appears for and represents the government before the Supreme Court. Moreover, no appeal may be taken by the United States to any appellate court without his approval.

As a result of Watergate, a special prosecutor was created within the Department of Justice to investigate and prosecute offenses arising out of the 1972 presidential election, allegations involving the president, members of the White House staff, or presidential appointees. Although appointed by President Nixon with the consent of the Senate, and a part of the Department of Justice, because of the political realities surrounding the Nixon administration, the special prosecutor and his office have had a considerable measure of independence from the attorney general. When the first special prosecutor, Professor Archibald Cox (on leave from the Harvard Law School), was dismissed by Nixon, Attorney General Richardson resigned in protest. When Nixon nominated Leon Jaworski, the Senate insisted on even more assurances that he would be allowed to proceed independent of the president and the Department of Justice. Jaworski carried on the Watergate investigation and prosecutions, including the successful challenge before the Supreme Court of President Nixon's attempt to withhold tapes and documents of presidential conversations. The Supreme Court denied Nixon's contention that since the special prosecutor was merely a member of the Executive Department and subject to presidential direction, he had no standing before a court of law to challenge the actions of the president. The office of special prosecutor continued and completed the Watergate prosecutions.

In the aftermath of Watergate there was some discussion about taking the Department of Justice and the attorney general out of the cabinet and making it an agency along the model of the General Accounting Office under the comptroller general. That is, putting it under the control of a career officer responsible to Congress, or at least not directly responsible to the president.[32]

The arguments for such an organizational structure are these: to minimize the danger that justice will be administered for partisan or political reasons, and to protect the independence of prosecutors and others investigating allegations of misconduct on the part of executive officials. On the other hand, the arguments for continuing to hold the president accountable for federal police and prosecutors are also compelling. There are grave dangers to a democracy from an independent, politically powerful prosecuting and police agency not directly accountable to the nation's elected chief executive.

All things considered, major changes in the structure of the Department of Justice or its relation to the president are not likely. More likely is that Congress will provide for the continuation of the office of special prosecutor, perhaps outside the Department of Justice to investigate alleged misconduct on the part of federal officials. It is also likely that as a result of Watergate, presidents will be more careful not to fuse the responsibilities of running political campaigns with the duties of the attorney general.

"Just say you were brought up on Spock, and throw yourself on the mercy of the court."

Drawing by Richter; © 1977 The New Yorker Magazine, Inc.

[32]Report of the National Academy of Public Administration, *Watergate: Its Implications for Responsible Government* (Basic Books, 1974), Chaps. 4 and 5.

Federal prosecutors are not the only lawyers provided by the national government. The Criminal Justice Act of 1970 provides funds for attorneys for poor defendants. Each district court has some discretion as to how to provide this assistance. Most districts have chosen to stay with the traditional system of assigning a private attorney to defend such people, but these attorneys are paid from public funds. Fifteen districts have elected to appoint public defenders paid a regular salary. The almost eighty public defenders operate under the general supervision of the Administrative Office of the United States Courts.

In 1974, Congress created a Legal Services Corporation to take over the responsibility for the work of the more than 2,500 lawyers previously employed by 900 federally funded local legal aid offices. The corporation was formed as a result of criticism that these legal aid offices had stretched their mandate to provide legal aid to the poor to using lawsuits and class actions to try to alter the distribution of political power. The Legal Services Corporation is limited to helping the poor with traditional problems such as back pay, bankruptcy, divorce. It is not given authority to challenge the existing power structures in cities and states.

The judges

The Constitution places the selection of federal judges in the hands of the president, acting with the advice and consent of the Senate. But political reality imposes constraints on the president's appointment power. The selection of a federal judge is actually a complex bargaining process. The principal figures involved are the candidates, the president, United States senators, the Department of Justice, the Standing Committee on the Federal Judiciary of the American Bar Association, and political party leaders.[33]

THE POLITICS OF JUDICIAL SELECTION

The practice of senatorial courtesy gives a senator veto power over the appointment of a judge who is to sit in his state, if that senator is a member of the president's party. Even if he is from the opposition party, he must be consulted. When the Senate is controlled by political opponents of the president, both senators from the state must be negotiated with regardless of their party affiliation. If negotiations between the senators and then between the senators and the Department of Justice deadlock, a seat may stay vacant for years.[34]

Since the end of World War II, the American Bar Association's Committee on the Federal Judiciary has come to play an important role in the appointment process. Federal appointments are sent to the committee for evaluation. Although its ratings do not stop a president from moving forward, any president is hesitant to submit to the Senate for confirmation a candidate rated unqualified by this group. The rule of senatorial courtesy does not apply to appointments to the Supreme Court and is less often applied to the selection of judges for the courts of appeals because these judges do not serve in any one senator's domain. So the president has con-

"You have a pretty good case, Mr. Pitkin. How much justice can you afford?"

Drawing by Handlesman; © 1973 The New Yorker Magazine, Inc.

[33]Harold W. Chase, *Federal Judges: The Appointing Process* (University of Minnesota Press, 1972), pp. 3–47; Henry J. Abraham, *Justices and Presidents: A Political History of Appointments to the Supreme Court* (Oxford University Press, 1974). See also Victor S. Navasky, *Kennedy Justice* (Atheneum, 1971), Chap. 5.

[34]Joel B. Grossman, *Lawyers and Judges: The ABA and the Politics of Judicial Selection* (Wiley, 1965), p. 27. See also Chase, *Federal Judges*, and the more provocative journalistic account, Joseph C. Goulden, *The Benchwarmers: The Private World of the Powerful Federal Judges* (Ballantine, 1976), Chap. 1.

Justice Oliver Wendell Holmes.

siderably more discretion in making these appointments than he does in appointments to the district courts. It is not surprising that judges in the district courts often reflect values different from those of persons appointed to the Supreme Court or to the courts of appeals.

Candidates for judicial office may "campaign" vigorously. Alphonso Taft wrote to Chief Justice Morrison R. Waite, for example:

> My dear Judge, I have sometimes hoped, that if Judge Swayne should retire, there might be a possibility of my being thought of for that place. I should like it. . . . If . . . you should think favorably, and should find opportunity [sic] to encourage it, I should certainly be under great obligation whatever the result might be.[35]

The chief justice promised to "lose no opportunity" to let the president know what a fine judge Taft would make. State and federal judges too are often active in promoting candidates. Sometimes their advice is solicited by the president, but it may well come uninvited.

The operation of the *political* process in the selection of judges may be shocking to some people. They may like to think that judges are picked without regard to party or ideology. But as a former Justice Department official, Donald Santarelli, has said: "When courts cease being an instrument for political change, then maybe the judges will stop being politically selected."[36]

THE ROLE OF PARTY

As Table 15–1 indicates, party considerations have always been important in the selection of judges. Presidents seldom choose a judge from the opposing party, and the use of judgeships as a form of political reward is openly acknowledged by those involved.[37] A state party leader wrote to the attorney general:

> If ———— is not named [to the court of appeals] this would damage seriously the Kennedy force in [this state.) ———— was openly for Kennedy before L.A. and stood strong and voted there. He is known as one of my

[35]Quoted in Alpheus T. Mason, *William Howard Taft: Chief Justice* (Simon and Schuster, 1965) p. 18.

[36]Jerry Landauer, "Shaping the Bench," *Wall Street Journal* (December 10, 1970), p. 1.

[37]J. W. Peltason, *Federal Courts in the Political Process* (Doubleday, 1955), p. 32.

15–1 Federal judgeships as political patronage		Number of judges appointed	
	President	**Democrats**	**Republicans**
	Roosevelt	203	8
	Truman	129	13
	Eisenhower	11	176
	Kennedy	113	11
	Johnson	170*	11
	Nixon-Ford	30	271

*One New York Liberal was appointed.
†As of May 1977.

SOURCE: Department of Justice

closest friends. He is an excellent lawyer—and on the merits alone, better qualified than Judge ——.

The Senators will give you no trouble, but we have put this on the line in public, and if —— is not appointed it will be a mortal blow.

The desired candidate was appointed.[38]

THE ROLE OF IDEOLOGY

But finding a party member is not enough. Presidents want to pick the "right" kind of Republican or "our" kind of Democrat. Especially when the appointment is to the Supreme Court, the policy orientation of the nominee is important. As President Lincoln told Congressman Boutewell when he appointed Salmon P. Chase to the Court, "We wish for a Chief Justice who will sustain what has been done in regard to emancipation and legal tender." (Lincoln guessed wrong on Chase and legal tender; historical analysis suggests that presidents guess wrong about a fourth of the time—that is, the men they appoint do not conform to their expectations.)[39] Theodore Roosevelt voiced this attitude in a letter to Senator Lodge about Judge Oliver Wendell Holmes of the Massachusetts Supreme Judicial Court, whom he was considering for the Supreme Court: "Now I should like to know that Judge Holmes was in entire sympathy with our views, that is with your views and mine. . . . I should hold myself guilty of an irreparable wrong to the nation if I should [appoint] any man who was not absolutely sane and sound on the great national policies for which we stand in public life."[40]

Roosevelt was even more specific in a letter to Lodge concerning the possible appointment of Horace Lurton: "[He] is right on the negro [*sic*] question; he is right on the power of the Federal Government; he is right on the insular business; he is right about corporations; and he is right about labor. On every question that would come before the bench he has so far shown himself to be in . . . touch with the policies in which you and I believe. . . ." Senator Lodge's reply is of equal interest: "I am glad that Lurton holds all the opinions that you say he does. . . . Those are the very questions on which I am just as anxious as you that judges should hold what we consider sound opinions, but I do not see why Republicans cannot be found who hold those opinions as well as Democrats."[41] The appointment went to a Republican, Attorney General William Moody.

Ideology is also significant in the creation of vacancies. Because federal judges serve for life, a judge may be able to schedule his retirement to allow a president whose views he approves to appoint his successor. Chief Justice Taney stayed on the bench long after his health began to fail to prevent Lincoln from nominating a Republican. Justice Holmes wrote to a friend that Chief Justice White had delayed having an operation, in part because of a "determination not to give the appointment to Wilson."

[38]Sheldon Goldman, "Judicial Appointments to the United States Courts of Appeals," in Thomas P. Jahnige and Sheldon Goldman, eds., *The Federal Judicial System: Readings in Process and Behavior* (Holt, Rinehart & Winston, 1968), p. 19.

[39]Robert Scigliano, *The Supreme Court and the Presidency* (Free Press, 1971), pp. 146–47. Quoted in Peltason, *Federal Courts in the Political Process*, p. 41.

[40]Henry Cabot Lodge, *Selections from the Correspondence of Theodore Roosevelt and Henry Cabot Lodge* (Scribner's, 1925), 1, 518–19.

[41]Quoted in Glendon A. Schubert, *Constitutional Politics* (Holt, Rinehart & Winston, 1960), pp. 40–41.

Holmes himself was pleased by Calvin Coolidge's election in 1924, which "relieves my conscience from the doubt whether I ought to resign so as to give the appointment to him."[42] In 1929 Chief Justice Taft wrote, "I am older and slower and less acute and more confused. However, as long as things continue as they are, and I am able to answer in my place. I must stay on the court in order to prevent the Bolsheviki from getting control. . . ."[43] And as many assumed, Justice Douglas was following well-established precedent when he tried unsuccessfully to hold off his retirement while Ford was president, despite serious illness, in the hope that Ford would be replaced by a president more likely to nominate someone who reflected Douglas' constitutional ideology.

THE CARTER ADMINISTRATION:
A NEW DAY?

When campaigning, President Carter proclaimed: "All federal judges and prosecutors should be appointed strictly on the basis of merit without any consideration of political aspects or influence."[44] He promised to appoint "independent blue ribbon judicial selection committees" to give him recommendations for filling judicial vacancies. Once elected, Carter proceeded by executive order to establish a United States Circuit Judge Nominating Commission consisting of thirteen separate panels, one for each federal circuit and two for the Fifth and Ninth circuits. Each eleven-member panel, some lawyers and some nonlawyers, is to go to work whenever the president asks its chairman to find a nominee for an appellate vacancy. Within six days, the panel is to give the president a confidential report on the five candidates it considers to be best qualified. Thirty days after it submits its report, the panel is to disband. None of the members is eligible to be a judicial nominee until one year after he or she has served on the commission.

This introduction of a "merit system" similar to that used in many states for the selection of state court judges is an important departure from past practices. But it is too soon to tell whether it will mean any real change from selection of judges based on partisan affiliation and ideological affinity with the president. We will probably have more public and broader prescreening than in the past, but through the screen are likely to come Democrats reflecting President Carter's constitutional orientations.

At the district court level, despite his campaign statements, President Carter discovered, as had his predecessors, that their selection remains firmly a part of the senatorial patronage system. As Attorney General Bell said, "The creation of selection commissions for appellate is traumatic enough experience. . . . Politics is the art of the possible and you can't do everything in one fell swoop.[45] "How long do you think," he asked, "it would take judgeship vacancies to be filled if we disrupted the system? You know, we could get a lot of publicity, but then we wouldn't get any judges."[46] On their own initiative, however, a few senators have established nominating commissions to screen candidates for them. In Florida,

[42]Mark De Wolfe Howe, ed., *Holmes-Laski Letters* (Atheneum, 1963) I, pp. 264, 453.

[43]Letter to Horace Taft, November 14, 1929, quoted in H. Pringle, *The Life and Times of William Howard Taft* (Farrar, 1939), II, p. 967.

[44]Norman C. Miller, "The Merit System or Patronage," *The Wall Street Journal* (February 28, 1977), p. 12.

[45]*National Journal,* February 10, 1977.

[46]Miller, "The Merit System."

the two Democratic senators, Lawton Chiles and Richard Stone, have appointed three members each to a nominating commission and have asked the Florida Bar Association to appoint another three. These nine persons send five candidates every time there is a federal judgeship to be appointed in that state. The senators then hold public meetings before making their final recommendations to the president. And they have actually recommended some Republicans to fill these judgeships. Democratic senators in Massachusetts, Colorado, California, Georgia, and Iowa have set up their own plans for nominating commissions. But in most states, senators are using the traditional processes and defending their doing so by arguing that they are as well qualified as any citizens' committee to select qualified judges. They also defend the present system as providing an important link between the federal courts and the people. It works, they argue, to provide judges who reflect the general values of the political majority of the state from which they come. Partisanship and ideology are factors that ought to be taken into account in appointing federal judges.

Obviously, the process of judicial selection is being modified, but to what extent and with what results remains to be seen. It is unlikely, however, that with or without nominating commissions, the partisan and ideological character of the federal judiciary will depart too much from that of those who select them.

CREATION AND ABOLITION OF JUDGESHIPS AND ALTERING JURISDICTIONS

Party politics is intimately involved in the creation of new judicial posts.[47] One of the first acts of a political party once it gains control of the White House and Congress is to increase the number of federal judgeships. When one party controls Congress and the other the White House, there is likely to be a stalemate, so that relatively few new judicial positions are created. Even after President Eisenhower promised that half the additional appointments would go to Democrats, he was unable to convince the Democratic leadership of Congress that there was a need for more judgeships. But when President Kennedy took office, Congress promptly created new positions. During his five years in office, President Kennedy appointed eighty-five federal judges, of whom eighty-four were Democrats, the other a member of New York's Liberal Party. When Nixon became president, he was able to pry more than sixty additional judgeships out of Congress, but conflicts between the White House and the Senate kept a large number of them vacant. During Ford's administration, Congress considered legislation to authorize an additional one hundred judges, but they delayed approving it until Carter became president.

Congressional control over the structure and jurisdiction of the federal courts has been used to influence judicial decisions. Although stopped in their attempts to impeach the judges, the Jeffersonians abolished the circuit courts that the Federalist Congress had created just prior to leaving office. In 1869 the radical Republicans in Congress used their power to alter the Supreme Court's appellate jurisdiction in order to snatch from the Court a case it was about to review involving the constitutionality of certain legislation (*Ex parte McCardle*)[48]. They also reduced the size of the Court to prevent President Andrew Johnson from filling two vacancies.

Justice Felix Frankfurter

---

[47]Richard J. Richardson and Kenneth N. Vines, *The Politics of Federal Courts* (Little, Brown, 1970), p. 17.
[48]7 Wallace 506 (1869).

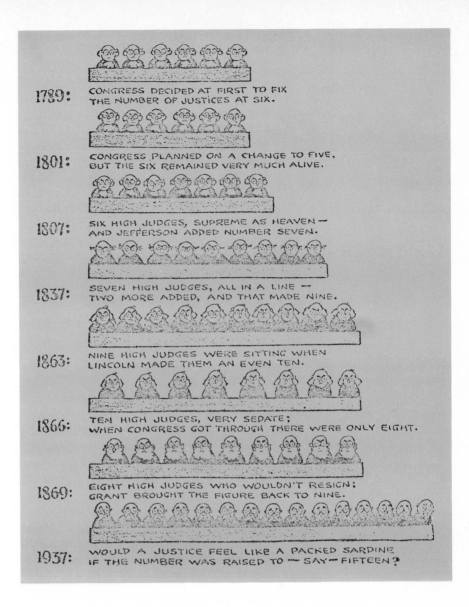

1789: CONGRESS DECIDED AT FIRST TO FIX THE NUMBER OF JUSTICES AT SIX.

1801: CONGRESS PLANNED ON A CHANGE TO FIVE, BUT THE SIX REMAINED VERY MUCH ALIVE.

1807: SIX HIGH JUDGES, SUPREME AS HEAVEN — AND JEFFERSON ADDED NUMBER SEVEN.

1837: SEVEN HIGH JUDGES, ALL IN A LINE — TWO MORE ADDED, AND THAT MADE NINE.

1863: NINE HIGH JUDGES WERE SITTING WHEN LINCOLN MADE THEM AN EVEN TEN.

1866: TEN HIGH JUDGES, VERY SEDATE; WHEN CONGRESS GOT THROUGH THERE WERE ONLY EIGHT.

1869: EIGHT HIGH JUDGES WHO WOULDN'T RESIGN; GRANT BROUGHT THE FIGURE BACK TO NINE.

1937: WOULD A JUSTICE FEEL LIKE A PACKED SARDINE IF THE NUMBER WAS RAISED TO — SAY — FIFTEEN?

Drawing by Herblock in the Washington News.

After Johnson left the White House, Congress returned the Court to its prior size to permit Grant to fill the vacancies.

The men Grant selected made it possible to reverse the Supreme Court invalidation of the Legal Tender Act. Historians are still debating whether Grant packed the Court. Certainly he was not unaware that his two appointees shared his sentiments about the desirability of reversing the earlier decision. President Franklin D. Roosevelt's battle with the Supreme Court in 1937 is a dramatic attempt by a political leader to influence judicial decisions by changing the size of the Court. Although Roosevelt did not succeed in packing the Court, it began to uphold New Deal legislation in the midst of the debate over his attempt to do so.

How the supreme court operates

The justices are in session from the first Monday in October through June. They listen to oral arguments for two weeks and then adjourn for two weeks to consider the cases and write their opinions. Six justices must participate in each decision. Cases are decided by a majority. In the event of a tie vote, the decision of the lower court is sustained, although the case may be re-argued.

At 10 A.M. on the days when the Supreme Court sits, the eight associate justices and the chief justice, dressed in their robes, file into the Court. As they take their seats — arranged according to seniority, with the chief justice in the center — the clerk of the Court introduces them as the "Honorable Chief Justice and Associate Justices of the Supreme Court of the United States." Those present in the courtroom are seated, with counsel taking their places along tables in front of the bench. The attorneys for the Department of Justice, dressed in formal morning clothes, are at the right. The other attorneys are dressed conservatively; sport coats are not considered proper. This is all part of what Richard M. Johnson has called the " 'dramaturgy' of the Court — the majesty of its courtroom; the black robes of the justices; the ritual of its proceedings at oral argument and on decision day; the secrecy and isolation of its decision-making conferences; the formal opinions invoking the symbols of Constitution, precedent, and framers' intent; and all the other elements of setting and conduct that distinguish the Supreme Court, a body of constitutional guardians, from all other officials . . ."[49]

WHAT CASES REACH THE SUPREME COURT?

When a citizen vows he will take his case to the highest court of the land even if it costs him his last penny, he perhaps underestimates the difficulty of securing Supreme Court review, overestimates the cost (although it costs plenty), and reveals a basic misunderstanding of the role of the Court. The rules for appealing a case to the Supreme Court are established by act of Congress and are exceedingly complex. Certain types of cases are said to go to the Supreme Court on appeal; in theory, the Court is obligated to hear these cases. Other appellate cases come before the Court by means of a discretionary writ of certiorari. In addition, the Constitution stipulates that the Supreme Court has original jurisdiction in specified situations. But one basic fact lies behind all the technicalities — the Supreme Court has control of its agenda and decides which cases it wants to consider. The justices closely review fewer than two hundred of the thousands of cases annually presented to them.[50]

It is not enough that Jones thinks he should have won his case against Smith. There has already been at least one appellate review of the trial, either in a federal court of appeals or in a state supreme court. The Supreme Court will review Jones's case only if his claim has broad public significance. It may be that there is a conflict between the rulings of two courts of appeals on a legal point. By deciding Jones's case, the Supreme Court can guarantee that one rule is followed throughout the judicial system. It may be that Jones's case raises a constitutional issue on which a state supreme court has presented an interpretation with which the Court

[49]Richard Johnson, *The Dynamics of Compliance* (Wiley, 1967), pp. 33–41. This summary of Johnson's comment is taken from David Adamany, "Legitimacy, Realigning Elections," p. 792. See also J. Harvie Wilkinson III, *Serving Justice: A Supreme Court Clerk's View* (Charterhouse, 1974), chaps. 2–4.

[50]Detailed figures as well as a review of the Court for the preceding term can be found in an annual article by the *Western Political Quarterly*, in each November issue of the *Harvard Law Review*, and in an annual analysis of important decisions edited by Philip Kurland under the title *The Supreme Court Annual Review*, published by the University of Chicago Press.

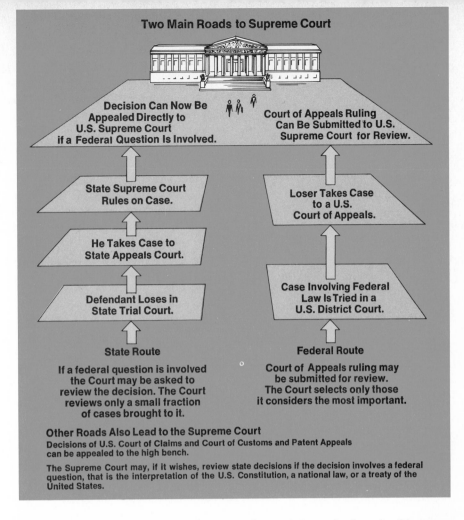

Two Main Roads to Supreme Court

Decision Can Now Be Appealed Directly to U.S. Supreme Court if a Federal Question Is Involved.

Court of Appeals Ruling Can Be Submitted to U.S. Supreme Court for Review.

State Supreme Court Rules on Case.

Loser Takes Case to a U.S. Court of Appeals.

He Takes Case to State Appeals Court.

Defendant Loses in State Trial Court.

Case Involving Federal Law Is Tried in a U.S. District Court.

State Route

If a federal question is involved the Court may be asked to review the decision. The Court reviews only a small fraction of cases brought to it.

Federal Route

Court of Appeals ruling may be submitted for review. The Court selects only those it considers the most important.

Other Roads Also Lead to the Supreme Court
Decisions of U.S. Court of Claims and Court of Customs and Patent Appeals can be appealed to the high bench.

The Supreme Court may, if it wishes, review state decisions if the decision involves a federal question, that is the interpretation of the U.S. Constitution, a national law, or a treaty of the United States.

justices disagree. The crucial factor in determining whether the Supreme Court will hear the case is its importance not to Jones, but to the operation of the governmental system as a whole.

The court accepts cases under the rule of four. If four justices are sufficiently interested in a petition for a writ of certiorari, the petition will be granted and the case brought forward for review. Denial of a writ of certiorari does not mean that the justices agree with the decision of the lower court, and such denials of writs of certiorari do not necessarily establish precedents. Refusal to grant such a writ may indicate all kinds of things, including that the justices do not wish to become involved in a political "hot potato" or that the Court is so divided on an issue that it is not yet prepared to take a stand.

The rule of four also applies to cases presented to the Court *on appeal*, that is, under its mandatory obligation to review. Most appeals are dismissed "for want of properly presented federal question," or "for want of a substantial federal question," or "for want of jurisdiction." Such dismissals, unlike those for a writ of certiorari, do have value as precedents. Lower court judges are supposed to take note that not even four members of the Supreme Court thought the issue raised any question of conflict with the Constitution or federal law or federal treaty.[51]

[51]*Hicks* v. *Miranda*, 422 U.S. 332 (1975).

Before the case is heard in open court, the justices receive printed *briefs*, perhaps running into hundreds of pages, in which each side presents legal arguments, historical materials, and relevant precedents. In addition, the Supreme Court may receive briefs from *amici curiae* — friends of the court. These may be individuals, organizations, or government agencies who claim to have an interest in the case and information of value to the Court. This procedure guarantees that the Department of Justice is represented if a suit between two private parties calls the constitutionality of an act of Congress into question. Although a brief brought by a private party or interest group may help the justices by presenting an argument or point of law that the parties to the case have not raised, often the briefs are filed as a means of "pressuring" the Court to reach a particular decision. In the 1954 school desegregation cases, twenty-four amicus briefs were filed. In the Bakke case, thirty-seven amicus briefs were filed for the University, sixteen of these were for Bakke, and five did not take sides.[52]

Formal oratory before the Supreme Court, perhaps lasting for several days, is a thing of the past. As a rule, counsel for each side is limited to a one-hour argument — in some cases even less — and the Court enforces the time limits. (Extremely important cases will occasionally be given additional time.) Lawyers use a lectern to which two lights are attached; a white light flashes five minutes before time is up and when the red light goes on, the lawyer must stop instantly, even in the middle of an "if."[53]

The entire procedure is formally informal. Sometimes, to the annoyance of the attorneys, the justices talk among themselves or consult briefs or legal volumes during the oral presentation. Justice Holmes occasionally napped during oral argument. When he found a presentation particularly bad, he would frequently and ostentatiously consult his watch.[54]

The justices freely interrupt the lawyers to ask questions, and to request additional information. If a lawyer seems to be having a difficult time, they may try to help him present a better case. Occasionally the justices bounce arguments off a hapless attorney, at one another. During oral argument in the school desegregation cases, Justice Frankfurter was grilling an NAACP lawyer: "Are you saying that we can say that 'separate but equal' is not a doctrine that is relevant at the primary school level? Is that what you are saying" he demanded. Justice Douglas tried to help the lawyer out. "I think you are saying," he ventured, "that segregation may be all right in streetcars and railroad cars and restaurants, but . . . education is different from that." The lawyer found the Douglas paraphrase to his liking. "Yes, sir," he replied. Douglas continued, "That is your argument, is it not? Isn't that your argument in this case?" Again a grateful "yes" from counsel. Frankfurter, however, was not even moderately impressed. "But how can that be your argument . . .?" he cried, and the lawyer was once again on his own.[55]

[52]Samuel Krislov, "The Amicus Curiae Brief: From Friendship to Advocacy," *Yale Law Journal* (March 1963), pp. 694–721.

[53]Edwin McElwain, "The Business of the Supreme Court," *Harvard Law Review* (1959), pp. 5–26.

[54]Henry J. Abraham, *The Judicial Process*, 3rd ed. (Oxford University Press, 1975), pp. 190–91.

[55]Berman, *It is so Ordered: The Supreme Court Rules on School Segregation* (Norton, 1966), p. 69.

The participants in oral argument are by no means equal. The solicitor general, who represents the federal government, enjoys an advantage as the result of his more frequent, more intensive contact with the justices. Similarly, though to a lesser extent, lawyers of great reputation can communicate with the Court more effectively than a young lawyer who is specially admitted to the Supreme Court bar to make his first appearance.[56]

THE CONFERENCE

Each Friday the justices meet in conference. During the week they have heard the oral arguments, read and studied the briefs, and examined the petitions. Before the conference, each justice receives a list of the cases that will be discussed. Each brings to the meeting a red leather book in which the cases and the votes of the justices are recorded. The Friday conferences are secret affairs; what goes on in these meetings has to be pieced together from the comments of members of the Court.

Although the procedure varies, the conferences are marked by informality and vigorous give-and-take. The chief justice presides. He usually opens the discussion by stating the facts, summarizing the questions of law, and making suggestions for disposing of the case. He then asks each member of the Court, in order of seniority, to give his views and conclusions. After full discussion, a vote is taken. The case is decided by majority vote, and one justice is designated to write the *opinion of the Court.* If the chief justice votes with the majority, he decides who writes the opinion. If he does not, the senior justice among the majority makes the decision. More often than not the justice will assign the opinion either to himself or to the justice whose position is closest to his own.[57] Justices who are among the minority normally select one of their number to write a *dissenting opinion*, although each dissenter is free to write his own. If a justice agrees with the majority on the decision but differs on the reasoning, he may write his own opinion; this is known as a *concurring opinion.*

OPINION WRITING

The justice selected to write the Court's opinion is faced with an exacting task. He must produce a document that will win the support of at least four — and hopefully eight — intelligent, strong-willed men, all of whom may have voted the same way he did but perhaps for very different reasons. Assisted by his law clerks, recent honor graduates from law school, the justice tries his hand at a draft and sends it to his colleagues for their comments. If he is lucky, the majority will accept his version, perhaps suggesting minor changes. But it may be that his original draft is not satisfactory to the Court. If this is the case, he is forced to redraft and recirculate his opinion until a majority can reach agreement.

There is considerable room for change in the process at this point.[58] In fact, there are "numerous instances on record in which the justice assigned the opinion of the Court has reported back that additional study had convinced him that he and the rest of the majority had been in error.[59] Sometimes he is able to convince the Court to change its mind. A dissenting justice can sometimes persuade the opinion writer of merits of his pro-

[56]Glendon A. Schubert, *Quantitative Analysis of Judicial Behavior* (Free Press, 1959), p. 109.

[57]David W. Rohde, "Policy Goals, Strategic Choice and Majority Opinion Assignments in the U.S. Supreme Court," *Midwest Journal of Political Science* (November 1972), pp. 652 ff.

[58]J. Woodford Howard, "On the Fluidity of Judicial Choice," *American Political Science Review* (March 1968), pp. 43–56. See also Murphy's *Elements of Judicial Strategy.*

[59]Howard, *ibid.*, p. 44.

test. For example, shortly after Harlan Fiske Stone came on the Court, the justices divided seven to one in a particular case, with Stone the lone dissenter. He did not give up. He took to Chief Justice Taft (who had assigned the opinion to himself) relevant articles from a dozen volumes of the Columbia and Harvard law reviews and a memorandum requesting reconsideration. Taft's draft opinion was circulated some time later, with the following note appended: "Dear Brethren: I think we made a mistake in this case and have written the opinion the other way. Hope you will agree. W.H.T." The new revised Taft opinion became the decision of a unanimous court.[60]

If the initial version is not acceptable to a majority of the Court, an elaborate bargaining process occurs. The opinion ultimately published is not necessarily the opinion the author would have liked to write. Like a committee report, it represents the most common denominator. Holmes bitterly complained to Laski that he had written an opinion "in terms to suit the majority of the brethren, although they didn't suit me. Years ago I did the same thing in the interest of getting a job done. I let the brethren put in a reason that I thought bad and cut out all that I thought good and I have squirmed ever since, and swore that never again—but again I yield and now comes a petition for rehearing pointing out all the horrors that will ensue from just what I didn't want to say."[61]

The two major weapons a justice can use against his colleagues are his vote and his willingness to write a separate opinion that will attack a doctrine the majority wishes to see adopted. A dissenting opinion is often written and circulated for the specific purpose of convincing the majority. If the opinion writer is persuaded by the logic of the dissenter, the dissenting opinion may never be published. Sometimes, however, an unpersuaded justice will be forced to give in to the demands of one of his colleagues. Especially if the Court is closely divided, one justice may be in a position to demand that a given argument be included in—or removed from—the opinion as the price of his swing vote. Sometimes this can happen even if the Court is not closely divided. An opinion writer who anticipates that his decision will bring critical public reaction may very much wish to have it presented as the view of a unanimous court and may be prepared to compromise to achieve unanimity.

OPINIONS AS MEDIA OF COMMUNICATION

As a general rule, Supreme Court decisions are accompanied by opinions that state the facts, present the issues, announce the decision, and—most important—attempt to justify the reasoning of the Court. Judicial opinions are the Court's principal method of expressing itself to the outside world, and it addresses them to various audiences. Perhaps the most important function of opinions is to instruct the lower courts and the bar how to act in future cases.

Sometimes judicial opinions are used to "drum up trade." A statement in the form "Nothing in this opinion should be taken to preclude a case in which . . ." is an invitation to attorneys and lower court judges to act in a certain way. A dissenting or concurring opinion may be used to throw cues to the bench and bar. Judicial opinions may be directed at Congress

[60]Alpheus T. Mason, *Harlan Fiske Stone: Pillar of the Law* (Viking, 1956), p. 222. Murphy, *Elements of Judicial Strategy*, and Howard, *ibid.*, contain dozens of similar examples.

[61]Howe, *Holmes–Laski Letters*, II, pp. 124, 125.

or the president. If the Court regrets that "in the absence of action by the Congress, we have no choice but to . . ." or insists that "relief of the sort that petitioner demands can only come from the political branches of government," it is clearly asking Congress to act. Sometimes the Court will interpret existing statutes so narrowly as to render them ineffective, in the hope of forcing fresh legislative action. Such a hope once prompted the following dissent from Justice Clark: "Unless the Congress changes the rule announced by the Court today, those intelligence agencies of our government engaged in law enforcement may as well close up shop. . . ." Within three months, new legislation was on the statute books.[62]

Finally, the justices use published opinions to communicate with the public. A well-handled opinion may increase support among specialized publics—especially lawyers and judges—and among the general population for a policy the Court is stressing. For this reason, the Court delayed declaring school segregation unconstitutional until unanimity could be secured. The justices understood that any sign of dissension on the bench on this major social issue would be an invitation to evade the Court's ruling.

The various functions of a judicial opinion are nicely illustrated by the following memorandum that Justice Frankfurter sent to Justice Murphy, discussing a dissenting opinion:

> This is a protest opinion—a protest at the Bar of the future—but also an effort to make the brethren realize what is at stake. Moreover, a powerful dissent . . . is bound to have an effect on the lower courts as well as on the officers of the law. . . . And so in order to impress our own brethren, the lower courts, and enforcement officers, it seems to me vital to make the dissent an impressive document.[63]

THE POWERS OF THE CHIEF JUSTICE

The chief justice has only one vote, and in terms of formal power, he is merely the first among equals.[64] However, his position gives him a unique opportunity to exercise leadership. The chief justice presides in open court and over the conferences, where he usually presents each case to his associates—thus setting the tone of the discussion. Also, as we have seen, he assigns the writing of the opinion in all cases when he votes with the majority. This role—choosing the opinion writer—is significant because the writer determines whether an opinion is based on one ground rather than another and whether it deals narrowly or broadly with the issues. These choices may make a decision more or less acceptable to the public, may affect the decision of other justices to dissent, and may affect the value of a decision as a precedent. The chief justice is also the key figure in the Court's certiorari procedure. In practice, he is generally able to eliminate from the Court's docket those cases he considers trivial.

The ability of the chief justice to influence his Court has varied considerably. Chief Justice Hughes ran the conferences like a stern schoolmaster, keeping the justices talking to the point, moving the discussion along, and

[62]Berman, *It Is So Ordered*, p. 114; Murphy, *Elements of Judicial Strategy*, p. 66.

[63]Quoted in Berman, *ibid.*, pp. 60, 61.

[64]This discussion is based on David Danelski, "The Influence of the Chief Justice in the Decisional Process of the Supreme Court," in Jahnige and Goldman, eds., *Federal Judicial System*, pp. 147–60.

doing his best to work out compromises. Frowning on dissents, he tried to achieve a unanimous vote in order to give decisions greater weight. Chief Justice Stone, on the other hand, encouraged each justice to state his own point of view and let the discussion wander as it would. Chief Justice Burger has devoted much of his time to judicial reform, speaking to bar and lay groups and trying to build political support for modernizing the judicial structure. As Danelski reminds us, "the Chief Justiceship does not guarantee leadership. It only offers its incumbent an opportunity to lead. Optimum leadership inheres in the combination of the office and an able, persuasive, personable judge."[65]

AFTER THE LAWSUIT IS OVER

Victory in the Supreme Court does not necessarily mean that the person will get what he wants. As a rule the Court does not implement its own decision, but "remands" the case to the lower court with instructions to act in accordance with the Supreme Court's opinion. The lower courts have considerable leeway in their interpretation of the Court's mandates.

The impact of a particular ruling announced by the Supreme Court on the behavior of those who are not immediate parties to a lawsuit is even more uncertain. Many of the more important decisions require further action by administrative and elected officials before they become the effective law of the land. Sometimes Supreme Court decisions are simply ignored: Despite the Supreme Court's holding that it is unconstitutional for school boards to require prayers within the schools, many school boards continued their previous practices.[66] For years after the Supreme Court held public school segregation unconstitutional, a great number of school districts remained segregated. The Constitution may be what the Supreme Court says it is, but a Supreme Court opinion, for the moment at least, is what a trial judge or a police officer or a prosecutor says it is.

The most difficult Supreme Court decisions to implement are those that require the cooperation of large numbers of officials. For example, a Supreme Court decision announcing a new standard for police arrest procedures is not likely to have an impact on the way police make arrests for some time. Not many police officers subscribe to the *United States Supreme Court Reports*. The process is more complex: Local prosecutors, state attorneys general, chiefs of police, and state and federal trial court judges must all participate in giving "meaning" to Supreme Court decisions.[67]

Although Congress or a president has occasionally "ignored" or "construed" a Supreme Court ruling to avoid its impact, by and large decisions whose implementation requires only the action of a central governmental agency become effective immediately. For example, when the Supreme Court held that President Truman lacked constitutional authority to seize steel companies temporarily to avoid a shutdown during the Korean War, the president promptly complied. Of course other presidents can use discretion in determining how that particular precedent should be applied to their own behavior.

[65]*Ibid.*, p. 148.

[66]Theodore L. Becker, ed., *The Impact of Supreme Court Decisions* (Oxford University Press, 1969); and Stephen L. Wasby, *The Impact of the United States Supreme Court* (Dorsey Press, 1970), and the literature cited therein.

[67]Richardson and Vines, *The Politics of Federal Courts*, p. 161; Bradley C. Canon, "Reactions of State Supreme Courts to a U.S. Supreme Court Civil Liberties Decision," *Law and Society Review* (Fall 1973), pp. 108ff.

The Supreme Court

"We are very quiet there but it is the quiet of a storm center...."
—Oliver Wendell Holmes, Jr.

THE SUPREME COURT
Washington, D.C. 20543

1 Courtyards
2 Solicitor General's Office
3 Lawyers' Lounge
4 Marshal's Office
5 Main Hall
6 Court Room
7 Conference and Reception Rooms
8 Court Conference Room
9 Robing Room
10 Chief Justice
    Warren Burger's Offices

Chief Justice	Appointed
Warren E. Burger	1969

Associate Justices:

11	William J. Brennan, Jr.	1956
12	Potter Stewart	1958
13	Byron R. White	1962
14	Thurgood Marshall	1967
15	Harry A. Blackmun	1970
16	Lewis F. Powell, Jr.	1971
17	William H. Rehnquist	1971
18	John Paul Stevens	1976
19	Stanley Reed (retired)	1938
20	William O. Douglas (retired)	1939

Judicial power in a democracy

An independent judiciary is considered one of the hallmarks of a free society. As impartial dispensers of equal justice under the law, judges should not be dependent on the executive, the legislature, the parties to the case, the electorate, or a mob outside the courtroom. But the very independence essential to protect judges in their roles as legal umpires raises basic problems when a society decides—as has ours—also to make judges political policy makers. Perhaps in no other society do groups and individuals resort to litigation as much as they do in this nation in order to secure reallocation of political resources. The involvement of our courts, especially the Supreme Court, in political contests means, of course, that they are subject to political criticism. Throughout our history there has been a running debate both over what the Supreme Court does and what it should do.

Since 1937, speaking generally, and especially since the end of World War II, the Supreme Court, with some zigging and some zagging, has reversed its traditional conservative policy directions. It has removed most of the constitutional restraints on government regulation of business, but it has imposed many more in order to protect civil liberties and civil rights, most especially for the poor and black.[68] In recent decades, the Supreme Court has become much more involved in our political life. It has been much less reluctant to strike down laws: Fifty-nine provisions of the acts of Congress and 1,000 acts of state legislatures and city councils have been invalidated since 1943.[69] Although the Supreme Court under Chief Justice Burger has been less activist in some areas than under Chief Justice Warren, in other areas it has been more so. Despite President Nixon's attempt to "turn the Supreme Court around," it continues to play an active role. The Burger Court in its first seven years voided 15 federal laws and nullified "more national laws on First Amendment and equal protection grounds than all of its predecessors combined."[70]

As might be expected, groups whose policy preferences have been endorsed by the Supreme Court defend its active involvement in our political affairs. They argue that the justices should do what is right, even if such actions are not politically popular. They contend that courts have a duty to protect the long-range interests of the public, even against the short-range wishes of the voters. And also as might be expected, there are critics of the Court's more active role, especially among those who disapprove of the policies it has adopted. But even among those who agree with its conclusions, some argue that just as it was wrong for conservative justices prior to 1937 to strike down laws they did not like, so it is wrong for the progressive justices of today to strike down laws they dislike. These critics contend that even if the Court makes the "right" decision, it is not right for the Court to take over the legislative responsibilities of the people's elected representatives.

THE PEOPLE AND THE COURT

The Supreme Court has always been involved in making policy. It is inherent in its functions. But throughout our history, the Supreme Court has

[68]Robert J. Harris, "Judicial Review: Vagaries and Varieties," *Journal of Politics* (August 1976), p. 188.

[69]P. Allan Dionisopoulos, "Judicial Review in the Textbooks," *DEA NEWS* (Fall 1976). On the other side, Nathan Lewin, "Avoiding the Supreme Court," *The New York Times Magazine* (October 17, 1976), criticizes the Burger Court for its retreat in defending the "underdogs."

[70]*Ibid.* For a study of Nixon's controversial nominations, see the critical account by James F. Simon, *In His Own Image: The Supreme Court in Richard Nixon's America* (McKay, 1974).

been attacked for engaging in "judicial legislation." And its recent more active and open role has returned these issues to the forefront of public discussion. Why should the branch of government least accountable to the people have a right to veto the actions of the people's elected representatives?

We no longer find acceptable the explanation that it is right to give the power of judicial review to politically independent judges because their own policy views are irrelevant to the decisions they make. The absurdity of the assumption that all they are doing is carrying out the clear commands of the Constitution is indicated by the fact that the justices divide so frequently over the question of what the Constitution means. More acceptable is the explanation that although judges do choose between competing values they are not free to adopt whatever policies they wish. They are restricted by procedural limitations. The doctrine of *stare decisis* imposes some constraints, but the most significant restrictions are those of the political system of which the judges are a part.

In the first place, the president and the Senate are likely to appoint to the bench justices whose decisions will reflect contemporary values. In the second place, as we have noted, judges have neither armies nor police to execute their rulings. Their policies are effective only to the extent that they are supported by a considerable portion of the electorate. To win a favorable Supreme Court decision is to win something of considerable political value, but the policies reflected by that decision may or may not substantially alter the way people behave. If the Court's policies are too far out of step with the values of the country, the Court is likely to get "reversed" by Congress. It is also limited by the necessity of maintaining the allegiance of the judicial bureaucracy.[71] There are also important links between the Court and the people. Although the public lacks precise knowledge about, or even much awareness of, the work of the Supreme Court, and although it is doubtful if many voters cast ballots for presidential candidates because of their stand toward the Court and its decisions, the outcome of the presidential elections does affect the direction of judicial interpretations.

This connection between the public and the Supreme Court does not come about because of Mr. Dooley's celebrated charge, "The Supreme Court follows the illiction returns."[72] On the contrary, after major realigning elections when a new political coalition takes over the White House and Congress, the old regime stays on in the federal courts. Or as one unknown wit put it, "The good presidents do dies with them, the bad lives on after them on the Supreme Court." But despite initial clashes, the new electoral coalitions eventually also "take over" the federal courts. Before too long, new interpretations of the Constitution reflect the new dominant political ideology.[73]

[71]Walter F. Murphy, *Congress and the Court* (Chicago: The University of Chicago Press, 1962); John R. Schmidhauser and Larry L. Berg, *The Supreme Court and Congress: Conflict and Interaction, 1945–1968* (New York: Free Press, 1972); Archibald Cox, *The Role of the Supreme Court in American Government* (New York: Oxford University Press, 1976).

[72]Finley Peter Dunne, "Mr. Dooley's Opinions," in *Bartlett's Familiar Quotations*, 14th ed. (Little, Brown, 1968), p. 890.

[73]Robert Dahl, "Decision-Making in a Democracy: The Supreme Court as a National Policy-Maker," *Journal of Public Law* (Fall, 1957), pp. 279–95; Richard Funston, "The Supreme Court and Critical Elections," *American Political Science Review* (September, 1975), pp. 795–811. For a somewhat different view, see Jonathan D. Casper, "The Supreme Court and National Policy

Even if there is no realigning election, the voters still have an impact on the course of constitutional development. For example, both in 1968 and 1972 President Nixon made it perfectly clear that he opposed the constitutional interpretations of the Supreme Court under Chief Justice Warren, and that if he were elected he would appoint "strict constructionists" to the Court. Although his views toward the Supreme Court probably had little to do with his winning the elections, the voters did put him in office. As president, he proceeded to do as promised. He appointed to the federal courts in general, and the Supreme Court in particular, more conservative jurists, although the Senate refused to confirm his first two choices for the Supreme Court. Again in 1976, by putting Jimmy Carter rather than Gerald Ford in the White House, the voters had an important impact on the course of constitutional development. The Democratic Congress will create a considerable number of additional federal judgeships to which President Carter will nominate and the Senate will confirm persons reflecting the views of the Democratic majority and of the people who elected them. Once again, judges and the people will be brought closer.

THE GUARDIAN ETHIC UNDER ATTACK[74]

Recently, a variety of critics have challenged the rather comforting explanation that we have just given to attempt to reconcile the major policy-making role of the judiciary with its independence from direct political controls. These critics are of varying political persuasions and fall into two general camps.

First, there are those who argue that the Supreme Court, in its zeal to protect the people, especially the poor, has become unhinged from its political moorings in the system. It is running wild, and is imposing the judges' policy preferences on the nation. Second, there are those who argue that the Supreme Court has never been, and never will be, very effective in protecting the poor and the dispossessed because the judges will always reflect the wishes of the ruling coalition in Congress and the White House. The judges manipulate symbols, but they never really cause any major realignment of political values or economic goods.[75] Plainly, these two groups of critics tend to cancel each other out, but let us take up their arguments in more detail.

First, let us look at the arguments of those who charge that the Court is running wild and interfering too much and too often in our political life. According to these critics, although in earlier times the Supreme Court occasionally told other parts of government what could not be done, the most "distinctive characteristic" of the modern-day court has been to "*extend* the role of what the government could do, even when the government did not want to do it."[76] Thus, the Supreme Court has told Congress and state legislatures that they must provide attorneys for the poor, and adequate care to mental patients; modernize the prisons; reapportion

Making," *American Political Science Review* (March 1976), pp. 5–63; Adamany, *Legitimacy, Realigning Elections,* pp. 841–43; Stuart S. Nagel, "Court-Curbing Periods in American History," *Vanderbilt Law Review* (June 1965), p. 925; Goldman and Jahnige, eds., *The Federal Courts as a Political System,* p. 263.

[74]From Ward E. Y. Elliott, *The Rise of Guardian Democracy* (Harvard University Press, 1974).

[75]Stuart A. Scheingold, *The Politics of Rights* (Yale University Press, 1974).

[76]Nathan Glazer, "Towards an Imperial Judiciary," *The Public Interest* (Fall 1976), p. 109. See also Raoul Berger, *Government by Judiciary* (Harvard University Press, 1977).

legislative bodies; and do whatever is necessary and proper to bring about racial integration in the public schools including busing of pupils. The "highly activist and intrusive judiciary is now a permanent part of the American Commonwealth," it is argued. No longer can we anticipate a cycle of liberal and activist judges to be followed by conservative and restrained ones. The Burger Court is still more involved in policy making than any in our history, except perhaps the Warren Court.

What has happened to change the relations between the Court and the political system? According to these critics, three factors explain why the Court has become unhinged from the political restraints of the past: (1) Once the Court takes a stand on an issue, it starts a motion which is hard to reverse. (2) There has been an expansion of the role of government which brings with it a more active role for courts in all kinds of areas from measuring the validity of employment to tests to determine which books are obscene. (3) The third and most important reason is that the Court is no longer a reflection of public sentiments but a cause of them. The Court, of course, must have political support. But the present-day Court has created its own new and powerful constituency. Today, public interest law firms, professional organizations, and trade unions are engaged in constitutional litigation. These groups, which work to expand the scope and power of government, have replaced the "powerful business interest of the 1930's and 1940's that engaged in constitutional litigation to *restrict* the power of government."[77] And surrounding this entire array of groups are "action-minded intellectuals," believers in the "guardian ethic."

The "guardian ethic" assumes "anything new must be better than anything old, that action must be better than inaction, expert better than amateur, standard better than special, and administered better than unadministered."[78] The "guardian ethic" is "democratic in its stress on equality, but it is anti-democratic in its stress on administration and intellectual elitism."[79] These "action-minded intellectuals" who are now the Court's powerful constituency, so it is charged, write most of the newspaper editorials and law reviews, teach in the universities, and dominate the bench. They urge judges not to wait for legislative action or the political process but to do what must be done — to strike down segregation, get rid of capital punishment, secure better apportioned legislatures, place restraints on the police, outlaw segregation in private schools, get rid of prayer in public schools, strike down state abortion laws. These are desirable changes. No matter that they cannot be carried out through the electoral and legislative processes. No matter that most voters would be against some of these actions. No matter that the legislatures which more directly reflect immediate public views are unwilling to do so. The Supreme Court should be the people's guardian.

Now let us take up the arguments of the second set of critics. They argue that the Supreme Court is not now and probably never has been very effective in serving as a guardian of the rights of minorities and that all it does is to legitimize the status quo. It provides symbolic satisfactions, but it really does not have much to do with who gets what, where, when, and how much. The Supreme Court may declare prayers in public schools

[77] *Ibid.*, p. 120.

[78] Elliott, *The Rise of Guardian Democracy*, p. 2.

[79] *Ibid.*

unconstitutional, but in many districts prayers are still being said. The Supreme Court may declare segregation to be unconstitutional, but in many schools we still have segregation. The Supreme Court may declare third-degree police methods unconstitutional, but such methods are still being used by many police departments. In other words, litigation brings about symbolic changes but no major shifts in the distribution of public goods.[80]

These commentators, both those who contend that the Supreme Court is serving as an intrusive antidemocratic set of uncontrolled guardians and those who argue that it is merely manipulating symbols while political life goes on as before, are persuasive. But we remain unconvinced by either point of view. We remember that the most informed student of the Supreme Court, E. S. Corwin, predicted in 1934 that the Court's role in American politics was about to be limited, just a year before the Court entered into one of its most prominent periods in our history.[81] This reminds us that we tend to exaggerate the trends in the particular historical cycle in which we live and write. Perhaps it is true that the Supreme Court, even one in which a majority of the justices were selected by Presidents Nixon and Ford, plays a more active role than did Courts of prior times. And it is doubtless true that opinion makers today are more supportive of this active judicial role than opinion-makers in earlier periods. Nonetheless, pressures on the court as part of the fabric of our democratic system remain powerful.

It is an oversimplification to say that the Court is nothing but a part of the ruling coalition that controls Congress and the White House, and that its policies have no impact except insofar as they are agreeable to that coalition. It is equally simplistic to say that the Court's policies are irreversible and uncontrollable, that there are no effective checks on what the Court does. The policy-making process is a complex one. What Congress and White House and state legislatures and police officers do has an effect on what the Supreme Court does, and what the Supreme Court does has an effect on what Congress and the White House and the state legislatures and the police do. Most important of all, what all these agencies do is related to what the various parts of "the people" want done. One illustration: The economic and social developments that led to the growth of a black middle class led to political power for them, which led to presidents who began to care about their values, which led in turn to the appointment of judges who reflected civil rights values. And this led to action and reaction in city councils, school boards, and state legislatures, which led to pressures to change the character of the judge's decisions.

"The people" speak in many ways and with many voices. The Supreme Court—and the other courts—represent and reflect the values of some of these people. And although it is not the defenseless, weak institution portrayed by some commentators, and although it is as much a cause of public opinion as a reflection of it, ultimately the power of the Court rests on its retention of the support of most of the people most of the time. No better standard for determining the legitimacy of a governmental institution has ever been discovered.

[80]See, for example, Scheingold, *The Politics of Rights.*

[81]Edward S. Corwin, *The Twilight of the Supreme Court* (Yale University Press, 1934).

Summary

1. Judges in America play a more active role in our political life than in other democracies. Federal courts receive their jurisdiction immediately from Congress, which must decide the constitutional division of responsibilities among federal and state courts.

2. Federal judges apply statutory law, common law, equity, admiralty and maritime law, and administrative law. They apply federal, criminal, and civil law. Although bound by procedural requirements, including *stare decisis,* they have to exercise discretion.

3. Improvement in the administration of federal courts has become a major political issue, as has the improvement of the operations of the Department of Justice and federal prosecutors.

4. Partisanship and ideology are important factors in the selection of federal judges at all levels and ensure a linkage between the courts and the rest of the political system.

5. The Supreme Court, with almost complete control over the cases it reviews as they come up from the state courts and from the courts of appeals and district courts, is a revered but somewhat mysterious branch of our government. Its nine justices annually dispose of thousands of cases, but they concentrate most of their time on about two hundred which establish guidelines for lower courts and the country.

6. A continuing question of major importance is the reconciliation of the role of judges, especially those on the Supreme Court, as independent and fair dispensers of justice for the parties before them with their vital role as interpreters of the Constitution. This is an especially complex problem in our democracy because of the power of judicial review and the significant role courts play in the making of public policy.

Chapter 16

Bureaucrats: The Real Power?

Attacking the bureaucracy is as traditional for politicians as kissing babies and marching in July 4th parades. Jimmy Carter told us: "Our government in Washington now is a horrible bureaucratic mess. It is disorganized, wasteful, has no purpose, and its policies . . . are incomprehensible or devised by special interest groups with little regard for the welfare of the average American citizen." Ronald Reagan makes the same point when he says, "We need to get the bureaucracy off of our backs and out of our pocketbooks." Former president Richard Nixon once wrote his cabinet and White House aides complaining that most of the bureaucrats spend half their time writing notes to one another.

Big bureaucracy is plainly in disrepute. Bureaucrats are lazy, inefficient, timid, *and* too powerful all at the same time, or so at least we are told by those who run for political office. We would be a lot better off, they imply, with less bureaucracy and fewer bureaucrats.

The federal bureaucracy is an inviting target. There is hardly a citizen who has not been hassled, defeated, or offended at some point or another in dealing with the Internal Revenue Service, the Postal Service, the U. S. Army, the Department of Health, Education and Welfare, or one of the dozens of national regulatory agencies such as the Food and Drug Administration or the Occupational Health and Safety Administration. Moreover, career public servants really have no press secretary who can speak up for their side of the story.

But as with much of the oversimplified campaign talk in American politics, the "bureaucrats-are-bums" speeches are usually misleading. Of course we have a lot of red tape and overlap in our bureaucratic processes—probably too much of each. The real question, however, is not the size or the existence of bureaucracy but whether bureaucracy is responsive to the people who have real needs. We also want to know whether the bureaucracy is accountable to the president, the Congress, and ultimately the citizens.

Who are the bureaucrats?

In this chapter, we are mainly interested in the almost 5 million people (2.8 million civilian and about 2.1 million in uniform) who make up the executive branch of the federal government. Certain facts about these people need to be emphasized at the outset:

1. Only about 12 percent of the career civilian employees work in the Washington area. The vast majority are employed in regional, field, and local offices scattered throughout the country and around the world. California alone has nearly 300,000 federal employees.

2. Almost half of the civilian employees work for the Army, Navy, Air Force, or other defense agencies.

3. Only a small part of the bureaucracy—perhaps 15 percent—works for welfare agencies such as the Social Security Administration or the Rural Electrification Administration, and more than half of these work for the Veterans Administration. The welfare state may consume a sizable portion of our budget, but the size of the federal bureaucracy that administers it is relatively small. A still smaller proportion of government employees work in regulatory agencies such as the Interstate Commerce Commission.

4. Federal employees are not of one type. Indeed, in terms of social origin, education, religion, and other background factors, bureaucrats are more broadly representative of the nation than are legislators or politically appointed executives.

5. Federal civilian employment in the past twenty years or so has stayed at about the same level and, in comparison with state and local growth rates, has leveled off. State and local civilian forces, on the other hand, continue to grow (currently over 12 million—about 3,350,000 at the state level and nearly 9 million in local government).

6. Their work in government is equally varied. Over 15,000 different personnel skills—about two-thirds as many as are found in all private business—are repre-

The Coast Guard, a part of the U.S. Department of Transportation, is shown here checking on the transfer of fish between two Russian ships during a routine patrol of the U.S. Atlantic Coast.

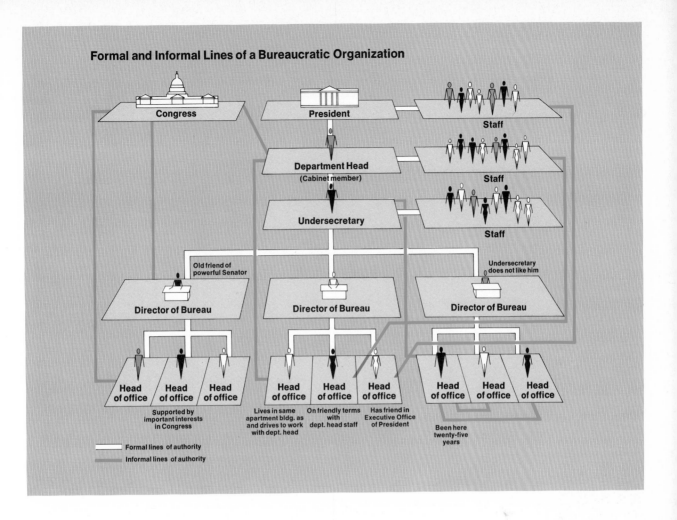

Formal and Informal Lines of a Bureaucratic Organization

Congress

President

Staff

Department Head
(Cabinet member)

Staff

Undersecretary

Staff

Old friend of
powerful Senator

Undersecretary
does not like him

Director of Bureau

Director of Bureau

Director of Bureau

Head
of office

Head
of office

Head
of office

Head
of office

Head
of office

Head
of office

Head
of office

Head
of office

Head
of office

Supported by
important interests
in Congress

Lives in same
apartment bldg. as
and drives to work
with dept. head

On friendly terms
with
dept. head staff

Has friend in
Executive Office
of President

Been here
twenty-five
years

Formal lines of authority

Informal lines of authority

sented in the federal government. Unlike Americans as a whole, however, most federal employees are white-collar workers—secretaries, clerks, lawyers, inspectors.

The vast number of bureaucrats are honest professionals, expert at their jobs. The bureaucrats may often be criticized, but presidents and the Congress ignore their advice at considerable risk. A compelling example is provided by the CIA's perceptive memos (many of them later published in the celebrated *Pentagon Papers)* arguing that the Vietnam War as President Johnson was intending to conduct it would be a disastrous failure. This was good advice, from an expert bureaucracy, that Johnson simply disregarded. The Nixon White House similarly chose to ignore or bypass the advice of the bureaucracy on matters of civil liberties—advice again that Nixon and his aides lived to regret not taking.

Structure

The bureaucrats or career government employees work in the executive branch, a cluster of twelve departments and more than fifty independent agencies embracing over 2,000 bureaus, divisions, branches, offices, services, and other subunits. In size, five big agencies—the Departments of Army, Navy, and Air Force, the Postal Service, and the Veterans Administration—tower over all the others. Most of the agencies are responsible to

361

White-Collar Workers	Number of Federal Workers
Secretaries and clerks	211,068
Postmen	202,262
Engineers (all types)	146,940
Scientists (all types)	85,501
Nurses and nurses' aides	67,904
Personnel administrators	35,331
Accountants	31,780
Teachers	26,284
Air-traffic controllers	26,005
Internal Revenue Service agents	21,155
Investigators	21,133
Inspectors	17,427
Forestry workers	14,624
Mathematicians and statisticians	13,550
Guards	13,477
Attorneys	12,761
Firemen	11,875
Computer operators	11,602
Key punchers	10,932
Doctors	8,033
Librarians	6,643
Telephone operators	5,059
Economists	4,798
Payroll clerks	4,553
Customs agents	4,301
Purchasing agents	3,959
Writers and editors	3,577
Psychologists	3,099
Photographers	3,061
Veterinarians	2,284
Pharmacists	1,439
Dentists	925
Chaplains	461
Blue-Collar Workers	
Mobile-industrial equipment workers	72,841
Manual laborers	57,383
Fixed-industrial-equipment workers	44,777
Service employes (all types)	43,706
Warehouse workers	42,344
Aircraft servicemen	32,074
Metal workers	29,765
Electronic-equipment workers	29,576
Machine-tool workers	19,547
Boat operators and servicemen	17,980
Ammunition and armament workers	16,213
Woodworkers	15,545
Plumbers and pipefitters	15,279
Printers	12,137
Painters and paperhangers	10,627

Note: Civilian workers. Latest totals available—white collar, October 1974; blue collar, October 1972.

SOURCE: U.S. Civil Service Commission

the president, but some are partly independent of him. Virtually all the agencies exist by act of Congress; legislators could abolish them either by passing a new law or by withholding funds.

FORMAL ORGANIZATION

The Cabinet departments are headed by secretaries (except Justice, which is headed by the attorney general). These secretaries are also cabinet members and thus are directly responsible to the president. Although

Attorney General Griffin Bell of the Department of Justice, speaks with Senators Kennedy and Laxalt prior to a Senate Judiciary sub-committee meeting on the effectiveness of anti-trust enforcement.

the departments vary greatly in size, they have certain features in common: Often a deputy or an undersecretary takes part of the administrative load off the secretary's shoulders, and several assistant secretaries direct major programs. Like the president, the secretaries have various subcabinet-level assistants who help them in planning, budget, personnel, legal services, public relations, and other staff functions. The departments are, of course, subdivided into bureaus and smaller units, but the basis of division may differ. The most common basis is *function*. For example, the Commerce Department is divided into the Bureau of the Census, the Patent Office, the Office of Minority Business Enterprise, and so on. The basis may also be clientele (for example, the Bureau of Indian Affairs of the Interior Department), or *work processes* (for example, the Economic Research Service of the Agriculture Department), or *geography* (for example, the Alaskan Air Command of the Department of the Air Force). The basis of organization of most departmental units—and indeed of the departments themselves—is mixed.

The score or more of government corporations, such as the Tennessee Valley Authority and the Federal Deposit Insurance Corporation, are a sort of cross between a business corporation and a regular government agency. Government corporations were designed to make possible a freedom of action and flexibility not always found in the regular federal agencies. These corporations have been freed from certain regulations of the Office of Management and Budget and the Comptroller General. They also have had more leeway in using their own earnings as they please. And yet the fact that the government owns the corporations means that it retains basic control over their activities.

The independent agencies have many types of organization and many degrees of independence. Broadly speaking, all agencies that are not corporations and that do not fall under the executive departments (such as Treasury or Interior) are called independent agencies. Many of these agencies, however, are no more independent of the president and Congress than are the executive departments themselves. The huge Veterans Administration is usually not represented in the cabinet, for example, but its chief is directly responsible to the president.

Another type of independent agency is the independent regulatory board or commission—agencies like the Securities and Exchange Commission, the National Labor Relations Board, the Interstate Commerce Commission. Congress deliberately set up these boards to keep them somewhat free from White House influence in exercising their quasi-legislative and quasi-judicial functions. Congress has protected their independence in several ways: The boards are headed by three or more commissioners with overlapping terms; they often have to be bipartisan in membership; and the president's power of removal is curbed.

Within the departments, corporations, and independent agencies are many subordinate units. The standard name for the largest subunit is the bureau, although sometimes it is called an office, administration, service, and so on. Bureaus are the working agencies of the federal government. In contrast to the big departments, which are often mere holding companies for a variety of agencies, the bureaus usually have fairly definite and clear-cut duties, as their names show: the Bureau of Customs and Bureau of the Mint of the Treasury Department, the Bureau of Indian Affairs of the Interior Department. All this elaborate organization of the executive branch gives order and system to administration. It assigns certain functions to certain units, places officials at the head of each unit and makes them responsible for performance, allows both specialization and coordination, permits ready communication, and in general makes our far-flung administration somewhat controllable and manageable. But this formal organization can be highly misleading.

INFORMAL ORGANIZATION

People differ—in attitude, motive, ability, experience, and political influence. And their very diversity leads to all sorts of complications. Relationships among officials in an agency may be based on influence rather than on formal authority, on expertise or political clout with constituency interest groups. Leadership may be lodged not at the top but in a variety of places. A certain group of officials may have considerable influence, whereas another group, with the same formal status, may have much less. The loyalties of some officials may cut across the formal aims of the agency.

Informal organization can have a great effect on administration. A subordinate official in an agency might be especially close to the chief simply because they went to the same college or play poker together, or because the subordinate knows how to ingratiate himself with the chief. A staff official may have tremendous influence not because of formal authority, but because experience, fairness, common sense, and personality lead people to turn to him for advice. In an agency headed by a chief who is weak or unimaginative, a vacuum may develop that encourages others to try to take over. Such informal organization and communication cutting across regular channels is inevitable in any organization, public or private, civilian or military.

The case against big bureaucracy

"This is brief, clear, concise and to the point. Try again and remember this is a U.S. government office."

Reprinted from Federal Times, with permission.

Big bureaucracy is that part of the government that you dislike. If you are not directly concerned about a matter one way or the other, it is easy to say that the national government should stay in Washington and mind its own business. And it is easy to agree with President Carter, who claims we need to pare some 1,900 federal agencies down to about 200. "We must not drift in the direction of bigger and bigger government" is the message from every recent president.

On the other hand, "When government is doing something you consider important, that's just an instance of society organizing itself to perform an urgent task."[1] A subject you are especially interested in deserves all the attention it can get. The public is almost always critical of big government and big bureaucracy in the abstract, but they will howl in protest whenever some national program that aids them is threatened. "It's a funny thing," said a Department of Agriculture official to an interviewer. "Rural people are against big government more than anybody. But just try to reduce one of their crop subsidy programs or close down an agricultural extension county office and they'll scream bloody murder."

In the abstract, everyone is against waste, but one person's waste is another's means of survival. There is little agreement on precisely what is wasteful or unnecessary. Whether or not one concludes that aid to the farmers, Head Start programs, welfare assistance, aid for the arts and humanities, or funds for more neutron bombs are a waste *or* ought to be

[1]Allen Large, "Is Big Government a Phoney Issue?" *The Wall Street Journal* (April 15, 1976), p. 14. See also Robert Samuelson, "Good For Nothing Government." in Alan Shank, ed.. *American Politics, Policies and Priorities*, 2nd ed. (Holbrook Press, 1977), pp. 287–94.

top national priorities depends upon differences in political values. Still, campaign-year images of national bureaucracy are largely negative. At one and the same time we condemn the nation's civil servants for being ineffective clerks *and* for being too powerful. Below are two lists of the time-honored criticisms aimed at the federal bureaucracy:

Bureaucrats as Paper-Shuffling Clerks:
1. Timid and indecisive
2. Flabby, overpaid, and lazy
3. Ruled by inertia
4. Unimaginative
5. Devoted to rigid procedures
6. Slow to accept new ideas
7. Slow to abandon unsuccessful policies
8. Impersonal and lacking individualism
9. Red tape artists
10. On "one long coffee break"

Bureaucrats as the Real Power in Washington:
1. "A self-anointed elite in our nation's capital"
2. "An oppressive foreign power"
3. "The fourth branch of government"
4. "Intolerably meddlesome"
5. "A demanding giant"
6. "The permanent government"
7. "The Super-Bureaucrats wield vast power"
8. "They have enormous power to do great injury"
10. "Intrusive, arrogant empire-builders"

Bureaucrats at work at U.S. Bureau of Census (above) and Internal Revenue Service (below). One group is storing data; the other is disposing of excess mailing debris.

Plainly, there is a cultural hostility to bureaucracy. The "organization man" or "bureaucratic man" has never been a hero in America. The lone cowboy or individualist is the cultural hero for most of us and always has been. But it is possible too that we blame the bureaucrats today for being *ineffectual* on the one hand and apparently *too effective* at what they want to achieve on the other. These lists, of course, sum up our worst fears and the extremes of our hostility.

Much of the hostility toward bureaucrats is part of the larger anti-Washington sentiment that developed in the wake of the Vietnam War and Watergate. Citizens have lost some of their confidence in the national government to which they had turned so often in the past for the solution of pressing problems. Public opinion polls taken in the late 1970s suggest the public is tired of waiting for solutions. Nearly 60 percent say they believe the national government is unresponsive. An even higher percentage say that "those people in Washington can be trusted only some of the time."

Big government: how big?

When Jefferson was president, the federal government employed 2,120 persons—Indian commissioners, postmasters, collectors of customs, tax collectors, marshals, lighthouse keepers, and clerks. Today, by latest count, the president heads an executive branch of nearly 3 million civilians and well over 2 million military employees, who work in at least 2,000 units of federal administration.

It is widely assumed that the federal bureaucracy is growing at an alarming rate and by 1984 will control nearly every aspect of our lives. Figures can be presented that make the federal establishment appear as a mushrooming giant. For example:

1. In 1929, federal spending amounted to about 2.5 percent of the gross national product. Today, the federal share is about 20 percent of the GNP.
2. The estimated annual cost of federally mandated paperwork is about $40 billion.
3. In the last fifteen years or so, nearly 250 new federal agencies or bureaus have sprung into being, while less than two dozen have been disbanded.
4. The latest catalogue of federal domestic assistance programs lists some 1,025 different programs.
5. One company alone, Kaiser Aluminum and Chemical Corporation, submits at least 10,000 reports a year to all levels of government, costing about $5 million a year in labor and overhead costs. Eli Lilly and Co. reports that the costs of its government paperwork is about $15 million a year.[2]
6. The national government owns one-third of the nation's land—and nearly 50 percent of the land west of Denver, Colorado. The Department of Defense alone owns land equivalent to the size of the state of Virginia. The government holds title to more than 400,000 buildings that cost well over $90 billion. It pays more than $663 million a year for rent for another 54,000 buildings.
7. The national government today provides the cash for more than one-quarter of the total spending of state and local government, and this percentage is likely to increase in the coming years.

After digesting figures like these, no wonder people often conclude that the government is trying to do too many things, to make too many decisions, in too great detail, on too many subjects, for too many separate purposes. Soon people begin advocating "birth control" for bureaucracy and federal programs. Or, as the editor of *Science* magazine proposed, "Congress should adopt the procedure that before a new law could be enacted two existing ones must be repealed."[3]

Defenders of the federal bureaucracy—and there are some—counter by pointing out that despite all the talk of a bloated bureaucracy, the federal workforce has scarcely grown in the past thirty years. In 1946 there were 19 federal civil servants for every 1,000 Americans; now there are only 13. Those who defend the size of government also like to say the proportion of our economic output consumed or distributed by the national government has remained pretty much the same for the past twenty-five years or more. Thus, in 1952, the nation's budget amounted to 19 percent of the GNP. Nowadays, about 20 or 21 percent of the GNP is usually accounted for by the national government.

ARE GOVERNMENT
BUREAUCRACIES IMMORTAL?

We have all heard stories about government agencies being constantly created, but we virtually never hear of any being abolished. Unlike old soldiers, they never die and never fade away either.

Herbert Kaufman, a political scientist at the Brookings Institution, set out a few years ago to study whether any old government agencies ever do

[2]See Paul H. Weaver, "The Crusade Against Federal Paperwork Is a Paper Tiger," *Fortune* (November 1976), p. 118. See also "Paperwork Commission: Into High Gear," *Congressional Quarterly* (March 26, 1977), pp. 553–56.

[3]Philip H. Abelson, *Science* (December 24, 1976), p. 1379.

16–2
Several
yardsticks for
measuring the
growth of
government,
1949–76

	1949	1976	Percent change from 1949 to 1976
Dollar expenditures (in billions)			
Federal	41.3	390.6	845.7
State-local	18.0	185.0	927.3
Total	59.3	575.6	870.7
Public expenditures as a percent of GNP			
Federal	16.0	23.2	45
State-local	7.0	11.0	57.1
Total	23.0	34.2	48.7
Public sector employees (in millions)			
Federal	2.075	2.850	37.3
State-local	3.906	12.229	213.1
Total	5.981	15.079	152.1
Public sector employees per 1,000 population			
Federal	13.9	13.2	−5.1
State-local	26.1	56.8	117.6
Total	40.0	70.0	75.0
Public expenditures as a percent of GNP adjusted for price changes*			
Federal	17.6	22.8	29.5
State-local	9.3	10.9	17.2
Total	26.9	33.7	25.3
Tax burden for the middle income family†	1953	1975	From 1953 to 1975
as percent of income	11.8	22.7	92.4

*Expressed in 1972 dollars.
†$5,000 in 1953 and $14,000 on 1975, assuming all income was based on wages and salaries.
SOURCE: Advisory Commission on Intergovernmental Relations, *Intergovernmental Perspective* (Fall, 1976), p. 9.

die. He began by looking at 175 agencies in selected areas of the national government that existed in 1923 and then traced them for the next fifty years. All but 27 of them were alive and well in 1973. In the meantime, 246 new agencies had been created to work in these same areas, for a new total of 394. Kaufman found that death of a bureaucracy is the exception rather than the rule. Further, he discovered that the birth of new bureaucratic units continued apace regardless of whether a Democrat or a Republican occupied the White House. New bureaucracies seem to be encouraged either by sudden shifts in economic conditions or new international tensions or by a "built-in thrust that . . . assists the even finer division of labor in organizations."[4] Excessive workloads in existing agencies, pressure by groups who believe a new agency will be more sympathetic to their point of view, and a variety of societal change factors all work in the direction of creating more units of government.

[4]Herbert Kaufman, *Are Government Organizations Immortal?* (The Brookings Institution, 1976), p. 67. See also Carl Grafton, "The Creation of Federal Agencies," *Administration and Society* (November 1975), pp. 328–65.

Doubtless we often ask too much of our government and sometimes give it problems that are impossible to solve.[5] Senator Gary Hart (D., Col.) suggests we definitely have a problem with big government, but is is not simply a problem of size or spending or taxes:

> The central problem of big government springs from our attitudes and and expectations. The problem of big government is big promises that cannot be backed up by performance. The problem of big government is inflated expectations that generate disillusionment rather than hope and progress. The problem of big government is the myth that it can solve every problem and meet every challenge. The problem of big government, frankly, is the demand placed upon it by every interest group in our society.[6]

What about the red tape problem? One way to look at red tape is to see it as a hopeless tangle of rules and regulations that keep public servants from doing anything but stamping papers. Another way is to see it as countless rules and regulations that require public servants to act impartially. A student who is told by her dean that she cannot drop a course after eight weeks without a penalty except with a doctor's excuse is apt to complain about "red tape" and unfeeling bureaucrats. But the rule was adopted so that all students would be treated alike. The dean was not given discretion so that he could allow students he likes to drop the course, but not others. In other words, red tape stems in large part from our desire not to give public servants too much discretion and to hold them accountable. After all, they are spending other people's money. Red tape means following prescribed and established rules. Red tape can also mean the endless signing of names and finding excuses for inaction. In other words, one person's red tape is another's proper procedures.

The more complex problems of bureaucracy center around questions of whether governments, especially big national ones responsive to political pressures, are the best instruments for administering certain types of programs. Can a government, for example, allocate gasoline or other scarce resources through federal agencies, or should we allow the market mechanism to handle such matters? Is the problem that bureaucracies are not properly organized and that we can make them more efficient by better organization? Or is there something inherent in governmental processes that makes them inappropriate for certain functions? Do bureaucracies tend to represent special interests rather than the general public interests? These difficult questions are at the heart of much public and political discussion these days.

At the Federal Records Center in East Point, Georgia, workers use bicycles to get around the huge document storage facility.

The United States Civil Service: a brief history

Until the middle of the nineteenth century, the federal civil service was based mainly on the spoils system. To ensure responsive government, it was believed that a new president should be free to put his own followers into office. Besides, it was thought that government should not be that

---

[5]For an excellent general treatment of the growth and necessity of bureaucracy, see Anthony Downs, *Inside Bureaucracy* (Little, Brown, 1967), and Frances E. Rourke, *Bureaucracy, Politics and Public Policy*, 2nd ed. (Little, Brown, 1976).

[6]U.S. Senator Gary Hart, "Big Government: Real or Imaginary?" *Civil Service Journal* (July–September 1976), p. 19.

complicated, that almost anybody could do the job. Later in the nineteenth century, however, a sharp reaction set in against the spoils system. In response to a series of events, including the assassination of President James Garfield in 1881 by a disappointed office-seeker, Congress passed the Pendleton Act. This set up a merit system under a three-person bipartisan board, the Civil Service Commission.

Nowadays senior government administrators must work closely with the Civil Service Commission in staffing their agencies. With about 8,600 employees of its own, the commission acts as a central clearinghouse for recruiting, examining, and appointing government workers.[7] It advertises for new employees, prepares and administers oral and written examinations throughout the country, and makes up a register of names of those who pass the tests. When an agency wishes to employ a person, the commission certifies to it three names taken from the top of the appropriate register. The senior administrators have some voice in the type of examination given, and some freedom of choice among the three job applicants.

So far have we come from the spoils system that in 1939, through the Hatch Act, Congress made it illegal to dismiss non-policy-making federal officials (those below cabinet and sub-cabinet rank) for partisan reasons. More recently, the Supreme Court has declared that it is unconstitutional to dismiss a public employee for partisan reasons. At the same time Congress, while protecting federal civil servants from dismissal for political reasons, also placed restraints on their active participation in partisan politics.

The Hatch Act was also designed to neutralize the federal civil service. Federal employees may vote but may not take an active part in politics. The Supreme Court has ruled that such limitations are constitutional, but pressure to abolish or remove most of the restrictions on partisan action is growing. (Democrats tend to favor removing the limits because most federal employees appear to be Democrats. Republicans, of course, tend to oppose repeal.)

The Hatch Act was passed to ensure impartiality and integrity, and to protect federal bureaucrats from coercion or threats by their superiors.[8] Differences over whether the Hatch Act should be modified have touched off heated exchanges in the Congress, especially in the 94th and 95th Congresses. Those defending the Hatch Act usually contend that it protects career public servants against having to donate money to parties or candidates in order to retain their jobs. Other defenders fear the growing influence of the government employee unions and say that a weakened Hatch Act could encourage these unions to extort from Congress the right to strike and even greater pay raises and fringe benefits. Those who favor modifying the Hatch Act say it is unwise and unfair to isolate so many people from active involvement in the nation's political processes. The Hatch Act also applies to state government employees whose salaries are

---

[7]Standard treatments of the Civil Service Commission are Donald B. Harvey, *The Civil Service Commission* (Praeger, 1970); and John W. Macy, Jr., *Public Service: The Human Side of Government* (Harper & Row, 1971).

[8]For discussion of the Hatch Act, see Henry Rose, "A Critical Look at the Hatch Act," *Harvard Law Review*, 75 (1962); and John R. Bolton, *The Hatch Act: A Civil Libertarian Defense* (American Enterprise Institute, 1976).

Bureaucracy in action: the classical or textbook model

paid even in part with federal funds. And many states have passed "little Hatch Acts" to govern their own public employees in a similar manner.

Early in this century, several scholars developed a formal model of administration from which they derived certain principles: (1) *Unity of command.* Every officer should have a superior to whom he reports and from whom he takes orders. (2) *Chain of command.* There should be a firm line of authority running from the top down and of formal responsibility running from the bottom up. (3) *Line and staff.* The staff advises the executive but gives no commands, whereas the line has operating duties. (4) *Span of control.* A hierarchical structure should be established so that no individuals supervise more agencies directly than they can effectively handle. (5) *Decentralization.* Administrators should delegate decisions and responsibilities to lower levels.

Woodrow Wilson, while still a professor, adopted many of these views and argued too that *politics* and *policy administration* should be carefully separated. Leave politics to Congress and management to government administrators who would adhere to the laws as passed by Congress. Followers of the noted German sociologist Max Weber argued that a properly run bureaucracy could be a model of efficiency. Together with Weber's model, these textbook principles of public administration were thought to promote rational and impartial management.

According to the textbook model, bureaucrats should not have unlimited discretion in making independent judgments. They should be closely controlled by established rules and regulations. And this is generally true in reality. Administrators are not free to make any rules they wish or to decide disputes any way they please. Limitations are of several kinds:

1. The agencies interpret and enforce laws of Congress; if they misinterpret a statute, Congress can always amend it to make its intent clearer. The basic legislative power of Congress compels the agencies to identify the will of Congress and to interpret and apply laws as Congress would wish. Congress can also exercise this control through investigations, and especially through appropriations.
2. Congress has closely regulated the procedures to be followed by regulatory agencies. Under the Administrative Procedures Act of 1946, agencies must publicize their machinery and organization, must give advance information of proposed rules to interested persons, must allow such persons to present information and arguments, must allow parties appearing before the agency to be accompanied by counsel and to cross-examine witnesses.
3. Under certain conditions, final actions of agencies may be appealed to the courts.
4. Other federal agencies place limits on the administrator's activities, for example, the Office of Management and Budget and the General Accounting Office. In addition to reviewing an agency's budget requests annually in the name of the president, OMB has a management section to review management, organization, and practices on a more or less continuous basis. The GAO conducts audits of agency spending, and in recent years has moved into investigations of the effectiveness of alternative programs designed for similar ends.
5. Administrators are also surrounded by informal political checks. They must keep in mind the demands of professional ethics, the advice and criticism of experts, and the attitudes of Congress, the president, interest groups, political parties, private persons, and so on. In the long run, these safeguards are the most important of all.

© 1958 United Feature Syndicate

The textbook or **classical model** (sometimes also called the rational man approach) remains an influential ideal for those engaged in government administration. It describes a part of the reality of bureaucracy, but *only* a part. We need to emphasize here, however, that laws passed by Congress are not just important, they are central. Most scholars and practitioners agree that the more they see of the bureaucracy, the more impressed they become with the fact that the agencies and the career public servants are very much the creatures of the enabling laws they work under. So this model is also, in part, the reality.

The real bureaucracy

Today it seems naive to think that we can separate the administration of policy from *political conflicts* over what the policy should be. Congress could not possibly spell out exactly what needs to be done in every instance. Our political system is, as we have noted in earlier chapters, always marked by a fair amount of compromise and ambiguity. Put another way, we often can agree on something only by leaving the matter a little vague. Since this is so often the case, a considerable amount of discretion is often left to the thousands of senior bureaucrats who administer federal programs.

The power of bureaucrats and their involvement in the politics of national policy is a dominant fact of life in contemporary American politics. Public employees are always called upon for advice and policy judgments during the policy process. For example, suppose Congress passes a law setting federal standards for automobile safety and designates the Department of Transportation to carry out the program. But conflicts over standards—or politics—do not stop with the adoption of the law. Or a president announces that we are about to become "energy self-sufficient," and Congress creates a Department of Energy to carry out certain programs and appropriates funds. Politics—conflicts over who is to get what and who is to do what—do not stop. Of course the policy established by the Congress counts; it alters subsequent political conflict in profound ways. But political decisions still need to be made as the policy is applied to changing economic or environmental conditions. Hence certain political decisions are merely transferred or delegated from the legislators to the bureaucrats.

PRESSURES AND PROBLEMS

A federal administrator must understand what is expected by superiors, by fellow professionals, and by the dictates of conscience. Career administrators are in a good position to know when a program is not operating properly and what action is needed. But that career administrators often do not go out of their way to "make things better" is one of the major complaints about bureaucrats. The problem is that bureaucrats often learn by hard experience that they are more likely to get into trouble by attempting to improve programs than if they just do nothing. In fact, despite the charge of administrative aggressiveness, scholarly investigation indicates that the hardening of administrative arteries is more likely.

When administrators are aggressive, they probably seek to increase the size and scope of their agency. Often the fiercest battles in Washington are not over principles or programs but over territorial boundaries, personnel cuts, and fringe benefits. "Career officials come naturally to believe that the health of their organization is vital to the nation's security."[9] Admin-

[9]Morton Halperin, "Why Bureaucrats Play Games," *Foreign Policy* (May 1971). See also I. M. Destler, *Presidents, Bureaucrats, and Foreign Policy* (Princeton University Press, 1972).

istrators become more skillful at building political alliances to protect their organization than at building alliances to protect the programs the organization is supposed to administer.

Career government workers, like all those who work in complex organizations, tend to use the resources at their command on flashy programs, and to give priority to issues that help focus attention on their activities. We hear much of the Defense Department's efforts to "sell the Pentagon," but except for the sheer size of its efforts, it is not exceptional. All organizations, public and private, work to promote a favorable image.

Organizations, again public and private, also tend to resist change and to resent "outside" direction by the president or other "external" central controls. A department head, whether he works for the government, a large corporation, or a university, is likely to consider the president to be an outsider whose authority in matters affecting his or her bureau is always suspect.

ADMINISTRATORS AS POLITICAL ALLIANCE BUILDERS

In the real bureaucracy, career administrators often become intricately involved in politics. They often have more bargaining and alliance-building skills than the elected and appointed officials to whom they report. In one sense, agency leaders are at the center of action in Washington. Over time, administrative agencies come to resemble entrenched pressure groups in that they continually operate to advance *their* interests.

Career bureaucrats develop a keen sensitivity to the political pressures playing on their bureaus. The degree to which administrators become attorneys for their clientele varies with the policy area, with personality, and other circumstances. But many bureau chiefs no longer meekly submit to superiors, if they ever did. If they are not defending some specialized constituency, they are arguing that government should be helping the weak and the underprivileged. The picture of the bureaucrat as subservient and timid is therefore misleading. Their influence can be substantial: "Bureaucratic politics rather than party politics has become the dominant theatre of decision in the modern state."[10]

The bureau chief, then, is at the center of what has been described as a "subgovernment," "policy whirlpool," or "cozy little triangle"—the lines linking bureaucrats with key congressional committees and their staff and with their clientele groups.[11]

It is such alliances that cause bureaucracy's resistance to change and direction from appointed or elected political "superiors." A bureau chief's loyalty to his agency and programs often competes with loyalty to his administrative superiors. Some people view these external relations as a sort of administrative guerrilla warfare—and as a serious roadblock in the way of fulfilling electoral or party responsibility or of holding elected leaders to account. Others see merely an inevitable clash over values in a system that should provide ample opportunities for such clashes. After all, the bureaus themselves are merely one more forum for registering the many demands that make up the people's will.

[10]Rourke, *Bureaucracy, Politics and Public Policy*, p. 153.

[11]See Ernest Griffith, *Congress: Its Contemporary Role*, 3rd ed. (New York University Press, 1961); J. Leiper Freeman, *The Political Process*, rev. ed. (Doubleday, 1965); Douglass Cater, *Power in Washington* (Random House, 1964); Dorothy James, *The Contemporary Presidency* (Pegasus Books, 1969); and Carol Greenwald, *Group Power Lobbying and Public Policy* (Praeger, 1977), esp. chap. 9.

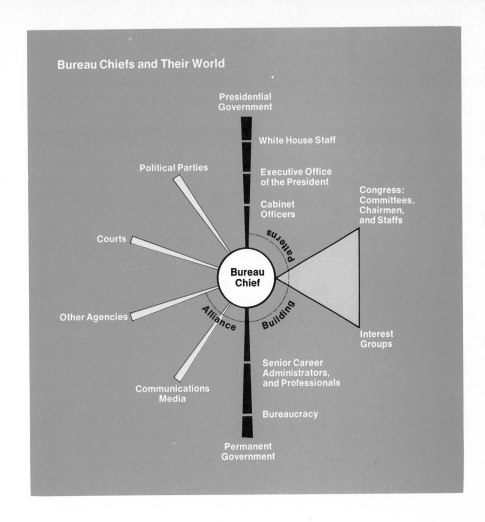

Bureau Chiefs and Their World

Members of Congress are also heavily involved. They pressure and cultivate bureau officials just as special interests nurture close ties with both Congress and bureau heads. Congress has control of agency budgets and the power to approve or deny requests for needed legislation. A bureau is especially careful to develop good relations with the members of the committees and subcommittees handling its legislation and appropriations, as is seen from the following exchanges at hearings:

OFFICIAL OF THE FISH AND WILDLIFE SERVICE: Last year at the hearings . . . you were quite interested in the aquarium there [the Senator's state], particularly in view of the centennial coming up. . . .

SENATOR MUNDT: That is right.

OFFICIAL: Rest assured we will try our best to have everything in order for the opening of that centennial.

SUBCOMMITTEE CHAIRMAN: I wrote you gentlemen . . . a polite letter about it . . . and no action was taken. . . . Now, Savannah may be unimportant to the Weather Bureau but it is important to me. . . .

WEATHER BUREAU OFFICIAL: I can almost commit ourselves to seeing to it that the Savannah weather report gets distribution in the north-eastern United States [source of tourists for the subcommittee chairman's district].[12]

Administrators in action: case studies

We have seen the complex of pressures and loyalties amid which bureaucrats must work. We have seen how they build alliances; sometimes they become so powerful that they defy presidents and Congress and seem to be little empires unto themselves.

The late J. Edgar Hoover, as chief of the FBI, was nominally subject to direction from the attorney general and the president of the United States. In fact, he was so popular with Congress and the public that he was practically immune from control. That immunity served the country well when he was able to defy President Nixon's requests for action that turned out to be designed to protect the Nixon administration from exposure of its wrongdoings. But how safe is it in a democracy for the head of the major policy agency to be so politically powerful that he can defy even the elected president?

Of course bureaucrats come in all shapes and sizes, with all kinds of political clout and alliances. Let's look at two case studies. One is real; the other is realistic but fictionalized here.

ADMIRAL RICKOVER'S NAVY

The career of Hyman G. Rickover points up the sharp limits on the authority of presidents and cabinet members over some bureaucrats. For about thirty years, Admiral Rickover has worked with powerful members of Congress to build a nuclear powered Navy, often in complete and open defiance of the chief of naval operations, the secretary of defense, and the president. In fact, he has outlasted thirteen secretaries of defense, thirteen secretaries of the navy, and at least ten chiefs of naval operations. He has lasted so long that today one of his protégés has become president of the United States. Yet Rickover is an admiral in the U. S. Navy and as such is presumably subject to the authority of many of those whom he has defied.

Time and again, Congress chose to listen to Rickover rather than Rickover's bureaucratic superiors, even when they had vigorous backing from various presidents.

On the face of it, there is something extraordinary about an engineer who is essentially an expert in nuclear propulsion playing such an important role in defense policy. Rickover, who has never held a major Navy command, has risen from captain to four-star admiral in two decades of doing exactly what he does now. On paper he is a bureaucrat whose two offices are so obscure that they are hard to find on government organization tables. As deputy commander of the nuclear power directorate in the Naval Sea Systems Command, and director of naval reactors in the Energy Research and Development Administration, Rickover has only about 250 employees in Washington plus another 100 or so in the field.

Through these two posts, Rickover, backed by a loyal band of powerful congressmen, has wrought an astounding transformation of our naval forces. Since the *Nautilus* sent its epic message ("Under way on nu-

President Carter and Admiral Rickover talk over the quality and condition of the navy fleet. Carter worked for Rickover in the 1950s; now Rickover "works" for Carter.

[12]Quoted in Aaron Wildavsky, *The Politics of the Budgetary Process*, 2nd ed. (Little, Brown, 1974), pp. 80, 81.

clear power") . . . Congress has entrusted Rickover with $27 billion to build what some Senators like to call "Rickover's Navy."[13]

Rickover's success stems from the unwavering support he has had from the members of the Armed Services Committees of both the House and the Senate and from members of the Joint Committee on Atomic Energy. "Rickover's skill at cultivating Congress — he works the hallways of congressional office buildings as assiduously as any lobbyist for a cause — has given his supporters on the Hill a sense that they also played a key role in creating the nuclear fleet.[14] He has been a frequent expert witness at congressional hearings and a notoriously tough manager with his employees. Part of his success is also due to the fact that his ships worked better than he promised.

GEORGE BROWN,
BUREAU CHIEF

The following fictional case, based on actual experiences, illustrates a more typical bureaucrat's existence. It also illustrates some of the painful choices bureaucrats may have to make, whether they are in Washington or in the field.

George Brown is chief of the Bureau of Erosion in the Department of Conservation. He is still in his early forties; his appointment to the post was a result of both ability and luck. When the old bureau chief retired, the president wanted to bring in a new chief from outside the agency, but influential members of Congress pressed for the selection of a former senator who had represented a farm state. As a compromise, Brown, then a division head, was promoted to bureau chief. A graduate of a Midwestern agricultural college, Brown is a career official in the federal service.

Early in March of Brown's second year in the new post, his boss, the secretary of conservation, summoned him and the other bureau heads to an important conference. The secretary informed the group that he had just attended a cabinet meeting in which the president, in order to fight inflation, had called on each department to effect at least a 10 percent cut in spending in the coming fiscal year. The president, the secretary reported, was convinced that there was a great popular demand for federal fiscal restraint.

Brown quickly calculated what this cutback would mean for his agency. For several years, the Bureau of Erosion had been spending about $90 million a year to help farmers protect their farmland. Could it get along on about $80 million, and where could savings be made? Returning to his office, Brown called a meeting of his personnel, budget, and management officials, and his four division chiefs. After several hours of discussion it was agreed that savings could be effected only by decreasing the scope of the program — which would involve ending the jobs of about 1,200 of the bureau's employees. He asked his subordinates to prepare a list of employees who were the least useful to the bureau. He would decide which to drop after checking with the affected congressmen.

---

[13]Juan Cameron, "Admiral Rickover's Final Battle," *Fortune* (November 1976), p. 193. For a critical view of Rickover's defiance of his superiors and his cozy relations with well-placed members of Congress, see Elmo R. Zumwalt, Jr., *On Watch: A Memoir* (Quadrangle, 1976), chap. 5.

[14]*Ibid.*, p. 200.

A few weeks later Mr. Brown presented an $80 million budget to Secretary Jones, who approved it and passed it along to the White House. The president then went over the figures in a conference with the director of the Office of Management and Budget, and a few weeks later the White House transmitted the budget for the whole executive department, incorporating the Erosion Bureau's $80 million, to Congress.

Meanwhile Brown was running into trouble. News of the proposed budget cut had leaked immediately to the personnel in the field. Nobody knew who would be dropped if the cut went through, and some officials were already looking around for other positions. Morale fell. Hearing of the cut, farmers' representatives in Washington notified local farm organizations throughout the country. Soon Brown began to receive letters asking that certain services be maintained. Members of the farm bloc in Congress were also becoming restless.

Shortly after the president's budget went to Congress, Representative Smith of Colorado asked Brown to see him. Smith was chairman of the Agriculture Subcommittee of the House Appropriations Committee and thus was a powerful factor in congressional treatment of the budget. Brown immediately went up to the Hill. Smith began talking in an urgent tone. He said that he had consulted his fellow subcommittee members, both Democrat and Republican, and they all agreed that the Erosion Bureau's cut must not go through. The farmers needed the usual $90 million and even more. They would practically rise up in arms if the program were reduced. Members of Congress from agricultural areas, Smith went on, were under tremendous pressure. Leaders of farm groups in Washington were mobilizing the farmers everywhere. Besides, Smith said, the president was unfair in cracking down on the farm program; he did not understand agricultural problems, and he failed to understand that programs designed to increase agricultural output were the best way to fight inflation. Besides, the cuts in federal programs should be made elsewhere.

Then Smith came to the point. Brown, he said, must vigorously oppose the budget cut. Hearings on appropriations would begin in a few days, and Brown as bureau chief would of course testify. At that time he must state that the cut would hurt the bureau and undermine its whole program. Brown would not have to volunteer this statement, Smith said. He could just respond to leading questions put by the committee members. Brown's testimony, he felt sure, would help clinch the argument against the cut because the committee would respect the judgment of the administrator closest to the problem.

Smith informed Brown that other bureaucrats were fighting to save their appropriations. Obviously, said Smith, they are counting on public reaction to get them an exemption from the 10 percent cutback. Brown would be foolish not to do the same.

Brown was in an embarassing position. He had submitted his estimates to the secretary of conservation and to the president, and it was his duty to back them up. An unwritten rule demanded, moreover, that agency heads defend budget estimates submitted to Congress, whatever their personal feelings might be. The president had appointed him to his position, and had a right to expect loyalty. On the other hand, he was on the spot with his own agency. The employees all expected their chief to look out for them. Brown had developed happy relations with "the field," and he squirmed at the thought of having to let more than a thousand employees go. What would they think when they heard him defend the cut? More important, he wanted to maintain friendly relations with the farmers, the farm organizations, and the farm bloc in Congress. Finally, Brown was committed to his program. He grasped its true importance, whereas the president's budget advisers were less likely to understand it. And he knew that his pet project—aid to rural poverty areas in Appalachia—would be most likely to be sacrificed because it was not supported by a powerful constituency.

Brown turned for advice to an old friend in the Office of Management and Budget. This friend urged him to defend the president's budget. He appealed to Brown's professional pride as an administrator and career servant. He reminded him that the chief executive must have control of the budget and that agency heads must subordinate their own interests to the executive program. He argued that the only way to stop inflation would be for all agencies to make program cuts. As for the employees to be dropped—well, that was part of the game. A lot of them could get jobs in defense agencies; civil service would protect their status. Anyway, they would understand Brown's position. In a parting shot he mentioned that the president had Brown in mind for bigger things.

The next day Brown had lunch with the senator, wise and experienced in Washington ways, who had helped him get his start in government. The senator was sympathetic. He understood Brown's problem, for many similar cases had arisen in the past. But there was no doubt about what Brown should do, the senator said. He should follow Representative Smith's plan, of course being as diplomatic as possible about it. This way he would protect his position with those who would be most important in the long run.

"After all," the senator said, "presidents come and go, parties rise and fall, but Smith and those other congressmen will be here a long time, and so will these farm organizations. They can do a lot for you in future years. And remember one other thing—these people are elected representatives of the people. Constitutionally, Congress has the power to spend money as it sees fit. Why should you object if they want to spend an extra few million?"

Leaving the Senate Office Building, Brown realized that his dilemma was worse than ever. The arguments on both sides were persuasive. He felt hopelessly divided in his loyalties and responsibilities. The president expected one thing of him. Congress (he was sure Smith reflected widespread feeling on Capitol Hill) expected another. As a career man and professional administrator, he sided with the president; as head of an agency, however, he wanted to protect his team. His future? Whatever decision he made, he was bound to alienate important people and interests. There was no way to compromise, because he would have to face a group of astute congressmen.

It was Brown's realization that the arguments in a sense canceled one another out that in the end helped him to make his decision. For he decided finally that the issue involved more than loyalties, ambitions, and programs. Ultimately it boiled down to two questions. First, to whom was he, Brown, legally and administratively responsible? Formally, of course, to the chief executive who appointed him and who was accountable to the people for the actions of the administration. And second, which course of action did he feel was better for the welfare of all the people? Looking at the question this way, he felt the president was right in asking for fiscal restraint. As a taxpayer and consumer himself, Brown knew of the strong sentiment for doing something about inflation. To be sure, Congress must make the final decision. But to make the decision, Brown reflected, Congress had to know the attitude of the administration, and the administration should speak with one voice for the majority of the people or it should not be speaking out at all. With mixed feelings, Brown decided to support the president. Being a seasoned alliance-builder, however, he hedged his bets somewhat. He came out strongly for the president's budget, but at the very same time he sent to friendly congressmen some questions to be asked of himself in future hearings, so that he might be able to give some hints of the impact of the cutbacks.

Who controls the bureaucrats?

The case studies we have just considered lead to three important generalizations:

1. Bureaucrats are people, not robots, and as people they are subject to many influences.
2. Bureaucrats do not respond merely to orders from the top but to a variety of motives stemming from their own personalities, formal and informal organization and communication, their political attitudes, their educational and professional background, and the political context in which they operate.
3. Bureaucrats are important in government. Some of them have tremendous discretion and make decisions of great significance. The cumulative effect of all their policies and actions on our daily lives is enormous.

Put these factors together and a crucial question arises. To which people should the bureaucrats be held accountable — the majority who elected the president, the majority as reflected by Congress, or the organized interests?

BUREAUCRATS AND THE POLITICAL SYSTEM

One school of thought is that the president should be placed clearly in charge, for he is responsive to the broadest constituency. The president, it is argued, must see that popular needs and expectations are converted into administrative action. If the nation votes for a conservative president who favors restricted intervention in the economy by federal agencies, that policy can be carried out only if the bureaucracy responds. Or if the electorate chooses a president who favors a more vigorous regulation of business, the majority's wishes can be translated into action only if the bureaucrats support the presidential policies.

Yet, as we have seen over and over again, under the American system of checks and balances a single political majority winning a presidential election does not acquire control of the national government, not even of the executive branch itself. For under our Constitution the president is not the undisputed master of the executive structure. Congress too has its say and wishes to keep it. Congress sets up the agencies, broadly determines their organization, provides money, and establishes the ground rules. Congress constantly reviews the activities of the bureaucrats by appropriations hearings, special investigations, or informal inquiry. And as we have seen, the Senate helps choose the people who run the agencies. Then, too, a presidential "mandate" is hard to apply directly to specialized issues.

Moreover, it is not Congress as a whole that shares the direction of the executive structure with the president. More accurately, it is individual members to whom Congress has delegated its authority. These people, primarily chairmen of committees, usually specialize in the appropriations and policies of a particular group of agencies—often the agencies serving constituents in their own districts. But some legislators stake out a claim over more general policies. The late Congressman Carl Vinson, for example, made the Navy Department his specialty. Members of Congress, who see presidents come and go, come to feel that they know more about agencies than the president does (and often they do). Although Congress as an institution may prefer to have the president in charge of the executive branch so it can hold him responsible for its operation, senior congressional leaders often prefer to seal off the agencies from presidential direction in order to maintain their own influence over public policy. Sometimes this is institutionalized—the Army chief of engineers, for example, is given authority by law to plan public works and report to Congress without going through the president.

Congress has deliberately decided that the independent regulatory agencies should not be under the president's control. Because these agencies make rules and decide disputes, Congress wants them to be arms of Congress. So in addition to making these commissions multiple in membership, Congress has given commissioners long and staggered terms. The president fills vacancies with the consent of the Senate, but Congress has restricted his right to remove the members of these quasi-legislative, quasi-judicial agencies.

Important as these institutional breaks in the president's chain of command are, they are only part of the picture. In addition, *political* checks block the president. Some of the agencies have so much support among interest groups and Congress that a president would hesitate to move against them. The U.S. Office of Education, for example, and the so-called clientele agencies such as the Law Enforcement Assistance Administration or the Veterans Administration have powerful backing.

Another important factor limits the extent of presidential control. Every day thousands of bureaucrats are involved in making thousands of decisions. The president has limited time, limited resources, and limited political influence. He and his staff can become involved only in matters of significant political interest. Members of Congress can operate in areas far from the presidential spotlight.

SOME ALTERNATIVES?

To many people, the federal administrative structure seems to be a self-defeating morass of contradictions. Sometimes it seems that virtually no one, anywhere, can establish priorities and exert leadership.

The president is often looked to as a counterweight to the otherwise powerful competing forces within the executive bureaucracy. But as we have seen, this is more of a wish than a reality. And presidential direction also presupposes that a president knows what he wants. Again, often as not, we are faced with a political rather than a technical problem. The same confusion and conflict within the country over values, ends, and priorities are likely to be reflected within the bureaucracy.

Blaming bureaucracy and damning bureaucrats for our troubles are not likely to make for more effective or responsive administration. Reforming the bureaucracy and the bureaucrats, another fashionable pastime, has led to a variety of proposals. Two deserve mention.

Some propose that we develop, along the English pattern, an *independent senior civil service* of career officials who would be moved from agency to agency in order to ensure that they develop no strong attachments to any particular agency. We have made some progress in this direction, but more than half of the senior civil servants serve most of their careers within one agency or bureau. Specialization is, of course, vital to modern organization. But rotation, some contend, would be a useful device. It might loosen up stiffened joints, bring new blood to agencies, encourage a sense of breadth rather than fixed routines. It might even break alliances among senior civil servants and outside client groups. "A profession of public administration, as distinct from a career with a specific agency, is vital to the proper centralization of a democratic administrative process."[15] But before Congress or presidents are likely to give much support to establishing an independent corps of civil servants, they will want a clear idea of what the creation of such a group might do to the power structures in our political system.

A second proposal goes to the very heart of the democratic process. It is concerned not with making bureaucrats more effective, but with ensuring that they are responsive to the electorate. The emphasis is upon *strengthening the political parties* as devices to link what the electorate wants done with what the federal administrative agencies do. As V. O. Key noted,

> The problem of bureaucracy is in part not a problem of bureaucracy at all. It is rather a question of attracting into party service an adequate supply of men competent to manage and control the bureaucracy from their posts as the transient but responsible heads of departments and agencies. . . . It is through such persons who owe their posts to the victorious party that popular control over government is maintained.[16]

Reorganizing the executive branch bureaucracy

As a presidential candidate, Jimmy Carter pledged, "It's time for us to take a new look at our government, to eliminate waste, to release our civil servants from bureaucratic chaos, to provide tough management." This has always been a good campaign theme and in the past other presidents have also announced that they were going to tackle the "bureaucracy problem." But meanwhile, the bureaucracy has continued to grow. There are hundreds of separate health programs, hundreds of separate education programs, and separate housing and transportation programs. Federal regulations today fill 60,000 pages in the *Federal Register*.

Expecting the bureaucracy to reform itself, said one observer, is like asking a whale to fly. From the days of FDR, conservatives and business groups have tended to attack big government (except the FBI and the military) as inefficient and as too much of an interference with the private sector. Liberals and union leaders, who until recently looked with favor upon big government, are not so sure about their views these days. Some liberals are now all too aware of the threat of big government to personal liberties, although they continue to support the basic functions of the national government. But even many liberals are questioning the effectiveness of large social service bureaucracies in easing poverty and welfare dependency.

---

[15]Theodore J. Lowi, *The End of Liberalism* (Norton, 1969), p. 304. See also Hugh Heclo, *A Government of Strangers: Executive Politics in Washington* (Brookings Institution, 1977), for a discussion of the relationship between political appointees and senior level bureaucrats and how they might be improved.

[16]V. O. Key, Jr., *Politics, Parties and Pressure Groups*, 5th ed. (Crowell, 1964), pp. 711–12.

"Now, all I hafta do is prune out all th' bad branches, without disturbin' any of th' good 'uns."

Haynie in *Louisville Courier-Journal.*

Back in the early 1970s, President Nixon proposed to Congress that it abolish seven departments (Labor, Commerce, Transportation, Agriculture, HEW, and Housing and Urban Development) and replace them with four new departments organized in broader categories such as natural resources, human resources, and economic development. Nixon argued that this restructured national bureaucracy could provide coherent planning, resolve interdepartmental conflicts, and deliver governmental services more efficiently.

Congress did not approve Nixon's recommendations. Spokesmen for particular departments opposed Nixon's reorganization (and remain likely to oppose any bold, sweeping reorganization that Carter will propose) because it threatened to lessen their influence. In any given field, the people in interest groups and in the bureaucracy have formed deep personal friendships. They have traded countless favors. And they have a durable alliance that cranks out legislation and assistance in behalf of projects they deem to be in "the public interest." Furthermore, congressional committee leaders are always sensitive to the fact that if they restructure the federal administration, they may have to reorganize their own committee system. This would upset the balance of power in Congress. In short, changing the shape of an administration is more than a matter of efficiency and economy. It also involves policy outcomes—who gets what, how, and why? The shape of the bureaucracy is both a cause and a consequence of political realities and public needs.

To gain control over the federal executive branch and make it work with the White House is both a crucial and a frustrating presidential responsibility. Because President Nixon's reorganization plans failed even to win serious consideration in Congress, the Nixon team employed a wide array of tactics to try to cut through entrenched programs and procedures and gain some measure of control over the bureaucracy. Thus they centralized more power in the White House, impounded program funds that were not in tune with the president's policies, and placed various White House aides in senior posts under cabinet members. Nixon apparently concluded that much of the day-to-day management of domestic programs — writing regulations, approving grants, and dividing up the budget in such major departments as HEW and HUD — actually involved important policy considerations. Therefore, these activities should be more directly under the control of the White House. An ironic aspect of all this was that Nixon was following the script generally prescribed by traditionally liberal advocates of strong presidential leadership, but for different policy ends.

Nixon's attempts in this area were short-lived, for he soon became swallowed up in Watergate and was forced to resign.[17]

Now it is President Carter's turn. Carter likes to portray himself as a manager, a planner, and a successful businessman. He boasts that in Georgia he helped to abolish 278 of the existing 300 agencies. "We developed and implemented," he says, "a remarkably effective system of zero base budgeting. We instituted tough performance auditing to insure proper conduct and efficient delivery of services."[18] Carter has emphasized that nothing as complex as the reorganization of the bureaucracy will be achieved overnight and that it would take at least a year or more to develop a blueprint for reorganization.

Almost a year after Carter took office, Washington is still full of skeptics about Carter's chances to change the shape of the bureaucracy. Most analysts agree that the federal government is unlikely to divest itself of major responsibilities. Even under Presidents Nixon and Ford, the trend was in the other direction. Government intervention in the nation's social and economic affairs has nearly always been dictated more by the needs of the time than by political campaign slogans. So long as President Carter remains an activist who wants government to respond to the problems of health care, urban blight, unemployment, environmental protection, and a variety of other problems, government involvement seems destined to grow.

ZERO-BASE BUDGETING AND SUNSET LAWS

What can be said of Carter's promise to bring about a leaner, more efficient, and more responsive government? In the abstract, he has considerable support. But it will be difficult for him to fulfill the promise. He seems to believe that his two chief tools are the zero-base budgeting technique and the so-called sunset laws.

Zero-base budgeting requires each bureau, agency, or department to justify each one of its functions every year and place them in order of priority. Ideally, according to this method, each department offers the president and the Office of Management and Budget a complete list of programs and priorities ranked in such a way that the weak programs are easily spotted for elimination. Critics say it may be naive to expect the bureaucracy to present an honest ranking of priorities. They will protect what they already have, perhaps by offering up essential functions as

---

[17]For a useful case study of Nixon's administrative strategies, see Richard P. Nathan, *The Plot That Failed: Nixon and the Administrative Presidency* (Wiley, 1975). See also Richard Rose, *Managing Presidential Objectives* (Free Press, 1976) for a study of the Nixon administration's efforts to introduce managerial techniques used in business to assess government programs.

[18]"Jimmy Carter on Bureaucracy and Government Inefficiency," statement released at the Democratic National Convention, New York, July 1976.

"low-priority items" in the knowledge these vital elements will not be cut. According to one story, for example, the Department of Interior might offer up the Washington Monument, one of its most popular and profitable projects, as a so-called low-priority item. Imagine the dilemma of the Carter staff trying to reduce the budget of Interior by cutting that "low-priority" item.

Defenders of ZBB, as zero-base budgeting is called, say that its main advantage is to examine those programs that generally escape scrutiny under traditional budget methods. The idea is to curb spending on government programs that have outlived their purpose. And Jimmy Carter has faith that what has been good for Georgia will be good for the country. "Zero-base budgeting has been well received in Georgia," says Carter. "It has become an important planning tool to insure that we are placing our priorities on the proper programs and are constantly seeking the maximum services for every state dollar."[19]

Sunset laws place government agencies or programs on limited life cycles, forcing them to justify their own existence every six or seven years or face abolition. Sunset laws have been passed in over a dozen states. Their chief purpose is to weed out ineffective programs and make room for new ones. The technique gets its name from a group in Colorado who proposed that the sun should set on programs that have outlived their original purpose or whose benefits are outweighed by other considerations. The burden would be on bureaucracies to perform well and prove themselves worthy of staying in business at the end of their targeted life of six years or so. Advocates of the sunset idea like to quote from former Supreme Court Justice William O. Douglas, who once said that "The great creative work of a federal agency must be done in the first decade of its existence if it is to be done at all. After that it is likely to become a prisoner of the bureaucracy."

Sunset is criticized by those who say that beneficiaries of programs seldom like to give up. Others say that the sunset idea is too simple for the complicated and subtle evaluation work that needs to be done. Still others argue that the sunset provisions would create more jobs and require enormous amounts of time and added paperwork from bureaucrats who will have to justify their existence every few years. Only time and experience will show whether Carter and Congress can achieve their goals with this new change.

INCREMENTALISM:
PROS AND CONS

Jimmy Carter's zero-base budgeting reminds many students of government of Lyndon Johnson's experiments with PPBS (Planning, Programming and Budgeting System) and Richard Nixon's MBO (Management By Objectives) notion. Both planning systems were an attempt to require agencies to specify more precisely their objectives—that is, program goals—and then to relate to these objectives the resources that were needed. But neither system made much of an impact in most governmental agencies, except perhaps in evaluation of a few weapons systems.

Most observers were skeptical of these two systems. They provided, it was said, a misleading impression of being "scientific" and gave an

[19]Jimmy Carter, "Planning a Budget from Zero," Jimmy Carter presidential campaign release, 1976, originally a speech delivered at the National Governors Conference, June 1974. See also Donald F. Haider, "Zero Base; Federal Style," *Public Administration Review* (July–August, 1977), pp. 400–407.

aura of quantification to what are basically qualitative issues. After more than a decade and a half of PPB and MBO, and prior to ZBB, planning and evaluation decisions in the government remain a patchwork. "We pass a law and let it go," laments Senator Hubert Humphrey. "It's a little like fathering a child and turning him over to the neighbors to raise, and not bothering to wonder how he's growing up."

A major challenge to the rational or systems-planning approach to decision-making is incrementalism. The incrementalists are people who question the idea that we can approach problems with definite objectives in mind and with a good sense of alternative ways of reaching those objectives. Individuals simply do not know enough about the alternatives. Their own goals and values are not clear enough, and the situations they face are too complex for a systematic approach. Rather, they are likely to go one step at a time, to feel their way, to cling to one familiar method rather than to consider carefully all other methods. The incrementalists say that they are merely being realistic, and that it is better to adjust and compromise with institutions than overturn them. Not only is this the way people *do* act, but this so-called muddling through approach is the way people *should* act if they wish to go about their affairs in a sensible and effective manner.[20]

Beyond the dispute between advocates of drastic reform strategies, such as ZBB and those who favor an incrementalist approach, is the concern that Congress does not pay sufficient attention to how its laws are implemented, and that it delegates too much authority to bureaucrats. It is charged that Congress, anxious whenever possible to avoid conflict, adopts such sweeping legislation and delegates so much authority to bureaucrats that they in effect have become the nation's lawgivers.

But could the Congress pass laws with very precise wording all the time? It would get too bogged down in the necessary details to complete its work. For example, imagine that Congress is concerned that there be enough truck lines in operation to ensure prompt tranportation service for shippers, but not so many as to lead to ruinous competition. If it attempted to specify the exact circumstances under which a new truck route should be licensed, the statute would have to read as follows:

> Keokuk, Iowa, needs four truck lines unless the new superhighway that they have been talking about for ten years gets built. Then they will need five unless, of course, Uncle Charlie's Speedy Express gets rid of its Model T and gets two tractors and vans. Then they will only need three as long as two freight trains a day also stop there.
>
> On the other hand, Smithville, Tennessee, needs eight truck lines unless. . . .[21]

Of course, Congress seldom writes laws like these. Instead, it declares its policy in general terms, and empowers the Interstate Commerce Commission to license new truck lines when such action would be warranted

[20]Examples of incrementalist thinking can be found in David Braybrooke and Charles E. Lindblom, *A Strategy of Decision* (Free Press, 1963); Charles E. Lindblom, *The Policy-Making Process* (Prentice-Hall, 1968); and Aaron Wildavsky, *The Politics of the Budgetary Process*, 2nd ed. (Little, Brown, 1974).

[21]Martin Shapiro, *The Supreme Court and Administrative Agencies* (Free Press, 1968), p. 4.

by "public convenience and necessity." The regulatory commissioners then judge the situation in Keokuk and Smithville, and make specific rules.

Still, Congress is under fire these days for encouraging the development of a bureaucratic state. People everywhere complain about overregulation, too many rules, too many incidents of governmental interference in their lives. Congress has gradually increased its efforts to limit administrative discretion. Yet the rules and regulations grow anyway. The executive and legislative branches will continue to have conflicting claims as will the bureaucrats among themselves, each insisting that the administrator act "in the public interest," but each with a different definition of that interest. *Defining the public interest is the crucial problem.*

Summary

1. We regularly condemn our bureaucracy and our bureaucrats, but we continue to turn to them to solve our toughest problems and to render more and better services. A survey of our bureaucratic agencies, then, is also a survey of how our political system has tried to identify many of our most important national goals.

2. The American bureaucracy is not, strictly speaking, organized according to the textbook model of management organization. This is because our bureaucracy is not fully subordinate to any branch of government. It has at least two immediate bosses—Congress and the president—and it must pay considerable attention as well to the courts and their rulings, and of course to the views of the well-organized interest groups. In many ways, the bureaucracy is a semi-independent force—a fourth branch of government—in Washington politics.

3. The debate and controversy over big government and big bureaucracy and how to reorganize it is likely to continue for several years before a resolution, if any, is found. Meanwhile, most analysts agree that the range and importance of the bureaucracy will expand and not contract in the years ahead. However, compared with other nations and their centralized bureaucracies, the hand of the bureaucracy probably rests more gently and less oppressively on Americans than on other peoples.

4. Who and how the government hires and what discretion or powers it grants its employees will always be a controversial topic. Still, to work in the career public service is often to have the opportunity to work on projects that offer countless ways to serve people, solve problems, and earn psychological satisfaction while trying to bring about a better society.

Chapter 17

Government by the People? Summary and Reappraisal

We have covered a great deal of ground in this book. Here let us try to summarize the essentials of "government by the people" and then return to the question, is it really government by the *people?*

The essence of our Constitution is that it both grants power to and withholds power from the national, state, and local governments. It does so in ingenious and effective ways. Fearing national weakness and popular disorder, the framers granted enough power to the national government to do its basic jobs, such as national defense and financial stability. Valuing above all the principle of individual liberty, the framers also wanted to protect the people from too much government. Believing in a representative republic, they proposed to make Congress and the presidency responsive to the people but not *too* responsive. How to achieve all these key aims, and some lesser ones, in a single instrument of government was the problem.

The first step was to distribute power among the three branches of government—legislative, executive, and judicial. The second step was to leave extensive authority with state and local governments. These two constitutional moves were nothing new, and the framers realized that they were not enough. All government officials, whether in the legislature, judiciary, or executive, whether in national, state, or local government, might join together to take away individual liberties. So the framers took a third step, the most brilliant and successful of all. Aware that officials always want to stay in office, the framers provided them with *different and competing constituencies* to satisfy. They also assumed that the constituents themselves would be divided—northerners vs. southerners, rich vs. poor, city people vs. country people. By their arrangement of offices, powers, and elections, the framers guaranteed that officials would compete and conflict with one another as they sought to please the voters.

The contrasting sizes of these two political parties reflect the wide variety of interest groups and individuals that a representative form of government must be responsive to: top, all five members of the Farmer-Labor Party met for a hearing on farm relief in 1933; (bottom) this 1923 meeting of the New Party packed the Philadelphia convention hall with members.

This does not sound like a very efficient system. But efficiency was not the main goal of the framers. They wanted a government that was *safe*, and only after that a government that would *work*. As the decades passed, however, the national government came under greater and greater pressure to perform effectively. The twentieth century in particular brought American involvement in vast global wars, depressions, and huge migrations of Europeans from abroad. There were also migrations of blacks and other rural people into northern cities; dramatic technological changes in transportation, communications, medicine, and education. Divided governments have trouble pulling themselves together, but the American experiment had even more trouble. It was too easy for leaders to "pass the buck." Certain arrangements also increased *minority* power: the filibuster in the Senate, for example, or the power of the Supreme Court to declare national or state laws unconstitutional. The power of organized minorities to obstruct sharpened the whole question of a representative republic. If leaders acting for a majority of the people could not act—could not pass a wages and hours law, for example, or obtain a constitutional amendment protecting the rights of women—was this really "government by the people?"

The pressure on government to *act* also produced changes, formal and informal, in our constitutional system. Americans tended to turn to whichever branch or level of government *could* act. Sometimes this was state government, more often it was national. Years ago, Congress was often the main seat of action, as in the great compromises between North and South over slavery before the Civil War. In this century people have tended to turn to the presidency for action. And men like Franklin Roosevelt, John Kennedy, and Lyndon Johnson were eager to respond. Soon we had an "imperial presidency" on our hands. More recently, the Supreme Court—the least democractic or "representative" of the three branches—has moved into the vacuum that surrounded such touchy issues as segregation, busing, abortion, and separation of church and state. The decisions of the Court may have been good or bad—but is this government by the *people?*

Through all these changes one great beacon has continued to shine—Americans' commitment to liberty. Often the beacon has flickered or even seemed to go out, as in the long tolerance of slavery; the suppression of the rights of blacks, women, and others; the inquisitions of Joe McCarthy. But always the light was renewed. Today our commitment to liberty is perhaps stronger than ever. But we define it differently. The Framers felt that individual liberty was a goal above all to be protected *against* government; today many feel that vital liberties or freedoms must be gained *through* government, in order to achieve another great goal, *equality.*

Liberty (or freedom) today means the right to a job, to a good education, to decent housing and medical care, not merely the ancient and basic liberties of speech and press and religion. As Franklin D. Roosevelt said, an *economic* bill of rights must supplement—and strengthen—the original one. This idea puts enormous burdens on government. It also intensifies the problem of how to protect the right of the great majority and at the same time the rights of minorities, who are also people.

Americans now want a government that is efficient and effective—that gets things done. We want to maintain our commitment to liberty or freedom. We want to achieve a large measure of equality. We want a government that acts for the majority but also protects minorities. We want to safeguard our nation in a world full of change and violence. Many Americans have profound doubts that our present government, with all its checks and balances, its dispersed power centers and power vacuums, is adequate. We live in an era of rising demand on resources and declining supply, of widening concepts of the rights of the poor, the elderly, women, and others. They fear that a social or political or economic elite, not the people as a whole, will run the system. Several types of fundamental change have been proposed to achieve an effective, representative, and safe system of representative government.[1] Let us examine these proposals.

Governmental reform

The framers, we noted, were far more interested in making government moderate and balanced and safe rather than *efficient* (though they wanted a more efficient set of leadership arrangements than those provided by the Articles of Confederation). But as the federal government took on more and more burdens, especially in this century, Americans have demanded that the government be made efficient and economical. Again and again commissions have been appointed, laws have been passed, and bureaus have been juggled around, in order to try to improve the president's management of the bureaucracy and ease the burden on the taxpayer. The reformers have been trying to unite administratively or governmentally what the framers tried to separate constitutionally.

In the immediately preceding chapters we have outlined how the Congress, the judiciary, and the executive attempt to reorganize and streamline their organizational processes to strengthen and renew themselves. Institutional reform and revitalization constantly take place as these institutions try to keep pace with changing policy demands and new political challenges.

Constitutional reform

Some Americans bent on strengthening the national government are skeptical about governmental reform. Reorganizing Congress or the presidency, shuffling bureaus around, centralizing power within the House or the Senate or the White House will do no good because they cannot overcome the fragmenting effect of the separation of powers and the checks and balances. What the framers carefully put apart in the new Constitution of 1787, these critics contend, cannot be put together except through *constitutional* reform. If we really want to make our government more effective and more democratic (that is, more directly representative of the mass of people), we must forget about tinkering and get down to fundamentals — *constitutional* fundamentals.

REFORMING THE ELECTORAL COLLEGE

One of the main targets of constitutional reformers worried about direct popular representation is the electoral college. We have seen (Chapter 11) that the electoral college distorts the representative process in choosing presidents. Critics argue that (1) small states and large "swing" states are overrepresented; (2) the winner-take-all aspect distorts equal representation of all voters and could elect a candidate who received fewer popular votes than his opponent; (3) electors could (and do) vote for some other

[1]On the historic commitments of Americans, and the conflict among them, see Robert A. Dahl, "On Removing Certain Impediments to Democracy in the United States," *Political Science Quarterly* (Spring 1977), pp. 1–20.

person than the candidate they were pledged to vote for; (4) if no candidate won a majority, the issue would be thrown into the House of Representatives. There each state delegation, no matter how large or small, would have one vote, thus distorting the representative process even further.

Defenders of the electoral college system say that opponents exaggerate the possible dangers, that the system has not broken down so far and probably never will. And if the electoral college is anti-popular or anti-majoritarian—so what? "The electoral college promotes unity and legitimacy by helping to generate majorities that are not narrow, geographically or ideologically, and by magnifying (as in 1960, 1968, 1976) narrow margins of victories in the popular vote," says George F. Will.[2]

The simplest and least drastic reform is to abolish the individual electors while retaining the winner-take-all method of counting the electoral vote. This proposal has never gotten very far, mainly because it does not deal with the main issue of "misrepresentation." Another reform proposal is the proportional plan, under which each candidate would receive the same proportion of the electoral vote of a state as he or she won of its popular vote; actual electors would be abolished. Thus if a candidate got one-third of the popular vote in a state having 12 electoral votes, he or she would win 4 electoral votes. Liberal Democrats fear that this proposal would increase the influence of rural, smalltown conservatives. Since the present system forces presidential candidates to fight especially hard for the big, urban states, many liberals feel that the president must be especially responsive to the needs and hopes of working-class, black, ethnic and other lower-income groups who make up the urban electorate.

The most important and controversial reform is direct popular election of the president. Presidents would be elected directly by the voters just as governors are; the electoral college and individual electors would be abolished. This kind of plan usually provides that if no candidate receives at least 40 percent of the total popular vote, a runoff election would be held between the two contenders with the most votes. The arguments for this plan are that it would give every voter the same weight in the presidential balloting, in accordance with the one person, one vote doctrine. The winner would take on more credibility or "legitimacy" because of his or her clean-cut popular victory. And of course the dangers and complications of the present electoral system would be replaced by a simple, visible, and decisive method. Opponents argue that the plan would require a national election system, thus further undermining federalism; that it would encourage naked, unrestrained majority rule and hence political extremism; and that the smaller states would be submerged and lose some of their present influence. Some fear also that the plan would make presidential campaigns more remote from the voters; candidates might stress television and give up their present forays into shopping centers and city malls.[3]

In 1977 President Carter recommended that Congress adopt a constitu-

[2]George F. Will, "Don't Fool With the Electoral College," *Newsweek*, April 4, 1977, p. 96.

[3]Neil R. Peirce, *The People's President* (Simon & Schuster, 1968) describes and advocates the direct-vote alternative. Nelson W. Polsby and Aaron B. Wildavsky, *Presidential Elections*, 4th ed. (Scribners, 1976) essentially favors the present system. Lawrence D. Longley and Alan G. Braun, *The Politics of the Electoral College Reform* (Yale University Press, 1972) is a comprehensive treatment.

tional amendment to provide for direct popular election of the president: "I do not recommend a Constitutional amendment lightly," he said. "I think the amendment process must be reserved for an issue of overriding governmental significance. But the method by which we elect our President is such an issue."[4] The battle was quickly joined. Two years later it seemed doubtful that, even if Congress (by the necessary two-thirds vote in each house) approved the amendment, the necessary three-fourths of the state legislatures would ratify this measure.

RECASTING THE CONSTITUTION

Reform of the electoral college, some critics say, would be only a small first step. They would rebuild the structure of our national government by recasting the Constitution. They would follow the strategy of the framers of the Constitution but "stand the Founding Fathers on their heads" by using constitutional change to *knit the government together.* Many proposals have been put forth over the years, but one by Rexford Tugwell, former New Deal brain-truster and governor of Puerto Rico, is especially interesting. His "model Constitution" would provide for a less powerful president, with a nine-year term; a vice-president in charge of internal affairs and another vice-president in charge of general affairs; a more powerful House of Representatives which, with strengthened leadership, would serve as the basic lawmaking branch; and an enlarged Senate composed of elder statesmen but with far less legislative power, much like the House of Lords in Great Britain.[5]

Other critics would go much farther and adopt parliamentary government. Under this form, the voters elect only a legislature at the national level, and the legislature in turn choose the prime minister, usually the head of the winning party. He or she then selects a cabinet from the rest of the party leadership and proceeds to run the country. The prime minister has a five-year term (in Britain) but may resign or be removed from office at any point during that term. Parliamentary government makes the long and often agonizing process of impeachment unnecessary. Indeed, if Richard Nixon had been prime minister, he would have had the opportunity to resign, call an election, take his case to the people, and let the voters decide. Of course, Watergate was an exceptional situation; but typically, when prime ministers run into trouble, there is a way for them either to leave office or to gain a fresh mandate from the people.

Thus the parliamentary form of government seems simple and fair. Why not adopt it in America? The easy answer to this question is that the American people, whatever their current disillusionment with the presidential (or better, presidential-congressional-judicial) form of government, simply are not dissatisfied enough to go through the long and complex process of so drastically changing the Constitution. But even if it were possible, most people doubt that parliamentary government would work here. It might give the United States the kind of "hair-trigger" government that caused weak and unstable regimes in Europe before World War II. Further, the parliamentary form, to be effective, depends on a relatively strong party system to make it work, and this is precisely what the United States lacks.

[4]Message to Congress, March 22, 1977, Office of the Vice-President, The White House, p. 8.

[5]Rexford G. Tugwell, *The Emerging Constitution* (Harper's Magazine Press, 1974); a less sweeping but equally thought-provoking argument for a new constitution is Charles M. Hardin, *Presidential Power and Accountability* (University of Chicago Press, 1974).

Political reform?

It is this final point—the absence of a strong party system—that troubles still another school of critics. They argue that *neither governmental nor constitutional reform* will make our political system stronger and more representative. The genius of the framers, they remind us, was not merely in the constitutional separation of powers; it was the *political* fragmenting of the new government. Leaders were divided by making them responsive to different constituencies. The solution must be to bring these leaders together politically, not just constitutionally.

That is precisely the job of the political party, these critics claim. One of the key results of the rise of the two-party system a century and half ago was a degree of "party government."[6] That is, a strong majority party, under the leadership of a strong national leader, might win a series of presidential elections, win control of both houses of Congress, and eventually win a majority in the Supreme Court. Because party leaders would be following a broadly similar philosophy, as reflected in the party platform, the national government would act in a somewhat unified way.

This is far different from what parties actually are today. As we have noted (Chapter 10), the parties have been declining in voter affiliation, organizational vitality, and influence on election outcomes. Parties have a much smaller role in pulling government together. They have a smaller part in recruiting leadership. Parties are no longer the center of action except during national conventions. Young people interested in issues are more likely to turn to groups such as Common Cause or environmental groups. Others concerned with issues look to interest groups like labor or veterans' or professional associations to carry the battle into Congress. Ambitious politicians today are more likely to attach themselves to widely known presidential candidates or other national figures. Candidate organizations and cause or interest group associations have replaced party organization at the grass roots.[7]

But for some, the decline of party means that: (1) Organized minorities will run the government, for the party system underlies majority rule, which is the key principle of democracy; (2) the national government will be divided among interest group pressures rather than unified by party principle and organization; (3) American politics will be dominated even more than it is now by the mass media, money, election technology, and "personalistic" candidates riding the television air waves and lacking real roots in local or state parties. These observers believe that democracy and the parties are so closely intertwined that the decline of parties quite simply means the decline of democracy in the United States.

[6]The classic work presenting the "party school" of government is E. E. Schattschneider, *Party Government* (Farrar and Rinehart, 1942).

[7]See Gerald M. Pomper, "The Decline of the Party in American Elections," *Political Science Quarterly* (Spring 1977), pp. 21–41.

Doonesbury

Efforts to revive American parties collide with two opposite tendencies. The first is the lack of support among Americans for parties as such. People may be strong Democrats or Republicans but still complain about "party politics" or "party hacks." Parties have rarely had a good press in America; at best they have been seen as necessary evils. So it is not surprising that many efforts to reform politics have ended up weakening the parties.[8] The direct primary took from the parties much of their control of the party label—that is, who could run as a Democrat or Republican—and thus of party influence over those elected to office. Civil service reformers took from the party its power over patronage. Recent campaign finance reforms have provided government subsidies directly to candidates and not to parties, for the most part.

The other great obstacle to party renewal has been recent reform efforts that have either bypassed the party or weakened it. The fact is that many of those who have become active in politics behind Barry Goldwater or Eugene McCarthy or George McGovern or Ronald Reagan or Jimmy Carter have not been especially interested in parties. They have been interested in *issues* and *candidates.* Hence their efforts have been devoted to winning office or reforming politics rather than renewing or "modernizing" the parties. Most of the reform efforts have centered on improving the ways in which presidential nominees are chosen in state primaries and caucuses and in national conventions. After decades of reforming the parties by weakening them, reformers have now turned to the last great citadel of national party strength, the national convention.

REFORMING THE NATIONAL CONVENTION

The national presidential convention has long been one of the most criticized parts of our election system, but the criticism has changed over the years. When the convention was the decisive stage in the nomination process, it was charged that candidates were picked by party bosses in smoke-filled rooms; that the state delegations were traded like chips on the gaming table; that the convention often came up with a compromise candidate who represented the dead level of party mediocrity. Defenders of the convention disagreed especially with this last criticism. They pointed to the caliber of men that conventions had brought before the country: Lincoln, Wilson, Al Smith, both Roosevelts, Willkie, Eisenhower, Kennedy. Such men not only made—or would have made—good presidents, but as proved representatives of the party consensus they would enjoy the support of a united party in the election campaign and in the White House.

Criticism of presidential conventions has declined in recent years, in part because conventions today rarely serve as key decision-making units. Presidential candidates now are mainly chosen in the state presidential primaries held before the convention meets; the convention ratifies the choice. Presidents running for reelection are almost automatically renominated by their parties; President Ford's defeat of Reagan took place in the earlier primaries rather than in the convention itself. In most other recent elections a strong contender has virtually "sewn up" the nomination well ahead of the convention. The convention merely ratifies the choice on the

[8]See Austin Ranney, *Curing the Mischiefs of Faction* (University of California Press, 1975), which also summarizes attitudes toward parties in the last century.

first, or at least very early, ballot. This was true of Kennedy in 1960, Goldwater in 1964, Nixon in 1968, McGovern in 1972, Carter in 1976.[9]

As the convention itself has declined in importance, attention has centered more on how delegates to the convention are chosen; that is, on the primaries and party meetings that decide the make-up of state delegations to the convention. Partly as a result of the ferment over the war in Vietnam, the 1960s produced debate and conflict over our political institutions, including the two big parties. During the early 1970s the momentum for reform peaked in the Democratic party under the leadership of Senator McGovern. Reformers were especially eager to open the party up to persons they felt had been prevented from playing their full role in the party—especially women, the young, and minority groups. In a bold move, it was decided in effect that state delegations must include such persons "in reasonable relation to the groups' presence in the population of the state." In some states this provision was interpreted in such a way that mandatory quotas were imposed. This became an explosive issue, for long-time Democratic leaders and union officials were kept off slates in favor of housewives, college students, and others who had had little experience in the party.

The conflict between reformers and regulars reached a climax in the 1972 convention in Miami. Established labor, black, and other group leaders looked on in helpless rage while the "new politics" dominated the convention. Following McGovern's defeat, the pendulum swung back against reform. There were no more mandatory quotas. But the push for reform was still strong. Instead of quotas, Democrats backed "affirmative action programs" under which state party officials were required to welcome and recruit women, young people, and minority group members into the party.[10] Winner-take-all presidential primaries were barred in favor of choosing most delegates in congressional districts, which had the practical result of producing split delegations. In many cases, these delegations gave their convention votes to several candidates. One result in 1976 was to produce delegations so divided that a form of proportional representation seemed in operation. Carter won in many states with pluralities, not majorities.

Republicans too have been reform-minded. They have taken steps to democratize internal procedures, to make governing organs more representative of the rank and file, to make party meetings more public and visible. For the Republicans, as for the Democrats, the thorniest issue has been how to open the party up to participation by more women, minority group members, youth, and poor persons.[11] But the Republicans have a special problem, which is the belief that the national leadership must not dictate to the state parties. This might be called "party federalism." The result is that the national committee can only recommend, not require,

[9]William R. Keech and Donald R. Matthews, *The Party's Choice* (Brookings, 1976), examines the impact of primaries on the convention decision in detail.

[10]On these and other aspects of Democratic convention reform see Denis G. Sullivan, Jeffrey L. Pressman, and F. Christopher Arterton, *Explorations in Convention Decision Making* (Freeman, 1976).

[11]Reform efforts in the Democratic and Republican parties are fully described in William J. Crotty, *Political Reform and the American Experiment* (Crowell, 1977), esp. chap. 8.

0

0

0

that lower party units ensure broader participation. The lingering impact of Watergate, however, and electoral setbacks in 1974 and 1976 indicated that reform would continue in the Republican party, unless it moved in radically new directions.

A NATIONAL PRESIDENTIAL PRIMARY?

But piecemeal reforms, in the view of some critics, will neither democratize the presidential nominating process nor strengthen the party system. The whole nominating process is too expensive, too complex, too long, and too exhausting for the candidates, they say. Some propose a sweeping change: a one-shot, nationwide, same-day presidential primary in each party, with a second runoff election if no candidate won 50 percent (in some proposals 40 percent) of the vote. This would be substituted for the present blend of state primaries, state conventions and caucuses, and national conventions. The national primary would be held around the beginning of September, the runoff (if one was necessary) around the beginning of October, and the general election at the usual time. Such a national primary would be simple, brief, and—above all—highly representative of the mass of voters.

The proposal has been criticized on the grounds that it would (1) favor wealthy candidates by enlarging the role of the mass media, since an enormous amount of money would be spent for advertising, especially television; (2) attract celebrities, like movie stars or religious leaders, who would attempt to convert their fame into presidential power; (3) typically require a runoff, with the result that voters would have to take part in *three* national elections in a row. The proposal would produce "low turnout, a confused voting public, little policy coherence, a tendency toward emphasizing demagogic and personal excesses, a lack of accountability by office-holders to organized party electorates, an undue emphasis on media influence, high personal expenses, and disorganized public relations-type campaigns," in Crotty's summary of the objections.[12]

A variation on the national primary is a proposal for a series of regional primaries. Candidates would run in clusters of states, beginning perhaps in the Northeast and moving to the South, the Midwest, the Plains States, and the Far West during spring and early summer of the presidential election year. The proposal has been criticized as having no advantages over the present system: the nominating process would still be long and expensive, and it would still require both state primaries and a national convention.

In his 1976 campaign for president, Ronald Reagan met with delegates to seek their support at the Republican National Convention.

Those who believe in party renewal more than reform are especially critical of the national primary. The great need, they contend, is to revitalize the party system, not purify it. They are pressing for three fundamental changes in party organization. The first is the renewal of the party caucus, not the boss-controlled caucus of the past but an open, participatory, and democratic "neighborhood" caucus. At such caucuses party members could debate issues, take positions on policy questions, and choose delegates to party caucuses or conventions. Any party member who wished could take part in the caucus, and everyone whether a grizzled party veteran or a college sophomore would have one vote. A second organizational change would be the strengthening of the party at the congressional district level, through better funding and staffing of the party headquarters for a congressional district. The congressional party could help its nomi-

[12]*Ibid.*, p. 229.

nee get elected, serve as a link between the party rank and file and the candidate (or member of the House), and exert pressure on the member if he or she strayed too far from the party platform.

The third organizational step might be the most decisive. This would be further strengthening of the party at the top. Already the office of the national party chairperson has been expanded to some degree; and the national party committees have been made somewhat more representative. The Republicans have established a kind of shadow cabinet to monitor the Carter administration and offer alternatives; the Democrats have held a midterm "charter conference" (see Chapter 10).[13] It is the future of the Democratic party midterm conference—and perhaps someday a Republican counterpart—that may be the best test of party renewal. The Democrats have scheduled a midterm conference for 1978. But will that conference be sufficiently independent of the Carter White House? Will it freely debate and decide on policy issues without undue pressure from the top Democratic leadership in White House and Congress? Will future Democratic midterm conferences be scheduled? These and other straws in the wind may indicate whether party renewal remains a real possibility.

Toward a new politics? leadership and disarray

At the opening of this chapter we summarized some key *constitutional* decisions and trends starting back in 1787. Remarkably, the Constitution of 1787 is still our Constitution of 1978. The various branches still cooperate and compete with one another—the president with Congress, the Senate and House with each other, the Supreme Court with the other two branches—just as the framers planned. Political developments have, of course, changed the constitutional system to some degree, but the structure stands essentially intact.

We will now summarize the major *political* trends of recent years. Note, however, that these trends seem to be changeable and unpredictable, compared with the constitutional structure. Party and public opinion and other political forces beat against the old structure, like storms and seas around an old castle, but the result seems to be more the disruption of the political forces than of the constitutional structure.

A POLITICS OF PERSONALITY?

Some recent key political developments are these:

1. A heightened interest in national issues, both the old bread and butter issues such as jobs and taxes, and the new social issues like crime, abortion, gun control.[14]
2. The continuing impact of the "new politics" of the last decade. That is, the entrance into the political arena of a large number of one-time "amateurs" who take strong positions on national issues, either on the left or the right, supporting candidates like Goldwater and McGovern.[15] These political amateurs include large numbers of college students and women.
3. A sharp rise in the number of "cause" groups, such as the Right to Life movement and the task forces led by Ralph Nader. Organized around compelling national is-

[13]On the 1974 charter conference, see Jeffrey L. Pressman, Denis G. Sullivan, and F. Christopher Arterton, "Cleavages, Decisions, and Legitimation: The Democrats' Mid-Term Conference, 1974," *Political Science Quarterly* (Spring 1976), pp. 89–107.

[14]Warren E. Miller and Teresa Levitin, *Leadership and Change* (Winthrop, 1976) treats the growth of issue voting; the second edition (1977) notes a drop in issue voting in 1976.

[15]Jeane Kirkpatrick, *The New Presidential Elite* (Russell Sage Foundation and Twentieth Century Fund, 1976) discusses the role of amateurs, especially in the 1972 presidential conventions.

During the early 1970s, the momentum for reform in choosing party delegates to attend the National Convention peaked in the Democratic party under the leadership of Senator George McGovern.

sues, these groups, along with traditional interest groups such as labor, business, and farmers, have invaded the policy-making process.

4. The spread of presidential primaries to more states, with the possibility that even more states will adopt such primaries by 1980. Some have contended that such wide use of the presidential primary will mean that we have to a great extent adopted the national primary, but through the back door.

5. A corresponding decline in political parties as organizations that can recruit candidates, mobilize voters in support of party nominees, integrate public policy making, and hold both their own leaders and opposition leaders responsible.

The sum total of these and other related trends, some observers fear, is a heavily *personalistic* politics dominated by media-projected celebrities. Television is suspected of shifting popular attention from issues to personalities, especially to the horserace between candidates.[16] Nationally known personalities with heavy financial backing can buy media space and time, election technology, large staffs, mailing lists, and firms specializing in massive telephone campaigns and promotional stunts. It is feared that a heavily personalistic politics might lead the way some day to would-be dictators and strongmen.

The politics of personality flowers in the context of a shifting, volatile, disorganized public opinion, and this was perhaps the most striking aspect of American politics in the 1970s. Public opinion analysts agreed that popular attitudes were in a state of disarray. The last few years, wrote Dawson, "have witnessed the rise of a growing disquiet, and even a sense of frustration, among many people. This disquiet has been associated with alterations in basic opinion relationships and with the breakup of some of the social and political coalitions that have given meaning and structure to political life over the past decades. There is a sense of change or pressure for change, but a lack of focus and structure to the various pressures. . . ."[17] Vietnam and Watergate have contributed heavily to this sense of a loss of direction.

NEW LEADERS, NEW PARTIES?

A key task of political parties is to provide some coherence and order to public opinion. Parties "aggregate" popular attitudes on the Right, Left, or Center and channel that support toward their nominees. Ideally parties sharpen alternatives, clarify choices, and stabilize opinion trends. This is precisely the role American parties have *not* been playing in recent years. In particular, neither major party has captured the loyalties of the young liberals and young conservatives who have entered the political arena.[18] Millions of people intensely involved in policy questions see no relation between issues and parties—or at least between issues and their own involvement in parties. Some complain that parties still divide over the old "boring" economic issues, not over the new "social" ones. Like the dinosaur of old, the two big parties have simply failed to adapt to a new environment. And no third party has risen to fill the gap.

Given such a fluid and frustrating situation, conditions might seem ripe for a realigning of the parties so that they would offer voters a meaningful

"Well, Senator, we've sharpened your image, and your recognition factor is way up. Unfortunately, they're all against you."

Drawing by Stevenson, © 1976. The New Yorker Magazine, Inc.

[16]See the symposium on "TV News and Politics," *The Wilson Quarterly* (Spring 1977), pp. 73–90.

[17]Richard E. Dawson, *Public Opinion and Contemporary Disarray* (Harper & Row, 1973), p. 3; see also Louis Harris, *The Anguish of Change* (Norton, 1973).

[18]Miller and Levitin, *Leadership and Change*, pp. 202ff.

choice on such issues as busing, law and order, and homosexual rights. Some people have proposed that American conservatives "form a new party that will replace the Republican party *in toto* as one of America's major parties."[19] Others hope that the GOP itself will become a clearly conservative party. Some liberals urge that the Democratic party become an explicitly liberal or even radical party. At critical times in the past, as in the Civil War period, the 1890s, and the 1930s, the two parties realigned the foundations of their support in the face of changing attitudes toward issues. Why not again in the 1980s?

Others are dubious about the prospects for party realignment. Many officeholding Democrats in 1976 and 1978 preferred to stick with the safe old economic issues on which they had won office for years. Many Republicans fear that their image as a party that protects the taxpayer and opposes big government will be blotted out if they bring in workers taking the "right" position on law and order but also favoring more social welfare and protection for labor. Still others fear that the two major parties will "decompose" or even die before they can be realigned. They note, for example, that Republican conservatives were not picking up party strength in the South — especially in state and local elections — even though strong southern support would be vital to the creation of a more conservative GOP.[20]

Americans tend to disagree about the need for stronger parties — and so do the authors of this book. Burns believes that we need stronger, more responsible leadership, and that strong parties provide foundation for such leadership.[21] Parties can give such leadership the support it needs in elections, legislatures, and bureaucracies. Peltason, however, doubts that the difference between "real" leaders and leaders who ignore what the people really want is all that clear. He believes, moreover, that whether or not our parties become better agencies for policy making will depend more on what happens in the workplace and schoolplace than in party circles or government offices. Party strength, in short, can be built only from the bottom up, not at the top. Cronin doubts that the parties will be revitalized by political leaders or anyone else. More likely, he expects, politicians will follow the lead of various interest groups or movements. Any change that does occur is likely to stem from civil rights, environmental, and other movements with causes, rather than from parties or party leaders.

AGAIN — ENDS AND MEANS

The debate over basic reform in the United States raises in acute form the issue of the differences between *principle* democrats and *process* democrats first discussed in Chapter 1. If the framers combined brilliantly the perspectives of both process and principle democrats, can Americans today equally well appreciate the linkage of ends and means in considering changes in the processes of democracy? The process democrat is willing to abide by constitutional procedures even when he loathes the result — for

[19]William A. Rusher, *The Making of the New Majority Party* (Sheed and Ward, 1975), p. xviii.

[20]On party realignment, see Everett Carll Ladd, Jr., with Charles D. Hadley, *Transformations of the American Party System* (Norton, 1975); Miller and Levitin, *Leadership and Change*, pp. 230ff; and the recent writings of Walter Dean Burnham.

[21]On the political and psychological foundations of leadership, see James MacGregor Burns, *Leadership* (Harper & Row, 1978).

example, the impeachment and removal of a president. The principle democrat believes that processes must always be tested against their actual consequences for the resolutions of short-term issues and immediate policy outcomes.

These conflicting views provide a useful test for democratic leadership. Is a leader a person who can override established processes in pursuit of some higher goal, who can withstand current majority feeling when he is convinced that that feeling violates fundamental democratic principles? Or does a leader try mainly to protect democratic processes? Can a leader do both?

Process democrats reason as follows: A governmental system should be tested basically on *how* it governs rather than on *what* it does. Does it protect the right of everyone to take part in the choice of policies and of leaders? Does it broadly represent the views of the people in what it does? Does it ensure that due procedure is observed in the enactment of policy — for example, that measures are fully debated in Congress and that citizens can challenge enacted measures in the courts? Process democrats may disapprove of the actions that result from all these due procedures. But they believe that in the long run that good procedures on the "input" side of government will lead to good policies on the "output" side.

Principle democrats reason as follows: Leaders must be concerned about the general welfare of the whole nation in the long run, not just the immediate interests of their constituents at any one time. Leaders must meet the test not only of current majorities but also of history. In the first decade of this century, not many Americans were concerned about conservation. But Theodore Roosevelt was, and we feel he acted responsibly in setting aside areas for recreation for all the generations that followed. Most Americans in 1941 were either isolationist or unaware of the menace of Hitlerism; Franklin Roosevelt acted on the basis of principle, not representation, when he prepared the country as much as possible for war. Vice-President Nixon wanted the United States to intervene to help the French in Indochina back in 1954; by the hindsight of history most feel that President Eisenhower did the right thing by not sending in the bombers. Various senators have recently been urging a substantial redistribution of income, though they have not felt much pressure for this policy from the poor in their states.

Process democrats are skeptical of all this. How does one know at the time where virtue lies, on whose side history (which, after all, is written by historians with all their own defects of vision) will be written? Was Herbert Hoover acting responsibly when he stuck to his principle of limited government action in the Depression, when many people wanted him to act? Did President Nixon act responsibly in ordering the secret, unauthorized bombings in Cambodia? Beware, say the process democrats, of sticking to your principles because you think you know better than the people and their current leaders who work through the usual processes of government. History has seen many examples of reactionary and revolutionary groups that have gained power under the banner of some grand doctrine but then come to believe that they know better than the people and end up imposing their will *on* the people.

Principle democrats concede the force of this point. But they insist that they are not talking about just *any* set of principles. A Joseph McCarthy might be wholly sincere in his inquisitorial and bullying tactics, but his "principles" would violate both the premises and the processes of American democracy. There must be some test of principle—some higher standard, some "public philosophy" in Walter Lippmann's term—against which the actions of leaders must be measured. The measuring rod must be the long-term, fundamental, deep-seated principles of a people. In the American case, there are the ideas of freedom, individual liberty, due process, fair representation, and equality of opportunity that have been spelled out in countless speeches and doctrines since the beginning of the republic. To be sure, these principles are hazy and often disregarded. But they are the only yardsticks we have for measuring what governments do.

Part Five

The Politics of National Policy

A Problem Guide

IN Part Five we come to what the national government actually does. Here we will reappraise the more important federal policy functions, ranging from decisions about defense weapons systems and SALT negotiations to taxation, consumer protection, and inflation. As we analyze policies and performance in these areas, we shall see that they raise anew many of the themes already explored in this book. Chapter 18 introduces the subject of policy-making processes and examines policy formation and implementation strategies.

In these times of crisis, can there really be a government by the people? Do the tasks now carried out by policy makers prove that democratic government is actually rule by the few rather than by the people as a whole? Do the complex operations of the federal government suggest that a democratic system cannot effectively perform the critical tasks of managing an industrial economy? That it cannot protect and enhance national resources, cope with the energy crisis, provide for an adequate and fair system of national health insurance? Chapters 21, 22, and 23 provide the factual background necessary for considering these charges.

Is our nearly two-hundred-year-old Constitution still viable in this age of international tensions and increasing world scarcities? The early 1970s witnessed heightened expectations for an era of detente, but more recently we hear mainly of the world population crisis, world food shortages, continuing energy and precious minerals shortages, and, of course, extreme inflation. Presidents seem to have the power to mobilize and manage our armed forces without getting the consent of the voters or even the consent of Congress—and sometimes without announcing their plans ahead of time. Under these new conditions, what happens to traditional constitutional processes of open debate and deliberative action? Does the unity of purpose and action required in an age of nuclear diplomacy make democratic processes obsolete? Or can new processes of foreign and military policy making be developed? What about the traditional supremacy of civilian over military leaders? What about the counterrevolutionary activities of the CIA? These are some of the problems addressed in Chapters 19 and 20.

Americans have always been quick to criticize their country's foreign policy, but no one seriously questions that foreign policy must be made by the national government. Even the most conservative critic has never urged that foreign affairs be turned over to business leaders, for example, or that the job of defending the country be turned over to state governments. But on domestic questions, people differ not only over what policies should be adopted, but also over whether government should act at all and, if so, which government. And if they agree that government should act, the dispute shifts to how far government should go and what kinds of control or procedure it should use.

What about the people—how do they get taken into account in the way our government functions? The increasing role of the national government in almost every aspect of our lives raises the basic question of whether big government narrows or enhances individual liberty and initiative. Are we more free today, or less? In our quest for greater equality and affirmative action do we risk a leveling down that may deprive us of creativity and individuality? And for whom does the national government perform its immense variety of tasks? Does it serve major needs of the people as a whole, or does it actually operate on behalf of well organized elite interests? Does federal regulation and taxation, supposedly undertaken for the general welfare, actually turn out to protect the industry or profession being regulated and taxed? Chapters 21, 22, and 23 investigate these and related questions.

What ensures that national policy makers will act responsibly? Those administering federal policies and programs have great power. In matters of foreign and defense policy, should officials be accountable to the people merely through elections, or is something else needed to prevent the abuse of power? Can the political system, as it is now designed, be made to work for underrepresented groups such as women, blacks, the elderly, and the poor? Do we need policy makers who are instructed by their parties as to what is to be done and how it should be done? Or should our governmental system allow our leaders more leeway to act quickly and comprehensively when such action is needed? This section will also treat how various interests, institutions, ideas, and individuals interrelate in the policy-making process. Does policy result from planning and rational analysis of all the alternatives? Or does it result from bargaining among individuals and groups to work out acceptable compromises? Or is policy the result of changing coalitions in which groups and individuals combine to give one group what it wants in return for what another group wants?

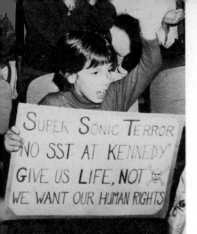

Chapter 18

Making Public Policy

The English playwright George Bernard Shaw once suggested that progress comes about because unreasonable people dream dreams of a different kind of world. Reasonable people, he observed, would adjust themselves to reality and merely cope as best they could. But the unreasonable people try to adapt the world to themselves. Thus when progress does come it is often due to the efforts of these unreasonable and often disagreeable people. Shaw's observation seems appropriate for looking at how important policy change is brought about in the United States.

The founding fathers were disagreeable persons, or so the British felt. Similarly, some of the major policy changes in the last half of the twentieth century have been begun by those unwilling to adjust themselves to the old ways of doing things. The civil rights movement, the women's movement, consumer protection activities, the ecology efforts, and the anti-Vietnam War protests all typify what Shaw was talking about. Policy change in the United States often has as its source persons who are impatient outsiders. Even the world of Washington policy makers is made up of all kinds of people—reasonable and unreasonable, smug and dissatisfied.

Public policy is the substance of what government does. This chapter will examine national public policy processes. The chapters that follow will examine the basic policy functions of the national government. We are interested here in how policy issues get placed on the public agenda. What are some of the major characteristics of our policy formulation, adoption, and implementation processes? We shall also give special attention to the role of interest groups, lobbyists, and public interest organizations. By *policy politics*, we refer to the way in which an issue of public policy is defined, discussed, and resolved.

Getting things done in Washington

Contests between the branches and often *within* the branches (House vs. Senate, cabinet officer vs. White House staff) capture our interest much as do sports events. We can identify with the side we want to win and then follow the contest to wait for a final outcome.

If we follow the way national policy is made as reported in the newspapers or on television, we rarely see behind bill-signing ceremonies, press conferences, or formal statements. And, very often, we mainly hear about the struggles and contests between the branches. Congress refuses to go along with the president. The courts overrule presidential impoundment of highway trust funds. Or the president vetoes a bill passed by Congress. These contests are of great news interest.

Washington journalism feeds on such contests because it makes for more interesting copy than the numerous cooperative and collaborative efforts to make policy. Box scores indicating how few of the president's legislative measures pass Congress often conceal as much as they reveal. They are helpful up to a point, but they do not really tell us why a president has not been successful. Neither do they tell us much about the quality of measures proposed, passed, and rejected. A president with an eye solely on the box score, for example, can avoid endorsing measures that are unlikely to pass. Moreover, the higher box score successes may be due more to rapidly increasing federal revenues than to presidential leadership with the Congress. But the box score approach to stories about the president and Congress is likely to remain popular because it helps simplify reporting.

Another example of this contest watching is the concern over the character of voting blocs within the Supreme Court. How many five-to-four decisions? Who are the judicial activists? Who are the practitioners of judicial restraint? And who are the swing voters?

THE ROLE OF EXPERTISE AND STAFF

Beneath and behind "the governing class," thousands of individuals are at work in the Washington policy-making process. They help resolve conflicts and facilitate cooperation *across* institutions. Only by understanding these people can we appreciate the patterns of national policy making.

Sometimes just being in the right place at the right time enables an individual to contribute to policy decisions. Usually, however, people who make a difference have formal positions or command needed knowledge, or both. Specialists from various professional communities are often looked to for advice in the early stages when policy makers are assigning relative importance to various competing issues. Thus, they are often in a strategic position to define what the issues are. It is, of course, also essential to be familiar with the rules of the Washington game.

Senior Congressional committee staff positions, which before 1946 were filled on a patronage basis, are increasingly filled on the basis of competence. The ability of these professional staffs to analyze information for hearings and legislation gives them considerable impact on policy making. They become a major center of communication that links Congress, executive branch, interest groups, and constituencies around the nation.[1]

[1] See, for example, Samuel C. Patterson, "The Professional Staff of Congressional Committees," *Administrative Science Quarterly* (March 1970), pp. 25ff. See also Michael J. Malbin, "Congressional Committee Staffs: Who's in Charge?" *The Public Interest* (Spring 1977), and David Price, *Who Makes the Laws: Creativity and Power in Senate Committees* (Schenkman, 1972).

Federal biomedical policy was remade in the 1960s by a small group of medical researchers, philanthropists, and members of Congress assisted by staffers both in Congress and the White House. Writers, academics, and professional entrepreneurs are often the catalysts for policy change: "The development of the Economic Opportunity Act, the Family Assistance Plan, the Safe Streets Act, the Tax Reform Act of 1969, the Model Cities Program, revenue-sharing, the TVA, . . . the National Traffic and Motor Vehicle Safety Act, and the Consumer Credit Protection Act ("truth-in-lending") all illustrate an essentially nonorganizational policy-development process."[2]

Some policy-making entrepreneurs are economists, lawyers, or scientists who have risen to positions of importance in government. Sometimes within a few years they can become strategic information brokers, knowing a vast amount about ongoing operations, actual practices, and plausible alternatives for change. They are likely to keep informed of professional developments in their disciplines, to meet with their counterparts in other departments and branches, and to maintain acquaintances in the trade associations and at the state level.

Washington is full of staff specialists who have served long periods within a policy area and in a variety of strategic government as well as nongovernment positions. The career ladders are neither tidy nor predictable. An economist at the OMB moves to the nongovernmental Brookings Institution and a few years later is back in government service within the Congressional Research Service. An aide to a senator goes to HEW and then back to elective state government positions. Later he returns to cabinet posts at HEW, Defense, and Justice, then becomes ambassador to Great Britain, again becomes a cabinet officer, and then once again becomes an ambassador. A young lawyer works in the office of the secretary at the Department of Defense, then joins the White House National Security Council Staff, leaves to become counsel for the Senate Armed Services Committee, three years later enters private practice in Washington, D.C., and three years later becomes Undersecretary of the Navy.[3]

These illustrations are by no means unusual. Mobility in Washington is extensive and career ladders diverse. As a result, complex networks of *friendships*, *influence*, and *loyalties* characterize the policy-making process.

One of the more fascinating aspects of Washington politics is the way in which policy activists in different branches of government, or associated with various nongovernmental organizations (such as research institutes, foundations, lobbyist units, or media), join forces in working alliances. Policy subsystems grow up around a set of interrelated issues, as much a response to the process of getting things done as to the issues. Age and formal position are less important than information, imagination, energy, and persistence. Policy activists learn how to capture support from members of Congress and senior White House aides. This, it turns out, is not difficult, for certain members of Congress and White House aides are always looking for new ideas with which to promote their careers.

Then, too, there is usually some newspaper or journal willing to provide a forum for debate of a new issue. There are countless opportunities for testifying at hearings, bringing suits in court, or convincing staff people

Some policy-makers, such as former Secretary of State Henry Kissinger, come from a group of highly educated economists, lawyers, or scientists.

[2]James Q. Wilson, *Political Organizations* (Basic Books, 1973), p. 331.

[3]These illustrations are real-life cases.

who serve cabinet or high Executive Office officials. There are many access points, or "cracks," in the larger political system.

Policy-making models

There are almost as many approaches used to study public policy making as there are political scientists who conduct research on our policy processes. Much depends on which policies are being studied or on the observer's political values. No matter how objective scholars try to be, the biases and assumptions they bring into a study usually influence what they find or conclude. Other differences come about because of the researcher's focus on only one stage of the policy process. There is a certain amount of agreement, however, about the various stages of the policy process — stages through which an issue gets attention and later becomes the subject of debate, deliberations and governmental action.

1. *Problem identification:* What is the problem? Does the government need to help out, intervene, regulate, or make some kind of decision? Should the issue or problem be placed on the agenda of government? For example, if air pollution somewhere is making people sick, is this a matter for governmental attention?

2. *Policy formulation:* What should be done? What are the alternatives that might help the government to alleviate the problem? Who should be involved in the planning and design of the policy? For example, if air pollution requires government action, what action is preferable? Should we ban automobiles and build or expand public transportation facilities, or merely tax those cars that are heavy polluters? Or invent and promote a car operated by electricity? Or, possibly, just inform the business community that they should somehow handle the matter themselves?

3. *Policy adoption:* What branch of government (or branches) need to act? What constitutional, legal, or political requirements must be met? How specific or how general must the decision be? For example, should Congress pass a clean air act, or should some regulatory body like the Environmental Protection Agency be asked to hold hearings on the matter and come up with recommendations? Or should this matter be one for presidential leadership — for the president to issue an executive order and give major addresses to the public?

4. *Policy implementation:* What is to be done, if anything, to carry out the policy? How much is to be spent where and how? How will the process of administration affect the policy? For example, should the government tax gasoline-guzzling automobiles on the basis of the more the guzzle the more the tax? Or should there be a price rise for gasoline in general? And what difference will it make to the policy goals?

5. *Policy evaluation:* How is the effectiveness or impact of the policy measured? Who evaluates the policy? What are the consequences of policy evaluation and congressional oversight of the policy? For example, are the antipollution laws really improving air quality? And are there demands for change or repeal of the antipollution regulations that arise out of evaluations of how they are working?[4]

Among the variety of approaches used to study policymaking in the United States are these: the rational man model, the power elite model, the bureaucratic politics model, the policy systems model, and the incrementalism or gradualist approach. These are not all the ways various people think the policy making system operates, but by examining them briefly we gain useful perspectives on how policy is shaped and made in the United States.

[4]See the helpful discussion of these and related questions in James E. Anderson, *Public Policy-Making* (Praeger, 1975), p. 26. See also Charles O. Jones, *An Introduction to the Study of Public Policy* (Wadsworth, 1970); and Richard I. Hofferbert, *The Study of Public Policy* (Bobbs-Merrill, 1974).

THE RATIONAL MAN MODEL

The rational man as policy maker tries to protect or maximize his own personal interests. This could also be said of the rational group. Groups are out to protect their interests and advance only those policies from which they will profit. The rational approach suggests *a calculating* strategy, with participants constantly asking what they will get out of government action or inaction, how much effort and time they should spend learning about the issues, and how much they might lose or gain by various actions of the government in response to an issue.

Faced with an issue, rational participants will first clarify their goals or objectives and rank them. They will then list all the important possible solutions and investigate the likely results of each. After considering each likely outcome, the persons then choose the policy with consequences most closely matching their goals.

THE POWER ELITE MODEL

The power elite approach to the study of policy making generally interprets what happens in the policy arena as the product of the political influence of powerful economic interests. They hold that we have a government of the rich, by the friends of the rich, and for the rich. If 5 percent of families in United States control 30 percent of the wealth, this is because our public policies favor the wealthy. If poverty programs seldom succeed in achieving their objectives, it is because the wealthy interests in the nation prefer these programs to be more symbolic than real.

The power elite school holds that we should study government *inaction* as much as government action. They claim that powerful business interests often are able to keep certain issues *off* the agenda of government. And these powerful interests generally do not want any kind of governmental interference in the economy unless they stand to gain from it. In short, the power elite school believes that there is a "ruling class" in America and that its influence and power are based upon the national corporate economy and the institutions that economy nourishes. Congress, presidents, and regulatory agencies are generally viewed as serving the interests of the powerful, monied class.

Critics of the power elite approach say that if researchers start with the assumption that elites account for policy changes or the lack of change, then they are likely to find evidence to support it. If you start, however, with the assumption that the policy process is far more complicated, then researchers will find evidence of a more complicated and subtle set of influences.

THE BUREAUCRATIC POLITICS MODEL

There is an older theory of American politics which holds that our politics and our public policies are the product of the struggle among *competing interest groups*. As groups gain and lose power, public policy will be changed in favor of those who are on top at the moment. But more recently scholars have concluded that this theory overstates the role of outside interest groups and underestimates the role of public bureaucracies. So they now suggest that what needs to be studied is the relative power and the political strategies of the large bureaucracies in Washington. What bureaucracy one belongs to will determine one's policy views, they claim. This approach contends also that standard operating procedures, and concern for larger budgets and expanding mission, all affect the information a bureaucracy will present to a president and to Congress. These same factors will also affect the way the policies are implemented.

This approach recommends that students of public policy give very close attention to the way the bureaucracy functions and the way bureaucrats become involved in the various stages of the policy process. We will be able to understand and explain policy outcomes, they say, only with a detailed understanding of the power of these bureaucracies and how they clash among themselves over different policy objectives.

THE POLICY SYSTEMS APPROACH

A more ambitious but more general approach to the study of policy making is offered by those who want to place all the factors and all the stages of the process into a *systems* framework. They claim that everything is interrelated and that a full understanding of how policies are made or changed can only come from a comprehensive look at these relationships. Borrowing from engineering and biological models, these researchers examine the "inputs" of the policy system and stress the way the policy process translates inputs into outputs and then how the *outputs*—the initial beginnings and programs—get converted into policy *outcomes*, or the results of the policy.

The diagram shown below conveys much of the policy systems approach. Note that the feedback and interaction loop linking policy outcomes with the other aspects of the system implies that policy results, and how the public reacts to the results, will in turn affect the future of this and other policies.

INCREMENTALIST MODEL

Incrementalism is an approach that suggests there is no single right answer for a given problem, but that various gradual adjustments need to be tried to deal with it. Unlike the rational man model, the incrementalist model suggests that only some of the alternatives are examined. More attention is devoted to seeking mutual agreement about what small steps can be taken than to finding a single, comprehensive answer. Our system of separation of powers and dispersal of authority promotes piecemeal

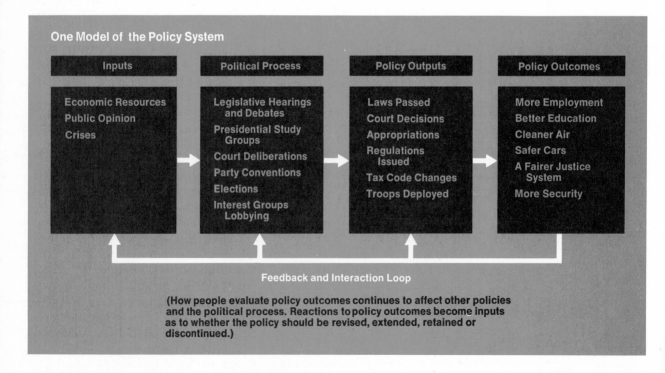

One Model of the Policy System

Inputs	Political Process	Policy Outputs	Policy Outcomes
Economic Resources	Legislative Hearings and Debates	Laws Passed	More Employment
Public Opinion	Presidential Study Groups	Court Decisions	Better Education
Crises	Court Deliberations	Appropriations	Cleaner Air
	Party Conventions	Regulations Issued	Safer Cars
	Elections	Tax Code Changes	A Fairer Justice System
	Interest Groups Lobbying	Troops Deployed	More Security

Feedback and Interaction Loop

(How people evaluate policy outcomes continues to affect other policies and the political process. Reactions to policy outcomes become inputs as to whether the policy should be revised, extended, retained or discontinued.)

policy change. Planning comprehensively is difficult in a system such as ours, which is glued together with alliance politics, majorities of the moment, and constant compromising.

Thinking comprehensively, however, is not impossible in our system. The problem is that in order to get something done and enforced, it takes the approval of lots of different and often differing people. As we develop consensus, there is much compromising and bargaining. The democratic process makes comprehensive and integrated action more difficult than in nondemocratic systems like the Soviet Union. Action in our society is especially difficult, compared with small countries such as Sweden, where there is a more homogeneous population and hence usually a broader consensus. We have to get by so many different veto groups that the policy proposals which result are almost always different from what the sponsors desired.

Policy makers bend over backwards to design programs in such a way as to cultivate interest-group support and to neutralize possible opponents. This results, not surprisingly, in watered-down objectives and laws that are extremely general and vague. To be sure, laws often are complex and detailed; yet they are deliberately written to permit discretionary interpretation. And objectives are seldom spelled out clearly.

There is also the fact that in a democracy political leaders are not likely to be risk takers and to call on the people to sacrifice today in order to avoid some problem decades from now. We don't do much about a fuel crisis until we run out of gasoline, or don't do much about air pollution until people start coughing and choking. But then again, as we look around the world, other nations are not doing much better at solving long-range problems either. All industrial nations have nearly the same problems; and even the old standard we measured ourselves against, England, with its disciplined parties, no separation of powers, and concentration of responsibility, is not making much progress with inflation or pollution or race (and religious) relations. In recent years there has been a growing recognition that direct governmental intervention in the form of command and control approach is not the only way to intervene or even the best and that modifying or using the market approach may often be more effective. Thus for pollution control we can either have the Environmental Protection Agency adopt rules and regulations for the hundreds of thousands of different businesses or we can make adjustments in the tax system or in the market system to give industries an economic incentive to avoid pollution.

The move to decentralize authority to states and localities also fosters incrementalism. With such strategies, Washington officials are in effect saying, "Let local elites decide what is proper policy in their locality. Let us not interfere." Some people argue, and they are partly correct, that efficiency and promoting a smaller federal bureaucracy are the prime motivations. But decentralization and "disaggregation" (dividing up policy making into fragmented, functional units) are also a means of getting Congress and federal bureaucrats to give up their power over federal funds. Thus, local policy making is still another way for Washington officials to make people happy. Yet it is often at the expense of national objectives, comprehensive planning, swift action.

Policy-making processes in democratic countries are, except in matters of foreign relations, rarely insulated from localism. Our party system and popular values concentrate power at the state and local levels. Numerous case studies document how our structural arrangements of government in general are better suited to protect the local status quo than to force unpopular activities or controls on local governments. Even when the national government is quite unified in its views, localities are often able to delay or greatly modify federal policies by local administrative manipulations.[5]

From past experience it seems that politicians count on a little real or symbolic change to satisfy the demands of most people. The very exercise of working on some new plan or legislating some additional initiative takes the edge off public alarm. "Don't just stand there: Do Something!" But the *something* does not have to be very much. And even radical actions by one set of policy makers can be restrained or pared back elsewhere in the system. This is the essence of incrementalism. Critics yearn for a better way to get things done. Defenders of incrementalism suggest that it is not a policy choice, but a fact of life.

Most of these models for studying policy making have some evidence to back them up, but it seems obvious that no single approach will explain everything. Perhaps it is best to borrow from several of them to help explain how our policies are made. By and large, then, policies are shaped by a combination of events, the availability of resources, past experience, and the ideas of concerned public officials and activist citizens. Elections, public opinion, and the competition among groups and bureaucracies, as well as the struggles among the branches of government, all become involved in the way policies are defined and settled. We now turn to a more detailed examination of what takes place in some of the key stages of the policy-making process.

Policy formulation

Who sets the agenda for national policy making? Policy is certainly not formulated in a vacuum. Organized interests representing varied points of view press claims and counterclaims. Some groups and persons clearly enjoy more access, most opportunities to get their cases heard, and more possibilities for vetoing measures that would hurt their interests. Still, why some issues become national controversies and others do not is unpredictable.

Some issues are given considerable attention, others are slow to win it, and still others seem victims of neglect. Some critics hold that "The most significant fact about the distribution of power in America is not who makes such decisions as are made, but rather how many matters of the greatest social importance are not the objects of anyone's decision at all."[6] That is, matters of great importance to some people sometimes do not get on the public agenda.

When government is inactive in some area, however, it does not mean it is without a policy in that area. Undeveloped or even unconscious though it may seem *inaction is still a policy.* Inattention to issues can be as important as decisive governmental action. Indifference to racial or sexual discrimination clearly was policy—very important policy for those affected by it.

[5]Gary Orfield, *The Reconstruction of Southern Education* (Wiley, 1969), p. 356.

[6]Robert Paul Wolff, *The Poverty of Liberalism* (Beacon Press, 1968), p. 118. See also M. A. Crenson, *The Un-Politics of Air Pollution* (Johns Hopkins Press, 1971); and Peter Bachrach and Morton S. Baratz, "Decisions and Nondecisions: An Analytical Framework," *American Political Science Review* (September 1963), pp. 632–42.

A former White House domestic advisor, Daniel P. Moynihan, once called for a policy of "benign neglect" toward minority problems, not because he was indifferent to racial discrimination, but rather because he felt that less governmental assertiveness was a better way to handle discrimination problems. Hence, we must distinguish between the instances when there is a plain lack of national attention to certain problems and those when the indifference is the result of a policy decision. Thus in the South for many decades the government did nothing about racial segregation, but the policy surely received plenty of attention. In short, everything has political consequences, including doing nothing.

SHARED LEADERSHIP

Inaction by some policy makers often forces an issue to another part of the political system. All three branches of the national government as well as the bureaucracy, media, and interest groups seem to take turns initiating public policy changes: The Supreme Court's *Brown* v. *Board of Education*[7] (1954) is a classic example of a landmark civil rights and education policy decision with implications for the other components of the political system. This same court decision was itself the result of a variety of economic, social, and political changes in the country; and it in turn triggered actions and reactions that ricocheted back on the Court.

One of the virtues of our separation of powers is that when things get clogged in one part of the system, a safety valve can often be found elsewhere. The safety valve is sometimes found in the courts, sometimes in a president, sometimes in the regulatory agencies. Groups pressing for policy changes will seek to exert influence where they are most likely to succeed. If you have large sums of money to contribute to a political campaign, you are more likely to have influence with Congress and the presidency than with the courts. If you lack funds and a large political base, you may find it more effective to resort to litigation. The NAACP, for example, has won numerous cases in its long-term efforts to improve the legal protection of blacks. Litigation is also now a standard weapon in the arsenal of community groups working for reform. Public-interest groups have gone to court frequently seeking to gain compliance with laws already on the books.

The president delegates policy-making power to various cabinet members and administrators, such as those shown here: top, Commerce Secretary Juanita Kreps and Labor Secretary F. Ray Marshall testify before the Joint Economic Committee; bottom, National Security Advisor Zbigniew Brzezinski, left, hosts Israeli Prime Minister Begin in Washington.

Just as Congress delegates extensive legislative power to the president, so he delegates policy-making power to administrators down the line. Obviously, a secretary of state can have a distinct influence on policy, as do other department heads and bureau, division, and section chiefs. In a sense, there is no level in the administrative hierarchy at which discretion ends. At any time the most routine matter may be called to the public's attention, perhaps by a newspaper columnist or a member of Congress. Then the matter will be given consideration by a bureau or department chief—perhaps even by the White House.

In short, there are thousands of people throughout the government (and millions more such as editors, lobbyists, and activist citizens, outside) who exert direct pressure on legislators, legislation, and policy. Control of legislation cannot be diagramed neatly. We find, instead, a president and Congress cooperating on some matters, fighting over others, and both influencing—and being influenced by—administrators throughout the government and political forces outside.

[7]347 U.S. 483 (1954).

Presidents share policy-making power not only with Congress but also with administrators in the executive branch. The extent to which presidents wield legislative power turns not only on their formal constitutional position and powers but also on their political position and powers. How effective is a president in appealing to the public? How good is his timing? How active and articulate are his lieutenants—his cabinet members and key agency heads? How close are his relations with congressional leaders? Can he mobilize public opinion? Does his influence reach into states and districts throughout the country? Does his party control Congress? Is the country in a depression?

Obviously a president's power turns to a great extent on his public prestige and standing. But in the daily task of getting things done in Washington, his effectiveness turns also on his professional reputation. Because the president's power, and his use of it, is customarily the most important single influence in Washington, these professionals watch him closely. Does he carry through on his promises? Does he reward those who help him and punish those who do not? How well does he bargain with other power centers? To what extent, in short, is he on top of the struggle for power, or submerged in it, or remote from it? The president's political skill and his political power are interrelated; Washington politicians must anticipate as best they can his ability and will to make the most of the advantages he has. Out of what others think of him and his power come his opportunities for influence with them.[8]

THE ISSUE-ATTENTION CYCLE

The span of the public's attention is short. Shifting public moods and the publicity needs of elected officials encourage the adoption of new policies rather than restructuring of existing policies. To rally support for a new program is easier than to cut back on-going programs. Too many beneficiaries, both the target of the programs and those who administer them, will usually fight any changes in programs already on the books. Thus, reworking or even rethinking old programs becomes subordinate to what might be called an "add-on" approach to public policy making.

In Anthony Downs' words, "Each of these new problems suddenly leaps into prominence, remains there for a short time, and then—though still largely unresolved—generally fades from the center of public attention."[9] Public boredom, he suggests, often sets in when large numbers of people realize the cost of solving the underlying problem would be very high indeed. (Perhaps boredom is the most underrated force in history.)

Policy makers, especially those in a democracy, do not like to make anybody mad if they can help it. There is not much point to losing votes. Therefore, they would rather enlarge the size of the national economic pie and give new groups funds without having to take them from old groups—that is, to increase the pie rather than to redistribute it. Like fathers and mothers and university administrators, anybody who has the responsibility for allocating scarce resources would rather make everybody happy than take allowance back from one child and give it to another, or take funds from one university department and redistribute them to another. The more likely the electorate is to have some way of controlling

---

[8]Richard E. Neustadt, *Presidential Power* (Wiley, 1976), Chap. 3.

[9]Anthony Downs, "Up and Down with Ecology—The Issue-Attention Cycle," *The Public Interest* (Summer 1972), p. 38.

those who govern, the more likely those who govern are going to be sensitive to these matters. But if the group that is presently getting "the short end of the stick" lacks political clout, it is likely not to get its fair share of the economic goods of the society.

Washington lobbyists and policy adoption politics

Lobbying is an old weapon. Generations of Americans have been stirred by exposés of the "invisible government." Indeed the very term "lobby" is a carryover from the days when representatives of economic interest groups stationed themselves in the hallway or entranceway of the state legislatures to request favors. From the time of the land frauds 180 years ago, when a whole legislature was bribed and the postmaster general was put on a private payroll as a lobbyist, to the milk scandals in the Nixon Administration or the Tongsun Park "influence buying" scandal of 1977, Americans have been periodically outraged at lobbyists.

Thousands of lobbyists are active in Washington today, but few of them are glamorous, unscrupulous, or very powerful. Most of the organizations maintaining lobbyists are highly specialized, such as the National Fertilizer Association, the Retired Officers Association, and the Institute of Shortening and Edible Oils. Lobbyists for these associations are often attorneys whose job is to watch a handful of bills and to keep in touch with a few administrative officials. Because lawmaking today is a highly technical matter, these lobbyists — or legislative counsels, as they like to be called — play a useful part in modern government. The harried congressman or administrator, threading his way through mountains of paper and seeking to appease conflicting interests, gladly turns to them for their views and information.[10]

Lobbyists for well-financed economic interests operate on a bigger scale. Their specialty is knowing just how to throw their political weight around. These lobbyists are better known throughout the country than some legislators, better paid, better staffed, and more secure in their position. Some of them are former members of Congress. The groups they represent have such broad interests that lobbyists must watch a wide variety of bills and regulatory agencies touching every phase of government. They are expert in raising such a clamor that they seem to be speaking for vast numbers of people.

They exert pressure in Congress wherever they can find vulnerable points — regular committees, appropriations committees, individual legislators, even on the floor of the House and Senate. They know how to mobilize their organizations back home to send a storm of letters, telegrams, and petitions down on Washington. They know how to draw up laws, to testify before committees, to help speed a bill through or to slow it down. They are experts in the art of influence. They also have the money to contract out some of their work to Washington law firms that specialize in legislative matters.

The Tobacco Institute, Inc., a lobbying-public relations organization, is an example of how an industry organizes to combat government regula-

[10]On lobbying as a communication process, see Lester W. Milbrath, *The Washington Lobbyists* (Rand McNally, 1963). Also see L. Harmon Zeigler and C. Wayne Peak, *Interest Groups in American Society*, 2nd ed. (Prentice-Hall, Inc., 1972); Lewis A. Dexter, *How Organizations Are Represented in Washington* (Bobbs-Merrill, 1969); and Carol S. Greenwald, *Group Power: Lobbying and Public Policy* (Praeger, 1977), and Jeffrey M. Berry, *Lobbying for the People* (Princeton University Press, 1977).

tion.[11] The Institute is comprised of fourteen of the leading tobacco producers. Presidents of the major tobacco companies sit on its board; and it is financed by these companies, who contribute according to their share of the market.

The Tobacco Institute's major efforts have been to overturn, modify, and delay government warnings to the public about the hazards of smoking. Led by retired members of Congress, it has battled, often successfully, to weaken regulations that would ban cigarette sales. And it continues to battle against more stringent regulation of cigarette usage. It hires top Washington lawyers and contracts work to noted public relations firms. It also hires its own experts to conduct studies that often run counter to reports put out by the government.

An advanced form of persuasion today is cooperative lobbying. A number of "specialized" organizations form a "peak" association to press for legislation—or to block it—in a general policy area. The Food Group, for example, a twenty-eight-year-old informal conference group in Washington, represents more than sixty business associations such as the National Canning Association and the International Association of Ice Cream Manufacturers. It works closely with the National Association of Manufacturers and the National Farm Bureau Federation. This group spawned an Information Committee on Federal Food Regulations to fight truth-in-packaging legislation. Sixty food groups would seem to be a pretty formidable coalition, but a study of cooperative lobbying indicates the frustrations as well as the opportunities involved in cooperation. The various specialized organizations differed over priorities, with the result that strong and unified pressure on Congress and government agencies was often hard to achieve.[12]

THE WASHINGTON "SUPERLAWYERS"

Lobbying is often defined as any intentional effort to influence *legislation*. But the Washington law firms that specialize in selling influence and insight concern themselves with all kinds of government activity. Their clients want early warnings about government action that might weaken their economic position. They also want any information that can improve their tax circumstances, win federal licenses or contracts, or lessen troublesome federal regulation.

Thousands of Washington lawyers specialize in helping clients to advance their interest before various agencies of the federal government. They are generally well educated, well connected, and well heeled. The successful ones work very hard and are much sought after. Much of what they do is not easily recognized as practicing law. Sometimes they serve almost as political science instructors: They educate their clients about how a bill becomes a law, about the politics of regulatory commissions, or about the significance of White House executive orders and budgetary priorities. Often, too, they merely stay in touch with friends who work in key government positions. Said one prominent lobbyist who serves Wall Street interests:

Lobbyists wear red cards to identify themselves when they visit Senate and Assembly chambers in the state of New Jersey on behalf of their causes.

[11]See the useful case history, A. Lee Fritschler, *Smoking and Politics: Policymaking and the Federal Bureaucracy* (Appleton-Century-Crofts, 1969).

[12]Donald R. Hall, *Cooperative Lobbying—The Power of Pressure* (University of Arizona Press, 1969).

You can't practice securities law from your desk in New York. You must get down to Washington at least once a week. . . . I'll go see a Commissioner even when I don't have anything specific to talk about. Hell, you can't let them forget who you are, because the time may come when you want to get a message across in a hurry. And I'm not talking about "fixing" any proceedings, either, so don't get any wrong ideas. But there are times in a securities practice when you want to get something through the Commission in a hurry, and, my boy, that's when you'd better have close acquaintances. And I don't mean any GS-13 staff attorney, either; I mean a mover.[13]

Public interest groups and policy making

The American people are organized in all kinds of ways: by occupation, by nationality, by race, by ethnic origin, by hobby. There is an organization speaking for almost everything and everybody. All organizations, of course, insist that what they want is in the public interest and that they are representing "the people," or at least what is in the people's interest.

Washington has also long seen so-called "public interest" groups, groups speaking for no particular economic class, no particular occupation. The League of Women Voters, the Americans for Democratic Action, and the Sierra Club are examples of such groups. In recent years Ralph Nader, Common Cause, the Environmental Defense Fund, and Friends of the Earth have popularized the public interest lobby. Many of these newer groups have often resorted to litigation. They turn to the lawsuit in part because they lack a mass base and because they feel inadequately represented in state and national legislatures. Motivated by a mixture of principle, ideology, and perhaps a need for recognition, these groups see themselves as representing the unrepresented or at least the underrepresented. They also view themselves as dedicated to winning benefits available to everyone as opposed to special, or parochial, benefits.

Groups also gain a forum for presenting their points of view by seeking permission to file amicus curiae (friend of the court) briefs even in cases in which they are not direct parties. Thus, the American Civil Liberties Union files many such briefs with the Supreme Court in cases that raise questions of constitutional liberty. Another technique is to publish in legal periodicals. Most judges read these journals to keep abreast of legal scholarship and sometimes even cite them as authority for their rulings.

John Gardner, the founder of Common Cause, talks to reporters about some of the group's congressional and lobby reform measures.

[13]Quoted in Joseph C. Goulden, *The Superlawyers: The Small and Powerful World of the Giant Washington Law Firms* (Weybright and Talley, 1972), p. 8. See also Mark Green, *The Other Government: The Unseen Power of Washington Lawyers* (Grossman, 1975).

"That ought to satisfy Ralph Nader!"

Drawing by Ed Fisher;
© 1970 The New Yorker Magazine, Inc.

The media, represented here by TV reporters Dan Rather and Bill Moyers (center and right) and columnist and commentator Jack Anderson (left), often function as a public interest lobby by keeping controversial issues constantly before the public eye.

These groups are dependent on a favorable press. Their reports and court battles are often prepared with a close eye on generating publicity. Some temptation doubtless exists for them to oversimplify and resort to moralistic rhetoric. In one such encounter Nader pointed out that "The best way to build government is to attack government." These strategies quite naturally grate on those in government and sometimes provoke stubborn opposition, especially among those who are trying to make programs work under difficult conditions. Criticism of Nader's Raiders comes from both Right and Left. Nader has learned how to use the techniques of investigation, publicity, and litigation, and he has captured the imagination and support of lots of people. He has had unquestionable impact. Some think it is a constructive impact, but obviously those who have been affected adversely think Nader is a troublemaker. Defenders argue that most of the criticism he gets is unfair and misleading. Nader pursues his objectives on many levels and through many stages of action, including hard pressure for fundamental legislative and administrative reforms. He has helped mobilize thousands of people at all levels of government. And thousands of people in government agencies and corporations have been affected by his studies. Thus, Nader is given credit by many on Capitol Hill for doing much to strengthen or initiate such legislation as the Natural Gas Pipe Line Safety Act, the Federal Coal Mine Health and Safety Act, the Wholesome Meat Act, the Radiation Control Act, and the Occupational Safety and Health Act.

PUBLIC INTEREST LOBBIES

A public interest lobby is one that seeks to represent general interests or those of the whole public rather than representing some specific economic or professional interest. There is, however, no agreement about who really represents *the public interest.* Thus the National Rifle Association claims that it represents a large segment of the public and doubtless it does. Plainly, the so-called public interest groups do not always represent the points of view held by the majority of the people. For example, some of

416

the environmental public interest groups in the 1970s helped delay for four years the building of the Alaska pipeline despite the fact that most Alaskans and most U.S. citizens favored it.

The problems of using this term are nicely described by a scholar who has studied these groups extensively:

> Thus, public interest groups do not always represent public intersts; special interest groups sometimes represent public interests; environmentalists, using public interest rhetoric, frequently are defending a type of natural law. The term *public interest lobby* masks considerable confusion. I will continue to use this term throughout the rest of the volume because it is the one commonly used, but a better term would be *citizens' lobby*. If we used that term we could avoid the tangle of arguing about who *really* represents public interests. A citizens' lobby could be said to be mistaken in its judgment that some position is representative of public interests without generating so much of an emotional charge as one does in saying that a public interest lobby is not really representing public interests.[14]

By whatever name they are called, however, well over a million people regularly contribute $15 to $25 to nationally organized "good government," pro-consumer, pro-environment and conservation lobbies. To cite just five examples and their 1977 membership gives an idea of their strength:

Year Begun	Name	Members
1892	Sierra Club	175,000
1920	League of Women Voters	140,000
1969	Friends of the Earth	25,000
1970	Common Cause	255,000
1971	R. Nader's Public Citizen Inc.	65,000

Who joins and sustains these groups? Members are mostly well-educated, middle and upper income and white. Most also are active in partisan politics, vote regularly and are important public opinion leaders in their home cities and states. They are willing to speak out on public issues and they believe things can be improved even if they may be skeptical about the quality of leaders currently in governmental offices. Most of them believe that unless citizens get together and form new institutions for representation, American government will be too influenced by economic and bureaucratic interests who will control public policy for their own benefit rather than for the benefit of the public-at-large. Thus they attempt to band together to reform government and advance issues through the politics of *ad hoc* coalitions around particular policies. Many of these groups have clearly been successful in initiating new policy ideas, building support for them and bringing about change. Through their efforts have come a whole host of automobile safety regulations, restrictions on the financing of political campaigns, new lobbying regulations and improved ways of analyzing the public benefits of major public works programs such as

[14]Andrew S. McFarland, *Public Interest Lobbies* (American Enterprise Institute, 1976), p. 43. See also Jeffrey Berry, *Lobbying For the People* (Princeton University Press, 1977).

dams. There can be little doubt that in the last few years public interest groups have been more influential in national politics than at any time since the Progressive Era. As they have become influential, they have also become controversial.

Many people feel that the citizen lobbies have begun to balance the scales of justice in Washington. But these organizations are seldom a match, either in numbers or influence, for the far better financed and well-established interest group lobbies. Most citizen lobbies exist on a month to month financial base. Turnover among staff is high due in part to low salaries and the fact that moral gratifications are not enough to motivate most people to stay. Moreover, the issue-attention span of even the attentive public is relatively short. Concern with government integrity and consumer protection can lapse after a while, quite apart from whether the fundamental problem has been addressed. Then too, many of these reform movements depend on supplies of recent college and law school graduates; yet young people form an unstable base for long-term support of policy change. Most are lured, by mood or necessity, to move on after a while.

Among the major organizational problems facing the public interest lobbies are the maintenance of high morale and avoiding the deadening effects of bureaucratization. There is a tendency among high-minded organizations either to talk or organize themselves to death. For a time, however, many of these groups do act as guardians of that valued human trait—the sense of righteous outrage. Still, those who are merely committed but not particularly competent soon find that outrage is not sufficient, especially if, as often is the case, they are middle- or upper middle-class individuals who really do not have that much personally to be outraged about. Blacks, American Indians, and groups with direct serious personal grievances—that is, self-interested groups, and the well-established special interests such as oil companies, Dow Chemical, and the AMA—are likely to be there long after the more generally outraged have turned to something else. In short, the more intense the interest, the easier to organize and sustain the interest group.

We have a long and rich history of reform movements that build up after some scandal, but then all returns to "normal." Even so, reformers eventually did "knock over" the corrupt city machines, and Nader and other consumer and environmental lobbies have forced several of the regulatory agencies to change their ways. Campaign reforms did come about in 1974 as contemporary reformers took advantage of the public outrage toward the Watergate scandals. Moreover, President Carter has appointed quite a number of persons to top positions in his administration who formerly were activists and lobbyists for these public interest groups.

These self-designated guardians of the public interest sustain themselves because substantial numbers of people are willing to support them. This support comes precisely because enough people believe in the need for what the Swedish have called an ombudsman—a person who will handle citizen complaints. These outside groups undoubtedly will carry on, bringing suits, issuing reports, and more generally, exposing what they feel are unfair, corrupt, or inefficient government practices.

These groups have become important in mobilizing and directing political efforts and attention. They are different from both political parties and the more conventional interest groups. They generally operate outside the parties, and for some segments of the population they may have replaced political parties in terms of group identification and allegiance. Some of this indifference or even antagonism to parties comes from the more populist nature of these groups—they are less concerned with winning elections and staying in office than with ideals of peace, environment, and equal rights.[15]

CONTROL OF LOBBYING

In general, Americans have been far more concerned about concentrated private power than divided government power. And the obvious problem of overrepresentation of some groups at the expense of others is a source of deep concern. For years reformers have been trying to curb the excesses of "pressure groups." The attempt to control lobbying—the primary weapon of interest groups—is a revealing example of the difficulties involved in trying to regulate groups in a democracy.

Attempts to control lobbying began at least a century ago. In 1877 Georgia wrote into its constitution the simple provision that lobbying is a crime. Early in this century a number of states passed acts to regulate lobbyists. Under the Federal Regulation of Lobbying Act of 1946, persons hired to influence or defeat bills in Congress must register and disclose the name and address of their employer, how much they are paid, and who pays them. Every three months they must file a further statement listing the names of publications that have carried their publicity and the bills they support or oppose. Organizations whose main purpose is to influence legislation also must furnish information that is printed regularly in the *Congressional Record.*

The aim of such legislation is to turn the spotlight of publicity on the expenditures and activities of lobbyists. The national lobby law has furnished a vast amount of detailed information about lobbyists—who they are, who sponsors and finances them, what bills they seek to pass or block. This information has given the public some idea of the amounts and sources of money involved, although the loopholes in this legislation are great.

Some hold that publicity is not enough, that what we need is actual regulation of lobbying. Most lobbysits, these critics argue, not only have no fear of publicity but, on the contrary, actually welcome it. Supporters of a new law to regulate lobbying say it is needed to ensure that the true picture of lobbying activity is made available to the public. One of the groups calling for lobby disclosure legislation feels that the following five ingredients should be part of the new law:

1. A two-tiered approach to reporting requirements that would retain comprehensive reporting for most organizations but would allow less active lobbying groups to file abbreviated reports requiring virtually no paper work
2. Reporting provisions that will include coverage of indirect lobbying (i.e., the efforts of national organizations to stimulate lobbying efforts by their members, affiliates, employees, shareholders, etc.)
3. Requiring the reporting of basic information about significant contributions to lobbying organizations
4. Coverage of lobbying activity directed at the executive branch, aimed at obtaining large federal contracts
5. Strong enforcement provisions with oversight and administration assigned to the General Accounting Office.[16]

[15]The power and strategies of the full range of interest groups are discussed in Greenwald, *Group Power: Lobbying and Public Policy.*

[16]*Legislative Report* (Common Cause, July 1977), mimeo, p. 2.

Opponents of these new regulation proposals claim they might drive the lobbyists underground, where their influence might be more hidden but just as effective. Regulation might also run into serious constitutional objections based on the rights guaranteed by the First Amendment.

These observers point out that lobbyists are a sort of "third house" of Congress. While the Senate and House are set up on a geographical basis, lobbyists represent people directly in terms of their economic or other interests. Small but important groups can get representation in this third house that they might not be able to get in the other two. In a nation of large and important interests, this kind of functional representation, if not abused, is highly useful as a supplement to geographical representation.

Group conflict and direct action

Policy issues often arise because people feel they are being cheated or threatened. So they band together with like-minded people. Invariably they discover other groups either within or outside of government who oppose their point of view. Trying to win friends and influence politicians becomes a prime goal.

Government is both a struggle among those already holding considerable political power and a struggle between those who hold it and those who *want* it. Politicians and policy-making administrative officials become conflict brokers and conflict managers not so much because they want to, but because this is the very heart of policy politics. Skillful policy makers usually understand interest group dynamics and know when and how to arbitrate among conflicting interests. To effect change they usually need to (1) identify the combination of interest groups that will produce enough support to win agreement with their proposal; (2) marshal the symbolic and real support of the identified groups; (3) fight off opposition groups; and (4) sustain their own capacity to play an effective role.[17] Governmental civil servants themselves serve increasingly as major sources of policy initiative as they guide the development of knowledge and mobilize public support for policy change.

PROTEST POLITICS

Policy change rarely happens without agitation, pressure, and visions of how conditions can be improved. Rational arguments, coalition building, compromise, and bill writing are the conventional ways to secure policy change. But the tactic of protest also has a rich legitimate history in America. Political scientist James Q. Wilson points out that protest occurs for one or more of several reasons:

> First, it may be a strategy designed to acquire resources with which to bargain. . . . Second, protest may be a strategy designed to make credible the willingness of a group to use the bargaining resources it already has. . . . Third, a protest may be designed to activate third parties. . . . Finally a protest activity may be carried on in order to enhance the protesting organization.[18]

---

[17]Drawn from Eugene Bardach, *The Skill Factor in Politics: Repealing Mental Commitment Laws in California* (Berkeley: University of California Press, 1972). See also R. W. Cobb and C. D. Elder, *Participation in American Politics: The Dynamics of Agenda-Building* (Allyn & Bacon, 1972).

[18]Wilson, *Political Organizations*, pp. 282–83.

Dramatic direct action is sometimes required to win recognition of a grievance or to gain attention from policy-making elites. Direct action embraces a variety of activities ranging from passive resistance and mass demonstrations to sit-ins, strikes, and heckling of speakers. Traditionally, strikes have been used in the United States mainly by unions to win concessions from employers; but strikes and other kinds of economic pressure can also be used for political purposes. The different forms of direct action have been used by many types of groups. In some places blacks active in the civil rights movement have been denied credit or dismissed from their jobs and blacklisted. White and black civil rights activists have counterattacked by organizing boycotts of buses and stores.

Protest against the war in Vietnam in the late 1960s stimulated direct action throughout the nation, especially on college campuses. In dozens of communities mass demonstrations and marches dramatized suppression of the right to vote, police brutality, or denial of job opportunity. Using nonviolent methods as their guide, some leaders sought to restrain their followers from violence; but, like the great Gandhi, they sometimes created situations in which violence easily erupted.

President Nixon's invasion of Cambodia in 1970, along with the Kent State and Jackson State killings, brought direct action to a new pitch on and off campuses. Students struck their classes, closed many colleges and universities, organized demonstrations, massed in Washington. Like much direct action, however, the early momentum soon dissipated.

VIOLENCE

The Whiskey Rebellion of 1794 and the Civil War are reminders that force is an old weapon in trying to bring about change. For decades labor disputes were marked by bloodshed. The history of the relations between the black and white races is marked by episodes of the use of force. Violence has been used to repress blacks; lynching and persecution were once a way of life. And the fear and threat of violence remain part of race relations.

A few advocate that force and violence should be major instruments of politics. Terrorists in Northern Ireland and the Middle East are examples. Even fewer argue that these tactics are appropriate in the United States. They contend that without violent action, the poor and the dispossessed will not be able to seize enough power to influence the course of events. However, the use of violence has not been productive in American politics; more often than not it has been counterproductive.

Direct peaceful action should not be confused with the use of force and violence. The former is protected by our Constitution; the latter is not. A peaceful march on city hall or a school or even the Pentagon can lead to violence but should not be confused with it. Similarly, a strike or a boycott is the application of economic coercion, but is different from violence or acts of terrorism.

Policy implementation: how policy is carried out

Once public policy has been decided upon, the process of governmental action begins. Even if we know what to do, can get political leaders to agree to it, and can devise an appropriate strategy, we may still not be able to ensure that the strategy will be carried out.[19] After the president has

---

[19]See Eugene Bardach, *The Implementation Game: What Happens after a Bill Becomes a Law* (The MIT Press, 1977).

signed a bill into law or a regulatory agency has completed its rule-making procedures, the government must act. Money must be spent and rules must be enforced if goals are to be met. The stage of the policy process that occurs after a bill becomes a law is the *implementation phase.*

Although the other parts of the policy process are well publicized, the implementation of a policy is often hidden within the vast bureaucracy and the months, years and sometimes decades over which a program is supposed to be carried out. A great number of federal programs fail to accomplish desired goals because of problems that show up during the implementation phase. The Kennedy administration's economic reform programs in Latin America, the Johnson administration's Model Cities program, and the Nixon-Ford programs in crime control all illustrate programs whose problems were not fully understood until long after they had been put into operation. When such failures occur, it is relatively easy to blame the original legislation rather than examine what happened after the bill became a law. Of course, poorly written legislation and badly conceived policy yield poor results. But policy analysts have begun to realize that even the best legislation can fail owing to problems encountered during the implementation.[20] Sometimes these problems can lead to the outright failure of a program, but more often they mean excessive delay, underachievement of desired goals, or costs far above those originally expected.

Why are there problems in carrying out federal policies?

A basic reason for problems at the implementation stage is that the coalition that comes together to get a bill through Congress often does not stay together after the bill has been enacted. Congress often passes ambiguous legislation which conceals serious policy differences. Rather than set clear goals, Congress, reflecting differences among the supporters of the policies, sets confusing goals and then turns over their regulation to the bureaucrats. Bureaucrats get the blame but they are merely trying to carry out unclear policies — deliberately left confused — and they must act in a political atmosphere of conflicting groups.

Take civil rights legislation, for example. Often the differences among women's groups, black groups, employer groups, trade unions are momentarily resolved and compromised and a bill becomes law. But after the bill has been enacted the coalition falls apart and the pressures are felt on the agencies trying to implement the policies. Conflicts arise and increase. Employers insist, for example, that the agency's regulations are unrealistic and interfere with their rights; women's groups argue that the agencies are failing to enforce the law vigorously; black groups claim that the agencies favor the women's groups but ignore the wishes of the blacks, and so it goes. Thus the more controversial the issue, the greater the chance of delay as powerful interest groups clash over a program and force officials charged with implementation to move cautiously.

Implementation is a process involving a long chain of decision points,

[20]Many of the political scientists and economists who study policy implementation publish their articles and findings in the following quarterly publications: *The Public Interest, Policy Analysis,* and *Public Policy.* The Brookings Institution and the American Enterprise Institute for Public Policy Research, which are both nonprofit, nongovernmental organizations located in Washington, D. C., publish books and reports in this same area. We will be quoting and making use of publications from these sources throughout the following chapters on national policy making.

all of which need to be cleared before a program can be successfully carried out. At each decision point is a public official or community leader who holds power to advance — or delay — the program. According to Pressman and Wildavsky, the more decision points a program needs to clear, the greater the chance of failure or delay.[21]

Special problems result if the successful implementation of a national program depends on the cooperation of state and local officials. One state or community may be eager to help; another might be opposed to a program and try to stop it.

Clearly, policy makers must consider the problems of implementation when they propose legislative solutions to national problems. One way to achieve this is to design policies and programs that are able to withstand buffeting by a constantly shifting set of political and social pressures. Another is having public officials or consultants of some kind ready to serve as "fixers" to repair damage as it is detected. Still another means to overcome some of the problems of implementation is to write legislation that does not depend for its success on the need to persuade people to help with it. For example, changes in the tax code are sometimes favored over complex public jobs programs by those seeking to stimulate the economy. In the one case, the apparatus for accomplishing a goal is already in place (the tax structure); in the other, a large new administrative structure would have to be established, staffed, and supervised. More and more, legislators are thinking past the problems of passing legislation and are examining the chances of successful implementation.

Policy evaluation: how effective is the policy?

As we have noted, the adoption of a policy is only the beginning of the policy process. After Congress passes a law and the president signs it, policy implementation takes place. But what happens next? Who watches, who evaluates, who decides whether it is working or not? The answer, or so it often seems, is everybody and nobody.

An ideal public organization, some think, would be one that continuously monitors and evaluates its own activities to determine whether it is accomplishing its goals and whether the goals are worth achieving. But this is obviously utopian. Organizational leaders, like the rest of us, are sometimes not the best ones to evalualate their own accomplishments.

Those favoring programs and those responsible for administering them often prefer to concentrate on getting the programs through Congress (and also funded fully) rather than evaluating their own success. Funds are scarce. *Bring us the success stories!* Crudely put, that seems to be the standard operating procedure. And then the success stories are paraded before the Office of Management and Budget and appropriate congressional committees.

Bureaus and agencies often cast their proposals in such a way as to persuade, not to report systematic evaluation. Program "evaluation" reports coming into the White House or the Congress from the bureaucracy have long been suspect, since the success of the programs they administer puts their own performance on the line. In this sense, evaluation can never be,

[21]Jeffrey Pressman and Aaron Wildavsky, *Implementation* (University of California Press, 1973). Other useful studies of policy execution include Martha Derthick, *New Towns In-Town: Why a Federal Program Failed* (The Urban Institute, 1972); and Charles O. Jones, *Clean Air* (University of Pittsburgh Press, 1975).

and probably should not be, entirely nonpolitical: It will be used by one party or branch of government against another. Evaluation will also be used by one department or agency against another. This in-fighting within the executive branch gives an agency additional incentives to politicize its evaluation efforts.[22]

Some bureaus become so involved with activities that enhance their prestige that they neglect the work which makes up their true purpose. Delays and deficiencies in evaluation sometimes occur because an agency wants to hide the real cost of its operations. Sometimes, however, the problem arises because it is difficult and expensive to develop outcome or impact measures. Also, it is difficult to relate governmental expenditures with policy outcomes, or to be precise about what has caused social change if change can even be noticed. The problem is to develop agreement on the measures to be used by the participants. Evaluation is clearly a political problem because whoever controls the evaluation process controls the outcome of any analysis.

Political and social scientists have turned their attention to the *product* side of public policy. Instead of being concerned only with what affects government, or with what goes on inside governmental institutions, more attention is being given to what comes out of the policy-making processes. Defining success becomes a major concern. And the test of a program is not input but *outcome.* "It is interesting, and at times important, to know how much money is spent on schools in a particular neighborhood or city. But the crucial question is how much do the children learn. Programs are for people, not for bureaucracies."[23]

Why have Congress and the White House not insisted on more systematic planning and evaluation? The short-term political incentives seem to propel their energies in an opposite direction. *Pass now, plan later!* The election is just around the corner. Presidents, especially, are ever eager for fast results. They sometimes do not realize the need for more analysis, testing, small-scale experiments, and systematic reappraisal of ongoing programs. They say they were elected not to study and research policies, but to get things done, and to put ideas into operation.

As Congress has been eclipsed by the executive in more and more policy formulation areas, there has been a move to strengthen it as a focus for **program oversight.** Congress has gradually accepted both its policy-initiating eclipse as well as its new after-the-fact assessment role, although even its staunchest defenders readily admit Congress performs this responsibility with only modest success.

The Legislative Reorganization Act of 1946 assigned to each standing committee the responsibility to "exercise continuous watchfulness of the execution by the administrative agencies concerned of any laws, the subject matter of which is within the jurisdication of such committee." Oversight is neither constant nor systematic, however, for a variety of reasons. Comprehensive oversight of all federal programs would demand all the time of all the staff and members of Congress.

Members of Congress exercise the oversight function when they are

"**Remember, son, if at first you don't suceed, re-evaluate the situation, draw up various hypotheses for your failure, choose reasonable corrective measures, and try, try again.**"

Copyright © 1974.
Reprinted by permission of Saturday Review /World and Randy Glasbergen.

---

[22]Aaron Wildavsky, "The Self-Evaluating Organization," *Public Administration Review* (September–October 1972), pp. 509–20. Our discussion draws from this article.

[23]Daniel P. Moynihan, "Policy vs. Program in the '70's," *The Public Interest* (Summer 1970), p. 100.

Senator Jacob Javits (R-N.Y.) directs a question to an oil company executive during an investigation into the energy crisis. Members of Congress may also exercise the oversight function to counter the force of the executive branch.

particularly upset with the way they are being treated by executive branch officials and when it serves their constituents in a direct way. Certain standing committees have created specific oversight subcommittees, but there is little knowledge of whether such subcommittees make any difference in the quality of policy making. What is frustrating, of course, is not that oversight is performed only selectively but that too often it comes only after some mishap or tragedy such as when the Air Forces' C-5A had its motor fall off and its landing gears collapse.

Evaluation of programs, however, is not primarily a technical problem, but a political one. Of course, all agree that there is something wrong with Defense Department procurement when the cost of buying a weapons system is much more than Congress anticipated, but for many evaluations the issues are choices between costs and benefits for which there is no expert answer. Is the welfare program worth the expenditures? Should we abolish subsidies to farmers? Has the highway program produced good or bad results for the nation? Are the funds spent on grants for students to attend medical schools worth it to the taxpayer? If experts could tell us whether these programs were "successful" or not, we would need a government of experts. But there are no precise answers, and this is why we rely on the democratic system and on politicians chosen by popular vote.

Many within and outside Congress feel Congress should not yet perform merely oversight functions. They feel that program oversight has a low priority compared with the need to strengthen Congress in other ways. Yet oversight, properly conducted, can be a major means for Congress to retain its role in policy making. For the present, however, incentives for conducting more comprehensive program oversight are great in the abstract but modest in concrete situations.

Summary

1. Public policy is the *substance* of what government does. It is a process. Public policy is never made, but is always in the process of being made. Public policy is often expressed but only in part, by a law, then by a court decision interpretation of that law, then by a law modifying that court decision, then by an agency regulation implementating that law, then by a presidential executive order, and then by another law of Congress, and on and on.

2. Policy making in the United States is neither simple nor tidy. There is not a "top down" structure of authority and hence policy is not made "on high." Rather, it takes form gradually with large numbers of persons helping to formulate a new response to a public problem. Policies change slowly, reflecting gradual changes in public opinion. Each shift in policy is a conscious action, as reflected in a new election, law, court decision.

3. Policy decisions are made by public officials who give direction to the government's actions. Policy outcomes are the consequences for society, the "so-what" or "bottom line" of what the government is doing and the way citizens respond to governmental action. Policy making can be studied through five stages — the identification of a problem, the formulation of policy solutions, the adoption or enactment of a new policy response, the implementation or application of the policy, and the evaluation of the policy.

4. Making public policy cannot be easily described in the abstract. For how policies change depends very much on what kinds of policies are being discussed, and who and how many persons they affect. The five chapters that follow describe and analyse foreign, military, regulatory, promotional and taxing and spending policies and how they are made. It will be seen that our policy-making processes permit large numbers of groups and individuals to join battle both to protect their own private interests and to enhance the public interest. Our political system, like all large systems, is weighted in favor of the status quo and against swift or sweeping change. But those who know better ways of doing things and are willing to take part in the pulling and hauling of the policy-making process can make a difference.

5. Knowledge, political skills, the ability to build coalitions of like-minded supporters and attract extensive press coverage are often critical preconditions for changing public policy. All of these, together with unusual stamina, are needed to place new issues on the public agenda and to get persons throughout the political system to cooperate in effecting change.

Chapter 19

Making Foreign Policy

Dramatic changes in recent years have transformed America's position in the world. For a generation we were preoccupied with preventing the Cold War from escalating into a hot war. Our interventions in Cuba, Vietnam, the Dominican Republic, Cambodia, and elsewhere antagonized other nations and deeply divided our own. In the 1970s, in the wake of almost ten years of war in Indochina, most Americans in and out of public office welcomed an end to the war. We also became cautious about overextending our influence abroad.

The substance and effect of American foreign policy is widely debated today. What officials and agencies actually make foreign policy? Have we relied too heavily on presidential leadership? Is American foreign policy overly dominated by military considerations? What role do and should intelligence agencies assume in our relations with other nations? Does foreign policy making differ from domestic policy making in regard to the role of experts, the news media, and the public?

The United States in a changing world

The chief objective of American foreign policy has been to preserve the security of the United States. To be sure, American politicians have often preferred to speak in high moral terms about human rights and safeguarding world peace. But beneath the high-flown rhetoric, the central purpose of protecting national interests has been fairly consistent.

But promoting the national interests of the United States provides no better guidelines to foreign policy makers than the standard of "the public interest" furnishes to those who make domestic policies. Total security is never obtainable, much less definable. Our policy makers try to influence, direct, and shape events—but the rest of the world shapes and influences us. And in recent decades the world about us has been in a process of constant upheaval.

427

The world continues to grow smaller in the late 1970s. Technical progress — satellite communications, for example — and growing food, fuel, and mineral shortages have profoundly changed the international scene. Common interests and mutual problems are forcing traditional conflicts and rivalries aside. Resource scarcities are creating new ones. The old order is changing.

Western Europe, gradually moving toward greater economic integration, is a vital force in world affairs. African and Middle Eastern nations have cast off their colonial ties. In Latin America, more than 300 million people are combating poverty, disease, and political chaos in an attempt to gain prosperity and dignity. Japan has risen from ashes to become the economic giant of Asia. China has established diplomatic ties with the West. Relations with Cástro's Cuba have mellowed. And the various accords among Middle Eastern nations seem, at least temporarily, to have achieved a foundation for stability there. There are hopeful signs about some old problems. But other unresolved problems and new crises abound.

By the late-1970s hopes for a "full generation of peace" seemed overly optimistic. Tension continued to characterize Soviet-Western relations. In Africa racial hatred threatened to ignite half the continent. Energy needs and poverty still fanned the conflict in the Middle East. In Southeast Asia three decades of war diminished chances for a lasting peace.

There was a widespread conviction on the part of many Americans that their government had misinformed them about the events and reasons leading to our involvement in Indochina. The publication of the classified *Pentagon Papers* opened a new phase in the debate that so often follows an unsuccessful war: who caused it, who is to blame, how can we avoid it in the future?

American involvement in Vietnam had clearly eroded the faith, especially of younger Americans, in the competence and fairness of their public leaders. They charged that the "foreign policy establishment" was fearful of dissent and that it had manipulated public opinion.

Previously, most Americans felt enormous wealth and power markedly increased their responsibilities to make the world safe for democracy. Now, growing numbers of people appear to favor more cautious, less interventionist policies. However, many others feel that while our wealth and power should be used with restraint, we still have a great responsibility for constructive action on a global level.

The makers of foreign policy must face all the facts of domestic and internal politics. In deciding what to do, they must consider the political situation in the nations throughout the world and the uncertainties and complexities of politics at home. At this time, when American power makes us the leading actor on the world scene whether we wish the role or not, and when our mistakes may have catastrophic and irreversible consequences, foreign policy making is one of the most critical tasks facing Americans.

The policy machinery

It is the responsibility of those who formulate our foreign policies to determine the basic objectives vital to our national interests and to devise programs to achieve these objectives. American foreign policy makers do not control the events that create problems and set limits to solutions. But to the best of their ability and resources these people must decide how to use (or not use) the instruments available to them: bargaining or negotiation, persuasion or progaganda, economic assistance or pressures, and the threat or actual use of armed force.

The responsibility for foreign policy making was fixed in the Constitution at the national level. However, it did not divide the powers over foreign relations cleanly and evenly. In England control over foreign relations had been given to the king and his ministers. The framers tried to redress the balance a bit. Many of the powers given to Congress by the Constitution reflect the decision to take them from the executive branch; the framers wanted to make what had been a prerogative of the executive into a more shared relationship with the legislature. Congress was given the power to declare war, to appropriate funds, and make rules for the armed forces. But the president was left as commander in chief of the armed forces and the director of those who negotiate in behalf of this nation with other countries. The courts have the power to interpret treaties, but by and large they have ruled that our relations with other nations are matters for the executive to negotiate.

Executive domination of foreign policy making is a fact of the political life of all nations, including democratic ones. Presidential dominance over American foreign policy has been constant in our history. Since the dawn of the nuclear age it has become one of the central issues of our time. To appreciate this phenomenon we will look at the people within the executive departments who make up the foreign policy establishment—the men and women and organizations through which the president acts.

AT THE TOP—THE SECRETARY OF STATE

The president's chief foreign policy adviser is usually his secretary of state. Officially the secretary of state helps a president make decisions. In actual practice the secretary sometimes formulates a great deal of foreign policy himself and then secures the president's backing. Just how much influence the secretary has depends largely on the president's personal desires. Presidents Harding, Coolidge, Hoover, Eisenhower, and Ford, turned over to their secretaries of state almost full responsibility for making important decisions. Other presidents—for example, Wilson, both Roosevelts, Kennedy, Nixon and Carter—have taken a more active part themselves. Indeed, at times they were their own secretaries of state. Even so, important decisions on foreign policy are so numerous that both president and secretary of state play important roles.

The secretary has the Department of State to administer and multiple roles to fill. He receives many visits from foreign diplomats. He attends international conferences and usually heads our delegation in the General Assembly of the United Nations. He makes key statements on foreign policy, sometimes speaking directly to the people. He appears before congressional committees to explain and justify administration policies. He visits other nations to confer with chiefs of state and foreign ministers, sometimes for explicit diplomatic negotiations, as in the case of Henry Kissinger's Middle East "shuttle diplomacy."

The secretary of state, as a leading member of the president's cabinet, sometimes has a hand in shaping general administration policy. He attempts to serve as the president's chief agent in coordinating all the governmental actions that affect our relations with foreign nations. This role is one that secretaries of state have nearly always found difficult to perform, especially when they must deal with the president's own staff or some

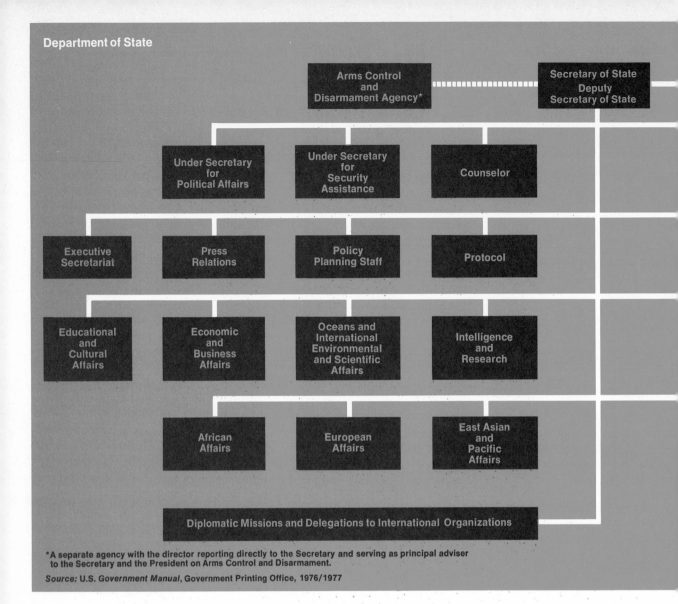

Department of State

Arms Control and Disarmament Agency* ···················· **Secretary of State / Deputy Secretary of State**

- Under Secretary for Political Affairs
- Under Secretary for Security Assistance
- Counselor

- Executive Secretariat
- Press Relations
- Policy Planning Staff
- Protocol

- Educational and Cultural Affairs
- Economic and Business Affairs
- Oceans and International Environmental and Scientific Affairs
- Intelligence and Research

- African Affairs
- European Affairs
- East Asian and Pacific Affairs

Diplomatic Missions and Delegations to International Organizations

*A separate agency with the director reporting directly to the Secretary and serving as principal adviser to the Secretary and the President on Arms Control and Disarmament.

Source: U.S. *Government Manual*, Government Printing Office, 1976/1977

powerful agency head who has close ties with the president.

The secretary of state is dependent on the support of the president, but he must also have considerable backing in the Congress. Unless he enjoys congressional confidence, the foreign policies proposed by the president may have rough going on Capital Hill.[1] For this reason, one of the secretary's top assistants is assigned to keep Congress in touch with the secretary's policies and to serve as a channel of communication between legislators and the secretary. Broadly speaking, however, the secretary is at the mercy of power relationships in Washington.

OTHER ADVISERS

Decades ago, the president called only on the secretary of state for advice in formulating foreign policies. Today, foreign policy is intimately affect-

[1]For an illustration of how important congressional confidence in the secretary of state is for the president's program, see Richard F. Fenno, Jr., *The President's Cabinet* (Harvard University Press, 1959), pp. 203ff. For a useful study of Henry Kissinger's secretary of state years, see Roger Morris, *Uncertain Greatness: Henry Kissinger and American Foreign Policy* (Harper & Row, 1977).

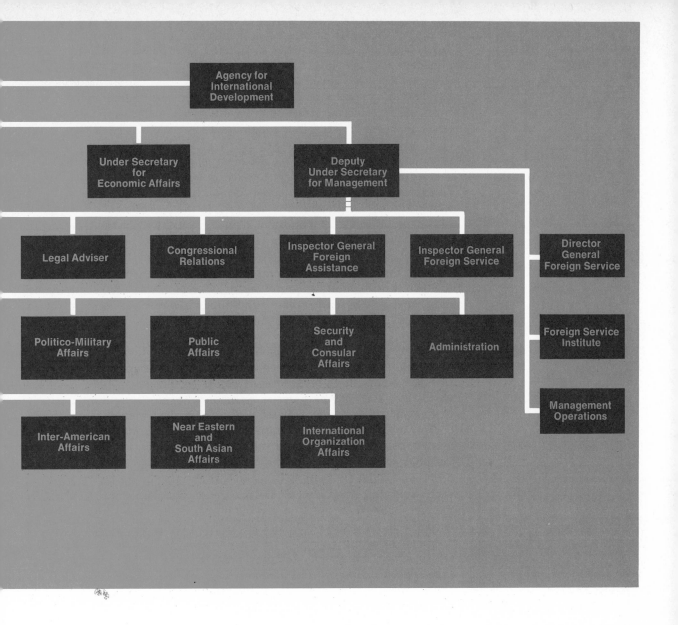

ed by every phase of governmental activity—finance, education, agriculture, commerce, energy, and, of course, military affairs. Suppose, for example, the president has to make a decision on a matter of international trade. The specialized knowledge and help he needs are scattered throughout the executive structure, in the Departments of Treasury, Energy, Commerce, Labor, and Agriculture, in the Federal Trade Commission, and in the United States Tariff Commission. Fifty agencies are concerned with foreign policy, and all of them are called upon from time to time to furnish advice and make decisions.

In addition to the secretary of state, the secretary of defense is also a major source of advice to a president. Because a main goal of American foreign policy is adequate security for the United States, it is not surprising that the military and defense agencies have a strong voice in the shaping of that policy. Moreover, the line between military and foreign policy is almost impossible to draw; indeed, the National Security Council was created to help integrate and coordinate the two.

THE PRESIDENT'S FOREIGN POLICY STAFF

The secretaries, agency chiefs, and their subordinates are chosen by the president and are expected to support and carry out his decisions. Yet at the same time they retain a measure of independence; they naturally tend to reflect the views of and to defend the departments and agencies they head.[2] As a result, our presidents have found a need to appoint personal advisers whose loyalties in the making of foreign policy lie solely with the chief executive. Since each president views responsibility in a personal way, the special adviser has played a loosely defined role.

Heading a staff of about fifty to sixty professionals, the national security policy assistant is assigned advisory, coordination, and sometimes negotiation duties. Originally, this assistant to the president merely kept the president informed of important developments within the government and around the world. President Nixon gave Henry Kissinger much more responsiblity while he served in this post, so much so that he served pretty much as a deputy president for foreign affairs. More often, however, the national security aide serves as a top staff person helping to keep the president constantly briefed and assisting him in his frequent communications with the secretaries of state and defense, the CIA director and others.

INTELLIGENCE AND FOREIGN POLICY

Policy makers must have some idea of the direction in which other nations are going to move in order to be able to counter those moves. They need, in other words, high-level foreign policy intelligence. Therefore, those who gather and analyze material are among the most important assistants to the policy makers. They often become policy-makers themselves.

What is the significance of yesterday's coup in Uganda or Angola? How many trained infantrymen are there in Czechoslovakia? What are the weapons and air strength of the North Korean military? What should we do about Soviet pressure on Poland? Before policy makers can answer such questions, they want to know a great deal about other countries—their probable reactions to a particular policy, their strengths and weaknesses, and, if possible, their strategic plans and intentions. Moreover, the makers of foreign policy must be familiar with the geographical and physical structure of the nations of the world; with the people—their number, skills, age distribution; the status of their arts, technology, engineering, and sciences; and their political and social systems.

Although most of the information comes from open sources, the term *intelligence work* conjures up visions of spies and undercover agents. Secret intelligence occasionally does supply the crucial and coordinating data. Intelligence work involves three operations—surveillance, research, and transmission. *Surveillance* is the close and systematic observation of developments the world over; *research* is the attempt "to establish meaningful patterns out of what was observed in the past and attempts to get meaning out of what appears to be going on now,[3] and *transmission* is getting the right information to the right people at the right time.

Many agencies engage in intelligence work, among them the State Department's Bureau of Intelligence and Research, the Defense Intelli-

President Carter with senior advisors, from left, U.N. Ambassador Andrew Young, National Security Council staff head Zbigniew Brzezinski, and Economic Advisors Council chairperson Charles Schultze.

[2]See Morton Halperin, *Bureaucratic Politics and Foreign Policy* (Brookings Institution, 1974).

[3]Sherman Kent, *Strategic Intelligence for American World Policy* (Princeton University Press, 1949), esp. p. 4. On the limits and abuses of intelligence activities, see R. H. Blum, ed., *Surveillance and Espionage in a Free Society* (Praeger, 1972).

gence Agency, the supersecret National Security Agency/Central Security Service (which works on code-breaking and electronic communications systems), the FBI, and the Central Intelligence Agency. These agencies form the United States Intelligence Board, which prepares intelligence surveys on most countries of the world.

The CIA was created in 1947 to coordinate the gathering and analysis of information that flows into the various parts of our government from all over the world. Yet organization alone cannot ensure that our policy makers will know all they need to know. As an expert on intelligence operations has pointed out:

> In both the Pearl Harbor and Cuban crises there was plenty of information. But in both cases, regardless of what the Monday morning quarterbacks have to say, the data was ambiguous and incomplete. There was never a single, definitive signal that said, "Get ready, get set, go!" but rather, a number of signals that, when put together, tended to crystallize suspicion. The true signals were always embedded in the noise or irrelevance of the false ones.[4]

Employing more than 15,000 persons, the CIA spends over $800 million annually. The CIA director, as head of the U.S. foreign intelligence community, oversees research, military intelligence operations, spy satellites, and U-2 and SR-71 exercises that may cost $7 billion annually. Critics charge, with reason, that CIA operations amount to a secret foreign policy insulated from public control and public scrutiny. In some nations the local CIA chief has more staff, more agents, a larger budget, and more influence than the U.S. ambassador.

Since its creation in 1947, the CIA has left a trail of covert activities and deposed governments such as those in Iran and Guatemala. The ill-fated 1961 Bay of Pigs invasion of Cuba was CIA directed. Later the CIA organized and trained anticommunist forces in Laos, and contributed considerable support to the anti-Allende forces in Chile. Because of its past record and because it must act when our government cannot officially intervene in another nation's affairs, there has been a growing tendency to credit (or blame) the CIA for any coup, purge, and revolt whether or not it was actually involved.

In 1967 several CIA "front groups" were discovered supporting a variety of research and political action programs, both domestic and foreign. In the mid-1970s it was revealed that the CIA had kept illegal files on 10,000 domestic dissidents. Some observers feel these activities represent an "integral part of our diplomacy and preparedness." Others have denounced them as "jeopardizing the very values we are resolved to defend."[5]

As long as the United States must deal with other nations, our policy makers need up-to-date, concise intelligence. Because the intelligence

---

[4]Roberta Wohlstetter, *Cuba and Pearl Harbor: Hindsight and Foresight* (Rand, 1965), p. 36.

[5]Christopher Felix, "Secret Operations Are an Integral Part of Our Diplomacy," and J. William Fulbright, "We Must Not Fight Fire with Fire," in Young Hum Kim, ed., *The Central Intelligence Agency: Problems of Secrecy in a Democracy* (D. C. Heath, 1968), pp. 36–46, 96–108. See also T. M. Franck and E. Weisband, eds., *Secrecy and Foreign Policy* (Oxford University Press, 1974).

must be collected and evaluated before it is usable, those who supply such information will remain powerful. The CIA's political leverage, its information, its secrecy, its speed in communication, its ability to act, and its enormous size make it a potent force. In the face of severe CIA criticism, Congress now has resolved that this power will be used by publicly accountable decision makers, and will not itself become a source of politically unaccountable decision making. There are now committees in both the Senate and the House whose primary purpose is to hold the CIA accountable to Congress.

COORDINATING THE FOREIGN POLICY ESTABLISHMENT— THE NSC

With so many officials and agencies involved in foreign policy, the problem of coordination is immense. One of the key coordinating agencies is the National Security Council, created by Congress in 1947 to help the president integrate foreign, military and economic policies that affect national security. It consists of the vice-president, secretary of state, secretary of defense, and such other officers as the president shall appoint. The chairman of the Joint Chiefs of Staff usually attends meetings of the council, as does the CIA director (on organizations charts, the CIA is an agency of the National Security Council). The assistant to the president for national security affairs serves as the executive secretary for the council staff.

President Kennedy, partly in response to charges that the system had become too rigid, and partly because of his desire to maintain firm personal control over national security policy, came to use the NSC much less than did his predecessor. Kennedy abolished most of the subcommittees of the NSC and relied heavily on his special assistant for national security affairs and a small personal staff.[6] Yet before his administration was over he found it necessary to create a variety of special task forces working under the NSC. President Johnson continued the Kennedy pattern. President Nixon revived the NSC as the principal forum for the consideration of policy issues, but he seemed to rely more on the NSC staff than on formal meetings. President Carter relies heavily on the NSC system but tries to work closely with each of his cabinet officers as well.

The history of the National Security Council suggests that it has been built more around people than organizational principles. Each president has shaped its structure and adapted its staff procedures to suit personal preferences. The NSC has been less important for the subjects it has treated than as an arena where options are lined up, opinions expressed, and predictions made. Under different administrations since 1947, and often within the same administration, the NSC has been the center stage for foreign policy deliberations, relegated to the wings, or tolerated as an "educational" forum to which issues were brought after decisions had already been made. The need for a National Security Council seems inescapable. "Yet," as a former NSC staff member aptly said, "what logic makes necessary, it does not necessarily make effective."[7]

The role of the state department

The United States Department of State has been variously called "a fudge factory," "a machine that fails," or "a bowl of jelly." Yet it is also the key agency in the day-to-day routine of foreign affairs. This executive department has five traditional duties:

[6]For an example of President Kennedy's use of the staff system, see Robert F. Kennedy, *Thirteen Days: A Memoir of the Cuban Missile Crisis* (Norton, 1969).

[7]Robert H. Johnson, "The National Security Council: The Relevance of the Past to Its Future," *Orbis* (Fall 1969), p. 709.

1. To negotiate with other nations and international organizations
2. To protect U.S. citizens and U.S. interests abroad
3. To promote U.S. interests and commercial enterprises
4. To collect and interpret intelligence
5. To represent a U.S. "presence" abroad

ORGANIZATION

As the diplomatic arm of a superpower, the State Department has responded to our new global concerns with continuous growth and reorganization. Many critics insist, however, that the more it changes, the more it stays the same. One detractor diagnoses the State Department's ills as chronic "elephantiasis and fragmentation."[8] However, among the cabinet departments, State's annual budget is the lowest—less than 1 percent of that of the Department of Defense. Considering the State Department's role and prestige, its staff of 23,000 is still among the executive branch's smallest, especially when compared with the more than 3 million civilian and military in the Defense Department.

But even though the State Department is relatively small, it is probably oversized. Virtually anybody who has ever been in the foreign service admits this. As one former State Department employee told one of us: "There are too many people chasing too few jobs in a system where there is no job tenure. The result is massive insecurity and an attempt to define even the most pathetic job as earthshakingly important as well as finding meaningful work for high level people where none really exists."

Helping the Secretary of State perform his several functions are a deputy secretary, undersecretaries for political affairs, for economic affairs, and management. These five officials are supported by about fifteen assistant secretaries and a staff of several hundred specialists, and a planning and coordination staff that formulates long-range programs. An executive secretariat coordinates work between the policy-making and advisory levels and maintains the Operations Center, the State Department's crisis room. It was established in 1961 when the Bay of Pigs invasion exposed critical communications problems within the department and between our posts overseas. The twenty secretaries, all political appointees, often meet to discuss current developments.

The day-to-day operations of the department are organized along functional and geographic lines. Responsible for activities that cut across geographic boundaries are nine bureaus, each headed by an assistant secretary: International Organizations Affairs, Security and Consular Affairs, Economic Affairs, International Scientific and Technological Affairs, Intelligence and Research, Public Affairs, Educational and Cultural Affairs, Congressional Relations, and Legal Adviser.

Five geographic bureaus, also headed by assistant secretaries, embrace specific regions: Inter-American Affairs, European Affairs, East Asian and Pacific Affairs, Near Eastern and South Asian Affairs, and African Affairs. These bureaus are divided into offices headed by country directors, and these are subdivided into about five hundred desk officers who cover specific countries and functions. This "layering" has plagued efficiency; the State Department has become top-heavy with administrators, who now comprise almost 40 percent of the personnel in each bureau. When in-

[8]Paraphrase of George F. Kennan in Stanley Hoffmann, *Gulliver's Troubles, or, The Setting of American Foreign Policy* (McGraw-Hill, 1968), p. 254, cited in John Franklin Campbell, *The Foreign Affairs Fudge Factory* (Basic Books, 1971), p. 13. But see also Graham Allison and Peter Szanton, *Remaking Foreign Policy* (Basic Books, 1976).

formed of this "management-labor" imbalance, Secretary Rusk retorted, "We're a policy business. We *need* more Chiefs than Indians."[9]

Conducting and managing foreign affairs is a big business. Foreign affairs create great problems and require precise workable solutions. Red tape and disorder in the State Department have caused modern presidents to create "bypass mechanisms"—personal state departments of their own. When this occurs, other agencies such as the CIA and the Department of Defense become more independent of traditional sources of foreign policy making.[10] In emergency, officials cannot wait for decisions to travel up and down the bureaucratic ladder. Organization, speed, and efficiency are needed. If they are frustrated by the Department of State, decision makers act through alternative means. The result, as an anonymous Washington official complained, is that "State is being run all over town."[11]

SPECIAL AGENCIES

Within the Department of State, but with only loose ties, is the Agency for International Development (AID), which operates under a director who reports directly to the secretary of state. With a staff of over 6,000, AID handles the nation's economic and technical assistance and coordinates most military aid programs. AID operates on the assumption that using our economic power to strengthen independent nations will improve our own security.

Economic assistance, or foreign aid, as it is commonly called, is a controversial and unpopular program. In the post-Vietnam years, many people wondered why we become so involved in other people's affairs. Others contend that the United States too often subordinates serious economic and social development goals to short-term political objectives, such as buying diplomatic support and strengthening friendly governments. Critics charge, too, that much of our aid is given with difficult "strings" attached, one of which is that the recipient country buy only U.S. products with our aid monies.

Many people also claim that economic and military aid is often used as a weapon to force less developed countries to accept policies they otherwise would not accept. Thus Johnson cut off economic aid until the Indian government agreed to reform its agricultural programs and, among other things, agreed to use vast supplies of fertilizers sold by U.S. firms. "I kept the 'short tether' on," said Johnson as he placed Indian aid on a month-to-month rather than year-to-year basis. "I decided to reshape our policy to meet the changed situation in the world. We would insist that our friends make a concerted effort to help themselves before we rushed in with food, money and sympathy."[12]

The Arms Control and Disarmament Agency (ACDA), officially independent but housed in the State Department, is another major special agency. ACDA's director reports to the secretary and the president on arms control and disarmament negotiations. Created in 1961 to cope with the wide range of disarmament problems, the ACDA conducts research, briefs our disarmament negotiators, and participates directly in disarma-

[9]Campbell, *Foreign Affairs Fudge Factory*, p. 123.

[10]Richard Holbrooke, "The Machine that Fails," *Foreign Policy* (Winter 1970–71), p. 70. On problems of "red tape" in Washington, see Herbert Kaufman *Red Tape* (Brookings, 1977).

[11]Quoted in Campbell, *Foreign Affairs Fudge Factory*, p. 228.

[12]Lyndon B. Johnson, *The Vantage Point* (Holt, Rinehart & Winston, 1971), p. 223.

ment talks and projects. The 1963 test-ban treaty was based on an ACDA draft. The agency promoted and secured the hot line communication system between Washington and Moscow. It helped shape the Antarctic Treaty, the Nuclear Nonproliferation Treaty, and the Outer Space Treaty. The ACDA is a major participant in the SALT talks and related détente negotiations. The agency, often viewed as both an arms limitation advocate and a "State Department orphan," is not a policing agency; its patient efforts are often undone by larger and more powerful interests within the government.

Americans overseas: the foreign service

American diplomacy is older than the United States. Even before the Revolution, Benjamin Franklin was sent as our representative to France by the Continental Congress. Today the United States maintains nearly three hundred posts abroad, with missions in the capital cities of almost all nations with whom we have diplomatic relations. In addition, we maintain permanent missions at the North Atlantic Treaty Organization, the Organization of American States, European regional organizations, the United Nations, and other units such as the International Civil Aviation Organization.

During our early years as a nation, the caliber of our overseas representation was high. Men like John Adams, Thomas Jefferson, and James Monroe served American interests in foreign capitals. But, following the War of 1812, diplomatic posts were used mainly as rewards for political activities. High diplomatic assignments were given to wealthy men who had contributed to the campaigns of victorious presidents. Because the salaries of diplomats were small and their expenses large, only such men could afford to take posts in the more important nations. Various minor reforms were made, but it was not until 1924 that a modern career service was established. In that year, a Foreign Service of the United States was established on a career basis. The service was further modernized and reorganized by the Foreign Service Act of 1946.

The American Foreign Service is the eyes and ears of the United States in other countries. Although a part of the State Department, the service represents the entire government and performs jobs for many other agencies. Its main duties are to carry out foreign policy as expressed in the directives of the secretary of state, gather data for American policy makers, protect Americans and American interests in foreign countries, and cultivate friendly relations with foreign peoples.

The Foreign Service is composed of ambassadors, ministers, officers, reserve officers, and staff. At the core of the service are the Foreign Service officers, comparable to the officers of the regular army in the military services. They are a select, specially trained body who are expected to take an assignment any place in the world on short notice. There are approximately 3,500 such officers; in recent years less than one hundred junior officers won appointment.[13]

The Foreign Service is one of the most prestigious and most criticized branches of the national government. Back in the 1950s the criticism seemed to outweigh the respect, and morale suffered accordingly. In loyalty-security hearings, officers were asked to justify remarks sometimes tak-

[13]See the perceptive assessment by James Fallows, "The Foreign Service as Mirror of America," *Washington Monthly* (April 1973), pp. 5–14.

en out of context from confidential reports made years before to superiors. Critics accused the service of being infiltrated by Communist sympathizers; others charged that it was dominated by a high-society elite who were still under the impression that diplomacy was the near monopoly of gentlemen. The charges about Communist infiltration were obviously overdrawn, as were claims that the service was preoccupied with refined manners. Still, most of the personnel of the service did come from the same general social background. This fact cut down on the effectiveness of their reporting, for every reporter, not matter how objective, selects and reevaluates what he sees on the basis of personal attitudes and life experiences.

In more recent years, criticism of the Foreign Service has come as much from within as from outside.[14] Most of the criticism claims the Foreign Service: (1) stifles creativity with its clannish "don't-rock-the-boat" and "minimize risk-taking" mentality; (2) attracts officers who are, or at least become, concerned more about *being* or *becoming* somebody than *doing* something; and (3) requires its new recruits to wait fifteen to twenty years before being considered for positions of responsibility. These problems are recognized in Washington, and the task of improving the Service continues. More women and minorities have been recruited in recent years, and other managerial innovations have been tried. But the career service features of the Foreign Service Corps—entry at the bottom, rank in the person rather than in the position, resistance to lateral entry, advancement through grades as determined by senior officers' evaluations, and the tendency toward self-government—make it resistant to change.

Criticism of the Foreign Service because of social class homogeneity is probably overstated. Most of the media and members of Congress come from pretty much the same better-educated, middle- and upper-income classes. And, plainly, there are individuals within this group who are of an independent mind. Some of the best congressional staff in recent years are former Foreign Service officers. More likely it is the structural characteristics of the State Department that prevent independent reporting and creativity. There is an old saying in the Foreign Service that there are old Foreign Service officers and there are bold Foreign Service officers, but there are no old bold Foreign Service officers. So we can expect the Foreign Service exposés to keep coming. Its problems of overstaffing, empty jobs, and tedious apprenticeships are in fact common in most bureaucracies. It is just that "The Foreign Service's situation is exaggerated—because its prestige is so high, and the value of its work inherently so hard to quantify. . . ."[15]

Drawing by Engleman.
Federal Times, August 16, 1976.

The United States and international organizations

The United States belongs to all the important world organizations, and its representatives attend all major international conferences. These organizations and conferences are major instruments of American diplomacy. In addition to the United Nations and its related agencies, the United States is a member of more than two hundred international organizations of various types. Slowly but steadily, certain functions are being transferred from the national to the international level. In its own hemisphere, the

[14]See, for example, Chris Argyris, *Some Causes of Organizational Ineffectiveness Within the Department of State* (Department of State Occasional Paper, U.S. Government Printing Office, 1967); John E. Harr, *The Professional Diplomat* (Princeton University Press, 1969), and *Toward a Modern Diplomacy* (1968), a report of the American Foreign Service Association.

[15]Fallows, "Foreign Service as Mirror," p. 14.

United Nations' delegates from Greece hold a press conference prior to the convening of the General Assembly.

TALK! TALK! TALK!

MAYBE SO, BUT IF THEY EVER **STOP** TALKING THEN THERE'S NO USE TALKING—

6-7 BRICKMAN

Drawing by Brickman. *The Evening Star* (Washington, D.C.), 1966.

United States is a member of the Organization of American States (OAS), a regional agency of twenty-four American republics. In addition to fostering economic and social progress, the OAS seeks to preserve unity and harmony among the American republics—no easy task.

The United Nations was set up by the victorious superpowers immediately after World War II in an effort to control the postwar world and to promote peace. But when the superpowers, which of course included both the U.S. and the USSR, ceased to be friendly, the UN was doomed to political impotence. It has retained a certain usefulness because of its technical agencies and limited peacekeeping activities, but it is far less successful than many people hoped it might be. They feel the United Nations was destined to bring nations together, to maintain international peace and security, to achieve international cooperation in solving world problems, and to promote and encourage respect for human rights.

The United Nations' failure to solve each and every dispute among nations and its inability to end global problems such as famines or the arms race have caused some Americans to become disillusioned with it. The organization suffers also from "creeping irrelevance" and a rigid international civil service that makes our Foreign Service look healthy. We witness the "defeat of an ideal," says one critic—the members pay lip service while at the same time pursuing their short-term interests at its expense. Timidity, bureaucracy, and "geographical" appeasement reign supreme. As one former ambassador to the UN put it, "The United Nations has become an assembly line of mass production of resolutions which have little relevance to the substance of the problem under discussion."[16] Thus, the sniping definition of a UN delegate as a person who has a problem for every solution, has become increasingly accurate.

The United Nations, like every other agency of international politics, is dominated by the fact the world is divided into separate nations acting, most of the time, in their own self-interest. The United States, like most nations, cites the UN Charter when it suits its short-term interest and ignores it when it does not. The U.S. has usually found that on important matters it is easier to deal with involved nations directly. The United Nations, with 149 member nations, can only do *what the member nations want it to do*. Rarely can it move fast. And rarely can it achieve solutions if there is no broad consensus.

Where is the United Nations headed today? It appears to be taking on a new role as the focus shifts from the Security Council, dominated by the super powers, to a General Assembly that increasingly expresses the strident demands of the Third World. In the General Assembly the voting is by nations, so that a nation representing 200,000 people has as much of a vote as one representing 200 million people. And the General Assembly has become dominated by Third World nations, especially those of Africa and the Middle East. They have voted to admit the Palestine Liberation Organization (PLO) and to take restrictive actions against Israel. Parliamentary democracies are hopelessly outnumbered and often outvoted in the United Nations. As these actions have taken place, support for the UN within the United States and the Western World has begun to decline. In

[16]Personal interview. See also Shirley Hazzard, *Defeat of an Ideal: A Study of the Self-Destruction of the United Nations* (Little, Brown, 1973). See also, Mahdi Elmandjra, *The United Nations System: An Analysis* (Faber and Faber, 1973). For a different view, see the diary by William F. Buckley, Jr., *United Nations Journal* (Putnam, 1974).

many ways, the UN has become a focus of the effort at economic redistribution between the less well developed countries (LDC's), and the more developed ones. This struggle is supplementing the old bloc conflicts of East versus West with one of North versus South.

Certain conservatives have long opposed our involvement in the UN, fearing the U.S. would risk being trapped or outvoted by the Communists or the Third World nations. Some of the U.S.'s disillusionments has come about because the UN is so large and unwieldy and seems to accomplish so little. There are many who feel the UN fails because we have had so little faith in it. They counsel us to expect more: *try to make it work.* Plainly, they add, the UN is a useful and perhaps a necessary organization for diplomatic consultation. Meanwhile, the UN remains a sometimes helpful forum for working out joint programs on the law of the sea, economic development, world population problems, global energy supplies, and the protection of the international environment.

The politics of foreign policy making

Foreign policy flows through much the same institutional and constitutional structures as does domestic policy. Public opinion, pressure groups, political parties, elections, separation of powers, federalism are also part of the politics of foreign policy making. But they operate somewhat differently from the way they do in internal affairs.

PUBLIC OPINION AND FOREIGN POLICY

Different foreign policy issues evoke different degrees of public involvement. In crisis situations — the Cuban missile crisis or the 1973 Arab-Israeli war — decisions are made by a small group of persons. Yet even in these situations the president and his advisers make their decisions with the knowledge that what they decide will ultimately have to have support from the public and its institutions, especially Congress.

In noncrisis situations the public appears to consist of three "publics." The largest, comprising perhaps as much as 75 percent of the adult population, is the mass public. This group knows little about foreign affairs, despite the grave importance of the subject.[17] During the Berlin Crisis in 1959, a *New York Times* survey showed that many people did not even know where Berlin was.[18] In 1964 the Survey Research Center found that 28 percent of the people interviewed did not know there was a Communist regime in China. And studies in 1970 revealed that even during the widely publicized Vietnam War, most Americans remained ignorant of major events abroad.[19]

The second public is the attentive public. Comprising perhaps 15 to 20 percent of the population, it maintains an active interest in foreign policy. The opinion makers are the third and smallest public. They transmit information and judgments on foreign affairs and mobilize support in the other two publics. To illustrate the relationship between these three publics, one analyst has developed this instructive analogy of a huge theater with a tense drama being played out on the stage:

[17]Alfred O. Hero, *Americans in World Affairs* (World Peace Foundation, 1959), p. 10. On patterns of information and participation in American politics, see Sidney Verba and Norman Nie, *Political Participation* (Harper & Row, 1972).

[18]*The New York Times* (March 22, 1959), Part IV, p. 8.

[19]Don D. Smith, " 'Dark Areas of Ignorance' Revisited: Current Knowledge about Asian Affairs," *Social Science Quarterly* (December 1970), pp. 668–73. See also John Mueller, *War, Presidents, and Public Opinion*, (Wiley, 1973).

Officials place their signatures on the Panama Canal treaty. Seated from left, President Carter, Organization of American States Secretary General Alejandro Orfila, and Panama's head of state General Omar Torrijos.

The mass public, occupying the many seats in the balcony, is so far removed from the scene of action that its members can hardly grasp the plot, much less hear all the lines or distinguish between the actors. Thus they may sit in stony silence or applaud impetuously, if not so vigorously as to shake the foundations of the theater. Usually, however, they get thoroughly bored and leave. . . . The attentive public, on the other hand, is located in the few choice orchestra seats. Its members can not only hear every line clearly, but can also see the facial expressions of the actors. Thus they become absorbed in the drama, applauding its high spots and disparaging its flaws. Indeed, their involvement is such that during the intermission they make their views known to any occupants of the balcony who may have wandered into the lobby. As for the members of the opinion-making public, they are the actors on the stage, performing their parts with gusto and intensity, not infrequently in an effort to upstage each other. Many are directing their performance at some specific portion of the orchestra audience. Others, those with especially strong vocal cords, try to make themselves heard as far as the balcony. All are keenly aware that the quality of their performance will greatly affect their bargaining power when they seek higher salaries or better parts in future productions.[20]

Why are so many people indifferent or uninformed? First, foreign affairs are usually more remote than domestic issues. People have more firsthand information about inflation than about Chilean land reform or Turkish political problems. The worker in the factory and the boss in the front office know what labor-management relations are about, and they have strong opinions on the subject. They are likely to be less concerned about the internal struggles for power within Ethiopia or our policy on Cambodia—or to feel that they could not do much about it anyway. Only when American soldiers, especially drafted soldiers, are being killed does the mass public become concerned with foreign affairs. And the relatively fewer citizens trying to influence foreign policies is not unique to the United States—it is found in other democratic nations also.[21]

Lack of widespread concern, knowledge, and involvement in the poli-

[20]James N. Rosenau, ed., *Public Opinion and Foreign Policy* (Random House, 1961), pp. 34–35.

[21]Gabriel A. Almond and Sidney Verba, *The Civic Culture: Political Attitudes and Democracy in Five Nations* (Princeton University Press, 1963).

tics of foreign policy should not be confused with lack of intense feelings about aspects of the international scene. Since World War II, questions about our relations with other nations have been high on the list of public concerns. And when issues such as the Vietnam conflict become domesticated—that is, when they visibly, directly, and immediately affect the people of the United States—the debate over such policies produces demonstrations, campaigns, hearings. In other words, there are all the trappings of the ordinary political process.[22] Until a foreign policy issue becomes critical, most Americans are unconcerned with it. But when they can see that it directly affects them, they can and often do become highly and intensely concerned about it.

PUBLIC MOODS: AN UNSTABLE BASE?

The movement from no interest to intense feeling means that the public reaction to foreign policy issues is often based on moods.[23] It has been traditionally held that the mass public oversimplifies the problems of foreign politics. It tends to reduce all issues to the one that is most urgent at the moment. It thinks of the participants in terms of heroes and villains. It favors quick and easy remedies—fire the secretary of state, or lower trade barriers and all will be well. Although this "mood theory" has been challenged, it is conceded that Americans are extremely "permissive" with U.S. foreign policy makers on international issues.[24] And although members of the attentive public and the decision makers are also subject to mood responses and oversimplification, as the level of interest and information rises so does the degree of sophistication.[25]

Popular indifference toward international politics means that policy makers often have to dramatize issues in order to arouse public support. On the other hand, in periods of public excitement, fear of rash public opinion causes policy makers to be overcautious. To secure American participation in the United Nations, for example, the State Department carried on an intensive publicity campaign. But, in so doing, it gave many people the impression that the United Nations would ensure peace and order in the world.

Too much has been made, however, of the American people's ignorance about foreign policy when contrasted to their knowledge of domestic issues. There is a growing view among scholars that the idea of the public as being moody and therefore providing an unstable base for foreign policy is vastly exaggerated. The instability of public moods, to the extent that it does exist, probably does not affect policy makers all that much. Most policy makers do not consider the public mood unless it is likely to be hostile

[22]Rosenau, *Domestic Sources of Foreign Policy*, p. 49.

[23]See Gabriel A. Almond, *The American People and Foreign Policy* (Harcourt, 1950); Rosenau, *Public Opinion and Foreign Policy;* and Hero, *Americans in World Affairs*. In a more recent edition of his book (Praeger, 1960), Almond has noted a "greater stabilization in foreign policy awareness and attention" in recent years.

[24]William R. Caspary, "The 'Mood Theory': A Study of Public Opinion and Foreign Policy," *American Political Science Review* (June 1970), pp. 536–46. See also Eugene J. Rosi, "Public Opinion and National Security Policy" in E. J. Rosi, ed., *American Defense and Détente* (Dodd, Mead, 1973).

[25]Rogers et al detect no significant increase in awareness among the college educated in their study of the general public's knowledge of foreign affairs. William C. Rogers et al., "A Comparison of Informed and General Public Opinion on U.S. Foreign Policy," *Public Opinion Quarterly* (Summer 1967), pp. 242–52.

to a foreign policy decision. Then the problem is not instability of mood but the public's distaste for a given decision. Moreover, issues are usually defined by policy makers; the public merely reacts to them. The public hardly determines issues. Policy makers shape the national agenda of issues. The State Department makes an effort to keep people informed about those areas of policy it thinks should be talked about publicly and makes an effort to keep itself informed about public opinion. Sometimes State Department officials give the impression that they do not care what the public thinks. This is perhaps misleading. Yet almost all negotiations in which the State Department has a major role are conducted in secret. Both the public and Congress are frequently kept at a distance.

Still, public opinion determines the broad limits within which others make decisions. Public attitudes determine the political possibilities open to policy makers. The president and his advisers know they must eventually secure active public support for programs that call for large expenditures of money or for commitments that involve grave danger to national security.

THE ATTENTIVE PUBLIC AND FOREIGN POLICY

Group and opinion leaders sprinkled through society—priests and preachers, newspaper editors, radio and TV commentators, professors, and public speakers—form an attentive public whose support is actively sought by the official policy makers. They have an influential voice in the shaping of foreign policy. These persons serve as a national pulse for our decision makers. One source calls these opinion-making elites "the decent, kindly cross that democratic governments carry around their necks in the contest with the dictatorships."[26]

The press is powerful in shaping public opinion, a fact reflected in frequent disputes between the "fourth estate" and the government. Hostility between the press and the Department of State is an issue of long standing. The press gets especially upset when the government's excessive use of classification or secrecy is used to bury its mistakes. According to some observers there are not one but three foreign offices in Washington—one at the *New York Times*, another at the *Washington Post*, and one at the State Department.

Another segment of the attentive public consists of citizens' organizations dedicated to increasing public awareness of U.S. foreign policy. The Foreign Policy Association designs community and media programs to encourage citizens to study and discuss major foreign policy controversies. The Council on Foreign Relations, sometimes called the cornerstone of the Eastern Establishment, publishes *Foreign Affairs* magazine and several books a year; it also provides a forum for bringing business leaders and government elites together for talks on new directions in foreign policy. Groups like the World Federalists argue for world government. The Navy League, comprised of friends of the Navy, devotes its energy to increasing the strength of the Navy believing this to be essential for the nation's security. Defense contractors also sometimes try to promote certain kinds of foreign policies. Religious and national-origin publics are particularly interested in certain phases of foreign policy. These groups sometimes have intense feelings about issues, and they are often strategically located to affect the outcome of elections.

[26]"The Way We Go to War," *The Economist* (June 26–July 2, 1971), p. 16.

It is difficult to generalize about the impact of special interest groups on American foreign policies. Their influence appears to vary by type of issue and from time to time. At moments of international crisis a president is able to mobilize so much public support that special groups find it difficult to exert much influence. And outside the crisis areas, careful investigations into some areas of policy such as reciprocal trade, find that special groups rarely have had a decisive role in the formulation of foreign policy.[27] One investigation came to the conclusion that "interest group influence on foreign policy is slight,"[28] weaker than in domestic policy. Of course, what is more difficult to determine is the impact on policy caused by policy makers' *anticipations* of group reactions.

PARTIES AND FOREIGN POLICY

Parties, as such, do not play a major role in shaping foreign policy, for two reasons: First, many Americans would still prefer to keep foreign policy out of politics. Second, parties take less clear and candid stands on foreign policy than they do on domestic policy. All the party weaknesses discussed in Chapter 10 operate in full measure in foreign policy making. Party platforms often obscure the issues instead of highlighting them; many congresspersons fail to follow even a very general party line; and the parties fail to discipline even the most outspoken rebels.

Should parties be concerned with foreign policy? At the end of World War II sentiment grew stronger for a bipartisan approach to foreign policy. An ambiguous term, bipartisanship seems to mean (1) collaboration between the executive and the congressional foreign policy leaders of both parties; (2) support of presidential foreign policies by both parties in Congress; (3) withdrawal of foreign policy issues from debate in political campaigns. In general, bipartisanship is an attempt to remove the issues of foreign policy from partisan politics. It is argued that despite the internal differences that divide Americans, we share a common interest with respect to other nations. During times of national danger we should unite behind policies necessary to preserve the national well-being, and such unity is needed to support our foreign policies. American foreign policy was ineffective following World War I because it became entangled in the partisan struggle between Democrats and Republicans.

Bipartisanship has appeal. In this era of chronic crisis, it seems to symbolize people standing shoulder to shoulder as they face an uncertain and potentially hostile world. It provides more continuity of policy, and it ensures that a wider variety of leaders and interests are consulted in policy making. Psychologically, it helps to satisfy the instinct of people to turn to one another for reassurance. Its motto—partisan politics stops at the water's edge—is comforting to the many Americans worried about disunity.

But the idea of bipartisanship has come under sharp attack. Some feel that bipartisanship is merely a smokescreen for presidential domination in foreign policy making. They suggest that it obscures the fact that foreign policy is made by a relatively small, self-perpetuating elite of national

[27]Raymond A. Bauer, Ithiel de Sola Pool, and Lewis Anthony Dexter, *American Business and Public Policy: The Politics of Foreign Trade* (Atherton, 1963), p. 396. See also Bernard C. Cohen, *The Press and Foreign Policy* (Princeton University Press, 1963), p. 2.

[28]Lester W. Milbrath, "Interest Groups and Foreign Policy," in Rosenau, *Public Opinion and Foreign Policy*, p. 251. See also the analysis of group influence on foreign policy in Bernard C. Cohen, *The Influence of Non-Governmental Groups on Foreign Policy-Making* (World Peace Foundation, 1959).

security managers who are essentially nonpartisan *and* unelected. Other critics charge that it denies a basic tenet of democracy—the right of a people to choose between alternative lines of action. According to this argument, in a free society people should be allowed and even encouraged to differ. The need in a democracy is not to stifle differences, or to ignore them. The need is to express the differences in a meaningful way, to find the will of the majority, to permit the government to act and the opposition to oppose.

Major divisions have also developed *within* the political parties. Thus, debates over our role in Indochina, when they finally did take place, occurred primarily within the Democratic party, not between Democrats and Republicans. And recent presidents seeking renomination have been challenged from within their own parties by candidates who advocate alternative directions in foreign policy. If our major parties do not always present us with a clear *choice*, they at least offer us *a chance* for changing officials and policies. To win as many votes as possible, the major parties search for common denominators among the voting public. They strive to find a basis for agreement from the medley of conflicting opinions. And when the winning party takes office, the losing party has the equally important task of furnishing "loyal" opposition.

Thus parties—and partisanship—are vital to democracy. "Why should we abandon them at the water's edge?" ask the opponents of bipartisanship. Certainly not because Americans are agreed on foreign policy: the nation abounds with different opinions, as recent crises have made clear. Surely not because we hope to show a united front to the rest of the world. We cannot deceive others with a pretense of agreement; they know our differences as well as we do. Besides, our party divisions should be something to flaunt with pride, not something to be hidden in the closet whenever foreigners seem to be looking at us.

Even more serious, critics conclude, bipartisanship erodes responsibility. A great virtue of partisan government is that those in office can be held to account simply because they hold authority. But when the leaders of both parties work together, responsibility fades. After things go badly, the leaders of each party maintain that it was the other party's fault. Instead of a sober consideration of alternative courses of action, there is a frantic hunt for scapegoats.

CONGRESS AND FOREIGN POLICY

It may seem strange to discuss our national legislative body as part of the attentive public rather than as part of the formal foreign policy establishment. But despite the importance of foreign policy, despite the fact that Congress can block the president's policy and undermine his decisions, Congress as an institution seldom directly *makes* foreign policy. In the making of foreign policy, the power of Congress is mainly *consultative*, although it sometimes does take the initiative in foreign economic and military assistance questions. It is also a link between the policy makers and the public. Like many of us, however, Congress wants a meaningful relationship, especially "meaningful consultation" with the president in matters of foreign relations.[29]

[29]Jacob K. Javits, "The Congressional Presence in Foreign Relations," *Foreign Affairs* (January 1970), p. 233. See also Alton Frye, *A Responsible Congress: The Politics of National Security* (McGraw-Hill, 1975); and James A. Nathan and James K. Oliver *United States Foreign Policy and World Order* (Little, Brown, 1976), Chap. 13.

Because of members of Congress' sensitivity to public opinion, because of their expertise, and because of their prominence, individual members (in contrast to Congress) are sometimes included within the circle of those who make the decisions. For example, the chairman of the Senate Committee on Foreign Relations has been involved at times, though usually his main role is either helping to educate the public or educating the president on what will or will not run into congressional opposition. When the chairman is out of sympathy with the policies of the president, as former Senator Fulbright was on Vietnam, he may use the committee to focus attention on the differences.

During the 1930s and after World War II, the almost unanimous opinion of academics and the attentive public favored strengthening the hand of the president and limiting the role of Congress in the foreign policy area. It was generally thought that *only the president* had the knowledge, the political base, and the broad, global perspective from which to develop coherent and sensible foreign policies. Congress was thought to be too responsive to the parochial and uninformed attitudes of the public. When conservative leaders tried to alter constitutional arrangements in order to limit the president's power to make executive agreements and to implement treaties, they ran into solid opposition from the intellectual and academic elites.

But in recent years, with popular sentiment and intellectual opinion so opposed to the Vietnam policies of Presidents Johnson and Nixon, Congress, especially the Senate, has become more assertive: The restriction by Congress on the use of funds for ground warfare in Laos, the 1973 vote to cut off funds for bombing in Cambodia, and the War Powers Resolution of 1973 were clear signs of a growing restiveness over presidential supremacy.

Can we have a democratic foreign policy?

A great paradox exists in conducting the foreign relations of a modern democracy. In the last century Tocqueville wrote that foreign relations "demand scarcely any of the qualities which are peculiar to a democracy; they require, on the contrary, the perfect use of all those in which it is deficient.[30] Morgenthau has observed more directly that policy makers in our democracy "either . . . must sacrifice what they consider good policy upon the altar of public opinion, or they must by devious means gain support for policies whose true nature is concealed from the public."[31] Not a few voices have charged our leaders with misleading the people, the experts with misleading our leaders, and ideologies with blinding all of us, especially in Indochina.

Where shall we draw the line? How *do* our policy makers reconcile public rights with political realities?

In Vietnam our apparent policy was to stop Communist expansion. Our policy makers guessed wrong in thinking gradual military pressure would deter the North. They miscalculated the character of the war as well as the commitment of those who opposed the Saigon governments.[32] Finally they

[30]Alexis de Tocqueville, *Democracy in America* (Knopf, 1945), I, 224–35.

[31]Hans Morgenthau, "The Conduct of American Foreign Policy," *Parliamentary Affairs* (Winter 1949), p. 147.

[32]For an excellent on-the-scene account of this miscalculation by a young marine officer who fought there, see Philip Caputo, *A Rumor of War* (Holt, Rinehart & Winston, 1977).

tried to get out with some face-saving gestures. And because they recognized mistakes or believed that the American people and Congress might not support them in what they thought necessary, they sought to conceal difficulties.

Perhaps our biggest disappointment—as a system of government—was that our institutions did not make up for these failings or at least did not warn us of them sooner. Students of government must ask themselves and search for the answer to the central, lingering question: How can we fashion our institutions and processes so as to prevent these human failings from exacting such a large toll again?

If one believes that the American people were kept in the dark, then one ignores the fact that no group of citizens has ever had access to more information about a war than we had about Vietnam. We did not have all the information, but, because of a free press and independent judiciary, more was shown, written, and said about Vietnam than in any other war from the Revolution to Korea: "We knew what we were doing when we went into Vietnam."[33]

Summary

1. Foreign policy is not made according to any set formula, but represents various traditions, organized interests, and constitutional processes. Our democracy has given the primary responsibility for making foreign policy to the chief executive. But he in turn is dependent on accidents of history, on his advisers, and in the long run, on the American people. When there are no obvious solutions to international problems, our decision makers must predict, act, and wait—sometimes successfully, but sometimes with unforeseeable and catastrophic consequences.

2. A president can usually act swiftly and decisively. He is often in a good position to see the nation's long-run interests above the tugging of bureaucratic and special interests. He must face the people in elections, but not so often that he must follow public opinion instead of leading it. Yet the desired presidential accountability between elections can only be achieved if the people are willing to inform themselves and demand answers, explanations, and honest reporting from their leaders.

3. War is merely the extension of diplomacy by other means. Perhaps future generations will be able to eliminate this alternative entirely, but in our own time our leaders must deal with realities, not dreams; with the world as they see it, not as they wish it. Greater restraints upon decision makers might undermine our security, and fewer restraints might endanger our freedom. In the end, if the Vietnam War has had any value, it is to make us aware of the limits of our power as a world *policeman* and to reappraise the balance of power among our institutions.

[33]See an essay so titled by Henry Fairlie in the *Washington Monthly* (May 1973), pp. 7–26.

Chapter 20

Providing for the Common Defense

When he ran for the presidency, Jimmy Carter often suggested that the Cold War was coming to a close, and sometimes added that he would never get the United States "militarily involved in the affairs of another country unless our own security was directly threatened." But in his first year in office it was clear to everyone, including President Carter, that strained Soviet-American relationships were still the overriding issue for American diplomacy and American military strategy. For example, there was Carter's willingness to support the production of neutron bombs (which use intense radiation to kill people without damaging buildings), urged on him by Pentagon officials as the most effective means of stopping the Soviet Union in the event of a ground attack in Central Europe.

Q. *Reporter:* How much do you think there is to the argument that if you have a cleaner weapon [the neutron bomb], as you define it, it makes war more possible, that it might be used, and secondly, where do you stand on the age-old question of nuclear weapons in Europe, for instance, as to whether if you start using them it wouldn't automatically escalate into a full-scale nuclear war?

A. *Carter:* I think one of the concepts that must be avoided is an exact description ahead of time of what I, as President, would do under every conceivable circumstance.

The ownership of atomic weapons and their potential use is such a horrifying prospect—their use—that it is a deterrent to a major confrontation between nations who possess atomic weapons.

I believe that the nation that uses atomic weapons first would be under heavy condemnation from the other people of the world unless the circumstances were extremely gross, such as unwarranted invasion into another country. . . .

In a nationwide television and radio address in October 1962, President Kennedy advised the American people that the U.S. was setting up a naval blockade against Cuba.

To answer the other part of your question, my guess is that no one would certainly know that the first use of atomic weapons might very well quickly lead to a rapid and uncontrolled escalation in the use of even more powerful weapons with possibly a worldwide holocaust resulting. This is a prospect that is sobering to us all and that's why the Soviets and we and others have worked so hard to try to reach an agreement in the prohibition against atomic weapons.[1]

The implication is that Carter reserves the right to use the neutron bomb in the event of an invasion by a Communist bloc nation. It is a position that raises again the specter of nuclear holocaust, and presents a tough U.S. stance to the Soviets.

The push for new bombs and more effective weapons continues at an alarming pace. At last count the U.S. if it unleashed its arsenal of missiles, could destroy the Soviet Union 44 times. The USSR could destroy us at least 22 times. Is it any longer possible for nations to fight each other and survive? President Kennedy once estimated that as many as 500 million deaths would have occurred during the first hours of a nuclear exchange between the U.S. and the USSR. In this age of absolute weaponry, this "fail-safe" era of "overkill" and *"second strike capability,"* some are optimistic. They believe that our recognition of the horror and destruction of nuclear war will enable us to bring these weapons under international control. For others, the proliferation of nuclear warheads portends the end of civilization.

The politics and strategy of defense

Both president and Congress are responsible for the common defense, and both have constitutional authority to discharge that responsibility. Congress appropriates the money and determines the size, structure, and organization of the fighting forces; the president is the commander in chief of these forces and determines when and how military power will be used. In defense as in foreign policy emergency situations, the president is the decision maker of last resort.

THE NATION'S DEFENSE OBJECTIVES

The defense goals of the nation change over time and are subject to a variety of constraints and the political mood of the nation. In the 1970s most Americans are less willing to support the use of American ground forces in overseas conflicts than they had been during the 1950s and 1960s. Public willingness to use nuclear weapons on behalf of our allies is much lower than in earlier periods. Support for cutbacks in defense spending is higher in the 1970s than in the earlier Cold War period. These changes in mood are probably due to related factors: the disillusioning experience of the Vietnam War, a lowered confidence in the military, and a reduced fear of both nuclear war and the spread of communism.[2] Plainly, however, we expect the president, Congress, and the military to protect us from attack.

[1]*The New York Times* (July 13, 1977), p. A–10.

[2]These findings are reported and discussed in Bruce Russett and Miroslav Ninic, "American Opinion on the Use of Military Force Abroad," *Political Science Quarterly* (Fall 1976), pp. 411–31; and John E. Mueller, "Changes in American Public Attitudes Toward International Involvement," in Sam C. Sarkesian, Morris Janowitz and Ellen Stein, eds., *The Consequences and Limits of Military Intervention* (Sage, 1977).

We also may expect them to do everything in their power to prevent war.

Beyond deterring war, however, our military or defense policies are intertwined with foreign policy objectives. These too change from era to era, but at present they include the following:

1. To preserve the United States as an independent nation
2. To safeguard our institutions and values
2. To maintain ability to deter aggression
4. To reduce the perils of nuclear war
5. To help resolve regional conflicts that imperil global peace
6. To revitalize our bond to allies who share our traditions, values, and interests
7. To build more rational relationships with potential adversaries
8. To protect as best we can our supplies of energy, strategic resources, and food

Critics sometimes charge that the military conspires with defense contractors and other strategic elites to maintain a vast network of bases and fleets around the world. They contend that the defense budget is deliberately being used to increase federal spending in order to keep the economy from a recession. This is the view that the military-industrial establishment has a life of its own, is too big to be effectively managed or controlled, spends too large a share of our national wealth, and is dedicated to exaggerating the "Soviet menace."

President Eisenhower once asked Nikita Khrushchev how he decided the question of funds for military expenses in his nation. Eisenhower began by saying:

> Perhaps first I should tell you how it is with us. It's like this: My military leaders say, "Mr. President, we need such and such a sum for such and such a program." I say, "Sorry, we don't have the funds." They say, "We have reliable information that the Soviet Union has already allocated funds for their own such program." So I give in. That's how they wring the money out of me. Now tell me, how is it with you?

Khrushchev responded:

> It's just the same. They say, "Comrade Khrushchev, look at this! The Americans are developing such and such a system." I tell them there's no money. So we discuss it some more, and I end up giving them the money they asked for.[3]

Military leaders scoff at charges of a military-industrial establishment. They point to the reduced size of the military and note that since its wartime peak in 1968, the U.S. defense budget has decreased in real dollars by more than one-third. Military personnel strength has dropped from 3.5 million to 2.1 million. There are fewer people in uniform now, they add, than at any time since 1950, and fewer U.S. troops abroad since 1940. Further, our active fleet of Navy ships has dropped by more than half. The chairman of the joint chiefs of staff—and thus the ranking military leader in the U.S.—refutes the charge of a military-industrial complex this way:

> The United States military establishment has no life of its own. Its existence does not generate its needs. Quite the opposite. The needs of na-

---

[3]Quoted by Clayton Fritchey, June 16, 1973, syndicated column, cited in Robert Sherrill, *Why They Call it Politics*, 2nd ed. (Harcourt, Brace, Jovanovich, 1974), pp. 58–59.

tional security generate the requirements for a national defense establishment. The size, composition, equipage, deployment, and state of readiness of our military forces are dictated by three factors: one is the tasks to be performed; two is the threat to our national security; the last is the degree of risk judged acceptable.[4]

We hear much about the military-industrial elite. And it exists. But it is not all-powerful and it is not the only elite that operates in our democracy. There is also a scientific-intellectual elite, an agribusiness elite, a public employees elite, a trade union elite. In short, our government is built on interest group-public agency-immediate benefit coalitions, all seeking to define the public interest.

The classical problem in determining defense objectives and the needed defense budgets is *how much is enough?* How to tell whether we are sufficiently strong? Most U.S. leaders would agree that in addition to the general objectives outlined above, our major defense programs must ensure we have the military strength (1) to maintain a strategic balance with the USSR, (2) to maintain naval forces adequate to deter attacks and keep essential sea lanes open, and (3) to maintain conventional combat forces that enable us to defend against likely threats to our security and that of all our allies elsewhere, especially in Europe.

"Twenty-five nuclear submarines, twelve hundred ICBMs, two hundred and seventy-five cruise missiles—oops, wrong list."

Drawing by Lorenz. © 1976 The New Yorker Magazine, Inc.

CONTROLLING THE DEFENSE BUDGET

The sheer magnitude of our defense establishment is difficult to comprehend. The Department of Defense will spend well over $135 billion in fiscal year 1980. More than half the people employed by the national government work in the Department of Defense. Nearly three-quarters of federal purchases of goods and services originate in the defense budget. This makes the Pentagon the biggest purchaser in the United States, absorbing over 6 percent of the total national output of goods and services.

Moreover, there are about 4,000 defense installations scattered across the country. Contracts in excess of $60 billion result in defense-related nongovernmental civilian employment of over 2 million. There are nearly 1.5 million retired defense department personnel drawing pensions and other fringe benefits. Clearly, the defense department's size and impact on our society raises questions about how it can be controlled.

Foreign policy expert George Kennan addresses the problem aptly when he writes that this vast flow of "military spending comes to constitute a vested interest on the part of all those who participate in it and benefit from it." The number of people who have a stake in the continuation of high defense spending is enormous and their political punch is usually very powerful. "This includes not just the industrialists who get the money and the Pentagon purchasers who get the hardware and services," says Kennan, "but also all those who benefit from the arrangement in other ways: not only the uniformed personnel of the armed services but those who serve the Pentagon directly as civilian workers, and beyond them the many more who, as workers in defense plants or in other capacities, share in the spin-off from these vast expenditures."[5]

[4]General George S. Brown, "National Security Policy and the Nation's Armed Services at 200 Years," in *Presidential Studies Quarterly* (Fall 1976), p. 4.

[5]George F. Kennan, *The Cloud of Danger* (Atlantic Little, Brown, 1977), p. 13. See also Adam Yarmolinsky, *The Military Establishment* (Harper & Row, 1971); and Sidney Lens, *The Military-Industrial Complex* (Pilgrim Press, 1970).

Year	Too Much	Too Little	About Right	No Opinion
1976	36%	22%	32%	10%
1974	44	12	32	12
1971	49	11	31	9
1969	52	8	31	9

Gallup Poll Index, April 1976.

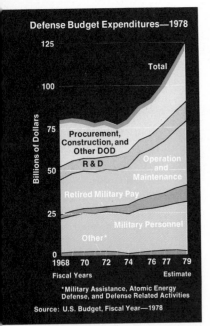

Defense Budget Expenditures—1978

Billions of Dollars

Procurement, Construction, and Other DOD
R & D
Operation and Maintenance
Retired Military Pay
Military Personnel
Other*
Total

1968 70 72 74 76 77 79
Fiscal Years   Estimate

*Military Assistance, Atomic Energy
Defense, and Defense Related Activities

Source: U.S. Budget, Fiscal Year—1978

In recent years, almost a half of the American people have felt that we spend too much on defense. This view was held by a majority toward the end of the Vietnam War. But as we ended that war and decreased defense spending in relation to other priorities, there has been a gradual increase in those who feel we may be spending too little on defense, as shown in Table 20–1.

Can President Carter control defense spending? During his campaign he declared that "without endangering the defense of our nation or commitments to our allies, we can reduce present defense expenditures by about $5 billion to $7 billion annually." However, Carter's first year budget increased defense spending by about $16 billion.

Some advisers have urged that Carter reduce troop strength and certain civilian support offices by about 100,000 per year over a five-year period. But such sharp cuts are vigorously opposed by the joint chiefs of staff. Others have suggested a bolder program of closing and consolidating domestic military bases. But base closings anger politicians and take a long time because the Defense Department must hold extensive public hearings before it can close a base. The fiercest antiwar doves in Congress often shout the loudest when a base closing is suggested for their district or state. Many analysts are skeptical of Carter's ability to reduce defense spending. They claim inflation, soaring military pensions, the increasing sophistication of new weapons, the need to match the Russians, and even simple bureaucratic inertia all make actual cuts unlikely.

It is commonly agreed that Soviet strategic nuclear capabilities have increased five or six fold since 1964. The Soviet Union maintains a high rate of growth in defense spending. This includes, we are told, new intercontinental and submarine-launched nuclear missiles, advanced ground and air combat equipment, and dramatically strengthened naval forces. As a Brookings Institution expert put it, "The Russians have been steadily building away while we were diddling away in Indochina."[6]

So Carter will have to study pay and pension costs, trim unneeded weapons programs, and make smaller gradual cuts in a considerable number of places. And of course military outbreaks anywhere in the world or a worsening of relations with the USSR could force Carter to abandon any hope of reducing defense spending by 1981. Then, too, even if the president succeeds in cutting defense spending, he can be overruled by a Congress that insists on further increases.

[6]Barry M. Blechman, quoted in Louis Kraar, "Why Defense Costs Are Headed Up," *Fortune* (December 1976), p. 164. See also Barry M. Blechman, "Manning an Affordable Defense," *Saturday Review* (December 11, 1976), pp. 11–14.

Making defense policy: Carter's B-1 bomber decision

Modern defense aircrafts: the Russian Mig 21 (top) and the U.S. B-1 bomber.

THE B-1	
Crew:	Four
Speed:	Supersonic (High Altitude) Near Sonic (Treetop Level)
Range:	Intercontinental
Length:	151 Feet
Wingspan:	137 Feet (Forward) 78 Feet (Swept)
Engines:	GE F101 Smokeless (30,000-Pound Thrust)

Source: Rockwell International (1976)

Heading into the 1960s, Air Force officials pushed for presidential and congressional approval to build a high-flying manned bomber that could travel at supersonic speeds. Research and planning was begun on the B-70 bomber, a large supersonic craft. But when the U-2 was shot down in 1960, so was the idea of a high-flying bomber, because of its vulnerability to Russian surface-to-air missiles (SAMs). Bureaucratic politics and inertia kept the B-70 going through the mid-1960s. Two prototypes were built: one crashed; the other is in a museum.

But research continued and in 1969 President Nixon's secretary of defense stepped up the program to develop a new bomber. This time it was a low-flying bomber that could penetrate Soviet airspace at low altitudes and thus avoid being shot down by SAMs. By 1970 the Rockwell International Corporation had won a contract to develop what was to be called the B-1 bomber. In 1973, congressional appropriations for the B-1 passed the $400 million mark.

The B-1 is a 151-foot swing-wing aircraft whose prime mission is to penetrate to targets at high subsonic speed while presenting a very small radar image. Its wings can change position and thus allow it to fly both at supersonic speeds at high altitudes and just under the sound barrier at treetop altitudes. Traveling with a crew of four, the B-1 was built to carry a payload of 24 short-range attack missiles (SRAMs).

Supporters of the B-1 claim that the bomber force is an important part of our nuclear deterrent; opponents contend bombers are the outmoded "battleships of the air force" and no longer serve a useful purpose in a world of intercontinental rocket-fired missiles. Opponents also note the Soviet's apparent disinterest in development of a long-range manned air bomber as evidence it is no longer a necessary weapon. Proponents of a B-1 bomber force pointed to its importance as part of the so-called triad of (1) land-based missiles, (2) sea-based missiles and (3) manned bombers with missiles. In this scheme, any Soviet action to destroy one arm of the triad will allow the United States to retain the capacity to retaliate. Defenders of the B-1 pointed out that the bombers are controlled by humans and, once sent to their targets, can be recalled and can thus be used as a threat.

There was considerable agreement in Congress and in the executive branch that the U.S. should maintain a bomber force. As Carter came to the presidency, the major issue revolved around the form of our bomber force. The central point was whether we needed to modernize the air fleet and if so, whether the B-1 bomber was our best alternative.

In the 1976 presidential campaign Gerald Ford gave his unqualified support to the B-1 bomber, campaigned at Rockwell's California plant, and had himself photographed in a B-1 pilot seat there. Candidate Carter said he opposed the production of the B-1 bomber "at this time." He added, however, "I believe that research and development should continue." He said the final decision on the B-1 should be up to the next president; whoever was president should study the matter carefully and decide the question of B-1 production sometime in mid-1977.

Meanwhile, Congress voted, by large majorities in both houses, to continue research and development of the B-1. Congress did agree, however, to hold off mass production until after the election, so that the newly elected president could have a say in this costly project. The Air Force wanted 244 B-1 bombers. Production costs alone were expected to run to about $24 billion, or nearly $100 million for each plane. Over a twenty-year period the B-1 program would cost about $100 billion to build, maintain, and operate.

These were the arguments Carter had to weigh in early 1977. The Air Force claimed that by the late 1980s, when the B-1 force would be ready to operate, the B-52 fleet would be twenty-five years old and in need of replacement. It was argued, too, that by the mid-1980s Soviet air defenses would be developed to the point that the B-52 would not be able to penetrate to targets. The B-52 also does not have the ability to fly at very low altitudes; it may not be able to take off and escape an enemy attack fast enough and may also be vulnerable to certain effects of nearby nuclear blasts.[7]

Critics of the B-1 argued this way: It costs too much. It is an environmental threat. It would need a fuel tanker to help it fly to and from the USSR. But by far the most telling criticism comes from those who feel there are more cost-effective alternatives to the B-1. A noted physicist who had served for many years on the president's science advisory committee summed it up as follows:

> The B-1 is a superexpensive way to obtain a particular capability. It costs more to buy, it costs more to operate, and it provides less-certain results than an achievable alternative. It also needs a new advanced [fuel] tanker if it is to fulfull the promises made for it. The cheaper, better way is a wide-bodied commercial jet aircraft equipped with intermediate-range, air-launched, nuclear-armed cruise missiles of about 1,500-nautical-mile range.[8]

A Brookings Institution team came to the same conclusion, saying that while a bomber force is needed, our current force will be "more than adequate" in the forseeable future. They saw a marked economic advantage in studying a standoff missile system.[9] Such a system would involve an airplane like the 747 flying to the Soviet borders and launching missiles that would penetrate to their targets. One such system is the air-launched cruise missile (ALCM). A cruise missile is an unmanned 14-foot long, 2-foot in diameter drone that could fly from 700 to 1,700 miles to targets at very low altitudes.

What was Carter to do? Most had expected him to take the easy way out and compromise with the B-1 proponents by approving production of perhaps 120 of the 244 planes requested. Moreover, Carter was a military man himself, and the overwhelming weight of military opinion favored the B-1. But he was also the candidate who promised he would balance the budget by 1980. Throughout the spring of 1977, Carter collected information and consulted all sides. The Defense Department provided a steady flow of reports and briefing books for his appraisal. Three options emerged:

The Strategic Air Command monitors the movement of an Air Launched Cruise Missile during a test. The ALCM serves as a less costly alternative to the B-1 bomber.

[7]Extensive debates on the merits of the B-1 bomber took place in the United States Senate in 1976. Senator Barry Goldwater championed the B-1 while Senator William Proxmire argued against it. These can be found in the *Congressional Record* at various dates throughout 1976. A compilation of arguments favorable to the B-1 is found in a widely distributed Rockwell International booklet, *Point of Fact* (Summer 1976).

[8]Richard L. Garwin, "You Can Do the Job Better and for Less Money," interview, *U.S. News and World Report* (April 26, 1976), p. 63.

[9]Alton H. Quanbeck and Archie L. Wood, *Modernizing the Strategic Bomber Force* (Brookings, 1976).

1. Build between 150 and 244 B-1s.
2. Refit the newest models of the fifteen-year-old B-52s to carry cruise missiles.
3. Modify the wide-bodied C-54 Galaxies or Boeing 747s to carry cruise missiles.

Carter retired to Camp David, a presidential vacation retreat in the western Maryland mountains, to go over the options one last time during the final weekend before his decision. Washington officials said his views on the B-1 were the best-kept presidential secret since the atom bomb. Carter himself called the decision "one of the most difficult" he had made since taking office.

Then the surprise. President Carter decided to kill the Air Force's request for the B-1s and move ahead with option 2 outlined above. Washington was surprised over Carter's decision because officials had become accustomed to pragmatic presidents who were inclined to opt for some simple "split-the-difference" solution. Carter had had such an option open. Instead, by killing the B-1 program, he upset conservatives and won substantial praise from liberals. Representative Barry Goldwater, Jr. (R-Calif.) reflected conservative reaction: "I am astounded." Goldwater added: "To my deep regret and concern, the decision to terminate the B-1 program confirms what I have feared all along—President Carter has surrounded himself with some of the most misguided but vociferous soft-liners on national defense in the Nation. Make no mistake about it. In one gesture, Mr. Carter has placed this Nation at a tremendous disadvantage."[10] Senator John Culver (D-Iowa) joyously spoke for opponents of the program, saying Carter's move was a "victory for common sense—the most constructive and courageous decision on military spending in our time."[11] Others pointed out that no one will know for sure, maybe even for decades, whether Carter made the right decision.

Analysts pointed out that never before had a president canceled so large a weapon system so close to production. The debate over the B-1 had been long and intense. There was heavy lobbying in Congress. Members of Congress were impressed with the fact that production of the B-1 would create 40,000 to 50,000 jobs. Rockwell and other contractors saw to it that the work was to have been spread out to nearly all the states and countless congressional districts.

Carter's way of immersing himself in the data conveyed in the end the impression of a systematic engineer and manager. It showed again that a president can stand up to the military and powerful military contractors. It confirmed Carter's tendency to opt for sweeping, sometimes controversial choices rather than limited ones. And his decision to kill the B-1 altogether also served as a partial rebuttal to those who felt Carter devotes more attention to style than substance. A *New York Times* White House reporter assessed the decision this way:

It was also doubtful that political motives really played a highly significant part in Mr. Carter's choice. Rather, with apparent relish, he seemed to have turned what could have been a compromise into the kind of difficult "yes or no" question that sorely tests Presidents and that can be

"Well, I bet if it wasn't a gas-guzzler he wouldn't have killed it!"

Reprinted courtesy of the Chicago Tribune.

[10]Barry Goldwater, Jr., *Congressional Record* (June 30, 1977), p. H6767.

[11]John Culver, quoted in *Time* (July 11, 1977), p. 9.

decided only by them. With apparent serenity he told his news conference simply that the B-1 "is not necessary."[12]

Many people view it as a hard, unequivocal decision, the kind that gives meaning to the old Oval Office slogan, "The buck stops here."

Organizing for Defense

The president, Congress, the National Security Council, and the State Department make overall policy and attempt to integrate our national security programs. But the day-by-day work of organizing for defense is the job of the Department of Defense, the DOD. The Pentagon, its headquarters, is the world's largest office building, and houses within its miles of corridors nearly 30,000 military and civilian personnel. The offices of several hundred generals and admirals are there, as is the office of the secretary of defense (OSD), symbolizing civilian control of the armed services.

Prior to 1947 there were two separate military departments, War and Navy. But the difficulty of coordinating them during World War II led to demands for unification. In 1947 the Air Force, already an autonomous unit within the War Department, was made an independent unit. The three military departments—Army, Navy, Air Force—were placed under the general supervision of the secretary of defense.[13] The Unification Act of 1947 was a bundle of compromises between the Army, which favored a tightly integrated department, and the Navy, which wanted a loosely federated structure. It also reflected compromises between members of Congress who felt that disunity and interservice rivalries were undermining our defense efforts, and those men who feared that a unified defense establishment would defy civilian control and smother dissenting views.

The 1947 act had not been long in operation before it became apparent that the Department of Defense, which was supposed to be the nation's sword, looked more like a pitchfork. All the act had really accomplished was to bring the military services under a common organization chart. Instead of moving from two military departments to one, we had ended up with three.

In 1958, Eisenhower urged Congress to appropriate all funds to the secretary of defense rather than to the separate military departments. He also wanted to give the secretary full control over the armed services, including the authority to transfer or abolish functions and to establish direct lines of command between his office and operational forces in the field. The president also asked that the joint chiefs of staff be strengthened by giving its chairman a vote, that the staff be enlarged, and that each service chief be allowed to delegate his command duties so that he could devote most of his time to the work of the joint chiefs.

The president's plan to unify the Defense Department by increasing the authority of the secretary of defense and by centralizing the joint chiefs was subjected to heavy congressional fire. Many in the Congress, fearful of creating a Prussian military establishment, argued that instead of concentrating greater authority in the secretary, what was needed was a streamlining of the civilian staffs, and all their attendant red tape.

[12]Charles Mohr, "Carter in the Role of Manager," *The New York Times*, July 1, 1977, p. A-11; see also Dom Bonafede, "Going Out on a Limb," *National Journal* (July 9, 1977), p. 1087.

[13]For a comprehensive analysis, see Paul Y. Hammond, *Organizing for Defense: The American Military Establishment in the Twentieth Century* (Princeton University Press, 1961). See also Samuel Huntington, *The Soldier and the State* (Vintage, 1964).

Eisenhower felt so strongly about his proposals for reorganization that he used the prestige and influence of his office to promote their acceptance. In the end, the Defense Department Reorganization Act of 1958 gave the president most of what he wanted. Congress, however, refused to approve the appropriation of funds to the secretary of defense. Further, at the prompting of the Naval Air Force, Marine Corps, and National Guard, Congress insisted that the secretary of defense notify the House and Senate armed services committees if he contemplated any major change in combat functions.

Congress also refused to repeal a provision, which Eisenhower called legalized insubordination, authorizing a secretary of a military department or a member of the joint chiefs to make any recommendations he wishes to Congress about Defense Department matters even if his recommendations are contrary to department policy. Eisenhower's view, like that of other presidents, was that he was the commander in chief, that the secretary of defense was his deputy, and that it was the duty of all military officials to support the policies of the Defense Department regardless of their own judgment.

DOD IN THE 1960s AND 1970s

Under Presidents Kennedy and Johnson, Secretary of Defense Robert McNamara proceeded to coordinate the supply and intelligence activities of the services, create unified military commands, and bring more unification to the department than Congress had been willing to provide by legislation. McNamara and his "Whiz kids," young economists and systems analysts, had their own ideas about strategic policies. Unlike many past civilian leaders of DOD, they raised questions about military strategy and overruled military leaders when they felt the "top brass" lacked sound reasons.[14]

Nixon and Ford and their defense secretaries gave the military chiefs a stronger voice in budget and weapon system decisions. Yet, for much of their eight years, Nixon and Ford imposed Henry Kissinger between themselves and the Pentagon. Kissinger acted as an alternative source of information and options on a broad range of military and national security policies. He served as a channel for various kinds of military advice and often found himself in battle with secretaries of defense and top military officials. Some people think Kissinger did an extraordinary job of balancing interests and serving the presidents. Others, like Admiral Elmo Zumwalt, concluded that Kissinger was sometimes deceptive.[15]

President Carter appointed as his secretary of defense Harold Brown, a physicist who had served as secretary of the air force under McNamara in the 1960s. Brown restored some of the McNamara innovations, but the issues of the late 1970s and early 1980s are significantly different from those of the 1960s.

DEFENSE DEPARTMENT:
CONTEMPORARY ISSUES

Has the political influence of the military and Pentagon been reduced after Vietnam? Some people think so. This was due to a general public reaction to Vietnam, a somewhat heightened antimilitarism, and the hope that the

[14]Two of the best accounts of the McNamara period at defense are: William W. Kaufmann, *The McNamara Strategy* (Harper & Row, 1964); and Alan C. Enthoven and K. Wayne Smith, *How Much Is Enough? Shaping the Defense Program, 1961–1969* (Harper & Row, 1971).

[15]Elmo R. Zumwalt, Jr., *On Watch* (Quadrangle, 1976), p. 397. For a lengthier and more favorable treatment, see Marvin and Bernard Kalb, *Kissinger* (Little, Brown, 1974).

U.S. Defense Secretary Harold Brown reviews a Guard of Honor during a visit to the Defense Agency in Toyko.

20−2 Military Personnel (1978)	
Army	790,000
Air Force	572,000
Navy	536,000
Marine Corps	192,000
Total	2,090,000

politics of detente would lead to an era of negotiation rather than confrontation. Those who feel the military wields less influence point to the vastly lower troop levels of the late 1970s, nearly 1.5 million lower than a decade earlier (see Table 20−2), and Pentagon defeats at the White House, such as the Carter B-1 bomber decision and the decision to have an all-volunteer military service. But others point to the growing defense budget despite peacetime conditions. They note that several recent presidents agreed to future funding for very expensive major weapons programs in exchange for the military's support of arms control agreements.

A major problem for the military as we enter the 1980s is the fact that the nation is running short of 18-year-olds. The World War II baby boom is over, and potential recruits in proportion to the total population will soon be the smallest in our entire history. Manpower costs and pension programs are eating up ever higher percentages of the defense budget. The all-volunteer army that began in the mid-1970s has contributed to rising costs. It is under continuing review in the Defense Department. Critics charge it isn't working. Defenders say it works well enough and that its problems are outweighed by the political uproar that would arise from an attempt to restore the draft. One way the military is solving some of its personnel shortages is by accelerated recruitment of women. About 40,000 women join the services each year now, and the U.S. Army has concluded that 20 to 35 percent of its positions could be filled by females. Only combat assignments and other especially hazardous positions are restricted to males. Some analysts predict the military may be 30 to 35 percent female by the mid or late 1980s.

Military leaders are also concerned about our preparedness to handle conventional war situations. Most of the headline discussions revolve around strategic nuclear weapons. But strategic nuclear spending is only 20 percent of the national defense budget. The threats to national security which we know least about are those that lie outside the strategic area. For example, consider the difficulties of regional balances of power, or possible disruptions of patterns of economic interdependence, as in oil transport. The problem of terrorism also worries the Pentagon. In short, there is more to peace and defense than the prevention of nuclear war. These substrategic issues are likely to be as important as strategic nuclear policy during the 1980s.

THE JOINT CHIEFS OF STAFF

The joint chiefs of staff (JCS) serve as the principal military advisers to the president, the National Security Council, and the secretary of defense. They comprise the military heads of the four armed services and a chairman, all appointed by the president with the consent of the Senate for a two-year term and eligible in peacetime for only one reappointment. The joint chiefs shape strategic plans, work out joint supply programs, review major supply and personnel requirements, formulate programs for joint training, make recommendations to the secretary of defense on the establishment of unified commands in strategic areas, and provide American representation on the military commissions of the United Nations, NATO, and the OAS.

The chairman of the joint chiefs takes precedence over all other military officers. He presides over the meetings of the joint chiefs, prepares the agenda, directs the staff of some 400 officers in an overall JCS organization of about 2,000 people, and informs the secretary of defense and the president of issues on which the joint chiefs have been unable to reach agreement.[16]

At times, the joint chiefs are unable to develop united strategies or to agree on the allocation of resources. There is more to disputes among military services, however, than mere professional jealousies. The technological revolution in warfare has rendered obsolete existing concepts about military missions. In the past, it made sense to divide command among land, sea, and air forces. Today, technology makes a mockery of such distinctions. Defense research and development is constantly altering formerly established roles and missions. Yet the individual services are reluctant to give up their traditional functions. Each branch supports weapons that bring it prestige. This often leads to interservice rivalries such as the Army and Air Force quarrel over which should provide air support for ground troops, and the Air Force and Navy dispute over land versus sea-based missiles.[17]

Sometimes interservice rivalries break out in the Congress and the press. Organizations such as the Association of the United States Army, the Navy League, and the Air Force Association lobby openly in behalf of their particular service. Behind the scenes the military men themselves are active. The president tries to keep interservice disputes inside the administration, but the military commander who feels that administration policy threatens the national security has a problem. He is taught to respect civilian supremacy and to obey his civilian superiors. But which civilian superiors? The president as commander in chief? Or should he—as he has a legal right to do—report to Congress, which is also a civilian superior? A few officers resolve the dilemma of conflicting loyalties to president, Congress, and conscience by resigning so that they will be free to carry their views to the nation. More commonly, military personnel who wish to dissent from official policy get their views to Congress by resorting to the Washington practice of "leaking" information to the press. Further, when testifying before congressional committees it is not difficult for officers to support the policies of the Defense Department only in a formal sense and to allow their real views to come across.

The continuation of interservice differences has led some to advocate the replacement of the joint chiefs by a single chief of staff, the complete integration of all military into a single branch, and the reassignment of forces in terms of strategic missions. Although such a system has had the support of many high-ranking Army and some Air Force officers, it is opposed by most Navy officers and most members of Congress.

Strategic defense policy, much like policy in any other area, is the result not of a collective process of rational inquiry but of a mutual process of give and take.[18] Whether strategic policies are worked out within the De-

The nation's top military commanders and defense department officials meeting in the National Military Command Center at the Pentagon to discuss plans, policies, and procedures.

[16]One of the best recent studies of the operations of the JCS is found in Lawrence J. Korb, *The Joint Chiefs of Staff: The First Twenty-five Years* (Indiana University Press, 1976). Korb contends the JCS has a marked tendency to adapt to and coalesce behind the policies of their political leaders more often than is generally presumed.

[17]Bruce M. Russett, *What Price Vigilance? The Burdens of National Defense* (Yale University Press, 1970). An excellent illustrative study of interservice rivalries as well as of bureaucratic caution is Edmund Beard, *Developing the ICBM: A Study of Bureaucratic Politics* (Columbia University Press, 1976).

[18]Samuel P. Huntington, *The Common Defense: Strategic Programs in National Politics* (Columbia University Press, 1961), preface and *passim*.

U.S. Military Stationed at Overseas Bases: 462,850

WESTERN EUROPE 266,700
W. Germany 208,500; Great Britain 20,300;
Italy 11,600; Spain 9,200; Turkey 4,400;
Greece 3,300; Iceland 3,100; Belgium
and Netherlands each 2,000; Portugal 1,400;
Morocco 900;

SOUTH KOREA
40,400

JAPAN AND
OKINAWA
45,300

CANADA
800

TAIWAN
2,200

GUAM
9,600

LATIN
AMERICA
15,800
(Bermuda,
Cuba, Canal
Zone, Puerto
Rico)

THAILAND
250

PHILIPPINES
14,600

Afloat (Stationed Overseas) 58,300
Other: 8,100

Source: Department of Defense, 1977

fense Department, the White House, or Congress, the decisions result from a political process in which some measure of consensus is essential. And some conflict among the participants is not necessarily evil. As one admiral put it: "How curious it is that the Congress *debates*, the Supreme Court *deliberates*, but for some reason or other the Joint Chiefs of Staff just *bicker!*"[19]

The joint chiefs engage in the same type of logrolling tactics used in Congress. On budget issues, they tend to endorse all the programs desired by each service. On questions relating to Vietnam, the joint chiefs nearly always simply endorsed the recommendations of Generals Westmoreland and Abrams. "When forced to choose on an issue of policy, the Chiefs compromise among the different service positions rather than attempting to develop a position based on a unified military point of view."[20]

Arms control and national defense

People have dreamed for centuries of a world in which conflicts would be resolved without force. But in reality, as long as the United States exists in a world of sovereign, independent nations, it will look to its own defenses. The policy of deterrence suggests that a strategic equilibrium between the

[19]Quoted *ibid.*, p. 170 See also David W. Tarr, "Military Technology and the Policy Process," *Western Political Quarterly* (March 1965), pp. 135ff.

[20]Morton H. Halperin, "President and Military," *Foreign Affairs* (January 1972), p. 321.

U.S. and the USSR, or mutual deterrence is the best realistic safeguard of U.S. security. (Effective deterrence is commonly measured by the usable strength of the survivable second-strike force.) The policy of deterrence is based on the idea that a conflict in values is the root cause of the East-West confrontation, and that military force is a reflection of that basic conflict. Moreover, proponents argue, we need to have a reserve military strength to back up our position in arms control negotiations.

Proponents of disarmament argue that armaments themselves are a fundamental cause of international tension. They warn of the immense risks of the deterrence system: human error, a failure in the warning network, a misguided missile, the inevitable expansion of the number of nations with nuclear weapons. But they paint an even grimmer picture of a future without arms control: heightened tension as the result of the development of more devastating nuclear warheads and longer-ranged, more accurate delivery vehicles; the threat of biological, chemical, and neutron-radiation weapons; the constant surveillance of spy satellites; ever-increasing defense budgets and commitments of human resources to weapons technology.[21]

Some advocates of disarmament feel this possibility can be forestalled only by general and complete renunciation of force and the elimination of all military power. The Soviets have favored disarmament in general terms, but until recently avoided specific proposals. A vocal minority in the West proposes that in order to save the world from nuclear destruction, the West must take a significant first step in disarmament. A skeptical majority suspects that the Soviet Union would not reciprocate but rather take advantage of our vulnerability.

A more practical alternative to the arms race is limited disarmament, generally known as arms control. Beginning with nuclear weapons, gradual arms reduction by both sides has two immediate objectives: first, to reduce the likelihood of war; second, to diminish the violence of armed conflict. Within this policy, mutual arms reduction would be accomplished through negotiations.

On August 5, 1963, the United Kingdom, the Soviet Union, and the United States agreed on a treaty to ban nuclear explosions in the atmosphere or in any other place where there was danger of radioactive debris. The treaty permits nations to test underground and has an escape clause allowing any signer to withdraw on three months' notice. Its ratification by the United States and the Soviet Union and the subsequent adherence to it by more than one hundred nations was viewed as a first step toward nuclear disarmament.

The test-ban treaty was followed in 1967 by the International Treaty on the Peaceful Uses of Outer Space, banning the use of satellites as vehicles or platforms for the launching of nuclear weapons, and in 1968 by the signing of the Nonproliferation Treaty and its presentation to the U.S. Senate for ratification. The Nonproliferation Treaty pledges the nuclear powers not to disseminate nuclear devices to nonnuclear powers for at least twenty-five years and the nonnuclear nations not to seek to acquire such devices.

---

[21]Ralph E. Lapp, *Arms Beyond Doubt: The Tyranny of Weapons Technology* (Cowles, 1970). See also Alva Myrdal, *The Game of Disarmament, How the United States and Russia Run the Arms Race* (Pantheon, 1977).

Strategic Arms Limitation Talks, and SALT negotiations, began in Helsinki, Finland, in November 1969. Discussions lasted two and a half years. They produced two agreements that were signed by Nixon and Leonid Brezhnev on May 26, 1972, in St. Catherine's Hall in the Kremlin. The United States and the Soviet Union agreed by treaty to limit their defensive nuclear arsenal of antiballistic missiles to 200 ABMs and no more—one system of 100 to defend the national capital and the other to defend an offensive missile site (see Table 20–3). In July of 1974, Nixon and Brezhnev agreed to limit the ABM defensive systems to one location in each nation.

Nixon and Brezhnev also signed an interim agreement to freeze each country's offensive missile forces for a five-year period. Pressures in both nations to restrict war expenditures led many people to hope the SALT talks would lead to a major breakthrough in curbing the arms race. Most observers feel that the record of "round one" SALT talks is neither reassuring nor disappointing; it is inconclusive.[22] Modest steps were taken, but military budgets continue to rise.

Meanwhile the Pentagon added some very costly items to its strategic force, including Trident submarines, a fleet of cruise missiles, and the experimental MX-missile, which is viewed as the replacement for Minuteman III missiles. Critics question the need to push ahead with construction of these expensive and dangerous weapons. Two specific charges are made. First, that in the name of accumulating bargaining chips for further SALT talks, we are really making negotiations on arms control more difficult by creating powerful vested constituencies for the preservation of weapons. Second, that our most important problems today are domestic ones; unnecessary defense spending will contribute to a further loss of confidence in America's financial and economic integrity.

Defenders of our military budgets say that SALT I provides a foundation of confidence and a process for more extensive and permanent agreement on arms limitation. Still, they argue, the key factor in the present policy is a perceived balance of strategic nuclear power between ourselves and the Soviet Union. If either felt vulnerable, detente would simply be out of the question.

[22]John Newhouse, *Cold Dawn: The Story of SALT* (Holt, Rinehart & Winston, 1973).

20–3
The U.S.–USSR
Strategic Balance

Weapon Category	Mid-1973 Estimates		Maximum Permitted by 1977 under First SALT Accords	
Offensive:	**U.S.**	**U.S.S.R.**	**U.S.**	**U.S.S.R.**
ICBMs	1,054	1,527	1,054	1,618 1,408
				+ or +
SLBMs	656	628	710	740 950
Total long-range missiles	1,710	2,155	1,764	2,358
Submarines equipped with nuclear missiles	41	48	44	62
Strategic bombers	442	140	(not covered by SALT)	
Deliverable warheads	6,560	2,280	(not covered by SALT)	
Defensive: ABMs	0	64	200*	200*

*Amended to 100 by 1974 accords.

Nixon and Brezhnev met again in the summer of 1974 in Moscow to sign additional accords and agreements. They sought a relaxation of tension in general and arranged a partial underground nuclear test ban accord. Nixon and Brezhnev also signed a ten-year agreement to facilitate economic, industrial, and technical cooperation. Clearly they were trying to find some way of putting the Cold War behind us and to improve relations through a series of agreements that were in the mutual interests of both countries. Ford met again in late 1974 with Brezhnev, this time at Vladivostok. They negotiated agreements about arms limitations which would take effect after SALT I in 1977 and run through 1985. Reaction to the Vladivostok accords was at best mixed. Henry Kissinger hailed them as a great breakthrough, but others contended that they merely allowed both sides ten more years of competitive buildup before agreeing to cut back.

Since 1974, it has become the declared policy of the United States to give a nuclear strategic response to a conventional attack in Europe and perhaps elsewhere. The United States has funded and prepared an extensive first-strike nuclear capability; the increased accuracy and numbers of strategic weapons deployed or being readied will augment the deliverable megatonnage of the U.S. by a factor of 10 by 1985.

PRESIDENT CARTER AND THE POLITICS OF ARMS SALES ABROAD

Jimmy Carter has set out to devise a comprehensive policy for controlling the sale of conventional arms overseas. Speaking to the United Nations, he declared that "there must be a wider effort to reduce the flow of weapons to all the troubled spots on this globe." In an effort to curb arms sales, he has said his administration will view such sales as "an exceptional foreign policy implement, to be used only in instances where it can clearly be demonstrated that the transfer contributes to our national security interests." Whether this will dampen U.S. exports remains to be seen.

> For the purchasers, modern weapons not only beef up their defenses, but also constitute a form of international and domestic prestige. Among sellers, the pressures grow out of economic and political considerations. Defense contractors squeezed by rising costs and declining military budgets may need foreign orders to survive. Defense officials, both civilian and military, view overseas sales as one way to defray the enormous costs of equipping a modern defense establishment. For diplomats, arms represent a tempting tool for cementing relations. For everyone, the advantages of a sale are many, the complications of a lost or blocked sale obvious. In such a climate, comprehensive guidelines of the sort Carter may try to produce can easily fail.[23]

What kinds of arms are sold? Among the more popular weapons sold in the past decade have been F-4, F-5, and F-14 fighter aircraft, helicopters, tanks, Hawk surface-to-air missiles, antitank missiles, and armored personnel carriers. When the U.S. occasionally tries to curb sales, overseas customers say they'll take their business elsewhere.

Total international sales of weapons for an average year in the late 1970s ran to well over $20 billion, with the U.S. responsible for at least $10 billion of that. The extremely scarce public resources of many Third World na-

---

[23]"Muffling the Arms Explosion," *National Journal*, special report (April 2, 1977), p. 497. See also Anthony Sampson, *The Arms Bazaar* (Viking, 1977).

tions, according to some critics, are being diverted from crucial human re-source or agricultural priorities to weapons. Thus, despite arms control initiatives and the various SALT talks, the arms race remains a very real and very expensive fact of life:

> The money devoted each year to military expenditures is more than the total income of all the peoples of Africa and South and Southeastern Asia. It is nearly three times what all the world's governments spend on health, nearly twice what they spend on education, and nearly thirty times what industrialized countries give in aid to developing countries. These massive military expenditures have continued to rise over the years despite the arms control agreements. Arms control has managed to slow down the mad momentum toward nuclear death, but not to arrest it.[24]

In passing the International Security Assistance and Arms Export Control Act of 1976, Congress called on the president to develop a more sensible arms trade policy. Its provisions include the congressional authority to veto any sale whose value is more than $25 million or that includes more than $7 million in major defense equipment by passing a resolution in both the House and Senate within thirty days of notification by the executive branch. It also provides for the prohibition of arms sales to any country that engages in a "consistent pattern of gross violations" of human rights, except in cases of overriding security importance. Still, in the end, what the United States does may make little difference. Although we and the Soviet Union are by far the largest suppliers and sellers of arms, Britain, France, Germany, and China also are significant exporters of arms and equipment. But as the *National Journal* concludes: "Worldwide limitations on sales will require mutual restraint, but the United States may have to gamble by taking unilateral steps to encourage others to join in."[25]

Security and liberty: not by power alone

What should be the role of the military in a democratic society? A fear of the military is deeply rooted in American traditions. And the unpopularity of the Vietnam War, together with the belief that vast military expenditures are giving undue influence to the military and their allies in the industrial community, has aroused concern about how to ensure civilian control over the so-called "military-industrial complex."[26]

The framers, recognizing that military domination is incompatible with free government, wove into the Constitution several precautions. The president, an elected official, is the commander in chief of the armed forces; with the Senate's consent, he commissions all officers. Congress makes the rules for the governance of the military services; and appropriations for the army are limited to a two-year period. Congress has supple-

---

[24]John G. Stoessinger, *The Might of Nations*, 5th ed. (Random House, 1975), pp. 392–393. See also William Epstein, *The Last Chance: Nuclear Proliferation and Arms Control* (Free Press, 1976).

[25]*National Journal*, "Muffling the Arms Explosion," p. 497.

[26]For opposing views on this issue, see John Kenneth Galbraith, *How to Control the Military* (Signet Broadside, 1969); and Albert L. Weeks, "The Pentagon's Alliance with Industry," *American Legion Magazine* (June 1971), pp. 24ff.

mented these precautions by requiring that the secretary of defense and the heads of the military departments be civilians and by devising elaborate procedures to prevent the military from controlling the selection of men and women for West Point, Annapolis, and the Air Force Academy.

Maintaining civilian supremacy over the military today is harder than it has ever been before. There is no longer a clear separation between military and civilian spheres of activity. As national security problems are brought to the fore, the generals are called upon to pass judgment on issues that in the past have not been thought to be within the scope of their competence. At the same time, their civilian superiors find it more difficult to secure the information they need to exercise control. In many cases it is the military who decide what information must remain top secret. Members of Congress and the general public are thus sometimes at a disadvantage. When a nation maintains a large military establishment, there tends to be an increase in centralization and in executive power, and a corresponding reduction in judicial and legislative control. A nation preoccupied with defense is also more likely to suppress dissent and to label critics as unpatriotic or subversive.

Yet it may be less the case that the military is to blame for pushing large budgets than that civilian leaders, elected and appointed, go along with military requests too readily. Congress has the power to control defense policy and defense spending, but it has apparently encouraged the tremendous growth in military responsibilities. Leading members of Congress have by and large followed the line of reasoning of the military leaders.[27]

Defenders of the defense budget feel that those who want to reduce it are naive. They point out that with the help of more analytical GAO audits, military procurement has been improved. They argue that defense programs in recent fiscal years have exacted the smallest percentage of the gross national product and the smallest percentage of the federal budget since 1950. They explain that the military budget must include the increasing expenditures necessary to maintain an all-volunteer army.

National debates about the military budget, weapons systems, force levels, and troops in Europe or Korea are now common. The objectives of a leaner, less costly, and more efficient military force are being pressed upon the military. This is true particularly since we have moved into an era of negotiations and away from the Cold War. Basic to most of these trends is the recognition that true national security lies in something more than troops and hardware.

In his last official address to the nation, President (and former General of the Army) Dwight D. Eisenhower warned against "the acquisition of unwarranted influence . . . by the military-industrial complex."[28] President Eisenhower's faith in the nation's future lay with "an alert and knowledgeable citizenry," who would guard against "the disastrous rise of misplaced power."

Summary

1. Providing for the nation's defense is one of the fundamental functions of the national government. But it is also one of the most costly and controversial functions. Nearly everything the nation's military does becomes enmeshed in politics, as it

[27]James Clotfelter, *The Military in American Politics* (Harper & Row, 1973), p. 234.

[28]*The New York Times* (January 18, 1961), p. 22.

should. For example, public opinion imposes severe constraints on the future uses of our military forces.

2. Americans are often bewildered by the complicated weapons systems and the almost foreign language of the military appropriations debates. In the late 1970s the prevailing attitude of Americans toward defense spending and the military establishment was one of modified toleration. We want to deter war. We want military strength that will assist the achievement of our foreign policy objectives. But we are concerned about the high cost of arms, and the possibility of either a nuclear war or nuclear proliferation that some day will lead to war. Many are also critical of our apparent encouragement of a reckless buildup of arms throughout the developing world.

3. Our system is designed to provide for civilian control over the military. This is always a challenge, for it is only natural for professional military officers to believe that the first claim on American resources should be our national security. Presidents, Congress, and the secretaries of defense, however, must weigh national security against competing claims. This inevitably causes a certain amount of strain. The military may disagree with decisions such as a presidential decision to eliminate production of the B-1 bomber, but they accept and live with them. The military in any society has enormous potential for direct political involvement, but this has not been the case in the United States. It is unlikely that the military will become involved in the future any more directly than has been the case in the past.

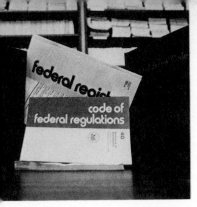

Chapter 21

Government as Regulator

As late as the 1950s, the national government had a major regulatory responsibility in only a handful of policy areas, primarily antitrust, financial institutions, transportation, and communications. But by 1980, nearly a hundred commissions, agencies, services, and administrations will direct, limit, or control what we can produce or do. About twenty of these are called independent regulatory agencies. They are outside the regular executive departments, enjoy a certain independence from White House influence, and are headed by a group usually composed of seven members. Most of the other regulatory organizations are located within the executive departments.

If just the basic federal regulations of the government were compiled into a book, a shelf of over 15 feet would be needed to hold the more than 60,000 pages of fine print. Federal agencies send out over 10,000 different forms a year and business spends an estimated $20 billion completing them. The total annual cost to the consumer of all regulatory activity is put at over $100 billion a year. Of course no society is ever unregulated. Yet the extent of regulation in the United States today alarms many people, especially business leaders. Nearly everything that gets done is controlled in some way or another by one or more governmental regulatory agencies. These agencies are legislature, judge, and jury all wrapped up in one.

Critics say we have far too much regulation. Most economists agree. The new regulatory mechanisms established in recent years—for pollution control, pension laws for employees, consumer product safety, industrial health and safety, bans on discrimination in hiring and so on—have generated fierce resentment. Why do we have so much regulation? Has regulation become too costly compared to the benefits it produces? This chapter is an introduction to the regulatory idea. It contains an analysis of the objectives of regulation, an estimate of costs and consequences, and a discussion of the need for curbing regulation.

The regulatory idea

Despite appearances to the contrary, regulatory agencies represent a uniquely American effort not to discard the idea of a competitive economy, but to perfect it while at the same time achieving valued social objectives. The United States operates with a competitive market economy. This means that wages, prices, the allocation of goods and services, and the employment of resources are generally regulated by the laws of supply and demand. Put another way, we rely on private enterprise and market incentives to carry out most of our production.

Regulation is government stepping in and altering the natural procedures of the open market to achieve some desired goal. The main economic regulatory role of the national government is to improve markets or to supplant markets only when they do not or cannot function effectively. In this sense regulation is a middle ground between socialism or government ownership and a laissez-faire or "hands off" policy. The open market is characterized by self-adjustment or natural regulation. Regulation by government is the interjection of political goals and values into the economy in the form of rules that direct behavior in the marketplace in certain specified ways.

Government regulation means setting restraints on individuals and groups, directly compelling them to take, or not to take, certain actions. Government regulation is closely related to government promotion, which means encouraging, strengthening, or safeguarding the interests of particular individuals or groups. Sometimes to regulate one interest may be to promote another. Regulation generally involves the government's use of its *police* power, and promotion usually involves the government's use of its *economic* power. (Government promotion is discussed in detail in the next chapter.) Often, either regulation or promotion, or a combination, can be used to carry out public policy.[1]

There have been four major waves of regulatory legislation in American history: at the turn of the century, in the 1910s, in the 1930s, and in the late 1960s through the present. Changing political intentions and forces have given rise to regulation. Among the primary reasons for regulation are these:

To control monopoly and oligopoly To achieve many economic goals, including optimal allocation of resources, it is necessary to encourage competition. Monopoly and oligopoly describe economic systems where power is concentrated in the hands of a few and there is no competition. Through antitrust regulation, the government works to ensure competition. When monopoly and oligopoly exist, as in the case of power companies for example, government steps in to regulate these industries to prevent them from taking advantage of their position. Thus government regulates prices in some markets and sets standards of performance.

To compensate for market imperfections The market does not always work to solve every problem, especially the problem of *externalities* or side-effects. Take pollution, for an example. There was no price imposed on a business for using the air and the water to store or discharge its waste. Therefore, the cost to the society of polluting the air was not taken into

[1]See James E. Anderson, ed. *Economic Regulatory Policies* (Southern Illinois University Press, 1976).

account by market forces. Or take the case of commuters who use their cars to go to work. The more who do so, the more difficult it is for commuters to get to work. (That is why commuters frequently favor mass transportation—so the other person will use it and thus open the roadways for them.) But present market forces do not place much emphasis on using the bus as against taking a car to work.

It is under these conditions where the market fails to set appropriate costs and benefits that pressures develop for the government to step in. It can do so by passing regulations that impose costs on using the air to pollute, or by taxing gasoline to make it more likely that people will leave their cars at home and so on.

Another market imperfection involves the case of natural monopoly. A natural monopoly exists when it would be grossly inefficient to have competition in a particular industry. If competition existed in electric utilities, the price of power might be much higher to the public than if just one company supplies all the power and saves money because of the size of its operation. When such a natural monopoly exists, the government regulates it.

To defend the economically weak. In order to protect the general well-being the government has involved itself directly in the economy to protect those who lack economic power. Thus the government has worked to establish a minimum wage and prevent abuses such as child labor. The government has also sought to control the conflict between labor and management and to protect workers' right to organize. In its role as the protector of the weak, the government has sought especially to ensure equal opportunity (a topic discussed at length in Chapter 6).

Regulating business

Business has never been altogether free of restrictive legislation, but during much of the latter part of the nineteenth century our national policy was to leave business pretty much alone. Indeed, a "hands-off" or laissez-faire policy was in effect. With considerable freedom, business leaders set about developing (as well as exploiting) a nation that was enormously rich in natural resources. The heroes of the 1870s and 1880s were not politicians but the business magnates—the Rockefellers, Morgans, Carnegies, and Fricks. "From rags to riches" became the nation's motto.

Yet many businessmen in the late nineteenth century were not just given their freedom, they often were given prime sections of land to subsidize expansion of rail systems, tariffs to protect infant industries, and implicit if not explicit police assistance to prevent rapid unionization. Government was helping to *promote* many of these businesses.

Toward the end of the century, a reaction set in. Sharp depressions rocked the economy and threw people out of work. Millions labored long hours in factory and field for meager wages. Muckrakers revealed that some of the most famous business leaders had indulged in shoddy practices and corrupt deals. A demand for government regulation of business sprang up, and a series of national and state laws were passed attempting to correct the worst abuses. Such laws were adopted on the pragmatic assumption that each problem could be handled as it arose. On balance, however, these laws did reflect a commitment to competitive markets, plus a notion of intervention for the purpose of remedying the defects of markets.

Social critics and reformers in the late nineteenth century argued that consumers of monopolized goods and services, especially in the oil, sugar, whiskey, and steel industries, were being cheated. At the same time, people began to have mixed feelings about big business. Americans have always been impressed by bigness—the tallest skyscraper, the largest football stadium, the biggest corporation—and the efficiency that often goes

**21—1
Some Regulatory
Agencies****

Organization	Year Established	Primary Function
Interstate Commerce Commission (ICC)	1887	Regulates rates, routes and practices of railroads, trucks, bus lines etc.
Federal Trade Commission (FTC)	1914	Administers certain antitrust laws concerning advertising, labeling and packaging to protect consumers from unfair business practices
Food and Drug Administration (in the Department of HEW) (FDA)	1931	Establishes regulations concerning purity, safety, and labeling accuracy of certain foods and drugs; issues licenses for manufacture and distribution
Federal Communications Commission (FCC)	1934	Licenses civilian radio and television communication; licenses and sets rates for interstate and international communication by wire, cable, and radio
Civil Aeronautics Board (CAB)	1938	Regulates airline routes, passenger fares, and freight fares
Animal and Plant Health Inspection Service (in Department of Agriculture)	1953	Sets standards, inspects, and enforces laws relating to meat, poultry, and plant safety
Environmental Protection Agency (EPA)	1970	Develops environmental quality standards approves state environmental plans, and rules on acceptability of environmental impact statements
Occupational Safety and Health Administration (OSHA) (in Department of Labor)	1971	Develops and enforces worker safety and health regulations
Bureau of Alcohol, Tobacco and Firearms (in Department of the Treasury)	1972	Enforces laws and regulates legal flow of these materials
Consumer Product Safety Commission	1972	Establishes mandatory product safety standards and bans sales of products which do not comply

**Examples of the nearly 100 services, commissions, agencies or administrations that have a significant national regulatory function.

with it. On the other hand, we have also been skeptical about the power and side effects of giant enterprises. Moreover, we often believe that our economic system functions best under conditions of fair competition among small—or reasonably small—businesses. These mixed views have long been reflected in our attempts to prevent monopoly and the restraint of competition through antitrust legislation.

In 1890 Congress responded to this new mood by passing the Sherman Antitrust Act. Designed to foster competition and stop the growth of private monopolies, the act made clear its intention "to protect trade and commerce against unlawful restraints and monopolies." Henceforth, persons making contracts, combinations, or conspiracies in restraint of trade in interstate and foreign commerce could be sued for damages, required to stop their illegal practices, and subjected to criminal penalties. The Sherman Antitrust Act had little immediate impact. Presidents made little attempt to enforce it, and the Supreme Court's early construction of it limited its scope.[2]

During the Wilson administration Congress added the Clayton Act to the antitrust arsenal. This act outlawed specific abuses such as the charging of different prices to different buyers in order to destroy a weaker competitor, granting rebates, making false statements about competitors and their products, buying up supplies to stifle competition, bribing competitor's employees, and so on. In addition, interlocking directorates in large corporations were banned and corporations were prohibited from acquiring stock (amended in 1950 to include assets) in competing concerns if such acquisitions substantially lessened interstate competition. At the same time, 1914, Congress established a five-person Federal Trade Commission (FTC) to enforce the Clayton Act and to prevent unfair competitive practices. The FTC was to be a traffic cop for competition.

But antitrust activity continued to be weak during the 1920s. Times were prosperous: Republican administrations were actively pro-business. The FTC consisted of men who opposed government regulation of business. The Department of Justice, charged with enforcing the Sherman Act, paid little attention to it.

Then came the Depression. Popular resentment mounted against big business as abuses were revealed. At first the Roosevelt administration tried to fight the Depression by setting aside the antitrust laws. But by the late 1930s the modern period of trustbusting began in earnest. Since then the Supreme Court has shown a more sympathetic attitude toward the purposes of the Sherman Act, and the FTC has acted with more vigor. The "beefed-up" Antitrust Division of the Department of Justice has won some notable victories.

But how effective has all this activity been? Have antitrust suits and FTC proceedings and the fear of them kept our system more competitive than otherwise might have been the case? It is difficult to give a precise answer, even to find out what is happening to the economic marketplace. But there is considerable agreement that business concentration still exists today pretty much as it has in the past: about one-third of the nation's manufacturing capacity is controlled by fifty companies, and well over two-thirds of all manufacturing assets are owned by only five hundred corporations.[3]

"It so happens, Gregory, that your Grandfather Sloan was detained by an agency of our government over an honest misunderstanding concerning certain anti-trust matters! He was not 'busted by the Feds'!"

Drawing by W. Miller;
© 1971 The New Yorker Magazine, Inc.

[2]*United States v. E. C. Knight Co.*, 156 U.S. 1 (1895).

[3]John Blair, *Economic Concentration: Structure, Behavior and Public Policy* (Harcourt, Brace, Jovanovich, 1972).

Monopolies have virtually disappeared from the economic arena (except for governmentally regulated natural monopolies like the telephone company). In place of the monopolies of old, two threats have emerged: the oligopoly, where a few firms dominate a market, like the automobile industry; and the conglomerate, a firm that owns businesses in many unrelated industries, like ITT. Antitrust tools have been seriously put to the test by these developments. Federal prosecutors have generally believed that the Sherman Act and the Clayton Act could be applied only to the traditional single-firm monopoly. But in recent years, the FTC and the Department of Justice have begun to expand the interpretation of existing legislation to attack oligopolies. They have moved against the major breakfast cereal producers and large oil companies, for example. Some critics view these actions as political "potshots" attacking once again the "economic royalists" because it is good politics. Others view these actions as cosmetic. They believe that if the goal is to break up large concentrations of economic power, it can be accomplished only if Congress enacts new legislation.

CONTROLLING BIG BUSINESS

What should the government do about big business? Few policymakers agree on the answer to this question. Some say we are doing too much. And even those who think we are doing too little do not agree on the solutions. Economist Neil Jacoby, for example, sees no need for new initiatives. He feels that the alleged damage done by big business is vastly overestimated, that even the extent of concentration is exaggerated. He rejects the view that the United States has become a corporate state as pure myth. He sees the increasing size of business as an indication of increased economies of scale. The market is still as competitive as before, only the companies are bigger. According to Jacoby, we, as consumers, benefit from the technology provided by the large modern corporation.[4]

Another view, held by John Kenneth Galbraith, among others, agrees with Jacoby that bigness contributes to efficiency, provides the capital necessary for innovation, and spurs economic growth. But this view also recognizes the abuses that can occur when economic power is concentrated in the hands of a few corporate managers. The critics want benefits of size channeled more toward the needs of society. Galbraith suggests three new tasks for government:

1. Provide assistance to the segment of our economy that is still considered to be competitive—for example, the corner grocery store or the independent TV repair shop.
2. Manage the economy directly by implementing wage-price controls in all the industries that are dominated by big business and big unions.
3. Control the direction of big business by restricting the use of resources in areas that are already overdeveloped; by setting limits on the use of technology; and by establishing stringent standards on the by-products of industry—for example, pollution—and enforcing the standards once set.[5]

"But this would be socialism!" exclaim many economists and policymakers. "No," says Galbraith. He argues that government already plays a

[4]Neil H. Jacoby, *Corporate Power and Social Responsibility* (Macmillan, 1973), pp. 138, 145, 249.

[5]John Kenneth Galbraith, *Economics and the Public Purpose* (Houghton Mifflin, 1973), pp. 221–22.

major role in the development of individual firms, and in the distribution of economic rewards between different industries. All Galbraith calls for, or so he claims, is the *redirection* of government subsidies. "If these proposals are socialism," he would reply to his critics, "socialism already exists."

Still another group of reformers wants to break up large corporations, not just regulate them. These individuals believe that the market can work, that all it needs is a chance. They are against bigness, charging that bigness leads to irresponsibility and misconduct.[6]

Are the nation's antitrust laws, drawn up several decades ago, still practical for a 1980s economy? This question evokes markedly different responses. At the center of activity in this area is the Justice Department's Antitrust Division. About 320 lawyers spend all their time preparing cases in an overall effort to protect the free enterprise system. In one recent four-and-a-half-year period, this division brought nearly 350 civil and criminal cases. Corporate conduct that may be illegal comes to their attention through complaints by a competitor, customer, or supplier.

Veteran observers feel the Antitrust Division does a reasonably fair and adequate job. Many say it is understaffed, and considering its responsibility it must work with an exceedingly small budget. In recent years the Federal Trade Commission also has been active in investigating the structure of concentrated industries. Many of the FTC's important cases, as with the Goodyear Tire and Rubber Company case in 1973, are settled during consent negotiations. Consent decrees are orders to cease anticompetitive conduct (although things other than anticompetitive conduct are sometimes specified in consent decrees).

Antitrust politics, like most economic controversies, resemble a tug of war. Major new battles in this arena are inevitable. Leading participants will include private antitrust lawyers, the FTC, the Justice Department, Senate and House Antitrust and Monopoly Subcommittees, the courts, lawyers representing corporate interests, and various public interest and consumer advocate lawyers. Each participant will have a different idea of what should — or should not — be done to deal with the problem.

Regulating labor-management relations

Governmental regulation of business has been essentially restrictive. Most of the laws and rules have curbed certain business practices and steered private enterprise into socially useful channels. But regulation cuts two ways. In the case of American workers, most laws in recent decades have tended not to restrict but to confer rights and opportunities. Actually, many labor laws do not touch labor directly; instead, they regulate its relations with employers.

LABOR AND THE GOVERNMENT

Labor leaders generally favor federal regulation. They fear labor would fare less well if regulation did not exist. Moreover, the federal government in recent years has become a major ally in the campaign to improve job safety and working conditions.

During the first half of this century, governmental protection and promotion were gradually extended over the whole range of labor activity and organization. This was the result of two basic developments: labor's growing political power, and the awareness of millions of Americans that a

---

[6]See, for example, Ralph Nader, et al., *Taming the Giant Corporation* (Norton, 1976).

healthy and secure nation depends in large measure on a healthy and secure labor force.

Labor's basic struggle was for the right to organize. For many decades trade unions had been held lawful by acts of state legislatures, but the courts had chipped away at this right by legalizing certain antiunion devices. The most notorious was the yellow-dog contract, by which antiunion employers, before they would hire new workers, made them promise not to join a labor organization. If labor organizers later tried to unionize the worker, the employer, on the basis of yellow-dog contracts, could apply for court orders to stop the organizers. Labor in 1932 secured the passage of the Norris-La Guardia Act, which made yellow-dog contracts unenforceable in federal courts. Granting labor the right to organize, the act also drastically limited the issuance of court orders against labor in other circumstances.

By 1932 unions had won other kinds of protection from the federal government, especially over conditions of labor. Almost a century before, in 1840, the government had established the ten-hour day in its navy yards. Later Congress shortened the working day of government employees to eight hours and required the eight-hour day for railroad employees and for seamen. Nevertheless, progress was slow. Then came the New Deal. Congress began to enact a series of laws to protect workers and their right to form trade unions.

PROTECTING WORKERS

Among the more important areas of federal regulation designed to protect workers are the following:

1. *Public contracts.* The Walsh-Healey Act of 1936, as amended, requires that all contracts with the national government in excess of $10,000 provide that no worker employed under such contracts be paid less than the prevailing wage; that he or she be paid overtime for all work in excess of eight hours per day or forty hours per week.
2. *Wages and hours.* The Fair Labor Standards Act of 1938 set a maximum work week of forty hours for all employers engaged in interstate commerce or in the production of goods for interstate commerce (with certain exemptions). Work beyond that amount must be paid for at one and one-half times the regular rate. Minimum wages, first set at 25 cents an hour, have been progressively increased to $2.90 in 1979 and this will rise to $3.35 in 1981.
3. *Child Labor.* The Federal Labor Standards Act prohibits child labor (under sixteen years of age or under eighteen in hazardous occupations) in industries that engage in, or that produce goods for, interstate commerce.
4. *Industrial safety and occupational health.* The Occupational Safety and Health Act of 1970 created the first comprehensive federal industrial safety program. It gives the secretary of labor broad authority to set safety and health standards for workers of companies in interstate commerce. This act is discussed in detail later in this chapter.

PROTECTING UNIONS

Do unions need federal laws to protect their right to organize? Much of the record of union efforts before 1933 suggests that organizing without federal protection was extremely difficult. Indeed, union membership and strength was waning fast until New Deal measures granted workers the right to organize and bargain collectively. The National Labor Relations Act of 1935 made these guarantees permanent. In the preamble, this act, usually called the Wagner Act, declared that workers in industries affecting interstate commerce (with certain exemptions) should have the right to organize and bargain collectively and that inequality in bargain-

Federal acts prohibiting child labor and regulating industrial safety and occupational health came too late to protect these boys who were put to work in an Indiana glassworks in 1908.

ing power between employers and workers led to industrial strife and economic instability. The act made five types of action unfair for employers (1) interfering with workers in their attempt to organize unions or bargain collectively, (2) supporting company unions (unions set up and dominated by the employer); (3) discriminating against membership in unions; (4) firing or otherwise victimizing an employee for having taken action under the act; (5) refusing to bargain with union representatives. The act was intended to prevent employers from using violence, espionage, propaganda, and community pressure to resist unionization of their plants.

To administer the act, a board of three (now five) members, holding overlapping terms of five years each, was set up. Under the act, the National Labor Relations Board (NLRB), a regulatory commission, has the ticklish job of determining the appropriate bargaining unit—that is, whether the employees may organize by plant, by craft, or on some other basis. The board operates largely through regional officers, who investigate charges of unfair labor practices and issue formal complaints, and through trial examiners, who hold hearings and submit reports to the board in Washington.

STRIKING A BALANCE

From the start, the Wagner Act was a center of controversy. It strengthened the unions and helped them seize greater economic and political power. In 1936 a committee of noted attorneys declared it unconstitutional. In 1937, the Supreme Court by a five-to-four vote upheld the constitutionality of the act.[7] The fight then shifted to Congress, where senators and representatives attacked the NLRB through denunciations, investigations, and slashes in its appropriations.

What caused all this uproar? First, from the outset the board vigorously applied the prolabor provisions of the act. Second, the board got caught in the struggle between AFL and CIO. Whichever way it decided certain cases, it was bound to antagonize one labor faction or the other. Third, the purpose of the act was widely misunderstood. Employers and editorial writers solemnly charged the measure and the board with being biased in favor of labor, when the very aim of the act had been to improve the workers' bargaining power.

Most unions were run honestly and responsively. Nevertheless, public opinion seemed to swing against labor after World War II. Not only labor excesses but a wave of great industrywide strikes intensified demands in Congress for a law that would equalize the obligations of labor and management. In 1946 the Republicans won majorities in both the House and Senate, paving the way for modification of the Wagner Act.

THE TAFT-HARTLEY ACT

The result was the Labor-Management Relations Act of 1947, commonly called the Taft-Hartley Act. This act, which applies with certain exceptions to industries affecting interstate commerce:

1. Outlaws the **closed shop** and permits the **union shop** (under which newly employed workers must join the union within a stated time period) only under certain conditions.
2. Outlaws jurisdictional strikes (strikes arising from disputes between unions over which has the right to do a job), secondary boycotts, political expenditures by unions in connection with federal elections, excessive union dues or fees, and strikes by federal employees.

475

[7]*National Labor Relations Board* v. *Jones & Laughlin Steel Corp.* 301 U.S. 1 (1937).

3. Makes it an unfair labor practice for unions to refuse to bargain with employers.
4. Permits employers and unions to sue each other in federal courts for violation of contracts.
5. Allows the use of the labor injunction on a limited scale.

Organized labor greeted the new measure as a "slave-labor" act and vowed it would use its political power to wipe the act from the books. Senator Taft saw the bill as "an extraordinary reversal along the right lines toward equalizing the power of labor unions and employers." Since 1947, organized labor has kept up its drive to repeal the Taft-Hartley Act, especially the section that permits states to outlaw union shops. Union leaders contend that these laws undermine their organizing efforts, especially in the South, where most of the states have taken advantage of it to pass so-called right-to-work laws.

The Taft-Hartley Act also set up machinery for handling disputes affecting an entire industry or a major part of it, where a stoppage would threaten national health or safety. When such a strike breaks out, the following steps are authorized:

1. The president appoints a special board to investigate and report the facts.
2. The president may then instruct the attorney general to seek in a federal court an eighty-day injunction against the strike.
3. The court grants this injunction if it agrees that the national health or safety is endangered.
4. If the parties have not settled the strike within the eighty days, the board informs the president of the employer's last offer of settlement.
5. The NLRB takes a secret vote among the employees to see if they will accept the employer's last offer.
6. If no settlement is reached, the injunction expires, and the president reports to Congress with such recommendations as he may wish to make.

How successful has the Taft-Hartley Act been in helping maintain labor peace? It has been invoked several times, against strikes in vital sectors of the economy such as atomic energy, coal, shipping, steel, and telephone service. Sometimes a president and the secretary of labor attempt to mediate strikes without resorting to the act. Its effectiveness is difficult to assess because legislation is only one of the many factors that affect industrial peace.

Still, the basic issue remains unresolved. Strikes are part of the price we pay for the system of collective bargaining. But under what conditions does the price become so high that the federal government should intervene, stop the strike, and force a settlement? The country will be dealing with this issue for a long time and increasingly so with the rapid spread of unionism among government workers.

The policies of collective bargaining are but part of a broader set of issues. Labor is deeply concerned not only with the traditional conditions of work such as hours, wages, and pensions, but also with job security itself, now threatened by technical change and automation. Business faces not only rising costs but intense foreign competition. The public is directly affected by altered patterns of competition, quality of goods, prices, and unemployment. The impact of monopoly power of either a business or a union is felt throughout society. A healthy labor-management climate

President Truman's seizure of the steel industry, in the midst of the Korean War in April 1952, in order to prevent a strike, rocked the business world. The Supreme Court ruled the seizure unconstitutional and a prolonged strike followed.

seems to require a willingness on the part of the immediate participants, the people, and their government to take a broad view of specific problems.

Regulating occupational safety and health: a case study

Perhaps the most criticized of all federal regulatory agencies in recent years is the Occupational Safety and Health Administration (OSHA), a unit in the Department of Labor created in 1970 and in operation since early 1971. If you have read about it in the newspapers, you have doubtless come across some report of its endless rules or its alleged arrogant or patronizing warnings to business operators. OSHA has approximately 4,400 rules on about 800 pages of the Code of Federal Regulations. It employs 2,200 persons, 1,400 of whom are safety and health inspectors.

OSHA was set up because too many people were dying in factory accidents or becoming disabled from work-related injuries. During World War II, for example, more Americans were killed in factory accidents than were killed in combat. As of 1970, 14,000 people were dying each year in industrial accidents and an estimated 100,000 people a year were being permanently disabled in workplace injuries.

The mandate of OSHA is nothing less than to protect the health and safety of more than 65 million workers in over 5 million workplaces. It is also asked to issue compulsory safety and health standards and to monitor compliance. To achieve these objectives, OSHA is empowered to inspect businesses and to issue notices of violation and fines. In recent years, it has conducted about 110,000 inspections.

CRITICISM OF OSHA

In business circles, OSHA has become a four-letter word. Many business executives criticized OSHA's standards as having only nuisance value. They also contend that the inspectors are not familiar enough with their business operation to make criticisms. Further, they believe that many of the OSHA regulations do not protect the worker. Some regulations, they add, force costly changes without good reason to believe the change will help. There is a widespread view that the costs of many of the OSHA changes have an inflationary effect. Large costs in meeting the regulations are passed on to the consumer in the form of higher prices. General Motors reported that it spent $79 million in 1974 to meet OSHA standards.

Small business operators (55 percent of industrial fatalities occur in businesses employing 25 or fewer workers) complain that OSHA has made too many rules; a small business simply cannot keep track of them. The regulations, they say, are too complex and too technical. The costs of compliance are prohibitive for the small business and in any event end up increasing the costs of production to an unacceptable level. They may even force a business to close.

Labor groups serve as OSHA's major source of support because of a belief in the goals of OSHA. But they still criticize the agency. They say it has been ineffectual and not strict enough with industry. Too much attention is given to trivial violations, but OSHA has not been quick to issue standards to protect workers from exposure to dangerous chemicals. There have not been enough inspectors (one estimate concludes that there are only enough to visit an "average" business once every 77 years). Finally, labor officials say OSHA enforcement generally lacks force. The average fine for a minor violation (which account for 98 percent of all violations) is

$13. Major violations average about $600. Labor does feel, however, that OSHA is a place a worker can go to force an employer to correct unsafe conditions.

But committees of Congress criticize it. President Ford condemned it. President Carter's economic advisers have suggested abolishing it. Much of OSHA's bad reputation comes from the feeling by business that OSHA is an intrusion into their private affairs. But there are additional factors, such as some unfortunate rules OSHA has issued. For example, they insisted for a time that taxi drivers must wear uniforms and that all toilets have U-shaped seats. And one employer was cited for "allowing ice to come into contact with water."

OSHA also became the victim of irate business leaders who have bombarded Congress and the White House with complaints. A conservative political group embarked on a Stop OSHA drive. OSHA was caught off balance in its attempts to respond to Congress. During the 1976 campaign, President Ford cited OSHA harassment of citizens and suggested that many would like to "throw OSHA into the ocean." He implied that he would do everything possible to curb its influence.

OSHA has not been as bad as its critics maintain, but neither has it been as effective as it should be. It deserves credit for its effective action against vinyl chloride and other serious threats to workers' health. But in the mid-1970s it came so close to alienating business and Congress that its very existence was threatened. Later Carter's advisers suggested that OSHA's safety regulations be dropped and replaced with a system of higher compensation benefits for accidental injury or a system of fines for companies or industries where accident rates were high.

In mid-1977 the Secretary of Labor, Ray Marshall, concluded that OSHA needed a major overhaul. As a result, he announced that OSHA would concentrate its limited energies on severe health hazards and make more use of an emergency power to restrict use of dangerous substances. OSHA will drop many of its trivial safety rules and focus on four major industries (construction, heavy manufacturing, transportation, and petrochemicals) that are considered especially hazardous. It will also attempt to keep the pressure on a few industries it considers potentially dangerous, such as auto repair, dry cleaning, and building materials. Marshall announced too that simply written guideline books would be used and paperwork would be simplified.

As the OSHA overhaul proceeds, more controversies are bound to arise. Perhaps they cannot be avoided as the government faces up to some of the tough issues of industrial health in a world of complex technology. An editorial in the *Washington Post* poses the political and technical problems well:

> If pursued with enough determination, this sensible strategy should make OSHA much more effective—but not necessarily more popular. Indeed, a vigorous regulatory campaign, especially against health hazards, is bound to take OSHA even farther into areas full of scientific uncertainty and political strain. Workers these days are exposed to a host of substances whose effects on human health are not fully understood. Even where something is known to be toxic, the precise degree of risk—or an acceptable amount of exposure—may be very hard to calculate and the costs of full protection can run very high. There are no sim-

ple formulas for weighing all the variables and determining how much a company, an industry or society in general should invest to safeguard a given number of lives.[8]

In short, the problem of OSHA arises because it is an attempt by government to intervene by command-control type of devices rather than economic incentives. This is why increasing numbers of liberals are joining conservatives in believing that instead of trying to write detailed rules and regulations, the government should impose certain general obligations on businesses and unions and provide a reasonably easy way for fines to be imposed. The idea here is to make it costly for businesses not to adopt safety standards, but to allow the details of administration to be worked out by the thousands of businesses rather than try to have some government agency do so. Thus the changes to be brought about during the Carter presidency are sensible not so much because the Carter administration is enlightened, but because as a nation we are becoming disillusioned about trying to regulate behavior by control and command devices.

Regulation to protect the environment

Pollution is an issue that has drawn much attention in recent years. Critics of strict controls on air, water, and noise pollution argue that our pursuit of a clean environment has damaged our economy and will continue to cause high unemployment. They repeatedly call attention, for example, to the disastrous consequences of the shutdown of an industry (or even of one large company). Proponents of tough antipollution laws have argued that we must now pay the price of decades of environmental abuse. They further argue that the longer we delay, the greater the costs to society—both in dollars and in lives.

[8]*The Washington Post* (May 26, 1977), p. A14.

Cowboy after O.S.H.A. Mythical supersafe cowboy illustrates what many business people think of the practicality of federal health-and-safety rules. Union leaders, however, complain regulation is lax.

J. N. Devin
in *National Safety News.*

By its very nature, the private sector of the economy tends to ignore pollution. Since everyone benefits from a pollution cleanup whether they pay for it or not, it is in no one's interest to pay the cost. Consequently, the government steps in to control environmental damage. While people usually agree that the government should do something about pollution, there is far less agreement about what it should do, how much, to whom, and who should pay the cost. These questions take on increased importance because of the special nature of the pollution issue. The cost of pollution control tends to fall on the polluter, so we would expect opposition to pollution control action from industry. The benefits of pollution control, on the other hand, go to everyone. Thus the issue of pollution control evokes concentrated opposition but diffuse or weak support. Antipollution legislation attempts to assign costs to a specific group of people in order to bring relief to a large, highly dispersed, and unorganized group of people.

Historically, environmental issues were discussed by local and state governments. In his study of the pollution question, Crenson finds that municipal *in*action has been a regular response to the air pollution problem in communities throughout the nation: "The federal government has taken on new responsibilities in the field of pollution abatement not so much because these local officials demand it, but because these lower levels of government have often failed to take action themselves."[9]

In its attack on pollution, the national government has chosen a regulatory and promotional approach, and has tended to ignore the possibility of self-regulating methods such as effluent charges that would force polluters to pay for the right to pollute. Using its power as a promoter, the government finances research into pollution control devices and assists states in maintaining their own pollution control programs and in building waste treatment facilities. The primary federal agencies concerned with the environment are the Council of Environmental Quality and the Environmental Protection Agency. Other federal agencies also hold power over the environment, including the Interior Department, the Food and Drug Administration, and the Department of Transportation. The Council on Environmental Quality, in the Executive Office of the President, develops and recommends policy options to the president and Congress. The Environmental Protection Agency is responsible for the enforcement of federal environmental laws and regulations.

The federal government today administers rules and regulations covering many forms of pollution. Laws cover air, water, and noise pollution as well as dangers to the environment from harmful chemicals in food. Arguments in the area of pollution control are rarely centered around the question of whether to act or not, but around the issue of *what price* we are willing and able to pay for a clean environment.[10] The Council on Environmental Quality estimates that the cost of cleaning up the environment could be $271 billion over the next ten years. The bulk of this spending would have to come from private sources. It is estimated that laws already on the books will cost the average homeowner an extra $15 a month in electricity costs by the year 1985. Some private interests, including the

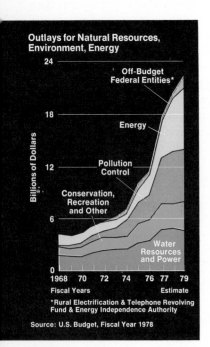

Outlays for Natural Resources, Environment, Energy

Billions of Dollars

Off-Budget Federal Entities*

Energy

Pollution Control

Conservation, Recreation and Other

Water Resources and Power

1968 70 72 74 76 77 79

Fiscal Years   Estimate

*Rural Electrification & Telephone Revolving Fund & Energy Independence Authority

Source: U.S. Budget, Fiscal Year 1978

---

[9]Matthew A. Crenson, *The Un-Politics of Air Pollution* (Johns Hopkins Press, 1971), p. 10.

[10]See John C. Whitaker, *Striking a Balance* (American Enterprise Institute/Hoover Institution, 1976); and Walter A. Rosenbaum, *The Politics of Environmental Concern,*, 2nd ed. (Praeger, 1977).

automotive industry and the chemical industry, have been hit hard by pollution control laws.

Is pollution control too costly? Environmentalists answer by pointing to the high costs of pollution itself. Dirty air and water and hazardous chemicals have costs to society in the form of burdensome health care costs and lost worker productivity due to poor health. In the asbestos industry it is estimated that a worker has a one out of five chance of developing cancer, and certain other job situations pose similar dangers.

Legislative progress in environmental control has been swift in the past ten years. The National Environmental Policy Act of 1969 set up the controversial requirement of environmental impact statements. The law required the filing of statements that would assess the potential effect of a federal action on the environment. This has been interpreted to require the filing of a statement for any project utilizing federal funds. Since 1970, thousands of statements have been filed. Critics claim that the environmental impact statements simply represent more government interference. Supporters argue that the statements have pointed out major flaws in projects and have led to cost savings along with greater environmental awareness.

Environmental impact stories and jokes are now widespread. Typical is the good news/bad news tale: "I have good news and bad news," said God. "Give me the good news first," said Moses. "I'm going to part the Red Sea so you and your people can walk right through it and escape from Egypt," said God. "Then when the Egyptian soldiers come after you I'm going to send the water rushing back and drown them all." "Great," said Moses. "What's the bad news?" "You write the environmental impact statement." God responded.

One of the most significant pieces of environmental legislation in recent years is the 1970 Amendment to the Clean Air Act of 1967.[11] This law establishes national air quality standards for the states that would ensure every American healthy air to breathe. It establishes strict pollution standards for new automobiles. Specifically, the law requires 1975 cars to be 90 percent cleaner than 1970 autos. The law also forces states to clean up stationary sources of pollution. The Clean Air amendments have met with mixed results. Many of the areas that did not meet healthy air standards in 1970 meet them today. Environmentalists, though, point to the extensions granted to auto manufacturers that have prevented the goals of the law from being met. Support for easing the burdens on the auto industry comes from those who feel it is more important to achieve better fuel economy and a lower priced car than to make a clean engine. In this case, the environmental goals of the 1970 law have been modified to meet the energy and economic concerns of the late 1970s.

The Water Quality Improvement Act of 1970 imposes liability for clean-up costs for oil spills on those responsible for them, and supplements other federal acts by stimulating investment by states and localities in water control and sewage treatment facilities. In recent years the government has also taken strong action against those who pollute rivers and streams. In one case, the Allied Chemical Corporation was fined $13.2 million for dumping the poisonous chemical Kepone in the state of Vir-

Results of an unclean environment: birds coated with oil off the coast of Santa Barbara, California, and New York City covered with a heavy blanket of smog.

[11]Charles O. Jones, *Clean Air: The Policies and Politics of Pollution Control* (University of Pittsburgh Press, 1975) offers a detailed analysis of national and local clean air legislation.

ginia's James River. Other corporations have been similarly fined. The Toxic Substances Control Act of 1976 requires more rigorous testing and control of new chemicals than has ever been required. It was a reaction to the thousands of chemical substances in use in American industry and agriculture. Many of these substances have recently been linked to several human diseases. Pesticides are a boon to farmers, but some, like DDT, have been banned after harmful effects have been found to outweigh their benefits in killing insects and weeds.

Concern about the possible harmful environmental effects of nuclear power plants mounted in the late 1970s. In Seabrook, N.H., hundreds of demonstraters were arrested after a march protesting the construction of a "nuke," as the plants have come to be called. Some environmentalists fear that failure of plant safety systems might lead to an explosion and many deaths, though the chances of have been estimated to be very small. Others fear that the radioactive waste of the power plants will have detrimental effects on the environment. Most recently, however, the nuke's biggest enemy has been economic. High construction and maintenance costs have made them less economically attractive than they once were.

A Mayor's Revenge

Businessmen, local officials, and other victims seething over the burdens and insults of federal paperwork may find balm for their spirits in a nonfederal document that is floating around. It's a letter from Ernest Angelo Jr., mayor of Midland, Texas. Some time ago, Mayor Angelo went through the ordeal of applying for a grant from the U.S. Department of Housing and Urban Development, a process that lasted over ten months and turned into a red-tape nightmare. Not long afterward, he received from the Dallas regional office of HUD a request for a reserved parking space at Midland's municipal airport. Seizing the opportunity to give the feds a taste of their own medicine, he replied in a letter that read, in part, as follows:

1. You must obtain from the U.S. Government Printing Office, or the National Archives, or the Library of Congress, or someplace, a supply of application form COM-1975. You must submit three executed and fourteen conformed copies of this application. . .
2. With the application submit the make and model of the proposed vehicle together with certified assurances that everyone connected with the manufacture, servicing, and operation of same [was] paid according to a wage scale that complies with the

requirements of the Davis-Bacon Act.
3. Submit a genealogical table for everyone who will operate said vehicle so that we can ascertain that there will be a precisely exact equal percentage of whites, blacks, and other minorities, as well as women and the elderly.
4. Submit certified assurances that this plan has been discussed at length with the EEOC and submit that commission's certification that requirement 3 above has been fully complied with.
5. Submit certified assurances that all operators of said vehicle and any filling station personnel that service same will be equipped with steel-toed boots, safety goggles, and crash helmets and that the vehicle will be equipped with at least safety belts and an air bag to show compliance with the Occupational Safety and Health Act.
6. Submit an Environmental Impact Statement . . . The statement should show the number of times the vehicle will be operated, times of day, the name of the operator of the vehicle, the number of other vehicles that might be coming into or leaving the parking lot at the same time, as well as the number and type of aircraft that might be landing or taking off at the airport at the same time and an exact conclusion as to the effect this will have on the atmosphere in West Texas.

7. In order to obtain approval of a negative Environmental Impact Statement, you will not be able to:
  (a) operate the car on gasoline produced from domestic oil because that would require that someone discover it, process it, and deliver it, and it is possible that some private person, firm or corporation might realize a profit as a result of such activities. . .
  (b) operate the car from energy produced by coal because this might require digging a hole in the ground. . .
8. Submit a certificate from the Attorney General of the United States that all of the certifiers of the above assurances are duly and legally authorized by Congress to make such certificates . . . and that the United States of America is a duly organized and legally existing independent nation with the full right, power, and authority to operate automobiles in the first place.

Upon receipt of the foregoing, rest assured that the application will be promptly referred to someone for approval. We cannot state at this time who that someone will be because whatever department he or she is in will be undergoing ... reorganization. . .

Reprinted by permission of *Fortune*, November 1976.

Many analysts claim that the great bulk of environmental legislation is too much too fast, with too little concern for the cost of the cleanup and its effect on the energy situation and the economy. Pollution control is now looked upon by most observers as a matter of tradeoffs. They ask how much pollution reduction is desired in light of other social policy goals. Environmentalists fear that decisions made now will sacrifice the progress of the last ten years. The issue of pollution control will remain at the center of the political battle for years to come as judgments are made of just how clean an environment Americans want and can afford.

Regulatory outcomes and issues

Positive accomplishments of regulation usually get overlooked. Considerable progress has been made in air pollution control. Lead paint poisonings and accidental aspirin poisonings have markedly decreased as a result of new regulatory efforts. Childproof bottle tops, automobile seat belts, and federally insured bank accounts are all by-products of federal regulation. The absence of thalidomide babies can be credited to regulatory activity, as can the safety of airline travel. The decrease in airplane hijackings and the banning of many cancer-producing pesticides is a direct result of national regulation.

But the positive accomplishments are somewhat offset by the costs. The cost of trucking or airline travel to the consumer is considerably higher as a result of certain regulatory rules. For example, price regulation has in recent years kept air fares 25 to 30 percent higher than they would otherwise have been. The official estimate of the cost of these artificially higher prices is over $1.5 billion per year. There has been a sharply lowered rate of new drug development and introduction of new drugs to the market since the 1962 amendments to the Food and Drug Act. There is also little doubt that get-tough pollution regulations have had an inflationary impact. Other studies argue that the Interstate Commerce Commission killed the railroad industry, that Federal Communications Commission regulations have caused more drab uniformity in programming, and that auto safety devices have caused drivers to drive less safely. There are fewer deaths and injuries to drivers and passengers, but more deaths and injuries to pedestrians.

The major problems and criticisms of regulation can be listed and briefly discussed as follows:

Regulation distorts and disrupts the operation of the market Sometimes governmental intervention upsets the normal adjustment processes of the market and thus encourages higher prices, the misallocation of resources, and inefficiencies.

Regulation can discourage competition Some forms of regulation (often the kind desired by industry) actually have a reverse effect. This is especially true where the government grants operating licenses and charters and seeks to maintain a certain level of quality or stability in the market. This exists in trucking and air travel, where the federal government exerts control over entry into markets. Regulatory red tape has also been charged with discouraging entry into industries and driving small businesses out of an industry. The regulatory approach "tends to impose costs on institutions in less than direct proportion to their size; the current approach tends to penalize small institutions and reward bigness."[12] United Airlines which apparently believes it can take care of itself opposes deregulation of air transportation. The less economically secure airlines are lobbying in favor of it. Another example of why it is sometimes too simple to speak of "the industry" position, for even within the same industry there are conflicting points of view.

Regulation may discourage technological development It is argued that if the reward for a new innovation is a new set of rules and a struggle for permission to use a new product, it may not be worth the effort.

Regulatory agencies are sometimes "captured" by the industries they regulate It is suggested, especially by those on the political Left, that some regulatory bodies are controlled by the big businesses they are supposed to be regulating. This is of course a popular view among those who see big business as a great power in our society. This view of industry "capture" may describe a few of the older regulatory bodies, but it has been discredited by many scholars. This is how one student of regulation explains what usually happens:

> An agency is established, sometimes with industry support and sometimes over industry objections, and then gradually creates a regulatory climate that acquires a life of its own. Certain firms will be helped by some of the specific regulatory decisions making up this climate, others will be hurt. But the industry as a whole will adjust to the climate and decide that the costs of shifting from the known hazards of regulation to the unknown ones of competition are too great; it thus will come to defend the system.[13]

The newer regulatory bodies probably will not get captured because they deal with many industries and are intentionally harder for any one of them to capture. Still another reason is that public interest groups are increasingly on the lookout for potential conflicts of interest in nominees to regulatory boards. A number of presidential nominees to regulatory positions have been defeated or withdrawn because of interest group opposition of this kind. A strict series of general standards have been suggested against which to measure these nominees. These include the following:

> 1. Nominees should be persons of high integrity, whose past records demonstrate that they have conducted their affairs honestly and fairly and conscientiously complied with the law, and that any previous government service was not used for personal financial gain.
> 2. Nominees should be firmly committed to basic principles of accountability in the Executive Branch, such as strong conflict of interest regulations, financial disclosure, open meetings, and checks on inordinate influence by regulated interests over agency policy.

[12]William Lilley III and James Miller III, "The New 'Social Regulation,'" *The Public Interest* (Spring 1977), p. 51. See also Rush Loving, Jr "The Pros and Cons of Airline Deregulation" *Fortune* (August, 1977) pp. 209–217.

[13]James Q. Wilson, "The Dead Hand of Regulation," *The Public Interest* (Fall 1971), p. 47.

3. Nominees should be knowledgeable about the industries they will regulate, without being inextricably intertwined with them.[14]

Still, some evidence of the capture thesis does exist in the "revolving door" problem of federal regulators leaving their jobs to take high-paying posts with the industries they previously regulated. There is ample evidence that people see jobs in regulatory agencies as stepping stones to lucrative careers in private industry. And the industries obviously benefit in several ways from hiring some of the abler regulators. President Carter came to office promising to "break up the sweetheart arrangement between regulatory agencies and the businesses they regulate." Carter said, "We obviously need federal legislation to restrict the employment of any member of a regulatory agency by the industry being regulated."

Although the "capture thesis" may be rejected by many scholars, Common Cause, a citizens' interest lobby, found that such commissioners meet ten times as often with industry representatives as with consumer representatives.[15] The Senate Government Affairs Committee, in a 1977 report, agrees with this finding and feels that the greatest cause of this disparity is financial cost. The consumer cannot afford a Washington lobbyist. This Senate committee also noted that the agency rules and regulations often are so confusing or obscure that the average citizen is unable to understand them and thus is ill-equipped to take part in regulatory agency actions.

Regulation has a high cost to industry and to the consumer   Various analysts have attempted to evaluate costs other than direct administrative costs. Environmental regulation alone is estimated to cost from $50 to 60 billion a year. Health, safety, and product regulations have an estimated cost of over $10 billion. The remainder of the economic rules have been estimated to cost consumers from $40 to $60 billion. Regulation is costly.

Regulation has often been introduced without cost-benefit analysis   Many critics argue that too little attention is given to the question of whether the benefits of a particular piece of regulation are great enough to justify its cost. Is it worth it to clean up automobile emissions 95 percent if the cost is many times that of an 85 percent cleanup? The answer to this question may be yes, but regulatory agencies are criticized for failing to ask, let alone to answer, such questions such as these.

Regulatory agencies lack qualified personnel   Critics of regulation and the heads of regulatory agencies themselves complain that the regulators lack the expertise to do their jobs properly. Regulatory agencies complain that they need larger budgets to attract more qualified staff. Critics argue too that government should not meddle in complex chemical or technological industries it knows little about.

[14]Adapted from David Cohen, President, Common Cause, testimony opposing the nomination of Robert McKinney to be chairman of the Federal Home Loan Bank Board, before the Committee on Banking, Housing and Urban Affairs, of the United States Senate (July 18, 1977), pp. 2–4.

[15]*With Only One Ear, A Common Cause Study of Industry and Consumer Representation Before Federal Regulatory Commissions* (Common Cause, August, 1977), 42 pages.

The deregulation debate

For the last twenty-five years, every president has proposed in some degree or another a program for regulatory reform. Economists from the conservative Chicago school on the one side to the most liberal pro-George McGovern and pro-Fred Harris school are all but unanimous that much regulation is unnecessary, and some of it uses the wrong strategy. Both Presidents Ford and Carter initiated regulatory reform efforts.

Although deregulation and regulatory reform have different meanings to different people, they are generally used to describe a cutback in the amount of regulation attempted by the federal government. There is agreement that some form of regulatory reform is needed, but it is more difficult to find agreement on specific actions. For example, President Carter has called for significant cutbacks in federal regulation of the airlines, but many airline officials have opposed the proposed changes. They claim that service would suffer and costs would increase: "It would, in one fell swoop, destroy a system that has produced the finest airline-transportation network in the world, with fares in the U.S. being about half what they are in foreign countries."[16] Proponents of airline or Civil Aeronautics Board (CAB) deregulation contend that the airlines and airline worker unions oppose greater reliance on the free market system because they fear the uncertainties of competition.

Many industries obviously look at regulation from the perspective of self-interest. If regulation imposes hardships and burdens, they oppose it. If regulation encourages order and stability in a market (often translated as less competition), they favor it. Thus, some industries are currently campaigning for more regulation, especially in the form of protective tariffs. For the most part, however, regulatory reform or deregulation efforts provide a general umbrella under which a great many companies seek to eliminate government-imposed operating cost increases *and* shield themselves from increased competition.

In the late 1970s, the battle over regulation has been thrown in with the more general fight to reduce the size of government. There is strong support for Congress to reshape the federal regulatory apparatus to make it less burdensome and more beneficial to the public. Among the proposals that have attracted attention are these:

1. A bill that would require the regulatory agencies to evaluate the effects of proposed regulations on competition. The bill would require regulatory agencies to issue pro-competition rules.
2. A number of bills that would require congressional approval of all major regulations adopted by the regulatory agencies. Some would give either house of Congress a veto over unpopular rules and regulations.
3. Legislation to lessen the amount of regulation in the airline industry.
4. Legislation in light of the energy crisis for higher prices for gas to reduce consumption and encourage more exploration.

Meanwhile, President Carter continues to pledge vigorous leadership in regulatory reform: "If I accomplish one thing in my administration, it's going to be to cut down the volume, the complexity of regulations, guide-

---

[16]Frank Borman, president of Eastern Airlines, quoted in *U.S. News and World Report* (May 9, 1977), p. 75. But see also the excellent public document *Civil Aeronautics Board Practices and Procedures*, Report of the subcommittee on Administrative Practice and Procedure of the Committee on the Judiciary, U.S. Senate. (Government Printing Office, 1975).

lines, directives, and required reports that afflict the business community of this nation".[17] A skeptical nation waits to see.

Summary

1. Regulation in America is neither socialism nor laissez-faire but rather a kind of pervasive intervention into the private sector built upon a commitment to a market economy. We often think of politics as the pursuit of private power and private interests. But it is plainly also an effort to define the public interest. We set up regulatory agencies in an effort to interpret the public interest and to achieve various goals.

2. Independent regulatory agencies, even though their members are nominated by the president, their powers derive from legislative delegation, and their decisions are subject to review by the courts, have a scope of responsibility in the American economy that often exceeds that of the three regular branches of government.

3. Despite the fact that few people have a kind word to say about regulation, we shall doubtless have a good deal more of it in the future. Regulation is a means of controlling or eliminating some of the abuses and problems generated by the private economy while avoiding government ownership and the risks of too much centralization. Increasing regulation is an inevitable by-product of a complex, industrialized, high-technology society.

[17]Carter, quoted in *Congressional Quarterly* (June 4, 1977), p. 1120.

Chapter 22

Government as Promoter

It is no longer clear where the public sector ends and the private sector begins. The government promotes agriculture, business, industry, education, exports. It also aids the poor, the sick, and the hungry both here and abroad — and foreign governments as well. Government promotion did not start recently: In his first annual address to Congress, George Washington called for a tariff to protect business. Alexander Hamilton, Washington's secretary of the treasury, proposed that government give financial assistance to new business ventures. The new government promoted commerce in numerous ways: by establishing a money system and a postal service, granting charters, enforcing contracts in court, subsidizing roads and waterways.

What should be the proper role of government in the economy? Conservatives answer that we need more economy in the government and less government in the economy. Others say that governmental "giveaway" programs are undermining our "way of life." Critics from the Left condemn subsidies to industry as "welfare for the rich." They charge that the so-called welfare state is merely a symbolic gesture in which the powerful interests in the United States hand out a few crumbs to keep the powerless quiet.

The why and the how of subsidies

Subsidy programs are more than just payoffs to organized interests: they are almost justified in language of "public purposes." Almost no group argues that it wants a subsidy merely to enrich itself, but argues that the subsidy is "good for the public." For example, magazine and book publishers argue for mail subsidies on the grounds that this will enhance public knowledge and democratic discussions. Many groups also "put the hayseed" in their mouth and argue that a subsidy to them will enhance the small farmer, an important cultural concept in our life. Government subsi-

488

dies to small business need to be understood not merely as an attempt to promote an economic policy but as part of the strongly held conviction that we need to preserve small business and the small farmer in order to strengthen democracy even if such units are not economically the most effective. College students are the beneficiaries of large subsidies both directly and indirectly because of the widespread conviction that the public also benefits from the education the students receive and that this justifies the use of tax dollars. And so it goes.

The government defines a subsidy as "the provision of federal economic assistance, at the expense of others in the economy, to the private sector producers or consumers of a particular good, service or factor of production." One committee in Congress estimates that federal subsidies in the late 1970s amounted to well over $125 billion a year. Computing how much is spent on government promotion is difficult because many federal subsidy programs are called something else. They may be called grant-in-aid, price support, tax incentive, stabilization program, and loan guarantee.[1] Government subsidy programs include:

1. *Cash benefits.* The government pays the sugar beet and cane growers to protect the welfare of the domestic sugar industry, and pays sheep raisers to improve the quality of American wool. Cash payments also help to support artists, to pay airlines part of the cost of carrying mail, and to support the privately owned U.S. merchant marine.

2. *Tax incentives.* The recipients of these subsidies receive no cash. But they are permitted to pay lower taxes than would normally be required. Tax incentives to business to encourage oil exploration and production are examples. So too, are the lower taxes on capital gains (profits made on stock or real estate held for over nine months) and the tax deductibility of interest on homes occupied by their owners. All these subsidies mean that while the government makes no expenditure, it loses revenue.

3. *Credit subsidies.* These involve government participation in loan transactions that give lower rates of interest than prevailing market conditions would allow. Credit subsidies range from loans to finance a student through college, the financing of a major public works project at a fraction of prevailing interest rates, to the financing of New York City.

4. *Benefit-in-kind subsidies.* Recipients receive a product or service paid for by the government. Food stamps for the poor or Medicare for the elderly are examples.

These are not all the ways in which the federal government has a direct impact on the economy. The government also sets tariffs on imports that allow domestic producers to earn higher prices than free markets would bring. In fact, almost all groups at one time or another have benefited from government help. Many business and economic conservatives openly seek government aid to fund an SST, to bail out Lockheed Aircraft, to support government-backed loans to railroads, to subsidize the merchant marine industry, and so on.[2] Just as plainly, spokespersons for the poor seek a larger government role in providing health services, in establishing a floor below which incomes are not allowed to fall, and in subsidizing improved housing and employment opportunities. Clearly, governmental promo-

---

[1] Philip Shabecoff, "U.S. Subsidizes Nearly Everything," *The New York Times* (March 30, 1977), p. E.3. We have drawn on this article for some examples here.

[2] See Louis Fisher, "Big Government, Conservative Style," *The Progressive* (March 1973), pp. 22–26.

Foodstamps are a form of federal subsidy program that provides aid for a wide range of needy people, such as the aged and infirm, and heads of families who cannot find work.

tion can be used to help any group. But who shall be aided in what way, and with what consequences are important questions.

Helping business

A government that protects property and enforces contracts enables owners of business to operate in a stable situation where agreements can be enforced. A government that promotes a prosperous economy enables businesses to enjoy a large volume of sales and good profits. The kind of monetary policy established by government—for example, tight or easy money—is of direct interest to business. Aside from these obvious aids, the national government supplies a number of specific services and assists individual sectors of the business community.

THE DEPARTMENT OF COMMERCE

The Department of Commerce is the nation's "service center" for businesses. Its secretary is nearly always a person with an extensive business background. The department assists business in many ways: Its Social and Economic Statistics Administration reports on business activity and prospects at home and around the world. The National Bureau of Standards makes scientific investigations and standardizes units of weight and measure.

The Bureau of the Census has been called the greatest fact-finding and figure-counting agency in the world. The Constitution requires that a national census be taken every ten years; the results of this census supply valuable information on business and agricultural activity, incomes, occupations, employment, housing and homeownership, and governmental finances.

The Patent Office is also in the Commerce Department. A patent, conferring the right of exclusive use of an invention for seventeen years, is a valuable property right. On receiving an application for a patent, the Patent Office must study its records to see if any prior patent might be infringed and if the invention is sufficiently original and useful to be patentable. Meanwhile, the applicant marks the product "patent pending." Patent policy also invokes such broad problems as the stimulation of invention and the threat of monopoly and economic concentration.

Through the Maritime Administration, the government directly and indirectly subsidizes the American merchant marine by several hundred million dollars a year. For financial and security reasons the federal government has determined that we must have a domestic merchant marine capable of carrying a sizable part of our oceangoing trade. It is generally agreed that without these special arrangements there would be just about *no* U.S. fleet and *no* U.S. shipbuilding industry. There are few industries in whose affairs the government has played so active a role. Nearly every aspect of the merchant marine industry is affected by a public measure or action intended to promote the U.S.-built fleet.[3] For example, the government has been paying operating subsidies to selected U.S. flag steamship companies since 1936. By the mid-1970s, this program had cost about $4 billion. The government also subsidizes the construction side of the maritime industry and since 1936 this has cost nearly $2 billion.

Critics point out that these subsidies discourage competition and raise the cost of ships to more than double the price of those built in foreign

[3]This promotional program is explained in Gerald R. Jantscher, *Bread upon the Waters: Federal Aids to the Maritime Industries* (Brookings, 1975), p. 10.

shipyards. They contend that this government promotion causes more problems than it solves. The maritime industry, of course, denies these charges and maintains that we need these capabilities, especially during wartime. The maritime workers also fight through their unions, to retain these subsidies. They, as much as the shippers and shipbuilders, are beneficiaries of this program.

OTHER HELP FOR BUSINESS

In addition to the activities of the Department of Commerce, the government assists business through such other agencies as the Small Business Administration, an independent agency headed by an administrator appointed by the president. The SBA with 4,300 full-time employer across the country is designed to aid small companies through such services as financial counseling, research, and loans to victims of natural disasters such as floods and hurricanes. SBA has about twenty loan programs to meet varying needs. As of 1978, it has some 240,000 loans outstanding, totally nearly $11 billion.

The government also aids business through research and experimentation carried on by a variety of agencies. Examples include new commercial wood products resulting from work done in the laboratories of the U.S. Forest Service and diversified uses of bituminous coal arising from research in the Department of the Interior.

Through a wide range of tax benefits for certain segments of the population government encourages certain types of activity and investment. The money given up by the government through provisions in the tax code is now called "tax expenditure." The government defines a tax expenditure as a loss of tax revenue, "attributable to provisions of the federal tax law that allow a special exclusion, exemption or deduction from gross income or provide a special credit, preferential rate of tax, or a deferral of tax liability."

Tax expenditures are one means by which the government pursues public policy objectives. Nearly all tax expenditures are meant to encourage certain economic activities. Among the economic activities encouraged by tax expenditures are investment, exporting, petroleum exploration and development, spending by state and local governments, and support of charitable institutions. Every nation's tax laws are in part a reflection of economic and social policy. They create incentives and disincentives for the use of capital and for the allocation of wealth between current consumption and investment (future consumption). Estimated tax expenditures of this kind in fiscal 1978 were about $10 billion for corporate business investment credit, over $6 billion for charitable and educational contributions, $6 billion for deductibility of home mortgage interest, and $5 billion for deductibility of property taxes. The concept of tax expenditures is still a controversial one, but the Congressional Budget Act of 1974 requires a listing of tax expenditures in the budget.[4]

Delivering the mail: a case study

The government assumed the responsibility for the delivery of the mail even before the Revolution. For many years, the postmaster general was more important for his political than for his administrative responsibilities. The president appointed to this post the national chairman of his own

[4]See the discussion and analysis in *Special Analyses: Budget of the United States Government Fiscal Year 1978* (Office of Management and Budget, 1977), 119–142. See also Irving Kristol, "Taxes, Poverty and Equality," *The Public Interest* (Fall 1974).

party or one of his key campaign managers. The reason was obvious: The Post Office Department had thousands of patronage jobs to give to local party workers. Over the years postal employees were gradually brought under the Civil Service, and there have been continuing efforts to restructure the Post Office as a self supporting business enterprise. Yet the Post Office is still heavily subsidized, and many people believe it always will be.

In 1970, in response to the recommendations of a presidential commission, and after two years of debate in Congress in which postal workers and their unions bargained hard to protect their positions, Congress abolished the Post Office Department and created a new independent agency, the United States Postal Service.

The Postal Service is governed by an eleven-member board of governors, nine of whom are appointed by the president with the consent of the Senate. No more than five may be from the same political party. These nine members in turn appoint a postmaster general, and he in turn joins them in selecting a deputy postmaster general. These two administrative officers also serve on the board of governors. The appointed members serve for staggered nine-year terms, but the postmaster general and the deputy serve at the board's direction.

Postal employees retain their Civil Service status, but the board has authority to set salaries and determine fringe benefits. Employees are permitted to engage in collective bargaining, but may not legally strike. In the event of a deadlock between the board and its employees, there is to be compulsory arbitration.

The United States Postal Service is the biggest nonmilitary department of the national government. It handles about 90 billion pieces of mail every year, operates about 30,000 post offices, and has 540,000 permanent employees.

In time, the Postal Service is supposed to become self-supporting. But during the transitional period which will run at least to 1984, Congress is to make appropriations from tax funds. Like a business, the Postal Service is permitted to sell bonds to purchase capital equipment. Unlike a business, however, it may set its charges only after a recommendation from presidentially appointed five-member Postal Rate Commission. The Civil Aeronautics Board and the Interstate Commerce Commission retain power to approve payments to air and rail carriers of the mails.

The new business organization reflects the businesslike nature of the Postal Service's functions. But it also reflects the fact that the decisions made by the Postal Service have a major impact on our economy and our political system. Its structure is designed to promote proper consideration of these political factors, and to avoid the service's making its decisions solely from a perspective of how to maximize profits.

Has the Postal Service experiment worked? Some say it works remarkably well. They point to the fact that the U.S. Postal Service provides the cheapest first class rate of any nation in the world except Canada. It handles more pieces of mail per employee than any nation in the world. Moreover, it has made substantial cost savings through employee cutbacks and has eliminated patronage in the appointment of postmasters and carriers. The purpose of the post office is not to make money but to perform a service, and the USPS is doing that more efficiently than ever before.

Others disagree—and usually with fervor. Since its creation, they complain, costs of providing mail service have soared. Labor costs have risen

This postal employee handles hundreds of packages that flow past him at the 30th Street Post Office in Philadelphia, Pennsylvania.

greatly, as has the cost of fuel to run the USPS's massive fleet of vehicles. They dislike the financial set-up. The USPS pays its operating expenses from its revenues, from government subsidies, and from borrowed money. As of 1978, it is receiving over $1.5 billion annually from the government, and is over $3 billion in debt.

The libertarian solution, advocated by those who want a pure free-market solution to problems, is for the government to give up a postal service altogether and to let private enterprise tackle the job. The Postal Service is suffering increasingly from competition from private carriers of second and third class mail and parcel post. Some utilities are now delivering their own bills to save postage costs, several newspapers and magazines are experimenting with other delivery services. A major legal obstacle to private mail delivery is that only a uniformed U.S. postal carrier is allowed by law to open a private mailbox.

The major policy questions facing Congress are (1) should the USPS continue to strive to break even at the expense of service; (2) should federal subsidies be increased; (3) should the USPS be abolished and responsibility for the postal service returned to Congress or the president? Some, including the postal service management, believe that the present system will work but that subsidies will be needed for the foreseeable future. They also suggest that small rural post offices should be closed down, postage rates increased and Saturday service dropped. Many members of Congress oppose these suggestions, for their constituents complain when services are curtailed.

The future of the postal service is less than bright. The increasing use of electronic communications (and electronic "money") creates less and less demand for the mail. Some suggest that, in order to survive, the Postal Service itself must get involved in electronic communications. But "Should Congress grant the United States Post Service a legal monopoly on electronic mail similar to the one it enjoys with conventional mail in the hope that such an extension could subsidize the sagging fortunes of the Postal Service and guarantee the continuation of first-class mail delivery? Or should electronic mail, like the telephone, be operated by private industry?"[5]

It is plain that the public must either pay the higher price of traditional services or be willing to give up something. And Congress will be continually faced with this blunt reality: to provide more money or to agree to cuts in services.

Promoting trade versus protectionism

Rapid changes in the world have brought several new external challenges to American trade policies. First, if we are to maintain our economic growth and high standard of living, we must increase our exports. But, economic development in certain segments of the world has introduced intense foreign competition. In Europe, American business faces an established and growing European Common Market. This entity has a potential industrial capacity equivalent to our own, and a population—and a market—significantly larger than ours. Japan, which has experienced tremendous industrial expansion, already competes with many American manufacturers.

[5]David Burnham, "Nation Facing Crucial Decisions over Policies on Communications," *The New York Times* (July 8, 1977), p. A10.

Communist bloc nations have also made some significant industrial advances and have begun to make inroads in world trade. The less developed nations pose yet different challenges. They want economic, social, and technical assistance and also markets for their products. Smaller, less developed countries have been concerned about U.S. companies operating within their borders. Some countries want to impose higher taxes or even nationalize such firms. Then, too, some of the world's less industrial nations have discovered that they can charge higher prices for a few of the raw materials needed by the U.S. (About 20 percent of the raw materials we use are now imported, and this percentage is rising.) The OPEC nations demonstrated this with dramatic oil price escalation.

Other developments affecting U.S. trade policy have been balance of payments deficits and major trade deficits which in recent years have run into the billions. The rise of the multinational corporation has also jolted the way we view our trade agreements. A multinational corporation is a company that through direct foreign investments organizes subsidiary production or marketing offices in other nations. ITT, Singer, Colgate-Palmolive, National Cash Register, and Goodyear, for example, have half of their fixed assets outside the United States. Critics, especially from affected labor unions, call such overseas investing the exporting of American jobs. Others charge that the interdependence of the world economy as well as its health is dangerously dependent upon the investments and decisions of multinational corporate managers. Leaders of big business say that multinational corporations are essential to the health of our economy and to growth in the third world. They actually help our balance of payments problem, and generate new kinds of jobs at home. Debate over proper controls and taxation on multinationals is likely to continue for some time to come.[6]

Has the United States turned isolationist? Its new economic policies of the late 1970s raised fundamental questions, but they must be understood in the perspective of long-term strategies.[7] The principal device used by all governments to aid their nation's business has been the tariff, and Congress has often favored interests that desire high protective tariffs. We have often criticized the restrictive and protectionist policies of other nations as an infringement on freedom of trade. Yet over the years, when our own businesses were threatened by foreign competition, they and their employees successfully petitioned Congress to curb competitive imports.

By the beginning of this century, many industries protected by high tariffs had expanded to a point where they needed sales in foreign markets. And Americans discovered that foreign trade is a two-way proposition: if you want people in a foreign market to buy your goods, you must be willing to buy theirs.

In 1934 Congress gave the president power to negotiate mutual tariff reductions with other nations, subject to certain restrictions. By 1970, tariffs on industrial products had been substantially reduced. But restrictions

[6]For different views, see Anthony Sampson, *The Sovereign State of I.T.T.* (Stein and Day, 1973); Hugh Stephenson, *The Coming Clash* (Saturday Review Press, 1972); Raymond Vernon, *Sovereignty at Bay* (Basic Books, 1971); and the Emergency Committee for American Trade, *The Multinational Corporation: American Mainstay in the World Economy* (1973). Also, R. J. Barnet and R. E. Muller, *Global Reach: The Power of the Multinational Corporations* (1975).

[7]C. Fred Bergsten, "The New Economics and U.S. Foreign Policy," *Foreign Affairs* (January 1972), p. 199.

on agricultural commodities remain, along with nontariff limitations such as quotas, minimum import prices, and prohibitions on sales of certain kinds of products. American business firms are finding it more difficult to compete in certain markets, especially in Japan and inside the Common Market. They also face competition from industrial giants in countries where there are no antitrust regulations. Because of restrictions on American sales abroad and tougher competition from foreign products inside the United States, protectionist feelings have revived.

The struggle over tariffs and international trade policies reflects some unusual interest group alignments. The Chamber of Commerce, the AFL-CIO, and the Farm Bureau have in general opposed measures that would limit foreign trade. Yet pressures to restrict imports arise from both organized labor and management in industries such as textiles, where foreign competition is especially severe.[8] Thus the issue cuts across and within interest groups and usually winds up one way or another on the president's desk.

Aiding farmers

American farmers grow an amazing variety of crops. There are big farmers employing many workers on hundreds of acres of land; there are farmers operating family-sized farms of 100 to 200 acres, with the help of one or two hired hands; there are tenant farmers working other people's farms for a share of the produce and profits: there are the farm laborers, thousands of whom move from farm to farm as the seasons change.

The principal agricultural role of the federal government during the nineteenth century was to promote production. In 1862 the Homestead Act gave settlers 160 acres of public land in exchange for a promise to occupy the land for five years; Congress granted huge tracts of land to the states for the establishment of agricultural and technical colleges; and it created the Department of Agriculture. In later years agricultural research stations were set up, conservation and reclamation programs undertaken, and farm cooperatives encouraged.

World War I increased government intervention in agriculture. The prices of food, cotton, and farmland skyrocketed, and the farmers enjoyed a boom. In 1920 the bubble burst. Prices fell and millions of farmers were left with surplus land, high taxes, and debts. Congress responded by passing measures to police the trading in contracts for future delivery of agricultural commodities, to encourage agricultural cooperatives, and to ease credit. But these efforts did not stop the agricultural depression.

The Great Depression sharply intensified agricultural problems. Most of the farmers' expenses continued at the same level no matter what the state of the market. So when the price of agricultural commodities dropped, the farmers tried to grow even more. Prices fell even further. And farmers were so numerous there was no way that they could control markets.

The Roosevelt administration tried to do for farmers what business people were doing for themselves — restrict production in order to increase or maintain prices. It tried to create new demands and shift farm production toward commodities for which there was a better market. Since the 1930s, the federal government has developed a whole arsenal of devices to bring some order into agricultural markets, sustain farm incomes, and

[8]See Raymond A. Bauer, Ithiel de Sola Pool, and Lewis Anthony Dexter, *American Business and Public Policy: The Politics of Foreign Trade* (Atherton, 1963), pp. 73–81, for the broad context in which trade policy is made.

achieve a balance between supply and demand. Some of these devices or subsidies are the following:

1. *Price supports.* The government, through loans, may take commodities off farmers' hands if it appears that excess production may cause prices to fall below a certain minimum. The farmers store their commodities in government warehouses and allow loans to expire if the market falls below the loan price; the government then takes over the commodities. By discouraging farm commodities from flooding into the market after each harvest, these loans encourage orderly marketing and eliminate sharp price changes.
2. *Conservation payments.* These are grants to farmers to induce them to take certain lands from production and plant them in grass or trees or to adopt other soil-conservation practices.
3. *Food for the poor.* Through the food stamp program, the National School Lunch Act, and the school milk program, government-purchased food is distributed to the needy.

Who benefits from government farm subsidies? Whatever the merits of our farm policies, subsidies seldom amount to a welfare program in the sense that they transfer income to poor farm families. The bulk of the subsidies go to the 20 percent whose net incomes already average $20,000 or more. ". . . They tend, at least roughly, to be distributed in proportion to the volume of production on each farm. The more a farm produces, the greater the value of price supports. Moreover, most of the cash payments a farmer receives from the government depend on the size of his acreage allotment or his production, both of which vary directly with the size of his farm."[9]

The most important policy development in the 1970s was the Department of Agriculture's sharp reductions of restrictions on production and its equally sharp reduction in direct farm subsidies. The worldwide upsurge in the demand for U.S. farm products that began in 1972 raised farm incomes and assets. The Agricultural Act of 1973 eliminated the hard to manage and often uneconomic government restrictions and controls on wheat, feed grains, and cotton. This permitted most farmers to respond quickly to the incentives of the market. Crop production during the 1970s has expanded tremendously. Exports of food products rose from $6.4 billion in 1967 to over $24 billion ten years later. Farmers export more than any other U.S. industry. This new role of America as a major food source for the world and the elimination of costly production adjustment programs have been important in reducing farm subsidy costs.

Government agricultural programs have been summarized as follows:

Market prices of the major farm crops and dairy products are supported by the federal government by means of nonrecourse commodity loans (loans which may be repaid in full through sacrifice of the loan collateral) and for product purchases at prices established by law or by the Secretary of Agriculture within the limits prescribed by law. In addition, target prices (prices determined by the Congress to be reasonable) are established by law for wheat, feed grains, cotton and rice. If market prices average below target prices over specified periods of the year,

Budget Outlays for Agriculture

Billions of Dollars

Total

Farm Income Stabilization

Agricultural Research and Services

1968 70 72 74 76 77 79
Fiscal Years   Estimate

Source: U.S. Budget, Fiscal Year 1978

[9]Charles L. Schultze, *The Distribution of Farm Subsidies: Who gets the Benefits?* (Brookings, 1971), p. 2.

farmers holding acreage allotments for those crops receive payments. These are based on the differences between the target price and the average price multiplied by the quantity of the crop normally produced on farmers' acreage allotments.[10]

There are likely to be short run periods where there will be surpluses of agricultural commodities in terms of farmers' ability to sell and make a profit, and thus pressures for continuation of farm subsidies. However, the long run trends are for food shortages. For a variety of reasons—improving health conditions and rising populations—the United States will be called upon to supply the peoples of the world with food and fiber. This external demand for our agricultural products is likely to soon overtake our short-run economic problems.

Energy conservation and development

Energy research and development have been a major responsibility of the national government, especially since World War II. The Department of Energy was established in 1977. Most people now agree that the energy resource problem must be dealt with by the government. The Carter administration has put forward a national energy plan with a goal of reducing dependence on foreign oil and to develop renewable and inexhaustible sources of energy for sustained economic growth.

The Carter plan called for conservation and fuel efficiency, more rational pricing and production policies, substitution of abundant energy resources for those in short supply, and the development of new technologies that will encourage new supplies of energy. The administration's plan sets these seven basic goals for 1985:

[10]*Perspectives on the Fiscal Year 1978 Budget* (Office of Management and Budget, 1977), p. 114.

By permission of Jeff MacNeilly.
Originally appeared in Harper's
Magazine, May 1977.

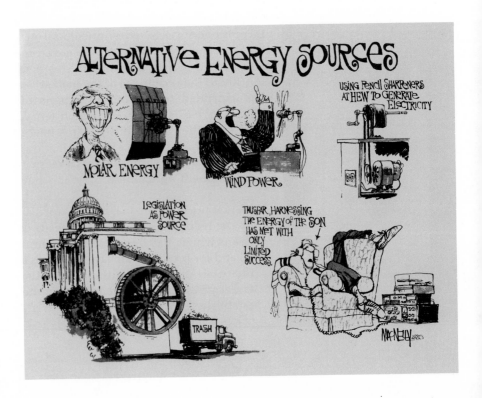

1. Reduce the annual growth of total energy demand to below 2 percent
2. Reduce gasoline consumption 10 percent below its current level
3. Reduce oil imports to 6 million barrels per day
4. Establish a strategic petroleum reserve of 1 billion barrels
5. Increase coal production by two-thirds, to more than 1 billion tons per year
6. Bring 90 percent of existing homes and all new buildings up to minimum energy efficiency standards
7. Use solar energy in more than two and a half million homes.

Many in Congress were skeptical that Carter's plan could achieve these objectives. Others in and out of Congress believed we needed to rely more on nuclear power. Carter's plan does give increased attention to lightwater reactor safety, licensing, and waste management, so that nuclear power could be used to help meet the U.S. energy deficit. But Carter did not propose to subsidize the nuclear industry. Nuclear energy will remain the object of intense public interest because of opposition by environmentalists, the effects on the economy of the location of nuclear facilities, overlapping federal and state safety codes, competition from private nuclear enterprises, and the impact of this energy source upon other power sources. Nonetheless, it is safe to assume that developing nuclear energy for both military and peaceful purposes will continue to be a multibillion-dollar enterprise managed directly by the federal government.

Providing for the poor

Until the Great Depression, except for veterans and a few special groups the national government had no responsibility for taking care of persons in need. America was thought to be a land of unlimited opportunity. Millions of acres of free land, enormous resources, and technical advances all helped take care of people who otherwise might not have made a go of it. When persons failed to get ahead, people said, it was their own fault. The "worthy poor," widows and orphans, were taken care of through private or county relief. During the early twentieth century, the state governments extended relief to needy old people, blind, and orphans, but the programs were limited. No work, no food was the ruling ethic.

Then the nation was struck by the Great Depression. In the early 1930s between 10 and 15 million people were without jobs. Breadlines, soup kitchens, private charity, meager state and local programs were pitifully inadequate gestures. The Roosevelt administration created on elaborate series of emergency relief programs.

What started as an emergency response to what was seen as a temporary condition has become a permanent feature of our governmental system. During the past forty years the national government has become progressively and deeply involved in welfare activities. Most welfare programs are administered by state and local governments, but funded by the national government and thus subject to Washington's control. The complex tangle of programs has produced an administrative maze. Even after three decades of national economic expansion, there are over 20 million Americans receiving some kind of welfare. At least 7 million families live on incomes below the poverty line. And the numbers being added to welfare rolls, and the cost of the programs, are increasing.[11]

---

[11]See the book by Gilbert Y. Steiner, *The State of Welfare* (Brookings Institution, 1971) an analysis of welfare programs on which we have drawn in this section.

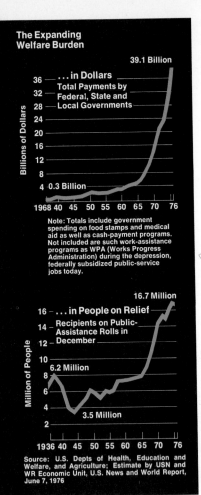

The Expanding Welfare Burden

...in Dollars
Total Payments by Federal, State and Local Governments

39.1 Billion

Billions of Dollars

36
32
28
24
20
16
12
8
4 — 0.3 Billion

1968 40 45 50 55 60 65 70 76

Note: Totals include government spending on food stamps and medical aid as well as cash-payment programs. Not included are such work-assistance programs as WPA (Works Progress Administration) during the depression, federally subsidized public-service jobs today.

...in People on Relief
Recipients on Public-Assistance Rolls in December

16.7 Million

Million of People

16
14
12
10
8 — 6.2 Million
6
4
2 — 3.5 Million

1936 40 45 50 55 60 65 70 76

Source: U.S. Depts of Health, Education and Welfare, and Agriculture; Estimate by USN and WR Economic Unit, U.S. News and World Report, June 7, 1976

While it is generally accepted that the national government should do something about poverty, it is much debated just what it should do. There is not even agreement about the dimensions of the problem—how many poor exist, who they are, and why they are poor. But it is clear that a substantial number of Americans, perhaps 30 million of them, do not have access to the life style we think of as comfortable. These are often the hidden poor. They remain invisible to the majority of Americans because they exist in the dark slums of the city and in the mountains and valleys of rural America.

A third of the poor are from families in which the breadwinner has been without a job for a long time. Some are headed by a father or mother whose skills are so meager that he or she cannot support the family. A large portion of the poor live in families headed by a person over sixty-five years of age or one with little or no education. Because black Americans have been subject to discrimination and denied opportunities for education, a greater percentage of blacks than whites are poor. Nevertheless, 70 percent of the poor are white.

Almost everybody is unhappy about the present state of national welfare policies, especially the largest of the so-called categorical relief programs, Aid to Families with Dependent Children. (There is little criticism of programs providing help for the aged, the blind, the disabled.) Conservatives argue that the drain on the taxpayer is beyond endurance and that welfare creates and perpetuates dependency. Liberals argue that it is immoral for a rich nation to spend billions for defense, to put men on the moon, to build highways, to subsidize wealthy farmers, and to assist business when millions are in want. Liberals argue too that welfare will in many cases improve opportunities for the poor and compensate for disadvantages imposed by society. Radicals argue that the poor are in poverty because of the deliberate design of the powerful or the natural workings of capitalism.

The National Advisory Commission on Civil Disorders (the Kerner Commission) summarized much of this dissatisfaction when it concluded: "The Commission believes that our present system of public assistance contributes materially to the tensions and social disorganization that have led to civil disorders. The failures of the system alienate the taxpayers who support it, the social workers who administer it, and the poor who depend on it. As one critic told the Commission: "The welfare system is designed to save money instead of people and tragically ends up doing neither."'[12]

In short, as Theodore Marmor points out:

What this crisis consists of differs from analyst to analyst, but the following issues emerge: (a) inadequacy of payment levels; (b) disparity of payments between one geographical area and another . . . , and among various categories of public assistance recipients; (c) administrative injustices and arbitrariness, including the alleged stigma of being on welfare, which also serves to deter eligible and deserving persons from applying; (d) the financial costs of increasing the benefits . . . ; (e) the unfortunate effects of public assistance upon family cohesiveness and work behavior; (f) the social divisiveness and inequity of welfare pro-

[12]*Report of the National Advisory Commission on Civil Disorders* (U.S. Government Printing Office, 1968), p. 252.

grams aiding only certain groups of the poor and excluding others, most notably the working poor.[13]

The celebrated exchange between F. Scott Fitzgerald and Ernest Hemingway continues to set the framework within which we debate welfare policies. Fitzgerald is reported to have said, "The rich are different from the poor." Hemingway responded, "Yes, they have more money." On the Fitzgerald side of the argument are social scientists like Herman Miller, Oscar Lewis, and Michael Harrington, who believe that we must make a distinction between those without money and the poor. A student at college from a middle-class background or a space scientist out of work may be without much money, but he or she is not poor. To be poor is to be part of the "culture of poverty." This subculture, with its own system of values and behaviors, makes it possible for those living in poverty to exist but difficult for them to "succeed" in the larger society. As Harrington has written, "There is . . . a language of the poor, a psychology of the poor, a world view of the poor. To be impoverished is to be an internal alien, to grow up in a culture that is radically different from one that dominates the society."[14] Although modern Fitzgeraldites vary in their political ideologies, they tend to emphasize that welfare is unlikely to be reduced unless people are given the education, training, and skills they need to break out of the culture of poverty. They also tend to favor measures to increase the political power of the poor so that they can secure their share of society's sources.

Those who take the Ernest Hemingway position—argue that what the poor need most is money. With more money they will be able to provide decent housing, secure education for their children, and in time become capable of taking care of themselves.

During the last several decades we have had several waves of welfare reform. They can be loosely categorized as having had the following purposes:

1. *Trying to substitute work for welfare.* In November 1934, President Roosevelt wrote, "What I am seeking is the abolition of relief altogether. I cannot say so out loud yet but I hope to be able to substitute work for relief."[15] He hoped that, with economic recovery and full employment, people would move from relief to employment. And many did so. But five presidents later, Richard Nixon announced, "What America needs now is not more welfare but more workfare."[16] The Carter administration is also trying to do this.

More jobs would benefit those who are temporarily unemployed. But the problem is that many of those on welfare are unemployable or unskilled.

2. *Trying to substitute social services.* In the early 1960s the major aim of reform was to provide professional help for those on welfare. It was believed that with this kind of assistance, those in need could learn to take care of themselves. For example, if the problem appeared to be illness, a caseworker was to see to it that

[13]Theodore Marmor, "On comparing Income Maintenance Alternatives," *American Political Science Review* (March 1971), pp. 84–85.

[14]Michael Harrington, *The Other America* (Penguin, 1963), pp. 23–24.

[15]Quoted in Steiner, *The State of Welfare*, p. 1.

[16]Quoted in Daniel P. Moynihan, *The Politics of a Guaranteed Income: The Nixon Administration and the Family Assistance Plan* (Random House, 1973), p. 225.

adequate health care was provided. If a family was about to lose its breadwinner because of a marital dispute, a caseworker would be assigned to see what could be done to keep the family together.

The difficulty, however, is that there are not enough trained caseworkers to provide help for all those on welfare. Even more discouraging is that experiments in which one group received services and another group merely received welfare payments demonstrated that the former group was not any less dependent on welfare than the latter.

3. *Trying to increase the political influence of the poor.* Strayer has written: "As the political power and the political resources of the affected public in the area of poverty and ghetto problems are minimal, likewise their success in generating remedial action is minimal. . . . Those who need to use government the most so as to regulate the environment, are the least able to do so."[17]

A primary thrust of Johnson's War on Poverty was to involve the poor in community action programs, to create structures outside the regular channels that the poor could use to claim a more adequate share of governmental services, and to mobilize the poor for political action.

4. *Trying to increase the cash income available to the very poor.* These reforms, the most recent, involve some kind of income maintenance program such as a family allowance, a negative income tax, or a guaranteed minimum annual income. Here the emphasis is on providing those in need with more dollars.

Forty-five years of experimentation, tinkering, and development have brought us a system that reflects all these approaches and more. What is the national government doing now?

UNEMPLOYMENT INSURANCE

This income maintenance system is operated jointly by the national and state governments. All employers of four or more employees pay a payroll tax. These funds are paid out to the states to give to workers who are not covered by other unemployment compensation programs. It is estimated that an average of 3.2 million persons received benefits each week in 1978. By the late 1970s, more than 75 percent of the workforce was covered by some kind of unemployment insurance.

SOCIAL SECURITY AND
RETIREMENT PROGRAMS

Social security, railroad retirement, and federal employee retirement programs support an estimated 35 million retired and disabled persons each year. These risks are covered by a nationwide system into which employers and employees each pay a certain amount. When workers reach the age of sixty-two, or older if they retire later, they receive monthly benefits that vary according to their contributions and the number of those in their family entitled to other benefits.

Social security, the world's largest "insurance" program for retirement, survivors, and disability, covers over 90 percent of the American workforce and will cost well over $150 billion in fiscal year 1979. Social security provided an estimated average payment of $242 per month to retired workers in 1978. Full benefits are paid between the ages of sixty-two and seventy-two only to those not presently earning wages of more than a certain amount. After age seventy-two, people are entitled to retirement benefits regardless of wage earnings.

The social security system, which used to be one of the least controversial federal programs, is now one of the most controversial. It was well on

[17]John Adrian Strayer, "The American Policy Process and the Problems of the Ghetto," *Western Political Quarterly* (March 1971), pp. 50–51.

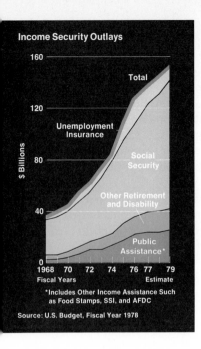

Income Security Outlays

$ Billions

160 — Total

120 — Unemployment Insurance

Social Security

80 —

Other Retirement and Disability

40 —

Public Assistance*

0 —
1968 70 72 74 76 77 79
Fiscal Years   Estimate

*Includes Other Income Assistance Such as Food Stamps, SSI, and AFDC

Source: U.S. Budget, Fiscal Year 1978

its way to going broke until changes were made in its financing. Benefits had risen so high, in part because they have had to keep up with the cost of living, that they exceeded revenues. Most of those now collecting benefits entered the system when tax and benefit rates were very low. The social security system's members were expanding rapidly. Now they receive far more in benefits than they paid in taxes—in fact, many of them receive their total tax contributions back within three years. The number of people in the social security system is no longer expanding; thus starting in 1978 the required tax contribution will go higher, and will continue to rise throughout the mid 1980s. Some economists are now suggesting that social security is a questionable investment.

Another criticism of the social security system is that the burden of paying for social security falls more on the poor in proportion to their ability to pay than on the rich. In other words it is a "regressive tax." The higher the earned income, the lower the percentage of payroll tax for social security. This tax is therefore regressive, unlike, for example, the individual income tax, for which rates go up as income goes higher.[18]

Considerable controversy erupted in 1977 over how to build up the social security trust fund. The Carter administration and Congress examined several options for putting the trust back on a solid base and finally resolved to raise payroll tax rates and to raise the taxable wage base. Most observers feel that the system is not only worth preserving but that nobody in their right political mind is going to jeopardize a system that benefits so many voters. Plainly, the president and the Congress will always find a way to keep it going.

SHOULD THE FEDERAL GOVERNMENT PROVIDE A GUARANTEED INCOME?

When social security began in 1935, there were millions of people for whom the insurance benefits were of little help. So the national government also made substantial grants to the states to help make welfare payments to certain needy persons. That there would always be some who would need welfare—those too handicapped to work, for example—was anticipated. But it was expected that, with the return of prosperity and the buildup of social security insurance benefits, the federal government could eventually leave to the states the burden of providing assistance to the blind, the handicapped, and orphans. This has never happened.

In good times as well as bad, one out of every nineteen Americans receives some kind of public assistance. Unemployment insurance is of little help to someone too unskilled to get a job or earn enough for his family to live on; old-age insurance is not enough for those who have no other resources. And a mother with small children finds it difficult to support her family when her husband dies or deserts her.

Aid for families with dependent children The fastest growing, most costly, and most controversial public assistance program is Aid for Families with Dependent Children. A dependent child is one under eighteen who has been deprived of parental support but who is living with the other parent or with a close relative. AFDC helps over eleven million persons, most of whom are children. The program's aim is to keep families with children together. Many critics charge that because families with fathers are not

[18]See Roger LeRoy Miller, "Social Security—The Cruelest Tax," *Harper's Magazine* (June 1974); and John A. Brittain, *The Payroll Tax for Social Security* (Brookings Institution, 1972).

eligible for assistance, AFDC encourages fathers to desert so that their wives and children may receive help. The program has also been charged with encouraging immorality and making welfare a way of life. Some states have tried to deny assistance to families where the mother is unwed, where there is a man living in the house, where a family has just moved to the state, or where the family is headed by an alien. But Congress and the Supreme Court have ruled against such restrictions on AFDC. The Court has even ruled that a recipient may not have welfare taken away without first being provided with a hearing. The state must show why the recipient should be ineligible and give him or her an opportunity to confront any adverse witnesses.[19]

Congress has passed amendments requiring mothers of children over six years old to participate in job-training or work programs to qualify for federally assisted welfare. It has increased federal grants for child care centers and has exempted from taxation a certain percentage of a mother's income so that she is not penalized because of earning a salary. The trouble is that nearly half of AFDC mothers have gone no further than the eighth grade in school. As Steiner has pointed out, even if AFDC children under six years of age were given a place in every licensed day care facility in the country, there would still be one million such children left over. "After a few years," he concludes, "it will inevitably be discovered that work-training and day-care have had little effect on the number of welfare dependents and no depressing effect on public relief costs. Some new solution will then be proposed, but the more realistic approach would be to accept the need for more welfare and to reject continued fantasizing about day-care and 'workfare' as miracle cures."[20]

In contrast to AFDC, which requires applicants to demonstrate a need before they are qualified to receive help, there are other welfare-type programs such as aid to student housing. As a result of this federal program, thousands of college students get subsidized rent whether they are in need or not.

"If God hadn't wanted there to be poor people, He would have made us rich people more generous."

Drawing by Dana Fradon; © 1973, The New Yorker Magazine, Inc.

A minimum income Effective in 1974, the federal government guaranteed a minimum income to Americans at least sixty-five years old, and to the blind and disabled of any age. This guarantee is an "absolute right": An eligible individual may receive $146 a month, and a couple both of whom are eligible will receive $219 per month. This program replaces state-administered programs of assistance to the aged, blind, and disabled. About 4 million aged, blind, or disabled people are covered. This program, called the Supplemental Security Income Program, is administered by the Social Security Administration. Its money, however, will come not from the Social Security Trust Fund, but from general funds of the U.S. Treasury.

Is this income guarantee a major step toward a universal cash income guarantee? Some people think so. "Supplemental Security Income, for the first time, makes the cash income of millions of Americans—the aged, the blind, the disabled—*a legal obligation* of the Federal Government. For a bewildering and unfair variety of state rules to decide who is 'needy' enough to be helped, SSI substitutes objective and national standards of

[19]*Goldberg* v. *Kelly* 397 U.S. 254 (1970).

[20]*The State of Welfare*, p. 74.

income and resources. In philosophy, procedures, and financing, the new law represents a quiet revolution in American welfare."[21]

Promoting equality

Welfare politics and welfare policies have remained high on the public agenda for more than a decade. Improvements have been realized. The number of families living below the poverty line has been reduced substantially since 1964. The number of substandard housing units has also been lowered markedly. More and more minority persons have entered and graduated from colleges. But the welfare and antipoverty offensives have always been controversial. And many measures once proposed have been allowed to die, later scuttled, or are still on the congressional agenda for action. The beleaguered War on Poverty, the unsuccessful battle to pass a family assistance program, and the campaign for national health insurance are illustrative.

THE WAR ON POVERTY

The Economic Opportunity Act of 1964 created the Office of Economic Opportunity, within the Executive Office of the president, as a command post to distribute federal funds to other agencies and to operate a variety of programs through its own staff. Each program was aimed at a specific condition or group. Among the more important of these programs were these:

1. *Operation Headstart.* Designed to get preschool children into school before the impact of a disadvantaged environment so disabled them that they would be unable to profit from formal instruction.
2. *Neighborhood Youth Corps.* For teenagers who dropped out or were in danger of dropping out of high school. Operated by the Department of Labor, the corps provided work experiences after school and during the summer.
3. *Community Action Programs.* This was an attempt to overcome what the drafters of the act thought to be the basic weaknesses of welfare programs—fragmentation and middle-class bias. The federal government made grants to local community action groups covering most of the costs for coordinated programs "that are developed and administered with maximum feasible participation of the residents of the areas and members of the group for whose benefit the Act was passed."

In its first ten years, the Economic Opportunity Act was subjected to intense criticism from many quarters. Some charged that the programs did not call for enough participation by the poor and provided inadequate funds for a serious attack on the overwhelming problems of chronic poverty. Some said the act was used to support unsavory "ripoffs." Others contended that much of the federal money never really benefited the poor for whom it was intended. Much of the criticism of the Great Society programs and the War on Poverty is exaggerated. Recent scholarship has found that many of these federal programs and services have aided the individuals involved and society as a whole.[22]

[21]Vincent J. and Vee Burke, "The Minimum Income Revolution," *The Progressive* (December 1973), p. 36. For a general treatment of new welfare and social insurance programs, see Joseph Pechman, ed., *The 1978 Budget: Setting National Priorities* (Brookings, 1977), chaps. 7 and 8.

[22]See, for example, Sar A. Levitan and Robert Taggart, *The Promise of Greatness: The Social Programs of the Last Decade and Their Major Achievements.* (Harvard University Press, 1976).

President Nixon for a time made a minimum or guaranteed income plan his top domestic priority. He proposed that the bulk of the existing welfare system, with its differing benefit levels, eligibility rules, and procedures, be abolished and replaced with a federally administered plan. The federal government would provide benefits on a uniform basis ensuring that every family, including those with working fathers, received at least a minimum income. (For a family of four, the proposed figure was $2,400). As earned income increased, federal assistance would be gradually reduced. States could supplement federal grants if they wished, but would not be required to do so. But the Nixon Family Assistance Plan was defeated in Congress.[23]

Now it's the Carter administration's turn. Carter says he is for a compassionate, adequate, fairly uniform and simplified welfare system. But, once in office, he soon realized no solution to welfare and poverty is going to satisfy everybody.

Carter's program to revise the welfare system included the following measures:

1. The government would assist workers from low-income families to find jobs in the private and public sectors. If jobs could not be found, up to 1.4 million public service jobs would be created.
2. Aid for Families with Dependent Children, Supplementary Security Income and the food stamp program would be replaced by a new work benefit and income support system. Under this plan, two-parent families, single people, childless couples and single parents with no child under the age of 14 would be expected to work full time and required to accept available work.
3. The current earned income tax credit program would be expanded to provide more tax relief to the working poor.

This Carter initiative immediately ran into political trouble, just as Nixon's had in the early 1970s. Welfare reform almost always gets attacked on one side by those who feel the proposals are too generous and on the other side by those who find them too stingy. Carter's program is no different in this respect.

Since the Depression, the federal government has helped Americans rent or build decent housing. The Federal Housing Administration (FHA), by insuring mortgages, makes it possible for lower middle-income people to buy homes. And the government, by guaranteeing (through the Federal Deposit Insurance Corporation) the savings accounts of depositors in savings and loan institutions, helps these institutions to provide mortgage funds to millions of Americans. But what about the other millions who are unable to purchase a home or pay rent for a house or an apartment? What about urban decay? What about blacks who are trapped in ghettos?

Since 1937 the federal government has had a public housing program. But what Catherine Bauer wrote more than twenty years ago is still true today: "Public housing, after more than two decades, still drags along in a kind of limbo, continuously controversial, not dead but never more than

[23]Theodore R. Marmor and Martin Rein, "Reforming the Welfare Mess: The Fate of the Family Assistance Plan, 1969–72," in Allan P. Sindler, ed., *Policy and Politics in America* (Little, Brown, 1973), p. 19. For another view, see Moynihan, *Politics of a Guaranteed Income*.

half alive."[24] Public housing has been called "high-rise slums for the poor." Tenants in these housing projects often do not like them; neighbors are often opposed. The destruction by city authorities of the huge Pruitt-Igoe complex in St. Louis in 1973 was an example of the disillusionment with traditional high-rise public housing projects. Most people do not want public housing in their neighborhoods; they fear reduction in property values and increased school taxes, and they want to remain segregated from black people or the poor.

Reforms of the 1970's include rent subsidies for the poor and scattered site location for public housing instead of high-density projects. It will be difficult to secure any considerable expansion of public housing, however, as long as governmental authority in the metropolitan areas is scattered among so many different agencies and suburbanites keep public housing confined to the central cities. As more and more communities require a public referendum before accepting a public housing project, the obstacles become even greater. For these reasons, many people now advocate that, instead of trying to provide subsidized housing, governments should make cash payments to the poor so they can compete for housing in the regular market.[25]

Congress also makes funds available to cities for urban renewal and rehabilitation. Cities are to acquire and clear slum properties, then resell the land to private builders who agree to develop it according to an approved plan. Federal grants and loans are also available to improve municipal services such as mass transit systems.

Urban renewal, despite some success, is criticized for replacing the slum homes of the poor with units that the poor cannot afford to rent or buy. And whatever is being done is not enough. Until recently, more housing units were being destroyed for highways and other civic projects than were being built. Federal laws now stipulate that no federal funds will be granted for any project that will displace persons from homes unless assistance will be given to those displaced and replacement homes found.

In 1966, through the Demonstration Cities and Metropolitan Development Act, Congress tried a new technique: Certain cities (Model Cities) were invited to submit plans for federal support for a coordinated attack on certain target areas. The plans were to be developed with the aid of the people living in those areas. This approach, similar to that of the War on Poverty, recognized past failures in which housing, education, transportation, and recreation were handled in an uncoordinated way. It was hoped that a coordinated attack on all phases of the urban environment would result in more progress.

In 1968, Congress tried another tactic. The Housing and Urban Development Act called for 6 million new or rehabilitated housing units a year for ten years for persons of low incomes. Again more was authorized than was appropriated. The most recent, but clearly not the last, approach is the Housing and Community Development Act of 1974. It provides a direct subsidy for low-income tenants in an amount that limits the rent they must pay to 25 percent of their incomes. The Carter Administration programs call for more of the same.

An example of high-rise, low-income housing built with the help of federal funds in the 1950s. Many of these projects deteriorated rapidly and became crime-ridden only a few years after they were built.

[24]"The Dreary Deadlock of Public Housing," *Architectural Forum* (May 1957), p. 140, quoted in Steiner, *Social Insecurity*, pp. 134–35.

[25]See, for example, Henry J. Aaron, *Shelters and Subsidies* (Brookings, 1972), chap. 10.

Throughout the debates over low-income housing runs the question: Should federal housing subsidies be concentrated in the inner city or spread out in the metropolitan areas? Ethnic and racial implications are obviously part of the debates. Concentration of families with the lowest incomes and often the least education in densely populated inner cities invites high rates of crime, vandalism, mental illness, delinquency, and drug addiction. Many well-to-do suburbanities oppose a strategy of dispersed economic integration. They see it as a proposal to tax the middle-income brackets to disperse "slums" to the suburbs. A leading proponent of locating the poor in housing in the suburban areas, Anthony Downs, contends that the opening of the suburbs would produce:

1. Better access to expanding job opportunities for workers in low- and moderate-income households—especially the unemployed.
2. Greater opportunities for such households to upgrade themselves by moving into middle-income neighborhoods, thereby escaping from crisis ghetto conditions.
3. Higher quality public schooling for children from low-income households who could attend schools dominated by children from middle-income households.
4. Greater opportunity for the nation to reach its officially adopted goals for producing improved housing for low and moderate-income households.
5. Fairer geographic distribution of the fiscal and social costs of dealing with metropolitan-area poverty.
6. Less possibility of major conflicts in the future caused by confrontations between two spatially separate and unequal societies in metropolitan areas.[26]

People may well agree that these benefits are desirable; there is considerable disagreement on how to attain such goals.

Summary

1. The role of government as promoter is not new; it is as old as the federal union itself. The intention was embodied in the preamble to the Constitution, which stated that "We the people" have as one of our aims to "promote the general welfare." We are now witnessing the latest of several surges of intense governmental concern with health, education, and welfare.

2. Many disagree with efforts by the national government to improve the quality of life, to focus resources and attention on the problems of the poor, to improve the urban environment. They view with distaste the bureaucracy required for these programs, and they allege that the programs are ineffective and interfere with individuals' initiative. But although most of these programs have been begun under Democratic presidents, they have secured bipartisan support. Regardless of the party in power in Washington, these activities of the national government are destined to become more significant.

3. The pressures are usually for more, not less, involvement by the national government. In one way or another, the United States government subsidizes nearly everyone. Government promotion policies are far more than payoffs to segments of the population. They reflect interpretations of the public interest. There are, as we have seen, public purposes at work in government promotion, as well as private interests.

[26]Anthony Downs, *Opening Up the Suburbs: An Urban Strategy for America* (Yale, 1973), p. 26.

Chapter 23

The Politics of Taxing and Spending

We have looked at two of the main methods by which government influences society—regulation and promotion. Through *regulation*, government lays down the rules that control what people may and may not do. Through *promotion*, government directly or indirectly advances the interests of certain groups or organizations. We have also looked at a third method, namely, the direct management of certain enterprises such as delivering the mail and developing nuclear energy. The government could allow a private company to process and deliver the mail; it could regulate the company in the public interest, or subsidize it, or both. Instead, the government itself took over the job.

But perhaps the most important influence the government has on the economy is the way in which it *taxes* and *spends* money. Enormous sums are involved. With a current national budget well over $450 billion, our government spends about 20 percent of the Gross National Product, more than one-fifth of the value of everything the country produces. Government has come to intervene in the economy in so many ways that governmental leaders are to a very real extent economic leaders as well.

Tax and budgetary decisions are especially important because they determine the division of resources between public and private goods and the distribution of private resources among different families and individuals. Tax and budget choices determine the government's priorities. Will domestic spending be cut? Will defense spending be increased? Should we have tax reform? The politics of taxing and spending centers about the questions of what we want to accomplish as a nation and who will actually bear the burden of paying for it.

By the late 1970s, the ability of the national government to control inflation without at the same time creating massive unemployment had become perhaps the most important domestic question. Worldwide inflation, a change in balance of international economic power as the oil-producing nations began to accumulate billions, growing problems of international exchange, and questions about the nature of international credit and banking mechanisms were the issues on the agendas of all the major nations. Obviously, the government of the United States could not escape the basic responsibility of trying to maintain the economic health of the nation.

Raising money

Big government is expensive. Federal, state, and local governments spend almost $700 billion yearly. This is about a third of the income of all Americans. The national government is the biggest spender of all. In recent years, Washington has disbursed more than all state and local governments combined.

Where does all this money come from? The federal government gets most of its funds from taxes. The rest comes from loans, commercial revenues from governmental enterprises, income from special fees and fines, and grants and gifts.

A third source of federal funds consists of administrative and commercial revenues. The fee paid to the State Department for a passport and the fine paid by a criminal are administrative revenues that account for a small portion of federal income. More important are the funds paid to the federal government in exchange for direct services—payments to the Post Office for stamps, to the Park Service for recreation, to the Government Printing Office for pamphlets.

Finally, some public-spirited people actually give money or property to the government. Mr. Justice Oliver Wendell Holmes, who did not mind taxes, left the government almost his entire estate when he died. But gifts, needless to say, are an infinitesimal source of federal revenue.

LEVYING TAXES

"In this world," Benjamin Franklin once said, "nothing is certain but death and taxes." Tax collecting is one of the oldest activities of government. Putting power over taxation into the hands of the people was a landmark in the rise of self-government. "No taxation without representation" has been the war cry not only of early Americans but of the people in countries the world over.

The new Constitution in 1787 clearly provided that Congress "shall have power to lay and collect taxes, duties, imposts, and excises." But duties and excise taxes had to be levied uniformly throughout the United States; direct taxes had to be apportioned among the states according to population; and no tax could be levied on articles exported from any state. Except during the Civil war, the federal government for a century relied on the tariff for most of its revenue. This hidden tax—which many people mistakenly thought to be a tax on foreigners—fluctuated with the rise and fall of trade and tariff levels. Congress supplemented these taxes with excise taxes on the manufacture or sale of certain goods. In 1894 an income tax law was enacted (such a tax had been used during the Civil War but given up shortly afterwards). The 1894 tax was not drastic—only 2 percent on all income over $4,000. One opponent of the bill scorned it on the floor of the Senate as "an attempt to array the rich against the poor, the poor against the rich . . . Socialism, communism, *devilism*." The next year, in *Pollock v. Farmers' Loan and Trust Co.*, the Supreme Court declared the tax unconstitutional on the ground that it was a direct tax and therefore had to be

"You BET I'm hopping mad! When inflation begins to affect the well-to-do, it's time something was DONE about it!"

Reprinted by permission of NEA

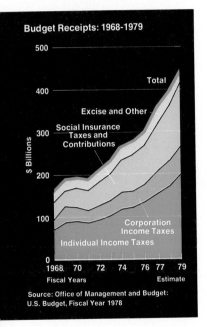

Budget Receipts: 1968-1979

Total

Excise and Other

Social Insurance Taxes and Contributions

Corporation Income Taxes

Individual Income Taxes

$ Billions

1968 70 72 74 76 77 79

Fiscal Years   Estimate

Source: Office of Management and Budget: U.S. Budget, Fiscal Year 1978

THE POLITICS AND MACHINERY OF TAXATION

apportioned among the states according to population.[1] About twenty years later, in 1915, the Sixteenth Amendment was adopted authorizing Congress "to lay and collect taxes on incomes, from whatever source derived, without apportionment among the several States, and without regard to any census or enumeration."

Raising money is only one important objective of taxation. Regulation and, more recently, promotion of economic growth and controlling inflation are others. Taxation as a device to promote economic growth will be discussed later. In a broad sense, all taxation regulates human behavior. For example, a graduated income tax has a leveling tendency on incomes, and a tariff act affects foreign trade. Congress has used its taxing power to prevent or regulate certain practices. Years ago, Congress laid a 10 percent tax on the circulation of notes by state banks, immediately putting an end to such issues.

Today federal taxes are as follows:

1. *Income taxes on individuals.* Taxes on the income of individuals account for more than 40 percent of the federal government's tax revenue. Originally set at a low rate, the income tax was greatly increased during World War I and went to new heights during World War II and the Korean conflict. Over the years the income tax has grown increasingly complex. Congress has responded to claims for differing kinds of exemptions and rates, but the tax has one great advantage in its flexibility. The schedule of rates can be raised or lowered in order to stimulate or restrain economic activity. The income tax is moderately progressive. People with high incomes generally pay larger fractions of their income than lower-income people, though many of the wealthy do benefit from tax loopholes.[2]

2. *Income taxes on corporations.* These account for about 13 percent of the national government's tax dollar. As late as 1942, corporate income taxes amounted to more than individual income taxes, but returns from the latter increased more rapidly during World War II.

3. *Social insurance or payroll taxes.* This is the second largest and most rapidly rising source of federal revenue. From a mere $4 billion in 1950 this tax has grown to raise nearly $150 billion in fiscal year 1979. These are the monies collected mainly from payroll deductions to finance social security and other insurance programs discussed in the previous chapter. They are, economists point out, highly regressive. Low-income people generally pay larger fractions of their income than do high-income people.

4. *Excise taxes.* Federal taxes on liquor, tobacco, gasoline, telephones, air travel, and other so-called luxury items account for about 4 percent of total tax revenues each year.

5. *Customs duties.* Though no longer the main source of federal income, these taxes provided in recent years an annual yield of more than $5 billion.

Most of us complain that our tax load is too heavy and that someone else is not carrying his fair share. People with large incomes naturally grumble about income taxes as high as 60 percent or more of their net income. Low-income people point out that even a low tax may deprive them of the necessities of life. People in the middle-income brackets feel that their situation is the worst of all—their incomes are not high but their taxes are.

What is the best type of tax? Some say the *graduated income tax:* it is rela-

[1]158 U.S. 601(1895).

[2]See Philip M. Stern, *The Rape of the Taxpayer* (Random House, 1973); and Joseph Pechman, *Federal Tax Policy*, rev. ed. (Brookings, 1971).

tively easy to collect, hits hardest those who are most able to pay, and hardly touches those at the bottom of the income ladder. Others argue that excise taxes are the fairest, because they are paid by people who are spending money for goods and thus obviously have money to spare. Furthermore, by discouraging people from buying expensive goods, excise taxes sometimes have a deflationary effect in time of rising prices. On the other hand, excise taxes are more expensive to collect than income taxes; and in some cases, such as the tax on tobacco, they may hit the poor the hardest. Most controversial of all taxes is the general sales tax, which is levied against the sales of all goods. Labor and liberal organizations call this form of tax regressive—that is, it hurts poor persons more than rich persons because the poor use a large portion of their earnings to buy goods. Proponents of the sales tax stress its potential anti-inflationary effect and point to its successful use in a number of states.

A recent tax bill illustrates the impact of taxes on a variety of individuals and groups. Testifying on proposed tax changes before a congressional committee, 138 witnesses expressed their views. The printed testimony covered more than sixteen hundred pages. Business representatives opposed new taxes on corporations. Small businessmen complained that existing taxes favored big business. Spokesmen for tobacco growers, transportation interests, the wine and spirits industry, movies, and legitimate theater, candymakers, telephone companies, and bowling alley proprietors argued that the proposed tax would discriminate against them. Labor demanded a lighter burden for low-income groups and higher taxes on business. Unorganized workers and consumers, however, were not represented.

Although the Constitution provides that all revenue bills must be initiated in the House of Representatives, it is usually the president who originates tax legislation. With the help of tax experts on his staff and in the Treasury Department, he draws up a tax program designed to meet the government's revenue needs for the coming fiscal year. It also takes into consideration the current and projected state of the economy. Often representatives of interest groups are consulted while the bill is being drawn up. Then the president submits his tax program to Congress, often along with his budget message. The powerful House Ways and Means Committee next holds hearings on the bill. Administration representatives, headed by the secretary of the treasury, usually lead off the parade of witnesses, followed by representatives of interested groups, taxation experts, and others. Then tax measures go through Congress in much the same way as other bills. Although the Senate cannot initiate tax legislation, it is active in tax matters. It often differs with the House and forces extensive changes in bills. Sometimes Congress refuses to follow the president's recommendations and works out a tax measure largely on its own.[3]

The Treasury Department has the job of collecting the taxes. One of the original departments set up in 1789, the Treasury today employs about 115,000 people. The actual tax-collecting job falls mainly to the Internal Revenue Service. Fifty-eight district directors are located throughout the country, and taxes are paid into district offices rather than directly to Washington. Customs duties are collected by the Treasury Department's

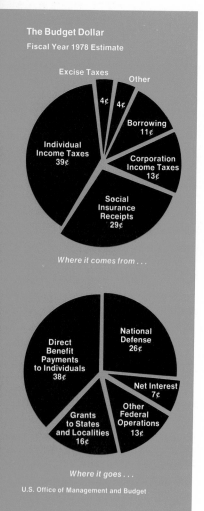

The Budget Dollar
Fiscal Year 1978 Estimate

Excise Taxes

Other

4¢   4¢

Borrowing
11¢

Individual
Income Taxes
39¢

Corporation
Income Taxes
13¢

Social
Insurance
Receipts
29¢

Where it comes from . . .

National
Defense
26¢

Direct
Benefit
Payments
to Individuals
38¢

Net Interest
7¢

Other
Federal
Operations
13¢

Grants
to States
and Localities
16¢

Where it goes . . .

U.S. Office of Management and Budget

[3]See John F. Manley, *The Politics of Finance* (Little, Brown, 1970); and Lawrence C. Pierce, *The Politics of Fiscal Policy Formation* (Goodyear, 1971).

Bureau of Customs, which maintains ports of entry, inspects cargo, assesses the value of merchandise, and with the United States Coast Guard, prevents smuggling.

The customs agent shown here uses some canine help to detect packages containing marijuana, one of the duties of the Treasury Departments Bureau of Customs.

When persons are suddenly faced with expenses too heavy to meet out of their regular income, they often have to borrow money. The same is true of government. During military and economic crises, the federal government has gone heavily in debt. It borrowed $23 billion during World War I, about $13 billion more during the 1930s, and over $200 billion more during World War II. By 1979 the gross federal debt was more than $785 billion.

Borrowing costs money. The federal government can borrow at a relatively low rate. Nevertheless the interest on the federal debt is about $40 billion a year. The size of the debt and of the interest payments alarms many Americans. How long can we allow the debt to grow at this staggering rate? Two considerations must be kept in mind. In the first place, the government owes most of the money to its own people rather than to foreign governments or persons. Second, the economic strength and resources of the country are more significant than the size of the public debt.

How does the government borrow money? The Constitution says that Congress may "borrow money on the credit of the United States"; it puts no limit on either the extent or method of borrowing. Under congressional authorization, the Treasury Department sells securities to banks, corporations, and individuals. Usually these securities take the form of long-term bonds or short-term treasury notes. Some bonds may be cashed in at any time, others not until their maturity. Because the United States government guarantees these bonds, they are in great demand, especially by banks and investment companies.

Spending the money

All the billions of dollars the government takes in are funneled into the treasury and then move out through hundreds of channels. Nothing reflects the rise of big government more clearly than the change in the amounts and methods of its spending. As recently as 1933 the federal government spent only $4 billion, about $30 per capita. By 1979 the respective figures were more than $490 billion and about $2000. The machinery for spending has changed, too. At one time spending was loosely administered. Records show, for example, that in an early year of the republic one Nicholas Johnson, a Navy agent of Newburyport, Massachusetts, was handed several thousand dollars to supply "Cpt. Brown for recruiting his Crew."[4] Today Mr. Johnson would have to make out detailed forms and wait for a check.

Where does the money go? Much of it, of course, is for national defense. In recent years about 26 percent to national security; 7 percent to interest on the national debt; 38 percent to social insurance, education, and other major social programs. Much of the federal debt is for payments for past wars. Defense-related expenditures such as veterans' pensions and benefits are buried in non-"national security" categories.

The sheer fact of spending more than $490 billion a year is most significant of all. Years ago, federal revenues and outlays were so small that national taxing and spending had little impact on the overall economy. Today the federal government cannot drain billions of dollars from certain

Federal power projects are a major form of outlay to develop or create (though some say destroy) regional resources.

[4]L. D. White, *The Federalists* (Macmillan, 1948), p. 341.

areas of the economy and pump them back into others without having a profound effect on the economy of the nation and of the world. This problem will be considered later in the chapter. First we must see how the federal budget is drawn up and made into law.

FORMULATING THE BUDGET

As we have seen, Congress must authorize the spending of funds, but the initiation of appropriations is a responsibility of the president. The first step in preparing a federal budget is for the various departments and agencies to estimate their needs.[5] This process starts early. While Congress is debating the budget for the fiscal year immediately ahead, the agencies are making budget estimates for the year following. The estimating job is handled largely by budget officers working under the direction of agency chiefs. The agency officials must take into account not only their needs as they see them, but also the overall presidential program and the probable reactions of Congress.[6] Departmental budgets are highly detailed; they include estimates on expected needs for personnel, supplies, office space, and the like.

The Office of Management and Budget handles the next phase of budget making. A staff agency of the president, the OMB examines each agency budget to see if it is in accord with the president's plans. This job is done by experienced budget examiners. Hearings are then held to give agency spokesmen a chance to clarify and defend their estimated needs. The OMB director and his aides, who make the final decision, frequently prune the agencies' requests rather severely.

For months the director has been conferring with the president and top

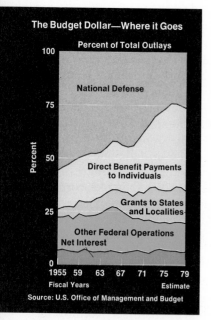

The Budget Dollar—Where it Goes

Percent of Total Outlays

National Defense

Direct Benefit Payments to Individuals

Grants to States and Localities

Other Federal Operations
Net Interest

1955 59 63 67 71 75 79
Fiscal Years   Estimate

Source: U.S. Office of Management and Budget

[5]For a discussion and graphic presentation of the budgetary cycle, see Aaron Wildavsky, *The Politics of the Budgetary Process*, rev. ed. (Little, Brown, 1974).

[6]*Ibid.*, Chap. 2; and Richard F. Fenno, Jr., "The House Appropriations Committee as a Political System," *American Political Science Review* (June 1962), pp. 310–24.

23—1
Budgetary process timetable

This is the timetable the President and Congress will try to follow as they enact the annual federal budget:	
Action to be completed	**On or before**
President submits current services budget to Congress	Nov. 10
President submits annual budget message to Congress	15 days after Congress meets
Congressional committees make recommendations to budget committees	March 15
Congressional Budget Office reports to budget committees	April 1
Budget committees report first budget resolution	April 15
Congress passes first budget resolution	May 15
Legislative committees complete reporting of authorizing legislation	May 15
Congress passes all spending bills	Seven days after Labor Day
Congress passes second budget resolution	Sept. 15
Congress passes budget reconciliation bill	Sept. 25
Fiscal year begins	Oct. 1

presidental aides and trying to keep the agencies below their budget ceilings. Finally, the director arrives at the White House with a single consolidated set of estimates of both revenue and expenditures, the product of perhaps a year's work. The president has reserved a day or two for a final review of the budget, and the two check the consolidated figures. The budget director also helps the president prepare a budget message that will stress key aspects of the budget and tie it in with broad national plans. By January, soon after Congress convenes, the budget and the message are ready for the legislatures and the public.

PROCESSING BUDGET PROPOSALS THROUGH THE EXECUTIVE BRANCH

Under the Constitution, only the Congress can appropriate funds. In 1974 Congress adopted the Budget Reform Act, which is designed to give it a more effective role in the budget process. The act calls on the president when submitting his proposals to include proposed changes in tax laws, estimates of amounts of revenue lost through existing preferential tax treatments, and five-year estimates of the costs of new and continuing federal programs. The act also calls on the president to seek authorizing legislation for a program a year before he asks Congress for the funds to do it. Preparation of the budget proposals is only the beginning. For as we saw in Chapter 14, the Budget Reform Act of 1974 also called for Congress to make important changes in the way it goes about appropriating funds.

CHECKING UP ON EXPENDITURES

After Congress has appropriated money, it reserves the right to check up on the way the money is spent. Under the Budget and Accounting Act of 1921, the General Accounting Office (GAO) does the national government's accounting job. The GAO is headed by a comptroller general, who is appointed by the president with the approval of the Senate. The comptroller general enjoys some measure of independence, however, for his term of office is fifteen years. He is not eligible for reappointment, and he can be removed only for specific cause by a joint resolution of Congress.

The comptroller general was originally intended to operate as an independent auditor serving as an arm of Congress to guard against improper and unauthorized expenditures. But as time went on, he was swamped by a gigantic accounting job that forced him to handle administrative matters in the executive branch even though he was not responsible to the chief executive. At the same time, overall management in the executive branch suffered, because daily accounting, an important instrument of administrative control, had been placed in a separate agency.

Improvements have been made in recent years. The GAO, with over 5,400 employees, now uses spot sampling methods to check vouchers and makes its audits in the field rather than in Washington. Although the comptroller general still has the authority to disallow expenditures, his approval is no longer needed prior to the disbursement of funds. Being relieved of personal responsibility for payments that may subsequently be disallowed, disbursing officers (provided they have acted in good faith and with reasonable diligence) have been encouraged to make their own decisions about the legality of expenditures. The General Accounting Office—as a result of the Legislative Reorganization Act of 1970—has taken on broader responsibilities in investigating and even evaluating programs. GAO has increasingly shifted from narrow fiscal auditing to what is called "performance auditing." Thus it is now checking upon the ade-

At Fort Knox, Kentucky, Representative John B. Conlan of Arizona, lifts a bar of gold from one of the vaults at the bullion depository.

quacy and effectiveness of a program's *performance* as well as the *honesty* of it.

It might seem that accounting is a technical matter that could be settled without much argument. But accounting is a political issue too, for it reflects two struggles in Washington: the attempt of Congress to maintain as much control as possible over the mushrooming bureaucratic machine, and the struggle of individual legislators to maintain a system that checks individual administrative payments.

Managing money

Today's economy is a money economy. We exchange commodities through a vast system of money and credit. We have seen the tremendous role the federal government plays in this system, simply because it gets and spends over $490 billion a year. But aside from its role as the biggest buyer and seller of goods and services, the federal government has a more direct impact on our money economy. It manufactures money; it regulates the value of money; it controls the nation's credit system; and it can devalue the dollar.

Manufacturing money is the easiest of these jobs. The Bureau of Engraving and Printing in the Treasury Department turns out millions of dollars in the form of bills, bonds, and postage stamps every week; this money is fed into general circulation through the Treasury and the Federal Reserve banks. In itself, this money is only so much paper. How does the government maintain its value?

THE CURRENCY SYSTEM

The Constitution gives the federal government the right to manage the nation's monetary system. Under the articles of Confederation, the national currency had consisted mainly of almost worthless paper money, and the individual states had maintained separate currencies. To correct this, the Constitution of 1787 gave Congress authority to coin money and to regulate its value, carefully withholding this power from the states. Thanks partly to Secretary of the Treasury Hamilton, Americans scrapped the confusing British system of guineas, pounds, shillings, and pence and adopted a decimal system.

Today the United States is on a highly modified gold standard. The unit of monetary value is defined in terms of gold. But all the currency of the United States is legal tender and cannot be freely exchanged for gold or silver. In short, the money of the United States is redeemable only for other money of the United States.

Money makes up only a part of the circulating medium and is less important to our economy than credit. In the expansion and contraction of credit, the most important institutions are the banks and the Federal Reserve System.

BANKS AND LENDING INSTITUTIONS

Banking, though a private business, is subject to close government supervision. There are over 14,000 banks in the United States; 4,600 are chartered by the national government, the rest by the states. The national banks have custody of 50 percent of all bank deposits. The comptroller of the currency in the Treasury Department supervises their operations. Each national bank must file reports on its financial condition four times a year and must permit bank examiners to inspect its books at least three times every two years.

Although state authorities have the primary responsibility for state-chartered banks, most of these banks are also subject to federal regulation because their deposits are insured by the Federal Deposit Insurance Corporation (FDIC). All national banks must participate in this program, and state banks that meet approved standards are also permitted to do so. All but a few hundred of the commercial bank and trust companies in the United States have their deposits insured by the FDIC, as do some mutual savings banks. The FDIC routinely examines banks that are not members of the Federal Reserve System (see below) and establishes rules designed to keep them from going bankrupt. When a member bank fails, the FDIC takes over its management and pays depositors.

The Federal Savings and Loan Insurance Corporation, operating under the supervision of the Federal Home Loan Bank Board, protects investors in federal savings and loan associations and those state-chartered institutions approved for participation. Like the FDIC, it guarantees savings up to $40,000 for each account.

THE FEDERAL RESERVE SYSTEM

In many nations, a central bank owned and operated by the national government makes monetary policy. The Constitution does not specifically authorize the national government to create such a bank—indeed, it says nothing at all about banking. But Alexander Hamilton believed that some such institution was necessary. In 1791, the United States Bank was incorporated by the national government and given a twenty-year charter. This bank was partly private and partly public; the national government owned a minority of the shares and had only a minority voice in its management. Jefferson and his supporters opposed the bank and refused to renew the charter in 1812. But Madison found it necessary to have the bank rechartered for another twenty years in 1816. In 1819 the Supreme Court in *McCulloch* v. *Maryland*[7] (see Chapter 3) upheld the constitutionality of the bank as a necessary and proper way for the national government to establish a uniform currency and to care for the property of the United States.

After the bank closed its doors in 1836, state banks, which had previously been restrained by the second United States Bank, began issuing notes that often could not be redeemed. A military crisis forced a house cleaning. To stabilize a war economy, Congress in 1863 authorized the chartering of national banks. These are privately owned corporations, not central banks or an institution like the United States Bank. State banks were permitted to continue in business, but a 10 percent federal tax on their notes quickly drove state bank notes out of existence.

The national bank system created during the Civil War was stable—indeed, so stable that it was inflexible. Financial crises during the late nineteenth century and in 1907 revealed a tendency to restrict loans and to contract the issuance of notes just when an *expansion* of money was needed. In order to furnish an elastic currency, and for other reasons, Congress in 1913 established the Federal Reserve System.

The act of 1913 was a compromise. Some wanted a strong central bank, but others feared this would centralize control over currency in too few hands. So a system was established that gives us a modified central banking program with considerable decentralization. The country is divided into twelve Federal Reserve districts, in each of which there is a Federal Reserve bank (most Federal Reserve banks have branches). Each Federal

[7] 4 Wheaton 316 (1819).

Reserve bank is owned by member banks. All national banks must join the system, and state banks that meet standards are permitted to do so. Today approximately 5,700 of the 14,000 banks are members of the system; these are the largest banks and have over 85 percent of total deposits.

Each Federal Reserve bank is headed by a board of directors. Six members are elected by the member banks, and three are appointed by the board of governors in Washington. Three of the directors elected by the member banks must be bankers, and three must be active in business and industry. The three directors appointed by the board of governors may not have any financial interest in and may not work for any bank. The board of governors designates one of its appointees chairman of the board of directors, and this board in turn selects a president to serve as chief executive officer.

A seven person board of governors sitting in Washington supervises the entire system. They are selected by the president with the consent of the Senate for fourteen-year terms. The president designates the chairman, who has a four-year term. The board of governors is advised by a federal advisory council, which is composed of a member from each Federal Reserve district. The board meets in Washington at least four times a year and determines general monetary and credit policies. It has four major devices to control the financial activities of the nation's banks and, in turn, the whole economy:

1. To increase or decrease within legal limits the reserves that member banks must maintain against their deposits in the Federal Reserve bank.
2. To raise or lower the discount rate charged by Federal Reserve banks to member banks. The discount rate is the price member banks must pay to get cash from the Federal Reserve banks for acceptable commercial notes that the banks hold.
3. Through the Open Market Committee (composed of all members of the board of governors and five representatives of the Reserve banks), to sell or buy government securities and certain other bills of exchange, bank acceptances, and so on.
4. To exercise direct control over the credit that may be extended in order to purchase securities (called margin requirements). From time to time Congress has given the board of governors temporary authority to fix terms of consumer credit.

Through these and other devices, the board of governors may affect the flow of money by tightening or loosening credit. For example, if inflation is threatening, the board can depress the economy by raising member-bank reserve requirements (thus cutting down on the cash they have available for lending); by raising discount rates (thus forcing member banks to raise the rates for which they will lend money); by selling government securities in the open market (thus absorbing funds from the economy); and by raising margin requirements (thus reducing credit available to bid up the prices of securities). In addition, the Federal Reserve banks serve as depositories for government funds, clear checks and transfer funds among member banks, and may, in case of economic emergency, lend money directly to businesses.

The Federal Reserve system is intentionally isolated from influence by the president. Because it does not depend on annual appropriations, even Congress exercises little control over it. "Devised as a service agency for banking and commerce—to achieve a semi-automatic adjustment of the money supply—the Federal Reserve has become as well a policy-making institution with major responsibility for national economic stabiliza-

Arthur Burns, a former economic advisor to Presidents Eisenhower and Nixon and more recently head of the Federal Reserve Board.

tion."[8] Many observers feel it is improper to give this important new responsibility to an agency so divorced from public accountability. The board of governors, for example, often has to make a choice between fighting inflation, which may cause unemployment, and promoting employment at the expense of increasing inflation. As Gardiner C. Means has said, "There is a good deal of question whether such a momentous decision should rest with the Federal Reserve Board."[9] Yet most bankers want to preserve the system's independence. They believe that only an agency insulated from political pressures can take the unpopular steps needed to prevent inflation.

The Federal Reserve Board grew in power and independence under the chairmanship of the politically astute, conservative economist Arthur F. Burns, a Nixon appointee. President Carter replaced Burns with G. William Miller in December 1977. Burns made a strong case that a major source of inflation is government overspending in response to demands from the electorate, and that one of the most important goals of the Federal Reserve Board is to control the rate of inflation. The Federal Reserve Board has the ability to counterbalance or aid any attempts by a president or Congress to stimulate the economy.

Today all agree that monetary policy must be considered as but one weapon to combat depression, control inflation, foster full employment, and encourage economic growth. Whether or not we can retain a system in which the central banking authorities "can legally . . . tell the head of [their] own Government to go fly a kite"[10] remains an unresolved issue.

Managing the economy

Does the government have the same direct control over the national economy that it has, say, over the U.S. military and national forests? No. Only if we had a socialized economy administered from Washington would we have a managed economy in that sense. We still have an economy in which a great deal of power is left to private individuals and enterprises. And yet the government keeps a firm hand on all the gears and levers that control the general direction in which the economy will head and the rate at which it will move. These gears and levers are taxes, spending, and credit.

It is only rather recently that Americans have recognized the part that government can play in stabilizing the economy. (There are still tremendous arguments over the part it *should* play.) The slow development of our understanding, the political struggle over the question of whether the federal government should take responsibility for full employment, the enactment of the Employment Act of 1946, and the Carter administration's economic stimulus and tax reform efforts in the late 1970s are fascinating episodes in the trend toward overall control of the economy by the federal government.

ECONOMIC GROPING

Depression is a hard teacher. The 1930s had a tremendous impact on American thinking about the role of government in the economy. We have had long, severe depressions before—for example, in the 1870s and 1890s.

[8]See Michael D. Reagan, "The Political Structure of the Federal Reserve System," *American Political Science Review* (March 1961), pp. 64–76, for a detailed analysis of the present structure and policy implications of the Federal Reserve System.

[9]Quoted in *ibid.*, p. 75.

[10]Elliot V. Bell, quoted in *ibid.*, p. 76.

The monetary policies set by the Federal Reserve Board are designed to control inflation and combat depressions, such as the one that occurred in the 1930s, when depositors gathered outside banks across the country in an attempt to withdraw their money.

But by 1929 the United States had become a rich and powerful nation. Then the Great Depression struck. Millions of unemployed, falling prices and incomes all added up to mass misery. "One vivid, gruesome moment of those dark days we shall never forget," wrote one observer. "We saw a crowd of some fifty men fighting over a barrel of garbage which had been set outside the back door of a restaurant. American citizens fighting for scraps of food like animals!"[11]

Despite a wide range of efforts on the part of the Roosevelt administration to cope with the Depression, it hung on. Faint signs of recovery could be seen in the mid-1930s; but the recession of 1937–38 indicated that we were by no means out of the woods. Eight or nine million people were jobless in 1939. Then came the war, and unemployment seemed cured. Millions of people had more income, more security, a higher standard of living. Lord Beveridge in England posed a question that bothered many thoughtful Americans: "Unemployment has been practically abolished twice in the lives of most of us—in the last war and in this war. Why does war solve the problem of unemployment which is so insoluble in peace?"[12] Worried that the economy might collapse after the war, thousands of people came up with plans to ensure jobs for all.

One school of thought was that the Depression lasted so long because the New Deal was hostile to business. Government intruded too long and too much into the economic life of the nation. Proponents of this theory urged the government to reduce spending, lower taxes, curb the power of labor, and generally leave business and the economy alone. Another large group said that the trouble with the New Deal was not that it had done too much but that it had done too little. The thinking of this group was deeply influenced by the work of John Maynard Keynes the English economist. In visits to the United States during the 1930s, Keynes warned that if people did not consume enough or invest enough, national income would fall. The way to increase national income is either to spend money on consumption goods (such as clothes or food or automobiles) or on investment goods (steel mills and dock facilities) or on both. Finally, *government must do the spending and investing if private enterprise by itself would not or could not.* Congress, through the passage of the Employment Act of 1946, accepted the Keynesian approach.

THE EMPLOYMENT ACT OF 1946

Passage of a law that specifically recognized the major role of the national government in the maintenance of full employment was bound to be difficult.[13] The bill as presented by the Truman administration had the support of organized labor, many senators, and members of several Senate committee staffs. Against the bill were such organizations as the National Association of Manufacturers, chambers of commerce, the American Farm Bureau Federation, and a number of key conservatives in Congress. Although the bill easily passed the Senate in close to its original form, the conservative House Rules Committee ensured that only a much weaker version would pass the House. Enacted in February 1946, the act declared:

[11]Quoted in F. L. Allen, *Since Yesterday* (Harper, 1940), p. 64.

[12]W. H. Beveridge, *The Pillars of Security* (Macmillan, 1943), p. 51.

[13]For the full history of the bill, see Stephen K. Bailey, *Congress Makes a Law* (Columbia University Press, 1950). For a history of national effects at economic planning since the 1930s, see Otis L. Graham, *Toward a Planned Society* (Oxford University Press, 1976).

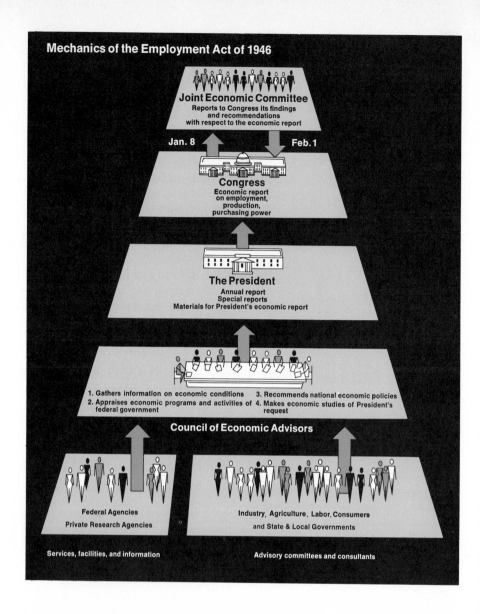

Mechanics of the Employment Act of 1946

It is the continuing policy and responsibility of the Federal Government to use all practicable means consistent with its needs and obligations and other essential considerations of national policy, with the assistance and cooperation of industry, agriculture, labor, and state and local governments, to coordinate and utilize all its plans, functions, and resources for the purpose of creating and maintaining, in a manner calculated to foster and promote free competitive enterprise and the general welfare, conditions under which there will be afforded useful employment, for those able, willing, and seeking to work, and to promote maximum employment, production, and purchasing power.

If this sounds like double talk, the reason may be that the bill had to be built on a series of compromises. In effect, the bill made the federal government responsible for maintaining high employment. Equally important, the act established machinery to carry out that responsibility:

1. *The Council of Economic Advisers* (CEA). This body is composed of three members appointed by the president with the consent of the Senate and located in the Executive Office of the President. It studies and forecasts economic trends, assesses the contribution of federal programs to maximum employment, and recommends to the president "national economic policies to foster and promote free competition, to avoid economic fluctuations or to diminish the effects thereof, and to maintain employment, production, and purchasing power."

2. *The Economic Report of the President.* Every January the president must submit to Congress an economic report based on the data and forecasts of the council. The report must include a program for carrying out the policy of the act; it can also include recommendations for legislation if the president sees fit.

3. *Joint Economic Committee* (JEC). This is a committee of Congress authorized by the act. Composed of seven senators and seven representatives, it must report early in each year its findings and proposals in respect to presidential recommendations. Aside from publishing various reports, the JEC is able to give Congress an overview of the economy. In this sense it is an anomaly in Congress: "a planning and theory group in a culture fiercely devoted to the short run and practical. It is committed to the panoramic view in a system that stresses jurisdictional lines. It signifies recognition that economic problems are related, in a body that deals with them piecemeal."[14]

How has the Employment Act worked in practice? The CEA has emerged as a high-level presidential advisory body. Its chairman serves both as an adviser to the president and as a spokesman for the president before Congress and the country. The annual economic report and the budget message are major presidential statements on the role governmental fiscal policies will play in the economy in the coming year. The JEC has played a significant role in developing information on important economic problems. The machinery established under the act is providing both the president and the Congress with the type of information and advice needed to shape the government's fiscal policy.[15]

The various mechanisms established by the act work, but is the information being utilized and the advice taken? Certainly the Employment Act is more significant for the basic ideas it embodies than for the procedures it created. The Keynesian economic underpinnings of the act gained acceptance in Washington and elsewhere, at least until it was found in the 1970s to be inadequate to deal with inflation *and* large scale unemployment. Governmental fiscal policy is being used in a straightforward fashion to stimulate the economy and cope with its fluctuations. No longer, for example, is a balanced budget viewed by Washington decisionmakers as a national goal always to be pursued. It is seen that in certain instances, it is better for the government to spend more than it takes in and to run a budget deficit. This is the course of action when the economy is not operating at full capacity. When the economy is operating at full capacity, other measures may be called for. A budget surplus, for instance, may be required to check inflationary pressures under conditions of full employment.

[14]Commission on Money and Credit, *Money and Credit: Their Influence on Jobs, Prices, and Growth* (Prentice-Hall), 1961), pp. 268–69.

[15]For an account of performance and politics under the Employment Act, see Harvey C. Mansfield, "The Congress and Economic Policy," in David B. Truman, ed., *The Congress and America's Future*, 2nd ed. (Prentice-Hall, 1973), Chap. 6.

The 1964 tax cut and the 1968 tax increase

This sort of Keynesian rationale provided the basis for the $12 billion personal income tax cut in 1964 and the early $2 billion cut in excise taxes in 1965. Although unemployment in 1964 was moving steadily downward, the economy was still not at full capacity; more stimulus from the federal government was required. The increased governmental spending and the lower taxes resulting from the 1964 cut put more money in the hands of the American people. They spent more money, thus creating more jobs. The economy boomed. Indeed, so successful was this action that though taxes were cut by $12 billion, $12.7 billion more was collected from personal taxes in 1964.

When the 1964 tax cut bill was passed, it was viewed by most people as a definite success. The "new" economics of the 1960s won praise from nearly all sides. But within just two years, new economic problems emerged. A growing economy usually means rising prices; when the expansionary effects of war are added, it means inflation. The increased purchasing power created by the tax cut, and the increased government purchases that occurred with greater Vietnam involvement, created a demand for goods that exceeded the supply. The CEA chairman, Gardner Ackley, warned President Johnson of the impending problem and suggested that a tax increase might be necessary.

Now Johnson was faced with the unpleasant side of Keynesian economics—taking dollars away from consumers. As the 1966 elections approached, however, few members of Congress wanted to campaign on a record of having just increased taxes. Johnson was reluctant to call for a tax increase. He, like most people, kept hoping the war might end soon.

Everyone nearly always dislikes tax increases. And the tax increase controversy in the late 1960s was made worse by political considerations. On what would the new tax revenues be spent? Liberal Democrats did not want to pass an increase if it was going to the Vietnam War. Conservatives did not want to support an increase if it meant more Great Society programs. Many liberals wanted *tax reform* to accompany the tax increase; conservatives wanted cuts in the federal budget to accompany the tax increase. Everyone wanted something, and with almost every group objectives differed. In the end Congress in 1968 passed a 10 percent surcharge tax and set out to cut budget expenditures by $6 billion.

The tax increase helped slow inflation—but only slightly. Most economists think the tax increase came too late. This kind of delay is a major problem in governmental management of the economy. While economists can sometimes determine fairly rapidly what the proper actions should be, the political process often responds more slowly. First, the economic ad-

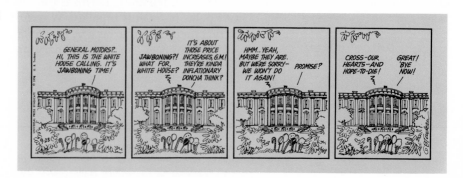

visers have to make the president aware of the problem and suggest policy responses. Second, the president must decide how and when to act. Next begins the formal presentation and unveiling of policy initiatives. Finally, Congress must be persuaded, and the measure guided through the legislative committees. Few shortcuts exist.

Known remedies are seldom as available as the Kennedy-sponsored tax cut was in the early 1960s. Moreover, we are limited because we must execute new policies by democratic procedures. And everything we do has consequences we never intend. The lessons of history show that we are seldom as smart as we think.

WHAT SHOULD BE DONE?

Some observers have suggested that the president be given standby authority to raise and lower taxes, within certain limits, without the approval of Congress. With such authority, for example, the tax increase of 1968 probably would have occurred a year earlier. But many in Congress see this proposal as taking away their constitutional responsibilities.

After the tax increase of 1968, inflationary pressures continued to build. The Federal Reserve tightened the money supply, but this did not stop the surging inflation. Nixon took office amid continued inflation. He sought for his first two years in office to curb inflation with traditional monetary and fiscal policies. Yet the rate of advance in prices and the cost of living climbed still higher, as did unemployment. Soon he faced the problem of inflation *and* rising unemployment occurring together.

What brought about these conditions? Many economists attribute it to the shift from *demand-pull* inflation to *cost-push* inflation. In the mid-1960s the demand for goods and services *pulled* up the price level; more people were willing to pay more for products. In the late 1960s, labor unions began to seek wage increases to compensate for the increased production costs, and as a result the increased cost *pushed* up the price level. Monetary and fiscal policies are not as good at slowing cost-push inflation as they are at halting demand-pull. Too, the power of many corporations allowed them to maintain high prices even when demand was declining. Thus, the car industry was able to keep prices high because the "big three" (GM, Ford, and Chrysler) together refused to lower prices. Consumers in turn had little choice—they either bought at the higher prices, or did without. Each of these choices posed an added problem for the managers of the nation's economy.

**President Carter and
tax reform**

In the past twenty-five years the share of the average family's income paid in direct taxes has doubled. Direct taxes for the average family rose twice as fast as for well-off and wealthy families. And despite our professed belief in equality, the money income of the top 10 percent of the population consistently averages twenty times more than the lowest 10 percent. All this has made many middle-income persons upset and has encouraged politicians to promise they will reform the tax system. Like apple pie and the flag, tax reform is an ideal issue for a candidate to support.

In the 1976 campaign, Jimmy Carter saved some of his strongest language for his criticism of the present tax structure. Carter called out national tax system a "disgrace." He added:

Carefully contrived loopholes let the total tax burden shift more and more toward the average wage earner. Some of our largest corporations with extremely high profits pay virtually no tax at all. The average family earning $10,000 per year pays a larger portion of its income in taxes than a family with an annual income of $1 million or more. When a business executive can charge off a $50 luncheon on a tax return and a truck driver cannot deduct his $1.50 sandwich—when oil companies pay less than 5% on their earnings while employees of the company pay at least three times this rate—when many pay no taxes on incomes of more than $100,000—then we need basic tax reform.

I am considering a drastic simplification of the income tax system that would *lower* taxes on middle and low income families. To do that you would eliminate hundreds of tax breaks and greatly reduce the tax rate . . . . Basically, subject to some exceptions, I favor a simplified tax system which treats all income the same, and a system which does not encourage corporations to locate plants abroad, while people who want to work are begging for jobs back home.[16]

But overhauling the tax system will be a tough promise to keep. To be sure, sweeping tax revision could save a lot of money. The tax breaks Carter seeks to close down now cost the government about $130 billion. These breaks, sometimes called tax loopholes or "tax expenditures," give special relief to certain individuals or organizations. But nearly every one of these tax breaks has its strong defenders who will fight any move to eliminate it. Most people want to abolish someone else's loopholes and keep their own. Perhaps this is why Carter was forced to postpone his tax "reform" effort in late 1977.

"An approach that concentrates on a limited number of specific proposals immediately runs afoul of those who stand to lose by the changes. Their cries are inevitably loud enough to drown out the praises of the few who are farsighted enough to perceive the potential gains for the general public."[17] A sweeping and comprehensive tax reform, as suggested by Carter, might mean significant gains for some and losses for others. But it may arouse more hostility than support as the majority of people, unsure of what will result, may prefer to bear the burdens they have now than accept the uncertain burdens of the alternative system. That is, unless a president and other national leaders could build a strong coalition of support around the measure, there is little chance of success. Whether Carter and his supporters are able to do this remains to be seen.

Most experts who share Carter's hopes believe he may be successful in ending the special treatment of *capital gains*. These are the gains on the sales of stocks or other assets such as real estate held over nine months. At present, individuals have only to pay taxes on capital gains profits at half the normal rate. Defenders insist that these lower rates are an important inducement to investment. Critics say this is unfair and moreover, that it complicates the tax system and distorts economic behavior.

Carter's critics say it is naive to call for elimination of the tax breaks. Their point is that tax incentives serve a variety of important public purposes, ranging from promoting business investment to encouraging private

"Remember, son, we are a government of loopholes, and not of men!"

Drawing by Dana Fradon; © 1976 The New Yorker Magazine, Inc.

[16]*Jimmy Carter on Tax Reform*, an issue sheet released by the Jimmy Carter Presidential Campaign (Summer 1976), mimeo.

[17]George Break and Joseph A. Pechman, *Federal Tax Reform: The Impossible Dream* (Brookings, 1975), pp. 13–15.

voluntary approaches to solve society's problems. Economist Murray Weidenbaum argues that the growth ot tax subsidies may be viewed as a reaction to the vast growth of government power and government regulations. He contends that despite the attractions of comprehensive tax reform and a simpler tax system, such "second best" alternatives as tax breaks are a reasonable means to be used for achieving public policy goals.[18]

So the battle over tax reform has been joined. Carter will have his hands full as he sets about to curb inflation, reform the tax system, *and* balance the budget by 1981. His reelection in 1980 would seem to be easily achieved if he succeeded in fulfilling these three goals, some say, but "Tax reform is like Eldorado. It stands gleaming somewhere over the horizon. But to get there, the Channel must be swum, the Sahara crossed, the Rockies climbed. No one has yet made it."[19]

Summary

1. In these last three chapters we have seen that economic and political life in our society are interwoven. There are no easily defined boundaries between private and public sectors of the economy. A few still insist that government and the economy must be kept strictly separated, that government should not interfere in private affairs. Whatever its theoretical merits, this view is unrealistic. In modern American society we have a political economy in which a decision in one area inevitably affects decisions in others. This political economy is a mixed economy: It blends private and public enterprise, individual initiative and government promotion, personal responsibility and public regulation, federal and state governments.

2. We have also discovered that government regulation, promotion, and economic management are not really distinct. Promotion may be used for regulatory purposes and regulation for promotional; government taxing and spending in the broadest sense always entails both.

3. One of the greatest challenges in a democracy is how to mobilize the government so that it can respond to changing economic conditions, but to do so in a fashion that keeps government accountable to the people. The problem in part is whether a governmental system such as ours can act effectively when action is needed. But the problem is also one of knowing what to do, and when to do it.

[18]Murray L. Weidenbaum, "In Defense of Tax Loopholes," *The New York Times* (June 26, 1977), p. 14 F.

[19]Robert J. Samuelson, "Tax Reform—Can Carter Help the Poor and Stimulate Investment Too?" *National Journal* (March 19, 1977), p. 427.

Part Six

State and Local Government

A Problem Guide

PART Six deals with entire systems of government at state and local levels. Americans in their states and localities face the same challenges that they face as a nation—the challenge of making democratic government a vital and indispensable way of ruling the people; of following basic constitutional principles, without letting government become stymied by internal disputes; of maintaining a balance between liberty and order; of achieving representation for all interests; of keeping state and local policy-makers responsible as well as responsive.

State and community governments, however, pose certain of these problems more sharply than others. Genuine political accountability is lacking in some states because of the splintering of executive power between governors and a host of independent administrative officials. The party system is often not strong enough to knit the official policy-making elites together as a team. In some states, special interest groups still have an unusual amount of influence; they take advantage of campaign finance loopholes and other influence-purchasing opportunities which are especially available to the well-organized and well-heeled.

Although some states seem unable to meet the demands of modern society, others are pointing the way to creative solutions. What spells the difference between effective and inadequate state governance? On the one hand, more and more functions are gradually being taken over by the federal government. Still, the lessons of the 1960s and 1970s suggest rather strongly that there are limits to what can be administered directly from Washington. Plainly, some kind of balance is needed, and revenue-sharing and other inter-governmental reform measures move in this direction. These and other critical questions of how states function are treated in Chapters 24, 25, 26, 27 and 28.

What about governments at the community level? It is hard to generalize about county and city government because of the enormous variety of political forms and cultures. Still the question of whether government by the people is a possibility remains central to our investigation. How much power, for example, does the local executive have? How much should he or she have, and to whom is he or she accountable? Are the various interests fairly represented in community policy-making processes? How well can local government mobilize the two indispensable tools of administration—able people and sufficient money—to do the job? Do our local governments have the capacity to carry on their functions efficiently and responsibly? These are the central questions raised in Chapters 29, 30, 31, 32, and 33.

The emphasis in this book has been on the political forces—parties, interest groups, public opinion, and so on—that shape policy making and policy outcomes. This is the emphasis in Part Six as well. To the student of American politics, the states and their subdivisions are fascinating political laboratories that allow comparison among different systems. How strong and unified is the party system? To what extent do state and local politics mirror national political tides? To what extent are they cut off from or wholly independent from national political influences? Does the political system foster competition between the two parties, or does one party clearly dominate? In the latter case, how much free and open competition exists among factions *within* the dominant party? In short, does the political system help the voters make meaningful choices? Do the policy makers respond to the needs and wishes of the great majority of citizens?

Chapter 24

State and Local Politics: Who Governs?

"Who really runs things around here?" This question is an ancient one. Not only philosophers but most people like to ask, "Who counts?" Nowhere, perhaps, has this question been asked more often and by more people than in the United States.

In 1924, two sociologists from Columbia University, Robert and Helen Lynd, decided that they would study a typical American city as though they were anthropologists investigating a tribe in Africa. For two years they lived in Muncie, Indiana, at that time a city of 381,000, asking questions and watching how people made their living, brought up their kids, used their leisure time, and joined in civic and social associations. The Lynds reported that despite the appearance of democratic practices, a social and economic elite was actually running things.[1] This started a series of studies by social scientists and journalists of all kinds of communities, all trying to find out how government works, and whether power is concentrated in the hands of the few, or dispersed among many.

In studying American state and local governments in the late 1970s to find out how they operate and who governs them, we are faced with unique problems. It is one thing to study the national system, vast and complex as it is: it is something else to study fifty separate state governments, each with its own legislature, executive, and judiciary, each with its own intricate politics and political traditions. Moreover, the government of each state is only part of a much larger picture. To discuss the government of Mississippi or the city of Detroit without mentioning white-black relations, the government of New York without noting the politics of ethnic groups, the government of Texas without referring to cattle and oil,

[1]Robert S. Lynd and Helen M. Lynd, *Middletown* (Harcourt, 1929). See also their equally brilliant treatment of Muncie ten years later, *Middletown in Transition* (Harcourt, 1937).

the government of Illinois without mentioning Chicago and Cook County politics, would be to ignore the dynamics of the political process. State governments, just like the national government, cannot properly be analyzed and assessed as organization charts rather than as systems of politics. And the great variations among the states—population, economic resources, environment—make comparisons and generalizations difficult.

Any governmental system is part of a larger social system. A government is a device that resolves or at least manages conflicts. Further, it distributes, regulates, and sometimes redistributes those things that are valued. It is also a device to achieve certain goals, to perform services desired both by those who govern and by those who are governed. Many factors outside the system itself are often more important than its structure or even the nature of its political parties. Some scholars have found that such factors as the economic system, the class structure, and the style of life are more important in determining the policies adopted by a particular state or municipality than the governmental structures it has adopted. However, the interrelations and mutual feedbacks between the economic, social, and political systems are so complex that it is difficult to unscramble them and to decide which is cause and which is effect.[2]

Complex as the picture of the state governments is, it is even more complicated by the thousands of cities, counties, towns, villages, school districts, water control districts, and other governmental units that are piled one on top of another within the states. If all states or cities or towns were alike, the task might be manageable; but of course they are not. Each city, each state is unique. While recognizing that our states, cities, and counties cannot be fitted into simplified categories, we must discover the patterns and search for the uniformities underlying all the variation. We need some tentative organizing concepts that will help us understand what is going on, whether we live in rural Vermont or downtown Los Angeles.

The location of power

How, then, can we understand the operations and problems of state and local government without becoming bogged down in endless detail? We can do so by restating the core problems of democratic governance—problems of citizen participation and liberty, constitutionalism, representation, responsible leadership. Further, we can emphasize a question that will throw light on all these problems—the question of *who governs.* Does political power in the states and localities tend to gravitate toward a relatively small number of elites? If so, who are these elites? Do they work closely together, or do they divide among themselves? Do the same elites dominate all decision making, or do some sets of leaders decide certain questions and leave other questions to other elites or simply to chance?

ANALYZING PATTERNS OF POWER

Relying on a rich mix of research methods, social scientists have focused on the pattern of power in communities, and they have, of course, come up with varied findings. Floyd Hunter, a sociologist who analyzed a southern regional city (Atlanta), found a relatively small and stable group of top policy makers drawn largely from the business class. This elite operated through shifting groups of secondary leaders, who sometimes modi-

---

[2]Thomas R. Dye, *Politics in States and Communities*, 3rd ed. (Prentice-Hall, 1977); Richard I. Hofferbert, *The Study of Public Policy* (Bobbs-Merrill, 1974); and Brian R. Fry and Richard F. Winters, "The Politics of Redistribution," *American Political Science Review* (June 1970), pp. 508–22.

fied policy, but the power of the elite was almost always there.[3] On the other hand, Robert Dahl, a political scientist at Yale, studying his own city of New Haven, concluded that while some people had a great deal of influence and most others had little, *there was no hard-core elite.* There were instead shifting coalitions of leaders who sometimes fell out among themselves and who always had to keep in mind what the public would bear when making their decisions.[4]

Of the two cities, Atlanta and New Haven, which is more typical of the distribution of influence in American communities? Could it be that the differences between Hunter's and Dahl's findings stem from the questions they asked? Plainly, the assumptions of investigators and the techniques they use produce differences in what they find.[5]

RULE BY A FEW OR RULE BY THE MANY?

One group of investigators, chiefly sociologists such as Hunter, is mainly concerned with social stratification. They assume that political influence is a function of the socioeconomic structure of the community. They try to find out who governs a community by asking a variety of citizens to identify the persons who are most influential in the community. Then these influentials are studied to determine their social characteristics, their role in decision making, the interrelations among them and between the influentials and the rest of the citizens. Those who use this technique report that the upper socioeconomic groups make up the power elite, that elected political leaders are subordinate to this elite, and that the major conflicts within the community are between the upper and the lower socioeconomic classes.

Another group of investigators, primarily political scientists such as Dahl, have questioned these findings and have raised objections to the research techniques. The evidence, they contend (even that contained within the stratification studies themselves), does not support the conclusion that communities are run by a power elite. Rather, the notion of a power elite is merely a reflection of the techniques used and the assumptions of the stratification theorists. Instead of studying the activities of those who are *thought* to have influence, one should study public policy to find out how, in fact, decisions are made. Those who conduct community studies in this manner usually find an open pluralistic power structure. Some people do have more influence than others, but influence is shared among a rather sizable number and tends to be limited to particular issues and areas. Those who have much to say about how the public schools are run may have little influence over economic policies. And in many communities and for many issues there is no identifiable group of influentials. Policy emerges not from the manipulations of a small group, but from the unanticipated and unplanned consequences of the behavior of a relatively large number of people. The social structure of the community, they find,

Governor James B. Longley of Maine, meets the press, accompanied by his budget commissioner.

[3]Floyd Hunter, *Community Power Structure* (University of North Carolina Press, 1953). For a reassessment of Hunter's findings, see M. Kent Jennings, *Community Influentials: The Elites of Atlanta* (Free Press, 1964).

[4]Robert A. Dahl, *Who Governs? Democracy and Power in an American City* (Yale University Press, 1961).

[5]See Nelson W. Polsby, *Community Power and Political Theory* (Yale University Press, 1963) for the perspective of a critic of social stratification theorists. See also Willis D. Hawley and Frederick Wirt, eds., *The Search for Community Power* (Prentice-Hall, 1969); and Raymond Wolfinger, *The Politics of Progress* (Prentice-Hall, 1974).

is certainly one factor, but it is not the determining factor in how goods and services are distributed within the community.

Here we have an example of how the questions we ask influence the answers we find.[6] If we ask strategically located citizens for their opinion of who is powerful, we will find that a relatively small number of people are the *real* holders of power. If we study dozens of local events and decisions, we will doubtless find that a variety of people are involved, different people in different policy areas. Still other students of local politics suggest that local values, traditions, and the way governmental organizations are structured may determine which issues get on the local agenda. They urge us to weigh carefully the possibility that defenders of the status quo can mobilize power resources in such a way that "nondecisions" may be more important than actual decisions. Study not only who rules, this school of scholars suggests, but also the procedures and rules of the game that operate to *prevent* issues from arising. Determine which groups or interests gain and which are handicapped by them.[7] This is a useful recommendation, although the task of studying nondecisions or nonevents is extremely complex.[8]

Community power studies, despite differences in approach and findings, have produced enough data about communities so that we can begin to generalize about how formal governmental institutions, structure of the society, economic factors, and other variables interrelate to create a political system that determines who gets what, where, when, and how.

The stakes of the political struggle

Events have given the national government enormous influence over the destiny of the American people. The advent of nuclear weapons has put into the hands of one person, the president, life-and-death control of the future of tens of millions of his fellow citizens. The assumption of responsibility for maintaining full employment, for fighting inflation, for regulating great economic power groups such as labor and business, and for subsidizing economically weaker sectors of the economy such as the poor has made the federal government .the custodian of the nation's economic strength and security. State and local governments cannot claim anything like this central a role. But the role of the states and localities is increasingly large in domestic policy questions, not only in absolute terms but even as compared with the national government. Since World War II, *state and local* governmental activities have increased much faster than the nondefense activities of the federal government. Today, two-thirds of the expenditures for domestic functions are carried by the states and their subdivisions.

Moreover, these governments generally have a more intimate relation with the average person than does Washington, for the neighborhood and housekeeping problems of Americans are closely regulated by state and local governments. The points where we come into contact with govern-

Mayors Maynard Jackson of Atlanta and Fred Hofheinz of Houston, exchange ideas about the job of urban government.

[6]However, see Robert E. Agger, Daniel Goldrich, and Bert E. Swanson, *The Rulers and the Ruled* (Wiley, 1964), for a study using the decisional approach that came to conclusions similar to those based on the reputational approach.

[7]See, for example, Peter Bachrach and Morton S. Baratz, *Power and Poverty: Theory and Practice* (Oxford University Press, 1970); Matthew A. Crenson, *The Unpolitics of Air Pollution: A Study of Non-Decisionmaking in Two Cities* (Johns Hopkins University Press, 1971); and Edward C. Hayes, *Power Structure and Urban Policy* (McGraw-Hill, 1972).

[8]Geoffrey Debnam, "Nondecisions and Power: The Two Faces of Bachrach and Baratz," *American Political Science Review* (September 1975), pp. 889–99.

ment most often are in school, on the highways, in a playground, at a big fire, in a hospital, in a courtroom. (But even in many of these policy areas, the mix of national, state, and local programs and responsibilities is such that it is often hard to isolate which level of government does what to whom. Also, there are some national-to-individual relationships that bypass state and local governments altogether, such as the mail service, social security, and tax collecting.)

Some things might seem far removed from any government—for example, having a dog or a cat as a pet. But dogs need a license, a collar, to be confined, and so on. And if anyone thinks that cats are beyond the reach of the law, one should remember Adlai E. Stevenson's famous veto of the "cat bill" when he was governor of Illinois. The bill would have imposed fines on cat owners who let their pets run off their premises, and would have allowed cat haters to trap them. The governor said:

> I cannot agree, that it should be the declared public policy of Illinois that a cat visiting a neighbor's yard or crossing the highway is a public nuisance. It is in the nature of cats to do a certain amount of unescorted roaming. . . . I am afraid this bill could only create discord, recrimination, and enmity. . . . We are all interested in protecting certain varieties of birds. . . . The problem of the cat versus bird is as old as time. If we attempt to resolve it by legislation who knows but what we may be called upon to take sides as well in the age-old problem of dog versus cat, bird versus bird, or even bird versus worm. . . .[9]

So the governor sided with cat lovers over bird lovers, while staying neutral between bird lovers and worm diggers. Such incidents illustrate how the complex working of modern society draws a maze of interests into the political process.

THE MAZE OF INTERESTS

Special interest groups are found, in varying forms, in all the states. Even industrial Rhode Island has farm organizations; even rural Montana has trade unions. And the big economic pressure groups operate in the states much as they do nationally. They try to build up the membership of their organizations; they lobby at the state capitol and at city hall; they propagandize the voters; they support their political friends in office and oppose their enemies. They also face the internal problems that all groups face: maintaining unity within the group, dealing with subgroups that break off in response to special needs, maintaining both democracy and discipline.

One great difference, however, is that group interests can be concentrated in states and localities, whereas their strength tends to be thinned out in the national government. Big Labor does not really run things in Washington, any more than Wall Street, the Catholic Church, or the American Legion does. But in some states and localities certain interests are clearly dominant because of the social and economic makeup of the area. Few politicians in Wisconsin will attack dairy farmers; candidates for office in Chicago will not shout their anti-Catholicism; most white officeholders in Boston and its suburbs are not likely to take a strong stand in favor of forced school busing.

[9]Veto message, Governor Adlai Stevenson, to members of the Senate Assembly, Springfield, Illinois, 1949.

It is the range and variety of these localized groupings that gives American politics its special flavor and excitement: auto unions and manufacturers in Michigan, corn and hog farmers in Iowa, French-Americans in northern New England, gas and oil interests in Texas, senior citizens in Florida, aircraft employees in southern California, copper miners in the Rockies, cotton growers in the South, Pennsylvania coal miners, sheep ranchers in Wyoming. The power of these groups, however, should not be exaggerated. Studying the urban politics of St. Louis, one political scientist concluded that the labor unions were sharply divided among the teamsters, building trades, machinists, auto workers, and so on; that the business community was divided between the big industrial, banking, and commercial firms on the one hand, and small downtown enterprises — shops, parking lot operators, and the like — on the other; and that such divisions had a direct impact on the governing of St. Louis.[10]

In New England, Irish and Italian fraternal societies have long expressed the opinions of their respective groups on various public issues, and there are also organizations to speak for the French-Canadians and the Poles. New England politicians have feared the power of such groups to influence elections, especially primaries. But, after a careful look, Duane Lockard downplayed such fears. He cites many examples of "Yankees" winning in heavily ethnic areas. Compared to the other considerations affecting the voter's choice, the ethnic factor is often small (although a minute percentage, of course, may still be decisive in an election). Much depends on the character of the candidates, on the appeals they create other than the ethnic.[11] Any group, no matter how strong, must cope with a variety of cross pressures, including a general sense of the rules of the game which suggest that the voter does not vote for "one of our own" merely on that ground alone.

Now, let us look further at the interests that are more specialized and that have a closer relation to local government. Many business people sell to the state or perform services for it: milk dealers, printers, contractors, parking meter manufacturers, makers of playground equipment, textbook publishers. Such people will often formally or informally organize in order to improve and stabilize their relations with purchasing officials. Another type of group intimately concerned with public policy is the professional association. The states license barbers, beauticians, architects, lawyers, doctors, optometrists, accountants, dentists, and many other groups. Associations representing such groups are concerned with the nature of the regulatory laws and with the makeup of the boards that do the regulating. They are especially concerned about the rules of admission to the profession and about the way in which professional misconduct is defined. Bar associations closely watch the appointment of judges and court officials.

The incredible number of groups represented in the capital of one large state can be seen in a partial list of business activities that registered their lobbyists with the Michigan legislature during a recent session: the Upper

State-licensed beauticians form one of the many interest groups that work to influence local government.

[10]Robert H. Salisbury, "St. Louis Politics: Relationships among Interests, Parties, and Governmental Structure," *Western Political Quarterly* (June 1960), pp. 498–507. For a related study that shows how labor leaders have only limited success in getting their members to vote for "their" candidate, see J. David Greenstone, *Labor in American Politics* (Knopf, 1969), Chap. 4.

[11]Duane Lockard, *New England State Politics* (Princeton University Press, 1959), Chap. 11. But see also Michael R. Levy and Michael S. Kramer, *The Ethnic Factor: How American Minorities Decide Elections* (Touchstone, 1973).

Peninsula Dairy Manufacturers' Association, the Society of Architects, the Beauticians' Aid Association, the National Association of Margarine Manufacturers, the Funeral Directors' and Embalmers' Association, the Cash-and-Carry Milk Dealers'' Association, the Institute of Dry Cleaning, the Association of Private Driver-Training Schools, and the Association of Civil Engineers and Land Surveyors in Private Practice.

After a survey of these and countless other lobbies in Michigan, one student of state government concluded that there was:

> An organization equipped to lobby for every business interest in the city, county, or state. A supermarket chain may, for example, have its interests represented generally by the state chamber of commerce, but the company may also belong to an association of chain stores (which must parry the thrusts of the corner-grocers' lobby), to a retail-food-dealers' organization, the package-liquor-dealers' association (if some of the stores have permits to sell same), and the company may itself register a lobbyist. In addition, if the chain is encountering labor problems, it may contribute to a "right-to-work" committee which lobbies against the union shop, and the executives of the company may choose to help support the state taxpayers' league. If the company owns its own fleet of semitrailer trucks or leases them, it may be represented by a company of additional groups dealing with the interests of this part of the business. A pluralistic society is simple in neither theory nor practice.[12]

Interest groups appear to have the most influence in the nonindustrial, nonurban states where a single party dominates political life and where party cohesion is not very strong within the state legislature.[13] In states with strong interest groups, the constitution tends to be long, frequently amended, with provision for a large number of elected (in contrast to appointed) officials. In such states interest groups appear to be better able to isolate governmental agencies from gubernatorial and legislative influence.[14]

LOBBYISTS AT THE
STATEHOUSE

There is a widespread conviction that lobbyists have a freer rein in state legislatures than they do in Congress, and what is more, bribery of state legislators by lobbyists is cruder, more basic, and more obvious. Kickbacks from highway contractors or other firms doing business with the state are exposed often enough to lend meaning to these claims. Spiro Agnew was forced to resign from the vice presidency because of kickback payoffs that came to him when he was governor of Maryland. Florida, Illinois, Louisiana, Massachusetts, New Jersey, and New York have all been plagued by indictments and convictions of state officials during the past several years. In New Jersey, approximately fifty public officials were convicted in the early 1970s, all on the charge of extorting kickbacks. Accord-

[12]Charles R. Adrian, *State and Local Government* (McGraw-Hill, 1960), p. 167. The list of Michigan lobbyists is drawn from the same source.

[13]L. Harmon Zeigler and Hendrik van Dalen, "Interest Groups in State Politics," in Herbert Jacob and Kenneth N. Vines, eds., *Politics in the American States*, 3rd. ed. (Little, Brown, 1976), p. 95.

[14]Lewis A. Froman, Jr., "Some Effects of Interest Group Strength in State Politics," *American Political Science Review* (December, 1966), p. 961.

ing to the U.S. district attorney's office there, "10 percent is the [kick-back] rate normally demanded by the politicians" from architects and engineers obtaining state contracts.[15]

Corruption of legislators and state officials is, of course, hard to prove. Insiders often charge that state legislators accept favors for votes. In some states it is a serious problem; in others considerably less so. Exposure of scandals in several states, especially in the post-Watergate era, pushed many legislatures to curb election abuses and pass ethics codes with more stringent conflict of interest statutes.[16] Still, few legislatures have enacted comprehensive financial disclosure laws and there appears to be widespread abuse of unused campaign funds. The persistence of the belief that the lobbyists with the most money have the most influence is itself significant.

In Washington, lobbyists tend to spend more time with legislators who are sympathetic to their points of view. In the state legislature, there appears to be more of an attempt to persuade, and lobbyists make a greater effort to pressure lawmakers to see the merits of the position they represent. President Carter, who served for a few years in the Georgia State Senate and then as governor, recalls that nearly all of the 259 members of the Georgia legislature were good honest men and women, that only a "tiny portion" were not good or honest. But Carter found that "It is difficult for the common good to prevail against the intense concentration of those who have a special interest, especially if the decisions are made behind locked doors . . . . In the absence of clear and comprehensive issues, it is simply not possible to marshall the interest of the general public, and under such circumstances legislators often respond to the quiet and professional pressure of lobbyists."[17]

In a few states a single corporation or organization has considerable influence; in others a "big three" or "big four" may dominate politics. But in most states there is wide-open competition among organizations, with no single group or coalition of groups standing out. In no state does any one organization exercise complete control of legislative politics, although the powerful Anaconda Company once came close in Montana.[18] Lobbyists are present in every state capital and they are there to guide through the legislature a small handful of bills their organization wants passed or defeated. Legislators are concerned with hundreds or even thousands of bills, in addition to doing casework in behalf of constituents and worrying about their party, district, and colleagues. The governor? "Governors come and governors go, but the lobbyists [or legislative representatives] stay on forever."[19] The shrewd lobbyist can usually get a chance—or several chances—to influence the fate of his few bills. He may not always be successful, but the odds are not bad.

"Here's a guy who wants to donate $200,000. What do I say?"

Drawing by Joseph Farris.
© 1974 Saturday Review/World.

[15]Monroe W. Karmin, "Throughout the U.S. Public Contracts Tied to 'Campaign Gifts,' " *The Wall Street Journal*, October 17, 1973, pp. 1, 29, and Martin Waldron, "Study Finds Contractors in Four States Help Politicians," *The New York Times*, August 26, 1973, p. 45.

[16]Herbert E. Alexander, ed., *Campaign Money: Reform and Reality in the States* (Free Press, 1976); and Larry L. Berg, Harlan Hahn, and John R. Schmidhauser, *Corruption in the American Political System* (General Learning Press, 1976).

[17]Jimmy Carter, *Why Not the Best?* (Bantam Books, 1976), p. 101.

[18]Zeigler and van Dalen, "Interest Groups in State Politics," pp. 98–101.

[19]Jesse Unruh, "A Reformed Legislature," *Journal of Public Law*, XVI (1967), 13.

Some groups have a special role both because of their relations to government and because of the size and importance of the work they are doing. Consider public school teachers, for example. They are both employees of the local government and an interest group exerting pressure on it. They must deal with many other organized groups in education: parents associated in local and state PTAs; principals and superintendents, who often have their own associations; parents of children attending private and parochial schools. Some teachers organize into unions and use the strike as a weapon for getting better wages and working conditions. All of them try to mobilize political influence as best they can.[20] Even local school boards often band together for better representation at the state capitol, as do community colleges, state universities, and vocational schools. The educational lobby can often put up a brave front on behalf of "educational progress," but when it comes to the details, its members may be badly divided among themselves.

CLUSTERS OF ATTITUDES:
A CASE STUDY

Analysis of the role of public opinion in the states and localities confronts us with the same problems as does the study of interest groups. On the one hand, the factors that apply on the national level apply locally as well. The people speak with many voices; there are many publics and subpublics. The interested public is always changing; the intensity of people's opinions varies; and opinion may be latent as well as open and noisy. Also, most states and communities have their own sets of opinion-making agencies: schools, churches, newspapers, radio and television stations, as well as their share of the audience of national television programs, best-selling books, popular magazines, nationwide newspapers like *The New York Times*, motion pictures, and newspaper columnists. Each locality has its own particular "mix" of these opinion-forming agencies, and powerful forces that are diluted nationally may be concentrated heavily in one area.

An example of this situation is the attitude toward states' rights in the South. Almost all Americans support states' rights in general, but in the South it has a political influence far greater than any pressure group or party. Quoted from the lips of such southern heroes as Jefferson and John Calhoun, bolstered by the trauma of civil war, resurrected in the face of northern civil rights programs and Supreme Court decisions on desegregation, states' rights has become a symbol that can be evoked for many purposes—state control of offshore oil, local determination of welfare standards, reduction of minimum wages. Only a daring southern politician would defy this symbol. The combat is waged *within* the symbol— that is, over its meaning and relevance rather than between it and other political concepts.

A citizen with sign takes his case to the New Jersey Assembly Chamber.

Another local variation of public opinion concerns the concentration of control of local media and the resulting conformity of political attitudes. The enormous variety of opinion-shaping forces throughout the nation may dwindle sharply in its impact on a particular locality, especially one that is some distance from a big metropolitan area. Here again local conditions vary so widely that generalization is dangerous. Perhaps a case study of one community might raise questions for other localities.

The newspaper situation in New Haven, Connecticut, is typical of that in many medium-sized cities of the United States. Compared with the last

[20]See Harmon Zeigler, *The Political Life of American Teachers* (Prentice-Hall, 1967), pp. 55–91.

century, when New Haven had three or four papers supporting different political parties, the city recently has had only two, a morning and an evening, both owned by the same family, both Republican in politics, and both heavily influenced by the family's conservative views. Most adults in New Haven read the evening paper, and almost all the politically active read the morning paper. Robert Dahl, analyzing the impact of the papers, concluded that their negativism and hostility to change, together with their biased reporting, may have reduced their readers' knowledge, understanding, and concern. They may have influenced their readers on specific policies, such as taxes; and they probably directly influenced the attitudes of politicians who exaggerated the newspapers' influence on public opinion.

But Dahl found definite limits to the power of this newspaper monopoly. For one thing, the publisher seemed more interested in immobilizing public opinion than in mobilizing it; he was less intent on initiating new policies than on stopping spendthrift politicians. For another, some politicians were skeptical of the newspapers' ability to influence opinion, and they were confident of their own political strength. But the main reason why the newspapers had limited influence was their competition. The more politically active the citizen was, the more likely he or she was to read an out-of-town newspaper such as *The New York Times*. Of the registered voters as a whole, only about four in ten said they got more information about political affairs from newspapers than from other sources. Another four out of ten got more from radio or television, or from talking with other people. Local opinion leaders had at least as much influence as the newspapers. Dahl was prompted to conclude:

> Word of mouth and personal experience are highly important sources of information that remain to a substantial extent beyond the reach of top leaders. . . . The extent to which an individual gains his information from other people than from the mass media is partly a function of his own experience. In some issue-areas, many citizens have *direct* experience; what happens there is happening to *them*, in a rather immediate way. In others, only a few citizens have any direct experience; at best the others have only derivative or vicarious experience. The more the citizens have direct experience, the more they seem to rely on talking with other people as a source of news; the more vicarious or indirect their experience, the more they seem to rely on the mass media.[21]

Direct experience, in short, could be not only a persuasive teacher, but a stubborn enemy of manipulative propaganda.

The newspaper organizations themselves were not monolithic. As is the case with many big newspapers, many of the reporters on the two papers were Democrats or personally friendly with politicians opposed to the publisher. Republicans sometimes complained that their stories were buried in the back pages while their Democratic opponents had much of the front page. Like many a party boss or interest-group leader, the publisher found he could not "deliver his precinct" even if he wished to do so.

[21]Dahl, *Who Governs?* p. 262. For a study which contends that a city's newspaper can be a major factor in who governs, see Hayes, *Power Structure and Urban Policy*. He finds that for years *The Oakland Tribune* enjoyed considerable influence over nominations, elections, and key appointments.

Newspapers have greater impact on local issues and elections than on national ones. Many citizens obtain a large part of their knowledge of the local political scene from the hometown newspaper. Voters are likely to have less rigid ideas about the merits of local candidates than about national or even state candidates. A strongly partisan Republican businessman, for example, is less open to persuasion by a Democratic candidate for Congress or the presidency than he may be by a Democratic candidate for the city council who is a friend or colleague. Attitudes toward local issues are also less likely to be rigid. For their consideration of national health insurance, U.S. involvement in the Middle East, federal income tax reform, or extensions of social security, citizens have many sources of information. But the local paper is almost the only medium that discusses school-board candidacies or the desirability of a community bond issue.

In cities like Los Angeles and Oakland, where political organizations are weak and authority is generally decentralized, newspapers play a more important part than in cities where political organizations are strong, such as Chicago. The influence of the newspapers also appears to be related to the class structure. Among better educated and upper income groups "there is a greater sense of ease, intimacy, and personal relationship between the reader and his paper. It seems as though the better educated reader is more likely to view his hometown paper as an institution made up of people doing a job." Less educated people generally read less and view the city's newspaper or newspapers as less important in their lives.[22]

APATHY

To discuss pressure groups and opinion shapers is always to run the risk of slighting the apathetic. But the political indifference that shows up as only a very general factor in a nationwide survey can be seen markedly in certain regions or localities. Nonvoting, for example, is greater in rural areas than it is in suburbia or the city. Migrant workers of the Southwest and poor whites and poor blacks in the South are among those who are less politically active.

It was in the small town and village that many American political thinkers, in an earlier day, saw the most hope for the practice of American democracy. Unhappily, many such communities today seem to lack an active political life. Although the small towns may be caught up in, and increasingly affected by, social and economic trends in the urban areas, the townspeople may shrink from adopting new ways of dealing with problems. Many of these small towns are slowly declining in population. Their young people often leave for better opportunities elsewhere, and their population is aging. Such political decisions as there are seem to be made by relatively few people, and these usually without much discussion. There is no clear confrontation of choices or options. Politics is highly personal and much affected by family and neighborhood relationships, petty favor-swapping, and minor deals. A town that is most in need of a searching examination of its future, culminating in a meaningful decision, may be lacking the means for such action.[23]

But big cities, too, can provide examples of apathy. Dahl found that even

[22]Leo Bogart, "Newspapers in the Age of Television," *Daedalus* (winter 1963), p. 124.

[23]See A. J. Vidich and Joseph Bensman, *Small Town in Mass Society* (Princeton University Press, 1958); and Laurene A. Wallace, *Carsonville: An American Village Viewed Sociologically* (University of Michigan Press, 1957).

At a town meeting in Durham, New Hampshire, citizens vote on a proposed oil refinery to be constructed in their town.

in New Haven, a relatively active city politically, "political indifference surrounds a great many citizens like impenetrable armor plate and makes them difficult targets for propaganda."[24] He cites as an example a campaign to revise the city charter. City politicians debated the matter vigorously; the newspapers took an outspoken position; a citizens' charter committee ran big advertisements; radio and television programs carried on the debate; fliers were even distributed from door to door. The result? Only 45 percent of those who voted in the regular election troubled to vote on the charter (and most opposed it).

Even the New England town meetings have difficulty getting people out to participate—despite the fact that their decisions have major consequences for the local tax rate and the quality of the schools, the police force, and the parks and recreational areas. Thomas Jefferson once proclaimed the town meeting to be the noblest, wisest instrument yet devised for the conduct of public affairs. Yet most towns find that only about 2 or 3 percent of their population care enough to come, unless there is a visit from President Carter (as happened in Clinton, Massachusetts, in March 1977), or a special town meeting session on some emotional issue such as the leashing of dogs. Clinton could not muster a quorum for its regular town meeting the month after Carter's celebrated 1977 visit. A town official in another Massachusetts community lists the causes for local apathy in his town this way:

Is it television? Conflict of time? Baby-sitter problems? The influx of new residents from outside New England where town meeting was never heard of and the difficulty of showing them that pure democracy still exists in the land? Feelings of individual impotence arising from suspected dominance by cliques or from the walloping impact of state and Federal conditions for funding and other restrictions on local choices? Pique arising from persistent potholes on certain streets or other unattended grievances? Even the positive excuse that the handful of regular attenders do a good enough job to save others from the bother of going? Or is it the lack of a feeling for community, the lack of reality of community?[25]

Doubtless all these are contributing factors, but students of political participation also generally conclude that the average person is not a political animal, that most people gladly leave politics and political responsibilities to a relatively small number of political activists.[26] For most people, personal concerns—arthritis, crabgrass, their bowling league, their son's Little League games, or helping their daughter apply for college— all come well ahead of becoming involved in their city's personnel board or planning and zoning commission. Of course for the many people who are quite satisfied with how local governments function, it may seem rational for them to sit on the sidelines and leave civic responsibilities to those who are interested and willing to handle them.

[24]Dahl, *Who Governs?* p. 264. See also Wolfinger, *The Politics of Progress*, esp. chap. 11.

[25]John W. Putnam, "Why Don't They Go to Town Meetings?" *The Boston Globe*, March 18, 1977, p. 23. See also Jane J. Mansbridge, "Town Meeting Democracy," in Peter Collier, ed., *Dilemmas of Democracy* (Harcourt, Brace, Jovanovich, 1976, pp. 148–79.

[26]See, for example, Sidney Verba and Norman H. Nie, *Political Participation: Political Democracy and Social Equality* (Harper & Row, 1972).

Cynicism about the effectiveness of local political processes is also reflected in the occasional use of the politics of protest—mass demonstrations, economic boycotts, even civil disorders—as a way of making demands on the governmental system. As certain issues become more intense, revitalized political activity often occurs. Blacks in the inner city form political organizations in order to present their grievances and organize their votes more effectively. Neighborhood organizations have been formed to work for better housing and enforcement of inspection ordinances. Although community organization work is exacting and the frustrations are many, these efforts have led to more active involvement of some of the poor in the politics of the city.[27]

State parties: a study in variety

The Democratic and Republican parties almost monopolize party activity in every state, just as they do the nation's politics as a whole. But the state political parties are not miniatures of the national parties. Each has its own special features. Not only does the different social and economic mix for each state make the parties different today, but the states have reacted differently to developments in American history. The Civil War left the South heavily Democratic and portions of the North heavily Republican. And the traumatic experience of the Great Depression, combined with the coming of the New Deal, helped produce a surge of Democratic strength in the big cities that still influences politics sharply.

THE INTERPLAY OF NATIONAL AND STATE POLITICS

The very structure of national party organizations grows out of the state parties. Not only are national and state party organizations interdependent, but their fortunes are also interdependent: swings at the national level help produce swings at the state and local level. Whenever the Democratic party, for example, wins a presidential and congressional sweep nationally, the number of Democratic governors, state legislators, mayors, and local councilmen tends to increase. Moreover, the relationship is usually constant—the greater the national party sweep, the greater the local party victories.

Many states have acted to avert the influence of national trends. For example, Kentucky, Mississippi, New Jersey, and Virginia have complete electoral "separation." They elect their governors and all state legislators in years when no presidential election is being held. More than two-thirds of the states will elect their governors and some legislators in off-year, that is, nonpresidential elections. This staggering of state elections is usually proposed as a way of concentrating the voters' attention on state issues. But it is often a tactical device of party warfare, used by local politicians of one party to prevent the opposition from benefiting by its national popularity. Of course, the tactic can backfire. Republicans in some states managed to get Republican governors elected during the Democratic 1930s and 1940s by having elections held when neither Roosevelt nor Truman was running; but when Eisenhower was winning in big sweeps during the 1950s, these same Republicans regretted that they were not running their statewide candidates in presidential years, for they had lost the chance to get pulled in on his coattails.

[27]Bryan T. Downes, *Politics, Change and the Urban Crisis* (Duxbury Press, 1976), esp. chaps. 7–9. See also Stephen C. Schlesinger, *The New Reformers: Forces for Change in American Politics* (Houghton Mifflin, 1975); and Norman I. and Susan Fainstein, *Urban Political Movements: The Search For Power by Minority Groups in American Cities* (Prentice-Hall, 1974).

A sample Massachusetts ballot, which lists nominees by office rather than by party.

Even when presidential and state elections are held simultaneously, the impact of national contest can be affected by the nature of the ballot. If, for example, the Republicans have as a presidential candidate an Eisenhower type who has great electoral drawing power, it will be to their advantage if the state has a party column, or *Indiana ballot.* To reduce the impact of the presidential candidate under such circumstances, the Democrats would prefer the office group, or *Massachusetts ballot.*[28] Despite all the ingenious efforts of politicians, national politics has a heavy impact on state and local government.

PARTY BALANCE AND IMBALANCE

The most important difference among the state party systems is the extent of two-party competition. State parties may be classified by three types on the basis of how the parties share state offices: the two-party type, in which the two parties share state offices rather evenly over the years and alternate in winning majorities; the modified one-party type, in which one party wins all or almost all the offices over the years, but the other party usually receives a large percentage of the votes, and surprises everybody—including itself—by sometimes winning; and the one-party type, in which one party wins all or nearly all the offices, and the second party usually receives only a small proportion of the popular vote. From the map of state party systems, based on voting patterns from 1962 to 1973, it can be

[28]Jerrold G. Rusk, "The Effect of the Australian Ballot Reform on Split Ticket Voting, 1876–1908," *American Political Science Review* (December 1970), pp. 1220–38.

seen that the modified one-party Democratic states are mainly the border states, but also Hawaii, Massachusetts, Rhode Island, and Florida. The seven one-party Democratic states are all in the South. There are no longer any one-party Republican states, since the former stalwart supporters of the Grand Old Party such as Vermont, North Dakota, and Kansas in recent elections have chosen some Democrats for state office.[29]

Since the end of World War II there has been an accelerating trend toward two-party politics. In the South, Republicans have begun to make a contest of general elections. The Republican resurgence in the South, so far, has shown mainly in voting for candidates for president and Congress, but Republicans are now regularly elected to the state legislature in southern states. Arkansas, Florida, Tennessee, and South and North Carolina have elected Republican governors, though most of these states did revert to the Democrats in recent elections. Republicans still have to make more significant gains in state and local elections before we can call most southern or border states two-party states, but the Solid South is no longer solid, especially within and around the larger cities, and in the mountain areas.[30] Outside the South there is also a gradual spread of two-partyism with the rise of Democratic strength in the formerly solid Republican

[29]This division of states is based on Austin Ranney's adaptation of the Dawson-Robinson measure in "Parties in State Politics," in Jacob and Vines, eds., *Politics in the American States*, chap. 2.

[30]One of the best recent books on the fast-changing political forces in the deep South is Jack Bass and Walter DeVries, *The Transformation of Southern Politics* (Basic Books, 1976).

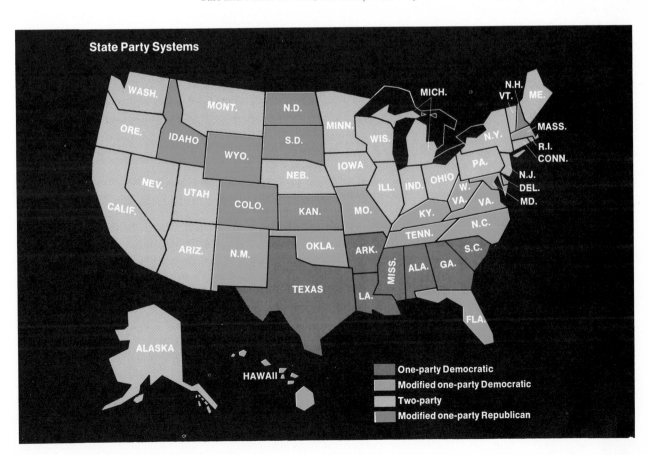

State Party Systems

- One-party Democratic
- Modified one-party Democratic
- Two-party
- Modified one-party Republican

states of Iowa, Maine, New Hampshire, and South Dakota. What the Democrats have lost in the South, they have gained in the Midwest and Northeast.

What are the consequences of a fairly even party balance? When parties and their candidates compete on an even basis, each is more likely to be sensitive to slight changes in public opinion, for the loss of even a fraction of the voters might tip the scales to the other side in the next election. Party competition tends to push leaders within each party to work more closely together, at least as elections draw near. Any defection may throw a victory to the opponents, so competition may produce more teamwork and efficiency in government.

Party imbalance may have a serious effect on the dominant party in a one-party state. Almost guaranteed a victory no matter how poor its record, the majority party may not keep itself in fighting trim. And the competition that otherwise would occur *between* the major parties often occurs *within* the majority party. Contests in some Southern states or in Massachusetts, which is fast becoming a one-party state, often are not between Democrats and Republicans, but among Democrats—sometimes a dozen or more of them—in the primary. In these intraparty fights, issues may not be clearly drawn. Personalities may dominate the campaign. Voters tend not to participate to the extent that they do where there are two-party contests. Here again one has to be careful in drawing connections, for lack of division within the community on major issues may cause the one-party situation as much as the other way around.

But if party imbalance disorganizes the dominant party, it pulverizes the minority party. Almost without hope of ever winning at all, minority leaders do not put up much of a fight. They find it difficult to raise the money for campaigns or to persuade people to become candidates for office. They have no state or local patronage jobs to give out in order to arouse hope within their ranks. Party workers and volunteers are slow to come forward. Young people wishing to succeed in politics tend to drift into the dominant party. And since the dominant party firmly controls the machinery of state and local affairs, the second party is likely to be concerned only with national politics and the patronage that could come their way if their party controls the White House.[31]

We have been discussing *state* party imbalance, but imbalance can be found in even more extreme form in cities and towns. Republicans hardly ever carry Chicago, Boston, Albany, Hartford, Pittsburgh, and many other cities throughout the industrial North. Democrats have only a ghost of a chance in numerous towns in the rural North. One result of this imbalance was the rapid growth, during the first half of this century, of nonpartisanship in local elections. Candidates were not able to run on major-party tickets, at least officially. The two great parties were, in effect, removed from open influence over local politics. Adopted in the name of good government, nonpartisanship's effect on the major parties was probably to weaken them further as organizations, for it sapped them at their foundations.

PARTY WEAKNESSES

The crucial fact about most states and localities is that *neither* party is organizationally very strong. Just as the national parties tend to break into

---

[31]The classic picture of this situation at its most extreme was drawn by V. O. Key, Jr., in *Southern Politics in State and Nation* (Knopf, 1949).

factions revolving around individual leaders in Congress and the White House, so the state and local parties tend to fragment into groups following individual candidates and officeholders. Most of the stronger leaders have personal organizations that often crowd the regular party organizations out of the picture. Regular party committees are supposed to remain neutral during primary fights, and often do, with the result that candidates have no feeling of obligation to the party organization once they win office. Candidates in the same party tend to run on their own. Each candidate sets up headquarters, puts up posters, sends out publicity, and taps sources of funds. Sometimes a candidate may deliberately keep clear of other candidates on the same ticket and even of the party label. The more offices to be voted on, the more candidates, and hence the greater the fragmentation of the party. Since most states have the long ballot (a ballot with numerous officers to be selected), they have fragmented parties.

What is the result? The late V. O. Key, Jr., a foremost student of state politics, expressed his concern about party organization at the state level. To paraphrase his conclusions:

1. State politics combined with constitutional arrangements, especially the dispersion of power in most of the statehouses, contributes to centralization of power in the national government by making the states unable to act.
2. The rapid growth of state responsibilities makes it even more important to modernize the organization of political forces within the states, which at the present time is usually erratic and atomized.
3. The political system places serious obstacles in the path of popular government by making it impossible for broad popular mandates to be expressed in some situations and at certain times.
4. Over the last half-century party organization has seriously deteriorated. This deterioration has been associated with the rise of the direct primary.[32]

In short, the problems presented by party weakness at the state level are the same as those presented at the national level — with this one difference: The national parties are roughly in balance, at least in presidential contests, while state and local parties often are highly noncompetitive, where they exist at all.[33] Many critics have suggested changes in the constitutional and administrative organization of the states, but the parties have received less attention. One reason may be that real reforms in party structure and balance are extremely difficult to bring about. No amount of tinkering with party structure can much alter the fact that most of the people of Kansas are Republicans and most of the people of the rural South are Democrats. As long as strong personal factions exist within a party, preaching about the need for party cohesion will have little effect. Attitudes and political behavior change slowly and grow out of basic social, economic, and psychological conditions that reformers can do little to change.

But to recognize that political forces are relatively stable is not to say that they are impervious to change. If such institutional forces as the long ballot help to make the state and local parties what they are, changes such as the

[32]V. O. Key, Jr., *American State Politics* (Knopf, 1956), pp. 266–67.

[33]For an excellent survey of the American party system and some commentary on the weakening of the Republican chances to control the U. S. Congress, see Everett C. Ladd with Charles D. Hadley, *Transformation of the American Party System: Political Coalitions from the New Deal to the 1970s* (Norton, 1975).

short ballot may also affect them; so may changes in legislative representation or in procedures for nominating candidates.[34]

A word about minor parties: Whatever their other differences, the Democrats and the Republicans who control state governments agree that minor parties should be discouraged. Although the Supreme Court has struck down as violations of the equal-protection clause requirements that made it especially difficult for minor party candidates to obtain places on the ballot,[35] in most states the laws continue to make it difficult for minor parties to become established and effective. In a few areas, such as in Minnesota, Maine, and New York City, third or fusion parties have on occasion been successful.

Elections: the struggle for office

The framers of the Constitution left the conduct of elections and other political matters largely in the hands of state government. This was one safeguard, they felt, against too much national power. Despite the fact that the Supreme Court has held that Congress can supersede state regulations for the election of presidential electors and members of Congress, and despite greater federal supervision of state and local elections to ensure compliance with the Fourteenth and Fifteenth Amendments, state control of elections remains a crucial fact.[36] Each state sets up its own way of managing elections, nominating candidates, regulating campaign contributions, preventing election fraud, and determining who shall be allowed to vote (always subject to limitations of the national Constitution). And states also administer the election of national officials, presidential electors, senators, and members of Congress.

NOMINATIONS

Almost all party nominations in the United States—with the exception of the nomination of the president—are made in party *primaries*. These primaries, however, are of different types—closed, open, runoff, and so on. The party primary is an almost uniquely American device that has had a great influence on the nature of state and local politics. Rather than review information, we might here raise some questions about the primary. Why was it adopted? What effect has it had on state and local parties and on the question of who governs? What are alternative ways of choosing nominees?

The primaries were not always the chief means of choosing candidates. Once our parties had attained full bloom in the 1830s and 1840s, candidates for most offices were chosen in conventions. These were like our national conventions, but in miniature. Delegates were called to order in a local hall or hotel, candidates nominated, speeches delivered, rollcall votes taken, and candidates finally chosen. Not only were statewise candidates, such as the gubernatorial nominee, selected in these conclaves; local conventions were also held to select candidates for district attorney, state representative, county commissioner, and even city offices, such as mayor. Whatever their shortcomings, these conventions provided a vitality at the grass roots that many observers find lacking today.

But conventions and caucuses had their shortcomings. In the late nine-

[34]Donald G. Herzberg and Alan Rosenthal, eds., *Strengthening the States: Essays on Legislative Reform* (Doubleday Anchor, 1972).

[35]*Moore* v. *Ogilvie* 394 U.S. 814 (1969); *Williams* v. *Rhodes* 393 U.S. 23 (1968).

[36]*Oregon* v. *Mitchell* 400 U.S. 112 (1970).

teenth century, as the rise of big cities provided lucrative contracts and franchises for politicians, local and state parties fell increasingly under the domination of bosses who used the convention as a means of control. The leaders often handpicked the delegates to conventions, refused to seat opposing delegates or ignored them if they were seated, and even used strong-arm methods. The great safeguard against such corruption was, of course, the opposition party, which could appeal to the people against bossism. But the creation of one-party states and districts as a result of the Civil War and the Bryan-McKinley fight of 1896 left most American states and localities with essentially one-party systems, especially in the South and the Northeast. So the great safeguard against oligarchy was gone.

The direct primary came largely as a result of this situation. During the first decade of this century, when reformers were attacking bossism, corruption, monopoly, and other conditions, the convention also came under fire. Nominations must be moved out of these boss-controlled conclaves, reformers declared, and put into the hands of the people. The means of democratizing nominations was at hand: the direct primary which had first been adopted in the South. Wisconsin enacted the first statewide primary law in 1901, and other states followed. Within a decade and a half, the direct primary had been adopted for most nominations in all but a few states.

How has the direct primary worked out? Like most institutional reforms, it has had mixed results. The primary has probably diminished somewhat the power of the party leaders. It is more difficult for a boss to influence several thousand voters going to the polls than a few delegates going to a convention. But the difference has been only one of degree, and varies widely from place to place. Some bosses survived the coming of the primary with ease. Participation in the primary is usually so light that they are able to control it by "delivering" votes. Still, the primaries often encourage people to challenge the bosses.

Some people, however, began to have second thoughts about the effect of primaries on party organization. After all, there were good party bosses as well as bad. Good bosses were threatened by factions supporting mediocre candidates and perhaps seeking to disrupt the party. The primaries have other weaknesses: Primary contest are often disorganized, bewildering, and heavily influenced by local considerations. Primaries make it impossible for the parties to balance their tickets. For example, the Democratic party in Massachusetts, largely made up of people of Irish descent, has sometimes found it difficult to nominate a balanced ticket because the decision was made in the primaries, heavily dominated by the Boston Irish. And primaries are especially hard on the minority party. Up-and-coming politicans naturally go to the major party primary, and the minority party nomination may even go begging. In short, primaries may work against competitive, orderly, meaningful, vigorous two-party politics.

Despite these drawbacks, the trend toward the primary continues. New York and Connecticut, long users of the convention for nomination of statewide officers, have now gone to the primary system, although they have tried to retain some of the features of the conventions. In both states the candidate who secures endorsement at the convention becomes the endorsed candidate and does not have to run in a primary unless another candidate who received 25 percent of the delegate votes (20 percent in Connecticut) wishes to challenge in a primary. Whether the adoption of this modified primary system will undermine the strong party systems of these two states is yet to be determined. In the past, the parties were able, under the convention system, to nominate some outstanding men. The fact that New York conventions have yielded such Republicans as Theodore Roosevelt, Charles Evans Hughes, Thomas E. Dewey, and Nelson Rockefeller, and such Democrats as Alfred E. Smith, Franklin Roosevelt, Herbert Lehman, and Averell Harriman is a tribute to the convention system.

The method of nominating candidates closely affects the organization of the party, and vice versa. The stronger the party — that is, the better led, the more vigorous and competitive and unified — the better are its chances of conducting its nominating fights through conventions. The weaker the party, the more likely are the voters to want to take nominating decisions out of the hands of party leaders and entrust them to voters in primaries. Hence it is quite logical that, given the fact that most state and local parties are weak, primaries are the typical method of choosing nominees. But the existence of primaries may be a major cause of the structural weakness of parties. Some day there may be a trend back to the convention method, but for the moment primaries rule the day.[37]

ELECTIONS: A CASE STUDY

Perhaps the most distinctive feature of American politics is the number and variety of elections. Western Europeans, who are used to voting for one or two candidates at the national and local levels, and voting only once every two or three years, are flabbergasted by the impression they receive that Americans engage almost continuously in elections. Selection of town and local officials in the late winter may be followed by primaries to choose delegates to conventions, followed by primaries to choose party candidates, followed by general elections, all interspersed with special elections, special town or state referenda, and even in some states recall elections to throw an official out of office. In many places, school board elections constitute still another separate election. Even more bewildering is the number of offices voted on at a particular election, from president to probate judge, from senator to sheriff, from governor to member of the library board. This is the long ballot in operation. Europeans are more accustomed to the election of a handful of key officials, who in turn appoint career officials.

While generalizing about the nature of this enormous variety of elections would be dangerous, experienced politicians might agree on the following rules of thumb: (1) By and large, the more local the election, the less the excitement and interest aroused among the electorate, and the less the participation. (2) Except in areas where strong party organizations exist, candidates usually run on their own; they win through their personal organizations rather than through efforts by the party (partly because there are so many candidates running for so many offices that the party cannot give much help to any one of them). (3) Voters' familiarity with names rather than issues is of relatively greater importance in local elections. (4) The candidate get most of their money from friends and from interest groups, not from their party. (5) While all kinds of propaganda are used, and often effectively, there is no substitute for personal

**"Well, that's democracy for you.
My vote nullifies your vote."**

Drawing by J. Marachi.
© 1967 Saturday Review.

[37]The most significant work on state party systems and nominating methods has been done by V. O. Key, Jr., and his students. See his *American State Politics* and his *Politics, Parties, and Pressure Groups* (Crowell, 1958), chaps. 11 and 14. See also Frank Sorauf, *Party Politics in America* (Little, Brown, 1972).

contact between the candidate and the voters, especially in local campaigns.

The 1974 campaign for governor of Connecticut exemplifies some of these rules of thumb. It also highlights a new pattern of women running for major elective offices. Connecticut Democrats held their nominating convention in July. Congresswoman Ella Grasso, a veteran of twenty-two years in politics, squared off against Connecticut Attorney General Robert Killian for the nomination.

The Irish ethnic voting blocks and many of their leaders sided with Killian while Italians generally supported Mrs. Grasso. Four years earlier the Democrats had lost both a Senate seat and the governorship because of deep-seated ethnic differences of the same kind within the party. Everyone wanted to avoid that this time, but, of course, that was far easier said than done.

Denied the blessing of state party leaders, Mrs. Grasso entered key local primaries, where delegates to the state convention were being selected, and she won several of these decisively. She also campaigned vigorously throughout the state in an attempt to convince party elites that she could win widespread support. "I took my case to the people," she later said. Her work paid off, for the convention was pretty much forced to nominate her. State party elders were indeed impressed.

By force of a strong personality and dogged campaigning she unified the Democratic party around her. Many claimed she was even a political artist — able equally to appeal to party regulars, independents, women, and younger voters. She had managed during her political career to remain philosophically liberal while still being acceptable to the party organization. Some joked that she did not look like a governor. A few party stalwarts worried, as one put it, "about how we were going to go into the governor's office and swear at her."

By this point in her political career, Mrs. Grasso had become hardened to the pushes and shoves of professional politics. She was also used to winning. This 55-year-old daughter of Italian immigrants had been running for elective office since 1952. She served in the state legislature and also, for twelve years, as Connecticut's secretary of state. A scholarship graduate from Mount Holyoke College, she had also earned a master's degree in economics and sociology. She had "paid her dues" to her party in innumerable ways; some people even considered her a protégé of aging party chairman John Bailey. But just as important, she had independently acquired substantial political and electioneering talents of her own. She was just now finishing her fourth year in the U.S. Congress.

Her Republican opponent, Congressman Robert H. Steele, sought to portray Grasso as a big liberal spender, and called her "Spenderella." Some of his supporters reportedly were distributing bumper stickers warning "Connecticut Can't Afford a Governess." Mrs. Grasso ignored most such charges and instead attacked recent utility rate hikes and promised effective state leadership on a broad range of issues.

Unquestionably, Connecticut voters were aware that the election of Mrs. Grasso would be a historic first. Although she would become the fourth woman governor in U.S. history, each of the others — Nellie Taylor Ross in Wyoming, Miriam Ferguson in Texas, and Lurleen Wallace in Alabama — were wives of former governors and came into office immediately after their husbands. Connecticut's Grasso would become the first woman elected in her own right. Ironically, in these years of women's move-

**Ella Grasso,
governor of Connecticut.**

ment breakthroughs, Mrs. Grasso was hardly the darling of the feminists. First, she was a hardened veteran of professional politics and admitted to some reservations about women's liberation activities. Moreover, she had taken a fairly firm stance in opposition to abortion measures.

On November 5, 1974, however, Ella Grasso won election by a rather comfortable margin. Indeed, her 59 percent total could be considered a rout. Immediately she became the most visible woman politician in elective office. Her victory will doubtless encourage more women to run for higher office. In November of 1976, Dixey Lee Ray won election as governor of Washington in a colorful and also decisive victory. Plainly, too, Governor Ray was hardly a women's movement candidate. The Grasso and Ray elections may signal a further opening up of the American political system. Still, the manner of their victories suggests that it requires a mix of the old politics and the new to win major victories over a sustained period.

Summary

Who governs? We return to our central question after the look we have taken at the shape of politics in American states and localities. It would be easy to evade the question by saying again that the answer to the question varies according to the state or locality, as of course it does. But the nature of local and state political systems, as we have seen them briefly, does permit some generalizations.

1. The striking fact is that American states and localities are characterized more by dispersion of political influence than by concentration. The tremendous diversity of elective offices gives influence to many different officials and tends to fragment political parties. In a positive vein this gives us more openings or "cracks" in the system for access purposes. In a negative vein it makes it hard to bring about changes and govern creatively.

2. The primary system of nominating candidates further diffuses power within the parties. A local newspaper publisher may, in effect, have a press monopoly, but he faces competition from many other media, such as television and radio, and he cannot even fully control the political influence of his own newspapers. The nominating system generally offers considerable access to the center of influence.

3. Most states and localities have reasonably open and porous systems that are a long way from oligarchy. This does not make them systems where every voter has roughly the same influence on political decisions.[38] Power tends to center in separate clusters of decision makers, and large numbers of people have very little role. The fact that under the American system they could have a more active one is not an adequate reply, for ignorance, lack of education, and other factors keep many voters from wielding much influence.

4. Students should look at their own state and communities and ask hard questions. Who has influence and who does not? Who is excluded from the system? What are the rules of the game? Under what conditions is influence exercised? *How* is it exercised — through authority, friendship, propaganda, deals, manipulation, coercion? And in whose behalf? What are the terms by which influence is pyramided and expended. What kind of influence do political leaders sacrifice in order to get the decision they want? In short, if most of these political systems are marked by deals, bargains, and exchanges, then who gains and loses what? Does fragmented power prevent leaders from making joint efforts on behalf of the great mass of people? Finally, what are the available means of keeping public servants, elected and appointed, accountable and responsive between elections?

[38]See Edward C. Banfield, *Political Influence* (Free Press, 1961). For a mayor's view of various power sources in Cleveland, see Carl Stokes, *Promises of Power* (Simon & Schuster, 1973).

Chapter 25

State Constitutions: Charters or Straitjackets?

Every state has a document known as the state constitution. It represents, at least in theory, the basic agreement of the people about the shape of their government and the distribution of power between them and that government. In reality, state constitutions are often highly detailed and overly long grab bags of rules and regulations. Over the years, they have become so loaded with trivia and amendments that they read more like legislative code books than statements of basic principles.

The state constitutions are the oldest documents in the political history of America. Outgrowths of the colonial charters, the early constitutions were themselves models for the national Constitution. Well before 1787, Americans adopted the practice of having state constitutions drafted and proposed by conventions specially called for that purpose. Upon completion, these conventions submitted their documents to the people for ratification.

The people of each state, subject only to the broad limitations of the federal Constitution, were and are free to create whatever kind of republican government they wish. And yet all state constitutions are similar in general outline. No state has established a parliamentary system; none has deprived its judges of the power of judicial review. As people moved westward across the United States, they copied the constitutions of the older states. The usual state constitution consists of a preamble; a bill of rights; articles providing for separation of powers, a two-house legislature, an executive department, an independent judiciary with power of judicial review, the form and powers of local units of government; an amendatory article; and miscellaneous provisions dealing with corporations, railroads, finances, and other specific topics.

State constitutions obviously tell us much about how power is distributed within our states, and from them we learn of the essential similarity in the structure of state governments. Yet the similarity of formal constitutions does not mean similarity in the actual governmental process. Much else has to be considered in determining who governs our states, as the preceding chapter suggests. The constitution is but a place to begin.

Constitutional rigidity and evasion

State constitutions contain more detail than the federal Constitution and are thus longer, less adaptable, require more frequent formal amendment, and remain effective for a shorter period.

California's much-amended constitution (403 amendments since 1879) goes into great detail about such matters as the taxation of fish, game, mollusks, or crustaceans; the disqualification from holding office or enjoying the right of suffrage of any person who participates in a duel; and the internal organization of several major departments. Article XX, Section 2, of Oklahoma's constitution proclaims, "Until changed by the Legislature, the flash test . . . for all kerosene oil for illuminating purposes shall be 115 degrees Fahrenheit; and the specific gravity test for all such oil shall be 40 degrees." Georgia's constitution details procedures to be followed by medical students in securing financial assistance. New Hampshire's sets the wages of its legislators in special session at a little over $3 a day. State constitutions vary in length from less than 8,000 words (Vermont) to 600,000 (Georgia).[1]

Although many of these detailed provisions deal with trivial subjects, others are concerned with important matters. The federal Constitution

[1]*The Book of the States*, 1976–77 (Council of State Governments, 1976), p. 174.

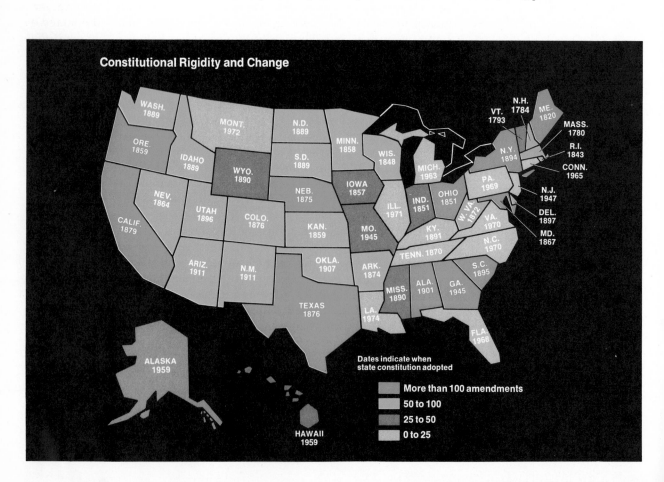

grants powers in broad and sweeping terms, letting future generations write in the details and adapt the basic charter of government to new conditions. The state constitutions are written in restrictive terms. Whereas the federal Constitution takes only a clause to authorize Congress to spend money, state constitutions require dozens of pages to specify the purposes for which the money may be spent, how much may be spent, and in what manner.

CONSTITUTIONS
AS ROADBLOCKS

A written constitution is an instrument of government that sets forth, among other things, the terms upon which public officials are authorized to act in behalf of the voters. The more detailed the constitution, the smaller the discretion the public officials enjoy. The earliest state constitutions had granted authority to the legislatures without much restriction on how their power should be exercised. But after the legislatures gave special privileges to railroads, canal-builders, and other interests, constitutional amendments were adopted to prevent these abuses. Reform groups, distrusting the legislatures, began to insist on having their programs incorporated into the constitution. In time, state constitutions became encrusted in layer after layer of detail.

What does this mean for democratic government? Most simply, it means that state constitutions often are less charters of self-government than strait jackets imposed on the living present by the dead past. Today's majorities find it hard to get the action they wish. For example, construction of the Delaware Bridge, linking Philadelphia with Camden, New Jersey, was delayed for five years because of restrictive clauses in the Pennsylvania constitution. For many years the Oregon legislature could not create a state college at Portland because the constitution forbade the founding of any new public institution outside Marion County.

The Delaware Bridge, linking the New Jersey and Pennsylvania turnpikes.

The detailed listing of powers soon throws constitutions out of date. Some outdated provisions of course do no harm, but more often they are roadblocks to effective government. The fixing of salaries, for example, makes it difficult to keep them geared to economic conditions. Prescribing a rigid administrative organization may make government incapable of adjusting to changing needs. Long constitutions usually need many amendments.

Under these conditions, the people's representatives—the legislature—cannot act on many problems; instead, the voters are called on regularly to pass upon constitutional amendments about which they know very little. Between 1921, when their last constitution was adopted, and 1974, when they adopted a new one, the voters of Louisiana were presented with about 750 proposed amendments, two-thirds of which they approved. In 1970 Louisiana voters were faced with 53 separate proposals for amendments. Thirty-one of these were strictly local in nature. Amendment No. 32, for example, would have raised from $20 to $50 the salary of secretaries to municipal fire and police civil service boards in certain communities.[2] Detail breeds more detail.

GETTING AROUND THE
CONSTITUTION

Does all this mean that state constitutions can forever prevent the wishes of the majority from being carried out? Not necessarily. The constitutional system of our states, like that of the national government, includes more

[2]*Voter's Guide to the 1970 Amendments* (Public Affairs Research Council of Louisiana, 1970), p. iii.

than the formal written document. The unwritten rules, the practices, the political parties, the interest groups also shape events. When large groups of people want their officials to act, they usually find some way to overcome formal barriers. One device is simply to ignore them; another rests on judicial interpretation. Judges can interpret the meaning of words so as to remove their restrictive force. Nevertheless, rigid state constitutions create a "constitutional autocracy" by making it more difficult for new majorities to achieve their aims.

Detailed state constitutions also increase the authority of the state judiciary. The more complex the constitution, the easier it is for the judges to veto legislation. One reason for the growing length of some constitutions is that amendments are often required to reverse judicial interpretations.

Amending the constitution

Constitutional amendments must be first *proposed* (initiated), then *ratified.* There are three ways to propose amendments: (1) by the legislature; (2) by initiative petition; and (3) by constitutional convention.

PROPOSING AND RATIFYING AMENDMENTS

Proposal of constitutional amendments by initiative petition from the people is permitted in approximately one-fourth of the states. Proposal of amendments by the legislature, the most common method, is permitted in all states except New Hampshire. Although provisions vary, the most general practice is to require the approval of two-thirds of the elected members in each chamber of the legislature in order to initiate an amendment. Some states require approval by a simple majority in two successive legislatures.

After an amendment has been proposed by one of these methods, it must be ratified. In all states except Delaware (where the legislature can ratify as well as propose amendments), ratification is by the voters. In most states, if a majority of those voting on the amendment approve it, the amendment becomes part of the constitution. In a few states, however, approval of a majority of all those voting in the election is required. Such a provision is a real obstacle, since many people who vote for candidates do not vote at all on amendments.

Amendments usually involve piecemeal change. Some observers, however, believe that most state constitutions are so bad that they cannot be salvaged by this kind of improvement. Rather than patching up the old model, they advocate trading it in for a new one. Former North Carolina governor Terry Sanford spoke for many governors when he wrote: "State constitutions, for so long the drag anchors of state progress, and permanent cloaks for the protection of special interests and points of view, should be revised or rewritten into more concise statements of principle."[3] How can the people get a new constitution if they want one?

CONSTITUTIONAL CONVENTIONS

The United States is the country of constitutional conventions.[4] Since the nation was founded, we have had over 225. Americans have always insisted on getting their constitutions down in writing. A constitution is an

[3]Terry Sanford, *Storm Over the States* (McGraw-Hill, 1967), 189.

[4]Albert L. Sturm, *Thirty Years of State Constitution Making, 1938–1968* (National Municipal League, 1970), p. 51. See also his *Trends in State Constitution-Making: 1966–1972* (Council of State Governments, 1973). An excellent comparative study is Elmer E. Cornwell, Jr., Jay S. Goodman, and Wayne R. Swanson, *State Constitutional Conventions: The Politics of the Revision Process in Seven States* (Praeger, 1975).

expression of popular will. It is fundamental law binding on all public officials, and it can be changed only by prescribed methods. Hence, we have
preferred to have our constitutions drawn up by some agency that would
be more in touch with the people's wishes than the legislature. The agency
we have chosen most often has been a constitutional convention.

Over four-fifths of the state constitutions authorize the legislature to
submit to the voters the question of calling a convention, and in the other
states the legislature is assumed to have the power to do so. In some thirteen states, the constitution requires the legislature to submit this question to the voters at fixed intervals.

If the voters approve the calling of a convention, the next step is to elect
delegates. Some constitutions contain elaborate procedures governing the
number of delegates, method of election, and time and place of the convention. Others leave the details to the legislature. After the delegates
have been chosen for the specific job of drafting a new constitution, they
usually assemble at the state capital.

When the convention has prepared a draft of the new constitution, it is
submitted to the voters. But first the delegates to the convention have to
make a difficult choice. Should the voters be asked to accept or reject the
new constitution as a whole? Or should they be given a chance to vote on
each section, as though it were an amendment to the old constitution? The
advantage of the first method is that one provision of a constitution ties in
with another, and in order to secure all the advantages of revision, the entire constitution should be adopted. The disadvantage is that a group that
takes issue with a particular provision may vote against the entire constitution in order to defeat the offending provision. When the convention
delegates know that one provision is controversial, they may decide to
submit at least that provision separately. Whichever method they choose,
the supporters of change must look to their political fences in order to get
their handiwork approved.

Instead of calling a constitutional convention, the legislature may appoint a small commission to make recommendations. A commission is less
expensive, does not require initial voter approval, and gives the legislature final control of what is presented to the electorate.

Florida, Virginia, California, and Louisiana have used the commission
procedure to bring about significant constitutional change. The California
constitutional revision commission, a bipartisan group of citizens representing a wide range of interests, has worked closely with the leaders of
the legislature. But its work has met with mixed success with the voters.[5] In
other states, the revision commission has not worked this well, perhaps
because it has not been responsive to political currents or representative of
enough interests. Commissions may have the advantage of providing
more objective consideration of amendments than either the legislature or
a convention, but as a result they may propose changes that will be rejected either by the legislature or by the voters. Still, revision commissions
have gained in popularity, and many experts feel they are a major new
resource to help modernize state constitutions.

The political struggle does not end once a constitutional convention has
assembled. Often those who dominate the legislature also dominate the

[5]Bernard L. Hyink, "California Revises Its Constitution," *Western Political Quarterly* (September 1969), pp. 637–54.

Government Under the Model State Constitution

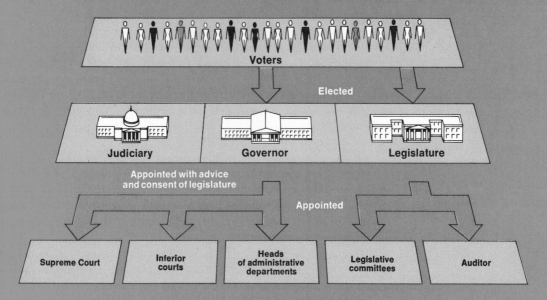

Government Under a Typical State Constitution

Adapted from charts prepared for the Committee on State Governments of the National Municipal League for the 1948 edition of the Model State Constitution, modified to reflect provisions of the 1967 revision.

convention, though sometimes other interests control it. Service in a convention carries greater prestige than a seat in the legislature, and many people are willing to interrupt their normal activities to spend some time at constitution making. For example, George Romney, when president of American Motors, played a vital role in the 1962 Michigan constitutional convention and went from there to the governorship and then to a cabinet position under Nixon. Since conventions may also attract greater popular attention, they usually can make fundamental changes that legislatures cannot or will not make.

Recent years have seen a renewal of interest in constitutional revision. The subject has become of such broad concern — partly, perhaps, because of much questioning of the whole governmental system in the past decade or so — that conventions have been called or commissions formed in more than two-thirds of the states. Arkansas, New Mexico, Illinois, Montana, Michigan, Maryland, New York, Tennessee, New Jersey, Connecticut, New Hampshire, Louisiana, and Texas, among others, have had constitutional conventions within the past several years. Revision commissions have been at work in many states: Examples are Alabama, New Hampshire, Ohio, North and South Dakota, Texas, Utah, and Washington.[6] Yet from all this activity, significant changes have resulted in only a few states.

CONVENTIONS: POLITICAL ASPECTS

If present constitutions are so bad, why have so few states modernized them? The answer lies in the nature of the political process. Constitutions are not a neutral set of rules perched above the world of rough-and-tumble politics. On the contrary, constitutions significantly affect who gets what from government. The way in which a constitution is changed can help or hinder various groups. "If the document is exceptionally innovative, those status quo supporting groups and interests, who have lost in the selection and convention process, will oppose and defeat the document. If the document is not innovative, those reform groups who initially lobbied for conventions will oppose and defeat the document."[7] Present state constitutions may be bad in the abstract or from the perspective of democratic theory, but they are not so bad for certain groups. And many people simply do not care. It is difficult to work up much excitement in a campaign for revision of a state constitution except among those with intense feelings, and they are more likely to oppose than to favor adoption. Those who like the status quo thus have a built-in advantage that, when combined with obstacles in the constitution itself, helps to explain the lack of action. Evidence from one state suggests that it is the voters with the most education and wealth who tend to favor revision, at least at first.[8] But as the history of constitutional revision shows, these reform leaders have usually not been successful in securing change.

The arrangement for the selection of convention delegates seems to have an impact on the kind of document the convention proposes. Nonpartisan multimember district selection devices are more likely to result in a "re-

[6]Albert L. Sturm, "State Constitutions and Constitutional Revision, 1974–75," *The Book of the States, 1976–77* (Council of State Governments, 1976), pp. 166–67.

[7]Elmer E. Cornwell, Jr., Jay S. Goodman, and Wayne R. Swanson, "State Constitutional Conventions: Delegates, Roll Calls, and Issues," *Midwest Journal of Political Science* (February 1970), p. 130. See also their longer treatment, *State Constitutional Conventions.*

[8]Norman C. Thomas, "The Electorate and State Constitutional Revision: An Analysis of Four Michigan Referenda," *Midwest Journal of Political Science* (February 1968), p. 129.

form" convention than those in which parties play a major role.[9] Let us look at some examples.

A convention called in Maryland in 1967 consisted of delegates elected on a nonpartisan basis. It selected its committee chairmen without regard to party, and was "one of the most carefully planned and efficiently managed constitutional conventions held in recent years."[10] The constitution it developed was endorsed by most business and civic leaders, and its supporters ran a well-financed campaign. The voters, however rejected it overwhelmingly, mostly because of a provision for nineteen-year-old voting and a strong nondiscrimination provision. New York's 1967 convention consisted of delegates selected on partisan tickets, and parties played a major role in its deliberations. Its proposed new constitution was also defeated decisively, primarily because of conflict over an article relating to church and state. In Rhode Island, voters turned down a draft constitution submitted to them by their constitutional convention, the longest one in history, primarily because of the opposition of the Republican governor and of those who objected to a provision relaxing prohibition of state lotteries.[11]

Constitutional revision also went down to defeat in Texas. Texas has a rather long constitution, to which more than 218 amendments had been added by 1973. The time appeared ripe to revise when political scandals in 1971 brought in a new governor, Dolph Briscoe, and a reform-oriented state legislature. The new leadership pushed through a variety of reforms dealing with ethics of officeholders, campaign practices, and registration of lobbyists. The legislature also called into being a convention to revise the 1876 constitution. The delegates worked for seventeen months. They came up with a much revised and shortened document that they thought would have modernized the many obsolete governmental practices still followed in the state. But the convention deadlocked over whether to give constitutional status to the state right-to-work law, which prohibits labor contracts that require union membership to hold a job.

The Texas AFL-CIO as well as Governor Briscoe withheld support for some of the convention's efforts. The governor warned that there would be higher taxes if the provision for annual sessions of the legislature was enacted as part of the revised constitution. Revisionists tried to salvage their work by offering substantial parts of the new charter to the voters as amendments to the existing constitution. The strategy did not work; in November, 1975, Texas voters rejected the new amendments by a 2 to 1 margin. Conservatives praised the old constitution as one that had served Texas well for a hundred years. Progressives complained that the old constitution was elitist, permitted only the narrowest of government objectives, and made real change nearly impossible.[12]

[9]Cornwell et al., "State Constitutional Conventions," p. 129.

[10]James E. Bebout, "State Constitutions and Constitutional Revision, 1965–67," *The Book of the States, 1967–68* (Council of State Governments, 1967), p. 8; John P. Wheeler, Jr., and Melissa Kinsey, *Magnificent Failure—The Maryland Constitutional Convention of 1967–1968* (National Municipal League, 1970).

[11]Bebout, "State Constitutions," p. 7; Elmer E. Cornwell, Jr., and Jay S. Goodman, *The Politics of the Rhode Island Constitutional Convention* (National Municipal League, 1970).

[12]See Beryl E. Pettus and Randall W. Bland, *Texas Government Today* (Dorsey Press, 1976), pp. 14–15.

Michigan is one of the very few states in which the voters have approved the work of a constitutional convention during the last twenty years, and in Michigan the new constitution, pushed by Romney in a spirited partisan campaign, is a simplified version of the old one.[13] In Tennessee, Connecticut, New Hampshire, New Jersey, and Pennsylvania, voters have approved the proposals from their constitutional conventions, but these conventions were restricted to consideration of only a few items, primarily reapportionment.

Substantial change was brought about in Louisiana in the early 1970s.[14] The Louisiana constitutional revision commission set out during 1973 and 1974 to write a streamlined "people's constitution," one the average person could understand. The AFL-CIO, NAACP, the League of Women Voters, a Committee for a Better Louisiana, the National Municipal League, and many other lobbying groups became involved in the shaping of the new constitution. It took well over a year to write and cost approximately $2.4 million. In the end, however, a readable 26,000-word document would replace the existing 256,500-word monster that contained detailed legislative items and some 536 amendments. The new constitution provides for "a strong bill of rights including a guarantee of equality of treatment; annual legislative sessions; single-member legislative districts; power of legislators to convene the legislature by majority vote; automatic veto sessions; removal of the lieutenant governor as president of the Senate; limitation of the number of principal executive departments to 20; strengthened authority for local government" and has some sensible tax reform provisions.[15] Governor Edwin Edwards, New Orleans Mayor Moon Lan-

Parties and special interest groups, such as these members of the Kootenai tribe in Idaho, often find ways to overcome formal constitutional barriers. In this case the Indians' efforts to collect tolls from vehicles passing through their area of the state were dramatic enough to win extensive financial assistance from the federal government.

[13]Robert S. Friedman, *The Michigan Constitutional Convention and Administrative Organization* (Institute of Public Administration, Ann Arbor, 1963).

[14]Cecil Morgan, "A New Constitution for Louisiana," *National Civic Review* (July 1974), pp. 343–56.

[15]Albert L. Sturm, "State Constitutions," p. 169.

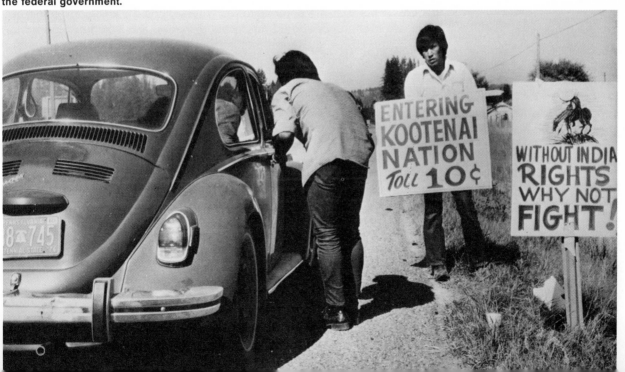

drieu, and several legislators supported ratification. Louisiana voters approved it at the polls by a large margin in April 1974, and it went into effect at the end of the year. No longer can the Louisiana constitution be cited as the chief example of unworkable state constitutions.

THE ILLINOIS CONSTITUTIONAL CONVENTION

Another notable exception to the pattern is Illinois, which in 1970 adopted the constitution submitted to it by the Sixth Illinois Constitutional Convention.

The 1870 Illinois constitution, like that of many states, placed substantial obstacles in the way of amendments, mainly by requiring extraordinary majorities for their approval. In 1965 the Illinois General Assembly created a study commission to determine how constitutional change could best be effected. The commission recommended that a convention be called. The General Assembly approved the recommendation, as did the voters in the 1968 general elections, in response to a well-supported bipartisan campaign.

The study commission, which had carefully avoided making recommendations on specific issues, then proposed ground rules for the convention. These were approved by the legislature. The commission and the General Assembly agreed that the delegates would be selected on a nonpartisan basis in a specially called primary and election, and that the delegates should be paid $12,500, to make it possible for interested persons to devote their full time to the task of revision.

On December 8, 1969, the delegates assembled in Springfield, and the convention began to work. After several months of deliberation by committees, the issues were taken to the floor. In the debates it became obvious that the major political interests of the state were well represented. Partisan positions were also evident, as was the traditional split between Chicago and downstate. But the nonpartisan election procedures reduced partisanship as compared with that of a traditional legislative session.

After nine months of deliberations (three times longer than it had taken the Founding Fathers), the delegates finally agreed on a document. Learning from the experiences of other states, they decided to submit the most controversial issues separately to the voters. Thus the electorate could decide whether judges should be elected or appointed, whether representation in the House of Representatives should be based on multimember districts with cumulative voting or on single-member districts, whether eighteen-year-olds should be made eligible to vote, and whether capital punishment should be abolished.

The "package" and the separate controversial questions were submitted to the voters, again at a special election. The main package had bipartisan support, including the endorsement of Democratic Mayor Richard Daley of Chicago and Republican Governor Richard Ogilvie. The mayor opposed the appointment of judges, the governor favored the idea. (He was to do the appointing.) They agreed that the multimember district system should be retained. Along with most other political leaders in the state, they avoided taking strong stands on the other controversial items. The voters overwhelmingly approved the "package," and favored elected judges and multimember districts. But they rejected eighteen-year-old voting and the abolition of capital punishment.

Illinois followed the prescription for success outlined by Cornwell, Goodman, and Swanson: Select delegates in special nonpartisan elections.

562

Produce a document somewhere between one that is "too innovative" and "too stand-pat," a document that does not antagonize major political factions and interests within the state. Submit controversial questions to the electorate separately in order to avoid creating a composite majority against the proposed constitution from among minorities offended by the controversial items.[16]

The new Illinois constitution provides much greater flexibility for the legislature, more home rule for the cities, greater power for the governor. How the legislative, executive, and judicial authorities use their new power will determine whether the effort to bring about constitutional revision will lead to significant change in the state.

CONSTITUTIONAL CHANGE BY POPULAR INITIATIVE

At the end of the nineteenth century, the prestige of state governments reached their lowest point. Out of this disillusionment came a variety of reforms, of which the constitutional *initiative* was one.[17] The initiative is a device that permits voters to force specific constitutional amendments onto the ballot. Seventeen states allow amendments to be proposed by such petitions. But the initiative method has not been the source of many important constitutional changes. In recent years, voters have rejected nine out of ten of the amendments that originated as the result of initiative procedures. Voters seem guided by the motto "When in doubt, vote no!" or "Be slow to change the handiwork of the past. The unforeseen consequences of revision may be worse than no revision at all."

Plainly, a variety of factors account for the low adoption rate of initiative measures, including these:

1. The process is difficult and expensive.
2. Initiatives tend to be used for controversial issues either already rejected by the legislature or which the proponents believe did not have a chance of passage in the legislature.
3. Initiatives are generally proposed by a small number of interest groups or by reform-minded elites who have yet to build a broad enough coalition of support for their views.[18]

Critics charge that the initiative asks the voters to make too many decisions for which they are not especially well prepared. Others argue that the use of the initiative petition can prevent elected representatives from exercising their proper authority. Still others hold that a constitution should be a blueprint that states not the rules for the moment but the overriding principles for an expanding future. It should certainly not, they say, get too specific about how governments are to operate on a day to day basis.

On the other hand, the initiative can be a valuable weapon against an unresponsive legislature. When a legislature is tied too much to certain

[16]Cornwell, et al., "State Constitutional Conventions," p. 130; see also Samuel K. Gove and Thomas R. Kitsos, *Revision Success: The Sixth Illinois Constitutional Convention* (National Municipal League, 1974).

[17]See John P. Wheeler, Jr., ed., *Salient Issues of Constitutional Revision* (National Municipal League, 1961), pp. 55–56.

[18]These are suggested by Mary F. Williams, "Politics and Voting Behavior in Statewide Referenda," paper delivered at the 1976 annual meetings of the American Political Science Association, Chicago, September 1976, p. 7.

special interests and refuses to acknowledge the legitimate demands of a majority of the citizens, the initiative is a desirable corrective. Properly used, it may educate the public on important policy issues and thereby serve to enlarge support for change — even though that change may have to wait for another time and some other means.

Summary

1. State constitutions are documents that attempt to spell out the fundamental law of a state. Although they vary considerably in detail, each outlines the organizational framework for that state and vests powers in the legislature and other departments and state officers. In addition, each describes the limits on state powers; provides for a bill of rights; and enumerates provisions for elections, local government, education, and state finances.

2. A constitution typically reveals little about the politics of a state. But to study the constitutional development of a state is to study its political heritage, the battles among interest groups, and the struggles to modernize and adapt to changing times.

3. Except for some of the newer ones, most state constitutions are not well written or organized. They are cumbersome documents that most people would hate to read. Although there are several ways to revise or completely rewrite state constitutions, no method has proved easy. Virtually all the methods are to one degree or another controlled by state legislatures. "Alterations that would undermine or threaten legislative power or challenge the conservative political values that often dominate American state legislatures have been difficult to achieve."[19]

4. Since 1900 only a handful of states have succeeded in making significant revisions. Voters and legislatures apparently fear change. Many of the groups that benefit from the existing arrangements work hard to preserve the status quo. Resistance to sweeping constitutional revision is likely to remain strong.

5. There is general agreement that most of the lengthy and highly detailed constitutions strengthen the position of conservative interests, frustrate officials with progressive tendencies, increase the need for court interpretation, and reflect the strength of dominant interest groups in the state at the time of adoption.

[19]Cornwell, et al., *State Constitutional Conventions*, p. 14.

Chapter 26

Under the Capitol Dome: The State Legislature

Mark Twain and Will Rogers always won easy laughs by poking fun at the antics of state politicians. The state legislature is still one of the public's favorite punching bags. In state after state, journalists assigned to the statehouse have been uncovering new stories about "extortion deals," "payoffs," and conflict of interest violations. Experts find that state legislatures are inefficient, badly organized, and rarely offer creative policy leadership. Governors complain that the legislature is uncooperative and ruled by autocratic leaders. The average person seldom thinks about the state legislature except to blame it when taxes go up and express relief when it adjourns. When did you last hear a kind word about state legislatures?

State legislatures, however, play a vital role in state politics. If most citizens are quick to point out their shortcomings, hardly anyone favors eliminating state legislatures. On the contrary, Americans want their legislatures to serve as a check and counterbalance on their governors and state bureaucracy. Moreover, even if the legislature is not the wellspring of policy leadership for the state, we want our legislatures to represent the views of the people and be a partner in passing the laws and in making and overseeing the implementation of public policy.

True, legislatures are often overshadowed by governors. This is the case in part because a legislature consists of a variety of voices which are often sounding off on dozens of different themes at once. Under the circumstances, it is difficult for such a divergent body to provide unified, swift policy leadership. State legislatures have also lost influence over policy making because they lack the staff and the time to compete with better-equipped and better-informed governors, bureaucrats, and interest group leaders. The typical state legislator is still very much a part-timer and "a bird of passage." That is, he or she has not been there for long, and will not stay for long (two or three terms is the average). Many states have raised the pay, increased staffs, and improved the operations, but these efforts to professionalize the legislatures are not yet enough to make legislatures dominant in policy making.

Their *political* functions, however, may be even more important now than their law or policy making functions. For the legislatures in our states are constantly settling conflicts and reconciling pressures among competing special interest groups. They represent local views at the state level and dramatize issues, so that they become the subject of open debate. In effect, then, a legislature serves as a lightning rod to which most of the conflicting pressures "of American society are drawn, and its primary job is to defuse these pressures so that the political system can function intact without blowing wide apart."[1] In short, as a former Vermont state senator put it, "The legislative process is a very complicated, but vitally important, way to air political issues in a manner that enables the public to be brought into the democratic decision-making process."[2]

The legislative branch

All states except Nebraska have a two-house—or bicameral—legislature. The lower and larger chamber is generally called the House of Representatives. Its size varies from a low of 40 in Alaska and Nevada to a high of 400 in New Hampshire; the typical number is around 100. In all but four states the representatives serve for a two-year term. The upper chamber, known in all the states as the Senate, is composed of about 40 members. State senators have a four-year term in about three-fourths of the states.

Forty-two states hold *annual* legislative sessions; in others, the legislature meets in regular session once every two years (biennial sessions), usually in January of odd-numbered years. In some states the constitution limits the legislature to a regular session of a fixed number of days, usually sixty or ninety days. Several means, such as going into a "special session," have been developed to get around this limitation. Such restrictions reflect the old distrust of government, the feeling that "the faster we get it over with the better." The governor has the power to call the legislature into special session (and in some states to determine the issues that may be discussed in the special session) a power frequently used because of the constitutional time limits on regular sessions.

The organization and procedures of the state legislature are similar to those of Congress. A speaker, usually chosen by the majority party, presides over the lower house. In several states speakers have more power to control proceedings than their national counterpart. For example, in addition to all the powers of the speaker of the national House of Representatives, they have the right to appoint committees, and thus theirs is a key role in determining policy. In about thirty states a lieutenant governor presides over the senate; in the others, the presiding officer is chosen by the majority party in the senate. The committee system prevails, as in Congress; but in some states, notably Massachusetts, joint committees are used to speed legislative action. However, state legislative committees are usually pale shadows of their congressional counterparts. They seldom have the same power over bills; they rarely have adequate professional assistance; the seniority system is not as stringently followed as in Congress; and turnover is much higher.

[1]Frank Smallwood, *Free and Independent: The Initiation of a College Professor into State Politics* (The Stephen Greene Press, 1976), p. 218.

[2]*Ibid.*, p. 218.

Although the formal structure and procedures of the legislatures are similar from state to state, this is not true of their actual operation. Some states, like New York, have strong political parties that take an active part in policy making. Here and in perhaps a dozen other states, the party caucus is an important part of the legislative machinery. In others, the parties assume no responsibility for the actions of their legislative members. In some states, governors lead the way; in others, they are relatively unimportant. The fairly competitive two-party system found in Congress exists in about ten states. In order to describe with any accuracy the actual functioning of a particular state legislature, one must be acquainted with the entire social and political environment in which the legislature operates.[3]

WHAT THE STATE
LEGISLATURES CAN—
AND CANNOT—DO

What do the approximately 7,500 state legislators do? They enact the laws that create state parks, specify the salaries for state officials, draw up the rules governing state elections, fix the state tax rate, and determine the quantity and quality of state correctional, mental health and educational institutions.

The state legislatures have all the governmental powers that are not given to some other agency. The Tenth Amendment to the federal Constitution makes it clear that governmental power not given to the national gov-

[3]John C. Wahlke, Heinz Eulau, William Buchanan, and LeRoy C. Ferguson's *The Legislative System: Explorations in Legislative Behavior* (Wiley, 1962) is a detailed analysis of the role and behavior of legislators in California, Tennessee, Ohio, and New Jersey.

How a bill becomes law

- Petitions are filed in the office of the House or Senate Clerk.
- Clerk assigns a number to the petition and refers it to a committee.
- Joint Committee holds public hearing before making report.
- An unfavorable report, if accepted by the House or Senate, kills the bill. A favorable report is considered the first reading.
- If the bill relates to state finances, it is referred to the Ways and Means Committee. When the Ways and Means Committee makes its recommendations, the bill is put on the next day's calendar for a second reading.
- Before voting on "ordering the bill to a third reading," a bill is subject to debate and amendment. If favorable action is taken and the bill is ordered to a third reading, it is then referred to the Committee on Bills in the Third Reading.
- Following a third reading, a vote is taken on "passing the bill to be engrossed." A favorable vote sends the bill to the other branch where it follows the same procedure.
- If a bill passes the second branch in an amended version, it is sent back to the originating branch for concurrence. If concurrence is rejected, the bill may go to a conference committee.
- When agreement is reached by both branches, the bill is prepared for final passage.
- Vote on enactment is taken in the House and then the Senate.
- The bill is sent to the Governor.
- The Governor, during the ten day period allotted him by the Constitution, may:
  — sign the bill into law
  — let it become law by taking no action
  — send it back with recommended amendments
  — veto it. A two-thirds vote of both branches is required to override a veto.
  — let it die by taking no action within ten days after the session has ended and the legislature has prorogued. This is called a pocket veto.

SOURCE: Prepared and published as part of pamphlet *Inside the State House* by the Massachusetts Legislature and The League of Women Voters of Massachusetts, 1974.

**State legislators enact laws that may affect inmates of correctional institutions.
In a new program at Hawaii State Prison, inmates have transformed
their dormitory into a day room.**

ernment or denied to the states lies with the states or with the people. The
state constitutions in turn give some of this reserved power exclusively to
*non*legislative agencies and specifically deny some of the legislature. What
is left is inherited by the state legislatures. To be sure, some state courts
have developed the doctrine of *implied limitations* on the legislatures by
ruling that when the constitution authorizes the legislature to do a particular thing, by implication it denies the legislature the power to do other
things.

Although subject to all these limitations, the legislature still has a
powerful voice in deciding the crucial political questions in the state.
Among other things, it levies state taxes, appropriates money, creates
agencies to carry out the tasks of government, allots functions among these
agencies, and investigates them to make sure they are doing what the
lawmakers intended them to do. State legislators, like their national counterparts, also participate in amending constitutions, have authority to
impeach and try public officials, and exercise some appointive powers.

Commonly, the state constitution prescribes the procedures legislators
must follow in order to make laws. In addition, limits on the rate of taxation, the kinds of tax, the subjects that may be taxed, and the purposes of
taxation are often detailed in the constitution. *Special legislation*—laws
dealing with particular persons or localities—is usually prohibited.

WHO ARE THE STATE
LEGISLATORS?

The typical American state legislator is a white, male, Protestant businessman or lawyer of Anglo-Saxon origin who had previous political experience—usually elective—at the city or county level. Some aspects of this
profile are changing, others are not. For example, lawyers continue to be
the largest occupational group in most state legislatures, just as they are in
Congress. Many young attorneys enter the legislature to perform a public
service, secure a reputation, and build up a practice. As one legislator put
it, "I don't consider myself a politician. I just availed myself of the opportunity because I was interested in legislative law in my capacity as a lawyer. It was an opportunity to expand my knowledge of the law. Also good
during the lean years of [my law] practice."[4]

[4]*Ibid.*, p. 103.

Real estate and insurance dealers, salespeople, and farmers are also found in legislatures in significant numbers. However, the number of farmers is decreasing as a result of reapportionment, the decline in the overall number of farmers, and the longer sessions of the legislatures. When legislatures used to meet just for a few winter months, farmers were able to fit their schedules to the legislative cycle. Still, farmers constitute a sizeable minority of legislators in all the farm states.

More and more women and blacks are winning election to state legislatures, but both are still notably in the minority. As of the late 1970s, there are about 700 women and nearly 300 black state legislators.[5] Women's political groups point out that it took 144 years for women to get the vote, but that more highly qualified women than ever before are beginning to run for statewide political offices. They are determined to have an equal voice in government.

Legislators almost have to be people with flexible schedules. Many of them are younger people right out of college, retired people, and those whose businesses or law practices have been so successful that they can afford to take the time off. In our more populous and wealthy states the trend is toward annual legislative sessions with reasonable salaries. Thus, California, Illinois, and New York all pay their legislators at least $20,000 a year, plus various expenses. (With expenses included, California legislators are now paid well over $30,000 a year.) A few other states, such as Michigan, Wisconsin, Ohio, and Pennsylvania provide "living wages." But in most states a legislator receives very little. In the typical state, legislators go to the capitol for only a few months a year and are paid so little that many are able to serve only if they are independently wealthy, can live off their parents, or have another job that can be readily combined with legislative service. The median compensation—including expense allowances—for a two-year legislative term is about $15,000.

Many nineteenth-century observers argued that legislators should not be paid, for salaries only served to attract people who had no interest in the job except the money. Today, most people believe the business of the state should be handled by professional legislators and not by part-time citizen legislators. They argue that inadequate salaries discourage qualified candidates from seeking office. Few business executives, teachers, or salaried workers, for example, can interrupt their lives to attend to legislative duties, and they cannot afford to give up their jobs and live on the salary the state pays.

What kind of men and women are the state legislators? State legislators are generally better educated, better employed, and more from the middle and upper middle income groups than the average person. They are usually hardworking, public-spirited citizens who feel serving in the legislature would be a good opportunity for service. Three state legislators gave these reasons for running for the job[6]:

They need people down here, laymen, that will represent the average

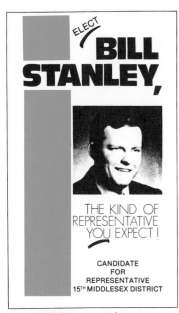

State legislators retain a powerful voice in the determination of crucial political questions.

---

[5]For an excellent study of women legislators and how they view the job, see Jeane Kirkpatrick, *Political Women* (Basic Books, 1974).

[6]From interviews with state legislators in Wahlke, et al., *The Legislative System*, p. 103 and pp. 115–16. A major study of why and how people ran for the state legislature in Oregon is: Lester G. Seligman, Michael R. King, Chong Lim Kim, and Roland E. Smith, *Patterns of Recruitment: A State Chooses Its Lawmakers* (Rand McNally, 1974).

viewpoint. The legislature needs people that aren't lawyers, that are for the common man. With my training and background in *labor*, I felt I could represent the average viewpoint, I mean the viewpoint of the people that work for a living. I thought I could do something that could better the position of the working man. I had no fancy slogans when I ran; this one thing was all I wanted.

A good many people urged me to run, with the argument that the *business* point of view represented in the legislature might be in the public interest. Many problems of legislation are identical with those of business—such as judicious spending of funds, efficient administration, a clear philosophy of government.

For eight years I served on the County Treasurer's Legislative Committee. During the course of that time I came down to the legislature often. While on the committee, I worked on bills such as the County Officials Pay Bill. I decided that I had some good experience and that I should run for the legislature.

"We need the measurement to be sure we have the right size loophole for our constituent in the new tax bill."

State legislators enjoy less prestige than do members of Congress, especially in states that have large legislatures. Discouraged by low salaries and the long hours the job requires—and by their relative lack of influence—many serve a term or two and then retire voluntarily. About a third of all legislators are newcomers, a percentage that has varied only slightly in recent years. There is some evidence in a few states, however, of a gradual increase in the number of legislators seeking reelection. Many are staying in the legislature for a series of terms.[7] Some state legislators doubtless call it quits after just a term or two because they get bored. They have to listen and pay attention to all kinds of matters that frankly do not interest them. As one one-termer advised, "In short, a great deal in the political process does not—repeat does not—involve the glamorous policy issues. Most of the work is sheer routine and hardly awe-inspiring."[8]

LOBBYISTS AND THE STATE LEGISLATURE

Those who dislike the laws that are passed, or who like the laws that are defeated, often claim that the fault lies with the integrity of the legislators. The state legislatures have their share of dishonest people, but it is probably no greater than in business, sports, or the entertainment field. A state legislature is surrounded by temptations. Many people who may be affected by decisions seek to bend these decisions to their advantage. Anyone who reads major state newspapers knows that certain contractors, road builders, developers, and large landholders have been known to seek contracts or special rulings by illegal means.

A larger problem has long challenged the integrity of representative government in America. "If there is any safe axiom in American politics," writes David Broder, "it is that our legislators get the funds with which they run from the very people who have the greatest direct stake in the legislation they will pass." Broder describes the problem well:

The arrangements are not subtle. Fund-raising dinners are held during the legislative sessions, and the distribution of campaign contributions

---

[7]See David Ray, "Membership Stability in Three State Legislatures: 1893–1969," *American Political Science Review* (March 1974), pp. 106–12.

[8]Smallwood, *Free and Independent*, p. 223.

is often done personally by the same lobbyists who are negotiating with those legislators on provisions of specific bills. The cynical remark of a Florida lobbyist, who had been "invited" to one of those mid-session "appreciation dinners" given by and for a key legislator, was that "you've got to appreciate someone for their past service—or their future service." At that point, the difference between a contribution and a bribe becomes so blurred as to be almost invisible.[9]

Open and unscrupulous lobbying still goes on in some states. But most people who have studied statehouse lobbying explain that obvious techniques are not as widespread or as effective as the public believes. Writing about his own experiences in the Vermont State Senate in 1973 and 1974, Frank Smallwood observes that as a general rule most of the lobbyists "were articulate, hard-working, and extremely well informed in their particular areas of expertise. This last attribute—information—represented their chief weapon and gave them real clout. As far as I could find out, the lobbyists didn't offer legislators any money or other direct inducements; at least, they never offered me anything, not even a sociable drink. Instead they relied on information."[10]

The effective lobbyists are specialists both in subject matter and also in legislative procedure. Lobbyists for organized interests know the schedule of the general hearings, committee meetings, floor debates, and social events. They are present and prepared when their interests are affected. Veteran lobbyists, in short, know how to win friends and influence. One of their rules of thumb is "It's a hell of a lot easier to kill a bill than to pass it." "If a bill hits the floor [of the Senate or the House] you don't have the foggiest idea how the vote will go unless you do an awful lot of homework. . . . To kill a bill all you need is a majority of a committee, but to pass it you need a majority of the House."[11]

On balance, probably too much is made of the negative aspects of lobbying. But even the occasional corrupt practices have done much to damage the faith Americans have in their state governments. Most state legislators would like to improve the image of the state legislature. Thus, nearly all the states, especially after a rash of political scandals in the early and mid-1970s, have intensified efforts to solve the problems of conflict of interest, regulation of lobbyists, and financing of political campaigns. Common Cause, the League of Women Voters, and other groups have helped to encourage the adoption of better financial disclosure, open-meeting, and campaign finance reforms. Not all of these have been easy to enforce, and not all of them have worked according to the original intentions.[12]

In many states attempts have been made to control lobbying and to regulate amounts that persons may spend to influence elections or the legislative process. These laws are difficult to enforce and raise constitutional questions if they infringe on the right of persons to petition their government or to spend their funds for political purposes. Those that rely primar-

Rep. Herbert A. Lesher, a member of the Delaware House of Representatives, performs his annual stunt of doing a complete somersault on top of a bucket as a final event for the General Assembly.

[9]David Broder, in Herbert E. Alexander, *Campaign Money: Reform and Reality in the States* (Free Press, 1976), p. 313.

[10]Smallwood, *Free and Independent*, p. 165. See also L. Harmon Zeigler and Michael A. Baer, *Lobbying Interaction and Influence in American State Legislatures* (Wadsworth, 1969).

[11]Lobbyist, quoted in Smallwood, p. 164.

[12]See Herbert Alexander, ed., *Campaign Money* (Free Press, 1976).

ily on reporting of what is spent and how or that limit the amounts legislators may receive have been more effective and raise fewer constitutional issues. Some people feel satisfactory legislative and enforcement solutions to these problems will be a long time in the making, simply because the distinctions between what is considered legitimate or illegitimate behavior are frequently so fine or debatable that they are nearly impossible to write into law.[13]

PARTIES IN THE STATE LEGISLATURES

The lieutenant governor presides over Nebraska's celebrated one-house legislature.

Except in Nebraska, where legislators are elected on a nonpartisan ballot — that is, a ballot without party labels — all candidates for state legislatures are nominated by political parties in primaries and elected as party members. However, the role of political parties in the management of legislatures and in policy making varies widely from state to state. In about a third of the states the political party is the most important factor in decision making; these tend to be the northern states east of the Mississippi and those with a high level of urbanization and industrialization. In other states, parties appear to have less significance as the major sources of conflict. Instead, rural-urban splits, or conservative-liberal coalitions, or regional blocs appear to be more prominent.

In state legislatures where the two major political parties are normally strong, parties serve as the basis for the organization and management of legislative business. The election of legislative officers and committees, for example, is made along party lines. Of course, party unity on *organizational* matters does not mean that members always vote together on *policy* issues before the legislature. Party voting is most often found in the two-party legislatures. Here party caucuses are most likely to formulate policy that members are expected to support in the legislative sessions. Some of the two-party legislatures, however, show little party cohesion, and even where cohesion exists, the role of the party in formulating policy may be exaggerated.

In states where a single party dominates the legislature but where the minority party has a sizable number of seats, the role of the party varies widely.[14] In some, both political parties are highly organized; in others, only the majority party has cohesion and the minority party is weak. But the most prevalent pattern in these states is for *both* parties to be weak. In legislatures where a single party has overwhelming control (until recently the Democrats traditionally held every seat in both houses in five southern states), parties are of little importance in conducting legislative business. Factions within the dominant party, however, are sometimes very active.

[13]For a useful review of the California experience in this area, see Larry L. Berg, Harlan Hahn, and John R. Schmidhauser, *Corruption in the American Political System* (General Learning Press, 1976), Chap. 7.

[14]For studies of party role in state legislatures, see Thomas A. Flinn, "Party Responsibility in the States: Some Causal Factors," *American Political Science Review* (March 1964), pp. 60–71; Hugh L. LeBlanc, "Voting in State Senates: Party and Constituency Influences," *Midwest Journal of Political Science* (February 1969), pp. 38–39. See also the discussion in Samuel C. Patterson, "American State Legislatures and Public Policy," in Herbert Jacob and Kenneth N. Vines, eds., *Politics in the American States*, 3rd ed. (Little, Brown, 1976), pp. 178–82. For a study which concludes that the impact of the political parties in campaigns for the legislature is negligible, see Jerome M. Mileur and George T. Sulzner, *Campaigning for the Massachusetts Senate* (University of Massachusetts Press, 1974).

In sum, parties are most likely to be strongest in the two-party legislatures, weakest in the one-party legislatures, and neither very strong nor weak in the modified one-party legislatures. In a few states, such as New York, Pennsylvania, and Massachusetts, parties play a more prominent role than they do in Congress, but they are considerably weaker in most state legislatures. Party control of legislation, in short, is even feebler in most states than it is in Congress.

OTHER INFLUENCES ON STATE
LEGISLATORS

The people elect their state legislators to represent them and their views at the statehouse. But few legislators feel that it is their job merely to mirror or re-present the views of their constituents. Most legislators prefer to see themselves as "trustees" of their constituents. The trustees generally claim to rely on their own conscience, on what they consider right, or on their considered judgment of the facts involved in the issues that come before them. This is in contrast to legislators who adopt the role of serving as a "delegate," following instructions from constituents. Scholars who studied four state legislatures concluded that the trustee role is not only the most popular, but also the easiest and most realistic: "Given the complexity of governmental problems, on the one hand, and the difficulty of finding out what clienteles may want, the delegate orientation is probably least functional from the point of view of effective representation."[15]

In fact, however, most state legislators rely on their colleagues—especially colleagues in their own party—to guide them in making decisions. "What a new legislator soon finds out is that there is no choice but to depend on his colleagues to inform him about issues assigned to their committees; and like it or not, he is reduced to following their advice unless he knows the subject well enough to have an opinion."[16] This is not only a convenient but a reasonable practice, for many legislators come to the statehouse with considerable experience in business, farming, the problems of cities, and so on. Veteran legislators develop expertise in controversial policy areas.

Members of a state legislature may also be influenced by what nearby states are doing. State legislators sometimes will travel to a nearby state noted for its "progress" or "innovations" in a particular policy area and study possible applications for their own state. Nowadays, too, the national government can have a powerful influence on actions in state legislatures: "When the California legislature passed the Pure Air Act of 1968, its actions were very much affected by decisions regarding air pollution control which had been and were being made in Washington. Similarly, when the state legislatures adopted legislation prescribing a 55-mile-per-hour speed limit in 1973, they were acting under very direct federal influence."[17]

In sum, most state legislators are influenced by their colleagues and legislative leaders and by a variety of forces outside the legislature itself, usu-

[15]Wahlke and Eulau, et al., *The Legislative System*, p. 286.

[16]Duane Lockard, *The Politics of State and Local Government*, 2nd ed. (Macmillan, 1969), p. 264. See also the useful discussion of influences on state legislators in James S. Lee, "Toward an Understanding of State Legislative Decision-Making," in Richard H. Leach and Timothy G. O'Rourke, eds. *Dimensions of State and Urban Policy Making* (Macmillan, 1975), pp. 156–75.

[17]Samuel C. Patterson, "American State Legislatures and Public Policy," in Jacob and Vines, eds., *Politics in the American States*, p. 187.

ally including leaders and opinion makers back in the district, the governor, local and state party leaders, interest group spokespeople, experts in the bureaucracy, and new ideas that are taking hold elsewhere in the nation.

Legislative modernization

The weaknesses of some of our state legislatures are much like those of Congress, but many analysts feel they run deeper. They find that legislative business is not conducted efficiently, that committee work is not well planned, that careful records are not kept, and that expert information is not systematically sought. It is felt too that introducing special and private legislation is too easy, and that parliamentary rules impede rather than expedite action and play into the hands of those who want only to cling to the status quo. Other weaknesses are peculiar to certain states: the length of sessions is unnecessarily restricted; salaries in many states are too low; the speakership is too powerful; and many legislatures lack the staff resources needed for policy making in today's complex society.

Many students of state government believe these structural or procedural inadequacies lessen the likelihood that state legislatures can perform their functions effectively. Low pay and short sessions, for example, are thought to guarantee too little deliberation on major issues. Lack of professional staff help leads, many feel, to an amateur committee system. On the other hand, "major reforms are likely" suggest two specialists in legislative studies, "to improve the quality of legislative life, making it a more desirable institution in which to work; to enhance the member's respect for the institution and to heighten their sense of political efficacy; to raise the attentive public's esteem for the institution; to increase the the legislature's effectiveness in overseeing the bureaucracy; to strengthen the legislature's position vis-a-vis the governor; to decrease its reliance on lobbies. . . ."[18]

IMPROVING STATE LEGISLATURES

Here are some specific recommendations made by one group of experts to improve legislative procedures in the states:

1. Constitutions should leave legislatures as unhampered as possible, encouraging the development of their own self-reliance. Limitations on a legislature's power to appropriate public funds, and to address itself to public questions, should be eliminated.
2. Use of popular initiative is inconsistent with representative government, except for the call of a constitutional convention.
3. Enactment of private bills, bills affecting few persons, local and special bills should be minimized.
4. As the principle of "one person, one vote" is applied, innovations in districting policies to improve patterns of representation should be devised and implemented.
5. State constitutions should provide for periodic reapportionment.
6. Adoption of a unicameral legislature may prove fruitful in some states. A small unicameral legislature may be especially appropriate in states where the cost of legislative operations is burdensome.

[18]William J. Keefe and Morris S. Ogul, *The American Legislative Process*, 4th ed. (Prentice-Hall, 1977), p. 454. For somewhat different interpretations, see Douglas C. Chaffey, "The Institutionalization of State Legislatures: A Comparative Study," *Western Political Quarterly* (March 1970), pp. 180–196; Leonard Ritt, "State Legislative Reform: Does It Matter?" *American Politics Quarterly* (October 1973), pp. 499–510; Albert K. Karnig and Lee Sigelman, "State Legislative Reform and Public Policy: Another Look," *Western Political Quarterly* (September 1975), pp. 548–52.

7. Legislatures should be of a small enough size to make the position of legislator more important and visible.

8. To develop more responsibility in legislative performance, and more independence, legislatures should be continuing bodies meeting in annual plenary sessions, without limitation of time or subject. Legislatures should be empowered to call themselves into session.

9. Competent professional staff should be provided the legislature, including staff for the leadership, both majority and minority.

10. State legislatures should utilize a strong system of standing committees, few in number, with broad, well-defined jurisdictions.

11. To expedite consideration of legislation, devices consistent with adequate opportunity for debate and deliberation should be adopted. These include electronic voting.

12. Codes of ethics should be adopted, applying to career, appointed, and elected officials, in all branches of state government.[19]

In the early 1970s, a group then known as the Citizen's Conference on State Legislatures used some of the standards contained in these recommendations to rank the fifty state legislatures.[20] They sought, for example,

[19]Alexander Heard, ed., *State Legislatures in American Government* (Prentice-Hall, 1966). See also Donald G. Herzberg and Alan Rosenthal, eds., *Strengthening the States: Essays on Legislative Reform* (Doubleday Anchor, 1972).

[20]Citizens' Conference on State Legislatures, *The Sometime Governments: A Critical Study of the 50 American Legislatures*, 2nd ed. (Citizens' Conference, Kansas City, Missouri, 1973), Chaps. 2–5.

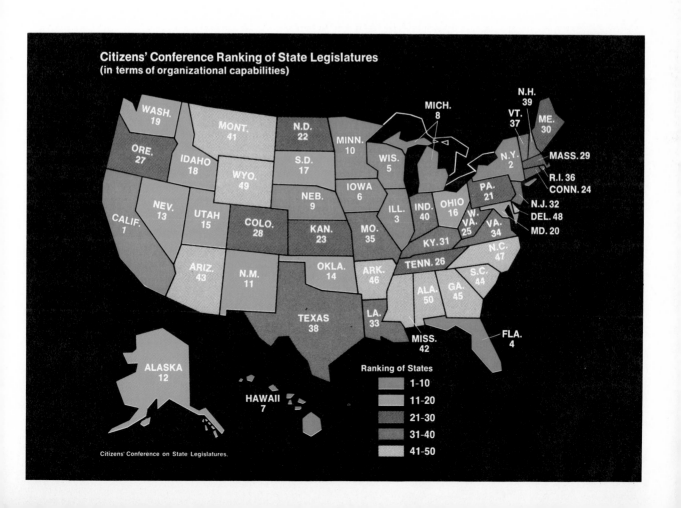

Citizens' Conference Ranking of State Legislatures
(in terms of organizational capabilities)

WASH. 19
MONT. 41
N.D. 22
MINN. 10
MICH. 8
N.H. 39
VT. 37
ME. 30
ORE. 27
IDAHO 18
WYO. 49
S.D. 17
WIS. 5
N.Y. 2
MASS. 29
R.I. 36
CONN. 24
NEV. 13
UTAH 15
COLO. 28
NEB. 9
IOWA 6
ILL. 3
IND. 40
OHIO 16
PA. 21
N.J. 32
DEL. 48
MD. 20
CALIF. 1
KAN. 23
MO. 35
W. VA. 25
VA. 34
KY. 31
N.C. 47
ARIZ. 43
N.M. 11
OKLA. 14
ARK. 46
TENN. 26
S.C. 44
ALA. 50
GA. 45
TEXAS 38
LA. 33
MISS. 42
FLA. 4
ALASKA 12
HAWAII 7

Ranking of States
1-10
11-20
21-30
31-40
41-50

Citizens' Conference on State Legislatures.

to measure how accountable, informed, independent, and representative each legislature was in relation to the other forty-nine states. Based on these measures, the California legislature ranked first, followed by New York and Illinois (see the accompanying map). Critics suggest that they used the California legislature as their model. In any event, this evaluation deals only with *structure* and *procedures*, and plainly does not rank the wisdom of their legislation. Evaluations of policy outputs, that is, what the legislatures enact and fund, are more interesting, but like evaluations of individual legislators, they often tell us more about the values of the evaluator than the performance of the legislator. Of course the fact that there are no objective standards to determine which policies are "best" is why we have democratically elected legislatures in the first place.

In recent years state legislators have sought to advance the effectiveness, independence, and accomplishments of the legislative branch of state government. Many of the recommended improvements of a decade or so ago have now been adopted in at least half the states. Thus, many legislatures now have longer sessions, more professional staff help, streamlined rules and procedures, fewer committees, and moderately increased salaries. About twenty states now employ joint legislative committees. More interstate cooperation has been brought about. Also, legislators in many states have taken advantage of the federal revenue-sharing program to broaden their scope of activities and expand their role in evaluating state and federal grant programs. In short, the largely amateur, part-time state legislatures of twenty years ago are being professionalized as their capabilities have been strengthened. All of this reflects a growing determination on the part of legislators—especially state legislative leaders—to be the bosses in their own houses.

TWO HOUSES OR ONE?

Bicameralism became the established pattern in the United States early in our history. During colonial days, the two chambers represented distinct interests—the upper house stood for royal authority, the lower house for the colonial cause. The desire to balance the aristocratic against the popular interest, and the belief in a government of checks and balances, led to the retention of bicameral legislatures after independence had been won. During the first decades of our republic, the requirements to vote for senator and the qualifications to serve in the Senate were stricter than those for the lower house. But by the middle of the nineteenth century, the same electorate was choosing the members of both houses. Today the two houses represent the same people (but usually in districts of different sizes). Why do we retain the two-house system? Is a "little U.S. Congress" structure really necessary at the state level?

Defenders of bicameralism insist that two chambers check hasty or ill-considered legislation. But, even in some states with two chambers, legislation is rushed through, especially in the closing days, with little consideration by either house. Sometimes the second chamber discovers errors in bills enacted by the other house and makes the necessary corrective amendments. Some bills proposed by one chamber are defeated by the other, but it is impossible to develop objective standards to determine whether the legislation so defeated was poor to begin with. Critics of bicameralism are persuaded that the governor's veto, the courts, and the electorate are better checks.

The case for a unicameral legislature has been made by those who feel that

1. A one-house legislature would be more efficient, avoid needless delays and duplication, and permit higher salaries.
2. A one-house legislature would permit the voters more knowledge about whom to blame and whom to credit and thereby increase accountability.
3. One strong, well-staffed house would be a more effective counterbalance to the governor.

George W. Norris, a longtime congressman and then U.S. Senator from Nebraska (1903–43) and the person most responsible for having his state adopt the one-house system in 1934, offered these two reasons for it:

> The legislature should be a business institution, with the state compared to a great corporation. The governor is its president; the legislature, the board of directors; the people, the stockholders. There is no more reason for a state to have a two-house legislature than there is for a bank to have two boards of directors or a city to have two boards of aldermen.
>
> The greatest evil of a two-house legislature is its institution of the conference committee. When a bill passes one house and is amended by the other, however slightly, it then must go to a conference committee, the source of numerous errors and frauds. And in this conference committee the "jokers" are placed in otherwise good laws. There the "bosses" and the special interests and the monopolies get in their secret work behind the scenes. There the elimination of a sentence or a paragraph, or even a word, may change the meaning of an entire law.[21]

Norris's arguments have been persuasive only in Nebraska, although good-government groups and some state conventions flirt with the idea from time to time. Nebraska voters appear satisfied with their forty-nine-person single-chamber legislature, but unicameralism attracts only limited interest elsewhere.

The case for the two-house legislature rests on these claims as well as on tradition:

1. A two-house legislature permits greater scrutiny of all new laws, reducing the chances of arbitrary or emotional action.
2. A two-house legislature provides for more access, more debate, and more representation of diverse points of view.
3. A two-house legislature makes it more difficult for any one person or interest in the state to dominate state decision making, for the chances are good that one of the houses will offer effective resistance.

Plainly, there are merits on both sides. But adoption of unicameralism is still viewed as a radical step. Moreover, it is a pretty safe bet that few state legislators will be attracted to a proposal that would put the majority of them out of office. In Nebraska, for example, before Norris's plan won at the polls, there were 33 senators and 100 house members. Afterward, there were just 49 senators. Reform action of this type would almost have to

---

[21]George W. Norris, *Fighting Liberal: The Autobiography of George W. Norris* (Collier Books, 1961), p. 343. See also the case for unicameralism made by Jesse Unruh, a former California Assembly speaker and the state's current state treasurer, in "Unicameralism—The Wave of the Future," in Herzberg and Rosenthal, eds., *Strengthening the States*, pp. 87–94. See also A. C. Breckenridge's evaluation of Nebraska's experience in *One House for Two* (Public Affairs Press, 1958).

come through the initiative petition (which we shall discuss at the end of this chapter). For as Norris points out, "Had we been forced to depend upon the submission of an amendment by legislative action in Nebraska, the plan never would have been submitted to the people."[22]

More hotly debated in the past twenty years than unicameralism versus bicameralism are the questions of how and on what basis legislators shall be elected.

The reapportionment revolution

One of the big issues of the 1960s was the battle over representation in the state legislatures, most of which gave to rural and smalltown voters more votes in the legislature than they would be entitled to on the basis of their share of the state's population. City officials complained bitterly that the smalltown and farm-dominated legislators were unsympathetic to their problems and were forcing rural notions of right and wrong upon them.

The complaint was an old one: George Washington Plunkitt, the Tammany Hall patriot of the turn of the century, charged in 1905: "Say, you hear a lot about the downtrodden people of Ireland. Now, let me tell you that they have more freedom and home rule than the people of this grand and imperial city. . . . In this state the Republican government makes no pretense at all. It says right out in the open: 'New York City is a nice big fat Goose. Come along with your carvin' knives and have a slice.' "[23]

The battle over reapportionment, however, was more complex than just a rural versus a city struggle. First of all, as the century proceeded, in many states the area that came to be most underrepresented was not the central cities but their suburbs. But even more to the point, many who live and do business within the city or live in its suburbs feel more akin politically with those who live on farms and small towns than they do with their fellow city dwellers. Many business interests located in cities nonetheless favored rural domination of the state legislatures because they felt that "cow country legislators" would be more responsive to their demands and less responsive to the social welfare schemes championed by many urban legislators.[24]

FEDERAL COURTS
TO THE RESCUE

But no matter how much they protested, those underrepresented in the state legislatures made little progress. Legislators from smaller towns and farmlands naturally did not wish to reapportion themselves out of a job, and their constituents did not wish to lose their influence. And even though the failure of state legislatures to reapportion often violated express provisions of state constitutions and raised serious questions under the federal Constitution, state and federal judges took the position that issues having to do with legislative districting were "political" and outside the scope of judicial authority. But there seemed to be no political remedy either.

Finally, the Supreme Court stepped in. In 1962, in the now famous case of Baker v. Carr, the Court held that voters do have standing to challenge legislative apportionment and that such questions should be considered by the federal courts. "Arbitrary and capricious" districts do deprive people of their constitutional rights and federal judges may take jurisdiction

[22]Norris, *Fighting Liberal*, p. 345.

[23]W. L. Riordon, *Plunkitt of Tammany Hall* (McClure, Phillips, 1905), pp. 38–39.

[24]Dean E. McHenry, "Urban vs. Rural in California," *National Municipal Review* (July 1969), p. 350.

over such cases.[25] *Baker* v. *Carr* started a small tidal wave. And in the years since, the following constitutional doctrines have been established.

In 1964 *(Wesberry* v. *Sanders)* the Supreme Court announced that as far as *congressional* representation is concerned, "as nearly as practicable one man's vote in a congressional election is to be worth as much as another's."[26] And in the same term it extended this principle to representation in the *state legislature*, although it has slightly modified it subsequently.

In *Reynolds* v. *Sims* (1964), the Court held that "the fundamental principle of representative government in this country is one of equal representation for equal numbers of people, without regard to race, sex, economic status, or place of residence within a state." This principle was applicable, in the court's view, not only to the *lower* house of the state legislature, which was usually based upon the population, but also to the *upper* house, where representation was often based upon area, such as counties or some other governmental unit. Defenders of this pattern had argued that so long as the lower house represented *population*, the upper house could represent *geographical units.* Look at the federal system embodied in the United States Constitution, they said. Is not representation in the United States Senate based upon area? Although many thought this to be a compelling argument, a majority of the Court did not. Chief Justice Warren explained: "Legislators represent people, not trees or acres. Legislators are elected by voters, not farms or cities or economic interests. . . . The right to elect legislators in a free and unimpaired fashion is a bedrock of our political system."[27] *The federal analogy, in short, does not hold.* Political subdivisions are not and never have been sovereign entities.

The constitutional requirement of one person, one vote has been extended to cover local units of government that exercise legislative functions, such as county commissions, city councils, junior college districts, and so on *(Avery* v. *Midland County,* 1968).[28] It has *not* been extended to cover judicial elections. States may continue to elect judges to multijudge courts from districts that are not based on the one person, one vote principle.[29] In addition, certain special purpose units of government, such as water control or irrigation districts, that perform limited functions affecting definable groups have been permitted to distribute votes according to the value of the land owned.[30]

Where the one person, one vote requirement does apply, the Supreme Court has been especially rigid about a state legislature's drawing of *congressional* districts. The legislature must justify any variance from strict mathematical equality among such districts by showing that it made a good-faith effort to come as close as possible to this standard. The desire to maintain specific interest orientations for particular districts, such as urban or rural, is no justification for a lack of mathematical equality; even a deviation of only 3.1 percent has been declared unconstitutional.

The Supreme Court is less insistent upon absolute equality as far as

---

[25] 369 U.S. 186.

[26] 376 U.S. 1.

[27] 377 U.S. 533.

[28] 390 U.S. 474.

[29] *Wells* v. *Edwards*, 409 U.S. 1095 (1973).

[30] *Associated Enterprises, Inc.* v. *Tolter District*, 410 US 743 (1973).

state legislative districts are concerned. The Burger Court has let it be known that it does not want to become "bogged down" in deciding state legislative reapportionment cases with "minor deviations."[31] But the requirement that the districts be established in accord with the one person, one vote principle remains. It does not make any difference that a majority of the voters in the state have specifically approved a constitutional amendment providing for the apportionment of one house of the state legislature by principles other than by population equality among districts: "an individual's constitutionally protected right to cast an equally weighted vote cannot be denied even by a vote of a majority of a State's electorate, if the apportionment scheme adopted by the voters fails to measure up to the requirements of the Equal Protection clause."[32]

The one person, one vote principle is applied less rigidly to local legislative bodies than it is to state or congressional legislative districts. At the local level "slightly greater percentage deviations" are tolerated in order to effect representation of distinctive units.[33]

UNANSWERED QUESTIONS

Even though the one person, one vote principle is firmly established, many other issues affecting the nature of legislative representation remain open. For example, in northern metropolitan areas, the most general pattern is for the core city to be Democratic and the surrounding suburbs Republican. If the legislative district lines are drawn like spokes from the central city to the suburbs, there will be fewer Republicans elected than if the district lines are drawn in concentric circles. It is possible to have multimember districts that are based on equal population but that, depending on how they are drawn, may over- or underrepresent minority groups or minor parties.

What of the use of racial or religious considerations in the drawing up of legislative districts? As we saw earlier, racial considerations are not per se — that is, automatically — unconstitutional. If district lines are drawn in order to protect the voting strength of blacks, and if they do not force white voters out of the process or unfairly minimize their voting strength, there is no constitutional violation. However, the Constitution does forbid the deliberate attempt to draw district lines in order to "impose a racial slur or stigma" or minimize the voting strengths of particular races or religions.[34]

CONSEQUENCES
OF REAPPORTIONMENT

In the more populous states of the North such as New Jersey, Michigan, Illinois, and New York, the suburban communities have gained legislative representation as the result of court-enforced reapportionment, at the greatest cost to rural districts, but at some cost to big cities. However, the traditional alliance between suburbs and rural districts against the big city appears to have been unchanged.

In the South, in such states as Georgia, Florida, and Tennessee (where Atlanta, Miami, and Memphis were so grossly underrepresented), reapportionment has had a dramatic impact. In Georgia it has increased the

---

[31]*Mahan* v. *Howell* 410 U.S. 315 (1973); see also Gordon E. Baker, "One Man, One Vote, and 'Political Fairness' — or How the Burger Court Found Happiness by Rediscovering *Reynolds* v. *Sims*," *Emory Law Journal* (summer 1974), pp. 701–23.

[32]*Lucas* v. *Forty-fourth General Assembly of Colorado* 377 U.S. 713 (1964).

[33]*Abate* v. *Mundt* 403 U.S. 182 (1977).

[34]*United Jewish Organization of Williamsburg, Inc.* v. *Hugh L. Carey*, 430 U.S. 144 (1977).

voice of Atlanta's citizens in the state legislature and provided opportunities for the election of blacks to that body. In Alabama, Birmingham and Mobile gained new political influence, and an alliance between these two cities could have a long-range impact on the politics of that state. In Florida, for the first time urban centers are the dominant voice in the legislature.

In the West, reapportionment seems to have had little impact, although it may be a factor in creating a more competitive two-party system in the more populous states such as California. "In Washington, reapportionment created the opportunity for change and the political actors have used that opportunity."[35]

Overall, the Democrats appear to be the net gainers from reapportionment.[36] It has tended to benefit suburban Republicans and city Democrats at the expense of rural Republicans in the North and rural Democrats in the South, with the effect of moving toward more competitive party systems in state legislatures.

What of the *policy* consequences of reapportionment? Many of its proponents were especially hopeful that it would lead to legislatures more sympathetic toward big-city people, more generous in support of the welfare, transportation, educational, and financial problems of the cities. It was also hoped that, with reapportionment, state aid and shared-tax formulas would be revised toward a more favorable distribution of state funds to the cities. Opponents of reapportionment were fearful that it would lead to a decline in the quality of legislators, an increase in taxation and spending, and a reduction of state support to rural areas.

So far neither the hopes of proponents nor the fears of opponents have been realized. In eleven states city officials feel their legislatures have been unaffected by reapportionment; in six states they are divided in their opinion; but in fifteen states they feel that their reapportioned legislatures are more sympathetic to their problems.[37] Studies of policies adopted by several state legislatures in the early 1960s failed to discover any correlation between legislative apportionment and welfare policies, distribution of state aid for public works, or support for education. Metropolitan and nonmetropolitan legislators seldom appeared to oppose each other in unified blocs. But the conditions of the early 1960s have been changed. Although it may be impossible precisely to correlate resulting policies with different patterns of representation, to alter the constituencies to which legislators are accountable is to make a major change in the political system. "Reapportionment is important on many scores, primarily because it eliminates *claims* of representative discrimination on the part of the urban areas, but it is not a panacea for the cities in their dealings with their respective legislatures."[38]

[35]James J. Best, "The Impact of Reapportionment on the Washington House of Representatives," in James A. Robinson, ed., *State Legislative Innovation* (Praeger, 1973), p. 180.

[36]Robert S. Erickson, "The Partisan Impact of State Legislative Reapportionment," *Midwest Journal of Political Science* (February 1971), pp. 57–71.

[37]Morley Segal and Lee Fritschler, "Emerging Patterns of Intergovernmental Relations," *The Municipal Year Book, 1970* (International City Management Association, 1971), pp. 34–35. See also Yong Hyo Cho and H. George Frederickson, "The Effects of Reapportionment: Subtle, Selective and Limited," *National Civic Review* (July 1974), pp. 357–62.

[38]Samuel K. Gove, *Reapportionment and the Cities: The Impact of Reapportionment on Urban Legislation in Illinois* (Loyola University Center for Research in Urban Government, Chicago, 1968), p. 34.

Direct legislation: policy making by the people?

Logos such as these reflect direct initiative measures by various interest groups to amend state constitutions. After a certain number of signatures are secured, the measure is placed on the ballot for approval or disapproval.

INITIATIVE

REFERENDUM

Does "We the People" mean the *people themselves* govern? Some of our states have given the people themselves the power to make their own laws. Around the turn of the century, one of the battle cries of the Progressive movement was to "return the government to the people" through the initiative, referendum, and recall. Give the voters the power to make or veto laws and to recall officials, they asserted, and the political machines will be destroyed and the special interests beaten. The Progressives had good reason to want to bypass their legislatures, for in several states the legislatures were indeed incompetent or under the domination of political machines. (The Southern Pacific Railroad's political machine in California had dominated the selection of state legislators and governors and United States senators for years.) The Progressives placed enormous trust in the wisdom of the individual and in the notion that voters would inform themselves about issues and make responsible decisions on a variety of policy questions put before them. Before we examine the experience of these direct democracy alternatives to the legislature, let us first describe them.

This procedure permits a designated minimum number of voters to propose a law that will be enacted if approved by a majority of the voters at a subsequent election. About twenty states, mostly in the West, authorize the making of laws by means of the initiative petition. In states like California, Oregon, Washington, and Colorado, the initiative has practically become a routine part of the legislative process.

The *direct* initiative applies in some states to constitutional amendments and to legislation; in some states it can be used for only one or the other. In a state that permits the direct initiative, any individual or interest group may, on their own initiative, draft a proposed law and file it with a designated state official—usually the secretary of state. The supporters have only to secure a certain number of signatures (often 5 to 10 percent of the total electorate), and then the measure is placed on the ballot at the next election for approval or disapproval.

In some states, the *indirect* initiative is used, which gives the state legislature an opportunity to act on the measure before it is referred to the voters. If the legislature enacts the measure without alteration, the law simply goes into effect. If the legislature does not approve, the proposed legislation is then placed on the ballot, although in some states additional signatures are required before it can be placed before the voters.

The referendum permits a majority of the voters to veto legislation or reject constitutional amendments. The referendum is simply a way of letting the people vote on proposed measures. It is required in every state except Delaware for the ratification of constitutional amendments. As applied to legislation, there are two general types of referenda, *mandatory* and *optional*. The mandatory referendum calls for a waiting period, usually sixty to ninety days, before legislation goes into effect. If during this period a prescribed number of voters sign a referendum petition requesting that the act be referred to the voters, the law does not go into effect unless a majority of the voters give their approval at the next election. The optional legislative referendum permits the legislature, at its discretion, to provide that a measure shall not become law until it has been approved by the voters at an election.

Although statewide referenda are used frequently in a few states, it is at the local level that referendum democracy flourishes. The annual volume of referenda presented to voters in school districts, cities, and counties, as well as states may run to several thousand, and many of these are on topics of considerable importance and heat—bonds for school buildings, fluoridation for water, the banning of bottles, restrictions on nuclear power facilities, and so on.

RECALL

Recall is the means by which the voters may remove elected public officials before the end of their terms. About twelve states provide for recall of state officers, but many others permit the recall of *local* officials. Recall also requires a petition, but more signatures are usually needed than in the case of the initiative and referendum. There are various kinds of recall election. In some, the official must stand on his or her record; in others, candidates are permitted to file and run against the incumbent.

In effect, the recall has the consequences of impeachment by the public. But in contrast with impeachment, there is no requirement that formal charges of wrongdoing be brought against the incumbent. Thus, recall permits throwing persons out of office merely because of policy differences; impeachment requires specific charges of wrongdoing. For recall voters must merely circulate their petitions and obtain the required signatures and the question gets put on the ballot. Recall is not used extensively at the state level, although when used it can lead to a bitter campaign. In the mid 1970s citizen groups tried in vain to recall Mayor Frank Rizzo of Philadelphia. In 1977 citizens in Madison, Wisconsin recalled a judge.

THE DEBATE OVER DIRECT DEMOCRACY

Political scientists differ, sometimes rather sharply, over the desirability of these direct legislation alternatives to reliance on representative government as manifested in state legislatures. The early opponents vehemently contended that direct democracy measures would undermine the legitimacy of representative government and also open the way for radical or special interest legislation. Critics of the initiative and referendum believe that the Progressives were overly idealistic and that these mechanisms would be used less as a citizen's weapon than as a vehicle for special interests. Only the well-organized interests, it was felt, could gather the appropriate signatures and mount the required media campaigns to gain victory.

There is some evidence that direct legislation, although championed as a liberal mechanism, has had conservative consequences. Thus, initiatives or referenda have been responsible for putting off busing and desegregation, delaying low-cost housing, and so on. It is generally thought that progressive reformers dealing especially with what might be called liberal issues—funds for schools, open housing legislation, metropolitan government and environmental efforts—are more likely to be successful before legislative bodies where the intensity of desires can be taken into account than through the devices of direct democracy. For issues such as civil rights, the referendum perhaps is becoming "an increasingly inappropriate political tool and process," for it fails to leave room, as does the legislative process, for calculation and compromise.[39] In effect, referendum results often mean total victory or total defeat.

[39]Raymond E. Wolfinger and Fred I. Greenstein, "The Repeal of Fair Housing in California: An Analysis of Referendum Voting," *American Political Science Review* (September 1968), p. 769. See also Howard D. Hamilton, "Direct Legislation: Some Implications of Open Housing Referenda," *American Political Science Review* (March 1970), pp. 124–37.

Critics of direct legislation also feel that the very fabric of legislative processes and representative government is at stake. To be sure, lack of faith in legislative bodies prompts the move to use the direct legislation devices. But it is an illusion, they say, to believe that the voter has the proper information to decide on countless complex, technical matters. The critics also suggest that the best way to restore faith in the legislature is not to bypass it, but to elect better people to it and rely on the deliberative processes and on their collective judgments. Three California political scientists point to yet another defect: "A disturbing feature of direct legislation—both the initiative and the referendum—is that it permits flashes of prejudice and emotion to sweep legislation onto or off the statute books. This is aided by the fact that sponsors can draft an initiative without being subjected to the modifying give-and-take normally involved in the legislative process. Moreover, the sponsors are not responsible for the political and social consequences of their proposals in the way elected officials are accountable to the voters."[40]

Still, for every critic of direct legislation, there are supporters of these policy-making-by-the-people options. Supporters argue that they have not given up on the legislative process. They only wish to employ direct legislation when legislatures prove unresponsive. Give us the opportunity, they say, if the legislature in our state won't act, of having our proposals debated in the open arena of election politics. Supporters further argue that the people *can* make decisions on complex and controversial matters. Thus, one scholar who has studied the initiative process questions the easy assertions about voter apathy, indifference, and susceptiblity. He reports that "recent California experiences with the initiatives suggest this may no longer be true. Clearly, poorly organized and less affluent California groups have been able to place measures on the ballot—the marijuana initiative, Proposition 18 in 1972; the coastal initiative, Proposition 20 in 1972; the environmental initiative, Proposition 9 in June, 1970; and others. Moreover, voters do not seem as easily misled by deceptive advertising as was once thought. In 1972 on a number of key initiatives, and in 1973 on Governor Reagan's tax initiative, the side with the most money actually lost. California's well-educated voters seemed far more able to cope with intricate initiatives than had been presumed by political scientists."[41]

Research on direct legislation as used in the state of Washington also provides support for the view that the initiative and referendum have worked pretty much as intended and can be useful additional channels for political expression. Bone and Benedict found that "Time and time again the sponsors have been ahead of the legislature. The initiative has been used to liberalize liquor laws, adopt daylight saving time, expand welfare benefits, authorize joint tenancies in property, protect game, advance and protect recreational opportunities, bring about reapportionment, and institute a number of government reforms including the state civil service, open meetings, and regulation of lobbying and campaign practices. "These supporters interpret their research findings by concluding that "the success at the polls of these measures and many others, often by large mar-

[40]Winston W. Crouch, et al. *California Government and Politics,* 6th ed. (Prentice-Hall, 1977), p. 127.

[41]Charles M. Price, "The Initiative: A Comparative State Analysis and Reassessment of a Western Phenomenon," *Western Political Quarterly* (June 1975), p. 260.

gins, can be interpreted to mean that the legislature was unresponsive to a widespread desire for these certain types of political change."[42]

Plainly, the experience suggests that neither the best hopes of the Progressives nor the worst worries of their critics have been realized. Yet, whatever the merits and desirability of the initiative, referendum, and recall, and the authors of this text disagree among themselves on this matter, it is apparent to all that there are severe limits to these mechanisms. They may be a cherished form of citizen-politics in those states that permit them, but they in no way replace a legislature. Representative government, especially the election of legislators, will continue to be the primary way for us to have our views regularly represented in state capitols, to enact our laws, and to make our public policy.

Summary

1. Americans greatly value the state legislature as a vital institution in our constitutional form of government, and yet they are invariably quick to criticize its imperfections. Perhaps we have overestimated the possibilities for responsive and representative legislatures. Or perhaps we make the legislatures the target of our complaints when the imperfections and the imperfectability of people are really at the heart of the matter.

2. The nation's more than 7,500 state legislators in the fifty states are called upon to represent our diverse views, to help formulate state public policy, to oversee the administration of state laws, and to help mediate political conflicts that arise in the state.

3. State legislators are asked to represent all the people in chambers that are constantly subjected to intense lobbying by organized interests. Lobbyists generally represent well-meaning interest groups but they often must express the most selfish aspect of the character of their clients. Often they are an important means of information. Sometimes the elected state legislator is the only effective representative and voice for the unorganized citizen. Many legislators feel this responsibility constantly and heavily.

4. Americans are demanding more of their state legislatures these days, Citizens turn to their state leaders for leadership in revitalizing the local economy, in conserving energy, in protecting the environment, and in bettering the quality of life. Increasing demands have been placed on the states by federal policies of revenue-sharing, which require states to provide more policy leadership both on a statewide basis and for cities and localities.

5. Legislative modernization is taking place in most of the states. The 1970s have witnessed a major wave of state political reforms and these have made most state legislatures somewhat more accountable and more prepared to do the public's business. Thus, most states now have some staff available to assist with their committee work. Most states now also have ethics commissions, open meeting laws, and many have reasonably good conflict-of-interest and financial disclosure laws.

6. Direct legislative procedures, especially the legislative or petition initiative, are an increasingly prominent part of the legislative process, especially in the West.

[42]Hugh A. Bone and Robert C. Benedict, "Perspectives on Direct Legislation: Washington State's Experience, 1914–1973," *Western Political Quarterly* (June 1975), p. 347.

Chapter 27

Governors: The Politics of Leadership

Nelson Rockefeller of New York, Ronald Reagan and Jerry Brown of California, James Thompson of Illinois, John Connally of Texas, Ella Grasso of Connecticut, and Jimmy Carter are national figures who have also been chief executives in their states. Governors are the most visible political figures in their areas. The chief executives of the larger states are usually national celebrities as well. President Carter is the first governor to be elected president since 1932, but the importance of the office as a launching pad for a national political career and as a forum for presenting policy views is well established. The great governors of earlier decades of this century—Theodore Roosevelt, Woodrow Wilson, Al Smith, Huey Long, Franklin Roosevelt, Robert LaFollette, Earl Warren, Adlai Stevenson—had a major impact on national politics. In the past twenty years or so, at least ten former governors have served in the national cabinet, two as vice-president, one as chief justice of the Supreme Court, and several dozen more in various judicial, subcabinet, or ambassadorial posts.

Today governors are expected to provide policy and administrative leadership. Even though only a few have as much constitutional power in their states as the president has in the national government, governors are judged by many of the same standards applied to presidents: Are their appointments good? Do they formulate policy effectively? Do they communicate their views forcefully? Are they able to get programs through the state legislature? Do they run honest and efficient administrations? Do they help raise the revenues needed to finance state programs? What of the tone and style of their leadership, of their relations with the people? In short, are they effective—do they know what needs doing and get it done?[1]

---

[1]John Bartlow Martin, *Adlai Stevenson of Illinois* (Garden City, N.Y.: Doubleday, 1976), p. 352. Chapters 6 and 7 of this volume present a detailed study of Stevenson as governor.

Before the American Revolution, the office of royal governor was deeply resented. At that time, the governor was appointed by the Crown and responsible to it, but he had broad veto powers over the actions of the colonial legislatures. As the Revolution neared, the governor became more and more unpopular with the colonists. The post-American Revolution office of governor was born in an atmosphere of distrust of a strong executive. The early state constitutions gave the governor few powers and in some instances even had his selection controlled by the legislature. Then, during the period of Jacksonian democracy (the 1830s), the idea spread that the voters should elect all top government officials, and the governor became only one of many elected officials.

Yet despite the suspicious environment in which the governorship was established, the demands of governing have gradually led to a strengthening of the role and authority of the governor, especially since the end of World War II. State constitutions have been changed to lengthen gubernatorial terms. As recently as 1950 nearly half the states had two-year terms for governors; now all but four have four-year terms. A decade or so ago many states forbade a governor from seeking immediate reelection; today only a few states do so. Twenty states have also strengthened the governorship by making the lieutenant governor run on the same ticket so that a governor is less likely to be faced with a hostile lieutenant governor. In most states governors have authority to restructure the state administrative machinery. Most important of all, in most states the governor presents the state budget to the legislature and controls spending after the budget has been approved. This means that state officials must look to the governor as well as the legislature for funds.

With more powers, governors of course also have more problems. This is especially true in recent years, as the states have taken on more responsibilities. At one time all the governor had to do was balance the state budget, make speeches about the virtues of the state, and criticize national officials, and a hostile mayor or two within the state. It was relatively easy to avoid hard decisions—or at least to postpone them. Not so today. Too many vital decisions were postponed. People now look to the governor for solutions and leadership. Governors can no longer merely preside; they must govern.

Becoming and remaining governor

Each state's constitution and laws spell out the rules for eligibility, tenure, and salary. In most states, to run for governor a person must be at least thirty years of age, a citizen of the United States, and a state resident for at least five years immediately preceding his or her election. The constitution typically reads: "The governor shall be elected, at the regular election every other odd-numbered year, by the direct vote of the people, for a term of four years beginning on the first day of January next following his election. Any qualified voter of the state who is at least thirty years of age shall be eligible to the office of Governor."

In practice, however, there are well-traveled career paths to the governor's office. Most governors begin their careers as lawyers and first win election to local office or as members of their state legislature. Two-thirds of the governors in the past fifteen years have been lawyers. Some, like Governors Thompson of Illinois and Teasdale of Missouri, won early visibility and reputations as hard-fighting prosecutors. The governors who are not lawyers usually have had prior business careers followed by service in the state legislature or in statewide elective or administrative posts. The most common career ladder to the governor's office is election to the state legislature followed by election to a statewide office such as attorney general, lieutenant governor, or secretary of state. But it is not unusual for a member of the national House of Representatives to run for governor. Governors Hugh Carey of New York, Ella Grasso of Connecticut, David Pryor of Arkansas, Edwin Edwards of Louisiana, and Pierre S. DuPont of Delaware typify this pattern.

Seldom does a person who has never held prior elective office become governor. When a newcomer to politics does win, the person has usually been given considerable publicity as a celebrity, as a well-known governmental advisor, or as a colorful maverick. Ronald Reagan, whose previous career had been as an actor and a television personality, is one example. Dixie Lee Ray, governor of Washington, also began her career in electoral politics at the top. But she had had a varied professional career mixed with considerable public service prior to becoming governor. She was a professor of marine biology for twenty-seven years at the University of Washington. During that time, she was a consultant to several levels of government. In 1972 President Nixon appointed her to the Atomic Energy Commission and she became chairman of that body the following year. Two years later she became assistant secretary of state of oceans and international environmental and scientific affairs. About a year later, she quit her post in protest and returned to Washington. Soon she was campaigning for governor. Her regular television appearances while she had been a faculty member at the University of Washington and her prominence as one of the nation's highest-ranking women officials helped her to overcome the "name recognition" problem that afflicts most new statewide candidates.

Governor James B. Longley of Maine, who was elected as an independent in 1974, is a most unusual case of a determined maverick who won a tight three-way race. Independent candidates, especially those who have never held any elective office, face the double problem of proving they can win, and proving they are not crackpots: "Longley overcame the first by the sheer intensity of the tide toward him, and the latter because he had built a personal reputation for years as a successful businessman and active civic leader. His striving for legitimacy was no doubt aided by the endorsement of the usually Republican *Bangor Daily News,* which has the largest circulation of any daily in the state. As another newspaper put it the day after election day, Longley was 'a *safe* maverick.' "[2] Longley's election bid was helped by his being a millionaire and by his strong stand against corruption in government, especially since he was running in the wake of the Watergate scandals. Longley had also served as chairman of the Maine Management and Cost Survey Commission, appointed by the previous governor to recommend budget cuts. "An idealist whose life might have been written by Horatio Alger, Longley was disappointed when the state's political leaders did not adopt many of his commission's recommendations, so he resolved to take his case directly to the voters. Campaigning on the slogan 'Think About It,' and hitting hard at the issue of budget-cutting, Longley" started slowly but pulled ahead of the Democrat and the Republican in the closing days of the race. He carried his home coun-

[2]Howard L. Reiter, "Who Voted for Longley? Maine Elects an Independent Governor," paper delivered at the 1975 Annual Meeting of the Northeast Political Science Association, New Brunswick, N.J., November 1975, p. 17.

ty, he picked up support from those who had voted for one of the losers of the Democratic gubernatorial primary. He also did well among ticket-splitters and high-income voters who were apparently ready for a change of pace in Maine.[3]

GOVERNORS ON
THE SPOT

Once elected, governors generally enjoy high visibility in their states. Most states boast an executive mansion. Salaries range from a high of $85,000 in New York to a low of $10,000 in Arkansas, with the average being about $40,000. In addition, most governors receive an expense allowance.

But just as governors have become increasingly important in recent years, they have also had to work between rising aspirations and the scarcity of resources. People want better schools, highways that do not require taking any land or spoil the environment, adequate welfare programs, aid to local school districts, civil rights and safe streets, clean air and streams. But they do not want higher taxes. The mid and late 1970's has been a period of austerity for most states, and the governors often are caught in the middle. Said Ella Grasso of Connecticut: "We can dream dreams, but if we can't pay the bill, we can't have new programs. The art of the possible makes it very difficult to be innovative."[4] Said Jerry Brown of California: "I'm trying to get everyone to realize that, yes, we may have to have money for more programs, but each item is in competition with another."[5]

Many governors complain, sometimes bitterly, that federal grant-in-aid programs, federal guidelines, and federal formulas shape so much of their activities that in many areas of public policy there is almost nothing left for them to decide. They would prefer to have the federal government give more dollars to the states, but give them without strings. Even more, the governors want federal dollars to be given to agencies that they control rather than directly to mayors, city councils, school boards, or welfare agencies. In short, most governors complain that they are faced with a whole range of problems, all of which they are expected to solve, yet few of which are within their authority. A governor "is forced to fight on all fronts—and is expected to emerge victorious" whether it is to prevent disorder at the state university, keep taxes from rising, decrease the rate of unemployment, or revitalize the state's economic climate.[6]

[3]*Ibid.*, p. 5.

[4]Ella Grasso, quoted in *The New York Times*, January 26, 1976, p. 38.

[5]Jerry Brown, quoted in *The Wall Street Journal*, February 24, 1976, p. 29.

[6]J. Stephen Turett, "The Vulnerability of American Governors, 1900–1969," *Midwest Journal of Political Science* (February 1971), p. 109.

Robert Grossman, *Mother Jones*, July 29, 1976. Reprinted by permission.

Plainly, governors have become a major political power in most states. They have also acquired the liabilities that come with the assets. One of the assets is likely reelection. At least in recent years, two-thirds of the governors who have sought reelection have won. Most elections for governor are now scheduled for nonpresidential election years. Reformers have successfully argued that presidential and gubernatorial elections should be separated so that governors are not subject to the tides of national politics. It may be that this alteration in the schedule of elections helps explain why incumbent governors are more likely to be reelected.

But not everyone is reelected. And incumbents often believe that to run after four years of making decisions and thereby gaining opponents is no advantage at all. Arkansas Governor Winthrop Rockefeller, defeated for reelection in 1970 by a "country lawyer," said of his opponent's strength: "He was new. He was fresh. He had no record." Massachusetts' Governor Francis Sargent blamed his 1974 defeat on the price of hamburger, meaning that inflation and soaring prices made people angry at incumbent politicians that year. Governor "Kit" Bond of Missouri blamed his surprise defeat in 1976 on his opponent's last-minute "negative" television advertising. His opponent, Bond said, made "appealing promises to lower or at least hold the line against utility increases and promised to stop increasing taxes for the working people and put more taxes on the corporations."

Most practical politicians believe that a governor who proposes new taxes will face the wrath of voters on election day. But studies by political scientists cast some doubt on this idea. Although defeated governors often claim that they lost because they had to raise taxes, "a governor who does not propose new taxes and new programs is often subject to a new-politics or issue-oriented campaign. And some governors have gone down to defeat this way."[7] The record indicates that "Voters will often bear taxes when they are convinced of the value of state services, just as they will often reject state services when they appear wasteful."[8]

Although there may be no inevitable punishment at the polls for raising taxes, if governors believe this is so they will ordinarily do everything to avoid it. The problem, however, is more complicated. Governors are "damned" if they do nothing, yet "damned" if they do the wrong thing. As Gerald Pomper puts it: "In state politics, governors have discretion to limit or raise taxes and spending, as their conception of the public's needs and desires indicates. The electoral consequences are uncertain, depending on the governors' commitments, the voters' changing concerns, and the quality of party competition."[9]

From a national perspective, one of the main political values of winning governorships is the development of national party leaders and officeholders. Republicans have recently had a difficult time winning governorships, especially compared to their much greater success a decade or more ago. As of 1978, Democrats controlled about three-fourths of the governors' offices. If the trend continues, it could further weaken the capacity of the Republican party to recruit leaders for national office.

[7]Thad Beyle and J. Oliver Williams, eds., *The American Governor in Behavioral Perspective* (Harper & Row, 1972), p. 31.

[8]Gerald Pomper, "Governors, Money and Votes," *ibid.*, pp. 63–64.

[9]Pomper, "Governors, Money and Votes," p. 64.

A governor's formal powers

"The executive power," says the federal Constitution, "shall be vested in the President of the United States." Compare this flat statement with its match in a typical state constitution: "The executive department shall consist of a Governor, Lieutenant Governor, Secretary of State, Treasurer, Attorney General," and perhaps other officials. In other words, the state governor shares executive power with other elected officials. Most state constitutions go on to say that "the supreme executive power shall be vested in the Governor, who shall take care that the laws be faithfully executed." And it is the governor to whom the public looks for law enforcement and the management of sprawling bureaucracies.

Governor Samuel W. Pennypacker, Pennsylvania's chief executive from 1903 to 1907, once told how he had come to office eager to ensure that the laws of the state were faithfully executed. Looking around to see what tools he had to carry out this responsibility, he discovered that the only persons to whom he could look for help were his secretary, the janitor, and his chauffeur. The prosecutors and police, locally elected and locally controlled, were subject to little or no gubernatorial supervision. The attorney general was elected independently by the voters and was not responsible to the governor. Of course, the governor could call out the National Guard, but that is a clumsy way to enforce the law. "So," said Governor Pennypacker, "I created the state police." Today all states have a police organization. In some states the governor has been given authority to supervise the activities of local prosecutors. Even so, most governors must rely on a variety of formal, informal, and *ad hoc* powers to see that "the laws be faithfully executed."

Exactly what powers does the typical governor have? That's a difficult

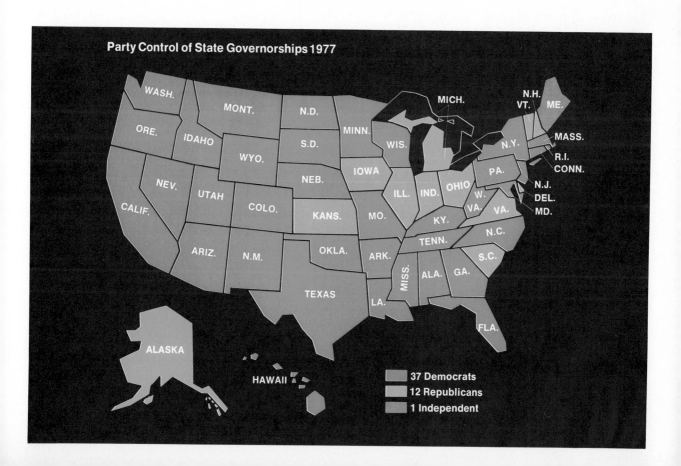

Party Control of State Governorships 1977

37 Democrats
12 Republicans
1 Independent

question to answer, for the powers of a governor vary widely from state to state. (See one attempted ranking of the formal powers of state governors, Table 27–1.) Moreover, the resources of governors inevitably depend on their capacity to persuade people to cooperate. This, in turn, usually depends on their reputation, their popularity, their knowledge of what should be done, and, of course, their ability to communicate clearly.

27–1
Rankings of states according to the formal powers of the governor (Based on budget powers, appointive powers, tenure potential, and veto powers)

Strong	Moderately strong	Weak
New York	North Dakota	Iowa
Illinois	Kentucky	New Hampshire
Hawaii	Virginia	Rhode Island
California	Montana	New Mexico
Michigan	Nebraska	North Carolina
Minnesota	Connecticut	Mississippi
New Jersey	Delaware	Indiana
Pennsylvania	Oklahoma	Florida
Maryland	Alabama	South Carolina
Utah	Wisconsin	West Virginia
Washington	Colorado	Texas
Massachusetts	Louisiana	
Ohio	Georgia	
Wyoming	Oregon	
Missouri	Nevada	
Alaska	Arizona	
Tennesse	South Dakota	
Idaho	Maine	
	Vermont	
	Kansas	
	Arkansas	

SOURCE: Adapted from Joseph A. Schlesinger, "A Comparison of the Relative Positions of Governors," in Thad Beyle and J. Oliver Williams, eds., *The American Governor in Behavioral Perspective* (New York: Harper & Row, 1972), p. 149.

Still, most governors have the following powers they can put to use in an effort to govern:

1. Appointive powers
2. The power to prepare the state budget
3. The right to help establish the legislature's agenda
4. Ordinance-making power or executive order powers
5. The power to command the state National Guard
6. The power to pardon or grant clemency
7. The right to veto legislation

Let us look briefly at each of these powers.

APPOINTIVE POWERS

Perhaps a governor's most important power is to recruit people to head the state's departments, commissions, and bureaus. Many governors now have a cabinet of advisors and major administrators. The recruitment of effective persons to this inner circle is plainly a real opportunity for a governor to provide direction for state government.

Some governors can appoint hundreds of key officials in their administration; others, such as those in Mississippi, South Carolina, Ari-

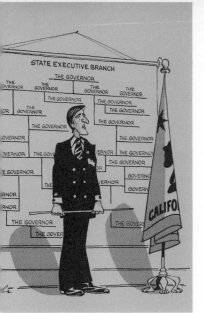

"I will explain our decision-making process . . ."

Renault, *Sacramento Bee*

zona, and Texas, have great restrictions on their appointive powers.[10] The governor is still one executive among many, with only limited authority over statewide *elected* officials. Governors neither appoint them nor can they dismiss them; if they are political enemies, they will not accept a governor's leadership. Governors have greater but still limited power over *appointed* administrative officials.

In most states, too, governors must share the appointive power with the state senate and may remove people only when they have violated the law or failed in their legal duties. There are some signs that the growing professionalism of state administrators whose programs are largely supported by federal funds is giving them a measure of independence from the governor and greater loyalty toward their counterparts at the national level than toward other state officials.

Three other problems face many governors in the use of their appointive powers. First, salaries are very low in many states, especially the smaller ones, and it is often hard to get people to leave better-paying jobs in private industry. This situation is even worse when the state capital is in one of the more remote or rural sections of the state. Second, the leadership in some state legislatures often demands that their friends be appointed to certain top posts in the state's executive branch. They will threaten to be uncooperative if the governor doesn't go along with some of their "suggested" nominees. Finally, turnover is relatively high in many state positions, and this often hampers a governor's efforts to carry out programs.

FISCAL AND BUDGETARY POWERS

A governor's fiscal or budgetary powers are potentially a key weapon in getting programs underway. In most states the governor now has nearly full responsibility to prepare the budget and present it to the legislature:

[10]See the discussion in Joseph Schlesinger, "The Politics of the Executive," in H. Jacob and K. N. Vines, eds., *Politics in the American States: A Comparative Analysis* (Little, Brown, 1965), pp. 227ff.

Gov. Dixie Lee Ray of Washington State; Governor Jay Rockefeller of West Virginia and Mrs. Rockefeller at the polls; Governor Richard Snelling of Vermont and Mrs. Snelling arriving at White House dinner; Governor James Thompson of Illinois delivering inaugural address.

Budget making involves bringing together the requests of all existing state agencies, calculating the costs of new state programs, estimating the probable income of the state, and evaluating these costs and income estimates in the light of program and policy objectives. The final budget document is submitted to the legislature for its adoption as an appropriations measure. No state monies can be spent without a legislative appropriation, and the legislature can make any alterations in the state budget it sees fit. Potentially, then, a legislature can control any activity of the state government through its power over appropriations, but as a practical matter, the legislature seldom reviews every item of the governor's budget. In practice, budgets tend to reflect the views of those responsible for their preparation, namely, the governor.[11]

Plainly, then, a governor who has control over the budget and uses this power effectively has a most important asset. This is even more true in states where governors can use the item veto; in such states they can control the flow of funds to the executive departments and thus shape their activities. "Without a favorable recommendation from the governor, an agency is unlikely to enjoy any substantial increase in its appropriations," although this is less true for agencies headed by elected officials.[12] Purchase, fiscal, and personnel matters, moreover, are frequently centralized under the governor. When implemented by a strong staff and backed by a strong political base, governors' fiscal powers are probably among the most important they have.

Fiscal problems, however, differ from state to state and from decade to decade. In the late 1970s, for example, most of the industrial states in the Northeast have been faced with serious unemployment, high welfare costs, and general fiscal trouble. They have been forced to take tough austerity measures that many legislators, party leaders, and interest group leaders found difficult to accept. On the other hand most of our oil- and food-producing states are doing much better. Texas in 1977 had a $3 billion surplus. The fiscal challenge there was not where to find money to spend, but how to spend wisely.

Budgeting problems for most states change over time. The 1960s and early 1970s saw new taxes and a high growth economy push up revenues so governors and legislatures could cut up an increasingly large budgetary pie. In the late 1970s, most states face tight money, high inflation, and pressing demands for new programs and expansion of existing activities. Now there is a new set of fiscal decisions. Where to cut? What are the tradeoffs? Governors Dukakis of Massachusetts, Brown of California, Carey of New York, and Lamm of Colorado, all of whom were elected as liberals or progressives, have chosen when in office to act as fiscal conservatives. Governor Dukakis, for example, often campaigned with pledges to increase services and lower taxes, only to find that once in office he seldom could do both and often could do neither.

[11]Thomas Dye, *Politics in States and Communities*, 3rd ed. (Prentice-Hall, 1977), pp. 176–77.

[12]Ira Sharkansky, "Agency Requests, Gubernatorial Support and Budget Success in State Legislatures," *American Political Science Review* (December 1968), pp. 1226, 1231. See also Thomas J. Anton, *The Politics of State Expenditures in Illinois* (University of Illinois Press, 1966), and Allen Schick, *Budget Innovation in the States* (Brookings Institution, 1971).

VETO POWERS

In all states except North Carolina, governors have relatively strong veto powers, usually much stronger than those of a president. In all but six states, the governor has, in addition to the regular qualified veto, the power to strike out — that is, *item veto* — individual items in appropriations measures while approving the rest. In a few states, the governor can even reduce a particular appropriation. The item and the *reduction veto*, like all vetoes, can be overridden by the legislature (normally the item veto by a two-thirds or three-fifths vote in both chambers, the reduction veto by a majority vote), but in many states most new laws and appropriation measures are sent to the governor after the legislature has adjourned. When a governor vetoes bills or items of appropriations, there is less chance for the legislature to override the veto. As state legislatures reassert their roles vis à vis the governor, just as Congress is doing with the president, they have adopted measures to allow the legislature to call itself into special session to reconsider a governor's vetoes. And now several states have established the veto session, a short session following adjournment so that the legislature can reconsider all measures vetoed by the governor.

Another interesting variation is the *amendatory* or *conditional* veto (which about fifteen states have) that allow governors to return a bill to the legislature with suggested changes or amendments that they want incorporated in it. The legislators must decide whether to accept the governor's recommendations or attempt to pass the bill in its original form over veto.

EXECUTIVE ORDERS

One of the long-standing powers of governors is their authority to issue executive orders that have the force of law. These differ from statutes or formal acts passed by the legislature, but they have almost the same binding effect.

Why do governors have this quasi-legislative power? Because state legislatures often pass highly general — some would say vague — laws, giving a governor or other executive officials authority to fill in the details. Thus, "When the legislature enacts a law providing for payments of state funds to local school districts, it may specify that state payments shall be conditional upon the maintenance of school standards to be established by the governor or one of his subordinates."[13] Sometimes the executive ordinances supplementing a law are both more detailed and more important, because the legislature has passed only a skeleton or outline of a law.

But just as Congress has become more assertive in recent years, so state legislatures have now enacted provisions for more supervision by the legislature of the rules and regulations issued by executive agencies. They want to see to it that what they intended to have done is in fact what is done.

COMMANDER IN CHIEF OF THE NATIONAL GUARD

Emergencies add to the authority of the executive, for they call for decisive action. The governor is commander in chief of the state's National Guard when it is not in federal service. The governor is responsible for using this force when local authorities are inadequate — in case of riots, floods, and other catastrophes. Hardly a year goes by in which the National Guard of some state does not see emergency duty. In most states, the state police are also available for emergencies.

[13]Austin F. MacDonald, *American State Government and Administration* (Crowell, 1948), p. 211.

The national government has the major responsibility of providing for national defense, but a governor is authorized to ensure public safety in times of emergency—for example, to regulate supplies of fuel and electric power and to issue orders for air raid protection. The civil defense program places the major responsibility on the states, and in almost all cases the states have turned the job over to the governor. Governors are normally advised by a civil defense council, which help them supervise and coordinate the civil defense activities of local government.

THE PARDON POWER

In half the states, governors have the pardoning power; in the others, they share this duty. Those who have violated state law look to the governor "to temper justice with mercy." The governor may, except in cases of certain specified crimes or in cases of impeachment, pardon the offender, commute a sentence by reducing it, or grant a reprieve by delaying the punishment. The governor is normally assisted by pardon attorneys or pardon boards who hold hearings and sift the evidence to determine whether or not there are reasons for a pardon. But it is the governor who has the responsibility for the decision. Many stories were told of governors keeping all-night vigils when men or women were condemned to death. With the reimposition of capital punishment the governor as the last judge has a task that few would envy.

POLICY-MAKING INFLUENCE

How much policy-making influence do governors have? Although their constitutional authority varies a good deal from state to state, their actual ability to influence legislative policy varies even more widely from state to state and from time to time than a reading of the constitutions might suggest.

Obviously governors may send messages to their legislatures and may argue for their programs. In some states they can trade appointive jobs for legislative support. They may use their veto powers to trade for votes. They can usually attract more public attention to their views than may any single legislator. But being the spokesperson for policy does not guarantee success. Much depends on a governor's ability, political base, personal popularity, and the political situation in which he or she operates. Some states have a long tradition of executive leadership. When governors have the support of powerful political organizations, they can guide policy. The governors of New York and Illinois, for example, have strong constitutional positions, and they are also likely to have party organizations behind them and close ties with their followers in the legislatures.

But even in states where governors are less likely to be national figures, they may derive power from a large popular following or a strong party organization. The governor of Mississippi has much less formal power than the governor of New York, and on the national political scene carries little weight. Yet within the state, his control over minor jobs, contracts, and patronage may make him a important figure. The governor of New York must operate through more formal machinery in a complex state containing many power sources able to compete with him on his own terms. Few governors of New York have ever been able to dominate their state legislature to the same extent as some of the formally weak but politically powerful southern governors.

Balanced against all these formal powers are great obstacles in the way of a governor. Among these can be a hostile legislature, a depressed economy, corrupt party or administrative officials, regional tensions in the state (downstate vs. upstate, or urban-rural splits), special interests and their lobbyists, a cynical press, an indifferent or apathetic public, the sheer inertia of what critics call "the vast immovable inherited bureaucracy of government," antique civil service systems, and the reluctance of most good individuals to care enough to get involved in state politics and government.

Ella Grasso of Connecticut probably spoke for many governors when she talked of her battles with the Connecticut state legislature: "I feel we are weathering the storm . . . I'm listening to their constituents. And if they were, we would be on the same wave length. [But] there is a very well developed sense of independence in the Assembly."[14] Pennsylvania's Milton Shapp has blamed the federal government for many of his problems and those of his neighboring governors: "Our problems do not stem from excess liberalism, dunderheaded state and local officials or businessmen hobbled with anti-business laws. [No, the chief culprit is] a misguided federal policy that has moved poverty from the rural South northward [and caused federal funds] to flow toward the Sunbelt." Governor Shapp adds, "There has been a diabolical political conniving in Washington against the Northeast. . . . Defense Department plans for construction this year allocate only $52 million to the Northeast and Mid-Atlantic states, out of a total of $1.6 billion."[15]

Governor Jerry Brown of California complains that the job of leadership in the states is a near-impossible one because no matter how much money is spent, or how many speeches are given, it seems to him that the problems keep outrunning the solutions. Brown concludes that merely because there's a problem does not mean governors or their advisors know what to do about it. Here is a typical Brown statement:

> The liberalism of the 60's is dead. The fact that there's a problem doesn't mean that more government will make it better. It might make it worse. The interventionism that we've seen in our society is analogous to Vietnam. With our money, power, and genius, we thought that we could make the people over there like us. Then we did the same thing to our cities. When problems don't go away we escalate the attack until someone gives up. I'm rethinking some of that escalatory social interventionism. Inaction may be the highest form of action.[16]

Thoughts like this recall the old saying that *the definition of a conservative politician is one who is currently in office.*

Plainly, governors today must be diplomats, negotiators, political-coalition builders, crisis managers, and much else. Much of their success depends on the support they can muster from their party, their friends, and the allies they can get among interest groups. The capacity to persuade

**Governor Edmund G. Brown
of California discusses
correspondence with his office
personnel at the Capitol.**

[14]Grasso, *The New York Times*, p. 38.

[15]Milton Shapp, quoted in *National Journal*, November 27, 1976, p. 1696, p. 1698. See also, on the sunbelt thesis, Kirkpatrick Sale, *Power Shift* (Random House, 1975). For a useful study of the increased role governors must play as representatives of their states in Washington, see Donald H. Haider, *When Governments Come To Washington: Governors, Mayors and Intergovernmental Lobbying* (Free Press, 1974).

[16]Governor Jerry Brown, *Thoughts* (City Lights Books, 1976), p. 56.

people, to think clearly and persevere are obvious assets — but even these will not guarantee success.

Although most scholars agree that governors are the most important policy leaders in the states, they differ over how much they can actually do. Some claim that social and economic conditions really determine both how much money is available and how it gets spent in the states. In fact, they say, governors have little leeway in budget and policy determination. Governors often come into office hoping to begin new programs but find they spend most of their time raising money just to keep things going. "Governors may be regarded as 'money providers' or as 'budget balancers'; only infrequently can they be viewed as 'decision makers' in the determination of state expenditures."[17]

Sara McCally Morehouse calls this the "counsel of despair": her research shows that a governor's "ability to provide political leadership will affect the quality and distribution of public policy. . . . The governor's role as leader of his political party has an important impact on the quality and distribution of policy. The coalitions that he forms within his political party aid him in putting into effect the policies that he desires." At any rate, governors will promote policies regardless of their success in getting everything they want. Morehouse is doubtless correct when she concludes that "The importance of an understanding of gubernatorial leadership cannot be exaggerated."[18] States will be playing a larger not a smaller role in planning and administering a wide range of social and economic programs. The ability of each governor is clearly important as a factor permitting states to solve problems and improve the quality of life.

Managing the state

Most governors come to office with no broad philosophy of management. They are usually pragmatic lawyers, handling each issue as it comes up, deciding it on its merits and then delegating the administrative responsibilities to their staff or department heads. Together the governors and their staffs must perform a whole range of functions, not all of which may be handled well.[19] These include such jobs as the following:

Changing or initiating policy
Maintaining a policy or a position under pressure
Settling disputes among different agencies or factions within agencies
Marketing
Recruiting
Allocating resources

In practice, most governors see their managerial duties as "unsexy" and as the least glamorous of their responsibilities. Many may like to give

[17]Thomas J. Anton, "Roles and Symbols in the Determination of State Expenditures," *Midwest Journal of Political Science* (February 1967), p. 34. See also Dye, *Politics in States and Communities*, pp. 178–79.

[18]Sara McCally Morehouse, "The Governor as Political Leader," in H. Jacobs and K. Vines, *Politics in the American States*, pp. 239–40.

[19]Martha W. Weinberg, *Managing the State* (MIT Press, 1977), p. 24. This is an excellent analysis of how one governor, Francis Sargent in Massachusetts, attempted to "manage" four major departments during his administration, 1969–75.

speeches and attend dinners and parades. And many others much prefer crisis management or the promotion of new programs to the day-to-day work of keeping government moving. But governors can hardly ignore their function as the state's chief executive. Voters expect their governors to make programs run more efficiently, to modernize governmental structure, and to be responsible for the approximately 3.2 million state employees throughout the nation. Of course, the style and quality of leadership varies from governor to governor and from state to state. Management can also vary greatly from one agency to another. And different kinds of programs demand different kinds of management. Martha Weinberg of MIT notes four kinds of state agencies in Massachusetts according to the ways in which some governors deal with them:[20]

1. Those agencies requiring constant scrutiny; e.g., Departments of Corrections and of Public Welfare
2. Those agencies that receive constant scrutiny because of the personal preferences of the governor; e.g., Department of Mental Health
3. Those agencies that receive gubernatorial attention because of a single crisis; e.g., Department of Community Affairs
4. Those agencies the governor leaves alone; e.g., Housing, Finance Agencies

Governors have also had to become more and more involved in grantsmanship, and in the planning and coordinating of federal grant-in-aid programs. The federal government has passed much legislation since the mid-1960s that specifically designates the governor as the chief federal planning and administrative officer in the state. Some examples are the Omnibus Crime Control and Safe Streets Act, the Economic Opportunity Acts, the Comprehensive Health Planning Act, the Land and Water Conservation Act, and regional development programs. This new role has led to more flexibility and more headaches for governors. On the one hand, it provides a governor with a new form of patronage—services and programs for influential professionals and local government communities. On the other hand, this new intergovernmental relations role requires more time, more staff, and constant negotiations both with the "feds" and local and interest group leaders who always want a bigger share of whatever money or services may be involved.

THE INFLUENCE
OF GOVERNORS ON STATE
AGENCIES

Governors are clearly the most important influence on most state agencies. In a survey of nearly 1,600 heads of state departments and administrative agencies, Deil S. Wright found that these senior state public servants looked upon the governors as the most important managerial and policy-

[20]*Ibid.*, pp. 66–70.

**27–2
Comparison of
gubernatorial and
legislative
influence on
agencies**

	Governor	Equal	Legislature
Who exercises greater control over your agency?	46%	26%	26%
Who exercises more detailed review of agency budget?	34	31	31
Who is more likely to reduce your budget requests?	30	23	41

Note: N = 1581.

SOURCE: Adapted from Deil Wright, David Kovenock, and Associates, *Assessing the Impacts of General Revenue Sharing in the Fifty States: A Survey of Administrators* (Chapel Hill: Institute for Research in Social Science, University of North Carolina, 1975).

making influence on their agencies. But state legislatures and interest groups also have significant power. (See Tables 27–2 and 27–3) Depending on the agency, a governor may well have to be careful to exert equal influence.

Plainly, agencies are not always responsive to their governors. Public agencies exist in a political climate that sometimes encourages them to be more responsive to interest groups, to the legislature, or to their own definitions of the public interest. Should all agencies be accountable to the governor all the time? Some reformers have long thought so. Others feel that we should examine the given task or tasks of an agency and ask: "How far should it be removed from having to respond instantly to public

**27–3
Comparison of
various influences
on agency
decisions**

	High	Moderate	Slight	None
Governor	50%	29%	12%	6%
Legislature	32	43	18	5
Client-interest groups	9	41	37	10

Note: N = 1581.

SOURCE: Adapted from Deil Wright, David Kovenock, and Associates, *Assessing the Impacts of General Revenue Sharing in the Fifty States: A Survey of Administrators* (Chapel Hill: Institute for Research in Social Science, University of North Carolina, 1975).

opinion or to a governor's perception of public opinion? What questions should be left in the hands of the political system, the electorate, and the governor to be 'managed' and which ones should be delegated to professional managers who are not directly accountable to any part of the political system?"[21]

MODERNIZING STATE
GOVERNMENT

Another important development giving the governor more of an impact on state government is the application of modern management techniques to state administration: planning, systems analysis, computers, zero-base budgeting. In fact, the whole modern system of professional management is gradually replacing the old back-scratching or buddy system of getting the state's business done.

The trend toward integrated administration is still strong. In the urban states with a competitive party system such as New York, Illinois, New Jersey, Pennsylvania, Washington, and California, governors have considerable formal constitutional authority. Even in more rural places such as South Dakota, there has been considerable streamlining of the executive departments, with hundreds of agencies consolidated into six comprehensive ones as the result of an executive order of the governor. But integrated administration is by no means an accomplished fact.

The wave of state reorganizations that followed World War I was repeated after World War II with a push from the national Hoover Commission —

[21]Weinberg, *Managing the State*, p. 227. For a classic study of what might best be called a charismatic state bureaucrat who achieved extraordinary independence from several governors as well as the state legislature in New York, see Robert A. Caro, *The Power Broker: Robert Moses and the Fall of New York* (Knopf, 1974).

a government modernization group led by former President Herbert Hoover. Most of the states appointed their own "Little Hoover Commissions" to recommend improvements in governmental structures. Their attempts to reorganize the state governments have not received universal praise. In many states, the commissions get together, make studies, and submit reports that are soon filed away and forgotten. Groups that profit from the existing structure—for example, those who have a pet bureau under their influence—can be counted upon to resist changes, and so can officials who fear loss of job or prestige. Legislators who suspect that recommendations will make the governor too powerful are often reluctant to approve them. And politicians who have lived within the existing structure and know their way around in it are naturally unwilling to give up a good thing.

Another group of critics opposes not so much the idea of reorganization as the basic principle that has dominated the movement. This is the principle of *executive power and responsibility*. During the past several decades, reorganizers have campaigned for the proposition that the governor should be made the manager of the executive branch. They have developed the following principles of reorganization.

1. All agencies should be consolidated and integrated into as few departments as possible, so that similar functions will be grouped together and the governor will be able to exercise real control.
2. Lines of responsibility should be fixed and definite.
3. Single-headed executives are to be preferred to boards and commissions.
4. The governor should have power to appoint and remove subordinates, including officers now elected, with the possible exception of the auditor.
5. The governor should have control over budgeting, accounting, reporting, purchasing, personnel, and planning, and should have the staff he or she needs to do these jobs.

But some critics, though they agree that centralized budgeting, purchasing, and the like are all good ideas, argue that conditions differ in each state and that no one pattern will fit all conditions. There is little evidence, they argue, to support these proposals except the opinions of the reorganizers themselves. What evidence do we have, they ask, that the people will hold the governor accountable and that the governor will devote time and energy to administrative matters? Most governors are chiefly interested in legislative problems, not in administrative details, and are seldom judged on their executive ability. There is a real danger that the reorganizers are overlooking basic values in their concern with saving money. As one critic put it: "Men invited to recommend a program which promises efficiency and economy for a state . . . have failed to warn their clients . . . of the enormous risk involved in creating a powerful chief executive in a state which has no responsible legislature and in many instances no effective opposition party."[22]

The reorganizers are quick to answer their critics. Of course it is ridiculous to make changes, they grant, without regard to local conditions and problems. But the basic idea—integrated authority, centralized direction,

[22]C. S. Hyneman, "Administrative Reorganization: An Adventure in Science and Theology," *Journal of Politics* (February 1939), pp. 74–75. For another presentation of this view, see Robert B. Highsaw, "The Southern Governor—Challenge to the Strong Executive Theme," *Public Administration Review* (Winter 1959), pp. 7–11.

simplified structure—is sound. There would be little danger of dictatorship. In fact, it is more likely that individuals not responsible to the voters will take over government when the administrative structure is cumbersome, confusing, and too spread out. The legislature can more effectively supervise an administration integrated under the governor's control than one in which responsibility is split.[23] In states where the governor's formal authority is not strong, special interests have found it easier to dominate administrative programs than in states where executive authority is strong.

EFFECTS OF REORGANIZATION

What have been the results of a half-century of reorganization? Some observers say that reorganization has not given us more efficient or democratic government. Others say it has. Still others say there is little evidence one way or another. Often the reorganizations result only in changes in organization charts but have no significant impact on actual operations. Large savings have been realized through centralized purchasing and the adoption of modern money management practices, but it is difficult to measure the results of the consolidation of departments, the creation of a governor's cabinet, establishment of an ombudsman office, or the strengthening of the governor's control over the executive branch. At the same time, the best-governed states do seem to be those in which the administrative structure has been closely integrated under the governor. Whether this integration has *caused* good government in those states is another, though closely related, question.

The basic idea of reorganization is to apply what we know to improve what we have. But to make reorganization pay the biggest dividends, it must be a continuous process. Recently some states (Michigan, Illinois, and Alaska) have recognized this truth and adopted reorganization procedures similar to the ones usually in effect on the national level. The governor is granted authority to submit to the state legislature reorganization proposals that if not disapproved within a certain period are automatically put into effect.

The reorganization of state administrative procedures is almost always justified in terms of efficiency and economy. Few would deny the importance of saving money, but it is doubtful that the costs of operating our state governments can be substantially reduced except by reducing their functions. Saving money and increasing efficiency are important, but these are not the only objectives of government nor the only standards for judging its operations. The question must always be: reorganization for what? Not merely to save money, but to serve public needs.

Overall formal reorganization is not the only way states modify and modernize their governmental structures. They often change piecemeal, copying innovations from other states. Certain states, in fact, serve as exporters of innovations. So is the federal government when it creates a department of housing and urban development, states often respond by creating departments of community affairs; when the federal government establishes a department of transportation, so do several of the states.

Other statewide elected officers

In many states the other executive officials elected by the people include the lieutenant governor, secretary of state, attorney general, treasurer, and auditor (see Table 27–4). What do they do?

[23]Coleman B. Ransone, Jr., *The Office of Governor in the United States* (University of Alabama Press, 1956), pp. 378–86.

Governor	50
Lieutenant governor	41
Attorney general	39
State treasurer	37
Secretary of state	37
State auditor	25
Superintendent of education	18
Controller	10
Agriculture commissioner	8
Public utilities commission	6
Insurance commissioner	5

SOURCE: *Book of the States, 1976—77*
(Council of State Governments, 1976),
pp. 114–15.

New York Governor Hugh Carey
delivers his "state of the state"
message, flanked by aides (rear
row, second from left) Assembly
Speaker Stanley Steingut,
Comptroller Arthur Levitt,
Lieutenant Governor Mary Ann
Krupsak, Attorney General Louis
Lefkowitz, and Senate Majority
Leader Warren Anderson.

The *lieutenant governor* often does very little. (An exception: the Texas lieutenant governor is sometimes as politically powerful as the governor.) In some states a lieutenant governor presides over the Senate, and, in case of the death, disability, or absence of the governor from the state, becomes governor or acting governor. The nine states that do not have a lieutenant governor do not seem to suffer any loss. Since the lieutenant governor is sometimes leader of a party faction different from that of the governor, and is occasionally even a member of the opposition party, he or she may become a thorn in the side of the chief executive. To try to avoid this, twenty states now provide for the election of the governor and lieutenant governor as a unit.

The *secretary of state* publishes the laws, supervises elections, and issues certificates of incorporation. In some states the secretary issues automobile licenses and registers corporate securities. This office is often the dumping ground for jobs that do not seem to belong to any other office and are not important enough to justify setting up a new agency. Yet several secretaries of state in recent years have begun modernization efforts in voter registration processes or have sponsored campaign finance and disclosure reforms. Several governors gained important statewide political visibility while serving as secretary of state, most notably Jerry Brown, Ella Grasso, and Jay Rockefeller.

The *attorney general* is the state's lawyer. He gives advice to state officials, represents the state before the courts, and supervises local prosecutors. Some attorneys general have real authority over local prosecutors and may prosecute cases on their own initiative. The office is often a steppingstone to the governorship, and occasionally attorneys general have made political capital out of their investigations of the state administration, or their pro-consumer litigation efforts.

The *treasurer* is the guardian of the state's money. Although in some states the job is largely ministerial, state treasurers generally have the vital responsibility to ensure that cash is available to meet obligations of the state and that all available funds are invested to maximize return.

The *auditor* has two major jobs: to authorize payments from the treasury and to make periodic audits of officials who handle state money. Before money can be spent, the auditor must sign a warrant certifying that the appropriation is authorized by law and that money is available in the treasury. This is the *pre-audit*, which many observers believe should be given to a comptroller appointed by and responsible to the governor. The auditing *after* the money has been spent, however, is a job that most believe should be given to an officer responsible to the legislature. The auditor is the one official who, even in the opinion of some of the most extreme advocates of centralized administration, should not be responsible to the governor.

As part of the trend toward integrated administration, the duties of elected state officials have generally been limited to the functions specified in the constitution, with the more important functions given to officials appointed by the governor. The budget directors and agency chiefs under the governor in many states have more important roles than the state treasurer or the secretary of state. Yet elected officers can often control patronage, attract a following, and thus develop a political base from which they can attack the governor's program and administration.

Disputes between attorneys general and governors can be political (different parties or conflicting ambitions), but they also can be over issues. So governors in many states have staff lawyers or hire a lawyer to work for them in a fight with the state's lawyer.

Some of the most progressive and controversial initiatives in state governments come from the other state constitutional officers. Attorney General John Hill in Texas helped design and pass the Texas Open Records Act, one of the broadest and most strictly enforced freedom-of-information statutes in the country.[24] Secretary of State Paul Guzzi in Massachusetts has modernized election laws, helped enact campaign finance laws, and championed conflict of interest reforms. State Treasurer Sam Brown of Colorado battled to transfer some of his state's revenue deposits from a few large Denver banks to smaller banks around the state. Brown also devised incentives for these banks to stimulate lending for student and small business loans and for low-income housing and family farms.

Can anyone really succeed in the job of governor? Many do not. But not long ago, Governor Daniel J. Evans of Washington state retired after an unusually successful twelve years in that office. He established an effective cabinet system, reorganized his executive branch, pressed for tax reform, helped enact pioneering environmental protection statutes, led other governors in strengthening the role of governors in national policymaking, governed for twelve years with a scandal-free administration, and pushed a variety of actions to involve the public in government. He set up a number of state intern programs and arranged numerous ways for young people to work part time in local service organizations, akin to Peace Corps work for minimal stipends.

In a program called Alternatives for Washington, his administration "invited the people themselves to set goals and priorities for the state's future development. In the past four years, over 100,000 Washingtonians have been suggesting and evaluating various options—through citizen task forces, local meetings, exhaustive mail and phone surveys, and other devices.

'THANKS DAN EVANS/JOB WELL DONE' says a bumper sticker distributed by some of the governor's friends here. It's a sentiment that can be echoed by many Americans grateful for politicians who really try to make government work."[25]

---

[24]Richard Hall, "State Government All-Stars," *The Washington Monthly* (September 1975), p. 47.

[25]Alan L. Otten, "Job Well Done," *The Wall Street Journal*, October 14, 1976, p. 22.

Summary

1. One of the strengths of the federal system is that the states can act as laboratories of democracy, testing ideas which, if successful, could be copied on a national level. So also the states are the testing place for many of our national leaders.

2. The job of the governor is one of the most difficult in American politics. Governors are usually lawyers, male (there are two women governors today), and middle-aged. Their chances for reelection are good, but their chances for accomplishing what they set out to do are nearly always overestimated by everyone—governors included. They have many formal powers. The most important are their budgetary and appointment powers. But a governor's formal powers will mean little if he or she is not naturally endowed with persuasive ability, as well as good judgment and the capacity to think clearly.

3. A governor is expected today to be the chief state policy-maker, the architect of the state budget, the chief manager of the state administration, and the political and symbolic leader in the state. Today, the governor also plays an increasingly complex role as the crucial link between the national and local governments. In short, governors are asked to be virtual miracle workers in this era of scarce resources and rising demands.

Chapter 28

Judges and Justice in the States

We hear more about the activities of federal judges, but it is the 1,200 state and municipal judges who actually do most of our judicial business. They preside over most of the criminal trials, settle most of the lawsuits between individuals, administer most of the estates. They interpret state constitutions and apply state laws, and from these interpretations ordinarily there is no further appeal. Of course, state judges must follow the federal Constitution, federal laws, and federal treaties "any Thing in the Constitution or Laws of any State to the Contrary notwithstanding." If in handling cases, state and local judges have to interpret what the federal Constitution, a federal law, or a federal treaty means — that is, if the case raises a federal question — that matter may be appealed from the state to the federal courts.

Most people know little about their state judges. They may not even know the name of the chief justice of their own supreme court. But these judges, perhaps even more than those of our federal courts, are important policy makers.[1] The legislature passes a law, but it is the judges who interpret it. State judges play a vital role in determining who gets what, where, when, and how. Judges make public policy. Nowadays state and local judges are coming in for closer attention not only because we have recognized their policy-making importance, but also because they are central links in the justice system, along with police, prosecutors, parole and probation officers, and correctional officials. And in not the least of their roles,

[1]Kenneth Vines and Herbert Jacob, "State Courts and Public Policy," in Herbert Jacob and Kenneth Vines, eds., *Politics in the American States* (Little, Brown, 1976); Kenneth Dolbeare, *Trial Courts in Urban Politics: State Court Policy Impact and Functions in a Local Political System* (Wiley, 1967); Henry Robert Glick and Kenneth Vines, *State Court Systems* (Prentice-Hall, 1971); and James R. Klonoski and Robert I. Mendelsohn, eds., *The Politics of Local Justice* (Little, Brown, 1970).

these judges help to settle the thousands of legal disputes between individuals ranging from divorces, through disputes over wages, to arguments about who was at fault in automobile accidents.

In this chapter we shall look at state and local courts first as policy-making agencies of state governments, and then as part of the justice system. Our focus will be on the courts, but we will also look at some of the closely related parts of the whole system of justice.

The shape of state courts

Each state has its own court system. These fifty systems vary, so that it is difficult to generalize about them. But for convenience, we may classify state courts into three categories: minor courts of limited jurisdiction, general trial courts, and appellate courts.

MINOR COURTS

Minor courts handle misdemeanors, that is, the less serious violations of local and state laws, and civil suits involving relatively small amounts of money. In some places they are also given the responsibility for holding preliminary hearings and setting bail for more serious charges. Decisions of these courts may be appealed and in most instances tried *de novo* — that is, tried all over again without reference to what happened in the minor court. In most places, these courts are financed and administered by the local unit of government — the township, the city, the county — but in some states the state governments have taken them over completely.

In cities, minor courts are known as municipal courts and often are divided into traffic courts, domestic-relations courts, small-claims courts, and police courts. These courts are likely to be presided over by paid magistrates trained in the law. In rural areas, the justice of the peace system still survives, although in many places the JPs are being stripped of more and more powers. The justice of the peace, like so many of our political institutions, was inherited from England. King John promised his barons in 1215 in Magna Carta that he would not "make men justices . . . unless they are such as know the law of the realm and are minded to observe it rightly." But many Englishmen were not then, and are still not now, persuaded that only those who are lawyers know the law. They saw no need to go to London or some other city just to take care of a minor legal dispute. They preferred to settle such matters in the neighborhood and to have them settled by neighbors in as easy, quick, and cheap a way as possible. To this day, lay magistrates are used more often in England than in this country to hear minor offenses, sometimes by themselves, sometimes serving with law-trained judges.

In this country nonlawyer judges, most of whom are justices of the peace, are under increasing attack. In a few states the courts have even gone so far as to declare such judges unconstitutional. It makes little sense, it is argued, to insist that everybody be represented by an attorney if the judge that hears the case has no legal education, and in some instances no formal education at all. The Supreme Court has not gone so far. It has ruled that at least in states where a defendant has a right to a new trial, he may first be tried in a court presided over by a lay magistrate.[2] But the Supreme Court ruled some time ago that it is a denial of due process if the magistrate who hears the case has his salary paid from fines collected by his court. More recently, the Court has held it violates due process if the mag-

---

[2]*North* v. *Russell*, 427 U.S. 328 (1976).

istrate is a mayor responsible for village finances whose court fines go into the village treasury.[3]

Justices of the peace are elected for a short term, most commonly from two to six years. Their authority is limited to performing marriages and notarizing papers, handling traffic violations, and hearing misdemeanors, usually those involving fines of less than $200. They also hear minor civil disputes. Since plaintiffs often have their choice among several justices of the peace in a county, they may pick the one most likely to decide in their favor. So it has been said that JP stands for "Judgment for the Plaintiff."

How does the JP system operate in practice? Sir Dennis Brogan, a celebrated English student of American politics, wrote of one of his adventures in America:

A justice of the peace is elected for a short term. His or her duties usually include performing marriages, notarizing papers, and handling misdemeanors.

> I had often heard of the "Jeddart justice" doled out by rural magistrates to motorists, of the iniquities of paying magistrates on a commission basis, of the insult to the law and its majesty which these methods involved. My host, whose car was moving rapidly down the great highway to the warm sun and true spring of Central Illinois after the rain, fog, and cold of the shores of Lake Michigan, had written on the subject. He had been the pupil and the collaborator of one of the greatest of American constitutional lawyers. His opinion was worth having. A car was backed off the road and a policeman signalled us in. I innocently assumed that there had been an accident, that we were being asked to take someone to hospital. How wrong I was! We were pinched for speeding. The traffic cop's not very smart uniform bore the words "Special Police." He had cartridges on his belt; they were of different colours and may have been dummies, but he was in complete command of the situation. He demanded the license which was fortunately available. He gave instructions. "Turn round and stop at the grocery store." "Can I make a U-turn?" asked my host ironically. "Sure." We entered the grocery store, and there was American justice at the receipt of custom.
>
> The magistrate was a bronzed jurist in a shabby shirt. He had one arm and no badge of office. This was not the Old Bailey. The representative of the "Senatus Populusque Illinoisensis" required no fasces, no mace to impress his customers. He duly pointed out that the accused could claim a jury trial, but that if he didn't, and pleaded guilty, the whole thing could be expedited.
>
> The policeman's complaint-sheet was produced; a conviction for speeding was duly entered in it; a receipt (a flimsy piece of paper) was issued. Ten dollars fine, $4 costs (which we believed went to the jurist). In two minutes it was all over. After all, there were other customers. My friend had "a record"; for the first time in his life he had been in an American police court.
>
> In a famous opinion Mr. Justice Frankfurter had laid it down that a court of the American system was not to be compared to the court of a Cadi sitting down under a tree. There was no tree, simply a third-rate village store. I recalled Mr. Frankfurter's dictum to my friend. He was not consoled. He thought of various points he might have made. The "esprit d'escalier" worked overtime. He recalled what he had written on

---

[3]*Tumey v Ohio*, 273 U.S. 510 (1927); *Ward v. Village of Monroeville*, 409 U.S. 57 (1972).

this aspect of the American judicial system. I tried to console him by pointing out that he had got down from his ivory tower as the song suggested. He was not amused. He had got out of the ivory tower all right, but as another song puts it, "Baby, it's cold outside."[4]

Unfortunately, this story is too typical of the way justice is administered in our minor courts. Of course, there is another side to the story. A basic principle of justice—the separation of the prosecuting from the judicial function—was observed. The fine was not out of proportion to the offense. Appeal to a higher court was allowed if desired. To be sure, the whole proceeding was informal and undignified, but great dignity and formality would have meant a more expensive court and probably higher costs for the defendant, or at least the taxpayers.

With the reduction of much of the work of many of the lay magistrates or their replacement by salaried and legally trained judges, criticism these days is directed more at the administration of justice in the minor courts of our large urban centers. Here the judge is a lawyer. Those accused of crime probably receive help from a public defender if they are unable to afford their own lawyer. But court calendars are so crowded that the cases are "processed" with little time for individual attention. Poor and ignorant defendants often spend days in jail waiting for their cases to come to trial. Although the fines may be small and the sentences less than a year, there is a growing concern and criticism about the operation of these courts.

A new and apparently effective reform is the establishment of "court-watching" groups. In some cities, these groups are sponsored by organizations like the American Civil Liberties Union, which is concerned with whether our courts are treating those charged with crimes fairly. In other cities the groups are sponsored by organizations concerned with whether judges are too easy on defendants. Whatever the reason, when a group of middle-class and relatively prominent citizens take turns watching the courts and reporting back their impressions, the public gets a look at what is otherwise likely to be a closed transaction among professionals. Prosecutors, public defenders, and judges too often become a comfortable "in group" with little or no public scrutiny. Court watchers make these professionals more sensitive to the views of the general public, since they know that what they are doing will be more widely reported.

TRIAL COURTS

Trial courts with complete original jurisdiction are variously called county courts, circuit courts, superior courts, district courts, and common pleas courts. They administer equity, criminal, common, and statutory law. Some states maintain separate courts for criminal and civil matters. More commonly, there are special probate courts to administer estates and to handle related matters. Although decisions of the general trial courts may be reviewed by appellate courts, in practice the trial court usually has final say.

The following story as related by Harry W. Jones shows the importance of trial courts in the administration of justice:

[4]"Down from the Ivory Tower," *Manchester Guardian Weekly* (May 31, 1956), p. 11. See also Isham G. Newton, "The Justice of the Peace—An American Judicial Dilemma," *Social Science* (April 1959).

A certain Bishop of Paris, known throughout Europe for his great learning and humility, came to the conclusion that he was unworthy of his high place in the Church and successfully petitioned the Pope for reassignment of service as a simple parish priest. . . . After less than a year of parish work, the former bishop was back in Rome with another petition, this one praying for his restoration to episcopal status, and for good and sufficient reason. "If I am unworthy to be Bishop of Paris," he said, "how much more unworthy am I to be priest of a parish. As bishop, I was remote from men and women of lowly station, my shortcomings and weaknesses concealed from them by distance and ecclesiastical dignity. But as a parish priest, I move intimately each day among the members of my flock, endeavoring by comfort, counsel and admonition to make their hard lot on earth seem better than it is. I *am* the Church to them; when my faith flags or my wisdom fails or my patience wears thin, it is the Church that has failed them. *Demote* me, Your Holiness, and make me bishop again, for I have learned how much easier it is to be a saintly bishop than to be a godly priest."

The trial judge is the parish priest of our legal order. The impression that prevails in society concerning the justice or injustice of our legal institutions depends almost entirely on the propriety, efficiency, and humaneness of observed trial court functions.[5]

APPELLATE COURTS

In most states, appeals from the trial courts are carried to the state supreme court, but twenty-five states have set up intermediate appeals courts that fit into the court structure in much the same way that the United States courts of appeals fit into the federal structure.

The court of final resort is usually called the supreme court. (In New York, the supreme court is a trial court, and the court of last resort is called the Court of Appeals.) Unless a federal question is involved, the state supreme courts are the highest to which a case may be carried.

The appellate courts of last resort vary from three to nine judges in membership, with seven being the most common number. State judges have the power of judicial review and may refuse to enforce state laws on the grounds that they violate the state or national constitution. They may also declare federal laws unconstitutional, although of course such decisions are subject to final review by the United States Supreme Court. All state judges take an oath to uphold the supremacy of the federal Constitu-

[5]Harry W. Jones, ed., *The Courts, the Public, and the Law Explosion* (Prentice-Hall, 1965), p. 125. See also David Neubauer, *Criminal Justice in Middle America* (General Learning Press, 1974).

Justices of the Oregon Supreme Court (sitting, from left) Justice Ralph Holman, Chief Justice Arno Denecke, Justice Thomas Tongue (standing, from left), Justices Berkeley Lent, Edward H. Howell, Dean Bryson, and Hans Linde.

tion, laws, and treaties, despite anything in their own constitutions or laws.

Some states permit the supreme court to give *advisory opinions* to the legislature or the governor upon request. Except in Colorado, these advisory opinions are not binding; they are regarded as opinions of the judges rather than as court decisions.

The judges

HOW ARE JUDGES CHOSEN

Judges are selected in four different ways. Popular election is used in about three-fourths of the states. Of these states, some have a nonpartisan primary for nominating and a nonpartisan ballot for electing judges; some elect judges on a separate day from other officers. In other states—primarily Eastern ones—judges are appointed by the governor (with the consent of the senate or executive council). In a few New England states the legislature elects the judges. California, Missouri, and other states have a modified appointment plan for some or all of their judges.

The modified appointment plan as used in Missouri, after which it is known, provides that whenever a vacancy occurs in a court to which the plan applies, a special nominating commission, composed of three lawyers elected by the bar, three citizens appointed by the governor, and the chief justice, nominates three candidates. The governor selects one, who then serves as a judge for at least a year. At the next general election the voters are asked, "Shall Judge———be retained in office?" If a majority assent, the judge gets a full new term; if not, another person is selected by the same procedure. At the end of his term, the judge does not have to be

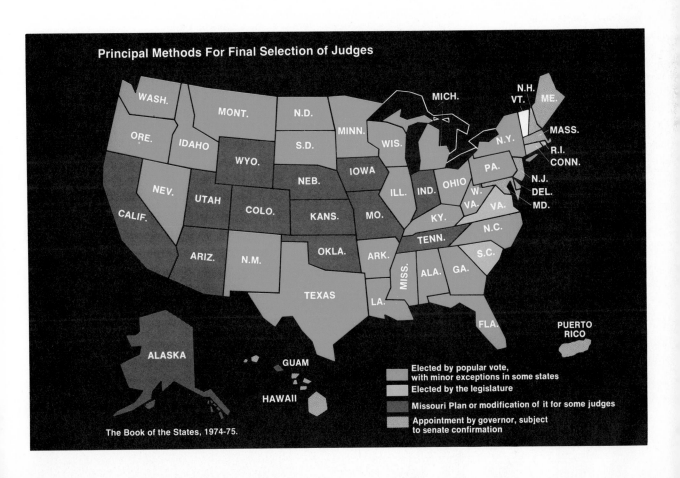

Principal Methods For Final Selection of Judges

Elected by popular vote, with minor exceptions in some states

Elected by the legislature

Missouri Plan or modification of it for some judges

Appointment by governor, subject to senate confirmation

The Book of the States, 1974-75.

renominated and reappointed. He merely certifies his wish to have his name placed on the ballot, and the voters are asked whether they want to retain him in office.[6]

Those who favor the appointive method argue that voters are not competent to assess legal learning and judicial abilities. Popular election, they assert, puts a premium on personality, requires judges to enter the political arena, and discourages many able lawyers from running for the office. Further, they insist, judges are often in effect appointed by party leaders despite the elective apparatus. Many lower court judges gain and retain office because of prior faithful party service. At the appellate level the governor often makes an interim appointment to fill vacancies created by resignation, retirement, or death of a sitting judge, and the appointee usually wins at the next election. In fact, more than half of all judges sitting on elective courts of last resort came there as appointees of the governor.[7]

Those who oppose the appointive system argue that the problem is not one of party but of *politics*. Judges should be accountable directly to the people. The governor's appointing them divorces them from the electorate, gives the governor too much power, and encourages them to become the governor's servants.

The dispute over the merits of appointive versus elective systems of judicial selection has continued for two hundred years. Yet only recently have we had any precise studies of what difference, if any, it makes in the decisions judges issue and the opinions they write. Even here we have to be highly tentative. But this is what we have found so far:

Chief Justice Virgil L. Kirk of the Tribal Courts of an Arizona reservation.

1. "Elected and appointed judicial systems do not differ as much in their results . . . as the debate literature would have us believe. . . ."[8]

2. The Missouri Plan as it has operated in that state has not eliminated partisan politics in the selection of judges, but it has altered the nature of the politics. It has "taken the partisan aspects of judicial selection out of the vortex of local political forces and leadership influence and projected them into the political world of the highest public official in the state."[9] There appears to be no difference, however, between the kinds of decisions made by judges selected through the Missouri Plan and those made by judges elected to office.

3. Partisanship may be dampened down through appointment: Studies indicate that Democratic judges tend to make more liberal decisions than do their Republican colleagues. These studies also show a less significant correlation between prior party affiliation and judicial voting in states with appointive judges than in states in which judges are elected.[10]

[6]Richard A. Watson and Rondal G. Downing, *The Politics of the Bench and the Bar: Judicial Selection under the Missouri Nonpartisan Court Plan* (Wiley, 1969), p. 13.

[7]James Herndon, "Appointment as a Means of Initial Accession to Elective Courts of Last Resort," *North Dakota Law Review*, XXXVIII (1962), 60–73; Emmett W. Bashful, *The Florida Supreme Court: A Study in Judicial Selection* (Florida Bureau of Governmental Research and Service, 1958); Kenneth N. Vines, "The Selection of Judges in Louisiana," in Vines and Jacob, *Studies in Judicial Politics* (Tulane Studies in Political Science, Volume VIII Tulane University, 1963), pp. 99–119; and Bancroft Henderson and T. C. Sinclair, *The Selection of Judges in Texas: An Exploratory Study* (Univ. of Houston Public Affairs Research Center, 1965).

[8]Stuart S. Nagel, *Comparing Elected and Appointed Judicial Systems* (Russell Sage, 1973), p. 36. Contains excellent bibliography.

[9]Watson and Downing, *The Politics of the Bench and the Bar*, p. 353.

[10]See footnote 19 in Sheldon Goldman, "Voting Behavior on the U.S. Courts of Appeals Revised," *American Political Science Review* (June 1975), for a review of the articles on the importance of partisanship and judicial behavior.

4. Courts to which judges are nominated and elected on a nonpartisan ballot show less partisan division than do those where judges are nominated by party conventions and elected in nonpartisan elections. Courts where judges live and work together in the same city show less partisan division than courts in which judges do not come together for deliberation or voting.[11]

5. State court judges, compared with those of the Supreme Court of the United States, tend toward unanimous decisions. This unanimity of decision making appears to be unrelated to the manner of judicial selection.[12]

At the moment about all we can say with assurance is that leaders of lawyers' groups tend to favor the appointive method. Yet there is little evidence that the method of judicial selection makes a real difference in the kinds of judicial decisions made.[13]

HOW JUDGES ARE JUDGED

Unlike federal judges who hold office during "good behavior," state judges are elected or appointed for fixed terms. But it is the states rather than the federal government that have taken the lead in establishing procedures to judge the judges in one manner or another. These procedures have been established because impeachment has been an ineffective and inappropriate means to remove unqualified judges. In most states there is a board, a commission, or a court to handle judicial discipline. Commissions are usually composed of lawyers and nonlawyers, despite the judges' objection to involving nonlawyers. The commissions investigate complaints and hold hearings for judges who are charged with improper performance either as a result of mental or physical disabilities or unethical or unfair conduct.

Some object to judicial disciplinary procedures on the ground that they undermine the independence of the judiciary so vital to the proper administration of justice. Those who think these procedures are necessary quote approvingly Philip Kurland, who wrote: "The provision for securing the independence of the judiciary was not created for the benefit of the judges but for the benefit of the judged."[14] And the general opinion among judicial reformers is that the growth of these commissions has helped to restore public confidence in the state judiciary.

The judicial reform movement

For the last half-century or so, and with a quickening pace in recent decades, judicial reform groups have been working to "institutionalize a broad range of structural and management improvements." As public criticism of and concern about the "crime problem," and about court delay has grown, a variety of reforms have been proposed. Many have been adopted. Here is what most reformers favor:

1. Judges should be selected by some kind of system that screens them in terms of

[11]David N. Adamany, "The Party Variable in Judges' Voting: Conceptual Notes and A Case Study," *American Political Science Review* (March 1969), pp. 72–73.

[12]Burton M. Atkins and Henry R. Glick, "Environmental and Structural Variables as Determinants of Issues in State Courts of Last Resort," *American Journal of Political Science* (February 1976), p. 97.

[13]Herbert Jacob, *Justice in America* (Boston: Little, Brown, 1965), pp. 206–7; Edward N. Beiser," A Comparative Analysis of State and Federal Judicial Behavior: The Reapportionment Cases," *American Political Science Review* (September 1968), pp. 688–98.

[14]Quoted by Frank Greenberg, "The Task of Judging the Judges," *Judicature* (May 1976), p. 467.

Punishment

Incapacitation

Deterrence

Rehabilitation

their qualifications, something like the Missouri Plan. Such plans have been adopted in fifteen states at the last count.

2. Judges should be paid adequately so that they have the financial independence they need to concentrate on their work and so that the more successful lawyers will be willing to serve on the bench. Salaries have been increased in most jurisdictions, but inflation has destroyed much of the progress that has been made. Judges are unable to earn anything beyond their salaries. They must be cautious about investments in order to avoid conflicts of interest. In many states, the salaries paid to judges are less than the average salary of the practicing attorneys of the same age and experience. This is an area where the reformers have not been and perhaps never will be successful.

3. Judges should serve for long terms. The arguments here are much the same as they are for tenure for college professors. They should be able to make decisions without fear of losing their jobs. Although there have been only a few constitutional changes extending judicial terms, actual tenure for judges is often longer than might appear from looking at constitutional provisions. Incumbent judges are ordinarily reelected. And in some states the constitution has been amended so that sitting judges merely run against their own records, which in effect gives them longer tenure in office.

4. Judges should be subject to discipline, including removal for cause. "A bad judge is worse than anything else," writes Donald Dale Jackson after a study of American courts. This is undoubtedly an exaggeration, but it makes a point.[15] As we have noted, in most states commissions have been created to investigate and evaluate judicial misconduct. Only a few judges have ever been removed from office, however.

5. State courts should be unified under the administrative supervision of the chief justice of the state supreme court. All judges should be subject to assignment where needed and not be appointed or elected to serve just in one particular district. Three-fourths of the states have some sort of unified court systems. In thirteen states the state government has taken over the entire responsibility for financing all the courts.

6. Rule-making powers should be given to the state supreme court or its chief justice. This is being done in more and more of the states. It permits judges to adopt rules relating to procedural matters, codes of professional conduct, even rules requiring lawyers to continue their education by taking refresher courses.

7. Court administrators should be appointed to assist in managing court business. Almost all states now have court administrators, a new profession with its own schools and conferences. (Like most professions such conferences tend to be held in warm climates during winter months.) The establishment of professional court administrators has gone so far that scholars are beginning to speculate, about a subtle transfer of authority that may be taking place away from the judges to their professional staff.[16]

The extent of adoption of these reforms has been dramatic, but the consequences have yet to be known. It is hoped that they will make for a quicker and more equitable delivery of justice. But to overcome some problems, for example that of delay, will require more than structural and organizational changes. The fact is that delay often works to the advantage of the participants in the system. For example, at times defendants and their attorneys find it to their advantage to hold off a trial. At other times prosecutors want delay to put pressure on defendants to accept

[15]Donald Dale Jackson, "Special Feature," *The New York Times*, quoted in *The Courier* (Champaign-Urbana), July 7, 1974.

[16]James A. Gazell, *State Trial Courts as Bureaucracies: A Study in Judicial Management* (Denellen, 1975), p. 145.

guilty pleas. Lawyers may seek delays because it may permit them to accept more clients and make more money. Further, no matter how modernized the management of court business, the flow of legal business grows and grows. And this leads to another and somewhat more controversial reform recommendation.

Some people propose that traffic violations, automobile injury cases, and victimless crimes should be handled by some procedure other than jury trials. New York is in the forefront of removing from the courts minor traffic offenses that do not involve serious moving violations. Other states are following. No-fault insurance programs should reduce the large number of cases stemming from automobile accidents. And when it is realized that half the people in prison and half of the trials involve victimless crimes, the "decriminalization" of these matters would substantially reduce the load on the courts. Six states have already repealed statutes on public drunkenness and now consider alcoholism a disease rather than a crime.

The reform of state judicial systems is difficult because it is mixed in partisan, ideological, and issue politics. Yet change is slowly coming, and court procedures and judicial selection methods are being altered—hopefully for the better.[17]

The justice system

Judge and jury are not the only ones involved in the processing of criminal charges. As we have noted, only a handful of those accused of committing a crime actually come up for trial. And only 10 to 15 percent of those who are convicted have been declared guilty as the result of a formal trial before either a judge or a jury. Most persons who go to prison or have to pay a criminal fine do so because they have pled guilty.[18] "Presiding" over this out of courtroom process is the prosecutor.

THE PROSECUTOR

Prosecutors are usually county officials, locally elected and subject to little if any supervision by state authorities. A prosecutor has "more control over life, liberty, and reputation than any other person in America."[19] (And by the way, the prosecutor is "largely an American invention," one of the few governmental positions we did not inherit from England. To this day in England, the administration of criminal justice is still based on the theory of private prosecution of criminals.) Our system puts the responsibility for prosecution on the government. The victims have no role, perhaps other than as witnesses. They are not consulted about what the charge should be or asked what they think might be an appropriate penalty. The matter is strictly between the state, represented by the prosecutor, and the accused, represented by an attorney.

When presented by the police with a case, the prosecutor must decide

[17]This section is taken from Alan V. Sokolow, "The State of the Judiciary," *The Book of the States, 1974–1975* (Council of State Governments, 1974), pp. 115–19. See also Frank H. Bailey and Jag C. Uppal, "The State of the Judiciary," *The Book of the States, 1976–1977* (Council of State Governments, 1976), pp. 87–91.

[18]Lynn M. Mather, "Some Determinants of the Method of Case Disposition: Decision-Making by Public Defenders in Los Angeles," *Law and Society Review* (winter 1974), p. 189.

[19]Robert H. Jackson, *Journal of the American Judicature Society* (1940), p. 28, quoted by Jack M. Kress, "Progress and Prosecution," *The Annals* (January 1976), p. 100.

first whether or not to file formal charges. He may divert the matter out of the criminal justice system and turn it over to a social welfare agency. He may dismiss the charges completely. Or he may take the matter before the grand jury, which almost always follows the prosecutor's recommendation. In many jurisdictions, for most offenses all he has to do is file an information affidavit.

The decision to charge or not to charge is "well nigh unreviewable in theory and even less reviewed in practice."[20] Of course there may be political consequences. A prosecutor who decides not to charge a person accused of some notorious crime is likely to be subject to political pressure and public criticism. But for routine crimes, the prosecutor is politically in a better position to dismiss a charge than are the police.

Police are supposed to enforce every law all the time. Of course it is impossible for them to do so, and they do exercise discretion. But an officer who failed to arrest a person alleged to have committed a crime might be subject to charges of failing in his duty. The prosecutor is the one with the discretion. In fact, the prosecutor is less likely to be criticized for dropping a case because of insufficient evidence than if he files a charge and fails to get a conviction.[21]

PLEA BARGAINING

A common practice is for the prosecution, or sometimes the judge, to offer either a reduction in the seriousness of the charge or a concession on the sentencing if a defendant will enter a plea of guilty to a particular crime. At one time this practice of plea bargaining was universally condemned. Apparently many people still feel that there is something "dirty" about it, like bartering away justice. However, many—but not all—of the several commissions of experts that have recently looked into the matter have endorsed plea bargaining.

Plea bargaining works. It produces "a result approximating closely, but informally and more swiftly, the results which ought to ensue from a trial, while avoiding most of the undesirable aspects of that ordeal."[22] Plea bargaining offers something to all those involved. Prosecutors are able to dispose of cases more quickly, avoid long-drawn-out trials, avoid the risk of losing a case, and build up a better "election-worthy conviction record."[23] The accused, by pleading guilty to a lesser offense, avoids the danger of being sentenced for a more serious charge. Defense attorneys avoid "the dilemma of either incurring the expense of going to trial with a losing case or appearing to provide no service whatever to their clients." By being able to handle more clients, they can also make more money.[24] Judges are able to dispose of cases on their dockets more easily.

Once the bargain between prosecutor and the defendant's attorney has been accepted, the matter is taken before a judge. The judge goes through a series of questions to the defendant: "Are you pleading guilty because

[20]Kress, p. 109.

[21]Lief H. Carter, *The Limits of Order* (D. C. Heath, 1974).

[22]American Bar Association Standards, "The Prosecution Function," p. 21 quoted by Kress, p. 11. For a contrary view, see National Advisory Commission on Criminal Justice Standards and Goals, *Report of the Task Force* (U.S. Government Printing Office, 1973).

[23]Thomas Church, Jr., "Plea Bargains, Concessions and the Courts: Analysis of a Quasi-Experiment," *Law & Society Review* (Spring 1976), p. 400.

[24]*Ibid.*

you are guilty? Are you aware of the maximum sentence for the crime to which you are entering a guilty plea? Were you coerced into pleading guilty or offering anything in return for it? Are you satisfied with the representation afforded by your attorney? The appropriate response must be given . . . and then the plea is accepted."[25] The Supreme Court has several times upheld plea bargaining. As long as the defendants knew what they were doing and entered into the bargain intelligently, by pleading guilty they have waived their constitutional rights to trial and may not subsequently back out of the arrangement. Prosecutors and judges also must live up to their side of the bargain.[26]

SENTENCING

Since police and prosecutors screen out a large proportion of the doubtful cases, "most left to be dealt with by courts are those in which there is no serious dispute over the guilt or innocence of the defendant. . . . This fact sets the tone for the process. . . . Everyone concerned—the defense lawyer, the prosecutor, the judge, the probation officer—becomes aware of the fact that he is involved in a process where the primary focus is on deciding what to do with the people who are in fact guilty."[27]

The traditional justifications for putting people in prison are as follows:

1. *Retribution.* Society is entitled to punish those who commit crimes, and if the state does not do so people will be tempted to take the matter into their own hands.
2. *Deterrence.* By putting those who commit crimes in prison, it warns others and keeps some who might otherwise violate the law from doing so.
3. *Protection of society.* There are persons who are so dangerous to the life and property of others that the only thing to do with them is to lock them into prison.
4. *Rehabilitation.* By placing convicted persons in a protected and controlled environment, we can work to rehabilitate them so that they will be able to return to society and become law-abiding and productive citizens.

Early in our national history retribution, deterrence, and social control were the primary purposes of sentencing. Then rehabilitation became the major goal and was thought to be the more humane approach. The *indefinite sentence* became popular. The idea behind the indefinite sentence is that each prisoner should be considered an individual suffering from an "illness." For each prisoner there should be a diagnosis of what made him or her act in an antisocial manner. A course of treatment should be prescribed, and if and when a "cure" is certified by experts such as psychologists and social workers, the prisoner should be released. Recently many have become disillusioned about our ability to effect "cures." And there has been a growing conviction that rehabilitation can be a screen behind which persons are kept confined. As a result, the time of the "indefinite sentence" reform of the last several decades appears to be coming to an end.

Judges still have considerable discretion in imposing sentences, for most penal codes do not set specific terms for specific crimes. Due process must be observed. Sentencing takes place in open court. The prisoner

Police officers are responsible for enforcing every law at all times. When presented by the police with a case, the prosecutor must decide whether to file formal charges.

[25]Jonathan D. Casper, *American Criminal Justice: The Defendant's Perspective* (Prentice-Hall, 1972) pp. 52–53.

[26]*Santobellow* v. *New York*, 404 U.S. 257 (1971).

[27]Edward Barrett, "The Adversary Proceeding and the Judicial Process," Lectures to the National College of State Trial Judges, quoted in Mather, "Some Determinants," pp. 187–88.

must be present and be represented by counsel. In many places, social workers are assigned to help the judge determine the appropriate sentence. In addition to these reports, the judge receives recommendations from the prosecutor, hears the arguments of the defense, and then sets the sentence.

An increasingly criticized feature of the criminal justice system is the fact that "different judges often mete out different sentences to similar defendants convicted of similar crimes, depending on the sentencing attitudes of the particular judge."[28] Some convicted offenders escape jail sentences altogether, while others convicted of the same crime go to jail for what is considered by many to be much too long. To ease the problems of differences in sentencing, several reforms have been suggested: reducing judicial discretion by more precise legislative fixing of standards; establishing advisory sentencing councils; adopting the English procedure of allowing appellate courts to review and modify sentences.[29]

Throughout the nation, the tendency is to send to prison only those convicted of the most serious crimes. During the 1960s the prison population actually declined, although since 1976 it has started to rise. There are 188,000 persons in state prisons, most of them in conventional closed prisons, although with the help of federal funds states are building more and more work farms and community centers for the less dangerous prisoners.[30]

Prisoners as a group do not have much political clout, but they are still entitled to certain constitutional protections, including the right not to have paroles revoked or probations terminated without a formal hearing.[31] Even inside the prison walls, discipline cannot be imposed without at least some type of hearing procedure.

Courts in crisis

There are at least two general models — that is, two general ways of thinking — about our system for the administration of criminal justice.[32] There is the *due process* model. It sees police, prosecutors, attorneys, judges, and correctional officials as adversaries. It focuses on the formal trial. Those who use this model tend to be most worried about an innocent person being convicted or about the poor and disadvantaged being unfairly treated. The fact that the system takes a long time to deal with an issue or to dispose of cases is of less concern than the fact that the system might not be just.

Others look at the system in terms of a *crime control* model. They see that people who commit crimes or get involved in disputes as "inputs" into the system. If it worked properly and efficiently, it should "process" these inputs and produce results. They are disturbed when they discover that the several parts operate with little central direction, that it is a "system"

---

[28]Edward M. Kennedy, "Criminal Sentencing: A Game of Chance," *Judicature* (December 1976), p. 210.

[29]Robert McKay, "It's Time to Rehabilitate the Sentencing Process," *Judicature* (December 1976), p. 227.

[30]James Q. Wilson, "Who Is in Prison?" *Commentary* (November 1976), pp. 55–56.

[31]*Morrisey* v. *Brewer,* 408 U.S. 471 (1972).

[32]Herbert Packer, "Two Models of the Criminal Process," *University of Pennsylvania Law Review* (November 1964), pp. 1–60. Herbert L. Packer, *The Limits of the Criminal Sanction* (Stanford University Press, 1968).

more in word than in fact. They are alarmed that the system is "jammed." They look to plea bargaining and more efficient management of court calendars as ways to improve the efficiency of the system.

But whether one is concerned about justice in the traditional way or about crime control, whether one believes the judges are too strict or too lenient, almost everyone agrees that the courts are in crisis. "Most agree . . . the time to do something about the criminal courts is now."[33] The trouble is there is less agreement about what should be done.

Summary

1. State and local judges, prosecutors, and correctional officials along with the police are key agencies in the administration of justice.

2. State and local courts are also important arenas for the making and carrying out of public policy.

3. For many years state and local courts operated with little public attention and not much public concern. Today, both as agencies for the making of public policy and as instruments for the administration of justice, they are the objects of many studies, and the recipients of large sums of money. But the problems are difficult, not the least being that there is no agreement about what the problems are. As in every other field, where actions have important consequences change is likely to be made by small steps, and will come about as the result of the push and pull of political pressures.

[33]George F. Cole and David Neubauer, "Courts Policy," *Policy Studies Journal,* 3 (August 1974), 61. See also "Reforming the Criminal Justice System," *Current History* (July/August 1976).

Chapter 29

Government at the Grass Roots

There are over 78,000 units of local government in the United States (about 77,000 too many, some people feel). Illinois alone has over 6,000. Rhode Island has about 100 (see Table 29–1). Cities, counties, school districts, townships, water control districts, park districts—all are crowded together and piled on top of one another. Average citizens live under five or six layers of government. They pay taxes to all of them—federal, state, county, municipal, and others—and are supposed to participate in the selection of the persons in charge of all these governments.

Why do we have such a patchwork of governments? The basic pattern was imported from England, like so many of our governmental forms. As the years passed, new governments were created to take on new jobs when the existing units were too small or were not up to the task. Also, people kept moving to or at least near to the large central cities and urbanization began to take hold. Decades of compromise and struggle among conflicting groups have given us our present system. It creaks and groans. It costs a lot of money. It is not very efficient. But there it is.

**29–1
Number and types
of local
governments**

	1942	1962	1972
Counties	3,050	3,043	3,044
Municipalities	16,220	18,000	18,517
Townships	18,919	17,142	16,991
School Districts	108,579	34,678	15,781
Special Districts	8,299	18,323	23,885
Total	155,067	91,186	78,218

SOURCE: U.S. Department of Commerce, *1972 Census of Governments*, Vol 1, p. 23.

Local governments vary in structure, size, power, and relation to one another. But in a constitutional sense they are all the same in that they all live on power "borrowed" from states. The states are basically *unitary* governments—that is, constitutionally all power is vested in the state government, with local units existing only as agents of the states and exercising power given to them by the state government.

"Little federalism": state-local relations

How does the *unitary* nature of state-local relations contrast with the *federal* nature of nation-state relations? The slicing up of governmental power among the various local units and the state government leads to many of the same problems that we have noted in the chapters on federalism. There is the same conflict between groups that want the state to do something and groups that fear an invasion of local rights. There is the same difficulty of constantly adjusting functions among the various units of government as economic and social conditions change. And there are the same disputes over whether a local majority or a statewide majority is to have its way. But there is a crucial difference:

In the beginning, the state legislatures were given almost unlimited constitutional authority over local governments and ran them pretty much as they wished. They granted, amended, and repealed city charters, established counties, determined city and county structure, set their debt limits, and passed laws for them. But by the end of the nineteenth century many state constitutions had been amended to forbid the legislature to pass laws dealing with particular local governments. In place of legislative enactments, constitutional provisions determined the structure—in some cases, even the process—of local governments.

However, since local governments are created by the state legislatures and have no constitutional authority in their own right, there are fewer constitutional obstacles against state interference in local matters than there are with respect to national-state relations. State officers participate in local government to a much greater extent than do federal officers in state politics. When doubt arises about the authority of local governments, the courts have generally decided against them.

The difference between the unitary state-local and the federal nation-state relations can be exaggerated; as in so many matters of politics, the difference is one of degree rather than of kind. Moreover, during the past several decades home-rule amendments have been added to about half the state constitutions. These amendments authorize many cities and some counties to run their own affairs and limit the power of state officials to interfere. Thus constitutional home rule in a small way introduces the federal principle into state constitutions.

The hedging in of the legislature's power did not put an end to state domination of local government. While the legislature's authority was being curtailed, the power of state administrative officials was being expanded. Problems once thought to be local came to be viewed as statewide. Many local governments lacked the money to do essential jobs. They could not afford specialists, and their administrative standards were notoriously low. Moreover, the states were encouraged to enter new fields by unfamiliar social and economic problems. Sometimes the states just took over a job previously handled by local people; sometimes the states offered local governments financial assistance, with certain strings attached.

Gradually, state officials were given more and more authority to supervise local officials. This tendency became especially evident in law enforcement, finance, health, highways, welfare, and election procedures.

The extent of state control over local units varies from state to state and, within each state, among the different kinds of local government. States supervise the activities of local governments by means of devices that give varying amounts of control to state officials. At one extreme—giving states the least amount of control—are requirements for reports by local officials to specified state officials. At the other extreme are requirements that local officials be appointed and removed by the state officers.[1]

The growing importance to the states of their relations with local governments is reflected in the establishment in about thirty of the states of a special office to deal with them. In some states it is a regular department: Illinois has a Department of Local Government Affairs. In other states it is a unit of the office of the governor: Tennessee has an office of urban and federal affairs. Although their functions vary, all these offices are concerned with the problems of local governments.

Our fair cities

What does the word "city" call to mind? Bright lights, crowded streets, museums, slums, skyscrapers, and lots of people. To some of us, the city may be Main Street, Courthouse Square, the old cannon, and farm families shopping and talking on Saturdays. For a city is not merely improved real estate. It is also people: men and women living and working together. Aristotle observed that people "came together in the cities for security but that they stayed there for the good life." The "good life" is defined differently by different people but it often includes these attractions found in the medium and larger cities:

1. Employment opportunities
2. Cultural centers
3. Diverse educational institutions
4. Entertainment and night life
5. Professional sport teams
6. Good restaurants
7. Diversity of people

Mayor Kenneth Gibson of Newark, N. J., serving as chief of the U.S. Conference of Mayors, speaks by phone to President Carter about federal aid to local government.

In our state statutes, this exciting thing, the city, is made to sound like a dull bit of lawyers' talk. For, in law, a city is a *municipal corporation*. There are over 18,500 of them in the United States. Some have millions of people, others a few hundred. Although not all densely populated places are governed as municipalities, the city is the major kind of local government for the urban dweller.

Each city has two major functions. One is to provide government within its boundaries in order that its citizens may maintain law and order, keep their streets clean, educate their children, purify their water, create parks, and in other ways make their area a good place in which to live. But the city has a second function—it is an instrument of the *state* to carry out *state* functions. It is distinguished from a county in the greater amount of discretion given to local officials and the greater emphasis on local functions.

[1]See Demetrios Caraley, *City Governments and Urban Problems* (Prentice-Hall, 1977), esp. chap. 3.

A county is supposed to operate primarily as an administrative unit of the state. The distinction is, of course, one of emphasis.

Each city has its own *charter*. This is not necessarily a single document; in some states one has to read the state statutes to discover the organization, powers, and functions of cities. The charter is to the city what a constitution is to the national or state government. It outlines the structure of government, sets the authority of the various officials, and provides for their selection. Where do the charters come from? Who draws them up?

In about ten states, the legislature writes a *special* charter for each city and may amend the charter as it pleases, although in a few of these states the charter must be submitted to the local voters for their approval. In practice, local groups often draft the charter in consultation with their legislative representatives; other members of the legislature usually defer to the delegation from the city. Since legislators need local support to stay in office, in practice the groups that dominate local politics often write their own charters, even though it is the state legislature that has the constitutional authority to do so. When the legislature is controlled by groups hostile to those in control of the city, however, a major battle may shape up.

In most states the constitution requires the legislature to classify cities (usually by size) and provide a charter for each class. If the legislature makes sufficiently refined classifications, it can, in effect, write a special charter for each city; in many states the constitution specifically permits special legislation for the largest city. Many legislatures permit the local citizenry to choose from among several kinds of charters. This is known as the *optional charter plan*.

HOME RULE

European cities can do anything that is not expressly forbidden; American cities have only those powers expressly conferred on them. State legislatures still exercise a great deal of control over city affairs. In addition to drawing up charters for the cities, the legislature allots functions to local officials and withdraws them at will. In case of conflict between a state and a local law, state law is enforced. In a few states, every time a city wants to put a stoplight on the corner of Broadway and High the city officials have to get permission from either the legislature or a state official.

Some states have legislative home rule. The legislature delegates authority over certain subjects so that the cities do not have to ask permission to deal with them. In about half of the states, however, the *constitution*, not the state legislature, delegates to citizens of certain-sized cities (a few extend the power to all municipalities) authority that they may exercise *regardless of the wishes of the legislature*. These are the *home-rule states*. The people of the city may elect a group of citizens who draw up a charter. After the charter has been approved by local voters (in some states it must also be approved by either the legislature or the governor, or both, to ensure that it will not conflict with the constitution), it becomes the city's basic instrument of government and may be amended by local citizens. Further, home-rule cities have the general power to dispose of matters of local concern without special authorization from the legislature.

Constitutional home rule thus introduces the federal principle. Two-thirds of our cities of over 200,000 population have some measure of home rule. It is a mistake to think of these cities as being really independent, however. Home-rule cities have some freedom in determining the general structure of their city government, but home rule often only slightly increases their substantive powers. Still, some cities such as those in Michigan, Ohio, and Colorado have acquired significant substantive powers from home rule provisions. And cities in Texas, Missouri, and California have done reasonably well for themselves.

Is home rule worth the struggle for it? Despite the small increase in local autonomy, and despite the fact that constitutional home rule introduces an element of rigidity into state-local relations and enhances the authority of state judges (who often have to determine which laws prevail), most reform groups favor its adoption. It frees the legislature from the necessity of dealing with some local matters. More important, it gives the voters of a particular city the power to decide for themselves the general structure of their municipal government.

FORMS OF CITY CHARTERS

The formal charters are good sources of information for beginning to learn how the people in our 18,500 cities govern and are governed. But to look at just a city charter can be very misleading. The actual constitutions—in the sense of the rules by which our cities are governed in contrast to their legal charters—vary from the narrowest rule by the few to the widest participation by the many. But until we have more comparative studies, classification of city governments by the form of their charter is still the best available.

The mayor-council charter The mayor-council charter is the oldest and the most popular charter in the smallest and largest of cities. Under this type of charter, the city council is usually a single chamber. The size of the council varies—a few have only two members, some as many as fifty. Seven members is the median in cities with over 5,000 people.

Many methods are used to select the council members—nonpartisan and partisan elections, by small wards, by large wards, from the city at large (see Table 29–2). It is not uncommon for special local political parties to participate in local elections: the Citizens party, the Taxpayers party, and so on. The way council members are chosen is an important factor in determining how power is distributed in a city. Large cities that elect members in partisan elections generally choose them by small districts or wards rather than at large. This combination tends to support strong party

Mayor Tom Bradley of Los Angeles meets with city residents one day a month to discuss problems and complaints.

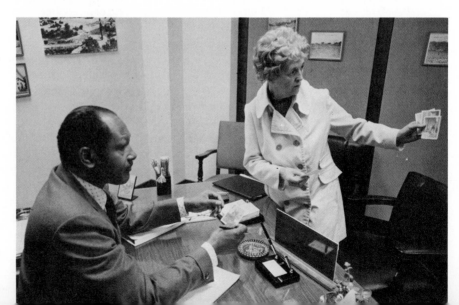

Mayor-Council Cities	Number at-large	Number by ward	Council Manager Cities	Number at-large	Number by ward	Commission Cities	Number at-large	Number by ward
Akron	3	10	Austin	6		Portland	5	
Atlanta	19		Cincinnati	9		St. Paul	7	
Baltimore	1	18	Dallas	3	8	Tulsa	5	
Birmingham	9		Fort Worth	8				
Boston	9		Kansas City	6	6			
Buffalo	6	9	Long Beach	8				
Chicago		50	Miami	4				
Cleveland		33	Norfolk	7				
Columbus	7		Oakland	8				
Denver	2	11	Oklahoma City		8			
Detroit	9		Phoenix	7				
El Paso	4		Rochester	5	4			
Honolulu		9	Sacramento		8			
Houston	3	5	San Antonio	1	10			
Indianapolis	29		San Diego	8				
Jacksonville	5	14	San Jose	7				
Jersey City	3	6	Toledo	8				
Los Angeles		15	Wichita	5				
Louisville	12		Tuscon		6			
Memphis	6	7						
Milwaukee		19						
Minneapolis		13						
Nashville	6	35						
New Orleans	2	5						
New York[a]	10	33						
Newark	4	5						
Omaha	7							
Philadelphia	7	10						
Pittsburgh	9							
St. Louis	1	28						
San Francisco	11							
Seattle	9							
Tampa	7							
Washington	4	8						

Source: *The Municipal Year Book* (Washington, D.C.: The International City Managers' Association, 1968), Table III and *The Municipal Year Book* (Washington, D.C.: The International City Management Association, 1972), Table 3/20.

[a]Two at-large seats for each of the five boroughs.

organizations. Nonpartisan at-large elections make party organization difficult. The larger the election districts, the more likely citywide considerations will be brought to bear in the selection of council members and the greater the influence of citywide institutions such as the local newspapers in the elections.[2]

The difference between at-large or large-district elections and the small single-member district can sometimes be quite significant in terms of what racial and ethnic groups you want to have represented on a city

[2]These generalizations are based on studies of Edward Banfield and James Q. Wilson, *City Politics* (Harvard Univ. Press, 1963) pp. 89–100. See also Heywood T. Sanders, *Local Elections and City Politics* (Urban Data Service, International City Management Association, January 1971), and Willis D. Hawley, *Nonpartisan Elections and the Case for Party Politics* (Wiley, 1973).

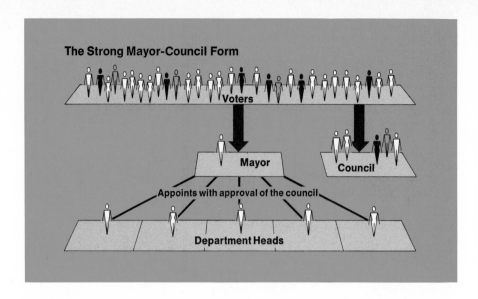

The Strong Mayor-Council Form

Voters

Mayor

Council

Appoints with approval of the council

Department Heads

council. Do you want the city's elite, white and black, to be on the council, or do you want the poor blacks, browns, or rednecks as well as the middle class? From the standpoint of the poor and disinherited, the at-large system is of little help. On the other hand, the single-member district is a crude method of proportional representation, and thus permits most groups at least a chance for representation.

The powers of the mayor vary from charter to charter (and even more widely from city to city and mayor to mayor). The mayor is elected by the people, but in some cases the charter assigns little more than ceremonial powers to him; he welcomes visiting dignitaries and gives them the key to the city. In some cities his appointive power is limited, and he shares administrative authority with the other elected officials and numerous boards and commissions. This is known as the *weak* mayor-council system.

Tracing the office of mayor through various charters, we find a general trend toward an increase in his authority. Like the presidency and the governorship, the office of mayor over the years has grown in importance. Many cities have altered their charters in order to give the mayor power to appoint and remove heads of departments and investigate their activities, to send messages to the city council, to prepare the budget, and to veto council ordinances. In other words, he has been given a share in policy-making, and city administration has been centralized under his direction. A recent development is the creation of a chief administrative officer, appointed by the mayor to assist him in directing city administration. In New York and Philadelphia, for example, these city administrators manage the housekeeping functions of the city government and provide professional administration, conferring some of the advantages that are thought to come with the adoption of the council-manager form of government, discussed below.

Many people believe that the *strong* mayor-council is the best charter for the large cities. This charter, they argue, gives the city a strong political leader, makes efficient administration possible, and, by centering authority in the hands of a few individuals, makes less likely the growth of "invisible government" by people who have power but who are not publicly accountable for its use.

The commission charter In 1900 the city of Galveston was flooded by storm driven tides. Over 6,000 people lost their lives, and property worth millions was destroyed. The mayor and aldermen seemed incapable of action. In the emergency, power began to fall into the hands of a group of businessmen who had been discussing methods of improving the harbor. They decided to act. After studying the charters of several cities, they went to the legislature with what was then almost a novel proposal for a new charter. They asked that control of the city be vested in five commissioners. The legislature approved.

About five years later, the attorney for the city of Des Moines, Iowa, took a business trip to Galveston. He was so favorably impressed with the commission government that he returned to Iowa with the proposal that the Iowa legislature permit cities to adopt commission charters.

The placing of all governmental powers in the hands of five people flew in the face of the traditional doctrine of separation of powers. Many felt that it was too dangerous to give a small group control over both administration and legislation. For this reason, the Des Moines Plan, as it was known, included the initiative, referendum, recall, and nonpartisan ballots for primaries and elections in addition to the ideas of the Galveston businessmen. The plan became very popular, and by 1917 over 500 cities were so governed. Since that time the number has declined, although St. Paul, Portland, Tulsa, and about 150 other cities with populations over 10,000 still have this kind of charter.

The commissioners, usually five, collectively constitute the city council; individually they are the heads of the departments of city administration. Most commissioners devote full time to their jobs and actively administer the affairs of their particular departments. One of the commissioners is selected as mayor, but in most cities the mayor has little more power than the other commissioners.

The commission charter was widely heralded as an introduction of safe

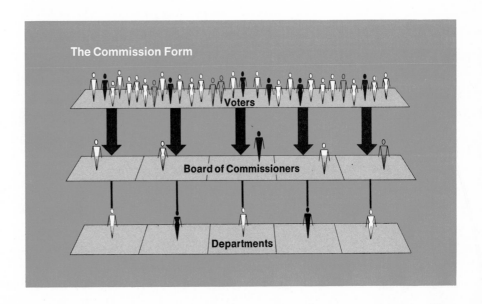

The Commission Form

Voters

Board of Commissioners

Departments

and sane business methods to city affairs. But after a brief wave of popularity, the new idea lost some of its glamour; the party bosses were suspicious and the city reformers disappointed. Although providing for more integrated control than the old mayor-council system, the commission charter left the city without a single responsible administrative head; in effect, a commission city has five mayors. Moreover, commissioners chosen because they represent major groups within the city often leave something to be desired as administrators of departments of public welfare, public safety, and so on. By 1917, reformers had discovered a new kind of charter which they believed had greater merit.

The council-manager charter   The council-manager, also known as city-manager, plan was acclaimed at the turn of the century as "the latest word in municipal reform." It is one of this nation's significant governmental innovations. In 1908 the small city of Staunton, Virginia, appointed a general manager to direct the city's work. Little note was taken of the step, but Richard Childs, an advertising man active in the short-ballot movement, became very much interested.

Childs was enthusiastic about the commission plan (discussed above) because it applied two basic ideas, *unification of power* and a *short ballot*, to city affairs. But it did not go far enough. Add to this a chief administrative officer, he reasoned, and the results should be even better.[3] The city-manager plan soon became the darling of both the reformers and the business elite. They liked the idea that the council would serve as a sort of "board of directors" in the business sense of setting broad policies, but a profession-

[3]On Child's contributions in this area, see John Porter East, *Council Manager Government: The Political Thought of its Founder* (University of North Carolina Press, 1965).

al executive would see that these policies were carried out with business-like efficiency.

Today about 2,200 cities with a total population of well over 50 million, located in every state except Indiana and Hawaii, operate under a council-manager charter. It is especially popular in California, which has more than 260 manager cities out of a total of 280 cities with a population over 5,000. The plan is used mostly in medium-sized cities. The largest city operating under a city manager is San Antonio, and the plan is also used by San Diego, Dallas, Kansas City, Cincinnati, Oakland, and Fort Worth.[4]

Under the council-manager charter, the council is usually elected in nonpartisan primaries and elections, either on a citywide basis or by election districts much larger than the wards in mayor-council cities. The number of council members varies, but there are usually fewer than in cities with mayor-council charters. The council appoints a city manager, supervises his activities, and fires him when he is unsatisfactory. It makes the laws, approves the budget, and—although it is not supposed to interfere in administration—supervises city government through the manager. A mayor is usually provided for the purpose of presiding over the council and representing the city on ceremonial occasions.

The city manager advises the council on policy and supervises the administration of city business. Since the council-manager cities try to attract the best available person, few of their charters require their councils to appoint a local citizen, nor do they prescribe detailed qualifications.

City-manager charters imply a *nonpolitical* city manager who merely carries out policies adopted by the council, and council-persons who refrain from interfering with the administration of city affairs. In fact, there is no such sharp distinction between policy-making and policy-applying.[5] Most city managers are the major source within the city government for the initiation of policies and programs:

> The city manager is a participant in the political process of the community whether he plays an active role in initiating policy, a passive role by merely drawing council attention to emerging problems, or a neutral role by refusing to commit himself publicly on a controversial question. . . . Refusal of a manager to commit himself can be interpreted by opposing groups as taking a position antagonistic to their own.[6]

The unavoidable involvement of the manager in the politics of the community means that when there is a change in the control of the council, managers sometimes are fired. The dismissal of a manager is usually explained in other than political terms—lack of sufficient management ability, a personality conflict. Or the manager may resign because of council meddling in administration. The explanations, however, are often only thin disguises for heated political struggles in the community.

---

[4]A useful political analysis of the forms of city government is found in Robert P. Boynton, "City Councils in the Legislative System," *The Municipal Yearbook, 1976* (International City Management Association, 1976), pp. 67–77.

[5]Ronald O. Loveridge, *City Managers in Legislative Politics* (Bobbs-Merrill, 1970).

[6]Gladys M. Kammerer, et al., *The Urban Political Community* (Houghton Mifflin, 1963), p. 5; see also Richard J. Stillman, *The Rise of the City Manager* (University of New Mexico Press, 1974).

How has the city-manager plan worked? Cities that adopted this kind of charter have generally enjoyed an improvement in standards of public employment, a reduction in costs, and better services. But some observers say it has also weakened *political leadership* in the city.

The political ethos "theory" and its critics

Some scholars contend that political *attitudes* and governmental *forms* are closely related. Thus, certain kinds of people will prefer certain forms of government. More specifically, it is argued that *council-manager* cities (the reform model) are generally upper-class or middle-class in character; few are mainly lower-class. *City-manager* government, according to this view, appeals to the concept of the public interest of these groups, a concept that stresses the "good" of the community at large, efficiency and economy, business methods and procedures, and nonpartisan civic participation. On the other hand, the city-manager form of government would have little appeal where low-income groups have more political influence. Lower-income groups and recently arrived immigrants, it is held, would more likely favor partisan elections, the mayor-council form of government, and the ward system of elections. These voters are more willing to trade their votes for the favors and the "friendship" offered by those in political office.[7]

Edward Banfield and James Q. Wilson conclude that knowing about the political character or "political ethos" of a city could help explain why the city is or was ruled by a political machine or by the council-manager (reform) model. They also held that the political ethos of a group was a function of income and ethnicity. WASPs and the better educated and better off would generally support the reform or "good government" model, whereas the poorer or more heavily immigrant a city's population, the more likely support for a strong mayor system and perhaps also a strong political machine.

In the cities a more general political ethos exists that may be classified in two general political orientations. The first, called the *public-regarding view*, looks upon city government as a means to perform, as economically and efficiently as possible, service for the general good of the community. Those who hold to the public-regarding attitude believe that partisanship at the city level should be minimized, that decisions should be based on careful calculation of the community good, and that civic, in contrast to political, organizations and issues call for participation by all good citizens in order to make the city a place where people can live in peace and harmony.

They called the second political culture *private-regarding*. This view sees the city government as an instrument designed to provide jobs, protection, and housing, and to meet the particular or more selfish needs of local groups and individuals. It views partisan politics as a useful and necessary device to secure one's fair share. It considers it fair play to have the appointment to office of one's friends who, in return for political support, should use their office to reward those who put them there. This private-regarding political ethos tends to deemphasize the possibility that all interests and groups within the community can be made equally happy and expects government to support those who support it.

'This year I'm not getting involved in any complicated issues. I'm just voting my straight ethnic prejudices.'

Drawing by Whitney Darrow Jr.:
© 1970 The New Yorker Magazine, Inc.

[7]Edward Banfield and James Q. Wilson, *City Politics* (Harvard University Press, 1963), Chap. 9, and a later restatement of their position (with slight modifications) in James Q. Wilson and Edward Banfield, "Political Ethos Revisited," *American Political Science Review* (December 1971), pp. 1048–62.

The main problem with the political ethos theory is that there is just too much variation in American cities. The closer scholars have examined the relationship between political attitudes and the structure of city government, the less convinced they are of any cause and effect linkages. The sharp differences in viewpoints between the upper and upper-middle income WASPs and other segments of the urban population was not usually as sharp as Banfield and Wilson have argued. The white middle and upper classes are not nearly as unified in outlook as most people have generally assumed, and probably never have been. Critics of this theory are now numerous, and they generally conclude that the concept of political ethos has led to too much simplification of the influence of sociocultural characteristics on political institutions.[8]

Government by the people, county style — country style?

For those who live outside the city, the county and township (in New England, the town) are the important units of local government. Although counties are not alternatives to city governments but additional layers, city people tend to look to city hall as the place where community affairs are managed. Where there is no city hall, the county courthouse is often the center of politics.

All states are divided into counties, though in Louisiana they are called parishes and in Alaska boroughs. With a few exceptions (such as Connecticut and Rhode Island, where counties have lost their governmental function), county governments exist in all the territory of the United States. Numbering about 3,100, they vary in size and population. Some are inhabited by few people and much desert: most of them are predominantly rural.

County governments are sharply divided into two major types: large urban counties like Los Angeles County, Cook County (Ill.), and Dade County (Fla.) and then the nearly 2,500 rural counties. The urban counties have many of the same offices as their rural counterparts, but they are very much intertwined with the problems of the urban centers. Here we are talking primarily about county governments outside the large urban centers.

County governments are least active in New England states, where the county is essentially a judicial district; county officials do a little road-building but not much else. Elsewhere the traditional functions of counties are law enforcement, highway construction and maintenance, tax collection and property assessment, recording of legal papers, and welfare. Despite assertion that the counties are dying governments, they have within recent years taken over more jobs than they have lost. Counties in some states have given up some of their responsibilities, but various states, especially in the South, are transferring urban functions such as transportation, water and sewer operations, and land use planning to their counties. Elsewhere certain cities are contracting with counties to provide

[8]For criticisms of the political ethos theory, see Raymond E. Wolfinger and John O. Field, "Political Ethos and the Structure of City Government," *American Political Science Review* (June 1966), pp. 324–26; Timothy M. Hennessy, "Problems in Concept Formation: The Ethos 'Theory' and The Comparative Study of Urban Politics," *Midwest Journal of Political Science* (November 1970), pp. 537–64; David R. Berman and Bruce D. Merrill, "Citizen Attitudes Toward Municipal Reform Institutions: A Testing of Some Assumptions," *The Western Political Quarterly* (June 1976), pp. 274–83; and Martin Shefter, "The Emergence of the Political Machine: An Alternative View," in Willis Hawley, et al., *Theoretical Perspectives on Urban Politics* (Prentice-Hall, 1976), pp. 14–44.

joint services such as manpower training, law enforcement, and correction. As Americans in the 1970s continue to stream to the suburbs beyond the city's border, they still want the government services to which they have grown accustomed. Thus, more and more they turn to the urban or suburban counties to provide urban functions and to secure a share of federal funds available to support these functions.[9]

COUNTY GOVERNMENT

How are counties organized to do their jobs?[10] Counties, even more than municipalities, exist to enforce state laws and to serve as administrative units of state government. In general, most counties have little legislative power. The typical county has a group of officials who act in some fashion as the governing body. These agencies have a variety of titles—board of commissioners, supervisors of roads, county court, commissioners' court, and so on. They vary in size from one to more than fifty members. They administer state laws, levy taxes, appropriate money, issue bonds, sign contracts in behalf of the county, and handle whatever jobs the state laws and constitution assign to them.

County boards, as we shall call these agencies, are of two types. The larger boards are usually composed of township supervisors or other township officials; the smaller boards are usually elected from the county at large.

County board members are often key political leaders and in some states control local affairs through their power over state patronage. They are much more important than a mere listing of their formal powers might suggest. Road problems and the granting of contracts to road contractors are frequently the major topics discussed at board meetings.

The county board shares its powers with a number of other officials, most commonly the sheriff, the prosecutor, the county clerk, the coroner, and the auditor. These are generally elected officials. Often, county treasurers, health officers, and surveyors are also found on the ballot. In general, county administration is an unwieldy collection of relatively independent agencies, and until recently there was seldom a single administrator or executive responsible for coordinating the activities of the county government. This is now beginning to change. Nearly 400 counties now appoint a chief administrative officer who serves at the pleasure of the county commissioners. And more than fifty relatively large counties now elect a county executive who is granted power over most administrative functions.

The county treasurer serves as auctioneer at this tax lien sale in Putnam County, New York.

WHAT DO COUNTY
OFFICIALS DO?

Sheriff Except in Rhode Island, where they are appointed by the governor, sheriffs are elected by the people of the county, usually for a two- or four-year term. They are charged with enforcing the law and keeping the county jail; in addition, they are the officers of the county's court of record. In some metropolitan counties in the North and in rural counties in the South, sheriffs are active as law-enforcement officers, but in most counties the sheriff lets the city police do the job within the cities, and the state police in the rural areas. In some of the latter, however, the sheriff

[9]See Rochelle L. Stanfield, "The Suburban Counties are Flexing Their Muscles," *National Journal* (May 7, 1977), pp. 704–9.
[10]For a comprehensive review of county government, see John C. Bollens et al., *American County Government* (Sage, 1969). See also Vincent L. Maranda and Robert D. Thomas, *The Forgotten Governments: County Commissioners as Policy Makers* (University of Florida Press, 1977).

and deputies are the only ones to keep law and order. If sheriffs meet serious trouble, they can summon a posse of local citizens to come to their assistance.

In addition to law enforcement work, sheriffs serve legal processes issued by the court, summon jurors, subpoena witnesses, and sell property to satisfy judgments.

Prosecutor   The prosecuting attorney—also known as county attorney, state's attorney, or district attorney—is commonly elected by voters of the county. Prosecutors aid the grand jury in preparing indictments, and in some states bring persons to trial by what is known as "information." They prosecute their state law violators and represent the state and county in civil suits. Their discretion is wide, and the decision whether or not to prosecute is often made by a prosecuting attorney alone. The job is especially attractive to young law graduates, and it often serves as a stepping-stone to higher political posts.

County clerk   The office of the county clerk is found in about half the states. In other states, the *clerk of the court* often performs this job. The county clerk is secretary to the county board and has such miscellaneous duties as supervision of elections, issuance of hunting, fishing, and marriage licenses, and the granting of permits for operation of amusement establishments outside city limits.

The "courthouse gang"   County governments are not always as headless as it might appear. In most of the counties in the United States, public affairs still "are in the hands of what the irreverent call the 'courthouse gang.' This 'gang' may be described as a more or less permanent group of elective and appointive officeholders together with private individuals whose business normally brings them into contact with public officials."

The offices of the county clerk and the county court.

Here are found road contractors, printers, purveyors of supplies, lawyers in criminal and probate work, and "ex-officials who have grown old in party service and who have become masters of the lower sorts of intrigue and so habituated to playing politics as to make residence at the county seat a psychological necessity."[11] The county is also an electoral district, and members of the state legislature are often graduates of the school of courthouse politics.

Frequently, one member of the courthouse elite is recognized generally as the boss. It may be the editor of the local newspaper, the president of the local bank, the chairman of the county farm bureau, the head of the oldest family, or the leader of a local party or faction. Occasionally, certain county officials are also recognized as having general, if informal, supervisory powers. Sometimes it is the chairman of the governing body. In Indiana, Ohio, Minnesota, and South Dakota, it is often the county auditor; in Illinois, the chairman of the board of county commissioners or supervisors; in Missouri, the judge of the county court; in Tennessee, Kentucky, and Alabama, the county or probate judge.

COUNTY REORGANIZATION

How well do the rural counties do their job? Not very well. In the first place, there are too many of them. When counties were first organized, the idea was to provide a county seat within a day's journey of everyone. A farmer could pile his family into the wagon and head for the courthouse. While he was attending to his business, the family could shop and pick up the local gossip. They could all get home in time to do the evening chores. Today, of course, farmers can drive through a dozen average-sized counties in a day.

The small area and population of many counties leads inevitably to inefficiency. Study after study has shown that money could be saved and services improved by *consolidating* counties. Though there is much talk about such action, very few consolidations have been achieved. County residents in rural America take pride in their county and do not like to see it lose its identity. Officeholders, their families, and their friends do not want county jobs to disappear. Businessmen at the county seat depend on officers, employees, and persons drawn to the city by business for much of their patronage.

The New England town meeting is an example of direct democracy.

Most county governments still lack modern fiscal and purchasing methods, and auditing practices often leave much to be desired. Even such an obvious moneysaving program as centralized purchasing has not been widely adopted. But progress is being made, slow as it is.

Several states now provide for county home rule. Typical of these states in Illinois, where a provision of the constitution provides that a county may receive home-rule powers if it creates the position of an elected county executive. The trend toward county home rule is growing.

Townships and towns

North of the Ohio, east of the Mississippi River (with minor exceptions), and outside of New England, the general practice is to subdivide counties into townships. The township is gradually losing many of its functions either to the counties or to the cities. Oklahoma, after whittling township functions down to almost nothing, abolished them altogether. In Iowa, townships still exist formally, but they have lost so many of their functions

---

[11]Quotations in this paragraph are from Lane W. Lancaster, *Government in Rural America*, 2nd ed. (Van Nostrand, 1952), pp. 57, 58, 59.

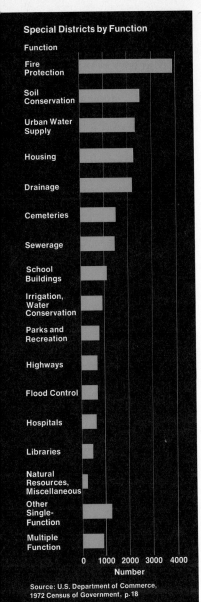

Special Districts by Function

Function

Fire Protection

Soil Conservation

Urban Water Supply

Housing

Drainage

Cemeteries

Sewerage

School Buildings

Irrigation, Water Conservation

Parks and Recreation

Highways

Flood Control

Hospitals

Libraries

Natural Resources, Miscellaneous

Other Single-Function

Multiple Function

0   1000   2000   3000   4000
Number

Source: U.S. Department of Commerce, 1972 Census of Government, p. 18

that the Census Bureau has stopped counting them. Where they exist, townships often handle outdoor relief, build and maintain roads, and sometimes serve as districts for school purposes. In some states, all the voters of the townships are entitled to attend an annual meeting to elect officers and to levy taxes and make appropriations. The township meetings are usually poorly attended.

A board of supervisors, a justice of the peace, and a constable are the typical township officials; all are elected. The township constable is to the justice of the peace what the sheriff is to the county courts. Since constables make their fees from court work, they do little law enforcement except for catching traffic violators.

The Middle Western and Middle Atlantic townships are often confused with the New England towns. But they are essentially different types of government. The town is the principal kind of rural or noncity government in New England. It is sometimes difficult for outsiders to understand that a New England town is an area of government that includes whatever villages there may be, plus the open country. Except where a municipality has been incorporated, the town does most of the things that a county does elsewhere.

Each town holds an annual meeting open to all voters. In the United States, this town meeting is the most frequently cited example of a *direct democracy*, where the voters participate directly in making the rules, passing new laws, levying taxes, and appropriating money. Before each meeting the selectmen issue a warrant designating the time and place of the meeting and setting forth the agenda. At the appointed time, a moderator is chosen to preside; the items on the agenda are then taken up, and the floor is open to citizens who wish to have their say.

The meeting may choose a board of selectmen, usually consisting of three or five members, who carry on the business of the town between meetings, have charge of town property, grant licenses, supervise other town officials, and call special town meetings. A town clerk, treasurer, assessor, constable, school board, and numerous other persons are elected by the voters or appointed by the selectmen. The town meeting often elects a finance committee to prepare the town budget.

The New England town meeting has long been a celebrated institution. The picture of sturdy and independent citizens coming together to talk over public affairs and speak their minds is a stirring one. The New England town is sometimes pointed to as the one place in the United States where there is no elite, where participatory democracy really exists. In fact, however, a recognized group of town "fathers" often provides leadership.

Special districts

Special districts are an organized unit of government usually established to provide one or more specific services, such as sewage disposal, fire protection, or pollution control, for a local area. They have nearly doubled in number during the past twenty-five years. They are often created for financial reasons, to enable an existing unit of government to evade established tax and debt limits, or to spread the tax burden over a wider area than that of the existing municipalities or counties. Many smaller special districts are formed in suburban areas to obtain urban services without having to create a city government or be annexed to one.

Although there is no consistent pattern in their organization and structure, special districts usually have a governing board appointed by officials of other governments or sometimes popularly elected. Special districts often are useful in dealing with urgent problems that overlap the boundaries of the existing units of government, but allow them to join together with this more flexible device.[12] Critics of the rapid increase of special districts claim that their existence undermines comprehensive planning. Further, the governing boards of these special districts usually enjoy low political visibility, and the typical citizen is generally uninformed about their decisions. All of this raises doubts about how accountable the special districts are to their constituents. Despite these and other complaints, however, special districts are hardly going to fade away. Too many problems are regional in character, and the special district mechanism can offer an economies of scale approach that will continue to be attractive to officials at the grass roots who are wrestling with local and regional problems.

Summary

1. Governmental forms at the grass roots in the United States come in a great variety of shapes and structures, but they have in common the fact that constitutional power is vested in the states, with the cities, towns, and counties acting as the agents of the state.

2. The most common governmental forms at the city level are the mayor-council or the council-manager (city manager) plans. Mayor-council governments generally have a strong mayor, have partisan city elections, operate with a ward system, and have reasonably short and simultaneous council terms. City-manager cities generally select the mayor from the council, operate with at-large and nonpartisan election arrangements, and have overlapping terms for council members. In general, city-manager cities are found in medium-large cities and in Western, especially sunbelt, cities.

3. We have a patchwork array of local governments but most of them enjoy considerable stability and continuity. Governmental consolidations seldom take place, except for school districts which have consolidated to take advantage of economies of scale. On the other hand, the past few decades have witnessed a tremendous growth in the number of special districts formed to provide special-purpose functions for several communities in an area.

---

[12]See Robert B. Hawley, Jr., *Self Government by District: Myth and Reality* (Hoover Institution Press, Stanford University, 1976.)

Chapter 30

Governing the Cities

Today it is metropolis, not the farm or the small town so beloved in American fact and fiction, where most of us live. Already about 75 percent of the American people are living on 5 percent of the land. Fifty-five percent of us live within fifty miles of coastal shoreline (Atlantic, Pacific, Gulf of Mexico, or along the Great Lakes and St. Lawrence River). By the year 2000 the nation will find itself with several large metropolitan regions of solid settlement: the Eastern Seaboard, the West Coast, and an urban Middle West uniting St. Louis, Chicago, Cleveland, Detroit, Indianapolis, and Buffalo.

Congestion, slums, smog, tension, rootlessness, shapelessness, loss of a sense of community, impersonal and unfriendly human relationships—all these terms have been used to describe the giant city of today. The big city has simply lost control of itself, many critics believe.[1] Even worse, it carries the seeds of the destruction of civilization. Historically, the city has grown from shelter to fortress to industrial center and to a mechanical way of life. *Polis*—the old Greek type of small city—gave way to metropolis and then to megalopolis.

Such criticisms of the city are in keeping with a long tradition of anticity bias on the part of major social critics, starting with Thomas Jefferson. These critics project the image of the city as an impersonal, cold, brutal environment in which crime flourishes and people lose their dignity. The big city is contrasted with the "wholesome" small community in which people live "whole lives" of total relationships. Some of the less sophisticated critics appear to measure the modern city against a small town inhabited by Anglo-Saxons who speak with a New England or Middle Western accent and spend their time sitting around the stove at the general store discussing local politics.

[1]Lewis Mumford, *The City in History* (Harcourt, 1961), pp. 543–44.

© 1976 National Geographic Society

"The town"—the Charlestown
section of Boston—is one square
mile of clean streets tightly
lined with brick houses
and wooden tenements.

But metropolis and urban values have their defenders. There are many who contend that the big city is not just a place of smog and sprawl. It is the center of innovation, excitement, and vitality. It is where social diversity can be found, where community pressures to conform are bearable. The large community is a meeting place for talent from all over the nation and the world: dancers, musicians, writers, actors, business leaders. Despite all the complaints, many people like living in the big city. And they point out that within metropolitan areas there are often fairly homogeneous smaller communities that retain some identity. Some of the best known are Greenwich Village in lower Manhattan, Georgetown in Washington, D.C., the Russian Hill and Chinatown sections of San Francisco, and the North End and South Boston areas in Boston.

Some people even challenge the idea of urban crisis. In a controversial but important book, political scientist Edward Banfield argues "There is . . . another side to the matter. The plain fact is that the overwhelming majority of city dwellers live more comfortably and conveniently than ever before. They have more and better housing, more and better schools, more and better transportation, and so on. By any conceivable measure of material welfare the present generation of urban Americans is, on the whole, better off than other large groups of people have ever been anywhere." He grants there is congestion, but he finds advantages in congestion as well as disadvantages. He contends that until very recently "most of the talk about the urban crisis has had to do with the comfort, convenience, and business advantage of the well-off white majority and not with the more serious problems of the poor, the Negro, and others who stand outside the charmed circle."[2] Banfield makes some useful points. Many of our cities are in good shape, especially in the West and the South. But the older cit-

[2]Edward C. Banfield, *The Unheavenly City: The Nature and Future of Our Urban Crisis* (Little, Brown, 1968), pp. 3, 5, 12. For some different views on Banfield's work, see the essays in H. M. Hocham, ed., *The Urban Economy* (Norton, 1976), Part Five.

ies from St. Louis north and east are in more serious trouble, not just in perceived crisis.

The suburban boom and its political implications

These luxury high-rise apartments in Fort Lee, New Jersey, are part of the suburban boom surrounding New York City.

In recent decades, the suburbs have been the fastest growing units in the United States. By 1980 about 40 percent of us will live in these communities on the fringe of the central cities. There is no typical suburb. There are commercial suburbs, and residential suburbs, and industrial suburbs, upper-income suburbs, middle-income suburbs, and working-class suburbs. More and more, there are highly urbanized suburbs that are hard to differentiate from the older cities.

The suburbs were brought about by a variety of factors: cheap land, more open space for recreational purposes, better highways that led out of the cities, and the changing character of the inner cities. In the post-World War II years, there was a massive migration of the poor and dispossessed—both black and white—from rural areas to the central cities, especially in the Northeast and North Central regions. By the mid-1970s three of every five blacks in the United States lived in the central city of a major metropolitan area. In many of these same metropolitan areas, more affluent whites fled to the suburbs in search of a more homogeneous community.

In charge of these metropolitan areas of cities and suburbs are dozens, in some cases even hundreds, of governments. There are over 1,000 governmental units in the Chicago area, and at least 1,400 in the New York City region. The four-county Pittsburgh metropolitan area illustrates the magnitude of fragmentation. In one recent count, it contained 704 local governments, 441 of which could levy property taxes. Within one of its counties—Allegheny—there are 84 municipalities, 42 townships, 62 school districts, and at least 129 school boards. Citizens of Whitehall, located in this metropolitan area, have sixteen layers of government between them and the state level.[3]

Layers of Governance, Whitehall, Pennsylvania, 1972

17. United States of America
  16. Commonwealth of Pennsylvania
    15. Air Quality Control Region
      14. Southwestern Pennsylvania Regional Planning Commission
    13. Western Pennsylvania Water Company
      12. Allegheny County
        11. Allegheny County Port Authority
          10. Allegheny County Criminal Justice Commission
        9. Allegheny County Soil and Water Conservation District
      8. Allegheny County Sanitary Authority
    7. City of Pittsburgh
      6. South Hills Area Council of Governments
    5. South Hills Regional Planning Commission
      4. Pleasant Hills Sanitary Authority
    3. Baldwin-Whitehall Schools Authority
  2. Baldwin-Whitehall School District
    1. Borough of Whitehall: Population 16,607

[3]"Substate Regionalism Today," Chap. 1 in *Regional Decision-Making: New Strategies for Substate Districts* (Advisory Commission on Intergovernmental Relations, 1973), p. 3.

On the average around the nation, there are at least 90 governments per metropolitan area, 50 per metropolitan county. There are many Clevelanders—that is, people who work in Cleveland, shop in Cleveland, read Cleveland newspapers—who do not *live* in Cleveland. By and large they tend to be whiter and wealthier than those who do live in Cleveland. Only about half the St. Louisans live in St. Louis. Again, those who do live there tend to be less well-off than those who live in the suburbs. "The Pennsylvania section of the Philadelphia metropolitan area contains five counties, Philadelphia included. Less than half that region's residents now live in the central city; less than half the labor force works there."[4] And so it is with most of our metropolitan areas.

Today many of those with young families who can afford it leave the crowded and blighted business areas and move out into more pleasant living quarters. They go in search of cheaper land, lower taxes, more room, better air. New shopping centers rise in outlying communities. Industries also move from the central city in search of cheaper land, lower taxes, and escape from city building and health codes. By 1980, about 90 million Americans will be suburbanites—that is, they will live outside the central cities in the approximately 280 regions designated by the Bureau of the Census as Standard Metropolitan Statistical Areas. Moreover, demographers predict a nearly 10 percent increase in suburban population by the year 2000. And most of the new jobs created in the United States will continue to be located in the suburbs. In short, "the evidence is overwhelming that suburbs have been by far the most economically dynamic parts of the nation during the past twenty years or more."[5]

Despite the fact that suburbanites often look on the politics of the central city as corrupt and something to escape from, the politics of the central city are very much a part of their lives. When they read their morning papers on the way to work, they find little news about the officials of their own suburbs, but much about Mayor Thomas Bradley or Mayor George Moscone or Mayor Michael Bilandic or Mayor Maynard Jackson, or of some other big-city mayor. Moreover, the major problems in which they are interested—transportation, crime, taxation of downtown businesses where they work—are more influenced by the decisions of the officials of central city than those of suburbia. And although suburbanites may have some influence in the central city through a business association or trade union, they have no direct vote in electing those whose decisions vitally affect them.

What of government and politics in the suburbs? It is dangerous to generalize. Individual suburbs vary greatly. Some differ much more from others than suburbs as a whole differ from central cities as a whole. Some suburbs, like Paradise Valley, Arizona, are the exclusive residences of the rich, governed by an efficient cluster of specialists. Still others are lower-middle-class neighborhoods of blue-collar workers. Some, like Compton and East Palo Alto, California, or Glen Arden and Seat Pleasant, Maryland, are predominantly black. And others are chosen by young professional families who have little interest in their community and view it as a stepping-stone from which to move with the next promotion.

[4]Charles E. Gilbert, *Governing the Suburbs* (Indiana University Press, 1967), p. 3; Committee for Economic Development, *Reshaping Government in Metropolitan Areas* (The Committee for Economic Development 1970), p. 13.

[5]Anthony Downs, *Opening Up the Suburbs* (Yale University Press, 1973), p. 22.

Some suburbanites tend to look at their local government as a device to protect their property, their schools, and their homes against "invasion" by minority groups. Occasionally, suburban dwellers become aroused over major local problems like educational policy or taxation, but in the absence of explosive issues suburban local politics tend to be low key. Most suburban communities are so limited in their jurisdiction that they seldom can cope with the major problems of urban life. As a result, even suburbanites who are active in state and national politics rarely have much interest in what happens at their local city hall. It is often difficult to find people to run for local office.

Various studies and surveys of suburban politics generally find that suburbanites are less politically active in home town politics than city residents are in central city politics. Political participation in small suburbs is especially low.[6] This is explained by the relatively homogeneous character of many suburbs, the "friends and neighbors" atmosphere, nonpartisan elections, and election dates that do not coincide with those of regular state and national elections. Of course some people are active, but the small-scale community of limited services does not have the compelling attraction of partisan elections in the large central cities. Nonetheless, suburbanites are more satisfied with their local governments than are residents of core city areas.[7]

The sheer complexity and fragmentation of government administration in suburbia often makes for confusion, if not frustration. Each suburban city has its own government, fire and police departments, school system, street-cleaning equipment, and building and health codes. And special-district governments piled on top of one another further complicate the situation. Also, many of the major tasks of suburban government are bound together with those of the metropolis. Criminals do not stop at city boundaries. The central city usually maintains an elaborate police department with detective bureaus, crime-detection laboratories, and an elaborate communications network, but its jurisdiction stops at the city line. Suburban police are fewer, and often untrained in criminology. Or consider traffic problems. Superhighways run through suburbia, with a number of access roads. These form a transportation unity, but in the midst of governmental disunity. In matters of health, too, there are often wide differences in health standards between parts of the metropolis. But germs, pollution, and smog do not notice city signposts.

Cities versus suburbs: how much of a contrast?

Many of us have grown up thinking that a suburb is a place where all the houses are alike, where all the husbands travel to the city to work, and where the life style is based on children, well-kept lawns, and single-family dwellings. Some of these stereotypes have a basis in reality, but the myths about suburbia greatly distort the fast-changing character of our diverse suburban areas. In fact, there are all kinds of housing patterns in

[6]Willis D. Hawley, *Nonpartisan Elections and The Case for Party Politics* (Wiley, 1973). Also, Fred Wirt, Benjamen Walter, Francine Rabinovitz, and Deborah Hensler, *On the City's Rim: Politics and Policy in Suburbia* (D. C. Heath, 1972), pp. 124–30.

[7]Kenneth Prewitt, *The Recruitment of Political Leaders: A Study of Citizen-Politicians* (Bobbs-Merrill, 1970); and Betty H. Zisk, *Local Interest Politics: A One-Way Street* (Bobbs-Merrill 1973). See also Sidney Verba and Norman Nie, *Participation in America* (Harper & Row, 1972). Karl Lamb, *As Orange Goes: Twelve Families and The Future of American Politics* (Norton, 1974).

suburbia; an increasingly large number of the residents of both sexes work in their own communities or in other nearby suburbs; and many of the suburbs now provide the diversity of services and economic opportunities once found only in the central cities. Older suburbs face mounting urban growth and aging problems. And while tax levels and tax rates generally remain higher in central cities, suburbs have experienced percentage increases in taxes and expenditures similar to those of the central cities. Moreover, as we noted earlier, not all suburbs are the same; many who live in the central city have the same life styles and concepts as those in the suburbs.[8] Still, many of the central cities find that their principal antagonists in the state legislature and in Congress are not the rural areas, but an alliance of the country and the suburbs. Thus, the long-standing lines of cleavage between city and suburbs persists as a major feature of political life in many of our major metropolitan areas.

But we must not draw too sharp a contrast between suburban and central-city problems. In the outlying areas the suburbanites may be feeling the bite of "suburbanitis." Many of them have discovered that the lower prices for land and the lower taxes are deceptive. Fire insurance rates are often higher; they have to pay more for garbage collection; they often have to build and maintain their own septic tanks. Moreover, as suburban real estate becomes improved, and as the suburb grows in size, new waterworks and other facilities are needed. The parks are inadequate, and part-time village government is unsatisfactory. So, common needs of government services, and their heavy expense, ultimately press on people both in the core city and in suburbia. This common problem raises the question of whether central city and suburbia can pool their resources in order to deal with it more effectively. We will return to this question after looking more closely at the politics and government of the core city.

The special problems of the central city

One of the fundamental problems of the core city in America is that while many of the upper-income families and high-tax-paying businesses have been moving out, low-income groups have been moving in. At the same time, the need for city services has greatly expanded. In the last century, masses of new immigrants arrived from Europe. In this century migrants have come from the rural areas, especially blacks and whites from the South. More recently, we have welcomed waves of newcomers from Puerto Rico, Cuba and Mexico and the number of immigrants from Latin American countries is on the rise. The majority of migrants settle first in the inner city, usually in the poorest, most decaying sections. Invariably, these new arrivals cause greater stress for the schools and community safety. High densities and substandard housing in these areas increase health and fire hazards.

Thus the burdens on central cities are growing. And in contrast to the middle and outer ring of suburbs, the central cities contain

1. More older persons
2. More substandard housing
3. More students from non-English-speaking backgrounds
4. More unemployment
5. Older buildings

Ravaged inner-city area of the South Bronx, New York.

[8]See John Kramer, ed., *North American Suburbs: Politics, Diversity, and Change* (The Glendessary Press, 1972); and *The Suburban Seventies, The Annals* (November, 1975).

6. Higher crime rates
7. Higher population densities
8. Much higher percentages of blacks and most other minorities
9. Higher costs per resident

Any picture of the central cities as composed exclusively of huddled and starving masses is, of course, misleading. Still, most students of central city-suburban differences conclude that the "judgment that the central city has the problems and the suburbs the resources, though oversimplified, is not unreasonable. The [central cities] have a concentration of 'high-cost citizens' and enterprises, whereas the [areas outside the central city] have the advantage of resources. Central cities, like the Red Queen in *Through the Looking Glass,* must run very fast to stay in the same place."[9]

Problems accumulate in the core city. The migration of persons lacking the job skills now needed for our automated and complicated economy puts heavy demands on welfare agencies. Crowding in segregated districts accelerates the process of urban decay and slum building. To meet stepped-up housing needs by people who cannot pay high rents, the city moves in with public housing programs. The building of public housing projects creates tensions among those who are forced to move out of the area as well as among those who are forced to move into the housing. People who live in congested areas require more police protection, but police problems grow when different racial groups live closely together in slum areas. And, as if these are not problems enough, there is also the movement of thousands of people into the core city in the morning and out to the suburbs in the evening, the congestion of streets, and the pollution of the air. Faced with all these problems, the big cities need a great deal of money; and this is precisely the resource they lack.

Does the fiscal crisis in the central cities mainly suggest that people hate to pay taxes and that by crying poverty they can shift their bills to someone else? This is the view of some, like Banfield.[10] And Norton Long argues that the cities' problems are not primarily due to their lack of money. Rather, he says, "major problems of the cities stem neither from the inadequacy of their resources nor even . . . from their inability to tax such resources as they may have, but from their failure to utilize quite significant resources (now being wasted) in a manner to promote and improve the viability of their local economies."[11] Most scholars, however, contend that economic burdens fall upon the central city quite differently from the way they do upon the suburbs, and that the movement of wealthier taxpayers to the suburbs compounds the problem. Central city mayors find it nearly impossible to increase revenues or to force suburbanites to pay a larger share of the bill. From the perspective of a mayor, the lack of a *politically available* tax resource is quite real. Thus, they say, the economic deterioration of the central city continues, except where central cities have

---

[9]Robert L. Lineberry and Ira Sharkansky, *Urban Politics and Public Policy* (Harper & Row, 1971), p. 32. See also Richard P. Nathan and Charles Adams, "Understanding Central City Hardship," *Political Science Quarterly* (Spring 1976); and Richard Child Hill, "Separate and Unequal: Governmental Inequality in the Metropolis," *American Political Science Review* (December 1974), pp. 1557–68.

[10]Banfield, *The Unheavenly City,* p. 9.

[11]Norton Long, *The Unwalled City* (Basic Books, 1972), p. vii.

Drawing by Timeniez, *Rocky Mountain News*, Denver Colorado.

gone after new industry by annexations (e.g., Kansas City and Houston) and city-county consolidations (e.g., Nashville and Jacksonville). This is the *economic* problem. The *legal* problem is that the states have not permitted the cities to get at income-wealth in any meaningful way with a local tax. One result has been the increased organization of cities to lobby for general revenue-sharing and other fiscal relief in their state capitals and especially in Washington.[12]

In an effort to recapture part of the tax base that escapes to the suburbs in the evenings, at least seventy beleaguered cities have imposed local payroll or other types of commuter taxes. These taxes seek to extract revenue from people who live in the suburbs but work and use central city facilities during the week. Some city officials feel this payroll or commuter tax is an effective way to shift some of the central city tax burden to those who benefit from the city but live beyond its borders. But some experts doubt whether this is a real solution. They point out that it is unlikely to provide significant long-run revenue growth, and they claim it may encourage even more businesses to leave the city.

Government of the central city

The core city may be decaying, but it remains the most important single governmental and economic unit within metropolis. And its politics are still the major concern of the citizens of metropolis. How are large cities governed? Like the federal and state governments, city government is divided into the executive, legislative, and judicial branches, with many more-or-less independent agencies, commissions, and authorities.

CITY HALL OFFICIALS

The most important and visible city official is the mayor.[13] Today the mayor must be the head of a huge bureaucracy as well as a politician. The typical mayor is a college graduate, usually with a legal or business background, and often in his mid-fifties. Few women serve as mayors of major cities, although more and more women are elected to city councils, and an increasing number of women now run for mayor. Blacks serve as mayors in over 120 cities, including Atlanta, Detroit, Los Angeles, Oakland, Newark, and Washingtin, D.C. Most mayors put in long hours, and sometimes seven-day weeks. They are frequently caught in the middle of public

[12]See Suzanne Farkas, *Urban Lobbying: Mayors in the Federal Arena* (New York University Press, 1971); and Donald H. Haider, *When Governments Come to Washington: Governors, Mayors and Intergovernmental Lobbying* (Free Press, 1974).

[13]But see the argument that the mayor is merely a temporary and partial leader and that the permanent leadership is provided by economic and labor union leaders: Jack Newfield and Paul DuBrul, *The Abuse of Power: The Permanent Government and The Fall of New York* (Viking Press, 1977).

employee strikes, tax controversies, city-suburb clashes, and an endless series of trips "with hat in hand" to their state and national legislatures. Central city mayors in the largest cities earn $30,000 to $60,000, and in middle-sized cities between $25,000 and $35,000. City managers, chief city administrators, and the top appointees at city hall sometimes make even more than their mayors. Indeed, the increased need for expert city planners, city finance directors, and city engineers has pushed up both the salaries and competition for such jobs, especially in cities with populations of 40,000 or more.[14]

The mayor of a large city has the same basic functions as any major executive leader. As chief of state he issues proclamations; receives important city visitors; appears at endless civic breakfasts, luncheons, and dinners; launches community and charity drives. As chief executive he appoints the heads of agencies, draws up the budget, checks up on administration, deals with sudden emergencies, mediates among warring department chiefs, tries to get rid of incompetents or misfits. As chief of party he usually dominates the city organization of his party. He helps recruit candidates for office, deals with revolts and opposition within the party, represents the party in Washington or the state capital. As chief legislator the mayor draws up proposed legislation and also makes a great deal of specific policy. Indeed, the only powers of the president that the metropolitan mayor does not hold at the city level are commander in chief and chief of foreign relations.

The mayor shares his legislative power with the city council. Typically, in the giant city the mayor has extensive power to recommend legislation and to participate in the legislative process; he has a broad veto power, for example, over both policy measures and appropriations. But the balance of power widely varies from city to city. Much depends on the basis on which the council is elected—for example, whether its members are elected by the same party organization that supports the mayor or by a personal organization of their own.[15] The mayor finds that his relations with the legislative branch are essentially a *political* problem, just as the president and the governors do. Sometimes the mayor must depend on his control of the party organization to ensure support in the council. For example, Chicago would seem to have a "weak" form of mayor because the city council consists of fifty members elected in small districts, but the late Richard Daley exercised considerable influence over the council because of his political strength in their districts.[16] Other cities may appear to have more streamlined executive-legislative relationships, but the mayor may be weak because he had little political influence over the council.[17]

Whatever the particular combination, the mayor and the council operate

Illinois Governor James Thompson (left) and Chicago Mayor Michael Bilandic.

[14]See Leonard I. Ruchelman, ed., *Big City Mayors: The Crisis in Urban Problems* (Indiana University Press, 1969); and Ronald O. Loveridge, *City Managers in Legislative Politics* (Bobbs-Merrill, 1971).

[15]The most comprehensive study of city councils is found in Heinz Eulau and Kenneth Prewitt, *Labyrinths of Democracy: Adaptations, Linkages, Representation, and Policies in Urban Politics* (Bobbs-Merrill, 1973). This is a study, however, primarily of medium-sized cities or suburbs in the San Francisco Bay Area.

[16]The best account of Mayor Richard Daley's dominant influence in Chicago politics for over two decades is Milton Rakove's *Don't Make No Waves, Don't Back No Losers* (Indiana University Press, 1975).

[17]See John P. Kottler and Paul R. Lawrence, *Mayors in Action* (John Wiley, 1974).

in terms of the separation of powers and the checks and balances that characterize other levels of American government. Hence the mayor must always deal with the problem of splintered and fragmented power, which in turn brings up the question of whether the big city can govern itself.

THE MAYOR AS CHIEF EXECUTIVE

One of the legendary mayors of the twentieth century, James Michael Curley of Boston, who also served in Congress, in the governor's office, and in jail.

The main job of the mayor is administrative in the broadest sense of that term. Under him are the big "line" agencies—police, fire, public safety, traffic, health, sanitation. There is also a host of special agencies, such as the board of elections, the city planning agency, and commissions that regulate particular occupations and professions. Big-city mayors usually have a staff that carries out typical executive office functions such as personnel, budgeting, and public relations. In this respect the mayor meets the same problems as all executives: coordinating a variety of different activities, assigning responsibilities, checking to see whether projects have been carried out, finding the ablest people to take charge, and allotting money through his control of the budget.[18]

The mayor has a special problem that is found on both the national and the state levels of government but not in so extreme a form as in the big city. This is the *public* or *special authority*. Essentially the same as public corporation, such as the Tennessee Valley Authority, these authorities have been set up to undertake important but specialized functions in the big cities; examples are the Metropolitan Water District of Southern California and the Port of New York Authority. As these suggest, the authority oversees functions lying outside as well as inside the boundaries of the metropolitan district. It has legal authority granted it by the state (or states) to raise money, hire experts, and take over some of the big-city jobs, such as transport, water, and housing.

Why public authorities? In part because state legislatures are often hostile to big-city mayors and prefer to place important functions outside their reach and that of their political "machines"; in part because the authority has great financial flexibility (for example, it can incur debt outside the limits imposed on the city by the state). But most of all, as suggested above, because many problems, such as transportation, are simply too big, and also cover too wide a geographic area, to be properly handled by the city itself. Robert Moses of New York City, a member of many public authorities, summed up the case for this kind of device: "The nearest thing to business in government is the public authority, which is business with private capital under public auspices, established only when both private enterprise and routine government have failed to meet an urgent need, and this device is often attacked because it is too independent of daily pressures, too unreachable by the boys and therefore essentially undemocratic."[19]

Whatever the general pros and cons of the authority—and the debate runs on and on—it poses a special problem for central city mayors. Not only are many of the vital functions of metropolitan government beyond their direct control, but even worse, a mosaic of special authorities and special districts that manage big functions like transit and sanitation con-

[18]See Jeffrey L. Pressman, "Preconditions of Mayoral Leadership," *American Political Science Review* (June 1972), pp. 511–24. In this excellent analysis Pressman examines the leadership resources and the constraints on the mayor of Oakland, California.

[19]Editors of *Fortune, The Exploding Metropolis*, (Doubleday, 1958), p. 99.

stantly come into contact—and conflict—with "line" agencies dealing with closely related problems such as intercity traffic and law enforcement.[20] It is hard enough for the mayor to coordinate and mediate among his own agencies; it is infinitely harder to deal with independent authorities. But if the authority is a problem for the mayor, it is also a temptation. By helping to sponsor these independent agencies, he can sometimes cut down on his direct load of administration. He can tap other sources of funds and hence keep his own city's tax rate lower than it otherwise would be. If things go wrong, he can more easily shift the blame by saying he did not have authority over a certain function and hence cannot be held responsible. But what might in certain instances make things easier for the mayor may not be necessarily good for the metropolitan welfare—or for the capacity of the city dwellers as a whole to govern themselves effectively.[21]

Summary

1. We live in a metropolitan nation. Most of us live in central cities or in outlying communities known as suburbs. There is considerable fragmentation of governmental units in the metropolitan areas, and this fragmentation tends to undermine citizen involvement in the problems of the metropolis.

2. There is no typical suburb. Although many suburbs are homogeneous, suburban America is highly heterogeneous. Suburbs are increasingly confronting urban problems, and the inner ring of suburbs often looks very much like the central city.

3. The standard of living in the central cities of the United States may be much better than it was fifty years ago, but the inequalities between many central cities and their middle and outer rings of affluent suburbs is increasing. The central cities, especially in the North and North Central sections of the country, are faced with economic hardships. The extraordinary fragmentation and dispersal of political authority in the metro areas and even in many of the central cities themselves has made it difficult to govern the big cities effectively.

"To the Housing Authority, Port Authority, Tunnel Authority, Transit Authority, Bridge Authority—to authority!"

Drawing by Dana Fradon; © 1976 The New Yorker Magazine, Inc.

[20]"Special Districts and Authorities," in *Regional Decision-Making: New Strategies for Substate Districts*, pp. 19–47.

[21]For studies of how some independent authorities have abused their autonomy and contributed to the economic problems of the central city, see the analysis of Robert Moses' many roles in Robert A. Caro, *The Power Broker: Robert Moses and The Fall of New York* (Knopf, 1974); and Newfield and DeBrul, *The Abuse of Power*.

Chapter 31

The Metropolis: Politics and Reform

Since city government touches personal and group interests at many points, these persons and interests continually mobilize as much influence as they can. The stakes and prizes of big-city politics are tremendous: appointments to city offices; the level of taxation; regulation of businesses, professions, and other activities; contracts from the city; allotment of various city benefits, like education and sanitation. Beyond all this is the general interest in honest, efficient, and far-seeing metropolitan government.[1]

Metropolitics: political life in central cities

Around all these stakes and prizes interest groups tend to form in varying degrees of size, solidarity, and effectiveness. The politicians of metropolis must deal with the basic group interests found anywhere in an industrial society—organized workers and business leaders, professional associations, good-government associations, ethnic groups. But all these are much closer to city officials than they may be for a governor or a president. The mayor of a big city is constantly operating in the eye of a political hurricane.

INTEREST GROUPS IN THE CENTRAL CITY

To a greater extent than a president or governor, the mayor must deal with special types of interest groups. One of these is the "problem group"—people who share a concern over a particular city problem even though they are members of many different economic interests. Groups concerned with halting highway construction or developing a park, when supported by the local newspapers, can mobilize a great deal of pressure on city hall. Once the problem is solved or somehow disappears, however, the

[1]For an excellent description of the "stakes and prizes" of one city's politics, see Wallace S. Sayre and Herbert Kaufman, *Governing New York City* (Russell Sage, 1960). Chap. 2.

group may disappear with it. Another special type of interest in the big city is the good-government, or reform, group. In some cities such as Cincinnati these groups have enjoyed such strong leadership and wide support that they have operated virtually as political parties. But in most big cities reform groups are simply one more pressure on city hall, and they are often divided among themselves. Their activities range all the way from trying to improve the whole metropolitan area, as the Citizens League of Minneapolis has done, to simply collecting facts and figures, as have the Cleveland Bureau of Governmental Research and the Milwaukee Citizens' Research Bureau.

Another interest group of growing importance is the association or union of city employees. Police, firefighters, streetcleaners, teachers, and other public employees are organized into unions, many of which are affiliated with the national AFL-CIO. These groups are more or less concerned about the city as a whole, but they are especially interested in specific matters such as pay, working conditions, and job security. Although in most states strikes by city employees working in vital services are prohibited by law, enforcement of the law is difficult. Teachers and municipal workers increasingly use the strike, or threat of strike, to force cities to increase wages and provide better benefits.[2]

Ordinarily, group interests in metropolis pursue their activities much like pressure groups anywhere; they put out press releases, hold meetings, write letters to the mayor and council, and mount all the pressure they can. Occasionally, a local interest group provides a striking example of the effective mobilization of influence. Several years ago, for example, the Exxon Corporation, which employed 1,800 people in Bayonne, New Jersey, and paid a fourth of the city's taxes, threatened to leave if local officials went ahead with a planned tax increase. The oil company, in combination with other businesses, channeled its efforts through citizens' and research organizations. Contending that the city's civil service was overstaffed, the

[2]Harry H. Wellington and Ralph K. Winter, Jr., *The Unions and the Cities* (Brookings Institution, 1971); and David T. Stanley, *Managing Local Government under Government Pressure* (Brookings Institution, 1972).

Deep in thought about a strike, former New York City Mayor F. H. LaGuardia (left) listens to a union representative at a conference of union leaders and employers in an effort to prevent stoppage of winter coal deliveries in the city.

businessmen asked for budget cuts as the price of staying in the city. The five city commissioners and the school board complied by cutting the pay of city laborers, effecting economies in textbooks and athletic programs, and reducing various city services. Exxon then announced that it would stay.[3]

Pressure groups often use the initiative, referendum and recall (which we discussed in Chapter 26) in making their influence felt. While the recall is only an occasional political weapon, there have been some memorable ones: an attempted recall of the mayor of Seattle in the mid-1970s, the Little Rock recall election (over desegregation) in the 1950s and the experience of a colleague of ours who remembers the time he and some friends came into a school board meeting in their home community in Michigan waving recall petitions and frightened the board into giving in to their demands. If the recall can be considered a colorful minor element in urban politics, the initiative and referendum must be considered central elements. Few major financial questions in a city or school system can be settled without a referendum. And now that public employee unions have begun to play a strategic role in several cities, it has become a union tactic to go directly to the voters with legislative proposals. Thus, sometimes a school board is by-passed altogether with an initiative petition.

Group interests must deal with many centers of power and decision. "Whether a city has a loose and many-centered politics or a powerful organization or political leader dominating the scene," Lockard says, "there is always bargaining between interests, bargaining between interests and leaders in government, bargaining between interests and the bureaucracy. Bargaining yes, but the patterns of bargaining vary with different kinds of political systems. In a city with focused leadership bargaining goes on in an atmosphere of deference to the power potential of the leadership. Direct negotiations with the leader or his deputies become common for all interests, and while other negotiations of course continue to be carried on, the fact that there is a central source of power conditions the manner and consequences of interest group demands. In a multicentered pattern of politics a more free-for-all kind of bargaining is common."

The interest group arrangements of the central city are in many ways similar to those of the national electorate now that this is an urban nation. However, within many of our central cities the electorate is biased in favor of the foreign-born, blacks, Latinos, and blue-collar workers. In national elections these groups support the Democratic party, and these partisan ties nearly always hold for local politics. But, to gain control of the central city the politicians must also appeal to the "outer wards," populated by the middle classes with interests much like those of suburbia and to upper-income apartment or townhouse areas on the waterfront or in the fashionable old neighborhoods.

Mayor George Moscone of San Francisco in negotiations with striking city workers.

The city machine

Who puts together these political arrangements? At the turn of the century the boss was the ruler of many of our larger cities and some of our smaller ones. After touring the United States, Lincoln Steffens, the famous muckraker, reported: "St. Louis exemplified boodle; Minneapolis, police graft; Pittsburgh, a political and industrial machine; and Philadelphia, general

[3]Duane Lockard, *The Politics of State and Local Government* (Macmillan, 1963), pp. 257, 258.

civic corruption."[4] Why were the big American cities boss-ridden? Many reasons were advanced: lack of public interest and the refusal of leading citizens to take part in public affairs; the influx of immigrants who found that the ward leaders and precinct men were their friends and that politics offered the main means of climbing the economic and social ladder; faulty structural organization of the city, leading to such weak government that some political leader had to take charge; and finally, business interests that stood behind the bosses and used them to secure favorable franchises and contracts and protection from regulation.

Few strong citywide political machines exist today.[5] But one that has existed recently, in Chicago, illuminates the methods of the past as well as the way America's second largest city has conducted its political affairs. A study of the city's politics showed that in a formal sense, as noted in Chapter 30, Chicago was run by a city council consisting of fifty aldermen elected on a nonpartisan ballot (although party affiliations were widely known) and by the mayor, who was its presiding officer. Actually it was run by the mayor and half a dozen of the most powerful Democratic aldermen. These Big Boys, as they were called, controlled the rest of the aldermen by granting or denying them good committee assignments, appropriations for their wards, and other important political favors. One of the big boys was chairman of the Council's Finance Committee and hence was able to control appropriations, even to the extent of having city services reduced in some ward if its aldermen refused to "play ball."[6]

Behind this concentration of governmental power is a disciplined party. An alderman has to work closely with the party leader in his ward; often he himself is the leader. Not only is he the elected representative of the local party members; he is commonly the "boss" of the ward; the party organization in the ward "belongs" to him. He decides who will run on the party's ticket within the ward, he appoints and dismisses precinct captains, and he dispenses patronage. Sometimes aldermen rebel against the city machine or form factional alliances or geographical blocs. But rarely does an alderman fight the machine successfully. "The leaders of the Central (Party) Committee could bring him into line by withholding patronage or discharging public employees from his ward, by denying him financial support from the party's general coffers at election time, or by allowing an investigation of graft and corruption to take place in his ward." The central committee can even destroy a whole ward organization, but it usually prefers not to use such disruptive measures.

[4]Lincoln Steffens, *The Shame of the Cities* (1904) (Peter Smith, 1948), p. 16. For a useful historical perspective on the beginnings of New York City's famed Tammany Hall machine, see Martin Shefter, "The Emergence of the Political Machine: An Alternative View," in Willis D. Hawley, et al., *Theoretical Perspectives on Urban Politics* (Prentice-Hall, 1976), pp. 14–44.

[5]For a useful discussion of political machines and the view that several forms of machine politics continue to flourish in many places, see Raymond E. Wolfinger, *The Politics of Progress* (Prentice-Hall, 1974), Chap. 4.

[6]The description of the Chicago machine, including the quotations, is from Martin Meyerson and Edward C. Banfield, *Politics, Planning, and the Public Interest* (Free Press, 1955), pp. 66–67. For a critical journalistic study of the Chicago machine, see Mike Royko, *Boss: Richard J. Daley of Chicago* (New American Library, 1971). For an excellent insider's analysis of the operation and values of the Chicago leadership, see Milton Rakove, *Don't Make No Waves, Don't Back No Losers* (Indiana University Press, 1975).

The key person in the organization is the precinct captain. A typical captain spends several evenings a week either visiting in the neighborhood or holding office hours to help his constituents cut through red tape or deal with parking tickets or property assessments. Many precinct captains act as social workers, providing countless services such as legal assistance for the destitute, intermediary help in negotiating with a landlord, getting broken street lights repaired, and talking with probation officers of youngsters who are in trouble. If the precinct captain cannot help, he will usually refer the person in need to the ward committeeman. New residents moving into the 25th ward in Chicago get a welcoming letter from their alderman-committeeman that illustrates how the system works:[7]

> **February 11, 1971**
>
> **Dear Friend:**
>
> **. . . The 25th Ward is fortunate in being represented at all levels of government by people of all ethnic backgrounds. We are truly a cosmopolitan organization. As members of our organization, we have the Honorable Frank Annunzio, who is Congressman for the Seventh Congressional District; Honorable Thaddeus V. Adesko, Judge of the Appellate Court; Honorable Charles S. Bonk, County Commissioner; Honorable Anthony Kogut, Judge of the Circuit Court of Cook County; Honorable Sam Romano, State Senator, Honorable Matt Ropa, State Representative. . . .**
>
> **I would like to point out to you that the next nonpartisan aldermanic election will be held on February 23, 1971. At that time I am sure you will be visited by your Democratic Precinct Captain who will be most anxious to discuss any problems of mutual interest.**
>
> **Our organization has always endeavored to meet the needs and wants of our people. I personally await the opportunity on behalf of all of the officials of the 25th Ward and myself, to be of assistance. Do not hesitate to let us know what your problems are, and if we can help, we are more than willing to extend our services.**
>
> **With every best wish, I am**
>
> **Sincerely,**
>
> *Alderman Vito Marzullo*
> **25th Ward Committeeman**

THE DECLINE OF THE BOSS?

There has been a decline in the number and power of citywide party bosses since the turn of the century. This decline is due in some part to a steady drumbeat of criticism and opposition by reform groups. It is due in part also to the shrinking of patronage as more and more city jobs come under civil service; the decrease in immigration; stricter supervision of the expenditure of funds by the state and national governments; a more affluent society, making city dwellers less dependent on the machine; and, above all, the rise of the welfare state, which supplies social security, unemployment insurance, medical assistance, and relief checks. The change should not be overdrawn. Ward bosses still dispense some of the old kinds of aid,

[7]This process is skillfully described in Milton L. Rakove, *Don't Make No Waves, Don't Back No Losers, An Insider's Analysis of the Daley Machine*, (Indiana University Press, 1975), pp. 116–17. © 1975 by Indiana University Press. Reprinted by permission of the publisher.

and their services are especially needed to help less-educated people to get around big-city regulations. There are some basic forces at work supporting the machines. The exodus to the suburbs is leaving the central city more and more in the hands of the less well-off: Latinos, blacks, southern whites, who are being "restricted" to the central city and who need and can profit from the help of a political machine.

If the political machine as it was known in earlier periods seldom exists today, what takes its place? To some extent the personal organizations of mayors, other powerful city officials, or organized public bureaucracies. Mayors like Robert Wagner of New York built their own "machines" that could often defeat the old type of boss. But more often the machine has been succeeded by a much less centralized system. Political influence may shift into the hands of many powerful and perhaps competing officeholders; or into the hands of state and federal officials from the metropolitan area; or into the hands of nonofficeholders such as newspaper publishers, union heads, bankers, leaders of ethnic groups.

Although the pattern of power varies widely from city to city, the problem is a central one that has occupied us throughout this book. Granted that bossism is of questionable desirability, how much better off is a metropolis that has no central system of power, that may be politically nothing more than a collection of warring fiefdoms or tongs? One virtue of the boss was that occasionally he did want to *do things* for the people, and at least he had the power to operate through the various units of government. A divided government might be more honest but less effective, especially in shaping and administering programs for lower-income groups and for the long-run improvement of the city. (This is not to say that a divided city, or one with decentralized governmental institutions, is necessarily less corrupt than other cities.)[8] A strong mayor can sometimes gather the reins into his own hands, but the difficulty with this is that his power is likely to last only as long as he holds office. LaGuardia was a strong mayor who built a personal organization in New York, as did Joseph Clark in Philadelphia; but neither man converted his personal organization into a lasting party organization. The late Richard J. Daley of Chicago did succeed in fashioning a well run party system, but part of his success was due to avoiding controversy and ignoring divisive issues. Still, with the aid of the party he was able to govern the city. How long the strong Democratic machine will last in Chicago, now that Daley is gone, is a topic occupying the thoughts of a good many politicians, not all of them in Chicago.

Party weakness is intensified by the fact that most central cities tend to favor one party, usually the Democrats. The absence of real two-party politics has somewhat the same effect on the city as it does on the South: One party is so big, and wins with such little effort, that it fails to keep in fighting trim, and sometimes disintegrates into factions. The minority party is too weak to have much hope of success, fails to provide a strong opposition or meaningful alternatives, and often plays a negative type of politics.

Mayors such as Robert Wagner of New York built their own "machines" that could often defeat the old boss machinery.

Types of big-city politics

Because there are so many cities and because only recently have scholars systematically studied these governmental and political units, it is difficult to generalize about city patterns. What is true in Chicago may or may not be an accurate picture of Cleveland or Detroit or Los Angeles. A few years

[8]See, on the contrary, John A. Gardiner, *The Politics of Corruption* (Russell Sage, 1970).

ago, a noted urban scholar, James Q. Wilson, classified big-city political systems this way:

1. *Machine politics*—Chicago and Albany. Wilson suggests that small districts or wards based on fairly homogeneous ethnic or religious neighborhoods, a large number of elective offices, and a polyglot, lower-income population in the city as a whole tend to promote organization or machine politics.
2. *Factional alliances or coalition of groups*—Kansas City, Boston, Cleveland, St. Louis, Jersey City, and Cincinnati. In these cities, although a single party, usually the Democrats, wins the elections, officeholders are not bound together by the party and are responsive to separate and independent political constituencies. One may represent a political club, another the civil servants, another the business community, another the black wards, and so on.
3. *Nonpolitical elite systems*—Houston, Los Angeles, Detroit. Control over public policy is in the hands of newspaper publishers, businessmen, labor leaders, lawyers, bankers, and so on. In these cities the party organizations have little to say in selecting candidates, and elective officials remain aloof from party affairs. As Wilson points out, in these "nonpartisan cities"—and here we refer to actual conduct, not to the formal charter provisions—city policies tend to favor the business community.[9]

Elements of all three types are, of course, found in all large cities. The differences are a matter of emphasis; it is also true that, in time, the political situation in cities changes. In almost all cities there are also to be found a variety of strengthened public employee organizations and reform groups, most working outside the established dominant party.

Many scholars believe that with the passage of the old machines, the greatest single locus of organized political resources now resides in public bureaucracies. Seldom do these "new machines" provide centralized leadership or direction for a city. But powerful public employee associations, as relatively autonomous islands of political power, can deny a mayor or anyone else the opportunity to lead. These bureaucratic "machines" are sometimes irresponsible, says Theodore Lowi. "That is, each agency shapes important public policies, yet the leadership of each is relatively self-perpetuating and not readily subject to the controls of any higher authority."[10]

Contemporary central-city politics, where political leaders must mediate and bargain among multiple interests no longer satisfied merely with a few jobs on the city payroll, often requires a new kind of political leadership.[11] Those who prove successful are often political brokers skilled at pyramiding the scarce political resources at their command and exploiting their own informal resources in dealing with the media, public bureaucracies, and other influentials. Another facet of the new-styled contemporary city politics has been the emergence of a new type, the amateur citizen-politician.

---

[9]Drawn from Wilson's "Politics and Reform in American Cities," in Ivan Hinderaker, ed., *American Government Annual, 1962–1963* (Holt, 1962), pp. 37–55.

[10]Theodore J. Lowi, "Machine Politics—Old and New," *The Public Interest* (Fall 1967), p. 86.

[11]See Alexander L. George, "Political Leadership and Social Change in American Cities," *Daedalus* (Fall 1968), pp. 1194–1217; and Jeffrey L. Pressman, "Preconditions of Mayoral Leadership," *American Political Science Review* (June 1972), pp. 511–24.

Adlai Stevenson's candidacy for president brought many of these amateur citizen-politicians into politics. Joining the Volunteers for Stevenson, and working at doorbell ringing and fund raising whetted the taste for politics of these enthusiastic homemakers, young public relations people, lawyers, and college professors. They organized political clubs to stay in politics. In 1968 the presidential nominating campaign of Senator Eugene McCarthy attracted a new group of amateurs from similar backgrounds, many of whom worked for George McGovern in 1972.

The amateurs consist largely of educated white middle-class people, cosmopolitan in outlook, under forty-five years of age, and articulate. They act in the tradition of an earlier generation of New Deal liberals and Progressive reformers. Concerned about the failure of the party professionals to emphasize issues and the inability of party leaders to develop programs, the new amateurs formed their own clubs. There they discussed civil rights, urban renewal, and education. But these were not merely debating societies; they were also action-oriented, working at the grass roots to secure the nomination of candidates, often against the leadership of the regular Democratic organizations.

That reform clubs will have staying power and will set the style for modern city politics is doubtful. Party professionals and most political scientists are skeptical. They accuse these amateurs of being more interested in talk than in action; of preferring to be right rather than effective; of intolerance toward those who do not share their own goals. The "pros" also contend that the amateurs are unrealistic in hoping to develop programmatic, cohesive, disciplined parties of liberal orientation within our large cities.

In fact, it is argued by some, the amateurs are making it difficult for the party professionals to secure the goals the amateurs say they want. The great mass of the urban population does not share these goals. If the amateurs force elected officers to follow the "new party line" and fail to recognize the compromises necessary to gain power, they will throw political control of the city to those who will exploit mass sentiments for illiberal purposes. In time, endorsement of candidates by a club may become a political liability. James Q. Wilson, a critic of the clubs, writes: "The debate over issues becomes, in a strict sense, a spurious debate, because it is not a responsible discussion of real policy alternatives but a device for generating incentives for party activities."[12] There is also a danger to the democratic process, according to some critics, of a too heavy infusion into our political system of people who are not motivated by personal political ambitions. They contend that high-minded persons with no concern for their political futures weaken the restraint that comes from the electoral process—that the people can throw you out at the next election if they don't like your views. As political scientist Joseph Schlesinger points out: "To slight the role of ambition in politics . . . or to treat it as a human failing to be suppressed, is to miss the central function of ambition in political systems. A political system unable to kindle ambitions for office is as much in danger of breaking down as one unable to restrain ambitions.

---

[12]James Q. Wilson, *The Amateur Democrat: Club Politics in Three Cities—New York, Chicago, Los Angeles* (University of Chicago Press, 1962), is an analysis of the goals, composition, and role of the clubs.

Representative government, above all, depends on a supply of men so driven; the desire for election and, more important, for reelection becomes the electorate's restraint upon its public officials. No more irresponsible government is imaginable than one of high-minded men unconcerned for their political futures."[13]

The political club members are not the only kind of amateur. Other kinds of local citizen politicians are the Sierra Club enthusiasts who press for better conservation laws, such as the passage of their state's bottle bills, or battle against the Winter Olympics. They are the Common Cause activists who fight for open meetings and financial disclosure changes at city hall. Or they are the leaders of the neighborhood association embroiled in a fight over zoning and one-way streets. They are members of a small group supporting or opposing a special-assessment program. They are not interested in going to the regular party organization's meetings and would find them boring and of little significance if they did go. But they are interested in changing things or conserving things and they are willing, in their own narrow and perhaps amateur way, to become involved. Moreover, even if these amateurs have a rather narrow perspective about politics and are at times too unwilling to accept certain political realities, they often are able to adapt and adopt some of the tactics used by the regulars. Sometimes they even win.

Can the mayor lead? a case study

The mayor is usually the most important and the most visible political figure in the big city. Like presidents, mayors are supposed to enunciate the city's goals, play the leading role in getting them accepted by the people and adopted by the city government, and carry them out. But, like the presidents, they are hemmed in on many sides. Big cities vary widely in their politics and mayors in their powers. We might explore the problem of mayoral leadership by taking one example—the mayor of New York. His job is considered by some as second only to the president's in complexity and manageability, for not only is New York the nation's biggest city and one of the financial, cultural, intellectual, and trading centers of the world, but it sprawls over parts of three states and hence continually faces problems of city-state-federal relationships.[14]

ADMINISTRATIVE CHIEF?

The mayor of New York City is supposed to be the administrative boss of the city government, and in some respects he is. For one thing, he appoints the heads of virtually all departments, such as police or fire; members of city boards and commissions, such as the parole commission; and city magistrates and justices. Unlike the president and most governors, he does not share his appointive power with legislative bodies. The mayor's authority to remove subordinates, despite numerous restrictions, is also fairly sweeping. In short, in his power to hire and fire, the mayor of New York is truly "the chief executive officer of the city," as the city charter says.

[13]Joseph Schlesinger, *Ambition and Politics: Political Careers in the United States.* (Rand McNally, 1966), p. 2.

[14]This case study, except where otherwise noted, is taken from Sayre and Kaufman, *Governing New York City;* modifications have been made to take into account charter and political changes. For a vivid account of "leadership" in New York City written by a personal aide to Mayor John Lindsay, see Barry Gottehrer, *The Mayor's Man* (Doubleday, 1975).

The mayor also has limited administrative power over the city's independent authorities. Some of the heads of authorities have won such wide recognition that they are politically effective in their own right. Most notable of these by far was Robert Moses, who might well have been called "Mr. Authority." His jobs suggest the variety of special agencies as well as the versatility of this brilliant, aggressive, and often controversial man. During the 1930s through the 1960s Moses was chairman of the Triborough Bridge and Tunnel Authority, commissioner of the Parks Department, a member of the City Planning Commission, chairman of the Mayor's Committee on Slum Clearance, a member of the New York City Youth Board, and president of the Jones Beach State Parkway Authority, besides holding many other jobs.[15] In all these positions he attracted friends (and enemies) within the city's administration as well as from the public. Clearly, in dealing with Moses the mayor was dealing with an independent leader who had his own "constituency." Relations between the two were often made more difficult because Moses was a lifelong Republican, and most New York mayors are Democrats.

The case of Robert Moses reminds us of a central fact of administration: Administrators are people, and they have interests, attitudes, and loyalties that may conflict with those of the mayor. This is certainly the case in New York City. Even the great "line" departments such as police and fire, theoretically under the direct control of the mayor, are not composed simply of persons deployed from the top. The heads of the departments are experienced people who have worked their way up from the ranks; who have strong loyalties and obligations to their colleagues and subordinates; who may entertain professional and perhaps political ambitions of their own; and who enjoy direct access to newspaper editors, party leaders, interest groups, and professional associations inside and outside New York. The rank-and-file employees—the firefighters, police officers, sanitation personnel, city hospital workers, guards at the city jails—have their unions or associations, desires for higher pay and shorter hours, all kinds of internal specializations, jealousies, and mutual defense coalitions against excessive interference from the top.

So we must forget the notion of the mayor as a real administrative "boss." He has great administrative resources, but he must ride herd on a collection of many thousands of human beings with cross-cutting interests and attitudes. And his powers are even more limited in his other roles.

LEGISLATIVE LEADER?

The mayor of New York, like any other mayor, finds his policy-making power splintered and fragmented from the moment he takes office. For he is working within a system of government that divides power among the national, state, and local governments, and among many officials at each level. Practically speaking, the mayor must coordinate or at least clear his major policies with the president, the governor of New York, one or two United States senators from the state, several members of Congress, state legislators from the city, and other officials, such as the state attorney general, members of Congress from the adjoining states of New Jersey and Connecticut, and perhaps a cabinet member or two. Within the city government his legislative power is further fragmented.

---

[15]Robert Moses is the subject of an instructive study by Robert A. Caro, *The Power Broker* (Knopf, 1974).

To be sure, the mayor has formal responsibility for shaping and presenting the legislative program. Indeed, formally or informally, he presents it several times—to the council, to the governor and the state legislature, and to other officials or bodies that must consider his policies. But the formal lawmaking power is vested in the city council, consisting of thirty-five members, twenty-five elected by districts, and ten boroughwide, two from each borough. On paper the council would appear to be virtually a little Congress; actually, it has played a rather passive role, allowing the mayor or other officials to take the leadership. The council fails to exercise the historic weapon of legislative bodies against executives—the appropriating power. It is almost monopolized by one party and hence lacks vigorous internal controversy in decision making. Weakness begets weakness; as the council has failed to exercise its power, it has failed to attract strong people who might convert it into a stronger agency.

The main fiscal control of the city is exercised neither by the mayor nor by the council, but by the Board of Estimate. This is a rather curious institution for a city that prides itself on modernity and streamlining in so many other areas of life. Composed of eight members with varying numbers of votes (four each for the mayor, the comptroller, and the president of the council; two each for the five borough presidents), the Board of Estimate is not elected directly by the people; its members are all elected to other positions. Still, it has an important role in budget making. Unlike the council, it does not follow the mayor's lead; usually it prefers to fight him. Sayre and Kaufman sum up its role as follows: "Its eight members are the most influential elected officials in the city government; it has developed a mode of operation which maximizes both its formal and informal powers; the relationships of its members with the party leaders are close and usually stable; it has high prestige with the other participants (in the city's political process), particularly with those to whom it provides a public forum; and its institutional life, especially its informal processes, is surrounded by a helpful amount of mystery."[16] Like Congress on the national level, the Board is the main countervailing power to the mayor.

A member of the city council need not automatically be hostile to the mayor. The extent to which a mayor can induce cooperation from a council member or a member of the Board of Estimate turns mainly on the extent to which the mayor can shape the political pressures working on the legislator in city hall and in the latter's district. In city hall the mayor can deal in jobs, favors, personal recognition, and the other usual currency of practical politics. But this may not be enough, just as it is often not enough in Washington. The usual currency of political influence is limited, and rival political leaders have some of that currency too. Ultimately, the mayor's power depends on the extent to which he can mobilize support for himself and his program that can be converted to support for, or threats to, the council member or member of the Board of Estimate. And this balance in turn depends on political organization.

New York City Mayor Abraham Beame announces he will seek a second term in city hall. He lost his bid and was suceeded in 1978 by Edward Koch.

PARTY LEADER?

A Democratic mayor of New York can be the most powerful single party leader in the city. Still, he must share his party power with other officials and with party leaders. There is no single citywide political party organization. Democrats are organized on the basis of county committees from

[16]Sayre and Kaufman, *Governing New York City*, p. 626.

the five boroughs, which in turn oversee vast hierarchies of precinct, ward, and assembly-district organizations. The mayor deals not with a unified party organization but with five county leaders, with members of the New York delegation to the United States Congress, with borough presidents (who have power in the Board of Estimate), and some traditional party bosses who hold no major office. Sometimes the mayor benefits from the absence of citywide unity, for he can follow the tactic of "dividing and conquering" the county leaders, but the party divisions may handicap him in pushing through a new program.

What a strong mayor must do is to build his own personal organization inside and outside the regular political party. This is a formidable task. He has considerable patronage, but jobs are not enough to build a political machine. Unlike the president, who can lean on the national party committee as well as his personal staff, the mayor has only a few political aides. He must deal with party committee officials who may be much more interested in working for other candidates and officeholders than for him. Usually the mayor finds that his personal organization is not enough by itself; he must supplement it by bargaining for allies among the other officeholders and heads of personal organizations.

The mayor and the party leaders often work together; the mayor "recognizes" the party leaders through patronage, and the party leaders help the mayor by ensuring his renomination and helping his reelection. Occasionally the mayor and the machine have a falling-out. In the past the mayor was often subordinated to the machine; Tammany chiefs like William Tweed and the more genteel Charles Murphy dictated key Democratic nominations. In 1961, making full use of the personal machine he had built up in his seven years in office, Robert Wagner beat the Tammany candidate in a bitter battle for renomination.

Wagner then announced he would take the leadership in reorganizing and strengthening the Democratic party. Following his election he proposed new rules under which the party would open its ranks to all interested citizens, improve its procedures for internal democracy, and play a more prominent role in drawing up and publicizing party programs. He forced some of the old party leaders out of their positions. Yet many were skeptical of any lasting improvement in the city's Democratic party.

LEADER OR CHIEF BARGAINER?

Plainly the mayor of New York is severely restricted, no matter how great his ability. Most of the time he must piece together a coalition out of various politicians and fragments of influence. He is less the leader who draws his sword, points out the direction, and rallies his battalions than the horse trader who talks and swaps and persuades and compromises. His governmental role tends to be more defensive than affirmative. He is continually involved in the process of building administrative, legislative, or party coalitions; and the price of such coalitions is usually weakened programs and policies. Usually he is in the middle of the political marketplace because little of importance can be done without his consent. But he finds effective action along a wide front, or even long-range planning, to be very difficult.

Whether or not one approves of this situation depends on one's views of the organization of political power. Some would contend that more progress comes of loose political arrangements like those of New York City than from a centralized and disciplined system. Lasting progress, they contend, comes here and there, two feet forward and one foot back, and is not dependent on direction from the top. Others hold that a city as sprawling and disorganized as New York needs a strong mayor and effective city government to lead it, and that too much bargaining and compromising will make impossible "mastery of the metropolis" by the city people as a whole.

Much more could be said about the difficulties of governing New York City. And indeed we will return in part to this discussion to take up the New York City fiscal crisis of the late 1970s in Chapter 33. A few cautions, however, are in order. New York has been cursed, many people feel, with a long succession of ineffective mayors in recent years, for reasons ranging from the vast number of public authorities to the existence and power of the Board of Estimate. But the situation is different in many other major cities. Mayors in Seattle, Los Angeles, Chicago, and Indianapolis have been able to provide leadership and have been able to make their cities governable. Also, city managers in Cincinnati, Kansas City, Dallas, and San Diego have enjoyed reasonable success in their efforts. So, although we can learn from the troubles in New York, New York is not the model for all American cities.

Can we govern the metro region effectively?

Most of this and the previous chapter would seem to answer with a big "yes" our theme question: Have the people of metropolis lost the power to govern themselves? The division between central city and suburbia, divided executive authority, fragmented legislative power, splintered and noncompetitive political parties, the absence of strong central government for the whole metropolitan region, the need for the mayor and other city leaders to bargain with so many national, state and local officials—all this would seem to suggest that the people as a whole cannot master these shapeless giants.

Who governs and what difference does it make who governs? At the turn of the century reformers were afraid of boss domination. But in the modern metropolis, the mayor of the central city, as we have seen, lacks authority even over many of the agencies within the city. Political machines do not run the central city, let alone the whole metropolis. The specialized urban bureaucrats may wield a lot of power, especially over wages and a few pet policies, but they do not offer leadership or direction for the metropolis. The "special interests" do not seem to control the metropolis, nor usually does a "business elite," nor any other kind of "they." Who, then, governs metropolis? Nobody? Or perhaps everybody? Upon closer analysis, the major problem seems to be not who governs, or who might be manipulating the people, but rather whether the dispersed political and physical arrangements in the metropolis prevent coherent leadership.

Over the years, scholars have proposed a variety of solutions to the nation's metropolitan governance needs. These include: city-county consolidation, metropolitan government (both one-tier or two-tier), annexation and even statehood. "But in the 170 years since the city of New Orleans and Orleans Parish marked the first major consolidation, there have been but 25 city-county consolidations. (The most recent consolidation took place when the city of Anchorage, Alaska combined with the Greater Anchorage Borough.) There are only a handful of metropolitan entities, from Dade County in the Miami area to the Twin Cities Metropolitan

Council covering Minneapolis and St. Paul, and few effective nonmetro-politan regional entities."[17]

The traditional solution to the problems of metropolitan areas has been to create governmental organizations for the whole metropolitan region. The idea was that if order could be brought about, fragmentation elimi-nated, and adequate services provided on a regional basis, rational and effective government would result. But one of the flaws of this solution was that many of the suburbs often opposed being politically united with other parts of the metropolitan area. Moreover, as Murphy and Rehfuss point out, another flaw is the basic assumption that "metropolitan prob-lems are essentially problems of metropolitan government. If this were true, then problems could be solved merely by reorganizing government." "Unfortunately," as they note, "problems like crime and housing segre-gation are not so easily solved. These and other problems exist and will continue to plague urban areas with or without governmental reor-ganization"[18]

As a kind of midway alternative to metropolitan government the na-tional government has urged states to create substate districts, essentially regional planning agencies, and require state funding to them, or through them to the localities. They also recommend that local units of government clear local programs that have a regional impact with these substate agencies, and that they authorize these new districts to assume operating roles over such areawide activities as waste disposal, transportation, water supply, and so on. It remains to be seen if the proposal for such regional units of government will be any more acceptable than have other schemes to provide effective areawide governance capabilities.

One of the specific schemes along these lines tried recently is the nationally encouraged creation of metropolitan-wide Councils of govern-ment (COGs). These are forums established throughout the country in the major metro areas to bring locally elected officials together. The COGS have devoted most of their time and resources to physical plan-ning and noncontroversial activities that do not touch central city prob-lems of race and poverty. The councils of government are set up, more-over, in such a way as to give the suburbs a veto over any project that would threaten their autonomy. Many people, in fact, consider the COGs to be barriers to solving metropolitan problems, just one more committee to deal with. In some respects the COGs suffer the same fate as the United Nations; it is a useful forum to which city officials may bring their prob-lems and exchange ideas, but little action ever results.[19]

Although we have had little success in the United States with metropoli-tan government, there have been countless efforts and experiments to seek solutions to the problem of fragmentation. One of these experiments has been the suggestion to make the *county* the major unit of government, especially for the approximately 100 metropolitan areas that are entirely

[17]Chairman's Introduction, *Regionalism Revisited: Recent Areawide and Local Responses* (Advi-sory Commission on Intergovernmental Relations, June 1977), p. 1.

[18]Thomas P. Murphy and John Rehfuss, *Urban Politics in the Suburban Era* (Dorsey Press, 1976), p. 236.

[19]See Melvin B. Mogulof, *Five Metropolitan Governments* (Urban Institute, 1972), and Mogulof, *Governing Metropolitan Areas* (Urban Institute, 1971).

within a single county. Erie County in New York has taken over health, hospital, library, and welfare services formerly handled by the cities within the county. Los Angeles County has assumed many functions for the hundreds of communities in that sprawling metropolitan region. Another and even more dramatic effort to fashion regional government is to abolish both city and county governments and merge them together. Since 1947, more than fifteen consolidated governments have been created, most by means of local referendum and two by state legislative action. The better known examples have occurred in Jacksonville, Florida, and Nashville, Tennessee. In both instances, voters in these areas agreed that the counties and the central cities would be abolished and entirely new governments would come into being: the Consolidated Government with a mayor and council in Jacksonville, and the Metropolitan Government with mayor and council in Nashville. Almost all recent efforts to get voters to approve county-city consolidations have failed. Defeats have been suffered in Portland (Oregon), Sacramento, Durham, Evansville (Indiana) and Charleston (South Carolina). Voters turned down the merger of Salt Lake City and Salt Lake County; so did voters in Ashland and Frankfort areas in Kentucky and in the Tallahassee and Lean County, Florida.

Examples of partial county consolidation brought about by the action of state legislatures are the Unigov in Indianapolis and the Twin Cities Metropolitan Council in Minneapolis–St. Paul. Unigov in Indianapolis operates under a single mayor and a twenty-nine member council.

> Citizens now receive most municipal and regional services from the consolidated government. . . . Beneath this areawide Unigov, . . . are several small cities and townships. Three cities were not affected by the consolidation, even though they are within Marion County, fourteen towns continue to elect governing officials and pass ordinances, although they must meet Unigov standards and the regional government must approve issuance of their general obligation bonds. Nine townships remain as they were before Unigov was formed, and provide welfare services.[20]

Unigov was created in 1970 by the state legislature without a referendum among the local units of government. This was a sharp departure from tradition and probably an essential procedure if such consolidations are to take place in many areas.[21] In some states, central cities have been able to annex large amounts of unincorporated territory, but after suburbs have become established, with their own governments, it is politically difficult to secure their consent to consolidation with the central city.

The Twin Cities Metropolitan Council was established in 1967 by legislative act. This fifteen-member council is appointed by the governor. Members are selected to represent population districts. "Prior to 1967

[20]League of Women Voters Educational Fund, *Supercity/Hometown, U.S.A.: Prospects for Two-Tier governments* (Praeger, 1974). See also York Wilibern, "UNIGOV: Local Government Reorganization in Indianapolis," in *Regional Governance: Promise and Performance* (Advisory Commission on Intergovernmental Relations, 1973), pp. 47–73. For a somewhat similar experiment, see Ted Kolderie, "Governance in the Twin Cities Area of Minnesota," *ibid.*, pp. 114–38.

[21]See Vincent L. Marando, "The Politics of Metropolitan Reform," in Alan K. Campbell and Roy W. Bahl, *State and Local Government: The Political Economy of Reform* (Free Press, 1976), pp. 24–49.

the Twin Cities region was plagued for many years by governmental fragmentation, tax inequities and disparities, and inconsistent provision of services throughout the region. The two central cities were ringed by over 130 incorporated suburban municipalities. This made central city annexation and city-county consolidation strategies useless for coping with metropolitan problems."[22] Today, the Twin Cities Metro Council which is in essence a new layer of government superimposed on top of the existing units of government, serves as a metropolitan planning and policy coordination agency with the following powers: It reviews all applications for federal funds from the region. It guides planning and development in the region, such as for airports and highways. It has the right to veto the legislative acts of communities or local special districts that endanger the overall welfare of the region. The Twin Cities model may be relatively easy to transfer elsewhere in the nation. On the other hand, it is not nearly as far-reaching a metropolitan government as are the city-county consolidation efforts in Jacksonville, Nashville, or the federated metropolitan plan that operates in greater Miami.

The federated city plan: a case study

Until 1957 the Miami metropolitan area was typical of many big cities: the population had mushroomed, but its political structure remained unchanged. The core city, was surrounded by twenty-five separate municipalities and wide expanses of unincorporated areas. Duplication of governmental services between Dade County and the several municipalities and inadequate service were all complicated by an inequitable tax structure. The first step toward improving the situation was taken in 1956 when the people of Florida approved a constitutional amendment giving Dade County constitutional home rule. The next year the voters of the entire county adopted a home-rule charter creating a countywide metropolitan government.

The new charter provided for a federated structure. The city of Miami and all the suburban cities retain their own identity and those functions not assigned to Metro. Metro has jurisdiction over such activities as fire and police protection, slum clearance, major transportation facilities, planning, and water and sewerage systems. It is governed by a board of commissioners elected on a countywide basis who in turn select a county manager.

During the first year of its operation under the new charter, Metro was sued 150 times by opponents of metropolitan federation, but it won all the decisive legal battles. In 1959 a move to amend the charter to reduce the powers of Metro and return many functions to the separate cities was soundly defeated.[23] But in 1968 a proposed charter amendment to transfer all municipal police and fire-fighting functions to Metro was defeated. Nonetheless, the visible success of the federated-city program in Dade County may encourage other areas to take the plunge.

---

[22]Murphy and Rehfuss, *Urban Politics in the Suburban Era*, p. 262. For an analysis of the early years of the Twin Cities Council, see Stanley Baldinger, *Planning and Governing the Metropolis: The Twin Cities Experience* (Praeger, 1971).

[23]A major source on the early years of the Dade County reform effort is Edward Sofen, *The Miami Metropolitan Experiment*, 2nd ed., (Doubleday, 1966). See also Melvin Mogulof, *Five Metropolitan Governments*, op. cit.

Nearly every metropolitan area today has a COG and other official and semiofficial bodies working to rationalize the maze of governmental structures. A remarkably high degree of cooperation already does take place, although much of it is informal. But progress in designing area-wide multipurpose, integrated metropolitan governing bodies has been slow. Why? In large part because metropolitan solutions must necessarily be gradual, depending upon specific needs and the physical and political context:

> Metropolitan reform that proceeds from the assumption that what is appropriate for Syracuse must also be best for San Antonio or Sacramento is likely to contain such simplistic premises as to be unworkable in any area. For example, city-county consolidation has been an effective solution for Nashville, but it could not get beyond the proposal stage in Pittsburgh or beyond the electorate in Memphis; annexation has worked well in Houston, Phoenix, and Oklahoma City, but would be of little help in larger cities ringed by incorporated suburbs. Similarly, the urban county approach, while serving the Los Angeles area reasonably well, almost surely would be ineffective in New England's traditionally weak counties. Basically, efforts to secure full-scale reorganization might be suitable only for many smaller metropolitan areas in which there are no sharp city-suburban cleavages and racial conflict is minimal. In such instances, it would represent a form of preventive medicine, designed to avoid the problems of larger metropolitan areas.[24]

From the Wall Street Journal.
Reprinted by permission of Joseph
Serrano.

In most metropolitan regions, to combine city and suburbs would be to shift political power to the suburbs. In most northern centers it would give Republicans control of city affairs. In other cases it would enable Democrats to threaten the present Republican one-party systems in the suburbs. Under these circumstances, neither Democratic leaders in central cities nor Republicans in control of the suburbs show much enthusiasm for metropolitan government schemes.

Blacks usually oppose area consolidation or similar reform proposals because it would dilute their political power, often rather severely. In the Jacksonville consolidation with Duval County, the black population as a percent of the total population was halved with the city-county consolidation. Moreover, over 120 cities now have black mayors, many of them large cities. Most of the black residents in these cities and in cities that might soon elect a black mayor understandably fear that metropolitan political reorganization would (1) undermine the political opportunities that have only recently come to blacks and (2) not result in structures that would be responsive to the social and economic problems of the poor.[25]

Apart from these political, social, racial, and economic differences which make metropolitan reorganization difficult, the fact is that most of the residents of metropolis are not sufficiently unhappy with the present governmental structure to favor major changes. Of course they want better

[24]Robert L. Lineberry, "Reforming Metropolitan Governance: Requiem or Reality," *Georgetown Law Journal*, Symposium on Restructuring Metropolitan Area Government (March–May 1970), p. 710. See also Willis D. Hawley, "On Understanding Metropolitan Political Integration," in Hawley, et al. *Theoretical Perspectives on Urban Politics*, pp. 100–145.

[25]Dale Rogers Marshall, Bernard Frieden, and Daniel Fessler, *Minority Perspectives* (Resources for the Future, 1972).

services, but these they hope to achieve by negotiation and other special devices. There is no rebellion against the existing governmental structure. It may not be the best arrangement but it does work, after a fashion.

COOPERATION IN PRACTICE

Drastic alteration of the constitutional structure of metropolis seems unlikely, at least in the near future. Through patchwork, piecemeal, pragmatic arrangements, the services the public want and are willing to pay for are being provided.

The special metropolitan districts, such as the Cook County Sanitary District and the Metropolitan District Commission for Eastern Massachusetts, have been mentioned. Central cities and county governments are providing services for the satellite cities. For example, about three dozen suburban communities buy water from Chicago. Los Angeles County supplies a variety of services to the smaller cities within the county on a contractual basis.[26]

The fiscal problems of metropolis remain severe. Metropolitan areas as a whole are wealthy, but many of their constituent parts are impoverished. The federal government, by grants to states and cities, is providing a larger portion of the funds to deal with city planning, to improve mass transportation to provide urban development, hospitals and welfare. Even so, the net result of intergovernmental grants to cities has been to reinforce the existing fiscal differences within the metro regions.[27]

A SOLUTION OUTSIDE METROPOLIS?

Many political scientists, for reasons we have discussed, believe that solutions to metropolitan problems are beyond the capacity of metropolis itself. They have advanced a variety of proposals. Some favor a strengthened role for the federal government with special emphasis on "equity" or on the goal that services should be directly related to needs. Some advocate vast increases in revenue-sharing, but they would give the revenue on the condition that states and local governments rationalize the governmental machinery of metropolis. Others believe the job must be done by the states, which hold the fundamental constitutional power. Still others put forward bold new proposals to establish *regional* governments that would rule over huge regions embracing many of metropolitan areas.

Big-city mayors have made it clear that in their judgment the urban condition is acute, and that we must rearrange our national priorities and allocate billions of dollars for massive aid to our large cities. For the cities themselves and their officials lack the resources and political jurisdiction necessary to attack the basic causes of urban pathology.[28] "We surrender," some mayors have been saying in effect to Washington. "Treat us like a conquered and occupied nation. Give us the kind of aid you gave Germany and Japan."

All these solutions have their opponents. Congress still does not show an overly sympathetic response to big-city mayors. State control? States

---

[26]Robert L. Bish, *The Public Economy of Metropolitan Areas* (Markham, 1971); and *Regional Decision-Making: New Strategies for Substate Districts* (Advisory Commission on Intergovernmental Relations, 1973).

[27]See Lineberry, "Reforming Metropolitan Governance," pp. 713–14; and also Norton Long, *The Unwalled City* (Basic Books, 1972).

[28]See Norton E. Long "A Marshall Plan for Cities?" *Public Interest* (Winter 1977), pp. 48–58.

are unable to deal easily with the problem of giant cities that stretch over state lines. New regional governments? A fascinating idea, but one that is probably beyond the reach of constitutional power and the capacity of the American people to engineer.

The issue, however, goes deeper than this; it goes back to the very heart of the question of government by the people. Can popular government best be effected through a strong executive leader of the La Guardia or Daley type—a person who wins or builds a strong position of political power and then tries to pull the divided city government together behind his program? Many would answer yes; they contend that progress can come only as a result of strong, central controls at the top, even though they want the leader to be willing to make concessions to particular groups and local areas. Not only can executive leadership bring about the drastic changes that may be necessary to metropolis, but only through a strong mayor can metropolitan government work for the benefit of the great majority of the people. Just as the nation has needed Jacksons and Lincolns and Roosevelts, so the cities need popular, even charismatic, leadership.

Others disagree. Progress in our great cities, they hold, will come from piecemeal efforts, from bargaining among leaders of all types, from community action, from exerting pressure here and there, from hammering out agreements or "treaties" among diverse groups. They grant that government by negotiation is often slow, and that makeshift arrangements sometimes result. But, given the nature of megalopolis, it is impossible to do better. Instead of grandiose schemes of regional government and city planning and disruptive urban renewal of whole blocks, they would like to see more moderate and prudent efforts. In the process they hope to hold on to some of the values of metropolis today—the unique streets, some of the older buildings, the little houses and apartment buildings that they prefer to the great hunks of concrete and glass and steel so beloved, they feel, by the city planners and reformers.

There are many positions in between these extremes. But certainly the extremes pose once again our crucial problem of central political control versus a more open and decentralized form of governance.

Summary

1. The politics of who governs and how to govern the metropolitan area are complicated by the fragmented political jurisdictions within most metro areas. Making matters even more difficult is the emergence of powerful public employee unions and the decline of central city political bosses and political party machines. Power has become dispersed as the problems of many of the central cities have become severe. American cities are in deep financial trouble; parts of urban United States are increasingly becoming "black, brown, and broke."

2. For a generation or more, reformers thought the answer to the problem of governance in the metropolis rested in finding and electing a strong central city mayor or establishing a regional government for the whole area. Both solutions have been difficult to achieve. Many of our central cities, certainly New York, seem designed to undermine strong mayoral leadership. And resistance to regionwide government continues to be great throughout the nation.

3. Still, interlocal cooperation does take place and a considerable range of experiments and initiatives have been tried to help overcome problems in metro regions. Most scholars and experts agree that state and federal leadership is required if we are to help leaders in central cities and their neighboring communities to face up to the cooperative strategies needed to improve the quality of life in metropolitan areas.

4. Various state and federal financial assistance and incentives will doubtless also be necessary to start knocking down the economic, political, and social barriers that too often separate the growing population of black and brown residents of our central cities from the remaining white population.

State and Urban Policy Making

In the fall of 1974, violence and protest broke out in two cities—Charleston, West Virginia, and Boston. In Charleston two men were shot and another beaten, coal mines and businesses were shut down, windows were smashed by rocks and bottles, highways were blocked, and the 44,500-student school system was closed. Ironically, all this was launched by a patriotic group who called themselves Concerned Citizens. At the heart of the dispute were a few dozen textbooks, approved by the local school authorities, that the Concerned Citizens had found anti-American.

In Boston, the school system was almost shut down, and violence erupted for several days. The issue was desegregation of the public schools. Like most northern urban centers, Boston's populations had become segregated into racial and ethnic neighborhoods. Now the people were being told that some of their youngsters would be bused into other neighborhoods while youths from distant neighborhoods would be bused to theirs. Boston school authorities had delayed until the last minute, and only under pressure from federal officials did they act. But their actions met with bitter protest. Parades were held, and windows were smashed. U.S. Senator Edward Kennedy, who had preached cooperation with the new policies, was shouted down by an irate crowd, and narrowly escaped after becoming the target of tomatoes and other flying objects.

Schools in both cities gradually resumed more normal activities. But these incidents demonstrate that the views and the power of the people can easily be underestimated. The people have many ways to oppose actions they dislike.

The roads we ride on, the schools we attend, the electric light bills we pay, the purity of the water we drink, the safety of the elevators we ride in, where we can park our cars, when we can marry—all these matters and many others are affected by state and local policy making. Listen to the debates in the state legislature, attend the meetings of the city council, watch candidates, and you come face to face with the problems of law enforcement, education, welfare, highways. Should the city close another school? Where? Will the voters approve a bond issue to construct a new hospital? Should the state superintendent of schools be given authority to establish minimum standards for teachers? What can be done about the traffic jam on Main Street? Hundreds of people—mayors, legislators, judges, ward bosses, civic commissions, unions, chambers of commerce—participate in the process of determining what officials will do, which ones will do it, and how they will do it.

It is obviously impossible to explore each activity of our states, cities, counties, school districts, townships, and so on. But we can at least review a few of the highlights. Table 32–1 indicates many of the priorities of government at the state and local level in terms of money expenditures. In this chapter, we examine many of the basic policy functions of the states and communities.

Government as educator

In ancient Greece, Plato and Aristotle insisted that education was a vital task of government. To them government itself was an educational institution. Thomas Jefferson was convinced that an educated citizenry was essential to democratic government. But only during the past century has the idea become generally accepted that government should provide tax-supported schools.

Many groups opposed "free" education. They argued that it would lead to social unrest, undermine the family, give government control over the minds of the young, require a huge bureaucracy, and result in a fatal mixture of education and politics. Was it fair, they asked, to tax people who could afford to educate their own children in private schools in order to educate others?

Today, compulsory public education is an established fact (although parents may, if they choose, send their children to approved private schools). A strong movement has developed to extend public education downward to kindergarten and nursery school, upward through college and adult education, outward to cover more subjects, and deeper to cover them better. Today more than a third of all state and local government expenditures are for education—more than for any other function. The richer states spend a larger proportion of their budgets on schools than do

**32–1
State and local
expenditures by
policy function,
1974–75**

Policy functions	State government	Local government
Education	39.1%	45.0%
Public welfare	18.5	7.0
Highways	12.6	5.8
Health and hospitals	7.3	7.0
Natural resources	2.6	0.6
Interest on debt	2.4	3.8
Housing and urban renewal	0.5	2.1
Other	17.1	28.8

SOURCE: *Governmental Finances in 1974–75,* Bureau of the Census, U.S. Department of Commerce (1976), Table 6, p. 20.

the poorer states, though the poor states make a greater tax effort (That is, poorer states have to tax themselves at a higher rate because they have less wealth to tax.)

THE GOVERNANCE OF
EDUCATION

In Charlestown, West Virginia, the Reverend Avis Hill led a group called Concerned Citizens in a protest against the use of textbooks that the group considered anti-American.

The city, the county, the township, or the school district has the chief responsibility for providing public elementary and secondary education. The school district, of which there are over 15,000, is the basic unit. In each district the voters elect a board of education. This board levies taxes, in most cases independently of the city or county. It appoints a superintendent of schools and other supervisory personnel, hires the teachers, and runs the schools from grade one through twelve.

Each state has a superintendent of public instruction or a commissioner of education. In about eighteen states they are popularly elected; in almost all states they share some authority with a state board of education. Although actual operation of the public schools is the responsibility of the local community, state officers have important supervisory powers. For one thing, they distribute financial assistance. State money is passed out according to many formulas, but the trend is definitely toward the equalization of resources. States are giving more money to poorer communities. Critics charge that methods of financing public schools in most states are chaotic and unjust, and reformers are pressing for more progressive formulas.

State officials often certify teachers and set minimum salaries. They are sometimes consulted by local authorities to ensure that new school buildings meet the minimum specifications set by the state. Some state officials have the authority to set the course of study and to determine what must be taught and what may not be taught. Generally in the South and West, state authorities determine which books will be used in the schools.

Until the 1950s, most local school districts provided only for elementary and secondary education, although some of the larger cities also supported junior colleges and universities. Since the end of World War II there has been a major expansion of community colleges. Students may attend the first two years of college or receive technical education within their own community. The trend is to create separate college districts with their own boards to operate and raise funds for the local community college; in some areas, however, the college is part of the regular public school system.

States support many kinds of universities and colleges, including land-grant universities created by the Morrill Act in 1862. These colleges and universities are governed by boards, in some states appointed by the governor, in a few elected by the voters.[1] These boards are designed to give public higher education institutions some independence, even though they depend on the legislature and governor for funds. A few states have even gone further and written into the constitution provisions to secure the independence of some universities.

With nearly 80 percent of the 11 million college students now attending publicly supported institutions, the control and support of higher education have become significant political questions. State after state has created either a superboard to take over the operation of all public universities or a coordinating board with varying degrees of control over operations and budgets. In addition governors are trying to impose controls on

[1]See Robert O. Berdahl, *State Coordination of Higher Education* (American Council on Education, 1971).

public universities which university administrators insist are appropriate for a highway department but not for a university. No longer do universities and faculties have the same degree of independence they once did to decide teaching loads, internal procedures, and how they spend and account for the funds given them.

What of the national government? The United States has a long tradition of leaving the control and funding of education to the states and local units. We do not have, as do many European countries, a ministry of education. In France, for example, it has been said that you can know what is being taught in every school class at the same time every day. Our national government has always provided encouragement and some help to the states. But since the 1960s, its educational role has grown. It makes grants for facilities, equipment, scholarships, loans, research, and general aid at elementary, secondary, and higher educational levels. With these federal dollars have come federal controls over how these dollars may be spent. Today federal regulations cover admissions, recordkeeping, employment practices, care of experimental animals, fiscal auditing, and so on. The secretary of HEW and the commissioner of education who heads the U.S. Office of Education have become national leaders in the formulation of educational programs.

Private schools still flourish at all levels. Several decades ago the Supreme Court made it clear that although a state may compel parents to send their children to school, parents have a right to educate their children in private schools if they prefer. Today most private universities and colleges also receive federal assistance and are thus subject to federal regulation as to how these dollars are to be spent. At the elementary and secondary levels, private schools receive much less assistance because most schools are operated by churches, and there are constitutional obstacles to their being given tax dollars.

Although in recent years state aid to inner-city schools has increased, more aid is needed to remove the disparity between suburban and inner-city educational opportunity.

EDUCATION ISSUES

Education and educational policy have long been part of the democratic policy-making process. What shall be taught and who shall teach are often hotly contested issues. Schools are favorite targets for all groups eager to have students taught the "right" things. Patriotic groups are concerned about "un-American" doctrines sneaking into textbooks or classrooms. Labor leaders want students to receive the right impressions about labor and its role in society. Business leaders want the children to see the free-enterprise system in the correct light. Spokesmen for minorities and women's groups want textbooks and other materials to reflect the history and contributions of the groups they represent. Educators, however, try to keep the schools isolated from the demands of outside groups. They argue that censors, whether public or private, must be prevented from determining what should be taught.

Some believe that the professional educators have too much authority over the schools. Others assert that only the professionals are qualified to determine teacher competence and school curriculum.[2] Controversies also rage over the desirability and constitutionality of religious education, the virtues of progressive education, and the ways and techniques of teaching, reading, spelling, and mathematics. There is growing concern over falling test and reading scores across the country. Some educators contend

[2]Harmon Zeigler and M. Kent Jennings, *Governing American Schools: Political Interaction in Local School Districts* (Duxbury Press, 1974).

that declining standards cheat students and society and that "out of a well-intentioned but inept concern with equality of opportunity, we have begun to reject anything that exceeds anyone's grasp."[3]

Today, however, the most acute problems and intense issues stem from the fact that inner-city schools are often rigidly segregated, underfinanced, and undersupported. As the Office of Education's report *Equality of Educational Opportunity*, generally known as the Coleman Report, stated, "Segregation has operated to reduce the quality of education provided in schools serving disadvantaged Negro neighborhoods."[4] Although in recent years state aid has increased at a greater rate for city than for suburban schools, states continue to contribute more per pupil to suburban schools than to inner-city schools. Federal help, while concentrated on the inner-city schools, has not been enough to remove the disparity: The children who need the most and best education are getting the least and the worst.

Many cities have fought battles over the question of busing students from one neighborhood to another. The Supreme Court has specifically rejected the idea that there is any constitutional requirement to achieve racial balance in the public schools. But if segregation has resulted from the deliberate attempt to isolate pupils by race, then officials have the duty to use appropriate means, including busing, to end the constitutional violation. However, federal court orders must address themselves to the constitutional violation and cannot be imposed upon governmental units that were not involved. In other words the Supreme Court has refused to permit judges to require busing across school district lines to overcome segregation that results from the concentration of blacks in the inner city and of whites in the suburbs.

Proponents of busing point to the Coleman Report findings that bringing minority pupils to a school attended by children from more advantaged families raises the achievement of the children from the depressed areas without impairing the accomplishment of others. Opponents of busing stress the desirability of maintaining neighborhood schools. Opponents also note that Coleman himself has in effect rejected his old report and now feels that the negative consequences of busing, such as white flight to the suburbs, outweigh the advantages. His change of mind in this controversial policy area has had no apparent effect, however, on the Supreme Court's relatively firm support of school busing.

Another lively issue in many cities is whether control over schools should be decentralized to neighborhoods. Some black leaders have argued that decentralizing control will help black parents identify with the schools and give black people control over the education of their children. New York City and Detroit have experimented with decentralization, with mixed results.[5]

[3]John Silber, "The Need for Elite Education," *Harper's* (June, 1977), p. 22.

[4]Department of Health, Education, and Welfare, *Equality of Educational Opportunity* (Government Printing Office, 1966), p. 20.

[5]See Mario Fantini and Marilyn Gittell, *Decentralization: Achieving Reform* (Praeger, 1973); Joseph F. Zimmerman, *The Federated City: Community Control in Large Cities* (St. Martin's Press, 1972); and Douglas Yates, "Political Innovation and Institution Building: The Experience of Decentralization Experiments," in Willis D. Hawley, et al., *Theoretical Perspectives on Urban Politics* (Prentice-Hall, 1976), pp. 146–75; and Norman I. Fainstein and Susan S. Fainstein, "The Future of Community Control," *American Political Science Review* (September 1976), pp. 905–23.

In the early 1970s, several investigations into the relationship between school financing, or school quality, and student achievement questioned the conclusions of the Coleman Report. It was generally agreed that, though high-quality teachers matter most, there is nothing that consistently and unambiguously makes a difference in student achievement. Children, reported one study, are far more influenced by what happens *at home* than by what happens *in school.* School desegregation and equalizing the quality of schools improve only very slightly the learning abilities of the less-advantaged students.[6] Still, whatever the form of organization and control, most people support the Kerner Commission, which recommended "a comprehensive approach designed to reconstruct the ghetto child's social and intellectual environment, compensate for disadvantages already suffered and provide necessary tools for development of essential literacy skills. This approach will entail adoption of new and costly educational policies and practices beginning with early childhood and continuing through elementary and secondary schools."[7] Clearly, the question of how much should be spent and for what kinds of programs to provide the poor with the education they need to become self-sufficient will be one of the continuing and controversial issues of the 1980s.

Another acute problem at the local level stems from the fact that schools are primarily financed by the property tax. This means that districts with the least valuable property have to tax themselves at the highest rates, and still are not likely to have as much money to educate their children as those living in districts where there is more valuable property. We shall discuss this further in the next chapter.

Another local educational issue flows from the growing militancy of teachers. They are organizing into unions at the same time that school authorities, faced with taxpayer resistance and inflation, struggle to find funds to operate schools. These fiscal pressures are becoming most acute just when, for the first time in decades, we are faced not with too many pupils, but too many teachers and buildings.

EDUCATION AND GOVERNMENTS

Whatever the arrangements to govern and operate our schools and colleges, elaborate attempts have been made to isolate from the rest of government school boards, boards of trustees, boards of regents, and other agencies that govern educational institutions. This isolation is strongly supported by well-organized groups such as the Parent–Teacher Associations, the National Education Association, the American Association of University Professors, the American Council on Education and other university and educational groups. It is also supported by the general conviction of most citizens that education should be kept out of the hands of the politicians. The special responsibility of educational institutions to search for the truth and to teach without fear of retribution makes it undesirable to govern them by the same kind of arrangements that are appropriate for institutions primarily concerned with power.

Education is, however, of such concern to so many people, and there are

---

[6]See Christopher Jencks, et al., *Inequality: A Reassessment of the Effect of Family and Schooling in America* (Basic Books, 1972). But see also *Financing Schools and Property Tax Relief: A State Responsibility* (Advisory Commission on Intergovernmental Relations, 1973).

[7]*Report of the National Advisory Commission on Civil Disorders,*p. 244.

so many different ideas about how the schools should be run, that it cannot be divorced from the political system. Educational policies, like those in agriculture, law enforcement, or any other field, are determined in our government by the political processes available and accessible to the people.[8]

Social services

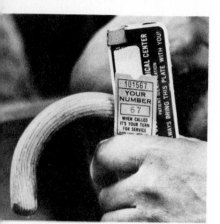

State and local government is still primarily responsible for welfare programs.

Welfare, despite sharply increasing federal involvement, remains a major state and local administrative responsibility. States and localities now pick up only about 20 percent of welfare and related social services costs, but this still constitutes the second largest expenditure for most states.

Today every state has some kind of department of welfare or human resources. This agency either directly administers welfare programs or supervises local officials who actually administer the programs. The county welfare departments, which in order to qualify for federal help must be staffed by persons selected on the basis of merit, determine which individuals are entitled to assistance and deal with clients. Within the limits of the federal program, each state is free to determine the size and details of its own welfare assistance.

General relief is almost entirely an activity of state and local government. General noninstitutionalized relief is essentially a county responsibility. Some townships do this job, but most welfare workers believe that townships are too small to support adequate welfare departments. A properly administered department requires trained caseworkers to process applications, make home visits, and help individuals and families.

Most states have assumed the responsibility for emotionally disturbed people, and have set up reformatories for juvenile delinquents. In some states, institutions for youthful lawbreakers have been placed under the jurisdiction of welfare rather than correctional authorities. In recent years there has been encouraging progress toward trained staff and more adequate facilities.

PUBLIC HEALTH

During a summer in the 1780s, the streets of Philadelphia were deserted. All who could afford to do so had taken their families and fled to the country. Every night the sounds of the death cart echoed through the empty city. Philadelphia had been stricken by a yellow-fever epidemic. Only when cool weather returned did the city resume normal activity. There were few families that did not lose a child, father, or mother.

Yellow fever, dysentery, malaria, and other diseases have periodically swept American cities. These catastrophes were one of the hazards of city life. As late as 1878–79, yellow fever struck the South. Memphis was nearly depopulated. State after state, following the lead of Louisiana and Massachusetts, established a board of health. Spurred by the medical discoveries of Pasteur and other scientists, authorities began programs for the protection of public health. Open sewers were covered and other hygienic measures instituted. In fact, it was not until contagious diseases had been brought under the control that the large city became a relatively safe place to live.

Today thousands of local governments—counties, cities, townships, special health districts—have some kind of public health program. Every state has an agency, usually called a department of health, that administers the state program and supervises local officials. The U.S. Public Health

[8]See Frederick Wirt and Michael Kirst, *The Political Web of American Education* (Little, Brown, 1972); and Zeigler and Jennings, *Governing American Schools.*

Government scientists aboard a helium balloon follow the movement of a mass of polluted air over Missouri and Indiana. They found that pollution originating in cities can foul the air in rural areas hundreds of miles away.

Service conducts research, assists state and local authorities, and administers federal grants to encourage them to expand their programs.

Prevention and control of disease is still a major public health activity. Doctors are required to report cases of communicable disease. Health department officials then investigate to discover the source of the infection, isolate the afflicted persons, and take whatever action seems to be called for. Most state health departments give doctors free vaccine and serum; many local departments give free vaccinations to those who cannot afford to go to private physicians. Since the public shows more enthusiasm for specific programs than for general disease control, some diseases have come in for special attention. The national government provides financial assistance for such activities as tuberculosis and venereal-disease control. Mobile X-ray units take free X-rays of schoolchildren, teachers, and the general public. Public health officials try to protect water supplies and see to it that waste and sewage are safely disposed of. They protect the community's food supply by inspecting hotels, restaurants, and food markets.

State and local governments are beginning to move on the environmental health front, and in fact several states have pioneered the way. California, New York, and Pennsylvania began state clean air programs before the federal government acted. Congress has followed the states' lead by gradually adopting more stringent federal regulations, but the primary responsibility for building facilities and enforcing regulations still belongs to the states. Pollution control agencies have been created in the states where there were none. Although pollution control spending accounts for only a small portion of total state spending, these allocations have risen sharply in the past twenty years.[9]

Unsafe streets and law enforcement

The famous Texas Rangers began as a small border patrol when they were organized back in 1835. In 1865 Massachusetts appointed a few state constables to suppress commercialized vice, a job the local police had been unwilling or unable to do. But it was not until 1905, with the organization of the Pennsylvania State Constabulary, that a real state police system came into being. This system was so successful that other states followed their example.

THE STATE POLICE

State police became a part of our law enforcement system for a variety of reasons. The breakdown of rural law enforcement, the coming of the automobile (demanding greater protection on the highways and a mobile force for apprehending fleeing criminals), and the need for a trained force to maintain order during strikes, fires, floods, and other emergencies all led to the creation of state police.

The establishment of the Pennsylvania State Constabulary marked a sharp break with traditional police methods. The force was a mounted and uniformed body organized on a military basis. Centralized control was given to a superintendent who, in turn, was directly responsible to the governor. This pattern has been followed by other states. These forces are now among the most respected police organizations in the world. They are well equipped, and they maintain high standards of conduct and discipline.

The military organization of these forces shields them from temptation,

[9]See Charles O. Jones, "Regulating the Environment," in Herbert Jacob and Kenneth Vines, eds., *Politics In the American States* (Little, Brown, 1976), pp. 388–427.

The 1936 Texas Rangers seem a
far cry from the modern state
police systems we know today.
The hats, however,
haven't changed much.

builds morale, and helps develop an *esprit de corps* that contrasts sharply
with the cynical attitude of some urban police. Because of their mobility
and professional character, state police are less accessible to "the smaller
fry of urban and rural politics." Moreover, they maintain rigorous systems
of recruitment and training.

Other state police systems have developed out of the rather modest
highway patrols of a few decades ago. During the 1930s traffic control in
rural regions became an acute problem, and state after state organized
highway patrols, usually as subordinate units of the highway or motor
vehicle department. Gradually their authority was extended from enforcing the rules of the road to exercising the usual powers of the police. Generally speaking, the state police that have grown out of highway patrols do
not have such effective training programs or such high standards as those
that have been modeled after the Pennsylvania force.

OTHER POLICE FORCES

State police are not the only law enforcement agencies maintained by state
governments. There are liquor law enforcement officials, fish and game
wardens, fire wardens, independent detective bureaus, and special motor
vehicle police. This dispersion of functions has been widely criticized, but
each department insists that it needs its own law enforcement agency to
handle its own special problems.

At the local level almost every municipality maintains its own police
force; a sheriff and his deputies work for the county; and some townships
have their own police officers. In fact, there are over 40,000 separate law
enforcement agencies, composed of more than 475,000 men and women.

Not many years ago the local law enforcement officials had little difficulty in dealing with crime. Everybody knew everybody else, and detection
of the guilty was relatively simple. Today in a mobile society where ano-
nymity makes capture difficult, criminals sometimes move swiftly across
the nation, cutting across jurisdictional boundaries. The existence of multiple police agencies, often with overlapping responsibilities, has undoubtedly increased the pressure for federal action.

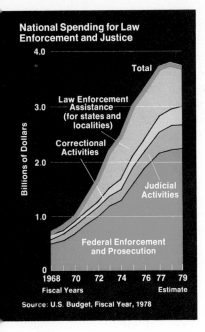

National Spending for Law Enforcement and Justice

Billions of Dollars

Total

Law Enforcement Assistance (for states and localities)

Correctional Activities

Judicial Activities

Federal Enforcement and Prosecution

Fiscal Years   Estimate

Source: U.S. Budget, Fiscal Year, 1978

Congress has gradually moved the national government further and further into a field traditionally reserved for state and local governments, although the national contribution to overall law enforcement spending is still very small. Today it is a federal offense to use the channels of interstate commerce to steal or to kidnap. The shipment of firearms to or by convicted felons across state lines, or of information or equipment used in illegal gambling, or of explosives for purposes of destroying churches or public buildings, and a variety of other activities affecting interstate commerce are also federal crimes. In each instance the demands for the extension of the police duties of the national government came about as a result of the failure or inability of the states and localities to deal with the problem. The failure of some state and local police to protect the rights of blacks added fuel to the demand for more vigorous federal police protection.

The Omnibus Crime Control and Safe Streets Act enacted in 1968 authorizes the FBI to increase its training activities for local police, provides grants to law enforcement students, creates within the Department of Justice a National Institute of Law Enforcement and Criminal Justice, and authorizes substantial block grants to the states to be used to improve programs, including those of the cities. The grants of nearly a billion dollars a year are administered by the Law Enforcement Assistance Administration. Evaluations of the LEAA "war on street crime" funds do not indicate that they have helped reduce the crime rate. Perhaps the crime rate would be higher without these funds, but this is doubtful.[10]

The long-standing conviction that control of crime is primarily a state and local responsibility made Congress reluctant to pass the 1968 act; it did so only because of growing public alarm about "crime in the streets." Even so, Congress built protections against federal control into the act.

Planning the urban community

Are our cities good places in which to live and work? Crowded shopping areas, dented fenders, shattered nerves, slums and blighted areas, inadequate parks, impossible traffic patterns—are all these evils and inconveniences necessary?

Many city people have asked these questions. Reorganization, city-manager charters, consolidated cities and counties—these are fine things, they argue, but the problem may lie deeper. Structural changes in the government are not enough; in addition, we need intelligent planning to avoid the kinds of problems that now confront us. Some have argued that we need to allocate billions of federal funds to make of our cities environments that encourage and enrich rather than discourage and alienate.

For many decades American cities were allowed to grow in a haphazard fashion: Industrialists were permitted to erect factories wherever they wished, towering buildings shut off sunlight from the streets below; traffic conditions transformed drivers into malevolent maniacs, pedestrians into traumatized wrecks. Schools were sandwiched in where the land was cheap or where the political organization could make a profit on the sale.

The most common method of assuring orderly growth is *zoning*—the creation of areas and the limitation on uses to which property may be put in each area. A community may be divided into areas for single-family

[10]See Thomas E. Cronin, "The War on Crime and Unsafe Streets, 1960–76: Policymaking for a Just and Safe Society," in Allan P. Sindler, ed., *America in the Seventies.* (Little Brown, 1977), pp. 208–60.

dwellings, two-family dwellings, multifamily dwellings, commercial purposes, and light and heavy industry. Other regulations restrict the height of building or their area, or require that buildings be located a certain distance apart and a certain distance from the front of the lot.

Zoning attempts to keep garbage dumps from being located next to residential areas, stabilizes property values, and enables the city or county government to coordinate services with land use. A zoning ordinance, however, is no better than its enforcement. This is usually the responsibility of a building inspector who makes sure that a projected building is consistent with building, zoning, fire, and sanitary regulations before he grants a building permit. In mose cases, a zoning or planning commission or the city council can amend the zoning ordinances and make exceptions to the regulations. These officials are often under tremendous pressure to grant exceptions, but if they go too far in permitting special cases, the whole purpose of zoning is defeated.

Zoning can also be used as a means of keeping "undesirables" out of a community, usually an upper-income white suburb. This is done merely by manipulating zoning requirements; for example, by mandating that all new homes be built on lots of an acre or more and by prohibiting the building of multifamily homes and apartments.[11]

Zoning is, however, only one phase of community planning. Until recently, planners were primarily concerned with streets and buildings. Today, many city planners are concerned with broader matters, and planning covers almost all the activities of people. Planners collect all the information they can about the city and then prepare long-range plans. Which sections are growing? Where should schools be built? Where should main highways be constructed to meet future needs? Will the water supply be adequate ten years hence? Are the parks accessible to all the people?

Today many communities are attempting to make order out of the chaos of random growth. Most cities have some kind of planning agency, especially under the stimulus of the present federal requirement that cities applying for community development assistance first develop a three-year community development plan. Further federal encouragement was provided by the 1974 Housing and Community Development Act in which cities receive federal help in the rehabilitation of their inner-city areas. Participating cities have to submit plans, local public hearing and citizen participation are required, and priority must be given to activities that benefit low-income families.[12]

Although housing is only one aspect of improving the urban community, it is a vital part of it. Millions of families are presently crowded into substandard dwellings, and the cost of such slums in terms of damage to the individuals is difficult to calculate. In addition, cities have a direct financial interest in improving urban housing. The costs of education, police and fire protection, and public welfare are considerably higher in slums than in other areas.

Obviously, planning must be built upon public support. No plan, how-

[11]See Michael N. Danielson, "The Politics of Exclusionary Zoning in Suburbia," *Political Science Quarterly* (Spring 1976), pp. 1–18.

[12]For an evaluation of what is achieved by these funds, see Richard P. Nathan, Paul R. Dornmel, et al., "Monitoring the Block Grant Program for Community Development," *Political Science Quarterly* (Summer 1977), pp. 219–44.

ever good it looks on paper, will be effective unless it reflects the interests and values of the major groups within the community. Effective planning is a product of the political process.[13]

Transportation policy

State and local governments build highways, public buildings, airports, parks, and recreational facilities. But by far the major program is building roads. State and local governments spend more money on roads than on anything else except education and welfare.

Until the advent of the automobile, canals and railroads were the major method of long-distance travel. Local roads were built and repaired under the direction of city, township, and county officials. Able-bodied male citizens were required either to put in a certain number of days working on the public roads or to pay taxes for that purpose.

By the 1890s bicycle clubs began to urge the building of hard-surfaced roads, but it was not until the 1900s and the automobile that road building became a major industry. It is not surprising that the function of road-building gradually was transferred from the township to larger units of government. But counties and townships still have important road-building and maintenance problems; nearly four-fifths of the rural road mileage is under their control. The other fifth, which includes almost all the main highways and most of the hard-surfaced roads, is built and maintained by the state.

Ever since 1916 the national government has supported state highway construction, but with the Federal Highway Act of 1956 and its supplements, especially the Highway Safety Act of 1968 and the Federal-Aid Highway Acts of 1968 and 1973, federal aid has increased. States do the planning, estimate the costs, get the construction done, even when they receive substantial federal assistance. In order to receive federal support, however, states must submit their plans to, and have their work inspected by, the Department of Transportation's Federal Highway Administration. All federally backed highways must meet certain standards governing the engineering of the roadbed, employment conditions for construction workers, and weight and load conditions for trucks using the roads.

Under the Federal Highway Act of 1956, the states have planned and built the National System of Interstate and Defense Highways. Now about 92 percent completed, the Interstate when finished will consist of 42,700 miles of superhighways linking almost all cities with a population of 50,000 or more. The federal government paid 90 percent of the costs. Most of the money came from user taxes—gasoline, tires, trucks—which are placed in a trust fund designated for that purpose. Funds are distributed among the states according to a formula that gives greater weight to population than has been given in other federal-aid highway programs.

Few aspects of government are more enmeshed in patronage politics than highway building. The large sums of money spent and the army of workers needed offer many opportunities for graft and favoritism. In some states the highway department is the chief means by which a political organization maintains its power; contractors are rewarded for their support and loyal party members are given jobs.

[13]See Alan Altshuler, *The City Planning Process* (Cornell University Press, 1965); Francine Rabinovitz, *City Politics and Planning* (Atherton, 1969); and Jeffrey L. Pressman, *Federal Programs and City Politics* (University of California Press, 1975).

Powerful interest groups support highway development. Automobile manufacturers, tire makers, oil companies, motel and restaurant associations, automobile and tourist clubs, trucking associations, and others join hands to protect their common cause. In most states they have been strong enough to persuade legislatures to allocate gasoline taxes, automobile drivers' license fees, trucking fees, and other user taxes for road purposes. But there is always conflict over how the money should be spent. Farmers want secondary roads developed, but truckers and tourists favor the improvement of main highways. Merchants want the roads to come their way, and their representatives try to get top priority for roads in their districts.

Recently, especially in the aftermath of the energy crisis more and more people have advocated that the federal government spend a sizable percentage of the highway trust funds on developing urban mass transit systems. The federal Aid Highway Act of 1973 authorized for the first time the use of the highway trust fund for purchasing buses and financing mass transit systems. In 1974, the passage of the National Mass Transportation Assistance Act expanded the national government's commitment to help the states and metropolitan areas develop better public transportation systems.

Regulation at the grass roots

Corporations receive their charters from the state. Banks, insurance companies, securities dealers, doctors, lawyers, barbers and various other businesses and professions are licensed, and their activities are supervised by state officials. State regulations range from measures to protect the public to mere window-dressing. Both farmers and workers—especially union members—are regulated as such. But of all the businesses, those that we designate as public utilities are the most closely restricted.

PUBLIC UTILITIES

It is easier to list than to define public utilities. Water plants, electric power companies, telephone companies, railroads, and buses are among the main ones. They are distinguished from other businesses by the fact that government gives them certain special privileges such as the power of eminent domain, the right to use public streets, and protection from competition. In return, public utilities are required to give the public adequate services at reasonable rates. Public utilities are used to render essential services in fields where normally competitive enterprise is not suitable.

In the United States, private enterprise subject to public regulation rather than public ownership has been the more general method of providing these essential services. Nevertheless, more than two-thirds of our cities own their own water works, about 100 operate their own gas utilities, and each year more and more are taking over the operation of their own transit systems. But other services—intercity transportation, railroads, airplanes, telephone, and telegraph—are almost everywhere provided by private enterprise subject to governmental regulation and some subsidization.

Since public utilities are not subject to the restraint of competition, the question of how they are regulated is important. Every state has a utilities commission to see that utilities operate in the interest of the public they serve. In most states utilities commissioners are appointed for overlapping terms by the governor with the consent of the senate, but in some southern and western states they are elected by the voters. In two, they are chosen by the legislature. The most common number of commissioners is three. The extent of commission regulation varies with the type of utility, but usually utility commissions have the authority to set rates, require uniform systems of accounts, approve issues of securities, pass on reorganization and merger plans, and permit abandonment of services. Most states have only one utilities commission, which combines the duties performed at the national level by the Interstate Commerce Commission, the Federal Communications Commission, the Federal Power Commission, the Civil Aeronautics Board, and (in some states) the Securities and Exchange Commission.

EMPLOYERS AND EMPLOYEES

Despite the expanded role of the national government, state and local officials still have much to say about working conditions. Here are some of the laws they enforce:

1. *Health and safety legislation.* States require proper heating, lighting, ventilation, fire escapes, and sanitary facilities in work areas. Machinery must be equipped with safety guards, and standards have been established to cut down occupational diseases. Health, building, and labor inspectors tour industrial plants to ensure compliance with the laws.

2. *Workmen's compensation.* Today all states have created workmen's compensation programs based on the belief that employees should not have to assume the costs of accidents. Like depreciation of machinery and other items, the costs of accidents are borne by the employer and are part of the price the consumer of the product must ultimately pay. No longer does the employee have to sue and prove that his employer was at fault. If they are injured or contract a disease in the ordinary course of employment, employees are entitled to compensation set by a prearranged schedule.

3. *Child labor.* All states forbid child labor, but laws vary widely in their coverage and in their definition of child labor. A good many states set the minimum age at fourteen. Higher age requirements are normal for employment in hazardous occupations and during school hours.

4. *Hours and wages.* Women and young people are protected by maximum-hours laws in most states. Men are covered only in certain dangerous occupations, or where the public safety is directly involved—operation of buses and trucks, for example. Sunday closing laws, and laws requiring that employees be allowed at least one day of rest in seven, generally apply to men as well as to women and children.

Minimum wage laws are in effect in most states, but in a few the laws apply only to women. Recently these laws applying only to one sex are coming under constitutional attack.

5. *Regulation of unions and collective bargaining.* National regulation of collective bargaining applies only to industries in, or affecting, *inter*state commerce. Although national law takes precedence over state enactments, states are left to impose their own regulations in many important areas of labor-management relations.

6. *Consumerism.* Citizens in many states are becoming more critical of the environmental havoc caused by industrial pollution, strip mining, and oil-shale extraction. Normally, their complaints soon turn into requests that the states set up some kind of regulatory and monitoring agencies with stiff penalties for violations. Consumer groups are similarly restless and often relentless supporters of state regulatory efforts. Take the example of auto repairs. The auto repair business is the biggest single headache for those who handle consumer complaints. In many areas there is a feeling that the licensing of auto mechanics by the state is needed to lessen the incidence of incompetent or dishonest practices. But the licensing of mechanics will not necessarily ensure that the repairs authorized are actually made or that all repairs are done competently and safely. Clearly, state regulatory authorities

**"Is there room for
both of us under there?"**

Reprinted with permission
from the *Rocky Mountain News*.

cannot be present in every service station or garage. But consumers are skeptical of
the suggestion that garage owners police their own businesses. Regulation is nearly always controversial and is always shaped by political forces.

Can we explain policy differences?

One of the most active research efforts of recent years by political scientists has been to try to identify the factors that explain why states do or do
not enact a variety of policies. These investigators visualize each state as
an economic and political system that produces certain "outputs," for
example, expenditures for welfare, a public housing program, a civil rights
law. They are trying to understand the dynamics of the political process, to
figure out why one state acts one way while another acts another.

These political scientists have looked at such phenomena as levels of
urbanization and industrialization, education, economic resources, home
ownership. They have studied "structural variables" such as types of party
systems and integration or diffusion of state administration, and political
variables such as the relevance of state politics to the citizen.

The early studies often suggested that factors such as urbanization,
wealth of the state, and geographical region accounted for public policy
differences much more than party systems or governmental structure.
Thus, the more urbanized and wealthy the state, the more likely it would
invest in human resources. Whether the state was a one-party state or had
competitive parties seemed not to matter. More recent studies suggest that
political and structural factors do indeed count. One study, for example,
concludes that a state's policy outputs are partially determined by the attitudes and behavior of those who participate actively in state politics.[14]
Other scholars find that creative leadership can make a difference. Thus a
governor who wants to encourage economic development can bring about
a change by going abroad on trade missions, opening up overseas offices,
and spending much time on promotion and development work. Through
determined leadership and skilled use of available resources, a governor
or a group of state leaders can overcome the constraints that traditionally
stifle change: "For instance, half a century after Huey Long's service as

[14]M. Kent Jennings and Harmon Zeigler, "The Salience of American State Politics, *American
Political Science Review* (June 1970), p. 535.

governor of Louisiana, that period is still termed Huey Long's Louisiana, with its combination of heavy taxation on mineral extraction and high expenditure for social services. In a similar way, LaFollette left his imprint on Wisconsin, Rockefeller on New York."[15]

If *policy outputs*—that which is spent on various functions—has long been of interest to political scientists, *policy outcomes*—the actual changes in what is done—are of special interest to contemporary students of state and urban policy making. Policy outcomes have been described as the "so what" or "the bottom line" of politics. A state's educational expenditures are its policy output, but often the citizen is concerned not just with the level of funding but with whether children are being better educated. In other words, *What difference does it make?* Political scientists are even asking how and to what extent policy outcomes in a state or community could be changed by changing some of the surrounding conditions over which we have some control.[16]

Plainly, this is a research frontier of political science, with conflicting conclusions on the part of investigators. But the analysis of policy outcomes and policy impact is much needed. The cumulative findings in this area of research will help us better to understand the dynamics of state and urban policy making and our complicated political environment.

Summary

1. We ask our state and local governments to do countless things for us, but the four functions of education, public welfare, highway building, and health and hospitals are the costliest services they provide. These account for more than three-fourths of state expenditures and about two-thirds of local government spending in the late 1970s.

2. In addition, we ask states and communities to make our streets safe, protect our natural resources, provide parks and recreation, encourage job opportunities, and protect the consumer. There are, of course, great differences in how states and communities set their priorities in these areas. For example, some states are so concerned about environmental quality that they are seeking selective growth even at the expense of job opportunities. Other states favor attracting jobs and industry despite pollution and the environmental costs.

3. Many political scientists today conduct research on the differences among the states and cities and their policy outputs. They are interested in why some states, for example, invest more in one policy function than another, and why policy benefits are distributed in the manner they are. There is a growing concern too about how citizens evaluate the way their governments provide and administer public services.

[15]Herbert Jacob, "Public Policy in the American States," in Jacob and Vines, eds., *Politics in the American States*, pp. 282–83. See also Richard Hofferbert, *The Study of Public Policy* (Bobbs-Merrill, 1974), and Robert Lineberry and Ira Sharkansky, *Urban Politics and Urban Policy*, 2nd ed. (Harper & Row, 1974).

[16]See, for example, Frank Levy, Arnold Meltsner, and Aaron Wildavsky, *Urban Outcomes* (University of California Press, 1974).

Chapter 33

Staffing and Financing State and Local Governments

For several days in April of 1976, the only police car on the streets of Mansfield, Ohio, was driven by Richard A. Porter. With a badge in his pocket and a deputized assistant at his side, Porter, who is also the city's mayor, filled in for a police force that was out on strike. They were sick with the "blue flu." Mansfield's 58,000 citizens were apprehensive. So were its 85 officers, but the police believed they deserved a substantial wage increase and felt this was the only recourse left to them. "It was the type of face-off that has become exasperatingly familiar in American cities, where public employees are striving to better their lot while municipal governments are striving to solve expanding problems with declining revenues."[1]

Government is very much a matter of people and money. People must be elected and hired, salaries must be negotiated and paid, materials purchased. The cost and quality of government depends partly on the ability of the people, and their ability in turn depends on how well they are paid and how much they have to spend.

Where do the people come from?

When we talk about the state, the city, or the county, we are simply using shorthand symbols for groups of people. Although we say that the government builds the roads or runs the schools, what we really mean is that a group of public officials or public employees build the roads or run the schools. About 12.5 million people work for our state and local governments. In a sense they *are* the state and local governments. How are these people chosen?

[1]Roger M. Williams, "The Clamor over Municipal Unions," *Saturday Review* (March 5, 1977), p. 12.

685

*Staffing and financing
state and local
governments*

A few of them are elected. The rest are generally appointed through some kind of merit system. The patronage system has not disappeared, and in many jurisdictions, it still helps to know the right people and belong to the right party. But these practices are no longer so common. The Supreme Court has declared it unconstitutional for a public employee to be dismissed for political reasons, affirmative action requirements are imposing on governments the need to recruit through open procedures, and unionization is being felt.[2]

STATE AND LOCAL MERIT SYSTEMS

Almost all states now use merit systems in choosing public servants. And in all the states welfare workers who administer grants under the national social security law are selected on the basis of merit, since this is a condition for receiving federal money.

The most general method of administering merit systems is by a civil service commission, usually composed of three members appointed by the governor, with the consent of the senate, for six-year overlapping terms. The commission prepares and administers examinations, provides "eligible" registers for various jobs from which appointments may be made, establishes job classifications, and prepares salary schedules. It also serves as a board of appeal for persons who are discharged. Commissions are becoming increasingly concerned with in-service training, collective bargaining, affirmative action programs, and the expanded need for top-level executives.

How well do the commissions do their job? Their many critics complain that they are too slow and wrapped up in red tape and clumsy rules. Eligible lists are not kept up to date; it takes weeks to fill vacancies, they say. But a more serious charge is that civil service commissions have deprived responsible officials of authority over subordinates. There is too much emphasis, it is argued, on "keeping the rascals out" and on insulating public servants from political coercion. As a result, employees enjoy so much job security that administrators cannot get rid of incompetents. Cases have been cited where it took months and several elaborate hearings to dismiss secretaries who could not type or librarians who could not read.

Merit systems vary greatly, and some of the so-called merit systems designed to foster ability and minimize political favoritism actually have the opposite effect: they discourage some persons from seeking public sector jobs. The commonly held belief that local personnel practices are dominated by political clearance factors is probably wrong. Yet in smaller communities family friendships and local residence usually still give certain applicants an advantage over others. "There have never been any studies that ranked civil service systems in local governments. Among professional personnel managers, however, Detroit, Los Angeles County, Milwaukee, and New Orleans have enjoyed good reputations, based on relatively strong staffing, community and political acceptance of merit principles, and rigorous competitive requirements for filling positions."[3]

---

[2]*Elrod* v. *Burns*, 427 U.S. 347 (1976).

[3]David T. Stanley, *Managing Local Government under Union Pressure* (Brookings Institution, 1972), pp. 9–10. See also Andrew Boesel, *Civil Service Commissions in City and County Government* (International City Managers' Association, 1973); and N. Joseph Cayer, *Public Personnel Administration in the United States* (St. Martin's Press, 1975).

Public worker unions have grown rapidly. They have become more important and are more militant in demanding better wages, hours, working conditions, and pensions for their members. They are also a rising political force in most states and many cities. States and local governments have learned to cope with this new political force and have been thrust into the position of acting as the "employer." This usually means the states and cities are involved in collective bargaining and voluntary or binding arbitration processes.

Roughly half of the 12 million state and local public employees are organized, compared with less than 25 percent of the workforce in the private sector. The American Federation of State, County and Municipal Employees, AFSCME, representing nearly 800,000 members, is said to be the fastest growing union in the country. Other public employee unions are the International Association of Fire Fighters, representing 175,000 fire personnel, and the National Teacher Association, which represents some 1,500,000 teachers. Firefighters are generally thought to be the most effective political activists among the public employee organizations. In Portland, Oregon, for example, "firefighters and their wives engage in telephone and door-to-door canvassing in campaigns for election of city commissioners. The local union also contributes money to candidates." In 1969, the police in that same city, affiliated with the AFSCME, "sent over 5,000 letters, individually typed by policemen's wives, to residents asking them to get their councilmen to vote for a wage increase formula favored by the union."[4]

Union pressures are a major reason the average pay of state and local government workers went up about 30 percent faster than that of those in private industry between 1955 and 1975. A number of inequities, including some almost inhumane wages, were corrected. This was certainly a major accomplishment for AFSCME and other public worker unions. In many areas of the country now, public employees are well paid; according to some people, they are overpaid.

What explains the success of these unions? The failure of the civil service system to meet many of the needs of public employees encouraged the growth of public worker unions. Also, of course, the widespread success of unions and collective bargaining in the private sector spurred those in the public sector to follow suit. But the political importance of the growing number of public employees was their special asset. Neal R. Peirce sums up their political clout this way:

> The public employee unions are succeeding so brilliantly because they can deliver the two most needed components of campaigns—money and manpower (not to mention the votes of their members, members' families and friends). Last year in California, government employee groups contributed $1.7 million, making them the biggest single contributor to elections in the nation's largest state. Moreover, government workers are literate, dedicated, go-to-meeting folks who can provide hard-pressed candidates with expert research, mailings and door-to-door canvasses.[5]

Public worker unions, such as the International Association of Firefighters to which the firemen shown here belong, have become more militant in demanding better wages for the services they provide.

[4]Jack Stieber, *Public Employee Unionism: Structure, Growth, Policy* (The Brookings Institution, 1973), p. 206.

[5]Neal R. Peirce, *The Boston Globe*, August 9, 1975, p. 7.

Deeply embedded in the democratic ethic is the idea that civil servants should not unionize and should not strike, especially employees like police and fire officials on whom the public depends for vital services. Many state and local elected officials, and certainly many people, feel it is wrong and dangerous for police, firefighters, and hospital workers to go out on strike. Calvin Coolidge when governor of Massachusetts became famous in 1919 when he opposed the Boston police strike by saying, "There is no right to strike against the public safety by anybody, anywhere, any time." But representatives of public employees argue that it is unfair for the government to guarantee workers the right to strike in the most vital sectors of private industry and deny all public employees the same right. And strikes in all these occupational areas have increased in recent years.

Strikes by public unions are illegal in all but four states, and even these states prohibit strikes for those who provide "vital and essential services." About twenty states have enacted legislation forbidding all public employee unions to use the strike as a weapon. In most instances, when strikes do occur local and state officials become more concerned with getting the workers back to work than sending them to jail for violating the law. Thus amnesty to the strikers has usually been the rule.

Union organizers refuse to see their strikes as defying the law; instead, they see the strike as a legitimate and useful weapon in a labor dispute. "Vowing not to strike," said one employee organizer, "is like sending a policeman into the streets without a gun." Still, the strike is generally viewed as a weapon of last resort, to be used only under intolerable conditions. AFSCME President Jerry Wurf puts it this way:

> I am opposed to strikes. I don't want strikes, they're bad. They are hard on the city; they're even harder on the workers. I'll fight bitterly for the right to strike. . . . But I don't think there is any principle involved in striking. Striking is a tactic to persuade an employer to deal with us. If it can be avoided almost any price ought to be paid in order to avoid a strike.[6]

The strike is not without political risks for the public worker unions. Adverse public reaction sometimes sets in; in some cities, such as San Francisco and Seattle, public backlash in the wake of strikes strengthened the hand of the mayors, who won recall votes or referenda, and who were then able to force the unions to back down on their demands.

Many union leaders now say they favor compulsory arbitration, and about twenty states have enacted laws that permit some form of arbitration. These union leaders see a chance to get something they might not get at a bargaining table without arousing the public backlash that usually comes with strikes. Binding arbitration is used in several states, mostly in public-safety areas of police and fire protection. A neutral third party or mediating board hears the arguments of both sides and devises what it considers a fair settlement. The verdict is final. An alternative is *last best offer arbitration*. This requires an arbitrator to consider the final offers of both sides and select one. The alleged advantages of this method is that it

Two teachers from Pittsburgh's West End fight winter cold as they picket in a strike that affected over 62,000 pupils. Some 3,700 teachers walked off their jobs over a contract dispute.

[6]Quoted in Sterling D. Spero and John M. Capazzola, *The Urban Community and Its Unionized Bureaucracies: Pressure Politics in Local Government Labor Relations* (Dunellen, 1973), p. 245.

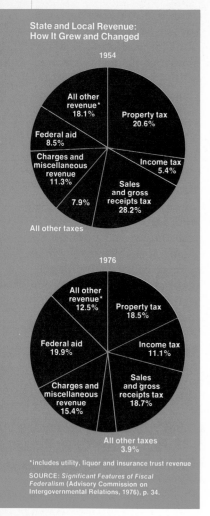

State and Local Revenue:
How It Grew and Changed

1954

All other revenue*
18.1%

Property tax
20.6%

Federal aid
8.5%

Charges and miscellaneous revenue
11.3%

Income tax
5.4%

Sales and gross receipts tax
28.2%

7.9%

All other taxes

1976

All other revenue*
12.5%

Property tax
18.5%

Federal aid
19.9%

Income tax
11.1%

Charges and miscellaneous revenue
15.4%

Sales and gross receipts tax
18.7%

All other taxes
3.9%

*includes utility, liquor and insurance trust revenue

SOURCE: *Significant Features of Fiscal Federalism* (Advisory Commission on Intergovernmental Relations, 1976), p. 34.

Firefighters and police picket in San Francisco in a fight for higher wages.

encourages realistic offers and voluntary settlement. Fearing that the other side's proposal may be chosen, both parties will trim their offers in the direction of being realistic. Binding arbitration has greatly reduced the occurrence of strikes in those states where it is practiced. It cannot guarantee that all public worker strikes will be avoided, but it can make the occurrence of legal strikes more predictable and make it easier to impose stiff penalties for illegal strikes.

The arguments against binding arbitration include the contention that it places too much power in the hands of a person who is not elected and not accountable to elected officials. The arbitrator is not necessarily a resident of the community or state involved. Settlements have often been expensive. It is probable too that each decision in a binding arbitration case has a ripple effect on the rest of a city or state administration. A pay raise and generous award to one group sets the standard for other public workers to aim at. It is common practice for one union to demand wage increases and benefits similar to those received by a previous union. In the cities, the police usually are the pacesetters in the politics of winning higher pay.[7] Thus, Sam Zagoria, director of labor-management relations for the U.S. Conference of Mayors, complains that binding arbitration "is a lot like leading the mayor and the city council into a large closet, locking the door and turning the key over to a stranger who came to town to clear up a personnel problem in one department and wound up preparing a plan for fiscal chaos."[8]

In an attempt to develop more public accountability, the use of a *public referendum* has been proposed in the case of a stalemate. The citizens, as the ultimate employer, determine which package is to be accepted. Union representatives oppose this method because they fear voters would generally vote down a settlement that would cost them more money. Other critics of the referendum proposal note that it would doubtless force the police, firefighters and others to become even more politicized than they already are. However, a Conference of Mayors official contends that "a public sector union is not entitled to more than the conscience of a community is willing to dictate. . . . If the community is not willing to pay for good teachers, for instance, then it has to face up to those consequences."[9]

These are likely developments in the near future:

1. There will be a continued strong push from the unions for compulsory binding arbitration to settle public labor disputes.
2. There will be continued unionization of public employees. The teachers' associations have grown very rapidly as teachers try to protect their jobs in the face of dwindling classroom enrollments.
3. The debate over the right of public employees to strike will continue, but will probably not be resolved.
4. State and local officials will become more skilled in collective bargaining and arbitration activities.

[7]This point is made in Frank J. Thompson, *Personnel Policy in the City: The Politics of Jobs in Oakland* (University of California Press, 1975), Chap. 3.

[8]"Compulsory Binding Arbitration," *State Legislatures* (April/May 1977), p. 15.

[9]Quoted in Neal R. Peirce, "Public Employee Unions Show Rise in Membership, Militancy," *National Journal* (August 30, 1975), p. 1244.

5. State and local politicians will continue to court public-worker union political support in their campaigns but be willing to appeal to the public to win showdowns with the public unions whenever governments face severe financial troubles.

6. Public-worker unions will play an important role in state and local politics above and beyond issues of pay and working conditions. They will be involved in who gets elected and they certainly will be consulted or at least heard on a whole range of public policy issues.

Where does the money come from?

State and local governments get most of their money through taxation. But, unlike the national government, they do not control the monetary machinery and often have to secure voter consent through a referendum before they can levy taxes. Still, state and local leadership has done a remarkable job in raising revenue. The state and local revenue system is now more diversified with the relative decline in reliance on property taxes and a relative increase in state income taxes and federal aid.

The duplication of governments by which the American people regulate their lives complicates the tax picture. Tax policies often conflict. When the national government is reducing taxes to encourage spending by the public, states may be raising taxes. Until recently, each level of government paid little attention to the tax policy of the other.

The number of taxing authorities also makes tax-gathering an expensive operation. National officials collect taxes on gasoline, state officials collect taxes on gasoline, and so do some local officials. Each maintains its own tax-gathering organization. Naturally, the taxpayer is confused. Taxpayers are allowed to deduct certain business expenses from their federal income tax, but not from their state income tax. Changes in state laws often affect the amount of federal tax a person must pay. For example, the national government permits taxpayers to deduct amounts paid for state taxes from their federal income tax return. Thus, if a state increases its taxes, the national government gets less money.

No matter who collects the taxes, however, all the money comes out of a single national economy. Each of the governments has a different tax base, and each of the taxes hits particular groups; but all government services rest on the productivity of the American people. And that productivity is increased by many of the activities of government. With their taxes the people buy police protection, parks and educational programs, highways, and other things that they think desirable. Who pays for these services?

WHO SHALL PAY THE TAXES?

A good tax might be defined as one the other person has to pay; a bad tax, one that I have to pay. Who shall bear the cost of state and local government is decided in the United States by politics. The people of any state are free to collect whatever taxes they wish from whomever (in that state) they wish, subject only to the restrictions imposed by the federal Constitution.

The Constitution forbids states to tax exports or imports, or to levy tonnage duties without the consent of Congress; to use their taxing power to interfere with federal operation; to discriminate against interstate commerce, unduly burden it, or directly tax it; or to use their taxing power to deprive persons of equal protection of the law or to deprive them of their property without due process. Constitutional lawyers and judges spend much of their time trying to apply these generalities to concrete situations. Out of hundreds of disputes, courts have decided, among other things, that states may not tax fixed and visible property located outside the state but may tax intangible assets located outside the state but owned by their own citizens. States may collect sales taxes from interstate sales, may collect income taxes from persons and corporations within the state even though the income was earned from interstate business, but may not tax the privilege of engaging in interstate commerce or the unapportioned gross receipts from interstate transactions.

State constitutions also restrict state taxing power. Certain kinds of property are exempt from taxation—property used for educational, charitable, or religious purposes, for example. State constitutions frequently list the taxes that may be collected, forbidding those not mentioned. The amount of tax that may be collected from various sources is also often stipulated.

The ability of people in a city, county, or other local unit to tax themselves is even more restricted. Their officials can collect only those taxes, in the amount, by the procedures, and for the purposes which the state constitution or the state legislature authorizes. What kinds of taxes can they collect?

GENERAL PROPERTY TAX

Widely criticized as "one of the worst taxes known to the civilized world," the general property tax is still the chief revenue source for local governments. It used to be the major state tax too, but in most states it is now of minor importance. The tax is difficult to administer, leads to favoritism and inequities, and takes little account of ability to pay.

A hundred years ago, wealth was primarily *real* property—land and buildings—which was relatively easy to value. Assessors could guess the value of the property a person owned, and this was a good test of his or her ability to help pay for government. Today wealth takes many forms. People own large amounts of *personal* property—both tangible, such as furniture, jewels, washing machines, expensive rugs, paintings; and intangible, such as stocks, bonds, money in the bank. A person can concentrate a large amount of wealth, difficult to value and easy to conceal, in a small rented apartment. Real property too has changed. It no longer consists mainly of barns, houses, and land, but of large industrial plants, great retail stores, and office buildings, the value of which is hard to measure.

Further, property ownership is less likely these days to correspond to ability to pay. The old couple with a large house valued at $55,000 may be living on Social Security payments and a small allowance provided by their children. They have to pay higher local taxes than does the young couple living in a rented apartment, both of whom work and have sizable incomes. Or compare the case of a person who borrows $20,000 to buy a $25,000 house and who is paying off the mortgage out of a $12,000-a-year job, and the case of the person who owns a $25,000 house debt-free and has a $12,000-a-year job. They both pay the same tax on their homes.

Although many communities stipulate that the general property tax be imposed on all property, the tax falls in fact on limited amounts of real property. Over 20 percent of real property in cities is exempt. Intangible personal property is seldom taxed. New Haven has only a little more than half its actual property on its tax roll. Some communities place a lower rate on intangible property in order to induce owners to announce their ownership. Tangible personal property, such as watches, rings, and so on, often escapes taxation or is grossly undervalued. In most cities an unwritten

691

*Staffing and financing
state and local
governments*

understanding develops concerning the kind of property the honest taxpayer should list. The good citizen who attempts to follow the written
word of the law is kindly advised by the assessor that it is not necessary.

The general property tax is also inflexible. During times of rising prices,
assessed values move up much more slowly than the general price level.
Thus, when governments need more money, the lagging tax bases fail to
provide it. Conversely, when prices fall, valuations do not drop at the
same rate. When persons cannot pay taxes, much property is thrown on
the market for tax delinquency. During the 1930s, for example, the general
property tax added to the miseries of many homeowners and to the problems of state and local officials.

The general property tax rate is difficult to compare from community to
community. The rate in one city may be only $10 per thousand; in another,
$40 per thousand. But in the second city valuation may be computed at
only a tenth of "real" value. Claims of local politicians that they have kept
down the tax rate must be looked at carefully. In some areas, property taxes are at such levels that to increase them may force businesses and middle-income families to move.

In recent years considerable controversy has been stirred up by the
heavy reliance on the property tax to support schools. As a result, the
amount of money actually available to finance the education of children
varies tremendously from area to area; rich suburban areas are able to
spend much more than poor areas such as central cities. And to compound
the problem, the places that can afford to spend the least, need the most.
Central-city districts have higher teacher and building costs and require
more expensive land purchases; and there are more students who need
expensive compensatory educational services than in well-to-do suburbs.

Some educational reformers have urged that the state take over the financing of public education, or assume a greater share of the burden, in
order to equalize money differences from community to community. This
is not a very popular idea. Although almost every state now does appropriate funds to local districts by formulas that provide more to the poorest
districts, attempts to ensure equal expenditures by greater state financing
have been defeated in several states in recent years.

Those hoping for greater state support for schools have turned to the
courts, alleging that reliance on the property tax results in a denial of equal
protection and violates the Constitution. Several state courts have ruled
that wide differences between school districts in per pupil expenditures
are inconsistent with the equal protection clause of the Fourteenth
Amendment to the Constitution. Thus the California supreme court
(*Serrano* v. *Priest*, 1971) agreed, but the U.S. Supreme Court in a five-to-four
decision (*San Antonio Independent School District* v. *Rodrigez*, 1973)[10] held
there is no constitutional requirement that the amount spent in each district per pupil must be the same. A majority in the Rodrigez case felt that
although states might wish to reassess their educational financial policies,
the combination of state aid and local property taxes does not deprive persons living in the less wealthy districts of any constitutional rights. The
Serrano decision is still applicable in California and that state has sought
to comply with it, though this has been a gradual process.

[10]411 U. S. 1 (1973).

**"It was just a sapling
when we moved in?"**

Reprinted with permission
from the *Minneapolis Tribune*

The issues raised are still open. The Supreme Court's decision has slowed the push toward intrastate equalization in school expenditures, but about 20 states have passed major school financing changes. State courts in New Jersey, Connecticut, and Washington have handed down decisions similar to the 1971 *Serrano* ruling. The relationship between the local property tax and the equitable support of public education will doubtless be at the center of controversy well into the 1980s.[11]

Despite its weaknesses, the general property tax will probably remain an important source of revenue for local government. Some people feel it is well suited because real rather than personal property is the chief beneficiary of many local services, such as fire protection. Alternative taxes are few, and they have their own disadvantages. Moreover, some of the bad features of the general property tax can be and are being corrected by improving property tax administration.[12]

One of the more recent efforts to reform the general property tax is the so-called circuit-breaker exemption by which about twenty-five states and certain cities give some form of tax relief to lower-income families. The term comes from the idea of protecting family income from property tax overload the same way an electrical circuit-breaker protects a family home from an electrical current overload. "That is, when the property tax burden of an individual exceeds a predetermined percentage of personal income, the circuit-breaker goes into effect to relieve the excess financial pressure."[13] The circuit-breaker property tax exemption seems to be most popular in the Great Lakes and Plains states, where residential property tax burdens are above average. They are least popular in the Southeast, where property tax burdens are low. Economists and tax authorities have argued about the merits and problems created by this reform. But until a negative income tax or some other comprehensive income maintenance plan is established to provide cash payments to the poor, circuit-breaker exemptions will probably be part of the state tax structure in a great many states.

Even with improved tax administration, the general property tax is not supplying local units of government with all the money they need to render the services their citizens want. Moreover, states have tended to leave the property tax to local units and thus need other sources for their funds. What other taxes do they collect?

OTHER TAXES

Sales taxes Born during the Great Depression, the sales tax is now one of the most important sources of money for many of the states. Today forty-five states impose some kind of general sales tax, normally on retail sales. Local sales taxes were uncommon until after World War II, but now about 4,500 communities impose a general sales tax. City sales taxes are unpopular with local merchants, who fear that they drive business away. Most

[11]Some important studies on this question are John E. Coons, et al., *Private Wealth and Public Education* (Harvard University Press, 1970); Arnold Meltsner, et al., *School Financing Reform— A Study of Political Feasibility: The Case of California* (Praeger, 1973); and Robert D. Reischauer and Robert W. Hartman, *Reforming School Finance* (Brookings, 1973).

[12]For a discussion of alternative revenue possibilities for local governments, see Joseph A. Pechman, *Federal Tax Policy*, rev. ed. (Brookings Institution, 1971), pp. 211–46; and James A. Maxwell and J. Richard Aronson, *Financing State and Local Governments*, 3rd ed. (Brookings, 1977).

[13]Maxwell and Aronson, *Financing State and Local Governments*, p. 158. See also U.S. Advisory Commission on Intergovernmental Relations, *Property Tax Circuit-Breakers: Current Status and Policy Issues* (ACIR, 1975).

693

*Staffing and financing
state and local
governments*

cities and states try to prevent evasion by imposing a use tax payable by persons who purchase items outside the city or state for use within the city or state. But most use taxes are difficult to collect.

Sales taxes, especially those levied by the state, are relatively easy to administer and produce large amounts of revenue. Despite their tendency to bear down hardest on the lower-income groups, their popularity is increasing. They seem relatively painless, since the consumer puts out the few cents on each item rather than paying a large tax bill at one time. Labor groups and those with small incomes are generally opposed to the sales tax and favor wider use of the progressive income tax. They argue that persons with small incomes spend a larger part of their budget for food and clothing than do the wealthy, and sales taxes fall heaviest on those least able to pay. In some states, food and drugs have been exempted from the sales tax. In others, passage of sales taxes has been coupled with an income tax.

Income taxes In constant dollars, state income tax revenues have increased by about 500 percent since 1950. Personal income is now taxed in forty-one states, but in most the income tax is a less important source of money than the sales tax. Income taxes are generally progressive or graduated—that is, the rate goes up with the size of the income. State income tax rates, however, do not rise as sharply as the federal tax and seldom go over 12 percent. In some states exemptions are generous. Corporation incomes are frequently taxed at a flat rate. Because of the importance and burden of the federal income tax, there is a strong feeling that states should go slow.

Some cities, following the lead of Philadelphia and Toledo, now collect a payroll tax. Philadelphia imposes a relatively small flat tax on salaries of all persons and net profits of unincorporated businesses and professions. The Toledo tax applies also to corporate profits. The municipal income tax enables hard-pressed cities to collect money from "daytime" citizens who use city facilities but live in the suburbs. This tax is especially popular among cities in Ohio and Pennsylvania, but is also being collected by New York City, Detroit, and Louisville.

Special excise taxes Almost all states tax gasoline, alcohol, and cigarettes. Since many cities also tax these items, the local, state, and federal levies often double the cost of these "luxury" items to the consumer. These are known as excise taxes. Gasoline taxes are sometimes combined with the funds collected from automobile and drivers' licenses and earmarked for highway purposes. Liquor taxes often consist of licenses to manufacture or sell alcoholic beverages and levies on their sale or consumption. Some states own their own liquor dispensaries, and the profits go to the state treasury. High taxation of liquor is justified on the grounds that it reduces the amount consumed, falls on an item that is not generally considered a necessity of life, and, through licensing, eases the task of law enforcement. Some states like North Carolina set aside some alcohol taxes for mental health programs and alcoholic rehabilitation. If the tax is raised too high, however, liquor tends to be diverted into illegal channels, and tax revenues fall off. High tobacco taxes in states like New York and Connecticut compared with low or no tobacco taxes in states like the Carolinas has led to interstate smuggling up and down the East Coast.

Suppose your state government must raise taxes substantially, which of these do you think would be the best way to do it?

	March 1972	March 1976
State sales tax	46%	45%
State income tax	25	25
State property tax	14	10
Other	5	6
Don't know	10	14

SOURCE: *Changing Public Attitudes on Governments and Taxes* (Advisory Commission on Intergovernmental Relations, 1976), p. 6.

This list does not begin to exhaust the kinds of taxes collected by states and local governments. Admissions taxes, stock transfer taxes, inheritance taxes, parimutuel taxes, corporate franchise taxes, license fees, and others are common. The tax on the privilege of "severing" natural resources such as coal, oil, and timber is important in some states. In Texas, New Mexico, Louisiana, and Oklahoma, for example, the severance tax on oil and natural gas accounts for more than 10 percent of state taxes.

NONTAX REVENUES

In addition to taxation, states derive some revenue from fees and special service charges. In fact, about 10 percent of the money collected by the state and local governments comes from these sources. Fees are charged for building inspection, recording of titles, court costs, licensing of professions, garbage disposal, and other special services. Parking meters have become an important revenue source for many cities. Special assessments against property owners whose property is benefited by public improvements, such as streets or sewers, are a general practice.

Some cities run business enterprises from which they make money (and sometimes lose it too). Municipally owned waterworks or gas and light companies often contribute to the city treasury. In some cases, utility profits are large enough to make other city taxes unnecessary.

More than thirteen states operate lotteries as a way of generating more revenue without raising taxes. Because lotteries take money from many people and return it to only a few, many economists say they are a form of tax, a very inequitable one. Critics of lotteries contend that through lotteries the government makes poor people poorer. Former U.S. Attorney Jonathan L. Goldstein adds that in New Jersey "the state lotteries make gambling respectable and thus create new clienteles for organized crime to prey upon. . . . [They] begin to blur people's ethical and moral values. It's a very grave error for states to participate and keep on promoting them."[14] The lottery operations are also criticized as inefficient revenue producers because prizes and administrative costs take up to 60 percent of the money collected. Nonetheless, perhaps as many as half of the states may try the lottery route as a painless way to raise money. This may be "the most oversold, misguided and morally reprehensible innovations in

[14]Quoted in Neal R. Peirce, "Making Book With Your State," *The Boston Globe*, June 11, 1977, Op. Ed. page.

695

*Staffing and financing
state and local
governments*

state policy this century," as Neal R. Peirce claims, but it is also likely to continue and expand as politicians and taxpayers seek an escape from new or higher taxes.[15]

Grants from one level of government to another have become increasingly important during the last several decades. As we have noted, the national government through grants-in-aid allots large sums to the states and to the cities. The states are giving more and more money to the local governments in the form of state grants to support particular programs or in the form of shared taxes. In the latter case, state officials return to local governments revenues collected from certain taxes, often without specifying the purposes for which the money shall be used.

When all the taxes and fees are added together, state and local governments collect large sums. But often they are still not enough to build the highways, or provide the amount of public assistance to the elderly, or perform the other functions the voters have insisted upon. What then? Even as you and we do, our governments often have to borrow money.

Borrowing money

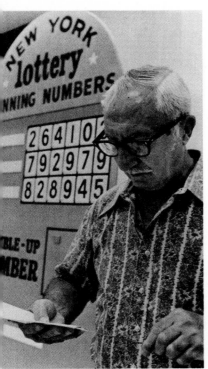

Lotteries are one source of revenue for many states.

During the early years of the nineteenth century, states and cities often subsidized railroad and canal builders. The money for this as well as for financing other public improvements came from bonds issued by the city or state. Bribery and favoritism were common. Provision for payment of debts was inadequate; at times, the people were burdened with old debts for improvements long after the improvements had lost their value. As a result, default on obligations frequently occurred, and city and state credit fell off.

Aroused by the legislatures' abuse of their powers, voters insisted on constitutional amendments reducing legislative discretion. Today most state constitutions put elaborate restrictions on the power of state and local legislatures to borrow money or pledge credit. In large measure, therefore, the power to borrow money for a long term has been transferred from the legislatures and city councils to the voters.

Fiscal planning to ensure that taxes are collected in time to cover necessary operating expenses has reduced the amount of short-term borrowing. Even so, officials sometimes need to borrow money for a short term. This floating debt consists of bank loans, tax-anticipation warrants, and other notes, and is paid out of current revenues.

States and cities sometimes need to borrow money for longer periods—fifteen or twenty years. During the Depression, money was needed for relief. Since the end of World War II, many states have gone into debt in order to pay bonuses to veterans. Expenditures for highway construction, school buildings, and slum clearance are so large that it is not feasible to pay for them out of current revenue. Moreover, these improvements have a long life and add to the wealth of the community, so it is desirable to pay for them by spreading the cost. For this purpose, governments issue bonds. The best practice—now required by many constitutions—is to issue serial bonds, a portion of which come due each year and are retired out of current revenues.

State and local bonds are especially attractive to wealthy investors, since the interest received from them is exempt from federal income tax. For this reason, these governments can borrow money at a lower interest rate than can private businesses. The credit of most cities and states is good, and

[15]*Ibid.*

they easily find buyers for their bonds. Some bonds are general obligation bonds and are backed by the credit of the issuing governments. Revenue bonds are backed only by the income from the particular project in which the money is invested. Governments are often permitted to issue revenue bonds beyond the limitations on their general indebtedness, and so use them whenever possible.

During World War II, with incomes high and tax collections good, many states were able to pay off much of their debt. Since the end of the war, state and municipal borrowing has increased to cover veterans' bonuses and to finance improvements postponed by the emergency. Debts of state and local governments have mounted sharply; recently state and local debt has increased faster than the federal debt.

New York City's money problems

In late 1975, New York City Mayor Abraham Beame admitted that his city was on the verge of having to default on its financial obligations. New York had been running its budget in deficit for several years and making up the deficit by short-term borrowing. In addition, New York, like most other cities, was having to borrow money for its capital projects. When there was a danger that New York could no longer honor its financial obligations, its credit in the borrowing market dried up. No one wanted to invest in a city about to go bankrupt.

Why did the New York financial crisis come about? Most analysts agree that New York's costly social services and welfare system and its high public employee salaries and benefits are a major part of the problem. New York City's wages, salaries, and other employee benefits are the highest in the nation. Moreover, one of every eight people in New York is on welfare.

As we discussed in Chapter 31, New York City leaders make decisions through compromise and extensive bargaining. The mayor must nearly always form temporary coalitions in order to exert any influence on policy

697

*Staffing and financing
state and local
governments*

matters. Further, he operates in a government that attempts to represent urban and suburban interests, the needs of the middle class, and those of the poor and the corporate executives. The mayor administers a city where agreement is an exception and not the rule and where conflict is a way of life.

It is this background of fragmented governmental structure that many believe has led to the sharp escalation of the cost of running New York. One area where evidence of this can be found is the growth of the political power of the city's municipal worker unions. In 1903, New York City employed 33,000 persons. By 1953 that number had risen to over 225,000. The 1960s saw the number of city employees pass the 350,000 mark; by 1972, the number had peaked at approximately 400,000. Through these years the cost of running the city rose step by step with the cost of personnel to run the city government. The 1960s saw major gains by the city's public worker unions as their power to force the city to yield to their demands grew with their numbers. The massive municipal unions demonstrated their ability to gain demands from a fragmented political structure that lacked the strength to fight the united employees. New York faced crippling strikes and work actions through the late 1960s and on into the 1970s by teachers, sanitation workers, transit personnel, and others. Many claim that the result has been settlements that bankrupted the city and forced it into future obligations in the form of generous pension benefits.

New York City plainly faced a large gap between the revenues it could expect from a strained tax base and the rapidly rising costs of running the city. It reacted by imposing more taxes and taking small steps toward paring its expenditures. Despite these efforts, the gap between income and outflow continued to grow. Borrowing was the only avenue available to make ends meet. While most cities borrow to allow for major capital expenditures, New York began to borrow heavily to meet current operating expenses. The city sold short-term bonds characterized by high interest rates and short payback periods. When these notes came due, the city would pay for them by issuing more bonds. The crisis surfaced in early 1975 when the big banks became unwilling to lend the hundreds of millions it took to run the city each month.[16] By June 30, 1975, New York City owed over $5.7 billion in short-term notes.

Defenders of the city point out that it always has been the home of incoming foreign immigrants as well as a refuge for Americans who have been discriminated against. The crisis has national not local causes, they say. New York, they argue, thus deserves special state and federal assistance. They also argue that the federal government takes more in taxes from New York than it gives back in welfare or other assistance.

President Ford disagreed. He blamed city officials for fiscal mismanagement and said he wanted no part of a national bailout for New York. He chided city leaders for allowing massive growth of the city's debt, a steady stream of unbalanced budgets, and large increases in public employee contracts. He stated: "During the last decade, the officials of New York City have allowed its budget to triple. No city can expect to remain solvent

[16]For an account of why New York City's financial situation worsened and of the role the big banks and bankers played both in helping to cause part of the problem and helping to alleviate it, see Jack Newfield and Paul DuBrul, *The Abuse of Power: The Permanent Government and the Fall of New York* (Viking Press, 1977).

if it allows its expenses to increase by an average of 12 percent every year, while its tax revenues are increasing by only 4 or 5 percent per year." Ford wanted New York City to file for bankruptcy before getting any national aid, and Congress, although divided, seemed to agree.

The president's "hard-nosed" stand prodded state and local officials, city labor union leaders, and creditors to review what they could do on their own to avert default and bankruptcy. The White House view was that without its tough stance, New York City would not have considered serious budget cutbacks and new taxes.

After some of the unions helped the city through the first of several bond payment crises, New York Governor Hugh Carey devised a plan that eventually won over the president and Congress. New York state imposed a $200 million dollar tax increase on the city. City officials agreed to require increased contributions to pension plans from city employees. Officials also pledged that they would continue to pare the city budget and would eliminate even more public jobs. (The mayor had already ordered cuts in the city work force of 22 percent.) The state levied added taxes on the estates of city residents, with proceeds to revert to the city. Union officials agreed to purchase $2.5 billion in city securities. They agreed to defer payments of $1.2 billion soon to come due. Several banks agreed to hold on to $1.6 billion of soon-to-mature notes and accepted reduced interest payments. In addition, investors in city bonds were asked to swap $1.6 billion of maturing notes for ten-year Municipal Assistance Corporation bonds.

In response to these pledges and the city's commitment to an austerity program that would help it achieve a balanced budget within three years, the federal government agreed to provide short-term loans of up to $2.3 billion annually for three years. More precisely, the national government

New York City's three daily newspapers carried these headlines on October 30, 1975, after President Ford refused to supply federal aid to bail the city out of its fiscal crisis.

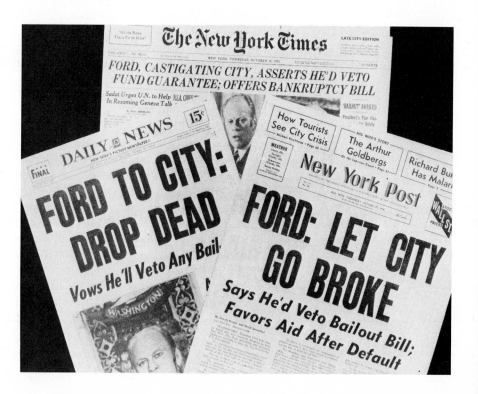

699

*Staffing and financing
state and local
governments*

would lend up to $2.3 billion a year to New York State to permit it to meet the city's seasonal short-term cash needs through mid-1978. These loans would have to be repaid by the close of each fiscal year and at an interest rate that actually would make the federal treasury a small profit.

Can this plan work? It is an intricate patchwork of pledges and promises, and its effectiveness will depend on a number of factors, including the willingness of the city's creditors and investors to accept its terms. The plan also is dependent on the ability of the state to shore up its own troubled financial condition. Meanwhile, the city's problems still are far from solved. The new taxes may drive businesses and upper-middle-income taxpayers out of the city. This possibility led some critics to wonder whether the hard medicine forced on New York City might actually make matters worse in the long run. In addition, some analysts questioned whether New York will be healthy enough even by 1978 to reenter the credit markets to meet future borrowing needs.

So the crisis is far from over for New York City. Many supporters of New York saw new hope in Carter's election and felt that a Democratic president would be more sympathetic to the city's needs. The 1978 budget for New York City was balanced but only with the help of more federal aid. Most officials concede that future budgets will again show deficits. The city's immediate future will depend on whether investors will have enough confidence to buy the city's bonds after the end of the federal governments massive loan programs. It will also depend on tough leadership. The election of Edward Koch as mayor in 1977, following a campaign in which he made relatively few promises to city employees, aroused hopes that the "Big Apple" might be able to solve one of its basic fiscal problems.

The near-default by New York obviously had a profound impact on mayors and governors (as well as investors) around the nation. There had been repeated warnings that a New York default would have grave consequences for the national economy and might undermine confidence in the dollar abroad. Many city and state officials worried that a default in New York would push the interest rates in the skeptical bond market even higher and thus beyond the limits within which they could afford to borrow.

New York's money problems prompted much-needed reappraisals of city and state financial practices. As the Washington Post observed, "[the New York crisis], more than anything politicians, or economists, or financiers could say, is forcing every unit of government to look more closely at its own financial condition. That, in the long run, will be highly beneficial to the country." However, the national loans for the 1975–78 period hardly constitute a lasting solution to the financial conditions of our large older cities. If other cities and states falter in the same direction as New York, we can be sure that the fabric of federalism as well as our system of intergovernmental relations will be subjected to searching reappraisal.

Summary

1. State and local governments have been the fastest growing part of government in the past twenty-five years. (Spending has risen from $18 billion in 1949 to state and local expenditures of about $300 billion in 1979.) But the tax burdens on the middle-income family, although also increased, are not much greater than they were twenty years ago, despite the fact that state and local governments have more responsibilities than they have ever had before.

2. One of the most controversial aspects of state and local government in recent years has been the unionization of nearly 50 percent of the public employees at the state and local levels. Unions have been increasingly successful in recruiting new members and helping to bargain for better wages, hours, working conditions, and pensions. The success of the unions has caused some public backlash, especially in those cities and states that have been financially pressed.

3. In the mid-1970s many cities and states were financially hurting because they borrowed too much, spent too much, and lost needed taxes to the suburbs or to other regions of the country. In the late 1970s, after tightening their belts, increased federal aid, and increased tax revenues, many of these same cities and states were enjoying surplus budgets.

4. The problems of many of the older cities and the energy-depressed states of the Northeast are obvious. Yet many state and local governments in the past twenty years have made considerable progress. Quite a few states and communities have modernized constitutions or charters, upgraded their personnel systems, professionalized their legislative processes, reorganized and strengthened their executives, passed ethics codes, instituted sunset and zero-based budgeting procedures, and invested in urban redevelopment or what might be called "city recovery." The flight from the central cities may be coming to an end, helped somewhat by the energy shortages and the fact that more people want to live closer to where they work. In countless cities there is a new psychology of hope that is breeding fresh investment and confidence. The cost of delivering public services and thus the tax rates is simply illustrated in our case study of New York City. But many optimists see America's inner cities on the verge of a comeback.

Epilogue: Citizen Politics

Ed Valtman '73, The Hartford Times

Government of, by, and for the people is the most exacting venture a large nation has ever undertaken. Exhilarating, demanding, and frustrating, the burden falls on each of us if we would make democracy work.

Some say democracy is merely a dream, an ideal that is unattainable. Others complain that politics is merely a con game, with the people getting fooled by their leaders. Still others say there is too much corruption in the American political system, that money and public relations too often distort and undermine the ideals of a democratic republic. These complaints have at least some validity. If government by and for the people in America is to be more than an abstract ideal, citizen activists must be willing to clarify the issues for debate, find out how the system works, demand accountability, form political alliances, and engage in action to change the system if necessary.

Citizen action

There is always the danger that political scientists will overvalue the contributions of the politically active and undervalue the contributions of those who choose to leave politics to others. In some societies the government actually compels people to engage in political action, attend political classes, and even makes the right kind of political response a precondition for getting a good job or attending college. In the United States, however, the choice of whether to be politically active belongs to each citizen. And those who choose to take care of the sick, grow the food, teach foreign languages, take care of the young, run service stations, and establish insurance agencies, but limit their politics to paying taxes and voting also make important contributions to our society.

Still, a democracy needs many people who are more involved in government. It needs individuals who care enough to give political matters a high claim on their talents and energies. We need especially to ensure that active citizenship is not concentrated in those who come only from a part of the community. Fortunately, the talents, time, and energies required for democratic government are not the monopoly of any particular group, class, sex, race, or section of the nation.

There is no recipe for preparing effective citizen-activists. Playing a part in politics depends on more than mere participation, commitment, and a desire to make things better. It demands political shrewdness and a comprehension of access points and political system slack. The possibilities for creative participation are numerous for those who are willing to work at it:

> In almost every area of social life [new activists] are certain to encounter entrenched and efficient bureaucracies which evade, resist and wear down, or simply absorb the force of their protest. The decline of political parties and of legislative authority has clearly reduced the accessibility of the political system and made the work of the newly activated citizens much harder than it once was. Nevertheless, there is abundant evidence to suggest that access is still possible and that bureaucracies can be pushed this way or that (even when they can't be seized and transformed).[1]

Many of the procedures of American politics may seem dull and complex—and they often are. The routines of both electoral and pressure politics can indeed be tedious, frustrating, and unrewarding. But there is much that is important, fascinating, inspiring—and even entertaining—in the patterns of American politics. Registration drives, for example, may seem unimportant until someone publicly challenges your right to vote, or your candidate loses an election by an especially slim margin. Limitations on campaign spending may seem unimportant—until the opposition accuses your candidate of trying to buy the election. And organizing protests and petitioning public officials may seem a waste of time—until finally the day comes when the officials in question come to see the merits of your complaints and reverse their policies.

To be sure, radical or revolutionary changes in our political system seldom occur, but the range of challenges and opportunities for the citizen-activist is plentiful: party politics, electoral politics, advisory politics, pressure, or movement, politics, and, of course, careers in the civil and military services.

Party politics

Though many people may have little interest in seeking political or career jobs in government, they can and should consider taking an active role in one of the two major or several fringe parties. As we have seen earlier, the American parties badly need strengthening at every level. The country

[1]Michael Walzer, *Political Action: A Practical Guide to Movement Politics* (Quadrangle Books, 1971), p. 122.

"That's the way our system works—each branch of government watches the other two, and the people watch dumbfounded."

Editorial cartoon by Frank Iterlandi. Copyright, Los Angeles Times. Reprinted with permission.

needs more party politicians to hunt our quality candidates and help elect them, and then to remind the elected of their responsibilities to the people.

Jeffersonians dreamed a great dream—that a party system could be effective, could raise issues for rational deliberation, and build coalitions to achieve a more just and decent society. Seldom have parties lived up to the Jeffersonian dream. Seldom have they served to discipline the whims of those in public office who have lost touch with the people. But if we have not lived up to the Jeffersonian hopes, it does not mean that parties are unimportant. We can still build a healthy, competitive party system that would recruit able public servants, spur provocative debates over national priorities, and inspire honesty and accountability in government.

The first step for the citizen-activist is to call local party officials, find out their views, objectives, and organizational routines. If you disagree with their views, your initial work is already cut out for you. If you agree with their views and intentions, they will doubtless welcome you and sign you up for some subcommittee or future campaign assignment.

One of the important jobs in party politics is enlarging the number of the party faithful. The task of getting people out to vote is equally important. Identification systems have to be devised. Names and addresses of those not registered must be obtained. Records of those who have moved away and those who have moved into the community must be continually updated.

Registration laws vary from state to state. The unregistered voter is sometimes apathetic, but our complex system of registration also inhibits many people who are interested in voting. They may not know when or where they can register, what the registration deadlines are, and when and how they must affiliate with a particular party in order to participate directly in party caucuses and primaries. The shrewd party activist will know the answers to these questions and will be able to provide both the cues and incentives needed to get people to participate more fully in party and election activities.

The heart of registration and voting drives lies in approaching the individual voter in person, but the approach is much more effective if it comes as part of a general effort. Often the best procedure is a nonpartisan communitywide program.

Much of this work would be simple drudgery under any other circumstances. In the heat of a campaign, however, this work often takes on an aura of the dramatic. Volunteers are part of a team engaged in a struggle. Party headquarters are always crowded; the phone seems always to be ringing. Crisis follows crisis. Candidates dash in to make arrangements for television spots and rush out to speak at the Kiwanis Club's annual barbecue. Rumors flow thick and fast.

Taking part in party politics can be a rewarding business, especially if, ideally, the names on the ballot are those of persons you have helped to nominate and—hopefully—elect. However, new activists should go into party politics with a realistic view of how parties operate. On the local level, organizations are often stagnant. Committees rarely meet, attendance is typically low. The parties are run, by and large, by small groups of people. Often the powers over crucial matters such as candidate selection, allocations of convention delegates, and campaign finances become centralized in the hands of a few city and state party veterans.

Party veterans often try to run campaigns offering something for everyone, while at the same time saying nothing that will offend anyone. Precisely because Americans are not strongly ideological, the two major parties usually have played down controversial issues. Instead they have tried to capture as many differing viewpoints and fence-sitting independents as they can. If parties today are often not very democratic in their internal activities, this does not necessarily have to be the case. If corruption and the influence of wealthy individuals or organized groups, such as trade unions, are in excess, this also does not need to be the case.[2]

Oldline leaders may try to close out newcomers to keep their organization as a kind of private preserve. They should not be allowed to succeed without a struggle. Turnover in local and state party posts is higher than most people think. New affirmative action rules are also helping to open the parties up. And in many states there are a variety of factions within the two major parties. So, if necessary, one can often work with another part of the organization, or join or form auxiliary groups like the Young Democrats or Young Republicans or the Ripon Society.

The tasks of rebuilding and reshaping the parties to become more effective in achieving their goals are tasks that cry out for concerned citizens.

Electoral politics

We will never have effective government at all levels until we can persuade many of our friends and neighbors that they must take personal responsibility for what happens. Just as a nation is never finished, so also nations and institutions can decay. Even the best structural processes and the most effective checks and balances cannot ensure free and just society. One of the persistent and usually fashionable traditions in America has been to joke about or put down the career politician. Intellectuals and foreign visitors say we lack brilliant and inspiring people in public life. Clergy and idealists despair of the lack of morality and vision in politics. And even major participants in politics laugh at the evasiveness toward critical issues. Said one: "a politician is a statesman who approaches every question with an open mouth."

It is well to remember, however, what Plato once noted: "What is honored in a country will be cultivated there." We need now, just as we did two hundred years ago, politicians who have objectives in view beyond the enlargement of their own careers. They will need to love politics, respect people, and delight in the tough give-and-take that should be the hallmark of democracy — the national conversations between leaders and the public. *Politics is not only the art of the possible, but also the art of making the difficult possible.*

A surprisingly large number of Americans have absolutely no interest in running for political office. There will always be many more who are willing to serve than to run. The personal sacrifices political life demands — less privacy, family life, and leisure, dangers to health, and so on — are far more than most people are willing to make. Thus, one of the major difficulties in our democracy is finding talented people to run for office.

---

[2]For studies of corruption and the excessive influence of money on state and local politics and what might be done about these problems, see Larry L. Berg, Harlan Hahn and John R. Schmidhauser, *Corruption in the American Political System* (General Learning Press, 1976); and Herbert E. Alexander, ed., *Campaign Money: Reform and Reality in the States* (Free Press, 1976).

Certainly chance plays an enormous role in determining whether one succeeds in a political career. This, along with the obvious lack of job security, often stops able people from even considering electoral politics. "One who enters politics must realize that he is to live dangerously," a former candidate has said. "In business, the line between the red and the black divides anxiety and comfort, but a businessman can survive a bad year; in politics 0.1 percent on one's biennial gross vote can mean the difference between prosperity and ruin."[3] It might be added that before entering politics, prospective candidates would be wise to reflect on their personal strengths and weaknesses. If they are sensitive to criticism, shy, short of temper, and prefer to lead a quiet, peaceful life, the chances are strong that they would neither be happy in politics nor be able to develop the kind of temperament so essential for elective public service today.

What can the citizen-activist do who chooses to seek political office? They can work actively in the campaigns of others and see first hand the ordeal of winning nomination and subsequent election. The would-be politician should also read widely in history, politics, and philosophy, know the use of parables, develop an excellent memory, study the major issues of the day, cultivate the leadership of major organizations in the region, and develop as fully as possible the capacity to listen and to learn.

Former U.S. Senator Hugh D. Scott, Jr., once listed the following personality traits as especially helpful for those who would like to be active in politics:

1. Be politically informed.
2. Integrity. Despite cynicism about politics, a dishonest politician is almost always exposed sooner or later.
3. Patience. Scott spent "twenty years or so of being stopped several times a day by people with something on their mind, of having my lapels seized so firmly or my sleeve tugged by someone who wants something done that he feels I may be able to do, of long interviews with people with a grievance, a petition, a plan, an invention, or just a two-way ball-bearing tongue."
4. Courtesy. "On Ballot Boulevard there's no market at all for the sour stuff."
5. Gregariousness.
6. Hard work. "To know your neighborhood and to help your neighbors is a 365-day-a-year job."
7. A sense of humor. Freshman members of Congress are warned by their elders, "Don't violate Rule Six." And what is Rule Six? "Don't take yourself too seriously." 'And Rules One to Five? "Don't take yourself too seriously." A sense of proportion, a sense of humor.
8. Courage.[4]

An important lesson learned time and again during the 1970s was that by finding out the rules and simply getting enough people to the right caucuses, preconvention meetings, party gatherings, and to the polls, new people can get themselves elected to important posts.[5] But the rules are

[3]Stimson Bullitt, *To Be a Politican* (Doubleday, 1959), p. 53.

[4]Hugh D. Scott, *How To Go Into Politics* (John Day, 1949), pp. 26ff.

[5]A few of the how-to-do-it books are Edward Schwartzman, *Campaign Craftsmanship: A Professional's Guide to Campaigning for Elective Office* (Universe Books, 1973); William T. Murphy, Jr., and Edward Schneier, *Vote Power: How To Work for the Person You Want Elected* (Doubleday, 1974); James Brown and Philip M. Seib, *The Art of Politics: Electoral Strategies and Cam-*

often difficult to figure out. Rarely is a candidacy successfully launched and brought to fruition in a few weeks, except in occasional special elections held to fill vacancies created by death or unexpected retirement. Long is the list of celebrated successful politicians who won office only after losing election bids one or several times.

A candidate for office should also learn how to use multiple advisers and know well the dangers of listening to only one set of counselors. Many younger politicians can find themselves surrounded by people who act more like cheerleaders than candid analysts. Of course winning power must always be subordinate to knowing the proper purposes to which it should be put.

Advisory politics

For many, party and electoral politics will not be the best way to contribute to government by the people. Those who have specialized knowledge that might improve governmental performance may prefer other alternatives. As the late Justice Robert H. Jackson suggested, "It is not the function of our government to keep the citizen from falling into error; it is the function of the citizen to keep the government from falling into error."

Public officials and career public servants at all levels of government usually welcome advice on public policy. If they don't welcome it, they should not be allowed to ignore new ideas or prevent open scrutiny of their operations. In practice, most officials conduct hearings, appoint study groups, establish advisory committees, and frequently have small sums of money available for consultant studies. For the citizen-activist who wants to change existing policies or help pass and establish new policies, there are many opportunities to obtain a hearing and press one's arguments.

It is important to remember, however, that especially in a democracy the academically well-researched argument may carry less weight than the political argument. That is, whether an adviser believes that a policy is "right" may be less important to many officials than how the policy will affect their career or reelection chances. Politicians fear being too much out in front or out of line with those who elect them.

Every community needs a loose coalition of people, willing to work together, often on a nonpartisan basis, to examine and offer policy advice on urgent city problems. City council members and their staffs cannot do it alone, nor can local business elites or minority leaders. What is needed are citizen-advisers who will apply their professional skills as well as common sense to such issues. Help is needed also in assisting those in office to promote equitable and effective programs. in areas such as tax reform, consumerism, jobs for those who want to work, and so on.

Citizen-advisers, to be sure, will often be disillusioned by the clumsiness with which politicians and bureaucrats use advice; but the adviser will learn, too, that knowledge is power. Most people holding public office are receptive to constructive ideas. Anyone willing to undertake systematic policy and program evaluations who can present a convincing rationale

paign Management (Alfred Publishers, 1976); David Hartman and Frank Dughi, Win Your Political Campaign (Pierce Publishing, 1976); and Donald G. Herzberg and J. W. Peltason, A Student Guide to Campaign Politics (McGraw-Hill, 1970). A perceptive and highly readable memoir by a man who has been active in political campaigns and politics at all levels of government is available in Lawrence F. O'Brien's No Final Victories: A Life in Politics from John F. Kennedy to Watergate (Ballantine, 1975).

for dealing with the realities finds a ready audience. Persons who can design cars that will cause less smog, invent better ways to produce energy and conserve natural resources, or formulate better foreign policies will find politicians knocking at their door.

Citizen-advisers learn too that once they have gained recognition and visibility in their field, their ability to influence officials and make governments more responsible is that much greater. They can help organize opposition coalitions of experts. Then, too, they can use their positions of acknowledged expertise to educate fellow citizens to support or oppose government programs. Citizen-advisers should also be concerned with the often inadequate means of putting programs into action. In the best of situations they will not only come up with new ideas, but also develop new ways of turning these ideas into successful programs.

Pressure or movement politics

The best insurance system for honest government is an alert citizenry, watchful of its leaders, and increasingly imaginative in developing new means to keep public officials and party leaders accountable and within the Constitution. Government by the people need not be a utopia unrelated to present-day processes and politics.

The difficulty with pressure politics is that not all the pressures are represented. The American political system is often biased in favor of producer interests against those of the consumers, in favor of the wealthy and educated as against the poor and ignorant. This has become well recognized, but it does not have to be accepted as the way things have to be. Those who claim to speak for the consumer and for the poor, the depressed, and the discriminated against have organized. "Public interest" lobbies, citizen-activist movements, and countless consumer groups have sprung into action in recent years. Their prime goal is not to elect people to office but to influence those who hold public office, to change policies, to increase accountability, and to lessen the secrecy that so often grows up as a barrier to the people's right to know.

"To choose pressure politics," writes Michael Walzer, "means to try to influence those people who already hold power, who sit in official seats, who may even be responsible for the outrages against which the movement is aimed."[6] Here again there are few established rules. Tactics differ markedly—from the SDS and Saul Alinsky kind of militance on the one hand to the more approved techniques of a Ralph Nader study report and of the League of Women Voters on the other. Certain general strategies are similar: Do not presuppose the hostility of all officials, media people, and outsiders. Neither look up to anyone nor down on anyone. Attack the people's leaders, not the people. (In politics, of course, everybody claims to speak for the public interest and to represent the people.) Alliances and coalitions with other related groups should be explored. Every effort should be made to increase the membership's understanding of how government works and what the issues are. What they do not know about, they can't object to. As H. L. Mencken said, "Conscience is the inner voice which warns us that someone may be watching."

On occasion, pressure groups and "public interest" lobbies support certain candidates with profit. The independent, single-issue candidate is another easy choice. He is unlikely to win, but his campaign can serve to

[6]Walzer, *Political Action*, p. 26.

spread the word, and a good vote can have significant demonstration effect. A single-issue campaign may also put considerable pressure on one of the major parties to make the cause its own and so win the support of whatever constituency is being mobilized. Educational campaigns, boycotts, petitions, strikes, marches, dissident writings, and nonviolent civil disobedience activities all must be considered. To paraphrase Alexander Solzhenitsyn, a great writer, for example, can serve in part as an opposition government.

Those who choose pressure politics do so in large part because they despair of realizing their main aims merely by electing new people to public office. As Common Cause's John W. Gardner ofter puts it, his group is not above politics, it is merely nonpartisan. It was his view that elected officials are limited by the accommodations they made to get elected, by their desire to be reelected, and by structural constraints in the institutions they must work with. Gardner added: "Clearly we cannot organize our society in such a way that we are dependent on inspired presidential leadership, because most of the time it won't be there. We must build creative strength in other parts of the system. And in fact that's the kind of system it was intended to be. It was never intended that we should seek a Big Daddy and lean on him. We shall save ourselves—or we won't be saved."[7]

Just as in election work, most citizen-action work will be tedious, routine, and repetitive. Stamina is essential. Membership maintenance and internal communications will sometimes seem urgent, exhilarating, and highly rewarding, but most of the time they will not. Strategies will vary from one region to another and from one set of policy issues to the next. But we have only to look at the considerable impact of Ralph Nader and the many public interest research groups he helped start to see that a few individuals—*when they know what they are doing*—can bring about significant change. These Nader-encouraged local student pressure groups have brought about such changes as the following:

1. The appointment of an ombudsman for prisoners in the St. Louis jails.
2. New regulations that forbid lumber companies to cut swaths of forest without federal approval.
3. A new plan in Detroit that forces landlords to repair dilapidated housing.
4. Successfully challenged utility rate increases in Massachusetts and Vermont.
5. The conception of a new Minnesota law that regulates the selling of hearing aids.
6. The passage of a truth-in-lending law in New York State.

Public service opportunities

Public employment has been the most rapidly growing segment of the American workforce. More than one out of every seven people in the workforce serve as employees of more than 78,000 governmental agencies at the federal, state, county, or municipal levels.[8] Most of the positions in government service are open to qualified people, regardless of their political persuasions. The career services at every level constantly need to recruit able newcomers.

Over 90 percent of the positions in the federal executive branch are open to qualified citizens by appointment. Most of these positions are filled through civil service examinations.

[7]John W. Gardner, *In Common Cause* (Norton, 1971), p. 84.

[8]John W. Macy, Jr., *Public Service: The Human Side of Government* (Harper & Row, 1971).

Positions calling for professional training are filled through interviews and questionnaires that enable the Civil Service Commission and the appointing agencies to examine the competence and experience of the individual.

Several federal agencies have their own personnel systems and are not covered by regular civil service rules. The TVA, FBI, National Security Agency, United States Information Agency, CIA, and Foreign Service Officer Corps, for example, recruit and hire their own employees.

The Foreign Service Office Corps deserves special mention because of its more specialized testing and its important diplomatic responsibilities. Written, oral, and language tests are required, and intensive interviews are used. Persons who wish to take the examinations may receive application forms from the Board of Examiners for the Foreign Service, Department of State, Washington, D.C. 20520.

Those who seek work in the federal career services should do so without illusions. Despite valiant efforts to make the merit system work, a tacit seniority system often takes root. Departments and bureaus do develop a political life of their own—a passion for size, growth, and jurisdictional integrity invariably develops.[9]

There has been considerable discussion in the 1970s about decentralization, or regionalization, of the federal government. Some authority has been given to federal regional offices or to state and local authorities. Still, most civil servants would agree that the key positions of power in the civil service are those at their respective headquarters offices in Washington, D.C. To move up the ladder, according to many now in the civil service, "you have got to be willing to move to Washington and work at the center. A whole raft of people get stuck in the provinces and become very frustrated." On the other hand, many of those in public service prefer to work in other parts of the country, and it is undeniable that people in a very real sense can make of their jobs what they want. The highly motivated public servant, no matter where he or she is located, nearly always can seize opportunities to improve the quality of government performance.

One of the fastest growing segments of public employment is in state and local governments. The positions of city manager and of city-planning director are especially challenging and demand talented executives with well developed political and managerial abilities.

Young people interested in sampling public service may participate in a variety of government internship programs. Intern programs provide people with short-term government experience and a first-hand look at the process. Many members of Congress take on college students as summer interns. Most states and many cities operate intern programs. Information about intern opportunities can usually be obtained from your department of political science or local student government officers.

Citizen-volunteer service

The Peace Corps recruits from a wide range of skilled Americans for overseas work. After screening and training, volunteers are assigned to countries that request Peace Corps services. Applicants must be eighteen years of age or older. Volunteers receive no regular salaries but get allowances to

[9]For some discussions about bureaucracy and career service, see John Franklin Campbell, *The Foreign Affairs Fudge Factory* (Basic Books, 1971); Anthony Downs, *Inside Bureaucracy* (Little, Brown, 1967); Edward Weisband and Thomas M. Franck, *Resignation in Protest* (Penguin, 1976).

cover the cost of clothing, housing, food, and incidental expenses so that they live at an economic level equivalent to their clients in the host country. Upon completion of service, Peace Corps volunteers receive a separation allotment based on time spent overseas.

Volunteers in Service to America (VISTA) is the domestic counterpart of the Peace Corps. Volunteers lend their talents for a year to the service of communities that are striving to solve pressing economic and social problems. After a training period that stresses supervised field experience, volunteers are sent to work in migrant worker communities, Indian reservations, rural and urban community action programs, hospitals, schools, and mental health facilities. In short, workers may be sent wherever poverty exists. VISTA volunteers are paid only subsistence expenses and a modest monthly stipend and personal allowance.

The several volunteer federal programs are consolidated in the national agency called ACTION. ACTION administers the Peace Corps, VISTA, the National Student Volunteer Program, Foster Grandparents, the Retired Senior Volunteer Program, and the Service Corps of Retired Executives. Inquiries about these programs should be addressed to ACTION Recruiting Office, Washington, D.C. 20525. Or, you may call ACTION toll free at 800–424–8580. A nationally sponsored Teacher Corps also exists for teachers or potential teachers who want to devote several years of service to poverty area schools. Inquiries about this program, which in addition offers teacher-training fellowships, should be directed to the Teacher Corps, U.S. Office of Education, Washington, D.C. 20202.

Last word

Citizen-activists can have an impact on governmental and political processes. Progress in civil rights, consumerism, ecology, women's liberation, campaign finance reform, and countless other areas came about only when concerned groups had acquired numbers and force that could no longer be ignored. To have impact, however, people must be willing to concentrate their energies, enlarge the number of those sharing their views, and work hard to channel their activities into effective political action. The essence of democracy is participatory and advocacy politics. Politics without party and partisan politics is really not democratic and open politics at all. Beware of those who try to remove critical policy issues from politics.

At the very least, people ought to exercise their right to vote. A better America will never result if tens of millions of us become spectators rather than active, informed participants. Ogden Nash once summed it up this way:

They have such refined and delicate palates
That they can discover no one worthy of their ballots
And then when someone terrible gets elected
They say, There, That's just what I expected!

Our ideals and aspirations are still valid. The trouble comes when we fail to live up to our own abiding values. Politics is the practical exercise of the art of self-government, and widespread participation is needed if we are to have meaningful self-government. Every individual in a democracy contributes to its success or failure. Speaking about his native Russia, Alexander Solzhenitsyn wrote, "We didn't love freedom enough." There are times here too, perhaps during the Watergate scandals and earlier during the McCarthy era in the 1950s, when it seems that many silent Americans do not cherish democracy enough. Stanford University biologist Paul R. Ehrlich put the case this way:

> I think the main thing that's wrong with our society is we've allowed people to think that in this day and age it is sufficient to vote a couple of times a year at most in order to be a good citizen. And I think if that's all we do, we're going to get exactly what we deserve. I think that all of us have to start doing what I call tithing to our society. Spending at least 10 per cent of our time trying to help run it. That doesn't necessarily mean being a politician, but it may. Getting involved in local government, getting involved in action organizations of certain sorts, informing yourself about issues and so on.

Plainly, the quality of commitment and concern of the people broadly determine the kind of government and leadership they get. Citizen politicians, critical and caring, can provide the vitality, vision, and clear thinking required for democratic self-government in the United States.

Keeping Informed: Reading and Research Sources

Newspapers, radio, and television are important sources of information, but the person who depends solely on these sources will have an imperfect picture of the world. They give only a disconnected story of the sensational — the newsworthy — events. They tell little of the whys and wherefores.

Magazines of general circulation contain useful material, but they do not go deeply into particular questions. Where do you find a law? How do you look up a court decision? Where can you find information on the United Nations? How do you find out how your congressman has voted? What are some good books on the USSR? Many aids and services have been designed to make such information readily available. An excellent place to begin is Clement E. Vose, *A Guide to Library Sources in Political Science: American Government* (1975) published by the American Political Science Association. Any respectable library should have copies. If yours does not, have the librarian order one by writing APSA, 1527 New Hampshire Avenue, Washington, D.C. 20036.

Important information-dispensing centers are the more than seventy-five hundred public libraries and the many hundreds of private libraries that are open to the public. In these libraries can be found, in addition to magazines of general interest, many specialized journals such as *The American Political Science Review*. There are also a number of periodical indexes, of which the *Public Affairs Information Service* is useful because it indexes books, pamphlets, and reports, as well as articles from hundreds of periodicals on topics in a broad range of current public interest. Major political science journals are included in the *Social Science and Humanities Index*. The *International Political Science Abstracts*, edited by the International Political Science Association, provides précis of articles from all major political science journals throughout the world. The *Reader's Guide to Periodical Literature* includes mainly popular magazines with mass or family circulation. The *Index to Legal Periodicals* and *Business Periodicals Index* are also useful.

The *Universal Reference System* is the most comprehensive reference to books, papers, journals, and reviews. Most of these indexes are published monthly and indexed cumulatively at the end of the year. They can help you locate materials on most subjects. In addition, Robert B. Harmon's *Political Science: A Bibliographical Guide to the Literature* (1965), which is kept up to date by supplements—No. 2 (1972), No. 3 (1974). See also by the same author, *Political Science Bibliographies*, Vol. 1 (1973), Vol. 2 (1976). Lubomyr Wynar's *Guide to Reference Materials in Political Science*, Vol. 1 (1967), Vol. 2 (1968), and the *ABS Guide to Recent Publications in the Social and Behavioral Sciences* (1965), also kept up to date with annual supplements, are useful. Other bibliographies you might consult are Frederick L. Holler's five-volume *The Information Sources of Political Science* (1975) and *ABC Pol Sci; Advance Bibliography of Contents: Political Science and Government*, a monthly service which reproduces the tables of contents of periodicals in the field of political science. The card catalog in the library will reveal the books that are available there. You may be able to learn something about an author's reputation or a particular book in the *Book Review Digest;* but reviews in this digest are taken from a limited group of publications. You will also find the *Book Review Index* helpful; it complements the *Book Review Digest* but is more current and complete. It lists sources of all reviews in periodicals indexed, and it comes in monthly and quarterly issues with annual cumulations. Most larger libraries also subscribe to *Perspective*, a thoughtful monthly journal that carries reviews of major new books on government, politics, and international affairs.

One of the most useful volumes is the *United States Government Manual*, an annual publication. This manual, which can be obtained from the Superintendent of Documents, U.S. Government Printing Office, Washington, D.C. 20402, covers the authority, organization, and functions of all branches of the government. It has up-to-date organization charts, tells who holds the higher executive positions, and gives a brief description of the work of each unit of government. The *Congressional Directory*, also published annually, has some of the materials found in the *Manual*, and it includes autobiographical sketches of members of Congress, lists of congressional committees and committee assignments, election statistics for the last several congressional elections, and maps of congressional districts. The *Directory* is the place to find out the name of your congressman, a short sketch of his life, what committees he is on, and the boundaries of the district he represents. The *Almanac of American Politics*, published by Gambit, contains current biographies, voting records, lobbying interests, as well as political and economic profiles on a member's district.

Of special interest to persons interested in social sciences is the *Encyclopedia of the Social Sciences*, published in 1930 under the editorship of Edwin R. A. Seligman and Alvin Johnson; it contains articles on various topics—political parties, sovereignty, representation, John Locke, for example—that are among the best short treatments to be found. The *International Encyclopedia of the Social Sciences*, edited by David L. Sills and published in 1968, complements its predecessor and brings the information up to date. Valuable review and survey articles can be found in the eight-volume series *Handbook of Political Science* (1975, 1976), edited by Fred Greenstein and Nelson W. Polsby.

Although both encyclopedias contain a great deal of biography, the *Dictionary of National Biography* and the *Dictionary of American Biography* are the prime sources for this type of data. Included are some outstanding articles; one by Carl Becker on Benjamin Franklin, for example, is found in the *Dictionary of American Biography*. In *Current Biography* you can find materials and background information on people in the news, and there is a companion set, *Biography Index*, in case specific information has not been written up fully in *Current Biography* for ten years or so. Also of help will be *Who's Who in American Politics* and *Who's Who in Government*.

Certain important tools for quick reference to current events are available, such as *Facts on File*, the *New York Times Index*, the *Wall Street Journal Index*, and *Keesing's Contemporary Archives*.

If you want raw figures, consult the *Statistical Abstract of the United States*, another yearly publication of the Government Printing Office. The reference librarian will be able to point out other useful tools of this nature, such as the *Historical Statistics of the United States*, the *Congressional District Data Book*, and the many publications from the Bureau of the Census. The *American Statistical Index* is a comprehensive guide to the statistical publications of the U.S. government. It is useful in locating which of the numerous publications issued by the government contain the statistics a student may be looking for. Phyllis G. Carter's *U.S. Census Data for Political and Social Research: A Manual for Students*, published in 1976 by the American Political Science Association, is also very helpful.

Where can you find a law? We often hear people talk about some statute without having seen it. Where can the actual text be found? The laws of the United States as passed by Congress are first printed individually and are known as slip laws. Each law has a number; in recent years public laws have been numbered according to the term of Congress in which they were enacted. At the end of each year the laws are collected and published by the Government Printing Office under the title of *United States Statutes at Large*. Each year's collection is separately numbered, though there are two separate parts of each number. Part One contains *public laws*—that is, laws affecting the people generally or having to do with governmental organization. Part Two contains *private laws*, those having to do with particular groups or individuals. The laws in the *Statutes at Large* are listed chronologically, each law constituting a separate chapter. The Taft-Hartley Act, for example, is Chapter 120 of Volume 61, on page 136; it is cited as 61 Stat. 136.

The volumes of *Statutes at Large* are useful for research, but they include many laws of only specialized interest. Further, many of the measures modify earlier legislation and are themselves modified by later legislation. To find *current* laws on a topic, it is best to go the *United States Code*, which contains the public laws of the United States that are in force at the present time. The official edition of the *United States Code* is published every six years. Supplements are issued annually between editions. The laws are arranged according to fifty titles; each title is divided into sections, and each section into paragraphs that are consecutively numbered for each title. The fifty titles cover such subjects as Congress, Title 2; Armed Forces, Title 10; Bankruptcy, Title 11; Labor, Title 29; and so on. The *Code* is cited by title and paragraph. The citation of the Taft-Hartley Act, for example, is 29 U.S.C. 141 ff.

The *Code*, like the *Statutes at Large*, is printed by the Government Printing Office, but there are also commercially published editions known as *United States Code Annotated* (USCA) and the *Federal Code Annotated* (FCA). These annotated editions include notes on judicial interpretations of the law as well as the law itself. If available, they are more useful than the *Code.*

The series *Treaties in Force* is the best source of information about treaties and executive agreements. These volumes are published annually and are organized chronologically.

Where does one find the rules and regulations issued by the president and the executive agencies? Every day except Sunday and Monday the government publishes the *Federal Register*, which contains executive orders, regulations, and proclamations issued by the president, as well as the orders and regulations promulgated by the executive agencies (including the independent regulatory commissions). These administrative rules and regulations are collected, codified, and kept up to date in the *Code of Federal Regulations*, organized on the same plan as the *United States Code.* The *Code of Federal Regulations*, the *Federal Register*, along with the *United States Government Manual* previously mentioned and the annual publication *Public Papers of the Presidents*, are part of what is known as the Federal Register System. The *Weekly Compilation of Presidential Documents*, which contains public messages, speeches, and statements of the president, is published every Monday.

The laws as they finally appear on the statute books give, however, only part of the story. Where do you find out what went on before the laws were passed or why certain laws were not passed? This information can, in part, be found in one of the most interesting items of American letters — the *Congressional Record*. The *Record* is issued every day Congress is in session and is bound and indexed at the end of each session. It contains everything that is said on the floors of the two chambers, plus a lot that is not said. Congress freely gives its consent to requests of its members "to revise and extend their remarks," which is a polite way of saying that congressmen are permitted to include in the *Record* statements they did not make before Congress. These speeches are then reprinted and distributed to the folks back home. Congressmen, with the unanimous consent of their colleagues, also place in the *Record* poems, articles, letters, editorials, and other materials they find interesting. Each day's *Record* is now accompanied by a *Daily Digest* that highlights the events both on the floor of Congress and in committees. Action on specific items can be traced by searching through the index. An easier method is to use the *Digest of Public General Bills*, which gives a brief summary of all the public bills and traces their progress.

There are several commercial services that provide convenient references to congressional activities. The *Congressional Quarterly Weekly Report* contains voting records, legislative action, reports on lobbying, and other materials about Congress in action. This is the best source for materials on lobbying activity. The materials are indexed and collected in the *Congressional Quarterly Almanac*, an annual publication. The *United States Code: Congressional and Administrative News* and the *Congressional Index* also provide ready reference to congressional activity. Another helpful way to monitor congressional activity is through the *CIS/Index*, an index to publications of Congress issued monthly with annual cumulations by the Congressional Information Service. It indexes and abstracts committee hearings, prints chamber reports and other congressional documents, and contains a brief summary of the statement of each witness in a hearing and includes page numbers on which particular testimonies appear.

Because most of the real work of Congress is done in committees, the reports of these committees and the printed records of hearings are important sources of information. The hearings and reports may be found in any of the 1,122 depository libraries in the United States. (A depository library is one that receives regularly publications issued by the Government Printing Office.)

Congress is not the only branch of the federal government that keeps a record of its work. All the other agencies have their own publications, describing their work and supplying the citizen with general and specialized information. These can be obtained from the Superintendent of Documents, Government Printing Office, Washington D.C. 20402, at a nominal price. They are indexed in the *Monthly Catalog of United States Government Publications*. One of the several general guides to government publications is Laurence F. Schmeckebier's and Roy B. Eastin's *Government Publications and Their Use*, 2nd. rev. ed. (Brookings, 1969).

Activities of the executive branch of the federal government as well as the Congress and the courts are analyzed in the *National Journal*, a weekly publication. This is the best single source on developments within the federal executive branch. *The Washington Monthly* and *The Public Interest* provide critical essays on policy politics and bureaucracy in Washington.

Where can you find the reports of the federal judiciary? Legal bibliography is a complex subject, but the law is too important to leave to lawyers. The decisions of the Supreme Court are published by the government in numbered volumes known as the *United States Reports*. Cases are cited by volume and page number. *Washington* v. *Davis*, 426 U.S. 229(1976), means that this case can be found in the 426th volume of the *United States Reports* on page 229 and that the opinion was handed down in 1976. Decisions of the Court prior to 1875 are cited by the name of the Supreme Court reporter. Thus *Marbury* v. *Madison*, 1 Cranch 137 (1803), can be found in the first volume of Cranch's Supreme Court reports on page 137; the opinion was announced in 1803. It now takes months before the official Supreme Court Reports are available, so to review recent opinions it is necessary to use editions of commercial publishers. The *United States Law Week* is the single most comprehensive review and the fastest off the press. Also available are the *Supreme Court Reporter*, published by West Publishing Company, and *United States Supreme Court Reports, Lawyers Edition*, published by the Lawyers Co-operative Publishing Company. Some of the federal district court rulings are now commercially published in volumes known as the *Federal Supplement*. Those of the federal courts of appeals are published by the same commercial publisher in volumes known as the *Federal Reporter*. These reports are available in many general libraries, and often can be found in special law libraries such as those located at the county courthouse.

You will get excellent assistance too from most university librarians, who will gladly direct you to the newest reference and document sources.

Glossary of Key Terms

We have tried to write a book about American politics and government that is highly readable. We realize, however, that certain legal terms and political science phrases may not be familiar. To make such words more understandable, we have compiled this glossary. Words or phrases that appear in the text in boldface color are defined here. We welcome suggestions for additions to the glossary.

Administrative law—That law which controls the authority and procedures of administrative agencies in their dealings with private interests; administrative law involves court review of how government agencies make and apply rules.

Admiralty and maritime law—Law derived from the general maritime law of nations, modified by Congress; applicable not only to the high seas, but also to the Great Lakes and all navigable rivers in the U.S.

Advisory Commission on Intergovernmental Relations—Created by Congress in 1959 to monitor the operation of the U.S. federal system and to recommend improvements, ACIR is a permanent national bipartisan board composed of representatives from the executive and legislative branches of federal, state, and local government and the public.

Amicus curiae—Literally, "a friend of the court"; an individual or organization that, with the permission of the court, gives testimony on a case already before the court to show the applications of the case beyond the particular instance at hand.

Antitrust—A policy that opposes the concentration of power in one for a few firms at the expense of competition.

Articles of Confederation—The first constitution of the newly independent American states, drafted in 1776, ratified in 1781, and replaced by the present Constitution in 1789.

Attentive public—Those who follow public affairs fairly carefully; who read newspapers and magazines to keep informed.

Autocracy—Government in which all power is concentrated in one person.

Baker v. *Carr*—Supreme Court ruling in 1962 that legislative apportionment could be challenged and reviewed by federal courts.

Balance of payments deficit—Total payments made to foreign nations by U.S. citizens and the U.S. government are higher than total receipts from foreign sources.

Bicameral—Two-house legislature; form for forty-nine of the states, as well as U.S. Congress.

Biennial session—Legislative session occurring once every two years.

Bill of attainder—A legislative act inflicting punishment on named individuals or a readily identifiable group.

Bipartisanship—A policy that emphasizes cooperation and a united front between the major political parties.

Block grant—Broad grant of funds made by one level of government to another level to be used in specific program areas—for example, health programs, or fighting crime.

Bureau—Generally, the largest subunit of a government department or agency.

Bureaucrat—Government official, normally one who gains office by appointment rather than election.

Categorical formula grant—Grant of funds made by one level of government to another to be used for specified purposes and in specified ways.

Caucus or conference—Meeting of members of each party in each chamber of the legislature for the purpose of selecting leaders and making decisions relating to party policy.

Classic model—Theory of organization developed early in this century, often referred to as the rational or textbook approach to bureaucracy.

Clear and present danger test—Constitutional doctrine that would permit legislatures to make illegal only those words that are used in such circumstances as to clearly and quickly lead to a serious substantive evil.

Clientele agency—Government bureau that performs a service or provides subsidies primarily for an identifiable special interest group.

Closed shop—A labor arrangement in which an employer must employ only people who are continuing union members.

Cloture (closure)—Procedure for terminating debate in the U.S. Senate.

Coattail influence—Influence a popular or unpopular candidate has on the electoral success or failure of other candidates on the same party ticket.

Collective bargaining—Method whereby representatives of the union and the employer determine wages, hours, and other conditions of employment through direct negotiation.

Commission charter—Form of city government in which a group of commissioners (usually five) serve as the city council and act as heads of departments in the municipal administration.

Common law—Judge-made law developed as courts decided cases; part of the English and American systems of justice.

Compulsory and binding arbitration—Process whereby a dispute between management and union is settled by an impartial third party. When the law dictates that a stalemated labor dispute must be turned over to an outside arbitrator, it is called *compulsory arbitration*. When union and management are required by law to accept the decision of the arbitrator, it is called *binding arbitration*.

Concurrent powers—Powers the Constitution gives to both national and state governments.

Confederation—Government in which member states delegate limited authority to a central government, and the central government lacks direct authority over citizens of the member states.

Conference committee—Committee appointed by the presiding officers of each house of the legislature to adjust differences on a particular bill. The report of the conference committee which goes back to each house, cannot be amended but must be accepted or rejected as it stands.

Conglomerate—A firm that owns businesses in many unrelated industries.

Consent decrees—Regulatory orders to cease anticompetitive conduct or to alter similar undesired economic behavior.

Constitution—Statement of the basis for the state; an instrument of government that specifies the manner in which public officials are authorized to act in behalf of the people.

Constitutional government—Government in which there are recognized and regularly enforced limits on the powers of those who govern.

Constitutional home rule—Constitutional authorization for local governmental units to conduct their own affairs.

Council-manager charter—Form of city government in which the city council hires a professional administrator to manage city affairs; also known as the city manager plan.

Cruise missile—Small, pilotless aircraft with an air-breathing jet engine; flies at altitudes of less than 250 feet, which makes it difficult to spot on radar; accurate enough to hit its target with either nuclear or nonnuclear warheads from more than 1,000 miles away; estimated cost in 1978 of one million dollars each.

Curtiss-Wright case—(*U.S.* v *Curtiss-Wright*, 1936) Supreme Court case in which the decision upheld the sovereignty of the national government in foreign affairs and declared the president to be its prime agent.

Dangerous tendency doctrine—Constitutional doctrine that would permit legislatures to make illegal words that have a tendency to lead to illegal action.

De facto segregation—Racial segregation created as a consequence of nonlegal actions.

De jure segregation—Racial segregation created by law or official actions; *see also* Jim Crow laws.

Delegate role—Concept of the role of a member of a legislature; that the legislator should represent the views of constituents even when the legislator may personally hold different views.

Demagogue—Leader who gains power by means of impassioned appeals to the prejudices and emotions of the masses.

Democracy—Government by the people, either directly or indirectly with free and frequent elections.

Detente—Relaxation of tension with another nation; conciliation or settlement with another nation.

Deviating election—Election in which the party out of power wins, but underlying voting patterns remain unchanged.

Direct primary—Voter participation in the nominating process by means of voting for candidates in primary election.

Discharge petition—Petition signed by a majority of the members of the House of Representatives to pry a bill from committee and bring it to the floor for consideration.

Economic Opportunity Act—Law that mapped out a many-faceted attack on American poverty.

Electoral college—Gathering in each state of electors from that state who formally cast their ballots for president on the basis of the electoral returns in that state; largely a formality.

Eminent domain—Power of governments to take private property for public use. The constitution requires governments to provide just compensation for property so taken.

Environmental impact statement — A government regulation that requires the filing of statements that would assess the potential effect of a federal action on the environment for any project utilizing federal funds.

Entitlement — Legal right or a legal title or a legal claim.

Equity — Judicial remedy used whenever suits for money damages do not provide adequate justice.

Establishment clause — First Amendment clause that, along with the Fourteenth Amendment, prohibits any governmental support for, or involvement with, religion or religious activities.

Excise tax — Consumer tax on a specific kind of merchandise, such as tobacco.

Exclusionary rule — Rule that evidence obtained in an unconstitutional or illegal manner may not be used at a trial against the person from whom the evidence was seized.

Executive agreement — International agreement made by a president that has the force of a treaty; does not need the approval of U.S. Senate.

Executive Office of the President — Cluster of staff agencies created by the Reorganization Act of 1939 to help the president. Currently the Executive Office consists of the White House Office, the Office of Management and Budget, the Council of Economic Advisers, the National Security Council, and a number of specialized offices.

Executive privilege — Claim of presidents that a president has the constitutional right to withhold information from Congress, courts, and the public, which the president thinks might be injurious to national security.

Ex post facto law — Retroactive criminal law.

Express powers — Powers specifically granted to one of the branches of the national government by the Constitution.

Extradition — Legal process whereby an alleged criminal offender is surrendered by the officials of one state to the officials in the state where the crime is alleged to have been committed.

Fairness doctrine — Requirement of the Federal Communications Commission that broadcasters and telecasters must take positive steps to ensure that differing points of view are heard.

Family Assistance Plan — The Nixon proposal for nationalizing and regularizing welfare payments.

Federal Deposit Insurance Corporation — The government agency that insures deposits in member banks up to $40,000.

The Federalist — Series of essays favoring the new Constitution, written by Hamilton, Jay, and Madison in 1787 and 1788 during the debate over ratification.

Federal Reserve Bank — One of twelve regional "banker's banks" that in combination make up the Federal Reserve System.

Federal system — Government with power divided by a constitution between a national and constituent governments.

Federated Metropolitan Plan — Plan that creates a government to handle common problems of the core city and suburbs while leaving other government functions with local units; sometimes also called a two-tier approach to metropolitan governance.

Fighting words — Words that by their very nature inflict injury upon those to whom they are addressed.

Filibuster — Holding the floor of the U.S. Senate to delay proceedings and thereby prevent a vote on a controversial issue.

Floating debt — Short-term government loans, in the form of bank notes or tax-anticipation warrants, that are paid out of current revenues.

Franchise — The right to vote.

Full faith and credit — Clause in the Constitution that requires each state to recognize the civil judgments rendered by the courts of the other states.

Gerrymandering — Drawing an election district in such a way that one party or group has a distinct advantage; the strategy is to provide a close but safe margin in numerous districts and concentrate (and hence waste) the opposition's vote in a few districts.

Government corporation — A cross between a business corporation and a government agency, created to secure greater freedom of action for a particular program.

Grand Old Party (GOP) — The Republican party.

Gross National Product (GNP) — Measure of the market value of all commodities and services produced by a nation in a year.

Hatch Acts — Laws of 1939–40 that barred federal employees from active participation in politics.

Implied powers — Powers given to Congress in the Constitution to do whatever is necessary and proper in order to carry out one of the express powers or any combination of them.

Incrementalism — Recent theory of public administration that deemphasizes comprehensiveness and insists that administrative decisions are and should be made piecemeal.

Independent agency — Government agency not subordinate to a regular executive department.

Indiana ballot — Ballot on which names of candidates are grouped together by party, facilitating voting by party.

Inflation — Rise in the general level of prices, which is the same thing as a fall in the value of money.

Initiative — Procedure whereby a certain number of voters may, by petition, propose a law and get it submitted to the people for a vote. Initiative may be direct (the proposed law is voted on directly by the people) or indirect (the proposal is submitted first to the legislature and then to the people if the legislature rejects it).

Intangible property — Certificates of ownership: stocks, bonds, savings.

Interstate compact — Agreement among states. The Constitution requires that such agreements must be approved by Congress.

Item veto — Grant of authority to the executive (usually the governor) to prevent certain legislative measures from being enacted despite their having been passed by the legislature.

Jim Crow laws—A once popular name for segregation laws.

Joint committee—Committee composed of members of both houses of a legislature; such a committee meets in order to speed legislative action or for efficiency purposes.

Judicial review—The authority, spelled out by Chief Justice John Marshall in *Marbury* v. *Madison* (1803), of the U.S. Supreme Court to examine federal and state legislative statutes and the actions of executive officials, in order to determine their validity, according to the Constitution.

Jus sanguinis—Citizenship acquired by citizenship of parents.

Jus soli—Citizenship acquired by place of birth.

Keynes, John Maynard—English economist who advocated a positive role for government in promoting national prosperity.

Lame duck—Official serving out a term after defeat for reelection and before the inauguration of a successor.

Legislative home rule—Power given by the legislature to local governments that eliminates the need for local governments to go back to the legislature for additional grants of power. State law still takes precedence over local ordinances, and powers given to the local government by the legislature may be rescinded.

Libel—Written defamation of another person. Especially in the case of public officials and public figures, the constitutional tests designed to restrict libel actions are very rigid.

Litigation—Carrying or pursuing a case or claim in the judicial process.

Long ballot—Ballot that came into general use in the late 1820s, with the belief that voters should elect all, or nearly all, the people who governed them; criticized as unwieldy and confusing because it contained too many offices and candidates.

McCulloch v. *Maryland* (1819)—Celebrated Supreme Court decision that established the doctrine of national supremacy and the doctrine that the implied powers of the national government are to be generously interpreted.

Maintaining elections—Election that shows a continuation of a pattern of partisan support.

Majority floor leader—Legislative position held by an important party member selected by the majority party in caucus or conference. The majority floor leader helps frame party strategy and tries to keep the membership in line. In the U.S. Senate the majority leader (in consultation with the minority floor leader) determines the agenda and has strong influence in committee selection.

Massachusetts ballot—Ballot on which names of candidates are grouped together by office, making independent voting easier.

Mass public—The general public, including a large segment of the population that is often uninformed about the details of political controversy and policy debates.

Mayor-council charter—The oldest and most common form of city government, consisting of either a weak mayor and a city council or a strong mayor and council.

Military-industrial establishment—Alleged alliance between top military and industrial leaders, who have a common interest in arms production and utilization.

Minority floor leader—Party leader in each house of a legislature elected by the minority party; generally an able spokesperson for the opposition.

Misdemeanor—Offense of lesser gravity than a felony, for which punishment may be a fine or imprisonment in a local rather than a state institution.

National debt—The long-term credit obligations of the government and its agencies and all interest-bearing short-term credit obligations.

Nationality—Legal allegiance to a nation, which in turn has an obligation to provide protection.

National Security Council—Planning and advisory board on matters relating to national security. Permanent members include the president, vice-president, secretary of state, secretary of defense, and the chairman of the joint chiefs of staff.

National supremacy—Constitutional doctrine that whenever there is a conflict between the constitutionally authorized actions of the national government and those of a state or local government, the actions of the national government take priority.

Natural monopoly—Exists when it would be inefficient to have competition in a particular industry; for instance in the case of a power company.

Necessary and proper clause—Clause of the Constitution setting forth the implied powers of Congress, which states that Congress, in addition to its enumerated powers, has the power to make all laws necessary and proper for carrying out all powers vested by the Constitution in the national government.

Nonproliferation Treaty—International agreement under which nuclear powers pledge themselves not to distribute nuclear devices to nonnuclear powers.

Obscenity—A work or expression that depicts sexual conduct in a patently offensive way as outlined by specific legislation or judicial interpretations; lacks serious literary, artistic, political, or social value.

Office group ballot—Method of voting in which all candidates are listed under the office for which they are running; sometimes called the "Massachusetts ballot" or the office-block ballot.

Office of Management and Budget (OMB)—Presidential staff agency that serves as a clearinghouse for budgetary requests and management improvements.

Oligarchy—Government controlled by a small segment of the people chosen on the basis of wealth or power.

Oligopoly—A few firms dominating an industry.

Ombudsman—Office in Sweden and elsewhere that handles citizen complaints against the government.

On appeal—Order issued by the Supreme Court to review those decisions of the lower courts, federal and state, which Congress has stipulated the Supreme Court is required to review.

Opinion leaders—Person in a family or neighborhood who influences local opinion.

Opinion maker—Person who influences how the general public views policy problems—for example, elected officials, editors, writers, teachers.

Parliamentary government—Government that gives authority to a legislature, which in turn selects the executive.

Party column ballot—Method of voting in which all candidates are listed under their party designation, making it easy for the voter to cast votes for all the candidates of one party; sometimes called the "Indiana ballot."

Party convention—Meeting of party delegates to pass on matters of party policy and in some cases to select party candidates for public office. Conventions are held on county, state, and national levels.

Party primary—Election for choosing party nominees; open to members and supporters of the party making the nomination.

Perceptual distortion—Looking at things from a subjective, personal frame of reference. Strong party adherents tend to look at people and events "through the eyes of their party."

Pluralistic power structure—The notion that some people do have more influence than others, but that influence is shared among many people and tends to be limited to particular issues and policy areas.

Political machine—Organized subgroup within a party consisting of a political boss and his supporting ward and precinct workers who get out the vote and perform a variety of "services" for local constituents between elections.

Poll tax—Payment made by a person; formerly required in some states as a condition of being allowed to vote.

Power elite—Term originally used by the sociologist C. Wright Mills, to describe the small group of people who he believed rule the country because of their socioeconomic status or high governmental positions.

PPBS—Budgetary system borrowed in the 1960s from industry that forces a government agency to define its objectives and budget in terms of specific programs.

Preferred-position doctrine—Constitutional doctrine that legislatures may not make illegal any purely speech activity unconnected with any action.

President pro tempore—Officer of the U.S. Senate chosen from the ranks, usually the senior member, in terms of service, of the majority party; serves as president of the Senate in the absence of the vice president.

Prior restraint—Censorship or other controls imposed on publications prior to publication.

Procedural due process—Constitutional requirement that governments proceed by proper means.

Program oversight—Process of monitoring and evaluating the details of how a program is being, or has been, carried out.

Public opinion—Cluster of views and attitudes held by people on a significant issue. Since any complex society has many groups, it is more precise to talk about publics, subpublics, and public opinions than about a single public opinion.

Quasi-judicial—The power held by some federal agencies to both execute and interpret regulations.

Quasi-legislative—The power held by some federal agencies to both make and execute regulations.

Quota sampling—Accounting for the variables in the population and assigning a quota for each variable to produce a representative cross-section.

Random sampling—Creating a representative sample through random selection; for example, shuffling housing tracts and interviewing individuals in every 5th, or 10th, or 15th house.

Realigning election—Election in which the basic partisan commitments of a significant segment of the electorate change, as in 1932.

Reapportionment—Redrawing of legislative district lines, to recognize the existing population distribution.

Recall—Removal of an official from office before the end of his or her term. A certain number of voters must petition for removal, after which the people vote.

Red tape—Procedures and forms used in carrying out policies and governmemt functions; a term often used to express dissatisfaction with especially slow and formal rules and procedures.

Referendum—Practice of submitting to popular vote measures passed upon by the legislature or proposed by initiative. Use of the referendum may be either required or optional.

Registration—Process of appearing before an official during a certain period of time before an election, in order to be eligible to vote.

Regressive tax—Tax that weighs most heavily on those least able to pay.

Regulation—A governmental order having the force of law, designed to control or govern the behavior of a business, union or similar organization.

Regulatory board or commission—Agency responsible for controlling some aspect of national life; generally has judicial, legislative, and executive powers.

Representative sample—A small but significant segment of a survey or polling universe reflecting a true cross-section of the views and attitudes of the group.

Republic—Form of government that derives its power from the voters; those chosen to govern are responsible to those whom they govern.

Republican form of government—System in which those who govern secure their authority to do so directly or indirectly from the voters.

Revenue sharing—The broadest possible grant of funds made by one level of government to another level;

the funds can be used at the discretion of the officials of the receiving unit.

Right to work law — A provision in state laws that prohibit arrangements between a union and an employer requiring membership in a union as a condition for getting or keeping a job.

Runoff election — Election held when no candidate receives a required percentage of the vote in an earlier election; the runoff election is usually held between the two candidates who got the most votes in the first election.

Safe seat — An electoral office, usually in a legislature, where the party or the incumbent is so strong that re-election is almost taken for granted.

Sales tax — General tax on consumer goods.

Salience — Significance of an event or issue.

SALT — Strategic arms limitation talks between the U.S. and Soviet governments to limit both defensive and offensive weapons systems.

Sampling error — The degree to which the sample is distorted and does not represent the "polling universe" to be measured.

Second strike capability — The surviving military force of a nation after it has suffered an all-out nuclear attack.

Sectional voting — Political bias revolving around a specific geographical region, such as the South, the Midwest, or the mountain states.

Sedition — Advocating the use of force to bring about political changes or overthrow of the government.

Selective perception — Tendency to pay attention to only those views, facts, and opinions that support our own biases; the inclination to distort messages according to our own preconceptions.

Severance tax — Tax on the privilege of "severing" natural resources such as coal, oil, and timber.

Shadow cabinet — The leadership of the party that is out of power, responsible for criticizing the party in power and ready to take its place if the opposition wins the next election.

Shays's Rebellion — Rural rebellion of 1786–87 in western Massachusetts protesting mortgage foreclosures; brought conservative support for a stronger national government.

Speaker — Presiding officer in the House of Representatives, formally elected by the House but actually selected by the majority party. The Speaker's powers include referral of legislation to committees, appointments to the House Rules Committee, recognition of members who wish to speak, ruling on questions of parliamentary procedure, and appointment of special conference committees.

Standing to sue — Doctrine that limits the right to bring legal action to persons who are adversely and immediately affected.

Stare decisis — The rule of precedent, whereby a rule of law contained in a judicial decision is binding on judges whenever the same question is presented.

Statutory law — Law enacted by a legislature.

Substantive due process — Constitutional requirement that governments act reasonably and that the sub-

stance of the laws themselves be reasonable.

Sunshine law — Law requiring public agencies to do most of their business in public.

Suspect classifications — Racial or national origin classifications created by law and subject to careful judicial scrutiny; likely to be declared unconstitutional unless they can be justified by overwhelmingly desirable state purposes that can be achieved in no other way.

Tangible property — Personal property, such as furniture and washing machine.

Titular leader — Nominal leader; leader by title only. The defeated presidential nominee is referred to as the titular leader of the party out of power, but the role is more honorary than it is a realistic power base.

Trustee role — Concept of the function of a member of a legislature: that of a legislator who feels he or she was sent to Washington or the state capital to think and vote independently for the general welfare, as they, not as their constituents, determine.

Unicameral — One-house legislature; Nebraska is the only state that uses this form.

Unitary system — Government with power concentrated by the constitution in the central government.

Universe — The entire population of a group about which information is sought.

Use tax — Equivalent tax payable by a person who purchases items outside a city or a state with a sales tax.

Virginia Plan — Proposal in the Constitutional Convention that provided for a strong legislature with representation in each house determined by population, thus favoring the large states.

Watkins v. United States — Supreme Court decision in 1957 holding that a congressional investigating committee has no power to "expose for the sake of exposure," that the rights of witnesses must be respected, and that "no inquiry is an end in itself."

Whip — Party leader who is the liaison between the leadership and the rank and file in the legislature.

White primary — Restriction of voting in Democratic primaries in the South to whites only; now unconstitutional.

Writ of certiorari — Writ used by the Supreme Court to review decisions of lower courts, federal and state, that are within the discretionary appellate jurisdiction of the Supreme Court.

Writ of habeas corpus — Court order requiring jailers to explain to a judge why they are holding a prisoner in custody.

Yellow-dog contract — A contract by an antiunion employer which forces prospective workers to promise they will not join a union after employment.

The Constitution of the United States

The Preamble

We the People of the United States, in Order to form a more perfect Union, establish Justice, insure domestic Tranquility, provide for the common defence, promote the general Welfare, and secure the Blessings of Liberty to ourselves and our Posterity, do ordain and establish this Constitution for the United States of America.

Article 1 — The Legislative Article

Legislative power

Section 1. All Legislative Powers herein granted shall be vested in a Congress of the United States, which shall consist of a Senate and House of Representatives.

House of representatives: composition; qualification; apportionment; impeachment power

Section 2. The House of Representatives shall be composed of Members chosen every second Year by the People of the several States, and the Electors in each State shall have the Qualifications requisite for Electors of the most numerous Branch of the State Legislature.

No Person shall be a Representative who shall not have attained to the Age of twenty five Years, and been seven Years a Citizen of the United States, and who shall not, when elected, be an Inhabitant of that State in which he shall be chosen.

Representatives and direct Taxes shall be apportioned among the several States which may be included within this Union, according to their respective Numbers, which shall be determined by adding to the whole Number of free Persons, including those bound to Service for a Term of Years, and excluding Indians not taxed, three fifths of all other Persons. The actual Enumeration shall be made within three Years after the first Meeting of the Congress of the United States, and within every subsequent Term of ten Years, in such Manner as they shall by Law direct. The Number of Representatives shall not exceed one for every thirty Thousand, but each State shall have at Least one Representative; and until such enumeration shall be made, the State of New Hampshire shall be entitled to chuse three, Massachusetts eight, Rhode-Island and Providence Plantations one, Connecticut five, New-York six, New Jersey four, Pennsylvania eight, Delaware one, Maryland six, Virginia ten, North Carolina five, South Carolina five, and Georgia three.

When vacancies happen in the Representation from any State, the Executive Authority thereof shall issue Writs of Election to fill such Vacancies.

The House of Representatives shall chuse their speaker and other Officers; and shall have the sole Power of Impeachment.

Senate: composition; qualifications; impeachment trials

Section 3. The Senate of the United States shall be composed of two Senators from each State, chosen by the Legislature thereof, for six Years; and each Senator shall have one Vote.

Immediately after they shall be assembled in Consequence of the first Election, they shall be divided as equally as may be into three Classes. The Seats of the Senators of the first Class shall be vacated at the Expiration of the second Year, of the second Class at the Expiration of the fourth Year, and of the third Class at the Expiration of the sixth Year, so that one third may be chosen every second Year; and if Vacancies happen by Resignation, or otherwise, during the Recess of the Legislature of any State, the Executive thereof may make temporary Appointments until the next Meeting of the Legislature, which shall then fill such Vacancies.

No Person shall be a Senator who shall not have attained to the Age of thirty Years, and been nine Years a Citizen of the United States, and who shall not, when elected, be an Inhabitant of that State for which he shall be chosen.

The Vice President of the United States shall be President of the Senate, but shall have no Vote, unless they be equally divided.

The Senate shall chuse their other Officers, and also a President pro tempore, in the Absence of the Vice President, or when he shall exercise the Office of the President of the United States.

The Senate shall have the sole Power to try all Impeachments. When sitting for that Purpose, they shall be on Oath or Affirmation. When the President of the United States is tried, the Chief Justice shall preside: And no Person shall be convicted without the Concurrence of two thirds of the Members present.

Judgment in Cases of Impeachment shall not extend further than to removal from Office, and disqualification to hold and enjoy any Office of honor, Trust or Profit under the United States: but the Party convicted shall nevertheless be liable and subject to Indictment, Trial, Judgement and Punishment, according to law.

Congressional elections: time; place; manner

Section 4. The Times, Places and Manner of holding Elections for Senators and Representatives, shall be prescribed in each State by the legislature thereof; but the Congress may at any time by Law make or alter such Regulations, except as to the Places of chusing Senators.

The Congress shall assemble at least once in every Year, and such Meeting shall be on the first Monday in December, unless they shall by Law appoint a different Day.

Powers and duties of the houses

Section 5. Each House shall be the Judge of the Elections, Returns and Qualifications of its own Members, and a Majority of each shall constitute a Quorum to do Business; but a smaller Number may adjourn from day to day, and may be authorized to compel the Attendance of absent Members, in such Manner, and under such Penalties as each House may provide.

Each House may determine the Rules of its Proceedings, punish its Members for disorderly Behaviour, and, with the Concurrence of two thirds, expel a Member.

Each House shall keep a Journal of its Proceedings, and from time to time publish the same, excepting such Parts as may in their Judgment require Secrecy; and the Yeas and Nays of the Members of either House on any question shall, at the Desire of one fifth of those Present, be entered on the Journal.

Neither House, during the Session of Congress, shall, without the Consent of the other, adjourn for more than three days, nor to any other Place than that in which the two Houses shall be sitting.

Rights of members

Section 6. The Senators and Representatives shall receive a Compensation for their Services, to be ascertained by Law, and paid out of the Treasury of the United States. They shall in all Cases, except Treason, Felony and Breach of the Peace, be privileged from Arrest during their Attendance at the Session of their respective Houses, and in going to and returning from the same; and for any Speech or Debate in either House, they shall not be questioned in any other Place.

No Senator or Representative shall, during the Time for which he was elected, be appointed to any civil Office under the Authority of the United States, which shall have been created, or the Emoluments whereof shall have been encreased during such time; and no Person holding any Office under the United States, shall be a Member of either House during his Continuance in Office.

Legislative powers: bills and resolutions

Section 7. All Bills for raising Revenue shall originate in the House of Representatives; but the Senate may propose or concur with Amendments as on other Bills.

Every Bill which shall have passed the House of Representatives and the Senate, shall, before it become a Law, be presented to the President of the United States; If he approve he shall sign it, but if not he shall return it, with his Objections to that House in which it shall have originated, who shall enter the Objections at large on their Journal, and proceed to reconsider it. If after such Reconsideration two thirds of that House shall agree to pass the Bill, it shall be sent, together with the Objections, to the other House, by which it shall likewise be reconsidered, and if approved by two thirds of that House, it shall become a Law. But in all such Cases the Votes of both Houses shall be determined by Yeas and Nays, and the Names of the Persons voting for and against the Bill shall be entered on the Journal of each House respectively. If any Bill shall not be returned by the President within ten Days (Sunday excepted) after it shall have been presented to him, the Same shall be a Law, in like Manner as if he had signed it, unless the Congress by their Adjournment prevent its Return, in which Case it shall not be a Law.

Every Order, Resolution, or Vote to which the Concurrence of the Senate and House of Representatives may be necessary (except on a question of Adjournment) shall be presented to the President of the United States; and before the Same shall take Effect, shall be approved by him, or being disapproved by him, shall be repassed by two thirds of the Senate and House of Representatives, according to the Rules and Limitations prescribed in the Case of a Bill.

Powers of congress

Section 8. The Congress shall have Power To lay and collect Taxes, Duties, Imposts and Excises, to pay the Debts and provide for the common Defence and general Welfare of the United States; but all Duties, Imposts and Excises shall be uniform throughout the United States;

To borrow Money on the credit of the United States;

To regulate Commerce with foreign Nations, and among the several States, and with the Indian Tribes;

To establish an uniform Rule of Naturalization, and uniform Laws on the subject of Bankruptcies throughout the United States;

To coin Money, regulate the Value thereof, and of foreign Coin, and fix the Standard of Weights and Measures;

To provide for the Punishment of counterfeiting the Securities and current Coin of the United States;

To establish Post Offices and post Roads;

To promote the Progress of Science and useful Arts, by securing for limited Times to Authors and Inventors the exclusive Right to their respective Writings and Discoveries;

To constitute Tribunals inferior to the supreme Court;

To define and punish Piracies and Felonies committed on the high Seas, and Offences against the Law of Nations;

To declare War, grant Letters of Marque and Reprisal, and make Rules concerning Captures on Land and Water;

To raise and support Armies, but no Appropriation of Money to that Use shall be for a longer Term than two Years;

To provide and maintain a Navy;

To make Rules for the Government and Regulation of the land and naval Forces;

To provide for calling forth the Militia to execute the Laws of the Union, suppress Insurrections and repel Invasions;

To provide for organizing, arming, and disciplining, the Militia, and for governing such Part of them as may be employed in the Service of the United States, reserving to the States respectively, the Appointment of the Officers, and the Authority of training the Militia ac-

cording to the discipline prescribed by Congress;

To exercise exclusive Legislation in all Cases whatsoever, over such District (not exceeding ten Miles square) as may, by Cession of particular States, and the Acceptance of Congress, become the Seat of the Government of the United States, and to exercise like Authority over all Places purchased by the Consent of the Legislature of the State in which the Same shall be for the Erection of Forts, Magazines, Arsenals, dock-Yards, and other needful Buildings;-And

To make all Laws which shall be necessary and proper for carrying into Execution the foregoing Powers, and all other Powers vested by this Constitution in the Government of the United States, or in any Department or Officer thereof.

Powers denied to congress

Section 9. The Migration or Importation of such Persons as any of the States now existing shall think proper to admit, shall not be prohibited by the Congress prior to the Year one thousand eight hundred and eight, but a Tax or duty may be imposed on such Importation, not exceeding ten dollars for each Person.

The Privilege of the Writ of Habeas Corpus shall not be suspended, unless when in Cases of Rebellion or Invasion the public Safety may require it.

No Bill of Attainder or ex post facto Law shall be passed.

No Capitation, or other direct, Tax shall be laid, unless in Proportion to the Census or Enumeration herein before directed to be taken.

No Tax or Duty shall be laid on Articles exported from any State.

No Preference shall be given by any Regulation of Commerce or Revenue to the Ports of one State over those of another: nor shall Vessels bound to, or from, one State be obliged to enter, clear, or pay Duties in another.

No Money shall be drawn from the Treasury, but in Consequence of Appropriations made by Law; and a regular Statement and Account of the Receipts and Expenditures of all public Money shall be published from time to time.

No Title of Nobility shall be granted by the United States: And no Person holding any Office of Profit or Trust under them, shall, without the Consent of the Congress, accept of any present, Emolument, Office, or Title, of any kind whatever, from any King, Prince, or foreign States.

Powers denied to the states

Section 10. No State shall enter into any Treaty, Alliance, or Confederation; grant Letters of Marque and Reprisal; coin Money; emit Bills of Credit; make any Thing but gold and silver Coin a Tender in Payment of Debts; pass any Bill of Attainder, ex post facto Law, or Law impairing the Obligation of Contracts, or grant any Title of Nobility.

No State shall, without the Consent of the Congress, lay any Imposts or Duties on Imports or Exports, except what may be absolutely necessary for executing its inspection Laws: and the net Produce of all Duties and Imposts, laid by any State on Imports or Exports, shall be for the Use of the Treasury of the United States; and all such Laws shall be subject to the Revision and Controul of the Congress.

No State shall, without the Consent of Congress, lay any Duty of Tonnage, keep Troops, or Ships of War in time of Peace, enter into any Agreement or Compact with another State, or with a foreign Power, or engage in War, unless actually invaded, or in such imminent Danger as will not admit of delay.

Article II – The Executive Article

Nature and scope of presidential power

Section 1. The executive Power shall be vested in a President of the United States of America. He shall hold his Office during the Term of four Years, and, together with the Vice President, chosen for the same term, be elected, as follows.

Each State shall appoint, in such Manner as the Legislature thereof may direct, a Number of Electors, Equal to the whole Number of Senators and Representatives to which the State may be entitled in the Congress: but no Senator or Representative, or Person holding an Office of Trust or Profit under the United States, shall be appointed an Elector.

The Electors shall meet in their respective States, and vote by Ballot for two Persons, of whom one at least shall not be an Inhabitant of the same State with themselves. And they shall make a List of all the Persons voted for, and the Number of Votes for each; which List they shall sign and certify, and transmit sealed to the Seat of the Government of the United States, directed to the President of the Senate. The President of the Senate shall, in the Presence of the Senate and House of Representatives, open all the Certificates, and the Votes shall then be counted. The Person having the greatest Number of Votes shall be the President, if such Number be a Majority of the whole Number of Electors appointed; and if there be more than one who have such Majority, and have an equal Number of Votes, then the House of Representatives shall immediately chuse by Ballot one of them for President: and if no Person have a Majority, then from the five highest on the List the said House shall in like Manner chuse the President. But in chusing the President, the Votes shall be taken by States, the Representation from each State having one Vote; A quorum for this Purpose shall consist of a Member or Members from two thirds of the States, and a Majority of all the States shall be necessary to a Choice. In every Case, after the Choice of the President, the Person having the greatest Number of Votes of the Electors shall be the Vice President. But if there should remain two or more who have equal Votes, the Senate shall chuse from them by Ballot the Vice President.

The Congress may determine the Time of chusing the Electors and the Day on which they shall give their Votes; which Day shall be the same throughout the United States.

No Person except a natural born Citizen, or a Citizen of the United States, at the time of the Adoption of this Constitution, shall be eligible to the Office of President; neither shall any Person be eligible to that Office who shall not have attained to the Age of thirty five Years, and been fourteen Years a Resident within the United States.

In Case of the Removal of the President from Office, or of his Death, Resignation, or Inability to discharge the Powers and Duties of the said Office, the Same shall devolve on the Vice President, and the Congress may by Law provide for the Case of Removal, Death, Resignation or Inability, both of the President and Vice President, declaring what Officer shall then act as President, and such Officer shall act accordingly, until the Disability be removed, or a President shall be elected.

The President shall, at stated Times, receive for his Services a Compensation, which shall neither be encreased nor diminished during the Period for which he shall have been elected, and he shall not receive within that Period any other Emolument from the United States, or any of them.

Before he enter on the Execution of his Office, he shall take the following Oath or Affirmation:-"I do solemnly swear (or affirm) that I will faithfully execute the Office of President of the United States, and will to the best of my Ability, preserve, protect and defend the Constitution of the United States."

Powers and duties of the president

Section 2. The President shall be Commander in Chief of the Army and Navy of the United States, and of the Militia of the several States, when called into the actual Service of the United States; he may require the Opinion, in writing, of the principal Officer in each of the executive Departments, upon any Subject relating to the Duties of their respective Offices, and he shall have power to grant Reprieves and Pardons for Offences against the United States, except in Cases of Impeachment.

He shall have Power, by and with the Advice and Consent of the Senate, to make Treaties, provided two thirds of the Senators present concur; and he shall nominate, and by and with the Advice and Consent of the Senate, shall appoint Ambassadors, other public Ministers and Consuls, Judges of the supreme Court, and all other Officers of the United States, whose Appointments are not herein otherwise provided for, and which shall be established by Law; but the Congress may by

Law vest the Appointment of such inferior Officers, as they think proper, in the President alone, in the Courts of Law, or in the Heads of Departments.

The President shall have Power to fill up all Vacancies that may happen during the Recess of the Senate, by granting Commissions which shall expire at the End of their next Session.

Section 3. He shall from time to time give to the Congress Information of the State of the Union, and recommend to their Consideration such Measures as he shall judge necessary and expedient; he may, on extraordinary Occasions, convene both Houses, or either of them, and in Case of Disagreement between them, with Respect to the Time of Adjournment, he may adjourn them to such Time as he shall think proper; he shall take Care that the Laws be faithfully executed, and shall Commission all the Officers of the United States.

Impeachment

Section 4. The President, Vice President and all civil Officers of the United States, shall be removed from Office on Impeachment for, and Conviction of, Treason, Bribery, or other High Crimes and Misdemeanors.

Article III — The Judicial Article

Judicial power, courts, judges

Section 1. The judicial Power of the United States, shall be vested in one supreme Court, and in such inferior Courts as the Congress may from time to time ordain and establish. The Judges, both of the supreme and inferior Courts, shall hold their Offices during good Behaviour, and shall, at stated Times, receive for their Services, a Compensation, which shall not be diminished during their Continuance in Office.

Jurisdiction

Section 2. The judicial Power shall extend to all Cases, in Law and Equity, arising under this Constitution, the Laws of the United States, and Treaties made, or which shall be made, under their Authority;-to all Cases affecting Ambassadors, other public Ministers and Consuls;-to all Cases of admiralty and maritime Jurisdiction;-to Controversies to which the United States shall be a Party;-to Controversies between two or more States; between a State and Citizens of another State; between Citizens of different States;-between Citizens of the same State claiming Lands under Grants of different States, and between a State or the Citizens thereof, and foreign States, Citizens or Subjects.

In all Cases affecting Ambassadors, other public Ministers and Consuls, and those in which a State shall be Party, the supreme Court shall have original Jurisdiction. In all the other Cases before mentioned, the supreme Court shall have appellate Jurisdiction, both as to Law and Fact, with such Exceptions, and under such Regulations as the Congress shall make.

The Trial of all Crimes, except in Cases of Impeachment, shall be by Jury; and such Trial shall be held in the State where the said Crimes shall have been committed; but when not committed within any State, the Trial shall be at such Place or Places as the Congress may by Law have directed.

Treason

Section 3. Treason against the United States, shall consist only in levying War against them, or in adhering to their Enemies, giving them Aid and Comfort. No Person shall be convicted of Treason unless on the Testimony of two Witnesses to the same overt Act, or on Confession in open Court.

The Congress shall have Power to declare the Punishment of Treason, but no Attainder of Treason shall work Corruption of Blood, or Forfeiture except during the Life of the Person attainted.

Article IV — Interstate Relations

Full faith and credit clause

Section 1. Full Faith and Credit shall be given in each State to the public Acts, Records, and judicial Proceedings of every other State. And the Congress may by general Laws prescribe the Manner in which such Acts, Records and Proceedings shall be proved, and the Effect thereof.

Privileges and immunities; interstate rendition

Section 2. The Citizens of each State shall be entitled to all Privileges and Immunities of Citizens in the several States.

A Person charged in any State with Treason, Felony, or other Crime, who shall flee from Justice, and be found in another State, shall on Demand of the executive Authority of the State from which he fled, be delivered up, to be removed to the State having Jurisdiction of the Crime.

No Person held to Service or Labour in one State, under the Laws thereof, escaping into another, shall, in Consequence of any Law or Regulation therein, be discharged from such Service or Labour, but shall be delivered up on Claim of the Party to whom such Service or Labour may be due.

Admission of states

Section 3. New States may be admitted by the Congress into this Union; but no new State shall be formed or erected within the Jurisdiction of any other State; nor any State be formed by the Junction of two or more States, or Parts of States, without the Consent of the Legislatures of the States concerned as well as of the Congress.

The Congress shall have Power to dispose of and make all needful Rules and Regulations respecting the Territory or other Property belonging to the United States; and nothing in this Constitution shall be so construed as to Prejudice any Claims of the United States, or of any particular State.

Republican form of government

Section 4. The United States shall guarantee to every State in this Union a Republican Form of Government, and shall protect each of them against Invasion; and on Application of the Legislature, or of the Executive (when the Legislature cannot be convened) against domestic Violence.

Article V—The Amending Power

The Congress, whenever two thirds of both Houses shall deem it necessary, shall propose Amendments to this Constitution, or, on the Application of the Legislatures of two thirds of the several States, shall call a Convention for proposing Amendments, which, in either Case, shall be valid to all Intents and Purposes, as Part of this Constitution, when ratified by the Legislatures of three fourths of the several States, or by Conventions in three fourths thereof as the one or the other Mode of Ratification may be proposed by the Congress; Provided that no Amendment which may be made prior to the Year One thousand eight hundred and eight shall in any Manner affect the first and fourth Clauses in the Ninth Section of the first Article; and that no State, without its Consent, shall be deprived of its equal Suffrage in the Senate.

Article VI—The Supremacy Article

All Debts contracted and Engagements entered into, before the Adoption of this Constitution, shall be as valid against the United States under this Constitution, as under the Confederation.

This Constitution, and the Laws of the United States which shall be made in Pursuance thereof; and all Treaties made, or which shall be made, under the Authority of the United States, shall be the supreme Law of the Land; and the Judges in every State shall be bound thereby, any Thing in the Constitution or Laws of any State to the Contrary notwithstanding.

The Senators and Representatives before mentioned, and the Members of the several State Legislatures, and all executive and judicial Officers, both of the United States and of the several States, shall be bound by Oath or Affirmation, to support this Constitution; but no religious Test shall ever be required as a Qualification to any Office or public Trust under the United States.

Article VII—Ratification

The Ratification of the Conventions of nine States, shall be sufficient for the Establishment of this Constitution between the States so ratifying the Same.

Done in Convention by the Unanimous Consent of the States present the Seventeenth Day of September in the Year of our Lord one thousand seven hundred and Eighty seven and of the Independence of the United States of America the Twelfth. In witness whereof We have hereunto subscribed our Names.

The Bill of Rights

[The first 10 Amendments were ratified December 15, 1791, and form what is known as the Bill of Rights]

Amendment 1—Religion, Speech, Assembly, and Politics

Congress shall make no law respecting an establishment of religion, or prohibiting the free exercise thereof; or abridging the freedom of speech, or of the press; or the right of the people peaceably to assemble, and to petition the Government for a redress or grievances.

Amendment 2—Militia and the Right to Bear Arms

A well regulated Militia, being necessary to the security of a free State, the right of the people to keep and bear Arms, shall not be infringed.

Amendment 3—Quartering of Soldiers

No Soldier shall, in time of peace be quartered in any house, without the consent of the Owner, nor in time of war, but in a manner to be prescribed by law.

Amendment 4—Searches and Seizures

The right of the people to be secure in their persons, houses, papers, and effects, against unreasonable searches and seizures, shall not be violated, and no Warrants shall issue, but upon probable cause, supported by Oath or affirmation, and particularly describing the place to be searched and the persons or things to be seized.

Amendment 5—Grand Juries, Self-Incrimination, Double Jeopardy, Due Process, and Eminent Domain

No person shall be held to answer for a capital, or otherwise infamous crime, unless on a presentment or indictment of a Grand Jury, except in cases arising in the land or naval forces, or in the Militia, when in actual service in time of War or public danger, nor shall any person be subject for the same offence to be twice put in jeopardy of life or limb; nor shall be compelled in any criminal case to be a witness against himself, nor be deprived of life, liberty, or property, without due process of law; nor shall private property be taken for public use, without just compensation.

Amendment 6—Criminal Court Procedures

In all criminal prosecutions, the accused shall enjoy the right to a speedy and public trial, by an impartial jury of the State and district wherein the crime shall have been committed, which district shall have been previously ascertained by law, and to be informed of the nature and cause of the accusation; to be confronted with the witnesses against him; to have compulsory process for obtaining witnesses in his favor, and to have the Assistance of Counsel for his defence.

Amendment 7 – Trial by Jury in Common Law Cases

In Suits at common law, where the value in controversy shall exceed twenty dollars, the right of trial by jury shall be preserved, and no fact tried by a jury, shall be otherwise reexamined in any Court of the United States, than according to the rules of the common law.

Amendment 8 – Bail, Cruel and Unusual Punishment

Excessive bail shall not be required, not excessive fines imposed, nor cruel and unusual punishments inflicted.

Amendment 9 – Rights Retained by the People

The enumeration in the Constitution, of certain rights, shall not be construed to deny or disparage others retained by the people.

Amendment 10 – Reserved Powers of the States

The powers not delegated to the United States by the Constitution, nor prohibited by it to the States, are reserved to the States respectively, or to the people.

Pre-Civil War amendments

Amendment 11 – Suits Against the States

[Ratified February 7, 1795]

The Judicial power of the United States shall not be construed to extend to any suit in law or equity, commenced or prosecuted against one of the United States by Citizens of another State, or by Citizens or Subjects of any Foreign State.

Amendment 12 – Election of the President

[Ratified July 27, 1804]

The Electors shall meet in their respective states and vote by ballot for President and Vice-President, one of whom, at least, shall not be an inhabitant of the same state with themselves; they shall name in their ballots the person voted for as President, and in distinct ballots the person voted for as Vice-President, and they shall make distinct lists of all persons voted for as President, and of all persons voted for as Vice-President, and of the number of votes for each, which lists they shall sign and certify, and transmit sealed to the seat of the government of the United States, directed to the President of the Senate;-The President of the Senate shall, in the presence of the Senate and House of Representatives, open all the certificates and the votes shall then be counted;-The person having the greatest number of votes for President, shall be the President, if such number be a majority of the whole number of Electors appointed; and if no person have such majority, then from the persons having the highest numbers not exceeding three on the list of those voted for as President, the House of Representatives shall choose immediately, by ballot, the President. But in choosing the President, the votes shall be taken by states, the representation from each state having one vote; a quorum for this purpose shall consist of a member or members from two-thirds of the states, and a majority of all the states shall be necessary to a choice. And if the House of Representatives shall not choose a President whenever the right of the choice shall devolve upon them, before the fourth day of March next following, then the Vice-President shall act as President, as in the case of the death or other constitutional disability of the President.-The person having the greatest number of votes as Vice-President, shall be the Vice-President, if such number be a majority of the whole number of Electors appointed, and if no person have a majority, then from the two highest numbers on the list, the Senate shall choose the Vice-President; a quorum for the purpose shall consist of two-thirds of the whole number of Senators, and a majority of the whole number shall be necessary to a choice. But no person constitutionally ineligible to the office of President shall be eligible to that of Vice-President of the United States.

Civil War amendments

Amendment 13 – Prohibition of Slavery

[Ratified December 6, 1865]

Section 1. Neither slavery nor involuntary servitude, except as a punishment for crime whereof the party shall have been duly convicted, shall exist within the United States, or any place subject to their jurisdiction.

Section 2. Congress shall have power to enforce this article by appropriate legislation.

Amendment 14 – Citizenship, Due Process, and Equal Protection of the Laws

[Ratified July 9, 1868]

Section 1. All persons born or naturalized in the United States, and subject to the jurisdiction thereof, are citizens of the United States and of the State wherein they reside. No State shall make or enforce any law which shall abridge the privileges or immunities of citizens of the United States; nor shall any State deprive any person of life, liberty, or property, without due process of law; nor deny to any person within its jurisdiction the equal protection of the laws.

Section 2. Representatives shall be apportioned among the several States according to their respective numbers, counting the whole number of persons in each State, excluding Indians not taxed. But when the right to vote at any election for the choice of electors for President and Vice President of the United States, Representatives in Congress, the Executive and Judicial Officers of a State, or the members of the Legislature thereof, is denied to any of the male inhabitants of such State, being twenty-one years of age, and citizens of the United States, or in any way abridged, except for participation in rebellion, or other crime, the basis of representation therein shall be reduced in the proportion which the number of such male citizens shall bear to the whole number of male citizens twenty-one years of age in such State.

Section 3. No person shall be a Senator or Representative in Congress, or elector of President and Vice President, or hold any office, civil or military, under the United States, or under any State, who having previously taken an oath, as a member of Congress, or as an officer of the United States, or as a member of any State legislature, or as an executive or judicial officer of any State, to support the Constitution of the United States, shall have engaged in insurrection or rebellion against the same, or given aid or comfort to the enemies thereof. But Congress may by a vote of two-thirds of each House, remove such disability.

Section 4. The validity of the public debt of the United States, authorized by law, including debts incurred for payment of pensions and bounties for services in suppressing insurrection or rebellion, shall not be questioned. But neither the United States nor any State shall assume or pay any debt or obligation incurred in aid of insurrection or rebellion against the United States, or any claim for the loss or emancipation of any slave; but all such debts, obligations and claims shall be held illegal and void.

Section 5. The Congress shall have power to enforce, by appropriate legislation, the provisions of this article.

Amendment 15 — The Right to Vote

[Ratified February 3, 1870]

Section 1. The right of citizens of the United States to vote shall not be denied or abridged by the United States or by any State on account of race, color, or previous condition of servitude.

Section 2. The Congress shall have power to enforce this article by appropriate legislation.

Twentieth-century amendments

Amendment 16 — Income Taxes

[Ratified February 3, 1913]

The Congress shall have power to lay and collect taxes on incomes, from whatever source derived, without apportionment among the several States, and without regard to any census or enumeration.

Amendment 17 — Direct Election of Senators

[Ratified April 8, 1913]

The Senate of the United States shall be composed of two Senators from each State, elected by the people thereof for six years; and each Senator shall have one vote. The electors in each State shall have the qualifications requisite for electors of the most numerous branch of the State legislatures.

When vacancies happen in the representation of any State in the Senate, the executive authority of such State shall issue writs of election to fill such vacancies: *Provided*, That the legislature of any State may empower the executive thereof to make temporary appointments until the people fill the vacancies by election as the legislature may direct.

This amendment shall not be so construed as to affect the election or term of any Senator chosen before it becomes valid as part of the Constitution.

Amendment 18 — Prohibition

[Ratified January 16, 1919]

Section 1. After one year from the ratification of this article the manufacture, sale, or transportation of intoxicating liquors within, the importation thereof into, or the exportation thereof from the United States and all territory subject to the jurisdiction thereof for beverage purposes is hereby prohibited.

Section 2. The Congress and the several States shall have concurrent power to enforce this article by appropriate legislation.

Section 3. This article shall be inoperative unless it shall have been ratified as an amendment to the Constitution by the legislatures of the several States, as provided in the Constitution, within seven years from the date of the submission hereof to the States by the Congress.

Amendment 19 — For Women's Suffrage

[Ratified August 18, 1920]

The right of citizens of the United States to vote shall not be denied or abridged by the United States or by any State on account of sex. Congress shall have power to enforce this article by appropriate legislation.

Amendment 20—The Lame Duck Amendment

[Ratified January 23, 1933]

Section 1. The terms of the President and Vice President shall end at noon on the 20th day of January, and the terms of Senators and Representatives at noon on the 3d of January, of the years in which such terms would have ended if this article had not been ratified; and the terms of their successors shall then begin.

Section 2. The Congress shall assemble at least once in every year, and such meeting shall begin at noon on the 3d day of January, unless they shall by law appoint a different day.

Section 3. If, at the time fixed for the beginning of the term of the President, the President elect shall have died, the Vice President elect shall become President. If a President shall not have been chosen before the time fixed for the beginning of his term, or if the President elect shall have failed to qualify, then the Vice President elect shall act as President until a President shall have qualified; and the Congress may by law provide for the case wherein neither a President elect nor a Vice President elect shall have qualified, declaring who shall then act as President, or the manner in which one who is to act shall be selected, and such person shall act accordingly until a President or Vice President shall have qualified.

Section 4. The Congress may by law provide for the case of the death of any of the persons from whom the House of Representatives may choose a President whenever the right of choice shall have devolved upon them, and for the case of the death of any of the persons from whom the Senate may choose a Vice President whenever the right of choice shall have devolved upon them.

Section 5. Sections 1 and 2 shall take effect on the 15th day of October following the ratification of this article.

Section 6. This article shall be inoperative unless it shall have been ratified as an amendment to the Constitution by the legislatures of three-fourths of the several States within seven years from the date of its submission.

Amendment 21—Repeal of Prohibition

[Ratified December 5, 1933]

Section 1. The eighteenth article of amendment to the Constitution of the United States is hereby repealed.

Section 2. The transportation or importation into any State, Territory, or possession of the United States for delivery or use therein of intoxicating liquors, in violation of the laws thereof, is hereby prohibited.

Section 3. This article shall be inoperative unless it shall have been ratified as an amendment to the Constitution by conventions in the several States, as provided in the Constitution, within seven years from the date of the submission hereof to the States by the Congress.

Amendment 22—Number of Presidential Terms

[Ratified February 27, 1951]

Section 1. No person shall be elected to the office of the President more than twice, and no person who has held the office of President, or acted as President for more than two years of a term to which some other person was elected President shall be elected to the office of the President more than once. But this Article shall not apply to any person holding the office of President when this Article was proposed by the Congress, and shall not prevent any person who may be holding the office of President, or acting as President, during the term within which this Article becomes operative from holding the office of President or acting as President during the remainder of such term.

Section 2. This article shall be inoperative unless it shall have been ratified as an amendment to the Constitution by the legislatures of three-fourths of the several States within seven years from the date of its submission to the States by the Congress.

Amendment 23—Presidential Electors for the District of Columbia

[Ratified March 29, 1961]

Section 1. The District constituting the seat of Government of the United States shall appoint in such manner as the Congress may direct:

A number of electors of President and Vice President equal to the whole number of Senators and Representatives in Congress to which the District would be entitled if it were a State, but in no event more than the least populous State; they shall be in addition to those appointed by the States, but they shall be considered, for the purposes of the election of President and Vice President, to be electors appointed by a State; and they shall meet in the District and perform such duties as provided by the twelfth article of amendment.

Section 2. The Congress shall have power to enforce this article by appropriate legislation.

Amendment 24—The Anti-Poll Tax Amendment

[Ratified January 23, 1964]

Section 1. The right of citizens of the United States to vote in any primary or other election for President or Vice President, for electors for President or Vice President, or for Senator or Representative in Congress, shall not be denied or abridged by the United States or any State by reason of failure to pay any poll tax or other tax.

Section 2. The Congress shall have power to enforce this article by appropriate legislation.

Amendment 25 — Presidential Disability, Vice Presidential Vacancies

[Ratified February 10, 1967]

Section 1. In case of the removal of the President from office or of his death or resignation, the Vice President shall become President.

Section 2. Whenever there is a vacancy in the office of the Vice President, the President shall nominate a Vice President who shall take office upon confirmation by a majority vote of both Houses of Congress.

Section 3. Whenever the President transmits to the President pro tempore of the Senate and the Speaker of the House of Representatives his written declaration that he is unable to discharge the powers and duties of his office, and until he transmits to them a written declaration to the contrary, such powers and duties shall be discharged by the Vice President as Acting President.

Section 4. Whenever the Vice President and a majority of either the principal officers of the executive departments or of such other body as Congress may by law provide, transmit to the President pro tempore of the Senate and the Speaker of the House of Representatives their written declaration that the President is unable to discharge the powers and duties of his office, the Vice President shall immediately assume the powers and duties of the office as Acting President.

Thereafter, when the President transmits to the President pro tempore of the Senate and the Speaker of the House of Representatives his written declaration that no inability exists, he shall resume the powers and duties of his office unless the Vice President and a majority of either the principal officers of the executive department or of such other body as Congress may by law provide, transmit within four days to the President pro tempore of the Senate and the Speaker of the House of Representatives their written declaration that the President is unable to discharge the powers and duties of his office. Thereupon Congress shall decide the issue, assembling within forty-eight hours for that purpose if not in session. If the Congress, within twenty-one days after receipt of the latter written declaration, or, if Congress is not in session, within twenty-one days after Congress is required to assemble, determines by two-thirds vote of both Houses that the President is unable to discharge the powers and duties of his office, the Vice President shall continue to discharge the same as Acting President; otherwise, the President shall resume the powers and duties of his office.

Amendment 26 — Eighteen-Year-Old Vote

[Ratified June 30, 1971]

Section 1. The right of citizens of the United States, who are eighteen years of age or older, to vote shall not be denied or abridged by the United States or by any State on account of age.

Section 2. The Congress shall have the power to enforce this article by appropriate legislation.

Proposed Amendment 27 — Equal Rights Amendment

[Proposed March 22, 1972]

Section 1. Equality of rights under the law shall not be denied or abridged by the United States or by any State on account of sex.

Section 2. The Congress shall have power to enforce, by appropriate legislation, the provisions of this article.

Section 3. This amendment shall take effect two years after date of ratification.

Index

WASHINGTON
Centers of Decision

Embassy Row Area

Massachusetts Ave.

Home of many of the major Washington law firms and interest group national headquarters

Pennsylvania Ave.

F St.

Fifteenth St.

18th St.

Virginia Ave.

Constitution Ave.

Seventeenth St.

Theodore Roosevelt Memorial Bridge

Arlington Memorial Bridge

← Dulles Airport

1 **The Capitol**
2 **Union Station**
3 **Senate Office Buildings**
4 **Supreme Court**
5 **Library of Congress**
Congressional Research Service
6 **House Office Buildings**
7 **FDA**
8 **FBI Identification Division**
9 **Dept. of Health, Education, & Welfare**

10 **Dept. of Housing & Urban Development**
11 **NASA**
12 **Department of Transportation**
13 **GSA Regional Office**
14 **Forrestal Bldg.**
Department of the Defense Office Building
15 **Smithsonian Institute**
16 **Dept. of Agriculture**
17 **Bureau of Engraving & Printing**
18 **Dept. of Labor**

19 **National Art Gallery**
20 **Federal Trade Comm.**
21 **Museum of Natural History**
22 **Dept. of Justice**
23 **IRS**
24 **Interstate Commerce Commission**
25 **Museum of History and Technology**
26 **FBI**
27 **U.S. Postal Service**
28 **General Accounting Office**
29 **Washington Monument**

30 **Dept. of Commerce**
31 **The Ellipse**
32 **National Press Clu**
33 **Treasury Dept.**
34 **U.S. Courts Buildin**
35 **Washington Post**
36 **New Executive Offi**
37 **White House**
38 **Executive Office of**
Office of Management and
Council of Economic Advise
National Security Council